W9-BIO-380

I. U. S. B.
BOOKSTORE
$35.20

Operations Management

ADDISON-WESLEY PUBLISHING COMPANY

Reading, Massachusetts ■ Menlo Park, California ■
Don Mills, Ontario ■ Wokingham, England ■ Amsterdam ■
Sydney ■ Singapore ■ Tokyo ■ Madrid ■
Bogotá ■ Santiago ■ San Juan

Operations Management

STRATEGY AND ANALYSIS

LEE J. KRAJEWSKI and LARRY P. RITZMAN
Ohio State University

Dedicated with love
to our families

Judie

Gary, Jeff,
Danny, and Jon

Virginia and Jerry;
Virginia and Larry

Barb

Todd and Karen

Kathryn and Paul;
Mildred and Ray

Sponsoring Editor Jim Heitker
Development Editor Christine Shuster
Production Supervisor Nancy Lasker Behler
Copy Editor Jerrold A. Moore
Text Design Curriculum Concepts; Quadrata, Inc.
Cover Design Marshall Henrichs
Technical Art Consultant Loretta M. Bailey
Illustrator Boston Graphics, Inc.
Permissions Editor Mary Dyer
Manufacturing Supervisor Hugh J. Crawford

Library of Congress Cataloging-in-Publication Data

Krajewski, Lee J.
Operations management.

Bibliography: p.
Includes index.
1. Production management. I. Ritzman, Larry P.
II. Title.
TS155.K788 1987 658.5 86-14087
ISBN 0-201-13480-2

Reprinted with corrections June 1987.

BCDEFGHIJ-HA-8987

PREFACE

Modern-day textbooks should reflect the strategic importance of operations management as well as its analytic nature and clearly define its role in the total organization. To this end we have written this textbook, which is intended for use in introductory courses in operations management at the undergraduate or graduate level. Just as the game of *Go* (alluded to on the cover of our text) requires a sound strategy, it is our firm belief that competitive organizations need a sound *operations* strategy and that the potential of operations management as a competitive weapon has not yet been fully realized. We believe that operations management is not merely a grab-bag of quantitative methods but rather a functional area on a par with accounting, marketing, and finance, and that it should be a full partner in the development of organizational objectives and strategies. It has taken the threat of international competition to awaken managers to the potentially powerful tool in operations management that they have had at their disposal for many years but have not used.

FEATURES OF THE BOOK

Based on our teaching, research, and consulting backgrounds, we have included in this text the most important problem areas faced by operations managers in the field and methods for dealing with these problems. There are some distinctive features worth noting.

Strategic Nature of Operations Management

Rather than just discussing operations strategy once and then forgetting it, we have woven the strategic nature of operations management into the fabric of each chapter. The intent is to reinforce the notion that the decisions in each topical area must be made in relationship to a common operations strategy. The strong analytical aspect of operations management is not forgotten. The tools and models now have more meaning and purpose, given the overall goals and objectives of the operations function.

Unique Material

In addition to traditional material found in operations management textbooks, we have included several chapters on topics of current interest in the field. Chapter 5 presents the latest developments in office, service sector, and manufacturing technology. Chapter 10 defines the important role of materials management, purchasing, and distribution in today's complicated world. Chapter 13 addresses master production scheduling, an important link between operations management, marketing, and finance in a manufacturing firm. Chapter 15 presents the highly touted just-in-time system for repetitive manufacturing situations as well as the unique problems of manufacturing in the process industries. Finally, we have devoted Chapters 18 and 19 to the very important topics of quality management and quality control. Regardless of the functional area of responsibility, managers and those aspiring to become managers should have a firm understanding of quality implications.

Manufacturing and Services

Operations managers are found in a variety of settings, both in manufacturing organizations and in service organizations. We have provided numerous examples of both settings throughout the textbook. We have tried to avoid categorizing manufacturing on the one hand and services on the other because in many cases the differences in management practice between the two are not very distinct. In some cases, however, a discussion of the issues in the service sector is unique enough to set it apart from the rest of the discussion.

Learning Aids

We have used a number of pedagogical devices to increase motivation and enhance the learning process. The cover page for each chapter presents some managerial issues to reinforce the importance of each topic. The subject matter of most chapters is motivated by case scenarios and the discussion flows from the strategic issues to the analysis of specific problems. Boxed material within the chapters contains real-life examples from sources such as the *Wall Street Journal, Business Week,* and *Fortune.* Each chapter ends with a list of chapter highlights, a list of key words, a series of thought-provoking study questions, and problems with realistic scenarios. An extensive list of selected references is also provided. A glossary can be found at the end of the textbook, where all key terms listed at the end of the chapters are defined.

Quantitative Methods

While we believe that quantitative methods are the backbone of analysis in operations management, we realize that not every school or university separates the instruction of quantitative methods from operations management. Consequently, we have put our discussion of the methods of financial analysis, queuing, simulation, and linear programming in appendices, *but* we have written them as if they were chapters. These appendices fully reflect the use of the tools in operations management, and can be inserted into the outline at any convenient spot.

SUPPORTING MATERIALS

Three types of materials have been prepared to supplement the book. Our *Instructor's Guide* and our *Lecture Notes,* available to professors, provide for each chapter a teaching note, answers to the study questions, solutions to the problems, test questions, and transparency masters. There is also a selection of short cases, in-class exercises, and worksheets tailored to the book.

A *Study Guide* can be purchased by the student as a book supplement. Each chapter includes an overview of the chapter concepts, learning objectives for each section, illustrative examples of complex problems, and several unsolved exercises and problems.

Finally, Addison-Wesley has prepared a software package which is complementary to the book. This package, consisting of a manual and a disk, contains analytical models with examples and chapter problems. Explanations include preparation of data and input as well as guides to reading and interpreting the computer output.

A NOTE TO THE STUDENTS

We have assumed that the users of this text do not have a background in operations management, nor an extensive background in mathematics or statistics. In addition, the textbook is written for the general business student and does not presume that everyone will become an operations manager some day. The thrust of the text is to demonstrate the interactive role that *all* functional areas must play to ensure an economically healthy organization. Thus, reading this textbook should be a valuable experience for any student contemplating a management career. It also provides comprehensive coverage of the material tested on the American Production and Inventory Control Society certification exams.

We urge you to take advantage of the features of this textbook in your study of operations management. Make use of the glossary when you encounter an unfamiliar term. Reread portions of chapters you do not understand and use the study questions to test your understanding of the topics. The references at the end of each chapter can be useful for term projects. In general, perseverance and a little common sense will overcome most of your difficulties in mastering this subject.

ACKNOWLEDGMENTS

We have written a textbook portraying the role that operations management plays in the organization and the consequences of the decisions made by operations managers, ranging from the "thrill of victory" to the "agony of defeat." No textbook, especially this one, could have been completed without the help of a great many people. The whole team at Addison-Wesley Publishing Company could always be counted on for support and encouragement, including Jim Heitker, Christine Shuster, Nancy Behler, Loretta Bailey, Mary Dyer, Mary Clare McEwing, Shirley Rieger, Connie Spatz, and Janis Jackson Hill. Special thanks go to Jerry Moore. As copy editor, he could transform what seemed to be a perfectly fine sentence into a much better one.

We wish to thank a distinguished group of reviewers who have provided countless suggestions for improving initial drafts of the text: Sumer Aggarwal, University of Massachusetts–Boston; William Berry, University of Iowa; John J. Castellano, Suffolk University; Chen Hua Chung, University of Kentucky; James A. Fitzsimmons, University of Texas–Austin; Stephen Goodman, University of Central Florida; Gene Groff, Georgia State University; Warren Hauck, Bowling Green State University; Vincent A. Mabert, Indiana University; Robert Meier, Western Washington University; Brooke A. Saladin, Wake Forest University; Carl Schultz, University of New Mexico; Linda Sprague, University of New Hampshire; Earle Steinberg, Touche Ross and Co.; and Urban Wemmerlov, University of Wisconsin–Madison.

We are indebted to our colleagues on the Faculty of Management Sciences for having provided valuable ideas as well as moral support for this project. We also wish to acknowledge the candid comments of many students, including our Ph.D. students and many others taking the introductory course in operations management at The Ohio State University. We have incorporated many of these suggestions in our final draft. Special thanks go to Sue Perrott

Siferd, who drafted the original versions of Chapters 4 and 5 and Appendix A at the time of our greatest need. When due dates were pressing and on-time delivery to the publisher seemed unlikely, she willingly joined in the project.

Finally, we wish to thank our families, who thought we left them to join a monastery for the past several years. Judie and Barb were marvelously supportive spouses, even after they learned that the elegant dinner at the Peppercorn Duck restaurant was just a ruse to tell them of our commitment to this project.

Westerville, Ohio

L.J.K.
L.P.R.

CONTENTS

Chapter 1

INTRODUCTION 1

Chapter 2
PRODUCT PLANNING AND COMPETITIVE PRIORITIES 29

Chapter 3
FORECASTING 71

Chapter 4 PROCESS DESIGN 119

Chapter 5 TECHNOLOGICAL CHOICES 169

Chapter 6 WORK MEASUREMENT 209

Chapter 17 PROJECT SCHEDULING AND CONTROL 639

Chapter 18 QUALITY MANAGEMENT 689

Chapter 19 QUALITY CONTROL 721

Chapter 20 OPERATIONS AS A COMPETITIVE WEAPON 757

Appendix A FINANCIAL ANALYSIS A1

Appendix B

QUEUING AND SIMULATION ANALYSIS B1

Appendix C

LINEAR PROGRAMMING C1

Appendix D

FINANCIAL AND STATISTICAL AIDS D1

Operations Management

CHAPTER

INTRODUCTION

Some Managerial Issues

- What are the causes of recent productivity trends and shifts in shares of world markets?
- What are the implications of recent employment and productivity trends in the service sector?
- What are the distinctions between manufacturing and service organizations?
- What types of decisions do operations managers face?
- How can managers identify and deal with environmental change when formulating corporate strategy?
- How does operations strategy relate to corporate strategy?
- Should management be concerned only with strategic issues?

Chapter Outline

Operations management deals with the production of the goods and services that we buy and use every day; its aim is to acquire and deploy resources efficiently to achieve an organization's mission. Every organization, whether private or public, manufacturing or service, has an operations function. In this book we focus on the management of this function. We present the role of operations within the total organization and highlight some of the newer tools and concepts used to support managerial decisions. We examine the strategic *and* the analytic dimensions of operations management because an effective manager must deal with both. We believe that operations management is one of the most challenging areas of a business—involving, as it does, most of the human and financial assets of an organization.

WHAT IS OPERATIONS MANAGEMENT?

Operations management is the systematic direction and control of the processes that transform inputs into finished goods or services. Production and operations management, taken together, comprise a system, as shown in Fig. 1.1. Inputs can be human resources (workers and managers), capital (equipment and facilities), materials, land, energy, and information. The circles in Fig. 1.1 represent *operations* where resources are utilized and transformations occur. Often a product passes through several such operations before being finished. An operation can be a machine center in a manufacturing plant, a teller station in a bank, a hospital ward, or a department in an office. The types of transformation vary widely and include physical or chemical (a factory), locational (an airline), attitudinal (a theater), educational (a school), physiological (an emergency room), informational (a computer center), exchange (a store), and storage (a distribution center).

Two other inputs are shown as dotted lines in Fig. 1.1. The first is the customer, who may come in direct contact with the production system and sometimes is an active participant in the transformation. Examples include the shopper in a store or the student at a university. The second is informa-

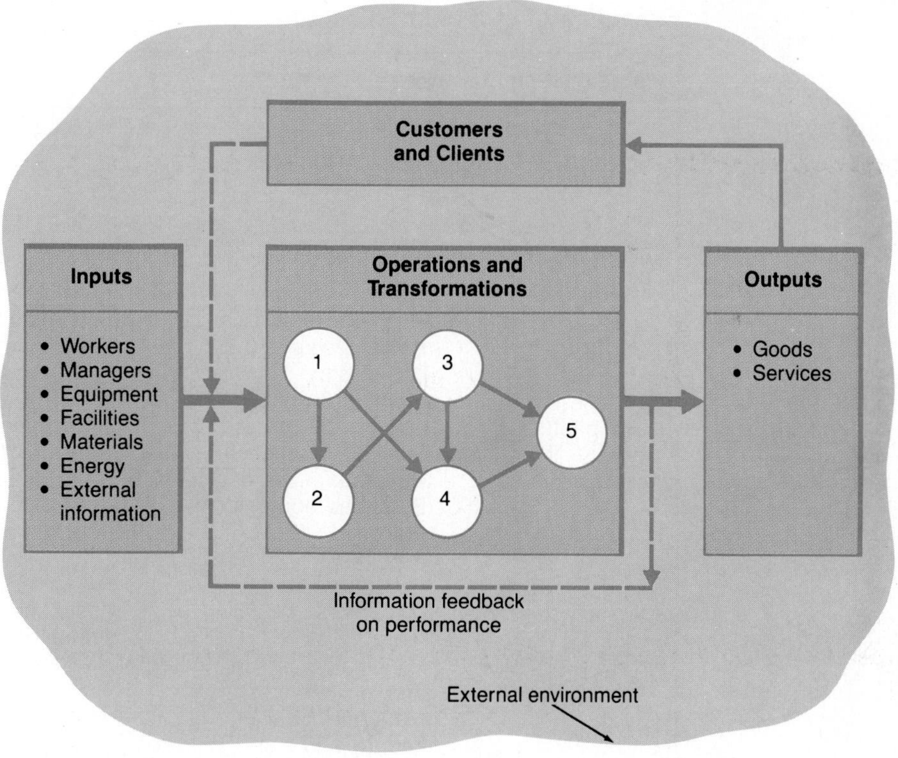

Figure 1.1

The Production and Operations Management System.

tion feedback. It can come from external sources, such as reports on economic trends, a telephone call from a vendor on past-due shipments, or new customer orders. It can also come from internal sources, such as reports on cost variances, customer service, or inventory levels. Information from both sources is needed to manage the production system.

Table 1.1 shows specific inputs and outputs for the systems in five different types of organizations.

Outputs from manufacturing operations are goods produced either for consumers or for other industrial firms, although auxiliary services can also be provided. Outputs from service operations range from delivered mail for a post office to a recovered patient for a hospital. Even though the inputs and outputs vary between industries, the underlying process of transforming inputs into outputs holds true for all production systems.

Table 1.1

Examples of Inputs and Outputs

Organization	Input	Output
• Jewelry store	Merchandise Store building Sales clerks Registers Jeweler Customer	Customer sales
• Post Office	Sorting machines Trucks Postal clerks and carriers Postmaster Mail	Delivered Mail
• Hospital	Doctors and nurses Staff Buildings Beds and equipment Power Supplies Patients	Recovered patient
• Manufacturing plant	Machines Plant Raw materials Workers Managers	Consumer goods Materials for purchase by other firms
• University	Faculty and staff Classrooms Library Supplies Students	Graduates Research Public service

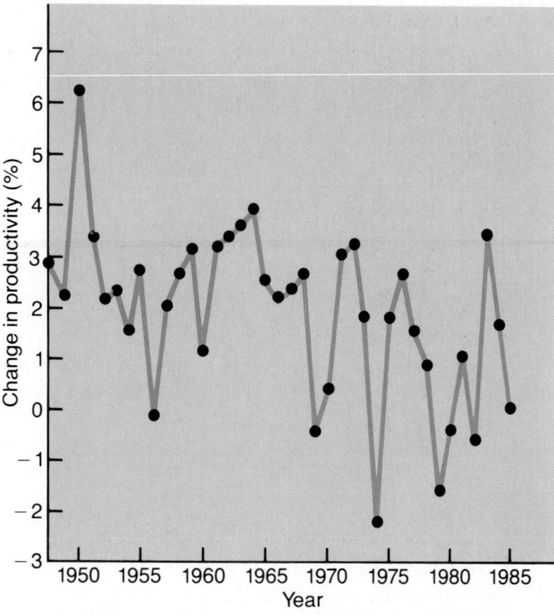

Figure 1.2

Productivity Trends: Percentage Changes in Total Output by the Nonfarm Business Sector (Valued in 1982 Dollars) per Hour Worked.

Source: Economic Report of the President, February 1986, p. 303.

SIGNIFICANT TRENDS IN PRODUCTIVITY AND SERVICES

Operations management is attracting increasing attention because of two significant trends: lagging productivity and the growth of the service sector. These trends are both recent and far-reaching.

Productivity Trends

In terms of total output, the United States is the most productive nation in the world. While only 5 percent of the world's population, it makes 22 percent of the world's goods and services. But this figure is down from 30 percent in 1970 and 52 percent in 1950. A major reason for this slippage is illustrated in Fig. 1.2, which shows changes in **productivity** since 1948 for the private business sector of the economy.* This graph shows how the dollar value of

* Farms are excluded from the graph. They represent less than 5 percent of U.S. output and employment.

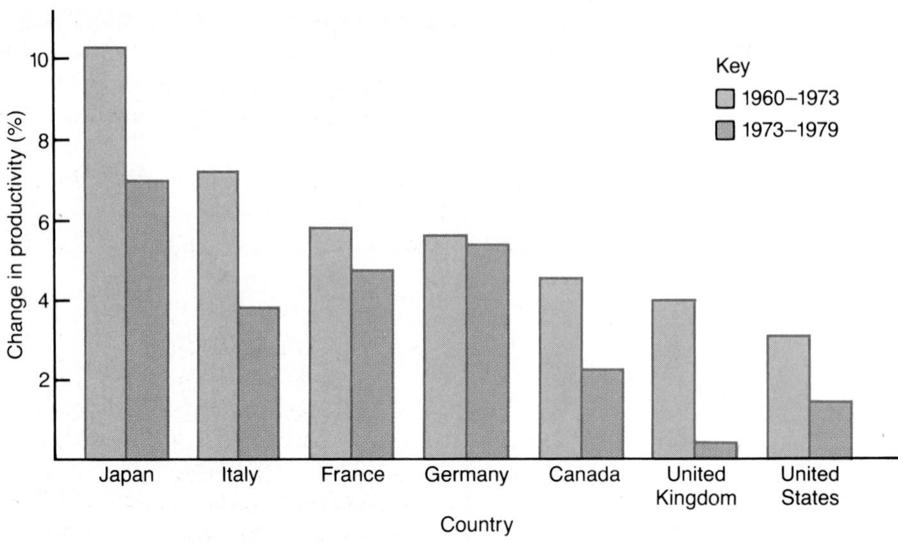

Figure 1.3

Annual Percentage Change in Manufacturing Productivity (Output per Hour Worked).

Source: Neef, A., and P. Capdevielle, "International Comparisons of Productivity and Labor Costs," *Monthly Labor Review,* U.S. Department of Labor, Bureau of Labor Statistics, December 1980, p. 33.

output per hour worked has changed from one year to the next. For example, productivity increased by more than 6 percent from 1949 to 1950 and almost $3\frac{1}{2}$ percent the next year, and so on. Evening out the peaks and valleys, you can detect a recent downward trend. The average annual increase was more than 2.5 percent through 1973 but only about 1 percent since then. Productivity rebounded somewhat in 1983, but the trend is still cause for real concern.

Even more unsettling are the statistics shown in Fig. 1.3, which compare productivity growth in manufacturing in seven industrialized countries. A cycle peak occurred in 1973, followed by a steep decline in 1974–1975; the productivity changes are shown both before and after the 1973 peak. You can see that productivity growth slowed after 1973 in all seven countries. However, the disturbing statistic is that, since 1960, the United States has had the lowest productivity growth (2.6 percent) of any country shown. (Japan is the leader at 9.2 percent.) As a result, U.S. firms are experiencing declining shares of the world market in aircraft, plastics, drugs, agricultural machinery, railway vehicles, and housing fixtures.

A number of Japanese manufacturers have penetrated markets within the United States. Examples include the automobile, semiconductor, steel, machine tool, consumer electronics, shipbuilding, and telecommunications industries. The Japanese competitive challenge applies to smokestack (heavy manufacturing) and high-tech industries alike. Fifteen years ago Japan accounted for only 8.5 percent of free-world automobile sales and 0.2 percent of U.S. sales. Now its share of the automobile market is 26 percent of free-world sales and 16.3 percent of U.S. sales. It is no wonder that D. E. Peterson, president of Ford Motor Company, concluded that "the passwords for the 80s will be productivity and quality."*

Many explanations are offered for lagging U.S. productivity. Federal (and sometimes state) government regulations such as OSHA† and EPA‡ requirements have increased costs, but safer jobs and cleaner air are not reflected in government statistics on the value of output. Net investment in new equipment and facilities has been only 6.6 percent of total output in the United States during the last decade. No other major industrial country devotes such a small share of total output to new capital investment. (Japan is the leader at 19.5 percent.) The composition of the work force is changing and attitudes toward work are shifting. Energy costs spiraled in the 1970s and only recently began to fall. Some experts argue that since the United States has a higher absolute level of productivity, further improvements are more difficult to achieve. High wages and stringent union contracts are sometimes identified as obstacles to productivity increases. During the last few years, Japan's wage rates averaged just over 50 percent of the U.S. average. Wage rates in Italy, France, and the United Kingdom are only 55–65 percent of those in this country. These rates represent quite a differential to overcome. High wage rates have been aggravated by a strong dollar, which makes U.S. prices and wages even higher relative to foreign competition.

Explanations such as these do not tell the full story. For example, Japanese firms successfully operate facilities in the United States, using U.S. workers. Productivity gains ultimately come from the managers and employees of individual organizations. Only when they find ways to increase productivity can high wages, salaries, and living standards be maintained. Increasing productivity is the central concern of operations (or production) managers. The connection between productivity and operations management is underscored in Box 1.1. This book conforms with the commission's recommendation for a strategy orientation in the study of operations.

Service Sector Trends

The findings presented in Box 1.1 relate to manufacturing firms. They produce goods or material products, which typically can be stored and transported. Nonmanufacturing firms, which are part of the service sector of the

* From remarks made at Annual Supplier Dinner, April 28, 1980.

† Occupational Safety and Health Administration.

‡ Environmental Protection Agency.

Box 1.1

PRESIDENT'S COMMISSION ON INDUSTRIAL COMPETITIVENESS

President Reagan established a Commission on Industrial Competitiveness to investigate lagging productivity. The commission recommended that the nation's business schools undertake a thoughtful response to the global challenge. Stating that U.S. firms are uncompetitive internationally because of not excelling in production, the commission concluded that:

> Production courses must deal with strategies of top executives, the translation of production strategies to live decisions of middle managers, and the tactical operations and procedures of lower-level managers.

Source: "President's Commission Enlists Business-Ed Forum Aid," *Higher Education and National Affairs,* Newsletter of the American Council on Education, October 22, 1984, p. 2. Reprinted by permission.

economy, produce services rather than goods. The service sector breaks down roughly into three equal components:

1. Local, state, and federal governments.
2. Wholesale and retail firms.
3. Health, financial service, real estate, insurance, repair service, business service, and personal service firms.

The service sector has been growing rapidly but suffers from a productivity record as bad as or worse than that in manufacturing. For example, the time an average person must work to pay for a washing machine is only 17 percent of the time necessary 30 years ago. Similarly, a television set can be purchased with only 4 percent of the work time needed then. Washing machines and television sets are manufactured goods. In the service sector the corresponding numbers are 73 percent for a cup of coffee at a restaurant and 105 percent for a haircut. These much larger percentages suggest low productivity growth in the service sector. Figure 1.4 shows that our examples are not the exception. Over almost a half century, the number of jobs in the service sector rose from 50 to 68 percent of total nonfarm jobs. Over the same time interval consumer expenditures for services (the measure of their output value) rose only from 41 to 47 percent. We can draw two conclusions from these figures:

1. Employment has been shifting out of manufacturing into services: 68 percent of the jobs are in the service sector, and only 32 percent are in

manufacturing. In 1940, manufacturing accounted for 50 percent of the jobs.

2. Productivity increases in the service sector are not even keeping pace with those in manufacturing. The upward trend in expenditures for services is not as steep as the upward trend in jobs. Thus the new service workers are not generating a proportional increase in output.

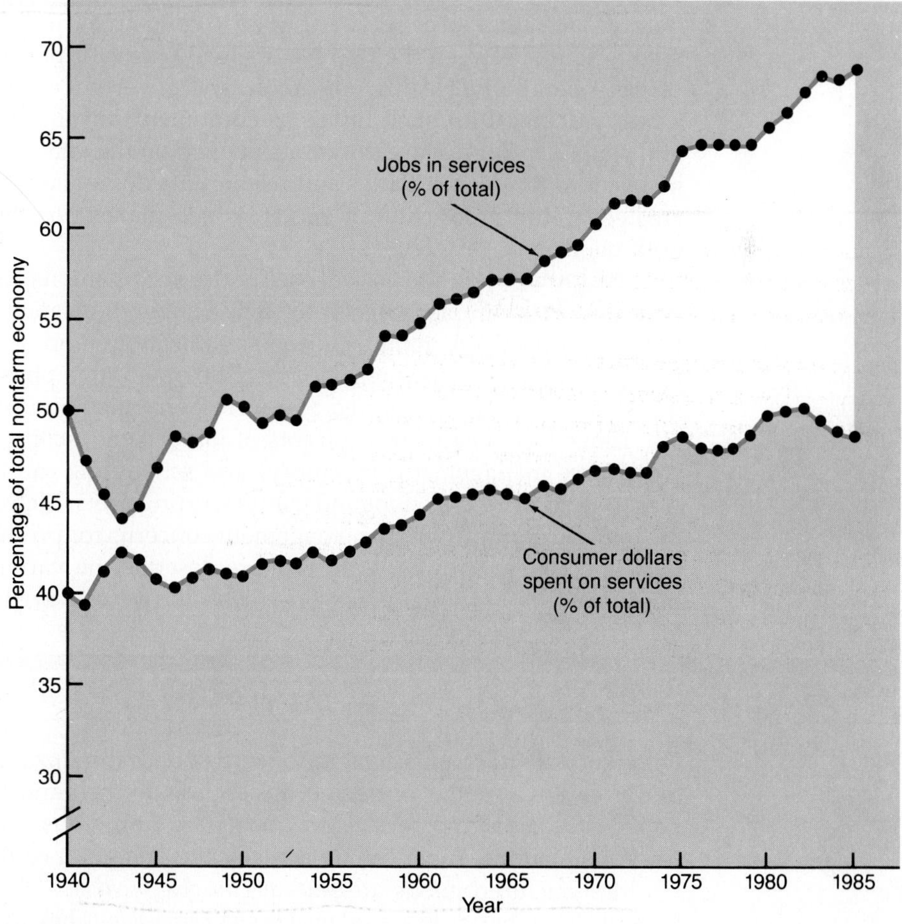

Figure 1.4

Employment and Consumer Expenditures in the Service Sector.

Note: Transportation and public utilities are not counted here as service-producers for employment statistics because of their heavy equipment requirements. If counted in the service sector, the number of jobs in services would grow by another 5 percent in 1985 and reach a total of 73 percent.

Source: Economic Report of the President, February 1986.

There is a temptation to project the trends shown in Fig. 1.4 into the next century and conclude that manufacturing will be an insignificant part of the U.S. economy. This is incorrect for two reasons. First, consumer expenditures and jobs have increased systematically in manufacturing. In real dollars, the value of manufacturing output has risen 257 percent since 1940. However, increases have been even more rapid in services. Second, the two sectors of the economy are complementary. For example, the output of many firms is purchased by other firms as inputs. Over 25 percent of these intermediate outputs are classified as services but go to companies in the nonservice sector. Another link between the two sectors is the heavy input of goods into many service operations. Health, education, and government institutions generate a heavy demand for such things as equipment, furniture, books, buildings, and materials. Service organizations depend on the vitality of firms producing goods, and vice versa. Banks and restaurants do not create wealth. Wealth is created by the production of goods, which makes possible the purchase of both goods and services.

The growing significance of the service sector and its lagging productivity have important implications for the field of operations management. The field initially focused on manufacturing organizations and was called *industrial management* or *production management*. The operations phases of service organizations were largely ignored and were performed almost at handicraft levels. Times have changed. Concepts of job design, facility location, capacity, work-force management, inventory, and scheduling can be applied equally well to service organizations and manufacturing firms. McDonald's restaurants are but one example where management concerns for productivity can pay off with spectacular growth. We therefore describe the various facets of operations found in both manufacturing firms and service organizations.

DIFFERENCES BETWEEN MANUFACTURING AND SERVICES

Differences between manufacturing and service organizations can be striking but often are a matter of degree. Exceptions to the general characteristics of goods producers and service producers are numerous. Thus the seven distinctions made in Table 1.2 are actually the ends of a continuum.

Manufactured goods are *physical, durable products*. We can see, feel, and inspect them. Services are *intangible and perishable*. They are often ideas, concepts, or information. This distinction gets cloudy when we try to classify an organization as either a goods producer or a service producer. Service organizations normally provide a bundle of both goods and services. Along with their services, a retailer delivers goods and a restaurant provides food. But a manufacturer also provides services, such as delivery-date concessions, technical advice, credit, or follow-up repairs.

Table 1.2

Continuum of Characteristics of Goods and Services Producers

More Like A Goods Producer ⟷	More Like A Services Producer
• Physical, durable product	• Intangible, perishable product
• Output can be inventoried	• Output cannot be inventoried
• Low customer contact	• High customer contact
• Long response time	• Short response time
• Regional, national, or international markets	• Local markets
• Large facilities with economies of scale	• Small facilities
• Capital intensive	• Labor intensive
• Quality easily measured	• Quality not easily measured

Because they are durable, goods usually can be *inventoried*. They can be stored and transported in anticipation of future demands, giving many manufacturers considerable flexibility. Peaks and valleys in demand can be handled by creating inventory and smoothing output levels. Services, however, cannot be preproduced. Without inventories to cushion the production system from erratic customer demands, service organizations are more constrained by time. This does not mean that inventories are unimportant to certain types of service organizations. In fact, wholesale and retail firms hold 44 percent of the economy's inventory. The difference is that these inventories are *inputs* (rather than outputs) to service systems. As inputs, these goods must be accompanied by further transformations before the service is completed. In addition, not all manufacturers produce finished goods inventory, particularly when final products are customized or have a limited shelf life.

A third distinction is *customer contact*. The customers themselves are inputs in many service organizations. Customers often provide much of the labor through self-service, producing and consuming a service at the same time. Hospitals, schools, jails, entertainment centers, and self-service facilities are places where the customer is present during most of the service operations. However, most customers for manufactured products have little or no contact with the production system. Primary customer contact is left to distribution and retail firms. In high-contact service organizations, the work force needs public relations skills to deal with customers. This sometimes blurs the boundaries between the marketing and operations functions. Many service producers have low customer contact at one level of the organization and high customer contact at other levels. Home offices (as opposed to branch offices) of insurance, banking, and postal service organizations have little direct customer contact. There can even be differences in the amount of customer contact at the same facility. The back-room operations of a jewelry store and baggage handling areas at an airport require little contact with customers, whereas the sales and ticket counter operations of these same organizations involve a great amount of contact.

Another distinction is the *response time* to demands. Manufacturers usually offer lead times measured in days or weeks, whereas many services must be offered within minutes of customer arrival. A customer at a supermarket grows impatient waiting more than 3 to 5 minutes in a checkout line, whereas the buyer of a forklift truck might be satisfied with a 16-week lead time. Since service customers usually arrive at a time of their choosing, there is more short-term demand uncertainty than in manufacturing. Arrival patterns are cyclical—on a daily and even an hourly basis—making it difficult to efficiently match capacity with demand. Exceptions on this response-time distinction can also be found. A surgeon might preschedule patients weeks in advance and a lawyer see clients by appointment only. Some manufacturers even expect same-day delivery from suppliers of high-volume parts.

Service organizations requiring direct customer contact must locate relatively near their customers in order to serve local markets. Services cannot be shipped to distant locations. A manufacturing facility, on the other hand, often serves *regional, national, or even international markets.* Manufacturing often involves *larger facilities,* more automation, and greater capital investment than service facilities. Location and size reflect market volumes, availability of transportation and distribution facilities, and economies of scale. Mail processing, public-utility, communication, and transportation organizations are exceptions to the general pattern. Technically, they are service organizations, but they are capital intensive and enjoy large-scale production. Supermarkets and franchised food operations also have these characteristics, in comparison with the corner grocery store or hamburger stand.

A final distinction is *quality.* Since services are usually a mixture of tangible goods and intangibles, measuring quality can be difficult. Individual preferences have much to do with assessing quality. Some customers prize a chat with the sales clerk during the purchase. Others rate quality high if the transaction takes place quickly. Still others assess quality by the firm's reputation for giving full customer satisfaction on all purchases.

THREE VIEWS OF OPERATIONS MANAGEMENT

We have defined operations management as the direction and control of processes whereby inputs are transformed at one or more operations into outputs. We have also stated that operations management is concerned about

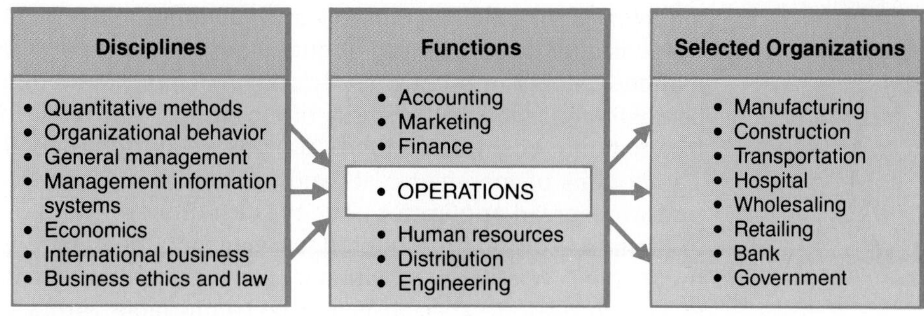

Figure 1.5

Operations Management as a Function.

productivity, in both manufacturing and service organizations. Further insight into operations management comes from three additional perspectives: We can view it as a function, a profession, and as a set of decisions.

As a Function

Operations can be identified in every organization. Figure 1.5 shows that operations is but one of several functions or departments in an organization. Each function or unit has primary responsibility for certain activities. Operations is concerned with the resources and processes that generate goods and services. Marketing is responsible for generating demand for the organization's output; finance deals with securing and investing the capital assets; human resources (often called *personnel*), with hiring and training; distribution, with transporting inputs and outputs; and engineering, with product design. These functions are often carried out by separate departments in the organization. However, in some cases an organization finds it more economical to contract for certain functions. A service organization, for example, may contract for engineering services when they are needed, rather than have an in-house engineering department. In other cases an organization may not need to perform certain functions. The Internal Revenue Service, for example, does not need a marketing department to stimulate demand. The operations function is not always performed by a separate department called *operations* or *production.* The owner of a small business, for example, may manage both marketing and operations and not have separate departments for these functions.

Operations management draws on a wide variety of disciplines, as shown in Figure 1.5. Quantitative methods of analysis provide an impressive set of modeling techniques to help solve production problems. The growing role of the computer makes the use of quantitative methods and management information systems important aspects of managing operations. Organizational behavior concepts aid the tasks of job design and work-force management. International business methods provide useful ideas about facility location. The notions of marginal costs and economies of scale from economics also find widespread application. The breadth of these—and other—contributing disciplines requires that operations managers be generalists, particularly at the higher levels in organizations. However, operations managers must also be able to relate to specialists and be comfortable with a variety of concepts and analytic techniques specific to operations.

Box 1.2

WANT ADS FOR OPERATIONS MANAGERS

Vice President of Operations
We offer an outstanding and highly visible opportunity for a pragmatic, results-oriented pro to join our headquarters staff. The successful candidate should have significant manufacturing experience with fabricated light metals in a labor-intensive environment. The position reports directly to the Division President.

Director of Operations
Expanding health maintenance organization needs a Director of Operations to function as Chief Operating Officer for a recently established regional component. Individual reports to the Chief Executive Officer of the parent organization health care delivery systems.

Director of Manufacturing
A rapidly growing medium-sized high technology manufacturing concern seeks the expertise of an experienced manufacturing professional. The candidate should have a minimum of five years experience in management, including production planning and control, materials management, MRP, and facilities management.

Operations Manager
Large brokerage firm seeks experienced Back Office Manager. Position involves all daily executing and settlement functions of a self-clearing NYSE member.

Plant Manager
An immediate position is available at our medium-sized manufacturing plant in the Chicago suburbs. Assembly, metal stamping, rubber molding, and flat surface lapping are all part of our process. Specific experience in these operations is not necessary, but a background in Industrial Management is. This is not a desk job. On-the-floor management of work force and total responsibility for the manufacturing facilities will be yours.

2. ## As a Profession — BIG demand

Operations management as a profession offers a range of jobs. The examples of want ads in Box 1.2 illustrate some of the variety available in manufacturing and services. In a manufacturing firm one of the upper level managers has the title of vice-president of manufacturing (or production). In a service organization, the corresponding title might be vice-president (or director) of operations. Other managers, who are responsible for particular facets of the production system, report to the operations manager. These other managers may be in the purchasing, inventory, quality control, or scheduling areas, to name a few.

Assistant Vice President
Materials Management
We operate two hospitals, four industrial medicine/urgent care facilities, and a retirement community. The basic function for the Assistant Vice President is to plan, implement, and control all phases of Pharmacy; Purchasing; Stores; Receiving, Distribution, and Transportation; Central Processing; Laundry; and Printing Services. Bachelor's degree in business preferred, master's degree a plus. Must have 5–10 years in materials management. Hospital experience is a plus.

Production Control Manager
An exciting opportunity for a results-oriented individual with a degree and proven track record. Responsible for controlling work-in-process to achieve on-time delivery and minimum inventory. Demands a self-starter who can coordinate major projects. The ability to interact with all levels of management is essential. A strong appreciation for systems development is needed.

Corporate Director of Purchasing
In this position you will service, select, and interface with a variety of vendors on a national and international basis. You will personally negotiate contracts, providing timely procurement of systems, equipment, materials, and services specified by company managers.

Manager of Quality Control
Local manufacturer needs Quality Control/Quality Assurance professional to direct the total QC/QA function. You must have 10 years experience in the QC/QA field with progressive managerial assignments. Also requires a BS degree. MBA preferred. Proficiency in a second language will be helpful.

Lower management and entry-level positions in manufacturing carry titles such as inventory control supervisor, first-line supervisor, buyer, scheduler, process analyst, production control analyst, time standard analyst, facilities planner, and value analyst. Corresponding titles in the service sector might be department supervisor (insurance), office supervisor (contractor), section head (government), purchasing agent (store), flight scheduler (airlines), operations analyst (bank), and scheduler (trucking).

One benefit of a profession is associations where practitioners can meet to exchange ideas. Key associations in operations are the American Production and Inventory Control Society (APICS), National Association of Purchasing Managers (NAPM), and Operations Management Association (OMA). The current demand for people trained or experienced in operations is quite good. The undergraduates majoring in operations management at one typical midwest university received the highest median starting salary of any business major in two of the last three years. At the MBA level across the country, graduate students majoring in operations management enjoyed an average starting salary of $28,900 in 1983, the highest of any for the seven majors surveyed. Operations has emerged as an excellent career path to the top levels in organizations. Biographies of 237 chief executive officers in 1984 showed that 36 percent "learned the ropes" in production. This proportion compares favorably with those for chief executives having backgrounds in finance (22 percent), marketing (21 percent), research (10 percent) and legal (9 percent). This situation is largely the result of the current productivity challenge. Promotions tend to come from areas where problems are the most severe and managers have been able to solve them.

As a Set of Decisions

Decision making is the basic part of all management activity, whether locating a new warehouse or dealing with a subordinate who is not meeting expectations. No standard process for making decisions can be applied to each individual and situation. However, we can think of decision making in terms of four basic steps: problem recognition; problem formulation; analysis of alternatives; and choosing and implementing an alternative.

Problem Recognition. A manager can often recognize problems and discover the need for improvement by observing, being inquisitive, and searching for symptoms of poor performance. This orientation helps a manager spot quality losses when they first start to go out of control, or question the work methods at a particularly inefficient operation. Sometimes this aspect of problem recognition is not necessary, as when routine decisions are made on a repetitive basis. Developing this month's production schedule or the annual budget are examples where the problems automatically come to the manager's attention.

Problem Formulation. The manager then defines the problem clearly and identifies alternatives available, constraints on the feasibility of choices, and the goals to be achieved by solving the problem. Problem definition is not as easy as you might think; it often involves sifting through a tangle of apparent problems to identify the real problem. The number of alternative solutions may be few or countless. Often the decisionmaker must consult with others to identify the full range of options. Constraints often are imposed by higher level decisions, such as available capacity or budgets. In some cases goals are quantitative in nature and objective measures, such as costs or percent on-time delivery, can be used to assess how well each alternative would meet the goals. In other cases goals are qualitative in nature and can only be assessed subjectively.

Analysis of Alternatives. Next, the manager collects information to help in the evaluation of alternatives. This information can come from computerized information systems, other people in the organization, or simply past experience. More often than not, the manager must deal with multiple objectives, which do not collapse neatly into a single performance measure. Cost, quality, and flexibility are three such objectives in operations. Confidence in the projection of outcomes of different alternatives can range from near certainty to considerable uncertainty. Multiple objectives and uncertainty of outcomes make this third step a challenging one.

Choice and Implementation of an Alternative. In some cases, a manager's selection of an alternative is based on nothing more than a list of pros and cons jotted on the back of an envelope. In other cases, the choice may be supported by a great deal of information and complex modeling techniques. In any case the selection, finally, is based on the best judgment of the manager about the likely outcomes of the decision. The decisionmaker often involves others in the process, particularly if he or she desires group consensus. Involving others affected by the decision often makes implementation more successful.

Decisions in Operations. The overall decision-making process is not unique to operations managers. What sets operations managers apart are the *types* of decisions they make. These decision areas are listed in Table 1.3, along with a sample question about each; they correspond to the major topics covered in the other chapters of this book and therefore are a good preview of things to come. Table 1.3 begins with long-range issues, such as choosing products or services to offer, determining competitive priorities, setting quality objectives, designing the process, making technological choices, establishing work-force policies, determining capacity, and locating and designing the physical layout of the facility. These types of decisions deal with the *design* of the production system. The remaining decisions, beginning with materials management, deal more with the *operation* of facilities after they are in place. Such decisions, sometimes called the *operations infrastructure,* deal with plan-

Table 1.3

Decisions in Operations Management

Decision Area	Sample Questions
Product plans	What products (goods or services) should we offer?
Competitive priorities	Should we excel on the basis of cost, quality, or flexibility?
Positioning strategy	Should we organize resources around products or processes?
Quality management	Should our goal be reliability or top-of-the-line quality?
Process design	What processes should we use to make our products?
Work-force management	How should we hire, train, and motivate our employees?
Technological choices	Is it time to automate some of our processes?
Capacity	What is the maximum reasonable size for our facility?
Maintenance	How much should we spend to maintain equipment and the facility?
Location	Should we be followers or leaders in picking new store locations?
Layout	How should we physically arrange desks and equipment?
Materials management	Who should be our suppliers? How do we evaluate and support them?
Production and staffing plans	What should be our output rates and staffing levels for this quarter?
Master production scheduling	Should we make-to-stock or make-to-order?
Inventory	How much inventory do we need? How should we control it?
Scheduling	What customers or jobs should we give top priority to?
Quality control	How do we best achieve our quality goals?

ning output levels over shorter periods of time, deciding when to release purchase or production orders, selecting vendors, managing inventories, scheduling resources, and maintaining quality.

CORPORATE AND OPERATIONS STRATEGIES

There is growing recognition of the importance of strategic issues for the organization as a whole, as well as the operations function in particular. As you read through this book, you will gain an appreciation of the strategic issues in operations management. At this point, however, we need to establish some basic concepts of strategy, beginning first at the organizational level.

Corporate Strategy

An organization can be a major corporation, federal agency, or bank. It can even be a business segment organized around a particular set of customers or clients who share common resources. Whatever the type of organization may be, its top management should deliberately relate the efforts of the whole organization to its future. Sometimes called long-range planning, **corporate strategy*** is the process of determining the organization's central purpose, deciding how best to acquire and allocate resources to carry out the mission, and establishing objectives against which to evaluate how well the mission is being achieved. This process involves defining the organization's mission, monitoring and adjusting to changes in the organization's environment, and identifying the organization's distinctive competencies.

The Mission. Determining an organization's mission requires answers to fundamental questions such as:

- What business are we in? What should it be ten years from now?
- Who are our customers or clients?
- What are our basic beliefs and philosophy?
- What are our greatest strengths? How can we use them to maximum advantage?
- What are our key performance objectives, such as growth or profits, by which to monitor success?

The Environment. An organization needs to continually adapt to its changing external environment. Adaptation begins with *environmental scanning*, whereby managers monitor the environment for opportunities or threats that need a response. One key environmental element is competition. Competitors may be gaining an edge by broadening product lines, improving quality, or lowering costs. New entrants in the market or product substitutes may pose a threat to continued profitability. The bargaining power of suppliers or customers can become a threat or an opportunity. In addition to competition, environmental elements include economic trends, technological changes, political conditions, social changes (such as attitudes toward work), and the availability of key resources.

The impact of these changes on current strategies can reveal shortcomings in planning and product development that need attention. Markets mature and decline, technology changes, and competitors find ways to achieve lower costs—all requiring adjustments in corporate strategy. Many businesses have faced a particularly turbulent environment during the last decade. Markets have grown more slowly, automation is more complicated and expensive, product life cycles seem shorter, and foreign competition is intensifying.

Distinctive Competencies. Environmental impacts cannot be "managed away." Corporate strategies must change to meet them, which means taking into account the organization's unique resources and strengths. A key concept is that few firms rarely succeed by meeting competition head-on, that is,

* Organizational strategy would be a more descriptive term since it applies to all types of organizations. We use the term corporate strategy only because of its widespread usage in practice.

by offering the same exact products and services. It is usually better to go after a *niche* in the market, taking advantage of what the firm can do particularly well. These **distinctive competencies** might include:

1. The size and ability of the work force. Employees gravitate to good jobs, but there is often a significant time lag between demand and supply. An available and competent work force is a strength.
2. Particularly efficient or well-located facilities such as offices, stores, or plants. The availability of such facilities is a major advantage because of the long lead time required to build new facilities.
3. The ability to easily change output levels, attract capital from stock sales, market and distribute the product, or differentiate the product from those offered by competitors.

Strategies versus Tactics. An important thing to understand about strategic planning is how it differs from tactical planning. Planning is future-oriented; that is, it involves making decisions today about tomorrow. Table 1.4 shows that every planning activity lies somewhere between the two ends of a continuum, with strategy at one end and tactics at the other.

The first difference between the two types of planning is the *time horizon* used. Strategic planning has a longer time horizon than tactical planning. Of course, what is considered long depends somewhat on the situation. Since it takes so long for a forest to grow, strategic plans of businesses in the forestry industry must look ahead as far as 100 years. A public utility might plan 30 years ahead. When firms enjoy shorter lead times in acquiring resources, but face a more volatile environment, a long time horizon may be only five years.

Because of their longer time horizons, strategic plans are made with *less certainty* about what the future holds. Making accurate forecasts of what will happen far into the future is very difficult. Strategic plans also are *less structured* for two reasons. First, they are more *ends-oriented*. The ends (or perfor-

Table 1.4

The Planning Continuum

Strategic Planning ◄——►	Tactical Planning
• Long time horizon	• Short time horizon
• Less certainty	• More certainty
• Less structured	• More structured
• More ends-oriented	• More means-oriented
• Poorly defined information requirements	• Well-defined information requirements
• Tends to have irreversible impact	• Tends to have reversible impact
• Focuses on the whole	• Focuses on parts

mance objectives) to be achieved must be established before the means of achieving them can be determined. Tactical planning focuses mainly on means. In effect, the ends used in tactical plans come from the means of strategic plans. Second, strategic planning is less structured because it has *poorly defined information requirements.* We can be less clear about the information we need now to make a strategic choice that may not have an impact for five years. Tactical planning, by contrast, is more routine and repetitive and requires very specific information. More formal and well-defined information systems are needed; they are often computerized because of the amount of information needed and its changing nature.

Strategic plans lead to decisions that are major commitments of present and future resources. As a result, they tend to have an *irreversible impact.* A tactical choice, such as how much to order this month from a certain supplier, has much less of an impact than the strategic decision to build a new warehouse. If a mistake is made on the order quantity, a supplemental order can be placed; if a mistake is made in the size, location, or timing of the warehouse construction, the firm is stuck with a costly, inefficient facility. Finally, strategic planning *focuses more on the whole* organization, cutting across functional areas and departments. This view of strategic planning recognizes that plans and decisions made in one area affect the plans and decisions made in other areas.

Operations Strategy

Strategy within the operations function is a natural extension of corporate strategy and is formulated in much the same way. The focus of **operations strategy** is on ways to achieve organizational goals and carry out the corporate strategy. Operational shortcomings are determined by comparing the current and projected capabilities of the production system with the requirements of the corporate strategy. Shortcomings are filled, taking advantage of distinctive competencies, by modifying strategies on such things as degree of automation, facility location, capacity, suppliers, and inventories. Only when these shortcomings cannot be overcome with available resources and distinctive competencies must the operations manager alert top management that corporate strategy must be revised.

Operations strategy is best understood within the context of individual decision areas. We therefore examine the strategic issues of operations management as they arise within the topics of later chapters. For now, we need to emphasize only three points:

1. Operations can be a competitive weapon or a millstone.
2. Decisions in operations should be linked.
3. The more fundamental (strategic) choices must be addressed first, but success also depends on tactical choices and detailed analysis.

Box 1.3

OPERATIONS AS A COMPETITIVE WEAPON

Competitors had to rethink their strategies when IBM's Personal Computer AT was introduced. It was high-powered as expected, with speed doubled and maximum memory tripled. What was not expected was the aggressive pricing. IBM's strategy is to become the lowest cost manufacturer in the personal-computer business, and in doing so become the most aggressively priced. Competitors had to adjust, concentrating on narrower markets, emphasizing overseas countries, selling "brandless machines" to be resold under other labels, or offering new features not in the PC AT. Some "clone" manufacturers have had to move out of the PC business entirely.

Source: "IBM's AT Computer Puts Pressure on Rivals and Rest of Its PC Line," *The Wall Street Journal,* October 17, 1984.

A Competitive Weapon. Operations concentrates on the resource side of corporate strategy, where the bulk of the organization's human and financial assets usually are committed. More than 15 years ago Wickham Skinner suggested that the production system can be either a competitive weapon or a millstone. He concluded that all too often it has become a millstone, with top management unknowingly abdicating large portions of corporate strategy to operations managers. For this reason, many operations policies reflect incorrect assumptions about corporate strategy. This lack of understanding can bind the firm to inappropriate resource mixes for years into the future.

Largely because of foreign competition and the technological explosion, attention is once again turning to operations. There is a growing recognition that a firm competes not only with new products, good marketing, and skillful finance, but also with unique competencies in operations. Finding ways to offer superior products and services at the same or lower prices is a formidable competitive weapon. Use of this weapon is illustrated in Box 1.3, which describes the introduction by IBM of the AT personal computer.

Linking Decision Areas. A key to success is the ability to link the various decision areas in operations to best meet overall corporate strategy. Plans, policies, and actions within operations must all be focused in the same direction and be mutually supportive if organizational goals are to be met successfully. Quality, automation, capacity, and inventory decisions must not be made independently; individual choices may make sense on their own but collectively may not add up to the best result.

Strategy and Analysis. Strategic planning suggests that our first concern is with *first-order* questions. We must decide whether to hold an item in inventory before deciding about how low the inventory should get before we reorder. Similarly, a first-order question is whether to expand on the same site or relocate, whereas a second-order question is the size of the new parking lot. To help you focus on such first-order questions, we introduce each chapter with some managerial issues that have a major impact on that aspect of operations management.

Look back at the decision areas in Table 1.3. The longer range (and more strategic) types of choices, such as product plans, competitive priorities, and the positioning strategy are listed at the top. We address such questions in the earlier chapters of this book. Even though we cover more tactical questions in later chapters, you should not conclude that they are unimportant. Taken together tactical decisions have a major cumulative effect. For example, millions of dollars are at stake in completing a power plant or a hotel on time. This issue is one of scheduling and appears near the bottom of the list in Table 1.3. Scheduling is a decision area that requires detailed analysis.

In fact, much of tactical planning depends on reasoned and careful analysis. The field of operations management draws on a wide variety of analytic techniques, ranging from simple lists of pros and cons to sophisticated linear programming models, simulation models, and computer-based information systems. Strategy and analysis are complementary and both are necessary. Each can be viewed separately but actually is part of a whole.

EVOLUTION OF OPERATIONS MANAGEMENT

Operations management has an interesting past and challenging future. Although the formal study of operations management began only in the twentieth century, the activity itself is ancient. The Egyptian pyramids, Greek Parthenon, and Great Wall of China represent significant production achievements. Particularly noteworthy milestones are repeatability, automation, scientific management, and the modern era.

Repeatability

One of the first steps taken toward efficiency was achieving some degree of **repeatability** in doing a task. One way to increase repeatability is to create more specialized jobs requiring only limited skills. The ancient Chinese and Greeks developed such specialization, with workers confining themselves to particular crafts or trades. Another way to increase repeatability is to standardize products and parts. Eli Whitney's manufacturing scheme for firearms in the early 1800s was based on interchangeable parts and went far to increase repeatability and standardize processes. While specialization and standardization can be undesirable if taken to extremes, the concept of repeatability is an important one to this day.

Automation

More repeatability, through standardized parts and specialized jobs, made automation possible. Automation means that capital is substituted for labor. Until the 1700s, manufacturing tended to be labor intensive and done on a small scale. This changed with the Industrial Revolution in England. Power-driven machinery was introduced to perform jobs previously done manually. Capital requirements for these power sources created the need for centralized facilities. Work shifted to factories from homes and craft shops. Automation and technological advances are still continuing; whereas the steam engine and double-entry bookkeeping were once the state of the art; today it is automatic teller machines, computers, lasers, and robots.

Scientific Management

The larger scale of production introduced by the Industrial Revolution created more complexity and with it the need for better management. Managing productive systems emerged as a field of study in the early 1900s. A new management philosophy called **scientific management** emerged. The key premise was that any operation could be improved by breaking it down into components, measuring the work content, and seeking ways to improve work methods. In the factory a middle-level production department gained much of the control over manufacturing issues formerly handled by the president and foremen.

The Modern Era

The complexity and scope of operations management have increased geometrically since World War I. Building on the early efforts of scientific management, operations management embraced a wide range of behavioral and quantitative techniques. The use of behavioral techniques began in 1925 with the famous study at Western Electric's Hawthorne plant. Productivity was found to depend not just on the physical environment but also on social norms and personal feelings. Designing and operating production systems that improve the quality of work life and long-run productivity still challenge operations managers. Another development has been the increasing application of mathematical and statistical models to the solution of management problems. Linear programming, inventory models, learning curves, and simulation are a few examples of these methods. Many of these techniques would not be feasible without the computer, which became a practical reality in the 1950s.

The field of operations management as it is now known had emerged by the 1950s. More recent developments include: (1) extension of management concepts, principles, and methods to the service sector; (2) growing recognition of the importance of the strategic side of operations; (3) rapidly changing technologies; and (4) intense pressure of foreign competition. These developments make operations management particularly challenging and vital now and for the years to come.

CHAPTER HIGHLIGHTS

This book is for an introductory course in operations management. It addresses the strategic issues of operations, without sacrificing the analytical side of decision making. Highlights of this first chapter are:

- Production processes transform inputs (workers, managers, equipment, facilities, materials, energy, and external information) into outputs (goods or services).
- Trends in productivity and the service sector offer new challenges to operations managers.
- Service systems, in contrast to manufacturing systems, tend to have intangible products that cannot be inventoried, more direct contact with the customer, shorter response times, local markets, more labor-intensive operations, and less measurable quality. Nonetheless, the distinctions are relative. When making decisions, managers of both manufacturing and service organizations must be fully aware of where their organizations are and should be on the continuum between goods producers and service producers.
- Operations management can be viewed as a function, a profession, and a set of decisions, concerned with the design and operation of production systems.
- A rational decision-making process includes problem recognition, problem formulation, analysis of alternatives, and choice and implementation of an alternative.
- Decision areas in operations management include product plans, competitive priorities, positioning strategy, quality management, process design, technological choices, work-force management, capacity, maintenance, location, layout, materials management, production and staffing plans, master production scheduling, inventory, scheduling, and quality control. Each succeeding type of decision has a shorter time horizon and is more tactical but has an important cumulative effect on system performance.
- Corporate strategy determines (1) the organization's mission; (2) how to acquire and allocate resources to achieve the mission; and (3) performance objectives. Top management must scan the external environment, guide the organization's adjustment to changes in the environment, and exploit distinctive competencies.
- Strategic planning, in contrast to tactical planning, means a longer time horizon, less certainty, less structure, an ends orientation, poorly defined information requirements, and a focus on the whole organization.
- Operations strategy is a natural extension of corporate strategy and involves three important concepts: (1) operations can be a formidable competitive weapon; (2) the various decisions in operations must be linked; and (3) first-order decisions are paramount, even though tactical decisions have a major cumulative effect.

- Historical milestones in the evolution of operations management include steps toward repeatability, automation, and scientific management. Since World War I, the scope and complexity of the operations function have escalated. A wide range of management concepts and tools, both behavioral and quantitative, has been built. Computer advances have had a major impact and are a continuing driving force behind rapid technological developments.

KEY TERMS

corporate strategy
distinctive competencies
operations management
operations strategy
productivity
repeatability
scientific management

STUDY QUESTIONS

1. Identify the inputs and outputs for four of the following firms.
   (a) hotel
   (b) public warehouse
   (c) paper mill
   (d) newspaper company
   (e) supermarket
   (f) home office of bank
2. What do the productivity trends in Figs. 1.2 and 1.3 mean? Do you expect them to continue? Explain.
3. Why is productivity of particular interest to the field of operations management?
4. Do the employment shifts to the service sector mean that the demand for goods is declining? Do you expect these employment trends to continue at the same pace? Why?
5. What are the usual distinctions between goods-producers and service-producers? Identify at least two types of firms that do not fit the pattern, explaining the reasons for your choices.
6. Which disciplines contribute significantly to the field of operations management? What does this imply for the necessary skills of operations managers?
7. What types of jobs are available in operations management?
8. List at least three types of decisions that deal with the design of a production system, along with a sample question for each one. Do the same for three types of decisions that deal with the operation of the production system.
9. What questions does an organizational mission statement answer?
10. How are environmental scanning, adjusting to environmental change, and distinctive competencies related?
11. What are the differences between strategic and tactical planning?
12. How can linking decisions better help make operations a competitive weapon? Can tactical decisions be ignored?
13. What are two ways of increasing repeatability?

PROBLEMS

1. Kathryn Shoemaker established the Grandmother's Chicken Restaurant in Middlesburg five years ago. It features a unique recipe for chicken, "just like grandmother used to make." The facility is homey, with relaxed and friendly service. Business has been very good during the past two years, both for lunch and dinner. Customers normally must wait about 15 minutes to be served, although complaints about service delays have increased. Kathryn is currently considering whether to expand the current facility or open a similar restaurant in neighboring Uniontown, which has been growing rapidly.

   (a) What types of strategic and tactical plans must Kathryn make?
   (b) What environmental forces could be at work at Middlesburg and Uniontown that Kathryn should consider?
   (c) What are the possible distinctive competencies of Grandmother's?

SELECTED REFERENCES

Berry, Steven, "Practitioner's Views on the Importance of Selected Production Management Topics," *Production and Inventory Management,* (Third Quarter 1979), pp. 1–17.

Chase, Richard B., and Nicholas J. Aquilano, *Production and Operations Management: A Life Cycle Approach,* 4th ed. Homewood, Ill.: Richard D. Irwin, 1985.

Collier, David A., "Managing a Service Firm: A Different Management Game," *National Productivity Review* (Winter 1983–1984), pp. 36–45.

Fitzsimmons, James A., and Robert S. Sullivan, *Service Operations Management.* New York: McGraw-Hill, 1982.

Groff, Gene K., and John R. Muth, *Operations Management: Analysis for Decisions.* Homewood, Ill.: Richard D. Irwin, 1972.

"Hard Times Push B-Schools into Basics," *Business Week* (August 30, 1982), pp. 23–24.

Hayes, Robert H., and William J. Abernathy, "Managing Our Way to Economic Decline," *Harvard Business Review* (July–August 1980), pp. 67–77.

Hax, Arnoldo C., and Nicolas S. Majluf, "The Corporate Strategic Planning Process," *Interfaces,* vol. 14, no. 1 (January–February 1984), pp. 47–60.

Mabert, Vincent A., and Michael J. Showalter, *Cases in Operations Management.* Plano, Texas: Business Publications, 1984.

Porter, Michael E., *Competitive Advantage: Creating and Sustaining Superior Performance.* New York: The Free Press, 1985.

"Schools Again Offer Courses in Production," *The Wall Street Journal* (January 26, 1981) p. 23.

Schroeder, Roger G., *Operations Management: Decision Making in the Operations Function,* 2nd ed. New York: McGraw-Hill, 1985.

Skinner, Wickham, "Manufacturing—Missing Link in Corporate Strategy," *Harvard Business Review* (May–June 1969), pp. 136–145.

Skinner, Wickham, *Manufacturing: The Formidable Competitive Weapon.* New York: John Wiley and Sons, 1985.

Stanbeck, Thomas M., Jr., P. J. Bearse, T. J. Noyelle, and R. A. Karasek, *Services: The New Economy*. Totowa, N.J.: Allanheld, Osmun and Co., 1981.

Starr, Martin, "The Performance of Japanese-Owned Firms in America: A Survey Report," Center for Operations, Columbia Business School, 1985.

Steiner, George A., *Top Management Planning*. New York: Macmillan, 1983.

Wheelwright, Steven C., "Manufacturing Strategy: Defining the Missing Link," *Strategic Management Journal*, vol. 5 (1984), pp. 71–91.

CHAPTER

PRODUCT PLANNING AND COMPETITIVE PRIORITIES

Some Managerial Issues

- What products (goods or services) should we offer?
- When should we enter and exit the market during a product's life cycle?
- When should we add or drop products?
- What should be our competitive priorities?
- Should we emphasize price, quality, or flexibility?
- What is our best positioning strategy?
- What impact does this choice have on our other decisions in operations?

Chapter Outline

In Chapter 1 you learned that corporate strategy defines the firm's mission, answering questions such as:

- What business are we in?
- What should it be 10 years from now?
- Who are our customers?

The answers define the products, whether goods or services, to be offered. **Product planning** is the whole spectrum of activities leading up to the introduction, revision, or dropping of products. Although product planning takes place primarily at the corporate-strategy level, it is the logical starting point for formulating operations strategy. When we know product characteristics we can effectively design and operate the production system.

Our coverage of product planning begins with a discussion of product life cycles, planning stages, and entrance–exit strategies. We then present the dimensions on which operations must excel in offering the chosen products. These dimensions are called *competitive priorities.* Next, we describe operations at two plants to show how actual operations are organized around competitive priorities. Finally, we show how an organization's choice of a process focus or product focus, called the *positioning strategy,* links decisions throughout the operations function.

PRODUCT PLANNING

Greater interest in product planning has been spurred recently by intense competition, expiration of patents, and the rapid pace of technological innovation. Product planning is an ongoing process—a job that is never finished—as shown in Box 2.1. When the shortwave radio market dried up, the R. L. Drake Company turned to marine radios and then satellite-television receivers. Competitive pressures are once again forcing the company to review its plans.

Many small companies start (as did R. L. Drake) with a limited number of products, often based on a process or product innovation of the founding entrepreneur. As time passes, though, the firm must add new products, either to replace those being phased out or to expand its market penetration. Larger firms, which have many more products, face the same challenge. More than $50 billion are spent each year to create new products or improve old ones. More than half of a firm's dollar volume typically comes from products introduced within the last ten years.

Box 2.1

NEW PRODUCTS AT R. L. DRAKE COMPANY

Mr. Drake's father founded the R. L. Drake Company at Miamisburg, Ohio, during World War II as a producer of shortwave radios. Although successful for over 30 years, the firm's revenues were dropping rapidly by 1978. Ham-radio sales were declining with little hope for resurgence. Mr. Drake, the firm's chief executive officer, altered the product for use on ships. However, Japanese producers began taking over this marine-radio market by 1981. Sales were still $7.3 million, but he knew the firm would soon be out of business if a new product wasn't found.

The new product idea of satellite-television receivers came from a distributor. Mr. Drake decided to bet the family business on making receivers for the consumer market. There wasn't a major company producing them and he believed the market was about to take off. Equipment for producing the earlier products, including a $250,000 machine to assemble circuit boards, was easily adapted to the new product. The company enjoyed fast success and the work force soon numbered 430 employees. There were only 340 employees earlier when ham-radio sales were at their peak. However, some bigger U.S. companies and Japanese firms are beginning to enter the market, forcing Mr. Drake to review his plans once again.

Source: "Losing Sales, Radio Company Finds Success in New Product," *The Wall Street Journal,* February 27, 1984.

Product Life Cycles

The concept of a **product life cycle,** as depicted in Fig. 2.1, best illustrates the need for introducing new products. If a firm does not introduce new products periodically, it will eventually decline. Since sales and profits from any given product eventually decrease, new products should be introduced before existing products hit their peak. The five stages of the product life cycle are product planning, introduction, growth, maturity, and decline.

During the *product planning* stage, ideas for new goods or services are generated, screened, and translated into final designs. Profits attributed to a product are negative at this point; sales have not begun and no revenues are coming in, yet development costs are being incurred. During the *introductory* stage, sales begin and profits are generated. Production efforts are still being refined and can best be characterized as fluid and evolving. Marketing efforts may be modest (as when introducing prescription drugs) or near their peak (as with new textbooks). Since sales volumes have not reached their high point, annual profits are relatively small, even though unit profit margins may be large. Successful products next enter a rapid *growth* stage. Sales and profits rise as in the introductory stage, but the jump in sales is particularly

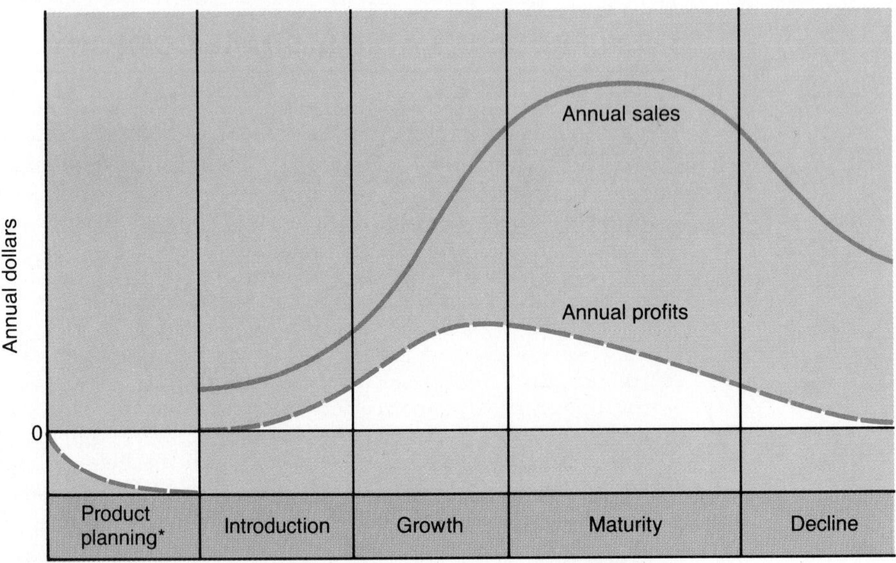

Figure 2.1

A Product's Life Cycle.

* There are negative profits during the product planning stage, since there are no revenues yet.

dramatic. The mandate for operations during this stage is somehow to keep up with demand; efficiency is less of a concern. Sales level off and profits begin to decline during the *maturity* stage. New competitors create pressures to cut costs and slow the squeeze on unit profit margins. Operations now must stress efficiency, although intensified marketing efforts to differentiate the product can ease the pressure. Ultimately, the product enters the *decline* stage and the product becomes obsolete. Sales and profits decrease to the point where the product is dropped by the firm. Either the demand for the product disappears or a better and/or less expensive product is now available to satisfy the demand.

The length of life cycles varies widely from product to product. The demand for shortwave radios from the R. L. Drake Company lasted for 30 years, whereas the demand for marine radios lasted only three years. Looking only at the time required to market a product after the idea was born (the first stage of the life cycle), we find that it took

- Eversharp only eight months to introduce ball-point pens;
- Gerbers only one year to introduce strained baby food; and
- Dictaphone Corporation less than two years to introduce the portable recording machine.

In contrast with these short time spans, it took 15 years for

- Xerox to introduce electrostatic copying machines;
- Polaroid to introduce the color-pack camera; and
- Bell Laboratories to introduce transistors.

Product life cycles have been particularly short in the high-tech computer and microchip industry. Products of companies such as Atari and Intel Corporation can become obsolete in months. The roller-coaster effect of short product life cycles requires special management skills. Quick, independent action is more highly prized in this type of situation than it is at companies enjoying longer product life cycles.

Entrance–Exit Strategies

The life cycle of a product can be quite different for a company than for a whole industry. The R. L. Drake Company may move out of the market of satellite-television receivers, even though these products may be produced by other firms for years to come. Table 2.1 shows the three basic strategies for entering and exiting the market. The choice of the **entrance–exit strategy** has important implications for the operations function.

Strategy A. The most natural strategy is for a firm to enter the market when the product is first introduced and stay with it until the end of its life cycle. Polaroid and Xerox are examples of companies that developed a new product

Table 2.1

Entrance–Exit Strategies

Strategy	Stage to Enter	Stage to Exit	Implications for Operations
A. Enter early and exit late	Introduction	Decline	Transition from low-volume, flexible producer to high-volume, low-cost producer
B. Enter early and exit early	Introduction	Maturity	Low-volume, flexible producer
C. Enter late and exit late	Growth	Decline	High-volume, low-cost producer

Source: Robert H. Hayes and Steven C. Wheelwright, "The Dynamics of Process-Product Life Cycles," *Harvard Business Review* (March–April 1979), pp. 127–136.

and grew with it throughout its life cycle. This strategy requires operations to evolve from a low-volume, flexible production system into a high-volume, low-cost system. Such a shift is always a challenge because it means changing over to a whole new way of doing things. The news item in Box 2.2 illustrates the strain of transition at Tallgrass Technologies. Similar growing pains have been experienced by companies (such as Apple, Atari, and Commodore Inter-

Box 2.2

GROWING PAINS AT TALLGRASS TECHNOLOGIES

Tallgrass Technologies Corporation is learning to cope with dazzling growth. When IBM entered the personal-computer market in 1981, the whole industry mushroomed, including the Tallgrass's new data-storage products. In two short years, the firm's annual sales jumped from $1 million to $60 million and the work force grew from 14 to 280 employees. Fat unit profit margins exceeded 60 percent and were a forgiving ally. However, times are changing. When Mr. Allen founded the firm, there were hardly any competitors. Now there are over 60. Mr. Allen is bringing in more management talent to equip the firm with a more formal organization to handle its larger size. Tallgrass must be ready for a possible shakeout in the industry as it enters a different phase.

Source: "High-Tech Firm Avoids Perils that Accompany Fast Growth," *The Wall Street Journal,* December 10, 1984.

national) in the personal-computer industry when they moved from a small, freewheeling venture to a large corporation. Strategy A can have a big offsetting advantage. By entering the market early, the firm gets a head start. This early learning and added experience may allow the early entrant to produce a better product at a lower cost than late entrants can produce initially.

Strategy B. Small, product-innovative firms often choose to stay in the low-volume, customized business. This strategy requires no painful transition. When the product reaches the maturity stage and profit margins begin to be squeezed, the firm drops the product and introduces new ones. Throughout the product life cycle, operations management maintains a smaller, flexible production system that is adaptable to changing products.

Strategy C. A firm waits in the wings until other innovative firms introduce a new product. After it is clear that the product has significant market appeal and will achieve high sales volumes, the firm enters the market with an automated, efficient production facility. Some companies even accompany their entry with *preemptive pricing,* setting their prices considerably lower than those of their competitors. This ensures the high volumes necessary for low unit costs. This strategy also avoids a transition and is likely to be selected by large firms, such as IBM when it entered the personal-computer market. Large firms can exploit their mass-marketing capabilities, established distribution channels, and easier access to capital markets to finance the massive investment needed for top efficiency in capital-intensive operations.

Product Planning Stage

Product planning is a four-step process, with corporate strategy exerting the guiding influence, as shown in Fig. 2.2. The process is most active during the first stage of the product life cycle.

Corporate Strategy. Product planning must fit the firm's strategic plans. Although it is an essential part of strategic planning, the definition of the firm's mission may be too narrow or too broad. If it is too narrow, promising growth opportunities will be missed. If the mission is too broad, the firm gets into areas where it has no distinctive competencies. The descriptions in Box 2.3 show that Gould, Inc. broadened its mission with considerable success; General Mills, Inc., first broadened its mission, then decided to narrow it and get back to what the company does best; and Cummins Engine Company considered broadening its mission but then decided to stay with its basic product line.

Step 1: Idea Generation. New product ideas can come from within the firm—from managers, employees, or Research and Development (R&D) laboratories. They can also come from the outside—from company distributors, outside licensers, and inventors. You may be surprised to learn that DuPont

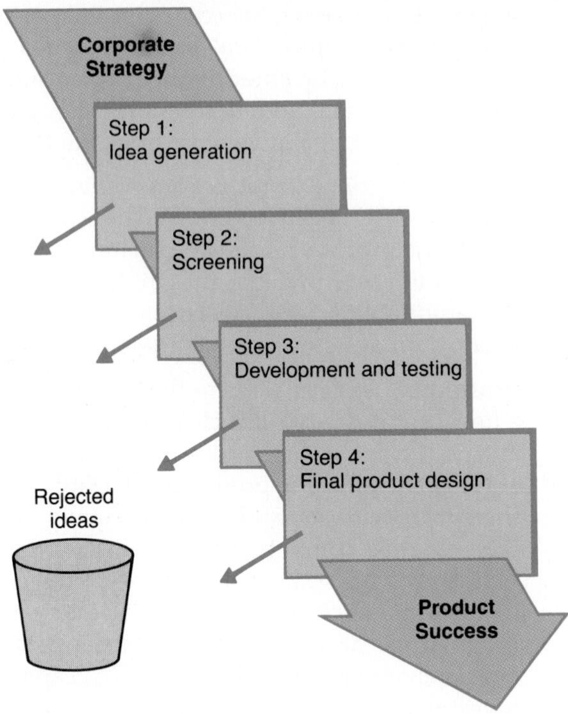

Figure 2.2

Steps in Product Planning.

Corporation, well-known for innovative new products, gets two-thirds of its new products from outside inventions.

New ideas can be either *market-oriented* or *technology-oriented.* The most obvious source of new ideas is marketing, which must be in tune with the needs of customers or clients. Market studies may reveal better ways of serving established markets or the chance to enter new markets. Examples of successful market-oriented ideas are dial-a-call services by psychologists, a new delivery service of fast foods to university students who live in dormitories, the five-minute single serving of Pizza Hut, and frozen vegetables in resealable plastic bags. Technology-oriented ideas include medical lasers to remove tumors, a compound of rubber and Teflon that might yield almost indestructible windshield wipers, or GM's diesel-engine innovation, which long ago put steam locomotive manufacturers out of business. Many such ideas come from the one-half million scientists whose research costs billions of dollars each year. Large firms do most of the industrial R&D work; 80 percent of R&D is done by firms employing more than 5000 people. Technological innovations can affect either the *product* or the *process.* Numerous inventions in the electronics and computer industries are spawning many new products. Inventions can also improve processes within the production system, which in turn may create new products. For example, automatic teller machines now make 24-hour service feasible for banks.

Step 2: Screening. There is never a dearth of new product ideas, so the real question is: Which ones are worthwhile? By one estimate, only one of every 60 ideas is actually commercialized, and only eight make it past the screening

Box 2.3

SHOULD THE MISSION BE BROADER OR NARROWER?

Make It Broader

Shedding a Rust Bowl image, Gould, Inc., expanded its mission beyond making batteries and engine parts. It now offers a wide range of high-tech electronics. When Mr. Ylvisaker took over as chairman in 1967, earnings were only $4.2 million. They have since swelled to $93.6 million and the "new Gould" has taken shape. The company now manufactures minicomputers, semiconductors, factory automation equipment, and test and measurement instruments. Skeptics questioned whether such diversity could be tied together as one company. However, the product lines are becoming complementary. One example is the minicomputers that can be used in the factory automation line.

Make It Narrower

General Mills, Inc., dropped its toy and fashion businesses to concentrate on its flagship of food processing and restaurants. The company left behind the two higher risk, capital-intensive businesses, since they demanded a more entrepreneurial style than the food company provided. For example, the Izod sportswear line wasn't keeping up with volatile consumer tastes. Narrowing their missions is a back-to-basics move made by several companies in the food industry that had difficulty with products that took them away from their distinctive competencies.

Cummins Engine Company decided to bet its future on just one product—diesel engines. It earlier flirted with diversification into products ranging from skis to computer equipment. With a preeminence as a diesel-engine producer, it has decided to concentrate on what it does best. To fend off foreign competition, Cummins spent over twice its net worth to retool its manufacturing facilities. It also developed new engine models and is moving into the lower horsepower market.

Sources: "Gould Reshapes Itself into High-Tech Outfit Amid Much Turmoil," *The Wall Street Journal,* October 3, 1984; "General Mills Inc. Will Spin Off Toy Group and Sell Fashion Units," *The Wall Street Journal,* March 27, 1985; "Cummins Decides to Go with Its Strength as It Pins Hopes on Diesel Truck Engines," *The Wall Street Journal,* July 3, 1984.

step. Some ideas do not fit the company's mission. Others are dismissed for failing to meet

1. marketing criteria,
2. operations criteria, or
3. financial criteria.

Marketing criteria include competition, effects on current products, marketability to present customers, patent status, promotional requirements, necessary after-market services, and changes in distribution channels. *Operations* criteria include technical feasibility and compatibility with current processes, work force, equipment, facility locations, and supplier capabilities. *Financial* criteria include required corporate size, investment requirements, risk, expected annual sales, profit margin per unit, and anticipated length of the product's life cycle. In a sense, the financial tests bring marketing and operations considerations together. Marketing criteria relate mainly to future revenues, whereas operations criteria relate directly to costs.

Step 3: Development and Testing. Next, the idea's technical feasibility is thoroughly pretested, which often involves considerable engineering work. Prototypes may be built for testing and analysis of the product's features. Beyond engineering, operations gets involved in assessing process, facility, and material needs. Finally, marketing tests are needed to obtain customer response and avoid the premature scrapping of a potentially good product. Trial tests in limited markets or with customer panels help to gauge customer reactions to the specific features of the product, packaging choices, and even promotional programs. Results of these tests may lead to changes in the product and the way it is presented before it is actually marketed. The end result should be reasonable assurance that the product is technically feasible, can be economically produced in quantity, and has customer appeal.

Product development and testing refine the exact features of the product. In the service industry three components of the "service bundle" (see Sasser, et al., 1978) must be clearly defined:

1. Facilitating goods.
2. Explicit services.
3. Implicit services.

For a restaurant, the facilitating goods include food, drink, table and chairs, and tableware. The second component includes characteristics defined by the five senses (such as taste, aroma, and atmosphere), speed of service, and quality of waiter service. The third component depends on the customer's preferences and is harder to define. It could be status, comfort, or a general sense of well-being.

In restaurant chains a prototype is usually built first. R. David Thomas started Wendy's Old-Fashioned Hamburgers in Columbus, Ohio, in 1969. At the first site, product features such as the menu, interior decor, and order processing service were carefully defined. Only after finishing this development and testing stage did Wendy's begin to expand and sell franchises.

Stage 4: Final Product Design. During final product design, product characteristics are defined in detail, often by lists of specifications, process formulas, and drawings. For a supermarket or an emergency service unit, maximum customer delay times may be established. For a utility boiler, detailed engineering drawings specify types of material and dimensions for each component. Substantial investments in financial and human resources are committed at this stage. Production begins, and marketing starts its promotional program with kick-off sales meetings and preview presentations at trade exhibits. In the case of multisite service firms (such as Wendy's), a limited number of facilities are added. If they prove successful, expansion to many new sites may proceed rapidly. In just one decade

- McDonald's went from 738 to 3750 units;
- Holiday Inns grew from 587 to 1750 inns; and
- Manpower, Inc.'s annual revenues grew from $47.3 to $161.2 million.

Life-Cycle Audits

Product planning is not limited to introducing new products. Other activities include revising existing products (a new mix for a faster rising cake or a lubricant that allows wire to be drawn faster) and eliminating products that are no longer an asset to the organization. Table 2.2 shows how companies in five industries (drugs, major appliances, food, clothing, and minor appli-

Table 2.2

Importance of Various Product Planning Activities

Activity	Importance*
Adding new products	41
Revising existing products	31
Finding new uses of existing products	15
Eliminating products	13

* Average score assigned by firms surveyed, where the highest possible score was 100.

Source: James T. Rothe, "The Product Elimination Decision," *MSU Business Topics*, Autumn 1970, pp. 45–52.

ances) ranked various product planning activities. Adding new products ranked first, followed closely by revising existing products.

To spot needs for revitalizing or eliminating products, **life-cycle audits** should be conducted. These audits evaluate a product in terms of changes (compared to the last several years) in sales and profits. Suppose that both sales and profits seem to be leveling off for a product. Looking back at Fig. 2.1, we can conclude that the product is entering the maturity stage. This is the time to rejuvenate the product, find ways to squeeze costs still more, stay with the product for a few more years, or simply drop it entirely. If both sales and profits were dropping, it would be in the decline stage. The only alternative would be to drop the product.

Product Screening Techniques

A critical step in product planning is screening, when most ideas are discarded. However, there is no guarantee that an optimal decision will be made at this stage, as the history of the following ill-fated products suggests.

- After painstaking market research, Ford launched the Edsel car with much fanfare. One enthusiastic dealer even unfurled a huge Edsel sign above San Francisco Bay. The company's high expectations were not met, and only about 100,000 cars were sold.
- IBM poured $40 million into promoting the PCjr. Production delays caused it to miss the Christmas season, and customers were dismayed at the high price and limited memory. Production of this model was discontinued, despite high initial expectations.
- Revlon, Inc., introduced a nail clipper that collected the clippings, but few customers decided that nail clippings were worth saving. The product was withdrawn.
- Extensive taste tests convinced Coca-Cola executives that customers would like the proposed change in the world's best-selling soft drink. They were surprised. We can now buy "New" Coke and "Classic" Coke.

There are two reasons for such failures. First, a great deal of *uncertainty* surrounds the choice. Making accurate forecasts of future sales, costs, and competitor reactions is difficult, if not perilous. Historical data for totally new products are nonexistent. Second, *multiple criteria* cannot be naturally merged into a single measure (such as dollars). Managers are hard pressed to estimate the dollar equivalent of operations compatibility or project risk.

Despite these obstacles, decisions must be made. At times some hard thinking in a quiet room is sufficient. At other times more formal procedures are needed. We will consider only two of these formal procedures: a preference matrix and break-even analysis.

Preference Matrix. Table 2.3 illustrates a **preference matrix** to evaluate a new product idea, thermal storage air conditioners. In this case let's say that management has chosen to evaluate new product ideas against six different criteria. The product's attractiveness is judged on a scale from 1 (worst) to 10 (best) for each criterion. Weights are assigned to the criteria in proportion to their perceived importance and sum to 100. Finally, a total score is obtained by summing the weighted scores (weight times score) for all the criteria. This score can be compared with those of other new product ideas or against a predetermined threshold. If management had established a threshold of at least 800, the thermal storage idea would not be pursued, since its score is only 750.

Not all managers are comfortable with this technique. It requires the manager to state the criterion weights before examining the alternatives. Sometimes the proper weights are not apparent until after the manager sees the scores for several alternatives. Only then can the manager decide what is important and what is not. The preference matrix also allows a low score on one criterion to be compensated for or overridden by high scores on others, which may or may not be realistic. The investment required for a new manufacturing process might exceed the firm's financial capability. In this case the new product idea must be dropped, no matter how high the scores were for the other criteria.

Break-Even Analysis. The **break-even analysis** technique deals primarily with the potential market volume and profit of a product idea. It helps the manager to answer questions such as:

1. Is the product's predicted sales volume sufficient to break even (neither earning a profit nor sustaining a loss)?

Table 2.3

Preference Matrix for Thermal Storage Air Conditioners

Performance Criterion	Weight (A)	Score (B)	Weighted Score (A × B)
Market potential	30	8	240
Unit profit margin	20	10	200
Operations compatibility	20	6	120
Competitive advantage	15	10	150
Investment requirement	10	2	20
Project risk	5	4	20
		Weighted score =	750

2. How low must the variable cost per unit be to break even, based on forecasts of sales and prices?
3. How low must the fixed cost be to break even?
4. How do price levels affect the break-even volume?

Break-even analysis assumes that total costs can be divided into fixed and variable components. If we let

$$p = \text{Price charged per unit sold,}$$
$$c = \text{Variable cost of each unit produced,}$$
$$F = \text{Fixed cost per year, and}$$
$$Q = \text{Number of units produced and sold per year,}$$

the variable cost, c, is the portion that varies directly with output. This cost is the incremental cost per unit for materials, labor, and usually some variable part of overhead. The fixed cost, F, is the portion of cost that remains constant for the relevant levels of output. This cost includes the equivalent annual cost of new equipment and facilities purchased (or rented) for the new product, including depreciation, interest, taxes, and insurance. The fixed cost can also include such items as the salaries of managers and staff, utilities, and portions of the sales or advertising budget. The difference between p and c is often called the *unit profit margin,* since it contributes both to profits and the covering of fixed costs.

Assume that the cost function is linear and consists of the fixed cost plus total variable costs ($F + cQ$). If we set total annual revenues (pQ) equal to the total cost and solve for Q, we get the break-even quantity:

$$pQ = F + cQ$$
$$(p - c)Q = F$$
$$Q = \frac{F}{p - c}$$

We can also find this break-even quantity graphically: It is the point on the graph where the total revenue line crosses the total cost line. Figure 2.3 demonstrates both the algebraic approach and the graphic approach for the case in which p is estimated at \$20, c at \$10, and F at \$100,000.

Break-even analysis cannot tell a manager whether to pursue or drop a new product idea. It does show what is likely to happen as a result of the forecasted costs and sales volumes. The manager can use different estimates for each variable to test the sensitivity of the decision to forecast errors. This technique is called **sensitivity analysis.** For example, suppose that the most pessimistic sales forecast for the product in Fig. 2.3 is 15,000 units, with the most likely level being 20,000. This means that the new product idea would do well, at least in terms of profits, if all other factors remain the same. Even the most pessimistic forecast lies above the break-even quantity.

$$Q = F/(p - c)$$
$$Q = 100{,}000/(20 - 10)$$
$$Q = 10{,}000$$

(a)

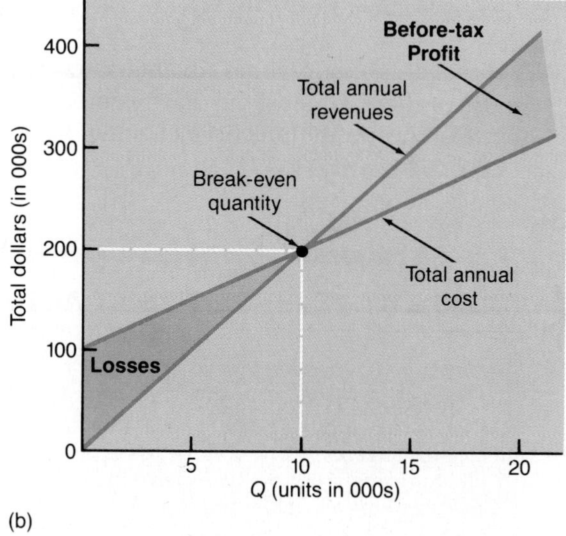

(b)

Figure 2.3

Break-Even Analysis: (a) Algebraic Solution; (b) Graphic Solution.

COMPETITIVE PRIORITIES

As important as choosing the products themselves is picking the dimensions on which to excel in producing those products. For example, deciding on the types of food to offer at a new restaurant is not enough. We must also determine and take advantage of our distinctive competencies, which set our restaurant apart from competitors. We have to decide how much to emphasize each of seven dimensions in operating the restaurant. These seven dimensions can be placed in four groups and collectively are called **competitive priorities**:

- *Cost*
  1. Low price
- *Quality level*
  2. High-performance design
  3. Fast delivery time

- *Quality reliability*
  4. Consistent quality
  5. On-time delivery
- *Flexibility*
  6. Product flexibility
  7. Volume flexibility

A firm gains a differential advantage by outperforming competitors on one or more of these dimensions. Each competitive priority is illustrated in Box 2.4 by reference to the practices of actual firms.

Box 2.4

COMPETITIVE PRIORITIES AT ACTUAL FIRMS

Low Price
Earl Scheib, Inc., of Beverly Hills operates 275 shops that offer a "no-frills" face-lift to cars at rock-bottom prices. Unit profit margins are protected by pinching every penny. Sales have increased at an annual rate of 15 percent and earnings are increasing at almost 50 percent per year.

High-Performance Design
The C. Hoare & Company, a bank founded in London in 1672, treats clients like royalty but charges a stiff price. Six descendants of the founder still run the family business. At least one is no more than an hour away, day or night. Customers are ushered in by a doorman in a frock coat. The teller counter is rimmed to easily handle umbrellas, with a drip gully carved below in the granite floor. The waiting room is lined with gold-rimmed ledgers in glass cases. Money is no object to the 8000 customers, whom most employees know by sight.

Fast Delivery Time
Fast-food wizard Donald Smith has taken a top position with Xian, a new Chicago-based Chinese restaurant chain. For Xian to succeed, Smith believes the maximum waiting time at the service counter must be cut from 80 to no more than 30 seconds. This speedup must be done without impairing the quality of food (which we define as performance design).

Consistent Quality
McDonald's restaurants are known for uniformly achieving their design specifications. The menu falls short of the delights of eating at a five-star restaurant, but you can expect that quality standards will be consistently met from one order to the next and from one restaurant to the next.

On-Time Delivery
Federal Express not only offers fast delivery time (overnight delivery), it also promises that the mail will be "absolutely, positively" delivered on

Low Price

Lowering prices squeezes unit profit margins, which can be partially offset by the higher volumes that may follow. The firm must also seek ways to minimize labor, materials, scrap, and overhead costs. But the ability to lower prices often means additional investment in facilities, equipment, and inventory. Lowering prices without jeopardizing quality usually occurs with undifferentiated products in the maturity stage of their life cycle. At that stage output levels tend to be high, and efficiency is likely to be at a peak with the

time. Meeting delivery promises comes at a cost. The same relatively inexpensive delivery by the U.S. Postal Service can cost as much as $25 if sent by Federal Express. Another example of on-time delivery is that of AT&T, which prided itself in installing 97 percent of new private lines by a promised date; this record slipped after divestiture.

Product Flexibility

When hit by an industry-wide slump, National Semiconductor Corporation decided to enter the growing market for custom-designed computer chips. They are made to suit the customer's specific requirements, rather than mass produced, and sold through a catalog. A custom-made chip can cost as much as $1 million.

Volume Flexibility

Thomas Woods, a 40-year-old contractor in Missouri, made it through the recent recession—the worst housing slump since World War II. He took some losses, but feels that he learned a good deal about how to control operations during the ups and downs of the housing market.

Sources: "Earl Scheib Is Still King of the No-Frills Paint Job," *Business Week,* May 27, 1985; "Bored with Queues? Some London Banks Let You Skip Them," *The Wall Street Journal,* October 26, 1984; "Fast-Food Whiz Donald Smith Is Hired to Make Chicago Firm National Chain," *The Wall Street Journal,* March 7, 1985; "Behind the Chaos in Phone Service," *U.S. News & World Report,* July 9, 1984; "National Semiconductor's Custom-Made Chips Are Bucking Company's General Sales Slump," *The Wall Street Journal,* February 12, 1985; "Builder Heeds Lessons Learned Surviving Last Housing Slump," *The Wall Street Journal,* November 19, 1984.

use of specialized equipment. In the context of break-even analysis, the fixed cost, F, is increased to achieve a sharply reduced variable cost, c.

Quality Level

The first of two quality level dimensions is *high-performance design*, which can mean superior features, close tolerances, and greater durability. It also includes the helpfulness and skill of the work force, whether sales clerks or gasoline attendants. After-sale support and financing may be part of the design specifications. For example, IBM now offers installment payment plans, credit cards, and equipment leasing. More than $1.5 billion worth of new IBM equipment is leased, which is a big boost to sales.

Fast delivery time is a different dimension of quality level. Delivery time is the elapsed time between receiving a customer's order and filling it. Industrial buyers often call this the lead time. A good delivery time can be a year for a major customized machine, several weeks for scheduling elective surgery, and minutes for an ambulance. Delivery times can be shortened by producing to inventory or having slack capacity.

Quality Reliability

Quality reliability reflects the consistency of the first two quality measures. *Consistent quality* measures the frequency with which the design specifications are met. A foundry might measure consistent quality as the percent of castings falling within the desired tolerances on selected dimensions. A cereal manufacturer might measure consistent quality as the frequency with which a box's contents match the nutritional information on the label. *On-time delivery* measures the frequency of meeting delivery time promises. Manufacturers measure on-time delivery as the percent of customer orders shipped when promised, with 95 percent often considered a good benchmark. A supermarket might measure on-time delivery as the percent of customers who must wait in the checkout line for less than three minutes.

Flexibility

Some firms give top priority to one of two types of flexibility. **Product flexibility** means that product designs are in a state of flux. Products are customized to individual preferences or have very short life cycles. Volumes for any individual product are low, since the firm competes on the basis of its ability to produce difficult, nonstandard products. The extreme case is one-of-a-kind production, where each new order is unique. Product flexibility can also mean the ability to make quick design changes and introduce new products quickly, such as in the high-tech industry.

Volume flexibility, on the other hand, is the ability to quickly accelerate or decelerate the rate of production to handle large fluctuations in demand. The time between peaks can be years, as with the cycles in the home-building industry or political campaigns. It can be months, as with a ski resort. It can even be hours, as with the systematic swings in demand from hour to hour at a major postal facility where mail is sorted and dispatched.

Trade-Offs

Sometimes a firm can improve cost, quality, and flexibility simultaneously. For example, it is not unusual for scrap and rework to account for 20–30 percent of a product's cost. A reduction in scrap and rework can sharply reduce costs and improve productivity. Improved quality can also help stimulate sales to the point where high-volume production is possible. Increased repeatability reduces unit costs, making higher quality possible at lower prices. Thus improved quality might actually be free.

Unfortunately, at some point further improvements on one dimension are accompanied by setbacks on one or more of the others. When design specifications are pushed to the top of the line, such as with Rolls Royce, premium prices are necessary. Higher prices reduce the firm's market share, which in turn cuts repeatability and increases costs. Higher prices also can be forced by shorter and more reliable delivery times (the $25 Federal Express package) and by increased product flexibility (the $1 million custom-made computer chip). Customization reduces repeatability, driving up costs. More customization can hurt delivery times. A customized product cannot be fully produced before its exact specifications are known. This condition applies equally to production of custom-made computer chips and "hold-the-pickle" hamburgers.

Thus managers must recognize the actual trade-offs that exist among the seven dimensions of competitive priorities. Much depends on the exact situation, including products, processes, distinctive competencies, and competition. Managers must judge which trade-offs are strongest in deciding which dimensions need particular emphasis. For example, it is easy for Earl Scheib, Inc., to emphasize not only low price but also quick (one-day) delivery times. Low product flexibility like that at McDonald's allows a fast mass-production process. The C. Hoare & Company enhances its top-quality image by also having fast delivery times. Loan inquiries are answered the day they are received, although this increases the price of the services provided.

Setting Competitive Priorities. It is intriguing to see how executives in North America (Canada, Mexico, and the United States), Europe (10 different countries), and Japan rate the importance of competitive priorities for their businesses. Figure 2.4 shows the average of responses to a survey of executives. They were asked to judge the importance of each dimension to their own businesses for the next five years. North American manufacturers rated

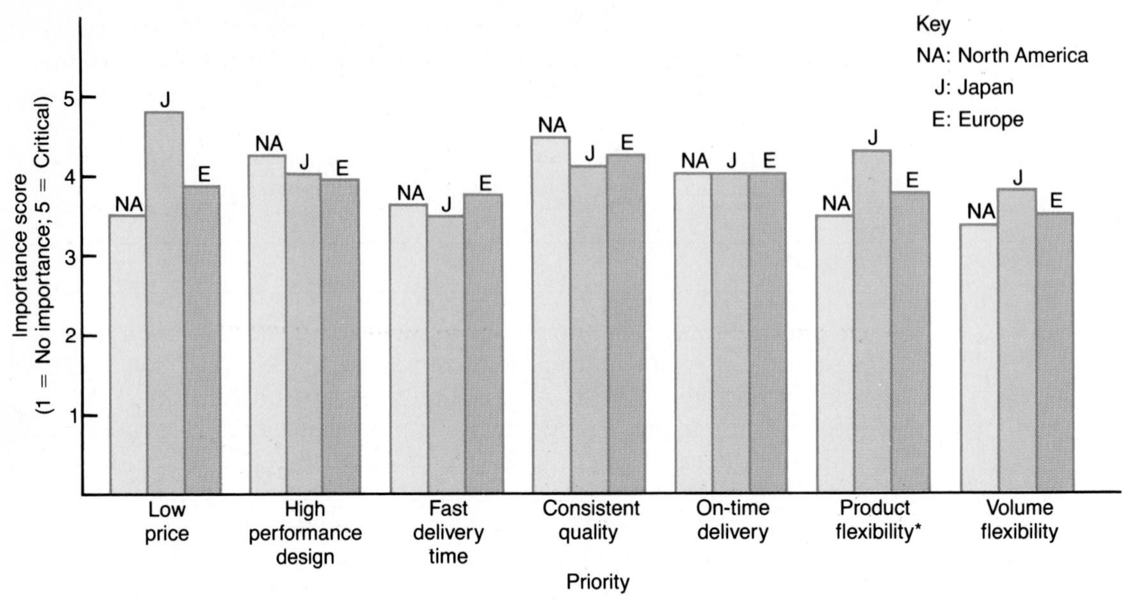

Figure 2.4

Competitive Priorities in North America, Japan, and Europe for the Next Five Years.

* Product flexibility is defined here as the ability to make rapid design changes or introduce new products quickly.

Source: Jeffrey Miller, Jinchiro Nakane, and Thomas Vollmann, "The 1983 Global Manufacturing Futures Survey" Research Report. School of Management, Boston University, April, 1983.

all four quality dimensions (high-performance design, fast delivery time, consistent quality, and on-time delivery) as the top priorities for the future, well ahead of price and flexibility. Their Japanese counterparts, in contrast, put low price at the top of the list by a wide margin, followed by product flexibility and consistent quality. Priorities of European executives tended to fall between the two extremes, with consistent quality ranked as the top priority. You should remember that Fig. 2.4 reflects priorities for the future, not current priorities. Japanese manufacturers rated consistent quality as a lower priority for the future, possibly because they are already doing well on this dimension.

Effective operations strategy begins with periodic reviews of competitive priorities. Managers should assess the firm's current performance in terms of the desired level on all seven dimensions. Performance should also be judged against the industry norm, a useful benchmark established by the firm's competitors. Then specific, measurable standards should be set. Examples of such standards for each competitive priority are

- reduce the price to $10 per unit;
- maintain the current tolerances on the product weight;
- promise deliveries within 3 weeks after receiving an order;
- decrease scrap losses by 10 percent;
- improve on-time delivery to 95 percent;
- increase the number of product options by 50 percent; and
- be able to double the production rate in just two months.

Figure 2.5 shows the results of a periodic review by one firm. Management decided that high costs were cutting into profits and, in order to achieve a significant price reduction, was willing to accept less product and volume flexibility. This type of decision has important implications for the choice of the positioning strategy for operations.

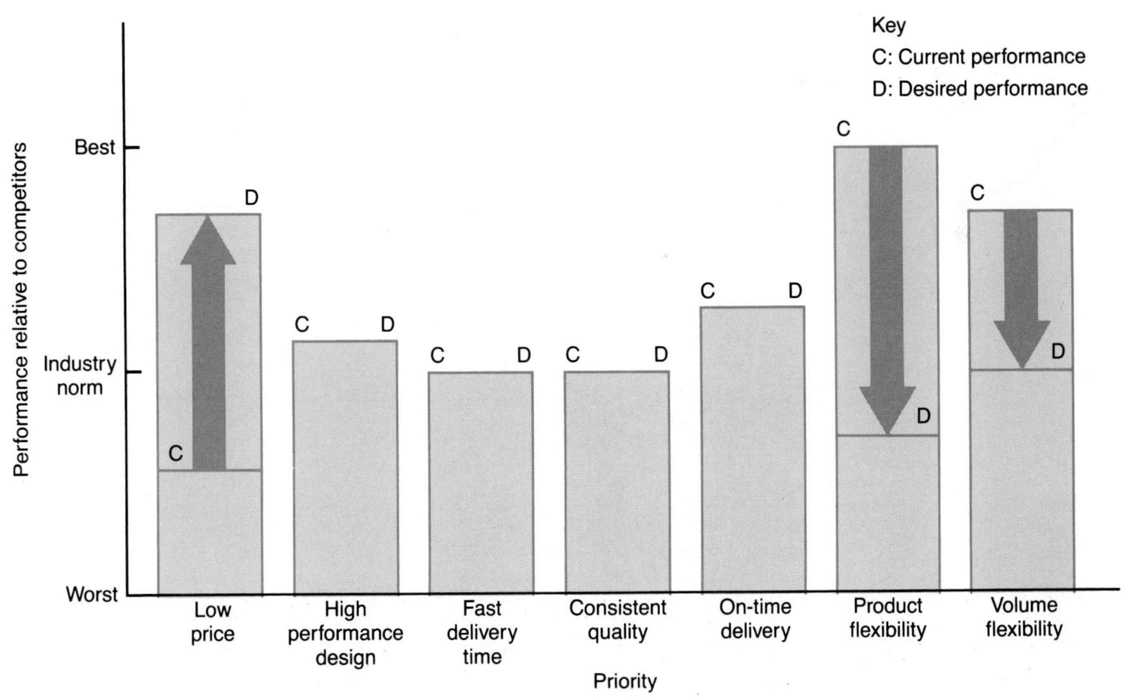

Figure 2.5

Setting Competitive Priorities.

POSITIONING STRATEGIES

For given product plans and competitive priorities, the operations manager must decide how to organize the production system. The choice the manager makes is called the **positioning strategy.** To understand this fundamental choice, look at Fig. 2.6. Each of three products has its own routing pattern (arrow), for a specified sequence of operations (circles).

Two entirely different positioning strategies are possible. With the **process-focused strategy,** shown in Fig. 2.6(a), the equipment and work force are

(a)

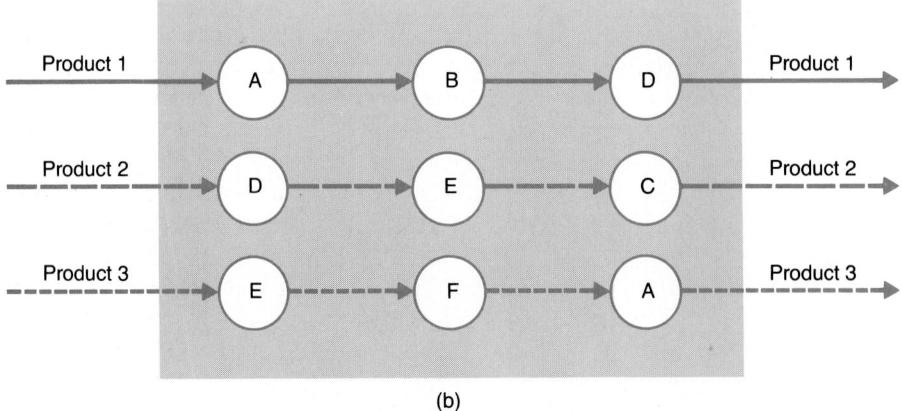

(b)

Figure 2.6

Two Different Positioning Strategies: (a) Process-Focused; (b) Product-Focused.

organized around the process. Only one area of the facility is set aside for operation A. This means that products 1 and 3 must share the same resources at operation A, while operation E must be flexible enough to handle both products 2 and 3. Thus product 1, for example, follows an A–B–D routing pattern. Turning to the **product-focused strategy,** shown in Fig. 2.6(b), you can see that resources are organized around the product. For example, there are two operation A's in the facility, one dedicated to product 1 and one to product 3. The routing pattern for each product is straightforward.

A Continuum of Strategies

Actually, there is a wide range of positioning strategies between these two extremes. This continuum of choices is represented in Fig. 2.7 by the diagonal from the process focus to the product focus. Figure 2.7 also shows how the choice relates to product volume (left to right) and flow pattern (top to bottom). Although a range of choices is available, few firms do or should position themselves too far off the diagonal. For example, a high-volume producer with a process focus can rarely compete successfully. Such a firm would have outdated, general purpose facilities providing needless flexibility but not top efficiency. Equally unlikely is a matching of customized production with the line flows of a product focus. Let's find out why this is so.

Process Focus. A process-focused strategy makes sense when a firm offers a wide variety of customized products, with many being one of a kind and made to order. Product volumes are too low to justify dedicating resources to individual products because resources would be idle too often. The only way to achieve reasonable resource utilization is to organize resources around similar processes. An overriding need for flexible operations usually results in less efficiency and repeatability. Owing to the uniqueness of the products, routings vary considerably from one order to the next; the flow pattern is jumbled and unpredictable. When visiting a process-focused facility, your first impression is likely to be one of chaos and confusion. Jumbled flows are apparent in Fig. 2.6(a), even with just three products. A production system with a process focus is often called a **job shop,** since it takes on a wide variety of small jobs and competes on the basis of resource flexibility. Process-focused businesses in manufacturing include aerospace firms, printing shops, and building contractors; and in the service industry, law firms, architectural firms, and general medical practices.

Intermediate Strategy. Halfway between a process focus and product focus is an intermediate strategy. Product or component volumes are larger than those in a process-focused firm. Some batching can be done by merging and handling several customer orders at the same time. If demand is sufficiently predictable, some standardized products or components can be made to stock. That is, they are produced in advance of receiving actual customer orders, when there is little risk of customers not wanting what has been produced. The flow pattern is still jumbled, but some dominant paths exist.

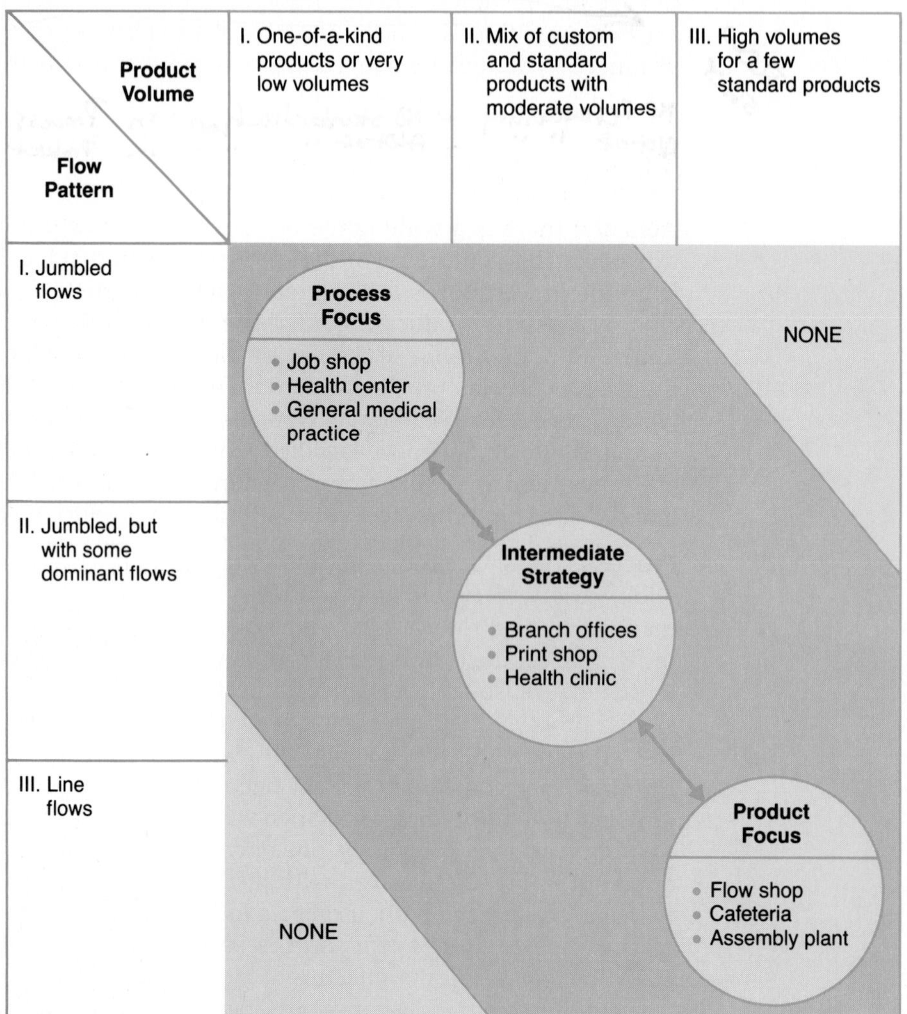

Figure 2.7

A Continuum of Positioning Strategies.

Source: Adapted from Robert H. Hayes and Steven C. Wheelwright, "Link Manufacturing Process and Product Life Cycles," *Harvard Business Review,* January–February 1979, pp. 133–140.

In some parts of the facility, for example, resources might be dedicated to one product or a group of similar parts. The types of businesses that utilize this strategy include heavy equipment manufacturing, garment manufacturing, catering, automobile repair shops, health clinics, and small-scale branch offices of service facilities, such as banks, brokerage houses, and advertising agencies.

Product Focus. A product-focused strategy fits high-volume production of a few standard products with line flows. With operations dedicated to just a few products, repeatability and specialization increase. Packaging and assembly options often make product diversity more apparent than real. The same product might be packaged in bottles or cans. Cars on an assembly line might go through the same basic operations, except the tire option: blackwalls for one car and whitewalls for the next. A product-focused production system is often called a **flow shop** because its routing patterns can be easily identified and follow the same path. Product standardization allows top efficiency. High-volume operations are highly specialized, with painstaking attention paid to each task. Examples of such efficiency are supermarkets (instead of the corner grocery store), credit cards (instead of individual bank loans), and medical clinics (replacing multiple trips to several doctors). Product-focused businesses include automobile manufacturers, manufacturers of electronic products, cafeterias, car washes, fast-food chains, and company home offices (supporting branch offices of service businesses).

High volumes and line flows lend themselves to highly automated facilities. Such facilities might operate around the clock to offset the huge capital investments required. Breweries, steel mills, food processing plants, oil refineries, public utilities, and some mail processing facilities are examples of continuous operations.

Customer Contact. In addition to product volumes and flow patterns, a third element is involved in the choice of a positioning strategy in the service sector. Service facilities normally have more customer contact than do manufacturing facilities. However, some service facilities have much more face-to-face customer contact than others. When such contact is high, operations are unbuffered from the customer, and services must be tailored to each customer's needs. The result is customized, low-volume production, which fits a process-focused strategy. An intermediate positioning strategy fits better when face-to-face and back-room work are more balanced. Customers interact with bank employees in the front office of a branch bank, while other operations are going on in the back office. In the back office more automation and batching of work is possible, increasing repeatability. Finally, some service facilities have virtually no face-to-face contact. Services are standardized and volumes are higher, as at home offices, distribution centers, and power plants, which fits a product focus.

LINKING PLANS, PRIORITIES, STRATEGIES, AND DECISIONS

Positioning strategy must be linked to product plans and competitive priorities, as shown in Table 2.4. A process focus meshes well with product plans favoring customized products, products with short life cycles, or early exit strategies. Volumes are low, but unit profit margins are high. Competitive priorities tend toward high-performance design quality, product flexibility, and volume flexibility. Less attention is paid to low price and quick delivery times. A product focus, on the other hand, makes sense when product plans call for standard products and long life cycles. Low prices, quick delivery times, and consistent quality are the top competitive priorities.

Positioning strategy also has a significant impact on other decisions and policies of an operations manager in process design, inventory, scheduling, and other areas. To gain insight into linkages, we now take a look at two entirely different companies: Longhorn Products and Suds Brewery. Each firm has a different positioning strategy, which has a far-reaching effect on how each facility is designed and operated. As you read along, watch for decisions that are linked and how they are linked at each plant.

Longhorn Products*

David Ream achieved his life-long dream in 1974 by starting his own company. It is a machine and fabrication shop located in San Antonio, Texas. After two difficult years, the firm has grown steadily. Sales in 1986 exceeded $500,000. Longhorn Products produces a wide variety of small metal parts that it sells to other manufacturers in the southwest. Some 50 percent of customer orders are one of a kind. The average order is for 35 pieces, and order quantities range from 1 to 500 pieces. Longhorn competes for orders through bidding processes, with the lowest bidders usually winning the jobs. Customer delivery lead times (which Mr. Ream calls "cycle times") vary from one to four months, depending on work content, material requirements, and capacity bottlenecks. Ream sees Longhorn's competitive priorities as producing a wide range of customized jobs, handling peaks and valleys in capacity, and consistently meeting due dates promised to customers. Although volumes are low, unit profit margins are high. The typical order brings in $2100 in revenue. Direct labor and material costs are approximately equal and total $960. The $1140 difference covers overhead costs such as employee benefits and equipment depreciation, as well as salaries for Ream, the accountant, and the shop supervisor—and goes to profit.

* A similar case on Norcen Industries can be found in Roger W. Schmenner, *Production/Operations Management: Concepts and Situations*, 2nd ed. Chicago: Science Research Associates, 1984.

Product planning at Longhorn takes the form of bidding on new designs. One of Ream's main tasks is to decide how the job will be manufactured, including the manufacturing operations to be performed and materials to be purchased. He responds to more than 100 requests per week and is awarded about 10 percent of the jobs bid on. The firm uses two sources of information when preparing bids. The first is a blueprint of the detailed design provided by the customer. If the order is repeat business, the blueprint is already on file. The second is a "routing sheet" listing each operation to be performed and time standards for it. The routing sheet also shows materials costs. If Longhorn has never produced the product before, Ream makes up a new routing sheet based on the blueprint and his estimates of time requirements. These estimates come from his experience with similar operations performed on other products.

Process Design, Technology, and Work-force Management. Time standards are updated to reflect actual experience. When a job is released, it is accompanied by the blueprint, routing sheet, and a "record card." Each worker posts on the record card the amount of time spent on each operation, along with the quantity produced. The accountant uses these to compute the labor cost of each job and to process payrolls. The record cards also serve as the basis for work measurement; time standards are revised, as necessary, for use in future bids.

Longhorn's equipment is general purpose, not technologically advanced, which is necessary to maintain flexibility. Ream estimates the value of the shop's 32 machines at only $350,000. Similarly, the work force is flexible; most workers are trained to operate several different machines. Hourly wages are

Table 2.4

Linking Positioning Strategy with Product Plans and Competitive Priorities

	Positioning Strategy	
High-Level Decision	Process Focus	Product Focus
Product planning	More customized products, with low volumes	More standardized products, with high volumes
	Shorter product life cycles	Longer product life cycles
	Products in earlier stages of life cycle	Products in later stages of life cycle
	An entrance–exit strategy favoring early exit	An entrance–exit strategy favoring late exit
Competitive priorities	High-performance design quality	Consistent quality
	More emphasis on product and volume flexibility	More emphasis on low price
	Long delivery times	Short delivery times

competitive, starting at \$5 per hour and ranging up to \$10 per hour for the most highly skilled workers. Incomes are supplemented by frequent overtime (at time-and-a-half) and by bonuses. The bonus plan increases pay by about 10 percent, depending on the last year's profits and worker seniority. Ream ruled out an individual incentive plan because of the variety of jobs and inaccuracy of time standards. Job variety affords workers considerable diversity in work activities. It also necessitates frequent interaction among the workers, shop supervisor, and Ream.

Almost as important to Ream as the bidding process is seeking out improvements in work methods that will reduce costs. He and the shop supervisor constantly look for new ways to reduce setup times (the time to change over a machine from one job to the next), improve tooling, perform an operation at a more efficient machine, make (rather than buy) a component, change routing sequences, or even redesign the product. Such improvements lead to perceptible drops in cost with repeat orders. Most improvements are incremental, with no big technological advances.

Capacity, Location, and Layout. Longhorn Products operates one full shift of 26 workers, augmented by a second shift of only six workers. Machine capacity is the main limitation; work overloads are handled with overtime and increased use of the second shift. Equipment capacity is not well balanced. Weekly usage per machine varies from 3 to 80 hours, with an average of 45. Because of variations in product mix, even the low-usage machines become bottlenecks from time to time. Ream describes the workload at most machines as "feast-or-famine." Bottlenecks shift from one machine to another, and it is difficult to anticipate these shifts. Equipment failures also contribute to the bottlenecks. However, they are not critical, since there is enough process flexibility to temporarily reroute jobs to other machines.

The current 50 × 100-foot building is leased. Space is cramped and Ream is looking over relocation options in San Antonio to gain more space. The current layout groups workers and equipment on a functional basis. For example, there is one area for drill presses, one for welding stations, and one for brake presses. A fair amount of space is needed to store in-process jobs on the shop floor. Since routing patterns vary from job to job, and since an order goes to an average of 12 different work stations, materials handling paths are complex, with considerable criss-crossing from one area of the plant to another. Materials are handled by the machine operators themselves.

Materials Management, Production Plans, and Inventory. In order to buffer operations and absorb floating bottlenecks, Ream quotes reasonably long delivery lead times to the customers. Delivery lead times average two months, even though the typical job takes only 100 work hours for all setup and processing activities. This approach creates considerable work-in-process (WIP) inventory. Most work stations have a queue of three or four jobs waiting to be started, which helps to decouple operations so that resources can be utilized more effectively.

Longhorn Products has little influence over its suppliers because of its low volumes. Vendor relationships are informal, with no long-term purchasing agreements. Very few purchased items are stocked in inventory. This minimizes inventory levels but lengthens product delivery times. Ream is currently considering stocking some high-usage raw materials and manufactured subassemblies to cut delays. Stockpiling can be carried only so far, since most products are customized. Owing to the customized nature of the business, products are not stocked in anticipation of future customer demands. Thus finished goods inventories are almost nonexistent, requiring no warehouses or distribution centers. As soon as an order is finished, it is shipped directly to the customer.

Production planning is not formalized or projected very far into the future. Ream keeps a record of the dollar volume of new sales received each week. Using lead time estimates and orders already booked, he projects total monthly output for three months ahead. However, these projections are not specific to each work station. The projections influence how aggressively he bids on new jobs and when to vary output levels. Overtime or expansion of the second shift is used to relieve excessive backlogs.

Scheduling and Quality Control. Ream uses a manual system to release and follow up on orders. After a bid is accepted, he reviews the routing sheet and blueprints. He orders needed materials from suppliers and any necessary tooling from the three tool and die makers in the shop. When all of the necessary materials and tooling are available, the order is released to the shop. The routing sheet, record card, and blueprint are placed in a folder and sent to the shop supervisor, signaling that work can begin.

Scheduling work in the shop is complex and chaotic, demanding much of Ream's time and that of the shop supervisor. The supervisor schedules worker assignments for only one or two days in advance. Longer schedules are of little value because of an unexpected **bottleneck operation,** rush orders, and rework problems. The supervisor paces the work, using four somewhat conflicting decision rules:

1. Try to have only one setup per job at a machine. Setup times range from 15 minutes to 5 hours, averaging 1.5 hours. About 30 percent of the work content of a job is setup, and the rest is processing. This first rule may be broken when a rush job arrives and preempts one already in progress.
2. Maximize the utilization of the "automatic" machines. These machines work automatically, requiring a worker only to load and unload them. One worker can operate several such machines simultaneously, cutting costs considerably.

3. Assign jobs to the most proficient workers. Workers are more adept at some jobs rather than others. During slack times, the supervisor may violate this rule to train less experienced workers on new tasks. Such cross-training is important in creating a flexible work force.
4. Toward the end of the month, expedite jobs closest to completion regardless of their due date. This helps Ream maximize the number of shipments made at the end of the month. Customers normally pay bills on a monthly basis. Although this rule causes what Ream calls the "end-of-month syndrome," it helps Longhorn's cash flow.

Longhorn workers are responsible for the quality of their own work, with spot checks made on outgoing shipments. Scrap and rework are sometimes a problem. In some cases, customers accept shipments deviating from the requested size. In other cases, scrap requires a second shop order to make up for the shortfall.

After an order is completed, the accountant calculates its actual labor and materials cost. When the actual cost deviates too much from standard, the accountant brings this result to Ream's attention. He investigates and often identifies ways to improve the process. In other cases, he adjusts the time standards to make them more realistic for use in future bids.

Suds Brewery*

The Suds Brewery in Detroit, Michigan, began production in 1978. It is one of six plants built throughout the country and services an eight-state region in the midwest. The brewery produces five million barrels of beer per year (one barrel is equivalent to 31 gallons). It produces two types of beer (regular and light), which are packaged in cans, bottles, and kegs. Different types of lids, bottle sizes and shapes, and cardboard containers generate more than 80 unique products. Each product is produced in high volume, although packaging can be made to order for large customers. The firm's customers are 105 wholesalers, who in turn sell to retailers in their respective areas. Although the 80 product options permit some product differentiation, the top priorities at Suds are on-time delivery, consistent quality, and competitive prices.

Process Design, Technology, and Work-force Management. The manufacturing process is capital intensive, with plant and equipment costing $175 million. With a work force of only 370, the plant investment is almost $473,000 per employee. More than one-third of the work force, including staff and

* A similar case on Jos. Schlitz Brewing Company can be found in Roger W. Schmenner, *Production/Operations Management: Concepts and Situations,* 2nd ed. Chicago: Science Research Associates, 1984.

managers, is salaried. Despite the art associated with brewing, automation has increased considerably over the last two decades. Without these advances, the work force at the Detroit plant would be four times as large. Equipment is now highly specialized and technologically advanced. The process flow is linear, following a one-directional routing. The two main production stages are brewing and packaging.

The *brewing* stage is under the control of the brewmaster. The cycle time to brew a batch is one full month. It begins by producing "wort" from malting barley and other grains. The grains are milled and then placed in huge stainless steel vessels, where brewing water is added. The "mash" is brought to a boil to break down the starches. The mixture is then transferred to a large, circular tub, where the liquid wort is separated from undissolved particles. The undissolved mash is sold to another company for livestock feed, and the wort is placed in a brew kettle. Hops are added and the mixture is boiled for two hours. The liquid is then separated in a whirlpool separator, cooled, and transferred into 50-foot-high fermentation tanks. Here the glucose in the wort is converted to alcohol, and carbon dioxide is introduced. The result is beer, which then passes through a series of filtering and storage processes. Most aging occurs at the ruh cellar, where the beer is held from seven to twelve days.

The *packaging* stage is continuous, with no buildup of inventory between successive operations. The process begins by piping beer to the two canning lines, three bottling lines, or single keg line. Equipment on each line fills, caps, and pasteurizes the beer. At the end of the can and bottle lines, the output is boxed into six-packs or cases and then placed on pallets for outbound shipment. These operations are performed at high speeds; the can-line rate is almost 100,000 cans per hour.

Most of the work force involved in the brewing and packaging processes play a monitoring role, watching the equipment and instrument panels. Workers tend to do the same job day after day, with much less diversity than at Longhorn Products. Employees may move from one packaging line to another, depending on the production schedule. However, there is little difference in the work. Pay is on an hourly basis, and since output is equipment-paced, there is no incentive system. Job changes are won on the basis of seniority and most involve workers moving from the night to the day shift. Union relations are satisfactory, with some 40 grievances per year. Owing to the high capital intensity of the brewery, management is particularly sensitive to achieving good labor–management relations. However, in contrast to Longhorn Products, information flows primarily from management to the workers and is provided less frequently. The main information flowing upward concerns equipment maintenance problems. Work measurement is also less important at Suds Brewery because output rates are well-known and routings are uniform.

Capacity, Location, and Layout. The Detroit plant is located on 156 acres of land and contains more than one million square feet of floor space. The plant operates three shifts per day, five days per week. Approximately 30 percent of the floor space is used for brewing; the remainder is used for the packaging lines and the warehouse. Equipment utilization is a top concern of management. Capacities are well understood and carefully balanced. The line fillers, which are particularly expensive at $500,000 each, are the limiting element in each line. Machines past the fillers in the lines have somewhat higher output rates, providing some cushion against temporary failure. Maintenance is a particularly vital function. The maintenance department monitors the design and upkeep of the equipment to minimize unexpected failures. Maintenance personnel respond quickly to failures when they do occur.

Although economies of scale are significant, Suds Brewery also has high enough sales volumes to warrant multiple plants, which are strategically located throughout the country. Having plants in several locations reduces the company's transportation costs and shortens transportation lead times to wholesalers. High volumes and transportation costs encouraged suppliers to build plants close to Suds's Detroit plant. Both inbound and outbound shipments are made by rail and truck. Docks can handle 30 freight cars and 19 trucks at the same time. The plant was designed so that 75 percent of the output could be shipped by either mode. Currently 60 percent of the shipments are made by rail.

The layout at Suds follows the product flow. Resources in the packaging area are grouped by type of product. Most materials handling is done by automated conveyors.

Materials Management, Production Plans, and Inventory. Production planning varies by manufacturing stage. The brewing operation produces to stock, whereas the packaging lines tend to produce to specific customer orders. Suds promises delivery times of from two to six weeks, but the brewing cycle itself takes four weeks. This forces the brewmaster to produce to forecast rather than booked customer orders. Forecasts are closely monitored, so that enough of each type of beer is available to support the packaging lines without creating excessive work-in-process inventory. One difficulty is seasonal demand; the peak demand in the summer months is double the demand in the winter. In order to smooth production rates and more fully utilize equipment capacity, Suds builds up excess inventory in the slack season and stores this inventory primarily in wholesaler warehouses. This strategy is feasible since pasteurized beer does not spoil.

Suds prefers to ship packaged beer directly from the line to wholesalers, even though the company has a plant warehouse. Approximately 60 percent of the output is shipped directly. The rest stays at the plant only a short time, and the average finished inventory there represents only two days of supply. Customer relationships are formalized. Each wholesaler orders once a month for delivery four weeks later. Each order specifies the desired product codes, quantities, and due dates. The Detroit plant uses a computer system to monitor the inventory of each wholesaler, to forecast future sales, and even to make suggestions to wholesalers on stocking policies.

Vendor relationships are long-term and formalized. Corporate headquarters negotiates long-term contracts for most major raw materials, although each plant contracts locally for miscellaneous MRO (maintenance/repair/operating) items. Firm orders are issued to vendors to cover output levels planned for the next month. Tentative orders for two more months are given to suppliers for forward visibility. Avoiding materials shortages is crucial, and raw materials inventories are carefully managed. Much depends on supplier lead times and dependability. Suds also takes advantage of some quantity discounts. Less than eight hours of supply is needed for bottles and cans. The inventory of bottle labels, on the other hand, averages a five-month's supply because of low holding costs and significant quantity discounts.

At the Detroit plant the same department that handles customer and vendor orders also plans production levels. Production planning goals are to meet customer orders as closely as possible, get full use of capacity, and maintain a stable work force. Monthly plans for exact lot sizes and sequences for each beer and packaging combination are developed in detail.

Scheduling and Quality Control. Each packaging line is scheduled one full month in advance. The scheduling process begins with the receipt of the next month's orders from wholesalers. Schedulers try to satisfy these orders, while maximizing equipment utilization and avoiding an excessive number of setups. Three basic decision rules are used:

1. Schedule the lines so that the packaging lines are working with the same type of beer.
2. For a given line, run together customer orders calling for the same packaging sizes and types (such as quart bottles), rather than frequently changing over from one size to another.
3. Run both canning lines at the same time; the number of workers needed on the second line is less than if it were operated when the first line is idle.

Using these rules, schedulers determine the start and finish time for the different runs on each line, while trying to satisfy all wholesaler requests. When the schedule is finalized, wholesaler delivery requests are acknowledged, and delivery times are specified. Some deviation from requested delivery times are inevitable: About 20 percent must be revised, but no deviation involves a shift of more than two weeks. Suds takes pride in filling over 98 percent of its acknowledged orders on time.

Even though schedules are planned a month in advance, some minor changes are tolerated in order to respond to revised customer requests. Usually, swaps between wholesalers can be arranged. Schedule modifications tend to be infrequent and minor. At no time are changes allowed that affect labor requirements scheduled for less than one week ahead.

Suds Brewery emphasizes quality control and has a quality control staff of 30 people who provide services around the clock. More than 1000 lab tests are performed on each batch brewed. Quality control personnel are authorized to stop production whenever there is a need for corrective action. For example, tests on the number of yeast cells during fermentation are made every three hours, while samples from the canning line are taken hourly. If a sample from a can fails to meet the standard, all output since the last inspection is systematically checked. All cans failing inspection are discarded. Because of the vigilance of the quality control department, large quantities are rarely lost.

All Suds plants are evaluated as cost centers rather than profit centers. The reason is that a plant has no control over sales, since its geographical market is fixed. A variety of performance measures are assessed weekly, comparing actual results with goals. The measures include barrels produced per week, cost per barrel, quality losses, worker absenteeism, complaints from wholesalers, a taste test, and on-time delivery.

Linkages at Longhorn Products and Suds Brewery

It is clear that the two companies employ different positioning strategies: Longhorn has a process focus, while Suds has a product focus. Product plans and competitive priorities on which the strategies are based are different also. The *product plans* at Longhorn are for low-volume, customized products, with 50 percent of the jobs being one of a kind. The product volumes at Suds are huge: 155 million gallons per year. There are only two types of beer, with 80 standard packaging options. The *competitive priorities* at Longhorn center on flexibility, whereas they are price and delivery time at Suds. The average delivery time at Longhorn of two months far exceeds the average work content of 100 hours. The opposite is true at Suds, where a delivery time of two to four weeks compares favorably with a four-week brewing cycle. The sharp contrast between Longhorn and Suds gives us a sense of how decisions in operations must mesh.

Congruent Operations Decisions. As shown in Fig. 2.8, the positioning strategy selected helps managers to translate product plans and competitive priorities into decisions throughout the operations function; in fact, it is the linchpin in congruent operations decisions. Table 2.5 contrasts decisions at Longhorn and Suds for a sample of these operations decision areas.

Technological choices depend on positioning strategy and can be quite different for the two strategies. To maintain flexibility, Longhorn selected more general-purpose equipment and is less capital intensive than Suds. Capital intensity can be measured by dividing the value of the equipment by the

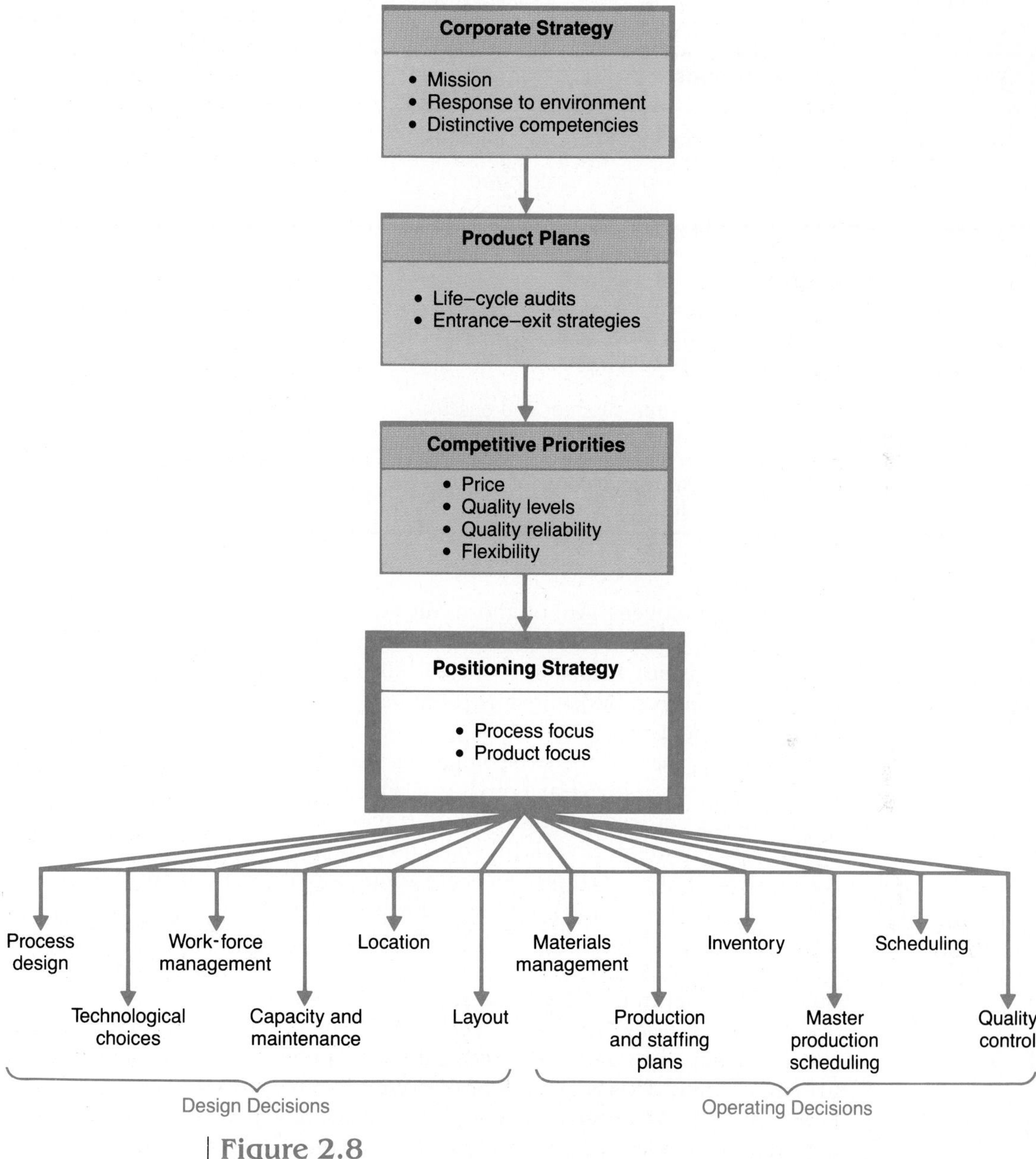

Figure 2.8

Positioning Strategy: The Linchpin in Operations Decisions.

Table 2.5

Linkages at Longhorn and Suds

Corporate Decision Area	Process Focus at Longhorn	Product Focus at Suds
Product plan	Low-volume, customized products	High-volume, standardized products
Competitive priorities	Product and volume flexibility	Low price and fast delivery
Operations Decision Area		
Technological choices	General-purpose equipment and labor intensive	Specialized equipment and capital intensive
Capacity	Lower utilization and big cushion	Higher utilization and small cushion
Materials management	Informal supplier and customer relationships	Formal supplier and customer relationships
Inventory	Considerable work-in-process (WIP) inventory	Little inventory tolerated
Scheduling	Fluid	Planned far ahead

number of employees. At Longhorn, the equipment is valued at $315,000 and the firm employs 32 workers, which translates into almost $10,000 per worker. This is but a fraction of the $473,000 per worker at Suds. In order to be cost competitive, Suds must use automation and technological advances to the fullest extent possible.

Capacity policies at the two companies also are quite different. Equipment utilization is much lower at Longhorn, with the average machine operating only 45 hours per week. Equipment utilization is much higher at Suds, which operates 120 hours per week (three shifts per day). Unexpected bottlenecks, rush orders, and rework problems are commonplace at Longhorn. Such uncertainties are rare at Suds, and less of a cushion is needed to guard against them. The capital intensity of a product focus makes slack capacity very expensive at Suds. With each filler line valued at $500,000, high capacity utilization is naturally a top concern of management.

Regarding *materials management,* Longhorn has only informal relationships with suppliers and customers alike. Its volumes are too small to give the firm much clout. This is quite a contrast with Suds, where the firm negotiates long-term contracts with suppliers of most major raw materials. The company requires customers (105 wholesalers) to place their orders one month in advance and can even modify delivery requests somewhat to maximize efficiency.

Inventory decisions also link directly to positioning strategy. To decouple operations and deal with the jumbled flows of a process focus, Longhorn allows large amounts of work-in-process inventory to accumulate on the shop floor. Such excesses are not needed or tolerated with the line flows at Suds. Forecasts are closely monitored to minimize WIP inventory. For the more expensive raw materials, such as bottles and cans, less than eight hour's inventory is held.

The process focus at Longhorn requires more fluid *scheduling* procedures. Detailed plans are not made for more than a day or two because of the uncertainties involved. This reactive, crisis-oriented scheduling process is not found at Suds. There, the concern for top efficiency and the simplicity of line flows demand elaborate scheduling and day-to-day monitoring of performance. Each packaging line is scheduled one full month in advance.

CHAPTER HIGHLIGHTS

- Product planning is an ongoing activity that defines the products (goods or services) to be produced.
- Product life cycles consist of five stages: product planning, introduction, growth, maturity, and decline.
- There are three strategies for when to enter and exit a product's life cycle. Each one places a different demand on the production system. Entering early and exiting late forces a transition from flexibility to low cost.
- The product planning stage involves idea generation, screening, development and testing, and final product design. These steps must fit the firm's mission, which may be too narrow or too broad.
- The preference matrix and break-even analysis, while not limited to product planning, are two techniques used to help screen new product lines.
- Competitive priorities state the dimensions on which the firm should excel. There are seven dimensions: low price, high-performance design, fast delivery time, consistent quality, on-time delivery, product flexibility, and volume flexibility. Trade-offs among them are often necessary. Management must judge which trade-offs are the strongest, along with the firm's distinctive competencies, when establishing desired levels for each dimension.
- The positioning strategy that meshes best with product plans and competitive priorities should be selected. The continuum of choices ranges from a process focus to a product focus.
- A process focus organizes resources around the process. This focus fits low volumes and jumbled flow patterns. A product focus dedicates resources to specific products, resulting in line flows. It fits high volumes and standardized products.
- The more the customer contact at a service facility, the greater is the tendency toward a process focus.
- Descriptions of two companies, Longhorn Products and Suds Brewery, demonstrate how the positioning strategy acts as a linchpin in operations decisions. Positioning strategy helps managers to translate corporate decisions into congruent decisions throughout the operations function.
- A process focus links with low volumes, high flexibility, general-purpose equipment, labor-intensive technologies, lower capacity utilization, informal relationships with suppliers and customers, large work-in-process inventories, and fluid schedules. The opposite is true of a product focus.

KEY TERMS

bottleneck operation
break-even analysis
competitive priorities
entrance–exit strategy
flow shop
job shop
life-cycle audits
positioning strategy
preference matrix
process-focused strategy
product flexibility
product life cycle
product planning
product-focused strategy
sensitivity analysis
volume flexibility

STUDY QUESTIONS

1. A sign on the way to an abandoned mine reads: "Choose your ruts carefully; you will be in them for the next 15 miles." How does this caution apply to product planning and choosing competitive priorities?
2. How does the concept of product life cycles illustrate the ongoing need for product planning?
3. How does the decision on when to enter and exit a product's life cycle affect the operations function? With which entrance–exit strategy would a product focus make most sense?
4. The Sealtight Company is a well-diversified manufacturer in the packaging business. It makes a variety of packaging materials and sells them to industrial buyers. Management is currently conducting a life-cycle audit to identify the current stage of each product in its life cycle. The profiles for two products are shown in Table 2.6.
   (a) In which stage is product A? Product B? Explain your choices.
   (b) For which product would low price be a higher competitive priority? Why?
5. Give an example of each component of the "service bundle" for each of the following products.
   (a) An insurance policy.
   (b) An airline trip.
   (c) Dental work.
6. What dimensions of competitive priorities seem to be the most important for each of the following companies?
   (a) McDonald's.
   (b) Toyota.
   (c) A manufacturer of specialty glues tailored to the needs of industrial buyers in the furniture and mobile-home industries.
7. What positioning strategy (process focus or product focus) seems best for each of the following situations? Briefly defend your choice.
   (a) A builder of skyscrapers and bridges.
   (b) A paper mill.
   (c) A microwave manufacturer.
   (d) A manufacturer of a wide variety of men's suits.

Table 2.6

Product Profiles

Product	Performance Measure	1986 Performance	Change Over Last Year	Average Annual Change Over Last Four Years
A	Annual sales	$30.8 million	+1.0%	+15.8%
	Unit price	1.12/lb	+2.2	+8.5
	Unit profit margin	0.16/lb	−0.3	+3.2
	Total profit contribution	4.4 million	+1.5	+22.5
B	Annual sales	5.4 million	+72.1	+35.0
	Unit price	1.30/lb	+7.0	+6.8
	Unit profit margin	0.70/lb	+12.1	+15.1
	Total profit contribution	2.9 million	+80.1	+37.2

8. Why do firms offering more customized, low-volume products tend to
   (a) compete less on short customer delivery times and low prices?
   (b) be less capital intensive?
   (c) maintain larger capacity cushions?

9. Why do firms with a product focus tend to
   (a) plan production and inventory levels further into the future?
   (b) have more formalized supplier relationships?
   (c) concentrate inventory less at the work-in-process level?

10. Table 2.5 describes seven ways in which corporate and operations decisions at Longhorn and Suds link with positioning strategy. State three other ways that decisions within the operations function are linked to positioning strategy. (See Fig. 2.8.) Explain your reasoning.

PROBLEMS

1. Frank Jennings has just patented a new device for washing dishes and cleaning dirty kitchen sinks, which he calls the "Easystik." This device has a tough, rubber head to scrub off difficult food deposits on dishes, and the handle is filled with a detergent that releases during use of the device. The Jennings Company, which Frank owns, has been in business since 1982 and now employs 35 people. Before trying to commercialize the Easystik and add it to his existing product line, Jennings wants reasonable assurance that it will be a success. After thinking through the production process and the cost of raw materials and new equipment, Jennings estimates the variable cost of each unit produced and sold at $7, with fixed costs per year at $56,000.
   (a) If the price is set at $25, how many units must be produced and sold to break even? Use both the graphic and algebraic approaches to get your answer.

(b) Jennings forecasts sales for the first year of 10,000 Easystiks, if the price is set at \$15. What would be the total contribution to profits from this new product during the first year?

(c) If the price is set at \$10 per unit, Jennings forecasts that first-year sales will double to 20,000 units. Which pricing strategy (\$15 or \$10) would make the greatest total contribution to profits?

(d) Cite two other considerations that would be critical to the final decision about producing Easystiks. Explain.

2. Another product, introduced at the Jennings Company in 1982, has experienced considerable growth during the last few years. Total sales in 1985 were 2400 units and total cost (fixed and variable) attributed to this product was \$258,000. In 1986, sales increased to 3600 units at a total cost of \$342,000.

(a) Assuming that the cost structure was the same in both years, what must be the variable cost, c, and fixed cost, F, for this product? *Hint:* Solve the following two linear equations for the two unknowns.

$$F + 3600c = \$342{,}000$$

$$F + 2400c = \$258{,}000$$

(b) What is the break-even quantity of this product if its price is \$115 per unit?

3. A third product at the Jennings Company has enjoyed reasonable sales volumes, but its contributions to profits have been disappointing. In 1986, 25,000 units were produced and sold. The price is \$8 per unit, c is \$6, and F is \$45,000.

(a) What is the break-even quantity for this product? Use both the graphic and algebraic approaches to get your answer.

(b) Jennings is considering ways to either stimulate sales volumes or decrease variable costs. He feels that it is possible to increase sales by 20 percent or reduce c to 80 percent of its current level. Which alternative leads to higher contributions to profits, assuming that each is equally costly to implement? *Hint:* Calculate profits for both alternatives and identify the one having the greatest impact.

(c) What is the percentage change in the unit profit margin generated by each alternative in (b)? How does this explain the result you obtained in (b)?

4. The Franklin Electronics Company is a small manufacturer of clock radios and other electronic products. Its executive committee is considering the possibility of introducing a novelty tape recorder. The market research department expects a growing interest in this type of unit, based on a recent survey of the market. The production department estimates that buying the necessary equipment would increase its fixed costs per year by \$20,000. The accounting department projects that the product would have to absorb another \$25,000 for the additional costs of executive salaries, rent, and taxes. The marketing department believes that the initial advertising budget would have to be \$15,000 per year and that its sales budget would increase by another \$30,000 per year. The new product would be priced at \$25 F.O.B. factory with no quantity discounts. The various operating departments expect the variable cost for labor and materials to be \$15 per unit.

(a) How many units must be produced and sold for the company to break even?

(b) If the advertising budget were increased to \$50,000, what would the break-even quantity be?

(c) A more automated production process could be used. It would triple production's fixed cost (from $20,000 to $60,000), while reducing the total variable cost per unit from $15 to $12. Would this more advanced technology decrease or increase the break-even quantity? Must this always be the case?

5. The Forsite Company is screening three new product ideas. Resource constraints allow only one idea to be commercialized at the present time. The following estimates have been made for the five performance criteria that management feels are most important.

Performance Criterion	Estimated Ratings		
	Product A	Product B	Product C
1. Demand uncertainty and project risk	0.3	0.9	0.2
2. Similarity to present products	0.7	0.8	0.6
3. Expected return on investment (ROI)	1.0	0.4	0.8
4. Compatibility with current manufacturing process	0.4	0.7	0.6
5. Competitive advantage	0.4	0.6	0.5

(a) Calculate a total weighted score for each alternative, using a preference matrix and assuming equal weights for each performance criterion. Which alternative is best? Worst?

(b) Suppose that the expected ROI is given twice the weight assigned to each of the remaining criteria? Does this affect the rankings of the three candidate products?

SELECTED REFERENCES

Chase, Richard B., and David A. Tansik, "Customer Contact Model for Organization Design," *Management Science,* vol. 29, no. 9 (September 1983), pp. 1037–1050.

Ferdows, K., and A. DeMayer, "The State of Large Manufacturers in Europe: Results of the 1984 European Manufacturing Futures Survey," INSEAD, 1984.

Hayes, Robert H., and Roger W. Schmenner, "How Should You Organize Manufacturing?" *Harvard Business Review* (January–February 1978), pp. 105–108.

Hayes, Robert H., and Steven C. Wheelwright, "Link Manufacturing Process and Product Life Cycles," *Harvard Business Review* (January–February 1979), pp. 133–140.

Hudson, R. G., J. C. Chambers, and R. G. Johnson, "New Product Planning Decisions Under Uncertainty," *Interfaces,* vol. 8, no. 1, part 2 (November 1977), pp. 82–96.

Leavitt, Theodore, "The Industrialization of Service," *Harvard Business Review* (September–October 1976), pp. 63–74.

Powell, Gary N., and George A. Johnson, "An Expectancy-Equity Model of Productive System Performance," *Journal of Operations Management,* vol. 1, no. 1 (August 1980), pp. 47–56.

Sasser, W. Earl, R. Paul Olsen, and D. Daryl Wyckoff, *Management of Service Operations.* Boston: Allyn and Bacon, 1978.

Schmenner, Roger W., *Production/Operations Management: Concepts and Situations,* 2nd ed. Chicago: Science Research Associates, 1984.

Skinner, Wickham, *Manufacturing in the Corporate Strategy.* New York: John Wiley and Sons, 1978.

Taylor, Sam G., "Are the Process Industries Different?" *23rd Annual Conference Proceedings,* American Production and Inventory Control Society (October 1980), Los Angeles, pp. 94–96.

Van Dierdonck, Ronald, and Jeffrey G. Miller, "Designing Production Planning and Control Systems," *Journal of Operations Management*, vol. 1, no. 1 (August 1980), pp. 37–46.

Wheelwright, Steven C., "Reflecting Corporate Strategy in Manufacturing Decisions," *Business Horizons* (February 1978), pp. 57–65.

Wheelwright, Steven C., and Robert H. Hayes, "Competing Through Manufacturing," *Harvard Business Review* (January–February 1985), pp. 99–109.

CHAPTER

3

FORECASTING

Some Managerial Issues

- Why is forecasting important to us?
- When can we best use time series models and when can we best use causal or qualitative models?
- What sort of controls do we have to impose on the forecasting system?
- How can we design the best forecasting system for a given situation?
- Is it always true that the most sophisticated forecasting system is the best for our use?

Chapter Outline

Many managers wonder how to predict with certainty what will happen in the future. The answer is simple: They cannot predict the future with certainty. Instead, managers use **forecasts** in their planning processes and accept the fact that forecasting involves errors. Forecasting makes use of historical data to anticipate future events. Forecasts are rarely perfect, regardless of the quantity of data and the extent of managerial experience on which they are based. Managers work with probabilities, or the likelihood that certain events will occur. Fortunately, forecasting methods have been devised and improved to the point that they provide useful estimates for planning purposes.

Many planning problems in operations management require forecasts of customer demand for products or services. Careers are made, or broken, on the basis of forecasting ability. In Box 3.1 we show some examples of forecasting successes and failures. Examples such as these emphasize the need for operations managers to learn about the advantages and limitations of the various forecasting methods available to them.

Box 3.1

THE UPS AND DOWNS OF FORECASTING

In mid-1985, General Motors offered 7.7 percent financing on leftover 1985 models. Competitors followed the lead, and, as a result, the industry had a seasonally adjusted annual sales record of 11 million units in September 1985. Inventories went to a two-year low. However, GM misread the increase in demand and forecasted continued high sales. The result was overstocked dealers, with inventories 67 percent above normal in January 1986.

The six largest producers of appliances spent some $300 million for plant and equipment in 1984, up 60 percent from 1983. This major level of investment was based on leading indicators of increased demand for 1985, including increased housing starts and the expected demand for appliances to replace some 200 million units purchased 15 years ago. Late in 1985, actual sales for 1985 were expected to be up 1 million units from 1984's record sales.

Based on forecasts in the late 1970s indicating price advantages of $6–$8 per barrel of heavy crude oil over light crude oil, U.S. companies spent $7 billion to refit their refineries to operate on the less expensive, heavier crude oils. However, oil-producing countries began pumping more premium-priced light oils and less heavy crude to maintain their incomes in the face of reduced demand for oil. In addition, the price differential between the oils narrowed. Many of the upgrading projects undertaken by the oil refineries may never pay for themselves.

In 1983, in order to get the Sunbeam Appliance Corporation into a more profitable position, management developed manufacturing schedules with improved sales forecasts. New forecast procedures were used and included getting sales estimates from some 200 top customers, projecting sales for a year ahead, and updating the forecast each month. The result was a 45 percent reduction in inventories.

Sources: "Detroit's Big Gamble," *Business Week,* January 13, 1986; "The Major-Appliance Industry Is on Fast Cycle," *Business Week,* September 2, 1985; "Heavy Crude Has Backfired on the Refiners," *Business Week,* November 7, 1983; "How Allegheny Is Rebuilding Sunbeam," *Business Week,* May 16, 1983.

CHARACTERISTICS OF DEMAND FOR PRODUCTS AND SERVICES

Why does forecasting customer demand pose a challenge? The answer is that the demand for a product or service can vary widely. The demand for letter sorting at a metropolitan post office peaks just before Christmas and again just before Easter. On the other hand, the weekly demand for haircuts at a local barbershop may be quite stable from week to week. The forecaster must act like a detective to uncover the underlying pattern of demand in a given situation, using whatever data and information are available. We first discuss the factors that affect demand in a given situation and then address the basic components of demand.

Factors Affecting Demand

What causes the demand pattern for a particular product or service? If we knew the answer to that question, forecasting would be much easier. Unfortunately, many factors have an impact on demand at any particular time. Table 3.1 shows that there are two major categories of factors: external and internal.

External Factors. Management cannot directly control external factors, particularly the general state of the economy. A booming economy exerts a positive influence on the level of demand, but the effect may not be the same for all products and services. A product or service may be affected by certain economic activities and not affected by others. Fortunately, a number of publications contain economic data that are useful for assessing the state of the economy.

Table 3.2 shows some common demand indicators and sources of information about them. **Leading indicators** are time series having turning points that typically precede the peaks and troughs of the general business cycle. For example, an upswing in residential building contracts may precede an in-

Table 3.1

Factors Affecting Demand for Goods and Services

External Factors
General state of the economy
Consumer tastes
Production service image in the eye of the public
Competitor actions
Government actions
Availability and cost of complementary products
Internal Factors
Product design
Price and advertising promotions
Packaging design
Salesperson quotas or incentives
Expansion or contraction of geographical market target areas
Product mix
Backlog policy

Table 3.2

Demand Indicators

Leading Indicators	Data Source
New corporations	Dun & Bradstreet
Business failures	Dun & Bradstreet
Residential building contracts	F. W. Dodge Corporation
Commercial/industrial building contracts	F. W. Dodge Corporation
Common-stock prices—industrial	Dow Jones
Wholesale commodity price index	Bureau of Labor Statistics
Average hours worked per week—manufacturing	Bureau of Labor Statistics
New orders for manufacturing durable goods	Department of Commerce
Coincident Indicators	
Gross national product (GNP)	Department of Commerce
Corporate profits	Department of Commerce
Unemployment	Bureau of Labor Statistics
Nonagricultural employment	Bureau of Labor Statistics
Nonfood wholesale prices	Bureau of Labor Statistics
Index of industrial production	Federal Reserve Board
Bank debits	Federal Reserve Board
Freight carloadings	Association of American Railroads
Lagging Indicators	
Personal income	Department of Commerce
Retail sales	Department of Commerce
Manufacturers' inventories	Department of Commerce
Consumer installment debt	Federal Reserve Board
Bank rates on business loans	Federal Reserve Board

crease in the demand for plywood by several weeks and homeowner's insurance by several months. **Coincident indicators** generally match the turning points in the business cycle and **lagging indicators** follow them, typically by several weeks or months. Just knowing that a series is a lagging indicator can be useful. For example, a firm interested in expanding and needing a business loan should realize that interest rates will reach their lowest point several weeks after the business cycle has reached its trough.

Returning to Table 3.1, let's look briefly at the other external factors that affect demand. Consumer tastes can change quickly, as they often do in clothing fashions. Also, the image of the product or service in the eyes of the consumer can be a big factor. In the late 1970s and early 1980s, foreign-car sales increased dramatically as a percentage of total car sales in the United

States. Why? Because consumers believed that foreign cars were more fuel efficient and were of superior quality.

The actions of competitors regarding prices, advertising promotions, and new products also affect sales. The Wendy's, Inc., advertisement featuring the question "Where's the beef?" definitely reduced the demand at the other leading hamburger franchises.

Local, state, and national governments can affect demand by passing legislation regarding taxes, interest rates, or environmental regulations. For example, limiting the sulphur content of coal used in steam-powered electric generating plants reduces the demand for coal produced in Ohio, which has a high sulphur content.

Finally, the success of complementary products affects demand. The location of a new Honda plant in Marysville, Ohio, stimulated the sales of many suppliers of automobile parts and components in the area. Future demand for products from these suppliers will depend on the overall success of Honda in that location.

Internal Factors. Decisions made internally also affect the demand for products or services and can be controlled by management. Recognizing that it can have an effect enables management to respond actively, rather than passively, to demand. The term **demand management** describes the process of influencing the timing and volume of demand or adapting to the undesirable effects of unchangeable demand patterns. Table 3.1 shows some of the ways in which management can affect demand.

Factors such as product design, price and advertising promotions, packaging design, salesperson quotas or incentives, and expansion or contraction of geographical market target areas can all contribute to changes in the demand volumes. However, the purpose of demand management goes beyond merely increasing customer demand.

Management must also consider and deal with the timing of demand, which is extremely important to the efficient utilization of resources and production capacity. Trying to produce for peak customer demand during the peak demand period can be very costly. In order to avoid this situation, firms often use price incentives or advertising promotions to encourage customers to purchase the product or service before or after traditional sales peaks. For example, telephone companies encourage customers to make long distance calls after normal business hours by offering lower evening and weekend rates. This practice reduces the amount of resources needed to handle peak demand.

Another tactic is to introduce a product that has a different heavy seasonal sales period. Firms with the technology to produce tractor lawn mowers might also produce snowmobiles to even out resource and production requirements over the year. In this way costly changes in work-force level and inventory can be minimized.

Finally, some companies use backlogs to stabilize resource requirements over time. When an inquiry or order is received for a product or service, the producer specifies a delivery date, which depends on the current workload and capacity. Doctors, dentists, and other professionals use this approach by asking patients to make an appointment for their services. Manufacturers of custom-built products also work to backlogs of demand.

Components of Demand

The five basic components of most business demand series are the average, trend, seasonal influence, cyclical movement, and random error. The first four of these components combine in varying degrees to define the underlying time pattern of demand and are affected by both external and internal factors. Fig. 3.1 shows the demand series for a particular product. The trend, seasonal influence, and cyclical movement components have a significant impact on the demand pattern for this product. Preparing useful forecasts for this product depends on the forecaster's ability to estimate accurately the effects of these components in the future. As you will see later in this chapter, estimating the average, trend, and seasonal influence is not too

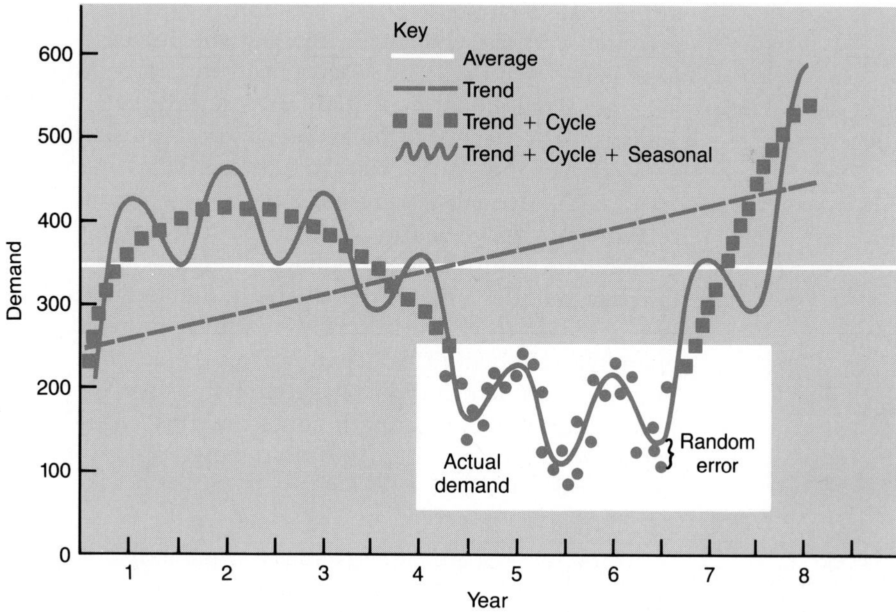

Figure 3.1

The Components of a Demand Series over Time.

difficult. Estimating cyclical movement is much more difficult. Often we do not know the duration of the cycle because we cannot predict the events that cause it. National and international events such as a presidential election, war in the Middle East, or an embargo on foreign-built machine tools can affect the demand for products or services. Our ability to make intelligent long-range forecasts depends on good estimates of cyclical movement.

The fifth component, random error, is the remaining demand after all known causes of demand (such as the average, trend, seasonal influence, and cyclical movement) have been identified. Random error is the component of demand that makes every forecast wrong. Random error is caused by chance variation and, by definition, chance variation cannot be predicted in advance. The insert in Fig. 3.1 shows the relationship of random error to actual demand.*

THE ROLE OF FORECASTING IN OPERATIONS MANAGEMENT

Because demand exhibits many different characteristics, several different types of forecasting methods are needed—and are available for use. The objective of the forecaster is to develop a useful forecast from the information at hand. In order to achieve this objective, the forecaster must select the appropriate technique. Sometimes this involves a trade-off between forecast accuracy and the cost of developing the forecast. Three general types of forecasting techniques are used for demand forecasting: **time series† analysis, causal methods,** and **qualitative techniques.** Time series analysis is a statistical approach that relies heavily on the use of historical data—a time series of demand—to project the future size of demand, recognizing historical trend and seasonality patterns. Causal methods mathematically express the relationship between the factor to be forecast and related factors such as promotional campaigns, economic conditions, and competitor actions. Qualitative techniques involve managerial judgment, expert opinion, and/or survey methods to convert qualitative information into quantitative estimates when relevant historical data are scarce. We describe each of these techniques in more detail later in this chapter. First, however, let's consider the conditions under which these techniques are most likely to be applied. Table 3.3 contains examples of demand forecasting applications and the typical planning horizon for each.

* If we make an error in estimating the trend, seasonal, or cyclical components, the error terms may be highly correlated with each other and consequently not a result of chance variation. In such cases we say that there is *autocorrelation* in the error terms.

† A time series is a list of repeated observations of a phenomenon, such as demand, arranged in the order in which they actually occurred.

Table 3.3

Demand Forecast Applications

Application	Time Horizon: Short Term (0–3 Months)	Medium Term (3 Months–2 Years)	Long Term (More than 2 Years)
Forecast quantity	Individual products or services	Total sales Groups or families of products	Total sales
Decision area	Inventory management Final assembly scheduling Work-force scheduling Master production scheduling	Staff planning Production planning Master production scheduling Purchasing Distribution	Facility location Capacity planning Process design
Forecasting technique	Time series Causal Qualitative	Causal Qualitative	Causal Qualitative

Short Term

In the short term (here, 0–3 months in the future) we are typically interested in forecasting unit demand for individual products or services. We are close to the point where we must satisfy the demand, and we need as much detail and accuracy as possible for planning purposes. Time series analysis is the method most often used for short-term forecasting. It is a relatively inexpensive way to generate the usually large number of forecasts required. The quality of these forecasts can be very good in the short term. Causal models, while potentially useful for individual item or service forecasts, are not used extensively for this purpose; they are much more costly than time series analysis and require more time to develop. In the short term, operations managers rarely can wait for development of causal models, even though they may be more accurate than time series models. Finally, qualitative techniques are used for short-term forecasts if historical data are not available for a specific item, such as when a new product is introduced. However, these forecast methods are also more expensive than forecasts generated from time series analysis.

Medium Term

The time horizon for the medium term is between three months and two years. For planning purposes the level of forecast detail required is not as great as for the short term. We typically forecast total sales demand in dollars or the number of units of an aggregation of products or services into similar groups or families. The need for medium-term forecasts arises from planning problems related to issues of capacity, such as those shown in Table 3.3. We often use causal models for medium-term forecasts. These models typically do a good job of identifying periods when the rate of growth of demand will change, such as when a period of slow growth in sales will turn into a period of rapid decline. The determination of these *turning points* is very important for the operations manager, particularly in the medium and long term. Some of the qualitative methods of forecasting are also good at identifying turning points. However, as we mentioned earlier, they are most often used in situations where no historical data exist. Time series analysis typically does not yield good results in the medium or long term, primarily because it relies on the assumption that existing patterns will continue in the future. This assumption may be valid for the short term, but for longer time horizons it rarely is.

Long Term

For time horizons exceeding two years, forecasts are usually developed for total sales demand in dollars or some other common unit of measurement, such as barrels, pounds, or kilowatts. Good long-term forecasts of demand for individual products or services are not only very difficult to make, but they also are too detailed for the planning problems that require long-term forecasts. The decision areas shown in Table 3.3 indicate the need to estimate market demand for an extended period into the future. Causal models and qualitative methods are the primary techniques used for long-term forecasting. However, even mathematically derived causal model forecasts have to be tempered by managerial experience and judgment because of the time horizon involved and the potential consequences of decisions based on them.

TIME SERIES ANALYSIS

In the simplest form of time series analysis, the only information we use is the historical record of demand for a product or service. We are not concerned with changes in the external and internal factors listed in Table 3.1, and we assume that what has occurred in the past will continue to occur in the future. Methods of time series analysis focus on the average, trend, and seasonal

Box 3.2

DUBLIN MEDICAL CLINIC

Henry Stamm, administrator of the Dublin Medical Clinic, was reviewing the operating reports for the past several months. He was disturbed to see that inventory supplies of some items were frequently out of stock. He decided to ask Ben Bruton, his assistant, if he had any ideas about remedying the situation.

"Ben, it seems to me that there must be a better way to manage our supplies. Take for example the blood-testing and urology supplies. In four of the last five weeks we had to place emergency orders to replenish those supplies. And you know how much more expensive it is to do that than to have sufficient stock."

"Henry, I realize we have been experiencing some disruptive stockouts, but I've been using the same ordering procedure for years. I base the ordering of all supplies on a weekly forecast of the number of patients we will process. I've been using the same forecast for each week: a constant 400 patients. We were doing fine until, as you point out, a few weeks ago. I would hate to just increase the forecast by some constant without knowing what effect that would have on our inventory of supplies."

Henry Stamm walked over to the chalkboard next to his desk. "Ben, I think we should review our forecasting procedures. What we have is a weekly time series of patient appointments, and I know there are useful methods for making forecasts in this sort of situation." He listed several techniques on the board, and Ben agreed to gather some historical data and test the techniques with the data. They decided to meet again in a week to discuss the results.

influence characteristics of time series; our task is to try to replicate these characteristics when projecting future demand. We can best illustrate time series analysis by using typical situations and data, beginning with an example of the need to analyze forecasting methods (Box 3.2).

Forecasting the Average

Consider Fig. 3.2, which shows patient arrivals at the Dublin Medical Clinic over the past 28 weeks. This graph is useful because it enables us to hypothesize the nature of and reasons for this demand pattern. However, for purposes of discussion let's proceed under the assumption that this series has only an average and random errors. (Those of you who feel that there is also a trend will have your chance later.) The simple moving average and exponential smoothing models are useful for forecasting the average of a time series.

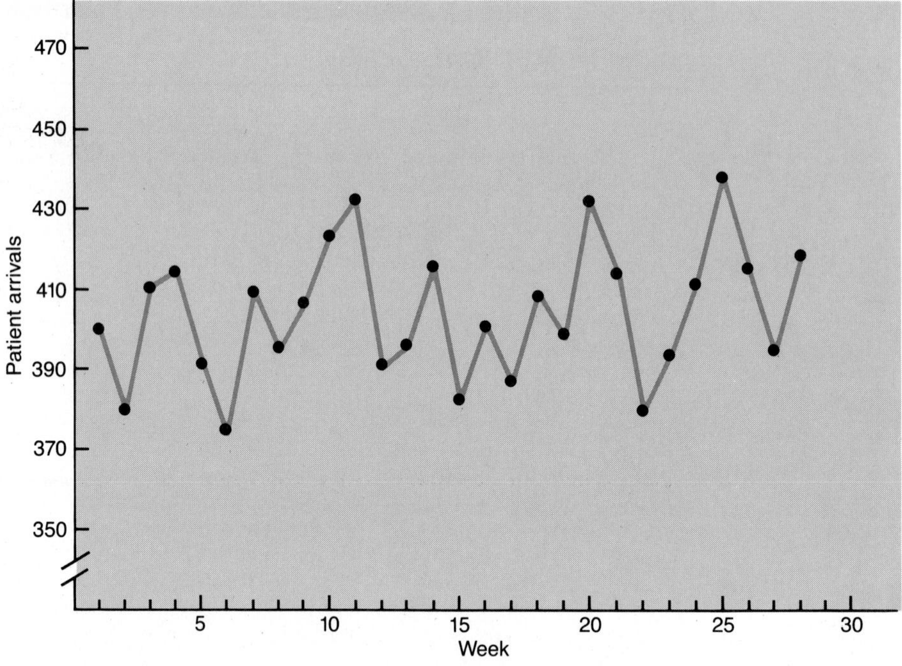

Figure 3.2

Weekly Patient Arrivals at the Dublin Medical Clinic.

Simple Moving Averages. We can use the simple **moving average method** to estimate the average of a demand time series and remove the effects of random fluctuation. This method is most useful when demand does not have a pronounced trend or any seasonal influences. To use a moving average model we simply calculate the average demand for the N most recent time periods and use it as the forecast for the next time period.* Specifically, the calculation involves

Average: $$A_t = \frac{D_t + D_{t-1} + D_{t-2} + \cdots + D_{t-N+1}}{N}.$$

Forecast: $F_{t+1} = A_t$.

Where: D_t = Actual demand in period t.

N = Total number of periods in the average.

A_t = Average computed for period t.

F_{t+1} = Forecast for period $t + 1$.

* In this section our forecast calculations are carried to one decimal place. If the time series is expressed in discrete units, such as patient arrivals, the forecast could be rounded to the nearest integer in practice.

The forecast is updated for each new period by averaging the same number of past demands. We keep the same value of N by replacing the oldest demand from the previous average with the most recent demand. Table 3.4 shows a three-week moving average forecast for the Dublin Medical Clinic data, while Table 3.5 shows a six-week moving average forecast for the same demands. Fig. 3.3 shows a comparison of the two forecasts. This information gives us some clues regarding the choice of the value for N. Note that the three-week moving average forecast varies more and reacts more quickly to large swings in demand. This sensitivity can be an advantage if, for example, the underlying average of the series is changing over time because of an unsuspected trend in the data. Conversely, the six-week moving average

Table 3.4

Three-Week Moving Average Forecast

Week (t)	Actual Demand (D_t)	Average (A_t)	Forecast (F_t)	Error ($D_t - F_t$)
1	401			Actual - Forecast
2	380			
3	411	397.3		
4	415	402.0	397.3	17.7
5	393	406.3	402.0	− 9.0
6	375	394.3	406.3	−31.3
7	410	392.7	394.3	15.7
8	395	393.3	392.7	2.3
9	406	403.7	393.3	12.7
10	424	408.3	403.7	20.3
11	433	421.0	408.3	24.7
12	391	416.0	421.0	−30.0
13	396	406.7	416.0	−20.0
14	417	401.3	406.7	10.3
15	383	398.7	401.3	−18.3
16	402	400.7	398.7	3.3
17	387	390.7	400.7	−13.7
18	410	399.7	390.7	19.3
19	398	398.3	399.7	− 1.7
20	433	413.7	398.3	34.7
21	415	415.3	413.7	1.3
22	380	409.3	415.3	−35.3
23	394	396.3	409.3	−15.3
24	412	395.3	396.3	15.7
25	439	415.0	395.3	43.7
26	416	422.3	415.0	1.0
27	395	416.7	422.3	−27.3
28	419		416.7	2.3

Table 3.5

Six-Week Moving Average Forecast

Week (t)	Actual Demand (D_t)	Average (A_t)	Forecast (F_t)	Error ($D_t - F_t$)
1	401			
2	380			
3	411			
4	415			
5	393			
6	375	395.8		
7	410	397.3	395.8	14.2
8	395	399.8	397.3	− 2.3
9	406	399.0	399.8	6.2
10	424	400.5	399.0	25.0
11	433	407.2	400.5	32.5
12	391	409.8	407.2	−16.2
13	396	407.5	409.8	−13.8
14	417	411.2	407.5	9.5
15	383	407.3	411.2	−28.2
16	402	403.7	407.3	− 5.3
17	387	396.0	403.7	−16.7
18	410	399.2	396.0	14.0
19	398	399.5	399.2	− 1.2
20	433	402.2	399.5	33.5
21	415	407.5	402.2	12.8
22	380	403.8	407.5	−27.5
23	394	405.0	403.8	− 9.8
24	412	405.3	405.0	7.0
25	439	412.2	405.3	33.7
26	416	409.3	412.2	3.8
27	395	406.0	409.3	−14.3
28	419		406.0	13.0

forecast is more stable because large swings in demand tend to cancel each other.

Including more historical data in the average results in a smoother forecast that is less susceptible to random variations. However, if the underlying average in the series is changing, the forecasts will tend to lag behind the changes for a longer period of time because it takes longer to get all the old data out of the forecast. A general rule is to use large values of N for demand series that are stable and small values of N for those that are susceptible to changes in the underlying average. We address other considerations for the choice of N when we discuss choosing the best method of forecasting.

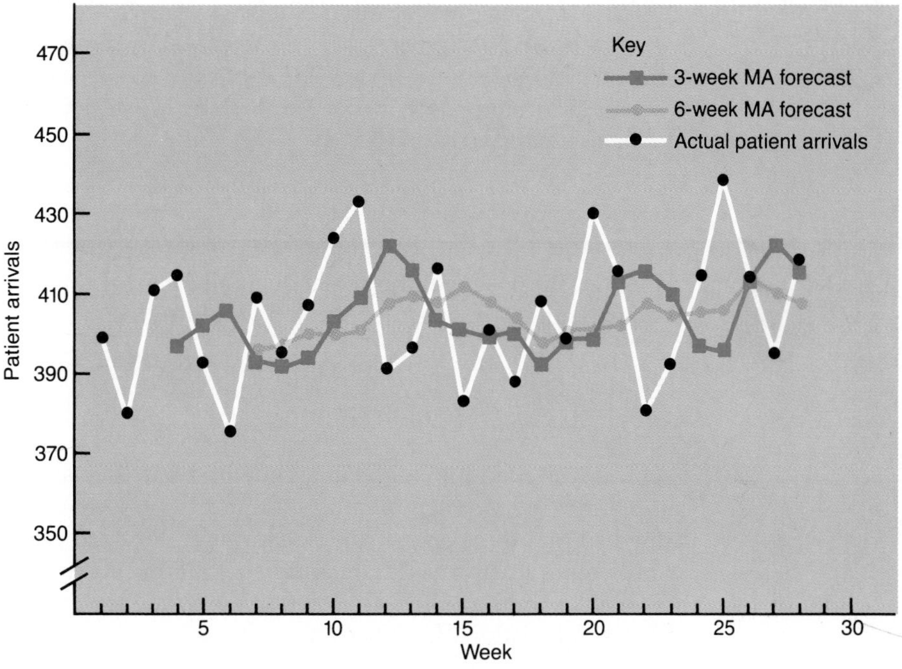

Figure 3.3

Comparison of Three-Week and Six-Week Moving Average Forecasts.

Weighted Moving Averages. In the simple moving average method each demand has the same weight in the average, namely, $1/N$. In the **weighted moving average method,** each historical demand in the average can have its own weight, so

$$\text{Average:} \quad A_t = W_1 D_t + W_2 D_{t-1} + \cdots + W_N D_{t-N+1}.$$

$$\text{Forecast:} \quad F_{t+1} = A_t.$$

$$\text{Where:} \quad \sum_{i=1}^{N} W_i = 1.$$

The weighted moving average method allows us to emphasize recent demand over earlier demand. The forecast will be more responsive to changes in the underlying average of the demand series. Alternatively, it allows us to put more emphasis on the levels of demand several periods ago, which have an impact on current demand. In this way "time-lag" effects can also be recognized.

For purposes of illustration, suppose that we are using a weighted moving average and assign weights of 70 percent of the most recent demand, 20 percent of the demand one week ago, and 10 percent of the demand two weeks ago. Using the data for the Dublin Medical Clinic, we calculate the average demand in week 3 to be

$$A_3 = 0.70(411) + 0.20(380) + 0.10(401) = 403.8.$$

The forecast for week 4 therefore is $F_4 = 403.8$ patients.

Now, suppose that the actual demand for week 4 is 415 patients. The new average and the forecast for week 5 would be

$$A_4 = 0.70(415) + 0.20(411) + 0.10(380) = 410.7;$$

$$F_5 = 410.7 \text{ patients.}$$

The weighted moving average method has the same shortcoming as the simple moving average method: data for N periods of demand must be retained so that the average can be computed for each period. This amount of data is not a great burden for simple situations such as our three-week and six-week examples. However, some time series are quite stable, and moving average calculations for 200 or more periods are not uncommon. For a company that has to forecast many different demands, data storage and update expenses can be costly.

Single Exponential Smoothing. Perhaps the most frequently used forecasting method is **single exponential smoothing** because of its simplicity and the small amount of data needed to support it. We call it *single* because we estimate only the average of the series. The basic premise of exponential smoothing is that recent demands should have more weight than earlier ones in computing the average for forecasting purposes. However, unlike the weighted moving average method, single exponential smoothing requires only three pieces of data: the average for the last period; the demand for this period; and a smoothing parameter, alpha (α). As before, we calculate an average of past demands at the end of the current period and use it as a forecast for the next period. However, we do not need much data in order to make the forecast, and we can adjust the amount of emphasis given to the most recent demand levels by simply adjusting the smoothing parameter.

The equations for the average of a demand series and the forecast using exponential smoothing are simply

Average: $A_t = \alpha D_t + (1 - \alpha)(A_{t-1}).$

Forecast: $F_{t+1} = A_t.$

Where: α = Smoothing parameter with a value between 0 and 1.

Table 3.6

Single Exponential Smoothing Weights

Demand	Weight	Numerical Weights for $\alpha = 0.1$	$\alpha = 0.2$	$\alpha = 0.8$
D_t	α	0.1000	0.2000	0.8000
D_{t-1}	$\alpha(1-\alpha)^1$	0.0900	0.1600	0.1600
D_{t-2}	$\alpha(1-\alpha)^2$	0.0810	0.1280	0.0320
D_{t-3}	$\alpha(1-\alpha)^3$	0.0729	0.1024	0.0064
D_{t-4}	$\alpha(1-\alpha)^4$	0.0656	0.0819	0.0013
D_{t-5}	$\alpha(1-\alpha)^5$	0.0590	0.0655	0.0003
D_{t-6}	$\alpha(1-\alpha)^6$	0.0531	0.0524	0.0001
D_{t-7}	$\alpha(1-\alpha)^7$	0.0478	0.0419	0.0000
D_{t-8}	$\alpha(1-\alpha)^8$	0.0430	0.0336	0.0000
D_{t-9}	$\alpha(1-\alpha)^9$	0.0387	0.0268	0.0000

Derivation of weight expressions

Let $t = 2$:

$$A_2 = \alpha D_2 + (1-\alpha)A_1$$

$$A_1 = \alpha D_1 + (1-\alpha)A_0$$

Substitute the expression for A_1 into the equation for A_2:

$$A_2 = \alpha D_2 + \alpha(1-\alpha)D_1 + (1-\alpha)^2 A_0$$

Let $t = 3$:

$$\begin{aligned} A_3 &= \alpha D_3 + (1-\alpha)A_2 \\ &= \alpha D_3 + (1-\alpha)[\alpha D_2 + \alpha(1-\alpha)D_1 + (1-\alpha)^2 A_0] \\ &= \alpha D_3 + \alpha(1-\alpha)D_2 + \alpha(1-\alpha)^2 D_1 + (1-\alpha)^3 A_0 \end{aligned}$$

Larger values of alpha emphasize recent demand and result in forecasts that are more responsive to changes in the underlying average; smaller values of alpha treat past demand more uniformly and result in more stable forecasts.* Exponential smoothing gets its name from the nature of the weights placed on each successive historical demand used to compute the average. Table 3.6 shows the general expressions for the weights to be placed on the ten most recent levels of demand in a series and the corresponding numerical weights for three assumed values of α. As with the weighted moving average method, the sum of the weights must equal 1, which is implicit in the single exponential smoothing equation. Table 3.6 also shows the derivation of the general expressions for the first three weights in the series.

In order to use the single exponential smoothing method we need an

* A_t can also be calculated using the forecast for period t: $A_t = \alpha D_t + (1-\alpha)(F_t)$.

initial value for the average. Suppose that we take the data for several weeks of past demand at the Dublin Medical Clinic and average them, arriving at a value of 400 as an estimate of the past average. To obtain the forecast for week 4, using single exponential smoothing with an assumed alpha of 0.10, we can calculate the average at the end of week 3 as follows:

$$A_3 = 0.10(411) + 0.90(400) = 41.1 + 360.0 = 401.1.$$

The forecast for week 4, F_4, would then be 401.1 patients. If the actual demand for week 4 turned out to be 415, the new average would be

$$A_4 = 0.10(415) + 0.90(401.1) = 402.5,$$

and the forecast for week 5, F_5, would be 402.5 patients. Table 3.7 shows a

Table 3.7

Exponential Smoothing Forecasts

Week (t)	Actual Demand (D_t)	$\alpha = 0.1$ ($F1_t$)	Error ($D_t - F1_t$)	$\alpha = 0.2$ ($F2_t$)	Error ($D_t - F2_t$)
1	401				
2	380				
3	411				
4	415	401.1	13.9	402.2	12.8
5	393	402.5	−9.5	404.8	−11.8
6	375	401.5	−26.5	402.4	−27.4
7	410	398.9	11.1	396.9	13.1
8	395	400.0	−5.0	399.5	−4.5
9	406	399.5	6.5	398.6	7.4
10	424	400.1	23.9	400.1	23.9
11	433	402.5	30.5	404.9	28.1
12	391	405.6	−14.6	410.5	−19.5
13	396	404.1	−8.1	406.6	−10.6
14	417	403.3	13.7	404.5	12.5
15	383	404.7	−21.7	407.0	−24.0
16	402	402.5	−0.5	402.2	−0.2
17	387	402.5	−15.5	402.2	−15.2
18	410	400.9	9.1	399.1	10.9
19	398	401.8	−3.8	401.3	−3.3
20	433	401.4	31.6	400.6	32.4
21	415	404.6	10.4	407.1	7.9
22	380	405.6	−25.6	408.7	−28.7
23	394	403.1	−9.1	403.0	−9.0
24	412	402.2	9.8	401.2	10.8
25	439	403.1	35.9	403.3	35.7
26	416	406.7	9.3	410.5	5.5
27	395	407.7	−12.7	411.6	−16.6
28	419	406.4	12.6	408.3	10.7

comparison of the performance of an exponential smoothing model for alpha values of 0.10 and 0.20.

Single exponential smoothing has the advantages of simplicity and minimal data requirements. It is inexpensive to use and therefore very attractive to firms that make thousands of forecasts each time period. However, its simplicity is also a disadvantage when the underlying average is changing, as is the case of a demand series with a trend. Like any method geared solely to the assumption of a stable average, single exponential smoothing results will lag behind changes in the underlying average of demand. Higher values of alpha may help to reduce forecast errors; however, the lags will still be there to some degree. Typically, if large values of alpha (greater than 0.50, for example) are required for a single exponential smoothing application, chances are good that a more sophisticated model is needed because of a significant trend and/or seasonal influence in the demand series. We address the issue of choosing the best value of alpha later.

Including a Trend

Let's now consider a demand time series that has a trend. Although a number of methods for recognizing a trend in making forecasts are available, we will focus on exponential smoothing here, since it is so widely used in practice. When a trend is present the average of the series is systematically increasing or decreasing over time. Single exponential smoothing approaches must be modified; otherwise, the forecasts will always be below or above the actual demand. An estimate of the current trend in a time series is the difference between the simple average of the series computed for the current period and the average computed for the last period. To obtain a better estimate of a long-term trend we can reduce the effects of random causes by averaging the current estimates. The method for arriving at the estimate of the trend is similar to the method we used to get the estimate of the average with single exponential smoothing.

The method for incorporating a trend in an exponentially smoothed forecast is called **double exponential smoothing** because we smooth the estimate for the average as well as the estimate for the trend. For each period we calculate the

Average:	$A_t = \alpha D_t + (1 - \alpha)(A_{t-1} + T_{t-1})$
Current estimate of trend:	$CT_t = A_t - A_{t-1}$
Average trend:	$T_t = \beta CT_t + (1 - \beta)T_{t-1}$
Forecast:	$F_{t+1} = A_t + T_t$
Where:	A_t = Exponentially smoothed average of the series in period t.

CT_t = Current estimate of the trend in period t.

T_t = Exponentially smoothed average of the trend in period t.

F_{t+1} = Forecast for next period.

α = Smoothing parameter with a value between 0 and 1.

β = Smoothing parameter with a value between 0 and 1.

We need an initial estimate for the average and the trend in order to get started. We can derive these estimates from past data or simply make an educated guess based on past experience.

Let's apply the double exponential smoothing method to the Dublin Medical Clinic data. Suppose that we are at the end of week 3, during which we had 411 patients. Our initial estimates of the average and the trend are 400 patients and 1 patient per week, respectively. Let's choose alpha (α) = 0.3 and beta (β) = 0.2. We proceed with the forecast for week 4 as follows:

$$A_3 = 0.3(411) + 0.7(400 + 1) = 404;$$

$$CT_3 = 404 - 400 = 4;$$

$$T_3 = 0.2(4) + 0.8(1) = 0.8 + 0.8 = 1.6;$$

$$F_4 = 404 + 1.6 = 405.6.$$

If the actual number of patients in week 4 turned out to be 415, the updated forecast for week 5 would be

$$A_4 = 0.3(415) + 0.7(404 + 1.6) = 408.4;$$

$$CT_4 = 408.4 - 404 = 4.4;$$

$$T_4 = 0.2(4.4) + 0.8(1.6) = 2.2;$$

$$F_5 = 408.4 + 2.2 = 410.6.$$

Table 3.8 shows the remainder of the forecasts for the 28 weeks and Fig. 3.4 shows the comparison of forecasts for one period ahead to actual demand. Several comments are in order at this point. First, we did not look very closely at possible values for alpha and beta, so we may be able to come up with a better forecast, using different values. We discuss how to choose the best values after covering forecast errors and their measurement. Second, we can make forecasts for periods beyond the next period by simply multiplying the

Table 3.8

Trend-Adjusted Exponential Smoothing Forecast (α = 0.3 and β = 0.2)

Week (t)	Actual Demand (D_t)	Forecast (F_t)	Error ($D_t - F_t$)
1	401		
2	380		
3	411		
4	415	405.6	9.4
5	393	410.6	−17.6
6	375	406.4	−31.4
7	410	396.2	13.8
8	395	400.4	− 5.4
9	406	398.5	7.5
10	424	400.9	23.1
11	433	409.4	23.6
12	391	419.5	−28.5
13	396	412.2	−16.2
14	417	407.6	9.4
15	383	411.3	−28.3
16	402	402.0	0.0
17	387	401.1	−14.1
18	410	395.2	14.8
19	398	398.9	− 0.9
20	433	397.7	35.3
21	415	409.6	5.4
22	380	412.8	−32.8
23	394	402.6	− 8.6
24	412	399.1	12.9
25	439	402.9	36.1
26	416	415.8	0.2
27	395	417.9	−22.9
28	419	411.7	7.3

trend estimate by the number of additional periods that we want in the forecast and add the result to the current average. For example, if we are in week 5 at the Dublin Medical Clinic and we want to estimate the demand for week 8, the forecast would simply be 408.4 + 3(2.2) = 415 patients (for α = 0.3, β = 0.2, and T_t = 2.2). However, the farther we project our trend estimate the more tenuous our forecast becomes. Thus the forecast for one period ahead for week 8 calculated in week 7 is 400.4 (see Table 3.8), which is much better than the forecast of 415 we made in week 5 for week 8. Even though this may not always be the case, this example indicates that the use of time series methods for forecasting should be restricted to the short term.

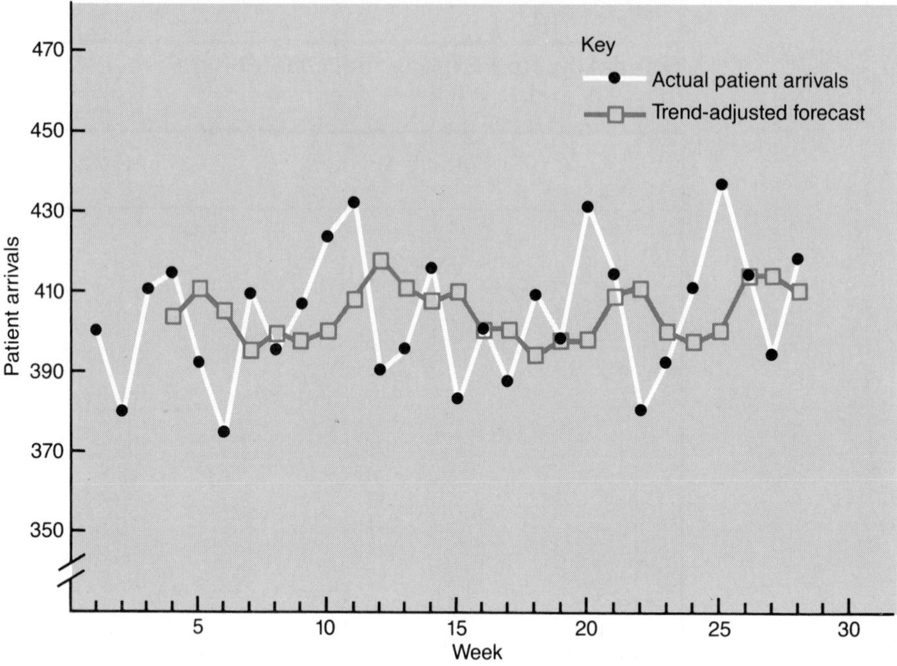

Figure 3.4

Trend-Adjusted Forecast.

Seasonal Influences

Many organizations experience seasonal demand for their products or services. The volume of letters processed by the U.S. Postal Service increases dramatically during the Christmas holiday period. Demands for products such as lawn and garden supplies, snow shovels, automobile tires, clothing, and construction supplies all have seasonal influences. Even the demand for telephone service is seasonal, as anyone trying to call relatives during holiday periods is well-aware. A number of methods are available for forecasting time series with seasonal influences. We present only the **multiplicative seasonal method** here because it is simple, and it introduces the notion of seasonal factors.

Consider Table 3.9, which contains historical demand data for a product experiencing seasonal influences. Typically, demand hits a trough in the first quarter and a peak in the third quarter. Let's examine 1983 more closely. The

Table 3.9

Calculation of Seasonal Factors

	1983		1984		1985		1986		
Quarter	Demand	Seasonal Factors*	Demand	Seasonal Factors*	Demand	Seasonal Factors*	Demand	Seasonal Factors*	**Average Seasonal Factors†**
1	45	0.18	70	0.23	100	0.22	100	0.18	0.20
2	335	1.34	370	1.23	585	1.30	725	1.32	1.30
3	520	2.08	590	1.97	830	1.84	1160	2.11	2.00
4	100	0.40	170	0.57	285	0.63	215	0.39	0.50
Total	1000		1200		1800		2200		
Quarterly average demand	250		300		450		550		

* Actual demand in a quarter divided by the average demand per quarter; subject to minor roundoff error.
† Average of the quarterly seasonal factors.

total demand for that year was 1000 units, or an average of 250 units per quarter. We can calculate a *seasonal factor* for each quarter by dividing the actual demand in a quarter by the average quarterly demand for that year. For example, in 1983 the first-quarter demand was 18 percent of the average demand of 250 units, which gives us an estimate of the seasonal factor for the first quarter in one year.

We repeat this process for each year of historical data. Table 3.9 shows the estimates of each quarter's seasonal factor for the years 1983–1986. A simple way to arrive at one seasonal factor for each quarter is to average the four estimates. These average seasonal factors appear in the right-hand column.

In order to use this method, we need to project total demand for 1987. We can make this projection in a number of ways, including the use of causal or qualitative methods, which we discuss later in this chapter. For now, let's suppose that after reviewing the historical trend of annual demand and the external and internal factors that could affect future demand, we believe that the annual demand for 1987 should be 2600 units. Our estimate of the average quarterly demand, then, is 2600/4 = 650 units. We make the quarterly forecasts by simply multiplying the seasonal factor for each quarter by the projected average quarterly demand, or

$$F_{1987,\,1} = 650 \times 0.20 = 130$$

$$F_{1987,\,2} = 650 \times 1.30 = 845$$

$$F_{1987,\,3} = 650 \times 2.00 = 1300$$

$$F_{1987,\,4} = 650 \times 0.50 = 325$$

At the end of each year we calculate the seasonal factors for that year. We can update the average seasonal factor for each quarter by calculating the average of all historical seasonal factors for that quarter, or by calculating a moving average or single exponentially smoothed average if we want some control over the relevance of past demand patterns.

The multiplicative seasonal method gets its name from the way we calculate and use the seasonal factors. When we multiply the seasonal factor by an estimate of the average period demand, we are assuming that the seasonal influence is dependent on the level of the series. The peaks and valleys are more extreme when the average demand level is high, a situation faced most often by organizations that produce goods and services having a seasonal demand. An alternative to the multiplicative seasonal method is the *additive seasonal method,* which assumes that the seasonal influence is a constant regardless of the average level of demand. Fig. 3.5(a) shows the pattern of additive seasonal influences, and Fig. 3.5(b) shows that of multiplicative seasonal influences.

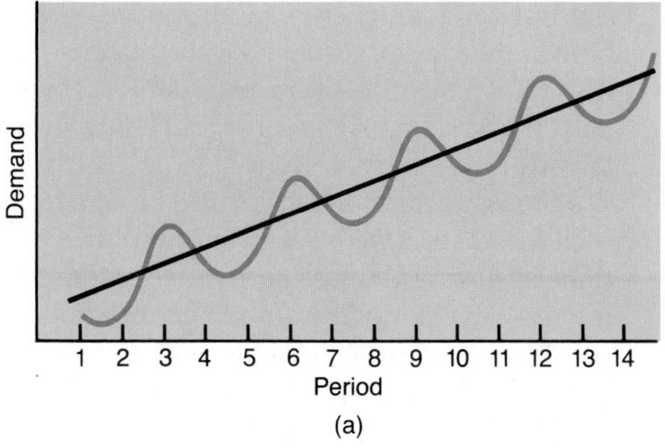

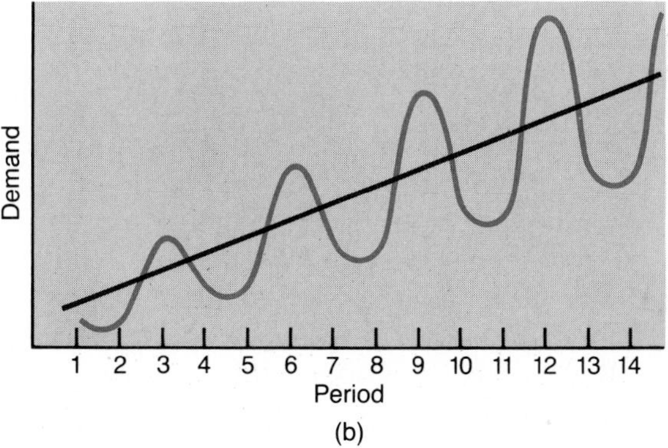

Figure 3.5

Comparison of (a) Additive and (b) Multiplicative Seasonal Influences.

Focus Forecasting

Is it always true that the more sophisticated the forecasting model is, the better the forecast will be? Is there one best forecasting technique for all products or services? The answer to both questions is no. In 1978, Bernard Smith, an inventory manager at American Hardware Supply, recognized these realities of forecasting and developed what he called **focus forecasting.**

Smith was responsible for an inventory of the 100,000 items purchased by the company's 21 buyers. Originally, the company used a basic exponential smoothing system with a curve-fitting method for projecting seasonal influences. These forecasts were used to determine purchase quantities. However, the buyers were changing 53 percent of the suggested purchase quantities. One of the major reasons that the buyers did not use these quantities was that they did not understand exponential smoothing and consequently did not trust the system. Their constant changes resulted in excessive purchases and levels of inventory.

Smith decided to survey the buyers to find out how they arrived at their own forecasts. One buyer computed the percentage increase in demand experienced during the last period and used it to project the increase in demand for the next period. Another buyer simply used the demand from the last period as the forecast for the next period. Other buyers used similar, simple methods for forecasting demand. Each buyer was responsible for a different group of items, and Smith had no reason to believe that any one of the methods would work well for all items.

Using the suggested methods from the buyers and adding some statistical methods, including exponential smoothing, Smith selected seven forecast methods as the basis for his focus forecasting technique. Every month all seven of the forecasting methods are used to make forecasts for each item. Historical data are used as the starting point for each method, and forecasts are made for recent demand. The forecasting method that produces the best forecast for recent demand data is chosen as the current method to be used to make the forecast for an item. The following month, the "best" forecasting method for an item may be different than the one chosen the current month.

Each month the computer prints the forecast for each of the 100,000 items. Buyers have the opportunity to override the computer forecast. However, Smith claims that his system provides excellent short-term forecasts for American Hardware Supply. The system is used for expensive as well as inexpensive items and has much more credibility with the buyers than the previous system.

Forecast Errors

There is a Chinese proverb that says, "To prophesy is extremely difficult, especially with respect to the future." And so it is with forecasting—there will always be errors. Forecast errors arise for many reasons, sometimes as a result of our inability to accurately assess the underlying components of demand and sometimes because of random causes outside of our control.

Measures of Forecast Errors. While it is logical to think in terms of minimizing forecast errors, we must have some means of measuring them first. Some commonly used measures of forecast errors are

Cumulative sum of forecast errors: $$\text{CFE} = \sum_{t=1}^{n} (D_t - F_t).$$

Standard deviation of forecast errors: $$\sigma = \sqrt{\frac{\sum_{t=1}^{n} (D_t - F_t)^2}{n}}$$

Mean absolute deviation of forecast errors: $$\text{MAD} = \frac{\sum_{t=1}^{n} |D_t - F_t|}{n}$$

Percentage forecast error in period t: $$P_t = \frac{100(D_t - F_t)}{D_t}$$

Where:

D_t = Actual demand in period t.

F_t = Forecast for period t.

n = Total number of periods.

$|\ |$ = Mathematical symbol used to indicate the absolute value, which disregards positive and negative signs.

The *cumulative sum of forecast errors* (CFE) is useful in measuring the *bias* in a forecast. Bias refers to the tendency of a forecast to always be too high or too low. For example, if a forecast is always lower than actual demand, the value of CFE will gradually get larger and larger. This increasingly large error indicates that there is some systematic deficiency in our forecasting approach. Perhaps we omitted a trend element or a cyclical influence, or perhaps the seasonality of the demand changed from its historical pattern. We explain later how we use CFE to develop a tracking signal to indicate when we should be concerned about forecast performance.

The *standard deviation* (σ) and the **mean absolute deviation** (MAD) measure the dispersion of forecast errors. If σ or MAD are small, the forecast is typically close to actual demand, whereas if they are large, there is the possibility of large forecast errors.* In practice, MAD is a popular measure of forecast errors because managers can easily understand it; it is merely the average error for each forecast. This measurement is also used in tracking signals and inventory control. You will see in Chapter 12 that MAD or σ can be used to determine safety stocks for inventory items. The greater that MAD or σ is, the larger the safety stock required, placing a premium on forecasting methods that result in small forecast errors.

* The standard deviation (σ) is a poor measure of forecast error variability if the forecasts are biased. For example, if all the forecast errors were +10, the standard deviation of forecast errors *should* be zero (no variation), but the formula for σ would yield some other value.

If forecast errors are normally distributed, which is the usual case if we properly specify the forecast model, there is a simple relationship between σ and MAD:

$$(1)\sigma = \sqrt{\frac{\pi}{2}}\text{MAD} \simeq 1.25\text{MAD} \qquad \text{or} \qquad (1)\text{MAD} = 0.7978\sigma \simeq 0.8\sigma,$$

where $\pi = 3.1416$. This relationship enables us to use the normal probability tables with MAD, which we discuss later.

MAD can be calculated each period as the simple average of all absolute forecast errors. However, MAD can be updated by using the single exponential smoothing method as well; that is

$$\text{MAD}_t = \alpha|D_t - F_t| + (1 - \alpha)\text{MAD}_{t-1}.$$

There are advantages to this approach: less historical data have to be retained for each estimate and recent forecast performance can be emphasized more heavily than past performance.

The *percentage of forecast error* (P_t) relates the forecast error to the level of demand and is useful in putting forecast performance into proper perspective. For example, an error of 100 would be considered large if the demand were only 200 units, whereas it would be insignificant if the demand were 10,000 units. Table 3.10 shows how P_t and the other measures of forecast error are calculated.

Table 3.10

Comparison of the Measures of Forecast Errors

Month (t)	Actual Demand (D_t)	Forecast (F_t)	Error ($D_t - F_t$)	Absolute Deviation $\lvert D_t - F_t \rvert$	Percentage Error (P_t)
1	200	180	+20	20	+10.0
2	240	250	−10	10	− 4.2
3	300	320	−20	20	− 6.7
4	270	250	+20	20	+ 7.4
5	230	240	−10	10	− 4.3
6	260	250	+10	10	+ 3.8

$$\text{Standard deviation } (\sigma) = \sqrt{\frac{(20)^2 + (-10)^2 + (-20)^2 + (20)^2 + (-10)^2 + (10)^2}{6}} = 15.8.$$

$$\text{Mean absolute deviation (MAD)} = \frac{20 + 10 + 20 + 20 + 10 + 10}{6} = 15.0.$$

$$\text{Cumulative forecast error (CFE)} = 20 - 10 - 20 + 20 - 10 + 10 = 10.$$

Table 3.11

Percentage of the Area of the Normal Probability Distribution within the Control Limits of the Tracking Signal

Number of MADs	Number of σ's*	Percentage of Area within Control Limits†
±1.0	±0.80	57.62
±1.5	±1.20	76.98
±2.0	±1.60	89.04
±2.5	±2.00	95.44
±3.0	±2.40	98.36
±3.5	±2.80	99.48
±4.0	±3.20	99.86

* The equivalent number of standard deviations is found by using the approximation of (1)MAD $\simeq 0.8\sigma$.

† The area of the normal curve included within the control limits is found in Appendix D.3. For example, the cumulative area from $-\infty$ to 0.80 is 0.7881. The area between zero and $+0.80\sigma$ is $0.7881 - 0.5000 = 0.2881$. Since the normal curve is symmetric, the area between -0.80σ and zero is also 0.2881. Therefore the area between $\pm 0.80\sigma$ is $0.2881 + 0.2881 = 0.5762$.

Tracking Signals. A **tracking signal** is a measurement that indicates whether a method of forecasting has any built-in biases over a period of time. If a correct forecasting system is being used, the cumulative sum of forecast errors (CFE) should tend toward zero. However, at any time, random errors can cause CFE to be nonzero. The tracking-signal formula is

$$\text{Tracking signal} = \frac{\text{CFE}}{\text{MAD}}.$$

Do Not Study

In this way the tracking signal measures the number of MADs represented by the cumulative sum of forecast errors. We can specify limits based on the normal probability tables, assuming that (1)MAD $= 0.8\sigma$. If the tracking signal falls outside the limits, we should check the forecast model that we are using because it no longer is tracking demand adequately. This approach is useful in computerized forecasting systems because it alerts us to forecasts that need attention. Table 3.11 shows the area of the normal probability distribution within the control limits of 1 to 4 MADs.

Choosing the limits for the tracking signal involves a trade-off between the cost of poor forecasts and the cost of checking for a problem when none exists. For example, suppose that CFE = 180 and MAD = 100; the tracking signal would be +1.8. If we had set the control limits of the tracking signal at ±1.5, we would check our forecasting method to see whether changes in the demand pattern indicate a needed change (1) in the model form (such as adding a trend estimate, or (2) in the values of the smoothing parameters. However, there is a chance that the value of +1.8 results from random variation only. In fact, with a limit of ±1.5, there is a probability of 0.115 (one-half the area outside the control limits) that we could get a value of the tracking signal greater than +1.5 as a result of random variation.

Choosing a Time Series Method

Another use of forecast error measurements is to provide input to the choice of the best forecasting method for a given product or service. For purposes of illustration, let's return to the Dublin Medical Clinic example and the models we developed for forecasting weekly patient arrivals. We will focus on MAD as a measure of forecast error dispersion in our discussion, but we could just as well use the standard deviation.

Criteria for Selection. Table 3.12 shows the forecast error performance of the models that we developed for the Dublin Medical Clinic. Choosing the best parameter values is closely related to choosing the components of demand for use in forecasting. In this example the latter choice involves including or excluding a trend component. The criteria to use in making choices of this sort include (1) minimizing MAD; (2) minimizing bias; and (3) meeting managerial expectations of changes in the components of demand. The first two criteria are statistical measures based on historical performance; the third reflects expectations of the future that may not have a foundation in the past.

Table 3.12

Forecast Error Performance of Various Forecasting Models for the Dublin Medical Clinic

Model*	Cumulative Sum of Forecast Errors (CFE—Bias)	Mean Absolute Deviation (MAD)	Tracking Signal (CFE/MAD)
Simple moving average			
a. Three-Week	23.1	17.1	1.35
b. Six-Week	69.8	15.5	4.50
Weighted moving average			
c. 0.70, 0.20, 0.10	14.0	18.4	0.76
Single exponential smoothing			
d. $\alpha = 0.1$	65.6	14.8	4.43
e. $\alpha = 0.2$	41.0	15.3	2.68
Exponential smoothing with trend			
f. $\alpha = 0.3, \beta = 0.2$	−7.9	16.2	−0.49
g. $\alpha = 0.3, \beta = 0.1$	−19.1	15.9	−1.20
h. $\alpha = 0.2, \beta = 0.1$	−29.5	15.6	−1.89

* The forecast performance of models a, b, d, e and f can be found in Tables 3.4, 3.5, 3.7, and 3.8, respectively.

The tracking signal is useful *after* you select a method—to identify when you should closely examine the model used in the assumptions.

Using Statistical Criteria. Let's begin by selecting the best value of N for moving average models based on MAD and bias considerations.* Regardless of the model, we would like to have forecasts with zero bias and zero MAD. Since this is impossible, we are often faced with a trade-off between bias and MAD, as demonstrated in Table 3.12. A value of $N = 3$ weeks gives us a lower bias but a greater MAD than does a value of $N = 6$ weeks. Normally, preference is given to lower values of MAD. However, in this example, the two values of MAD are not that much different, whereas the measures of bias are very different. A positive value of the cumulative sum of forecast errors indicates that, on balance, the forecasts have been too low. This can be very detrimental to operations at Dublin Medical Clinic, particularly if inventory supply ordering procedures and staffing schedules are based on the raw forecasts. If the difference in MAD is not significant, $N = 3$ seems like a good choice for the simple moving average model.

Similar considerations are involved in choosing alpha (α) for the single exponential smoothing model and alpha (α) and beta (β) for the double exponential smoothing model. Again, the differences in MAD are insignificant, but the differences in bias are significant. Larger values of alpha and beta seem to result in less bias than do smaller values in this example. Consequently, if we were to use the single exponential smoothing model, $\alpha = 0.2$ would be best. If we were to use the double exponential smoothing model, $\alpha = 0.3$ and $\beta = 0.2$ would be best.

Which model should we choose, based on the statistical measures of forecast errors? The differences between the MADs in our example are managerially insignificant, so the exponential smoothing model with trend does the best job. Thus the trend is a component of demand that we should consider in making our forecasts. There is some evidence in Table 3.12 to support the choice to include the trend. First, our choice of $N = 3$ for the simple moving average model and $\alpha = 0.2$ for the single exponential smoothing model over the other parameter values indicates a tendency to emphasize recent demand in the forecast. This condition occurs in a model designed to forecast only the average of a time series when a trend is actually present. Second, consider the tracking signal in Table 3.12. Suppose that we have set the limits at ± 2.5, which means that there is approximately a 2 percent probability that a tracking signal value will exceed 2.5 when nothing is wrong. If we had chosen a six-week moving average model or a single exponential smoothing model with $\alpha = 0.1$ or 0.2, the tracking signal would have indicated a problem with the assumptions used in the model. We might have decided to include a trend in the forecast at that time.

---

* No attempt was made to find the "best" models in Table 3.12. The results and our discussion should be viewed as illustrations of the uses that forecast measures have in the selection of a model.

Using Managerial Expectations. In Table 3.1 we indicated a number of external and internal factors that can affect demand. These factors can lead to changes in the nature of the components of demand, such as a change in the average level, the rate of trend, or the timing and size of peaks in a seasonal demand series. Such changes can cause historical data on customer demand to lose their relevance for projecting future demands. In some cases, management may use the parameters of a time series model as policy variables, depicting expectations of changes in the underlying components of demand. We can use two general guidelines in this regard:

1. For projections of stable demand patterns, low values of alpha and beta or large values of N give the best results and emphasize historical experience.
2. For projections of changing demand patterns, high values of alpha and beta or small values of N give the best results. When the historical components of demand are changing, emphasize recent history.

Regardless of the basis used for choosing the model parameters, forecast errors should be monitored and the parameters modified as needed. In this way a poor model choice can be detected.

CAUSAL METHODS

Causal methods are the most sophisticated forecasting tools. They are used when historical data are available and the relationship between the factor to be forecasted and other external or internal factors (such as those in Table 3.1) can be identified. These relationships are expressed in mathematical terms and can be very complex. Causal methods are by far the best for predicting turning points in demand and preparing long-range forecasts. A number of sophisticated causal methods are used, but we will focus on linear regression as an example.

Linear Regression

Linear regression is one of the best known causal methods of forecasting. In this approach one variable, called a **dependent variable,** is related to one or more **independent variables** by a linear equation. The dependent variable, such as demand or cost, is the variable we want to forecast. The independent variables are assumed to affect the dependent variable and thereby "caused" the results observed in the past.

To illustrate the use of linear regression we will use the simplest of models, in which the dependent variable is a function of only one independent variable. Such a situation is described in Box 3.3.

The linear regression method requires that we first hypothesize a relation-

Box 3.3

LINEAR REGRESSION AS A FORECASTING TOOL

Ohio Swiss Milk Products manufactures and distributes ice cream in ten communities located in Ohio, Kentucky, and West Virginia. The company wants to expand operations by locating another plant in northern Ohio. An issue of current concern is the size of the new plant because it will be a function of the expected demand for ice cream within the typical 900–square-mile area normally served by a plant. A market survey is currently underway, attempting to determine the demand for Ohio Swiss ice cream in the 900–square-mile area surrounding each of four potential sites. However, one of the major inputs to the final location decision is the manufacturing cost per gallon of ice cream (exclusive of raw materials costs), which depends on the size of the plant.

Ohio Swiss has experienced economies of scale in the production of ice cream, but the staff has never estimated the relationship between the manufacturing cost per gallon and the number of gallons produced in a year. The board of directors asked the staff to estimate this relationship so that the manufacturing cost per gallon for the new plant can be estimated when the demand has been estimated for each potential site.

The staff gathered data from each of the ten existing plants. The plants had outputs ranging from 238,100 gallons to 597,000 gallons per year and manufacturing costs ranging from \$967 to \$1068 per 1000 gallons produced. After examining the data, the staff concluded that the manufacturing cost per 1000 gallons produced could be approximated by

$$\begin{matrix}\text{Manufacturing cost} \\ \text{per 1000 gallons}\end{matrix} = a + b\begin{pmatrix}\text{Thousands of} \\ \text{gallons produced}\end{pmatrix},$$

where a and b are parameters to be estimated.

ship between the dependent variable and the independent variable. In the Ohio Swiss case, the staff hypothesized that the relationship would be a simple straight line:

$$Y_i = \alpha + \beta X_i + u_i,$$

where

Y_i = The actual manufacturing cost per 1000 gallons of ice cream at plant i.

X_i = The number of gallons of ice cream (expressed in thousands) produced at plant i.

α = The Y intercept of the line.

β = The slope of the line.

u_i = Random error.

Since we do not know the values of alpha and beta, we must estimate them from a sample of data. In this example, the sample consists of the manufacturing cost (Y_i) and the gallons produced (X_i) from each of the ten existing plants. These data are used to calculate a, the estimate of alpha, and b, the estimate of beta using a technique called *least squares*. The objective is to find values of a and b that minimize the sum of the squared deviations of the *actual* Y_i values from the *estimated* values, or

$$\text{Minimize} \quad \sum_{i=1}^{n} [Y_i - (a + bX_i)]^2,$$

where n is the number of data points in the sample.

The process of finding the values of a and b that minimize the sum of squared deviations is quite complex, so we will merely state the equations here.

$$a = \overline{Y} - b\overline{X} \qquad \text{and} \qquad b = \frac{\Sigma XY - n\overline{XY}}{\Sigma X^2 - n\overline{X}^2}$$

where

a = The estimate of the Y intercept.

b = The estimate of the slope of the line.

$\overline{Y}$ = The average of the Y values.

$\overline{X}$ = The average of the X values.

Linear Regression Analysis

Table 3.13 shows the linear regression analysis for the Ohio Swiss Milk Products problem. The data gathered from each plant are shown in the second and third columns. The last two columns contain the interim calculations needed for the computation of a and b. In order to determine the least squares regression line, we must first compute the slope b. When we have determined b, we can easily calculate a, as shown at the bottom of Table 3.13.

Just as in time series analysis, we can calculate a measure of forecast error. In this case it is called the *standard error of the estimate,* even though it is calculated in the same way that the standard deviation of forecast errors is calculated. The equation is

$$S_{YX} = \sqrt{\frac{\Sigma(Y_i - \hat{Y}_i)^2}{n}},$$

where $\hat{Y}_i = a + bX_i$ is the estimate of Y_i and n is the number of data points. In the Ohio Swiss problem, the standard error of the estimate is

Table 3.13

Linear Regression Analysis of the Manufacturing Cost of Ice Cream

Plant (i)	Cost per 1000 gal (Y_i)	Gallons Produced (000) (X_i)	(X_iY_i)	(X_i^2)
1	$ 1015	416.9	423,153.5	173,805.6
2	973	472.5	459,742.5	223,256.2
3	1046	250.0	261,500.0	62,500.0
4	1006	372.1	374,332.6	138,458.4
5	1058	238.1	251,909.8	56,691.6
6	1068	258.6	276,184.8	66,874.0
7	967	597.0	577,299.0	356,409.0
8	997	414.0	412,758.0	171,396.0
9	1044	263.2	274,780.8	69,274.2
10	1008	372.0	374,976.0	138,384.0
	$10,182	3,654.4	3,686,637.0	1,457,049.0

$$\overline{X} = \frac{\Sigma X}{n} = \frac{3654.4}{10} = 365.44$$

$$\overline{Y} = \frac{\Sigma Y}{n} = \frac{10,182}{10} = 1018.20$$

$$b = \frac{\Sigma XY - n\overline{X}\overline{Y}}{\Sigma X^2 - n\overline{X}^2} = \frac{3,686,637 - 10(365.44)(1018.20)}{1,457,049 - 10(365.44)^2} = -0.2819$$

$$a = \overline{Y} - b\overline{X} = 1018.20 - (-0.2819)(365.44) = 1121.2$$

$$S_{YX} = \sqrt{\frac{(1015 - 1003.7)^2 + (973 - 988.0)^2 + \cdots + (1008 - 1016.3)^2}{10}}$$

$$= 11.82,$$

and the estimated relationship for the manufacturing cost is

$$\hat{Y} = 1121.2 - 0.2819X.$$

We can easily plot the line by selecting two values of X, calculating the value of $\hat{Y}$ at these points, and connecting the points with a straight line. Suppose that we choose two extreme values of X from our data set, such as 238.1 and 597.0. The calculated values of $\hat{Y}$ at these points are 1054.1 and 952.9, respectively. The resulting line is shown in Fig. 3.6.

Note that the line has a negative slope, which indicates that the larger plants have lower per-unit manufacturing costs than smaller plants. In particular, costs are reduced by more than 28 cents per thousand gallons produced

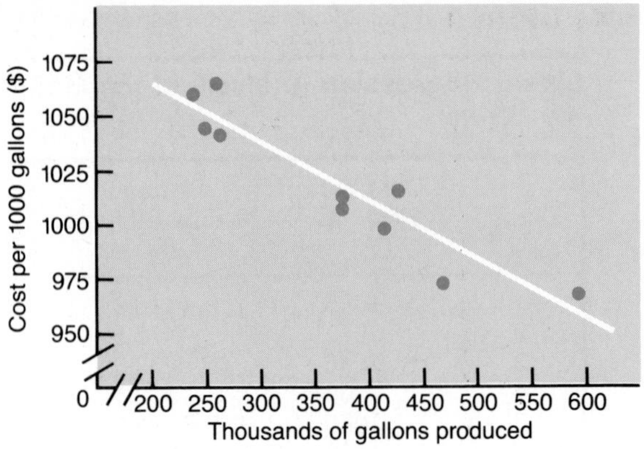

Figure 3.6

The Least Squares Regression Line of Manufacturing Costs for Ice Cream.

for each thousand gallons of capacity over the range of data used in the study. This reinforces the concept of economies of scale, which we discuss in Chapter 7. Our sample is limited to plants having capacities ranging from 238,000 to 597,000 gallons per year. We have no evidence to indicate the effects on costs for plant sizes outside that range; the relationship could even be nonlinear. Consequently, making cost estimates for plant sizes outside the range of our data would be very tenuous.

Suppose that the market survey data indicated an annual demand for Ohio Swiss ice cream of about 325,000 gallons in the 900–square-mile area surrounding Bucyrus, Ohio. The estimate of the manufacturing cost per thousand gallons for a plant producing 325,000 gallons a year would be

$$\hat{Y} = 1121.2 - 0.2819(325) = \$1029.58,$$

with a standard error of the estimate of 11.82.

This type of analysis can provide useful guidance for important operations management decisions. However, considerable amounts of data are needed in order to obtain useful relationships from linear regression models. This approach is relatively costly because of the amount of data gathering and analysis required to arrive at the proper model. In our Ohio Swiss example, we started with an assumption of linearity for the cost function. However, we could have made other assumptions, some of which may have been better than the one we chose. In addition, independent variables other than the number of gallons produced may also be important. Considerable analysis may be required before the final model is acceptable. Nonetheless, linear regression models are very good at predicting turning points and can be useful tools for solving many planning problems.

QUALITATIVE TECHNIQUES

The time series and causal methods of forecasting require a considerable amount of historical data to formulate a model. As we have shown, these techniques can produce good forecasts. However, situations arise in which good forecasts are needed, but historical data is lacking. Such is the case with the introduction of a new product or service or the need to forecast long-term technological change. Qualitative techniques have been designed for these situations. These techniques rely on judgment, experience, and other forms of qualitative information to generate the forecasts. In this section we discuss two of the more successful qualitative techniques currently in use: market research and the Delphi method.

Market Research

Suppose that you were in the process of planning a new business that would provide consumers the opportunity to do their grocery shopping by using a personal computer in their homes. They would hook up to your minicomputer through a telephone modem and your computer would show them all of the alternatives available, including price, for any food category of their choice. The customers would select the groceries they want and you would deliver them. Since this is a new service in your community, you are interested in the potential consumer demand for it. One way to determine consumer interest is to conduct a market research study. **Market research** is a systematic approach to creating and testing hypotheses about the market. Usually, data are gathered by conducting a survey.

Designing and conducting your market research study would include the following activities. First, you would need to design a questionnaire that would request the information you need. For example, you would like to obtain economic and demographic information from those interviewed. Such information might include (1) the store where they currently do their grocery shopping; (2) how far the store is from their homes; (3) their average weekly grocery bills; (4) whether they have a personal computer or terminal in the home; (5) annual family income; and, of course (6) whether they would be interested in your service. Second, in conjunction with the design of the questionnaire, you would need to decide how you will administer it. You have three choices: telephone polling, mailings, or personal interviews. If there are only a few questions, telephone calls are useful. More extensive questions are best handled by mailing the survey instrument to prospective customers. Questions involving some interpretation may require a personal interview.

A third activity is selecting a representative sample of households to survey. The sample should include a random selection of households within the market area of your new service. The size of the sample may depend on the cost of the method for administering the questionnaire as well as the time available for gathering the data. Finally, after the data have been collected, you must analyze it in order to answer the questions of interest. A considerable amount of judgment must be exercised in using the data to project demand for a new product because of economic or competitor factors that could not be included in the questionnaire. Also, the response rate on mailed questionnaires is typically low (30 percent is often considered good), and you must weigh the possibility that the respondents are an atypical group and no longer represent a random sampling of your potential market.

Market research can be used to forecast demands for the short, medium, and long terms. Accuracy is excellent for the short term, good for the medium term, and only fair for the long term. Although market research yields many benefits, actual results often fall short of expectations. Table 3.14 highlights some of these shortcomings.

Delphi Method

The **Delphi method** is a process of gaining consensus from a group of experts while maintaining their anonymity. This form of forecasting is useful when there are no historical data from which to develop statistical models; when judgment or opinion, based on experience and study of the market, industry, or scientific developments, are the only bases for making informed projections. The process involves a coordinator who conveys questions to each member of the group, who may not even know who else is participating. The experts respond to the questions and argue in support of their response. The coordinator pools the responses and prepares a report consisting of a statistical summary of the responses to the questions as well as a summary of arguments for particular responses to the questions. The coordinator sends the report to the same group for another round. The participants can repeat or modify their previous responses. Some form of consensus is usually obtained in two to four rounds. About two months are required to implement the process. The Delphi method can be used to develop long-range forecasts of product demands and new product sales projections; it is fair to good in identifying turning points in demand.

One of the more useful applications for the Delphi method is that of **technological forecasting.** The rate of technological change is increasing at a much greater pace than ever before. Medical science and computer science are just two examples of areas experiencing rapid technological change. Not too long ago, replacing a human heart with a mechanical heart was unthinkable. Computers become obsolete soon after they are produced. In addition,

Table 3.14

Ideal Goals Sought and Real Data Obtained from Market Research

Goals Sought	Actual Attainments
Unequivocal Findings: "Our product will find good customer acceptance."	*Hedged Findings:* "Good customer acceptance was revealed by our sampling survey, but we were unable to study the likely response for sustained periods when other competitive brands make their appearance."
Precision: "Exactly 80 percent of the market likes our product."	*Probability Estimate:* "It can be stated at a confidence of 90 percent (or 10 percent risk of error) that from 75 to 85 percent of the market likes our product."
Simplicity: Brief statements with readily understood implications are arrived at.	*Complexity:* Lengthy findings result, with numerous qualifications and involved implications that are often difficult to fully comprehend and interpret.
Definiteness: Planning can be based on solid expectations.	*Likelihood:* Findings are subject to risks and uncertainties of the marketplace.
Promptness: "Get the answer within the next 10 days."	*Delay:* Lengthy surveys and subsequent detailed analysis will be needed to come up with usable answers.

Source: Enrick, Norbert Lloyd, *Market and Sales Forecasting,* 2nd edition, Robert E. Krieger Publishing Company, Malabar, Florida, 1979. Reprinted by permission.

we have progressed to the point where an almost completely automated factory is possible. What is next? That question is the focus of technological forecasting. The Delphi method can be used to gain a consensus on the answer from a panel of experts. The panel members may be asked to specify the advancements that they believe will come from the scientific community, as well as changes in environmental and social forces such as quality of life, governmental regulations, and competitor actions. The questions are typically directed toward specific organizations or industries. The results of such a process can provide direction for a firm's research and development staff.

DESIGNING THE FORECASTING SYSTEM

We have discussed a number of forecasting methods in this chapter. It would seem that all we need to do is choose one, make our forecasts, and proceed to the next stage in analyzing operations management problems. Unfortunately, it is not that simple. The choice of method is certainly an important aspect of designing a forecasting system, but there are some other important considerations. When designing a demand forecasting system, we must determine (1) what we want to forecast; (2) what data to use; (3) what software package to use (for a computerized system); and (4) how the system can assist managerial decision making.

Deciding What to Forecast

It is not uncommon to hear operations managers say that forecasts of demand should be made for all goods or services produced by their companies. While some sort of demand estimate is needed for all items, it may not be necessary to expend the same energy and resources on each one. The sales volume of the item, the level of aggregation, and the unit of measurement are all considerations in determining what we should forecast.

Item Sales Volume. One way to identify those products deserving the most attention is to rank all the products sold on the basis of annual sales or profits. When the GAF Corporation ranked its products, it found that of 2000 film products, 45 accounted for 50 percent of the annual sales dollars; 125 accounted for 70 percent; and 385 accounted for 90 percent (Stratton, 1971). Consequently, more sophisticated forecasting methods and closer control of these 385 items was justified, while only a quarterly or semiannual review of the remaining 1615 items was needed. The process of relating the amount of control over an item to its sales volume is called an **ABC analysis.** A items are the most important, B items are of intermediate importance, and C items of least importance. The resources devoted to attaining accurate forecasts can be related to the importance of the item. The break-points for the A, B, and C categories are arbitrary but serve to focus attention on a select few. In Chapter 12 we discuss the ABC analysis in conjunction with inventory control.

Level of Aggregation. Very few companies have errors of more than 5 percent in their forecasts of total demand for all products. However, errors in forecasts for individual items range from −100 percent to +300 percent, or more (Plossl, 1972). Thus the greater the aggregation is, the more accurate are the forecasts. Many companies employ a two-tier forecasting system in which forecasts are first made for **product families;** then forecasts for individual items are derived in such a way that their sum equals the total forecast for the family. This approach maintains consistency between planning for the final stages of manufacturing (which requires the unit forecasts) and longer term planning for sales, profit, and capacity (which requires the product family forecasts).

Units of Measurement. Forecasts that serve as input to the planning and analysis of operations problems are most useful if they are based on product units, rather than dollars. Too often, forecasts given to operations managers are expressed in sales dollars. These forecasts are not very helpful because price can fluctuate and, even though the total dollar figure for sales could be the same from month to month, the actual number of units of demand could vary widely. It is often better to forecast the number of units of demand and then translate them to sales estimates by multiplying them by the price.

Sometimes it is not possible to forecast the number of units of demand for a product. Companies producing products or services to customer order face this problem. In such situations it is better to forecast the standard labor or machine *hours* required of each of the critical resources, based on historical patterns. For these companies estimates of labor or machine hours are important to scheduling and capacity planning.

Data Considerations

Suppose that you want to forecast the weekly demand for one of your high-volume products. Where would you get the historical demand data? Simply referring to company records is not sufficient. Would you look at the record of weekly shipments of your product and use those quantities as demand? This approach would be appropriate only if your company had no back orders of that product and all orders for a week were also shipped that week.

A better source of demand data is the record of orders booked. This first step in the **order entry sequence** occurs when a customer states the quantity desired and the date it is needed. Then, after a credit check and the proper documentation have been completed, the order is entered into the system. Next, total requirements are checked to determine whether capacity and materials are available to satisfy the demand. Finally, the order is accepted and the sales department can inform the customer. By this point the quantity or due date may have changed. Nonetheless, the real demand for the product was registered when the order was originally booked.

Selecting a Software Package (Computerized Systems)

Many forecasting software packages are available for all sizes of computers. These programs offer a wide variety of forecasting capabilities and report formats. Packages such as General Electric's *Time Series Forecasting System* and IBM's *Consumer Goods System* (COGS) and *Inventory Management Program and Control Technique* (IMPACT) contain forecasting modules used by many firms that have large computer facilities. Since the introduction of microcomputers, scores of software packages have been developed for virtually all of the popular personal computers. The applications range from simple to very sophisticated models. The prices of these microcomputer packages make them attractive alternatives to traditional mainframe packages.

Some techniques are more cost effective for short time horizons, while others are more appropriate for long time horizons. Thus selecting a forecasting software package is usually a decision made jointly by marketing and operations. Typically, an implementation team consisting of marketing and operations staff is charged with selecting a package from the wide variety available. The team may ask their departments for a "wish list" and then categorize the wishes as "musts" or "wants." Their final selection of the package will be based on considerations such as (1) how well the package satisfies the musts and wants; (2) the cost of buying or leasing the package; (3) the level of clerical support required; and (4) the amount of programmer maintenance required.

Considerations Involving Managerial Use of the System

Two aspects of managerial use of a computerized forecasting system deserve special mention. First, single-number forecasts are rarely useful because forecasts are almost always wrong. Consequently, a manager knows that if he or she gets a single number for the forecasted demand of a product, the actual demand will be anything but that figure. A far more useful approach is to provide the manager with a forecasted value and an error range, which can be done by using MAD. For example, suppose that the forecasted value for a product is 100 units, with a MAD of 10 units. Using Table 3.11, we could say that there is about a 95 percent chance that actual demand will fall within ±2.5 MADs of the forecast. We could tell the manager that the forecast is for 100 units and that we are 95 percent sure that actual demand will fall in the range of 75 to 125 units. Now the manager has a better feel for the uncertainty in the forecast and can better plan inventories, staffing levels, and the like.

The second aspect of managerial use worth considering is the expected amount of managerial interface with the system. Tracking signals should be computed for each forecast, and messages should be generated when the signals exceed the range selected. Managers should have the capability to override a computer-generated forecast with a forecast of their own or modify the models used when changes in the demand pattern dictate. The GAF Corporation, for example, generates a product-group forecast report that shows both the model's forecast and the forecast generated by the market staff based on experience and factors not included in the model. Managers are free to use either forecast, which helps them to gain confidence in the forecasting system.

CHAPTER HIGHLIGHTS

- Three general types of forecasting techniques are used for demand forecasting: time series analysis, causal methods, and qualitative techniques. All three types are useful for short-term forecasting, whereas causal methods and qualitative techniques are more appropriate for medium- and long-term forecasting.
- The five basic components of demand are the average, trend, seasonal influence, cyclical movement, and random error. An understanding of the external factors (outside of management's control) and the internal factors (within management's control) that affect the components of demand is essential for making good forecasts.
- Simple moving averages, weighted moving averages, and single exponential smoothing are techniques designed to forecast the average of a time series. The single exponential smoothing technique has the advantage of requiring a minimal amount of data to be kept for use in updating the forecast.
- Double exponential smoothing is a method for including a trend estimate in exponentially smoothed forecasts. Estimates for the series average and the trend are smoothed to provide the forecast.
- Although many techniques allow for seasonal influences, a simple approach is to derive seasonal factors for each period in the seasonal cycle from the average demand per period. These factors can be averaged for as many historical seasonal cycles as data are available. The seasonal factors can be applied to projections of the average future demand per period to obtain forecasts for each individual forecast period. This is an example of a multiplicative method, which is based on the assumption that the seasonal influence is proportional to the level of average demand.
- The cumulative sum of forecast errors (CFE), the standard deviation of forecast errors (σ), the mean absolute deviation (MAD), and the percentage forecast error (P_t) are all measures of forecast error used in practice. CFE and MAD are used to develop a tracking signal that determines when the forecasting model no longer is making good forecasts. Forecast error measures can also be used to select the best forecast model from available alternatives.
- Causal forecasting methods are more sophisticated than time series models and hypothesize a functional relationship between the factor to be forecasted and other internal or external factors. Linear regression is one of the more popular causal methods used in forecasting.
- Qualitative techniques of forecasting are useful in situations where there is a lack of relevant historical data. These techniques are based on the judgment, experience, and expertise of those who do the forecasts. Market research and the Delphi method are two examples of qualitative techniques. The Delphi method has been used to make forecasts of technological change.
- Considerations for designing a forecasting system include determining what to forecast, what data to use, what forecasting method and software package (in computerized systems) to use, and how the system can assist managerial decision making. Deciding what to forecast involves consideration of the value of the item, the level of aggregation required, and the units of measure.

KEY TERMS

ABC analysis
causal methods
coincident indicators
Delphi method
demand management
dependent variable
double exponential smoothing
focus forecasting
forecasts
independent variables
lagging indicators
leading indicators
market research
mean absolute deviation (MAD)
moving average method
multiplicative seasonal method
order entry sequence
product families
qualitative techniques
single exponential smoothing
technological forecasting
time series analysis
tracking signal
weighted moving average method

STUDY QUESTIONS

1. You have thousands of items in your product line and must forecast demand for each one on a weekly basis. Which of the three approaches (time series, causal, qualitative) would you use? Why?
2. You are the owner–manager of a new movie theater in town. The problem you face is that you get an overflow crowd of teenagers for your Friday and Saturday night showings of the horror movie "Bad Dreams on Mohican Way—Part 16" and very little attendance for other movies shown during the rest of the week. Discuss several ways in which you could use demand management to smooth the load on your facilities over the week and during the day on Saturday.
3. If you had to choose among simple moving averages, weighted moving averages, and single exponential smoothing to forecast demand for a product having no trend or seasonal components, which method would you choose? Why?
4. For what type of demand pattern is the single exponential smoothing model with a low value of alpha most appropriate? Explain.
5. You have just spent eight months developing a forecasting model of hourly check volumes to be processed by the encoding department of a large bank. Based on historical data, your model's forecasts resulted in a MAD of 500 checks. The first week you used the new model, the actual MAD was 1000 checks. Should you be concerned? Explain.
6. How can you use a simple regression model in conjunction with the seasonal factors approach to seasonal forecasting?
7. As a consultant, you have been asked to

look into the forecasting problems of a certain company. The company has been plotting the cumulative forecast error for each of their forecasts and using the results to judge the adequacy of its forecasting system. What are your reactions to their approach? What would you recommend?

8. As part of its product planning program, your company is interested in determining when the gasoline engine will be replaced by some other source of power for the automobile. How would you go about preparing such a forecast?
9. What are the trade-offs you must make in selecting a forecast model on the basis of forecast errors?
10. You have received two forecasts for a given product. The first says that demand next month will be 500 units. The other says that demand next month will be between 400 and 600 units. Which of the two forecasts would you prefer? Why?

PROBLEMS

1. Ted's TV sells and repairs television sets. The manager needs weekly forecasts of repair-service calls in order to plan required levels of repair personnel. The forecast for the week of October 3 was 50 calls. The manager uses a single exponential smoothing model with $\alpha = 0.2$. Find the forecast for the week of November 7, which is next week.

Week of	Actual Repair Calls
October 3	60
October 10	45
October 17	57
October 24	48
October 31	53
November 7	?

2. The Polish General's Pizza Parlor is a small restaurant catering to patrons with a European taste for pizza. One of its specialties is Polish Prize pizza. The manager must forecast weekly demand for these special pizzas so that he can order pizza shells weekly. Recent demand has been

Week of	Number of Polish Prize Pizzas
June 2	50
June 7	65
June 16	52
June 23	56
June 30	55
July 7	60

(a) Forecast the demand for Polish Prize pizza for June 23–July 7, using a three-period moving average model.

(b) Repeat part (a), using a weighted moving average model. The weights are 0.50, 0.30, and 0.20, where 0.50 refers to the most recent demand.

(c) Calculate the forecast errors for each method.

3. The Plushee Carpet Company sells and installs carpeting for all purposes, both indoor and outdoor. The manager is interested in forecasting the number of requests for carpet installation estimates, so

that she can better plan for the number of estimators required. The number of monthly requests for estimates during the past nine months are

Month	Requests for Estimates
January	30
February	40
March	23
April	27
May	40
June	47
July	35
August	38
September	40

(a) Using a four-month moving average model, forecast the number of July, August, and September requests.
(b) Using a six-month moving average model, forecast the number of July, August, and September requests.
(c) Compare the performance of the two models with a simple calculation of the forecast errors. Explain the relative performances of the two models.

4. The Northville Post Office experiences a "seasonal" pattern of daily mail volume every week. The following data for two representative weeks is expressed in thousands of pieces of mail.

Day	Week 1	Week 2
Monday	20	15
Tuesday	30	32
Wednesday	35	30
Thursday	50	48
Friday	70	72
Saturday	15	10
Sunday	5	8
Total	225	215

(a) Calculate seasonal factors for each day of the week.
(b) If the postmaster estimates that there will be 230,000 pieces of mail to sort next week, forecast the volume for each day of the week.

5. The monthly demand for units manufactured by the Acme Rocket company has been

Month	Units
May	100
June	80
July	110
August	115
September	105
October	110
November	125
December	120

(a) Use a single exponential smoothing model to forecast the number of units for June through December. The initial forecast for May was 105 units; $\alpha = 0.2$.
(b) Calculate the percentage error for each month from June through December and the MAD of forecast errors as of the end of December.
(c) Calculate the tracking signal as of the end of December. What can you say about the performance of your forecasting model?

6. The historical demand for a particular service is

Month	Number of Customers
June	5
July	15
August	10
September	20
October	50
November	15
December	35

(a) Assuming that the forecast for June was 10 customers, use a single exponential smoothing model with $\alpha = 0.1$ to forecast demand for December.

(b) Repeat part (a), but let $\alpha = 0.4$.
(c) Compare the two results using MAD.

7. The demand for Krispee Crunchies, a favorite breakfast cereal for people born in the 1940s, is experiencing a decline in demand. The company is interested in closely monitoring demand for this product as it nears the end of its life cycle. A double exponential smoothing model is used with $\alpha = 0.1$ and $\beta = 0.2$. For January, the estimate for the average number of cases sold per month was 900,000 and the trend was $-50,000$ per month. The following is the actual sales history for January, February, and March. Use the double exponential smoothing model to generate forecasts for February, March, and April.

Month	Sales
January	890,000
February	800,000
March	825,000

8. The materials manager of Columbus Coated Vinyl uses a forecasting model to estimate demand for one of the families of wall coverings the company produces. The forecast and the actual demand for the past 6 weeks are

Week	Forecast	Actual Demand
1	300	290
2	320	340
3	305	335
4	330	310
5	315	338
6	322	331

(a) Calculate the MAD of forecast errors.
(b) Calculate the tracking signal as of the end of week 6. What can you say about the forecasts generated by the model?

9. Consider the demand data for the product manufactured by the Acme Rocket Company in Problem 5.
(a) Use simple linear regression analysis to develop a forecasting model for monthly demand. In this application, the dependent variable is monthly demand (Y) and the independent variable is the month (X). For May, let $X = 1$; for June, $X = 2$; and so on.
(b) Use the model to forecast demand for January, February, and March. Here, $X = 9$, 10, and 11, respectively.

10. You are in charge of inventory control for your company. As part of your job, you must obtain forecasts of demand for the products stocked in inventory. Sales data for one of the products are

Week	Sales (000 Units)
1	264
2	116
3	165
4	101
5	209

(a) Use a single exponential smoothing model to forecast sales for week 6. The forecast for week 1 was 170, and $\alpha = 0.3$.
(b) During lunch with the marketing manager, you found out that there was a special advertising budget for this particular product. Advertising expenditures were

Week	Advertising ($000)
1	2.5
2	1.3
3	1.4
4	1.0
5	2.0

Use linear regression to develop a

forecasting model for this product. The marketing manager said that next week they will spend $1750 on advertising for that product. What is your demand forecast for week 6?

(c) Which of the two approaches—(a) or (b)—would you feel more comfortable with? Why? Discuss the advantages and disadvantages of your choice.

SELECTED REFERENCES

Adam, Everett E., "Individual Item Forecasting Model Evaluation," *Decision Sciences,* vol. 4, no. 4 (1973).

Box, George E. P., and Gwilym M. Jenkins, *Time Series Analysis: Forecasting and Control.* San Francisco: Holden-Day, 1970.

Brown, R. G., *Statistical Forecasting for Inventory Control.* New York: McGraw-Hill, 1959.

Chambers, John C., Satinder K. Mullick, and Donald D. Smith, "How to Choose the Right Forecasting Technique," *Harvard Business Review* (July–August 1971), pp. 45–74.

Eilon, Samuel, and Joseph Elmaleh, "Adaptive Limits in Inventory Control," *Management Science,* vol. 16, no. 8 (April 1970), pp. B533–B548.

Flowers, A. D., "A Simulation Study of Smoothing Constant Limits for an Adaptive Forecasting System," *Journal of Operations Management,* vol. 2 (1980), pp. 84–94.

Gardner, Everette S., "The Strange Case of the Lagging Forecasts," *Interfaces,* vol. 14, no. 3 (May–June 1984), pp. 47–50.

Gardner, Everette S., and David G. Dannenbring, "Forecasting with Exponential Smoothing: Some Guidelines for Model Selection," *Decision Sciences,* vol. 11, no. 2 (April 1980), pp. 370–383.

Huang, D. S., *Regression and Econometric Methods.* New York: John Wiley and Sons, 1970.

Mabert, Vincent A., "Forecast Modification Based on Residual Analysis: A Case Study of Check Volume Estimation," *Decision Sciences,* vol. 9, no. 2 (April 1978), pp. 285–296.

Makridakis, Spyros, Steven C. Wheelwright, and Victor E. McGee, *Forecasting: Methods and Applications,* 2nd ed. New York: John Wiley and Sons, 1983.

Plossl, George W., "Getting the Most from Forecasts." Paper presented at the APICS 1972 International Conference and reprinted in *Forecasting.* Falls Church, Va.: American Production and Inventory Control Society, 2nd ed., 1979.

Shiskin, Julius, Allan H. Young, and John Musgrave, "The X-11 Variant of the Census II Seasonal Adjustment Program," U.S. Bureau of the Census, Technical Paper No. 15, February 1967.

Smith, Bernard, *Focus Forecasting: Computer Techniques for Inventory Control.* Boston: CBI Publishing, 1978.

Stratton, William B., "How to Design a Viable Forecasting System," *Production and Inventory Management,* vol. 20, no. 1 (First Quarter 1979), pp. 17–27.

Trigg, D. W., and A. G. Leach, "Exponential Smoothing with an Adaptive Response Rate," *Operational Research Quarterly,* vol. 18, no. 1 (March 1967), pp. 53–59.

Whybark, D. Clay, "A Comparison of Adaptive Forecasting Techniques," *The Logistics and Transportation Review,* vol. 8, no. 3 (1972), pp. 13–26.

Wood, Steve D., "Forecasting Patient Census: Commonalities in Time Series Models," *Health Services Research,* vol. 11, no. 2 (1976), p. 158.

CHAPTER 4

PROCESS DESIGN

Some Managerial Issues

- What processes should we use to produce our goods and services?
- How much should we automate those processes?
- How capital intensive should our operations be?
- Do we need general-purpose or special-purpose equipment?
- How flexible should our work force be?
- How much should we vertically integrate?
- How much should we involve the customer in the production process?
- How do we fit the human element into process design?
- Should our jobs be specialized or enlarged?
- How should we select and train employees?
- What incentive systems can we use to best merge individual and organization goals?

Chapter Outline

Even after an organization's managers make choices concerning product plans, competitive priorities, and positioning strategy, many questions remain unanswered. One of the essential questions is: *How* should we make our products? The question is easy, but the answer involves many difficult choices in selecting the best mix of human resources, equipment, and materials. The examples in Box 4.1 underscore the variety of choices possible. General Motors, with its supersmart machines, and Saga Corporation, with its computer system, opted for more automation. Labor savings and better quality are gained from greater capital intensity. Equally important can be the choice of materials, as illustrated by the denim makers and Nucor Corporation. Changing the types of raw materials can lead to significant productivity gains.

Process design decisions are of strategic importance. The need for a close link with product design (the last step in product planning) is clear from GM's "simultaneous engineering" approach. Another reason for process design's strategic importance is that wrong choices can affect an organization's ability to compete over the long run. Process design is the foundation on which an organization will likely build for many years. It affects productivity, which is essentially the value of outputs divided by the value of the inputs (O/I =

Output/Input). Much of the input is set during process design. The AGV system at the new GM plant is a major commitment that cannot be quickly reversed. However, process design choices are not made once and for all because process design is an ongoing activity. The programs at the H. J. Heinz Company represent a relentless pursuit of ways to improve the production process. The principles and techniques that we present in this chapter apply to both first-time and redesign choices.

We begin by defining process design and considering four facets of process design: capital intensity, resource flexibility, vertical integration, and customer involvement. We turn next to some basic techniques frequently used to analyze new and existing processes: process charts, multiple activity charts, and flow diagrams. We conclude the chapter with a discussion of work-force management. This last section, concerning human resources, covers an essential element of process design and deserves careful consideration in any organization. The concern for employees is illustrated in Box 4.1 by the compensation plan at Nucor, the PEP program at H. J. Heinz, and the president's philosophy at Chaparral Steel. We cover job design issues related to employee selection, training, and compensation. We devote Chapter 5 to technological advances, which are another important aspect of process design, and the ever-widening array of choices they present.

WHAT IS PROCESS DESIGN?

Process design is the selection of inputs, operations, work flows, and methods used to produce goods and services. Input selection includes choosing the preferred mix of human skills, raw materials, and equipment consistent with an organization's positioning strategy and its ability to obtain these resources. This step involves determining which operations will be performed by workers and which by machines and the transformations (see Fig. 1.1) that will be used to meld human beings and machines into cohesive production processes. The examples in Box 4.1 suggest that the need for process design or redesign decisions arises for many reasons:

- A new or substantially modified product or service is being offered.
- Competitive priorities have changed.
- Volume of the product or service demanded is changing.
- Current performance is inadequate.
- Competitors are gaining a comparative advantage by using a different process, or a new technology is available.
- The cost or availability of inputs has changed.

Not all these situations lead to a change in the current process. In some situations, the costs of change clearly outweigh the benefits. Occasionally, as with a brand new product or the unavailability of a current input, a new process is mandatory. Most of the time, however, decisions in this area will not be so clear-cut. Even when they are, they must be carefully integrated with decisions about product design, product quality, capacity, and layout.

FACETS OF PROCESS DESIGN

Whether considering processes for offices, service industries, or manufacturers, we encounter four common facets of process design: degree of capital intensity, resource flexibility, vertical integration, and customer involvement. **Capital intensity** depends on the mix of equipment and human skills in a

Box 4.1

SOME PROCESS DESIGN EXAMPLES

- In a bid for Japanese-style efficiency, General Motors' new $5 billion Saturn plant in Spring Hill, Tennessee, will reflect many new cost-cutting ideas. The goal is to cut the 200 hours now required to assemble a small car to only about 35 hours. More complete modules, such as instrument panels and seats, will be built by outside suppliers. Old-fashioned conveyor lines will be replaced by an automatic guided vehicle (AGV) system. Cars mounted on carts will be guided from one operation to the next by a network of wires embedded in the floor. Supersmart machines will cut labor costs and improve quality. A process called "simultaneous engineering" is being used, which gets product design engineers, manufacturing engineers, and marketers to work jointly as the product is designed and the manufacturing process is selected.
- Saga Corporation, the leading operator of college dining halls, has entered the restaurant business. Since this is a low-margin industry, top efficiency is essential. A computer system is being considered for the "back room" operations of the restaurants. Waitresses would punch in orders at a dining room terminal. The computer would then print out orders in the kitchen, track the progress of the food orders, and prepare the next day's shopping list. The system costs $45,000 per restaurant, but would cut ordering time and deliver the dinner check sooner. Operations might be streamlined enough to handle overflows, which otherwise are turned away on busy nights.
- About 2500 churches in the United States now use computers for processes such as accounting, word processing, mailings, membership tracking, sermon writing, and bible study.
- Denim makers now have a new way to produce blue jeans with that prewashed look. Washed pants, which represent half of total sales, used to go through a process called "mill washing." A new fabric has been

production process; the greater the relative cost of equipment, the greater is the capital intensity. **Resource flexibility** is a measure of the ease with which equipment and employees can handle a wide variety of products, output levels, duties, and functions. **Vertical integration** relates to the supply chain from raw materials to final consumer; the more of the chain that is handled by a firm's own production system, the greater is the vertical integration. **Customer involvement** reflects how much and in what ways the customer becomes a part of the production process.

These four facets of process design are related. Choices made for one may significantly affect the choices for another. Fig. 4.1 represents these relationships as a triangular pyramid. The base of the pyramid is capital intensity. The other three facets are resource flexibility, vertical integration, and cus-

developed that looks and feels like it has been washed, even before being sewn. Savings range from 25 to 50 cents per pair.

- The Nucor Corporation in North Carolina uses scrap metal instead of expensive iron ore to make its steel. It uses the continuous-casting method to eliminate the intermediate process of making ingots. The work force is not unionized, but annual salaries and bonuses average $30,000 per worker.
- The H. J. Heinz Company has a "Profit Improvement Program" (PIP) to institutionalize the constant pressure for higher productivity in a price-competitive industry. Teams of *salaried workers* from different disciplines initiate projects having major cost-saving potential. Examples include new processes for peeling potatoes, reclaiming heat from blanching ovens, reducing the amount of can overfilling, automating tuna processing (even though fish come in different sizes), and taking staggered breaks at British plants (rather than completely shutting down the lines for the breaks). Another program, called "People Excellence Products" (PEP) encourages *hourly workers* to form teams to improve quality and cut costs.
- Chaparral Steel in Texas enjoys top labor productivity, requiring only 1.8 hours of labor per ton of steel. Its workers and supervisors seek out the latest equipment and methods. The president believes in a "classless society" at work, which is reflected by the profit-sharing plan in which everyone participates.

Sources: "Behind the Hype at GM's Saturn," *Fortune,* November 11, 1985; "The Dean of College Cuisine Smartens Up," *Fortune,* August 6, 1984; "Churches, Congregations Increasingly Use Personal Computers to Enhance Worship," *The Wall Street Journal,* December 12, 1984; "America's Best-Managed Factories," *Fortune,* May 28, 1984; "Heinz Pushes to Be the Low Cost Producer," *Fortune,* June 24, 1985.

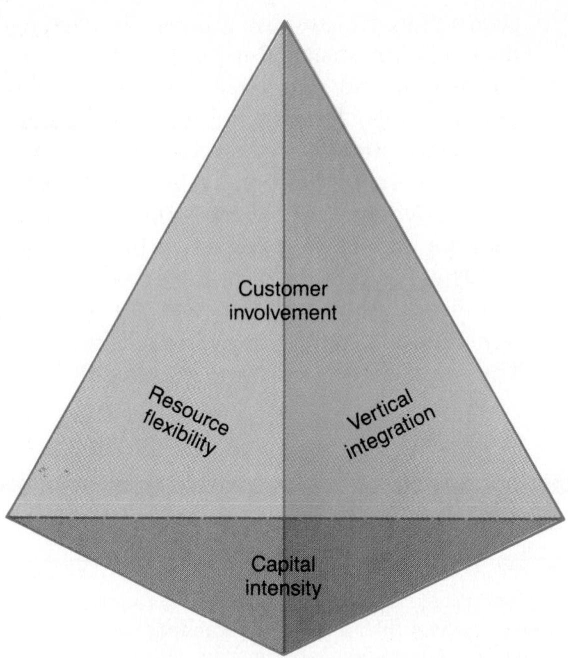

Figure 4.1

Facets of Process Design.

tomer involvement. Think of the edges as the linkages and trade-offs between pairs of the facets. The process design choices made about these facets depend on where products are in their life cycle, the competitive priorities, and positioning strategy selected.

The reliability of demand forecasts and management's views toward risk also affect the choices made. Present and projected market share, the volume of products or services to be produced over a specific period of time, and the ability of such products and services to command a price that will allow their profitable production must all be considered. Price and market share can be affected by the process chosen. For example, the automation of GE's dishwasher plant at Louisville, Kentucky, helped increase its market share from 32 to 40 percent.

Capital Intensity

Whether you are designing an entirely new process or redesigning an existing one, you have to determine what portion of the task will be performed by employees and what portion by machines. Clearly, GM's Saturn plant will be highly capital intensive in order to better combat the large gap between U.S. wage rates and those of the Japanese. Because of the great strides made in recent years in computer hardware and software, many types of equipment are now available to perform specific tasks with little human intervention. The process designer faces an ever-widening set of choices, ranging from a great deal of automation to very little. More capital intensity is not always best, as proved by E. T. Wright's shoemaking plant. It was selected in a recent survey as one of the ten best-managed factories, but the company still relies on skilled artisans and hand labor to make its arch preserver shoes. Competitive priorities call for a unique product of high quality, even if a pair of shoes retails for over $100. These priorities have not yet been achievable with high capital intensity.

Some types of equipment can be acquired a piece at a time, which allows the user to try it out without making a large and risky initial capital investment. Examples of such equipment are new photocopy machines and stand-alone word processors and printers. However, many technological choices involve large and costly systems—and a great deal more capital and risk. Another consideration is that different processes have different requirements for inventory and space. A process with a strong worker orientation may require more inventory to buffer differences in individual performance, and more space may be needed in order to meet health and safety requirements. Buffering against individual differences is one of the reasons for GM's AGV system, since each car can stay with the same worker until the job is done right.

Resource Flexibility

In Chapter 2, we discussed product flexibility and volume flexibility as competitive priorities. The ability to achieve either type of flexibility rests with the process design and choices made about employees, facilities, and equipment. These choices determine the *degree* of resource flexibility. When product plans call for short life cycles or when product flexibility must be high, equipment must be general purpose and employees need to perform a broad range of duties.

Until recently, there has been a strong inverse relationship between capital intensity and resource flexibility. Only when the volume of a particular product or service was high enough could a firm afford the capital investment needed for top efficiency. Fig. 4.2 illustrates this relationship for two processes. Process 1 calls for inexpensive, general-purpose equipment. It gets the job done, but not at peak efficiency. In terms of break-even analysis, the fixed cost, F_1, is relatively small, but the variable unit cost (slope of the total-cost line) is large. Process 2 is much more capital intensive, which drives up F_2. Its virtue is top efficiency and therefore a small unit cost. Unfortunately, this

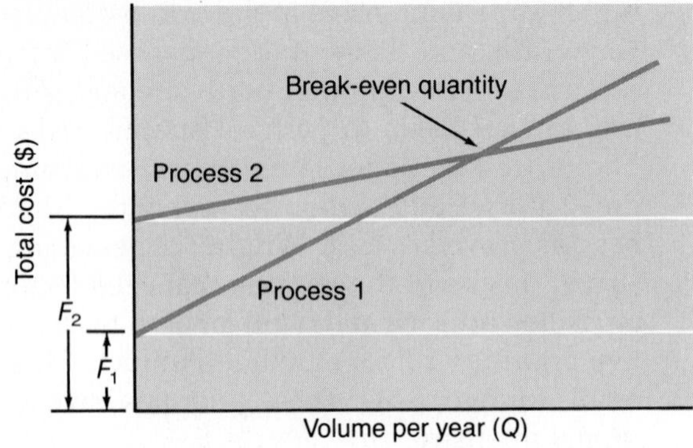

Figure 4.2

Relationship between Capital Intensity and Product Volume.

efficiency is often achieved only by dedicating special-purpose equipment to a narrow range of products or tasks. The break-even quantity in Fig. 4.2 is well to the right on the graph, which means that, unless volumes are high enough (which is less likely with high product flexibility), the capital intensity of process 2 is not warranted.

Exceptions to the inverse relationship between capital intensity and flexibility are beginning to emerge. For example, GM's Saturn system will have a computer system that will allow customers to order from a range of options at the dealership. The order will go to the computers of the Spring Hill plant, with production of the car beginning within hours. This example is but one of many where capital intensity (the computer system) and product flexibility (several product options) go together. As you will see in Chapter 5, newer technologies allowing certain types of flexible automation are available that are capital intensive but allow for more resource flexibility than was possible in the past.

Resource flexibility also has important implications for the work force. Operations managers must decide whether or not to have a **flexible work force.** If general-purpose equipment seems best, it may also be necessary for employees to be able to do different tasks at more than one work station or handle more than one type of customer. In this situation, decisions must be made about the type of skills, training, and education needed by workers and how much cross-training in other jobs to give them.

The union contract for GM's Saturn plant allows for considerable worker flexibility. There will be only four to six job classifications. Most automobile plants currently have dozens of job classifications, which severely limits resource flexibility. We showed in one study that worker flexibility is one of the best ways to achieve reliable customer service and alleviate capacity bottlenecks (Ritzman, King and Krajewski, 1984). Resource flexibility was found to be particularly crucial in environments calling for a process-focused positioning strategy. Low-volume production, jumbled routings, and fluid scheduling cause feast-or-famine workloads at individual operations, which resource flexibility helps absorb.

An example of worker flexibility issues concerns the staffing and specialization decisions faced by administrators of large urban hospitals. Many hospitals use an all RN nursing staff instead of a mix of registered nurses (RN), licensed practical nurses (LPN), and aides. Registered nurses have a higher education level and earn more than LPNs and aides, but they are more flexible because they can perform all nursing tasks and not just a selected subset of those tasks. Sometimes hospitals choose the opposite extreme (worker specialization) in an attempt to hold costs down. In Russia, for example, delicate eye surgery is performed on an "assembly line," which consists of patients on stretchers that glide past five work stations. A surgeon at each station has three minutes to complete a specific portion of the operation before the patient moves on to the next surgeon. Obviously, these surgeons are highly specialized. Resource flexibility has been sacrificed, but great speed and economy are attained.

The type of work force required also depends on the need for volume flexibility. When conditions allow for a smooth, steady rate of output, the likely choice is a permanent work force that expects regular full-time employment. If the process is subject to hourly, daily, or seasonal peaks and valleys in demand, the use of part-time or temporary employees to supplement a smaller core of full-time employees may be the best approach. However, this approach may not be practical if knowledge and skill requirements are too high for a temporary worker to grasp quickly.

Vertical Integration

A third facet of process design is vertical integration. All businesses buy some of the inputs to their processes. Purchased inputs may include raw materials, parts manufactured by someone else, or professional services. The degree of vertical integration reflects a firm's decisions about what to make itself and what to buy from others. Managers make vertical integration decisions by looking at the entire supply chain, including transactions and transformations, required for production—from the acquisition of raw materials until the finished product or service is delivered to the customer. The more vertically integrated a firm is, the more processes in the chain it chooses to control. *Backward integration* represents movement toward the sources of raw materials and parts. *Forward integration* means that the firm owns more of the channels of distribution, such as its own distribution centers (warehouses) or even retail stores. Examples of firms choosing varying degrees of vertical integration are shown in Box 4.2.

Extensive vertical integration is more likely to be attractive when volumes are high. A local restaurant simply does not have the volume to keep a team of six workers busy peeling eggs, even if they can process 10,000 in one shift, as at Atlantic Foods. Such efficiency comes from task specialization and high

Box 4.2

CHOOSING THE DEGREE OF VERTICAL INTEGRATION

More Integration

- Kroger Company, the largest food retailer in the United States during 1982, on the basis of domestic sales, has considerable backward integration. It operates dairies, a trout farm, and plants making peanut butter, crackers, coffee, and many other dry groceries. It sells these products under the Kroger label.
- Some of the largest U.S. corporations, such as Chase Manhattan, IBM, and GE, have joined together to start their own insurance company. The company offers to all of them high-risk coverage that big casualty insurers are reluctant to provide.
- General Motors paid $2.5 billion to acquire Electronic Data Systems (EDS), a company that specializes in overhauling computer systems. Looking at this acquisition as more than an investment, GM also wanted EDS to help solve its internal communication and data-processing problems. New information systems will help GM's suppliers, manufacturers, and employees communicate better with each other. By buying EDS, rather than contracting for services, a long-term contract cost of at least $3 billion was saved.

Less Integration

- While an old and controversial idea, more government work is being contracted out. Costs are often cut as much as 20 percent, without sacrificing quality. This goes beyond garbage collection, road repairs, and public transportation. Private industry is now under contract in some cases to staff control towers at small airports, operate prisons, run wastewater treatment plants, trim trees, and demolish buildings.
- Restaurants and food-service operators need hard-boiled eggs for salad bars and sandwiches. Many find it more efficient to buy precooked egg products than to process their own. Some suppliers use machines to peel their eggs, but Atlantic Foods feels that quality is improved by doing it manually. A team of six employees set a record of peeling 10,000 eggs in just one shift.

Sources: "Aggressive a Century, Kroger Is Retrenching to Stem Falling Profits," *The Wall Street Journal*, May 31, 1984; "Wall Street Eyes an Ultimate Junk Bond," *Fortune*, February 3, 1986; "Is Perot Good for General Motors?" *Fortune*, August 6, 1984; "When Public Services Go Private," *Fortune*, May 27, 1985; "Boiled-Egg Peelers Aim for Perfection, and That's No Yolk," *The Wall Street Journal*, July 9, 1985.

repeatability. Likewise, a corner grocery store does not have the sales volumes or resources to operate its own trout farm, as does Kroger. When high enough volumes are reached, a firm is more likely to pursue backward integration. This same principle applies to forward integration. For example, a firm that does not enjoy a large volume of deliveries is probably unable to economically justify its own network of regional warehouses.

Vertical integration can reduce resource flexibility. The necessary investment in facilities and equipment can be large and not easily reversed. For example, Kroger is experiencing problems caused by waning inflation. Customers are less enthusiastic about house brands and generic (no brand) products, turning more toward national brand groceries. This shift has created excess manufacturing capacity, which Kroger must fill; it is doing so by making ice cream or dough for frozen pizza for its competitors, which in turn sell the products under different labels. While this may be an ideal solution, excess capacity did limit Kroger's resource flexibility and range of acceptable business opportunities. Something had to be done about the resources tied up as idle equipment and facilities.

Make or Buy. Backward integration is often referred to as the *make-or-buy* decision. The costs and advantages of each approach must be studied. The make-or-buy problem for a fast-food restaurant adding salad to its menu is illustrated in Box 4.3. The economic analysis is straightforward in that the annual costs for both options must be estimated. All cost categories affected by a make-or-buy decision must be identified and all such costs should be included in the analysis. Equally important are qualitative factors. For example, customers might be willing to pay more for a salad that they can make to their own tastes (that is, more product flexibility). Another qualitative factor may be that the preassembled salad does not fit the image that customers have of Sandwich Castle. For these reasons, Rader chose to minimize risks by leasing the salad bar—the "make" decision. Although sizable capital investments are required for some "make" decisions, in other situations key considerations could be the availability and alternative uses of professional expertise, employee time, equipment, and space.

Own or Lease. When a firm decides on more vertical integration, it must also decide whether to own or lease the necessary facilities and equipment. These decisions frequently favor the lease option for items affected by fairly rapid changes in technology, items that require frequent servicing, or items for which industry practices have made leasing the norm, such as in the photocopier industry. Leasing is also common when a firm has a short-term need for equipment. For example, in the construction industry projects may take several months or years to complete, and heavy equipment is leased as needed.

Many firms lease payroll, security, cleaning, and other types of services, rather than employing personnel and using their other resources to provide these services. Frequently, an organization can hire a firm with the desired expertise and obtain a higher quality of service at a lower cost than it could obtain from a staff of its own.

Box 4.3

MAKE OR BUY AT SANDWICH CASTLE

The Problem

Mike Rader owns and operates Sandwich Castle, a fast-food restaurant with a menu limited to hamburgers and chicken sandwiches. He plans to add salad to the menu and has identified two feasible options. The "make" option is to install a salad bar stocked with various garden vegetables, fruits, salad dressings, and toppings and to let the customer assemble the salad. The "buy" option is to have several kinds of preassembled salads, such as Chef's salad, shrimp salad, and chicken salad, available for sale. Rader would buy the preassembled salads from a local supplier, although it would be necessary to install some additional refrigeration in the kitchen area for storing them.

Rader estimates the fixed cost of operating the salad bar at $12,000 per year, which includes leasing the salad bar from a local restaurant supply firm, the energy to operate the refrigerated unit, and another part-time employee to keep the salad bar stocked at the busiest times. Rader estimates ingredient costs, including the paper bowl for the salad, at about $2.00 for each salad made at the salad bar, although he thinks that will vary considerably from customer to customer. The preassembled salad alternative would have fixed costs of about $2,400 for leasing the additional refrigeration space and energy to run the units. The supplier charges $1.50 per salad. Rader expects to sell 20,000 salads per year.

Assuming that both salads will be sold at the same price, should Sandwich Castle let customers *make* their own salads on the premises or should it *buy* preassembled salads?

The Analysis

The Make Option

Added fixed cost and labor	$12,000
Cost of ingredients (20,000 × $2)	40,000
Total annual cost	$52,000

Cost per unit ($52,000 ÷ 20,000) = $2.60

The Buy Option

Added fixed cost	$ 2,400
Cost of preassembled salads (20,000 × $1.50)	30,000
Total annual cost	$32,400

Cost per unit ($32,400 ÷ 20,000) = $1.62

Choice of Materials. The decision to buy introduces still another round of choices. Several materials that could serve the same purpose are usually available. Differences in price, delivery time, quality, and vendor reliability all bear on the choice of materials. Cost differences can be significant to a firm because the typical manufacturer now spends some 60 percent of its total sales dollars on purchased materials and services. The trend toward disposables adds still another decision point: "dispose or reuse." One good example is the health care industry. Hospitals are high-volume users of such disposable items as syringes, scalpels, gloves, paper hospital gowns, and paper sheets for examination tables. Frequently, it is easier and cheaper to maintain sterile conditions with the use of disposable supplies. Their use, however, creates the problem of contaminated waste. Prevalent in other industries, concern over contaminated waste is now spreading to the health care industry. This concern on the part of the public may force hospitals to have their own incinerators and vertically integrate into the waste disposal business, as has occurred in Europe.

Customer Involvement

The fourth facet of process design is the extent to which the customer will be allowed to interact with the process. For service industries in which the service cannot occur without the presence of the customer, questions related to customer contact are critical. The two alternatives at Sandwich Castle (see Box 4.3) had different kinds of customer involvement relative to

1. self-service;
2. product selection; and
3. time and location.

Self-service. At a salad bar customers assemble the salad themselves. Self-service is a common process design choice of many retailers, particularly when price is a competitive priority. Self-service is also used to advantage by some product-focused manufacturers. Their customers become the final assemblers, as with inexpensive bicycles and furniture. Production costs are lower because the assembly process is simplified; shipping costs, inventory costs, and loss due to damage also are frequently lower. Some customers choose to take over parts of the process formerly performed by the manufacturer or dealer in order to save money. In other cases, competitive priorities require that customers receive full service and individualized attention. This type of situation has important implications for the work force, which needs strong social skills in dealing with the public. Such situations blur the boundaries between the marketing and operations functions.

Even industrial firms get involved with the process design decisions of their suppliers. Such participation is particularly true for long-term supply contracts, where a major customer wants to be sure of the quality standards and delivery reliability of the supplier. Japanese automobile manufacturers have worked with their suppliers on process design decisions for many years. As U.S. firms are moving to longer-term relationships with their vendors, it is not surprising to find major manufacturers exhibiting concern and offering advice to their suppliers about process design. Some suppliers are even soliciting input from their customers about these decisions.

Product Selection. The do-it-yourself salad bar at Sandwich Castle would give customers much more control over portions and ingredients. For a business that competes on the basis of product flexibility, the customer is involved by giving the order specifications or even doing the engineering design for the product. A builder of custom-designed homes is a good example of this approach. Customer involvement extends beyond the product design phase. During construction, the customer inspects the work-in-process at various points. Customer involvement with the builder's processes is not likely to end even when the owner occupies the house. Most builders guarantee their work for some extended time period, and most owners find reasons to exercise this warranty.

Timing and Location. Finally, the two salad options affect when and where the salad assembly takes place. For industries in which service cannot occur without the customer's presence, such issues affect the process design. If the service process calls for customers, clients, or patients to be met by appointment, decisions involving the location of such meetings become part of the process design decisions. Will the customers be served only on the suppliers' premises, or will the employees of the supplier go to the customers' premises? Will the service be provided at yet a third location? Operators of emergency ambulance services cannot predict when the next call for service will occur or where they will have to go and must design their processes accordingly. They cannot provide service without a patient. On the other hand, certified public accountants, in their role as independent auditors, frequently work on their clients' premises, a situation in which both the time and place are likely to be known well in advance.

High customer involvement tends to be less capital intensive and more resource flexible. These conditions are particularly true when there is a need for full service, customized orders, unpredictable demands, and service provided at customer locations. Exceptions can be found, such as with telephone exchanges, vending machines, and automatic bank tellers. However, these processes require a minimal amount of personalized attention.

Trade-offs between Facets

We have identified several trade-offs among the four facets of process design. We can use the three fundamental relationships (trade-offs) shown in Fig. 4.3,

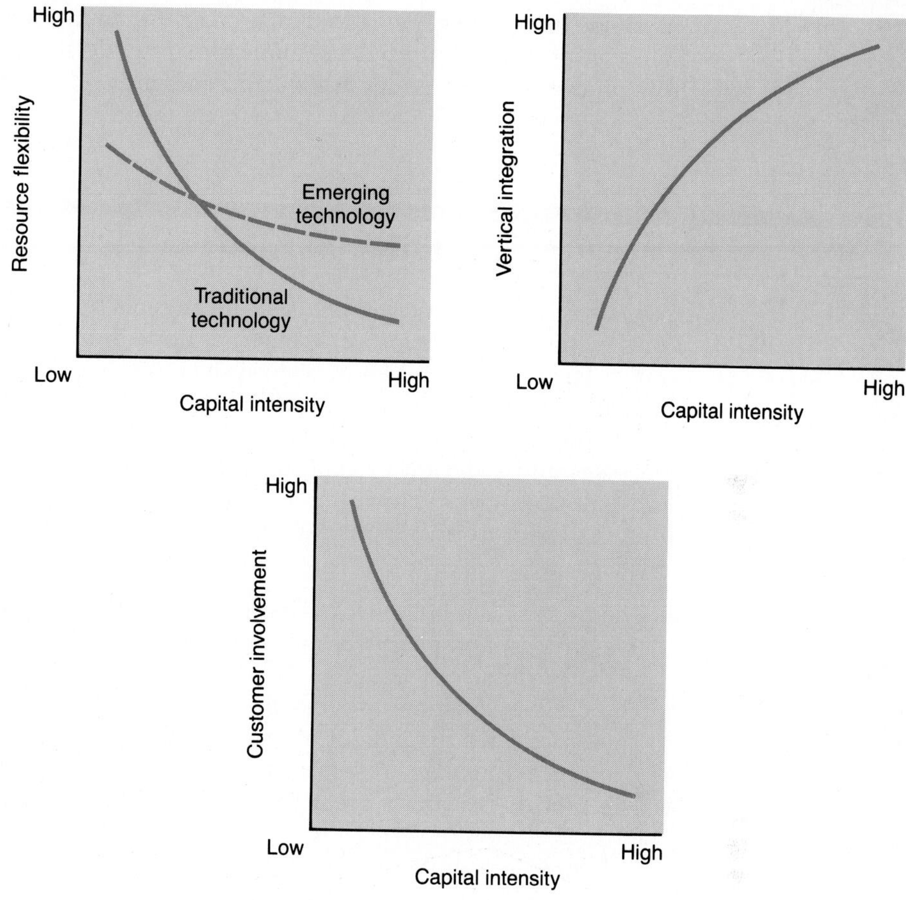

Figure 4.3

Trade-Offs in Process Design.

with capital intensity as a common facet, to infer trade-offs between the other pairs of facets not shown. For example, vertical integration and customer involvement relate oppositely to capital intensity. We can therefore conclude that there is an inverse relationship between them. Such relationships are not based on cause and effect. The underlying variable is repeatability, which comes from high product volumes, standardization of parts, task specialization, and low customer involvement. Increasing repeatability opens the door for

1. more automation (and therefore capital intensity);
2. less need for resource flexibility; and
3. more opportunities for vertical integration.

Of course, these are general tendencies rather than unbreakable laws. Exceptions can be found, but these relationships provide a way of understanding how process design choices are linked coherently.

ANALYTICAL TOOLS FOR PROCESS DESIGN

In this section we present three basic techniques for analyzing activities and flows within processes: process charts, multiple activity charts, and flow diagrams. These techniques allow us to systematically question the process itself and each detail of the process, highlighting areas where tasks can be simplified or productivity improved. We can use these techniques to design new processes and redesign existing ones and should use them periodically to study all operations. However, the greatest payoff is likely to come from applying them to operations having one or more of the following characteristics.

- The process is a bottleneck. That is, work piles up waiting to go through this process, and people or machines are idle while waiting for the output of the process.
- The process consumes a great amount of time.
- The process results in a lot of waste materials.
- The process involves disagreeable or dangerous working conditions.
- The process requires a great deal of physical movement.

All three techniques involve breaking a process into detailed components. In order to do this, we ask six questions:

What is being done?	*Where* is it being done?
When is it being done?	*How long* does it take?
Who is doing it?	*How* is it being done?

Answers to these questions are challenged by asking still another question: *Why?* Why is it even being done? Why is it being done where it is being done? Why is it being done when it is being done? Such questioning can often lead to some creative answers that can cause a breakthrough in process design.

These techniques are closely related to techniques presented in Chapter 6 (work measurement), since time estimates are needed for the different tasks in the process. However, time estimates are also needed in many other aspects of operations management, such as for capacity, production planning, staffing, and scheduling decisions.

Process Charts

A **process chart** is an organized way of recording all the activities that are performed by a person, by a machine, at a work station, or on a material. We can break these activities into five categories: operation, transportation, inspection, delay, and storage. An *operation* consists of changing something, creating something new, or adding to something. Productive work of some sort is being done. Examples of operations are mixing tar, stone, and sand to get asphalt; drilling a hole; or loading a railcar. *Transportation* (sometimes called materials handling) means that the subject of the study moves from one place to another. The subject can be a person, a material, a tool, or a piece of equipment. Examples of transportation are a customer walking from one end of a counter to another, a crane hoisting a steel beam from a truck bed to the spot where it is needed at a construction site, or a conveyor carrying a partially completed product from one work station to the next.* *Inspection* consists of checking or verifying something, but not changing it. Checking for blemishes on a surface, weighing a product, or taking a temperature reading are examples of inspections. *Delays* occur when the subject is held up awaiting further action. Time spent waiting for materials or equipment, time for clean-up, or time that workers, machines, or work stations are idle because there is nothing for them to do are examples of delays. *Storage* occurs when something is put away until a later time. Supplies being unloaded and placed in a storeroom as inventory, equipment put away after use, or papers put in a file cabinet are examples of storage. Depending on the situation, other activity categories may be used, such as "subcontracting/outside services" or distinguishing between "temporary storage" and "permanent storage."

In order to complete a process chart for a new process you must identify each step required for each activity. If the process is an existing one, you can actually observe the steps. Each step is categorized relative to the subject being studied. If the subject taken as the focal point changes (say, from the product being made to the worker) so might the category to which a step is assigned change. You then record the distance traveled and the time† taken to perform each step. When you have recorded all the activities and steps, you total time and distances, summarize the activities, and estimate the annual cost of the entire process.

Table 4.1 illustrates a process chart for making a batch of brownies at a bakery. The process begins with the baker removing preassembled brownie mix and ends when the large pan of brownies is removed from the oven. Raw materials (the brownie mix, water, and eggs) and equipment and container

* Materials handling processes, including packaging and storage, are discussed further in Chapter 5.

† See Chapter 6 on the various ways to establish time standards.

Table 4.1

Process Chart for Making Brownies at a Bakery

Process: making one batch of brownies
Subject charted: baker

Beginning: remove brownie mix from bin
Ending: remove brownies from oven

Summary			
Activity	Number of Steps	Time	Distance
Operation	18	22.5	
Transport	13	11.7	550
Inspect	2	0.2	
Delay	2	40.0	
Store	—	—	

Step No.	Time (Min)	Distance (Ft)	Operation	Transport	Inspect	Delay	Store	Step Description
1	1.3		X					Remove preassembled brownie mix from adjacent storage bin
2	0.2		X					Place mix on counter
3	1.2	60		X				Walk to cabinet
4	0.4		X					Remove bowl and mixer
5	1.2	60		X				Return the bowl and mixer to counter
6	0.2		X					Place bowl and mixer on counter
7	1.3		X					Open brownie mix bag and dump contents into bowl
8	1.2	60		X				Walk to cabinet
9	0.3		X					Remove pan and measuring container
10	1.2	60		X				Return with pan and measuring container to counter
11	0.2		X					Place pan and measuring container on counter
12	0.6	30		X				Walk to refrigerator
13	0.8		X					Remove eggs from refrigerator
14	0.6	30		X				Walk back to counter
15	0.1		X					Place eggs on counter
16	2.8		X					Break eggs into brownie mix; place egg shells on counter
17	2.2		X					Use mixer to stir eggs and brownie mix
18	0.9	40		X				Pick up measuring container; walk to sink
19	1.4		X					Turn on water faucet; fill measuring container; turn off faucet
20	0.8	40		X				Walk back to counter

Step No.	Time (Min)	Distance (Ft)	OPERATION	TRANSPORT	INSPECT	DELAY	STORE	Step Description
21	0.3		X					Pour water into brownie mix; put container on counter
22	4.3		X					Use mixer to thoroughly stir ingredients in bowl
23	0.1				X			Inspect mixture in bowl
24	1.9		X					Pour mixture into pan
25	0.1				X			Inspect mixture in pan
26	0.3		X					Discard egg shells in adjacent trash container
27	0.9	40		X				Take bowl, mixer, and measuring container to sink
28	4.0		X					Wash bowl, mixer, and measuring container; dry them
29	0.6	20		X				Return bowl, mixer, and measuring container to their cabinet
30	0.2	10		X				Walk to oven
31	10.0					X		Turn on oven; let oven preheat
32	1.0	50		X				Walk to counter
33	1.3	50		X				Pick up pan; walk to oven; place pan in oven
34	30.0					X		Wait 30 minutes while brownie batch bakes; turn off oven
35	0.5		X					Open oven; remove pan; close oven
	74.4	550						Totals

(bowl mixer, measuring container, and pan) must be assembled. The brownie mix must be prepared, the oven preheated, and the brownies baked. The analyst broke this process into 35 steps, which take an average of 74.4 minutes to complete. The subject of the study is the baker, who traveled a total distance of 550 feet.

It is helpful to know the annual cost of the process charted, which becomes a benchmark against which other methods for performing the process can be evaluated. The annual labor cost can be estimated by finding the product of the following factors.

- Time in hours to perform the process each time.
- Variable cost per hour.
- Number of times the process is performed per week.
- Number of weeks per year in which the process is performed.

Assuming that the baker earns \$17 per hour (including variable fringe benefits) and that the process is performed 12 times per week, we calculate the total labor cost to be

$$(74.4 \text{ min}/60 \text{ min}) \text{ hr} \times \$17/\text{hr} \times 12/\text{wk} \times 52 \text{ wk/yr} = \$13{,}154/\text{yr}.$$

Adding in costs for materials would result in a sizable total cost—and brownies are but one of many products made at the bakery.

A summary of the activities is shown in the upper right-hand corner of the process chart. Careful analysis of the process gives us three ideas for improvements:

1. Eliminate the preheating delay.
2. Combine the trips for equipment.
3. Eliminate the first mixing.

Preheating Delay. Although there are only two delays, they account for 40 minutes, which is more than 50 percent of the time needed for the entire process. The first delay is at step 31, when the baker waits 10 minutes for the oven to preheat. If the oven were turned on earlier, other activities could be performed while the oven preheats. The baker would then be productive during those 10 minutes. If the oven is turned on during the first trip to the cabinet (step 3), there is an added bonus: Since the oven is located on the way to the cabinet, some travel time is saved.

Trips for Tools. An analysis of transport activities reveals that the baker walks to the cabinet twice to get tools. This is inefficient, since the tools are not heavy or large enough to require two trips; even if they were unwieldy, a cart could be used. Combining steps 3–5 with steps 8–10 saves time, since all the tools are gathered at once, and eliminates 120 feet of travel.

First Mixing. Steps 16, 17, 21, and 22 can be rearranged to add the eggs and water to the brownie mix before mixing. This cuts out another step and a little time.

Other Changes. The improvements made so far are reflected in Table 4.2, a revised process chart for baking a batch of brownies. We have eliminated six steps and cut about 20 percent off the total time and distance traveled. There still may be other opportunities for improvement. In the revised process (Table 4.2) the delay time of 30 minutes (step 28) stands out. Perhaps the baker can start the next job while the brownies are baking, or make up more preassembled brownie mix for future batches.

Summary. This simple example illustrates how to use a process chart to analyze a process. In other manufacturing or service industry environments, the method is the same, even though the processes, materials, and equipment are different. To make a process more efficient, you should question each delay and then analyze the operation, transport, inspection, and storage activities to see whether they can be combined, rearranged, or eliminated. Improvements in productivity can be significant.

Multiple Activity Charts

A process chart describes the work being done by or on just one subject. In Tables 4.1 and 4.2, the subject is the baker. Sometimes it is more revealing to simultaneously track multiple subjects. This tracking is the purpose of a **multiple activity chart,** which shows the activities performed by or on several subjects over some time period. Multiple activity charts are useful in determining how work can be divided among members of a group on a more equal basis, how time for certain elements can be reduced, how elements can be rearranged to shorten the overall time for a job, and how people, work stations, or machines can be utilized more effectively. Finding ways to minimize idle time is a particular goal of analysts when they use multiple activity charts.

You begin by first determining the process to be studied. Divide a sheet of paper into columns, with one for each person, material, or work station. This form serves as the basis for your multiple activity chart, on which you then list each important element of the process. You next observe the process, establish a time standard for each element (see Chapter 6), and chart the time required to perform each element by using vertical bars having lengths that represent these times.

In Box 4.4, we describe a situation in which Dr. Wilson, an orthodontist, is trying to decide whether to continue with four patient work stations and two technicians or to increase capacity to six patient work stations and three technicians. A multiple activity chart is a good tool to use in analyzing this

Table 4.2

Revised Process Chart for Making Brownies at a Bakery

Process: making one batch of brownies
Subject charted: baker

Beginning: remove brownie mix from bin
Ending: remove brownies from oven

Summary

Activity	Number of Steps	Time	Distance
Operation	15	20.7	
Transport	11	9.6	430
Inspect	2	0.2	
Delay	1	30.0	
Store	—	—	

Step No.	Time (Min)	Distance (Ft)	Operation	Transport	Inspect	Delay	Store	Step Description
1	1.3		X					Remove preassembled brownie mix from adjacent storage bin
2	0.2		X					Place mix on counter
3	1.3	50		X				Walk to oven; turn it on for preheating
4	0.2	10		X				Continue walking on to cabinet
5	0.5		X					Remove bowl, mixer, pan, and measuring container
6	1.2	60		X				Return to counter with equipment
7	0.3		X					Place equipment on counter
8	1.3		X					Open brownie mix bag and dump contents into bowl
9	0.6	30		X				Walk to refrigerator
10	0.8		X					Remove eggs from refrigerator
11	0.6	30		X				Walk back to counter
12	0.1		X					Place eggs on counter
13	0.9	40		X				Pick up measuring container; walk to sink
14	1.4		X					Turn on water faucet; fill measuring container; turn off faucet
15	0.8	40		X				Walk back to counter
16	0.3		X					Pour water into brownie mix; put container on counter
17	2.8		X					Break eggs into brownie mix; place egg shells on counter
18	5.0		X					Use mixer to thoroughly stir ingredients in bowl

Step No.	Time (Min)	Distance (Ft)	OPERATION	TRANSPORT	INSPECT	DELAY	STORE	Step Description
19	0.1				X			Inspect mixture in bowl
20	1.9		X					Pour mixture into pan
21	0.1				X			Inspect mixture in pan
22	0.3		X					Discard egg shells in adjacent trash container
23	0.9	40		X				Take bowl, mixer, and measuring container to sink
24	4.0		X					Wash bowl, mixer, and measuring container; dry them
25	0.6	20		X				Return bowl, mixer, and measuring container to cabinet
26	1.2	60		X				Walk to counter
27	1.3	50		X				Pick up pan; walk to oven; place pan in oven
28	30.0					X		Wait 30 minutes while brownie batch bakes; turn off oven
29	0.5		X					Open oven; remove pan; close oven
	60.5	430						Totals

Box 4.4

PROCESS DESIGN IN AN ORTHODONTIST'S OFFICE

Dr. Edward Wilson is an orthodontist with a large, well-established practice. He sees current patients for biweekly adjustment of their braces on three mornings each week, from 7:00 A.M. until noon, and on two afternoons from 2 to 5 P.M. The procedure followed during these routine visits is for the receptionist to seat the patient in one of four chairs; Dr. Wilson then checks the patient. After this check, which takes about one minute, one of two orthodontic technicians adjusts the patient's braces. The adjustment procedure takes the technicians about eight minutes per patient. After the braces are adjusted, Dr. Wilson again checks the patient and makes any necessary final adjustment. This final check takes about two minutes. Dr. Wilson has developed very efficient procedures because many of his patients are students and professional business people who do not want to miss school or work for long periods. His objective is to get them in and out of the chair in 20 minutes or less.

Dr. Wilson currently has four chairs and employs two technicians. The technicians take about one minute between patients to wash their hands, and each technician is allowed to take a five minute break at the end of each hour. At their busiest, Dr. Wilson and the technicians are able to process twelve patients per hour. Many patients are referred to Dr. Wilson, and he would like to be able to expand his practice without expanding the hours he now devotes to routine brace adjustments. He is thinking of adding two more chairs and hiring one more technician. He wants to know how many more patients he can actually see in an hour if he continues to spend one minute with the patients before the technicians work on them and about two minutes with them after the technicians have finished.

situation because the orthodontist, the two technicians, and the four chairs may all be represented on the chart and their utilization determined. Fig. 4.4 is a multiple activity chart with columns for the orthodontist, technicians 1 and 2, and the four patient work stations A, B, C, and D. The receptionist seats the patients, but we are not interested in the receptionist's other activities here, so there is no column for the receptionist. Technician 1 works on patients in chairs A and B, and technician 2 works on patients in chairs C and D. This multiple activity chart is a typical representation of what happens during one of their busiest morning hours. The technicians are actually occupied for all but 7 minutes of the hour. Their utilization is a very high 88 percent, calculated by dividing the time they are occupied by the length of the time period being studied. Dr. Wilson's utilization is much lower. He is occupied only 36 minutes of the hour, for a utilization of 36/60 = 60 percent. You can also see on the multiple activity chart the amount of time that each

MULTIPLE ACTIVITY CHART

LOCATION: Dr. Wilson's Office DATE: 10-8-86 TIME: UNITS: Minutes

OBSERVER: S. Perry METHOD: ✓ PRESENT BEGIN: 7:06 AM

___ PROPOSED END: 8:06 AM

PROCESS: Routine check-up of patients - 4 chairs TOTAL ELAPSED: 60 Min.

SUMMARY:	TIME SPENT:			
ITEM	WORKING	IDLE	OTHER*	% UTILIZATION
Dr. Wilson	36	24		36/60 = 60%
Technician 1	53	7		53/60 = 88%
Technician 2	53	7		53/60 = 88%
Chair A	36	20	4	36/60 = 60%
Chair B	36	18	6	36/60 = 60%
Chair C	36	17	7	36/60 = 60%
Chair D	36	15	9	36/60 = 60%

*IDENTIFY OTHER: Chair is occupied, but patient is idle. Treat as idle time.

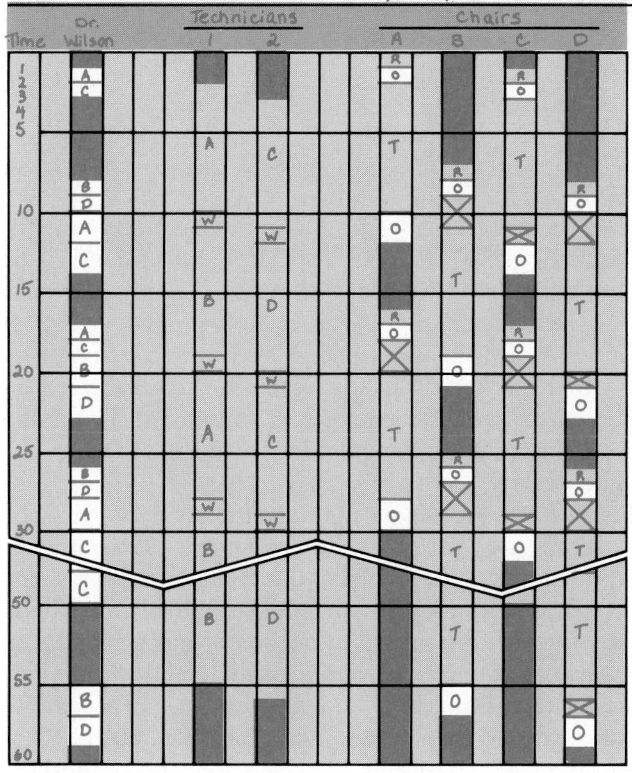

Key
A: Working on patient in chair A
B: Working on patient in chair B
C: Working on patient in chair C
D: Working on patient in chair D
O: Orthodontist working on patient
R: Receptionist seats patient
T: Technician working on patient
W: Washing hands
X: Chair occupied but patient idle
■: Idle time

Figure 4.4

Multiple Activity Chart for Orthodontist: Four Chairs.

chair is unoccupied, or occupied by a patient waiting for the next step in the process. On the morning of this analysis the patients in chair A had to spend only 4 minutes waiting, but the chair was unoccupied for 20 minutes of the hour (shown as idle time). Patients in chair D had to wait 9 minutes, but the chair was empty for only 15 minutes. Since this waiting time was spread over three patients, for three minutes each, it was probably acceptable to them.

Fig. 4.5 shows a hypothetical multiple activity chart for six chairs, three technicians and the orthodontist, under the same time constraints. The orthodontist now has as little unoccupied time as the technicians. All of them are busy for 53 minutes of 60, for utilization ratios of 88 percent. Even though almost every patient has to wait before and after seeing the technician, no patient's total time in the chair exceeds 20 minutes, so that goal can be met. It appears that Dr. Wilson can add two chairs and an additional technician to his staff and see 18 patients every hour instead of 12, but he and his technicians would be very busy.

Studies such as these have made dentistry a much different business than it used to be. The dental profession stands out in the health care industry as a leader in productivity improvement over the past several decades. These substantial gains are being studied carefully by the rest of the health care industry.

Flow Diagrams

When an operation involves a lot of movement of materials or people, a **flow diagram** is a useful analytical tool. It is the simplest of the three techniques and is a diagram of the flows of people, equipment, or materials through a process. To make a flow diagram, you first need a rough sketch of the area in which the process is performed. Make your sketch on a grid (graph paper or other paper marked off in squares). On the grid, trace the path followed by the person, material, machinery, or equipment. Finish the diagram by using arrows to indicate the direction in which the movement is made, that is, the direction of flow.

Fig. 4.6 shows a flow diagram for a car wash facility, illustrating the flows of cars and customers. Cars enter one of two lines from the street. The cars at the heads of the two lines alternate in forming a single line that rounds a sharp corner and into the washing bay. Just before the car enters the washing bay, the customer gets out of the car and walks through a separate door and hallway to the office where he or she makes payment. The car proceeds through the washing bay, and the customer proceeds through the hallway and out a second door to rejoin the car after it is rolled to an open area and wiped down. The customer gets back into the car and drives away. The car wash facility used to have only one waiting line, and, during peak periods, cars would extend into the street, blocking traffic. The car wash facility owner

MULTIPLE ACTIVITY CHART

LOCATION: Dr. Wilson's Office DATE: ______ TIME: UNITS: Minutes

OBSERVER: S. Perry METHOD: ___ PRESENT ✓ PROPOSED BEGIN: ______ END: ______

PROCESS: Routine check-up of patients - 6 chairs TOTAL ELAPSED: 60 Min.

SUMMARY:	TIME SPENT:			
ITEM	WORKING	IDLE	OTHER*	% UTILIZATION
Dr. Wilson	53	7		53/60 = 88%
Technician 1	53	7		53/60 = 88%
Technician 2	53	7		53/60 = 88%
Technician 3	53	7		53/60 = 88%
Chair A	36	17	7	36/60 = 60%
Chair B	36	16	8	36/60 = 60%
Chair C	36	14	10	36/60 = 60%
Chair D	36	13	11	36/60 = 60%
Chair E	36	11	13	36/60 = 60%
Chair F	36	12	12	36/60 = 60% (includes 1 min. of next hr.)

*IDENTIFY OTHER: Chair is occupied, but patient is idle. Treat as idle time.

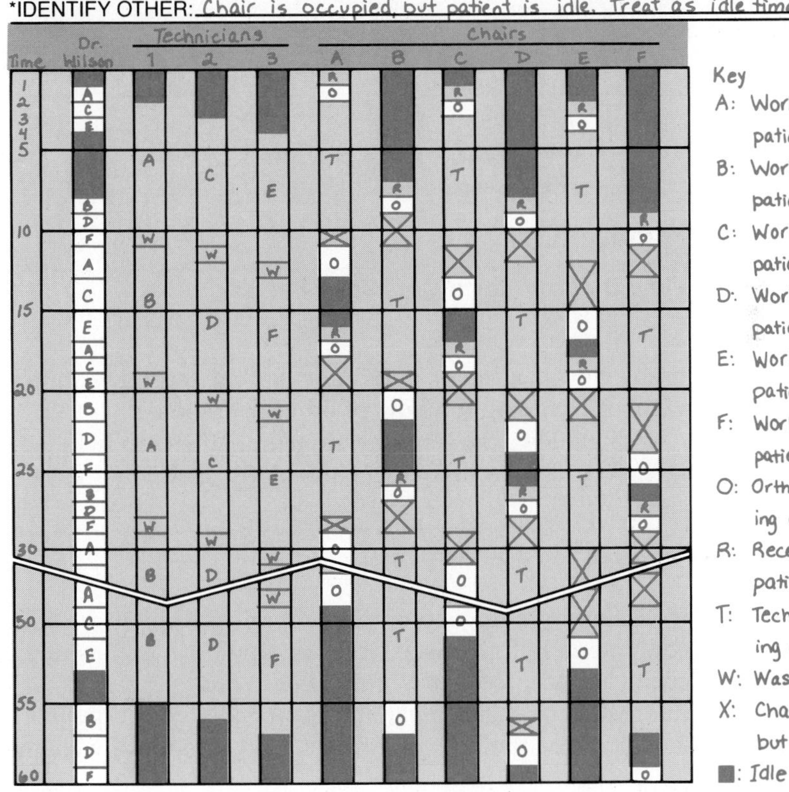

Figure 4.5

Multiple Activity Chart for Orthodontist: Six Chairs.

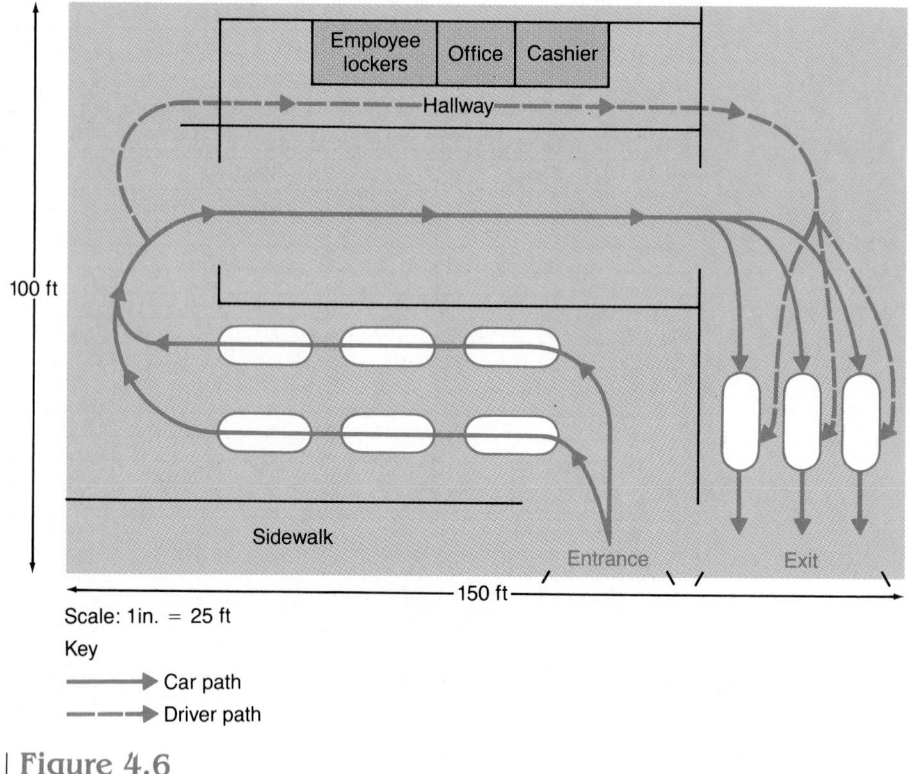

Figure 4.6

Flow Diagram for a Car Wash Facility.

used a flow diagram to determine that the second waiting line could be added without changing the flow of other operations.*

When flows are complex, sketching them can help you see clearly what is going on. This technique is particularly useful in analyzing bottlenecks.

Capital Budgeting

Ideas for improving a process often call for capital investment in facilities and equipment. In Dr. Wilson's case he would have to acquire space for two more chairs and the necessary equipment in order to gain capacity. Further vertical integration by a firm invariably requires more equipment and perhaps a new facility. Since the bulk of a firm's assets are usually committed to the opera-

* Queuing and simulation analysis, described in Appendix B, are more extensive methods to study waiting lines.

tions function, many ideas for capital expenditures and proposals for their inclusion in the firm's **capital budgeting** process originate there.

Operations managers must find ways to encourage innovative ideas for improving productivity. At the same time, they must screen out those ideas that do not fit with established operations strategy, or which do not generate enough benefits relative to the investment required. Benefits can be labor savings, materials cost reduction, less scrap, better quality, lower inventory, better customer service, or higher revenues. Benefits can also be more qualitative, such as greater resource flexibility, which expands opportunities for future products. The operations manager must estimate the costs, benefits, and risks involved in the proposed change. These estimates are then analyzed by means of one or more capital budgeting techniques, such as net present value, payback, or internal rate of return. A brief review of these financial techniques is found in Appendix A.

The final step in capital budgeting is taken by top management, or even the board of directors, when a major capital investment is proposed. They make sure that large investments in equipment and facilities are in line with current corporate strategies, particularly with respect to product plans and competitive priorities.

WORK-FORCE MANAGEMENT

Deciding *how* we are going to make products inevitably leads us to the human element, a fundamental part of process design. One reason is that process design affects the quality of work life and the level of employee satisfaction. Another reason is that payroll and employee benefits are major costs for most organizations. We illustrate this point in Table 4.3 with two petroleum companies, three automobile manufacturers, two large retailers, and two large grocery chains, all of whom have several thousand employees.

Table 4.3 shows the number of employees for each firm, its assets per employee, and its total reported net profits. The list is arranged in descending order of the rate of total assets per employee. This figure is a rough measure of the degree of an organization's capital intensity. The last column in Table 4.3 shows hypothetical minimum labor costs. Most of these firms have human resource costs far in excess of this hypothetical minimum. Comparison of the last two columns indicates that any firm on the list would welcome a 10 percent reduction in the hypothetical labor costs. For the less capital-intensive firms, such a decrease in labor costs would have a most favorable impact on net profits.

There are many issues to consider in work-force management, as illustrated in Box 4.5. The owner and operator of Today's Maid faces several such problems, and he is correct in thinking that many of them are interrelated.

Table 4.3

The Significance of Labor Costs

Name of Firm	Number of Employees (000)	Assets per Employee ($000)	Net Profit ($000,000)	Hypothetical* Minimum Labor Costs ($000,000)
Exxon	150	$422	$5528	$ 900
Mobil	178	234	1268	1068
Chrysler	100	90	1491	600
Ford	384	72	2907	2304
General Motors	748	70	4516	4488
J.C. Penney	178	46	435	1068
Kmart	270	34	499	1620
Safeway Stores	165	27	185	990
Kroger	160	23	157	960

* Hypothetical costs = Number of employees × 2000 hr/yr × $3.00/hr.
Source: "The Forbes 500," *Forbes*, April 29, 1985.

Because human beings are complex and somewhat unpredictable, there is no single set of best answers to all human resource problems. Whole books have been written on such topics as job design, unions, organizational behavior, motivation, leadership, and resistance to change. Because of space limitations, we must be content with a brief look at

1. concepts in job design;
2. job design practices;
3. employee selection and training; and
4. compensation.

Job Design Concepts

Job design is the starting point for considering work-force management issues. The design of a job determines the skills and training that an employee will need to do it and is one determinant of the compensation the employee will receive. Additionally, job content itself may be a motivating factor.

Scientific Management. Traditional job design got its real start more than 100 years ago when Frederick Taylor proposed an approach known as scientific management. Taylor believed that jobs should be studied scientifically, with careful analysis and experimentation, in order to find the most economic way to perform a task. After the most economic way has been discovered, workers should be chosen and trained in the new method and the new method installed in operations. Taylor stressed the need for teamwork between management and workers. He believed that management must accept the responsibility for coordinating work so that output is not restricted by poor planning and timing. Taylor also believed that scientific management would work only if the economic benefits of increased output were shared by both management and workers.

Box 4.5

TODAY'S MAID

Frank Edwards owns and operates Today's Maid, a residential cleaning service targeted toward middle-to-high income earners who do not want to clean their own homes. Edwards prides himself on providing a thorough, reliable service, consistently meeting high standards of cleanliness. He sends out teams of two or four workers, complete with equipment and supplies, who clean residences on a regular or one-time-only basis. He does not consider Today's Maid the low-cost competitor, but prefers to compete on quality. His employees must pass a "cleaning test" proving that they can recognize and produce cleaning that meets Edwards's personal standards. In addition, prospective employees must have personal references that show they are honest and reliable.

Recently, Edwards's business has been expanding. Work-force management problems are occupying more and more of his time. His ability to accept new customers has been limited only by his ability to find new employees that meet his standards for cleaning ability, personal honesty, and reliability. He is thinking of requiring that potential employees take a lie detector test and post a surety bond. He is also considering instituting a training course in residential cleaning, in order to clarify to employees just how to meet the required standards. Another problem he faces is how to integrate new employees with old ones. Should he place new employees on established teams, or form new teams with new employees? To what extent should he worry about how well co-workers get along? Should he include some kind of personality test as a screening device for new applicants?

Because good employees are as hard to keep in this business as they are to find, Edwards is also concerned about how to best motivate his employees to stay on the job. What is a fair amount to pay? What kind of benefits should he include in his employee compensation plan? What kind of incentives would inspire them to do a thorough, professional cleaning job, without squandering time and supplies? How can Edwards enforce his personal standards without inspecting every job? Edwards feels that somehow all these issues are related, and he would like to find the best set of answers.

Taylor's methods dealt primarily with the technical aspects of job design. His "engineering approach" was concerned primarily with ways to best reach, grasp, and move objects; the number of repetitions to be performed before a rest was needed; and the best physical position for the worker. Taylor began his work in the steel industry, but his theories spread through many industries and were widely practiced by the early 1900s. There is no doubt that scientific management techniques practiced by industrial engineers contributed greatly to the increase in productivity that took place in the United States in the first half of the twentieth century. Many of Taylor's concepts continue to be the first techniques applied when managers seek increased productivity.

Economic Trade-offs of Specialization. Whether to define a job in narrow or broad terms is one of the toughest decisions in job design. Engineers, sociologists, psychologists, economists, managers, and workers all have different ideas. The actual choice varies widely. Many U.S. industries have achieved tremendous economic success with narrowly designed jobs for their workers. This is particularly true for firms with a product focus. Other firms have had great success using work teams in which each member is capable of performing all parts of the task assigned to the team.

Arguments in favor of job specialization include:

1. It takes the worker less time to learn highly specialized, narrowly defined methods and procedures.
2. The potential work pace is much higher, leading to more output in less time.
3. The education and skill requirements of the work force are much lower, so it is not as expensive to hire workers.

Short learning time, a fast work pace, and low labor costs are all compelling economic arguments in favor of division of work into narrowly defined jobs. However, there are also arguments against narrowly defined jobs:

1. An imbalance of work is created by the inability to divide tasks perfectly, so that each worker is performing an equivalent amount of work. Consequently, some workers have idle time and others do not.
2. The need for coordination and materials handling increases.
3. Highly repetitive work can sometimes have adverse behavioral consequences, such as costly employee turnover, low output rates, and poor quality.

Idle time, increased coordination and materials handling, and adverse behavioral consequences are all *costs* of job specialization. Certainly the most puzzling part of finding a reasonable trade-off in costs lies in the behavioral dimension of job design.

Behavioral Considerations. Taylor considered only economic benefits in his theory of job design; people also work for other reasons. Social needs (that is, needs to be recognized, to belong to a group, and so on) and individual needs (that is, to feel important, to feel in control, and so on) all influence how people perform their jobs. In many work environments, workers lack opportunities to

1. control the pace of work;
2. receive gratification from the work itself, because of the narrowness of the tasks involved;
3. advance to a better position;
4. show initiative by developing better methods or tools for doing the job; and
5. communicate with fellow workers.

These opportunities are more likely to be lacking in narrowly designed jobs. Sociologists and psychologists contend that highly repetitive jobs lead to monotony, which leads to boredom and sometimes to poor job performance. Some symptoms of poor job performance are high rates of turnover, absenteeism, and tardiness; grievances; and intentional disruption of the production flow by workers. White-collar workers may exhibit many of the disruptive behaviors of blue-collar workers for the same reasons. Excessive personal illness, chronic tardiness, and incomplete work assignments may all be symptoms of job stress in white-collar workers who feel that they lack control over their work, have little or no opportunity for advancement, and receive no encouragement to show initiative. These behaviors may be more subtle to detect but may be even more costly to an organization to ignore.

The usual remedy suggested to overcome the boredom of highly specialized jobs is **job enlargement.** A job is *horizontally* enlarged if the worker is assigned a greater variety of tasks, say, eight or ten rather than one or two. A job is *vertically* enlarged if the worker gets more involved in the planning or inspection of his or her own work. More self-supervision is delegated to them. Job enlargement often includes both elements. For example, a worker may be given the responsibility for operating several machines, inspecting the output, deciding when machines need maintenance, and even performing some types of maintenance. Job enlargement is closely related to worker flexibility. A worker with an enlarged job knows how to do more tasks and can work in more places. Sometimes work teams are formed in order to enlarge the jobs of all members. Team members are expected to learn how to perform all the jobs for which the team is responsible. Work teams provide opportunities for communication and for the worker to feel a greater sense of accomplishment.

Many studies on the relationships among specialization, boredom, job satisfaction, and productivity have been made in the last 30 years. Unfortunately the evidence from them is mixed. One of the earliest studies showed that workers with more specialized jobs were more dissatisfied than those with jobs offering more diversity (Walker, 1950). In another study, attendance and job satisfaction were linked with job complexity (Turner and Lawrence, 1965). These results also indicated that city workers were more satisfied with low job complexity than were workers from a rural setting. In a study involving a change from assembly-line work to work teams (job enlargement) job satisfaction increased and productivity improved nearly 70 percent over a four-year period (Fisher, 1980). Other studies reported that productivity declined when jobs were enlarged.

In a study of bank employees, work was reorganized so that some jobs were vertically enlarged and some were simplified. Some of the employees with enlarged jobs had improved performance and some did not. The results seemed to be related to the psychological needs of the workers (Hackman, 1978). It appears that the need for job enlargement depends on the local culture, nature of the work, employee perceptions of the job, nature of group interactions, and type of supervision given.

Sociotechnical Theory. In the early 1950s, studies in the coal fields of Great Britain led to a theory of job design that combined technical elements with behavioral considerations. This theory holds that the job designer needs to recognize two dimensions in any productive system: the technical subsystem and the social subsystem. If one is emphasized and the other neglected, less efficiency will result. Work organizations are viewed as sociotechnical systems that exist to do work. These systems involve people using technology to carry out sets of tasks related to a specified purpose. People and equipment are input factors to the system. The fit of people and equipment determines the level of economic performance and job satisfaction, which are the output factors (Trist, 1981). Thus the entire work system, rather than its individual tasks, becomes the basic unit for analysis. Similarly, the work group becomes more important than the individual.

Eric Trist's studies in the 1950s showed that it is important in job design to consider the

1. role of the worker;
2. nature of task boundaries; and
3. autonomy of the work group.

These considerations are interconnected. In sociotechnical theory, workers are viewed as complementary to, rather than extensions of, machines. However, the job designer must decide whether the workers' roles are those of *producing entities,* or *variance controllers* of the equipment they operate. This distinction helps job designers to identify job requirements and determine the nature of task boundaries. This determination can be made on the basis of technology, time, or place. Usually, technical requirements determine the boundaries unless parts of the overall production task are separated by space or by time. The determination of task boundaries also influences how workers are supervised. Frank Edwards cannot possibly supervise all of his house-cleaning workers at once because each team will be cleaning a different home. One possibility for supervision is to place one team member in charge of the others, and give that worker responsibility for specific work assignments, distribution of tools and equipment, and inspection of the finished work. Another possibility, which requires advance familiarity with the work site, is for Edwards to make specific assignments to each team member, and give team members total responsibility for completion and inspection of their own work.

An autonomous or self-governing work group has the authority to make decisions about its work and the responsibility to carry out their own decisions. Job designers must consider how much autonomy work groups should have. Work groups probably need more autonomy when the jobs that members perform vary widely or require a great deal of cooperation from others in the group. Edwards might find it advantageous to let work teams have considerable autonomy in deciding how to clean individual homes. Each client's home and request list will be unique, and cooperation between team members is probably necessary.

Job Design Practices

Regardless of the theories of job design, it is finally necessary for the job designer to determine the job responsibilities of each group or individual. The first step in designing a job is to determine the objective to be achieved by the employee or work group and, second, to consider alternative ways to achieve that objective. This process may involve an analysis of existing jobs or may require the creation of a prototype job which can be studied.

Job Analysis. You can approach a job analysis in any number of ways. If employees are already doing a job similar to the one you want done, simply interview the employees about the job. One technique is a directed conference; its objective is to have employees describe verbally their own jobs. A second technique is similar to the first, except that employees are given questionnaires and asked to describe their jobs in writing. A third technique is to use a trained observer, or someone familiar with the job, to observe the work being done and ask informed questions. Some jobs, especially those involving **knowledge workers,** do not lend themselves to analysis by the third technique. Knowledge workers generate and disseminate information, including many nonclerical white-collar workers, nonmanagerial professionals, and managers.

Job Descriptions. The end result of job analysis is a job description containing

1. a job title;
2. a description of duties and responsibilities;
3. a set of working conditions;
4. a list of demands likely to be placed on the employee;
5. a suggested base pay rate; and
6. desired characteristics of the person who is to do the job.

The analyst should consider any strenuous manual, motor, or mental demands to be placed on an employee and guidelines for limiting these demands. Manual, motor, and mental limitations are the subjects of a field of study called *ergonomics,* which is concerned with how to design and arrange processes to enable people to work more safely and effectively. For example, if a job involves unloading heavy cargo, the physical strength and the amount of energy expended by the worker may limit the amount of cargo that can be unloaded in a certain period of time. However, if the worker uses a fork-lift tractor, the physical demands on the worker will be less, and the amount of cargo that can be handled will increase.

Many mental tasks place great demands on a person's information processing capability and judgment. In many jobs workers monitor screens and dials, looking for deviations from normal. Often these abnormalities have a low chance of occurring, but, when they do occur, a split second decision is needed. For example, the jobs of air-traffic controllers, power-plant operators, pilots, and intensive-care–unit personnel in hospitals require quick processing of information received from several dials and screens and rapid response if something is wrong. These intense demands may be limited by frequent breaks, rotation of personnel, more days off between work assignments, and other means.

On the other hand, many jobs require a minimum level of manual, motor, or mental capability. The job descriptions specify any such requirements. If a job involving typing or assembly work calls for motor skills, a minimum acceptable skill level is frequently set. For example, a person doing word processing might be expected to enter a certain number of lines of error-free text every hour, or a person assembling calculators might be expected to assemble 50 within a specified time. The job description for an accountant may specify a degree in accounting, a certain number of years' experience, and/or CPA status. Air-traffic controllers, power-plant operators, pilots, and intensive-care–unit personnel must be capable of a high level of concentration and fast thinking.

Employee Selection and Training

Having decided what jobs need to be done and what they involve, the manager's next step is to select people to do them and provide any necessary training.

The Selection Decision. If a position is being filled with a current employee, personnel records and recommendations of current and past supervisors will play a role in the decision. If a new employee is being hired, inputs might include:

1. Information from an application form.
2. Recommendations from previous employers and others.
3. Records of formal training or meeting of legal requirements, such as transcripts, certifications, or licenses to practice.
4. Results of personality tests, lie detector tests, and tests of various skills required to do the job.
5. Information and impressions from personal interviews with those to whom the employee would report and with whom the employee would work.

Of the items in this list, the personal interview probably carries the most weight in the job selection decision. In many large organizations, human resource specialists recruit and screen applicants for positions. The supervisor to whom the employee will report usually makes the final selection decision.

Training of Employees. Most large corporations devote resources to developing and updating employees' skills. Training may range from teaching employees very specific skills, such as how to use a certain piece of equipment, to more general skills, such as problem-solving techniques or time-management skills. Training may be formal or informal and may be accomplished in a variety of ways. Some methods used to train and further the education of employees are

1. on-the-job training;
2. courses given by staff personnel and others within the organization;
3. courses given by outside consultants and trainers; and
4. tuition reimbursement for technical school or college courses.

On-the-job training (OJT) programs provide a way for employees to learn jobs by actually performing them. A structured OJT program may include classes, exams, and formal checks of the employee's progress. In some OJT programs, employees are rotated among several jobs. Many banks give their entry-level white-collar workers the designation of "management trainee" and rotate them through several jobs during their first two years with the bank. They may serve in positions such as tellers or credit investigators before being assigned to a junior management position. The idea behind this type of rotation is that future managers should have first-hand experience in the positions under their supervision. Less structured OJT may consist only of supervisors or others showing employees how to do their jobs, leaving them to do the work, and then checking the results.

Many organizations have a department in charge of employee development. This is typically a staff function, and its role is to help line managers identify the training needs of their employees. When such needs have been identified, a development specialist prepares and presents or obtains from outside sources the needed programs. One common type of employee development effort is the orientation program. Many firms use orientation programs to introduce new employees to requirements of their jobs or organizational policies or both. Sometimes all new employees in certain jobs must take a set of courses within their first year on the job. For example, all customer service employees might be given courses in assertiveness training, dealing with irate customers, and the technical details of the company's products. These courses may be offered in formal classes taught by company personnel, or they may be given by means of video cassettes augmented by training manuals. Courses may take an hour or several weeks. The accounting department of a large company might hold training sessions several times a year to teach people throughout the organization the proper procedures for completing paperwork related to purchasing and other materials management matters. Anyone who deals with such paperwork would be expected to attend once a year.

Another way for people to enhance their job skills is to attend seminars, conferences and workshops given by professional trainers from outside their own organization. Some of these courses are designed to meet the continuing education requirements of various professional groups. Others are designed to meet needs of specific industries or to explain new technologies. The variety of courses available is endless.

A common way in which businesses promote increased levels of education among their employees is by means of tuition reimbursement. Many firms repay employees for some or all of the costs of technical school and college courses taken on the employees' own time. Some firms will even pay a salary to selected employees while sending them to school on a full-time basis. Such arrangements are usually accompanied by an agreement on the employees' part to work for the company for a specified length of time after receiving the schooling.

Many companies make large investments in employee training. When employees are being trained, they are usually being paid but may not be performing their jobs at the same time. Often, arrangements must be made to have someone else do the job while the regular employee is being trained. If a course is prepared in-house, there are costs of the time to develop and teach it; course materials, such as books and video tapes, are expensive to produce or buy. Companies sending employees to outside courses, workshops, and lectures usually pay for travel, lodging and food, as well as the course and the employees' time. For their investment in training, companies generally expect more productive employees in return.

Compensation

A final issue in work-force management is **compensation,** that is, the pay and employee benefits provided by an organization. As shown in Box 4.6, alternative approaches, such as bonuses at GE, special recognition at 3M, and profit sharing at GM, to standard pay and benefits packages are being used.

One desirable feature of a sound wage and salary structure is that it achieves both external and internal balance. *External balance* means that a firm's wages are in line with other wage rates in the geographical area and with other wage rates in the same industry. The supply of people available, willing, and able to do the job must also be considered. Wages or salaries should be set high enough to attract and hold people with the needed abilities. *Internal balance* means that compensation rates reflect the importance and difficulty of a job in relation to other jobs in the firm. One common method of determining compensation is to use a point ranking scale. Factors applicable to a job, such as skill, effort, responsibility, and working conditions, are each assigned points based on the required level of each factor. Points for each job

Box 4.6

VARIATIONS IN COMPENSATION PLANS

- While General Electric's chief executive rewards employees with bonuses for extraordinary contributions, Minnesota Mining and Manufacturing relies on ego-boosters such as trophies and certificates. Both companies act on the belief that their employees enjoy creating new ideas for its own sake.
- For the new GM Saturn plant, the United Auto Workers union agreed to give up restrictive work rules limiting worker flexibility. The UAW also accepted guaranteed salaries at 80 percent of the industry's average. The other 20 percent would be paid, or not paid, through profit sharing and incentive plans. In exchange, the majority of the workers are promised lifetime job security and a bigger role in decision making.

Sources: "Eight Big Masters of Innovation," *Fortune,* October 16, 1984; "Behind the Hype at GM's Saturn," *Fortune,* November 15, 1985.

are totaled, and jobs are ranked accordingly. Jobs with higher rankings receive higher compensation than jobs with lower rankings.

Compensation plans usually include *employee benefits.* Full-time employees usually receive paid vacation time and health care insurance. Other employee benefits may include life insurance, tuition reimbursement, stock plans, pension plans, use of company recreation facilities, use of company vehicles, and the right to buy company products at a discount. A benefits package is usually assembled in the same way that external balance for wage rates is determined, that is, by considering geographic and industry norms. In industries with large numbers of unionized employees, the entire compensation plan and many related job design issues are subject to negotiation between union and management.

Some industries, particularly in the service sector, rely heavily on part-time employees who receive little in the way of employee benefits. This practice lowers labor costs and provides greater flexibility in meeting varying levels of demand for services. Fast-food restaurants, retail stores, and banks have always relied on part-time employees. The health care industry is increasingly doing so.

Methods of Compensation. Some common methods of compensation are

1. pay for number of hours worked;
2. piece rate;
3. commission rate; and
4. salary.

Many firms compensate most of their employees strictly on the basis of *number of hours worked.* Under these plans, employees usually earn an hourly rate of pay for regular hours worked and an increased rate of pay, called overtime, for additional hours worked; the regular work week is usually 40 hours. Sometimes, overtime rates are paid for any hours worked on certain days of the week, regardless of the total worked during the rest of the week. For example, when the normal work week is Monday through Friday, manufacturing firms may pay extra for work on Saturday and Sunday. Overtime rates are often paid for work on official holidays. Premium rates are paid for many hazardous jobs.

Piece rate is a pay plan in which compensation is based on the number of units processed during a day or week. Machine operators are often compensated on the basis of output: The faster the operator, the higher the pay. Assembly workers are sometimes paid on the basis of the number of units they can assemble in a given period of time. Telephone workers may receive pay on the basis of the number of positive contacts made. Agricultural workers are often paid on the basis of the amount of produce picked. For these workers, output is sometimes graded; those receiving better grades receive a higher pay rate. One precaution must be taken in designing piece rate plans: Make sure that quantity incentives do not interfere with quality. A worker should not be rewarded for producing so quickly that product quality is unacceptable.

Commission plans are like piece rate compensation for sales personnel. Sales people who work on commission receive a percentage of total sales as their compensation. Therefore the more they sell, the more they earn. Although it is a fairly common plan, not all sales personnel are on straight commission.

Most supervisors, managers, nonmanagerial professionals, and other white-collar workers are usually paid a *salary*, which means that they receive a flat rate every pay period. They are expected to work 40 hours or more per week in order to earn the salary, and they often do not receive overtime pay for hours worked in excess of 40.

Individual Incentive Systems. Sometimes, incentive plans are used to motivate workers to perform. Such plans reward output that exceeds a predetermined base level. One plan is the 100 percent premium plan. Suppose that the base level is set at 50 units of output. Under a 100 percent premium plan, a worker who produces 60 units will receive an additional 10/50, or 20 percent of the base rate. If the incentive plan is a 50 percent premium plan, the worker will get a bonus equal to 50 percent of 10/50, or 10 percent of the base rate.

Some of the things to consider about an incentive plan are the ease of measuring the output, the record keeping required, the economic climate, dependencies among workers, and the attitude of the group toward highly productive individuals. If the output is machine-paced and individual operators cannot control the output rate, there is not much point in having an individual incentive plan. If quality and safety suffer because individuals work too fast in order to earn bonuses, an incentive plan may lead to decreased productivity.

Group Incentive Plans. If productivity is a function of an entire group, a group incentive plan might be better than an individual incentive plan. One type of group incentive plan is a Scanlon plan. A labor–management productivity committee is formed; its purpose is to solicit suggestions from employees on how to improve productivity and reduce costs. These suggestions may have to do with work methods, scheduling, arrangement of facilities, energy use, or anything the employees can think of to improve working conditions, save money, and increase productivity. Under this plan, any increased profits are shared between management and labor. Scanlon plans have been fairly successful in many plants.

Other Motivating Factors. Some sociologists, psychologists, and job-design theorists argue that money is not a primary motivator for many workers and that more important sources of motivation are inherent in the job itself. Some of these motivators are

1. a feeling of accomplishment;
2. recognition for a job well done;
3. the importance of the work itself;
4. responsibility;
5. advancement to a position of greater responsibility;
6. variety of the job;
7. autonomy;
8. knowledge or skill required to do the job;
9. opportunity to learn new knowledge or skills; and
10. a challenge

All these factors must be considered, along with the compensation package, if management is to give adequate attention to the total compensation for the job.

CHAPTER HIGHLIGHTS

Process design deals with *how* to make a product. Many choices must be made on capital intensity, resource flexibility, vertical integration, customer involvement, and the human element. The closely related topic of technological choices is discussed in Chapter 5.

- Process design is of strategic importance and is closely linked to the productivity levels a firm can achieve. It involves the selection of inputs, operations, work flows, and methods used to produce goods and services.
- Process design decisions are made when a new product is to be offered, an existing product modified, demand levels change, current performance is inadequate, new technology is available, costs or availability of inputs change, or competitive priorities change.
- Four facets of process design are: capital intensity, resource flexibility, vertical integration, and customer involvement. *Capital intensity* concerns the mix of capital equipment and human skills in a process. *Resource flexibility* reflects the degree to which equipment is general purpose and individuals can handle a wide variety of work. *Vertical integration* concerns the decisions to make or buy parts and services. Vertical integration decisions are made by looking at the entire chain of supply from raw materials to final consumer and determining which processes the firm itself wants to perform. *Customer involvement* is the extent to which customers are allowed to interact with the production process. Self-service, product selection, and the timing and location of the interaction must all be considered.
- Trade-offs among these facets are often necessary. For example, higher capital intensity is usually associated with lower resource flexibility, higher vertical integra-

tion, and lower customer involvement. The variable underlying these relationships is repeatability.

- Three techniques for analyzing process activities and flows are process charts, multiple activity charts, and flow diagrams. All are organized ways of studying the details of a process in order to design or redesign it.
- Process design choices often require investment in new facilities or equipment. Operations managers must assess benefits and costs of each investment proposed. After the necessary estimates have been made, a financial analysis can be made, using techniques such as net present value.
- Scientific management is an engineering approach to job design that is concerned with the most economic way to perform the job.
- Managers must decide whether jobs are to be narrowly or broadly defined. Advantages of narrowly defined jobs are short learning time, fast work pace, and low labor costs. Disadvantages are creation of more idle time for some workers, increased materials handling and coordination needs, and adverse behavioral consequences.
- Job enlargement, both horizontal and vertical, is the usual remedy suggested to overcome the boredom of highly specialized jobs. Results of studies of links among specialization, boredom, job satisfaction, and performance (productivity) have been mixed. The relationships seem to depend on the specific characteristics of the situation.
- The sociotechnical theory of job design considers both the technical requirements and the social requirements of a job. The focus is on the work group instead of the individual worker.
- A careful job analysis leads to a job description that defines the work to be done, working conditions, and employee capabilities required.
- Inputs to the employee selection process include application forms, personnel records, recommendations, transcripts, test results, and impressions from personal interviews.
- Some methods of employee training are on-the-job training, internal and external training courses, and tuition reimbursement for educational courses.
- Compensation plans may be straight salary, based on hours worked or output produced, or some combination of these methods. Some compensation plans include individual and group incentives for increased productivity. Most compensation plans provide employee benefits.
- Motivation factors may include the job itself and the opportunities for advancement, recognition, and feelings of accomplishment.

KEY TERMS

capital budgeting
capital intensity
compensation
customer involvement
flexible work force
flow diagram
job design
job enlargement
knowledge workers
multiple activity chart

on-the-job training
piece rate
process chart
process design
resource flexibility
vertical integration

STUDY QUESTIONS

1. When you registered for this course you had to go through a registration process. Think of this process from the standpoint of your university or college. Identify elements of the process for which process design or redesign is needed.
2. Compare the process of preparing and serving your own lunch at home with the process of preparing and serving lunch to others at a local pizza parlor. What inputs in terms of materials, human effort, and equipment are involved in each process? How are these inputs similar? How are they different?
3. Process design choices cannot be isolated from decisions in other areas of operations management. Comment on this statement from the standpoint of a manager of a bookstore. *Hint:* Look over the table of contents to get some ideas.
4. How much capital intensity do you recommend for a business having an extremely unpredictable product demand? How much vertical integration? Explain.
5. The number of mail-order businesses has increased dramatically in the United States in the last ten years. Compare the processes of a business selling ski equipment and clothing by direct mail to the processes of a retail store handling the same items. How do they differ in terms of capital intensity, resource flexibility, vertical integration, and customer involvement? How are they the same?
6. Suppose that you and a friend decide to start a business selling sandwiches and snacks in college dormitories late at night. What decisions must you make regarding vertical integration? How will your customers be involved in your process?
7. Suppose that a grocery store has decided to add an in-store bakery. The next decision to be made is whether to install a drive-in window for the bakery so that customers do not have to enter the store in order to purchase baked goods. The store manager expects that this window would do a high volume of business early in the morning, as people purchase donuts on their way to work. How is this window likely to affect other processes in the store? What processes will have to be performed by the employees in the bakery that they would otherwise not perform? How would customer involvement differ from that in the rest of the grocery operations?
8. Why are human resources critical to process design? Does this relationship depend on whether a firm is highly capital intensive?
9. What are the arguments for and against narrowly defined jobs?
10. What is the difference between horizontal and vertical job enlargement? How is the issue of job enlargement related to the arguments for and against narrowly defined jobs?
11. What opportunities do workers lack in some work environments? Compare an assembly-line worker in a highly automated plant and a secretary in a busy law office. Which opportunities are each likely to have? Which are they likely to lack?

12. What is sociotechnical theory? How does it differ from scientific management?
13. What are some techniques of job analysis? What are the elements of a job description? Consider a job you have held (or a friend's job), analyze it, and write a brief job description for it.
14. What are some of the methods used to train employees? For what kind of training is each of these methods appropriate? Which method are you most likely to find in a small business?
15. What is the objective in designing a compensation plan? What is meant by achieving external and internal wage balance? What happens if this balance is not achieved?
16. What are some common compensation plans? Why are managers usually compensated with a salary instead of by the number of hours worked? How are piece rate and commission plans related? In what situations is each method appropriate?

PROBLEMS

1. Two different manufacturing processes are being considered for making a new product that is to be introduced soon. The first process is less capital intensive, with fixed costs of only $50,000 per year and variable costs of $400 per unit. The second process has a fixed cost of $200,000 but would have a variable cost of only $150 per unit. What is the break-even quantity, beyond which the second process becomes more attractive?
2. Dr. Wilson (see Box 4.4) estimates that adding two new chairs will increase fixed costs by $70,000, including the annual equivalent cost of the capital investment and the salary of one more technician. Each new patient is expected to bring in $1500 per year in additional revenue, with variable costs estimated at $100 per patient. The two new chairs will allow him to expand his practice by as many as 200 patients. How many patients would have to be added for the new process design to break even?
3. Hahn Manufacturing has been purchasing a key component of one of its products from a local supplier. The current purchase price is $3000 per unit. Efforts at standardizing parts have succeeded to the point where this same component can now be used in five different products. Annual component usage should increase from 500 to 2000 units. Management is now wondering whether it is time to make the component in-house, rather than to continue buying it from the supplier. Fixed costs would increase by about $70,000 per year for the new equipment and tooling needed. The cost of raw materials and variable overhead would be about $2200 per unit, while labor costs would go up by another $550 per unit produced.
   (a) Should Hahn make rather than buy?
   (b) What is the break-even quantity?
   (c) What other considerations might be important?
4. Suppose that you are in charge of a large mailing to the alumni of your college, inviting them to contribute to a scholarship fund. The letters and envelopes have been individually addressed (mailing labels were not used). The letters are to be folded and stuffed into the correct envelope, the envelopes are to be sealed, and a

large commemorative stamp is to be placed in the upper right hand corner of each envelope. Make a process chart for this activity. Assume that it is a one-person operation. Estimate how long it will take to stuff, seal, and stamp 1000 envelopes. Assume that the person who is doing this work is paid $10.00 per hour. How much will it cost to process 1000 letters, based on your time estimate? Consider how each of the following changes individually would affect the process.

- Each letter has the salutation "Dear Alumnus or Alumna," instead of the person's name.
- Mailing labels are used, and they have to be put on the envelopes.
- Prestamped envelopes are used.
- Envelopes are to be stamped by a postage meter.
- Window envelopes are used.

(a) Which of these changes would reduce the time and cost of the process?
(b) Would any of these changes be likely to reduce the effectiveness of the mailing? If so, which ones? Why?

5. Prepare a multiple activity chart for a hypothetical worker whose job is to load and unload three dry-cleaning machines (call them machines A, B, and C). Use the following conditions.
   - It is the beginning of the day, and all machines are empty.
   - All three machines are identical.
   - Each machine takes one minute to load and three minutes to unload.

   The machines run for 12 minutes each time they are loaded. The worker starts by loading machine A, then machine B, and finally machine C. The machines are close enough together that the travel time from one to the other can be ignored. After the initial loading, the worker unloads and reloads each machine as soon as the machine stops running, or as soon as the worker is available. (In other words, the worker does not waste time.)
   (a) Complete the multiple activity chart for the three machines and for the worker for one hour. Calculate the utilization (percentage) for each.
   (b) Assume that the machines are not turned off until the end of the day. What is the utilization (percentages) of the machines and the worker for the second hour and every hour thereafter?

6. Suppose the dry-cleaning worker in Problem 5 is given four machines to tend. Complete a multiple activity chart for four machines and one worker under the same conditions.
   (a) What is the utilization (percentage) of the worker and the machines? Compare your answer to that obtained for three machines.
   (b) Is it possible, hypothetically, for a worker to be 100 percent utilized? Is it possible practically? What would you likely observe if you watched a person actually doing this work?

7. Make a multiple activity chart for a pizza baker who is assembling pizzas and baking them in two ovens that each hold two pizzas. Assume that demand for the pizzas is so high that all possible output will be used. Use the following conditions.
   - Each pizza takes 5 minutes to assemble.
   - Pizzas must bake for 17 minutes and be removed promptly.
   - It takes one minute to put a pizza in the oven and one minute to take it out. Assume that this does not prolong the baking time for any other pizza in the oven.

- An oven may be opened to put in a pizza or take one out, even if another pizza is baking.
- If a pizza is being assembled, and it is time to take another one out of the oven, the assembly process is interrupted to do so. The baker then continues assembling the first pizza.

Prepare a multiple activity chart for the baker and ovens from 5:00 P.M. until 6:30 P.M. Assume that the ovens are hot but empty at 5 P.M.

(a) How many pizzas can the baker turn out in this period of time?
(b) How many pizzas are in the oven at 6:30?
(c) What is the utilization (percentage) of each shelf?
(d) What percentage of the time is each oven being used (with one or two pizzas in it)?
(e) What is the utilization (percentage) of the baker?

Hint: You will probably need a column for each shelf of each oven and one for the baker. Use any symbols that you think are appropriate.

8. Diagrams of two self-service gasoline stations, both located on corners, are shown in Fig. 4.7 (a) and (b). Both have two rows of four pumps and a booth in which an attendant receives payment for the gasoline. At neither station is it necessary for the customer to pay in advance. The exits and entrances are marked on the diagrams. Analyze the possible directions of flows of cars and people through each station.
   (a) Which station has the most efficient flow from the standpoint of the customer?
   (b) Which station is likely to lose the most sales from potential customers who cannot gain access to the pumps because another car is headed the other direction?
   (c) At which of the gas stations can a customer pay without getting out of the car?

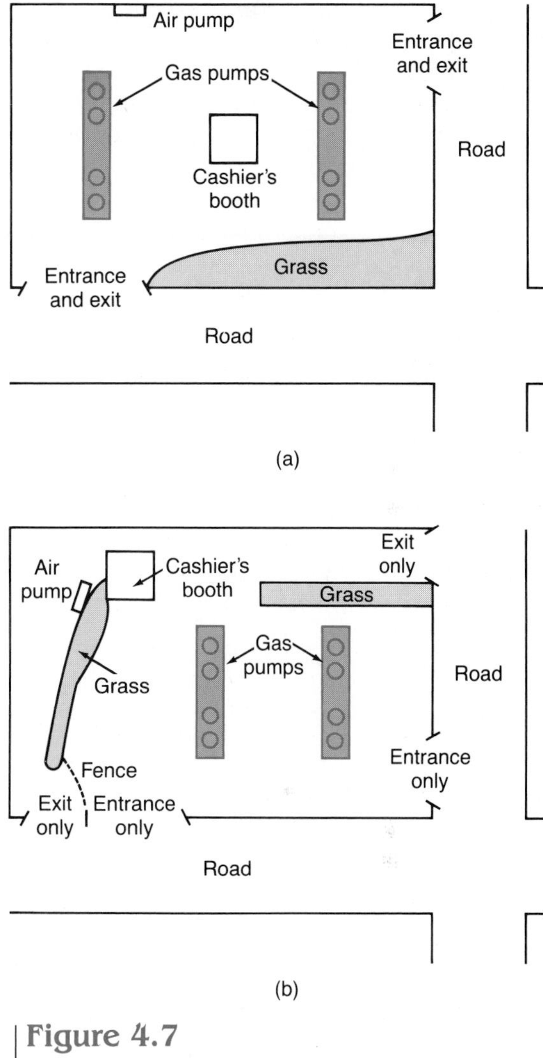

Figure 4.7

Flow Diagrams for Two Self-Service Gasoline Stations.

9. Refer to the process chart in Table 4.2. If the baker can be assigned other duties,

step 28 (waiting 30 minutes for the brownies to bake) does not have to be considered a delay.

(a) If the brownie baking process is thus reduced by 30 minutes, what is the new total time?

(b) What is the new labor cost per year?

(c) Think of one other way to make the operation more efficient. How much could your change save in time and dollars?

SELECTED REFERENCES

Abernathy, William J., "Production Process Structure and Technological Change," *Decision Sciences,* vol. 7, no. 4 (October 1976), pp. 607–619.

Chase, Richard B., "Where Does the Customer Fit in a Service Operation?" *Harvard Business Review* (November–December 1978), pp. 137–142.

Hackman, J. Richard, Jone L. Pearce, and Jane Camins Wolfe, "Effects of Changes in Job Characteristics on Work Attitudes and Behaviors," *Organizational Behavior and Human Performance,* vol. 21 (1978), pp. 289–304.

Hauck, Warren C., *Motivating People to Work: The Key to Improving Productivity.* Atlanta: Industrial Engineering and Management Press, 1984.

Hulin, Charles L., and Milton R. Blood, "Job Enlargement, Individual Differences, and Worker Responses," *Psychological Bulletin,* vol. 69, no. 1, 1968, pp. 41–55.

Kantrow, Alan M., "The Strategy–Technology Connection," *Harvard Business Review* (July–August 1980), pp. 6–21.

Kilbridge, Maurice, and Leon Wester, "An Economic Model for the Division of Labor," *Management Science,* vol. 12, no. 6 (February 1966), pp. B255–B269.

Knights, David, Hugh Willmott, and David Collison (Eds.), *Job Redesign.* Hants, England: Gower Publishing Company Limited, 1985.

Levitt, Theodore, "The Industrialization of Service," *Harvard Business Review* (September–October 1976), pp. 63–74.

Lovelock, Christopher H., and Robert F. Young, "Look to Consumers to Increase Productivity," *Harvard Business Review* (May–June 1979), pp. 168–178.

Nadler, Gerald, *Work Design.* Homewood, Ill.: Richard D. Irwin, 1970.

Niebel, Benjamin W., *Motion and Time Study.* Homewood, Ill.: Richard D. Irwin, 1976.

Paul, William J., Keith B. Robertson, and Frederick Herzberg, "Job Enrichment Pays Off," *Harvard Business Review* (March–April 1969), pp. 61–78.

Pierce, Jon L., and Randall B. Dunham, "Task Design: A Literature Review," *Academy of Management Review* (October 1976), pp. 83–96.

Ritzman, Larry P., Barry E. King, and Lee J. Krajewski, "Manufacturing Performance—Pulling the Right Levers," *Harvard Business Review* (March–April 1984), pp. 143–152.

Shostak, Arthur B., and William Gomberg, *Blue-Collar World.* Englewood Cliffs, N.J.: Prentice-Hall, 1964.

Skinner, Wickham, "Operations Technology: Blind Spot in Strategic Management," *Interfaces,* vol. 14 (January–February 1984), pp. 116–125.

Steers, Richard M., and Richard T. Mowday, "The Motivational Properties of Tasks," *Academy of Management Review* (October 1977), pp. 645–658.

Taylor, Sam G., Samuel M. Seward, and Steven F. Bolander, "Why the Process Industries Are Different," *Production and Inventory Management* (Fourth Quarter 1981), pp. 9–24.

Trist, Eric L., "The Sociotechnical Perspective," in A. H. Van de Ven and W. F. Joyce (Eds.), *Perspectives on Organization Design.* New York: John Wiley & Sons, 1981.

Walker, Charles R., "The Problem of the Repetitive Job," *Harvard Business Review,* vol. 28, (May 1950), pp. 54–58.

Wheelwright, Steven C., and Robert H. Hayes, "Competing through Manufacturing," *Harvard Business Review* (January–February 1985), pp. 99–109.

CHAPTER 5

TECHNOLOGICAL CHOICES

Some Managerial Issues

- What technologies would enhance the productivity of our knowledge workers?
- Is it time for us to have linked communication and information systems?
- How much should we automate the front office? Back office?
- How should our materials handling choices fit with our positioning strategy?
- How can one-worker–multiple-machines, group technology, and flexible manufacturing approaches help us achieve the benefits of repeatability?
- Should we have fixed or programmable automation?
- What types of computer assistance should we use for product design and manufacturing?

Chapter Outline

Just as the human element is an integral part of process design, so are the types of machinery, tooling, and equipment chosen. In this chapter we conclude the topic of process design by discussing the ever-widening array of choices in **technology** available to managers. Even the simple process of sawing lumber can involve a range of choices:

1. A worker using a simple hand saw.
2. A portable power saw driven by electricity but operated, guided, and controlled by a worker.
3. A rigidly mounted power saw, which requires a worker to set it up, load it, and unload it, with the material to be sawed automatically guided into the blade.
4. A very high-speed, continuously running power saw, with automatic material feeding and unloading and infrequent worker intervention.

In the search for higher productivity and quality, which is the key to maintaining or increasing our standard of living, continuing attention must be paid to emerging technologies. Additions to technological choices over the last 20 years have increasingly been related to advances in computer technology. Many new ways to do things involve microcomputers or combinations of computer networks that did not exist or were not economically feasible 20 years ago.

When you join a new organization, become familiar with its particular process technologies. Fellow employees and your own observations are excellent sources for learning about how something works. Suppliers of complex equipment and new technologies are usually eager to assist in providing an understanding of the benefits of their products. Professional organizations and journals are other sources of information about current and developing processes in various industries. By developing the habit of thinking about why something is done the way that it is, you can find many opportunities to improve processes. Discovering these opportunities requires good powers of observation, an inquiring mind, and a willingness to ask questions. Another payoff is a better understanding of the overall organization, even if your job is peripheral to process design decisions.

This chapter is divided into three main sections: office technology, technology in the service sector, and manufacturing technology. The dividing lines we use are approximate at best. For example, offices exist in all types of organizations, both in the manufacturing and service sectors, and some technologies are used in both sectors. Even so, our three-section organization of this chapter provides a convenient way to glimpse some of the exciting developments in and applications of technology. We begin with office processes, since they are so pervasive.

OFFICE TECHNOLOGY

Sixty million Americans work in offices. They work in main offices, branch offices, back offices, front offices, sales offices, department offices, head offices, field offices, home offices, and myriad other locations designated by the word *office*. Offices are everywhere in today's world of work. Telephone calls can be made from cars over cellular telephones. Portable microcomputers can be used at any location and, through a telephone, can access other computers. This combination—made possible by microtechnology—means that even a car can easily become a portable office in which written and verbal information may be received, processed, and transmitted. Clearly, choices for office processes are changing.

Office Processes and Operations

In the United States alone, more than $1 trillion is paid yearly to white-collar personnel. Because this level of expenditure is so large, more automation of office activities can lead to large productivity gains. Sixty percent of the trillion dollars is paid to managers and nonmanagerial professionals, so opportunities for productivity improvement are not limited to the clerical level. A year-long study of 300 knowledge workers in 15 different types of manufacturing and service businesses focused on how these workers spent their work time. Results showed that 25 percent of their time was spent in less productive activities such as traveling, waiting, filing, or making copies; 46 percent of their time was spent in meetings; and only 29 percent of their time was spent doing intellectual work such as reading, analyzing, or writing (Poppel, 1980). If office automation could be used to shift one hour per day per knowledge worker from less productive activities to more productive intellectual work, this improvement alone would increase overall worker effectiveness by 12.5 percent; as a result, U.S. businesses could save more than $75 billion annually.

Activities conducted in an office generally fall into one of six categories:

1. Exchange of written and spoken messages with others inside and outside the organization.
2. Collecting, analyzing, processing, filing, storing, and retrieving information.
3. Keeping a calendar.
4. Meeting with others.
5. Composing and preparing documents.
6. Assimilating information (reading, viewing, listening).

These activities themselves have not changed much in the past 100 years. On the other hand, during the past decade, rapid advances in communication and information systems technology have greatly changed the array of technological choices for carrying out these activities.

Technological Choices for Office Processes

Many electronic systems and microtechnical devices are available today to make office tasks easier, faster, or more accurate. They also reduce distance barriers and are likely to affect even small offices. Some technological possibilities for the office of the future are listed in Table 5.1.

Telephone Systems. Many of today's telephone systems allow a user to talk to several people at once, leave and receive recorded messages, automatically forward all incoming calls to another location, automatically redial a telephone number when a busy signal is reached, store and automatically dial frequently called numbers, and receive a signal when another call is waiting on the line.

In addition, telephone lines are a conduit for many other systems. For example, sophisticated *dictation systems* operate over phone lines, and a person may dictate over any touchtone phone, wherever it may be located. Using the buttons on the phone, the person doing the dictating can play back what was recorded, record over passages to change them, and, in general, use the dictation system as if it were in his or her own office.

Table 5.1

Some Technologies for the Office of the Future

Telephone Systems
Dictation systems
Message exchange systems
Electronic blackboards
Closed circuit telephone systems
Document transmission systems
Report Preparation Systems
Word processing systems
Electronic spreadsheets
Computer graphics software
Linked Communication and Information Systems
Electronic mail systems
Electronic work stations

Message exchange systems allow users to call their own numbers and receive any messages that have been recorded for them. This kind of system is designed to eliminate the annoying game of "telephone tag," where one caller leaves a message for another with a third party; the recipient of the first call returns the call, but now the original caller is out; and so on, until one of the callers reaches the other or gives up. If both parties have recorders on their phones it might be possible for them to complete the communication with just two phone calls, saving a great deal of time and annoyance.

Electronic blackboards and *closed circuit television systems* can be operated over phone lines to allow parties in different locations to exchange written information, as well as see each other while talking. The electronic blackboard is a device that can be written on, and the message will be transmitted and shown on the television screen in the other location. Dayton Power and Light Company, an electric utility in the midwest, uses electronic blackboards and closed circuit television to conduct meetings involving corporate executives at headquarters and plant managers located many miles away along the Ohio River.

Several systems now exist for transmitting facsimiles of documents quickly and accurately over phone lines. Other *document transmission systems* have their own lines. These systems typically require expensive equipment on both the sending and receiving ends but can be useful in filing last-minute bids, reports, and legal documents or making changes at the last possible minute.

Report Preparation Systems. A **word processing system** may consist of a single stand-alone unit, or many units linked together. These systems allow documents to be created, filed, retrieved, altered, and stored electronically. Most word processors can be programmed to produce the same letter to be sent to many people, addressing each letter individually. Mailing lists are much easier to maintain on word processors, especially if the word processor software can sort alphabetically. Authors of reports and letters prepared on word processing systems quickly become addicted to these systems, primarily because of the ease with which errors can be corrected and changes made.

Electronic spreadsheets have become a popular analytical tool, and almost any office with a microcomputer has spreadsheet software. Most spreadsheet packages have a large number of rows and columns into which data are entered and manipulated mathematically. Recalculations are quickly performed, or the spreadsheet format rapidly rearranged, should new or additional data be included. Contributing to the popularity of electronic spreadsheets is their ability to answer "what if" questions. The effects of alternative forecasts or cost changes on a proposal can be studied very quickly by revising a few numbers on an electronic spreadsheet and recalculating the result.

Very sophisticated *computer graphics software* is now available for large and small computers, as are word processing programs and spreadsheet packages. Many microcomputer systems offer software that links word processing and spreadsheets with graphics capabilities, thus providing integrated systems. These microcomputer systems frequently come in small modules that even small businesses can afford. Printing technology is also making rapid strides. Laser printers can be used to produce elegant documents. Photocopying technology continues to make breakthroughs. Copies of documents may be reduced, enlarged, copied on both sides, and copied in color—all at faster and faster speeds, at lower and lower costs, with higher and higher quality.

Linked Communication and Information Systems. More and more companies are linking microcomputers to mainframe computers in order to give authorized employees access to needed corporate information. Links between microcomputers are also common. The rapid growth of computer networks has led to concern over data security. A carefully designed integrated computer system contains user safeguards. They limit the unauthorized browsing of the merely curious, but a determined and knowledgeable data thief is almost impossible to stop. Managers should carefully consider security in the design of integrated systems. Such systems are valuable tools, providing timely and accurate information for decision making.

In some integrated systems portable computers are used to collect data and feed the data to microcomputers at distant locations; the microcomputers are then used to transmit the data to the mainframe computer. An example of this process is presented in Box 5.1. Dayton Power and Light enjoyed large gains in productivity and improved accuracy in its meter reading operation by

Box 5.1

METER READING—AN EXAMPLE OF AN INTEGRATED COMPUTER SYSTEM

Dayton Power and Light Company, an electric and gas utility in Ohio, uses portable computers for their meter readers to collect the daily meter readings. Each evening the files from these portable computers are then read into microcomputers at 14 different regional office locations. The data thus accumulated are transferred to the mainframe computer, and the customer accounts are updated nightly with the new meter reading information. The entire updating process, which used to take the better part of each night, is now done in minutes.

Data entry duties and chances for human error have been greatly reduced, as now only the meter readers enter the data into the system, and that is done by keying the data into the portable computer at the meter's site. The portable computer is programmed to check each entry against upper and lower limits, based on a customer's past usage. If the meter reader enters a reading outside these bounds, the portable computer will beep, signaling a possible error. The meter reader can immediately check to see if a mistake has been made.

Under the former system, the meter reader handwrote the daily meter readings on forms that were to be electronically scanned (like multiple-choice exam sheets). These forms were then accumulated at the same 14 locations, and transferred by courier each evening to the company's central data processing facility. There, scanners read the data sheets and transferred the data to a computer tape. The data tape was used in turn to update customer accounts nightly. The result of the new process is the same, but greater speed and accuracy have been attained.

Since the meter reading task is a high-volume operation with over 35,000 meters read daily, this task was a natural one to consider when the company began looking for ways to gain greater efficiency by increasing capital intensity. Microtechnology had dropped in price so that conversion to such an integrated system was feasible. The technology exists for an even more capital-intensive system. It is possible to install a system whereby meters are read at a central location by a computer, eliminating the need for a worker to read and transmit the data. Conversion to this process is very expensive at present. However, such a system would represent the ultimate in accuracy and timeliness and do away with almost all worker involvement in the meter reading process. In time this system, or one yet to be invented, will replace the current integrated system, just as the integrated system replaced the handwritten scanner sheet system.

Sources: "Utility-Bill Errors Could Soon Be Thing of Past with New Meter-Reading Devices," *The Wall Street Journal,* August 14, 1985; The Dayton Power and Light Company, *1984 Annual Report.*

linking the three levels of computer systems. Many other computerized systems involve integrated microcomputers and mainframe computers in order to support decision making at all levels in an organization.

Some large computer systems feature a communication method called electronic mail.* An **electronic mail system** allows users to exchange messages, through computers, with others who have access to the same computer network. A message may be sent to one user, to a specific group (such as all district managers), or to all employees with access to the system. Sending the same message at the same time to a large number of people is one of the biggest advantages of electronic mail. Organizations may use it to make announcements to employees who routinely use a specific computer system, such as customer service representatives who check the customer information system on a daily basis. If these employees need information about price changes or product availability, it is easy to send such information to all of them at the same time. In some corporations, electronic mail has become so popular that employees complain of receiving electronic junk mail.

Electronic work stations can be used to link all the components of an electronic communication and information system. Many firms are marketing electronic work stations for managers, analysts, and clerical workers. These work stations are desks or complete cubicles with built-in terminals, phone systems, and other electronic devices designed to make the user's work life easier and more productive.

Implications for the Future

The technology exists to eliminate most barriers of time and place in office activities. Telephone calls may be made from automobiles. A report may be dictated from Singapore or the office next door. A meeting can involve people in New York and San Francisco at the same time. Entire transactions may take place by means of phone recorders, without the participants ever speaking directly to each other. Corporate and other databases may be accessed from home or hotel room with a modem and computer terminal. Corporate news items may be simultaneously announced throughout the organization by electronic mail.

In almost any office today you are likely to find some components of an electronic communication and information system. In only a few offices would you find all of them. Because of investment costs or inadequate productivity measures, managers often find it difficult to justify the acquisition of these systems for offices. Sometimes decisionmakers do not fully appreciate the benefits or understand the workings of these newly developed systems.

* The term *electronic mail* may also apply to document transmission, described in the preceding section.

At other times, the projected marginal improvement in productivity is very small. However, most new technology does allow people to work with greater accuracy, higher quality, and more convenience. Many of these benefits are not always known in advance or easy to quantify. Nonetheless, capital investments *are* being made in office technology and are likely to increase. Many of you are tomorrow's decisionmakers who will be instrumental in buying and using new office processes and systems. You may already be familiar with computer keyboards, word processing, electronic spreadsheets, electronic mail, and other electronic technologies. Furthermore, some of these systems are available in modules that you can try before making a huge investment. All indications point toward greater office productivity in the future.

TECHNOLOGY IN THE SERVICE SECTOR

As you noted in Chapter 1, the service sector is a dominant force in the U.S. economy today. Recall that the service sector includes banks, utilities, government services, transportation services, education, health care, food service, hotels and motels, wholesale and retail trade, personal services, leisure services, and more. With so many organizations and people involved, the search for ways to improve productivity in the service sector is bound to have rewards.

An Example: Tax Returns

The range of technologies available to a tax preparation firm is illustrated in Box 5.2. The firm's front office has jumbled routings and high customer contact. Employees must be quite flexible, as they are required to handle a wide variety of tax preparation problems. The back office operation has no contact with customers, allowing more repeatability and specialization. The equipment provided there is more diverse than in the front office. The process reflects the typical inverse relationship between customer contact and capital intensity (see Chapter 4).

Let's see what kind of impact a hypothetical computerized tax preparation system might have on the process. To help preparers use the computer to prepare returns, we could install computer terminals on their desks. We also supply a program that runs at the terminal and prompts the preparer in the front office with the next question to ask the client, and the preparer types in the client's answers to each question in turn. The computer program then performs all necessary arithmetic and prints the completed tax forms for the client. The need for the math checker in the back office is eliminated. The need for concept checkers still exists, but the nature of their duties changes.

Now, if a preparer has a question about how to treat a particular item, the preparer queries a back-office expert directly through the computer when the question arises. Also, with extensive programming, we could have the terminal prompt the preparer not only for the next question, but also warn the preparer about answers that seem out of line, such as "Did this person really drive 100,000 miles on business last year?" Computerized office operations, including the electronic filing concept described at the bottom of Box 5.2, can be the next step up in the technology for preparing tax returns. Payoffs can be improved response time, accuracy, and productivity.

Box 5.2

TECHNOLOGICAL CHOICES AT H&R BLOCK

H&R Block is a large, low-priced tax preparation firm. The technology it uses in the front office differs from that in the back office. Furthermore, an entirely new technology may be right around the corner.

The Front Office

The front office consists of two areas: one area serves as a client waiting room, in which clients are greeted and assigned to a tax preparer; and another area in which the preparers work with clients. These two areas may be in the same or adjoining rooms. In the work area, the tax preparers interview clients and solicit the information necessary to prepare the client's tax return. In most cases, a complete draft of all forms needed for the return is prepared while the client is present, so that the client knows the approximate tax owed or refund due before leaving. The major work in the office is performed in front of the clients and would be impossible to perform without the clients' cooperation. Work flows are short—client to preparer—but jumbled, because each client in turn is sent to the next available preparer, who does all the work for that client, no matter how complicated the return might be or how many forms it might require. Front-office employees in this firm have broad general knowledge about the tax code, and are expected to be able to prepare all tax forms commonly used by individuals.

In terms of technology, front-offices might be equipped with desks, chairs for the preparer and clients, a pile of tax forms, pencils, erasers, pocket calculators, and little else. All tax preparers are similarly equipped. They are likely not to have private telephones because the tax preparers do not need to call each other or outside parties.

The Back Office

The clients leave the front office after the amount of their tax liability or refund has been established. However, the return is subject to further processing. All returns completed on a given day are collected and sent to the

Technological Choices in the Service Sector

Tax preparation is just one example of how computer technology can change processes in service industries. Some other applications of new technology in the service sector are

1. electronic funds transfer systems;
2. automatic teller machines;
3. bar coding;

back office, which may be located in another building. At this office, other employees scrutinize the returns for mathematical and conceptual errors, make required copies, and store copies for reference in case further information about the returns is required later. Other copies are sent back to the front office, where clients will pick them up. The back office has virtually no contact with clients and limited contact with other employees. Work may flow in a line from math checker to concept checker to copymaker to file clerk. Work in this office is somewhat easier to organize, predict, and measure than the work in the front office. Employees in the back office are much more specialized than those in the front office. Many have developed areas of expertise and are extremely knowledgeable about specific segments of the tax code.

In terms of technology, employees in the back office have a wider variety of equipment. Math checkers need a calculator capable of printing hard copy, so that discrepancies can be easily checked. Concept checkers are expected to be specialists who can answer questions about unusual situations, so these employees have access to volumes of the tax code and phone access to the Internal Revenue Service. Each employee in the back office is likely to have a phone.

Emerging Technology

The Internal Revenue Service is exploring a new technology: the electronic filing of returns. Returns would be prepared on a computer and then fed by telephone directly into an IRS computer for processing. This would eliminate several steps by IRS workers, cut errors substantially, and reduce the response time by several weeks. H&R Block offices in Cincinnati and Phoenix are participating in a test of electronic filing. One spokesman suggested that this approach is the wave of the future.

Source: "IRS May Electrify Us with Speedy Refunds," *The Columbus Dispatch*, February 14, 1986.

4. electronic data interchange;
5. integrated computer order systems; and
6. on-line databases.

The banking industry began to automate in the 1930s when check sorting machines were invented. Financial service institutions have continually improved operational efficiency in ways that are increasingly visible to the customer. Two of those ways are *electronic funds transfer (EFT)* systems and *automatic teller machines* (ATMs). The EFTs transfer money electronically between bank accounts; ATMs are computers that customers use to withdraw cash, make deposits, pay utility bills, and check their account balances without ever seeing a bank employee. Through ATMs, bank customers have access to their funds 24 hours a day. In spite of this round-the-clock convenience, banks are finding that employees alone do not influence the customer's perception of service. If an ATM swallows a bankcard or refuses a transaction, or, worse yet, if the computer is down and the customer desperately wants cash, the customer's impression of the service suffers.

Bar coding is a process having widespread implications for wholesaling, retailing, and warehousing in the service sector and for the manufacturing sector, as well. A bar code is a set of wide and thin black bars and spaces that can be read by an optical scanner. A great deal of information may be conveyed by bar codes, including product name, lot number, manufacturing location, shelf location, and price. A bar code may be printed directly on the package of a product, or it may be printed on a label or sticker that is affixed to the product or its package. Bar codes are also printed on cartons, so that products inside can be easily identified.

Bar codes have dramatically increased productivity in supermarkets over the past 10 years. A grocery checker using an optical scanner at the checkout counter needs to make sure only that the scanner has read the bar code label on the product (typically, the scanner beeps when it reads an item). The price and item are automatically recorded on a sales register, and inventory records are updated. Bar coding speeds the checkout process and makes inventory control much easier. The customer benefits from receiving a precise record of the transaction and quicker, more accurate service at the checkout counter. In addition to grocery stores, many other retailers are beginning to use optical scanners. Some public libraries use bar codes on library books and patrons' library cards. VCR rental stores are beginning to use bar codes on tapes and customers' credit cards to speed up the checkout process. Warehouse operators are finding bar coding extremely useful in keeping track of locations of specific products. Present applications of bar coding have just scratched the surface of the potential for this system.

Electronic data interchange (EDI) **systems** are integrated systems in which computers in one organization exchange information directly with computers in another organization. The transportation industry uses these systems to transmit specific shipping-related documents—invoices, freight bills, and other information—from one computer to another. EDI eliminates the sea of paperwork involved in most shipping transactions, improves accuracy, and saves time.

Many suppliers of various goods and services place computer terminals in their customers' offices, so that customers can order directly and conveniently from the supplier. Airlines place computer terminals in travel agents' offices, so that customers' reservations and tickets can be handled directly through the travel agent's terminal. American Hospital Supply has placed terminals in the purchasing agent's office in many hospitals. These terminals make it easy for a hospital to order supplies whenever it runs low and allow the hospital to keep smaller quantities on hand, thus lowering inventory carrying costs. *Integrated computer order systems* now link firms and their customers in many industries, allowing customers to order electronically, and in some cases reserve inventory in the supplier's warehouse. The availability of such systems is bound to have many effects on process design. Direct customer involvement with salespeople is one thing, but direct customer involvement with inventory by means of the computer is quite another. Discrepancies between real inventory and computer records become critical, and the firm selling the goods may lose control over the timing and quantity of sales. Customers with computer access to vendors' inventory records may reserve units they do not really need as a precaution against their own uncertainty and later cancel such orders if their needs do not materialize. This can wreak havoc with a supplier's inventory system.

A growing number of proprietary *on-line databases,* which subscribers may access in a variety of ways, are available. Most of these databases can be accessed through users' personal computers linked to telephone lines by means of a modem, but some can be accessed directly through terminals installed on the users' premises. In 1985, more than 2000 of these databases were commercially available, and the number is growing rapidly. Lawyers can look up regulations and legal opinions through a service called Lexis. Stockbrokers can get instant stock price quotations from several systems. Weather data, currency rates, ski conditions, the status of bills in Congress, and full texts of several major newspapers and magazines from around the world are among the databases available electronically. Thus managers and analysts can have at their fingertips information previously available only after hours of laborious manual search through libraries and other sources. Users of these services who are not located in major cities now have instant access to data never before available to them.

These are just a few of the many examples of new technology in the service sector. If you look around, you will see many more. It is difficult to predict the types of services that will be provided in the future and the technologies that will be used to provide them. However, we expect a greater variety of services with less human contact, available at a wider range of times and places. As with office technology, barriers of time and place will be reduced.

MANUFACTURING TECHNOLOGY

Whether in an office, a service sector firm, or a manufacturing plant, transformation processes convert inputs into outputs. Since manufacturing converts materials into goods that have a physical form, our discussion of manufacturing technology emphasizes two aspects of production:

1. Transformation processes in manufacturing focus on changing the properties of materials in one way or another.
2. Moving, packaging, and storing materials are important processes in their own right, making materials handling a special concern.

The same advances in microtechnology that are changing the office are also changing the factory. Robots are being used increasingly for welding, painting, riveting, bending, soldering, drilling, materials handling, and many other jobs. Computers are being used to control machine setups, loading, unloading, and routing of materials from one work station to another. Computers also are being used in product design, scheduling, and production and inventory planning. Box 5.3 contains a description of some of the new computer, robotic, and materials handling technologies used by Ford Motor Company to make the Aerostar minivan.

Before considering some of the more sophisticated technologies, let's begin with a survey of manufacturing processes and the factors to consider when making a specific technological choice. We then give specific attention to materials handling processes, as well as ways to achieve repeatability in the manufacturing process. Finally, we take a look at some of the newer computer-related technologies in manufacturing.

Manufacturing Processes

One way to classify manufacturing processes is by the objective of the process. In converting raw materials to finished goods, the objective usually is one or more of the following.

1. Change the material's physical properties.
2. Change the material's shape.
3. Machine parts to a fixed dimension.
4. Obtain a surface finish.
5. Join parts or materials.

Box 5.3

MANUFACTURING FORD'S AEROSTAR—ADVANCED TECHNOLOGY IN ACTION

Aerostar, Ford Motor Company's most versatile entry in the minivan market, is produced using some of the most sophisticated manufacturing technology in the world. Ford's assembly plant in St. Louis was enlarged and completely reequipped with new facilities and tooling to accommodate the Aerostar. Typical of this new technology are more than 550 computers linked in a network so that computer-controlled machinery can be monitored continuously. These computers, plus accurate robot welders and manufacturing innovations such as the use of one-piece body-side panels, make it possible to build vehicles of very consistent quality.

Aerostar's roof panel was totally designed using computer graphics. Using the electronic design data, computer commands for machining are produced and electronically sent to numerically controlled mills for machining sheet-metal dies and inspection tools. Roof panels stamped from the dies are then checked against the computer data from the original design. By using computer-aided design and manufacturing techniques, a uniform fit between body panels is ensured, leading to less wind and road noise and better weather protection.

Aerostar's underbody assembly line uses 40 welding robots, including 24 gantry models—Ford's first overhead-mounted robots in the United States. Gantry robots can carry up to 200 pounds of tooling and require less floor space than side-mounted models. Robots also are key elements in Aerostar's welding and painting processes. Ninety-seven percent of Aerostar's 4000 spot welds are done by robots or other automated equipment. Robots apply enamel to Aerostar's interior surfaces. The robots and automatic spray machines that apply paint to the exterior not only eliminate operations that are tedious and unpleasant for workers, but also produce a finish that is consistent in appearance and virtually defect free.

Aerostar's chassis and trim department uses a material handling system called power-and-free-conveyors. These conveyors eliminate conventional under-the-line floor pits, which separate employees from their co-workers and make it hard to reach parts. They also facilitate access to the vehicle by all employees.

A key element in the successful integration of these new manufacturing techniques was the involvement of plant employees in the design of the new systems. Early in the development phase proposed methods were reviewed with those who would be directly responsible for certain operations. Employees made 434 suggestions, about 60 percent of which were adopted.

Source: Ford Motor Company, *Second Quarter Report to Stockholders*, Summer 1985.

Table 5.2

Technical Classification of Manufacturing Processes

	Processes for Changing Physical Properties	
Chemical reactions	Hot working	Refining/extraction
Cold working	Heat treatment	Shot peening
	Processes for Changing the Shape of Materials	
Casting	Spinning	Forging
Stretch forming	Extruding	Roll forming
Rolling	Torch cutting	Drawing
Explosive forming	Squeezing	Electrohydraulic forming
Crushing	Magnetic forming	Shearing
Piercing	Electroforming	Plastics molding
Powder metal forming	Bending	
	Processes for Machining Parts to a Fixed Dimension	
	Traditional chip removal processes	
Turning	Sawing	Planing
Broaching	Shaping	Milling
Drilling	Grinding	Boring
Hobbing	Reaming	Routing
	Nontraditional machining processes	
Ultrasonic machining	Plasma-arc machining	Electrochemical
Optical lasers	Electron beam machining	Abrasive jet cutting
	Processes for Obtaining a Surface Finish	
Polishing	Lapping	Abrasive belt grinding
Metal spraying	Barrel tumbling	Sanding
Electroplating	Superfinishing	Honing
Painting		
	Processes for Joining Parts or Materials	
Welding	Pressing	Soldering
Riveting	Brazing	Screw fastening
Plugging	Adhesive joining	

Source: Amstead, B. J., P. F. Oswald, and M. L. Begeman, *Manufacturing Processes*, 7th ed. New York: John Wiley & Sons, 1977.

In Table 5.2, you can see some of the specific processes included in each of these five categories. It is beyond the scope of this text for us to fully define each process, but the list provides some understanding of the types in each category. Two points should be made about transformation processes. First, few processes are unique to one industry or applied to just one kind of raw material. The processes listed in Table 5.2 are found in the metal-working, wood-working, masonry, food, oil, and chemical industries. Second, there typically are several technological alternatives for each process. Consider a simple product, such as fudge. You can use a stove and a pan to cook a batch at home. A supermarket with a "home-made" candy counter might use large containers with special heat and temperature controls to make large batches of fudge once a day. A chocolate factory would use large vats, continuous flows, and highly automated processes to produce fudge round the clock. The raw materials, finished products, and types of processes are quite similar in all three situations. However, the specific technologies used are decidedly different.

Choosing a specific manufacturing technology requires consideration of many factors. Some of the factors of concern to those who choose, implement, and manage manufacturing technology are shown in Table 5.3. Many trade-offs must occur among these factors, so the correct choice for one organization is not necessarily the correct choice for another. The first factor listed, the match with competitive priorities and positioning strategy, is a crucial consideration. Think back to the choices for sawing lumber at the beginning of this chapter. Suppose that we are operating a sawmill; low price is our top competitive priority, and product focus is our positioning strategy. By choosing the most capital-intensive sawing technology within our budget constraints, we will be able to turn out high volumes of standardized products at a low cost per unit. On the other hand, suppose that we are operating a custom furniture shop; we compete on product flexibility and have a process focus. We have several general purpose saws, both hand and electric powered, which can perform any sawing task that might be needed. Our capital investment in sawing equipment is much lower, but employee skill requirements are much higher for the custom furniture shop than for the sawmill.

Table 5.3

Factors to Consider When Choosing a Manufacturing Technology

- Match with competitive priorities and positioning strategy
- Expected volume of the products for which the technology will be used
- Applicability of the technology to the manufacturing problem being addressed
- Ease of integration with existing technologies and systems
- Flexibility of the technology if
  - the system is changed
  - the volume of product is changed
  - the product is changed
- Ease of operation
- Cost of operation
- Capital investment requirements
- Reliability of the technology
- Required maintenance
- Availability of spare parts
- Labor requirements
- Raw-material requirements
- Likelihood of worker acceptance
- Complexity of training required
- Likelihood of supervisor acceptance
- Safety features and hazards
- Environmental requirements of space, temperature, and atmosphere
- Information system requirements

Materials Handling Processes

During the conversion from raw materials to finished goods, materials generally must be moved from one place to another. If delays are encountered in the manufacturing processes, goods must be stored. Goods may have to be packaged or placed in containers before they can be moved or stored. Moving, packaging, and storing are known as **materials handling processes.** These processes are necessary for materials to flow through other manufacturing processes. How, when, and by whom materials are handled is an important consideration in manufacturing. Materials handling takes time, costs money, and adds no value to the product. For these reasons, any handling that can be eliminated should be eliminated.

Moving. A rule of thumb in designing materials handling systems is "The best handling is no handling at all." Some guiding principles for developing or changing materials handling processes are listed in Table 5.4. These principles relate primarily to the movement aspects of materials handling.

Packaging. Materials are usually placed in containers or on pallets for moving and storing, as well as for shipping to customers.* Technological choices for packaging and containers cannot be separated from decisions regarding how and when to transport and store materials. Containers can range from very large storage tanks, railcars, or truck trailers to very small bottles, cans, or boxes. Packaging of individual items in a product-focus manufacturing environment may well be performed as the last step before the item rolls off the line.

Storage. Storage, either short- or long-term, occurs when the flow of materials through the manufacturing process is stopped. Stopped or stored material is called *work-in-process inventory.* Goods stored after processing has been completed are called *finished goods inventory.* Inventory costs money, but inventory costs can be reduced by decreasing the volume of materials held, by decreasing the time it is held, or both. Any reduction in materials handling can increase productivity. This increased productivity may come from more efficient movement of materials through the factory, reduced inventories, or lower packaging costs.

A Comparison of Materials Handling Needs. In Chapter 2 we considered the operations of two firms having very different materials handling needs. For Suds Brewery, materials literally flow along fixed paths, through pipes from one large vat to another. The handling of materials is very repetitious, structured, and automatic. The final packaging is an important part of the

* A pallet is a low, portable platform on which materials are placed for ease in materials handling, storage, or even machining.

Table 5.4

Design Principles for Materials Handling Systems

- Straighten and shorten moves whenever possible.
- Combine and eliminate moves and handling operations whenever possible.
- Materials being moved should be brought as close as possible to the next point of use before being halted.
- Whenever possible, preposition materials for the next operation before depositing them.
- Consider moving workers rather than materials.
- Use mechanical handling rather than manual labor when practicable.
- Use overhead space where possible.

Source: E. Ralph Sims, "Material Handling Systems," *Handbook of Industrial Engineering*, Chapter 10.3, G. Salvendy (Ed.) New York: John Wiley & Sons, 1982.

entire manufacturing process. The beer is automatically canned or bottled, placed in six- or twelve-packs, and finally put in heavy cardboard cases for immediate shipping by rail or truck. All materials handling is accomplished with as little worker intervention as possible.

In contrast, at Longhorn materials for a particular job are placed in reusable open-top containers called tote boxes. These containers are then carried to the next work station, where additional work is to be performed. Lift trucks and carts are used to transport materials that are too heavy for a person to carry. The flow of material through the shop is very jumbled, since no two jobs are likely to have the same path. As customer orders progress through the shop, individual parts are placed in and removed from the tote boxes several times. Stacks of tote boxes full of partially completed parts sit by some machines waiting to be worked on. Finished orders are shipped to customers in individually built crates because each customer's order is unique. Longhorn's materials handling processes are more informal and much less structured than Suds's. Longhorn's materials handling processes resist automation because the path of each job through the shop and the materials handled are unique. Because of its product focus and large volumes of identical products, Suds Brewery enjoys far more efficiency in materials handling operations than does Longhorn.

Repeatability in Manufacturing Processes

One of the characteristics of a product focus is a large volume of identical or very similar products, which leads to repeating the same process over and over. As first noted in Chapter 1, repeatability is one of the keys to increased productivity. With the higher volumes of a product focus, automation becomes more attractive, and labor costs are driven down as the need to set up for different products is minimized. With high volumes, one production line may be dedicated to a single product. Line flows of materials through the manufacturing process simplify materials handling. Inventories can be cut because there is less need to decouple one operation from the next. The Japanese refer to a product focus as *overlapped operations,* where materials move directly from one operation to the next without waiting in queues.

Unfortunately, product volumes are not always high enough to justify dedicating a single line to one product or even to several very similar products. In those situations, three alternatives still exist for achieving the benefits of high repeatability:

1. One-worker–multiple-machines.
2. Group technology.
3. Flexible automation.

One-Worker–Multiple-Machines Concept

If volumes are not sufficient to keep several workers busy on one production line, it may be possible to set up a smaller line that keeps just one worker busy. This is the theory behind the **one-worker–multiple-machines** (OWMM) **concept,** which is being applied widely in Japan. For example, Mitsubishi Electric Company since 1979 has converted the use of more than 25 percent of its machine operations to this concept. To make OWMM possible, a worker must be able to operate several different machines simultaneously. A typical situation is for the worker to operate four or five machines, each performing a different process. This approach is possible only when each machine operates on its own for much of the cycle. The worker must only load or unload each machine as needed. Sometimes, automatic feeds even eliminate the loading requirement. Suppose that an OWMM station consists of one worker and two different machines. The product made on the line passes through two processes, one performed by machine 1 and the other performed by machine 2. The sequence of steps for the worker would be as follows:

1. Unload the unit of product finished at machine 1, and place it on a conveyor going to machine 2.
2. Load machine 1 to make another unit, drawing from nearby raw materials.
3. While machine 1 is working, unload machine 2 as soon as it has finished. Put the finished product on the conveyor going to the inventory storage or shipping area.
4. Load machine 2, using the unit just finished at machine 1. This step

completes the full cycle for the worker, who returns to step 1, and repeats the sequence.

Figure 5.1 illustrates these four steps. Having a worker operate several machines is not uncommon. What is unique about OWMM is that several *different* machines make up a line flow. The more common approach is to have one worker operate several identical machines. An example of this approach can be found in the semiconductor industry. One worker may operate several saws that cut silicon bars into slices that ultimately become chips. Such an arrangement reduces labor requirements but not work-in-process inventory, unlike OWMM.

Group Technology

Another possibility for achieving repeatability with low-volume processes is the use of **group technology** (GT). Grouping several products (or parts) having common attributes into families is the first step in taking advantage of group technology. Product or part families may be formed on the basis of size, shape, manufacturing requirements, routing requirements, or demand. The idea is to find a set of products with enough similarity in processing requirements that little machine changeover or setup is required from one product to the next. For example, all bolts might be assigned to the same part family because they all require the same basic processing steps regardless of variations in size and shape. Figure 5.2 shows 13 parts that belong to the same family for manufacturing purposes.

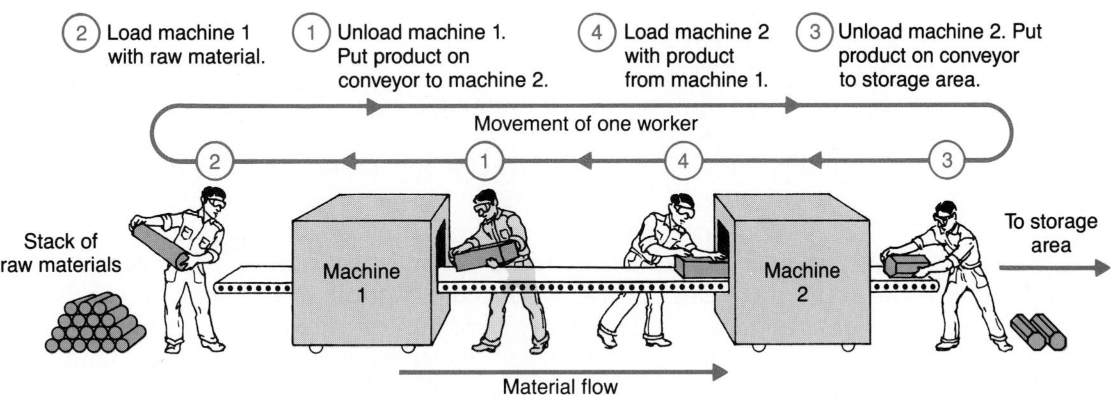

Figure 5.1

One-Worker–Multiple-Machines (OWMM) Concept.

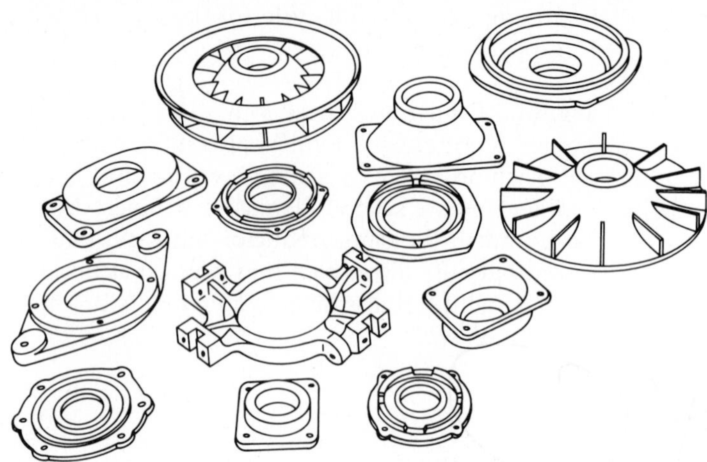

Figure 5.2

Thirteen Parts Belonging to the Same Family.

Source: Mikell P. Groover, *Automation, Production Systems, and Computer-Aided Manufacturing.* Englewood Cliffs, N.J.: Prentice-Hall, 1980, p. 540. Reprinted by permission.

The second step in using group technology is to create a separate area, called a *cell,* for the machine tools required to perform the basic processes. The machines are usually arranged to allow for line flows. Benefits resulting from GT cells are

1. less time lost to setups;
2. lower work-in-process inventory;
3. less materials handling;
4. reduced cycle time; and
5. increased opportunities for automation.

The machines in a GT cell will require only minor adjustments to their basic setups to accommodate each different batch from the same family of parts. Thus product changeovers are greatly simplified. In addition, GT cells simplify product routings and reduce cycle time, that is, the length of time the job is in the shop. Thus queues of materials waiting to be worked on are shortened or eliminated. Frequently, handling of materials is automated so that, after loading the GT cell with raw materials, a worker does not handle the machined parts until the job is complete.

Many job shops have been able to simplify some of their product routings and achieve higher efficiency by identifying product families and using GT cells. Figure 5.3(a) illustrates a shop floor where there are no GT cells. There

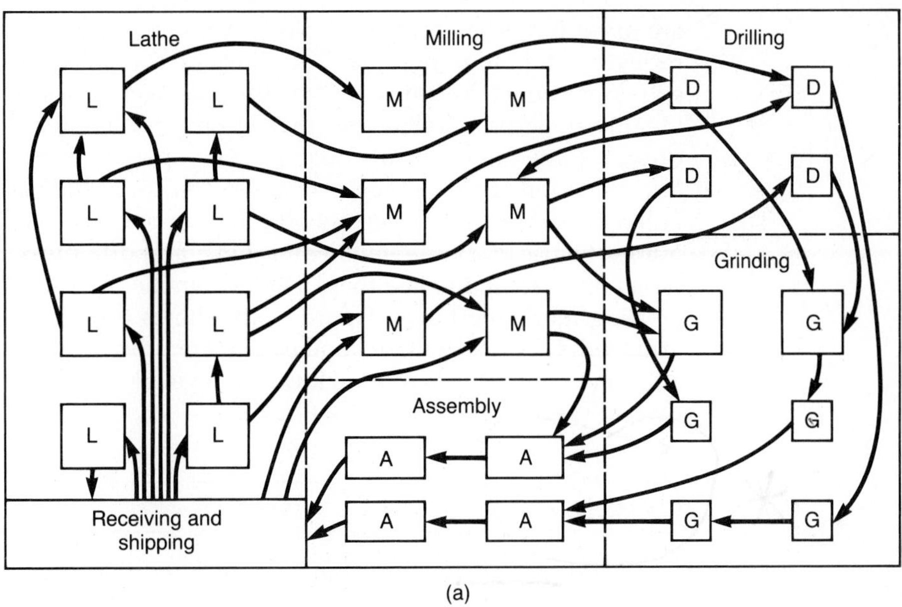

(a)

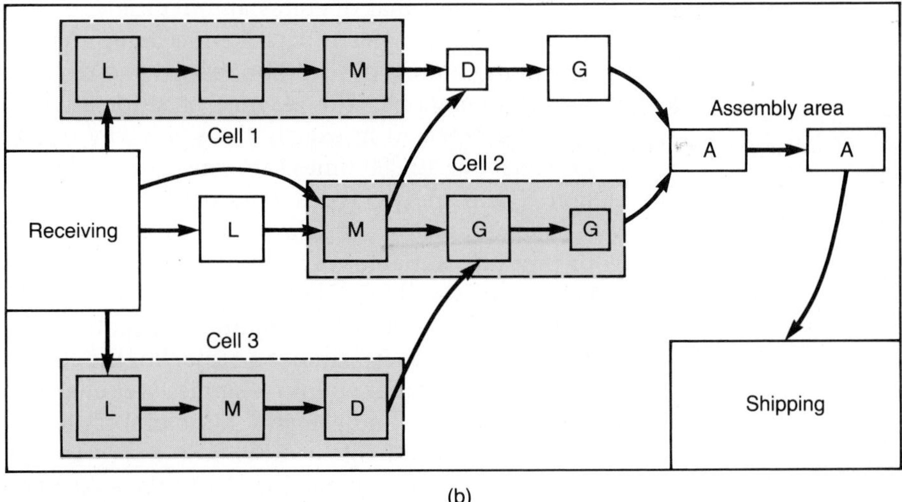

(b)

Figure 5.3

Process Flows before and after the Use of GT Cells: (a) Jumbled Flows in a Job Shop *without* GT Cells; (b) Line Flows Achieved in a Job Shop *with* Three GT Cells.

Source: Mikell P. Groover, *Automation, Production Systems, and Computer-Aided Manufacturing*. Englewood Cliffs, N.J.: Prentice-Hall, 1980, pp. 540–541. Reprinted by permission.

are areas for lathes, milling, drilling, grinding, and assembly, as well as a receiving and shipping area. The flows of materials through this shop are extremely jumbled. Suppose that the manager of this job shop is able to identify three product families that account for a majority of the firm's production. One family always requires two operations on lathes, followed by one operation at the milling machines. The second family always requires a milling operation followed by two grinding operations. The third family requires the use of a lathe, milling machine, and drill press. Three GT cells can be set up to accommodate these product families and simplify the routings by creating more line flows. Figure 5.3(b) shows how these GT cells might be arranged. Jobs not in these families that are processed outside these cells will still have jumbled routings. However, overall productivity still can be improved greatly by the use of a few cells.

Flexible Automation

The word *automatic* comes from the Greek work for self-acting and has been around for well over 200 years. In the late 1940s the automobile industry coined the word **automation.** We use this word to describe a system, process, or piece of equipment that operates automatically. Automation is a self-acting, or self-regulating, system because mechanical or electronic devices replace many of the human observation, effort, and decision-making functions in performing operations. The essence of automation is repeatability. If a process is to be repeated in exactly the same way two times, 10 times, 100 times, 500 times, or 10,000 times, at some point it becomes a candidate for automation. There are two types of automation: fixed and programmable.

With **fixed automation,** the flow lines are configured to produce one type of part or product. Variable costs per unit are very low, although the initial investment can be very high. High production rates can be achieved, making it suitable for products in high demand. Operations are performed in a fixed sequence in which each operation is simple, but the coordination and integration of many such operations into a single large machine is complex. Fixed automation is inflexible, and changes in the process to accommodate product changes are difficult and costly. Chemical processing and oil refineries are examples of this kind of automation. Until the mid-1980s, most automobile plants in the United States were dominated by fixed automation, and some still are.

Programmable automation also requires a high initial investment but (for a given installation) not usually as high as for fixed automation. This type of flexible automation is breaking down the traditional inverse relationship between resource flexibility and capital intensity (see Chapter 4). High capital intensity *and* high resource flexibility are now possible. The processes performed by programmable automation may be adapted to new product configurations by reprogramming the instructions to the machine or system. Once written, the programs can be reused, resulting in rapid changeovers. This type of flexibility is useful in both product-focus and process-focus operations. Suppose that a machine has been dedicated to a particular product (product focus), but the product has reached the end of its life cycle. The machine can be reused simply by reprogramming it for the sequence and type of operations needed for a new product. When there is a process focus, the machine makes a variety of products in small batches. The changeover, once a program has been written for each product, is made simply by retrieving and using the program for the next product.

Industrial robots and flexible manufacturing systems are sophisticated types of programmable automation, which have captured the attention of the press and public. Less glamorous, but used far more commonly, are numerical control machine tools.

Numerical Control Machines

Numerical control (NC) **machines** were first developed in the early 1950s at Massachusetts Institute of Technology through research sponsored by the U.S. Air Force. The objective of this research was to find more efficient methods of manufacturing jet aircraft. These large machine tools could be programmed to repeat a sequence of instructions, so that small to medium-sized batches of parts could be machined to closer tolerances. Parts in many sizes and shapes could be drilled, turned, bored, or milled as required. The instructions were fed to the machine by means of a punched tape or card. The machine operator needed to load the raw materials into the NC machine and unload the machined parts, but a semiskilled, rather than a skilled, worker could be used to operate the machine. To reconfigure the machine, only the instructions on the punched tape had to be changed.

Newer NC machines no longer receive their instructions from a punched tape or card but from a computer. **Computer numerical control** (CNC) **machines,** are usually stand-alone pieces of equipment, each controlled by its own microcomputer. A DNC system is a *direct numerical control* system of several NC machines controlled by one computer. In practice there is some overlap in the terminology in this area.

Industrial Robots

A robot is a form of programmable automation that relies heavily on microtechnology. **Industrial robots** perform highly repetitive tasks without tiring, complaining, needing a lunch break, or going to the restroom. They willingly accept poor working conditions and zero wages and perform hazardous tasks without complaint. They are more likely to be found in major automobile plants than anywhere else, but more firms are buying a single robot or a few robots, much as they first acquired NC equipment many years ago.

Robots have an arm, a hand, and sometimes fingers or even an eye. The hand (sometimes called an *end effector* or *tool*) actually does the work. There are several types of robot hands, including:

1. Magnetic hand.
2. Vacuum hand.
3. Photocell detectors on the hand.
4. A TV camera for inspection on the hand.
5. Microswitch sensors on the hand.
6. Extra-long fingers.
7. The palm only, for finger attachment.
8. Hooked hand for lifting heavy objects.
9. Spray-gun hand.
10. Welding-gun hand.

Robots were initially used mainly for welding. The basic features of a typical industrial robot are shown in Fig. 5.4*. This robot has six rotational joints and is popular for spot-welding applications. Figure 5.5 shows a large electric robot reaching in the front-door window to apply a sealant bead and seal the body of a pickup truck. It gives you some idea of robots' great mobility and ability to move their hands into difficult locations. Figure 5.6 shows a battery of robots spot welding bodies at an automotive plant. A close-up view of the same production line is shown in Fig. 5.7.

Robotic applications are not limited to welding at automotive or truck assembly plants. Robots are being used to pick fruit on trees, mix chemicals in chemistry labs, and wash windows. Although the full range of possibilities is still being developed, the most frequent current applications of robots in practice are:

1. Assembly (from nuts and bolts to welding and electronics assembly).
2. Spray painting.
3. Materials handling.
4. Inspection and electrical testing.

Except for spray painting, the trend is away from hydraulic robots to electric robots, primarily because of maintenance costs. Hydraulic robot maintenance requires workers from two different trade unions, while only one union is involved with electric robots.† The initial price of a robot varies depending on its size and functions. Other costs associated with acquisition

* Safety equipment has been removed or opened for some cases in Figs. 5.4–5.8 to provide a clear view of the robots. Safety equipment must be in place prior to operation.

† This illustration provides yet another example of how both employee and equipment choices are inseparable parts of process design.

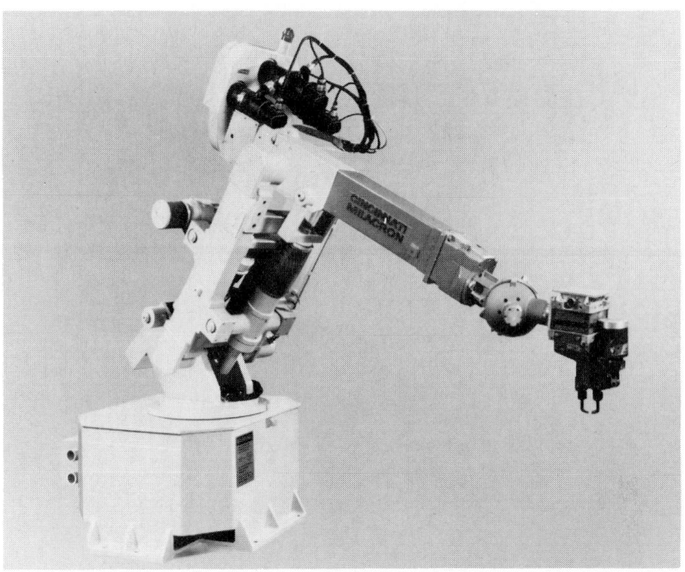

Figure 5.4

A Cincinnati Milacron 776 Robot for Spot-Welding Applications.

Source: Courtesy of Cincinnati Milacron. Reprinted by permission.

Figure 5.5

A Robot Reaching through an Automobile's Front-Door Window.

Source: Courtesy of Cincinnati Milacron. Reprinted by permission.

Figure 5.6

Robots Welding in an Automotive Plant.

Source: Courtesy of Cincinnati Milacron. Reprinted by permission.

Figure 5.7

Close-up View of Robot in Fig. 5.6.

Source: Courtesy of Cincinnati Milacron. Reprinted by permission.

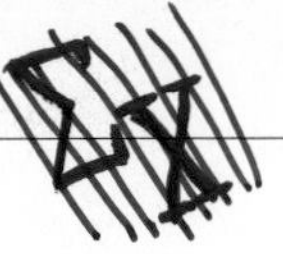

Table 5.5

Robots: Current Practice

Characteristic	Actual Experience
Number now used in the United States	From 10,000 to 12,000
Number expected to be in use in another five to seven years	From 30,000 to 100,000
Investment cost	From $20,000 to $100,000, depending on sophistication
Payback period	Typically less than three years
Return on investment	Typically from 12% to 18%, with some as high as 40%
Operating life	From 15,000 to 25,000 work hours
Annual maintenance cost	10% of initial investment cost; major overhaul after 10,000 hours
Best volume levels	More than 50,000 units per year and less than 500,000 units per year
Installation time	One to five days, depending on complexity

Source: Mitchell, Roger H., and Vincent A. Mabert, "Robotics: Myths and Realities for Smaller American Manufacturers," *Business Horizons,* July/August 1986. Reprinted by permission.

of a robot include modifying the design to match the robot to the desired task, preparing the site for the robot, installing and debugging the robot, modifying the rest of the process, and training and moving workers. Benefits from a robot installation include reduced materials waste, more consistent quality, and labor savings. Table 5.5 highlights some other interesting information about current experience with robots.

Flexible Manufacturing Systems

A third type of flexible automation is the **flexible manufacturing system** (FMS). Combining the best features of fixed and programmable automation, FMSs are becoming more technologically and financially feasible. An FMS can be highly capital intensive, requiring a large initial investment but few workers to keep it operating. The three key components of an FMS are

1. several work stations and a computer that controls their operations;
2. a computer-controlled transport system for moving materials and parts from one machine to another and in and out of the system; and
3. loading and unloading stations.

Each work station can perform a number of different operations. Integrated computer control links work station operations, which are performed by NC, CNC, or DNC machines, or even robots. The transport system connects the work stations to each other and to the loading and unloading points. Parts usually are produced in families, with one or a few families assigned to each FMS. Workers transfer raw materials for the part family to the loading points, where the FMS takes over and passes the materials through a set sequence of operations. The transporter carries materials to the work stations along a route determined by the control computer.

The short setup times for machines in an FMS are made possible by automatic tool interchange capabilities; that is, tools can be switched quickly to enable machines to perform a different process. Such flexibility often allows more than one machine to perform an operation, so production can continue even when a machine is down for maintenance. Also, bottlenecks in production do not develop because parts can be routed to another machine if one is busy. When the operations have been completed, the finished parts are returned to an unloading station, where a worker unloads them.

Figure 5.8 shows the layout of an FMS at the Mazak Corporation plant in Kentucky.* The plant produces turning and machining centers. Specific characteristics of this FMS (one of three at the plant) are:

1. The computer control room (upper right) is the location of the main computer, which controls the transporter and the sequence of operations.
2. Three CNC machines, each with its own microprocessor, control the details of the machining process.
3. Two automated guided vehicles (AGVs)† travel around a 200-foot-long oval track in the center of the layout, moving materials on pallets to and from the CNCs. The AGVs are controlled by the main computer and are guided by wires embedded under the floor. The AGVs are battery powered and go to certain spots on the track for recharging at the direction of the main computer.
4. Each CNC center has an indexing table between it and the track. An inbound pallet from the AGV is automatically transferred to the right-hand side of the table. An outbound pallet holding a finished part is automatically transferred to the left-hand side of the table for pickup by an AGV. The indexing tables prevent any delays at the CNC center or AGV.
5. A tool changer, which loads and unloads tooling magazines, is located behind each CNC center. Each magazine holds an assortment of tools;

* We are indebted to Vincent Mabert for much of the information about this FMS, including Figs. 5.8 and 5.9.

† Other methods of handling materials on pallets, such as powered roller conveyors and chain towlines, are also possible.

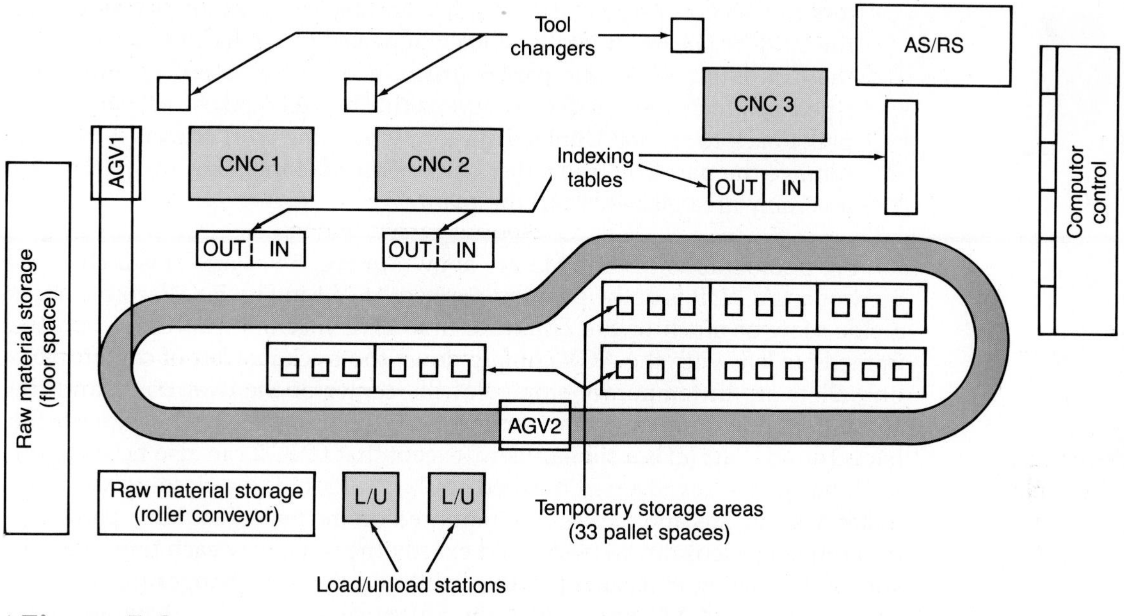

Figure 5.8

A Flexible Manufacturing System at Mazak Corporation.

Source: Courtesy of Vincent Mabert and Mazak Corporation. Reprinted by permission.

they are selected automatically for the next specific machining step. Changing from one tool to another takes only two minutes.

6. A family of seven different parts are made at the FMS. Machining times range from two to four hours per operation (called a *setting*), and a part normally goes through three settings.
7. There are two load/unload stations (lower left). A worker is assigned to each station during the shift when loading and unloading take place. To load a pallet the first time (for the first setting), the worker uses a crane to get the raw material for the part from the storage area and then positions and clamps it on the pallet. To reset a part after its first operation, the operator must unclamp the part, inspect the completed work, and reorient and reclamp the part. Loading takes 10 to 20 minutes.
8. During the evening and night shifts, the FMS operates automatically, without workers at the load/unload stations. Parts that need to be repositioned or unloaded are moved by the AGV to one of 33 pallet spaces next to the track for temporary storage. They are retrieved by workers during the next day shift.
9. Finished parts are stored in the automatic storage and retrieval system (AS/RS), shown in the upper right portion of the layout. The AGV trans-

fers the part on its pallet to an indexing table, which then transfers it to the AS/RS. The AS/RS automatically moves it to the location directed by the computer. When the part is finally needed for assembly into a finished product, this process is reversed. The AGV takes the part on its pallet back to the load/unload station, where the worker uses a crane to remove the part from the pallet. An overhead crane takes the part to the assembly area elsewhere in the plant.

Six photographs of the FMS are shown in Fig. 5.9. Part (a) is a close-up view of an AGV; it is at the position marked AGV 1 in Fig. 5.8. Part (b) shows a side view of much of the FMS; the first CNC machine (CNC 1) is on the immediate left, with the AGV coming down the track just left of center; parts on pallets are in temporary storage at the center of the oval track; and the computer control room on the second floor (behind the windows) is in the background. Part (c) is a similar view, except that CNC 2 can also be seen; the AGV has just received a part finished at CNC 1. Part (d) is a close-up view of a pallet; various jigs and fixtures are mounted on the pallet, so that a particular part (one of seven) can be positioned exactly the same way each time. Part (e) shows the tooling magazine (on the right) and the tool changer (on the left) assigned to each CNC; an arm (not shown) moves back and forth between the tooling magazine and the machine's spindle; it makes sure that the right tool is used for the next machining step; the tool changer holds a second tooling magazine ready, in case of either tool wear (sensed automatically) or the need for a tool not in the current magazine; in either event, the tool changer removes the current magazine from its position and replaces it with the other magazine; and the tool changer, in turn, is supplied with magazines from the tool room by a shuttle vehicle. Finally, part (f) shows the AR/RS in the background where finished parts are stored until needed for assembly.

This particular system is typical of the future envisioned by many for flexible manufacturing systems. Use of an FMS fits with an intermediate positioning strategy involving a medium-level of variety (5 to 100 parts) and volume (annual production rates of 40 to 2000 units per part). The system is flexible enough to simultaneously handle many products with very small batch sizes. In practice, an FMS can yield another benefit. At any specific time, some systems are producing low-variety, high-volume products, much in the same way that fixed automation does. However, when a product comes to the end of its life cycle, the FMS can be reprogrammed to accommodate a different product that is being introduced. This opportunity makes FMS very appealing even to firms tending toward a product focus, particularly when life cycles are short. Finally, you should not conclude that FMS concepts are limited to *machining* operations. Many of the current installations handle *assembly* operations, such as those for typewriters and associated printers at IBM's huge, automated factory in Kentucky.

Figure 5.9

Photographs of an FMS at Mazak Corporation: (a) An AGV; (b) Side View of FMS; (c) CNC 1, an AGV, and Temporary Storage; (d) Jigs and Fixtures on Pallet; (e) Tooling Magazine and Tool Changer; (f) The AS/RS

Source: Courtesy of Vincent Mabert and Mazak Corporation. Reprinted by permission.

Other Computer Assistance in Manufacturing

Computer-aided Design. In order to effectively practice group technology or utilize a flexible manufacturing system, a good way to store and retrieve information about parts is needed. In fact, a good parts classification system is crucial to the success of GT cells and FMSs. One way to obtain such a parts classification system is to use **computer-aided design** (CAD) for product design. Firms may apply group technology without using CAD, and CAD may be used without group technology, but the two systems are a natural marriage. With a CAD system, it is not so often necessary to reinvent the wheel when designing a new product. Old designs can be quickly accessed and modified as appropriate, often saving valuable development time. Computer-aided design systems offer many other advantages over conventional designing and drafting by hand. Drawings of parts are created on a video screen, and the computer is able to show several views of the parts when the dimensions are specified. A part may be subjected to tests of strength and stress by the computer without having to build expensive prototypes or models. Thus several alternative designs can be tested and rejected or accepted rather quickly. Plans and specifications can be prepared or modified and printed out rapidly by manufacturing engineers and others. Necessary changes in product design can be made easily and quickly.

CAD/CAM. In general, you will find that the term **computer-aided manufacturing** (CAM) is used to refer to CNC machines, DNC systems, use of robotics, GT cells that are computer controlled, or FMSs. On the other hand, the CAD/CAM designation has a special meaning. A CAD/CAM system links design and manufacturing functions through the computer. This system provides design specifications directly to the equipment and machines that will perform the manufacturing processes. One major advantage of CAD/CAM systems is that the latest design changes are easier to execute and can be put into effect instantly upon being approved. Figure 5.10 shows both CAD and CAM work stations. The CAD system (Fig. 5.10a) consists of the CAD computers, designing and drawing screens, and drawing plotters. The designer uses them to prepare drawings of the product design, do structural analysis of the product, and make parts lists. The CAM system, linked directly to the CAD computers, allows the designer to help in production engineering tasks, such as selecting cutting processes and tools, compiling the NC program instructions, and estimating time requirements.

Terminology. An abundance of terms relate to the use of computers in manufacturing, and all of them seem to have acronyms. Some of the more common terms used are computer-aided process planning (CAPP), computer-aided engineering (CAE), computer-aided manufacturing (CAM), and computer-integrated manufacturing (CIM). Computer-aided engineering generally refers to the strength and stress tests performed in CAD systems,

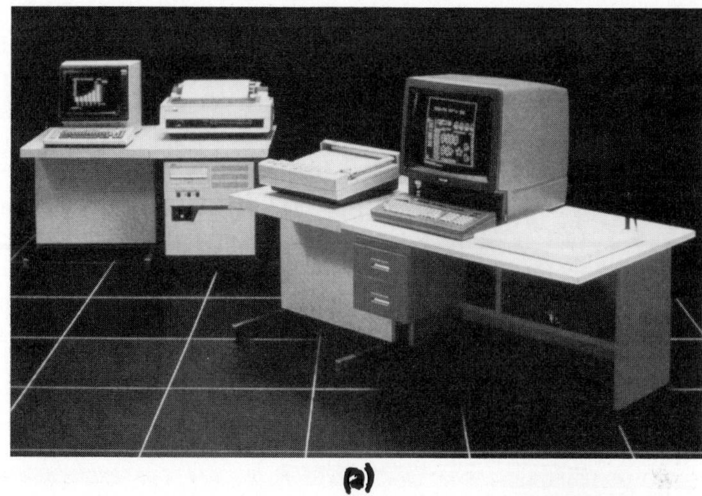

(a)

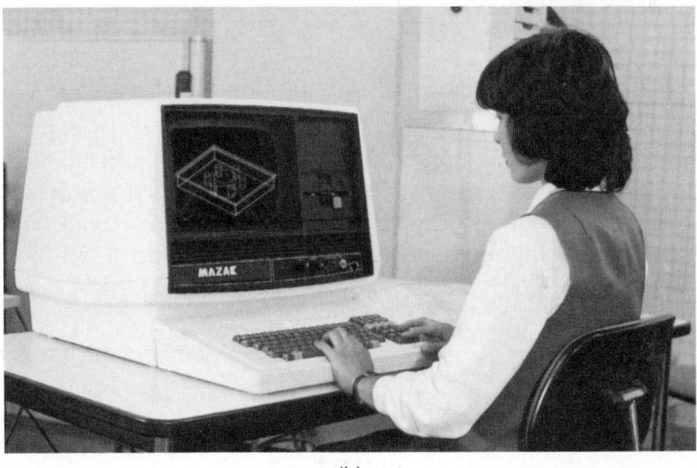

(b)

Figure 5.10

CAD/CAM Work Stations: (a) A CAD System; (b) A CAM System.

Source: Courtesy of Mazak Corporation. Reprinted by permission.

and CAPP refers to methods used to determine which processes will work best in the manufacture of a product. Thus CAE and CAPP are not only closely related to CAD, but they also are a part of the most sophisticated CAD systems. You will find that most of these terms and acronyms do not have unique meanings, and meanings can vary from vendor to vendor and firm to firm.

Computer-integrated manufacturing (CIM) is sometimes used interchangeably with FMS, but we prefer to think of CIM as an umbrella term that means a total integration of product design, engineering, process planning, and manufacturing through complex computer systems. Other computerized systems of inventory control, production planning, and scheduling can come under the umbrella of CIM. Twenty years ago some experts expected that most manufacturing would be done by CIM systems by now, giving us the factory of the future. That forecast did not come true. Adopting computerized technology takes time, patience, and a very large commitment on the part of top management, factory managers, and other employees. It frequently involves changing entire systems and may involve great risk. An even greater risk may be not to consider computer-integrated manufacturing at all.

CHAPTER HIGHLIGHTS

Just as the human element is crucial to process design, so are the technological choices that we considered in this chapter. In order to achieve better quality and higher productivity, continuing attention must be paid to the technological dimension of process design. Some of the chapter highlights are:

- Advances in computer technology have significantly broadened technological choices in offices, service industries, and manufacturing organizations.
- Improvements in telephone communication systems (for dictation, message exchange, and document transmission), report preparation (word processing, spreadsheets, and computer graphics), and linked communication systems (electronic mail) provide opportunities for increasing office productivity. Thus the technology exists to eliminate many barriers of time and space in current office processes.
- Decoupling some operations from direct customer contact so that similar operations can be batched helps increase productivity in a service organization.
- EFTs, ATMs, bar coding, EDI, integrated computer ordering, and on-line database systems are examples of newer technologies in the service sector.
- Manufacturing processes change the physical properties and shape of materials, machine materials to given dimensions, provide a surface finish, and join parts or materials.
- Many factors must be considered when choosing the specific technology for a process. No factor is more important than the fit with competitive priorities and positioning strategy.
- Materials handling processes deal with moving, storing, and packaging materials as they move through the manufacturing process and on to the final customer. When they fit with the positioning strategy, materials handling technologies can improve productivity.
- Repeatability is one of the keys to increased productivity. Higher product volumes allow for higher resource utilization because little time is lost to machine changeovers and materials handling is minimized.
- If product volumes are too low to justify

dedicating a production line to a single product, it may be possible to obtain line flows by using the one-worker–multiple-machines (OWMM) concept, in which one worker operates several different machines, or group technology (GT) cells, where machines are arranged to produce families of parts. Flexible automation is a third way to achieve the benefits of repeatability when volumes are not high.

- Programmable automation often costs less than fixed automation, but it is still costly. Flexibility is gained and setups are minimized because the machines can be reprogrammed to follow new instructions. Numerical control (NC) machines and robots are examples of programmable automation.
- Programmable automation includes flexible manufacturing systems (FMS), which consist of several computer-controlled work stations, an interconnecting transport system, and areas for loading and unloading. An FMS is very expensive to acquire but flexible enough to accommodate new product families.
- Another form of computer assistance for manufacturing is the CAD/CAM system, which links computerized product design and production engineering functions.

KEY TERMS

automation
bar coding
computer numerical control (CNC) machines
computer-aided design (CAD)
computer-aided manufacturing (CAM)
computer-integrated manufacturing (CIM)
electronic data interchange (EDI) systems
electronic mail system
electronic spreadsheets
fixed automation
flexible manufacturing system (FMS)
group technology (GT)
industrial robots
materials handling processes
numerical control (NC) machines
one-worker–multiple-machines (OWMM) concept
programmable automation
technology
word processing system

STUDY QUESTIONS

1. Why should decisions on technology and work-force management be made together?
2. What development over the last 20 years has contributed to widening technological choices in offices, the service sector, and manufacturing?
3. What activities are commonly conducted in offices? For each activity, name a technology available today that allows the ac-

tivity to be conducted differently than it was 20 years ago.

4. In what ways is an automatic teller machine (ATM) more flexible than a human bank teller? In what ways is the human bank teller more flexible? What are the advantages of an ATM system to the bank? What are the advantages to the customer? How does an ATM allow the bank to increase repeatability?
5. What are five objectives of manufacturing processes? Suppose that you are a manufacturer of men's suits. Which of those objectives do your manufacturing processes have? Which of those objectives would you find in the Ford Aerostar plant processes (see Box 5.3)?
6. What are factors to consider when choosing a manufacturing technology? Which of those factors would you consider when choosing technology in the service sector?
7. What are materials handling processes? Why do we say that "the best materials handling is no handling at all"? Compare materials handling in two industries: one with a product focus and one with a process focus.
8. What are the design principles for a materials handling system? What rationale leads to these principles?
9. What is the one-worker–multiple-machines (OWMM) concept? What is a group technology (GT) cell? What is a flexible manufacturing system (FMS)? What do they all have in common? How are they different?
10. Explain the difference between fixed and programmable automation. Give examples of each.
11. What do numerical control (NC) machines and robots have in common?
12. What are the elements of a flexible manufacturing system (FMS)? Why is this kind of system flexible?
13. What are some of the advantages of computer-aided-design (CAD)?

PROBLEMS

1. How do activities in front offices differ from those in back offices? What do they have in common? Compare the activities in an insurance agent's office to the activities in the insurance company's home office. Which office has the advantage in finding efficient ways to conduct their activities? Why?
2. Suppose an electric utility company contracts to have its meter readers read meters for the local water company in addition to reading its own. What productivity improvements might result if the electric utility company and the water company were viewed as a single entity? Could meter readers read as many of the utility's meters in a day if they read water meters too? If the utility uses an integrated system of computers in their meter reading (see Box 5.1), what additional links would be required in the network? What additional information would have to be stored in the meter readers' portable computers?
3. If a tax preparation firm (see Box 5.2) used computer terminals to prompt the preparer to ask the client the next question, why not let clients use the terminals directly and do away with the preparers? The firm described in Box 5.2 guarantees

that it will pay the penalty on any additional tax clients may be assessed because of errors made by the firm. How might this firm want to alter its guarantee if preparers used a computer to help them query clients? If preparers are eliminated, what additional responsibilities are placed on the clients? What are the advantages of using employees to conduct client interviews? What are the advantages of using computers?

SELECTED REFERENCES

Bylinsky, Gene, "The Race to the Automatic Factory," *Fortune*, February 21, 1983, pp. 52–60.

Collier, David A., *Service Management: The Automation of Services*. Reston, Va.: Reston Publishing Company, 1985.

Collier, David A., "The Service Sector Revolution: The Automation of Services," *Long Range Planning*, vol. 16, no. 6 (December 1983), pp. 11–13.

Doyle, Lawrence E., Carl A. Keyser, James L. Leach, George F. Schrader, and Morse B. Singer, *Manufacturing Processes and Materials for Engineers*, 3rd ed. Englewood Cliffs, N.J.: Prentice-Hall, 1985.

"Flexible Manufacturing Systems," *Modern Materials Handling*, September 7, 1982.

Gaimon, Cheryl, "The Optimal Acquisition of Automation to Enhance the Productivity of Labor," *Management Science*, vol. 31, no. 9 (1985), pp. 1175–1190.

Gerwin, Donald, "Do's and Don'ts of Computerized Manufacturing," *Harvard Business Review* (March–April 1982), pp. 107–116.

Gold, Bela, "CAM Sets New Rules for Production," *Harvard Business Review* (November–December 1982), pp. 88–94.

Green, Timothy J., and Randall P. Sadowski, "A Review of Cellular Manufacturing Assumptions, Advantages and Design Techniques," *Journal of Operations Management*, vol. 4, no. 2 (February 1984), pp. 85–97.

Groover, Mikell P., and E. W. Zimmers, Jr., *CAD/CAM: Computer-Aided Design and Manufacturing*. Englewood Cliffs, N.J.: Prentice-Hall, 1984.

Hausman, W. H., L. B. Schwartz, and S. C. Graves, "Optimal Storage Assignment in Automatic Warehousing Systems," *Management Science*, vol. 22, no. 6 (1976), pp. 629–638.

Hyer, Nancy, and Urban Wemmerlov, "Group Technology and Productivity," *Harvard Business Review* (July–August 1984), pp. 140–149.

"IBM's Automated Factory—A Giant Step Forward," *Modern Materials Handling*, March, 1985.

Jenkins, K. M., and A. R. Raedels, "The Robot Revolution: Strategic Considerations for Managers," *Production and Inventory Management* (Third Quarter 1982), pp. 107–116.

Levitt, Theodore, "The Industrialization of Service," *Harvard Business Review* (September–October 1976), pp. 63–74.

Mertes, Louis H., "Doing Your Office Over—Electronically," *Harvard Business Review* (March–April 1981), pp. 127–135.

Paprocki, Jeffrey T., "Flexible Manufacturing Systems—Automating the Factory." Technical paper presented at 2nd International Manufacturing Management and Technological Conference, Munich, Germany, June 1979.

Poppel, Harvey L., "Who Needs the Office of the Future?" *Harvard Business Review* (November–December 1982), pp. 146–155.

Rosenthal, Stephen, "Progress Toward the Factory of the Future," *Journal of Operations Management*, vol. 4, no. 3 (May 1984), pp. 203–229.

Roth, Aleda V., "Strategic Planning for the Optimal Acquisition of Flexible Manufacturing Systems Technology." Unpublished dissertation, Ohio State University, 1986.

Seligman, Daniel, "Life Will Be Different When We're All On-Line," *Fortune*, February 4, 1985, pp. 68–72.

Skinner, Wickham, "Operations Technology: Blind Spot in Strategic Management," *Interfaces*, vol. 14, no. 1 (January–February 1984), pp. 116–125.

Starr, Martin K., and Alan J. Biloski, "The Decision to Adopt New Technology—Effects on Organizational Size," *Omega*, vol. 12, no. 4 (1984), pp. 353–361.

Stecke, Kathryn E., and James J. Solberg, "Loading and Control Policies for a Flexible Manufacturing System," *International Journal of Production Research*, vol. 19, no. 5 (1981), pp. 481–490.

Stone, Philip J., and Robert Luchetti, "Your Office Is Where You Are," *Harvard Business Review* (March–April 1985), pp. 102–117.

Suresh, Nallan C., and Jack R. Meredith, "A Generic Approach to Justifying Flexible Manufacturing Systems," *Proceedings of the First ORSA/TIMS Special Interest Conference*, August 15–17, 1984.

Thomas, Dan R. E., "Strategy Is Different in Service Businesses," *Harvard Business Review* (July–August 1978), pp. 158–165.

White, Robert B., "A Prototype for the Automated Office," *Datamation* (April 1977), pp. 83–90.

CHAPTER

6

WORK MEASUREMENT

Some Managerial Issues

- How can we get the time standards we need to compare alternative process designs or project future capacity requirements?
- How can we estimate the amount of labor we will need for a new product or service?
- Which method of work measurement can we use most effectively in a given situation?
- How much total production do we need before the cost per unit is low enough to be competitive in a new market?
- How will our methods of work measurement change as more automation is introduced?

Chapter Outline

As we mentioned in Chapter 4, the scientific management movement was inspired by Frederick Taylor. In addition to blazing new trails in the area of work methods improvement, Taylor was the first to use a stopwatch to measure the output of manual operations. This pioneering work focused the attention of management on the importance of work measurement and learning to do jobs in better ways in order to improve performance. Work measurement is the basis for estimating an operating system's output, taking into consideration the effects of organizational and individual learning. As you will see, this information is a necessary input to the design of new systems or the management of existing ones. In this chapter, we first discuss the methods available for determining output standards and then explore the implications of learning for operations strategy and planning.

WHAT IS A STANDARD?

A standard is a commonly accepted basis for comparison. With respect to work measurement, we usually refer to *labor* standards or *machine* standards. A **labor standard** is the time required for a trained worker to perform a given task using a prescribed work method with normal effort and skill. Labor standards are more difficult to develop than machine standards because employee capabilities vary. Machines can be designed to perform a specific task, and factors such as effort and skill do not vary among machines of the same type. For example, a robot in a flexible machine cell will repetitively perform the same tasks with little time variation from unit to unit. In contrast, skill, effort, and stamina vary from employee to employee.

The key word in the definition of labor standard is *normal*. Consider the Italian Maiden Pizza Company example in Box 6.1, in which the owner is interested in the standard time to assemble a pizza. Normal effort in this case would be the pace that we would expect most workers to maintain in assembling pizzas throughout the day. Suppose that we observed one of the workers assembling a pizza in 20 seconds. If the worker continued this pace she could assemble 1440 pizzas in an eight-hour day. Before we could use 20 seconds as the standard, however, we would have to determine whether this worker was working at a reasonable pace. Perhaps she is a very energetic

Box 6.1

ITALIAN MAIDEN PIZZA COMPANY

Jack Spumoni owned a fast-growing company which manufactured frozen pizza for sale in major supermarket grocery stores under the brand name Italian Maiden. The production process was quite simple. A special sauce was spread over the pizza shell and then pepperoni and cheese were added. The pizza was put into a decorative box and fast-frozen using a CO_2 process. Periodically, the schedule would change and other varieties of pizza would be manufactured. Some would have Italian sausage instead of pepperoni, while others would have some combination of onions, green peppers, and mushrooms in addition to the meat. There were ten employees, with each employee assembling complete pizzas.

With sales increasing, Jack faced the problem of determining the work-force and freezer capacities that increased production rates would require. Assembling pizzas was a repetitive process of short duration, but he did not know how much time each pizza took a worker to complete or how many pizzas a worker could be expected to produce in a day. He instituted a time study of the assembly operation to develop a time standard that he could use for planning work-force requirements. He also realized that he would have to make some allowances for break periods and fatigue. In addition, no one had ever determined the minimum time required to freeze the pizzas. Consequently, a standard for the freezing time per pizza was developed for the freezer as well. Given the standards for the assembly operation and sales estimates for the products, Jack was able to get the estimates of the work-force and freezer capacity requirements he needed for operations planning.

person and the time it takes her to assemble a pizza is less than for the average worker. Also, her skill level may be above average. She may have considerable experience in pizza assembly and learned the work methods well. In addition, the estimate of 20 seconds per pizza does not reflect allowances for rest periods or fatigue during the workday. Consideration of factors such as pace, skill, and fatigue requires judgment. Generally, we cannot use the time per unit we observe over a short period of time for one employee as a standard for an extended period of time for all employees. Labor standards require some degree of modification of observed times, based on the judgment of skilled observers.

WORK STANDARDS AS A MANAGERIAL TOOL

Many companies that develop work standards experience productivity gains. Nonetheless, work measurement is one of the most controversial areas in the field of operations management because it is here that conflict often arises between management and labor. When output standards are used as the basis for pay, unions will object if the standards are set "too high" and management will object if the standards are set "too low". Of course, setting output standards either too high *or* too low makes planning for appropriate capacity levels difficult, increases costs, and reduces profits.

The controversy is not only between labor and management. Managers themselves often disagree on the use of engineered work standards. Some believe that the costs of large industrial engineering staffs and the hidden costs of resolving labor–management conflicts outweigh the benefits of elaborate standards; others believe that engineered standards actually defeat the purpose of increasing worker productivity when they are used for piecework incentives. Moreover, new work methods devised by the employee to increase output are kept secret, so that standards will not be raised.

The nature of controversies such as these point to the need for effective *work-force management* and the structure of appropriate incentives (see Chapter 4). Standards are often used to define a day's work and are usually set so that a motivated worker will be able to produce more work than the standard amount. Under an incentive compensation plan, such workers earn a bonus for output that exceeds the standard. However, work standards can be used in a variety of other ways in operations management:

1. *Comparing alternative process designs.* Time standards are useful for comparing different routings for an item or alternative layouts of facilities. They can also be used to evaluate new work methods and to estimate the advantages of purchasing new equipment.

2. *Scheduling.* Time estimates are needed in order to assign tasks to workers and machines, so that resources can be effectively utilized.

3. *Capacity planning.* Current and projected capacity requirements can be determined for given demand requirements with the help of time estimates for tasks. Long-term capital and work-force staffing decisions also require these time estimates.

4. *Pricing and Costing.* With labor and machine time standards as a base, cost standards can be developed for current and new products. Cost standards can be used to develop budgets and determine product prices. They can also be used in make-or-buy decisions.

5. *Performance appraisal.* A worker's output can be compared to the standard output over a period of time to determine how well the worker is performing. Work measurement methods can also be used to estimate the proportion of time workers are idle or otherwise unproductive.

Work measurement is used more for some of these applications than for others. A survey of 1500 firms indicated that the most frequent use of work measurement was for estimating and costing (89 percent of the firms), followed by incentive compensation plans (59 percent), scheduling (51 percent), and performance appraisal (41 percent). Only 2 percent of the firms used work measurement for staffing and capacity planning (Rice, 1977).

METHODS OF WORK MEASUREMENT

Because of the variety of uses for work measurement, the number of work measurement methods used is not surprising. The choice of which method to use may depend on the application. For example, we need a high degree of precision when comparing actual work method results to standards. A stopwatch study or predetermined times might be used here. Alternatively, the time estimates we need for the long-term planning of capital additions do not need to be as precise. Approaches based on historical data may be sufficient in this case. Consequently, a firm may use more than one work measurement approach to satisfy its need for time estimates. We present and discuss five of the more commonly used methods in this section.

Historical Data Approach

One of the simplest approaches to work measurement involves the use of historical data in two different ways. The first is the use of expert judgment to arrive at time estimates for a particular job or activity. For example, the owner of a machine shop might ask the shop foreman to estimate the time required to complete a certain operation on a new job. The foreman could make a reasonably accurate estimate in many cases because of past experience in similar situations.

Table 6.1

Historical Time Data for the Cutting Operation of a Gear

Part Number: G-1043A
Description: Large Transmission Gear

Order Number	Quantity	Setup Time (hr)	Total Run Time (min)	Moving Average*	
				Setup Time (hr)	Run Time per Unit (min)
B-325C	150	2.20	196	—	—
B-410A	175	2.10	231	—	—
F-101D	320	3.00	413	2.43	1.30
G-172A	160	2.30	203	2.47	1.29
M-372D	250	1.50	338	2.27	1.30
X-0534	100	2.00	130	1.93	1.31

* The three preceding orders are averaged. The run time per unit is calculated by dividing the total run time for the three orders by the total number of units produced for those orders.

The second makes use of actual data on the time required in the past to complete an operation for a particular product. For example, Table 6.1 shows the setup times and run times for the last six orders for a transmission gear. These data could be taken from employee time cards or from routing sheets. A simple moving average of the time required can also be calculated in order to track performance on the operation. In this example, some improvements apparently were made in the setup time per order.* However, the run time per unit is slowly increasing. The average for each factor could be used to estimate the time required to complete a new order. For instance, if a new order were for 275 units, the time estimate would be 1.93 hours for setup and (275)(1.31) = 360 minutes of run time.

Both methods used in the historical data approach have several advantages. First, this approach yields rough estimates that can be useful for product pricing or costing. Expert opinions can be used to develop standards for new products before production begins. The actual-data method can be used for estimating times for future work based on similar jobs done in the past. Second, this approach is quick and inexpensive, relative to other approaches. No stopwatches are needed and most of the data are already on time cards or in the heads of experienced personnel. Finally, the historical data approach can be used to identify trends in productivity, as demonstrated by the exam-

* The sample size in this example was kept small for demonstration purposes. In an actual application, more data would be needed before conclusions about setup time and run time per unit could be made. With small sample sizes, the randomness in the data could cause the effects you see in Table 6.1.

ple in Table 6.1. These trends could be tied to wage incentives for the work force or used to signal problems with materials, work methods, or personnel associated with a certain operation.

The historical data approach also has its disadvantages. The quality of the estimates made by experienced personnel is related to their ability to make good estimates. They can make errors because estimating times for new work is largely subjective. Also, the use of historical data for developing time standards assumes that past performance was "normal." In the transmission gear example shown in Table 6.1, the last two orders may have been processed by an inexperienced worker, accounting for the increase in the run times per unit. The historical data approach does not control for the work methods used or the normality of the worker's pace on each order. If such data are to be used for setting standards, some subjective adjustments may be needed to account for these factors.

Time Study Method

The method used most often for setting time standards for a task is the **time study.** A job is divided into a series of smaller work elements representing the accepted work methods for the job. An analyst uses a stopwatch to time a trained worker who performs the work elements for a number of work cycles; the analyst then calculates the average time for each work element. With this information and a performance rating based on judgment, the analyst develops a time standard for the task.

Selecting Work Elements. To illustrate the time study method, consider Fig. 6.1. It shows an observation sheet used to study the packaging of ceramic coffee cups, which requires only four work elements. Several considerations are involved in selecting the work elements for a time study. First, each work element should have definite starting and stopping points to facilitate taking the stopwatch readings. Second, work elements that take less than three seconds to complete should be avoided because they are difficult to time. For example, work element 2 could have been divided into three detailed elements: (1) pick up liner with left hand; (2) expand liner to open the holes for each cup; and (3) insert liner into carton. Since each of these activities is done very quickly, it would be difficult to get accurate times for each one. Finally, the work elements should correspond to the standard work method that has been running smoothly for a period of time in a standard work environment. Incidental operations not normally involved in the task should be identified and separated from the repetitive work.

Timing the Elements. After the work elements have been identified, a worker trained in the work method is selected for study. The worker is then timed for each work element for an initial set of observations. In Fig. 6.1, the

OPERATION: Coffee Cup Packaging	DATE 1/23	OPERATOR: B. Larson CLOCK NO: 43-6205	
OBSERVER: S. Johnson	START 9:00 (AM) PM	STOP 9:22 (AM) PM	ELAPSED STUDY TIME 21.68	TIME PER PIECE 21.68/10 = 2.168

ELEMENT DESCRIPTION		OBSERVATIONS 1	2	3	4	5	6	7	8	9	10	$\bar{t}$	RF	FREQ	NT
1. Get two cartons*	t	.48	+	.46	+	.54	+	.49	+	.51	÷5=	.50	1.05	0.5	.26
	r	.48		.85		9.14		.53		.83					
2. Put liner into carton	t	.11	.13	.09	.10	.11	.13	.08	.12	.10	.09	.11	.95	1.0	.10
	r	.59	.56	.94	.82	.25	.23	.61	.50	.93	.83				
3. Place cups into carton	t	.74	.68	.71	.69	.73	.70	.68	.74	.71	.72	.71	1.10	1.0	.78
	r	1.33	3.24	5.65	7.51	.98	.93	14.29	16.24	18.64	20.55				
4. Seal carton and set aside	t	1.10	1.15	1.07	1.09	1.12	1.11	1.09	1.08	1.10	1.13	1.10	.90	1.0	.99
	r	2.43	4.39	6.72	8.60	11.10	13.04	15.38	17.32	19.74	21.68				
NORMAL TIME FOR CYCLE															2.13

ALLOWANCES (% of normal time) 15% STANDARD TIME 2.45 Min/piece

Figure 6.1

Time Study Observation Sheet.

* This element occurs only on every other cycle.

continuous method of timing is shown. For each work element, the *r* row shows the stopwatch reading at the completion of that element, and the watch is not reset until the end of the study. To avoid unnecessary writing, whole numbers are shown only when they change from the last observation. For example, the stopwatch reading for the second observation of the element "put liner into carton" was actually 2.56, but only .56 was written on the form. In order to get the observed time for a work element, the observer merely takes the difference between two successive continuous watch readings after the timing part of the study is over. For example, in observation 1, the clock read 0.48 minutes after element 1 and 0.59 minutes after element 2. Consequently, the observed time for element 2 is $0.59 - 0.48 = 0.11$ min. These items are shown in the *t* row for each element. An alternative technique, called the *snap-back method,* involves resetting the watch to zero after each work element has been completed. Although this technique gives work element times directly for each observation, it requires the observer to read and record the times and to reset the watch at the end of each element. Sometimes, two watches are used, one for recording the previous work element and the other for timing the present work element. However, if some work elements are done quickly, getting accurate times may be difficult.

Determining the Sample Size. In our example we observed only 10 cycles of the packaging operation. Was this number enough? Typically, companies using the time study to set standards want an estimate for the average time that is within 5 percent of the true long-range average time 95 percent of the time. A formula, based on the normal distribution, allows us to determine the sample size required. Let

n = Required sample size;

p = Precision of the estimate;

$\bar{t}$ = Average observed time for a work element; and

s = Sample standard deviation of observed times for a work element.

Then, the required sample size is

$$n = \left[\left(\frac{1.96}{p}\right)\left(\frac{s}{\bar{t}}\right)\right]^2$$

The constant 1.96 represents the ± 1.96 standard deviations from the mean that leave a total of 5 percent of the normal curve in its tails. The term $s/\bar{t}$ is called the sample *coefficient of variation.* If you know the sample coefficient of variation for a work element, you can use Table 6.2 to find the required sample size for that work element for a precision of $p = 0.05$. For example, if you want an estimate to be within 5 percent of the true average time for a work element that has $\bar{t} = 0.60$ min and $s = 0.20$, you would calculate $s/\bar{t} = 0.20/0.60 = 33$ percent, and $n = 167$.

Setting the Standard. The final step is to determine the standard. First, the analyst determines the *normal time* (*NT*) for each work element. Here the pace of the worker being observed is judged. Not only must the analyst assess whether the worker's pace is above or below normal, but also *how much* above or below normal. The analyst assigns a performance *rating factor* (*RF*) to the worker's performance on each work element. For example, in Fig. 6.1 the performance rating factor for work element 3 was 1.10. A performance rating factor greater than one means that the worker was working at a faster than normal pace (that is, more work output in a given amount of time). In other instances, the worker was judged to be working at a slower than normal pace. The average observed time ($\bar{t}$), the frequency (*FREQ*) of the work element per

Table 6.2

Sample Size Requirements for Various Coefficients of Variation in a Time Study*

Coefficient of Variation (%)	Sample Size (*n*)	Coefficient of Variation (%)	Sample Size (*n*)
1	1	26	104
2	1	27	112
3	1	28	120
4	2	29	129
5	4	30	138
6	6	31	148
7	8	32	157
8	10	33	167
9	12	34	178
10	15	35	188
11	19	36	199
12	22	37	210
13	26	38	222
14	30	39	234
15	35	40	246
16	39	41	258
17	44	42	271
18	50	43	284
19	55	44	297
20	61	45	311
21	68	46	325
22	74	47	339
23	81	48	354
24	89	49	369
25	96	50	384

* These sample sizes allow us to state with 95 percent confidence that the estimate of the average time will be within 5 percent of the population average. The effects of cycle length or the number of repetitions of the job per year are not reflected in these figures.

cycle, and the rating factor are multiplied to obtain the normal time for a work element; that is,

$$NT = \bar{t}(FREQ)(RF).$$

For example, work element 1 occurs only once in every two cycles ($FREQ = 0.50$). Its normal time per cycle would be

$$NT = 0.50(0.50)(1.05) = 0.26 \text{ min.}$$

The normal time for the cycle (NTC) is the sum of the normal times for the individual work elements. In our example, $NTC = 2.13$ min. However, we cannot use that time as a standard. It does not account for fatigue, rest periods, or unavoidable delays that occur during an average workday. Consequently, we must add some *allowance time* to the normal time to adjust for these factors. Thus the *standard time* (ST) is

$$ST = NTC(1 + A),$$

where A is the proportion of the normal time to be added for allowances. For the coffee cup packaging operation, the normal time for the cycle is 2.13 minutes and $A = 0.15$, so

$$ST = 2.13(1 + 0.15) = 2.45 \text{ min/carton}.$$

This translates into $\dfrac{480 \text{ min/day}}{2.45 \text{ min/carton}} = 196$ cartons/day.

Judgment in Time Study. Several aspects of a time study require the use of judgment by the analyst. First, the analyst must take care when defining the work elements to be included in the time study. As we discussed previously, these work elements must not be too short and must have definite starting and stopping points. Also, some work elements may occur infrequently and irregularly. The analyst must be sure to include times for these work elements as well.

Second, the analyst may have to eliminate some observed times because the elements are nonrepresentative of the work. An obvious case would be one where the worker accidentally dropped a tool. However, nonrepresentative elements are not always that obvious. In some cases a chance happening such as a machine malfunction can distort the results. If these nonrepresentative times are not excluded, the standard will be incorrect. However, the analyst must use judgment in deciding which times, if any, are to be excluded.

Another area where judgment plays a role is in the amount of allowance time to be added to the normal time. Most allowances are in the range of 10 to 20 percent. They are intended to account for factors such as fatigue or unexpected delays that are difficult to measure. As you will see later in this chapter, *work sampling* can be used to estimate some of the factors in allowance time.

Finally, the aspect of time study that requires the greatest amount of judgment is that of performance rating. Usually only one worker is observed during a study, and worker performance will seldom conform to the notion of "normal" as used in the definition of standard. Thus an adjustment has to be made in the average observed time in order to estimate the time it would take a trained operator to do the task at a normal pace. Unfortunately, you cannot avoid the use of judgment or the need to arrive at a performance rating by studying all the workers and using their average time as normal. If the workers are fast, it would not be fair to set the standard based on their normal time, particularly if a wage incentive plan is involved. Conversely, if the workers are slow, basing the standard on their normal time would be unfair to the company. Further, the possibility that workers will slow their pace when they are being observed in a time study is very real. Consequently, the use of judgment in assigning performance rates seems to be a necessary, but often controversial, aspect of conducting a time study.

Overall Assessment of Time Study. Time study is the most frequently used method for setting time standards. Qualified analysts can typically set good standards using this method, and workers understand the process. However, the method has some limitations. Its use is not appropriate, for example, when setting standards for "thinking" jobs such as mathematicians solving a problem, professors preparing a lecture, or an automobile repairman diagnosing the cause of a problem. Nor is it appropriate for nonrepetitive jobs, such as nonroutine maintenance repair, where the nature of the task changes each time it is done. In addition, the use of a stopwatch is an art, and an inexperienced person should not conduct time studies; errors in recording information can result in poor standards. Likewise, an inexperienced person may not include all the work elements. Finally, unions may object to time study because of the judgment and subjectivity involved. Nonetheless, time study conducted by an experienced observer is usually a satisfactory, although imperfect, tool for setting equitable time standards.

Elemental Standard Data Approach

If thousands of work standards are needed in a plant, the amount of time and the cost required to use the time study method may be excessive. In such cases analysts often use elemental standard data in order to derive standards for various jobs. This approach is based on the notion that a high degree of similarity exists in the operations needed for certain jobs. The time standards for work elements that are common to a class of jobs can be stored in a database for future use. A work measurement approach such as time study can be used to compile standards for these common elements. Sometimes, the time required for a work element depends on certain variable characteristics of the jobs. In these situations an equation that relates these characteristics to the time required for the work element can also be stored in the database for later use.

To illustrate the elemental standard data approach, we show in Table 6.3 the normal times for some of the work elements of a core-making operation. A core is made of packed sand and is used to make the inner portion of a mold for a part; the core displaces the molten metal to form a cavity. Note that two variable characteristics may affect the normal times for job work elements: the core area (top box area) and the core volume. If you were to use the time

Table 6.3

Elemental Standard Data for a Core-Making Operation

	Work Elements (minutes)							Variable Characteristics	
Job Number	Sand in (1)	Peen (2)	Strike off (3)	Vent/ jar (4)	Position box (5)	Draw box (6)	Position core (7)	Core area (in^2)	Core volume (in^3)
2438	0.160	0.410	0.120	0.010	0.080	0.152	0.118	50	204
2562	0.132	0.400	0.101	0.011	0.078	0.133	0.121	15	8
3210	0.174	0.425	0.145	0.011	0.081	0.165	0.119	83	261
3784	0.104	0.413	0.117	0.010	0.082	0.140	0.120	25	40
4210	0.156	0.420	0.130	0.011	0.079	0.150	0.118	61	175

study method, you would have to observe each of the seven work elements for each new job if it differed from the others with respect to area and volume. For example, if a new job arrived that had an area of 42 square inches and a volume of 150 cubic inches, you would have to do a complete time study for it in order to have a standard for future use. More importantly, you could not predict the time it would take for the new job *before* production actually started, unless you used some subjective modification of a known standard.

From the data in Table 6.3, it appears that work elements 4, 5, and 7 are not affected by the variable characteristics of the jobs. The historical average of the normal times for these elements could be stored in a database for future use, unmodified for the variable characteristics. The other four elements, however, appear to be affected by the variable characteristics. For example, the plot of the normal times for work element 3 in Fig. 6.2 indicates a linear relationship between normal time and core area. You could use the data in Table 6.3 to develop a regression equation for estimating the normal time for this work element as a function of core area. In this example, the equation would be

$$NT = 0.0959 + 0.00057\,(CA),$$

where CA is the core area. This equation is represented by the dashed line in Fig. 6.2. Instead of storing a single normal time in the database for this element, the equation could be stored and used as needed to compute a normal time.

The equations for other work elements may be more complex than the one for element 3. The normal times for these other elements may be a function of both the core area and the core volume, or they may be nonlinear functions of these characteristics. Various statistical techniques can be used to

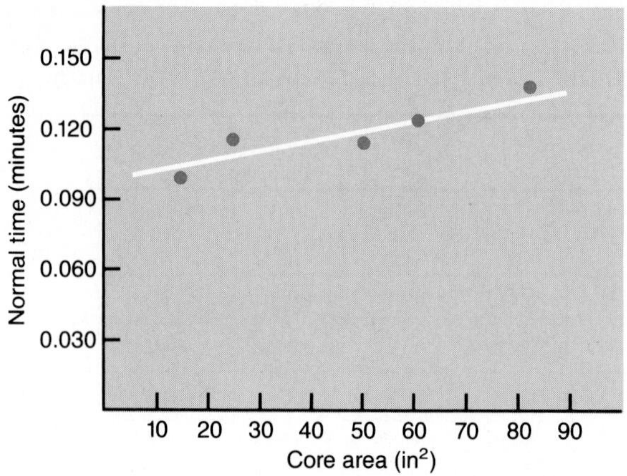

Figure 6.2

Work Element 3: Normal Time as a Function of Core Area.

find the best fit to the data. When the database has been established, it can be used to estimate the normal times for jobs requiring these work elements. However, allowances must still be added to arrive at the standard times for the jobs.

The elemental standard data approach has the advantage of reducing the need for time studies. In addition, the database can be used to develop standards for new work before production begins. This advantage is helpful in product costing and pricing as well as production planning. Also, when work methods change for a work element, it is much easier to determine the normal time for that element once and store it in the database than it would be to do a separate time study for each job requiring that work element.

However, this approach also has some disadvantages. Although the need for time studies is reduced, it is unlikely that they can be eliminated. In general, it is best to develop the normal times for the database using the time study method. Also, companies like to periodically check with time studies the standards that they developed by the elemental standard data approach. Another consideration is that it may be difficult to specify all the variable characteristics of jobs that affect times for each work element. Consequently, the fit of the functions to the data may not be very good.

Predetermined Data Approach

The predetermined data approach carries the elemental standard data approach one step further. Each work element is divided into a series of micromotions that are common to a wide variety of tasks. The normal times for these micromotions are stored in a database, along with modifications for variable characteristics, so that the normal time for any task can be developed by reference to the database.

The most commonly used predetermined data systems are the basic motion time (BMT) study and **methods time measurement** (MTM). Actually, there are a variety of MTM databases, but we will focus on the most accurate, MTM-1. In MTM-1 the basic micromotions are reach, move, disengage, apply pressure, grasp, position, release, and turn. The normal times for these micromotions, modified for various characteristics, were developed from the motion picture studies of a sample of workers in a variety of industrial settings. Trained observers applied performance ratings to the observations. Table 6.4 shows the *move* motion from the MTM-1 data. A time measurement unit (TMU) is 0.0006 minutes. For example, if an object weighing less than 2.5 pounds is to be moved 16 inches to an exact location (case C), the time estimate would be 18.7 TMUs, or 0.011 minutes. The weight allowances adjust the time estimates for different object weights. There are similar tables for the other motions.

Setting standards using predetermined data involves several steps. Each work element must be broken into its basic micromotions. Then, the degree of difficulty of each motion must be rated. Next, the normal times for each motion are found in the tables and added to get the normal time for the task. Finally, the normal time is adjusted for allowances to give the standard time.

The predetermined data approach offers some advantages over the other approaches we have discussed. First, standards can be set for new jobs before production begins, which cannot be done with the time study method. Second, it allows the comparison of new work methods without conducting a time study. Third, it provides a greater degree of consistency in the setting of time standards because the sources of error in time studies, such as data recording errors, are reduced. Finally, this approach defuses the objection of biased judgment in the performance rating because the ratings were performed by experienced persons outside the company. Performance ratings are no longer needed in order to derive a standard.

The predetermined data approach also has its drawbacks. The data may not reflect the situation in any specific plant. What is normal for one plant may not be so for another plant. The sample of workers used to develop the predetermined data may not be representative of workers in general. Further, performance time variations can result from many factors—too many to publish in tables such as Table 6.4. In some circumstances, the time needed to move an object may depend on the shape of the object, even though the MTM-1 charts do not recognize that. Then, there is the assumption that the times associated with the micromotions can simply be added together to get the total time for a task. This assumption disregards the possibility that the actual time may depend on the specific *sequence* of motions. Finally, there is a danger that the approach will be misused because, on the surface, it appears

Table 6.4

MTM Predetermined Data for the *Move* Micromotion

Distance Moved Inches	Time TMU A	Time TMU B	Time TMU C	Hand In Motion B	Wt. Allowance: Wt. (lb.) Up to	Wt. Allowance: Dynamic Factor	Wt. Allowance: Static Constant TMU	Case and Description
¾ or less	2.0	2.0	2.0	1.7				A Move object to other hand or against stop.
1	2.5	2.9	3.4	2.3	2.5	1.00	0	
2	3.6	4.6	5.2	2.9				
3	4.9	5.7	6.7	3.6	7.5	1.06	2.2	
4	6.1	6.9	8.0	4.3				
5	7.3	8.0	9.2	5.0	12.5	1.11	3.9	
6	8.1	8.9	10.3	5.7				
7	8.9	9.7	11.1	6.5	17.5	1.17	5.6	B Move object to approximate or indefinite location.
8	9.7	10.6	11.8	7.2				
9	10.5	11.5	12.7	7.9	22.5	1.22	7.4	
10	11.3	12.2	13.5	8.6				
12	12.9	13.4	15.2	10.0	27.5	1.28	9.1	
14	14.4	14.6	16.9	11.4				
16	16.0	15.8	18.7	12.8	32.5	1.33	10.8	
18	17.6	17.0	20.4	14.2				
20	19.2	18.2	22.1	15.6	37.5	1.39	12.5	C Move object to exact location.
22	20.8	19.4	23.8	17.0				
24	22.4	20.6	25.5	18.4	42.5	1.44	14.3	
26	24.0	21.8	27.3	19.8				
28	25.5	23.1	29.0	21.2	47.5	1.50	16.0	
30	27.1	24.3	30.7	22.7				
Additional	0.8	0.6	0.85		TMU per inch over 30 inches			

easy to use. Actually, considerable skill is needed to properly identify all the micromotions and accurately judge the difficulty of the motion. Considerable training and experience are required, and an inexperienced person will come up with poor standards.

Work Sampling Method

Work sampling is another method of work measurement. It is a broader approach, not concerned with timing detailed motions but with estimating the proportions of time spent (by people and machines) on activities such as producing a product or service, doing paperwork, waiting for instructions, waiting for maintenance, or being idle. To make these estimates you would take a large number of observations. The underlying assumption is that the proportion of instances the activity is observed in the sample will be the proportion of time spent on the activity in general. The size of your sample affects the degree of precision that you can expect from estimates for a given level of statistical confidence. Data from a work sampling study can also be used to estimate machine or labor utilization percentages and the allowances needed to set standards with methods such as time study, elemental standard data, and predetermined data; to determine job content; and to help assess the cost of jobs or activities. Work sampling would be useful in analyzing the problem described in Box 6.2.

Box 6.2

A PROPOSAL FOR A NEW MEDICAL RECORDS STORAGE AND RETRIEVAL SYSTEM

The hospital administrator at a private hospital is considering a proposal for the purchase of an automated medical records storage and retrieval system. The estimated annual equipment amortization cost and expenses for maintaining the new system will be $150,000, after the labor savings in the medical records department have been accounted for. However, the administrator does not know how much will be saved by reducing the amount of time spent by registered nurses (RNs) and licensed practical nurses (LPNs) accessing medical records. Presently, these nurses must either retrieve the records manually or have them copied and sent to their wards. The new system would allow the nurses to access the records directly through computer terminals located on each floor of the hospital. The vendor of the new system estimates that the system will reduce the amount of time the nurses spend accessing records by 25 percent. The total annual salary for RNs in the hospital is $3,628,000 and for LPNs, $2,375,000. The hospital administrator is willing to assume that the nurses could productively use any time saved by the new system. The problem is to estimate the proportion of the total time these nurses currently spend accessing medical records.

Source: A similar case can be found in Ralph W. Swain, *Health Systems Analysis*, Grid Publishing Company. Columbus, Ohio: 1981, pp. 148–154.

Work Sampling Procedures. Conducting a work sampling study involves the following steps:

1. Define the activities.
2. Design the observation form.
3. Determine the length of the study.
4. Determine the pilot sample size.
5. Randomize the observation times.
6. Determine the observer schedule and record the data.
7. Check to see whether additional sampling is required.

Figure 6.3 shows an observation form for the work sampling study at the hospital. Activities could have been more detailed, but the hospital administrator is mainly interested in the proportion of time spent on records by RNs and LPNs. The other data can also be useful for planning purposes and are included merely to provide a representative example of an observation form. Information on RNs and LPNs is recorded separately because they spend different amounts of time with medical records at this hospital. The form should provide enough space to record the observations as they are made. They can be summarized later for analysis.

It is important that the study be conducted over a representative period of time. Since we are using a sampling approach, we must be sure to give each activity a chance to occur a representative number of times. For example, if an activity occurs only once a week, it would not make sense to conduct the study over a period of one day because there is a good chance that we will not observe that activity. In such a case the study should probably span several

	Activity				
	Working with records	Attending to patients	Other support activities	Idle or break	Total
RN	卌 卌 卌 |	卌 卌 卌 卌 卌 卌	卌 卌 卌 卌 卌 |	卌 |||	80
LPN	|||	卌 卌 卌 卌 卌 卌 卌 卌 卌	卌 |||	||||	60

Figure 6.3

Observation Form for the Hospital Work Sampling Study.

months. In the hospital example, accessing records occurs continuously throughout the week and from week to week throughout the year. Consequently, our study should cover several weeks, the exact length of time depending on the number of observations made.

This initial study is called a pilot study because we may have to make more observations later. If we have a reasonable idea of the proportion of time an activity takes and the degree of precision required for the estimate, we can use Table 6.5 to determine the sample size for the pilot study. For example, suppose that we suspect that an activity takes about 25 percent of workers' time. To have 95 percent confidence that the interval 0.22 to 0.28 (± 0.03 absolute error) contains the actual proportion of time for that activity for the entire group (population) will require 800 observations. After the pilot study, if we find that the sample estimate for the activity is actually 0.30, we can use the table to determine the additional number of observations we would need for the same degree of absolute error. In this example it would be 96 more observations.

Often there is no real basis prior to the study for estimating the proportion of time for an activity. In these situations the sample size for the pilot study will be somewhat arbitrary. This is the approach we will use for the hospital example. The hospital administrator selected a typical ward for the study. This ward is staffed with 4 RNs and 3 LPNs. It was decided that the observer would make 20 trips through the ward and each time record the activity of each nurse. Thus RN activities would be observed 80 times and LPN activities, 60 times. The results of the pilot study are shown in Fig. 6.3.

The times of day the observer makes the trips to gather data should be randomized over the length of the study. This approach reduces the amount of bias in the data. For example, if employees know that they will be observed each day at 2:30 P.M., they may alter their behavior from normal patterns. If this happens, the data will not represent actual performance. After the observation times have been determined, a schedule for the observer can be developed.

Analysis of the Hospital Data. The hospital administrator would like to estimate the net savings of introducing an automated medical records storage and retrieval system. Mathematically, we have

$$\text{Net savings} = 0.25(\$3{,}628{,}000p_1 + \$2{,}375{,}000p_2) - \$150{,}000,$$

where

p_1 = Proportion of time spent by RNs with records; and

p_2 = Proportion of time spent by LPNs with records.

Recall that the vendor estimates that the system would save 25 percent of the time nurses spend with records and that the hospital administrator is assuming that any time saved can be productively used. From Fig. 6.3, the pilot

Table 6.5

Sample Size Requirements for Work Sampling Studies for Various Values of *p* and Absolute Error*

Proportion of Time for Activity or Delay, *p*	Absolute Error				
	±0.01	±0.02	±0.03	±0.04	±0.05
0.01 or 0.99	380	95	42	24	15
0.02 or 0.98	753	188	84	47	30
0.03 or 0.97	1117	279	124	70	45
0.04 or 0.96	1475	369	164	92	59
0.05 or 0.95	1824	456	203	114	73
0.06 or 0.94	2166	541	241	135	87
0.07 or 0.93	2500	625	278	156	100
0.08 or 0.92	2826	707	314	177	113
0.09 or 0.91	3145	786	349	197	126
0.10 or 0.90	3456	864	384	216	138
0.11 or 0.89	3759	940	418	235	150
0.12 or 0.88	4055	1014	451	253	162
0.13 or 0.87	4343	1086	483	271	174
0.14 or 0.86	4623	1156	514	289	185
0.15 or 0.85	4896	1224	544	306	196
0.16 or 0.84	5161	1290	573	323	206
0.17 or 0.83	5418	1355	602	339	217
0.18 or 0.82	5668	1417	630	354	227
0.19 or 0.81	5910	1477	657	369	236
0.20 or 0.80	6144	1536	683	384	246
0.21 or 0.79	6371	1593	708	398	255
0.22 or 0.78	6589	1647	732	412	264
0.23 or 0.77	6801	1700	756	425	272
0.24 or 0.76	7004	1751	778	438	280
0.25 or 0.75	7200	1800	800	450	288
0.26 or 0.74	7388	1847	821	462	296
0.27 or 0.73	7569	1892	841	473	303
0.28 or 0.72	7741	1935	860	484	310
0.29 or 0.71	7907	1977	879	494	316
0.30 or 0.70	8064	2016	896	504	323
0.31 or 0.69	8214	2053	913	513	329
0.32 or 0.68	8356	2089	928	522	334
0.33 or 0.67	8490	2123	943	531	340
0.34 or 0.66	8617	2154	957	539	345
0.35 or 0.65	8736	2184	971	546	349
0.36 or 0.64	8847	2212	983	553	354
0.37 or 0.63	8951	2238	995	559	358
0.38 or 0.62	9047	2262	1005	565	362
0.39 or 0.61	9135	2284	1015	571	365
0.40 or 0.60	9216	2304	1024	576	369
0.41 or 0.59	9289	2322	1032	581	372
0.42 or 0.58	9354	2339	1039	585	374
0.43 or 0.57	9412	2353	1046	588	376
0.44 or 0.56	9462	2365	1051	591	378
0.45 or 0.55	9504	2376	1056	594	380
0.46 or 0.54	9539	2385	1060	596	382
0.47 or 0.53	9565	2391	1063	598	383
0.48 or 0.52	9585	2396	1065	599	383
0.49 or 0.51	9596	2399	1066	600	384
0.50	9600	2400	1067	600	384

* These sample sizes yield a 95 percent confidence that the estimate for *p* is within a specific absolute error of the population average.

study yielded estimates of $\tilde{p}_1 = 16/80 = 0.20$, and $\tilde{p}_2 = 3/60 = 0.05$. With these figures,

$$\begin{aligned}\text{Net savings} &= 0.25[(\$3{,}628{,}000)(0.20) + (\$2{,}375{,}000)(0.05)] - \$150{,}000 \\ &= \$61{,}087.50.\end{aligned}$$

On the basis of pilot study results, the new system appears to be a good investment. But how confident are we in $\tilde{p}_1$ and $\tilde{p}_2$, our estimates of p_1 and p_2? We can find out by constructing 95 percent confidence intervals for each estimate based on the normal approximation to the binomial distribution. These calculations will indicate a range of values for the proportion that will contain the true proportion for the population 95 percent of the time. For p_1 we have

$$\tilde{p}_1 - 1.96\sqrt{\frac{\tilde{p}_1(1.0 - \tilde{p}_1)}{n}} \le p_1 \le \tilde{p}_1 + 1.96\sqrt{\frac{\tilde{p}_1(1.0 - \tilde{p}_1)}{n}}$$

$$0.20 - 1.96\sqrt{\frac{0.20(0.80)}{80}} \le p_1 \le 0.20 + 1.96\sqrt{\frac{0.20(0.80)}{80}}$$

$$0.11 \le p_1 \le 0.29.$$

Our confidence interval indicates that the proportion for the population could be as low as 0.11 or as high as 0.29.

We can similarly construct a confidence interval for p_2

$$0.05 - 1.96\sqrt{\frac{0.05(0.95)}{60}} \le p_2 \le 0.05 + 1.96\sqrt{\frac{0.05(0.95)}{60}}$$

$$0 \le p_2 \le 0.11.$$

The lower level of the confidence interval is zero because it is impossible to have a negative value for p_2.

Apparently from our pilot study results, the actual proportions could be as low as $p_1 = 0.11$ and $p_2 = 0.00$. If these proportions were true, the investment would result in a net savings of $-\$50{,}230.00$, or a significant annual loss to the hospital. This result indicates that we need more precision in our estimates for p_1 and p_2 before the administrator can make a decision.

What level of precision do we need? We can answer that question by first determining the break-even value for p_1 with $p_2 = 0$ as the worst case. We solve for p_1 when net savings are zero.

$$0.25[\$3{,}628{,}000p_1 + \$2{,}375{,}000(0.00)] - \$150{,}000 = 0$$

$$\$907{,}000p_1 = \$150{,}000$$

$$p_1 = \frac{\$150{,}000}{\$907{,}000} = 0.1654 \approx 0.17.$$

Since our best estimate of p_1 so far is 0.20, our next step is to find the sample size that would give us a 95 percent confidence interval of $0.17 \leq p_1 \leq 0.23$. The lower limit of the confidence interval is the break-even value for p_1. Since the break-even value is 3 percentage points lower than our best estimate, the upper limit must be 3 percentage points greater. Using Table 6.5 for $\bar{p}_1 = 0.20$ and a ± 0.03 absolute error, we find that the sample size should be 683. Thus for 4 RNs, we need to make 171 trips, or 151 more than we already have made. If our estimate for p_1 is still about 0.20 after making the added observations, we can be reasonably confident that there will be some savings regardless of the value for p_2. We could make a similar analysis for p_2; however, the sample size chosen for p_1 in this example should exceed that needed for p_2, assuming that the LPNs are observed along with the RNs. For confirmation, note in Table 6.5 that sample size requirements are less for values of p around 0.05 than they are for values around 0.20.

Overall Assessment of Work Sampling. The work sampling method is used frequently in practice. It offers certain advantages over other approaches. No special training is required for the observers; no stopwatches are needed, and several studies can be conducted simultaneously by the observer. It is more economical for studying jobs having long cycle times because less observer time is required; observations are made only at random times. The workers themselves often prefer this method of work measurement to other approaches.

The major disadvantage to work sampling is the large number of observations required. Even though each observation is short, a lot of them are needed to provide a reasonable degree of precision for the estimate. This method is usually not economical for setting standards for repetitive, well-defined jobs. The other approaches we discussed are more appropriate.

THE EFFECTS OF LEARNING

The approaches to work measurement that we have discussed so far are based on the assumption that the effects of future learning are negligible. The implication is that the work place is a stable environment where change does not take place. If such an environment exists, it is an exception rather than the rule. Where there is change, there is also learning. There are two major types of learning: individual and organizational.

With instruction and repetition, workers learn to perform their jobs more efficiently and thereby reduce the number of direct labor hours per unit. Such may be the case in Fig. 6.4, where the cycle time is continually reduced until the 140th unit is produced. At that point learning is negligible and a standard time for the operation can be developed.

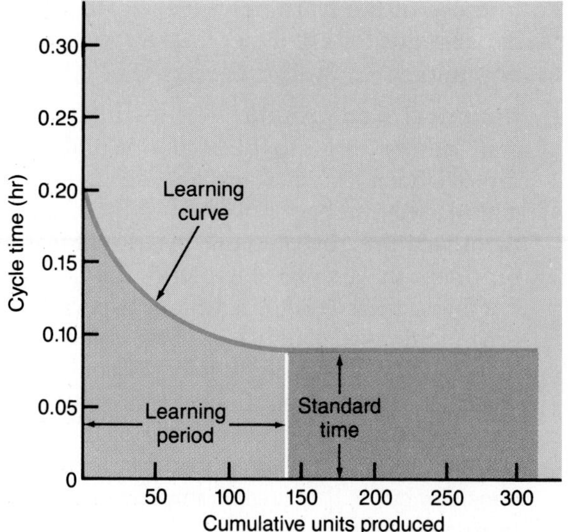

Figure 6.4

Relationship between the Learning Curve and the Standard Time per Cycle.

Organizational learning, in general, and management learning in particular, involve gaining experience in product and process design improvements, automation and other capital investments, and changes in administrative methods or personnel to improve the efficiency of operations. The cycle-time improvement shown in Fig. 6.4 could have resulted from better work methods, tools, product design, supervision of the operation, as well as from individual worker learning. Changes such as these in the workplace create the need for continually reevaluating existing standards and setting new ones, as necessary.

Projecting the Learning Effect

The learning effect can be represented by a line called a **learning curve**, which displays the relationship between the total direct labor per unit and the cumulative quantity of a product produced. The curve in Fig. 6.4 is an example of a learning curve for one operation. The terms *manufacturing progress function* and *experience curve* have also been used to describe this relationship, although the experience curve typically refers to total *value-added costs* per unit rather than labor hours. The principles underlying these curves are identical to those of the learning curve, however. We use the term *learning curve* to depict reductions in either total direct labor per unit or total value-added costs per unit.

Historical Background. The learning curve was first developed in the aircraft industry prior to the Second World War, when it was discovered that the direct labor input per airplane declined with considerable regularity as the cumulative number of planes produced increased. A survey of major airplane manufacturers revealed that a series of learning curves could be developed to represent the average experience for various categories of airframes (fighters, bombers, and so on). The unique aspect of these curves was that although the time required to produce the first unit differed by type of airframe, the rate of learning was surprisingly similar. For example, once production started, the direct labor for the eighth unit was only 80 percent that of the fourth unit, and the twelfth was only 80 percent of the sixth, and so on. In each case, each doubling of quantities reduced production time by 20 percent. Because of the consistency in the rate of improvement, it was concluded that the aircraft industry's rate of learning was 80 percent between doubled quantities of airframes. Of course, for any given product and company, the rate of learning can be different.

Learning Curves and Competitive Strategy. Learning curves enable managers to project the manufacturing cost per unit for a given cumulative production quantity. Firms that choose to emphasize low prices in their competitive strategy rely on high volumes to maintain profit margins. These firms strive to move down the learning curve (lower labor hours per unit or lower costs per unit) by increasing volume. This tactic makes entry into a market by competitors difficult. For example, in the electronics component industry, the cost of developing an integrated circuit is so large that the first units produced must be priced high. As cumulative production increases, costs (and prices) fall. The first companies in the market have a big advantage because newcomers, such as Korean firms, must start selling at lower prices and suffer large initial losses.

The incidents described in Box 6.3 show that projecting learning effects with learning curves or experience curves can be risky. It is all too easy to forget the dynamics of the environment, in which disturbances (such as new products or market changes) can disrupt the expected benefits of increased production. Nonetheless, the learning curve has many useful applications, as you will learn. Let's now turn to the problem of formulating a learning curve.

Development of Learning Curves

In our examples we will focus on direct labor hours per unit, although we could have used costs just as easily. We can develop learning curves in one of

Box 6.3

PROJECTING LEARNING EFFECTS CAN BE RISKY

From 1909 to 1923, the Ford Motor Company followed a strategy of cost minimization coupled with an aggressive pricing campaign to raise volume. Because of an 85 percent learning curve, Ford automobile prices fell dramatically. However, the mass-production strategy resulted in product inflexibility and, when the market shifted to closed body, more comfortable cars, Ford had difficulty responding. Following the learning curve and a cost-minimization strategy to its end cost Ford its market dominance. In this case product changes disrupted the progress of the learning curve.

Douglas Aircraft was forced to merge with McDonnell Company because of financial problems. Douglas assumed that it could reduce the costs of its new jet aircraft following a learning-curve formula and committed to delivery dates and prices with its customers. Continued modification of its plans disrupted the learning curve and the cost reductions were not realized.

International Business Machine's shipping schedules of its 360 series computers in 1965 were disrupted because of the company's efforts to attain high-volume production while it was undertaking a major product renovation.

The price of TV picture tubes dropped significantly from the late 1940s until 1963, when color TV entered the market. The cost of color TV tubes shot up, but then the learning curve reasserted itself and prices went down each year thereafter. Much of the manufacturing know-how was transferable from black-and-white to color TV tube production, so the transition was less severe than sometimes is the case.

Source: William J. Abernathy and Kenneth Wayne, "Limits on the Learning Curve," *Harvard Business Review* (September–October 1974), pp. 109–119.

two ways: (1) the spreadsheet approach, which is a simple arithmetic tabulation that can be displayed graphically to provide estimates of direct labor hours per unit; and (2) the logarithmic approach, which enables us to get time estimates without a complete tabulation of successive time–output combinations. When we develop a learning curve we make the following assumptions.

1. The direct labor required to produce the $n + 1$st unit will always be less than the direct labor required for the nth unit.
2. Direct labor requirements will decrease at a decreasing rate as cumulative production increases.
3. The reduction in time will follow an exponential curve.

Table 6.6

Unit, Cumulative Total, and Cumulative Average Direct Labor Hours

	80 Percent Learning Curve			90 Percent Learning Curve		
Cumulative Production (units)	Direct labor hours for last unit	Cumulative direct labor hours	Cumulative average direct labor hours	Direct labor hours for last unit	Cumulative direct labor hours	Cumulative average direct labor hours
1	50,000	50,000	50,000	50,000	50,000	50,000
2	40,000	90,000	45,000	45,000	95,000	47,500
4	32,000	157,104	39,276	40,500	177,812	44,453
8	25,600	267,296	33,412	36,450	328,688	41,086
16	20,480	446,000	27,875	32,805	601,984	37,624
32	16,384	733,920	22,935	29,525	1,095,552	34,236
64	13,107	1,196,224	18,691	26,572	1,985,344	31,021
128	10,486	1,937,152	15,134	23,915	3,588,352	28,034
256	8,389	3,123,712	12,202	21,524	6,475,008	25,293
512	6,711	5,023,232	9,811	19,371	11,672,064	22,797

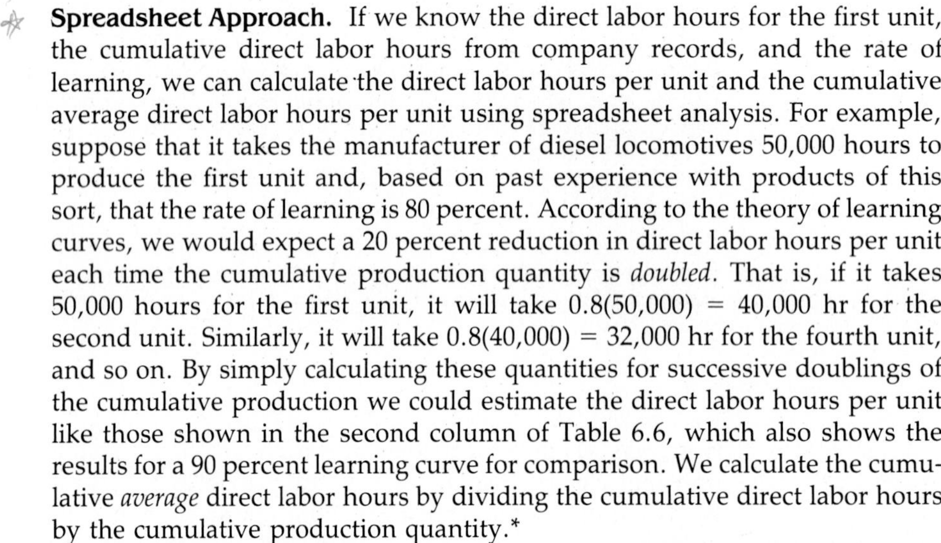

Spreadsheet Approach. If we know the direct labor hours for the first unit, the cumulative direct labor hours from company records, and the rate of learning, we can calculate the direct labor hours per unit and the cumulative average direct labor hours per unit using spreadsheet analysis. For example, suppose that it takes the manufacturer of diesel locomotives 50,000 hours to produce the first unit and, based on past experience with products of this sort, that the rate of learning is 80 percent. According to the theory of learning curves, we would expect a 20 percent reduction in direct labor hours per unit each time the cumulative production quantity is *doubled*. That is, if it takes 50,000 hours for the first unit, it will take 0.8(50,000) = 40,000 hr for the second unit. Similarly, it will take 0.8(40,000) = 32,000 hr for the fourth unit, and so on. By simply calculating these quantities for successive doublings of the cumulative production we could estimate the direct labor hours per unit like those shown in the second column of Table 6.6, which also shows the results for a 90 percent learning curve for comparison. We calculate the cumulative *average* direct labor hours by dividing the cumulative direct labor hours by the cumulative production quantity.*

Spreadsheets like the one in Table 6.6 can be prepared using pencil and paper or on the computer, using a commercial spreadsheet software package. The electronic spreadsheets have the advantage of giving the computer the task of calculating the entries in the spreadsheet by specifying the equations it should use to make the calculations.

* If the cumulative direct labor hours are not known, the logarithmic approach must be used to estimate the cumulative average direct labor hours.

The spreadsheet entries can be plotted so that estimates can be made for production quantities not tabulated in the spreadsheet. Figure 6.5 shows a plot of the 80 percent curves in Table 6.6. Plotting could also be done on a computer with the aid of a graphics software package. Unit times for non-tabulated quantities can be read from the graph.

Estimates for quantities not tabulated can also be made by interpolating the spreadsheet entries themselves. Suppose that we want an estimate for the direct labor per unit of the fortieth unit produced for the 80 percent learning curve in Table 6.6. It obviously must be between the 16,384 hours for the thirty-second unit and the 13,107 hours for the sixty-fourth unit. Interpolation would yield the following estimate.

$$\begin{aligned}\text{Interpolated}\\ \text{time for the 40th unit} &= 16{,}384 - \left(\frac{40-32}{64-32}\right)(16{,}384 - 13{,}107)\\ &= 15{,}566 \text{ hr.}\end{aligned}$$

Similarly, the cumulative average direct labor hours for 40 units would be 21,874 hours. Although these interpolations are easy to calculate, they should be used with caution. They are based on the assumption that the times vary *linearly* between the entries in the spreadsheet. However, as Fig. 6.4 shows, the times for the learning curve actually follow an *exponential curve.* Nonetheless, the interpolated figures are often adequate for most planning purposes.

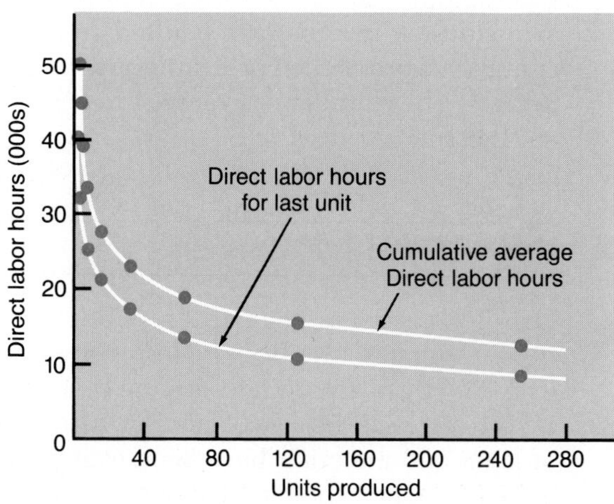

Figure 6.5

80 Percent Learning Curve.

Logarithmic Approach. A logarithmic model of the learning curve enables us to get the time estimates we need directly, without interpolation or reading a graph. The direct labor required for the nth unit, u_n, is

$$u_n = kn^b,$$

where

k = The direct labor hours for the first unit;

n = Total number of units produced;

r = The learning rate; and

$b = \log r/\log 2$.

For illustrative purposes, we will use this model to estimate the direct labor required for the fortieth diesel locomotive, assuming that the learning rate is 80 percent.

$$\begin{aligned} u_{40} &= 50{,}000(40)^{\log 0.8/\log 2} \\ &= 50{,}000(40)^{-0.322} \\ &= 50{,}000(0.30488) \\ &= 15{,}244 \text{ hr.} \end{aligned}$$

We can calculate the cumulative average number of hours per unit for the first 40 units with the help of Table 6.7. It contains conversion factors, which, when multiplied by the direct labor requirements for the first unit, yield the average time per unit for selected cumulative production quantities. For a cumulative production of 40 units and an 80 percent learning rate, the factor is 0.42984. The cumulative average direct labor hours per unit is 50,000(0.42984) = 21,492 hr.

Use of Learning Curves

Learning curves can be used in a variety of ways. One use is in bid preparation. Estimates of labor costs for large jobs facilitate the pricing of bids. Knowing the learning rate and the cost of materials for each unit, the estimator can arrive at the cost of labor by using a learning curve. After the total cost of labor and materials have been estimated, a desired level of profits can be added to obtain the total bid amount.

Learning curves can also be used in financial planning. The learning curve can help the financial planner determine the amount of cash necessary to finance operations. It provides a basis for comparing prices and costs and can be used to project periods of financial drain, when expenditures exceed

Table 6.7

Conversion Factors for the Cumulative Average Number of Direct Labor Hours per Unit

80 Percent Learning Rate (*n* = Cumulative production)						90 Percent Learning Rate (*n* = Cumulative production)					
n		*n*		*n*		*n*		*n*		*n*	
1	1.00000	19	0.53178	37	0.43976	1	1.00000	19	0.73545	37	0.67091
2	0.90000	20	0.52425	38	0.43634	2	0.95000	20	0.73039	38	0.66839
3	0.83403	21	0.51715	39	0.43304	3	0.91540	21	0.72559	39	0.66595
4	0.78553	22	0.51045	40	0.42984	4	0.88905	22	0.72102	40	0.66357
5	0.74755	23	0.50410	64	0.37382	5	0.86784	23	0.71666	64	0.62043
6	0.71657	24	0.49808	128	0.30269	6	0.85013	24	0.71251	128	0.56069
7	0.69056	25	0.49234	256	0.24405	7	0.83496	25	0.70853	256	0.50586
8	0.66824	26	0.48688	512	0.19622	8	0.82172	26	0.70472	512	0.45594
9	0.64876	27	0.48167	600	0.18661	9	0.80998	27	0.70106	600	0.44519
10	0.63154	28	0.47668	700	0.17771	10	0.79945	28	0.69754	700	0.43496
11	0.61613	29	0.47191	800	0.17034	11	0.78991	29	0.69416	800	0.42629
12	0.60224	30	0.46733	900	0.16408	12	0.78120	30	0.69090	900	0.41878
13	0.58960	31	0.46293	1000	0.15867	13	0.77320	31	0.68775	1000	0.41217
14	0.57802	32	0.45871	1200	0.14972	14	0.76580	32	0.68471	1200	0.40097
15	0.56737	33	0.45464	1400	0.14254	15	0.75891	33	0.68177	1400	0.39173
16	0.55751	34	0.45072	1600	0.13660	16	0.75249	34	0.67893	1600	0.38390
17	0.54834	35	0.44694	1800	0.13155	17	0.74646	35	0.67617	1800	0.37711
18	0.53979	36	0.44329	2000	0.12720	18	0.74080	36	0.67350	2000	0.37114

receipts. A contract price is determined, in part, by the *average* direct labor costs per unit for the number of contracted units. In the early stages of production, the direct labor costs will exceed the average used in determining the contract price, whereas in the later stages of production the reverse will be true. This information enables the financial planner to make necessary arrangements in advance with customers and the bank to finance the operations.

Another application of learning curves is estimating the direct labor requirements for a production schedule. Table 6.8 shows an example using a 90 percent learning curve. The number of direct labor hours needed for the first unit was 30,000 hours. Column 3 was derived from the factors in Table 6.7. (The figure for month 6 was interpolated.) The cumulative total hours were calculated by multiplying column 2 by column 3. The total hours per month, shown in column 5, were obtained by subtracting the successive monthly cumulative totals in column 4. (For example, for month 2, 130,175 − 57,000 = 73,175 hr.) Finally, column 6 was calculated by dividing the number of work hours per month into column 5. (For this example, we assumed that there are 200 work hours in each month.) This calculation gives us an estimate of the number of full-time direct labor employees needed. This information can be used to estimate training requirements and develop hiring plans.

Table 6.8

Estimating Labor Requirements Using a 90% Learning Curve

	Production Schedule		Estimates of Labor Requirements			
Month	Units per month (1)	Cumulative units (2)	Cumulative average time (3)	Cumulative total hours (4)	Total hours/month (5)	Total direct employees/month* (6)
1	2	2	28,500	57,000	57,000	285
2	3	5	26,035	130,175	73,175	366
3	5	10	23,983	239,830	109,655	548
4	8	18	22,224	400,032	160,202	801
5	12	30	20,727	621,810	221,778	1109
6	20	50	19,368	968,400	346,590	1733
7	14	64	18,613	1,191,232	222,832	1114

* Based on an assumed 200 labor hours in each month.

Estimating the Rate of Learning

It is not difficult to estimate the rate of learning if there are some historical data to work with. Table 6.9 shows a simple averaging approach and Box 6.4 shows how the logarithmic model can be used to make a reasonable estimate.

The estimates have to be more subjective when production has not yet started. In these situations, the analyst can either assume that the learning rate will be the same as for similar goods produced by the company in the past or that the learning rate will equal that of the industry as a whole for

Table 6.9

The Use of Historical Data to Estimate the Rate of Learning

Cumulative Production (units)	Direct Labor Hours, Last Unit (u_n)	Ratio (u_{2n}/u_n)
1	120	
2	95	$u_2/u_1 = 95/120 = 0.79$
4	78	$u_4/u_2 = 78/95 = 0.82$
5	73	
8	65	$u_8/u_4 = 65/78 = 0.83$
10	61	$u_{10}/u_5 = 61/73 = 0.84$
		Total = 3.28
		Average learning rate = 3.28/4 = 0.82.

Box 6.4

ESTIMATING THE LEARNING RATE WITH THE LOGARITHMIC MODEL

Consider a company that produces landing-flap assemblies for a large manufacturer of airplanes. Suppose that it takes 2500 hours to produce the first assembly. It is projected that it will take 402 hours to produce the 165th assembly. What is the learning rate for landing-flap assembly?

Using the equation for the direct labor required for a given unit, we have

$$u_{165} = 2500(165)^b = 402 \text{ hr.}$$

We can solve this relationship for b by using logarithms, or

$$(165)^b = \frac{402}{2500} = 0.1608$$

$$b \log 165 = \log 0.1608$$

$$b = \frac{\log 0.1608}{\log 165} = -0.35793$$

To find the learning rate, we use the definition of b:

$$b = \frac{\log r}{\log 2} = -0.35793$$

$$\log r = (-0.35793)\log 2 = -0.10774$$

$$r = 10^{(-0.10774)} = 0.78.$$

Consequently, the learning rate is 78 percent. This means that when production is doubled, the direct labor per unit is reduced by 22 percent.

similar applications. In either case actual performance should be monitored and revisions should be made in the learning rate as data are accumulated.

It is dangerous to blindly accept the industry learning rate because it can be quite different for a specific company. One factor involved is the mix of labor-paced and machine-paced operations. The opportunity to reduce direct labor hours on machine-paced operations is limited because the output rate is controlled by the capability of the machines, not the workers. The greater the ratio of labor-paced to machine-paced operations, the greater is the effect of learning on direct labor requirements.

Another factor affecting the rate of learning is the degree of complexity of the product. The learning rate for simple products is not as pronounced as it is for complex products. Complex products offer more opportunity to improve work methods, materials, and process design over the life of a product.

Closely associated with this factor is the experience of the organization with similar products. The greater the difference in the product, relative to anything the company has manufactured in the past, the greater is the expected learning rate.

The rate of capital inputs also affects the learning rate. Here we are referring to the overall reduction of direct labor hours because of the introduction of automation or general improvements in plant and equipment. Capital improvements are introduced at discrete points in time and typically have a significant effect. Thus they tend to make the actual learning curve uneven in contrast to a theoretical curve, such as the one shown in Fig. 6.5. Consequently, when estimating the learning rate based on previous experience or industry averages, an analyst must consider anticipated capital inputs.

MANAGERIAL CONSIDERATIONS IN WORK MEASUREMENT

Our discussion of work measurement methods would not be complete without introducing the managerial considerations associated with recognizing the quality of the production of goods or services in work standards and the ever-growing role of automation and its effect on work measurement in the future.

Quality and Work Standards

One of the uses of work measurement is to set standards that can be used for incentive pay plans. The purpose of incentive pay is to encourage high levels of output from employees. However, a high rate of output may come at the expense of quality. Where is the advantage to a company if a worker produces at 115 percent of standard but has a 20 percent defective rate?

It can be argued that management, not the worker, is primarily to blame for poor quality. However, we defer discussion on that topic until Chapter 18, where we more fully explore the issues of quality. Nonetheless, incentive plans that do not incorporate a consideration for quality may not motivate the worker to produce high quality goods. Somehow, quality must be tied to incentives.

Two basic approaches are used to recognizing quality in incentive plans. The first is the *autocratic approach:* either docking the worker's pay for defective production or requiring the worker to repair all defects at a lower rate of pay. The latter approach is not too popular with workers because in many cases the defects are not repairable, or they were not the fault of the worker.

The second is the *motivational approach,* which is based on the concept of extra pay for extra effort. In the following example there are actually two standards: one for daily production and the other for quality. Suppose that the daily production standard for an item is 1000 units. The daily wage rate is $50, but the operator gets an additional $0.30 for each unit produced over 1000 units. A daily production total of 1040 units would net the operator a bonus of $12.00, bringing daily work earnings to $62.00. However, there is also a quality standard of 95 percent defect-free production. If the operator produces at better than 95 percent quality, there is an added bonus of $0.10 for each defect-free unit produced beyond the standard. Suppose that 1009 acceptable items were produced. The quality bonus is 1009 − 0.95(1040) = 21 units. This adds a bonus of $2.10, bringing the total daily wage to $64.10.

Many variants of the motivational approach to incorporating quality issues into work measurement are used in practice. The point, however, is that quality should not be forgotten when work standards are being developed.

Impact of Automation

The advent of CAD/CAM factories in the future will offer a much different environment for the application of work measurement methods (Shell, 1982). First, there will be less need to actually observe an operation and rate the performance because of the increase in machine controlled processing cycles. Many cycle times will be determined by digital control devices and therefore will not have to be observed.

Second, although there will still be a need to determine allowances for fatigue, the nature of fatigue will be different. It will shift from physical fatigue to mental fatigue. Traditional values for allowance factors may not be appropriate for this type of fatigue.

Third, the method of work sampling will be simplified. An automated factory of the future will have the ability to electronically monitor the state of activity of many of the work units.

Fourth, predetermined time systems will still be useful. However, the need will be greater for analyzing robotic motions and the activities of knowledge workers than at present. Systems like robot time and motion (RTM) are useful for evaluating alternative robotic work methods. The emphasis on measuring the work of knowledge workers comes from the greater proportion of the work force that this type of worker is likely to represent.

Finally, standard data will probably be developed for major segments of the automated manufacturing system, as opposed to separate operations of an item's processing cycle. The times required for major manufacturing segments could be put into a CAD/CAM database, which would facilitate the simulation of alternative work methods and product cost estimates before production actually starts.

Even with automated factories, the major objective of work measurement will remain unchanged. Management then, as well as now, will still be interested in increasing productivity and reducing costs.

CHAPTER HIGHLIGHTS

Work measurement provides information necessary for many of the planning decisions faced by operations managers. This chapter presented the commonly used approaches to work measurement. Some of the chapter highlights are:

- Work measurement results are useful for comparing alternative process designs, scheduling, capacity planning, pricing and costing, performance appraisal, and developing incentive plans. The most frequent use of work measurement in practice is for estimating and costing, followed by incentive plan development, scheduling, and performance appraisal.
- The historical data approach to work measurement relies either on expert judgment or a historical data file to arrive at time estimates for a particular job or activity.
- The method most often used for setting time standards for a job is the time study. The job is divided into a series of smaller work elements. A stopwatch is used to time a trained worker using the prescribed work method for a number of cycles. The worker's pace is rated and allowances are added to arrive at a standard.
- The elemental standard data approach is an attempt to economize on the number of standards that must be derived and stored. The time standards for work elements that are common to a class of jobs can be stored in a database for future use in compiling time standards for jobs having these elements.
- The predetermined data approach further divides each work element into a series of micromotions. The normal times for these micromotions are stored in a database. Standards can be developed without a stopwatch.
- Work sampling is used most often to estimate the proportion of time spent on various broader activities associated with the production of goods or services. A large number of random observations are needed to make the estimates.
- In situations where significant learning takes place as production increases, learning curves can be used to prepare bids, decide on whether to make or buy a component, estimate the financial requirements over the life of a contract, and estimate the number of direct labor workers needed for a specific production schedule. If the learning rate is 90 percent, for example, each doubling of production volume reduces the labor required per unit by 10 percent.
- Firms using a low price strategy strive to move down the learning curve to reduce labor hours per unit and costs per unit by increasing volume. This makes entry into a market by competitors very costly.
- Labor standards used for incentive pay plans should include recognition for good product quality.
- The advent of automated factories will facilitate the process of work measurement because much of the work done will be machine-paced and monitored by computers. However, allowances will have to be made for mental fatigue in workers and there will be more of a need to develop predetermined time systems for knowledge workers.

KEY TERMS

labor standard
learning curve
methods time measurement (MTM)
time study
work sampling

STUDY QUESTIONS

1. An instructor for an introductory class in operations management positions all his students on the 50-yard line of the football field. He declares that anyone who does not reach the goal line in 5 seconds will fail the course. Discuss this intriguing way of grading a class from the perspective of the definition of a standard.
2. Consider the Italian Maiden Pizza Company example in Box 6.1. Suppose that there were plans to introduce a new deep-dish pizza product at Italian Maiden. How might Jack Spumoni develop time standards for producing this type of pizza?
3. The historical data approach to developing work standards in Table 6.1 utilized the moving averages technique. Single exponential smoothing could just as well have been used. Discuss the advantage of using single exponential smoothing and how tracking signals could be used in this application.
4. A colleague of yours comments that a time study with the use of a standard stopwatch is a precise method for determining work standards. What is your reply?
5. Your company builds concrete patio floors to customer specifications. The activities are (1) consultation with the customer to get the specifications; (2) drawing the plans; (3) digging the foundation; (4) building the forms; and (5) laying the concrete. Explain how you could use the elemental standard data approach to determine a time standard for each work element.
6. Two of your assistants are arguing over the precision required for a work sampling study. The proportion of time spent by a group of your employees manually filling out forms for customer orders turned out to be 0.28 in a recent pilot study. There is a proposal to bring in a network of microcomputers to speed this process. One assistant believes that the estimate should be within ± 0.01 of the true proportion, while the other thinks that a precision of ± 0.05 is sufficient. The pilot study had a sample size of 100. What would you consider in choosing a sample size here?
7. In Chapter 2, Fig. 2.7 depicts the continuum of positioning strategies. Relate what Fig. 2.7 shows to the concepts of learning curves and competitive strategy.

8. Which results in a lower number of direct labor hours per unit: an 80 percent learning curve or a 90 percent learning curve? Explain.

9. A friend of yours firmly believes that if the "factory of the future" is ever realized, there will be no need for work measurement. Comment.

PROBLEMS

1. A worker assembled 15 parts in 30 minutes during a time study. The analyst rated the worker at 110 percent. The allowance for fatigue, personal time and other contingencies is 20 percent. Calculate the
   (a) normal time for this job.
   (b) standard for this job.

2. You have just received the following data involving an assembly operation in your department. The data are expressed in minutes.

Work Element	Observation 1	2	3	4	*RF*
1	0.50	0.45	0.57	0.48	0.9
2	0.24	0.27	0.26	0.23	1.0
3	0.70	0.67	0.74	0.69	0.9
4	0.57	0.54	0.56	0.53	1.2

The allowances typically constitute 15 percent of the normal time. You have also been told that the schedule calls for 500 units per day for the foreseeable future. If each employee works 450 minutes per day, how many employees will you need?

3. The Saghuaro Leather Company produces leather goods for cowpunchers who work the vast Sonora Desert. One of the manufacturing operations involves three work elements. The second and third elements are not affected by the area of the leather component to be worked on. The normal times for these elements were easily determined: 1.34 and 0.73 minutes, respectively. However, the normal time for the first element, cutting the component from animal skins, is believed to be a function of the area of the component, so the following data were gathered.

Observation	Normal Time for Element 1 (min)	Area of Component (in^2)
1	0.07	5.00
2	0.10	7.50
3	0.13	15.50
4	0.20	25.00
5	0.24	34.00

The next job requires a component of 29.0 square inches. Use the concepts of the elemental standard data approach to find the normal time for the next job.

4. The following information has been gathered for the last four jobs at a certain work station. The most recent job was D.

Job	Production Quantity (units)	Setup Time (hr)	Total Run Time (min)
A	1100	4.15	2365
B	1500	4.50	3075
C	520	3.95	1009
D	900	3.90	1764

Using the concepts of the historical data approach and a moving average of the past 4 orders, make the following estimates.
   (a) Job E is scheduled to have 750 units.

Estimate the total time required at this work station.

(b) Job E actually took 4.05 hours in setup and 1515 minutes of run time. Job F is scheduled to have 1400 units. Estimate the total time required at the work station for job F.

5. A time analyst observed a job where the work methods have just been changed. The job is divided into four work elements. The element times for the first five cycles, recorded on a *continuous basis,* are shown in the following table with a performance rating (*RF*) for each element.

	Cycle Times (min)					
Element	1	2	3	4	5	*RF*
1	0.50	3.30	5.70	8.20	10.85	1.10
2	0.70	3.45	5.95	8.55	11.10	1.20
3	1.45	4.05	6.50	9.25	11.75	1.20
4	2.75	5.25	7.60	10.35	13.00	0.90

(a) Calculate the normal time for this job.
(b) Calculate the standard time for this job, assuming that the allowance is 20 percent.
(c) On the basis of the data available, what is the appropriate sample size to estimate the time for element 2 within ± 5 percent of the true mean time with 95 percent confidence?

6. Consider the recorded observations of 10 cycles of the coffee cup packaging operation shown in Fig. 6.1.
(a) Suppose that we want a sample size that gives an average time within 5 percent of the true average time 95 percent of the time. Did we make enough observations? If not, how many more should we make?
(b) Suppose that all we wanted was a precision of ± 10 percent. How many additional observations would we need now?

7. A library administrator wants to determine the proportion of the time the circulation clerk is idle. The following information was gathered on a random basis using work sampling.

Day	No. Times Clerk Busy	No. Times Clerk Idle	Total No. Observations
Monday	8	2	10
Tuesday	7	1	8
Wednesday	9	3	12
Thursday	7	3	10
Friday	8	2	10
Saturday	6	4	10

If the administrator wants a 95 percent confidence level and a degree of precision of ± 0.04, how many more observations will be needed?

8. As manager of an encoding department in a bank, you are concerned about the amount of time your encoder clerks are clearing their machines because of malfunctions. You were handed a proposal to modify the design of the machines for a price of $50,000. The modification will reduce the amount of time spent clearing the machines by 80 percent. You employ 20 encoder clerks at an annual salary of $12,000 each. It is safe to assume that any time saved from clearing the machines could be used to process more checks and reduce the interest charges the bank must pay. To help you decide whether the proposal is worth considering, you had a pi-

lot work sampling study made, which provided the following results.

Activity	Observations
Processing checks	50
Clearing machine	10
Waiting for checks	20
Breaks	5
Total	85

(a) If the life of the modification is 10 years and the tax rate is 50 percent, what is the simple payback period for the proposal based on your sample estimate? (Use straight-line depreciation.)

(b) What is the confidence interval for your estimate? Would you suggest a larger sample size? Why?

9. The Compton Company has kept the time records shown in Table 6.10 on a new product it is manufacturing.

(a) Calculate the rate of learning.

(b) Estimate the direct labor hours needed for the eightieth unit.

10. You have just been given the production schedule for a new product. This product is considerably different than any others your company has produced. Historically, the learning rate has been 80 percent on projects such as this.

Month	Units
1	3
2	7
3	10
4	12
5	4
6	2

The first unit took 1000 hours to produce. If your budget only provides for a maximum of 25 direct labor employees in any month and a total of 15,000 direct labor hours for the entire schedule, will your budget be adequate? Assume 200 work hours in each month.

Table 6.10

Cumulative Production	Direct Labor Hours, Last Unit
1	46
2	38
3	N/A
4	30
5	28
6	N/A
7	N/A
8	25.6
9	N/A
10	24

SELECTED REFERENCES

Abernathy, William J., and Kenneth Wayne, "Limits of the Learning Curve," *Harvard Business Review* (September–October 1974), pp. 109–119.

Andress, Frank J., "The Learning Curve as a Production Tool," *Harvard Business Review* (January–February 1954), pp. 1–11.

Barnes, Ralph, *Motion and Time Study: Design and Measurement of Work*, 7th ed. New York: John Wiley and Sons, 1980.

Graves, Clare W., "Deterioration of Work Standards," *Harvard Business Review* (September–October 1966), pp. 118–126.

Moore, Franklin G., *Manufacturing Management,* Homewood, Ill.: Richard D. Irwin, 1969.

Nadler, Gerald, *Work Design,* Homewood, Ill.: Richard D. Irwin, 1970.

Niebel, Richard W., *Motion and Time Study,* 6th ed. Homewood, Ill.: Richard D. Irwin, 1976.

Rice, Robert S., "Survey of Work Measurement and Wage Incentives," *Industrial Engineering,* vol. 9, no. 7 (July 1977), pp. 18–31.

Shell, Richard L., "The Impact of Automation on Work Measurement," *1982 Fall Industrial Engineering Conference Proceedings,* Institute of Industrial Engineers (November 1982), Cincinnati, pp. 348–353.

Sirota, David, "Productivity Management," *Harvard Business Review* (September–October 1966), pp. 111–116.

Yelle, Louis E., "The Learning Curve: Historical Review and Comprehensive Survey," *Decision Sciences,* vol. 10, no. 2 (April 1979), pp. 302–328.

CHAPTER

CAPACITY AND MAINTENANCE

Some Managerial Issues

- How should we measure capacity?
- What is the maximum reasonable size for our facility?
- How much capacity cushion is best for our processes?
- Should we follow an *expansionist* or a *wait-and-see* strategy?
- How should we link capacity to competitive priorities? To other decision areas?
- How intense should our maintenance effort be?
- How should our maintenance department be managed?

Chapter Outline

After deciding what products should be offered (product planning) and how they are to be made (process design), managerial attention turns to capacity. For purposes of these introductory remarks, **capacity** is defined as the maximum rate of output for a facility. The facility could be a work station or an entire organization. Later, we introduce two other definitions of capacity. Whatever the definition, the operations manager must provide the capacity to meet current and future demand or suffer the consequences of missed opportunities.

Figure 7.1 shows three types of alternative situations: increasing, maintaining, and decreasing capacity. Curve (*a*) represents increasing organizational capacity, for which long-term, medium-term, and short-term planning is needed. Long-term capacity planning looks into the future at least two years, but construction lead times alone can force much longer time horizons. It can take a decade to build an electric utility plant and more than half a century to grow a forest for the paper industry. Investment in new facilities and equipment often are sizable, requiring top-management participation and approval. Medium- and short-term capacity plans are constrained by the long-term plans. The focus of these shorter planning time horizons turns from capital investment toward work-force size, overtime budgets, inventory investment, and other aspects of operations. Decisions in these areas can be reversed more quickly and with less impact than capital investment decisions and are considered in later chapters.

Curve (*b*) represents the situation of maintaining current capacity. Capacity can be maintained by preventive maintenance programs, judicious replacement of existing equipment, or even by providing alternative means of output

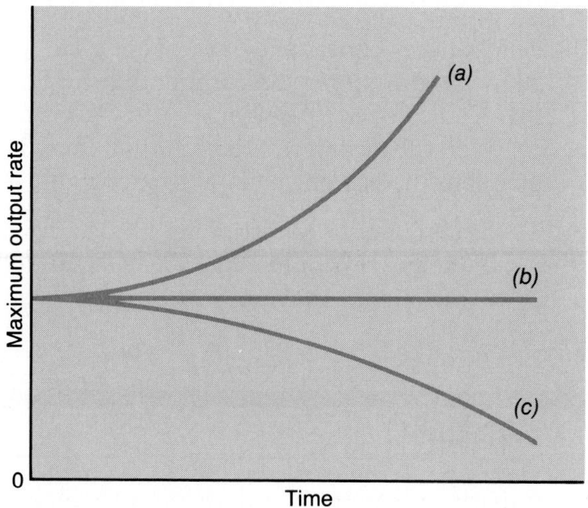

Figure 7.1

Three Alternative Types of Capacity Situations.

when the system experiences failure. System maintenance strives to maintain the maximum output rate of the organization whatever the level of capital investment. In this regard, the only difference between curve (*a*) and (*b*) is that curve (*a*) incorporates capital investment to expand capacity.

Curve (*c*) represents the situation in which capacity must be decreased, or allowed to erode. Capacity erodes when system maintenance programs are ineffective, no effort is made to replace aging equipment, or parts of the business are sold. Some industries and many firms have let capacity erode in the past—often with disastrous results. The U.S. steel industry is a case in point. Plant and equipment had been neglected to the point where U.S. steelmakers lost their international competitive advantage. This is not to say that old equipment should always be replaced by new equipment. Lincoln Electric Company was selected as one of the ten best managed companies by *Fortune* in 1984. Its plant and equipment are over 30 years old, but it has managed to hold its overwhelming market share in welding equipment for 50 years. Rather than replacing old, nonautomated equipment, Lincoln Electric uses employee incentives and a good maintenance program to keep output high.

Capacity reductions may reflect short-sighted management pursuing a quick return on investment and overlooking long-term investment that would help to secure or improve their position in the marketplace. Alternatively, capacity reductions may reflect restrictive government policies that increase the risk of long-term investment, such as reducing or eliminating investment tax breaks. Capacity cutbacks can also be caused by having too many products in the decline stage of their life cycle, process design choices that do not allow the firm to remain competitive, and overly optimistic demand forecasts that lead to overexpansion.

We will focus on situations where it is desirable to expand or at least maintain the current level of capacity and on two crucial capacity issues:

1. When should investments in facilities and equipment be made and by how much should capacity be expanded (long-term capacity planning)?
2. How should the system's capacity be maintained (maintenance)?

CAPACITY PLANNING

Capacity planning is a decision area central to the long-term growth of an organization. A poor job of capacity planning can be very costly, as the example in Box 7.1 shows. Managers have to consider many questions when choosing a capacity strategy, including: Should we have one large facility or several small facilities? Should we expand capacity before the demand is

Box 7.1

POOR CAPACITY PLANNING CAN RESULT IN MAJOR ORGANIZATIONAL UPHEAVALS

In 1980, Pan American World Airlines purchased National Airlines just when many airlines were engaged in money-losing fare wars on domestic routes. High fuel prices and a recession caused Pan Am huge deficits. The airline decided to use National to feed passengers from interior U.S. cities to the more profitable Pan Am international flights at Kennedy airport. This increased the average daily Pan Am departures at Kennedy from 33 in 1981 to 60 in 1984. According to a Pan Am official, this created a disaster at Worldport, the Pan Am terminal at Kennedy. The terminal lacked enough gates, the baggage handling system was inefficient, and leaking roofs and dimly-lit hallways reflected poor maintenance. Although the chairman of Pan Am was aware of growing delays at Worldport in late 1983 and was planning broad management changes to address the major problems, the spark that spurred the immediate changes happened when he took a Pan Am flight to Paris and was delayed at the terminal for one and a half hours. Shortly afterward, 23 vice presidents had been fired, forced to resign, or quit.

Source: "Pan Am Conducts Major Shake-Up to Improve Its Weak Performance," *Wall Street Journal*, August 16, 1984.

there, or should we wait until demand is more certain? A systematic approach is needed in order to answer such questions and develop capacity strategy appropriate for each situation.

Measuring Capacity

Capacity planning requires an indication of current capacity and its utilization, so that future additions can be properly scheduled. A statistic often used to indicate the degree to which equipment, space, or labor is currently being utilized is the *average utilization rate.* It is calculated as follows:

$$\text{Average utilization rate} = \frac{\text{Average output rate}}{\text{Capacity}},$$

expressed as a percentage. The average output rate and the capacity must be measured in the same terms, such as time, customers, and units. As you will see later in this chapter, the utilization rate is an indicator for deciding when to add extra capacity. However, in order to plan for proper utilization rates we first need to measure capacity.

Basic Capacity Measures. No single capacity measure is best for all types of situations. A reasonable capacity measure might be the number of patients that can be treated per day at a hospital, available seat-miles (ASMs) per month of an airline, or number of machines at a job shop. In general there are three basic capacity measures (illustrated for a restaurant):

1. Maximum output rate (customers served per day).
2. Maximum input rate (number of available employee hours per day).
3. Number of input units (number of seats).

The first measure is the definition of capacity that we used earlier. It is already expressed in the same terms as the average output rate. For multiple products, however, a complication arises: The capacity measure must also be accompanied by a statement on the *product mix.* For example, a restaurant may be able to handle 100 take-out customers *or* 50 sit-down customers per hour. It could also handle 50 take-out *and* 25 sit-down customers, as well as many other mixes of the two customer types. Product-mix assumptions also must be stated for the other two measures when multiple products share the same resources.

Managers of process-focused facilities with high product flexibility tend to express capacity in terms of inputs and often use the second measure, maximum input rate. In order to use it, however, we must convert the output rate into an equivalent measure. In our example, we would multiply the average output rate (customers per day) by the average processing time (employee hours per customer) to get average employee hours demanded per day. The third measure also requires a conversion before we can use it. In our example, we must translate customer demand into seat requirements, such as the average number of seats typically occupied during the day. In summary, any one of the three measures is acceptable so long as (1) product mix assumptions are stated; and (2) any necessary conversions are made to compare capacity and average output rate on an equivalent basis.

Defining *Maximum*. A complication in measuring capacity lies with the meaning of *maximum*. Capacity often can be expanded temporarily with such options as overtime or subcontracting. While helping with temporary peaks, these options cannot be sustained for long. Employees do not want excessive overtime for extended periods. Overtime premiums also drive up costs. Thus measures for both *peak* and *sustained* capacity levels are needed. When this distinction is overlooked, a firm can find itself making minimal profits when sales are at a record high, if prices were not increased to absorb the extra cost of operating at peak capacity.

Economies of Scale

Now that we have determined a measure for capacity, we turn to the issues relating to facility size. Historically, many organizations have subscribed to the concept of **economies of scale**. The concept seems simple: Increasing a facility's size (or scale) decreases the average unit cost. In Fig. 7.2, the 1000-bed hospital shows economies of scale because the average unit cost at its "best operating level" is less than that of the 500-bed hospital. If patient demand is sufficient, the larger size is the better choice. Economies (and diseconomies) of scale are also represented by each individual cost curve. As the output rate increases up to the best operating level, economies of scale are realized. Beyond that level, diseconomies set in. Although finding the best operating level is illusive, managers often set policies regarding the maximum size for any one facility. Employee ceilings of 300 are common for labor-intensive industries such as metal-working or apparel (Schmenner, 1982). The limits grow to as large as 6000 employees for capital-intensive industries such as transportation equipment or electronics. The real challenge in setting such policies is predicting how costs will change for different output rates and facility sizes. This assessment requires careful attention to the different causes of economies of scale for each situation.

Spreading Fixed Costs. In the short term, certain costs do not vary with changes in the output rate. These fixed costs include heating costs, debt service, and management salaries (see Chapter 2). Depreciation of plant and equipment already owned is also a fixed cost in the accounting sense. When the output rate—and therefore the facility's utilization—are increased, the

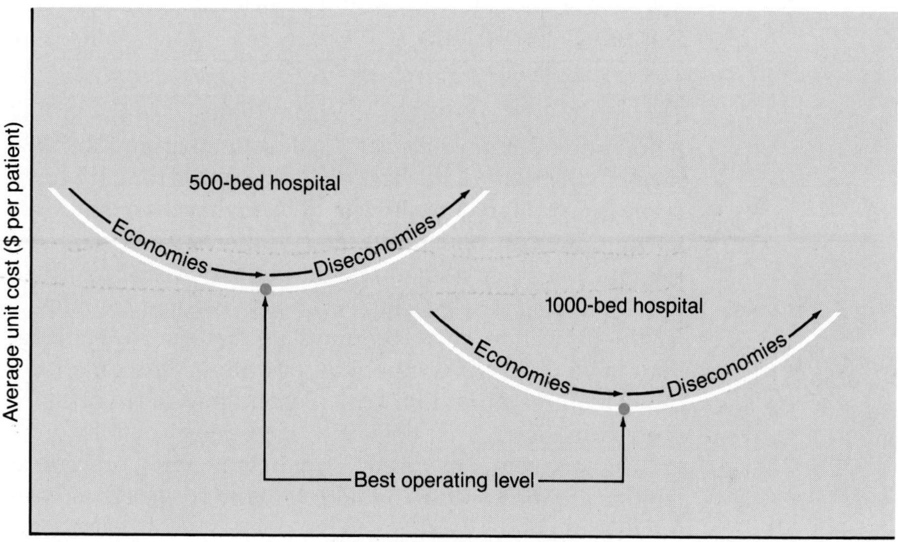

Figure 7.2

Economies and Diseconomies of Scale.

average unit cost drops because fixed costs are spread over more units. Increments of capacity often come in sizable amounts, forcing a firm initially to buy more capacity than it needs. Demand increases in subsequent years can be absorbed over a fairly wide range without adding fixed costs.

Construction Costs. A second reason for greater economies of scale for the 1000-bed hospital in Fig. 7.2 is that it costs less to build than twice the cost of the 500-bed hospital. The 1000-bed facility is therefore more economical, so long as demand is close enough to its best operating level.

Process Advantages. Repeatability and high-volume production provide many opportunities for cost reduction. A more efficient process technology may be possible and its capital intensity justifiable at a higher output rate. The process shifts toward a product-focused strategy, with resources dedicated to individual products. More specialized equipment replaces general-purpose machinery. Dedicating resources to individual products reduces changeovers and setups, which improves efficiency. Even if dedicated resources still are not possible, a higher output rate (to meet greater demand) means longer runs without a corresponding increase in inventory. Further benefits may include learning curve effects and a greater ability to find ways to improve process and job designs.

Focused Facilities

The concept of economies of scale typically leads to large plants. At some point, however, *diseconomies of scale* set in. Figure 7.2 shows average unit costs rising to the right of the best operating levels for both hospitals. Also, the cost curve for a 1500-bed facility could be higher than that for the 1000-bed facility. Having one consolidated facility, rather than several smaller ones carefully placed close to customers, could increase distribution costs for manufacturers. Managing larger facilities can also become complex. In order to increase facility utilization, more products are made at the same facility. The products may have different competitive priorities. One calls for top quality and another requires minimum cost. Scheduling and work-force management get more complicated. To help with increasing complexity more staff specialists and supervisors are hired, and bureaucratic procedures are added. Run lengths are increased to avoid too many costly changeovers, but this change inflates inventory, perhaps to the point where a warehouse is needed to store it. In short, the savings derived from spreading fixed costs can be dwarfed by these added costs.

Prior to 1970, even though large plants were difficult to manage, many firms were willing to endure the managerial headaches in order to compete on the basis of low prices in world markets. However, after 1970, the ground rules for competition changed and economies of scale no longer could guarantee an advantage. Quality and flexibility gained importance. Also, rapid technological changes shortened product life cycles, and managers of large plants found it increasingly difficult to maintain high volume. For many companies the time had come to reevaluate the usefulness of large facilities.

First proposed in the early 1970s, the concept of **focused facilities** has persuaded many firms to move away from large facilities trying to do everything (Skinner, 1974). The concept of focused facilities holds that narrowing the range of demands placed on a facility will lead to better performance because managerial attention can be concentrated on fewer tasks. For example, one plant attempting to satisfy all markets may give way to several smaller plants, each serving one market. Or, one plant producing all the components and assembling the final product may be split into two plants, one producing the components and one assembling the final product. Thus each can focus on its own individual process technology. Even with a large facility, focus can be gained by having "plants within plants." The competitive priorities, technology and work force are individualized. Boundaries may be established by physically separating subunits, even within the same building. The separation can even be less tangible than this, such as by means of revised organizational relationships.

The focused facilities concept has led some firms to tout the virtues of smallness. The General Electric Aircraft Engine Group once concentrated production in two large complexes but now has eight smaller satellite plants. Hewlett-Packard, S. C. Johnson and Sons Company, and American Telephone and Telegraph Company, to name a few, have also gone to smaller facilities and focused operations. Some managers feel that this minimizes risk because if a plant becomes obsolete sooner than expected, it is better to have a smaller investment in plant and equipment. Also, some companies feel that smaller plants provide a much better environment for employees. There are fewer layers of management, it is easier to use team approaches to problem solving, and there are shorter lines of communication between departments. In all of this the message is clear: Do not let the facility get too large and make sure that it has enough focus.

Capacity Strategy

Before we look at a systematic approach to capacity decisions, let's consider the three dimensions of capacity strategy:

1. Capacity cushions.
2. Timing and sizing of expansion.
3. Links.

Capacity Cushions. North American manufacturers recently picked low capacity utilization as one of their top three concerns (Miller, 1983). Japanese manufacturers, by contrast, are more likely to complain that capacity utilization is too high. The problems accompanying high capacity utilization in manufacturing are described in Box 7.2.

Average utilization rates should not get too close to 100 percent. When they do it is usually a signal to increase capacity or suffer the consequences of lost demand or poor delivery performance. The amount by which the average utilization rate falls below 100 percent is called the **capacity cushion.** Specifically,

$$\text{Capacity cushion} = 100 - \text{Average utilization rate},$$

expressed as a percentage. Mr. Rogers's plant had only a 3 percent capacity cushion. Although the paper industry is capital intensive, which argues for small cushions, 3 percent seems too small. Electrical utilities are also capital intensive and consider cushions of 15 to 20 percent to be optimal, but they do have to provide much shorter customer response times. Clearly managers must carefully weigh the factors arguing for both large and small cushions.

We begin with arguments for *large cushions.* A clerk in the human services department of a state government can handle as many as 50 clients per day. However, demand is not evenly spaced. Some days of the week have predictably higher demands than other days. There can even be an hour-to-hour

Box 7.2

CAPACITY UTILIZATION CAN BE TOO HIGH

George E. Rogers manages the Crown Zellerbach Corporation's paper mill in Louisiana. The industry is now operating at 97 percent utilization and Mr. Rogers is discovering that the boom is not an unalloyed blessing. Customers are frustrated by mounting backlogs. Prices have gone up 25 percent and some customers are on an allocation system. They receive only 90 percent of their orders. Some believe quality is being sacrificed for volume. Machines, which can cost hundreds of millions of dollars each, are being operated even though they should be shut down for preventive maintenance. The market's tightness is causing some customers to place orders earlier. Others are looking overseas to Finland and West Germany for additional supply. High capacity utilization is straining the equipment and management alike.

Source: "When an Industry Is Too Busy," *New York Times,* April 5, 1984.

pattern. At a typical fire department, the number of fire alarms peaks between 2 P.M. and 6 P.M., when the rate is three to four times higher than it is between 1 A.M. and 5 A.M. Such peaks cannot be smoothed out with inventories or by having the customer wait a long time for service. In order to give prompt customer service, an organization's capacity cushion must be big enough to handle peak demands, particularly in the service industry. Customers grow impatient if they have to wait in a supermarket checkout line for more than a few minutes, whereas the buyer of a forklift tractor considers a manufacturer's delivery time of two months to be excellent.

Large cushions are also necessary when future demand is uncertain. One large bank operated its computer for six months at an average 77 percent load on the central processing unit (CPU) during peak demand. Top management felt that the capacity cushion was more than ample and rejected a proposal to expand capacity. During the next six months, the average CPU utilization during peaks surged to 83 percent. Totally unexpected was the dramatic decline in customer service and missed due dates. The capacity cushion proved to be too small to meet the bank's customer service objectives, contrary to earlier expectations. Another type of demand uncertainty is a changing product mix. Total demand might be stable, but the load can shift unpredictably from one work center to another as the mix changes. Feast-or-famine conditions go along with high product flexibility. One example is a municipal criminal justice system, where the capacity (courtroom hours) varies with the nature of the trial and whether a jury is needed. The mix varies from one month to the next.

Other reasons for large capacity cushions lie on the supply (rather than the demand) side. Capacity often comes in large increments, so that expanding even by the minimum amount possible may create a large cushion. Allowances must be made for absenteeism, vacations, holidays, materials delays, work breaks, equipment failures, and scrap losses. Penalty costs for overtime or subcontracting can create the need for further increases in capacity cushions.

The motivation for *small cushions* is simple. Unused capacity costs money. For capital-intensive firms, it is vital to minimize the capacity cushion, as is evident in Table 7.1. Businesses with high capital intensity achieve a disappointing 7 percent return on investment (ROI) when the capacity cushion is high (and utilization low). The ROI increases to a more respectable 17 percent when the capacity cushion is low. However, this strong correlation pattern does not exist for labor-intensive firms. The ROI is about the same, regardless of utilization, because there is less investment in equipment, and changing the capacity cushion often does not entail significant capital expenditures.

Timing and Sizing of Expansion. The second dimension of capacity strategy is when to expand and by how much. Figure 7.3 illustrates two extreme strategies: The *expansionist strategy* involves large, infrequent jumps in capacity, compared to the *wait-and-see strategy*. The timing and sizing of expansion are related. When the length of time between increments is increased, so must be the size of the increments. The expansionist strategy stays ahead of demand. Even though this creates a large capacity cushion, it minimizes the chance that sales will be lost because of insufficient capacity. The wait-and-see strategy lags behind demand requirements, relying on short-term options to augment capacity. Table 7.2 lists some of these options, each of which has drawbacks. For example, overtime means time-and-a-half wages for nonexempt employees, the output rate might slip during overtime hours, and union agreements limit the amount of allowable overtime. Nonetheless, some

Table 7.1

Return on Investment for High Capital-Intensity Businesses

Capacity Cushion	Return on Investment (ROI)*
Low (less than 15%)	17%
Medium (between 15% and 30%)	11
High (above 30%)	7

* ROI measured as pretax income divided by average investment.

Source: Abell, Derek F., and John S. Hammond, *Strategic Market Planning: Problems and Analytical Approaches.* Englewood Cliffs, N.J.: Prentice-Hall, 1979.

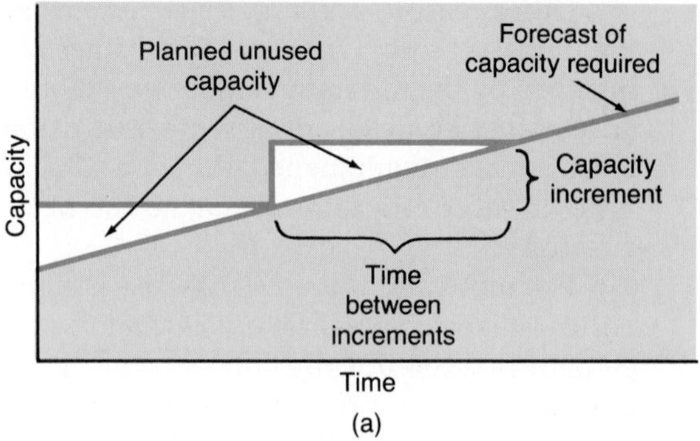

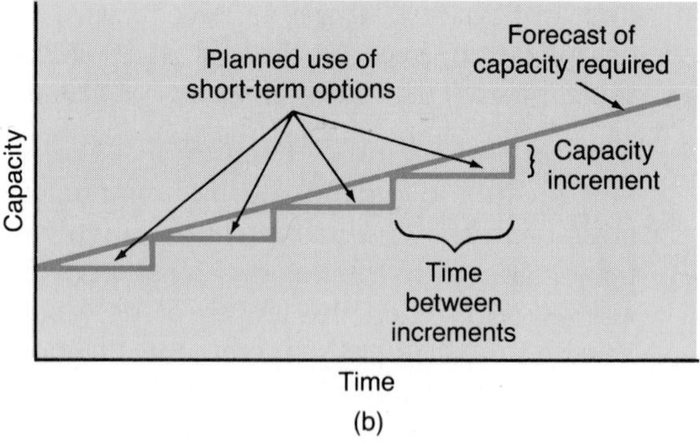

Figure 7.3

Two Capacity Strategies: (a) Expansionist Strategy; (b) Wait-and-See Strategy.

mix of short-term options might make the wait-and-see strategy best in certain situations.

Several factors favor the expansionist strategy. When economies of scale and learning effects are strong, a firm can reduce its costs and compete more on price. This strategy might increase its market share, with supply creating demand. The expansionist strategy becomes a form of preemptive marketing when a firm makes a large capacity expansion, or perhaps just announces that one is imminent. By making it clear that it will do whatever is necessary to compete on cost, the firm is using capacity as a competitive weapon, preempting expansion by others who must sacrifice some of their market share or risk glutting the industry with overcapacity. To be successful, the preempting firm must have credibility that it will carry out its plans and signal them before competition can act.

The wait-and-see strategy is conservative and minimizes risk. When a firm does expand, it might be to renovate existing structures rather than build new ones. The more a firm invests in any one facility, the more it depends on its success. The wait-and-see strategy reduces the risks of overly optimistic demand forecasts, technological change that makes the facility obsolete, and unpredictable competitive reactions. This strategy fits better with competitive priorities emphasizing flexibility and top quality and foregoes the larger market share of the lowest-cost producer. This strategy has been criticized by some who compare U.S. and Japanese management styles; U.S. managers tend to take fewer risks. They are on the *fast track* of the corporate ladder, spending only a few years in each succeeding job. They earn promotions by avoiding the big mistake and maximizing short-term profit and ROI. The wait-and-see strategy fits this style but can erode market share over the long haul.

Management must pick one of these two strategies or one of the many in between. The choice could even be a *follow-the-leader strategy* of expanding when others do. If the others are right, so are you, and nobody gains a competitive advantage. If they make a mistake and overexpand, everyone shares in the agony of overcapacity.

Links. A subsidiary of a large consumer goods manufacturer sold 85 percent of its output to other divisions in the company, with the remaining 15 percent going to outside customers. The capacity of one of its processes was being squeezed. One option was to make a major expansion, enabling the subsidiary to attract more outside customers. However, this would have caused a shift in competitive priorities. Rather than being a low-cost supplier to the

Table 7.2

Some Short-Term Capacity Options

Lease extra space temporarily.
Authorize overtime.
Staff second or third shifts with temporary workers.
Add weekend shifts.
Subcontract work.
Alternate routings, using different (and less efficient) work stations that have excess capacity.
Schedule longer runs to minimize capacity losses during changeovers, even though inventories become inflated.
Level output rates by building up inventory in a slack season.
Postpone preventive maintenance.
Use multiskilled workers to alleviate bottlenecks.
Allow back orders to increase, extend due date promises, or have stockouts.

other divisions, it would have to place higher priority on flexibility and quality. Management decided against the expansion, because of the poor coupling with other policies.

This is but one example of how capacity affects all parts of a firm. Capacity choices can affect market share, so marketing is involved. Expansion means capital investment, so finance is concerned. Capacity choices are also linked with various decision areas in operations. Table 7.3 suggests how considerations in several decision areas relate to a strategy favoring either small or large capacity cushions.

A Systematic Approach to Capacity Decisions

Although each situation is somewhat different, a four-step procedure can help managers make sound capacity decisions:

1. Estimate future capacity requirements.
2. Identify gaps by comparing requirements with available capacity.
3. Develop alternative plans for filling the gaps.
4. Evaluate each alternative, both quantitatively and qualitatively, and make a final choice.

Step 1: Estimate Capacity Requirements. The beginning point is a demand forecast. Since long-term decisions are involved, forecasts of demand, productivity, competition, and technological changes must extend well into the future. Unfortunately, forecast errors get larger as forecast time horizons become longer. The consequences of overestimating future demand or being surprised by the capacity expansions of competitors are illustrated in Box 7.3. A capacity glut results in a cost–price squeeze. Conversely, examples abound of firms losing market share and the cost advantages of the learning curve by failing to expand soon enough. Thus errors can be made in either direction. See Chapter 3 for a more detailed discussion of quantitative and qualitative forecasting methods.

A forecast of demand has to be converted into a number comparable with the capacity measure. Suppose that capacity is expressed as the number of available machines at a machining operation. With this particular measure, we must convert the demand rate into the number of required machines. We begin by calculating the machine hours required per year for each product:

Total machine hours required per year = Number of units of product forecasted for a year × Time to process one unit + Number of batches per year × Standard setup time per batch,

or

$$R = Dt_p + Bt_s.$$

Table 7.3

Linking Capacity with Other Decisions

Decision Area	Typical Capacity Strategy: Small cushion	Typical Capacity Strategy: Large cushion	Comments
Choosing competitive priorities			
Low price, high conformance to specifications	X		Typically involves high-volume production and high utilization.
High flexibility, fast delivery, on-time delivery		X	Greater capacity cushion needed to permit quick response.
Process design			
Capital intensive	X		Capital intensity usually calls for high utilization.
Labor intensive		X	Usually more output variability is coupled with a high priority on flexibility.
Yield losses			
Small, consistent	X		More certainty in plans permits high utilization.
Large, unpredictable		X	Larger variances in "good" output require more capacity than would otherwise be needed.
Job design			
More worker flexibility	X		Flexible work force increases capability to assist with operation overloads.
Less worker flexibility		X	Overloaded work stations need more capacity, while underutilized work stations have idle time.
Inventory			
Low inventory costs	X		Inventory can be stockpiled and used to meet peak demands as they occur.
High inventory costs		X	Peak demands must be met by increased production.
Scheduling			
Stable environment	X		Schedules can be made with a high degree of assurance that they will not need to be changed in the near term.
Unstable environment		X	Changing schedules causes disruptions and requires more capacity.

Box 7.3

FORECAST ERRORS AND EXCESS CAPACITY

- Despite the economic recovery, hotel and motel operators and investors are being hurt by the nationwide glut in rooms. In Houston and Miami, for example, overbuilding has caused rate wars and mothballed hotels. The industry's nationwide occupancy rate is down to 66.6 percent, six points less than a decade earlier. Rising room rates entice entrepreneurs to get into the business but overcapacity drives the rates down again.
- With just one week left until Christmas, retailers slashed their prices in order to sell off their merchandise. Many believe that there are too many retailers. Walter Loel, a Morgan Stanley and Company analyst, figured that there are 47 percent more stores than needed. Price cutting and market-share battles are expected until a shakeout trims the overcapacity.
- Cruise ship lines are now offering discount packages in response to overcapacity. The popularity of cruises in the late 1970s led many executives to order more ships. Now there is too much capacity and the profitability of the past is no longer available.
- When the farm economy dipped in 1980, the makers of farm machinery were taken by surprise and were slow to react. Now the industry is operating at less than 30 percent of its capacity for making tractors and combines. Prices are being slashed to move out expensive inventories, which in turn cuts profits. Mergers, company failures, and plant closings are expected to trim the overcapacity.

Sources: "U.S. Lodging Industry Is Staggered by Room Glut and Building Boom," *Wall Street Journal*, November 26, 1984; "Oversupply of Retail Outlets Is Seen as Big Cause of Holiday Price Cuts," *Wall Street Journal*, December 18, 1984; "Cruise Ship Lines Offer Discount Packages in Response to Overcapacity, Strong Dollar," *Wall Street Journal*, August 16, 1984; "Farm-Gear Makers' Severe Price Cutting Is Set to Intensity; More Mergers Are Seen," *Wall Street Journal*, December 10, 1984.

If more than one product is involved, we would calculate the machine hours required for each one and add them to get a final R value.

Next, we calculate the number of machine hours per year satisfied by one machine, which is

Hours per year from one machine = Hours operated on all shifts and all work days in a year × (100 − Capacity cushion)/100,

or

$$H = \frac{N(100 - C)}{100}$$

Knowing the total hours required (R) and the amount satisfied per machine (H), we obtain the number of machines required from their ratio, or

$$M = \frac{R}{H}.$$

This conversion process is not limited to machines. The input unit could just as easily be seats in a theater or teller stations in a bank.

Let's use a plant work station that produces two different products as an example of the conversion process. Table 7.4 gives information on these two products, X and Y. The plant operates 250 days per year, with two eight-hour shifts. Management believes that a capacity cushion of 15 percent above the allowance in the time standards is best. We need to calculate the number of machines needed at the work station.

We begin with R, which in turn needs a value for B. Since product X is made in batches of 40 units, 50 batches (or 2000/40) will be made during the year. This is the value of B for product X. Summing the machine hour requirements for both products, we get

$$R = [2000(4) + 50(5)] + [6000(3) + 100(8)] = 27{,}050.$$

The remaining calculations are

$$H = (250 \text{ days/year} \times 2 \text{ shifts/day} \times 8 \text{ hours/shift})\left(\frac{100 - 15}{100}\right)$$
$$= 3400;$$

and

$$M = \frac{27{,}050}{3400} = 7.96 \quad \text{or} \quad 8 \text{ machines.}$$

Step 2: Identify Gaps. We find capacity gaps by subtracting current capacity from projected capacity requirements. Any positive difference, or shortfall, is

Table 7.4

Selected Information about Products X and Y

Item	Product X	Product Y
Annual demand forecast (units)	2000	6000
Batch size (units)	40	60
Standard processing time (hr/unit)	4	3
Standard setup time (hr/batch)	5	8

a capacity gap. However, the correct capacity measure must be used. Complications arise when multiple operations and several resource inputs are involved. For example, when studying market-share statistics in the early 1970s many executives concluded that airlines having the larger share of seats flown get a larger share of the total passengers. In other words, fly more seats to get more passengers. The response by many airlines was to buy more jumbo jets. It soon became painfully evident that competitors flying smaller planes enjoyed more success. The key factor was the number of departures rather than the number of seats. The capacity balance between small and large planes had to be adjusted by selling or mothballing many of the jumbo jets. Another example of capacity imbalance is that of the resort operator who expanded the number of rooms in a lodge without expanding central services. The operator's reasoning was that room rentals, rather than parking lots or swimming pools, account for most of the revenue. Unfortunately, the number of guests turned out to be limited by these central services. Expanding only the number of rooms simply increased the vacancy rate. Capacity balance also applies to manufacturing. Expanding the capacity of some operations in a plant may increase overall capacity very little, if other bottleneck operations also are not expanded.

Consider Grandmother's Chicken Restaurant; we can use it to illustrate the correct approach. Grandmother's is known throughout Middlesburg for its unique chicken recipe and its homey atmosphere. Business has been excellent. Kathryn Shoemaker, the owner, expects total sales for this year (1987) to be $850,000, which strains the kitchen's capacity to its limit. If sales go any higher, customer service will be unacceptable during peak hours. Kathryn is putting together a capacity plan and has selected annual dollar sales as her capacity measure. Although the kitchen is operating at 100 percent utilization, the dining room still has some slack capacity. She estimates its average utilization rate to be 80 percent, which means that it can handle annual sales of up to $1,062,500 (or $850,000/0.80). Table 7.5 shows Kathryn's forecast of capacity requirements, along with how she figured the capacity gaps. Her

Table 7.5

Capacity Gaps at Grandmother's Chicken Restaurant

	Annual Estimates ($000)				
Projections	1988	1989	1990	1991	1992
Capacity requirements	920	995	1085	1175	1275
Capacity gaps:					
Kitchen (current capacity, $850,000)	70	145	235	325	425
Dining (current capacity, $1,062,500)	—	—	22.5	112.5	212.5

annual projections cover the period through 1992, when sales are expected to have increased by 50 percent over the current level.

Step 3: Develop Alternatives. The next step is to develop alternative plans for filling the projected gaps. Alternatives include the short-term options listed in Table 7.2, a number of timing/sizing options for adding new capacity, and expanding at a different location. Let's return to the Grandmother's Chicken example and suppose that Kathryn has narrowed her choices to two alternatives:

1. *Single-Stage Expansion.* Expand both the kitchen and dining area now, bringing their capacities up to $1,275,000 of sales per year. This level represents a 50 percent expansion of the kitchen and 20 percent expansion of the dining area. This alternative tends toward the expansionist strategy, in that capacity leads demand, and construction would be required only once during the next five years.
2. *Two-Stage Expansion.* Expand only the kitchen now, bringing its capacity up to that of the dining area ($1,062,500 of sales per year). If sales in 1988 and 1989 live up to expectations, expand both at the end of 1990 up to the $1,275,000 sales level. This alternative tends more toward the wait-and-see strategy. The initial expansion is less, but capacity would also lag behind forecasted sales in one year (1990), with the loss in potential sales being $22,500.

Step 4: Evaluate the Alternatives. In this final step, each alternative is evaluated, both quantitatively and qualitatively. *Quantitatively,* we estimate the changes in cash flows over the forecast time horizon. The cash flows into (cash inflows) and out of (cash outflows) the organization include revenues, costs, and changes in assets and liabilities. We are concerned here only with the increments of cash flows attributable to the project. Because these cash flows extend over several years, we would use a technique such as net present value to reflect the time value of money. (See Appendix A.) *Qualitatively,* we have to look at the fit of each alternative with overall capacity strategy and other aspects of the business that are not captured well by the net present value analysis. Of particular concern might be uncertainties about demand, competitive reaction, technological change, and cost estimates. Some of these factors cannot be quantified and have to be assessed on the basis of judgment and experience. Others can be quantified, and we can analyze each alternative, using different assumptions about the future. One set of assumptions could represent a worst case, where demand is less, competition is greater, and construction costs are higher than expected. Another set of assumptions could represent the most optimistic view of the future. This type of "what-if" analysis gives managers an idea of the implications of each alternative before making a final choice.

In Box 7.4, we show the assumptions and financial analysis for Grand-

Box 7.4

FINANCIAL COMPARISON OF CAPACITY ALTERNATIVES FOR GRANDMOTHER'S CHICKEN RESTAURANT

Kathryn Shoemaker estimates that her before-tax profit is 20 percent, which she arrived at by determining that, for each $100 of sales, $60 are required to cover variable costs and $20 to cover fixed costs (other than depreciation). Kathryn also made the following assumptions about the capital investment required for the two alternatives.

Alternative 1: Single-Stage Expansion	Alternative 2: Two-Stage Expansion
Initial investment of $200,000 at the end of 1987	Initial investment of $80,000 at the end of 1987 and an additional investment of $170,000 at the end of 1990
20-year life	20-year life for initial investment and 17-year life for the additional investment
Depreciation of $10,000 per year, with no salvage value	Depreciation of $4000 through 1990 and $14,000 ($4000 +$10,000) thereafter, with no salvage value

In addition, Kathryn assumed that federal and state taxes would be 50 percent of profits. The incremental cash inflows shown in Fig. 7.4 were calculated in the following manner (one example for each alternative).

1989 Cash Inflow for Alternative 1

Before-tax amount	$29,000	[($995,000 − $850,000)(0.20)]
Less depreciation	10,000	
Taxable amount	19,000	[$29,000 − $10,000]
Additional taxes	9,500	[$19,000(0.50)]
After-tax amount	19,500	[$29,000 − $9,500]

1991 Cash Inflow for Alternative 2

Before-tax amount	$65,000	[($1,175,000 − $850,000)(0.20)]
Depreciation	14,000	
Taxable amount	51,000	[$65,000 − $14,000]
Additional taxes	25,500	[$51,000(0.50)]
After-tax amount	39,500	[$65,000 − $25,500]

Each after-tax incremental inflow is then discounted using the factors in Appendix D.1 and the total is obtained for each alternative. The net present value for each alternative is calculated for the difference between the total discounted cash inflow and initial outlay. (See Appendix A for details.) For alternative 2 the initial outlay is equal to the initial investment of $80,000 plus the additional investment of $170,000 discounted for 3 years.

If the total discounted cash inflows exceed the initial outlay, the average return on investment exceeds the value used for the discount factor. Suppose that Kathryn has set a target for return on investment of 16 percent. Using 0.16 as the discount factor, we get the following net present values.

Single-Stage Expansion:	$12,518
Two-Stage Expansion:	$22,785

mother's Chicken Restaurant. Figure 7.4 shows the after-tax incremental cash flows for the two alternatives. The incremental cash inflows (above the horizontal line) are the profits enjoyed from higher levels of sales made possible by the increased capacity; the incremental cash outflows (below the horizon-

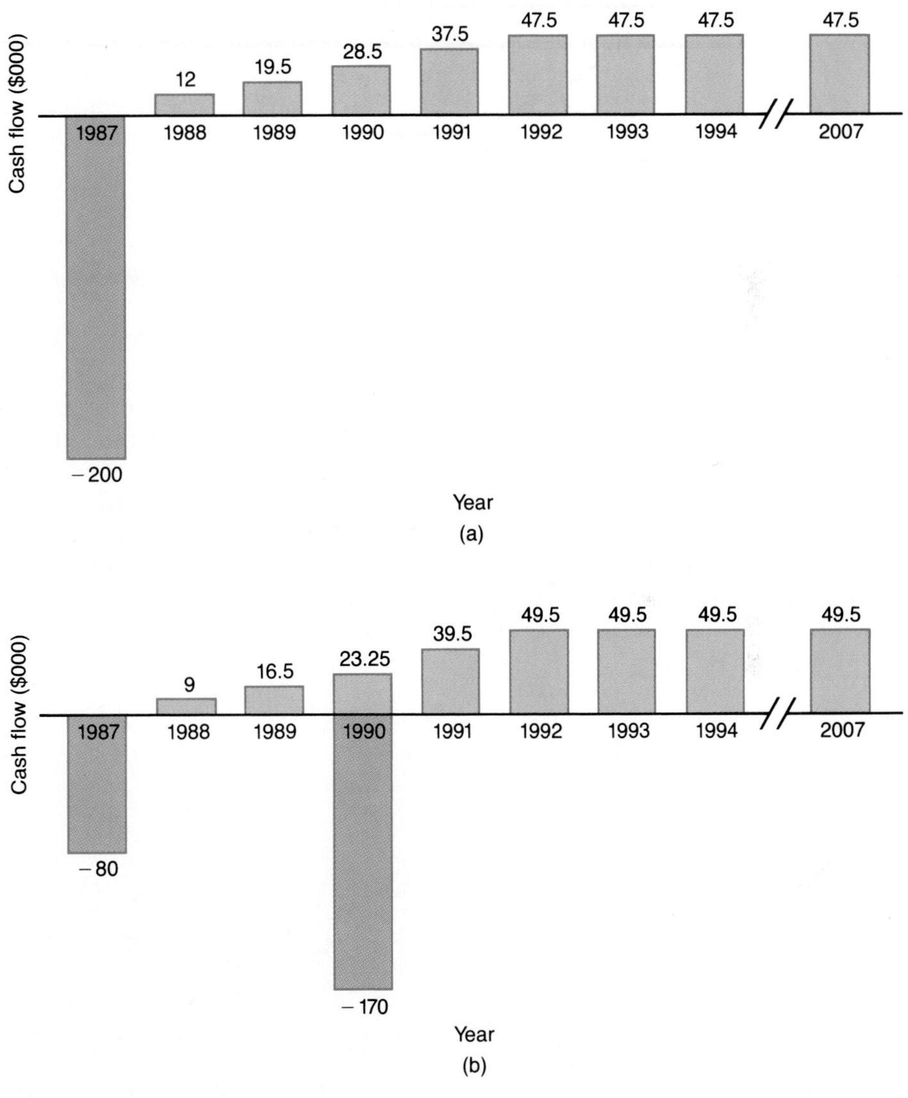

Figure 7.4

After-Tax Incremental Cash Flows ($000) for Grandmother's Chicken Restaurant: (a) Alternative 1 (Single-Stage Expansion); (b) Alternative 2 (Two-Stage Expansion).

tal line) represent the investment outlays for the expansion. Since the net present value of inflows minus outflows is positive, either alternative is better than not expanding at all. Of the two alternatives, the second is preferable. The disadvantages of higher construction costs and less revenue through 1990 are outweighed by having less excess capacity. Turning to qualitative considerations, the second alternative also has other advantages. Kathryn has more time to gauge demand. If her forecasts (Table 7.5) are wrong, she has a chance to adjust her plans before investing in a major expansion. The restaurant's "homey" image might be lost with a capacity much beyond the $1,062,500 sales level. Perhaps she should consider opening a second restaurant on the other side of town, rather than continuing to expand the first one. Alternative 2 also fits this possibility better.

MAINTENANCE

Maintaining the production capacity of an organization, regardless of the degree of capital intensity, is essential to long-term growth and profitability. The broad view of system maintenance includes, but is not limited to, machine maintenance. As you will learn later in this section, managers can choose from a number of other options in order to maintain a specific output rate. A basic problem in maintenance is to ensure adequate output performance while minimizing total operations costs. Obviously, some trade-offs must be involved. The graph in Fig. 7.5 reminds us of the automobile mechanic in the TV ad who says, "You can pay me now, or you can pay me later."

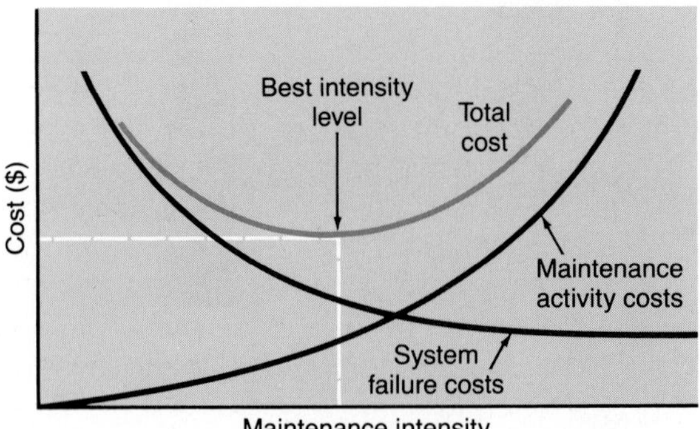

Figure 7.5

Maintenance Cost Trade-Off.

"Paying me now" equates to *maintenance activity costs*. These are the costs incurred in attempting to maintain the desired output rate. For an automobile, these costs would include oil changes, tune-ups, oil and air filter replacements, brake jobs, and tire balancing, rotation, and replacement. As maintenance intensity increases, so do maintenance activity costs.

"Paying me later" equates to *system failure costs*. These costs are incurred when the system fails to perform at the desired output rate. System failures never happen at a "good" time, typically require emergency measures, and can be costly. Hundreds of workers on a production line can be idled, along with expensive equipment, and customer shipments delayed just because one machine fails. Long-term disruption may require a firm to contract out work, rent equipment, hire more skilled workers, or pay overtime premiums. Disrupted or reduced customer service can also be costly in terms of dissatisfied customers and lost revenue. Airline customers may be delayed or rerouted because of equipment failure. An electric generating plant down because of equipment failure with no alternative means of power generation can lose customer revenues of as much as $1 million per day. Even in our automobile example, system failure resulting in an engine overhaul, a stalled car on a country road, or an accident because of faulty brakes can be very expensive.

The graph in Fig. 7.5 illustrates another important point: The objective is to minimize *total costs*. The intensity of the maintenance effort therefore should balance maintenance activity costs and system failure costs, so that their sum produces minimal total costs.

Varying Maintenance Intensity

Managers have several ways to intensify maintenance effort. Eight broad options are listed in Table 7.6. Some reduce the frequency of breakdowns, while others reduce the severity of a breakdown once it occurs.

Preventive Maintenance. One good way to help prevent breakdowns and poor performance is by **preventive maintenance** (PM). It can be triggered after a certain elapsed time or after so many hours of actual machine use. Preventive maintenance can also be triggered by inspections. For example, pilots and ground crews have checklists, which they use to spot problems. Preventive maintenance is especially attractive when the time between failures is fairly predictable and when breakdown costs are particularly high. Breakdowns are very costly to high-volume, capital-intensive manufacturers who operate with minimum inventory and work-force buffers. Such manufacturers use preventive maintenance extensively. Toyota operates only two production shifts, leaving a four-hour interval after each shift for preventive maintenance. This practice allows the production shifts to run with a minimum of disruption.

Table 7.6

Ways to Vary Maintenance Intensity

Option	Decreases Breakdown Frequency	Decreases Breakdown Severity
Preventive maintenance	X	
Early replacement	X	
Improved equipment and facility design	X	X
Operator involvement	X	X
Maintenance department capability		X
Redundancy		X
Resource flexibility		X
Inventory		X

Early Replacement. Replacing some parts in a machine before they fail is actually a form of preventive maintenance. This concept also applies to an entire machine. A point is reached where it is more economical to replace the machine with a new one. Savings in maintenance and operating costs pay for the investment outlay. The extreme case of replacement is the disposable product, such as the throw-away paper plates or inexpensive telephones now on the market. When it is time to service them, they are discarded for new ones.

Improved Equipment and Facility Design. Facilities and equipment designed for maintainability can be purchased. Although typically more expensive, they have more reliable components and are engineered to minimize maintenance. They are more trouble-free and easier to repair when trouble does arise. Modular TV designs mean quick repair with economically replaceable units. Another example is that of standardizing clearances, connections, and lubricants to simplify the repair process when the equipment fails. A third example is the practice in electronics industry to preuse or "burn in" components before final assembly. This minimizes the higher than normal chance for failure during the first few hours of operation, often called the "infant-mortality period."

Operator Involvement. Breakdowns are often caused by improper operation of equipment. Firms can increase maintenance intensity by providing better operator training. Operator involvement can also yield other benefits. For example, in some large Japanese manufacturing plants, operators' jobs are expanded to include routine inspection and care of their own equipment. They take pride in keeping their equipment in top shape, rather than leaving it to maintenance specialists. This form of horizontal job enlargement can help foster a committed and well-trained work force. The concept applies just as easily to workers in retail stores or offices.

Maintenance Department Capability. The capability of a maintenance department to maintain the desired output rate of the plant and equipment is reflected in several dimensions. Crew size might be much larger than needed *on the average* because of the unpredictability of breakdowns. Although this type of capacity cushion is expensive, the response to emergencies is quick. Another dimension is the skill mix selected by management. It can include highly trained technicians and state-of-the-art maintenance equipment. The department can then meet any contingency, rather than having to turn to outside contractors. A third dimension is scheduling. The department may have a sophisticated computer-based system to forecast workloads by skill category, schedule preventive maintenance, and react quickly to breakdowns.

Redundancy. The effects of breakdowns can be reduced through **redundancy.** We have already described how a capacity cushion helps absorb disruptions from equipment failures. Backup equipment that provides extra capacity is a form of redundancy. Another form is designing equipment with extra components in parallel. Thus if one component fails, the other can be activated. Suppose that there are two parts in a parallel configuration. Let the **reliability** of each one be 0.90, meaning that each one has a 90 percent chance of working at any time. This arrangement increases the system's reliability to 0.99. The system fails only if neither component works, which has a joint probability of only one percent [(1.0 − 0.9)(1.0 − 0.9)]. If these components were designed in series, where both must work for the whole system to work, the opposite occurs. The system's reliability is *less* than that of the components. The joint probability that both will work is only 81 percent [0.90(0.90)].

Resource Flexibility. The greater the flexibility of maintenance resources (work force and equipment), the quicker can be the response to service demands. Conversely, specialization results in more capacity bottlenecks. Resource flexibility also applies to the production facility itself. If products can be rerouted to alternative operations when equipment at one operation fails, the consequences of a breakdown are less. Cross-trained workers can move to other operations when their own equipment fails, rather than waiting idly until the repair is made. Of course, too much worker flexibility can prevent workers from mastering each job. If workers do not operate equipment correctly, even more maintenance problems might be created.

Inventory. Holding spare equipment parts in inventory shortens the time needed to fix a breakdown. It is a good idea to stock extra items that require long lead times for delivery, have a high rate of usage, and are relatively inexpensive, particularly if downtime costs are high. Production inventories can also help by meeting customer demand until production is restored. Air Force policy on jet engines is a good example. In order to have the planes ready when needed, a mix of repaired engines and new components is kept in inventory. Inventories are held at both the bases (where the planes are flying) and at a central depot.

Managing the Maintenance Department

Most organizations of any size create a maintenance department. It can be a single custodian in a small apartment building or several hundred employees in a large manufacturing plant. Nonetheless, the maintenance department is a miniature production system, cutting across the various decision areas in operations management. The questions in Box 7.5 are examples of the maintenance issues in each decision area. To be sure, there are issues unique to maintenance, including:

1. The type of information system needed.
2. The frequency of performing preventive maintenance.
3. When to replace equipment.

Box 7.5

DECISION AREAS AND ISSUES IN MAINTENANCE MANAGEMENT

- *Process design.* How much vertical integration, rather than contracting out maintenance jobs, is best? Are there better ways to do maintenance jobs?
- *Job design.* What should the lines of authority be? How much cross-training is best? Should production workers themselves become involved in equipment maintenance?
- *Work measurement.* How much effort should be spent getting good time standards for various routine work elements? What are the benefits that would result when scheduling work, controlling performance, and identifying areas for improvement? Should elemental standard data or work sampling methods be used?
- *Layout and location.* Should resources be positioned close to production areas (called "area maintenance") or at a centralized location?
- *Production and staffing plans.* How many workers are needed in each craft or specialty? Should more employees be hired or should more overtime and contracting be used to handle peak demands?
- *Inventory.* How much inventory is needed? Should it be in maintenance parts, production inventory, or some mix of the two? How are the key items to stock identified.
- *Scheduling.* How can response to breakdowns be quick, while still getting good resource utilization? Which jobs get priority?

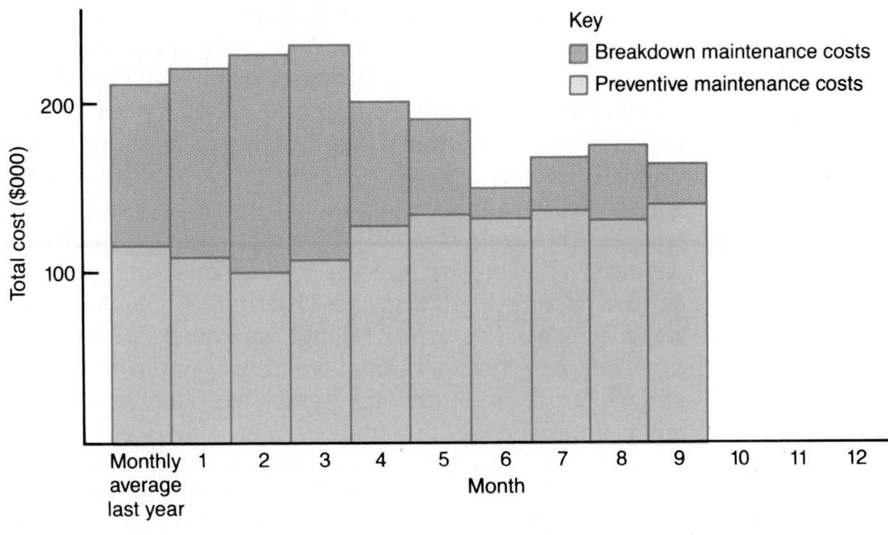

Figure 7.6

Comparative Maintenance Costs.

Information System. At the detailed level, information is needed about time standards, current inventory levels of spare parts, and the backlog of jobs to be scheduled. It is particularly important to keep records of the maintenance done on each piece of equipment. Only then can the machines causing high maintenance costs and breaking down often be discovered. Whether recorded on a manual or computer system, this detailed information is the necessary first step toward cost containment.

On a broader level, the information system should provide aggregate measures of performance, such as those shown in Fig. 7.6. The chart shows that the increase in preventive maintenance since the fourth month has paid off; breakdown costs are much lower. Other measures of interest are

1. Actual versus standard times of work elements performed by maintenance personnel.
2. Total downtime caused by breakdown repairs.
3. Allocation of maintenance costs to production.

Such information helps management determine whether costs are being controlled and whether the firm is getting full value from its maintenance effort.

Frequency of Preventive Maintenance. Senator Robert Byrd said, "Don't fix it if it ain't broke." But another saying is "Repair the roof before the rain falls." The best solution often lies somewhere in the middle.

Choosing PM frequencies to minimize costs is easier said than done because no one knows for sure when a piece of equipment might fail. If we did, we could schedule PM just before that time. Figure 7.7 shows two *failure distributions*. Curve (*a*) represents a rather typical situation: After a certain period of operating time the probability of machine failure increases rapidly. Curve (*b*) depicts a very complex machine, which has many components that are subject to failure. After an initial shakedown period, the probability of failure increases less rapidly. For each of these machines the problem is to determine the proper interval (in this case, measured in operating hours) between successive PM events. That interval could be very different for the two machines. The costs of doing scheduled PM must be balanced with the expected costs incurred from breakdowns and compared to the costs of other options for decreasing the frequency of system failure (such as early replacement, improved equipment design, and increased operator involvement). It is likely that some mix of these options will be best.

Whether the frequency of PM events is based on maintenance recommendations of the equipment manufacturer, historical data, or the maintenance supervisor's experience, the effect on the maintenance crew must be considered. With all the equipment that must be maintained in a plant, PM events should be scheduled to provide a level workload for the crew, allowing for some capacity cushion to handle unpredictable breakdowns. However, this may not always be possible.

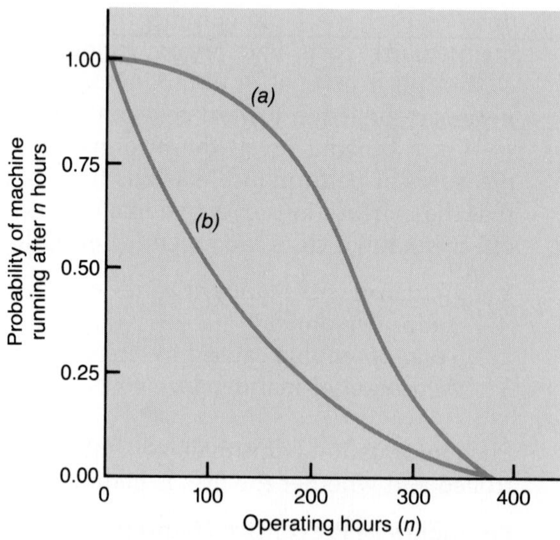

Figure 7.7

Failure Distributions for Two Different Machines.

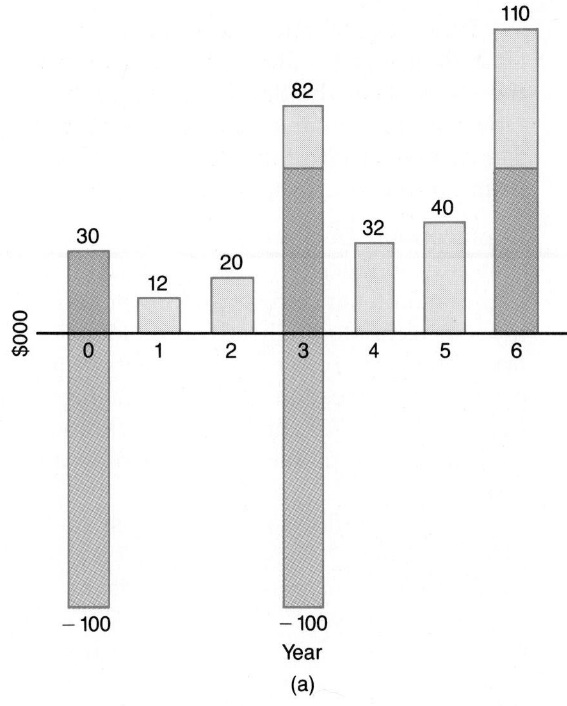

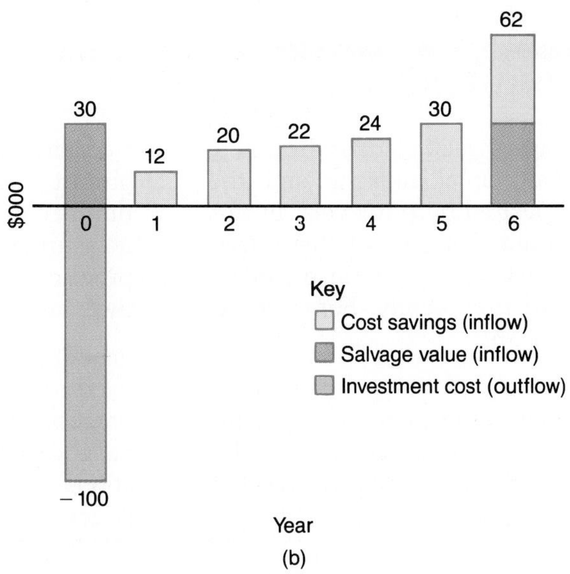

Figure 7.8

Two Replacement Options: (a) Replacement Every Three Years; (b) Replacement Every Six Years.

Preventive maintenance events should be scheduled during times that are least disruptive to operations. The most desirable time to schedule PM is after the last shift of the day or between shifts when two shifts are being used. However, firms that have three eight-hour shifts must use weekends as much as possible for PM. Sometimes, the only way to do PM is to take time away from production.

Replacement Decisions. It is important to know when to replace capacity that is economically or technologically outworn. Aging capacity brings on higher maintenance costs and lower efficiency, compared to the latest equipment or technologically advanced facilities. Savings in both maintenance and operating costs result from replacing equipment more, rather than less, frequently. The question is whether the higher capital investment is offset by the savings. Figure 7.8 illustrates cash flows from two different replacement policies: machine replacement every three years; machine replacement every six years.

The cash inflows are either cost savings or the salvage value of the replaced machine.* The data in Fig. 7.8 can be used to calculate present values for the two alternatives for comparison. The greatest difficulty lies in estimating the cash flows to begin with. The estimates depend on future demand, positions in product life cycles, technological advances, and maintenance costs, which pose a very complex forecasting problem.

CHAPTER HIGHLIGHTS

Operations managers must plan for the timely acquisition of additional capacity and the maintenance of desired output levels. In this chapter you learned that both of these decision areas are crucial to long-term organizational growth and profitability. Some of the chapter highlights are:

- Long-term capacity planning involves investment in new facilities and equipment, while maintenance strives to ensure a desired level of output rate for a given level of capital investment.
- Capacity can be measured as the maximum output rate, maximum input rate, or the number of input units. Complications in measuring capacity arise from changes in product mix and differentiation between peak and sustained capacity levels.
- Economies of scale derive from spreading fixed costs, reduced construction costs, and process advantages. Diseconomies of scale have forced many firms to focus their operations and move to smaller, rather than larger, facilities.

* Under both policies, a new machine is bought at the end of year 6, so cash flows need to be projected only that far. The salvage value, but not the investment outlay, should be included in year 6. The compensating benefits for an investment outlay in year 6 would begin after our planning time horizon.

- Capacity cushions can be small or large, depending on the cost of unused capacity, required delivery times, supply uncertainties, and uneven or uncertain demand.
- Three capacity strategies are expansionist, wait-and-see, and follow-the-leader. The expansionist strategy is attractive when there are economies of scale, learning effects, and a preemptive marketing approach. The wait-and-see strategy minimizes risk by relying more on short-term options. The follow-the-leader strategy maintains the current balance between competitors.
- Capacity choices must be linked to other operations management choices, ranging from competitive priorities to scheduling.
- The four steps in capacity planning are: (1) estimate capacity requirements; (2) identify gaps; (3) develop alternatives; and (4) evaluate the alternatives.
- Managers must select the right balance between maintenance activity costs and system failure costs. The intensity of maintenance can be varied along eight dimensions: preventive maintenance, early replacement, improved equipment design, operator involvement, maintenance department capability, redundancy, resource flexibility, and inventory.
- The maintenance department is a miniature production department cutting across the various decision areas in operations management. A maintenance information system is needed to discover what or who is causing high maintenance costs and breakdowns and also to provide aggregate measures of performance for top management.
- Choosing the best preventive maintenance intervals involves consideration of costs relative to other options for reducing the frequency of system failures, the workload of maintenance personnel, and the times available to perform the maintenance.
- Replacement decisions should include consideration of the cash flows for various replacement intervals using some type of present value analysis. Crucial input estimates for the analysis pose a very complex forecasting problem.

KEY TERMS

capacity
capacity cushion
economies of scale
focused facilities
preventive maintenance (PM)
redundancy
reliability

STUDY QUESTIONS

1. What factors make capacity planning a particular challenge?
2. What are the different ways of responding to capacity gaps?
3. What capacity measure would you recommend for a drive-in window at a bank? For an entire toy manufacturing plant? What complications might you run into when using these measures?
4. What types of estimates and forecasts are

needed for capacity planning? For maintenance planning?

5. A young boy has set up a lemonade stand on the corner of Speedway and Park. Temperatures get up to 110° during the summer. The intersection is near a major university and a large construction site. Explain to this young entrepreneur how his business might benefit from economies of scale.
6. Explain to the young entrepreneur in Question 5 the sorts of things that might lead to diseconomies of scale.
7. You are the manager of a small messenger service. Currently your average messenger utilization rate is 96 percent. Adding another messenger would reduce your average utilization rate to 85 percent. What factors would you consider in making a decision about this capacity increase?
8. We discussed the eight managerial options for total system maintenance shown in Table 7.6. Discuss each of them as they would relate to the operation of a ten-speed bicycle.
9. How does operator involvement relate to maintenance and job design? Worker flexibility?
10. Suppose that your automobile is ten years old. Discuss the cost trade-offs you would consider in replacing the car now versus waiting another year. Also, do you think that the best PM interval would change if you decided to replace your automobile every two years instead of every ten years? Explain.

PROBLEMS

1. Garden City had been burying all its residential trash in a landfill. Seven years ago the city built an electric generating plant to burn both residential and commercial trash. All refuse is burned, eliminating landfill costs entirely, and electricity is generated as a valuable by-product. Despite some initial controversy and start-up problems, the plant has been successful. However, its capacity of 80 megawatts (mW) will be reached next year. This capacity equates to 850 tons of trash per day, allowing for a capacity cushion needed for the peaking characteristics of customers. The capacity requirements in mW predicted for the next 20 years to burn all refuse are shown in Table 7.7.

   The mayor is considering three alternatives.

   Alternative 1: Expand enough at the end of year 0 to last for 20 years. This means a 50 mW increase (130 − 80).
   Alternative 2: Expand at the end of year 0 and at the end of year 10.
   Alternative 3: Expand at the end of years 0, 5, 10, and 15.

   Each alternative would provide a 130-mW

Table 7.7

Year	0	1	2	3	4	5	6	7	8	9	10	11	12	13	14	15	16	17	18	19	20
Capacity	80	82.5	85	87.5	90	92.5	95	97.5	100	102.5	105	107.5	110	112.5	115	117.5	120	122.5	125	127.5	130

capacity at the end of the 20-year time horizon. The value of the plant at that time will be the same, regardless of the alternative chosen. There are significant economies of scale in construction costs: A 12.5-mW expansion costs $25 million; a 25-mW expansion costs $36 million; and a 50-mW expansion costs only $54 million. The level of future interest rates is uncertain, leading to uncertainty about how much of a return should be expected from the expansions. The mayor believes that the necessary return could be as low as 10 percent and as high at 14 percent. (See Appendix A.)

(a) Compute the cash flows for each alternative. (*Note:* As a municipal utility, the operation pays no taxes.)
(b) Which of the three alternatives minimizes the present value of construction costs over the next 20 years, if the discount rate is 10 percent? 14 percent?
(c) Since the decision involves public policy and compromise, what political dimensions does the mayor face?

2. You have been asked to put together a capacity plan for a critical bottleneck operation at the Surefoot Sandal Company. Your capacity measure is number of machines. Three products (men's, women's, and unisex sandals are manufactured. The time standards (processing and setup), batch size, and demand forecasts are given in Table 7.8. Because of demand uncertainties, you obtained three demand forecasts (pessimistic, expected, and optimistic). The firm operates two eight-hour shifts, five days per week, and 50 weeks per year. Experience shows that a capacity cushion of 5 percent will suffice.

(a) What is the minimum number of machines needed? The expected number? The maximum number?
(b) If the operation currently has four machines and can expand capacity by 20 percent through short-term options, how many machines (if any) do you recommend be purchased?

3. Ivan M. Sharp owns a retail store that is experiencing significant growth. Ivan is trying to decide whether to expand its capacity, which currently is at $750,000 in sales per quarter. He is thinking about expanding to the $850,000 level. Construction costs would be $200,000. He estimates the investment life at 20 years, uses straight-line depreciation ($10,000 per year), pays taxes of 40 percent, and expects a return on his investment of at least 16 percent. Salvage value is assumed to be

Table 7.8

	Time Standards			Demand Forecast (000 pairs/yr)		
Product	Processing (hr/pair)	Setup (hr/batch)	**Batch Size (pairs/batch)**	Pessimistic	Expected	Optimistic
Men's	0.05	0.5	240	70	80	110
Women's	0.10	2.2	180	52	60	75
Unisex	0.02	3.8	360	80	120	170

negligible, and the before-tax profit from additional sales is 20 percent. Sales are seasonal, with peaks in the spring and summer quarters. Forecasts of capacity requirements expressed in sales per quarter are

Year	Qtr	Sales per Qtr ($000)	Year	Qtr	Sales per Qtr ($000)
1988	1	720	1989	1	800
	2	800		2	890
	3	780		3	860
	4	690		4	770

Demand in 1990 and beyond is expected to exceed $850,000 per quarter. Ivan believes the best time to expand is toward the end of the fourth quarter, either in 1987 or 1988, because this is the slowest part of the year.

(a) How much do 1988 after-tax profits increase if Ivan expands at the end of 1987? Does this benefit exceed the $32,000 opportunity cost [$200,000(0.16)] of investing at that time?

(b) Repeat (a) for the 1988 expansion option.

(c) Calculate the net present value of the 1988 expansion option, recognizing inflows for 1989 through 2008 (20 years). Should Ivan plan to expand at all? Explain.

4. The single milling machine at Stout Manufacturing has been severely overloaded during the last year. The plant operates eight hours per day, five days per week, and 50 weeks per year. Management prefers a capacity cushion of 15 percent. Two major types of products are routed through the milling machine.

Information	Product A	Product B
Annual demand forecast (units)	3000	2000
Batch size (units)	20	40
Standard processing time (hr/unit)	0.5	0.8
Standard setup time (hr/batch)	2	8

How many new milling machines are required if Stout does not resort to any short-term capacity options?

5. Two new alternatives have come up for expanding Grandmother's Chicken Restaurant. (See Table 7.5, Fig. 7.4, and Box 7.4.) Both alternatives would involve much more automation in the kitchen, featuring a special cooking process. Although the process is more capital intensive, the chicken tastes exactly like the original recipe. It also drives down the labor cost, so that the before-tax profit for *all* sales (not just the sales from the extra capacity added) goes up from 20 to 23 percent. This increases the pre-tax profit by three percent of each sales dollar through $850,000 and by 23 percent of each sales dollar between $850,000 and the new capacity limit. Otherwise, the new alternatives are much the same as the original two. The two new alternatives are:

- Expand both the kitchen and dining area now (at the end of 1987), bringing capacity up to $1,275,000 of sales per year. The construction cost, including the new automation, would be $335,000 (rather than the earlier $200,000). Assume a 20-year life, straight-line depreciation of $16,750 per year, and the same tax rate (50 percent).
- Expand only the kitchen now, bringing its capacity up to $1,062,500 of annual

sales. At the end of 1990, expand both the kitchen and dining area up to the $1,275,000 volume. Construction and equipment costs would be $424,000, with $220,000 at the end of 1987 and the remainder at the end of 1990. The initial investment has a 20-year life and the subsequent investment has a 17-year life. As with the first new alternative, the contribution margin goes up to 23 percent. Annual depreciation would be $11,000 through 1990 and $23,000 thereafter.

With both new alternatives, the salvage value will be negligible at the end of 2007 (20 years from now).

(a) Calculate the after-tax profits for each alternative.

(b) Calculate the net present value for each alternative, keeping the 16 percent discount rate. Which alternative is best?

(c) Should Grandmother's Chicken Restaurant expand with the new or the old technology?

6. An intricate part for a commercial airliner has a reliability of only 0.80, despite all engineering efforts to increase it. If four components are installed in parallel, and only one needs to function at a time, would you want to be a passenger on the airliner?

7. A new diagnostic machine costs $70,000 and has a life of 10 years. Riverside Hospital currently has a machine that is six years old. Annual maintenance and operating costs vary, depending on the age of such a machine. The information shown in Table 7.9 was gathered. The salvage values are after-tax inflows. Management is currently evaluating three policies:

- Keep the current machine for another four years, when its salvage value reaches zero.
- Buy a new machine now and every four years thereafter.
- Buy a new machine now and every two years thereafter.

Using the first policy as the "base case," an analyst calculated the following cash flows ($000) for the policy of replacing the machine every four years.

Year	Investment	Salvage Value	Annual Cost Savings
0	70	28	—
1			24 − 12 = 12
2			26 − 14 = 12
3			28 − 16 = 12
4		42	30 − 18 = 12

(a) What are the cash flows for the policy of replacing the machine every two years? Remember that the annual cost savings will be higher in the last two years, since maintenance and operating costs drop back to only $12,000 in the third year with the new machine.

Table 7.9

Age (yr)	Maintenance and Operating Costs ($000)	Salvage Value ($000)
1	12	63
2	14	56
3	16	49
4	18	42
5	20	35
6	22	28
7	24	21
8	26	14
9	28	7
10	30	0

(b) Calculate the net present value for replacing the machine every two or four years, compared to the base-case policy. Let there be straight-line depreciation; the discount rate, 12 percent, and the tax rate, 50 percent. Since the annual depreciation in this example will be the same for all three policies, depreciation does not shield the cost savings from taxes. Should the machine be replaced now? If so, is it better to wait two years or four years until the next replacement?

SELECTED REFERENCES

"America's Best Managed Factories," *Fortune,* May 28, 1984, pp. 16–24.

"Avoiding Plant Failures Grows More Difficult for Many Industries," *Wall Street Journal,* January 8, 1981.

Bott, Kevin, and Larry P. Ritzman, "Irregular Workloads with MRP Systems," *Journal of Operations Management,* vol. 3, no. 4, 1983, pp. 169–182.

Bowman, Edward H., "Scale of Operations—An Empirical Study," *Operations Research* (June 1958), pp. 320–328.

Buffa, Elwood S., *Meeting the Competitive Challenge: Manufacturing Strategy for U.S. Companies.* Homewood, Ill.: Dow Jones—Irwin, 1984.

Goldhar, J. D., and Mariann Jelinek, "Plan for Economies of Scope," *Harvard Business Review* (November–December 1983), pp. 141–148.

Hardy, Stan, and Lee Krajewski, "A Simulation of Interactive Maintenance Decisions," *Decision Sciences,* vol. 6, no. 1 (January 1975), pp. 92–105.

Hayes, Robert H., and Steven C. Wheelwright, *Restoring Our Competitive Edge: Competing Through Manufacturing.* New York: John Wiley and Sons, 1984.

Miller, Jeffrey, Jinchiro Nakane, and Thomas Vollmann, *The 1983 Global Manufacturing Futures Survey.* Working paper, School of Management, Boston University, 1983.

Sassar, W. Earl, "Match Supply and Demand in Service Industries," *Harvard Business Review* (November–December 1976), pp. 133–140.

Schmenner, Roger W., *Making Business Location Decisions.* Englewood Cliffs, N.J.: Prentice-Hall, 1982.

Skinner, Wickham, "The Focused Factory," *Harvard Business Review* (May–June 1974), pp. 113–121.

"Small Is Beautiful Now in Manufacturing," *Business Week,* October 22, 1984, pp. 152–156.

Wilkinson, John J., "How to Manage Maintenance," *Harvard Business Review* (March–April 1968), pp. 36–47.

CHAPTER 8

LOCATION

Some Strategic Issues

- Should we open facilities overseas? If so, how should they be managed?
- What factors should we consider to be dominant in picking a new location? Secondary?
- Should we expand on site, add a new facility, or relocate the existing facility?
- Should we locate near suppliers, the work force, or customers?
- How does the quality of life enter our location decision?
- Should we be leaders or followers in picking locations for new retail outlets?
- Should we organize multiple plants by product line, market area, or process? What about flexibility?

Chapter Outline

More than 3000 new plants are built and more than 7500 plants are expanded in a typical year in the United States. When we add to that the new stores, warehouses, office buildings, and medical facilities in the service industries, the importance of location decisions becomes apparent. Each time capacity plans call for expansion, the question of where to expand arises. The chief executive officer (CEO) of a midwest electrical supply company was flying across the southern United States when the needle on his jet's fuel tank suddenly plunged to empty. The pilot frantically radioed for help and landed at a nearby small airport in rural Arkansas. The CEO was extremely grateful and found the town much to his liking. Within a few weeks he picked the town as the site for his new manufacturing plant.

There are other such stories, but we should not conclude that location decisions are trivial and mainly based on executive whim. A poor location decision can negate wise choices made in the other areas of operations management. For example, plant location was critical for one small steel company. Kaiser Steel Corporation decided to close after having trouble with its steel operations for eight years. The major reason was that its only mill was in California where it faced the brunt of competition from Japanese imports.

Location decisions have strategic implications because they can assist in achieving company goals. For example, why are White Castle restaurants often located near manufacturing plants? Or, why do you often see many competing new-car sales showrooms grouped together? In the case of White Castle the strategy is to achieve market segmentation by catering to the blue-collar worker and thus locating near the target population and away from competitors like McDonald's or Wendy's. The strategy in locating new-car sales showrooms is to be close to the competition because new car purchases involve comparative shopping and customers prefer to do their shopping in one area. The strategies are quite different and the location decisions reflect this.

Recognizing the strategic impact of location decisions, we first examine the overall trends in location patterns and then consider the factors that influence location choices. Considering the strategic factors alone may not indicate the best specific location for a facility. Decisions are made quite differently, depending on whether a single facility or multiple facilities are involved. After considering both types of situation, we conclude the chapter with the special case of locating emergency units.

SIGNIFICANT TRENDS

It is fascinating to watch the changes in location patterns, which reflect changes in strategy. McDonald's had an urban strategy, but now is locating stores in some low-population centers. Holiday Inn followed a rural strategy but now is adding more units in urban locations. The steel industry is more dispersed than before. High-tech electronics firms are clustered to achieve a *critical mass,* but these concentrations are scattered across the country (California's Silicon Valley, Boston's Route 128 corridor, New York state, Phoenix, Colorado, Austin, Portland [Oregon], and Florida's "Gold Coast"). Four location trends are particularly evident: geographic diversity, movement to the growing Sunbelt, movement from declining urban areas, and the internationalization of production.

Geographic Diversity

The mix of business is broadening in most regions. Regions depend less than in the past on certain key industries. Electric and electronic machinery remains a key industry in New England, as do fabricated metals in the mideastern and textiles in the southeastern and food processing in the north central regions of the United States. However, these industries are relatively less important in those regions than just a decade ago. There are two causes of this trend. The first is *improved transportation and communication technology.* There has been a dramatic reduction in time to ship goods from Kansas City to New York City or from Osaka, Japan, to Kansas City. Air transportation also makes it easier for executives to visit branch plants. Telephone technology facilitates both voice communication between people and data communication between computers. The number of out-of-state phone calls doubled in one decade, standing at over 6 billion in 1980. This reduces the "friction of distance," so that a facility can service a larger market area and need not be close to its suppliers. In service industries, more back-room operations can be centralized at home offices, which can support a wider network of branch offices located near the customer.

The second cause of geographic dispersion, which widens the range of acceptable locations, is the *narrowing of regional wage differentials.* The Pacific region (California, Oregon, Washington, Alaska, and Hawaii) has enjoyed the highest income per capita, while the South (Maryland south to Florida and west to Texas) has suffered the lowest. In 1960, per capita income in the Pacific region was 120 percent of the national average, while in the South it was only 78 percent. However, by 1980, per capita income in the Pacific region stood at only 111 percent and the South moved up to 89 percent of the national average. The 42 percent difference [120% − 78%] dropped to 22 percent [111% − 89%] in just 20 years.

These factors expand the range of attractive locations. The *exact* location of a new facility is less critical today for many industries. However, it is still necessary to avoid "the big mistake." For example, the National Seating and Dimensional Company relocated to West Virginia for low labor rates, but went bankrupt trying to achieve the necessary worker skill levels. Other firms went bankrupt for *not* relocating, such as most of the textile companies that decided to stay in New England.

The Growing Sunbelt

Industry has tended to move south and west, away from the "Frostbelt" and into the "Sunbelt." Figure 8.1 shows how manufacturing employment shifted among regions from 1967 to 1977. Frostbelt employment decreased noticeably, particularly in the New England, mideastern and Great Lakes regions. For example, the Great Lakes' share of 28.3 percent of total manufacturing employment in 1967 dropped to 27.1 percent in 1977. The Sunbelt regions (southeastern, south central, southwestern and Pacific) compensated for these losses with 1–2 percent gains.

Several factors contribute to this movement. Reduced transportation and communication costs are two important factors, reducing the necessity for staying in the industrial heartland of the Great Lakes and mideastern regions. Some parts of the Sunbelt offer lower labor costs, less unionism, and possibly

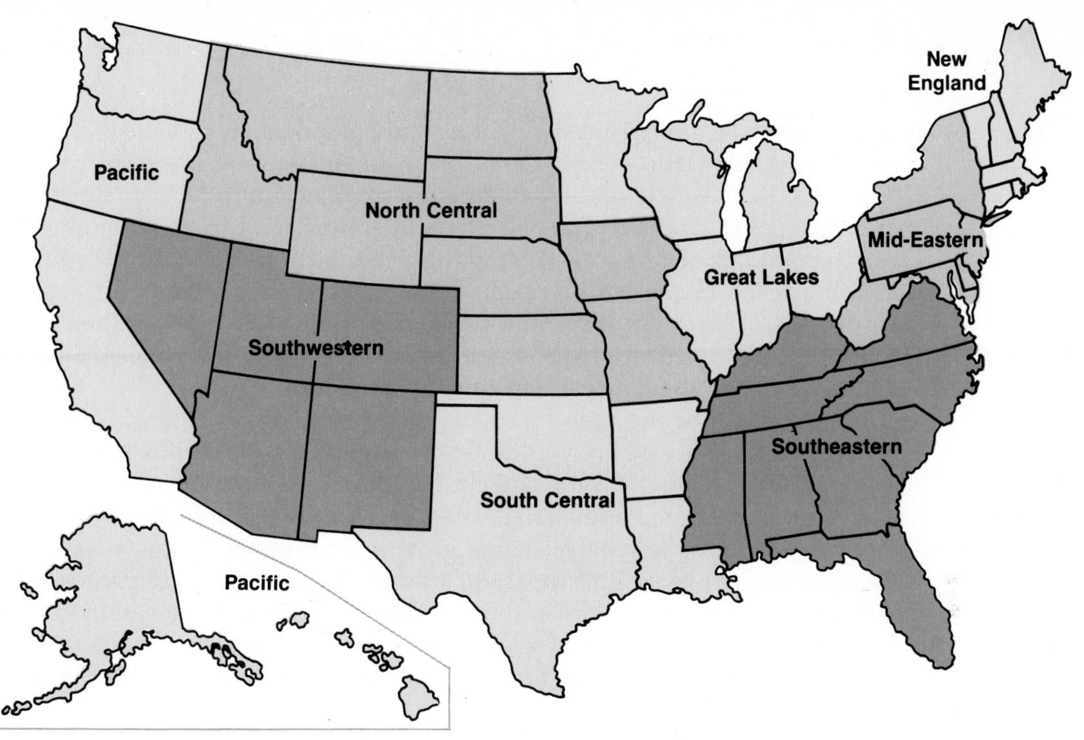

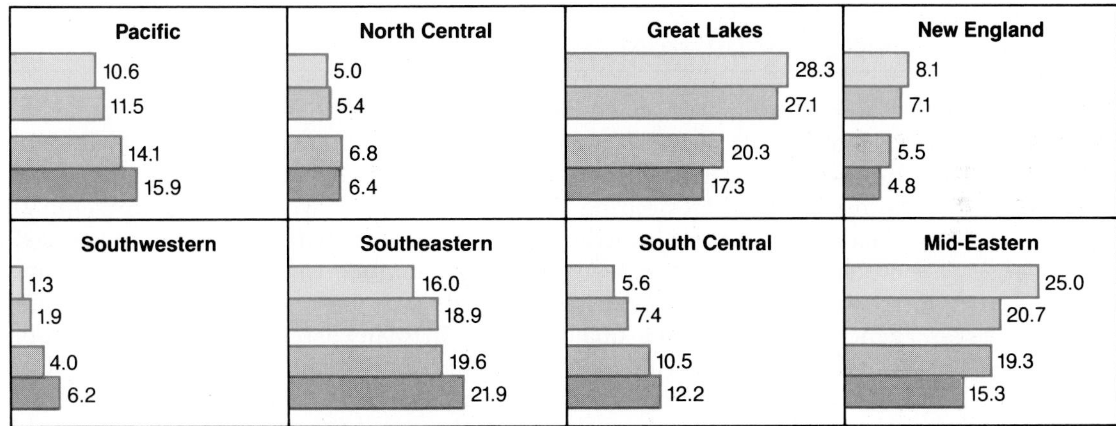

Key

- Percentage of total manufacturing employment—1967
- Percentage of total manufacturing employment—1977
- Percentage of total population—1980
- Percentage of total population projected—year 2000

Figure 8.1

Manufacturing Employment and Population Patterns.

Sources: Schmenner, Roger W., *Making Business Location Decisions.* Englewood Cliffs, N.J.: Prentice-Hall, 1982; "Where Growth Will Be Fastest, Slowest by 2000," *U.S. News & World Report,* September 19, 1983, p. 58.

a stronger work ethic. The advent of air conditioning and the increase in paid retirement have also favored the Sunbelt. Manufacturing has been concentrated in the Frostbelt, and manufacturers are reluctant to relocate their support and R&D activities. Sunbelt plants therefore tend to focus more on a specific product or process, allowing high-volume production, with products tending to be in the mature stage of their life cycles. This strategy takes advantage of labor cost differences, leaving products that are in their early stages for the Frostbelt plants and closer to R&D support activities. Sunbelt plants also tend to be newer and to be less unionized.

Figure 8.1 also shows forecasts of population changes between 1980 and the year 2000. Once again, you can see that the Sunbelt is attracting a larger share, at the expense of the Frostbelt. However, these projections should be viewed with caution. Population increases do not always bring large numbers of new businesses to an area. Rapid growth in areas with a low population base, for example, has little impact on location decisions, particularly for large retail chains. The mideastern and Great Lakes regions lead the nation in *sales density,* which is the dollars of retail sales per square mile. Since retailers need people with purchasing power in order to be successful, these regions remain the hottest retail markets.

Decline of Urban Areas

Manufacturing plants have also moved from the cities to rural areas (areas not including a city of 50,000 or more). A similar shift can be seen in Japan and the industrialized countries of Europe. Over 50 percent of the new industrial jobs in the United States during the last two decades went to rural areas—in all regions. Rural areas gained manufacturing employment even in the mideastern states. Gains have been particularly impressive in the southeastern and south central regions. Reasons for this shift include high crime rates and general decline of the quality of life in many large cities. Office location decisions are following suit. For example, IBM moved its corporate office from New York City to nearby Armonk, Ex-Cell-O Corporation moved from Detroit to nearby Troy, and Brunswick moved from Chicago to Skokie.

Internationalization of Production

Between 1976 and 1983, direct investment abroad of private U.S. assets increased from $136.8 billion to $226.1 billion, a 65 percent increase. At the same time, direct investment of private foreign assets in the United States jumped from $30.8 billion to $133.5 billion, a 333 percent increase. Many U.S. manufacturers also rely increasingly on foreign suppliers. Of the 20 most strategic materials, 17 are imported from four countries in southern Africa. Wage-rate differentials, expanding foreign markets, and improved transportation break down the barriers of time and space between countries. Having a local presence, with the product made where it is to be sold, can increase sales or decrease the threat of quotas. The result is a more linked world economy. In Box 8.1 we illustrate this trend with some specific companies. AccuRay, Ford, and Caterpillar are examples of manufacturing firms locating abroad. In the service industry McDonald's now operates 350 restaurants in Japan, while Allstate Insurance has 100,000 insurance policies in force there. In the second half of Box 8.1 we describe the activities of some foreign firms in a variety of industries (automobiles, electronics, and machine tools) that are building or acquiring facilities in this country.

Despite the advantages of more international production, a new set of problems arises, including differences in language, politics, and culture. Many firms are poorly equipped to handle these differences. For example, few U.S. managers know a foreign language. There are more English teachers in Russia than students studying Russian in the U.S. Such problems create three recurring issues for managers of international production:

1. Environmental adjustment.
2. Exporting techniques.
3. Organizing multinationally.

Environmental Adjustment. The overseas plant confronts the manager with unfamiliar labor laws, tax laws, and regulatory requirements. The role of government in foreign countries can be more dominant, requiring know-how to handle bureaucratic red tape. Hiring a foreign national to handle government contacts is not without problems, since this person is not well-versed on the firm's own policies and procedures. The economic environment can also be quite different. What seemed to be good policies on automation or inventory may be inappropriate overseas because of a different cost mix. Cultural differences are perhaps the most baffling. Foreign nationals comprise the work force and often much of the management team at an overseas plant. Their values, customs, and attitudes toward work can collide with policies adopted at the home office. These employees may not be sympathetic to what they consider to be strange approaches and may resist change.

Exporting Techniques. A second recurring issue is that of how much of the corporation's production methods to transplant overseas. If a firm totally accepts the approaches of the foreign managers and workers, some effective techniques and policies may be overlooked. The other extreme can be as bad, since some techniques and policies may not fit the new environment. Some compromise between the two extremes is normally best. For example, McDonald's menu (that is, its product plan) and restaurant layout are the same in Japan as in the United States. However, sites are selected and restaurants are built closer to adjoining buildings with Japanese preferences in mind. The

Box 8.1

INTERNATIONALIZATION OF PRODUCTION

Locating Overseas

AccuRay Corporation is a manufacturer of process control equipment headquartered in Columbus, Ohio. It is doubling its plant and work-force size at its plant in Ireland. One-third of its shipments are now finished at the Irish plant. AccuRay is one of 400 U.S. companies now operating in Ireland, where there is a skilled and low-cost work force.

Ford Motor Company moved the production of agricultural tractors from its Michigan plant to its plants in Belgium and England. Lower wage costs, the strong U.S. dollar, and the ability to consolidate production volumes saved enough to offset shipping costs to the United States.

Caterpillar Tractor Company shifted the production of bulldozers from Illinois and Iowa to Scotland, where more than 1000 Scots are now turning out bulldozers.

Influx of Foreign Firms

Several Japanese firms are locating production facilities in the United States. Honda located an automobile plant in Marysville, Ohio, with a work force of 2300. Mazda is building a plant in Flat Rock, Michigan, and will employ 3500 workers. Nissan Motor Company expanded its plant in Smyrna, Tennessee, to make the Sentra passenger car in addition to light trucks. These three facilities alone will have capacity of 780,000 cars and trucks per year. Moreover, a joint venture between Toyota and GM resulted in a new assembly plant in Freemont, California.

Four Japanese electronics companies (NEC, Fujitsu, Seiko, and Kyocera) are building five manufacturing plants in the Portland, Oregon, area. They will manufacture such products as personal computer printers and advanced fiber-optics telecommunications equipment.

The Le Blond Company has made metal working lathes since 1877. It is now called Le Blond Makino, after Japan's Makino Milling Machine Ltd. bought 51 percent interest in the company. Le Blond makes a wider range of products than before and is much more international. It now has a plant in Singapore and is selling lathes made by a West German firm. The machining centers assembled at its home base in Cincinnati, Ohio, will have half U.S. and half Japanese parts and labor.

Sources: "Three Columbus Firms Considering Ireland Plants," *Columbus Dispatch,* May 24, 1985; "Ford Will Move Production to Europe of Large Farm Tractors by End of Year," *Wall Street Journal,* February 15, 1985; "Jobs Lost at U.S. Caterpillar Plant Go to Scotland," *Wall Street Journal,* April 10, 1985; "First Sentra Due from U.S. Plant," *Columbus Dispatch,* March 25, 1985; "Why Oregon Suddenly Looks Good to High-Tech Companies," *Business Week,* November 5, 1985, pp. 138–140; "Making Machine Tools Increasingly Requires Ties to Foreign Firms," *Wall Street Journal,* September 4, 1984.

chain's trademark character is named Donald McDonald (rather than Ronald McDonald) because it is easier to pronounce.

Organizing Multinationally. Having multiple plants always raises the question of how much control the home office should retain. Language, cultural, and economic differences make this question that much more crucial for international operations. The home office can provide technical specialists to make decisions about equipment, inventory systems, quality control procedures, and the like. Such centralized control fits the strategy of doing things "our way" and can improve interplant coordination. The decentralized strategy of giving local managers more autonomy has its own advantages, such as adapting policies to local conditions, preserving incentives at lower levels, and minimizing the cost of a large central office.

FACTORS AFFECTING LOCATION DECISIONS

The desirability of a particular **facility location** depends on several factors. The description in Box 8.2 suggests that GM gave particular weight to union attitudes, outbound transportation costs, quality of life, and the availability of utilities when making its Saturn facility location decision. Comprehensive checklists have been developed to cover myriad factors that can be important in any specific situation. In order to pare the checklist to reasonable size, we can disregard some factors entirely if they do not qualify in at least one of two respects:

1. The degree of factor achievement must vary among the locations being evaluated. If the factor is not sensitive to location, it does not influence the choice.
2. The difference in the degree of factor achievement must be significant to management. A 50 percent differential is not that important if applied to a minor cost category.

Inbound transportation cost was of little importance to the Saturn plant decision because many parts are to be made on site. It was not a location requirement or even an important secondary factor.

We can designate some of the remaining factors as "*dominant*" and others as "*secondary.*" Dominant factors are derived from competitive priorities and are the factors that have a particularly large impact on sales or costs. Similarly, low wage costs might be a requirement for a labor intensive plant. Satisfying these requirements is mandatory if the facility is to be competitive. Secondary factors can also be quite important, but management may be willing to accept lower achievement on some of them to achieve higher scores on some others.

Box 8.2

GENERAL MOTORS LOCATES SATURN PLANT IN TENNESSEE

General Motors Corporation is locating its new $5 billion Saturn manufacturing complex for small cars in Spring Hill, Tennessee. Approximately 6000 workers will assemble 500,000 cars per year. The facility will be the most integrated car operation in the United States with many parts made by one of several feeder plants located on site. About 150 acres will be under one roof. The economic benefits from a $200 million annual payroll led governors and developers to offer over 1000 possible locations in more than two dozen states. The selection process was done partly by computer, but dragged out for more than the expected three or four months.

While the facility will be located in a historically anti-union state, it will be operated by a UAW work force. The contract is quite innovative, providing for an unprecedented degree of worker flexibility and more of a "consensus decision-making" structure. UAW officials welcome the close proximity to a Nissan plant, which they have been unable to organize to date. Spring Hill offers major rail and highway routes to most customers within 500 miles. While a Michigan site would be closer to existing suppliers, most major parts will be made on site. Locating close to the customer is more important than locating close to the supplier. Spring Hill is near Nashville, a metropolitan area offering a variety of educational and cultural activities. The state offers a stable economic climate, with adequate water and electric power. After considering 60 different location factors, GM concluded that Spring Hill offered the "best balance" of them. Saturn Corp. headquarters and the engineering staff, however, will be located in Michigan near Detroit.

Source: "GM Is Expected to Put Saturn Complex in Tennessee as UAW Board Votes Pact," *Wall Street Journal,* January 29, 1985.

Dominant Factors

Based on interviews and survey data, five clusters of factors were found to dominate location decisions for new manufacturing plants (Schmenner, 1982). The percentage for each factor cluster represents the proportion of those responding who picked it as a "must" when considering a new plant opening.

1. Favorable labor climate (76%).
2. Proximity to markets (55%).
3. Quality of life (35%).

4. Proximity to suppliers and resources (31%).
5. Proximity to company's other facilities (25%).

A favorable labor climate was a dominant factor for 76 percent of the new plant openings. This climate comes partly from low labor costs, which is a function of wage rates, training requirements, attitudes toward work, and worker productivity. Another aspect of the labor climate is concern about unionization. Many executives believe that a low probability of unionism is a major advantage. One indicator of this attitude is that, while 50 percent of U.S. industry is unionized, only 20 percent of new plant openings have unions. The only exception to this pattern is in the Great Lakes region, where 60 percent of new plants are unionized from the outset. Firms that emphasize labor climate are naturally more labor intensive, such as in the textile, furniture, and consumer electronics industries.

Proximity to markets is the next most frequently mentioned requirement. This relationship is particularly important when outbound transportation rates are relatively high, such as with commodity items that are relatively inexpensive to produce but are heavy or bulky. Paper, plastic pipe, cans, heavy metals, and processed foods are good examples of such products.

Quality of life in the area received a much lower rating from representatives of all but one of the industrial groups. The lone exception is high-tech executives, who rate it at the top of the list. Attracting and keeping a good engineering staff is much more important to them than the labor environment or transportation costs. A university in the vicinity or an attractive living style can make the difference.

Proximity to suppliers and resources was of relatively low importance to respondents from most industries, except for those relying on bulky or heavy raw materials. In such cases inbound transportation costs become a dominant concern and forced location near suppliers. For example, paper mills are located near forests and food processing facilities near farms. Nearby suppliers can offer other advantages as well, such as lower inventories.

The final dominant factor listed frequently is *proximity to the parent company's other facilities*. Some plants are feeders to others, or rely on other facilities for management or staff support. These ties require substantial amounts of coordination and communication, which distance makes more difficult.

Many other factors can emerge as important in any given situation, including the cost of shuffling people and materials between plants; utility costs (energy, water, and telephone); state, county, and local taxes; financing incentives offered by state or local governments; relocation costs; and executive preferences. After the location choice is narrowed from a region to a specific site, still other factors are introduced: room for expansion, land and construction costs, accessibility to the airport and expressway, rail service, insurance, competition from other firms for the work force, local ordinances (such as pollution or noise control), governmental help with roads and labor training, community attitudes, and many others. Community attitudes are sometimes difficult to measure, and it is unwise to overlook small but vocal protest groups. Even though the governor, mayor, and city council may give their blessings, those officials are temporary occupants of their positions, and the community mood can change with the next election.

Factors in the Service Sector

Warehouse location decisions are similar to those for manufacturing plants, with low transportation costs being a requirement. The difference is that proximity to markets begins to take on larger importance. Part of the reason for establishing warehouses, other than reducing transportation costs, is to position inventory closer to the customer. The influence of location on revenues is even more important for most other service facilities. In fact, it usually dominates all other factors for retailers, banks, supermarkets, dry cleaners, hotels, hospitals, restaurants, and local government services, which all strive to be close to their target customers and clients. Residential density, traffic volumes, and income levels are important aspects of estimating sales impact. Each of the six factors mentioned in Box 8.3 for a fast-food restaurant chain relates to impact on revenues. Another lesson from the information in Box 8.3 is that the dominant factors must fit a firm's product plans, such as having the lunch-hour crowd as its target market.

One complication in estimating the sales potential at various locations is the impact of competitor locations. Not only must their current locations be considered, but also competitor reactions to a firm's new locations should be anticipated, even though they may be difficult (if not impossible) to predict. Often customers buy at the nearest store, so it pays to avoid areas where competitors are already established. In other cases, just the opposite occurs, and it is advantageous to locate in a cluster near other competitors. This is clearly the case for new-car sales showrooms, as mentioned earlier, and for the fast-food chain in the Box 8.3 example. A critical mass is created, whereby the total number of customers attracted exceeds the total number who would be attracted to the same stores at scattered locations. Recognizing this effect, some firms use a follow-the-leader strategy when selecting new sites.

SINGLE-FACILITY LOCATION

For now, let's consider locating only one new facility. If it is part of a larger network of a firm's facilities, we will assume that there is no interdependence. This assumption holds in the case of the chain in Box 8.3, where a decision to open a restaurant in Tampa, Florida, is independent of where its restaurants are located in Paris, Texas.

Box 8.3

LOCATION FACTORS FOR A FAST-FOOD RESTAURANT CHAIN

In just a decade a fast-food restaurant chain grew from one to a thousand restaurants in North America and Japan. All units are built to company specifications for exterior style and interior decor. Twenty percent of the stores are company-owned, with the rest owned by franchisers. In either case, six factors are given primary attention in location decisions:

1. Area employment.
2. Retail activity.
3. Competitor locations.
4. Traffic flow.
5. Residential density.
6. Accessibility and visibility.

Area employment is crucial since the target market is 20- to 45-year-old employees eating during their lunch break. Shopping centers, manufacturing plants, and offices with large work forces are ideal, so long as the employees are allowed off premises during breaks. *Retail activity* in the area is important, since going to the restaurant is often an impulse-buying decision. Having the facility near other stores capitalizes on trips shoppers make to the area for other reasons. Being near *competitor locations* is seen as an advantage. Having successful food outlets nearby shows that a good market exists. Competitors can be observed to assess the intensity and direction of customer flows throughout the day. These flows can be compared with national averages to see if they are above or below average. *Traffic flows* are important because most of the business is from people in cars, and 40 percent of sales is from the drive-by window. Management considers a traffic flow of 16,000 cars per 24-hour period good. *Residential density* is another important factor, with 20,000 residents within a two-mile radius considered good. This population density ensures nighttime and weekend business. An upper-middle class population is preferred. *Accessibility and visibility* make up the last dominant factor. Possible backups of traffic into and out of the site during the noon rush hour are carefully considered. The volume and direction of traffic by time of day, traffic signals, intersections, and traffic medians are all part of accessibility. Visibility involves distance from the street and the size of nearby buildings and signs.

Data are collected for each site before management's review, including all information on the six dominant factors and much more. For example, an on-site evaluation form covering 16 characteristics is filled out by a manager. There are competitive analysis forms and a work map showing the location of current stores, competition, retail centers, plants, and the like. Management uses judgment and past experience to make a decision about each site. Consideration is being given to the use of more analytical methods to assist with the more difficult decisions involving potential market saturation.

On-Site Expansion, New Plant, or Relocation

The first thing to consider is whether to expand on site, build another facility, or relocate to another site. A survey of *Fortune* 500 firms during the 1970s showed that 45 percent of the expansions were on-site, 43 percent were at new plants, and only 12 percent were relocations (Schmenner, 1982). *On-site* expansion is favored for keeping management together, reducing construction time and costs, and not having to split up operations. At some point, a plant is expanded to the point where focus is lost and diseconomies of scale set in. Poor materials handling, employee "job bumping," the increasing complexity of production control, and simply the lack of space all argue for building a new plant or relocating the existing one. Those deciding to *build a new plant* cited additional reasons, such as not having to rely solely on production from a single plant, escaping unproductive labor, modernizing with new production technology, and reducing transportation costs. *Relocating* an existing plant also addresses the problems of continued on-site expansion. Most firms that relocate are small (less than 10 employees), single-plant companies cramped for space and needing to redesign their production processes and layouts. Over 80 percent of all relocations are within 20 miles of the first location, so as to retain the current work force (Schmenner, 1982).

A Systematic Selection Process

Selecting a new facility location involves a series of steps. The process is triggered, for example, by a retailer's perceived ability to increase profits with another outlet or perhaps a hospital's projection of a bed shortage. Those responsible for location decisions can be a joint division–corporate staff team for a large corporation or just the owner for a small company. With small companies, the decisions are made less formally and normally involve only a local search.

The next step is to identify the important location factors, often breaking them into dominant and secondary categories. These factors become the basis for evaluating different locations. Alternatives are first considered in terms of overall regions, then are narrowed down to communities, and finally to specific sites. Perhaps 5–15 sites are thoroughly evaluated. Data are collected from various sources, including location consultants, state development agencies, chambers of commerce, banks, electric power companies, land developers, realtors, and on-site visits.

The data are then analyzed. For quantifiable financial factors, cash flows can be projected, including a breakdown by each cost category (such as inbound transportation, outbound transportation, labor, construction costs, and utilities) and each revenue source (such as a stock or bond issue, sales, and interest income). These factors often are converted to a single measure of financial merit, such as present value or payback. (See Appendix A.) Qualitative factors pertaining to each site are then evaluated. Some managers, such as those in the fast-food chain (Box 8.3), are comfortable with seeing only the expected performance on each factor. Others prefer a more formalized way of dealing with multiple criteria. A weighted score can be calculated for each alternative site, provided that it has already passed the threshold for the dominant factors. The weighted score is calculated much the same as the preference matrix for product planning. (See Chapter 2.) Table 8.1 shows the calculation of the score for a hypothetical site. A weight is assigned to each factor, so that the weights in this case add to 100 percent. Factors are assigned scores of 1 for poor and 5 for excellent. The weighted score is obtained by multiplying each factor score by the factor weight and then adding the weighted scores. The scores and weights shown in Table 8.1 are arbitrary; many others may be equally as good.

The end result is a final report containing site recommendations and a summary of the data and analyses on which they are based. In large companies, an audio-visual presentation of the key findings of the site selection process is also made to top management.

Load–Distance Method

Looking back through the various location factors, you can see that many relate to distance. Proximity to markets, proximity to suppliers and resources, proximity to other company facilities, average distance to target customers, and even the response time of fire engines all have to do with distance. The **load–distance method** deals with proximity factors and can be used to sharpen the early stage of location analysis. Before using this method, you

Table 8.1

Weighted Location Score for a Site

Location Factor	Weight (*a*)	Score (*b*)	Weighted Score (*a* × *b*)
Total patient miles per month	25	4	100
Facility utilization	20	3	60
Average time per emergency trip	20	3	60
Expressway accessibility	15	4	60
Land and construction costs	10	1	10
Employee preferences	10	5	50
		Weighted Location Score =	340

must be able to express the distance between two grid coordinates on a map. You will also need this capability for layout planning in Chapter 9.

Distance Measures. Suppose that in Fig. 8.2 point A, at coordinates (20, 10), represents a possible location for a new warehouse. Point B at coordinates (80, 60) represents one of the plants supplying the new warehouse. What is the distance between the two facilities? The best answer is the actual travel distance, but this distance can be time-consuming to calculate. If shipments are by truck, the distance traveled depends on the highway system and the specific route taken. For rough calculations, which is the real purpose of the load–distance method anyway, you can use either a **euclidean distance measure** or a **rectilinear distance measure.** *Euclidean* distance is the length of the dotted line connecting points A and B in Fig. 8.2 and is the shortest possible distance between them. It is found by squaring the difference between the x-coordinates, adding this to the squared differences between the y-coordinates, and taking the square root of this sum. The mathematical expression, which is the formula for the length of the hypotenuse of a right triangle, is

$$d_{AB} = \sqrt{(x_A - x_B)^2 + (y_A - y_B)^2},$$

where

d_{AB} = Distance between points A and B;

x_A = x-coordinate of point A;

y_A = y-coordinate of point A;

x_B = x-coordinate of point B; and

y_B = y-coordinate of point B.

Using the coordinates in Fig. 8.2 and solving for d_{AB}, we get

$$d_{AB} = \sqrt{(20 - 80)^2 + (10 - 60)^2} = 78.1.$$

Rectilinear distance assumes that the trip is made with a series of 90° turns, as along city blocks. This distance is essentially the sum of the two dotted lines representing the base and side of the triangle in Fig. 8.2. The distance traveled in the x-direction is the absolute value of the difference in x-coordinates. Adding this result to the absolute value of the difference in the y-coordinates gives us

$$d_{AB} = |x_A - x_B| + |y_A - y_B|.$$

For our example, we get

$$d_{AB} = |20 - 80| + |10 - 60| = 110.$$

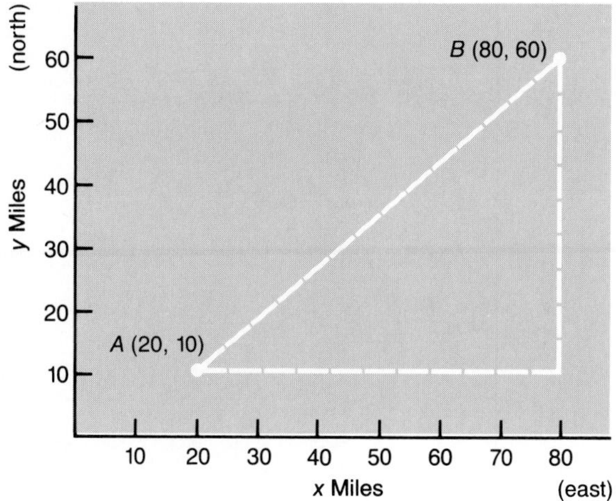

Figure 8.2

Distance between Two Points.

Calculating a Load–Distance Score. You can use either of the distance measures* to calculate a load–distance score for any location to be evaluated. You multiply the loads flowing to and from a facility by the distances traveled. The flows may involve shipments from suppliers, between plants, and to customers. They can represent travel to or from the facility by employees or clients. Some adjustments may be needed, as when an inbound trip is twice as costly per mile traveled as an outbound shipment. Expressed mathematically, the load–distance model is

$$ld = \sum_i l_{fi} d_{fi},$$

where

ld = Total load–distance score, summed over all flows;
l_{fi} = Load (such as tons or number of trips) between the facility being located (facility f) and some other facility (facility i); and
d_{fi} = Distance (actual, euclidean, or rectilinear) between facilities f and i.

Full-Grid Search. Intuitively, the location that minimizes ld is the one that has big loads going short distances. It is a relatively simple matter to cost out different locations with this model, following some systematic search process.

* The euclidean and rectilinear measures give quite different numbers: 78.1 versus 110, in our example. However, our interest is in the *relative* performance of different locations, and we use only one of the distance measures throughout the calculations. When it comes to finding the best location, the distortion caused by using one measure, when the other more closely approximates the actual distance, is relatively small.

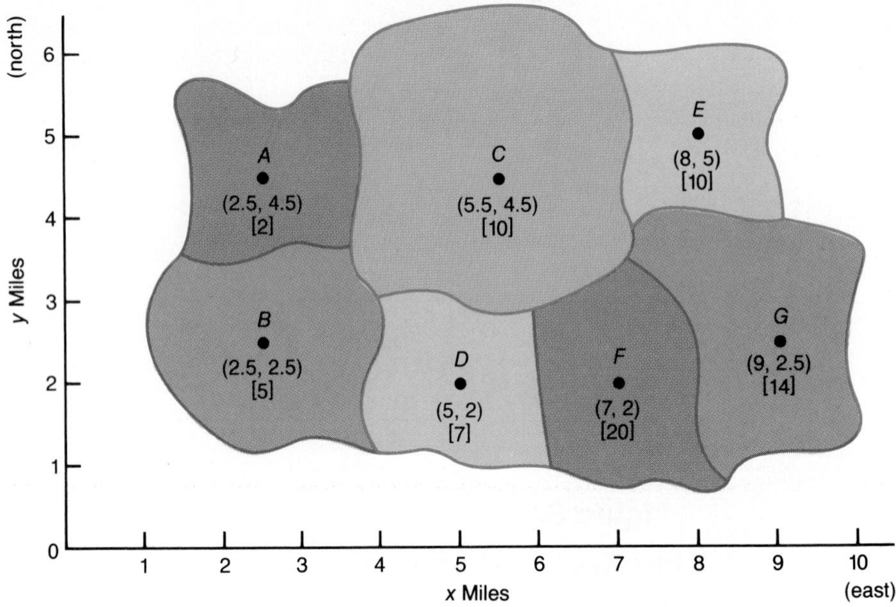

Figure 8.3

Census Tracts in a City.

Note: Numbers in parentheses are census tract coordinates; the number in the brackets is the population (000) of the census tract.

For example, suppose a medical facility is to be located in a fast-growing portion of a city. The facility is targeted to handle the seven census tracts shown in Fig. 8.3. The coordinates for the center of each census tract are shown, along with projected populations. With such data, you can calculate load–distance scores. Calculations for locating the medical facility at (7, 2), using the rectilinear distance measure, are shown in Table 8.2. For example, the distance between census tract A at (2.5, 4.5) and the proposed location at (7, 2) is 4.5 miles in the east–west direction, plus 2.5 miles in the north–south direction, or 7 miles. This distance multiplied by the population equals 14, or the *ld* score for census tract A. The sum of the *ld* scores is the total *ld* score for location (7, 2). Similar calculations were made for a grid search of several alternative locations; their scores are shown in Fig. 8.4. Of the points investigated, the (7, 2) location is best because its score of 168 is the lowest for the 15 points investigated. An acceptable medical facility site might not be available in the immediate area of (7, 2), but Fig. 8.4 also shows the implications of selecting a location elsewhere. For example, a two-mile deviation directly north to (7, 4) increases the score to only 197, which is less of a penalty than the same deviation to the east or west.

Table 8.2

Load–Distance Score for Location (7, 2)

Census Tract	Coordinates x	Coordinates y	Population (000) (l)	Rectilinear Distance (d)	$l \times d$ (000)
A	2.5	4.5	2	4.5 + 2.5 = 7	14
B	2.5	2.5	5	4.5 + 0.5 = 5	25
C	5.5	4.5	10	1.5 + 2.5 = 4	40
D	5	2	7	2 + 0 = 2	14
E	8	5	10	1 + 3 = 4	40
F	7	2	20	0 + 0 = 0	0
G	9	2.5	14	2 + 0.5 = 2.5	35
				Total ld =	168

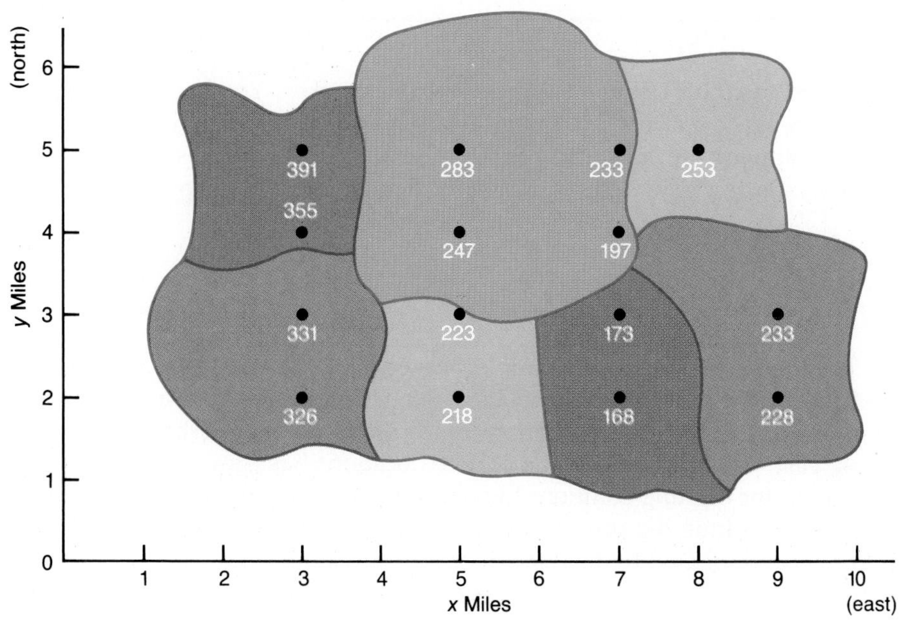

Figure 8.4

Load–Distance Scores from Grid Search.

Table 8.3

Calculating the Center of Gravity of a Target Area

Census Tract	Coordinates x	y	Population (000) (l)	lx	ly
A	2.5	4.5	2	5	9
B	2.5	2.5	5	12.5	12.5
C	5.5	4.5	10	55	45
D	5	2	7	35	14
E	8	5	10	80	50
F	7	2	20	140	40
G	9	2.5	14	126	35
			$\sum l_i = 68$	$\sum l_i x_i = 453.5$	$\sum l_i y_i = 205.5$

$$x^* = \frac{\sum_i l_i x_i}{\sum_i l_i} = \frac{453.5}{68} = 6.7$$

$$y^* = \frac{\sum_i l_i y_i}{\sum_i l_i} = \frac{205.5}{68} = 3.0$$

Patterned Search. Using a *patterned search* is quicker. You begin by locating the facility at the *center of gravity* of the target area. This location is usually not the optimum for the euclidean or rectilinear distance measures, but still is an excellent starting point.* Its coordinates, denoted x^* and y^*, are

$$x^* = \frac{\sum_i l_i x_i}{\sum_i l_i} \quad \text{and} \quad y^* = \frac{\sum_i l_i y_i}{\sum_i l_i}.$$

For the medical facility example, the center of gravity is (6.7, 3.0). The method of calculation is shown in Table 8.3. Using this location as the starting solution, you next evaluate locations in the vicinity, say, one-half mile north, south, east, and west of it. If one of these locations has a lower load–distance score than the starting solution, the best one becomes the new starting solution. You continue the process by searching in the near vicinity of this new starting solution. Eventually none of the directional changes uncovers a better solution. The current "starting solution" is then your final solution. Patterned

* If the distance measure is $\sum_i [(x_i - x^*)^2 + (y_i - y^*)^2]$, that is, the square of the euclidean measure, the center of gravity location is optimal.

search has the advantage of speed but does not have the added information provided by a full grid search and may result in a suboptimal solution.

MULTIPLE-FACILITY LOCATIONS

Sometimes a new facility must be located within a network of existing, interdependent facilities. This situation introduces new issues, such as plant charters and how to allocate work to each facility.

Plant Charters

When a company has several plants, management must figure out how best to divide responsibilities between them. At least informally, each has a **plant charter,** which clarifies its responsibilities and focuses its activities. Four plant charter strategies are listed below, with the percentage in parentheses indicating frequencies found in actual practice (Schmenner, 1982):

1. Product plant (58%).
2. Market-area plant (31%)
3. Process plant (9%).
4. General-purpose plant (3%).

Product Plant. The **product plant** strategy is the most popular. The demand for any one product is satisfied by one plant or just a few plants, which distribute goods to all market areas. Product specialization allows higher volume production than is possible otherwise. This strategy is particularly attractive when (1) production of certain products requires a favorable labor climate or proximity to suppliers and resources; and (2) outbound transportation costs are not excessive. For example, 83 percent of the companies reporting to be "labor-rate sensitive" (in textiles, furniture, and consumer electrical goods) have product plants, well above the industrial norm of 58 percent. Product plants tend to be nonunion, experience changing product mixes, and are more independent and self-sufficient, having their own staff and engineering capabilities.

Market-Area Plant. As its name implies, the **market-area plant** strategy is chosen when proximity to markets is the dominant location factor. Each plant produces all or most of the products for its assigned market area. This strategy makes sense when heavy or bulky products result in high outbound transportation costs, such as in the paper, plastic, pipe, glass, and oil refining industries. Producing these commodity-like goods requires little customization, which permits a product-focused strategy, lower worker skills, and higher capital intensity.

Market-area plants also make sense when fast delivery times and customized products (rather than low transportation costs) are crucial, such as for a company that makes architect-specified building products. A firm establishes small beachhead plants for each market area early in the product life cycle, which prevents it being blocked from certain market areas. Although initial costs can be high, so can the payoff as sales expand. The Trus Joist Company, which makes customized roof and floor support systems, followed this approach. It faced competition from small firms (that did not enjoy economies of scale) and large firms alike. By developing a manufacturing process that was efficient at low volumes, it built more than a dozen beachhead plants before total sales even reached $100 million (Hayes and Wheelwright, 1984).

Process Plants. The **process plant** strategy assigns to each plant a different segment of the production process. Each plant utilizes only a few technologies. This segregation provides higher volumes for each process, which is important when economies of scale are significant. Some plants become feeders to others, such as when components made at some plants are sent on to a final assembly plant. Process plants are more frequently chosen for producing complex products, such as computers. While only 9 percent of all companies reporting have process plants, 19 percent of the high-tech firms (office equipment, computers, electronics, and instruments) favor process plants (Schmenner, 1982). Even if a firm prefers less vertical integration, it may elect to perform some processes in-house. For example, it may have developed a special technology that gives it a competitive advantage, which is ideal for a process plant. Process plants tend to have the highest capital intensity and are the most dependent on the rest of the corporation.

High-technology firms often develop campuses with a hub-and-spoke layout. The hub is the main plant for technical development and prototype manufacturing. Other facilities—the spokes—spring up around it for component manufacturing and assembly. Hewlett-Packard's facility at Santa Rosa, California, is such a campus. There are six major modules, with each one limited to 1000 to 2000 employees. When any one complex gets too large, a market or product is spun off to become a new campus.

General-Purpose Plant. The **general-purpose plant** strategy deliberately maximizes each plant's product and resource flexibility. Department of Defense and NASA suppliers, such as in shipbuilding and aerospace, have such plants. Also, thousands of workshops in towns and cities across the country are general-purpose plants. This strategy is rare for multiplant firms. Normally, when a firm has grown to the point of having several plants, there is enough repeatability to emphasize a focus by product, market, or process.

Manual Methods of Location Analysis

When a new facility (branch bank, warehouse or plant) is to be added to a network of other facilities, the selection of a location becomes more complex.

As with single-facility decisions, you must decide where to put the new facility. However, you now must also decide how to reallocate work among facilities to take the best advantage of the new facility. Changing work allocations in turn affects the size (or capacity utilization) of the facilities. The multiple-facility location problem therefore has three dimensions—location, allocation, and capacity—which must be solved simultaneously. In many cases, by merely looking for patterns in the data and using some trial-and-error calculations, you can identify an attractive solution.

Manufacturing or Distribution Systems. In manufacturing or distribution systems, management can choose the sources of demand (plants, warehouses, distributors, retail outlets) each new facility will serve. One approach is to divide the total market into regions, with a facility located (or to be located) in each region. As the desired number of facilities increases, so does the number of regions. Dividing the market into regions determines each facility's capacity and work allocation: Each facility serves its region and it must have enough capacity to do so. A goal of management may be to make all facilities similar in size in order to obtain scale economies. The only remaining choice, then, is the location of each facility within its region, which can be done by single-facility location techniques such as full-grid or patterned search.

The first division of a market into regions may not be satisfactory, so the market should be divided different ways and the process repeated for each alternative. Specifically, the entire process involves the following steps.

1. Divide the total market area into n regions, one for each facility to be located.
2. Based on the demand in its region calculate the capacity required for each facility.
3. Find the best location for each facility within its region, using a single-facility location technique.
4. Calculate the total load–distance measure for the entire market, which is the sum of the load–distance measures for each region.
5. If the solution is acceptable with respect to capacity and the load–distance measure, stop. Otherwise, repeat the process for an alternative division of the market into regions.

Service or Retail Systems. In service or retail systems the customers often choose the facility to serve them. This condition requires a different approach to location, allocation, and capacity decisions. Using a simple trial-and-error approach, you would first select some tentative facility locations, then make an assumption about how customers select specific locations. This approach will determine allocation and capacity patterns. After evaluating the solution obtained, you can try other reasonable locations in the same manner. Specifically, the entire process involves the following steps.

1. Select n trial locations, one for each facility to be located.
2. Assign customer demand to each facility according to an assumed customer selection process such as "go to closest facility" or "go to the facility closest to other desired services or stores."
3. Based on the assigned demand calculate the capacity required for each facility.
4. Calculate the total load–distance measure (or some other measure reflecting the ways in which the customers would reach the facilities) for the n facilities.
5. If the solution is acceptable, stop. Otherwise, select new trial locations and repeat the process.

To illustrate this process, let's return again to the medical facility problem. (See Fig. 8.3.) Assume that two facilities, rather than one, are to be located. For the various location factors important to management, suppose that the choices have been narrowed to four locations, one each in census tracts B, C, D, and G. Table 8.4 provides a column of load–distance scores for each candidate location and each population center (census tract). For example, suppose that the population in census tract A chooses to be treated at a facility located at D. Still assuming *rectilinear distance,* you can determine that locations A and D are 5 miles apart. Multiplying this distance by A's population of 2 gives you a load–distance score of 10. You can verify all the other numbers in the table this same way.

Let the first trial solution be to open medical facilities at locations C and G (bracketed in Table 8.4). Next assume that patients choose the closest facility for treatment, which is the smallest number (circled) in each row in the bracketed columns. You can use the *load–distance* measure here because, for

Table 8.4

Load–Distances (000) for Four Candidate Locations

Population Center	Candidate Location			
	B	C	D	G
A	4	(6)	10	17
B	0	(25)	15	32.5
C	50	(0)	30	55
D	21	(21)	0	31.5
E	80	(30)	60	35
F	100	80	40	(50)
G	91	77	63	(0)

each row, the load is the same for all candidate locations; the only factor that changes across the row is distance. For example, A is closer to C than G, since its load–distance score is only 6 (or 2 × 3) rather than 17 (or 2 × 8.5). Adding the circled entries in both columns, you get a total load–distance score of 132. With this solution, the facility at C serves all population centers except F and G. Thus the allocation pattern for location C includes census tracts A–E, and a facility at that location must have the capacity to handle the total population of these tracts, which is 34. Similarly, a facility at location G would serve the total population of F and G; the necessary capacity for the facility at G also happens to be 34 in this example. You would evaluate several other pairs of locations in the same way. The results, coupled with the other important location factors, lead to the final choice of two locations.

Computer-Assisted Methods of Location Analysis

Many location analysis problems are far more complex than those discussed so far and call for computer assistance. Consider the complexity faced by a medium-sized manufacturer distributing through warehouses (often called *distribution centers*) to various demand centers. The problem is to determine the number, size, allocation pattern, and location of the warehouses for

1. thousands of demand centers;
2. hundreds of potential warehouse locations;
3. several manufacturing plants;
4. multiple product lines;
5. different transportation rates, depending on the direction of shipment, product, quantity, rate breaks, and geographical area;
6. operating costs that have both a fixed component and a component varying with the warehouse size; and
7. inventory levels varying from location to location.

This kind of complexity argues for the use of a computer to assist with the analysis. Three basic types of computer models have been developed for this purpose: heuristic, simulation, and optimization.

Heuristics. **Heuristics** are solution guidelines, or rules of thumb, that find good solutions to problems but not necessarily the best ones. Their advantages include efficiency and the ability to handle more general views of a problem. The patterned search procedure described earlier for single-facility location problems is one such heuristic procedure. One of the first heuristics to be *computerized* for location problems was proposed more than two decades ago to handle several hundred potential warehouse sites and several thousand demand centers (Kuehn and Hamburger, 1963). Many other heuristic models are available today for a variety of problem situations. However, this early one gives us another illustration of the nature of heuristics. It develops a sequence of warehouse locations, each of which is based on an evaluation of the previous solution. We begin by evaluating all potential warehouse sites to find the one that can serve all demand centers at the lowest cost. The best location becomes the site for the first warehouse. This location has the lowest transportation and operating costs for serving all demand centers. (In the context of our earlier medical facility problem, this is the candidate location in Table 8.4 that has the lowest total.)

Now that the first warehouse location has been determined, we repeat the process to find where to add the second warehouse to the network. The location that reduces total costs the most is chosen. Beginning with the second warehouse, we have to make allocation and capacity decisions. If we do not impose any capacity constraints, each demand center is assigned to the available warehouse that serves it at the lowest added cost. The process of locating one warehouse at a time continues until total costs are not reduced by another addition. The warehouses in the network at this point represent the final solution, although two final checks are made. The first check is to determine whether total costs can be reduced by dropping any of the warehouses. Some of the later facilities could have made an earlier one unwise. The second check is to determine whether costs are reduced by replacing a warehouse by one at a potential site that is not yet in the solution.

Simulation. **Simulation** is a modeling technique that reproduces the behavior of a system. It allows you to manipulate certain variables and learn the effect on operating characteristics of interest. (See Appendix B.) For location problems, simulation models allow you to evaluate different location alternatives by trial and error. It is up to you to seek out the most reasonable alternatives. Simulation handles more realistic views of a problem and involves the decisionmaker in the solution process itself. For each run, the decisionmaker inputs the facilities to be opened, and the simulator typically makes the allocation decisions based on some reasonable assumptions. One of the more sophisticated simulations was used by the Ralston Purina Company to assist in locating warehouses (Markland, 1973). There were 137 demand centers, 5 field warehouses, and 4 plants with their associated warehouses. Random demand at each demand center by product type was simulated over a period of time. Demand was met by the closest warehouse having available inventory. Data were produced through the simulation on inventory levels, transportation costs, warehouse operating costs, and back orders. The simulator showed that the least-cost alternative would be to consolidate the five field warehouses into only three. Ralston Purina made this change and saved $132,000 per year.

Optimization. In contrast to heuristic and simulation computer models, optimization procedures guarantee the "best" solution. Even though this approach might appear to be preferable, it has two limitations: (1) most optimization procedures utilize more simplified and less realistic views of a problem; and (2) they do not generate a variety of solutions, which is important to do because of the qualitative factors that are being ignored. One of the first optimization procedures for solving location problems was the *transportation method.* This technique finds the best allocation patterns for a set of location and capacity choices, assuming that costs increase linearly with the size of the shipments between facilities. The decisionmaker must try several choices, much as with simulation, but is assured that the allocation pattern for each one is optimal. Because of its importance to several areas of operations management, the transportation method is described more fully in Appendix C.

Undoubtedly the most sophisticated and realistic optimization techniques have been applied at Hunt-Wesson Foods, Inc. (Geoffrion, 1976). The solution procedure is complex: A nonlinear optimization method is used, along with the transportation method to solve subproblems. The model solved problems even more complex than the one just described at Ralston-Purina. This method's particular virtue is the ability to impose capacity limits on facility size. As a result of the analysis, five changes were instituted within the company's network, which reportedly saved millions of dollars.

LOCATIONS FOR EMERGENCY UNITS

Selecting locations for police services, fire stations, and ambulances resembles other location problems in service industries, since proximity to users is important. However, three differences deserve special mention:

1. Response time.
2. Minimum coverage.
3. Mobile locations.

Response Time

When time is of the essence, *response time* becomes a dominant location factor. Unfortunately, response time is not easy to estimate. It is a complex function of dispatching policies (how many and which units to send), time of day, volume of calls, and size of fleet. Simulation models have been developed to estimate response time under different location strategies. In Los Angeles a simulation model was developed to help relocate 9 of 14 ambulances (Fitzsimmons, 1973). The mean response time was cut by 9 percent. Even more important, the probability of a response taking more than 6 minutes was cut by 33 percent.

Minimum Coverage

With emergency services, averaging the proximity or response time across all areas can be misleading. A preferred goal often is achieving *minimum coverage* for all areas. This view is reinforced by government and insurance standards. For example, the American Insurance Association standards require that every point in "high-value districts" be within one mile of a fire engine company.

Locating emergency facilities is often called a "covering problem." Table 8.5 shows an example of coverage analysis; the rows represent population centers and the columns represent potential facility locations. If the location is close enough to cover the population center (either in terms of minimum time or distance standards), it receives a value of 1; otherwise, it receives a value of 0. For example, location A covers population centers A, B, and G. The objective is to cover all population centers with the minimum number of facilities. After careful inspection of Table 8.5, it becomes apparent that not all population centers can be covered with just two locations. Opening facilities at locations E and F comes the closest, but this solution still leaves population center A uncovered.

Mobile Locations

The notion of fixed locations gives way to *mobile locations* for ambulances and police patrol cars. Like fire engines, they go to the population, but ambulances and patrol cars often get dispatched from one incident to another before returning to their stations. Patrol cars travel around their assigned response areas, rather than staying at a particular location. Fire station loca-

Table 8.5

Coverage Analysis

Population Center	Candidate Location							
	A	B	C	D	E	F	G	H
A	1	1	0	0	0	0	1	0
B	1	1	0	1	0	1	0	0
C	0	0	1	0	1	0	0	0
D	0	1	0	1	0	1	0	0
E	0	0	1	0	1	0	0	0
F	0	1	0	1	0	1	1	1
G	1	1	0	0	0	1	1	0
H	0	0	0	0	0	1	0	1

tions are fixed, but engine and ladder companies can be shifted temporarily. This is a common practice in all large cities, where the number of fire alarms is high relative to capacity. When certain units are out fighting fires, a computer-based system decides how to relocate the remaining units into empty firehouses (Kolesar and Walker, 1974). The objective is to maximize the chance that firefighters and equipment will be available to respond to new calls.

CHAPTER HIGHLIGHTS

Location decisions have strategic implications. In this chapter we looked at recent industry trends, important factors, and several simple approaches to finding a good location. Some of the chapter highlights are:

- Four trends in location patterns are geographic diversity, the growing Sunbelt, the decline of urban areas, and the internationalization of production.
- Despite the advantages of international production, differences in language, politics, and culture introduce new problems. Three recurring issues are environmental adjustment, exporting techniques, and organizing multinationally.
- Location decisions depend on many factors. For a given situation some factors can be disregarded entirely; the remainder can be divided into dominant and secondary factors.
- Five clusters of factors dominate most plant location decisions: favorable labor climate, proximity to markets, quality of life, proximity to suppliers and resources, and proximity to other company facilities. Which ones are "musts" depends on the type of business.
- Proximity to markets, clients, or customers is a particularly dominant factor in service industries. A complicating factor in estimating the sales potential of a location is competition. Having competitor facilities nearby can be an asset or a liability, depending on the type of business.
- Most facility expansions occur on the same site; they are less disruptive and quicker. A point is reached, however, when focus is lost by not adding another facility or relocating the existing one. These alternatives have additional advantages, such as opportunities to modernize processes and reduce transportation costs. Relocation is chosen primarily by smaller firms, which typically move only short distances.
- One way of considering qualitative factors is to calculate a weighted score for each alternative location, using the preference matrix approach.
- The load–distance model is a way to bring together concerns on proximity (to markets, suppliers, resources, and other company facilities) during the early stages of location analysis. Either the euclidean or the rectilinear distance measure can be used to determine distances to reasonable locations. These alternatives can be assessed by making a full-grid or patterned search. The center of gravity of an area is a good starting point for making a patterned search.
- Firms can choose among four multiplant strategies. *Product plants* are favored when labor climate or proximity to suppliers (or resources) are crucial. *Market-area plants*

seek to (1) minimize outbound transportation costs; or (2) provide a quick, customized response to customers. With *process plants,* each plant performs a different segment of the production process. The plants tend to be more capital intensive, with larger scale economies. *General-purpose plants* are rare. They maximize flexibility without focusing on the product, market, or process.

- Multiple-facility problems have three dimensions: location, allocation, and capacity. Trial-and-error methods can begin with a candidate allocation and capacity plan and then determine the preferred locations using single-facility techniques. If customers pick the facility serving them, the location search process must be reversed.
- Location analysis for multiple facilities can be extremely complex. A variety of computerized heuristic, simulation, and optimization models have been developed over the last two decades to help in dealing with this complexity. The transportation method is a basic tool for finding allocation patterns.
- Selecting locations for emergency units has three distinctive features: response time, minimum coverage, and mobile locations. Coverage analysis and simulation are tools that can be used to assist in making these decisions.

KEY TERMS

euclidean distance measure
facility location
general-purpose plant
heuristics
load–distance method
market-area plant
plant charter
process plant
product plant
rectilinear distance measure
simulation

STUDY QUESTIONS

1. What factors have expanded the range of possible locations?
2. What are the attractions of the Sunbelt for manufacturing plants? What can make foreign locations attractive?
3. Why does an overseas location confront a manager with a different set of problems?
4. Describe briefly the five dominant factors in plant location. For each one, identify a business for which it would be especially crucial.
5. Which location factor is particularly important to service industries? How is it related to competitor locations?
6. Under what conditions does a firm usually choose to relocate rather than expand on site?
7. What are the advantages of building another plant versus on-site expansion?
8. What process can a firm use to pick a new facility location?
9. Financial analysis, such as net present

value or payback, can assist in making a location decision. Explain why it normally is insufficient as the sole basis for making the decision.

10. "Euclidean and rectilinear distances differ. Furthermore, neither are correct in terms of actual distance. Therefore neither should be used for location analysis." Comment on this statement.
11. A full-grid search is less efficient than a patterned search, but may be preferable. Why?
12. Under what conditions is each of the four multiplant strategies likely to be adopted?
13. At what point does a multiple-facility location problem break down into several single-facility location problems?
14. Why does the manual method for a multiple-facility problem depend on who decides how work is allocated?
15. What are the advantages and disadvantages of heuristic, simulation, and optimization computer models for multiple-facility location analysis?
16. How does selecting locations for emergency units differ from that for other facilities in the service industries?

PROBLEMS

1. The point has been reached where an electronics manufacturer must expand by building a second facility. The search has been narrowed to four locations, all of which are acceptable to management in terms of dominant factors. The assessment of these sites in terms of seven location factors is shown in Table 8.6. For example, candidate location A has a factor score of 5 (excellent) for labor climate. The weight for this factor (20) is the highest of any.
   (a) Calculate the weighted score for each location. Which location would you recommend?

Table 8.6

Location Factors	Factor Weight	Factor Score for Each Location			
		A	B	C	D
1. Labor climate	20	5	4	4	5
2. Quality of life	16	2	3	4	1
3. Transportation system	16	3	4	3	2
4. Proximity to markets	14	5	3	4	4
5. Proximity to materials	12	2	3	3	4
6. Taxes	12	2	5	5	4
7. Utilities	10	5	4	3	3

Scoring key: 5 = Excellent to 1 = Poor.

(b) What is your recommendation if factors 2, 4, and 6 are ignored (that is, given weights of 0)?

2. The following three points are the locations of important facilities in a transportation network: (25, 40), (50, 20), and (80, 40). The coordinates are in miles.
   (a) Calculate the euclidean distances (in miles) between each of the three pairs of facilities.
   (b) Calculate these distances using rectilinear distances.

3. The best location found so far in Figs. 8.3 and 8.4 was (7, 2), with a load–distance score of 168. Search in the neighborhood of this point for a better solution, trying (6.5, 2), (7, 2.5), and (7.5, 2). Continue using rectilinear distances. The best solution turns out to be the optimal one. *Note:* The x-coordinate of the optimal solution is equal to the x-coordinate of one of the demand points. Similarly, the optimal y-coordinate is equal to the y-coordinate of one of the demand points. This agreement is always the case when rectilinear distance is used.

4. Mailmanna, Georgia, is considering the relocation of its main post office. The current facility has been outgrown and needs modernizing. Besides, a lot of money is unnecessarily being spent transporting mail to and from the facility. Growing suburbs have shifted the population density from where it was 40 years ago, when the current facility was built. In addition, last year a new airport was built much farther from the main post office. Ralph U. Reddie, the current postmaster, asked his assistants to draw a grid map showing the new airport and ten aggregated mail-source points. These aggregated mail-source points are the result of grouping 40 substations in Mailmanna into 10 larger ones. They represent points where mail is picked up and delivered. Two major-highway entry points into the city for mail from surrounding areas were also included. The coordinates and trips per day to and from the 10 aggregated mail-source points, the two entry points (E1 and E2), the airport (A), and the current main post office (M) are shown in Table 8.7. In effect, M acts as a mail-source point even after relocation.
   (a) Calculate the center of gravity as a possible location for the new facility (round to the nearest whole numbers).
   (b) Compare the load–distance scores for the location in (a) and the current location using rectilinear distance.

5. A supplier to the electric utility industry has a strategy of market-area plants, since the product is heavy and transportation costs are high. One market area includes

Table 8.7

Mail-Source Point	Round Trips per Day (l)	xy-Coordinates (miles)
1	3	(3, 12)
2	3	(2, 8)
3	3	(3, 3)
4	3	(6, 1)
5	3	(8, 5)
6	2	(13, 5)
7	3	(13, 3)
8	3	(14, 6)
9	2	(15, 10)
10	2	(10, 10)
E1	5	(18, 1)
E2	10	(2, 5)
A	15	(6, 14)
M	3	(10, 3)

Table 8.8

Customer Locations	Tons Shipped (000)	xy-Coordinates
Three Rivers, MI	5	(7, 13)
Fort Wayne, IN	92	(8, 12)
Columbus, OH	70	(11, 10)
Ashland, KY	35	(11, 7)
Kingsport, TN	9	(12, 4)
Canton, OH	227	(13, 11)
Wheeling, WV	16	(14, 10)
Roanoke, VA	153	(15, 5)

the lower part of the Great Lakes region and the upper portion of the southeastern region. Over 600,000 tons are to be shipped to eight major customer locations, as shown in Table 8.8.

(a) Calculate the center of gravity (rounding to the nearest $\frac{1}{10}$ unit of distance).

(b) Calculate the load–distance scores for the four points that are 0.5 unit of distance north, east, south, and west of the center of gravity. Use rectilinear distances. Is there any improvement?

6. A manufacturer is investigating which location would best position its new plant relative to two suppliers (located in cities A and B) and two market areas (represented by cities C and D). Management has limited the search to those four locations. The following information has been collected.

Location	xy-Coordinates (miles)	Tons per Year (000)	Freight Rate ($/ton-mile)
A	(200,300)	3	1
B	(500,200)	4	2
C	(100,100)	3	3
D	(400,400)	4	5

(a) Which of the four locations gives the lowest total cost, assuming euclidean distances? *Hint:* The cost of inbound shipments from supplier B is $8000 per mile (4000 × 2) between location B and the new plant.

(b) Which location is best, assuming rectilinear distances?

(c) What is the center of gravity (coordinates)?

7. Reconsider the two-facility problem in Table 8.4. Find, by trial and error, a better solution than opening medical facilities at locations C and G. Limit your search to locations B, C, D, and G, staying with the rectilinear distance measure.

(a) What is the total load–distance score of your improved solution?

(b) How much capacity is needed at each medical facility in your solution?

8. Management wants to locate two facilities to serve two groups of demand points. The data shown in Table 8.9 were collected.

(a) Draw a grid map showing the locations of the demand points.

Table 8.9

Demand Point	*xy*-Coordinates (Miles)	Trips per Day (l)
A	(5, 12)	8
B	(12, 30)	8
C	(18, 18)	20
D	(18, 0)	20
E	(28, 28)	15
F	(35, 40)	10
G	(43, 28)	30

(b) Divide the points into two groups on a north–south basis. The north facility will serve B, E, F, and G, while the south facility will serve A, C, and D. Let the facility locations be the centers of gravity of the two areas, rounding to the nearest whole numbers. What is the total load–distance score for the entire system, assuming euclidean distance?

(c) Repeat (b) for an east–west division. The west facility will serve A, B, C, and D, while the east facility will serve E, F, and G. Is this solution better or worse than the one in (b)?

9. A firm plans to open two new facilities that maximize proximity to population centers. It is assumed that customers will go to the nearest available facility. A map of the area is shown in Fig. 8.5. The numbers are the actual distances between centers. Locations B and F are highway intersections, rather than population centers. Population densities and distances between each pair of points are given in Table 8.10. For example, the shortest distance from A to E (and vice versa) is 62.
   (a) Management wants to limit the locations to these eight points and is giving particular attention to a plan for locating facilities at C and H. Calculate the total load–distance score for this plan.
   (b) Try at least one other plan that you think might improve on this score.

10. You want to locate enough fire stations to ensure an average response time of 6 minutes to each of five population centers.

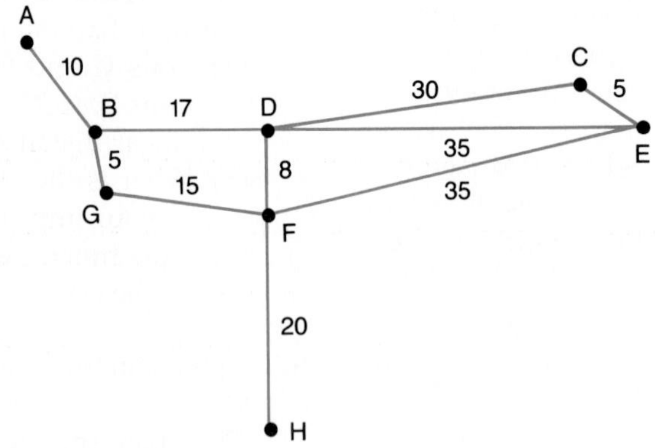

Figure 8.5

Table 8.10

From	A	B	C	D	E	F	G	H	Population Density
A	0	10	57	27	62	30	15	50	5
B	10	0	47	17	52	20	5	40	0
C	57	47	0	30	5	38	52	58	10
D	27	17	30	0	35	8	22	28	20
E	62	52	5	35	0	35	50	55	30
F	30	20	38	8	35	0	15	20	0
G	15	5	52	22	50	15	0	35	4
H	50	40	58	28	55	20	35	0	20

(Columns A–H are under the spanning header "To".)

The response times are shown in Table 8.11.

(a) Set up a table showing which locations cover each population center.

(b) What is the minimum number of facilities needed? Where should they be located?

11. A city manager wants to set up a municipal ambulance system to provide emergency medical service. The 5-mile by 6-mile service area has been divided into 14 population centers. Their coordinates (in miles) are shown in Table 8.12. The standard for acceptable service is a minimum of 2.5 miles. Of these 14 locations, the manager considers only 7 to be acceptable sites (for qualitative reasons): C, D, G, I, J, L, and M.

(a) Set up a table showing the locations that cover each population center, assuming euclidean distance.

(b) What is the minimum number of ambulance sites needed? Where should they be located?

Table 8.11

Population Center	Response Time (min) by Candidate Location				
	A	B	C	D	E
A	1	2	8	20	15
B	2	1	3	12	10
C	8	3	1	16	5
D	20	12	16	1	4
E	15	10	5	4	1

Table 8.12

Population Center	xy-Coordinates	Population Center	xy-Coordinates
A	(0, 6)	H	(0, 2)
B	(3, 6)	I	(1, 2)
C	(2, 5)	J	(5, 2)
D	(3, 4)	K	(3, 1)
E	(4, 4)	L	(1, 0)
F	(5, 4)	M	(4, 1)
G	(3, 3)	N	(5, 0)

SELECTED REFERENCES

Chaiken, Jan M., and Richard C. Larson, "Methods for Allocating Urban Emergency Units: A Survey," *Management Science,* vol. 19, no. 4 part 2 (December 1972), pp. 627–636.

Fitzsimmons, James A., "A Methodology for Emergency Ambulance Development," *Management Sciences,* vol. 19, no. 6 (February 1973), pp. 627–636.

Fulton, Maurice, "New Factors in Plant Location," *Harvard Business Review* May–June 1971), pp. 4–17, 166–168.

Geoffrion, Arthur M., "Better Distribution Planning with Computer Models," *Harvard Business Review* (July–August 1976), pp. 92–99.

Hamel, Gary, and C. K. Prahalad, "Do You Really Have a Global Strategy?" *Harvard Business Review* (July–August 1985), pp. 139–148.

Harms, Craig S., "A Comparison of Facility Location Techniques." Unpublished doctoral dissertation, The Ohio State University, 1984.

Hayes, Robert H., and Steven C. Wheelwright, *Restoring Our Competitive Edge: Competing Through Manufacturing.* New York: John Wiley and Sons, 1984.

Khumawala, Basheer M., and D. Clay Whybark, "A Comparison of Some Recent Warehouse Location Techniques," *The Logistics Review,* vol. 7, no. 3 (Spring 1971).

Kolesar, P., and W. E. Walker, "An Algorithm for the Dynamic Relocation of Fire Companies," *Operations Research,* vol. 22, no. 2 (March–April 1974), pp. 249–274.

Kuehn, Alfred A., and Michael J. Hamburger, "A Heuristic Program for Locating Warehouses," *Management Science,* vol. 9, no. 4 (July 1963), pp. 643–666.

Markland, Robert E., "Analyzing Geographical Discrete Warehousing Networks by Computer Simulation," *Decision Sciences,* vol. 4, no. 2 (April 1973), pp. 216–236.

Schilling, David A., "Dynamic Location Modeling For Public-Sector Facilities: A Multicriteria Approach," *Decision Sciences,* vol. 11, no. 4 (October 1980), pp. 714–724.

Schmenner, Roger W., *Making Business Location Decisions.* Englewood Cliffs, New Jersey: Prentice-Hall, 1982.

Schmenner, Roger W., "Multiple Manufacturing Strategies among the *Fortune* 500," *Journal of Operations Management,* vol. 2, no. 2 (February 1982), pp. 77–86.

Skinner, Wickham, *Manufacturing in the Corporate Strategy.* New York: John Wiley and Sons, 1978.

CHAPTER

LAYOUT

Some Managerial Issues

- Should we have a process, product, hybrid, or fixed layout?
- What performance criteria do we need to emphasize?
- What centers should we work into the layout?
- How much should we involve employees in the layout process?
- What type of layout pattern makes sense for our warehouse?
- What is the best trade-off between proximity and privacy for our office layout?
- Should we have a paced or unpaced line?
- What is the desired output rate for our assembly line?
- Should we consider a mixed-model line?
- What should we do to humanize product layouts?

Chapter Outline

We already have considered such issues as *what* products to offer, *what* positioning strategy to use, *what* types of work to do within the firm, *what* types of employees and technology to employ, *how much* capacity in plant and equipment to provide, and *where* to locate facilities. Facility layout also deals with questions concerning what, how much, and where. Layout decisions translate these other decisions into actual physical arrangements of people, equipment, and space for the purpose of producing goods and services. In this chapter we examine layout in a variety of settings, along with techniques of layout analysis.

WHAT IS A LAYOUT?

The example in Box 9.1 describes an actual layout problem. The office tower was originally built near the state capitol to house many state government operations. Because of rapid growth, the layout must be revised to accommo-

Box 9.1

A LAYOUT FOR THE OFFICE OF BUDGET MANAGEMENT

You are the director of the office of budget management, which is a department in a large state government. Your department consists of 120 employees assigned to eight different sections. It is one of several departments occupying a relatively new office tower. This building was constructed to bring together under one roof most of the departments in the state government. It was justified also by the substantial cost reduction resulting from vacating leased space elsewhere. The building was designed to accommodate growth expectations, so that more space was allocated to your department than justified by its original size. Currently, however, workloads have expanded to the extent that 30 new employees must be hired and somehow housed in the space allocated to your department. While changing the layout, it also makes sense to review it to make sure that it is arranged as effectively as possible. Your hope is to improve communication among people who must interact, find a way to include all 150 employees in the department's assigned area, minimize adverse reactions to space reductions or relocations, and create a good work environment. How will you proceed?

date more employees. This need raises the question of what a layout is, and how we can recognize a good layout when we see one.

Layout planning involves decisions about the physical arrangement of centers of economic activity within a facility. A *center* can be anything that consumes space; a person, group of people, machine, workbench, work station, reception area, department, timecard rack, stairway, aisle, storage area, cafeteria, or conference room, and the like. The words *physical arrangement* in our definition introduce four choices:

1. *What centers should be included in the layout?* A central storage area for tools makes sense for certain processes, but keeping tools at individual work stations makes sense for others. A special display area of generic brands in a grocery store may be most effective.
2. *How much space and capacity is needed for each center?* Inadequate space can hurt productivity and create a perception of no privacy. Excessive space is wasteful and can isolate employees unnecessarily.
3. *How should each center's space be configured?* The amount of space, shape, and the elements to be placed in it are interrelated. Placing the desk and chair relative to the file cabinet and other furniture in a person's office is determined by the activities to be performed there, as well as its size and shape. The office can be private and carpeted or more utilitarian.

Original layout		
A	E	C
B	E	D

Revised layout		
C	E	A
D	E	B

Figure 9.1

Identical Relative Locations and Different Absolute Locations.

4. *Where should each center be located?* Location in the middle of a facility or in a backroom can be important in terms of productivity.

There are two dimensions to the fourth question: *relative* location and *absolute* location. Look at the plan on the left in Fig. 9.1. It shows the location of five departments (A–E) on a floor, where department E has been allocated twice the space of the others. The location of A relative to B is identical to the relative location of C to D. This means that the distance between A and B is equal to the distance between C and D. Relative location is normally the crucial issue in materials handling cost or communication effectiveness. Now look at the plan on the right. Although relative locations are unchanged, the revised layout might be much worse, since the absolute locations have been changed. For example, in considering a revised layout, the cost of moving department C to the northwest corner may be excessive; C might be a dock, but the railroad spur currently comes in on the northeast side of the building, and extending the spur could be expensive.

STRATEGIC ISSUES

Layout choices must be closely tied to higher level decisions, as clearly shown in Box 9.2. The three retailers are shifting their product plans and competitive priorities toward higher quality (and higher priced) merchandise. This must be communicated by the "spatial language" of a facility's layout. The upgraded atmosphere of the stores conveys a sense of being more exclusive and luxurious. Several other fundamental (and strategic) choices must be made in layout planning. We begin with the choice of a layout type.

Choosing a Layout Type

A fundamental choice in planning any layout is that of layout type. This decision depends largely on positioning strategy. There are four basic types of layout: process, product, hybrid, and fixed.

Process Layout. When positioning strategy calls for a process focus, resources (employees and equipment) must be organized around the process. (See Fig. 2.6 in Chapter 2.) A **process layout** accomplishes this purpose by clustering in one center the resources that perform similar functions. For example, all grinding is done in a grinding department, all drills are located in the same area of a shop, all bills are processed in an accounts payable section, and all budget apparel is displayed in one area of a department store. This format is most commonly used when many different products (customers) must be produced (served) intermittently at the same work stations. Demand levels are too low or unpredictable to allow human and capital resources to be set aside exclusively for a particular product line or type of customer. Resources are relatively general purpose, flexible, and less capital intensive. The process layout is less vulnerable to changes in product mix or new marketing strategies. Equipment utilization can be higher than it would otherwise be, since the requirements for all products or services can be pooled. In addition,

Box 9.2

LARGE RETAILERS CHANGE STRATEGY AND LAYOUTS

Three large retailers are changing their strategy and the focal point is layout. While keeping their separate identities, all three will offer merchandise of better quality in more attractive stores. Bottom-of-the-line quality still is offered, but the overall price mix is rising. The new layouts have striking graphics and use "racetrack" aisles to guide customers past more of the merchandise.

J. C. Penney spent $3.2 million on its Glenbrook Mall store in Fort Wayne. Some departments were eliminated, such as paint, hardware, and major appliance. Other departments were expanded, such as apparel, jewelry, luggage, and housewares. The image was upgraded by better carpet, potted plants, and more mannequins. Sales increased by 40 percent. The plan is to revise layouts at 550 of the largest Penney stores at a cost of about $1 billion.

Sears, Roebuck & Company finds that customers are browsing more at its remodeled stores, rather than just buying one item. Store layouts are patterned after how people shop. Similar items are located in one place, rather than displayed at several departments. Merchandise is arrayed from left to right, with the most expensive items on the right. Sears plans to spend $1.7 billion on 622 stores.

K mart Corporation wants to change its image to include high-quality, name-brand goods. There will be departmental "modules," such as kitchen shops and electronics displays. Over $2.25 billion will be invested in remodeling many of its 1024 full-sized stores.

Source: "Large Retailers Are Changing Strategy and Image by Remodeling Stores, Upgrading Products Lines," *Wall Street Journal*, July 10, 1984

employee supervision can be more specialized, which is important when the job content requires a good deal of technical knowledge.

As you saw in Chapter 2, a process focus (and the accompanying process layout) also has its disadvantages. Processing rates tend to be slower, and productive time is lost in changing over from one product to another. More space and capital is tied up in inventory, which is needed to decouple work stations from variations in output rates. Cycle times, the time lag between when jobs are started and finished, are longer. Materials handling tends to be costlier. Variable path devices, rather than gravity drops or conveyors, must be used because of the diversity in routings that result in jumbled flows. As you will soon see, a major challenge in designing a process layout is to locate centers so that they bring some order to the apparent chaos of the process-focused operation.

Product Layout. When the positioning strategy calls for a product focus, resources are dedicated to individual products. A **product layout** achieves this purpose by arranging resources around the product's routing, rather than sharing them across many products. An automated car wash is a good example of a product layout. Product layouts rely more on specialized, capital-intensive resources and are riskier for products with short or uncertain product lives. Their advantages are the mirror image of the disadvantages to process layouts. Faster processing rates, lower inventories, and less unproductive time lost to changeovers and materials handling are examples of these advantages.

Whereas one of the mysteries in process layouts is where to locate centers, this issue is trivial for product layouts. If a product's routing is A–B–C, it is easy to see that the layout should place A next to B and B next to C. This arrangement, which simply follows the product's routing, makes sure that all pairs of centers that interact with each other are as close together as possible (have a common boundary). The challenge of product layouts is to group activities to form work stations and achieve the desired output rate with the least resources. The composition and number of work stations are crucial decisions. All jobs flowing along the line have the same routing and there is minimal inventory decoupling. The output of the line can only be as fast as the slowest work station, so balancing capacities is essential.

We need to make two final points about product layouts before going on. First, several different items belonging to the same general family can be made on the same line. These **mixed-model assembly lines** are quite common. For example, an automobile assembly line may make a wide variety of Bonnevilles in terms of color, trim, and engines. Producing all of them on the same line is possible so long as the routings and work requirements at different work stations are sufficiently similar. In such cases, high-volume production is possible even with more product flexibility.

Second, straight-line flows may not be best, or even feasible, for product layouts. A straight-line flow might imply that the receiving and shipping docks are separated, which could cause inefficient use of space or of the shipping and receiving crew. Perhaps the dimensions of the building do not even permit straight-line flows. In such cases, product layouts can be arranged in L, O, S, or U shapes. Such shapes can still maintain the adjacent interactions required by the routing.

Hybrid Layout. More often than not, a positioning strategy combines elements of both a product and process focus. This is an intermediate positioning strategy, which calls for a **hybrid layout**. Some portions of the facility are designed as a process layout and other portions are designed as a product layout. This treatment is often applied when group technology cells, one-worker–multiple-machine stations (OWMM), or flexible manufacturing systems (FMS) are introduced (see Chapter 5). These "islands of automation" represent miniature product layouts, since all resources needed to make the family of parts are brought together as one center. At the same time, not all production can be handled this way, and the rest of the facility represents a process layout. Hybrid layouts also are found when facilities have both fabrication and assembly operations. Fabrication operations, where components are made from raw materials, tend to have a process focus. Assembly operations tend to have a product focus.

Another example of a hybrid layout is a retail store. Similar merchandise may be grouped so that customers have a fairly good idea of where to find desired items (a process layout). At the same time customers often are routed along fairly predetermined paths, such as up and down the "racetrack" aisles mentioned in Box 9.2 (a product layout). The motive is to maximize exposure to the full array of goods, thereby stimulating sales.

Fixed-position Layout. The fourth basic type of layout is the **fixed-position layout**. When a product is particularly massive or bulky it does not make sense to move it from one work station to another, as with process, product, or hybrid layouts. Such is the case in shipbuilding, assembling airplanes or locomotives, making huge pressure vessels, building dams, or repairing home furnaces. Workers, along with their tools and equipment, come to the product to work on it until it is finished, or at least until much of the work is completed. This layout type minimizes the number of times that the product must be moved and often is the only feasible solution. We will not consider fixed-position layouts any further. When management decides on this format, the layout problem is basically solved. The operations manager's attention turns to other questions, such as process design, inventory, and scheduling.

Performance Criteria

Another fundamental choice to be made in layout planning is that of performance criteria. Materials handling costs may be the driving force. The plant may be strictly utilitarian or take on more of a campus-like appearance. The mandate may be to squeeze all the operations into a small space or to provide a more spacious work environment. Such alternatives must be considered before and during the analysis of different layouts. What to emphasize is situational and requires managerial judgment. Table 9.1 shows the performance criteria that might get the most attention in terms of four different settings.

Capital Investment. Floor space, equipment needs, and inventory levels depend in part on whether a process or product layout format is selected. When volumes are low, higher resource utilization is possible with a process focus. This focus reduces equipment and space needs, although the possible disadvantage of more space and investment in inventory must also be considered. Capital investment is an important criterion in all settings. If privacy is increased by allocating more space to centers or by adding partitions, the amount of investment required rises. If an existing layout is to be revised, renovation costs can be significant. The remodeling plans at Penney, Sears, and K mart stores (see Box 9.2) have a total price tag of almost $5 billion.

Materials Handling. Relative locations of centers should allow large flows to go short distances. Frequent trips or interactions between work centers should be recognized by locating these centers close to each other. In a manufacturing plant, this approach minimizes *materials handling costs.* In a warehouse, *stockpicking costs* are reduced by storing items typically needed for the same order next to each other. In a retail store, *customer convenience* is im-

Table 9.1

Performance Criteria for Four Different Settings

Manufacturing Plant	Office
Capital investment Materials handling Flexibility Labor productivity Maintenance Work environment Employee attitudes	Capital investment Communication Flexibility Atmosphere Organizational structure Employee attitudes
Warehouse	**Retail Store**
Capital investment Stockpicking Flexibility Work environment Shelf life	Capital investment Customer convenience Flexibility Atmosphere Sales

proved if items are grouped predictably to minimize customer search and travel time. In an office, *communication* and cooperation often can be improved by putting people or departments who must interact frequently near each other. Telephone calls and memos can be poor substitutes for face-to-face communication.

Flexibility. A *flexible* layout is a better layout for many situations. Layout flexibility can mean one of two things. It may mean that a layout remains desirable even after significant changes occur in the mix of customers served by the store, products made at the plant, item space requirements in a warehouse, or organizational structure in an office. Making a layout flexible in this first sense depends in part on management's ability to forecast the future. The second meaning of layout flexibility is that the layout is designed so that the cost of changing it at a later date, to meet new conditions, is minimal. Having modular furniture and partitions, rather than permanent load-bearing walls, is one way to minimize the cost of layout changes in an office.

Other Criteria. Table 9.1 shows other criteria that can also be important. *Labor productivity* can be affected if certain work stations can be operated by common personnel in some layouts but not others. Downtime spent waiting for materials can be caused by materials handling difficulties resulting from poor layout. Equipment *maintenance* can be made difficult by inadequate space or poor access. The *work environment*, including temperature, noise level, and safety, can be layout-related; its counterpart in an office or store is the *atmosphere* created by the layout. Office layouts can reinforce the *organizational structure* by putting all members of the same department in the same area. Encouraging *sales* is an important criterion for a store layout. Some warehouse layouts make it easier to pick stock on a FIFO (first-in, first-out) basis, so as to minimize loss due to spoilage or limited *shelf lives*. Finally, *employee attitudes* may depend on whether the layout allows workers to socialize with each other, reflects equitably the employee's level of responsibility, or puts the worker under the watchful eyes of the supervisor.

Four More Choices

After selecting a layout type and the key performance criteria, management still faces four fundamental choices: center definition, timing, building design, and level of employee participation.

Center Definition. The types of centers to be included in the layout is a first-order question. A receptionist area for a group of offices provides insulation from unscheduled interruptions. A sporting goods section in a store can capitalize on the fitness craze. An entire department can be treated as one center, mandating contiguous space for everyone in it. Or it can be split into several centers, allowing those with greater interaction with the public to be located elsewhere. Perhaps departmental or job boundaries should even be reorganized in order to create effective centers.

Timing. What might be best for this year can be unsatisfactory in the future, owing to growth or short product life cycles imposed by marketing strategy. As the future becomes less predictable, some managers tend to discount it and place more weight on present operations. Another response is to maximize flexibility, such as having wide bays (fewer columns), heavy duty floors, or extra electrical connections (unused for the present) and extra space for future expansion.

Building Design. The fixed and variable costs of a productive system are directly related to building design. Some designs may cost as little as $30 per square foot, whereas others are twice that amount. Single-story plants are now the trend: They require less nonproductive space for stairways and elevators, allow horizontal moving of materials, and utilize special foundations only where needed for heavy equipment. Single-story construction can also have disadvantages: Land costs can be prohibitive for such buildings in a downtown area; lighting and air conditioning can also be more costly.

Employee Participation. Whether employees are involved in the layout process may affect employee attitudes more than the features of the layout itself. The amount of involvement needs to dovetail with work-force management policies. (See Chapter 4.) Rightly or wrongly, professional employees and higher level managers are normally allowed considerable input into the layout process when it affects their work areas.

PROCESS LAYOUTS: A THREE-STEP PROCEDURE

Having addressed the more strategic issues of layout, it is time to consider actual designs. The approach differs, depending on whether a process layout or product layout has been chosen. We begin with an approach to process layouts, which also applies to the parts of hybrid layouts that have a process focus. Three basic steps are involved, whether you are designing a new layout or revising an existing layout:

1. Gather information.
2. Develop a block plan.
3. Design a detailed layout.

Gather Information (Step 1)

Figure 9.2 illustrates the type of information needed to begin designing a revised layout for Longhorn Products. If necessary, refer back to the description of the company's operations in Chapter 2.

Department	Square feet
1. Burr and grind	1000
2. NC equipment	950
3. Shipping and receiving	750
4. Lathes and drills	1200
5. Tool crib	800
6. Inspection	700
Total	5400

(a)

2	4	3
6	5	1

60′ × 90′

(b)

From – To Matrix (trips/day)

From \ To	1	2	3	4	5	6
1. Burr and grind						70
2. NC equipment	20				45	
3. Shipping and receiving		10		15		20
4. Lathes and drills	20				40	
5. Tool crib		30		30		
6. Inspection	10		70			

(c)

1. Shipping and receiving (department 3) should remain where it is, since it is next to the dock.
2. Keep lathes and drills (department 4) at its current location because relocation costs are prohibitive.

(d)

Figure 9.2

Layout Information for Longhorn Products: (a) Space Requirements by Center; (b) Available Space and Current Block Plan; (c) Closeness Ratings; (d) Other Considerations.

Space Requirements By Center. As shown in Fig. 9.2(a), Longhorn has grouped its processes into six different departments, or centers. For example, department 1 is the burr and grind area, and department 6 is the inspection area. The exact space requirements of each department, expressed in square feet, are shown in Fig. 9.2(a). You can calculate space requirements in various ways, but you must tie them to capacity plans. Itemize all equipment and specific space needs for each center. Add enough "circulation" space to provide for aisles and the like. It is not unusual for circulation space to be at least 25 percent of the center's total space requirement.

Available Space. Figure 9.2(b) shows the available space and dimensions of the facility, along with a rough allocation of space for each department.

Whenever there is an existing layout, as there is at Longhorn, it is called the *current block plan*. Available space at the Longhorn plant is 90 feet by 60 feet, or 5400 square feet. You could start by dividing the total amount of space into six equal blocks of space (equivalent to 900 square feet), one for each department. This amount of space is too much for inspection (needing only 700 square feet) and too little for lathes and drills (needing 1200 square feet). However, the approximation is good enough until you reach the last step of process layout design (detailed layout).*

Closeness Ratings. Another type of information required is the need for locating different centers close to each other. This helps us determine the best relative location for each department. Either a From–To matrix or a REL chart provides the needed information. Figure 9.2(c) shows a **From–To matrix** for Longhorn. The estimated number of materials handling trips from each department to every other one is shown. The greatest number of one-way trips is from department 1 to department 6 and from 6 to 3 (70 in both cases). Thus department 6 should be located near both 1 and 3, which certainly is not true in the current layout. You can estimate the number of trips from the routings and ordering frequencies for typical items made at the plant. Statistical sampling or polling of experts (such as supervisors or materials handlers) are other ways to obtain this information.

A **REL chart** (REL stands for relationships) is a different way to express closeness ratings. The ratings are qualitative judgments of managers or employees. An A could signify the judgment that it is *absolutely necessary* to locate two departments close to each other, an E could represent the judgment that it is *especially important*, and so on. Being qualitative, the A rating is higher than the E, but we do not know by how much.

Other Considerations. The last information gathered for Longhorn, other considerations, is shown in Fig. 9.2(d). Some performance criteria depend on the *absolute* location of a department (such as not moving it because of relocation costs, noise factors, or management preference). These criteria cannot be reflected in a REL chart. Similarly, a From–To matrix tends to focus only on materials handling. Other considerations, such as those shown in Table 9.1, must be handled qualitatively and listed separately.

Develop a Block Plan (Step 2)

The second step in layout design is to develop a block plan that satisfies performance criteria and area requirements insofar as possible. The most

*If this approximation is too rough, we can use a finer grid, say, with four rows and six columns. The larger departments (such as lathes and drills) could then be assigned more block spaces than the smaller departments.

From \ To	1	2	3	4	5	6
1. Burr and grind		20		20		80
2. NC equipment			10		75	
3. Shipping and receiving				15		90
4. Lathes and drills					70	
5. Tool crib						
6. Inspection						

Figure 9.3

Merged Closeness Ratings.

elementary way to do this is by trial and error but depends on your ability to spot patterns in the data. There is no guarantee that you will identify the best or nearly best solution. However, one study showed that such an approach, at least when supplemented by the use of a computer to evaluate solutions, often compares quite favorably with more sophisticated techniques (Scriabin and Vergin, 1975).

A good place to start is with the closeness ratings shown in Fig. 9.2. To make it easier to identify significant interactions, you should merge the flows between department pairs in both directions.* The results are shown in Fig. 9.3, and only the upper right half of the matrix is used. For example, the total number of trips between departments 1 and 6 is 80 (or 70 + 10). Looking at the greatest interactions (say, 70 and above), a good block plan would locate:

1. Departments 3 and 6 close together.
2. Departments 1 and 6 close together.
3. Departments 2 and 5 close together.
4. Departments 4 and 5 close together.
5. Departments 3 and 4 at their current locations because of the other considerations listed in Fig. 9.2.

It is not clear that all five requirements can be achieved. If after several attempts you cannot make them work, drop one or more and try again. If all five can be easily achieved, add more requirements (such as for interactions below 70). Fortunately, finding a good block plan for Longhorn turns out to be fairly easy. The plan in Fig. 9.4 was worked out by the trial-and-error

*This approach assumes that material handling costs do not depend on the direction of flow. If this is not true, the numbers would have to be weighted differently.

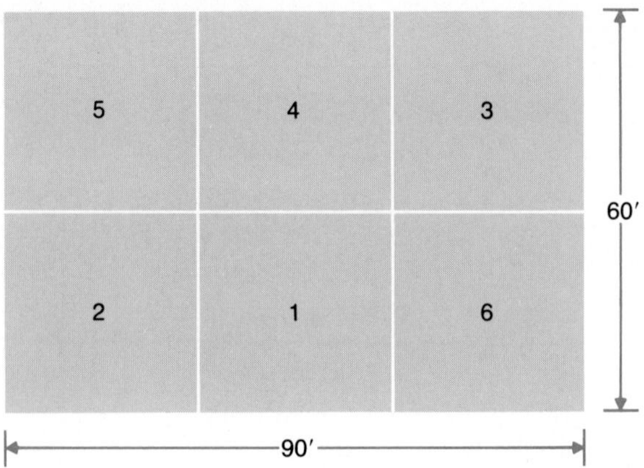

Figure 9.4

Proposed Block Plan.

method and satisfies all five requirements. Start by placing departments 3 and 4 in their current positions. Since the first requirement is to locate departments 3 and 6 close to each other, you can put 6 in the southeast corner of the layout; this location minimizes the distance between 3 and 6. The second requirement is to have departments 1 and 6 close to each other. You can achieve it by putting 1 in the space just to the left of 6, and so on.

It helps to have a total desirability score for at least some aspects of a layout in order to see how much better one plan is than another. You can easily adapt the load–distance model for location problems (see Chapter 8) to this purpose when *relative* locations (such as material handling, stockpicking, and communication effectiveness) are a key concern. In terms of material handling costs,

$$ld = \sum_{j=i}^{n} \sum_{i=1}^{n} l_{ij} d_{ij}.$$

where

ld = Total load–distance score measuring the materials handling difficulties of the block plan;*

l_{ij} = Load, measured as the number of trips between departments i and j in both directions;†

* A more elaborate treatment of l_{ij} is to multiply the number of trips by the cost to move one load for one unit of distance. The cost depends on the materials handling methods used for transfers between departments, as well as the type of materials to be moved.

† Since l_{ij} represents the merged flow between department pairs in both directions, j needs only to be summed from i (rather than 1) to n.

d_{ij} = Units of distance (actual, euclidean, or rectilinear) between departments i and j, where $d_{ij} = 0$ if $i = j$ (see Chapter 8 for distance computations); and

n = Total number of departments.

Table 9.2 shows the results of applying this formula to the current and proposed block plans. The *ld*-score drops from 785 to 400, which represents an almost 50 percent improvement with the proposed plan. You must now decide whether this improvement is worth the cost of relocating four of the six departments (all but 3 and 4). If relocation costs are too much, you must come up with a less expensive proposal. Looking at the calculations for the current plan in Table 9.2, you can get some clues. Much of the 785 score comes from the trips between departments 3 and 6 (270) and between departments 1 and 6 (160). One possibility is just to switch the locations of departments 5 and 6. This solution puts department 6 closer to both 1 and 3. Additional calculations will show that the *ld*-score for this plan drops to 610, and only two departments have to be relocated. Perhaps this is the best compromise.

Design a Detailed Layout (Step 3)

After a satisfactory block plan is found, it should be translated into a detailed representation showing the exact size and shape of each center, the arrange-

Table 9.2

Load–Distance Scores: Current and Proposed

Department Pair (ij)	Merged Closeness Rating (l_{ij})*	Current Plan: Distance (d_{ij})†	Current Plan: $l_{ij}d_{ij}$	Proposed Plan: Distance (d_{ij})†	Proposed Plan: $l_{ij}d_{ij}$
1, 2	20	3	60	1	20
1, 4	20	2	40	1	20
1, 6	80	2	160	1	80
2, 3	10	2	20	3	30
2, 5	75	2	150	1	75
3, 4	15	1	15	1	15
3, 6	90	3	270	1	90
4, 5	70	1	70	1	70
			ld = 785		ld = 400

* All of these nonzero ratings come from Fig. 9.3.

† Rectilinear distances are calculated from the current plan (Fig. 9.2b) and the proposed plan (Fig. 9.4). In the current plan, departments 1 and 2 are at the southeast and northwest blocks of the plant, respectively. The distance between the centers of these blocks is three *units* of distance (two horizontally and one vertically); each unit actually measures 30 ft.

ment of elements (such as desks, machines, or storage areas) within it, and the location of aisles, stairways, and other unproductive space. These visual representations can be 2-dimensional drawings, 3-dimensional models, or even computer-aided graphics. This last step in the layout design process is important because it helps decisionmakers to grasp the essence of the proposal and even spot problems that might otherwise be overlooked. If others in the company are to be involved in layout decisions, the detailed layout becomes the focus of the discussion.

AIDS FOR PROCESS LAYOUT DECISIONS

Finding a good block plan becomes complex with realistically sized problems. A 20-department problem has 20! possible layouts, which means 2.43×10^{18} possibilities. If a computer evaluated one possibility each microsecond, 8 hours a day, it would take 250,000 years for the computer to arrive at the final solution. Fortunately, several aids for making process layout decisions that are computationally feasible are now available.

Automated Layout Design Program (ALDEP)

Representative of the kind of computer-based models available is the **automated layout design program** (ALDEP). It is a heuristic method and generally provides good solutions, although not necessarily the best. Many solutions can be generated quickly, and those having better scores are displayed. The ALDEP method can be best explained with an example. Suppose that Bregman Manufacturing is building a new plant. Todd Paul, the vice-president of manufacturing, has pulled together the information shown in Fig. 9.5 for the departments to be located on the first floor of the plant. Todd has divided the floor into 9 rows and 12 columns. Each block represents 100 square feet, which means that 13 blocks should be allocated to materials storage, 5 blocks to forming, and so on. Productive space is lost to the elevator, stairs, office, and aisle. In contrast to Longhorn (see Fig. 9.2), Todd is using a REL chart rather than a From–To matrix. The letters indicate the closeness score, whereas the numbers in parentheses help to explain the reason for the rating. For example, it is absolutely necessary (rating = A) for the forming department and the assembly department to be close to each other, since personnel are shared and supervision is easier. Seven scores are shown for each department; for example, for department 5, four scores are recorded in department 5's column and the other three in its row.

The version of ALDEP illustrated here randomly picks the first department to be added to those that have been prepositioned (1, 6, 82, 83, 84, and 99). In our example, we selected department 5 first. We insert it as a strip 2 columns wide, beginning with the first available space in the northwest cor-

	Department	Square feet
1	Materials storage	1,300
2	Forming	500
3	Machining	1,000
4	Painting	600
5	Assembly	1,400
6	Stamping	1,200
7	Saw	800
8	Inspection	700
82	Elevator	100
83	Stairs	200
84	Office	800
99	Aisle	2,200
	Total	10,800

(a)

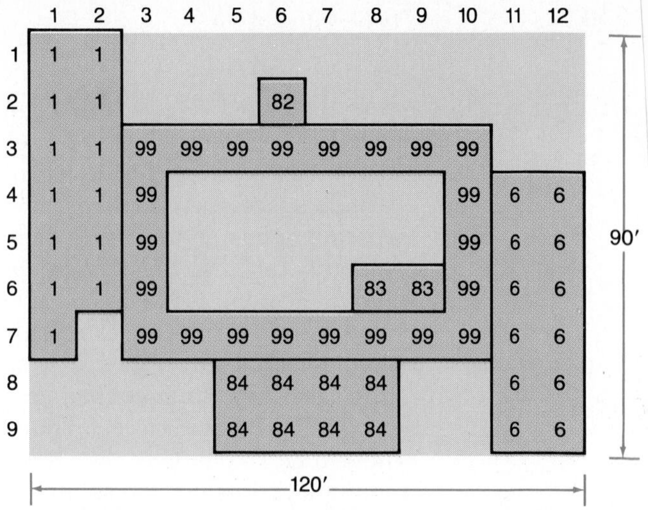

	1	2	3	4	5	6	7	8	9	10	11	12
1	1	1										
2	1	1				82						
3	1	1	99	99	99	99	99	99	99	99		
4	1	1	99							99	6	6
5	1	1	99							99	6	6
6	1	1	99					83	83	99	6	6
7	1		99	99	99	99	99	99	99	99	6	6
8					84	84	84	84			6	6
9					84	84	84	84			6	6

120′ × 90′

*Productive space lost to elevator, stairs, office, and aisle is shown, along with required locations for departments 1 and 6.

(b)

	Department	2	3	4	5	6	7	8
1	Materials storage	O (1)	O (1)	U	E (1)	U	O (1)	E (1)
2	Forming		E (1)	U	A (2,3)	U	I (1)	O (1)
3	Machining			I (1)	O (1)	U (1)	I (1)	U
4	Painting				E (2,3)	O	U (1)	E (4)
5	Assembly					X (5,6)	I (1)	I (1)
6	Stamping						I (1)	O (1)
7	Saw							I (1)
8	Inspection							

Closeness ratings

Rating	Definition
A	Absolutely necessary
E	Especially important
I	Important
O	Ordinary closeness
U	Unimportant
X	Undesirable

Explanation codes

Code	Meaning
1	Materials handling
2	Shared personnel
3	Ease of supervision
4	Space utilization
5	Noise
6	Employee attitudes

(c)

1. Owing to noise factors and the need for special foundations, the stamping department should be put in the southeast corner.
2. Materials storage should be on the northwest side, since this is where the shipping and receiving dock will be placed.

(d)

Figure 9.5

Layout Information for Bregman Manufacturing: (a) Space Requirements by Center; (b) Available Space;* (c) Closeness Ratings (REL Chart); (d) Other Considerations.

ner of the layout (Fig. 9.5b). When we reach the bottom of the layout, we move the strip to the right and back up the diagram. In our example department 1 has been prepositioned in the northwest corner and so the first available space open for department 5 is actually in the southwest corner. Department 5 is not finished when the strip finishes its downward move in columns 1 and 2, so the department is finished on the strip's way back up in columns 3 and 4. It fills in around department 99, which has been prepositioned. After we have allocated enough space (14 blocks) to department 5 we search the REL chart (Fig. 9.5c) to see if the department just added has a high rating (A or E) with any remaining department. If we find one, we insert it next. Otherwise, we select at random one of the departments yet to be added. When ALDEP completes the layout in this manner, it assigns a score to the layout and prints out the solution, if it looks promising. For a given layout problem, ALDEP can generate many solutions because of the random character of its logic.

Figure 9.6 shows the sequence in which the departments were entered, the strip pattern, and the trial block plan printed out by the computer for one such solution; the score for this solution is 41. The score was computed differently than was the *ld*-score used earlier. First, the letter ratings were converted into a numerical equivalent of 6 for A, 5 for E, 4 for I, 3 for O, 2 for U, and 0 for X.* Second, these numerical equivalents were added to the total score whenever they belonged to departments that touched somewhere along their borders. For example, department 3 touches departments 4, 5, and 8. The corresponding closeness ratings are I, O, and U respectively, which increases the total score by 9 (or 4 + 3 + 2).

Other Computer Models

Among the computer software packages developed in recent years, one of the most powerful heuristic methods is used in the **computerized relative allocation of facilities technique** (CRAFT). Working from an initial block plan (or starting solution), it evaluates all possible paired exchanges of departments. The exchange that helps the most (that is, causes the greatest reduction in the total *ld*-score) is made, creating a new starting solution. This process continues until no other exchanges can be found to reduce the *ld*-score. The starting solution at this point is also the final solution, which is printed out, along with the *ld*-score.

Other models have been developed to handle multiple floors and relocation costs (see Cinar, 1975 and Hicks and Cowan, 1976). Goal programming, a special form of linear programming, has been used to optimize a solution

* These numerical equivalents are arbitrary, and others could be used. After numerical equivalents have been established, it is also possible to compute *ld*-scores as done earlier.

Department	Reason
5	Random
2	A between 5 and 2
3	E between 2 and 3
4	Random
8	E between 4 and 8
7	Only one left

(a)

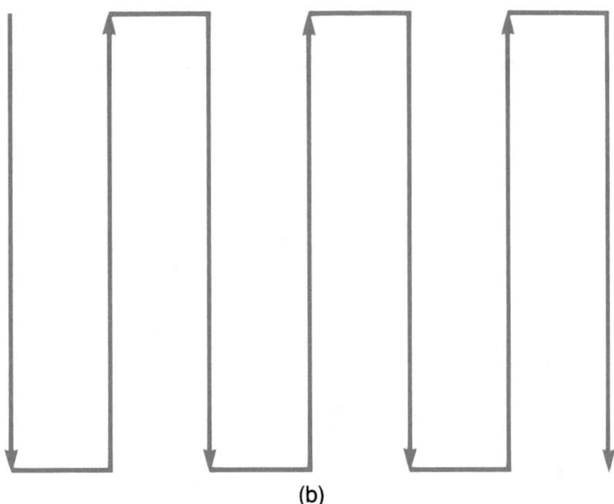

(b)

1	1	2	2	2	2	4	4	4	8	7	7
1	1	5	5	2	82	4	4	8	8	7	7
1	1	99	99	99	99	99	99	99	99	7	7
1	1	99	5	3	3	3	4	8	99	6	6
1	1	99	5	3	3	3	3	8	99	6	6
1	1	99	5	3	3	3	83	83	99	6	6
1	5	99	99	99	99	99	99	99	99	6	6
5	5	5	5	84	84	84	84	8	8	6	6
5	5	5	5	84	84	84	84	7	7	6	6

Score = 41

(c)

Figure 9.6

Application of ALDEP to Bregman Manufacturing: (a) Sequence of Entering Department; (b) Strip Pattern; (c) One Trial Block Plan.

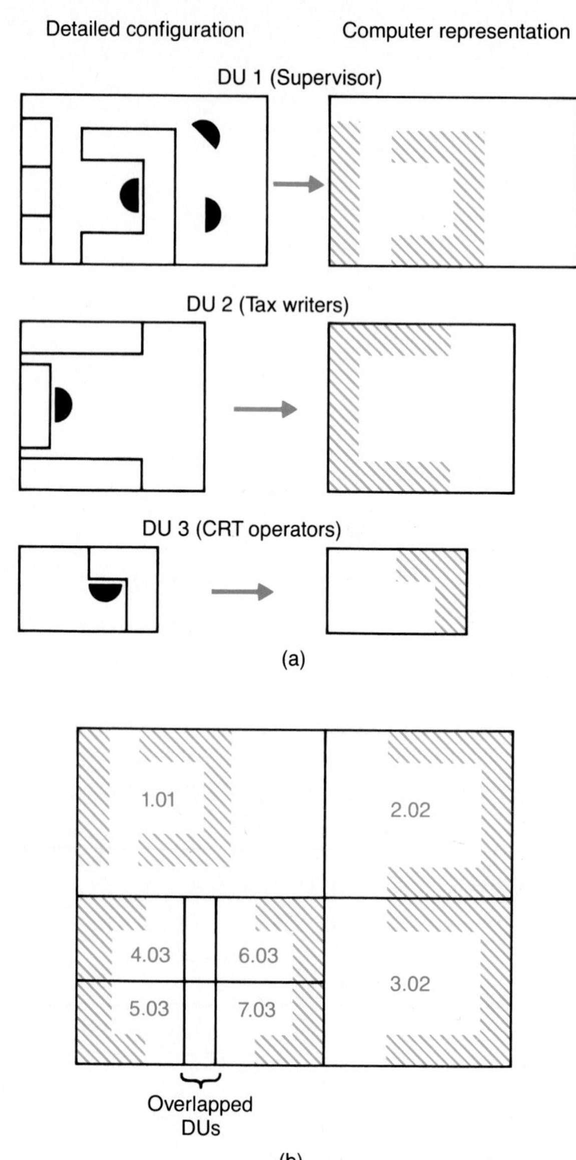

Figure 9.7

Design Unit Representation of Personal Property Tax Section in County Auditor's Office: (a) Design Units; (b) One Possible Layout.

Source: Jacobs, F. R., "A Multi-Criteria, Multi-Constrained Layout Planning System." Unpublished Ph.D. dissertation, Ohio State University, 1979.

with several criteria simultaneously (see Ritzman et al., 1979). One particularly intriguing development is a method to better integrate the last two steps of layout planning (the block plan and detailed layout). A detailed configuration (called a *design unit*) is preassigned to each center and must be maintained throughout the solution process. This constraint prevents unusual shapes from occurring and helps the manager better visualize the final layout. Figure 9.7 illustrates this approach. Design unit 1 is assigned to the supervisor, 2 to each of the two tax writers, and 3 to each of four CRT operators (Fig. 9.7a). One possible layout displayed by the computer plotter is shown in Fig. 9.7(b). The tax writers are positioned along the east side of the building. The circulation space (unshaded area) is overlapped for the CRT operators to conserve space, which is one of the several layout criteria used. The computer considers mirror images and rotations of the design units, as done with the supervisor's office.

More interactive software packages are being developed, which involve the decisionmaker throughout the solution process. With one package (Liggett and Mitchell, 1981), a solution is generated from scratch, much as with ALDEP. The difference is that the decisionmaker (not the computer) decides which center to add next, in order to best respond to the spectrum of performance criteria unique to each specific facility. When a center is chosen and added, the computer helps by displaying a color or gray-scale contour map superimposed on the block plan. The better locations for the center (in terms of the *ld*-score) are shown in darker tones.

PROCESS LAYOUTS: TWO SPECIAL CASES

We conclude the discussion of process layouts with two special cases: warehouses and offices. Much of the preceding discussion still applies, but each of these two special cases has unique aspects.

Warehouse Layouts

Warehouses are similar to manufacturing plants in that materials are moved between activity centers. The transformation at the centers is one of storage, rather than a physical or chemical change. Figure 9.8 illustrates the simplest type of warehousing situation. At A-1 Distribution Systems, items are received at the dock and then moved to a storage area. At a later date, stockpickers withdraw inventory to fill individual customer orders. For example, 280 trips per week are made between the dock and the storage area for toasters. This analysis can be made as it was for Longhorn Products.

A Simpler Method. We can use an even simpler method, which is guaranteed to minimize the *ld*-score. A short cut is possible because all travel is

Department	Trips to and from dock	Area needed (blocks)	Ratio (trips to area)
1. Toasters	280	1	280
2. Room air-conditioners	160	2	80
3. Microwaves	360	1	360
4. Stereos	375	3	125
5. TV's	800	4	200
6. Radios	150	1	150
7. Bulk storage	100	2	50

(a)

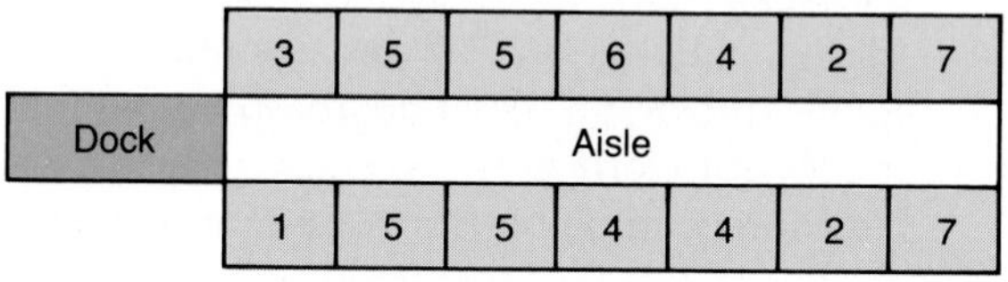

	3	5	5	6	4	2	7
Dock	Aisle						
	1	5	5	4	4	2	7

(b)

Figure 9.8

A Layout for A-1 Distribution Systems: (a) Layout Information; (b) Best Block Plan.

between the dock and individual departments (no travel between departments). The decision rule is as follows:

1. *Equal areas*—If all departments require the same space, simply place the one generating the most trips closest to the dock, the one generating the next largest number of trips next closest to the dock, and so on.
2. *Unequal areas*—If some departments need more space than others (as is true for A-1), give the location closest to the dock to the department with the largest ratio of trip frequency to block spaces. At A-1, microwaves (department 3) has the greatest ratio. Only 360 trips per week are involved, but it takes up only one block of prime space. Toasters (department 1) gets second preference, and so on.

Some Qualifications. A warehouse layout designed in this way may not be best, for three reasons. First, the demand for different items is often seasonal. A good layout might place radios close to the dock for Christmas and move air conditioners close to it in the summer. Second, the crucial issue might be space utilization at A-1, which brings other dimensions of a layout into play. An 82,000-square-foot, 32-foot-high, racked warehouse can handle the same volume as a 107,000-square-foot, low-ceiling warehouse. Productivity gains of as much as 50 percent in order picking have been reported, which can help offset the added rack and equipment costs of such high-density designs. Another possibility being experimented with is a warehouse where incoming materials are assigned to the nearest available space, rather than a predetermined area where all like items are clustered. The location of each item is entered into a computer. When the time comes to retrieve an item, its location is printed out on the shipping bill. When more than one item is on the bill, the computer is programmed to identify the shortest route for the order picker.

A third reason why the proposed layout might not be best is that another layout *pattern* might be better. A-1 is using an *out-and-back selection pattern,* where one item is picked at a time. On a *route collection trip,* the order picker selects a variety of items to be shipped to a given customer. When *batch picking,* the order picker gathers the quantity of an item that is needed to satisfy a group of customer orders that are to be shipped by a common trucker. Finally, in the *zone system,* each picker is assigned to a zone. The picker gathers all items needed from the zone and places them on a powered conveyor line. Figure 9.9 illustrates the zone concept for a warehouse serving several toy supermarkets (such as Children's Palace). The conveyor line con-

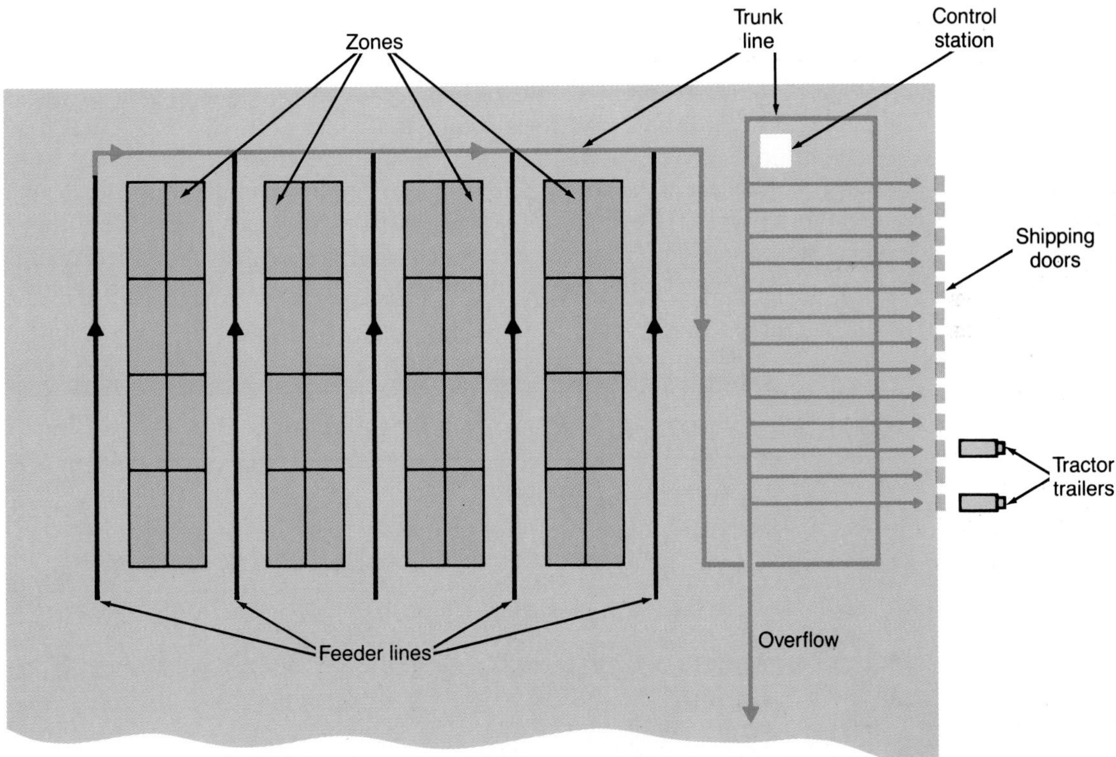

Figure 9.9

A Zone System for a Warehouse.

sists of five feeder lines and one trunk line. When the merchandise arrives at the control station, an operator directs it to the correct destination (tractor trailor) for outbound shipment. The advantage of the zone system is that pickers do not need to travel throughout the warehouse to fill orders; they are responsible only for their assigned zones.

Office Layouts

Over 40 percent of the U.S. work force is employed in offices. The extract of the newspaper article in Box 9.3 suggests that layout affects both productivity and the quality of work life. In a recent survey three-fourths of the 1400 employees polled said productivity could be raised by improvements in their work places.

Proximity. Being accessible to co-workers and supervisors can enhance understanding and mutual interests. Conversations get more formal when people are farther away from each other. Sometimes, face-to-face communication is essential. The famous Hawthorne study in 1939 showed (among other things) that the physical work setting influences group formation (Homans, 1950). The original intent of the research was to find out how a physical variable (lighting intensity) affects productivity. An early discovery was that when lighting intensity was lowered by mistake, productivity increased. This led to a redirection of the study, with the focus on how small groups form and affect work norms. The impact of layout on behavior was obscured, but there clearly was one. Management used *spatial language* to tell the experimental group of workers that they were important. Both their absolute and relative

Box 9.3

OFFICE LAYOUTS AFFECT PRODUCTIVITY

First Bank of Edina, Minnesota, changed its layout. Gone are the lack of privacy and frequent distractions of its prior "bullpen" office arrangement. In its place are work stations with modular units and partitions. Overall efficiency increased by 15 percent in 30 months, partly due to the new layout design.

Design experts surveyed recently believe that better layouts (including lights, acoustics, and climate control) can help both productivity and morale.

Source: "Productivity Jumps in Some Offices after an Interior Redesign," *Wall Street Journal*, September 25, 1984.

locations were changed. The workers were moved to a separate room away from the watchful eyes of a supervisor. The revised layout made contact between workers and the setting of group norms easier. More recent studies confirm that proximity to others can be beneficial, such as helping clarify what is expected of a person on the job.

Most formal procedures for designing office layouts try to maximize the proximity of workers whose jobs require frequent interaction. Data are collected on the frequency and importance of interactions between individuals or groups. Such data are obtained from questionnaires or are based on the judgment of managers. The data can then be used in a REL chart or a From–To matrix. Procedures are even available to identify natural clusters of people, which then can be treated as a center in a block plan (see Jacobs et al., 1980). The goal of such approaches is to design layouts around work flows and communication patterns.

Privacy. Another key factor in office design, although somewhat culturally dependent, is privacy. A child in Great Britain does not expect the privacy of an individual bedroom, whereas a child in the United States does. Sometimes, employees need quiet in order to do their work. Overstimulation from outside disruptions, crowding, and being one of many can hurt performance. When a newspaper company went from private work spaces to an open-plan office to improve worker proximity, the results were disappointing (see Oldham and Brass, 1979). Employees felt like they were in a fishbowl, with little control over their environment. The link between privacy and satisfaction (with the supervisor and the job) was also found to be strong at several departments of a state government (see Schuler et al., 1981).

Some Options. Providing both proximity and privacy for employees is a dilemma. Privacy is gained by more liberal space standards, baffled ceilings, doors, partitions, and thick carpeting to absorb noise. These features can be expensive and reduce layout flexibility. Proximity is gained by opening up the work area. Thus a trade-off between proximity and privacy is usually made. Four different trade-off strategies are available: traditional layouts, office landscaping, activity settings, and electronic cottages. Managers must be environmentally competent in choosing a strategy, since none is best for all offices. The choice requires an understanding of work requirements, the work force itself, and management's working philosophy.

Traditional layouts mean closed offices for some employees and open areas (or bullpens) for all others. The closed offices, with their solid doors and floor-to-ceiling walls, go to management and those employees whose work requires privacy. A typical result is considerable isolation and long hallways lined by closed doors. The open areas mean rows of desks, often in military-like uniformity. Each person has a designated place in traditional layouts. The location, size, and furnishing of the place correlate closely with the person's status in the organization. This contrasts sharply with the more egalitarian settings in Japan.

An approach developed in Germany in the late 1950s puts everyone (including top management) in an open area. Desks and equipment are arranged in smoothly flowing patterns. An extension to this concept is called *office landscaping:* Plants, screens, and portable partitions increase privacy; they help to cluster and separate groups, while adding attractiveness, and flexibility is maintained with movable work stations and accessories. The work stations (or cubicles) are semiprivate, which can make concentration or holding sensitive discussions difficult. Construction costs are as much as 40 percent less than for traditional layouts, and rearrangement costs are even less. Employee reactions to open offices at Sperry Rand's and McDonald's world headquarters were quite favorable. Open offices are also used at Hewlett-Packard, but the corporate nurse keeps earplugs in inventory!

Activity-settings represent a relatively new concept for achieving both proximity and privacy (Stone and Luchetti, 1985). Multiple work places cover the full range of work needs: a library, teleconferencing facility, reception area, conference room, special graphics area, shared terminals, and the like. Employees move from one activity setting to the next as their work changes during the day. Each person also gets a small, personal office as a home base. While much smaller than in the first two strategies, the semiprivate nook provides a sense of territoriality.

Some futurists expect more and more employees to work at home, connected to the office through the computer. Called *electronic cottages,* they are a modern-day version of the cottage industries that existed prior to the Industrial Revolution. The privacy of the home may be ideal for certain kinds of routine work. However, electronic cottages are a poor choice when face-to-face contact and supervision are needed.

PRODUCT LAYOUTS

We now turn from process layouts to product layouts, which raise entirely different issues for management. The two types of product layouts are the production line and the assembly line. In both cases the work stations are arranged serially, and the product moves from one station to the next until the work is finished. Employees at one station work on a unit forwarded from the preceding station on the line. Although similar to an assembly line in most respects, a **production line** is different in one essential respect. Production-line work is more capital intensive, and specialized equipment is used at each station; work cannot be partially shifted from one machine to an entirely different one, just to balance workloads. An **assembly line,** on the other hand, is more labor intensive, giving it much more flexibility for repackaging work elements and better balancing loads; this flexibility is an advantage, but it also adds complexity. We therefore begin with production lines.

Production Lines

Designing a production line would be simple if desired output rates never varied, equipment capacity could be added in small increments, processing times were constant, and there were no unexpected capacity losses (such as for scrap, rework, or equipment breakdowns). Unfortunately, such an environment is difficult to find. Several items belonging to the same product family might be produced on a line, but their processing times may not be identical at certain work stations. Customer demands fluctuate, creating either capacity or inventory problems. Yield losses *do* occur. These instabilities are particularly challenging in product layouts because of the serial dependency of work stations. Capacity and pacing decisions are crucial.

Capacity. One question concerns the best capacity for each station. Should there be one, two or three machines at the station? The greater its capacity cushion, the less likely it will delay production at downstream stations. The answer depends largely on the increments possible in adding capacity, the cost of adding capacity increments, and management's strategy on workforce flexibility. There is some evidence of a *bowl phenomenon* in production lines, which means that extra capacity helps more at the center of a line, even though cushions are cut at the beginning or end of the line to compensate. Such a line might actually perform better than a perfectly balanced one, where the amount of capacity cushion is equally distributed.

Pacing. Another question is whether to use inventory to decouple work stations. *Paced lines* have no buffer inventory, making them particularly susceptible to unexpected capacity losses. With *unpaced lines,* inventory storage areas are placed between stations. These storage areas reduce the likelihood that unexpected downtime at one station will delay work downstream but do increase space and inventory costs. If unpaced lines seem to be a good strategy, they introduce the tactical question of how big the storage areas should be. A station can be held up for two reasons:

1. The first station has fallen behind to the point where the inbound inventory for the second station is depleted. The second station is delayed.
2. The second station has fallen behind to the point where its inbound storage area is temporarily full. The first station is delayed until there is room for the inventory.

The second delay is called *blocking*. It seems to happen more often at stations near the beginning of a line.

Assembly Lines

The additional complexity of assembly lines is illustrated in Box 9.4 for Green Grass, Inc. Its management wants to set up an assembly line that will produce 2400 Big Broadcaster spreaders per week and operate one shift per day. The work elements and the times required to do them for each spreader are known. For example, bolting the leg frame to the hopper takes an average of

Box 9.4

ASSEMBLY-LINE BALANCING AT GREEN GRASS

Green Grass, Inc., is expanding its product line to include a new concept in fertilizer spreaders called the Big Broadcaster. This spreader cuts fertilizer application time to 30 percent of that required with traditional methods. The Big Broadcaster is to be made on a new assembly line in one of the Green Grass plants. Most parts are to be purchased from outside suppliers. Management decided against further vertical integration until customer response to the new spreader is better known. Karen Annay, the plant manager, has just received marketing's latest forecasts for the next year. She wants the line to be designed to make 2400 spreaders per week for at least the next three months. The plant will operate 5 days per week, 1 shift per day, and 8 hours per shift. A few utility workers are used in the plant to relieve others for breaks, cover for absenteeism, and help at temporary bottlenecks. Since equipment failures will be negligible, the line should be operating practically 40 hours per week.

The plant manager's staff has already identified the work that must be performed to assemble the spreader. The work is broken down into work elements which are the smallest units of work that can be performed independently. Each element is listed in the table to the right with its corresponding performance time.

The plant manager has decided on a paced line because of materials handling and space considerations. With no inventory storage, each operator will have the same time to complete the assigned work elements. It also means that the whole line can move only as fast as the slowest station. In order to maximize productivity, Karen wants a line with the minimum number of stations (and therefore workers) that will assemble the required 2400 Big Broadcasters per week. The design problem is to determine the number of stations needed and the work elements to be performed at each station.

51 seconds. More than one work element can be performed at a station, but each work element is assigned to only one station. One worker at each station does the same work over and over. After the worker at one station finishes the assigned work for one unit, a conveyor moves the unit to the next station. The basic question is: "How many stations are needed and what work elements are to be assigned to each one?" Answering this question is called **assembly-line balancing.**

Work Element	Description	Time (sec)
Attach leg frame		
1	Bolt leg frame to hopper	51
2	Insert impeller shaft into hopper	7
3	Attach agitator to shaft	24
4	Secure with cotter pin	10
Attach axle		
5	Insert bearings into housings	25
6	Slip axle through first bearing and shaft	40
7	Slip axle through second bearing	20
Attach drive wheel		
8	Slip on drive wheel	35
9	Place washer over axle	6
10	Secure with cotter pin	15
11	Push on hub cap	9
Attach free wheel		
12	Slip on free wheel	30
13	Place washer over axle	6
14	Secure with cotton pin	15
15	Push on hub cap	9
Mount lower post		
16	Bolt lower handle post to hopper	27
17	Seat post in square hole	13
18	Secure leg to support strap	60
Attach controls		
19	Insert control wire	28
20	Guide wire through slot	12
21	Slip T handle over lower post	21
22	Attach on–off control	26
23	Attach level	58
24	Mount name plate	29
	Total	576

Precedence Diagram. If the work elements had to be performed in the exact sequence listed in Box 9.4, the preceding question could be easily answered. While most assembly lines must satisfy some technological precedence requirements among work elements, there usually is a fair amount of latitude and more than one possible sequence for doing them. Figure 9.10 shows a *precedence diagram* for assembling the Big Broadcaster. Each circle represents a work element, with the time to do it shown below the circle. The arrows show the precedence requirements. For example, either work element 2 or 5 can be done after 1. If the choice is 2, then either 3 or 5 can follow next. It also shows that 7 cannot start until after 4 and 6 are done. Work elements 4 and 6 must be assigned either to the same station as 7 (and performed by the same worker before starting 7) or to a prior station (and done earlier by another worker).

Desired Output Rate. The plant manager at Green Grass has decided on an output rate of 2400 Big Broadcasters per week. While closely related to demand forecasts, the output rate also depends on policies on rebalancing frequency, capacity utilization, and job specialization. All else being equal, production rates should match demand rates as closely as possible. Matching ensures on-time delivery and prevents the buildup of unwanted inventory. The disadvantage is that it increases *rebalancing frequency*. Each time a line is rebalanced, the jobs of many workers on the line must be redesigned. If the line is speeded up, a worker is given fewer work elements. If the line is slowed down, a worker is given more work elements. Time spent relearning jobs temporarily hurts productivity. The changeover may even require a new detailed layout for some stations. A good example of avoiding frequent changes is given in Box 9.5. When demand fell, GM eventually laid off a whole shift, rather than gradually scaling back its output rate.

Capacity utilization is another factor that has to be considered. Multiple

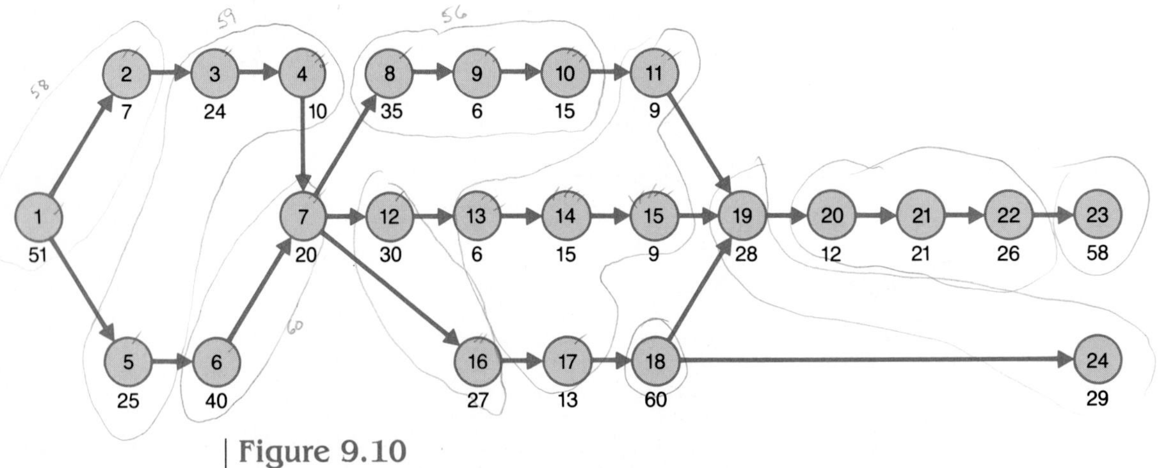

Figure 9.10

Precedence Diagram for Assembling the Big Broadcaster.

Box 9.5

REBALANCING FREQUENCY AT GENERAL MOTORS

General Motors Corporation announced that its assembly plant in Orion Township, Michigan, will add a second shift, recalling 2300 laid-off workers. The line is designed to build 67 cars an hour (Cadillac de Ville and Oldsmobile 98 models).

Source: "GM Plant Will Add Shift, Recalling 2,300," *Wall Street Journal*, May 14, 1984.

shifts increase equipment utilization, which is crucial for capital-intensive facilities, but they may be unattractive because of higher pay rates or low demand. A third policy area related to the desired output rate is the degree of *job specialization.* As the desired output rate from a line increases, fewer work elements can be assigned to a station and jobs become more specialized. (See Chapter 4.) The GM line in Box 9.5 has an output rate of 67 cars per hour, which implies considerable job specialization.

Cycle Time. After the desired output rate for a line has been chosen, its cycle time can be computed. An assembly line's **cycle time** is the maximum amount of time allowed for work on a unit at each station.* If the time required to do the work elements at a station exceeds the line's cycle time, the station will be a bottleneck, preventing the line from reaching its desired output rate. Returning to Green Grass, Inc., let's convert the desired output rate (2400 units per week) to an hourly rate. Dividing by 40 work hours per week (one eight-hour shift, five days per week), we get 60 units per hour. The cycle time is the reciprocal of the desired hourly output rate. We need to convert it to seconds because work-element times at Green Grass were also expressed in seconds, which gives us:

$$\begin{aligned} c &= \left(\frac{1}{r}\right)(3600 \text{ sec/hr}) \\ &= \left(\frac{1}{60}\right)(3600) \\ &= 60 \text{ sec/unit.} \end{aligned}$$

where

c = Cycle time in sec/unit; and

r = Desired output rate in units/hr.

* Except in the context of assembly-line balancing, *cycle time* means the time that elapses between starting and completing a job. Some researchers and practitioners use the term *lead time* in connection with this latter meaning.

Thus no station can have more than 60 seconds of work per unit assigned to it, if the line is to assemble 2400 units per week.

Theoretical Minimum. If we set c to achieve the desired output rate, the assembly-line balancing problem is to assign every work element to a station, satisfy all precedence requirements, and minimize the number of stations (n) formed. If each station is operated by a different worker, minimizing n also maximizes productivity. The ultimate in balance is when the sum of the work-element times at each station equals c; the workload at each station is perfectly balanced and no station has any idle time. Normally, this goal is impossible to achieve in real applications, owing to the unevenness of work-element times and the loss of flexibility caused by precedence requirements. However, assuming perfect balance gives us a benchmark on the smallest number of stations possible. It is called the *theoretical minimum* (TM) number of stations, since it may not be achievable. For the Big Broadcaster line,

$$
\begin{aligned}
TM &= \frac{t}{c} \\
&= \frac{576}{60} = 9.6 \qquad \text{or} \qquad 10 \text{ stations,}
\end{aligned}
$$

where t is the total amount of time required to assemble each unit, or the sum of all work-element times. Since it is impossible to have a fractional station, we round 9.6 up to 10 stations, the theoretical minimum number of stations at Green Grass, Inc.

Three Related Goals. Minimizing n ensures automatically that we (1) minimize idle time; (2) maximize efficiency; and (3) minimize balance delay. These goals are used interchangeably in line balancing, so you need to be familiar with each one:

$$
\begin{aligned}
\text{Idle time} &= nc - t \\
\text{Efficiency (\%)} &= \left(\frac{t}{nc}\right)(100) \\
\text{Balance delay (\%)} &= 100 - \text{Efficiency}
\end{aligned}
$$

Idle time is the total unproductive time for all stations in the assembly of each unit. Each of the n stations spends c seconds per unit, which means that nc is the total time (productive time and idle time) spent per unit. Subtracting the productive time t gives us the idle time. Efficiency is the ratio of productive time to total time, expressed as a percent. Balance delay is the amount by which efficiency falls short of 100 percent. So long as c is fixed, we can optimize all three goals by minimizing n.

Finding a Solution. An overwhelming number of assembly-line solutions are possible, even for this small problem, and the number of possibilities expands as quickly as for process layouts. Once again, computer assistance is available. One software package, for example, considers every feasible combination of work elements that do not violate precedence or cycle time requirements when forming a new station. The combination that minimizes the station's idle time is selected (see Hoffman, 1963). If any work elements remain unassigned, a second station is formed, and so on.

The approach we will use is even simpler. At each iteration, a work element is selected from a list of candidates and assigned to a station. This process is repeated until all stations are formed. Two commonly used decision rules for selecting from the candidate list are:

Rule 1. Pick the candidate with the *longest work-element time.* Intuitively, this tends to assign the more difficult work elements to stations as quickly as possible. Work elements having shorter times are easier to fit into a station and should be saved for fine tuning the solution.

Rule 2. Pick the candidate having the *largest number of followers.* Figure 9.10 shows, for example, that work element 18 has six followers and 21 has two followers. Intuitively, this rule helps to keep your options open for forming subsequent stations. Otherwise, precedence requirements may leave only a few possible sequences of work elements, and all of them may require an unnecessary amount of idle time.

Returning to Big Broadcaster, let's develop solutions manually using these rules. Our overall solution procedure is much like the logic that would be used in computer programs:

Step 1. Let $k = 1$, where k is a counter for the station being formed.

Step 2. Make a list of candidates. Each work element included in the list must satisfy three conditions:

(a) it has not yet been assigned to this or any previous station;
(b) all its predecessors have been assigned to this or a previous station; and
(c) the sum of its time and those of the work elements (if any) already assigned to this station does not exceed the cycle time.

If no such candidates can be found, go to step 4.

Step 3. Pick a candidate using one of the two decision rules. Assign it to station k. Go to step 2.

Step 4. If some work elements are still unassigned, but there are no candidates, a new station must be started. Increment k by 1 and go to step 2. Otherwise, you have a complete solution. Stop.

Figure 9.11 shows a solution that begins with picking candidates at step 3, using decision rule 1. Let's follow the first few iterations until the second station is formed to see the pattern.

- (Step 1) Start with station 1 ($k = 1$).
- (Step 2) Figure 9.10 shows us that only work element 1 can be a candidate. It is a predecessor to all others.

Station	Work elements assigned	Total time per cycle	Station slack
S1	1, 2	58	2
S2	5, 3, 4	59	1
S3	6, 7	60	0
S4	8, 9, 10	56	4
S5	12, 16	57	3
S6	17, 11, 13, 14, 15	52	8
S7	18	60	0
S8	24, 19	57	3
S9	20, 21, 22	59	1
S10	23	58	2
		Total =	24

$$\text{Efficiency} = \frac{576}{10(60)}(100) = 96\%$$

$$\text{Balance delay} = 100 - 96 = 4\%$$

(a)

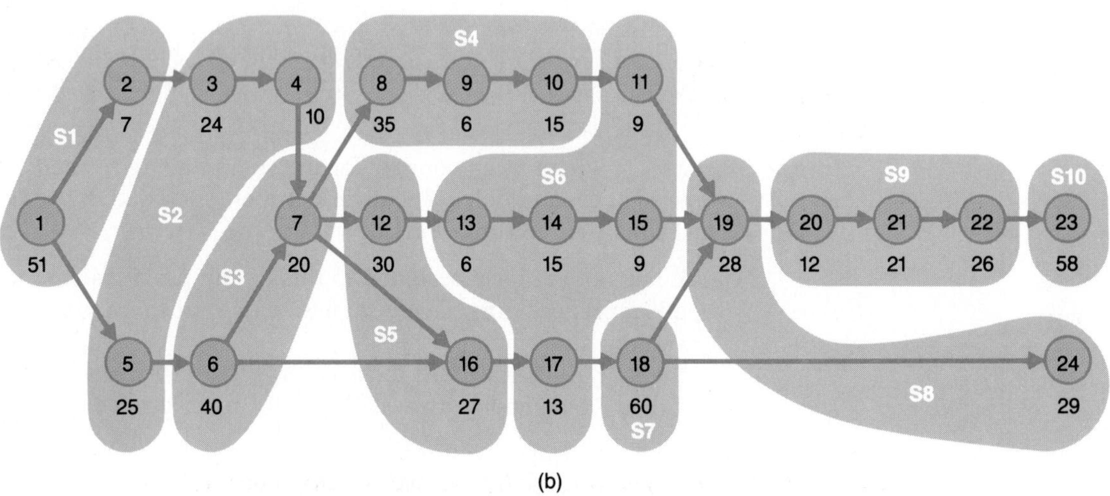

(b)

Figure 9.11

Big Broadcaster Solution Using Longest Work-Element Time Rule: (a) Stations Formed; (b) Precedence Diagram Showing Solution.

- (Step 3) Work element 1 is the first one assigned to station 1.
- (Step 2) Only 2 is a candidate. Work element 5 would exceed the station's cycle time of 60 seconds.
- (Step 3) Thus 2 is the second work element assigned to station 1.
- (Step 2) No candidates can be found, since adding either 3 or 5 would exceed the cycle time.
- (Step 4) Move on to station 2 ($k = 2$).
- (Step 2) The candidates are 3 and 5.
- (Step 3) Pick 5, since its time is longer (25 versus 24). This is the first instance of a real choice because there was only one candidate for each previous iteration.
- (Step 2) Work element 3 is the only candidate. The time for 6 is too long to fit into station 2.
- (Step 3) Thus 3 is the second work element assigned to station 2.
- (Step 2) Only 4 is a candidate, again because of cycle time.
- (Step 3) Thus 4 is the third work element assigned to station 2.
- (Step 2) No candidates exist, since adding 6 would exceed the cycle time. Station 2 is completed, consisting of work elements 5, 3, and 4.

Continuing on in this manner, we find that the final solution shown in Fig. 9.11 calls for only 10 stations. The efficiency is 96 percent and balance delay only 4 percent. Our calculation of the theoretical minimum number of stations told us that we could do no better than this. It is impossible to produce 2400 spreaders per week with less than 10 stations. Such a happy ending does not always occur, and, sometimes, another procedure would do better. Computer-based techniques tend to give good, although not necessarily optimal, results. Human judgment and pattern recognition often allow us to improve on computer generated solutions. In fact, manual methods are still the most prevalent in practice.

A Larger View of Assembly Lines

To this point, we have held to a narrow view of assembly lines. Table 9.3 brings out some of the diversity found in practice. Product weight for the light manufacturing group (toys, pens, hearing aids, and clocks) averages only 3 pounds, whereas it averages more than 2 tons for products in the tractors and engines group (farm tractors, generators, and compressors). Even more importantly, management options go far beyond that of balancing a line for a given cycle time.

Modify Cycle Time. It is important to remember that a line's cycle time depends on the desired output rate. In turn, the maximum efficiency possible

Table 9.3

Assembly-Line Characteristics by Industry

	Industry						
Characteristic	Overall	Light manufacturing	Small appliance	Auto parts	Lawn and garden	Large appliance	Tractors and engines
Sample size							
Number in sample	95	17	19	12	15	19	13
Product weight (lb)	NA	3	11	27	108	1075	5647
Work force							
Average age of line worker	33.2	36.9	31.8	41.0	31.9	28.1	32.0
Percentage of female workers	39.3	83.1	70.2	30.0	20.7	16.6	0.0
Grouped percentage of unionized shops	79.3	61.5	72.7	85.7	85.9	78.5	100.0
Percentage of firms using utility workers	70.6	46.1	63.6	71.4	85.7	78.5	83.0
Rebalancing frequency							
Number of major rebalances per year	3.1	1.3	3.0	5.0	1.8	2.9	5.6
Days after major rebalance before achieving full production	5.4	8.8	4.1	3.0	4.8	5.8	5.4
Behavioral factors							
Absenteeism (average number of days per worker per year)	5.9	7.3	4.8	4.3	6.2	6.5	6.1
Turnover (average percentage of line work force per year)	28.9	3.5	46.3	9.4	25.6	40.1	42.3
Formal grievances (per 100 workers per year)	51.9	63.1	39.5	54.4	66.7	46.1	44.2
Percentage of firms using job rotation on the line	27.0	46.1	20.0	14.3	42.8	21.4	14.0
Percentage of firms attempting job enlargement	38.2	45.5	60.0	14.3	14.2	50.0	29.0

Source: Chase, Richard B., "Survey of Paced Assembly Lines," *Industrial Engineering,* vol. 16, no. 2 (February 1974), pp. 14–18.

from the line varies considerably with the cycle time selected. This second point can be illustrated with Big Broadcaster. The total time required for all work elements is 576 seconds. Recall that its cycle time is 60 seconds and the theoretical minimum number of stations possible is 10. This means that the maximum efficiency* we *might* be able to reach is 96%, or [576/(10)(60)](100).

If we reduce the cycle time to 57 seconds, which is just enough to force the theoretical minimum of stations up to 11, the highest efficiency that we can hope for is 92 percent. If we reduce the cycle time still more, but not to the point where the theoretical minimum number of stations goes up to 12, the maximum possible efficiency actually increases. For example, a cycle time of 53 seconds with 11 stations would bring the maximum possible efficiency that might be achieved up to almost 99 percent.

These calculations suggest exploring a range of cycle times, while still approximating the output rate originally desired. Suppose that we are fortunate enough to find a solution with only 11 stations, if the cycle time is cut to 53 seconds. The line's output would be 68 (or 3600/53) spreaders per hour rather than the 60 originally desired. This still might be the best choice, since efficiency is so high. To avoid inventory buildups, we could change the number of hours the line is operated by reducing overtime, having a shorter shift, or transferring employees periodically to work elsewhere in the plant.

Another possibility is to let the finished inventory build up for some time and then rebalance the line at a lower output rate to deplete the excess. Management's policy on the frequency of rebalancing applies here. The Japanese automobile manufacturing strategy calls for rebalancing lines about 12 times a year. Table 9.3 shows that this frequency is much greater than in the United States, where the overall average is only 3.1 times per year. The Japanese strategy minimizes inventories and balance delay. The major disadvantage of the Japanese approach is that it disrupts production when changing from one line configuration to another. Table 9.3 shows that it takes 5.4 days, on the average, before full production is achieved after a change. Greater work flexibility, cross-training, and job rotation, which are additional elements of the Japanese approach, can help to minimize this disruption.

Identical Lines or Stations. It is not always desirable to have just one line produce all of a product's output. For example, the Big Broadcaster could be made on two lines. Each line could have five stations and a cycle time of 120 seconds. Even if the idea of multiple lines is discarded, some work elements on a single line might best be performed at more than one station. Two identical stations could be formed, with each one assembling alternate spreaders as they move down the line. This approach is mandatory if a work-

* We are dealing here with the *theoretical* maximum efficiency, since we used the theoretical minimum number of stations in the calculation. The *actual* efficiency of an assembly line depends on the number of stations (n) actually formed.

element time exceeds the cycle time and the work cannot be efficiently subdivided.

Workers at identical stations have more time to assemble each unit and more work content. Greater work content increases variety and enlarges jobs horizontally. It also makes line-balancing problems easier to solve. In fact, imbalances between stations can be totally eliminated with identical stations, if each one performs *all* the tasks. This extreme ignores the fact that when job variety goes beyond some limit, performance times increase. The economies of line production and specialization are lost. Equipment needs and wage rates can also increase. A common practice is to pay workers according to the highest skill level required at the station. With more variety (and less specialization) it is less likely that work elements warranting premium pay can be grouped into the fewest number of stations.

The point here is clear: The option of identical lines or stations gives management considerable latitude. The impact of job enlargement on attitudes and behavior must be assessed along with the economic aspects in selecting the best strategy.

Mixed-Model Lines. Sometimes several models belonging to the same product family are produced on the same line. The reference in Box 9.5 to both Cadillac de Ville and Oldsmobile 98 models is a good example. While it has important advantages, such as having both high-volume production *and* product flexibility, mixed-model production can seriously complicate scheduling. Every industrial group in Table 9.3 ranked this problem ahead of line stoppage, quality, parts supply, or absenteeism. Information must be communicated for each unit about the specific parts to be assembled at each station. Care must be taken to alternate from one model to another, so as not to overload some stations for too long. Despite these difficulties, the mixed-model line is often the only reasonable choice, as when product plans call for many customer options; there may not be enough volume to justify a separate line for each model.

Line Pacing. Just as with production lines, assembly lines can be paced or unpaced. Unpaced lines use materials handling devices only to move the product from one station to another—not also for pacing. Inventory storage is provided between stations to decouple them. Since this method increases inventory and possible materials handling costs, you might wonder why it may be an attractive option. One important reason is that it helps to absorb the variability in work-element times at different stations. These times vary from one unit to the next, owing to alignment problems, component shortages, or alternating models. If management decides on a paced line, variability in work-element times must be absorbed in some other way. The line might be slowed down to allow more time for each station. Unfinished work might be completed later, off the line. More idle time might be allowed in the middle of the line, as with production lines, to account for the bowl phenomenon. Finally, the idle time at individual stations might be better equalized.

Behavioral Options. The most controversial aspect of assembly lines is behavioral. The absenteeism, turnover, and grievance statistics in Table 9.3 identify lines as a likely place for personnel problems to occur. High specialization (say, cycle times less than 2 minutes) and paced production are frequently identified as reasons for low job satisfaction. Modifying the cycle time or creating identical stations (two managerial options previously considered) can be used to enlarge jobs. Table 9.3 shows that almost one-third of the companies surveyed are exploring job enlargement and rotation to increase job variety. Such efforts are not always successful. Some cases have been reported where workers reacted unfavorably to enlarged jobs. Workers generally favor inventory buffers as a means to avoid mechanical pacing. One study even showed that productivity increased on unpaced lines.

Another option for humanizing assembly lines is that of involving worker groups more in decisions about who is assigned to each station, when jobs are rotated, which specific work elements are assigned to a station, and even how these tasks are performed. In Europe, Volvo allows considerable group control. Management identifies for each group the work to be done, specifies the desired daily output rate, and provides the necessary resources. Each group decides the rest. The quality circles of Japan, which are now becoming more widespread in the United States, are another example of employee involvement.

Other behavioral options include arranging station layouts to facilitate social interaction, creating stations where two or more people work together, and giving particular attention to personnel selection. Some workers, such as those from rural communities, are likely to be more averse to assembly-line work. Others seem to actually prefer routine work.

Eliminating Bottlenecks. It may be better to select a line balance that overcycles some stations initially, that is, to allow the total work time at some stations to exceed the cycle time. Then steps can be taken to eliminate these bottlenecks, so that the line's desired output rate is met. A methods study or encouraging worker suggestions can often uncover ways to reduce individual work-element times or find better ways of integrating work elements at bottleneck stations. If the line is unpaced, the number of hours worked at a bottleneck might be increased. Finally, worker assignments can sometimes help to level out imbalances because of individual differences in productivity.

CHAPTER HIGHLIGHTS

- Layout decisions go beyond where to place centers of economic activity. Equally important are which centers to include, how much space they need, and how to configure their space.
- There are four layout types: process, product, hybrid, and fixed. Management's choice must be coupled with its positioning strategy. A process focus requires a process layout, while a product focus calls for a

product layout. Hybrid layouts, such as OWMM, group technology cells, and FMS, implement an intermediate positioning strategy.

- Capital investment, materials handling cost, and flexibility are important criteria in judging most layouts. Entirely different criteria, such as sales or communication, might be emphasized for stores or offices.
- Four other fundamental choices are center definitions, timing, building design, and employee participation.
- Three steps in designing a process layout are gathering the necessary information, developing a good block plan, and translating it into a detailed layout. Information needed for process layouts includes space requirements by center, available space (including the current block plan if there is an existing layout), closeness ratings, and other considerations. Closeness ratings can be tabulated on either a From–To matrix or a REL chart. A manual approach to finding a block plan begins with a listing of key requirements, based on large closeness ratings or other considerations. Trial and error is then used to find a block plan that satisfies most of the requirements. A load–distance score helps evaluate the plan for relative location concerns.
- Several computer-based models, such as ALDEP and CRAFT, are now available for decision support. Recently developed software programs can handle multiple criteria, provide a visual representation of the layout, and involve the decisionmaker more throughout the solution process.
- The simplest warehouse situation is the out-and-back selection pattern. Departmental proximity to the dock depends on the ratio of trip frequency to space needs. Other patterns are the route collection trip, batch picking, and the zone system.
- The effect of a layout on people is particularly apparent in offices, affecting productivity and the quality of work life. Four strategies for making proximity–privacy trade-offs are traditional layouts, office landscaping, activity settings, and electronic cottages. Managers must be environmentally competent in picking a strategy, since no single one is best for all situations.
- A product layout can serve as either a production line or an assembly line. Production lines require decisions about capacity and pacing. Assembly lines have the additional dimension of forming stations out of clusters of work elements.
- The assembly-line balancing problem is to assign tasks to stations so as to satisfy all precedence and cycle-time constraints, while minimizing the number of stations required. This in turn minimizes idle time, maximizes efficiency, and minimizes balance delay. The desired output rate from a line depends not only on demand forecasts, but management's policies on the frequency of rebalancing, capacity utilization, and job specialization. One approach to assembly-line balancing is to create one station at a time. A work element selected from a list of candidates is added to a station at each iteration. Two decision rules for making this choice are the longest work-element time and largest number of followers rules.
- Management must look beyond the narrow view of line balancing. Changing the cycle time, creating identical lines or stations, single or mixed-model lines, line pacing, behavioral options, and eliminating bottlenecks are options that are available to ensure the success of a product layout.

KEY TERMS

assembly line
assembly-line balancing
automated layout design program (ALDEP)
computerized relative allocation of facilities technique (CRAFT)
cycle time
From-To matrix
fixed-position layout
hybrid layout
layout planning
mixed-model assembly line
process layout
product layout
production line
REL chart

STUDY QUESTIONS

1. What are the types of choices that must be made in designing a layout? Which ones are the most strategic?
2. How does a process layout differ from a product layout? Illustrate each with an example that you have encountered at work or where you live.
3. With which other decision areas is layout strongly connected? Explain.
4. Identify the types of layout performance criteria that might be most important in the following settings.
   (a) Bank.
   (b) Parking lot.
   (c) Law firm.
   (d) Small metal fabricator.
5. How would you go about developing the layout for the office of budget management described in Box 9.1?
   (a) What information would you gather? How?
   (b) How would you analyze this information?
   (c) How much employee involvement would you recommend? Why?
6. Consider the layout of a retail store you recently visited as a customer. What criteria seemed most important to those who designed it? Why?
7. Think of a small- to medium-sized class that you have taken where there was no assigned seating. Did you tend to sit in the same seat each time? Which criterion discussed for office layouts were you implicitly satisfying?
8. Layouts are often designed to fit current work activities and interaction patterns. These, in turn, are partially shaped by the existing layout. Comment on this apparent circularity.
9. What are the differences between production lines and assembly lines? The similarities?
10. What information is needed before you can solve a line-balancing problem?
11. Suppose a line's desired output rate is 20

units per hour. Why might management consider cycle times other than 180 seconds?

12. Why might employee dissatisfaction be higher on assembly lines? What steps might help to alleviate this problem? Will these steps always lead to higher satisfaction and productivity? Explain.

PROBLEMS

1. The Cleghorn Tool and Machine Company is a job shop specializing in precision parts for aerospace markets. Figure 9.12 shows the From–To matrix and the current block plan for the key manufacturing centers of the 50,000-square-foot facility. Using rectilinear distance (the current distance from inspection to shipping and receiving is 3 units of distance), calculate the change in the load–distance (*ld*) score if Cleghorn exchanges the locations of the tool crib and inspection.
2. Use trial and error to find a layout for Cleghorn Tool and Machine which has a load–distance score even lower than the one found in answering Problem 1.
3. Eastern Electronics makes various products for the communications industry. One of its manufacturing plants makes a device for sensing when telephone calls are placed. A From–To matrix and the current layout are shown in Fig. 9.13. Management is reasonably satisfied with the current layout, although it has heard some complaints about the placement of departments D, G, K, and L. Find a revised block plan for moving only these four departments, using trial and error. Show that the load–distance score is improved, assuming rectilinear distance.
4. Reconsider the office of budget management in Box 9.1. A From–To matrix was developed from questionnaires sent to each of the 120 current employees (Fig. 9.14). It contains section names and area requirements and represents the relative importance of interactions between each of the sections.

From \ To	1	2	3	4	5	6
1. Burr and grind						70
2. NC equipment	20				45	
3. Shipping and receiving		10		15		20
4. Lathes and drills	20				40	
5. Tool crib		30		30		
6. Inspection	10		70			

(a)

NC equipment	Lathes and drills	Shipping and receiving
Inspection	Tool crib	Burr and grind

(b)

Figure 9.12

(a) From–To Matrix (trips/day); (b) Current Block Plan.

From \ To	A	B	C	D	E	F	G	H	I	J	K	L
A. Network lead forming												80
B. Wire forming and subassembly									50	70		
C. Final assembly						120						
D. Coil and terminal eyeletting					40							
E. Presoldering				80							90	
F. Final testing							120					
G. Inventory storage		30						40	50			
H. Coil winding									80			
I. Coil assembly			70		40						60	
J. Network preparation	90											
K. Soldering			80									
L. Network insertion			60									

(a)

L	H	B	K
F	I	J	A
C	D	E	G

(b)

Figure 9.13

(a) From–To Matrix (trips/day); (b) Current Block Plan.

From \ To	1	2	3	4	5	6	7	8	Area needed (blocks)
1. Administration		5	1	3	5	6	5	8	3
2. State Controlling Board	3						1		1
3. Program clearing house	2					1			3
4. Social services	3				6	2	1		2
5. Institutions	3			7		3	7		2
6. Accounting	2				1				1
7. Education	4	1	1	1	8	3			1
8. Internal audit	8						1		3

Figure 9.14

Table 9.4

Storage Section Data

Section	Distance to Assembly Line	Section	Distance to Assembly Line
1	50	7	920
2	60	8	930
3	200	9	940
4	210	10	1680
5	220	11	1690
6	230	12	1700

(a) Develop a square block plan (4 rows and 4 columns) for OBM. Calculate its score, as would be done by ALDEP.

(b) What behavioral issues need to be addressed when revising the layout?

5. Big Reaper plans to produce several new and larger truck models on an assembly line at its Barbville manufacturing facility. Four major warehousing areas in the plant, divided into 12 equal sections, will be used to store the parts and components needed for the new models. Based on current inventory and output plans, the average number of trips per day between storage and the assembly line have been estimated for each of seven basic part categories. The number of storage sections needed for each one (Table 9.4) and the distance from each section to the assembly line (Table 9.5) have also been calculated. Assign each part category to one or more storage sections, so as to provide the right amount of space for each. Find the assignment that minimizes travel from storage to the assembly line. Owing to size restrictions, part category G cannot be assigned to section 1 or 2.

Table 9.5

Parts Data

Part Category	Trips per Day	Number of Sections Needed
A	150	3
B	75	1
C	120	2
D	150	1
E	80	2
F	140	2
G	25	1

6. Table 9.6 has been partially completed from the information in Box 9.4 and Fig. 9.10 for the Big Broadcaster.

(a) Complete Table 9.6 by filling in the last column.

(b) Find a line-balancing solution using the largest number of followers rule. Break ties using the largest work-element time rule. If a tie remains, pick the work element with the highest numerical label.

(c) Calculate the efficiency and balance delay of your solution.

7. An assembly line has been devised to make electric can openers, as shown in Table 9.7.

90 (a) What is the maximum output rate of this line in can openers per hour?

Table 9.6

Work Element	Number of Followers	Work Element	Number of Followers
1	23	13	
2	20	14	
3	19	15	
4	18	16	
5	19	17	
6	18	18	
7	17	19	
8	8	20	
9	7	21	
10	6	22	
11	5	23	
12	8	24	

Table 9.7

Station	Work Element Assigned	Work-Element Time (min)
S1	1	2.8
S2	3, 4	1.5, 1.4
S3	2, 5, 6	0.5, 1.5, 0.7
S4	7	2.3
S5	8	2.5
S6	9, 10, 11	1.7, 0.8, 0.3
S7	12, 13	1.2, 1.8

(b) What cycle time (in minutes) corresponds to this rate?

(c) If there is a worker at each station, how many hours of idle time are lost during each 8 hour shift?

(d) What is the line's efficiency?

(e) What station is the bottleneck operation?

8. Klondike, Inc., has developed a new camera that even a child can operate with minimal instruction. Beautiful shots are possible simply by pressing a button. Management wants to establish two assembly lines to make the camera. Each line includes 11 work elements and must produce 30 cameras per hour. Only *immediate* predecessors are shown in Table 9.8.

Table 9.8

Work Element	Work-Element Time (sec)	Immediate Predecessor
1	12	—
2	60	1
3	36	—
4	24	—
5	38	3, 4
6	72	2, 5
7	14	—
8	72	—
9	35	7, 8
10	60	9
11	12	6, 10

For example, work elements 2 and 5 are immediate predecessors of work element 6. Work element 2 in turn must be preceded by 1, while 5 must be preceded by 3 and 4. You can therefore conclude that the full list of predecessors to work element 6 includes work elements 1 through 5.

(a) Construct a precedence diagram.
(b) What cycle time (in seconds) corresponds to 30 cameras per hour?
(c) What is the theoretical minimum number of stations for each line?
(d) Use the longest work-element time rule to balance the line.
(e) What is the efficiency of your line?
(f) Can you find any way to improve it?
(g) Why might management decide to use two smaller lines, rather than one large one?

9. The *trim line* at Universal Engines is a small subassembly line that, along with other such lines, feeds into the final chassis line. The entire assembly line is to make Universal's new E cars and will be composed of more than 900 work stations. The trim line itself involves only 13 work elements and must handle 15 cars per hour. In addition to the usual precedence constraints, there are two *zoning constraints*. First, work elements 11 and 12 should, preferably, be assigned to the same station; both use a common component and assigning them to the same station conserves storage space. Second, work elements 8 and 10 cannot be performed at the same station. Work-element data are shown in Table 9.9. For a definition of *immediate* predecessors, see Problem 8.

(a) Draw a precedence diagram.
(b) What cycle time (in minutes) results in the desired output rate?
(c) What is the theoretical minimum number of stations?
(d) Using trial and error, balance the line as best you can.
(e) What is the efficiency of your solution?

Table 9.9

Work Element	Work-Element Time (min)	Immediate Predecessor
1	2.4	—
2	0.5	—
3	2.1	—
4	2.0	1
5	1.0	1
6	0.7	5
7	1.1	2
8	2.0	3
9	1.8	4
10	1.9	6, 7
11	0.6	8
12	1.4	10
13	1.0	9, 11, 12

Table 9.10

Work Element	Work-Element Time (sec)	Immediate Predecessor
1	20	—
2	60	1
3	30	2
4	40	2
5	5	2
6	35	1
7	17	4, 5
8	50	3, 6, 7

10. Balance the work elements for assembling bathroom scales shown in Table 9.10, if the cycle time is 90 seconds. Use the longest work-element time rule. See Problem 8 for a definition of immediate predecessors.

SELECTED REFERENCES

Arcus, A. L., "COMSOAL: A Computer Method of Sequencing Operations for Assembly Lines," *International Journal of Production Research*, vol. 4, no. 4 (1966).

Buffa, Elwood S., G. C. Armour, and Thomas E. Vollmann, "Allocating Facilities with CRAFT," *Harvard Business Review* (March–April 1964), pp. 136–158.

Chase, Richard B., "Survey of Paced Assembly Lines," *Industrial Engineering*, vol. 6, no. 2 (February 1974), pp. 14–18.

Cinar, U. "Facilities Planning: A Systems Analysis and Space Allocation Approach." In C. M. Eastman (Ed.), *Spatial Synthesis in Computer-Aided Building Design*. New York: John Wiley & Sons, 1975.

Eastman, C. M., *Spatial Synthesis in Computer-Aided Building Design*. New York: John Wiley & Sons, 1975.

El-Rayah, J., "The Efficiency of Balanced and Unbalanced Production Lines," *International Journal of Production Research*, vol. 17, no. 1 (1979), pp. 61–75.

Ghosh, Soumen, and Roger Gagnon, "A Comprehensive Literature Review and Hierarchical Taxonomy for the Design and Balancing of Assembly Lines." Working Paper Series, College of Administrative Science, Ohio State University (January 1986).

Hicks, P. E., and T. E. Cowan, "CRAFT-M for Layout Rearrangement," *Industrial Engineering*, May 1976.

Hoffman, T. R., "Assembly Line Balancing with a Precedence Matrix," *Management Science*, vol. 9, no. 4 (July 1963), pp. 551–562.

Homans, G. C., *The Human Group*. New York: Harcourt Brace, 1950.

Jacobs, F. Robert, John W. Bradford, and Larry P. Ritzman, "Computerized Layout: An Integrated Approach to Spatial Planning and Communication Requirements," *Industrial Engineering*, vol. 12, no. 7 (July 1980), pp. 56–61.

Kilbridge, M. D., and L. Wester, "A Heuristic Method of Assembly Line Balancing," *Journal of Industrial Engineering*, vol. 12, no. 4 (July–August 1961), pp. 292–298.

Kottas, J. F., and H. Lau, "Some Problems with Transient Phenomena When Simulating Unpaced Lines," *Journal of Operations Management*, vol. 1, no. 3 (February 1981), pp. 155–164.

Liggett, R. S., and W. J. Mitchell, "Interactive Graphic Floor Plan Layout Method," *Computer Aided Design*, vol. 13, no. 5 (September 1981), pp. 289–298.

Muther, Richard, *Practical Plant Layout*. New York: McGraw-Hill, 1955.

Oldham, G. R., and D. J. Brass, "Employee Reactions to an Open-Plan Office: A Naturally Occurring Quasi-Experiment," *Administrative Science Quarterly*, vol. 24 (1979), pp. 267–294.

Pinto, Peter D., David Dannenbring, and Basheer Khumawala, "Assembly Line Balancing with Processing Alternatives," *Management Science*, vol. 29, no. 7 (July 1983), pp. 817–830.

Ritzman, Larry P., John W. Bradford, and F. Robert Jacobs, "A Multiple Objective Approach to Space Planning for Academic Facilities," *Management Science*, vol. 25, no. 9 (September 1979), pp. 895–906.

Schuler, Randall S., Larry P. Ritzman, and Vicki L. Davis, "Merging Prescriptive and Behavioral Approaches for Office Layout," *Journal of Operations Management*, vol. 1, no. 3 (February 1981), pp. 131–142.

Scriabin, M., and R. C. Vergin, "Comparison of Computer Algorithms and Visual Based Methods for Plant Layout," *Management Science*, vol. 22, no. 2 (October 1975), pp. 172–181.

Seehof, J. M., and W. O. Evans, "Automated Layout Design Program, *Journal of Industrial Engineering*, vol. 18, no. 12 (December 1967), pp. 690–695.

Steel, F. I., *Physical Settings and Organization Development*. Reading, Mass.: Addison-Wesley, 1973.

Stone, Philip J., and Robert Luchetti, "Your Office Is Where You Are," *Harvard Business Review* (March–April 1985), pp. 102–117.

CHAPTER 10

MATERIALS MANAGEMENT

Some Managerial Issues

- What are the various planning levels in materials management and how should we coordinate them?
- Should we move to a more integrated organizational structure?
- How should we select, evaluate and support suppliers?
- Should we do more centralized buying? Should we use long-term contracts?
- Should we add distribution centers and position inventory closer to the customer?
- What modes of transportation are best for us?
- Are our inventories and other cushions too high or too low?
- What are our best options for reducing inventory wisely?
- How should we link materials management to competitive priorities?

Chapter Outline

We have finished presenting the longer-term decisions in operations management, which deal with the *design* of production facilities. Positioning strategy, process design (including work-force management and technological choices), capacity, location, and layout are all part of facility design. We now turn to the shorter-range decisions in operations management. **Materials management** deals with the *operation* of facilities after they have been designed and built. Managing supplies, production levels, staffing patterns, inventories, schedules, and distribution all come under the umbrella of materials management. Decisions in these areas affect the management of materials either directly or indirectly.

IMPORTANCE OF MATERIALS MANAGEMENT

Since materials management decisions have shorter time horizons, they are by definition more tactical than strategic. (See Chapter 1.) However, they still have a major cumulative effect and attract considerable managerial attention. Top executives at manufacturing firms in North America, Japan, and Europe picked materials management (specifically production and inventory control) as the area receiving the most attention in recent years with regard to improving manufacturing effectiveness (Miller, et al., 1983). This choice was made from 39 possibilities spanning the full range of concerns in operations management. There are two reasons why tactical decisions about materials are considered to be so important: (1) the central role of materials in production; and (2) the impact of inventories on company success.

Central Role of Materials

Managing materials is common to organizations in every segment of the economy. Materials are necessary inputs to churches, governments, manufacturers, wholesalers, retailers, and universities. Manufacturers make products from materials purchased from outside suppliers. Service industries also need materials in the form of physical items (facilitating goods) purchased from suppliers—one of three components of a service bundle. (See Chapter 2.) The cost of purchased materials is substantial: The typical U.S. manufacturing firm during the last 30 years has spent some 55 percent of its total sales dollars on purchased materials and services. Actually, the share has been increasing: from 40 percent in 1945 to 50 percent in 1960 to 60 percent today. Only about 15–20 percent is now spent on labor (wages, salaries, and benefits), with the remainder contributed to net income, depreciation, taxes, and retained earnings. The proportion spent on purchased materials varies from industry to industry. At one extreme, the petroleum refining industry spends over 80 percent of its sales dollars on materials; the pharmaceutical industry is at the other extreme, at only 25 percent. There is also some variability between countries. Owing to the lack of natural resources, Japanese firms must spend, on the average, 5 percent more of their sales dollars for materials than firms in North America and Europe. Despite such variability, one conclusion is clear: Most firms fall within the 45–65 percent range, giving materials a very high profit-making potential. The example in Box 10.1 illustrates this potential. In order to increase gross profits by $1 million, the company could increase sales by *10 percent* or reduce labor costs by *5 percent*. A third alternative is to reduce materials costs, which requires only a *2 percent* change to achieve the same increase in profits. Since smaller percentage changes normally are easier to achieve, materials are a prime target for cost reduction efforts; a small percentage change in this area makes a significant difference in profits.

Impact of Inventory

Materials also are important because of the investment tied up in them. In 1985, $859.1 billion in inventory were held in the U.S. economy. The ratio of final business sales revenue to inventory cost was only 3 : 1, the lowest ratio

Box 10.1

PROFIT-MAKING POTENTIAL OF MATERIALS

The K. K. Welsh Company manufactures small machines for intermittent use in offices or small firms, such as retail stores or gas stations. This year's sales will be approximately $100 million. Materials costs represent 50 percent of the sales dollar, and 20 percent goes for salaries, wages, and benefits. A 10-percent gross profit (before taxes) is expected, which is typical of prior years at K. K. Welsh.

The business plan calls for gross profits to be increased next year by $1 million, from $10 million to $11 million. Three options are being reviewed for achieving this goal. The calculation for each option is shown in the following table.

Alternative	Percent Change
1. Increase sales by $10 million (10% of which yields $1 million in gross profits).	$\left(\frac{\$10 \text{ million}}{\$100 \text{ million}}\right)(100) = \underline{\underline{10\%}}.$
2. Reduce labor costs by $1 million.	$\left(\frac{\$1 \text{ million}}{\$20 \text{ million}}\right)(100) = \underline{\underline{5\%}}.$
3. Reduce materials costs by $1 million.	$\left(\frac{\$1 \text{ million}}{\$50 \text{ million}}\right)(100) = \underline{\underline{2\%}}.$

over the last four decades.* Consider a second ratio: Inventory investment in the U.S. economy is more than double all business investment (by both the manufacturing and service sectors) in new plants and equipment each year. Each dollar tied up in inventory is a dollar unavailable to invest in new products, technological improvements, or capacity increases.

Figure 10.1 shows that most inventory is held by manufacturers, wholesalers, and retailers. Since only 40 percent is held by the manufacturing sector, materials management is of concern throughout the entire economy.

FUNCTION OF MATERIALS MANAGEMENT

Having a better appreciation for the pivotal role of materials management, we now consider more carefully the types of decisions actually involved. It would be ideal if one person in a firm could make all materials management decisions centrally, since they are so interrelated. However, the sheer magnitude

* This ratio for the economy as a whole is lower than for the typical firm. The reason is that only *final* sales to the ultimate consumer are considered, excluding intermediate sales from one firm to another.

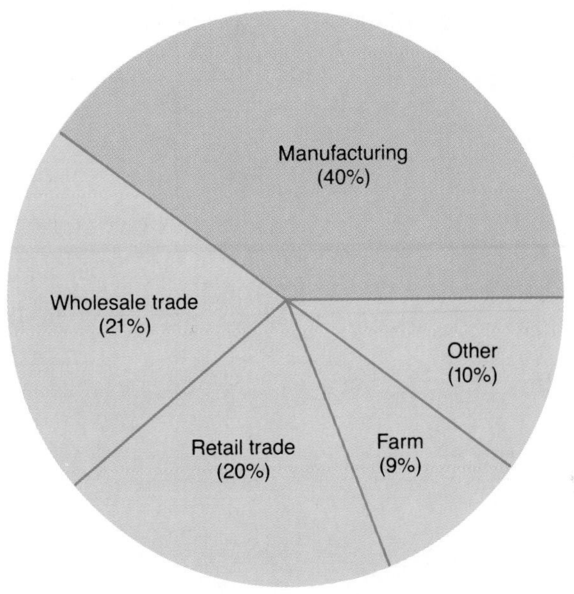

Figure 10.1

Where Inventories Are Held.

Source: Economic Report of the President, 1986, p. 272.

of this task makes it impossible. It is not unusual for a business unit to be responsible for thousands of employees and product items, hundreds of work centers, several plants, and hundreds of suppliers. Having one person develop weekly plans even three months into the future for purchasing, inventory, output rates, work-force levels, and shipping schedules is mind boggling. In practice, decisions are made hierarchically, top-down, with feedback loops to handle problems not anticipated at higher levels.

A Decision Hierarchy

A typical hierarchy for making materials management decisions is shown in Fig. 10.2. A block diagram is presented for both the service (Fig. 10.2a) and manufacturing (Fig. 10.2b) sectors, since the terminology used is not quite the same. The functions associated with materials management are located in the two large shaded areas at the bottom of the figure.

Figure 10.2 also represents a roadmap of this chapter and the next seven, showing how they relate to the first nine chapters. Beginning at the top of the hierarchy, corporate strategy sets the general direction of the organization for years ahead. Decisions are made about the mission and the acquisition and

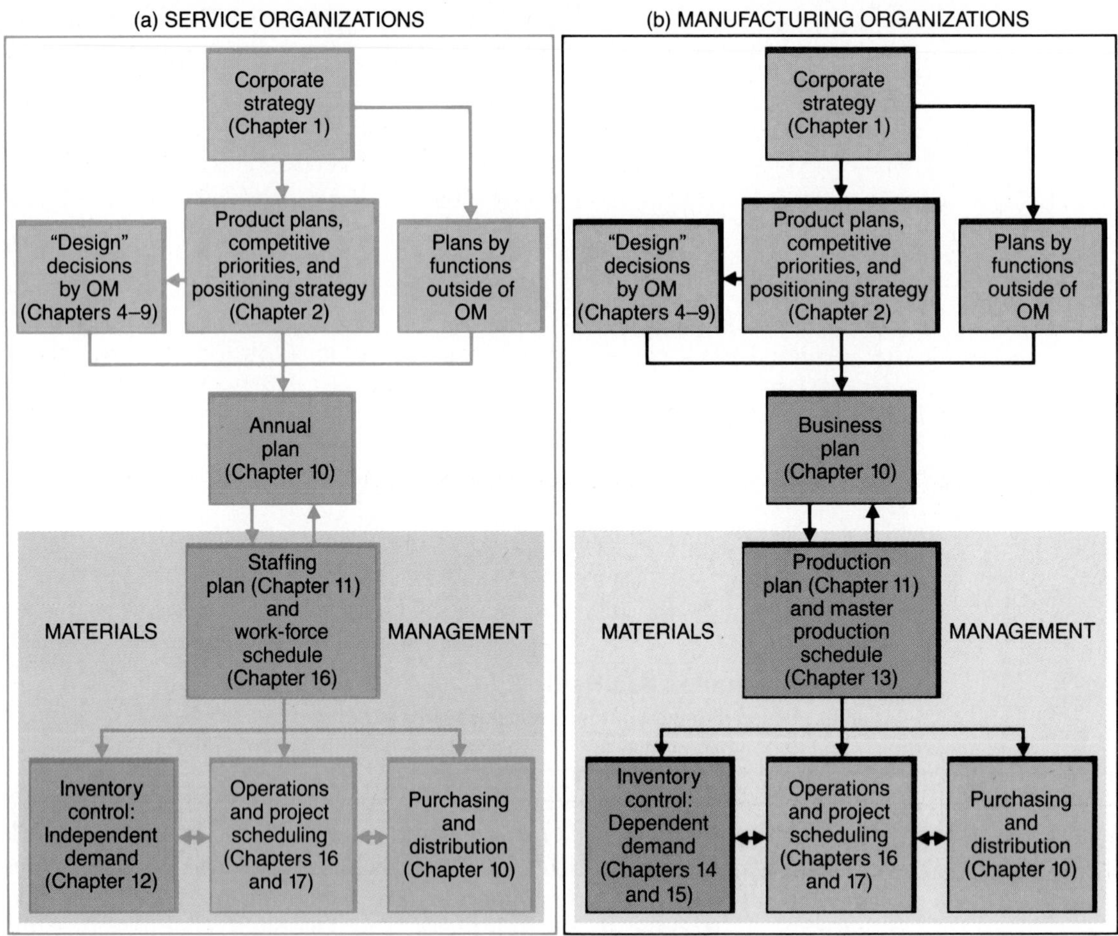

Figure 10.2

Materials Management Decision for (a) Service Organizations; and (b) Manufacturing Organizations.

deployment of resources to meet it. Goals are established for growth, market share, and profit margins. Product plans and competitive priorities are selected, which then shape

1. plans made by managers of other functions, such as marketing, finance, engineering, and human resource management;
2. the way that operations managers select a positioning strategy (Chapter 2); and

3. design decisions made by operations managers about the work force, technology, processes, long-run capacity, location, and layout. (See Chapters 4–9.)

At this point, top management needs a financial assessment of the organization's near future, that is, for one or two years ahead. This assessment is called either a business plan (in manufacturing) or an annual plan (in service industries). A **business plan** is a projected statement of income, costs, and profits. It is usually accompanied by budgets, a projected balance sheet, and a projected cash flow statement, showing the source and application of funds. The business plan brings together into one coherent package the plans and expectations of a firm's operations, finance, and marketing managers. Service organizations, such as a hospital, retail store, or government agency, also prepare such a plan. Since some service organizations are in the public sector and are not even businesses, we call their plan an **annual plan**. This terminology is not universal, and other terms commonly used are the *financial plan* or *budget*.

Figure 10.2 shows that the level in the hierarchy below the business or annual plan moves us into the domain of materials management. In a service organization, preparation of a *staffing plan* begins the planning process by setting the basic activity and personnel levels for one or two years ahead, often on a monthly basis. Since facility and equipment capacities are fixed by now, changing staffing levels (such as hiring) and personnel utilization (such as overtime) are the main ways left to adjust capacity. The staffing level is particularly important in the service sector because payroll (including employee benefits) tends to dominate the budget and demand cannot be satisfied with preproduced inventories. The work force must be there when needed, or customer service slips. Turning to the manufacturing sector, preparation of a *production plan* launches the operational planning process. More complex than the service-sector staffing plan, the production plan sets the monthly output rate for major groups (or families) of items, say, for the next year ahead. Staffing levels, inventory projections, and demand forecasts are all part of the plan.

A staffing plan does not specify the days and times of day each person will be on duty. Similarly, the production plan is not specific as to the weekly output for each item. To achieve this level of detail, we must go one step lower in the hierarchy of Fig. 10.2. A *work-force schedule* (Chapter 16) is developed within the guidelines of the staffing plan to specify the on-duty hours and work assignment of each employee. This step is crucial for service organizations such as police departments, hospitals, and retailers who operate around the clock. The work-force schedule breaks down the staffing plan and makes it operational. In like manner, the *master production schedule* (Chapter 13) makes the production plan specific. It states the weekly output quantity for each item, projected weeks or months into the future.

Figure 10.2 shows that the final level of operations planning consists of three areas:

1. Inventory control.
2. Operations and project scheduling.
3. Purchasing and distribution.

The best system for *inventory control* depends on the type of demand involved. In Chapter 12, we cover demand situations of particular interest to service industries. We devote Chapters 14 and 15 to a presentation of several systems for managing inventories at manufacturing firms. Inventory control is closely related to scheduling issues. After a shop order is released (an inventory control decision), someone must decide when the item is to be processed at each of the work centers in its routing (a scheduling decision). *Operations scheduling* (Chapter 16) and *project scheduling* (Chapter 17) both deal with establishing starting and completion times for activities, jobs, or customers. This brings us to the functions of *purchasing* and *distribution*, which deal with the flow of materials into and out of the production system.

This hierarchical process allows senior managers to make top-level decisions using aggregate data. Their decisions constrain the more detailed plans developed at lower levels. The process is not only a practical necessity, but helps management to delegate more effectively. Two examples of the process are given in Box 10.2.

Organizing the Materials Function

The departmental structure in many organizations resembles parts of Fig. 10.2. Distinct departments for purchasing and inventory control are frequently found in service industries. This structure is less likely for staff planning, work-force scheduling, and operations scheduling. These tasks are usually done on a decentralized basis. For example, branch managers at retail stores or banks develop their own schedules.

Departmental structure in manufacturing firms fits Fig. 10.2 even more closely. Except for very small firms, there usually are separate departments for production planning, inventory control, production control, purchasing, and distribution. The production planning department prepares the production plan and master schedule. The inventory control department manages inventory levels and maintains records of the amount and location of inventory by item. The production control department schedules operations, the purchasing department manages inbound shipments of raw materials and purchased parts, and the distribution department (sometimes called the *traffic*, or *shipping*, department) handles outbound shipments.

Table 10.1 gives you an even better idea of how companies organize the full range of tasks in materials management. Each task is assigned to one of

Box 10.2

TWO EXAMPLES OF HIERARCHICAL PLANNING

A Tire Company

A large U.S. tire company has a plant in each of four regions in the country—eastern, north central, south central and western. Each plant makes all of the high-volume product lines. This is not true for low-volume products, which are made at only one or two plants. A warehouse, often called a "distribution center" (DC), is located at each plant. It receives tires made in-house as well as at the other three plants and then ships out mixed loads to the customers.

Hierarchical planning begins with corporate management, who establish the distribution regions served by each plant, working only with annual forecast totals. At the next level, plant managers put together monthly output, manpower, and inventory plans. These plans are still aggregated, since they are for groups (families) of items. Finally, shop managers break these plans down into shorter term plans for each individual item. These detailed plans must satisfy the higher level plans, as well as provide good customer service.

A Paper Company

International Paper operates 24 paper mills, 100 other manufacturing plants, and 100 DCs. It markets its products of pulp, paper, and paper products worldwide. Top management makes decisions such as whether to invest in new production facilities for new lines and, if so, where to put them and at what size. One level lower, a business plan is prepared annually to assess yearly profit levels for each business unit.

One difficult problem is scheduling customer orders at the paper mills to meet new demand and back orders. Scheduling begins with a divisional manager who oversees several plants. Decisions are made about the monthly allocation of work to each plant, so as to get the best balance between production costs, transportation costs, and on-time delivery. At the plant level, a new set of plans is worked out. Batch sizes, production sequences, and start/finish times are determined for each item, as well as which ones are assigned to each machine. Finally, these plans are the basis for preparing final shipping schedules.

Sources: Paul S. Bender, William D. Northup, and Jeremy F. Shapiro, "Practical Modeling for Resource Managment," *Harvard Business Review*, March–April 1981, pp. 163–173; Harlan C. Meal, "Putting Production Decisions Where They Belong," *Harvard Business Review*, March–April 1984, pp. 102–111.

five departmental groupings, as reported in a 1978 survey of 137 U.S. manufacturers. For example, vendor selection was assigned to the purchasing department more often than to any other department. As interesting as the work content of each department is the level at which the tasks are performed. Table 10.1 also shows whether a materials management task is done

Table 10.1

Materials Management Task Assignments

Department	Task Assignment	Organizational Level*
Purchasing	Vendor selection	G
	Issuing purchase releases	L
	Inbound transportation	L
Manufacturing	Manufacturing/distribution systems development	G
	Receiving	L
	Factory stockroom operation	L
	Finished goods warehousing at the plant	L
Production planning, inventory control, and production control	Assigning delivery due dates to orders	G
	Finished goods inventory control (plant)	G
	Master scheduling	G
	WIP inventory control	L
	Raw materials inventory control	L
	Detailed production scheduling	L
Distribution and traffic	Finished goods inventory control (DCs)	G
	Outbound transportation: DCs to customer	G
	Shipping	L
	Outbound transportation: Plant to DCs	L
Marketing	Forecasting	G
	Processing incoming customer orders	G

* L = tasks done locally, at plant site.
G = tasks done globally, at divisional or corporate level.

Source: Jeffrey G. Miller, Peter Gilmour, and Roland Van Dierdonck, "Organizing for Materials Management." Working Paper HBS 80-23, Graduate School of Business Administration, Harvard University, 1980.

mainly at the individual plant site (local) or at the divisional or corporate level (global).

Two findings are clear from Table 10.1:

1. Some tasks are performed at higher organizational levels than others. This reinforces the notion of the decision hierarchy in Fig. 10.2. Tasks done at higher levels tend to involve high-impact areas, rather than the

day-to-day planning of materials flows. They also tend to relate more directly to the customer, such as assigning due dates and controlling finished goods inventory.

2. Not all materials management tasks are handled by the same department. Even though Table 10.1 somewhat arbitrarily clusters production planning, inventory control, and production control into one department, considerable dispersion of tasks across departmental lines remains.

Since the early 1960s, there has been growing sentiment for (1) grouping most materials management tasks under one roof; and (2) elevating the manager of this new group to a higher position in the company. This new department is typically called *materials management*, although the term *logistics management* is used sometimes. At one organizational extreme is the *segmented structure*, which is the arrangement traditionally used. Of particular concern is the placement of three departments: (1) purchasing; (2) production planning, inventory control, and production control; and (3) distribution and traffic. In a segmented organization the manager of each of these departments reports to a different person. At the other organizational extreme is the *integrated structure*, which creates a materials management department headed by a key executive. This structure not only elevates the materials function, but recognizes that the various materials management tasks are all part of the same broad activity. It brings together all tasks related to flows of materials beginning with the purchase of raw materials and ending with the distribution of the finished product or service.

In a 1978 survey, only 10 percent of the firms responding still used a segmented structure; 40 percent placed the three key departments together in an integrated structure. The remaining 50 percent used hybrid structures, with only two of the three departments reporting to the same executive. The department most likely to be left out was distribution, which continued reporting to marketing.

PURCHASING AND DISTRIBUTION

Although subsequent chapters deal with most of the materials management tasks, they do not include a discussion of certain aspects of purchasing and distribution. Entire books have been written about each of these functions, so we must settle for a brief introduction to each one.

Purchasing

Purchasing is the starting point in the materials management cycle of acquisition, storage, conversion, storage, and distribution. Its main task is acquisition, that is, placing purchase orders with selected vendors in response to requests (called *purchase requisitions*) from others in the firm and then following up open orders until they are received. Purchasing normally gets authority to buy from the production and inventory control department, at least at a manufacturing firm. For a retailer, the decision about what to buy is the same as the decision about the merchandise to be sold; product planning and purchasing decisions are intermixed.

It is a mistake to conclude that purchasing's role is limited to placing orders and then expediting them until delivered. Expediting means to follow up with the supplier on the status of orders placed but not received by writing, sending a telex, or calling by telephone. Purchasing is of strategic importance and therefore must go beyond meeting these day-to-day requirements. Its prime function is to satisfy the firm's long-term supply needs, so as to best complement the firm's production capabilities. This task is crucial for any organization, whether retailer, hospital, or manufacturer. Purchasing departments in the private sector of the U.S. economy account for expenditures of $2 trillion per year, and the federal government accounts for another $159 billion. Purchasing's role can be better understood if we look at selected decision areas beyond the order placing and expediting activities. We begin with vendor selection.

Vendor Selection. Purchasing is the eyes and ears of the organization in the supplier marketplace, continuously seeking better buys. This process begins with the vendor selection decision. Purchasing agents for some companies establish formal rating procedures to help them select new suppliers or periodically review current suppliers. Three of the many criteria considered in a selection decision almost always are price, quality, and delivery. Beginning with *price,* recall that a typical firm is now spending 60 percent of its total sales dollars on purchased items. Finding suppliers who charge lower prices is a key to healthy profit margins.

As important as it is, price is not the only consideration. The *quality* of materials from a supplier can be very important, as illustrated by the example in Box 10.3. The Defense Department suffered because its suppliers delivered parts and materials that did not conform to specifications. The hidden costs of poor quality can be high, particularly if the defects are not detected until after considerable value has been added by subsequent manufacturing operations. The hidden costs of poor quality are not limited to manufacturers. For a retailer, poor quality can mean loss of goodwill and future sales. Quality problems are particularly devastating if a firm's competitive priority is production of top-quality merchandise. (See Chapter 18 for more discussion of quality.)

The last criterion considered here for vendor selection is *delivery*. Shorter lead times and on-time delivery help the buying firm to maintain its customer service with less inventory. Maimonides Medical Center, a 700-bed hospital in Brooklyn, buys much of its materials from one supplier. The supplier offers very short lead times from a nearby warehouse. This has allowed

Box 10.3

WHY VENDOR QUALITY MAKES A DIFFERENCE

Semiconductor chips are used in almost every computer-equipped weapons system. Recently some were supplied to many defense contractors from a major supplier without adequate testing. There were irregularities in testing procedures for about 200 chip types. The Defense Department was forced to delay accepting shipment of any arms containing the suspect microchips. Shipments worth millions of dollars were held up, while prime contractors and smaller subcontractors checked their products and inventories for problems. This hurt the cash flow of many contractors and caused late shipments to the Defense Department.

Source: "Chips Testing Causes Delay on Weapons," *Wall Street Journal*, October 25, 1984.

Maimonides to pare its inventory from about $1200 to only $150 per bed. The benefits of fast and on-time deliveries also apply to the manufacturing sector. Many manufacturing firms seek *just-in-time* (JIT) delivery from their suppliers in order to minimize inventory levels. (See Chapter 15.) This constraint requires selecting vendors who have local plants or are willing to build new ones nearby. Almost half of the U.S. plants owned by Japanese firms rely on local suppliers for more than 70 percent of their components. Another example of the use of JIT is Kasle Steel Corporation. It is building a steel-processing plant adjacent to GM's Buick facility in Flint, Michigan, even though it already has two plants only 70 miles away. This new plant is part of a planned complex (called "Buick City") at which almost all parts will be supplied to the GM facility by nearby plants. These clustered suppliers will ship very small quantities frequently, so that inventory at the assembly plant will be negligible.

Vendor Relations. A second purchasing issue of strategic importance is the type of relations maintained with vendors. A firm can relate to a supplier either competitively or cooperatively. The *competitive orientation* is particularly prevalent in North America. Negotiations between buyer and seller are viewed as a zero-sum game: Whatever is lost by one side is gained by the other; for every winner there is a loser. There is little mutual trust, and short-term advantages are prized over long-term commitments to each other. The buyer may try to beat the supplier's price down to the lowest survival level, while demanding high quality and excellent customer service. The buyer may also expect the supplier to provide high volume flexibility, pushing demand to high levels during boom times and ordering almost nothing during recessions. The supplier, on the other hand, presses for higher prices for specific levels of quality, customer service, and volume flexibility. Which party wins depends largely on the balance of power between the buyer and supplier. The buyer has the upper hand when

1. the buyer represents a significant share of the supplier's sales;
2. the purchased item is not unique, but rather highly standardized with many substitutes offered by competing suppliers;
3. the buyer is in a credible position to integrate backward into the supplier's business;
4. the supplier lacks credibility in being able to integrate forward into the buyer's business; and
5. the cost of switching to a new vendor is relatively low.

Conversely, the supplier is more powerful if these factors are reversed. To gain leverage, for example, a supplier may attempt to increase the buyer's cost of switching to another supplier. One tactic is to encourage more customized design of the parts it makes for the buyer's products. The more this tactic succeeds, the greater is the deterrent to switching to a new supplier.

The *cooperative orientation* to supplier relations is attracting more attention, particularly because of the success certain Japanese firms have had with it. The buyer and seller are seen as partners, with each helping the other as much as possible. One important variable in fostering a cooperative spirit is the number of suppliers from which a buyer chooses to buy the same item. A competitive orientation argues for multiple suppliers, with six suppliers being better than three. This minimizes switching costs and keeps each supplier off balance. The premise is that the increased competition creates a built-in pressure for low prices, high quality, and fast delivery times. Multiple sources also ensure backup capability in the event that one source is disabled by a strike, capacity shortage, or quality problem. In contrast, the cooperative orientation favors few suppliers for a particular purchased item, with just one or two suppliers being the ideal number. One big advantage is increased volumes. The supplier gains repeatability, which helps movement toward the product-focused strategy of a high-volume, low-cost producer. (See Chapter 2.) When contracts are large, the supplier may even have to build a new facility and hire a new work force. Being assured of a long-term relationship may make the difference in whether the supplier builds a new facility, particularly if it is to be located in close proximity to the buyer's plant. Fewer suppliers may also benefit the buyer. The buyer gains clout by becoming one of the supplier's major customers. The supplier becomes almost an extension of the buyer. The trade-offs between single and multiple sources are highlighted by the two opposing positions in Box 10.4.

A cooperative orientation means more than reducing the number of suppliers: It means sharing more information on future buying intentions. This forward visibility improves the ability of suppliers to forecast future demand,

Box 10.4

COMPETITIVE VERSUS COOPERATIVE ORIENTATIONS

Competitive

The Air Force divided a huge jet-engine contract between General Electric and the former exclusive contract-holder, Pratt & Whitney. The Air Force expects the competition to save costs. A warranty system also shifts some costs for materials failures back to the supplier.

Cooperative

Toyota has 300 major suppliers, compared with GM's nearly 4000. Chairman Smith said GM is planning to pare the number of suppliers in its network, leaving only the most efficient ones. Suppliers who pass muster will get long-term contracts. This benefit helps ensure that suppliers will get enough volume to recoup any investments in cost-saving equipment and new capacity. Higher repeatability also should create economies of scale.

Sources: "Procurement Success Story," *Wall Street Journal*, February 6, 1984; "Auto Companies Push Part Makers to Raise Efficiency, Cut Prices," *Wall Street Journal*, July 31, 1984.

which makes them more efficient and reliable. Better forecasts allow inventory to be cut and on-time delivery to be improved. In long-term and stable relationships, the purchasing agent visits vendors' plants, cultivates cooperative attitudes, and jealously guards the relationships. A cooperative orientation may even lead the buyer to suggest ways to improve the supplier's operations. This approach not only reduces supply problems, but also allows quicker resolution of problems when they do occur. Trust in a supplier can mean that the buyer does not even have to inspect incoming materials. It can also mean looser specifications on purchase orders, involving the supplier more in designing parts, implementing cost reduction ideas, and sharing in cost savings. For example, Rockwell is the major contractor for the B-1 bomber program. It saved $500 million on a fixed-priced incentive program, under which the government and contractor split the savings when an item comes in under budget.

Length of Contracts. Purchasing must decide how to contract for each item it buys. No one procedure is best for the thousands of items purchased by most firms. The procedure selected depends a great deal on volume and usage rates. When there is *low demand,* as with customized items not held in inventory, a buyer has three options:

1. Competitive bidding.
2. Sole source contracting.
3. Vendor catalogues.

Competitive bidding means that several suppliers are asked to submit formal quotations. The lowest *and* best (most capable) bidder receives the contract. This method is not mandatory in the private sector but is prudent when the expenditure to be made is great, as with new heavy equipment or a computer system. If the dollar value of the purchase is low or time is of the essence, there are two other options. One is sole source contracting, in which a company negotiates a contract with a single supplier. Purchasing lead time is reduced, but the best buy may not be obtained, particularly if the buyer is unaware of comparative prices. The other option is simply to look through several vendor catalogues and make a selection. The cost of any further search outweighs the benefits.

Contracting procedures can be quite different with *high demand,* as with standardized items for which there is continuous demand. There are two options: (1) preselected vendors; or (2) long-term contracts. With the first option, competitive bidding is not done for each order placed. When requisitions are received from production and inventory control, purchasing immediately sends to the preselected vendor a purchase order specifying the product, quantity, and delivery due date. There is no delay because of vendor selection.

If demands are high enough, the second option may be used. It really is a special case of using preselected vendors. Long-term contracts covering one or more years are negotiated, with delivery dates, quantities, and often prices left open. The buying firm commits to a supplier for the agreed-on period of time, often sending periodic estimates of future needs to the supplier. When a new order is placed, purchasing does not even need to write a purchase order. The requisition often goes directly to the supplier, bypassing purchasing entirely. The requisition specifies the quantity and due date. If price was left open in the long-term contract, then it is set at whatever is in effect at the time of purchase. Most long-term contracts are called *blanket* or *open-end* contracts. A blanket contract covers a variety of items, whereas an open-end contract allows items to be added or the contract period extended. Long-term contracts have several advantages. The buyer saves paperwork and reserves capacity with a supplier. Since the annual volumes negotiated on the contract are large, price concessions are possible. Vendors prefer long-term contracts because they make future demand more certain. Long-term contracts are consistent with the cooperative orientation to supplier relations.

Centralized Buying. When an organization has several facilities (stores, hospitals, or plants), a decision must be made about whether to buy locally or centrally. There is a trend away from complete decentralization by major organizations such as Du Pont, General Foods, PPG Industries, Quaker Oats, and Westinghouse. Some items are best purchased centrally, while others should be left to local initiative. In deciding which strategy is best for a particular item, management must weigh the advantages and disadvantages of each.

Centralization has several advantages, some of which are identical to those of long-term contracts. When two or more local facilities use the same standardized items, centralized buying can increase purchasing clout. Savings can be significant, often on the order of 10 percent or more. Increased buying power can help in other ways, such as getting better service to buyer locations, ensuring long-term supply availability, or developing new supplier capability. As an example of getting better service, centralized buying at General Foods helped immensely with the energy shortages experienced in 1973–1974. By dealing on a corporation-to-corporation basis, the company was able to ensure an adequate supply of scarce materials to each of its facilities. Two trends favor more centralization: (1) growth of multinational business operations, which makes specialized knowledge and skills desirable when items must be purchased from foreign sources; and (2) growth of computer-based information systems for materials management, which allows specialists at headquarters to have access to data previously available only at the local level.

Despite these advantages, centralized buying for all items would be a mistake. Items unique to a particular facility should be purchased locally. The same holds for purchases that must be closely meshed with production schedules because purchasing lead times may be longer, with another level in the hierarchy involved. When quality or short shipment (quantities received are less than ordered) problems arise, centralized buying can prevent local managers from responding quickly. Probably the biggest disadvantage of centralized buying is loss of control at the local level. Plant or division managers may be evaluated on a profit or cost center basis, and yet a major cost item is not under their control. It is possible to lose some of the entrepreneurial spirit at local levels, which is essential to organizations such as General Motors. Perhaps the best solution is a compromise strategy, whereby local autonomy and centralized buying are both possible. For example, the corporate purchasing group at IBM negotiates contracts on a centralized basis only at the request of local plants. Then, one of the facilities takes over as the prime plant in monitoring the contract. General Motors also has a mixed strategy, buying some items centrally while purchasing others locally through its 100 purchasing offices. To help identify opportunities for centralized buying, GM publishes lists of items purchased by each local office.

Distribution

Purchasing deals with *inbound* materials, whereas **distribution** is concerned with the *outbound* flow of materials from the manufacturer to the customer. Distribution deals with storing and transporting products and broadens the marketplace for a firm, adding time and place value to its products. Transportation makes up a substantial share of an item's price, with over 10 percent of the U.S. labor force engaged in transportation or transportation-related industries. Here we briefly consider three issues faced by distribution managers.

Positioning Finished Goods Inventory. A fundamental choice is where to stock inventory of finished goods. *Forward positioning* means locating stock closer to customers at a warehouse (now usually called a *distribution center* or DC), wholesaler, or retailer locations. *Backward positioning* means holding the inventory at the manufacturing plant or maintaining no inventory. Forward positioning can have two advantages: (1) fast delivery times; and (2) possible reductions in transportation costs. Forward positioning cuts delivery times, which can be an important competitive priority. Dubbed the "warm puppy effect," proximity to a stocking point can give customers a more comfortable feeling (see Vollmann, et al., 1984), which, in turn, can stimulate sales. The second advantage can be savings in transportation costs. The premium rates of less-than-carload (LCL) shipments might be avoided. Shipments out of the plant are concentrated on a few routes (to the DCs), rather than fragmented for scattered customer locations. Even outbound shipments from DCs to customer destinations may now be large enough to achieve full carload (CL) rates more frequently, particularly if several plants are providing a variety of products to the DCs. For example, General Foods mixes products received from various plants at its distribution centers and reships to customers at full CL rates.

Forward positioning is not always possible or advisable. If competitive priorities call for product flexibility and customized products, it does not make sense to even have any finished goods inventory. The risk of creating unwanted products is too great. Specific customer orders must be placed before the manufacturer can know exactly what to produce. A second argument against forward positioning is the *pooling effect.* The demand in any one region can be unpredictably high one month and low the next. If demand in several such regions is pooled, as would be the case with less forward positioning, the highs at some regions tend to cancel the lows at others. Demand is less erratic and more predictable when inventory is positioned at a centralized point, rather than at a DC for each small region. Inventories for the whole system can be lower, and costly reshipments from one DC to another can be minimized. The description in Box 10.5 provides a good example of the pooling effect. Ethan Allen originally positioned inventory as far forward as possible: with retailers. By creating DCs as intermediate stocking points, inventories dropped dramatically. If management does decide on a strategy of having DCs, it must next decide on their number and location. (See Chapter 8.) It must also design and operate an inventory replenishment system (Chapters 12 and 14).

Selection of Transportation Mode. There are several modes of transportation from which to choose, and technological change in transportation is fairly rapid. For example, most pipelines move petroleum, but some companies use

Box 10.5

DISTRIBUTION CENTERS AT ETHAN ALLEN

Originally each of the 40 retailers of Ethan Allen products in the New York metropolitan area maintained its own inventory. The aggregate inventory value averaged $3 million. Unfortunately, the inventory levels still were not enough to satisfy most customer orders. The probability that all items in a customer's order were on hand was only 0.25. This meant back orders and long customer response times.

Ethan Allen solved this dilemma by creating one large field warehouse to serve all 40 retailers. The retailers no longer needed to carry separate inventories, except for display purposes. The aggregate inventory value dropped to $700,000 and the probability of filling a customer's order from DC inventory increased to 0.80. This success in New York led to the establishment of several DCs in other metropolitan areas.

Source: Thomas E. Vollmann, William L. Berry, and D. Clay Whybark, *Manufacturing Planning and Control Systems,* Homewood, Ill.: Richard D. Irwin, 1984.

them to transport fish and coal. Railroads move 30 percent of U.S. freight (down from 50 percent in 1947), while truckers now haul 40 percent. The five basic modes are highway, rail, water, pipeline, and air. Each has its own advantages and limitations.

Highway transportation provides the flexibility of shipping to almost any location served by existing highways. No rehandling is needed for pickup and delivery. Transit times are good and rates are usually less than rail for small or short hauls. *Rail* transportation can move large quantities very cheaply, but transit times are long and variable. This mode is usually best for shipping raw materials, rather than finished goods. Rail shipments often require additional transportation modes for pickup and delivery. *Water* transportation provides high capacity at low unit cost, but transit times are slow and large parts of a country are inaccessible to waterborne carriers. *Pipeline* transportation is a highly specialized mode with limited geographical flexibility. It is limited to liquids, gases, or solids in slurry form. However, no packaging is needed, and operating costs per mile are low. *Air* transportation is the fastest and most expensive mode. Although increasing geometrically, it still represents only 1 percent of all freight moved. It is limited by the availability of airport facilities and requires another mode for pickup and delivery.

In addition to these primary modes, special service modes and hybrids, such as parcel post, air express, bus service, freight forwarder, and piggyback, are available. Transportation companies are organized under different ownership and management forms. A firm may decide to be a *private carrier,* owning and operating its own fleet. It may select a *contract carrier,* negotiating with a carrier for a specified amount, type, and frequency of shipment. A contract carrier does not provide service to the general public, but instead serves specific customers under negotiated contracts. A third option is to select a *common carrier,* which must serve all customers without discrimination. This option gives the firm the least control over carrier availability but makes sense for low volume producers with geographically dispersed markets.

Scheduling, Routing, and Carrier Selection. Several activities are involved in the day-to-day control of freight movement. The shipping schedule must mesh with purchasing and production and inventory control schedules. It also reflects the trade-off between transportation costs and customer response times. By delaying a shipment for another two days, it may be possible to achieve full carload (CL) rates for a rail shipment or full truckload (TL) rates for truck shipments. Routing choices must also be made. A central post office, operating its own fleet to collect mail from outlying areas, must determine the trip route to each pickup point. A manufacturer may select a routing that combines shipments to multiple customers and gains lower freight rates. The firm may even negotiate lower rates if it develops routings where large volumes can be shipped on a regular basis. These choices are complex. Even before deregulation, the U.S. freight rate structure seemed chaotic to the uninitiated. Now rates and services vary markedly, depending on the specific mode and carrier chosen.

INVENTORY CONCEPTS

It is now clear that materials management is a central influence on company success, requiring coordination among several decision areas and departments. We now introduce some basic inventory concepts and definitions that are needed for subsequent chapters. **Inventory** can be defined as a stock of materials created to satisfy some eventual demand. Inventory is created when the rate of receipts exceeds the rate of disbursements. It is depleted when disbursements exceed receipts.

Inventory Categories

Inventory can be held at many possible locations or stocking points, as shown in Fig. 10.3. Inventory for the manufacturing plant exists in three accounting categories: raw materials, work-in-process, and finished goods. In the system shown in Fig. 10.3, *raw materials* are maintained at two stocking points: the supplier's facility and the plant. The raw materials at the plant then pass through one or more processes where they are transformed into various levels of *work-in-process* (WIP) inventory. When this inventory is processed at

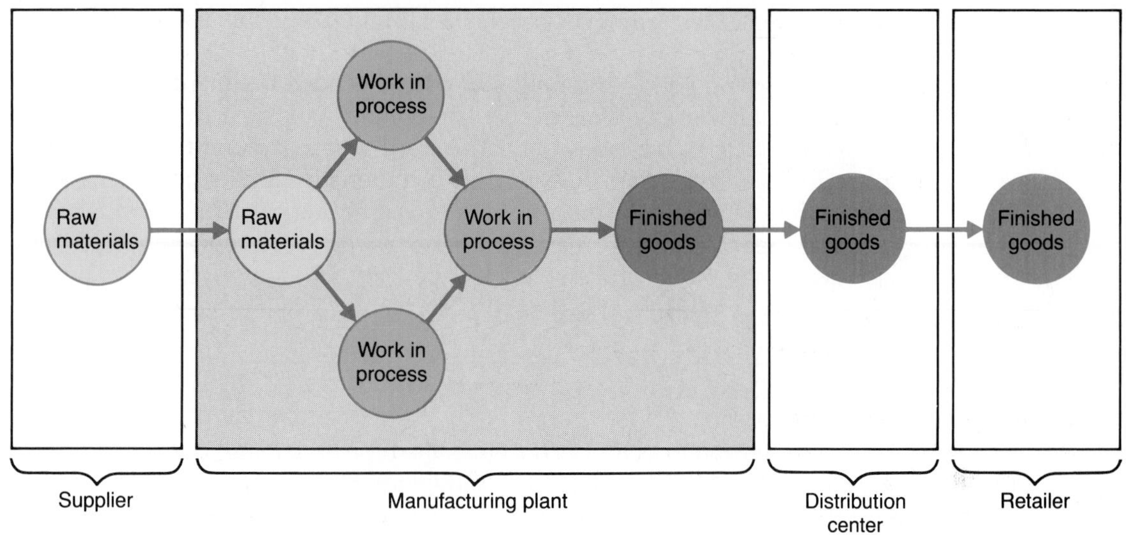

Figure 10.3

A Materials Flow System.

the final operation, it becomes *finished goods* inventory. This can be positioned at the plant, DC, and retail locations. Materials flow systems can be more or less complex than shown in Fig. 10.3. A small retailer must manage only the inventories at the local store, making the system seem quite simple. A large retailer, such as Kroger, often integrates backward to include distribution centers and even manufacturing plants, which creates a more complex system. A process-focused manufacturer such as Longhorn (Chapter 2) ships directly to the customer, creating a simple system with no intervening DCs or retail stocking points. A product-focused manufacturer may integrate backward to the point where it has its own feeder plants, which in turn supply its assembly plants. A multiplant setting is particularly challenging to materials management, since inventories must be coordinated at even more stocking points.

Inventory can be broken down into more than the three categories of raw materials, WIP, and finished goods. One frequent distinction made in manufacturing is whether an item is a parent or a component. A **parent** is an item manufactured from one or more **component** items. The chair in which you are sitting is made up of several components, such as legs, arms, a seat, and fasteners. Many items are both a parent and component. A **subassembly** is made up of several components, which makes it a parent, but, since it is one of several items going into the final product, it is also a component. In contrast, raw materials are never parents and finished goods are never components.

A concept related to the notion of parents and components is **part commonality,** which exists whenever a component has more than one parent; that is, the same part is used to manufacture several different subassemblies or products. A giant step toward part commonality took place in the early 1800s, when Eli Whitney introduced interchangeable parts for manufacturing firearms. (See Chapter 1.) Part commonality increases repeatability, which has several advantages for process design. (See Chapters 4 and 5.) You will also see that it helps to reduce inventory.

Types of Demand

Another important inventory concept is the type of demand, which can either be independent or dependent. The **independent demand** of an item is influenced by market conditions and is generated directly by customers. It is independent because it is not related to the demand for any other item held in stock. In manufacturing, only items at the finished goods level have exclusively independent demand. Components at the WIP level can experience independent demand only when customers ask for spare-part replacements. In a service setting, as with merchandise at a single site, parent–component relationships do not exist. There are no parents and the merchandise only experiences independent demand.

Dependent demand is related to the ordering of parent items. Suppose that component B's only parent is item A. In order to make one unit of A, we need one unit of B. If a production order of 100 units of A is to be released three weeks from now, we can expect the demand for B to be zero for the next two weeks and 100 units in the third week. Demand for dependent demand items can be *derived* in this way from the production plans for parent items. For independent demand items, the future demand can only be *forecast*. Entirely different production and inventory control systems must be applied, depending on whether demand is independent (being forecast) or dependent (being derived).*

Measures of Inventory

You have already learned that inventory levels can have a significant impact on profits. Suppose that it costs a firm 35 percent of the dollars tied up in inventory to maintain this level of inventory for a year. If the inventory level averages 30 percent of sales, the cost to hold inventory is 10.5 percent (or 0.35

* Chapter 12 deals more with independent-demand systems, while Chapters 14 and 15 cover dependent-demand systems.

× 0.30) of total sales. This cost is sizable, when you realize that gross profit margins often are less than 10 percent. For this reason, managers closely monitor inventories to keep them at an acceptably low level. Inventories are reported to them in three basic ways:

1. Aggregate inventory value.
2. Weeks of supply.
3. Inventory turnover.

All inventory measures begin with a physical count in units, volume, or weight. However, one unit of item A may be worth only pennies, whereas one unit of item B may be valued in the thousands of dollars. We can obtain the **aggregate inventory value** for a group of items by multiplying the number of units of each item on hand by its per-unit value and adding the amounts for all items included. This value tells managers how much of a firm's assets are tied up in inventory. Manufacturing firms typically have about 25 percent of their total assets in inventory, while wholesalers and retailers average about 75 percent. To some extent we can evaluate the aggregate inventory value historically, by industry data, or by managerial judgment. However, we cannot do so realistically without taking demand into account. We can include demand rates by using the measures: weeks of supply and inventory turnover. **Weeks of supply** (or days of supply) is the aggregate inventory value divided by the sales per week at cost. Although the numerator includes the value of all items (raw materials, WIP, and finished goods), the denominator is only the cost of the finished goods sold. **Inventory turnover** (or *turns*) is found by dividing annual sales at cost by the average aggregate inventory value maintained during the year. It can also be calculated by dividing the number of business weeks in a year by the weeks of supply.

To illustrate these calculations, suppose that a company averaged \$2 million in inventory last year, and the cost of goods sold was \$10 million. Assuming 52 weeks per year, we measure inventory as:

$$\text{Weeks of supply} = \frac{\$2 \text{ million}}{\$10 \text{ million}/52}$$
$$= 10.4 \text{ wk},$$

and

$$\text{Turnover} = \frac{\$10 \text{ million}}{\$2 \text{ million}} \quad \text{or} \quad \frac{52 \text{ weeks}}{10.4 \text{ weeks}}$$
$$= 5 \text{ turns/yr}.$$

The "best" inventory level, even when expressed as turnover, cannot be easily determined. Although 5 or 6 turns per year is typical, high-tech firms settle for only about 3 turns. At the other extreme, some Japanese automobile firms report 40 turns per year.

Inventory Costs

Table 10.2 indicates why the best turnover rate varies so much. Conflicting costs and pressures argue either for low or high inventories. A manager must assess each one before reaching any conclusions about appropriate inventory levels. Let's examine each of these costs, beginning with holding costs.

Holding (Carrying) Cost. The central reason for keeping inventories low is that inventory represents money invested temporarily in goods for which a firm must pay (rather than receive) interest on the investment. This cost is called the **inventory holding** (or carrying) **cost.** Companies usually calculate this cost for an item as a percentage of its value. The cost to hold an item in inventory for a year typically ranges from 25 to 40 percent of the item's value. Suppose that the annual holding cost per unit held is 30 percent of the item's value. If the average inventory of a $100 item is 10 units, the annual holding cost would be $300 [or 0.30($100)/unit × 10 units].

Table 10.2 shows the components of holding costs. The largest component usually is the interest or opportunity cost, whichever is larger. Suppose that a company wants to increase its investment in inventory but would have to obtain a loan at 15 percent interest to do so. To increase inventory, the company would also have to delay some automation that promises a 20 percent after-tax return per year. The anticipated 20 percent return is the opportunity cost. In this case, it is also the true cost of holding inventory, since it exceeds the 15 percent interest rate for the loan.*

Then there are storage and handling costs. Inventory takes up space and must be moved into and out of storage. Several years ago, managers at Ford Motor Company were amazed at the small size of certain Japanese plants. Toyota's Kamego engine plant occupies only 300,000 square feet, but achieves the same output rate as the 900,000-square-foot Ford plant recently built in Europe. The essential difference is that Toyota has found ways for getting by with much less inventory. Determining how much to increase holding-cost estimates to account for storage and materials handling is not a clear-cut procedure. We are tempted to calculate an *allocated cost* for the space and materials handlers, that is, to simply multiply the annual depreciation of the storage facility by the proportion of that space required to store one unit. Suppose that we do this and the result is $10 per unit. Does it really cost $10 more in storage to increase average annual inventory by one more unit? The answer, most likely, is no. In the short run, in fact, we may be able to increase inventory well beyond its current level without incurring any new *out-of-pocket* costs for either storage space or the materials handling crew. In order to

* In practice, a firm should equalize its opportunity and interest costs. In this particular case, it would pay for the firm to get an even larger loan to finance the automation project, since the anticipated return exceeds the rate of interest.

Table 10.2

Conflicting Pressures on Inventory Levels

Pressures for Small Inventories ⟵⟶	Pressures for Large Inventories
Interest or opportunity cost	Customer service
Storage and handling cost	Ordering or setup cost
Property taxes	Labor and facility utilization
Insurance premiums	Transportation cost
Shrinkage costs: Pilferage, obsolescence, and deterioration	Cost of purchased items

decide whether the true cost is $10, zero, or somewhere in between, we should follow one guiding principle: Include only those costs that actually change because of the decision being made. Thus the $10 storage cost is relevant to determining facility size. If we decide to store short-term inventories in public warehouses, where we are charged according to the amount of space used, the storage cost charged by the public warehouse is relevant. However, if we decide to store short-term inventories in our own facilities, there is no real storage cost when space is abundant and has no other short-term value.

The final components of holding cost are taxes, insurance, and shrinkage (pilferage, obsolescence, and deterioration). Taxes and insurance are self-explanatory, but the three forms of shrinkage need further explanation. *Pilferage* is theft of inventory by either customers or employees and is a significant percentage of sales for many businesses. *Obsolescence* occurs when inventory cannot be used or sold at full value, owing to model changes, engineering modifications, or unexpectedly low demand. Just as the previously useful items accumulating in your garage often end up as junk, so there also is a risk that an item placed in inventory will never be sold. The risk of obsolescence is particularly great when competitive priorities favor product flexibility. *Deterioration* is the third form of shrinkage. Value is lost through physical spoilage or damage. Food and beverages, for example, lose value and may even have to be discarded when their shelf life is reached. When the rate of deterioration is high, build up of large inventories may be unwise. Inventory records must be more extensive because it is not enough to know total on-hand inventory. It must be broken down by age, so that a FIFO (first-in, first-out) system can be used to minimize loss.

If these components of holding cost were the only measures affecting inventory choices, holding inventory would not be rational. The fact that inventory held in the U.S. economy is approaching the $1 trillion mark suggests that other performance measures must exist. The pressures for large inventories listed in Table 10.2 are the reasons why inventory exists despite its expense. We begin with customer service.

Customer Service. Creating inventory, particularly at forward positions, speeds up delivery times and can also improve on-time delivery. Inventory reduces the chance of a stockout or the need for a back order, which are key measures for wholesalers and retailers. It also increases the percentage of on-time deliveries, which is a key performance measure for manufacturers. Translating such measures into a dollar equivalent, as done for inventory holding cost, can be difficult if not impossible. What will customers do if there is a stockout? They can wait for a back order to replenish the inventory, buy elsewhere this one time, or shift to another supplier permanently. This wide range of possibilities makes dollar estimates little more than a guess. Lack of measurement precision does not diminish the importance of customer service and managers must carefully watch all aspects of customer service.

Ordering or Setup Costs. Whenever a batch (lot) of an item is ordered, certain managerial or clerical costs are involved. **Ordering cost** is the same, regardless of the order size. For a purchased item, someone has to take the time to decide about the lot size, select a vendor, and negotiate terms. Time is also spent on paperwork, follow-up, and receiving. Most of the same activities are involved in placing a production order for a manufactured item, but the type of paperwork changes. Here it is often necessary to send along with the shop order such additional information as a blueprint and a routing sequence. Otherwise, the workers would not know how to make the product. In contrast to customer service, it is common to assign a dollar estimate to the cost of placing an order. As with holding costs, we must take care to include only relevant ordering costs.

Setup (or changeover) **cost** is similar to ordering cost, since it also is independent of order size. This cost is for labor and equipment time lost changing over from the prior job: new tooling, jigs, or fixtures may be needed, and the machine may have to be cleaned. Scrap or rework may be substantially higher at the start of a run, making scrap a function of setup frequency. Setup times can be substantial, as in the case of U.S. automobile manufacturers, which need an average of four hours to change the dies for large hood and fender presses. A manufacturer of glue, which integrated backward to make its own plastic bottles, faces setup times of 14 hours for some machines that make and decorate the plastic bottles. Combined with its inventory policies, 25 percent of the company's capacity is lost to setups.

Labor and Equipment Utilization. Management can increase work-force productivity and facility utilization in three ways by creating more inventory. First, setup time is unproductive because it does not add value to a product. Setup-time losses can be reduced by placing larger production orders less frequently. Although inventories increase, downtime for setups decreases.

Second, productivity drops when a parent order must be rescheduled for lack of components. Many actions may be taken to cope with component unavailability, but each has a cost. For example, one option is to make an extra setup and do another job. The delayed job could then be done on overtime (at time-and-a-half rates) after the component inventories have been replenished. Perhaps accountants should create a "confusion account" to which mistakes could be charged. If this were done, we can be sure that (1) the account would be sizable; and (2) unavailable components would be a major contributor. The third way that inventories can improve resource utilization is in helping to stabilize a manufacturer's output rate, even when demand is cyclical or seasonal. Inventory built during slack periods can handle the extra demand in peak seasons. Varying the work force through extra shifts, hiring, layoffs, and overtime can be minimized. Equipment capacities can also be less, since capacity does not need to match peak demand.

Transportation Cost. Sometimes, *outbound* transportation cost can be reduced by increasing inventory levels. Large inventory allows more time to help ensure CL shipments and minimizes the need for expedited shipments by more expensive modes of transportation. As you have already seen, more forward positioning of inventory can reduce outbound transportation cost, even though the pooling effect is lessened and more inventory is necessary. *Inbound* transportation cost may also be reduced if more inventory is allowed. Sometimes, several items are ordered from the same supplier. Combining these orders and placing them at the same time may lead to CL rather than LCL rates. Ordering several items at the same time can increase total inventory, but the holding cost can be outweighed by savings in transportation cost.

Cost of Purchased Items. A firm can often reduce total payments to suppliers if it can tolerate higher inventory. Suppose that a firm learns that a key supplier is about to increase prices. It might be cheaper for the firm to order a larger quantity than usual, in effect delaying the price increase, even though the inventory temporarily increases. Similarly, a firm can take advantage of **quantity discounts,** where the price per unit drops when the order is sufficiently large, if it is willing to increase the average inventory.

Types of Inventory

Inventory can be viewed as a necessary evil. Although it costs money to hold, inventory helps with customer service and resource utilization and reduces ordering, setup, transportation, and purchased materials costs. Another perspective on inventory is to classify it by functional purpose. Inventory's primary purpose is to *uncouple* activities, providing some degree of independence at various points in a materials flow system. Inventories of purchased items uncouple a manufacturer from its suppliers. Placing inventory between two work centers in a plant uncouples them, making scheduling more manageable. Merchandise inventory at a store uncouples a retailer from its customers. In the context of uncoupling, there are four types of inventory: cycle, safety, anticipation, and pipeline.

Cycle Inventory. Savings in most of the costs listed in the right-hand column of Table 10.2 are gained if orders are placed less frequently. Unfortunately, these savings come at a cost: The required **cycle inventory** will be larger. Two principles are involved:

1. The lot size or batch size, which we refer to as Q in this and subsequent chapters, varies in direct proportion with the elapsed time between orders. The longer the time between orders, the larger must be Q. For example, if an order for an item is placed monthly, the average Q will be equivalent to one month's demand. If the cycle is increased to three months, Q must also be tripled.
2. *The amount of cycle inventory held, on the average, can be estimated as one-half of Q.** For example, the average cycle inventory is 50 if Q is 100. One-half of Q is the average of the maximum and minimum amounts of cycle inventory. At the beginning of the interval, cycle inventory is at its maximum, since the order of 100 just arrived. At the end of the interval, just before a new order arrives, cycle inventory drops to its minimum, or 0. Assuming that the demand rate is constant, the average of 100 and 0 is 50, or $Q/2$.

Now consider the advantages of large cycle inventory: better customer service, less frequent orders and setups, and reduced transportation and purchasing costs. Increasing Q (and therefore cycle inventory) normally improves customer service because (1) the possibility of a stockout exists only at the end of a cycle; and (2) there are fewer cycles per year when Q is larger.† Thus a higher Q means fewer risks of stockout. For example, suppose that an item's lot size Q is increased from one to four weeks of demand. This decreases the number of potential stockouts from 52 to only 13 per year. Following similar reasoning, increasing Q also reduces the annual cost of orders and setups, since fewer are made per year. Larger lot sizes also might make CL

* The value $Q/2$ formula is exact only when the demand rate is constant and uniform. Fortunately, our simulation research showed that the formula still provides a reasonably good estimate for dependent demand situations, where demand rates are not constant. Factors other than the demand rate, such as scrap losses, can also cause estimating errors when this simple formula is used.

† We found exceptions to this relationship between Q and customer service in manufacturing. Larger lot sizes can create more feast-or-famine capacity requirements, which hurt a manufacturer's ability to ship on time. In such cases, larger lot sizes hurt on-time delivery performance.

rates or quantity discount prices possible, thereby decreasing the cost of transportation or raw materials.

Safety Stock Inventory. A second purpose of inventory is to protect against uncertainties in supply, lead time, and demand. **Safety stock inventory** can improve customer service and reduce the hidden costs of unavailable components. The greater the uncertainty in the *demand during lead time* (DDLT), the more safety stock can be justified. If a vendor is unreliable, deviating frequently from the requested lot size or from the promised delivery time, safety stock is desirable. If a manufactured item is subject to significant and frequent amounts of scrap or rework, safety stock is needed.

There is a simple way to create safety stock: Place an order for delivery earlier than when the item is typically needed.* The replenishment order therefore arrives ahead of time, giving a margin of error to cushion against uncertainty. For example, suppose that the average lead time from a supplier is three weeks, but a firm does not let inventory drop below five weeks of supply, just to be safe. This policy creates a safety stock equal to two (or 5 − 3) weeks of supply.

Anticipation Inventory. The use of **anticipation inventory** helps to absorb uneven rates of demand or supply. A business often faces fluctuating demands for its products. Manufacturers of air conditioners can experience 90 percent of their annual demand during just three months of a year. Demand for furniture during the late summer can be double the average monthly rate. About 60 percent of the annual customer demand for toys occurs in the six weeks before Christmas. Such unevenness in demand rates may lead a manufacturer to stockpile inventory during periods of low demand, so that output levels do not have to be increased much when demand rates hit their peak. These anticipation inventories may be held by the manufacturer or pushed forward toward retailers. Smoothing output rates with inventory can increase productivity because varying output rates and work-force size can be costly. Anticipation inventory also can help when supply, rather than demand, is uneven. A company may stock up on a certain purchased item if its suppliers are threatened with a strike or severe capacity limitations.

Pipeline (Transit) Inventory. Materials must be moved forward from point to point in the materials flow system. Materials move from vendors to the plant, from one operation to the next in the plant, from a plant to a DC or a customer, and from a DC to a retailer. Because this movement is time consuming, **pipeline inventory** is necessarily created. It is the amount of inventory held between the originating and receiving points. More technically,

* When orders are placed at fixed intervals, there is a second way: Place an order for more than we think is needed up through when the next order should be received. (See Chapter 12.)

pipeline inventory is the sum of all **scheduled receipts** (sometimes called **open orders**), which are orders that have been placed but not yet received. Pipeline inventory can be in three stages: inbound, outbound, and within the plant. The inbound stage includes scheduled receipts of raw materials, which are not yet available for use. Inventory in the outbound stage consists of finished goods that have been shipped but not yet received and paid for by the customer. Within the plant, the pipeline includes all scheduled receipts for production orders sent to the shop. Thus pipeline inventory in the plant represents WIP inventory. This inventory category often is the firm's largest, particularly in a job shop with its many customized products, few part commonalities, and process focus.

Holding pipeline inventory generally costs the same as cycle, safety stock, or anticipation inventory. Purchased materials in the pipeline can be an exception. A firm sometimes does not pay for materials until they are received and inspected. Only then does the inventory investment occur. Just as the amount of cycle inventory can be estimated as $Q/2$, the pipeline inventory between two points can be estimated as DDLT. This amount is an average, and it is zero when there are no scheduled receipts. When there is one scheduled receipt, pipeline inventory equals the size of the open order. Suppose that a plant makes monthly rail shipments to a wholesaler for a particular item in average lots of 280 units. The average demand experienced by the wholesaler is 70 units per week, and the lead time from the plant is three weeks. The estimated average pipeline inventory, or DDLT, is 210 [or 3(70)]. Note that the lot size does not directly affect the size of the pipeline.* Increasing Q does inflate the size of a scheduled receipt, but this increase is canceled by a proportionate decrease in the number of orders placed per year.

Reducing Inventory Levels

Particularly with higher interest rates, managers are eager to find cost-effective ways to reduce inventory levels. Later, we examine various ways for finding optimal lot sizes. (See Chapter 12.) However, it is important not to lose sight of the basic tactics that can lead to inventory reduction, which we call *levers*. Table 10.3 shows levers for each type of inventory. A *primary lever* is the one that must be activated if inventory is to be reduced. A *secondary lever* decreases the penalty cost of applying the primary lever and reduces the need for having inventory in the first place.

Cycle Inventory. Since the cycle inventory level is approximately equal to $Q/2$, the primary lever is simply to reduce the lot size Q. Several Japanese

* There can be an indirect effect, however. If the lead time gets longer with larger lot sizes, then DDLT (and therefore pipeline inventory) will increase.

Table 10.3

Levers for Reducing Inventory

Type of Inventory	Primary Lever	Secondary Lever
Cycle	Reduce Q	Reduce ordering and setup cost Increase repeatability
Safety stock	Place orders closer to the time when they must be received	Improve forecasting Reduce the lead time Reduce supply uncertainties Increase equipment and labor buffers
Anticipation	Vary the production rate to follow the demand rate	Level out demand rates
Pipeline	Cut production–distribution lead time	Forward positioning Selection of suppliers and carriers Reduce Q

firms have reduced Q to the point where it is only a fraction of a shift's supply. These lots are extremely small, when traditionally they have been equal to several weeks (or even months) of supply. Making such reductions in Q without making any other changes can be devastating. For example, setup costs can skyrocket, which leads us to the two secondary levers. Managers and the work force should find ways to streamline methods for placing orders and making setups. Such improvements can reduce ordering and setup costs per job, which then allows Q to be reduced.

Increased repeatability can also help to reduce cycle inventory. Perhaps resources can be devoted exclusively to the same product, so that changeovers are no longer needed. Or, at least, the increased volumes may justify new setup methods. Other possibilities are the one-worker–multiple-machine concept, group technology, or flexible automation. (See Chapter 5.) Part commonality might increase volumes to the point where transportation costs and quantity discounts no longer stand in the way of small lot sizes. Another way to increase repeatability and volume is to centralize buying.

Safety Stock Inventory. Recall that safety stock inventory can be created by releasing orders well before materials or parts are needed. Table 10.3 shows that the primary lever for reducing this type of inventory is to release orders closer to the time when they must be received. This approach can lead to unacceptable customer service, unless demand, supply, and delivery uncertainties can be minimized.

There are four secondary levers that can be used. First, do a better job forecasting demand, so that there are fewer surprises from customers. Perhaps customers can even be encouraged to preorder items before they need them. A second possibility is to find ways to cut the lead times. Cutting lead times cuts the uncertainty in DDLT. For example, local suppliers could be selected whenever possible. A third option is to reduce supply uncertainties. Vendors may be more reliable if production plans are shared with them, permitting them to make more realistic forecasts. Surprises from unexpected scrap or rework can be reduced by improving manufacturing processes or adding inspection stations. Preventive maintenance can minimize unexpected downtime caused by equipment failure. A fourth secondary lever for reducing safety stock is to rely more on equipment and labor buffers. In fact, these are the only buffers available to businesses in the service sector, since they cannot inventory their services. One example of an equipment buffer is when a manufacturer buys more equipment and increases its capacity cushion (see Chapter 7) to help absorb the disruptions from equipment failures. When this is done, there is less need for inventories to decouple operations. An example of a labor buffer is cross-trained workers, who provide a more flexible work force. An idle worker in one area can switch to operations where demand is unusually high.

Anticipation Inventory. Table 10.3 shows that the primary lever to reduce anticipation inventory is simply to match the demand rate with the production rate. This strategy can be more successful if customer demand can be leveled out by adding new products with different demand cycles, promotional campaigns, or seasonal pricing plans.

Pipeline Inventory. An operations manager has direct control over lead time but not the demand rate. Since pipeline inventory is a function of DDLT, it can be cut only by reducing the lead time. Various secondary levers can help managers to cut lead times. First, we have already established that forward positioning of inventory cuts lead time. Second, a firm might find more responsive suppliers, select new carriers for shipments between stocking locations, or improve materials handling within the plant. Introducing a computer system could shorten information delays between a DC and retailer. Third, decreasing Q may help, at least in those cases where lead time depends on lot size. Smaller jobs require less time to complete.

Materials Management and Operations Strategy

Having covered the basic concepts in materials management, we conclude with a discussion of its links with operations strategy. In relation to a process-focused firm, a product-focused firm (see Chapter 2) tends to have

1. less tolerance for "cushions";
2. less pressure for an integrated structure;

3. longer planning horizons;
4. more formalized vendor and customer relationships; and
5. information systems oriented to forecasts and inventory records.

Cushions. One strategy for capacity planning (see Chapter 7) favors large capacity cushions that require extra equipment and result in lower utilization rates. Two types of materials management cushions are extra workers and high inventories. All firms use these cushions, but in varying degrees. A firm with a product focus has less tolerance for cushions for three basic reasons. First, there is less *complexity* to buffer against. Complexity results from (1) low repeatability; (2) high product and volume flexibility; (3) jumbled routings; and (4) using the same equipment for many low-volume products or parts—all characteristics of a process focus. Second, there is less *uncertainty* to buffer against. On the demand side, the higher volumes of a product focus make forecasting customer demand easier. There are fewer last-minute design changes from the customer or engineering, since product flexibility is low. On the supply side, higher volumes give a firm more clout in finding reliable suppliers. Within a firm's own plant, high volumes reduce the uncertainty in lead times and production quantities, caused by capacity bottlenecks, rework, and scrap. Short lead times mean small WIP inventories. Third, a firm with a product focus is likely to emphasize low price as a competitive priority. A key to productivity improvement and lower costs is minimal cushions. Large safety stock inventories and extra workers are too costly a luxury.

Integrated Structure. We have already considered the trend toward an integrated organizational structure, in which three key departments (purchasing, production and inventory control, and distribution) report to the same executive. Integration requires a high degree of coordination and cooperation among these departments, as well as with manufacturing and marketing. While integration seems to be a good idea, those firms that have an integrated structure and those that do not are fairly evenly split. Integration comes at a cost and should be done only when benefits exceed costs. *Benefits* are greatest in the uncertain environment of a process focus. Demand and supply uncertainties mean unexpected changes and updates, which in turn call for more coordination. When uncertainty is low, an organization can afford to be more compartmentalized and fragmented. Turning from benefits to *costs*, some aspects of the distribution function are simplified with a process focus, since there is little finished goods inventory and few, if any, DCs to manage. Making the distribution department part of an integrated structure therefore does not add much complexity in a process-focused firm. Finally, the greater ability to create finished goods inventory with a product focus uncouples operations from distribution. Distribution is more likely to be housed with marketing and separated from purchasing and production planning.

Planning horizons. Production plans and schedules are developed farther into the future when there is a product focus for two reasons. First, forward scheduling is feasible. The increased certainty in demand and supply means that schedules can be developed without having to change them almost immediately because of unexpected events. Recall that Suds Brewery allowed few of the last-minute disruptions that were commonplace at Longhorn. (See Chapter 2.) Therefore it was feasible at Suds to schedule the packaging line a month in advance, while the supervisor at Longhorn could schedule worker assignments only one or two days ahead. Second, a product focus creates a strong incentive to plan ahead. Maximizing facility and equipment utilization is a top goal because the facility is so capital intensive. High utilization rates depend on forward scheduling.

Vendor and Customer Relationships. Both vendor and customer relationships are more formal and extensive with a product focus. Firms negotiate annual supply contracts with key suppliers, rather than using the full purchasing cycle for each new purchase. Contract terms tend to be more attractive than terms for individual purchases. With high volumes, a firm can exert more control over suppliers, and, conversely, suppliers naturally cater to larger customers. Distribution channels also are more formal. Markets are more scattered, requiring an elaborate network of regional DCs. With a process focus, where product flexibility is high, it is impossible to position inventory at DCs close to the customer. Typically, shipments are made directly from the plant to the customer.

Information Systems. Information requirements for a product focus are oriented to demand forecasts and current inventory levels. This situation differs from that of process-focused firms, where information is oriented to the bidding process and specific customer orders. Here, output plans are communicated by releasing jobs with detailed routing information.

CHAPTER HIGHLIGHTS

- Materials management deals with purchasing, production plans, staffing plans, inventories, schedules, and distribution. Managing materials is a common function in organizations in every segment of the economy.
- Purchased materials now represent about 60 percent of the total sales dollars for a typical manufacturer. The ratio of final business sales to inventories is only 3 : 1 for the U.S. economy. Inventory investment is more than double annual business investments in new equipment and facilities. These three statistics are strong motivators for managing materials better.
- Decisions in materials management by necessity are made hierarchically. In a *service* organization, an annual plan is translated into a staffing plan, which is then converted into a work-force schedule. In a *manufacturing* firm, a business plan is translated into a production plan, which then is converted into a master production schedule. In either case, the final decision levels are

inventory control, scheduling, purchasing, and distribution.

- There is growing sentiment for integrated organization structures, bringing purchasing, production and inventory control, and distribution into one department headed by a key executive.
- In addition to order placing and expediting, purchasing makes vital decisions such as vendor selection, vendor relations, length of contracts, and centralized buying.
- Distribution decides such issues as the positioning of finished goods inventories, transportation mode selection, shipping schedules, routings, and carrier selection.
- Forward positioning of inventory at DCs can cut delivery times and transportation costs, although the pooling effect is less and can result in higher inventory levels. Forward positioning is not advisable if product flexibility is high.
- Inventory falls into three accounting categories: raw materials, work-in-process, and finished goods. Inventory can be measured by aggregate inventory value, weeks of supply, or inventory turnover. Components of holding costs are interest (or opportunity cost), storage and handling, taxes, insurance, and shrinkage.
- An item can be a parent, a component, or both a parent and a component. If a component has more than one parent, part commonality exists, which increases repeatability.
- Whether an item is subject to independent or dependent demand is a key to how its inventory is managed. Dependent demand can be derived from production plans of parents, while independent demand must be forecast.
- Pressures working against minimal inventory are customer service, ordering or setup cost, labor and equipment utilization, transportation cost, and purchased materials cost. These pressures argue for higher inventories.
- There are four types of inventory, depending on their purpose: cycle, safety stock, anticipation, and pipeline. Levers can be used to reduce each type of inventory. For example, the primary lever for reducing cycle inventory is the lot size (Q), whereas it is the lead time for pipeline inventory. Secondary levers have to be used in conjunction with the primary levers.
- Choices in materials management must fit operations strategy. When competitive priorities favor a product focus, there tend to be: (1) less tolerance for cushions; (2) less pressure for an integrated structure; (3) longer planning horizons; (4) more formalized vendor and customer relationships; and (5) information systems oriented to forecasts and inventory records.

KEY TERMS

aggregate inventory value
annual plan
anticipation inventory
business plan
component
cycle inventory
dependent demand
distribution
independent demand
inventory
inventory holding cost
inventory turnover

materials management
open orders
ordering cost
parent
part commonality
pipeline inventory
purchasing
quantity discounts
safety stock inventory
scheduled receipts
setup cost
subassembly
weeks of supply

STUDY QUESTIONS

1. Some people call inventory the "root of all evil." Tying money up in inventory lessens opportunities to improve productivity. The reasons that make inventory attractive are the same ones that stand in the way of substantial improvements in efficiency. Do you agree or disagree with this position? Why?
2. Since organizations in the service sector do not manufacture products from raw materials, materials management concepts do not apply to them. Do you agree or disagree? Why?
3. Working down from the annual plan (business plan for manufacturing firms), describe each of the planning levels in materials management for both service and manufacturing organizations.
4. It has been said that "if not controlled, work will flow to the competent people until they are submerged." What does this imply for centralizing all materials management functions under one key executive?
5. Suppose that you are a buyer charged with selecting one or more suppliers of an expensive, high-volume part going into a new product line. How would you proceed?
6. What steps would you take to make vendor relations more cooperative? Is a cooperative orientation always best?
7. When would you favor
   (a) long-term purchase contracts?
   (b) centralized buying?
8. Ethan Allen *reduced* inventory by creating more DCs. (See Box 10.5.) Does positioning inventory forward at DCs not *increase* inventory, since there is less of a pooling effect?
9. You have been asked to review the policies of a company for which the dollar value of inventory now exceeds 40 percent of total sales. How would you go about identifying opportunities for inventory reduction? To what extent can some of your ideas help improve delivery times and reduce transportation costs?
10. The purpose of safety stock inventory is to protect against uncertainty in demand and supply. What is the purpose of cycle inventory?
11. What can be done to reduce the cost of buying and holding materials purchased from suppliers?
12. Give three examples of how competitive priorities can affect choices made in materials management.

PROBLEMS

1. John Stout, the Materials Manager at Hendler Enterprises, is beginning to look for ways to reduce inventories. A recent accounting statement showed inventories at the following levels.

Raw materials	\$2,540,000
Work-in-process	1,860,200
Finished goods	2,420,800

This year's cost of goods sold should be about \$19.2 million. Assuming 52 weeks per year, express total inventory as
(a) weeks of supply.
(b) inventory turns.

2. One of Hendler's product lines is experiencing 6.2 turns per year, and its annual sales volume (at cost) is \$750,820. How much inventory is being held?
3. John Stout has decided to establish three DCs in different regions of the country. For one of the major product lines at Hendler Enterprises, he expects the average weekly demand to be 50 units per DC. The product is valued at \$650 per unit. Average shipment sizes from the factory warehouse to the DCs will be approximately 350 units per trip. Each DC should experience fairly steady demand from its customers. Average lead time (including ordering delays and transit time) will be about two weeks. The average DC will carry one week's supply as safety stock, since the demand during the lead time sometimes exceeds its average of 100 units [(50 units/wk)(2 wk)]. Anticipation inventory should be negligible.
(a) Calculate the average aggregate value of inventory that will be held at the three DCs with Stout's new positioning strategy.
(b) What type of inventory (cycle, safety stock, or pipeline) is the greatest component of the aggregate value? What is the primary lever available to John for reducing it?
4. Suppose that a product has an annual demand of 390 units per year. The lot size is 130 units, and the lead time is four weeks. The firm has 52 business weeks per year.
(a) If 390 units must be ordered over the course of a year, at a rate of 130 units per order, how many orders will be placed?
(b) Multiply your answer in (a) by both the lot size and lead time. This number is the *unit-weeks* of pipeline inventory held at one time or another during the year.
(c) Divide your answer in (b) by 52 to get the average pipeline inventory (in units) per week.
(d) Now set up a mathematical expression for pipeline inventory, using D for annual demand, Q for lot size, and LT for lead time. How does your final expression, simplified, relate to the notion that pipeline inventory is approximated by DDLT?
5. A subassembly is produced in lots of 120 units. It is assembled from two components worth \$50. The value added (for labor and variable overhead) in manufacturing one unit from its two components is \$40, bringing the total cost per completed unit to \$90. The typical lead time for the item is 6 weeks and its annual demand is 936 units. There are 52 business weeks per year.
(a) How many units of cycle inventory are held, on the average, for the sub-

Table 10.4

Performance Criterion	Weight	Rating		
		Vendor A	Vendor B	Vendor C
1. Price	0.2	0.6	0.5	0.5
2. Quality	0.3	0.7	0.2	0.8
3. Delivery	0.2	0.6	0.4	0.7
4. Production facilities and capacity	0.1	0.7	0.6	0.7
5. Warranties and claims policies	0.1	0.9	0.6	0.8
6. Financial position	0.1	0.7	0.5	0.9

assembly? What is the dollar value of this cycle inventory?

(b) How many units of pipeline inventory are held, on the average, for the subassembly? What is the dollar value of this inventory? *Hint:* Assume that the typical job in pipeline inventory is 50 percent completed. Thus one-half the labor and variable overhead costs has been added, bringing the unit cost to $70 (or 50 + 40/2).

6. The Foresite Company periodically evaluates its vendors to spot problem areas. One of its essential raw materials is supplied by three vendors. Purchases currently are equally distributed among the vendors. Ratings (high values mean good performance) based on six weighted performance criteria are shown in Table 10.4 for the vendors.
   (a) Calculate a total weighted score for each vendor using a preference matrix. (See Chapter 2.)
   (b) What changes, if any, do you recommend in the company's purchasing policy?

SELECTED REFERENCES

Ammer, Dean S., *Materials Management*, Homewood, Ill.: Richard D. Irwin, 1962.

Banerjee, Avijit, "An Integrated Inventory Model for a Purchaser and a Vendor," *Proceedings of the 1985 Annual Meeting*, American Institute for Decision Sciences (November 1985), pp. 746–748.

Buffa, Elwood S., *Meeting the Competitive Challenge*, Homewood, Ill.: Dow Jones-Irwin, 1984.

Burt, D., *Proactive Purchasing*, Englewood Cliffs, N.J.: Prentice-Hall, 1984.

Clark, James T., "Inventory Flow Models: Preparing for Zero Inventory." Fall Seminar on Zero Inventory Philosophy and Practices, St. Louis, Missouri, American Production and Inventory Control Society, October 1984.

Corey, E. Raymond, "Should Companies Centralize Procurement?" *Harvard Business Review* (November–December 1978), pp. 102–110.

Dobler, Donald W., Lamar Lee, Jr., and David N. Burt, *Purchasing and Materials Management*, New York: McGraw-Hill, 1984.

Miller, Jeffrey G., and P. Gilmour, "Materials Managers: Who Needs Them?" *Harvard Business Review* (July–August 1979), pp. 143–153.

Miller, Jeffrey G., Jinchiro Nakane, and Thomas Vollmann, "The 1983 Global Manufacturing Futures Survey." Working Paper, Boston University, April 1983.

Narasimhan, Ram, "An Analytical Approach to Supplier Selection," *Journal of Purchasing and Materials Management* (Winter 1983), pp. 27–32.

Pittiglio, Rabin, Todd, and McGrath, "Assessing High Tech Inventory Management," *P&IM Review and APICS News* (July 1984), pp. 52–55.

Schonberger, R., and J. Gilbert, "Just-In-Time Purchasing: A Challenge For U.S. Industry," *California Management Review*, vol. 26, no. 1 (Fall 1983), pp. 54–68.

Van Dierdonck, Roland, and Jeffrey G. Miller, "Designing Production Planning and Control Systems," *Journal of Operations Management*, vol. 1, no. 1 (August 1980), pp. 37–46.

Vollmann, Thomas E., William L. Berry, and D. Clay Whybark, *Manufacturing Planning and Control Systems*, Homewood, Ill.: Richard D. Irwin, 1984.

CHAPTER 11

PRODUCTION AND STAFFING PLANS

Some Managerial Issues

- What is the relationship between our positioning strategy and production plan?
- How can we adjust the pattern of demand to reduce the costs of operations?
- Should we use a level work-force strategy or some variable work-force strategy?
- Should we use subcontracting to achieve short-term capacity increases or some combination of overtime and the hiring of seasonal employees?

Chapter Outline

The overall strategy of an organization must somehow be translated into detailed operating plans. In Chapter 10 you learned that the materials management decision hierarchy begins with a plan that links strategic goals and objectives with more detailed and specific plans. For manufacturing organizations, the production plan links the business plan with the master production schedule. For service organizations, the staffing plan links the annual plan with the detailed work-force schedule. In this chapter we focus on production and staffing plans and their relationship to the hierarchy of plans in manufacturing and service organizations.

THE NATURE OF PRODUCTION AND STAFFING PLANS

Box 11.1 contains examples of the need for production and staffing plans. Specifically, a **production plan** is a managerial statement of time-phased production rates, work-force levels, and inventory investment, which takes into consideration customer requirements and capacity limitations. It balances the typically conflicting objectives of maximizing customer service, minimizing inventory investment, maintaining a stable work force, minimizing production cost, and maximizing profit. It also provides valuable information for

Box 11.1

TYPICAL PRODUCTION AND STAFFING PROBLEMS

Clearwater Post Office

The director of a large sectional center post office in Clearwater must prepare a staffing plan for next year. His concern for the moment is focused on the part-time work force that supports the mail-sorting system. Some mail must still be sorted manually, but much of it can be sorted with the help of machines. The part-time work force fills in for absent full-time clerks and helps move the mail from station to station as needed. In some cases part-time employees staff manual sorting stations during peak demand periods. The director has a good estimate of the number of part-time workers he needs for each of the 13 accounting periods of the year. An accounting period is four weeks long. The need for part-time workers peaks at the Christmas and Easter seasons and troughs in the summer.

The budget he received from the annual planning process at the regional headquarters indicated that he had $100,000 to use for part-time help this year. The first step is to develop a staffing plan for part-time help, showing the desired number for each accounting period. There are many possible plans, ranging from keeping a stable work force to allowing a lot of hiring and firing to match seasonal requirements. Nonetheless, he has to know how many part-time workers he will have during each accounting period before he can begin to work out their daily schedules.

Tru-Rainbow Paint Company

The Tru-Rainbow Paint Company produces a wide variety of paint products for both commercial and private use. Hundreds of raw materials are used to produce the thousands of individual products, which may vary by color, texture, size of container, and base (oil or latex). The demand for paint is highly seasonal, with the peak months in the summer. The several hundred employees are flexible in that they can be assigned to work on any part of the paint manufacturing process.

Judie Tower, manufacturing manager, just received her budget guidelines from the business plan for next year. They put limits of $3,300,000 on labor (including overtime, hires, and layoffs), an average monthly finished goods inventory investment of $1,350,000, and little or no back orders. Judie knows that these figures are still somewhat negotiable but that she has to get the support of marketing and finance if changes are to be made. She first has to evaluate production rates and work-force levels to see if she can meet the budget constraints. After she has done so, Judie can then begin to schedule individual products for production, set up a work-force schedule for each week, and project her needs for raw materials.

other plans, such as the master production schedule and the materials requirements plan to be covered in later chapters.

The **staffing plan** is to service organizations what the production plan is to manufacturing organizations. It is a managerial statement of time-phased staff sizes and labor-related capacities, which takes into consideration customer requirements and machine-limited capacities. It also must balance conflicting objectives involving customer service, work-force stability, cost, and profit. The staffing plan is useful for developing the specific work-force schedule assigning workers to shifts and daily schedules. Table 11.1 gives some examples of the types of employees that have to be included in a variety of problem settings.

Aggregation

Both the production plan and the staffing plan are useful because they are general. The planner can devise a course of action, consistent with strategic goals and objectives, without having to deal with a lot of detail. For example, if you had to schedule each of the thousands of products and hundreds of employees at Tru-Rainbow just to find out whether your plan would satisfy budget guidelines, you would face a hopeless task. Even if you could prepare such a plan, it would lose much of its usefulness because of the time and

Table 11.1

Examples of Types of Employees Included in a Staffing Plan

Service	Employee Type
Airline	Flight attendants
	Pilots
Airport operations	Baggage handlers
	Skycaps
Banking	Tellers
	Encoding clerks
Defense	New enlistees
Emergency	Police officers
	Firemen
Health care	Nurses
Municipal sanitation	Refuse collectors
	Truck drivers
Municipal transportation	Bus mechanics
	Bus drivers
Telephone	Installers
	Linemen
	Operators

effort required to update the details contained in it. For this reason, production and staffing plans are based on aggregated quantities. With respect to production and staffing plans, aggregation is performed along three dimensions: products (or services), labor, and time.

Product Families. A group of products or services that have similar demand requirements and common processing, labor, and materials requirements is called a **product family.** Sometimes, these families relate to market groupings or, in the case of production plans, to specific manufacturing processes. A firm's products or services can be aggregated into a set of relatively broad product families in order to avoid too much detail at this stage of the planning process. In addition, a common and meaningful measurement should be used, such as units, dollars, standard hours, gallons, or pounds.

For example, the Clearwater Post Office can combine the demand for all services into two categories: letter-size mail services and parcel services. The unit of measurement could be standard processing hours. Alternatively, the Tru-Rainbow Paint Company could reduce all its products to gallons of paint and develop the production plan as if it had only one product. In each of these examples greater detail can be introduced by creating more product families; however, the planning effort increases as well. Each organization must decide on the level of detail that is needed for its planning purposes.

Labor. Labor can be aggregated in various ways, depending on the flexibility of the work force in producing the product families. For example, if the entire work force is used in the production of every product family, the work force can be considered a single aggregate group for planning purposes—as in the Clearwater Post Office and Tru-Rainbow examples. Alternatively, the work force can be aggregated by product family. An automobile manufacturer would find this approach useful because, under the concept of focused facilities, groups of production lines and even entire plants are devoted to a given product family. (See Chapter 7.) Economic conditions and changes in consumer preferences may cause production cutbacks in one product family and production increases in another. Such was the case in the late 1970s when the price of gasoline rose substantially and consumers shifted from buying full-sized cars to buying smaller, fuel-efficient cars. Often, labor is not interchangeable because of the scattered locations of the plants processing the product families. In this case, planning for changes in staffing levels and the use of overtime is more useful on a product family basis.

Labor can be measured in terms of number of employees or labor hours. When working with the number of employees, you must take care to account properly for part-time employees: The number of employees should be expressed in *full-time equivalents* (FTE). One FTE represents one employee who works the normal number of hours per shift in a work week. Suppose that Tru-Rainbow employs 90 full-time and 40 part-time employees. In a normal shift, the part-time employees work only half the number of hours the full-time employees do. Thus the plant would have 110 (or 90 + 20) full-time equivalent employees for planning purposes.

Time. A planning horizon is the length of time into the future covered by the production or staffing plan. Typically, the planning horizon is one year, although this can differ in various situations. Planning decisions must be made about several factors, such as production rates for each product family and labor levels for each work-force group. But how often should these decisions be made during the planning horizon? Daily is too frequent because of the expense and disruptive effect on production rates and the work force. Once a year is not frequent enough to allow for adjustments to reflect seasonal demand or updated forecasts. Thus decisions such as these are usually made monthly or quarterly. Some companies use monthly planning periods for the near portion of the planning horizon and quarterly periods for the portion farther out. In practice, planning periods reflect a balance between the needs for (1) a limited number of decision points to reduce planning complexity; and (2) flexibility to adjust production rates and work-force levels when demand forecasts exhibit seasonal variations.

Relationship to Other Plans

Figure 11.1 illustrates the relationships among the production (or staffing) plan, the business (or annual) plan, and more detailed plans. In the manufacturing sector top management sets the direction and strategies of the company for the next year and beyond in the business plan. It provides the overall

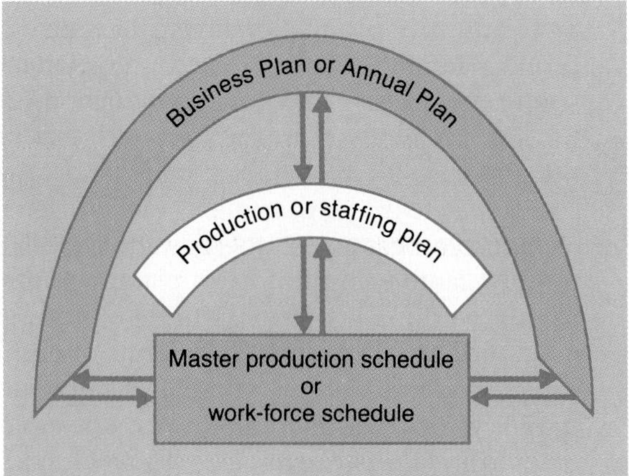

Figure 11.1

Relationship of Production and Staffing Plans to Other Plans.

framework of demand projections, functional area inputs, and capital budget from which the production plan and the master production schedule are developed. The production plan specifies corresponding product family production rates, inventory levels, and work-force levels. The master schedule, in turn, specifies the timing and size of production quantities for each product in the product families (Chapter 13). Thus the production plan plays a key role in translating the strategies of the business plan into an operational plan for the manufacturing process.

In the service sector, top management sets the direction and objectives of the organization in the annual plan. It provides the framework for developing the staffing plan and work-force schedule. The staffing plan presents the number and types of employees needed to meet the objectives of the annual plan. The *work-force schedule,* in turn, details the specific work schedule for each employee in each staffing plan category. For example, a staffing plan might allocate 10 police officers for the day shift in a particular district; the work-force schedule might require 5 of them to work Monday through Friday and the other 5 to work Wednesday through Sunday to meet the day-to-day needs for police protection in that district. In this way the work-force schedule implements the staffing plan in much the same way that the master production schedule implements the production plan. (A more complete discussion of the work-force schedule is presented in Chapter 16.)

Besides the *top-down* planning process described in the preceding discussion, Figure 11.1 indicates that information flows from lower level planning to higher level planning. If a production plan that satisfies the directives of the business plan cannot be developed, the business plan may have to be adjusted. Similarly, if a feasible master production schedule cannot be developed, the production plan or the business plan may have to be adjusted. A similar situation exists for the annual plan, staffing plan, and work-force schedule. It is important for you to realize that the top-down planning process is dynamic and that the plans, in particular the production and staffing plans, are based on two-way information flows. We present the details of these information flows in the remainder of this chapter and the following chapters.

MANAGERIAL IMPORTANCE OF PRODUCTION AND STAFFING PLANS

Production and staffing plans play an important role in achieving the organizational objectives. The extract from a newspaper article in Box 11.2 is a case in point: It demonstrates that the costs associated with various production strategies play a major role in the profitability of a firm. In this section we concentrate on the managerial inputs, objectives, and strategies associated with production and staffing plans.

Box 11.2

THE IMPACT OF PRODUCTION PLANNING AT FIRESTONE

Profits at the Firestone Tire and Rubber Company for the first quarter of 1984 dropped 12 percent despite a 15 percent rise in sales. In addition to a shortage of tires for Firestone's expanded store and dealer network and some tire price discounting, overtime and other expenses related to increasing tire production were blamed for the profit decline. Firestone planned to increase its output by going to a seven-day-week operation at its tire plants and subcontracting the manufacture of some of its tires. An increase in training costs related to the addition of a fourth work crew was also expected.

Source: "Firestone Profit from Operations Fell in 1st Period," by Ralph E. Winter, *Wall Street Journal*, February 22, 1984.

Managerial Inputs

Table 11.2 shows the various functional areas that supply inputs to production or staffing plans. Because of the importance of the plan, a high ranking

Table 11.2

Managerial Inputs to Production and Staffing Plans

Area	Typical Inputs
Engineering	New product (or service) development
	Major product (or service) changes and their impact on resources
	Labor and machine standards
Finance	Cost data
	Financial condition of firm
Human Resources	Labor market conditions
	Capacity of training programs
Manufacturing (or operations)	Current machine capacities
	Work-force productivities
	Current work-force staff levels
	New equipment plans
Marketing	Forecasts
	Economic conditions
	Competitor behavior
Materials	Raw materials availability
	Current inventory levels
	Subcontractor capabilities
	Storage capacities

person in each area should provide the inputs. One way of ensuring thi. participation is to create a committee consisting of representatives of each area. For example, the Bendix Corporation has such a committee, which is chaired by the General Manager who has the overall responsibility to see that company policies are followed, conflicts are resolved, and a final plan is approved. Each representative furnishes information that is essential to the development of the plan.

Typical Objectives

The many and varied inputs from the functional areas in an organization make the production or staffing plan an organization plan, not a functional area plan. However, it is typically the case that the various functional areas have conflicting objectives for the use of the organization's resources. Table 11.3 shows six objectives commonly considered during development of a production or staffing plan.

A little reflection on these six objectives reveals their conflicting nature. For example, fast delivery times and on-time delivery can be improved by increasing the stock of finished goods. A staffing plan at the Clearwater Post

Table 11.3

Typical Objectives in Production and Staffing Plans

Objective	Comments
Minimize costs/maximize profits	If customer demand is not affected by the plan, minimizing costs will also maximize profits. Many service organizations are nonprofit and seek to minimize costs.
Maximize customer service	As discussed in Chapter 2, delivery time and on-time delivery are two dimensions of quality. Improving these dimensions requires additional work-force, machine capacity, or inventory resources.
Minimize inventory investment	Large accumulations in inventory are expensive because the money could be used for more productive investments.
Minimize changes in production rates	Frequent changes in production rates can cause difficulties in coordinating the supplying of materials and require production line rebalances.
Minimize changes in work-force levels	Fluctuating work-force levels may cause lower productivity because the new hires typically need time to be fully productive.
Maximize utilization of plant and equipment	Firms with a product focus require uniformly high utilization of plant and equipment.

Office that minimizes costs may not minimize changes in the work-force levels or maximize customer service. Also, a manufacturing firm that uses a stable production rate will necessarily build inventories of finished goods in the face of a seasonal demand for its product families.

Although these objectives can all be collapsed into one of cost minimization, with the choice of appropriate costs for the objectives, nonquantifiable factors usually require modification of any plan. Methods for resolving multiple, conflicting objectives are available but are beyond the scope of this book. Nonetheless, the relative importance of each objective must be considered and the plan modified until the entire set of important objectives are reasonably satisfied.

Balancing these various objectives in order to arrive at an acceptable production or staffing plan involves consideration of various decision alternatives. The two basic types of decision alternatives are reactive and aggressive.

Reactive Alternatives

Reactive alternatives are actions that can be taken to cope with demand requirements. That is, we accept forecasted demand as a given and modify staffing and inventory levels.

Adjust Work-Force Levels. A work-force level can be adjusted by hiring or laying off employees. The use of this alternative can be attractive if the work force is largely unskilled or semiskilled and the labor pool is good sized. However, for a particular company, the size of the qualified labor pool may limit the number of new employees that can be hired at any one time. Also, new employees must be trained and the training facilities themselves may limit the number of hires at any one time.

Overtime and Undertime. An alternative to adjustment of the work force is the use of overtime and undertime. Overtime can be used to satisfy production requirements that cannot be completed on regular time, although there are limitations on its use. It is expensive (typically 150 percent of the regular-time pay rate), and in many cases workers do not want to work a lot of overtime for an extended period of time.

Undertime is used when labor capacity exceeds demand requirements. Workers are kept on the payroll, rather than laying them off. This option is often used by companies, such as those firms with a process focus, that have highly skilled employees who are hard to replace.

Vacation Schedules. A firm can shut down during an annual lull in sales, leaving a skeleton crew to cover operations and perform maintenance. Depending on the duration of the shutdown, employees would take all, or part, of their allowed vacation time during this period. Use of this alternative depends on the extent that the employer can mandate the vacation schedules of its employees. If this authority is limited (say, by union contract) and if part-time or seasonal labor can be substituted for full-time personnel, employees could be encouraged to take vacations during periods when these sources of labor are most abundant.

Anticipation Inventory. When a plant faces a seasonal demand for one or more of its product families, anticipation inventory can be stocked during light demand periods and used during heavy demand periods. This alternative has a stabilizing effect on production rates and work-force levels but may be very costly. Stocking finished goods is the most expensive form of inventory investment because the value of the product is greatest in its finished state. Plans to stock components and subassemblies that can be assembled quickly when customer orders come in might be preferable to stocking finished goods.

In general, service organizations cannot use anticipation inventory because services cannot be stocked. However, in some instances services can be performed prior to actual need. For example, telephone company workers can lay cables for service to a housing development before construction begins. They could do this work during a period when the workload for scheduled services is low.

Subcontractors. A short-term capacity source that can be used to overcome capacity shortages is subcontracting. Subcontractors can supply services and build components, assemblies, or even an entire product in some cases. Arrangements with subcontractors can be more permanent if the subcontractor can supply the components or assemblies cheaper than the company can produce them itself. Such is the case with the major automobile manufacturers, who typically subcontract for underbody frames, steering linkage components, and other items. (See the discussion on vertical integration in Chapter 4.)

Backlogs, Back Orders, and Stockouts. Another way to cope with a given demand forecast is to plan for order backlogs. A **backlog** is an accumulation of customer orders that have been promised for delivery at some future date. Delivery lead times typically increase during seasonal peaks in demand. Organizations with a process focus often use this method. The customer places an order for a customized product or service and it is promised for delivery later. Job shops, TV repair shops, and automobile repair shops work to varying degrees to backlogs.

A **back order** is a customer order that is not ready for the customer when promised or demanded. The customer has not canceled the order, so the net effect is to push demand requirements to later periods. A **stockout,** on the other hand, is simply a matter of not satisfying the demand for a stock item when it occurs. This alternative may be used by firms with a product focus. The customer may return later when there is a new supply or go to a competitor, in which case the customer may never return, resulting in a lost opportunity for sales. Planned stockouts would only be used when the expected loss in sales and customer goodwill is less than the cost of adding the capacity needed to satisfy demand.

The reactive alternatives collectively serve to define the production rate. When decisions have been made regarding each of these methods for coping with a given demand forecast for each period of the planning horizon, the production rate for each period has been specified. In other words, the production rate is a function of the factors of production addressed by these alternatives.

Aggressive Alternatives

Attempting to cope with seasonal or volatile demand patterns using reactive alternatives can be costly. Another approach is to attempt to adjust the demand pattern in order to achieve efficiency and reduce costs. **Aggressive alternatives** are actions that attempt to modify demand and, consequently, resource requirements. Box 11.3 contains an example of two of the three aggressive alternatives we discuss in this section.

Complementary Products. One way to even out the load on facility resources is to produce **complementary products** or services having similar resource requirements but different demand cycles. For example, a company producing garden tractors can also produce snowmobiles, making requirements for major components, such as engines, reasonably uniform year round. In the service sector, a city parks and recreation department can counterbalance seasonal staffing requirements for summer activities by offering evening creative workshops and indoor sports such as basketball, volleyball, and indoor soccer during the winter and spring. The key is to find products or services that can be produced with existing resources, yet have the property of leveling the need for resources over the year.

Promotional Campaigns. Advertising can be used to modify seasonal demand patterns by generating customer demand in other than the traditional peak periods. Beer sales in the winter months can be stimulated with aggressive advertising, for example. General Motors announced a promotional sales program with a reduced interest rate on company-financed automobile loans and, coupled with an advertising campaign, stimulated lagging automobile sales during traditionally poor sales periods. Carpet-cleaning companies promote the sales of their services by offering reduced rates during the off-season.

Creative Pricing. Closely allied to the promotional campaign is creative pricing. Discounts can be offered to customers if they buy products outside traditional peak sales periods. Automobile rebate programs, price reductions for

Box 11.3

AGGRESSIVE ALTERNATIVES IN THE MATZOH INDUSTRY

Producers of matzoh for the Jewish Passover holiday are in a seasonal business. Each autumn, Brooklyn's Satmar Hasidim begins making 100,000 pounds of the crisp, unleavened bread for the following spring using an assembly line of 30 workers. In Long Island City, Queens, the Horowitz Margareten factory is also at peak production in the fall. It is more automated than the Satmar bakery, producing 1250 sheets of matzoh a minute. Also, the B. Manischewitz Company, a kosher foods manufacturer in Jersey City, experiences 40 percent of its annual sales for the eight-day Passover holiday alone. Nevertheless, companies such as these have decided not to settle for a seasonal product and are gradually shifting toward markets with year-round appeal and broader market segments. Manufacturers are still hiring extra workers for the spring crunch, but they are also utilizing the following aggressive alternatives.

- *Complementary products*

  Manischewitz entered the market for Hispanic foods with several canned soups and crackers.
  Several of the companies also make borscht, gefilte fish, candies, cake mixes, duck sauce, and macaroons, some of which are available year round.

- *Promotional Campaigns*

  Margareten had a radio campaign to interest other ethnic groups in traditionally Jewish products, such as matzoh.
  Some companies are promoting matzoh for diet plans and capitalizing on the national craze for fitness foods.

Source: "New Matzoh Markets Sought," *New York Times*, April 9, 1984.

winter clothing in the late summer months, reduced rates for long distance calls after 5 P.M., and "two for the price of one" automobile tire sales are examples of creative pricing alternatives.

Planning Strategies

We have discussed many different decision alternatives for production or staffing plans. These alternatives are combined in various ways to arrive at an acceptable plan. For the remainder of this chapter, let's assume that the expected results of the aggressive alternatives have already been incorporated in the demand forecasts of the product families or services. This assumption allows us to focus on the reactive alternatives that serve to define the production rates and staff levels. In this regard a planning strategy amounts to selecting the particular alternatives to use in a given situation. There are two *pure strategies:* the chase and the level strategies.

A **chase strategy** adjusts production rates or staff levels to match the demand requirements over the planning horizon. There are many ways in which this can be accomplished. For example, workers can be hired or laid off, or overtime and subcontracting can be used during peak periods. The key point is that anticipation inventory or undertime is not used. Thus, the chase strategy has the advantage of low inventory investment or backlogs but at the expense of adjusting production rates or staff levels for every period of the planning horizon.

A **level strategy** maintains a constant production rate or staff level over the planning horizon. In manufacturing firms a constant production rate is often accomplished by maintaining a stable work force and building anticipation inventory to satisfy peak seasonal demands. Hiring, overtime or subcontracting can be used if the work force is subject to attrition, but the production rate remains constant. In service firms a level strategy usually involves maintaining a stable work force and using undertime, overtime, and backlogs. The distinguishing feature of a level strategy is that anticipation inventory or undertime is used to help maintain a constant output capability. The advantages are level production rates and a stable work force at the expense of increased inventory investment, undertime, overtime, and backlogs.

Obviously, a range of strategies is bracketed by the chase strategy at one extreme and the level strategy at the other. For example, the best strategy for the Tru-Rainbow Paint Company may be to use a *mixed strategy* of anticipation inventory buildup during slack periods, only a few work-force level changes, and overtime to meet projected manufacturing requirements. Regardless of whether a company chooses a pure strategy or some mix, the important point is that the strategy must be chosen in light of the planning objectives discussed previously. The production plan or staffing plan not only is a product of the inputs of many people representing various functional areas, but also has an *impact* on the operations of these people and the functional areas they represent. Thus the production or staffing plans, which affect the course of the firm over the near and intermediate future, have a high degree of managerial significance.

THE PLANNING PROCESS

Figure 11.2 shows the planning process for production plans and staffing plans. The overall process is dynamic and continuing; aspects of the plan are updated periodically as new information becomes available and new opportunities emerge.

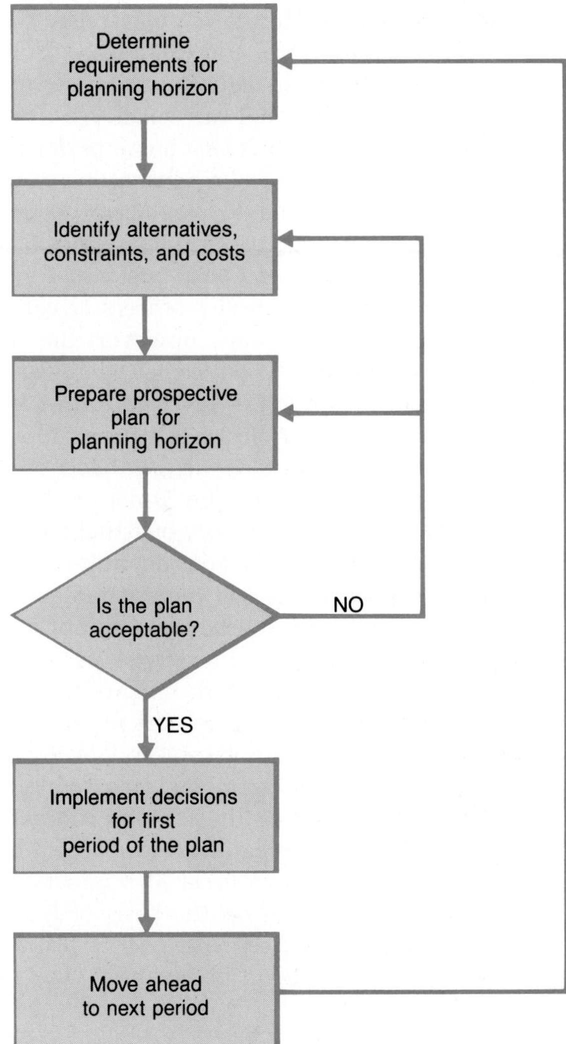

Figure 11.2

The Production and Staff Planning Process.

Demand Requirements

The first step in the planning process is to determine the demand requirements for each period of the planning horizon. We can estimate these requirements in various ways (many of which we have already discussed). For staffing plans, we base forecasts of staff requirements for each work-force group on historical demands and existing backlogs for services. We often express these requirements in labor hours or in terms of FTEs. For example, a director of nursing in a hospital can develop a direct-care index for a nursing staff, translating all the activities a nurse performs into an equivalent total amount of time required, based on a projection of patient census (Wolfe and Young, 1965). Also, a formula developed for police patrol staffing accounts for such factors as the number of calls for service by type, the number of street miles patrolled, and the number of businesses in the community to determine the workload in terms of police officers or vehicles (Chaiken and Larson, 1972).

For production plans, however, the requirements could represent the demand for finished products, as well as external demand for components or parts. We can derive the expected future requirements for finished products from backlogs, if the firm has a process focus, or from forecasts for product families made to stock, if the firm has a product focus. Sometimes dealers or warehouses that handle the firm's products indicate their requirements for finished products in advance of actual orders. These advance orders are commitments to purchase various quantities of products in the future and provide a more reliable forecast of requirements from those sources.

Two sources of external demand for components or parts are *service-part orders* and *interplant orders*. Service parts (or assemblies) are used to replace worn-out or damaged parts in products previously sold by the company. Examples include electric motors for automatic washers or dryers, electronic components for television sets, and gears for automobile transmissions. Interplant orders for components or assemblies are those generated by other plants in a multiplant division of a company. For production planning purposes, we can aggregate service-part and interplant demand into product families as we do with finished products. We can forecast both service-part and interplant orders on the basis of historical demand; however, we can make a much better estimate of interplant orders if the production plans of other plants are known in advance.

Alternatives, Constraints, and Costs

We presented the alternatives used in production or staffing plans when we discussed the managerial importance of these plans. We now focus on the basic relationships, constraints, and costs that have to be considered.

Basic Relationships. It is important for you to understand two basic relationships, so that you can evaluate and compare prospective plans. The basic relationships are: (1) the equation for the number of workers in production or staffing plans; and (2) the equation for the inventory level in production plans.

The equation for the number of workers in the work force in a given period is

Workers in current period	=	Workers at end of last period	+	Hires at start of current period	−	Layoffs at start of current period.

Any decisions made about hiring or laying off employees during the current period will affect the number of workers on hand. For example, if the director of the Clearwater Post Office has ten part-time clerks at the end of the third accounting period and decides to hire five new part-time employees at the start of the fourth accounting period, the total number of part-time employees for the fourth accounting period would be fifteen clerks. In general, an equation such as this is needed for each work-force group in the production or staffing plan.

The equation for the inventory level in a given period is

Inventory at the end of current period	=	Inventory at the end of last period	+	Production in current period	−	Demand requirements in current period.

The production decision for the current period affects the inventory level at the end of the current period. For example, suppose that Tru-Rainbow has an inventory level of 600,000 gallons of paint at the end of January, has a forecasted demand for 100,000 gallons in February, and has decided to produce 250,000 gallons in February. The expected inventory at the end of February would be 600,000 + 250,000 − 100,000 = 750,000 gallons.

If the use of back orders is an alternative being considered, the equation for the inventory level is a little more complicated:

Inventory at the end of current period	=	Inventory at the end of last period	+	Production in current period	+	Back orders in current period
	−	Back orders in last period	−	Demand requirements in current period.		

The back-order quantity in the last period is considered to be a requirement in the current period, and, if it cannot be satisfied along with the demand in the current period, the total unsatisfied requirements will be back ordered for the next period. As with the equation for the work force, we need an inventory equation for each product family in the production plan.

Physical and Policy Constraints. Constraints can represent physical limitations on the use of certain planning alternatives or managerial policies associated with the production or staffing plan. For example, the training center at a particular company may be capable of training a maximum of 50 new hires in a given period. Other physical limitations might include machine capacities that limit the maximum output in any given period or space for inventory storage. Policy constraints for any period might include limits on the amount of back ordering, the use of subcontracting or the quantity of overtime, and minimum inventory levels to achieve desired safety stocks.

We must satisfy physical and policy constraints before we can consider a production plan or staffing plan to be acceptable. Unfortunately, merely choosing alternatives that satisfy the constraints does not ensure that the *best* plan will result. Typically, many plans can satisfy a specific set of constraints.

Costs. In addition to identifying reasonable alternatives and relevant constraints, we must gather data on applicable costs. We usually consider several types of costs when preparing production or staffing plans:

1. *Regular-time costs.* These costs include the wages paid to employees on regular time plus any fringe-benefit contributions. Fringe benefits typically include health insurance (hospital, surgical, eye care, dental care); Social Security and retirement funds; and paid vacations, holidays, and certain other types of absence.
2. *Overtime costs.* Overtime wages are typically 150 percent of regular-time wages, exclusive of fringe benefits. Some companies offer a 200 percent rate for working overtime on Sundays or holidays.
3. *Hiring and layoff costs.* Hiring costs include the costs of advertising jobs, interviews, training programs for new employees, and initial paperwork. Layoff costs include the costs of exit interviews and severance pay. In some companies, when a reduction in the work force is made, senior employees whose jobs have been eliminated have the right to "bump" less senior employees from their jobs. In the process, a considerable number of employees may change jobs, with the least senior people actually getting laid off. In this case, layoff costs should also include all costs of training and lost productivity caused by bumping.
4. *Inventory holding costs.* Inventory holding costs include the costs of capital tied up in inventory, variable storage and warehousing costs, pilferage and obsolescence costs, insurance costs, and taxes. Only costs that vary with the *level* of inventory investment should be included.
5. *Back-order and stockout costs.* The cost of not satisfying customer demand is difficult to assess. In the case of a back order, costs are incurred for expediting the past-due order, and there is the potential cost of losing the customer's sales to competitors in the future. This latter cost is sometimes called *loss of goodwill.* In some cases, back orders are not allowed. In other words, the customer is not identified with a specific order that is past due. In these situations, the stockout cost is essentially a *lost sales cost* consisting of lost profit from the sale plus the loss of goodwill.

An Acceptable Plan

Figure 11.2 indicates that developing an acceptable plan is an iterative process. First, a *prospective* plan is developed. For a production plan with monthly periods, monthly production rates, inventory and backlog accumulations, subcontracted production, and monthly work-force levels (including hires, layoffs, and overtime) must all be specified. The requirements are similar for a staffing plan, except that no inventory accumulation is projected. The plan is prospective at this point because it must now be checked for feasibility relative to constraints and then evaluated relative to the objectives to determine whether it is acceptable. If the plan is not acceptable, a new prospective plan must be developed, which may include new alternatives or changes in physical or policy constraints. If the plan is acceptable, implementation begins.

Implementation and Updating

Implementation requires the commitment of top management. This commitment begins with the creation of a planning committee, as we suggested earlier, which makes inputs into and reviews the proposed production or staffing plan. The committee discusses the current proposed plan and recommends changes to better balance conflicting objectives. In the final analysis, a commitment to the plan does not necessarily mean that everyone is in total agreement, but it does imply that everyone will work toward achieving it.

As new information comes in, the plan must be updated. One updating procedure is called a **rolling planning horizon.** Suppose that we have a 12-month planning horizon for a production or staffing plan. It is currently the beginning of January, and we have just developed an acceptable plan for January through December. We would implement only the decisions for January. At the end of January, we would update the plan for February through December and *add* January of the following year to the plan. If the February plan is acceptable, we would implement the decisions for February. This process maintains our 12-month planning horizon and allows us to incorporate the latest forecasts of requirements in the plan.

ILLUSTRATIVE PRODUCTION AND STAFFING PLANS

In this section we demonstrate the development of production and staffing plans. In some situations the correct set of alternatives is reasonably obvious. Table 11.4 shows some examples of fitting strategy to environment. The strategies listed make sense, even though the extent of their application in any

Table 11.4

Examples of Fitting Strategy to Environment

Organization	Environment	Possible Strategy
City street repair	Labor intensive Unskilled workers Seasonal requirements Ample labor supply	Variable work-force levels Low overtime No subcontracting
Outboard motor company	Costly equipment Skilled labor Costly inventory	Complementary products Off-season promotions Level production rate Limited hires/layoffs Low inventory investment
TV repair service	Steady, increasing demand Skilled employees Tight labor market	Overtime Gradual hires Increase backlog for short-term demand surges
Men's shoe manufacturer	Labor in short supply Low inventory holding cost	Level work force Build up anticipation inventories Low overtime Subcontracting

specific situation would still be subject to analysis. In general, firms that have a process focus find volume flexibility easier and tend to meet variable demand with overtime, subcontracting, or work-force level changes, unless highly skilled, hard-to-find labor is involved. On the other hand, firms that have a product focus find volume flexibility difficult and tend to meet fluctuating demand with anticipation inventory, scheduled vacations, or plant shutdowns.

Most often, however, the development of production or staffing plans involves economic considerations. In the remainder of this section we develop plans for the Clearwater Post Office and Tru-Rainbow. We use a trial-and-error method, which involves tables and graphs and is widely used in practice.

The Clearwater Post Office Staffing Plan

Box 11.4 shows the data for the Clearwater Post Office. The director would like to develop staffing plans consistent with two alternative strategies:

1. *Level strategy.* Determine a stable work-force level without the use of backlogs or subcontractors but minimize the use of undertime. The resulting plan is called Plan 1.

2. *Chase strategy.* Adjust work-force levels as needed to achieve requirements. Do not use overtime, undertime, or subcontractors. Using this strategy results in Plan 2.

These strategies are at the extreme points of the range that could be evaluated for planning purposes. We evaluate some mixed-strategy plans when we discuss Tru-Rainbow.

Box 11.4

DATA FOR THE CLEARWATER POST OFFICE STAFFING PROBLEM

Requirements

Work-force requirements are shown as the number of part-time employees required for each accounting period. The fiscal year begins on July 1 and ends on June 30. For example, in accounting period 6, it is estimated that 20 part-time employees will be needed to help the full-time work force during the Christmas holiday season.

	Accounting Period													
	1	2	3	4	5	6	7	8	9	10	11	12	13	Total
Requirement	5	6	8	15	17	20	15	15	10	16	14	14	12	167

Ten part-time clerks are presently on the work force. These employees have not been netted out of the requirements shown.

Constraints

1. Physical:

   No more than 10 new hires in any period because of limited training facilities.

2. Policy:

   No backlogs of mail; demand must be met each period.
   Overtime cannot exceed 25 percent of the regular-time capacity in any period.

Costs

Regular-time wages	$500 per accounting period
Overtime wages	150% of the regular-time rate
Hires	$600 per person
Layoffs	$100 per person

Table 11.5

Plan 1 Using Level Strategy for the Clearwater Post Office Staffing Problem

	Accounting Period													
	1	2	3	4	5	6	7	8	9	10	11	12	13	**Total**
Requirement	5	6	8	15	17	20	15	15	10	16	14	14	12	167
Staff level	16	16	16	16	16	16	16	16	16	16	16	16	16	208
Hires	6	—	—	—	—	—	—	—	—	—	—	—	—	6
Layoffs	—	—	—	—	—	—	—	—	—	—	—	—	—	0
Overtime	—	—	—	—	1	4	—	—	—	—	—	—	—	5

Level Strategy. Since we cannot use backlogs or subcontractors, we must satisfy demand as it occurs in each period. One way to satisfy work-force requirements is to find the peak requirement and staff the facility year round just to meet the peak. This approach would require 20 part-time employees (period 6). However, this would give us a lot of undertime (idle capacity) for most of the year.

A better way is to find the work-force level that, when it is fully used on overtime, the peak requirement is met. Since the most overtime that we can use is 25 percent of the regular-time capacity (w), we have

$$1.25w = 20 \text{ employees}$$

$$w = \frac{20}{1.25} = 16 \text{ employees.}$$

This staff size minimizes the resulting amount of undertime. Since there already are 10 part-time employees, the director must immediately hire 6 more.* Table 11.5 shows the resulting hires and overtime for Plan 1.

Chase Strategy. This strategy simply involves adjusting the work force as needed to meet demand. The director would plan to immediately lay off 5 part-time employees, then steadily build the work force to 20 by period 6. After that, we find that the work force can be reduced except for the secondary peak in period 10, when the director must hire 6 more employees. Table 11.6 shows the staff level along with the hires and layoffs for Plan 2.

Cost Comparisons. Table 11.7 shows the costs for each plan. You should not be surprised to see that Plan 2 using the chase strategy is less expen-

* An even better plan would be to wait until period 4 to hire employees, however this would not be consistent with a level strategy.

Table 11.6

Plan 2 Using Chase Strategy for the Clearwater Post Office Staffing Problem

	Accounting Period													
	1	2	3	4	5	6	7	8	9	10	11	12	13	Total
Requirement	5	6	8	15	17	20	15	15	10	16	14	14	12	167
Staff level	5	6	8	15	17	20	15	15	10	16	14	14	12	167
Hires	—	1	2	7	2	3	—	—	—	6	—	—	—	21
Layoffs	5	—	—	—	—	—	5	—	5	—	2	—	2	19
Overtime	—	—	—	—	—	—	—	—	—	—	—	—	—	0

sive for this situation. Plan 1 using the level strategy calls for a lot of undertime and, unless the director can find productive work for these people during slack periods, it is too costly to have them on the payroll. Intuitively, use of the chase strategy in this situation makes sense—and the economics of the case verify it. Recall (Box 11.1) that the director only had $100,000 to use for part-time staffing; thus the chase strategy would satisfy the budgeting limitations imposed by the regional annual plan.

The Tru-Rainbow Paint Company Production Plan

The staffing problem that we just analyzed had some relatively simple alternatives to evaluate. The Tru-Rainbow problem involves the use of more of the reactive alternatives that we discussed earlier. Data for the production planning problem are shown in Box 11.5. Note that the demand for paint is highly seasonal, with the peak months in summer. In order to prepare a prospective production plan, the following strategies have been proposed for consideration.

Table 11.7

Cost Comparisons for the Clearwater Post Office Staffing Plans

Cost	Plan 1 Using Level Strategy		Plan 2 Using Chase Strategy	
Regular time	208 Worker periods @ $500 =	$104,000	167 Worker periods @ $500 =	$83,500
Overtime	5 Worker periods @ $750 =	3,750	0 Worker periods @ $750 =	0
Hire	6 Workers @ $600 =	3,600	21 Workers @ $600 =	12,600
Layoff	0 Workers @ $100 =	0	19 Workers @ $100 =	1,900
Total		$111,350		$98,000

Box 11.5

DATA FOR THE TRU-RAINBOW PAINT COMPANY PRODUCTION PROBLEM

Requirements

Production requirements are expressed in thousands of gallons of paint.

	Month												
	Jan	Feb	Mar	Apr	May	June	July	Aug	Sept	Oct	Nov	Dec	Total
Requirement	50	100	150	200	250	400	600	550	350	200	100	50	3000

The company currently employs 110 workers. The current inventory of 400,000 gallons of paint has not been deducted from the requirements shown.

Constraints

1. Physical:

   The maximum storage capacity is 900,000 gallons.

2. Policy:

   The maximum overtime in any month is 20 percent of the regular-time capacity in that month.
   Subcontracting is not allowed.

Costs

Regular-time wages	\$2000 per employee per month, including fringe benefits.
Overtime wages	150 percent of the regular-time rate, excluding fringe benefits, which amounts to \$2400 per employee-month.
Hires	\$1000 per employee, including paperwork and training.
Layoffs	\$500 per employee, including severance pay.
Inventory	40 percent of average inventory value per year. Inventory is valued at \$3.00 per gallon for materials and labor. Consequently, it costs \$1.20 to hold one gallon in inventory for a year, or \$0.10 per month.
Back orders	\$0.50 per gallon per month to reflect expediting costs and possible loss of future goodwill.

Other Data

Each employee can produce 2000 gallons of paint per month.
There is no loss of productivity for overtime work.

1. *Level strategy*. Maintain a level production rate throughout the next 12 months and build an ending inventory of 400,000 gallons. Do not allow any back orders or stockouts and do not use overtime or subcontracting. The resulting plan is called Plan 1.
2. *Chase strategy*. Hire and lay off as dictated by production requirements and build an ending inventory of 400,000 gallons. Do not allow any back orders or stockouts and do not use any overtime or subcontracting. Using this strategy results in Plan 2.
3. *Mixed strategy 1*. Maintain a base work force of 75 employees, hire seasonal employees for June through August, and build an ending inventory of 400,000 gallons. Do not allow any back orders or stockouts and do not use any overtime or subcontracting. Plan 3 is the outcome.
4. *Mixed strategy 2*. Maintain a level work force of 110 employees over the next 12 months. As more capacity is needed, first use overtime to the maximum allowed. If more capacity is required, use back orders as needed. Do not use subcontracting or allow stockouts, and build an ending inventory of at least 150,000 gallons. Plan 4 reflects this strategy.

Level Strategy. Given the beginning and ending inventory levels, we can develop a prospective production plan for this strategy by using the equation for inventory; that is

$$\text{Inventory at the end of December} = \text{Inventory at the start of January} + \text{Total annual production} - \text{Total annual demand.}$$

If we let

i_{12} = Inventory at the end of December (in 12 months),

i_0 = Inventory at the start of January (now),

p = Monthly production rate, and

r = Total annual demand,

we have

$$i_{12} = i_0 + 12p - r.$$

Since we do not know p, we can rearrange terms to get a relationship for p:

$$p = \frac{i_{12} - i_0 + r}{12}.$$

Substituting the values of the variables into this relationship yields

$$p = \frac{400{,}000 - 400{,}000 + 3{,}000{,}000}{12} = \frac{3{,}000{,}000}{12}$$

$$= 250{,}000 \text{ gal/mo.}$$

Table 11.8

Plan 1 Using Level Strategy for the Tru-Rainbow Paint Company Production Problem

	Month											
	Jan	Feb	Mar	Apr	May	Jun	Jul	Aug	Sep	Oct	Nov	Dec
Requirement	50	100	150	200	250	400	600	550	350	200	100	50
Production plan	250	250	250	250	250	250	250	250	250	250	250	250
Workers required	125	125	125	125	125	125	125	125	125	125	125	125
Hires	15	—	—	—	—	—	—	—	—	—	—	—
Inventory	600	750	850	900	900	750	400	100	—	50	200	400

Note: Requirement, production plan, and inventory quantities are thousands of gallons of paint.

The monthly work force required would be 125 employees, since each employee can produce an average of 2000 gallons per month. This requirement means that the company would have to hire 15 employees immediately.

Before we can accept Plan 1 as feasible, we must check to be sure that no back orders, stockouts, overtime, or subcontracting will be needed. We construct Table 11.8 and check to see whether sufficient capacity is available each period. We calculated the inventory position by using the equation for the inventory level. Note that Plan 1 does not require back orders, stockouts, overtime or subcontracting. If this were not the case, a level production plan would fail to yield the desired ending inventory position. The ending inventory position would have to be increased on a trial-and-error basis until a feasible plan could be found. Note that the projected inventory position in September is zero, even though there are no back orders or stockouts.

Table 11.9

Plan 2 Using Chase Strategy for the Tru-Rainbow Paint Company Production Problem

	Month											
	Jan	Feb	Mar	Apr	May	Jun	Jul	Aug	Sep	Oct	Nov	Dec
Requirement	50	100	150	200	250	400	600	550	350	200	100	50
Production plan	50	100	150	200	250	400	600	550	350	200	100	50
Workers required	25	50	75	100	125	200	300	275	175	100	50	25
Hires	—	25	25	25	25	75	100	—	—	—	—	—
Layoffs	85	—	—	—	—	—	—	25	100	75	50	25
Inventory	400	400	400	400	400	400	400	400	400	400	400	400

Note: Requirement, production plan, and inventory quantities are thousands of gallons of paint.

Chase Strategy. Using the chase strategy, the company would merely hire and lay off employees to match seasonal demand. We divide the forecasted requirements by 2000 gallons per month to get the number of workers required each month; a constant inventory level of 400,000 gallons is maintained throughout the year. Table 11.9 shows the results of the calculations for Plan 2. Figure 11.3 contrasts the level strategy, which uses anticipation inventory to meet variable demands, and the chase strategy, which adjusts

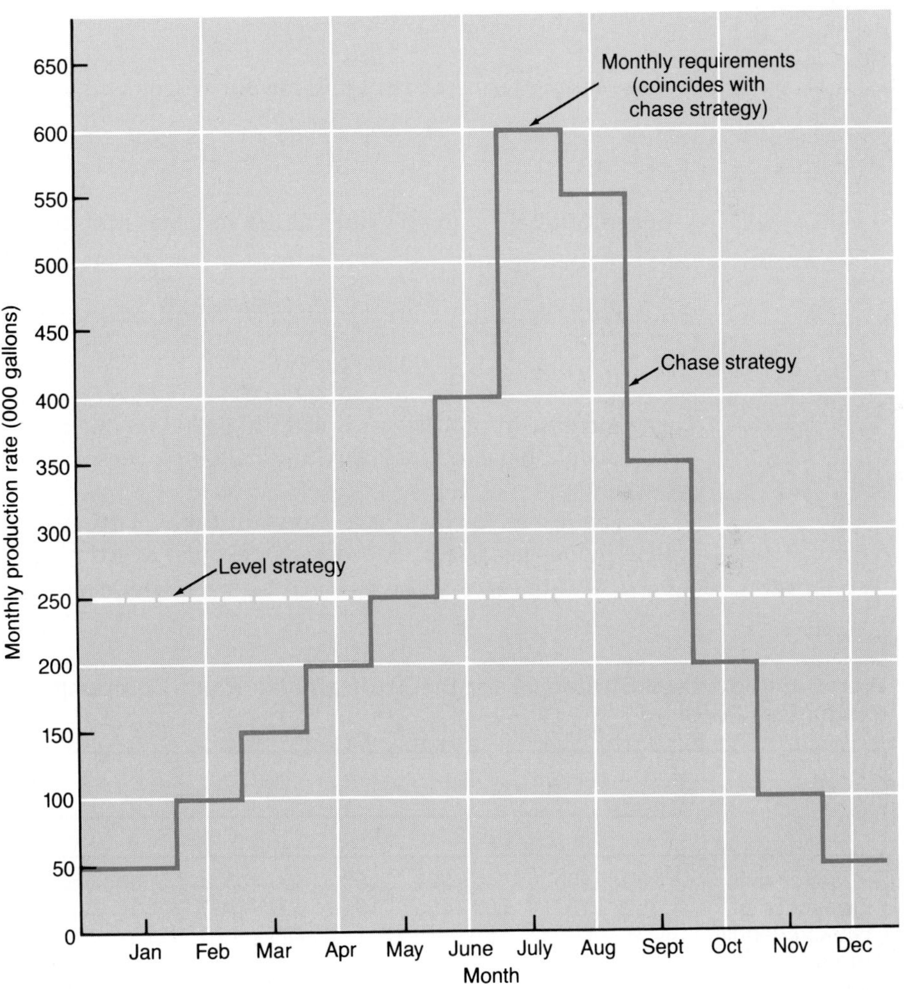

Figure 11.3

Comparison of Pure Strategies for the Tru-Rainbow Paint Company Production Problem.

capacity to meet those same demands. If the company were to use the chase strategy, it would have to fire 85 employees immediately.

Mixed Strategy 1. Since we are to have 75 employees as a base work force, this strategy calls for production of 150,000 gallons a month for January through May and September through December, a total of nine months. It also calls for a greater production rate in the three months of June, July, and August. If we let p_1 be the given nine-month production rate, and p_2 be the unknown three-month production rate, the relationship for the desired ending inventory position is

$$i_{12} = i_0 + 9p_1 + 3p_2 - r.$$

Rearranging terms and solving for p_2, we get

$$p_2 = \frac{i_{12} - i_0 - 9p_1 + r}{3}.$$

Substituting the known values of the variables into the relationship for p_2, we get

$$p_2 = \frac{400{,}000 - 400{,}000 - 9(150{,}000) + 3{,}000{,}000}{3}$$
$$= 550{,}000 \text{ gal/mo.}$$

The increase in production is 400,000 gallons, which indicates that Tru-Rainbow would have to hire 200 additional employees in June and lay them off in September.

The results for Plan 3 are shown in Table 11.10. A quick check reveals that Plan 3 does not use back orders, stockouts, overtime, or subcontracting. We

Table 11.10

Plan 3 Using Mixed Strategy 1 for the Tru-Rainbow Paint Company Production Problem

	Month											
	Jan	Feb	Mar	Apr	May	Jun	Jul	Aug	Sep	Oct	Nov	Dec
Requirement	50	100	150	200	250	400	600	550	350	200	100	50
Production plan	150	150	150	150	150	550	550	550	150	150	150	150
Workers required	75	75	75	75	75	275	275	275	75	75	75	75
Hires	—	—	—	—	—	200	—	—	—	—	—	—
Layoffs	35	—	—	—	—	—	—	—	200	—	—	—
Inventory	500	550	550	500	400	550	500	500	300	250	300	400

Note: Requirement, production plan, and inventory quantities are thousands of gallons of paint.

Table 11.11

Plan 4 Using Mixed Strategy 2 for the Tru-Rainbow Paint Company Production Problem

	Month											
	Jan	Feb	Mar	Apr	May	Jun	Jul	Aug	Sep	Oct	Nov	Dec
Requirement	50	100	150	200	250	400	600	550	350	200	100	50
Production plan	220	220	220	220	220	220	220	264	264	264	220	220
Workers required	110	110	110	110	110	110	110	110	110	110	110	110
Overtime used	—	—	—	—	—	—	—	44	44	44	—	—
Inventory	570	690	760	780	750	570	190	—	—	—	2	172
Back order	—	—	—	—	—	—	—	96	182	118	—	—

Note: Requirement, production plan, inventory, overtime, and back-order quantities are thousands of gallons of paint.

could consider many other plans. For example, a constant production rate of 100,000 gallons for the nine months would also work; however Tru-Rainbow would have to hire 300 employees in June. It may not be possible, or desirable, to hire that many employees at one time.

Mixed Strategy 2. Table 11.11 shows the results of a mixed strategy that allows overtime and back orders. To construct the details of Plan 4, we must calculate the inventory position period by period. When we get to August, we see that the projected inventory position would be negative unless we take some corrective action. Using the inventory equation, the inventory position at the end of August would be 190,000 + 220,000 − 550,000 = −140,000. The maximum amount of overtime for the work force of 110 employees is 44,000 gallons per month [or 0.20(2000)(110)]. Since we need to make up 140,000 gallons, we can use the maximum overtime to increase the production rate in August to 264,000 gallons and allow the remaining 96,000 gallons to be back ordered. In September, the effective demand is 446,000 gallons (or 350,000 + 96,000). If we again use maximum overtime, the production rate is 264,000 gallons, but we must back order the remaining 182,000 gallons (or 446,000 − 264,000). The plan for October is calculated similarly. When we get to November and December, we start to build inventory again.

Graphic Presentation. We show the four plans graphically in Fig. 11.4. If a plan is not too complicated, we find it useful to graph cumulative production and compare it to cumulative requirements over the planning horizon in order to identify inventory buildups or back orders. For example, Plan 1 shows that considerable inventory is accumulated through May and slowly depletes to zero by September, when the cumulative production and beginning inventory equal the cumulative manufacturing requirements. We can

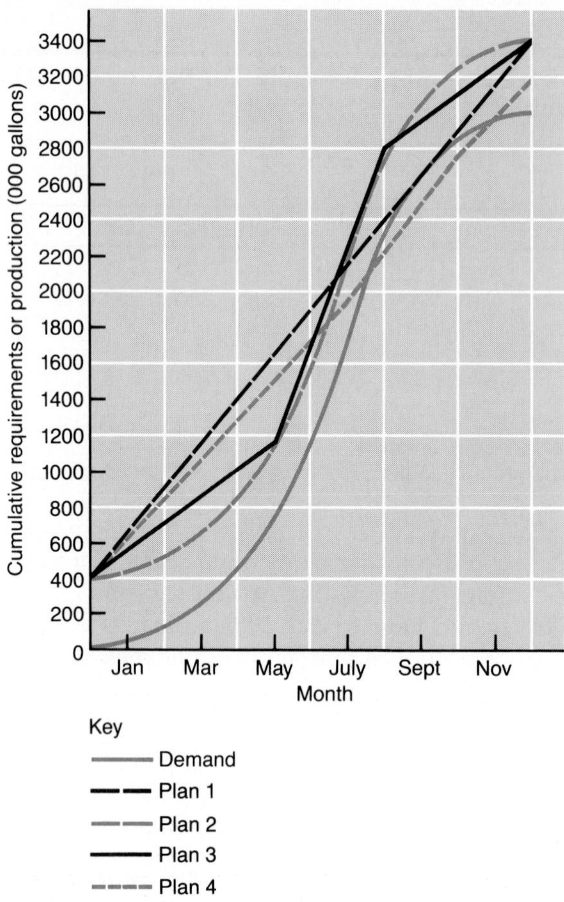

Figure 11.4

Graphic Comparison of Plans for the Tru-Rainbow Paint Company Production Problem.

even graph various plans on a trial-and-error basis and then put the data in tabular form, as in Tables 11.8–11.11, for more detailed analysis.

Comparing Plans. The acceptability of a prospective plan depends on balancing objectives like those we discussed earlier. Table 11.12 provides a cost comparison of the plans. If the sole objective is to minimize total quantifiable costs, Plan 4 would be the best of the four plans.

However, certain aspects of Plan 4 may be undesirable. Table 11.13 shows a comparison of the plans against several criteria. Here the average inventory

Table 11.12

Cost Comparison for the Tru-Rainbow Paint Company Production Plans

Cost	Plan 1 Using Level Strategy	Plan 2 Using Chase Strategy	Plan 3 Using Mixed Strategy 1	Plan 4 Using Mixed Strategy 2
Regular time	$3,000,000	$3,000,000	$3,000,000	$2,640,000
Overtime	—	—	—	158,400
Inventory	590,000	480,000	530,000	448,400
Hire	15,000	275,000	200,000	—
Layoff	—	180,000	117,500	—
Back order	—	—	—	198,000
Total	$3,605,000	$3,935,000	$3,847,500	$3,444,800

investment is the average monthly inventory level in units multiplied by the value per unit, $3. The average back orders are merely the total back orders divided by 12. If we are only considering average back orders, Plan 4 is the *worst* of the four plans. In fact, none of the four plans dominates the other three in terms of the criteria used. Each plan meets at least one criterion better than any of the other three. Consequently, unless management specifies an overriding objective criterion, the final selection process must reconcile a number of conflicting objectives.

Table 11.13

Comparison of the Tru-Rainbow Paint Company Production Plans Against Various Criteria

Criterion	Plan 1 Using Level Strategy	Plan 2 Using Chase Strategy	Plan 3 Using Mixed Strategy 1	Plan 4 Using Mixed Strategy 2
Total cost	$3,605,000	$3,935,000	$3,847,500	$3,444,800
Average inventory investment per month	$1,475,000	$1,200,000	$1,325,000	$1,120,000
Average back orders per month	0	0	0	33,167 gal
Number of changes in production rate	0	12	2	2
Number of changes in work-force level	0	12	2	0

MATHEMATICAL APPROACHES

The major advantage of the trial-and-error approach we used to demonstrate the development of an acceptable production or staffing plan is its simplicity. The approach can also be easily programmed for a spreadsheet analysis on a microcomputer. Many alternative production rates or work-force levels could be tried and the results tabulated and even graphed. Nonetheless, the key to using such a procedure is the ingenuity of the planner who, in the first place, must devise good plans for evaluation. The "best" plan may never be found; and the approach becomes difficult to work with when numerous constraints are imposed. Several mathematical models have been developed to assist in the analysis of complex planning problems. We briefly highlight the characteristics of a selected few.

Linear Programming Models

Linear programming models seek to find the optimal production or staffing plan for a linear objective function and a set of linear constraints. These models are capable of handling a large number of decision variables and constraints. Their major disadvantages are that you must use a single objective, and the relationships between variables must be linear. In addition, the models are sometimes difficult to formulate. See Appendix C for more details on linear programming.

Goal Programming Models

Goal programming models are used to help resolve the typical conflicting objectives present in the production or staff planning process. The objectives are first ranked in order of priority. Then the model, based on linear programming, proceeds sequentially to find a plan that satisfies the objectives in order of priority until all have been satisfied or it finds one that cannot be satisfied. In addition to the advantage of explicitly ordering multiple objectives, these models have the same advantages and limitations as linear programming models. (See Lee and Moore, 1974.)

Search Decision Rule

The **search decision rule** (see Taubert, 1968) is one of the many heuristic methods that have been devised for the production planning problem. A *heuristic method* cannot guarantee an optimal solution because it consists of rules of thumb, or guidelines, that embody common sense and the experience of decisionmakers in solving problems. The result is typically a good solution, but not necessarily the best. The search decision rule finds the values of the production rate and work-force level for each period of the planning horizon that minimize total costs, using a computer search method. The technique does not depend on specific assumptions about the shape of the objective function. In an iterative fashion, the procedure can arrive at a low cost solution to the problem.

Although mathematical approaches can be useful in evaluating production or staffing plan alternatives, they are only an input to the final plan. You have seen in this chapter that the planning process is dynamic and often complicated by conflicting objectives. Mathematical models can help managers evaluate changes in plans and resolve conflicting objectives. Nonetheless, managers, not the models, make the decisions.

CHAPTER HIGHLIGHTS

In manufacturing organizations, the production plan links the business plan and the master production schedule. In service organizations, the staffing plan links the annual plan and the work-force schedule. In this chapter we showed how these plans can be developed in a manner consistent with the strategies and objectives of top management. Some of the highlights of the chapter are:

- Production and staffing plans are managerial statements of time-phased production or service rates, labor requirements, and, in manufacturing, inventory investment that consider customer demand and physical capacity limitations.
- Products or services, labor, and time are aggregated to reduce the level of detail in the planning process.
- Inputs are required from the various functional areas in the organization. This approach typically raises conflicting objectives, which must be reconciled in the plan. One of the typical manufacturing objectives not considered in a service organization is to minimize investment in finished goods inventory.
- The two basic types of decision alternatives are *reactive* alternatives, which take the customer demand as a given quantity, and *aggressive* alternatives, which seek to change customer demand to achieve efficiency in providing the goods or services.
- Two pure planning strategies are the *level* strategy, which maintains a constant work-force size or production rate, and the *chase* strategy, which allows work-force levels and production rates to vary according to customer demand.
- Production and staff planning is an iterative process, which involves the determination of requirements; identification of relevant constraints, alternatives, and costs; preparation of a prospective plan; checking for acceptability to top management; and implementation of the first period of the plan.
- Mathematical approaches to aggregate planning can be categorized as either optimizing or heuristic. They can be used to generate prospective plans that may have to be modified during the planning process to reconcile various conflicting objectives or to incorporate nonquantitative factors.

KEY TERMS

aggressive alternatives
backlog
back order
chase strategy
complementary products
goal programming models
level strategy
linear programming
product family
production plan
reactive alternatives
rolling planning horizon
search decision rule
staffing plan
stockout

STUDY QUESTIONS

1. What is a production plan? Why must quantities be aggregated?
2. How do the production plan and staffing plan relate to other plans of an organization?
3. Consider the following statement. "Production planning is the responsibility of our manufacturing personnel because it deals with the resources they are responsible for." Comment on that statement in light of the strategic importance of production planning.
4. Give reasons why executives representing the following areas should be interested in production planning.
   (a) Marketing
   (b) Manufacturing
   (c) Materials
   (d) Finance
   (e) Human resources
   (f) Engineering
5. What are the typical objectives to be considered in production and staff planning? Comment on the conflicting nature of these objectives.
6. What is the difference between *reactive* alternatives and *aggressive* alternatives in production and staff planning? Provide several examples of each.
7. The *chase* strategy and the *level* strategy represent two extremes in production or staff planning. Define each one and describe the type of environment in which each would work best.
8. Briefly describe the production and staff planning process and explain how inputs from functional areas in the organization are solicited and incorporated in the process.
9. Compare and contrast the staff plan in a service organization with a production plan in a manufacturing organization. In what ways are the objectives, alternatives, and planning processes different?
10. The Hometown Bank currently employs eight tellers to staff lobby stations for customer transactions. Customer demand for banking services is variable, with peaks coinciding with the end of the week, end of the month, and holiday seasons. Because of this variability the tellers are idle

much of the time; however, during the rush periods customers experience lengthy delays. Suppose that you are the operations manager of this bank.

(a) What staff planning alternatives would you consider?
(b) What data would you need?
(c) What objectives would you consider?

PROBLEMS

1. The Crop-Chemical Company produces chemical fertilizers. The projected manufacturing requirements (in thousands of gallons) for the next four quarters are 20, 10, 40, and 50. Stockouts and back orders are to be avoided. A level production strategy is desired.
   (a) Determine the quarterly production rate required to meet total demand for the year. Beginning inventory is zero.
   (b) Specify the anticipation inventories that will be produced.
   (c) Suppose that the requirements for the next four quarters are 10, 40, 50, and 20. The total demand is the same, but would the production rate in part (a) have to be changed? If so, what rate would be needed now?

2. The Cranston Telephone Company employs workers who lay telephone cables and perform a number of other construction activities. The company prides itself on good service and strives to meet all commitments on time. Company policy is to complete all service orders within the quarter during which they were placed. Each worker puts in 600 hours per quarter regular time and can work an additional 100 hours overtime. The operations department has estimated that the following work-force requirements for such services will be needed next year.

	Quarter			
	1	2	3	4
Hours	12,000	24,000	30,000	6,000

   Wages are \$6000 per quarter, with an overtime pay rate of \$15 per hour. It costs \$8000 to hire, train, and outfit a new employee. Layoff costs are \$2000 per employee. Currently, 40 employees work for Cranston in this capacity.
   (a) Find a level work-force plan that allows for no delay in service and minimizes undertime. What is the total cost of the plan? How many hours in undertime does your plan call for?
   (b) Use a chase strategy without overtime. What is the total cost of this plan?
   (c) Propose a plan of your own. Compare your plan with those of parts (a) and (b) and discuss its comparative merits.

3. The Little Shoe Company makes sandals for children. Management has just prepared a forecast of sales (in pairs of sandals) for next year and now must prepare a production plan. The company has traditionally maintained a level work-force strategy. Currently there are 10 workers, many of whom have been with the company for a number of years. Each employee can produce 25 pairs of sandals in a two-month period of time, the planning period used by Little Shoe. Every year managment authorizes overtime in periods 1, 5 and 6 up to a maximum of 20 percent of regular-time capacity. Management wants to avoid stockouts and back orders and will not accept any plan that calls for such shortages. At present there

are 200 pairs of sandals in finished goods inventory. The demand forecast is

	Period					
	1	2	3	4	5	6
Sales	400	220	100	300	500	450

(a) Is the level work-force strategy with the current work force feasible, assuming that overtime is used in periods 1, 5, and 6? Explain.

(b) Find two alternative plans that would satisfy management's concern over stockouts and back orders disregarding costs. What are the trade-offs between these two plans that must be considered?

4. The Bull Grin Company produces a feed supplement for animal foods produced by a number of companies. Sales are seasonal, but Bull Grin's customers refuse to stockpile its product during slack sales periods. In other words, the customers want to minimize *their* inventory investments, insist on shipments according to their schedules, and will accept no back orders.

Bull Grin employs manual, unskilled labor; little or no training is required. The hiring and layoff plans are made on a quarterly basis. It costs $150 to hire a new employee and $300 to lay off an employee who is on the payroll. At present there are 100 employees at Bull Grin. An employee earns $1620 in regular-time wages per quarter. The overtime rate is 150 percent of the regular-time wage; however, no employee is allowed to produce more than 750 pounds of feed supplement on overtime in a quarter. The average worker can produce 2000 pounds during a quarter on regular time.

The management of Bull Grin does not want finished goods inventory to fall below 40,000 pounds, the current inventory level. It costs $90 to hold *1000 pounds* of feed supplement in inventory per quarter. New annual forecasts are now available:

Quarter	Demand (lb)
1	100,000
2	410,000
3	770,000
4	440,000
Total =	1,720,000

The following production planning strategies have been proposed.

- Level work-force strategy without overtime.
- Chase strategy without overtime.
- A level work force of 200 employees, with authorization to use overtime in Quarters 2 and 3.

(a) Compare each of the three strategies on a cost basis, making sure that Quarter 4 ending inventory is exactly 40,000 pounds and that no quarter has an ending inventory of less than 40,000 pounds.

(b) How much would the inventory carrying cost of $90 per 1000 pounds per quarter have to increase before the best strategy in part (a) changes?

(c) How much would the layoff cost of $300 per employee have to decrease before the best strategy in part (a) changes?

5. Consider again the Bull Grin Company described in Problem 4. Suppose that management is willing to negotiate some price concessions with customers, which would give them an incentive to stockpile feed supplement prior to actual need in their production schedules. Bull Grin management estimates that demand for feed supplement resulting from this new arrangement would be

Quarter	Demand (lb)
1	200,000
2	540,000
3	540,000
4	440,000
	Total = 1,720,000

(a) For the new demand schedule, which strategy described in Problem 4 is best on a cost basis?

(b) Compare the plans you developed with the new schedule to those you developed in part (a) of Problem 4. With the change in schedule, is there a change in the best strategy? Explain.

(c) How much could Bull Grin afford to reduce annual revenues to get the new demand schedule?

6. The manager of Gretchen's Hamburger Paradise must prepare an annual staffing plan. The Hamburger Paradise shop is a fast-food shop located in an ideal spot near the local high school. The only products the shop sells are hamburgers, chili, soft drinks, shakes, and french fries. A sample of 1000 customers taken at random revealed that they purchased 2100 hamburgers, 200 pints of chili, 1000 soft drinks and shakes, and 1000 bags of french fries. Thus, for purposes of estimating staffing requirements, the manager assumes that each customer purchases 2.1 hamburgers, 0.2 pints of chili, 1 soft drink or shake, and 1 bag of french fries. Each hamburger requires 4 minutes of labor. A pint of chili requires 3 minutes, while a soft drink/shake and a bag of fries each take 2 minutes of labor.

Gretchen's Hamburger Paradise currently has 10 employees who work 80 hours a month. They are high school students who work part-time on staggered shifts. Wages are $400 per month for regular time and $7.50 per hour for overtime. It costs $250 to hire and train a new employee and $50 to fire an employee.

The manager realizes that building up seasonal inventories of hamburgers (or any of the products) would not be wise because of customer taste preferences. Also, any demand not satisfied is a lost sale and must be avoided. Three strategies have come to mind:

- Level work force and use of up to 20 percent of regular-time capacity on overtime in any month.
- Maintain a base of 10 employees, hiring and firing, as necessary, to avoid any overtime.
- Chase strategy, hiring and firing employees as demand changes to avoid overtime.

When performing her calculations the manager always rounds to the next highest integer for the number of employees. She also follows a policy of not using an employee more than 80 hours per month, except when overtime is needed. The projected demand by month (number of customers) for next year is:

Jan	Feb	Mar	Apr	May	Jun
3000	2800	3200	3500	3800	4500

Jul	Aug	Sep	Oct	Nov	Dec
4800	4200	3800	3600	3500	3000

(a) Develop the schedule of service requirements for the next year.

(b) Which of the three strategies is most effective?

(c) Suppose that an arrangement with the high school enables the manager to identify good prospective employees without having to advertise in the local newspaper. This reduces the hiring cost to $50, which is mainly the cost of charred hamburgers during training. Will this change the manager's strategy on a cost basis? *Should* the manager change strategies, considering other objectives that may be appropriate?

SELECTED REFERENCES

Bowman, E. H., "Consistency and Optimality in Managerial Decision Making," *Management Science*, vol. 9, no. 2 (January, 1963), pp. 310–321.

Chaiken, J. M., and R. C. Larson, "Methods for Allocating Urban Emergency Units: A Survey," *Management Science*, vol. 19, no. 4 (December, Part 2, 1972), pp. 110–130.

Hanssman, F., and S. W. Hess, "A Linear Programming Approach to Production and Employment Scheduling," *Management Technology*, vol. 1 (January 1960), pp. 46–51.

Holt, C., C. F. Modigliani, and H. Simon, "A Linear Decision Rule for Production and Employment Scheduling," *Management Science*, vol. 2, no. 2 (October 1955), pp. 1–30.

Jones, C. H., "Parametric Production Planning," *Management Science*, vol. 15, no. 11 (July 1967), pp. 843–866.

Kinsey, John W., "Master Production Planning—The Key to Successful Master Scheduling." *Proceedings of the 24th Annual APICS Conference*, Boston (October 1981), pp. 81–85.

Krajewski, L., and H. Thompson, "Efficient Employment Planning in Public Utilities," *The Bell Journal of Economics and Management Science*, vol. 6, no. 1 (Spring 1975), pp. 314–326.

Lee, S. M., and L. J. Moore, "A Practice Approach to Production Scheduling," *Production and Inventory Management* (1st Quarter 1974), pp. 79–92.

Lee, W. B., and B. M. Khumawala, "Simulation Testing of Aggregate Production Planning Models in an Implementation Methodology," *Management Science*, vol. 20, no. 6 (February 1974), pp. 903–911.

McClain, J. D., and L. J. Thomas, "Horizon Effects in Aggregate Production Planning with Seasonal Demand," *Management Science*, vol. 23, no. 7 (March 1977), pp. 728–736.

Mellichamp, J., and R. Love, "Production Heuristics for the Aggregate Planning Problem," *Management Science*, vol. 24, no. 12 (August 1978), pp. 1242–1251.

Silver, E. A., "A Tutorial on Production Smoothing and Workforce Balancing," *Operations Research* (November–December 1967), pp. 985–1010.

Smith, Linda M., "Marketing's Role in a Manufacturing Environment." *Proceedings of the 23rd Annual APICS Conference*, Los Angeles (October 1980), pp. 248–251.

Taubert, W. H., "A Search Decision Rule for the Aggregate Scheduling Problem," *Management Science*, vol. 14, no. 6 (February 1968), pp. 343–359.

Vollmann, Thomas E., "Capacity Planning: The Missing Link," *Production and Inventory Management* (First Quarter 1973), pp. 61–73.

Wolfe, H., and J. P. Young, "Staffing the Nursing Unit—Part 1: Controlled Variable Staffing," *Nursing Research*, vol. 14, no. 3 (Summer 1965), pp. 236–243.

CHAPTER 12

INDEPENDENT-DEMAND INVENTORY SYSTEMS

Some Managerial Issues

- How large should be our cycle and safety stock inventories?
- What type of system—a *Q* system, *P* System, or some hybrid—should we use to control inventories?
- Should we use a manual or computerized system?
- Which items demand our closest attention and control?
- How much effort must we spend to maintain accurate inventory records?
- How often should we update our lot sizes, safety stocks, and lead times?
- How do we handle quantity discounts and should we hedge against price increases?

Chapter Outline

In Chapter 10, you learned that demand for an item can be either independent or dependent, that independent demand is influenced by market conditions, and that an independent-demand item has no parents. Figure 12.1 shows the key feature of independent demand. The demand from any one customer can be "lumpy," but the total demand from all customers can be fairly constant from one week to the next. Low demand from some customers is offset by high demand from the rest. Total demand follows a fairly smooth pattern, with some random fluctuations. This pattern does not hold for a dependent-demand item. In that case, demand for an item occurs only when an order for one of its parents is released. Such orders tend to be relatively infrequent, unless the item has many parents and they have small lot sizes. The result is a lumpy, on-again, off-again pattern.

The best way to manage inventory differs for the two cases. In this chapter, we cover the case of independent demand, which includes

1. wholesale and retail merchandise, amounting to 40% percent of the economy's inventory;

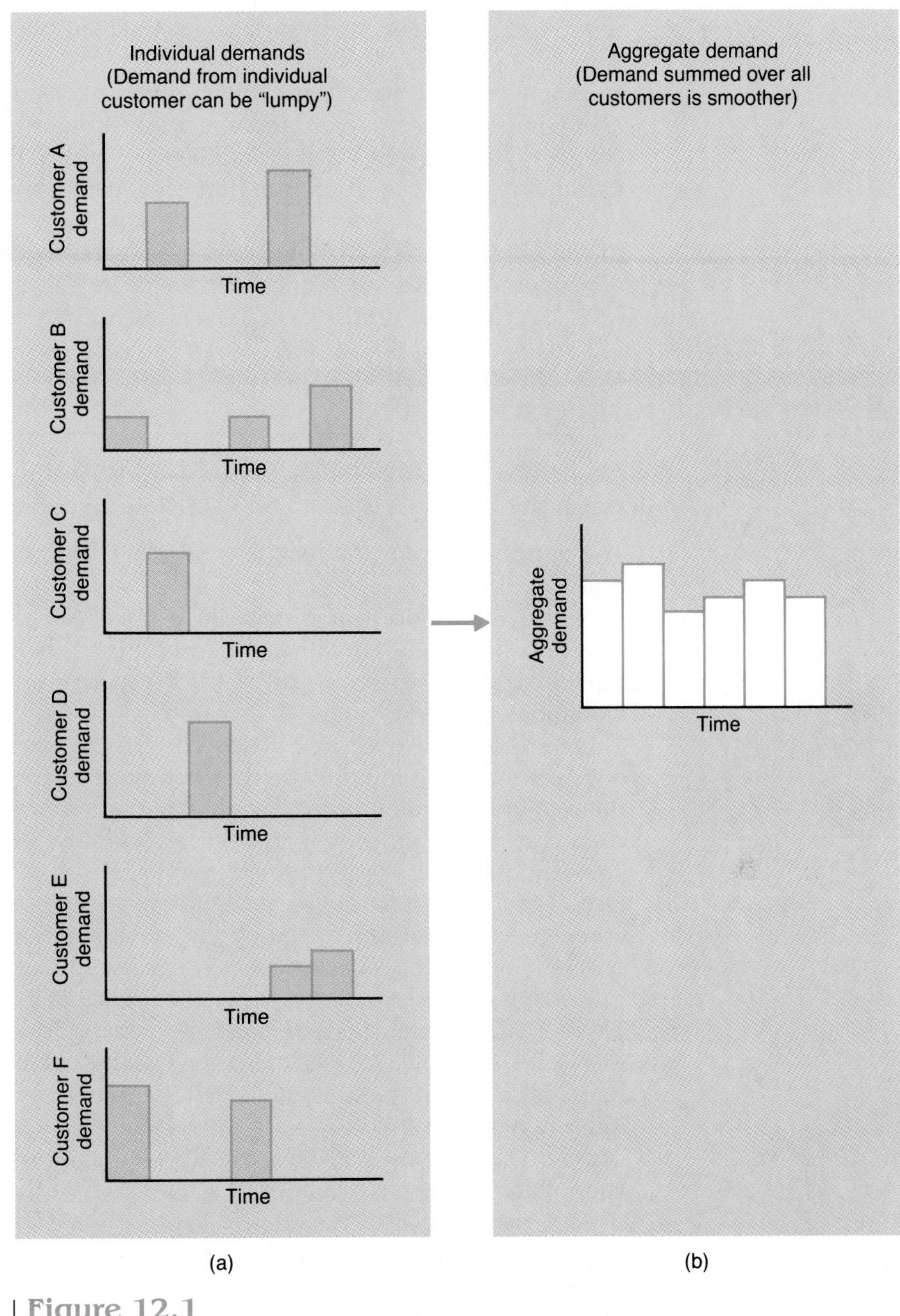

Figure 12.1

Key Feature of Independent Demand: (a) Individual Demand can be "lumpy"; but (b) Aggregate Demand is smoother.

2. service-industry inventory, such as hospital supplies, book publishing, and office supplies at a bank;
3. end-item and replacement-part inventories at a manufacturing firm; and
4. MRO (maintenance, repair, and operating supplies) at a manufacturing company, that is, items that do not become part of the product, such as machine repair parts, employee uniforms, paint, towels, and fuel.

The description in Box 12.1 illustrates a typical situation facing a manager of independent-demand inventories. Any manager such as Lois faces a range of issues. Let's begin with the basics: the size and frequency of new orders.

ECONOMIC ORDER QUANTITY

A good starting point for finding reasonable lot sizes is with the **economic order quantity** (EOQ). It is based on the following assumptions.

1. The demand rate for the item is constant. For example, it is always 10 units per day.
2. The item is produced or purchased in lots. An order for the item is received all at one time, rather than piecemeal. There are no constraints on the size of each lot, such as truck capacity or materials handling limitations.
3. There are only two relevant costs. The first is inventory holding cost, which is found by multiplying the average inventory level (in units) by the cost to hold one unit for a specific period of time. The second is the fixed cost per lot for ordering or setup. Quantity discounts for large lot sizes and price increases expected in the near future are not considered.
4. Decisions for one item can be made independently of decisions made for other items. For example, there is no advantage in combining several orders going to the same supplier, or in coordinating the orders for a group of items to level out capacity requirements in the shop.
5. There is no uncertainty in demand, lead time, or supply. The demand rate is not only constant (see first assumption), but also known. The lead time is also constant and known. For example, the time from placing an order to receiving it is always 14 days. Finally, there is no uncertainty in supply. The amount received is exactly what was ordered. This rules out short shipments from a vendor or scrap losses in the shop. Given complete certainty, no stockouts arise because the planner can determine exactly when to order to avoid them.

Total Inventory Costs

Based on the EOQ assumptions, on-hand inventory behaves as shown in Fig. 12.2. The straight-line depletion of inventory during the period results in an

Box 12.1

INVENTORY MANAGEMENT FOR A RETAILER

The Columbus Museum of Natural History opened a gift shop two years ago and named Lois Henry as the shop manager. Lois's product plan calls for ten general groups of merchandise: containers, art works, Eskimo crafts, Indian goods, geological items, paper goods, books, regular jewelry, scientific instruments (such as binoculars or barometers), and seasonal goods. Each group in turn breaks down into more specific categories. For example, the containers group consists of ceramic, glass, wood, metal, bookend, basket, and birdfeeder items.

Lois is pleased with many aspects of the gift shop, such as the merchandise offered, the store layout, and the work force (sales clerks). Annual sales now exceed $230,000 and are still climbing. However, inventory-related problems have proved to be a thorn in her side.

- *High Inventories:* Inventory turnover is much too low, which squeezes profit margins and causes cash-flow problems. High inventories are caused by overestimating future sales for some items and by her current strategy of reviewing most items only every five months. At the present time, Lois has no way to spot slow-moving or obsolete items, let alone monitor pilferage.
- *Stockouts:* Despite the high aggregate inventory, many items are sold out before replenishment orders arrive. Lois gets several stockout notices from the sales clerks each week and suspects that lost sales are becoming a significant factor.
- *Seasonal Sales:* Perhaps the most puzzling inventory problem of all is with the seasonal goods group, which includes men's clothes, women's clothes, Christmas gifts, and toys. These are "one-time" inventory decisions, since any merchandise not sold during the season is sold later at a loss or held for a whole year until the next season. If she does not order enough for the season, sales opportunities are lost. There is not enough time left in the season to get in a second order and have it filled. Both overages and stockouts therefore are costly, with demand uncertainty making one of the two outcomes almost inevitable.

In reflecting on these three problems, Lois believes that it is now time to improve her inventory policies and introduce a more systematic inventory control system. At present, she reviews the status of two of the ten merchandise groups each month, on a rotating basis, so that each group is reviewed once every five months. This frequency may seem to be overly long, but the process is time-consuming. It begins with a physical count of on-hand inventory for each item. Next, she intuitively judges whether the current supply is adequate. If it is not, she places a replenishment order for enough units to cover the expected demand until the next review. The only exception to this procedure is when a sales clerk reports a stockout. So long as the item does not belong to the seasonal goods group, she places a new order for it as soon as possible, rather than waiting for the next review. Lois is uncertain about what type of new system would be best. Perhaps a written record is needed to continuously update the inventory level of each item. This step, at least, would help her make replenishment decisions and provide the basis for monitoring the overall inventory situation.

average cycle inventory (see Chapter 10) equal to one-half the lot size Q. Consequently, the total cost of ordering Q units each time we place an order is given by the following function.

$$\text{Total cost} = \text{Annual holding cost} + \text{Annual ordering or setup cost},$$

or

$$C = \frac{Q}{2}(H) + \frac{D}{Q}(S),$$

where

C = Total cost per year;

D = Annual demand, in units per year;

H = Cost to hold one unit in inventory for a year;

S = Cost to order or setup one lot, in dollars per lot; and

Q = Average lot size, in units.

The annual holding cost is the average inventory over the course of a year multiplied by the cost to hold one unit for a year. This cost increases linearly as Q increases. The second term on the right-hand side of the equation is the number of lots ordered per year multiplied by the cost to place each order. We find the average number of orders per year by dividing the annual demand by Q. For example, if 1200 units must be ordered each year and the average lot size is 100 units, then 12 orders would be placed during the year. The annual ordering or setup cost decreases as Q increases because fewer orders are placed.

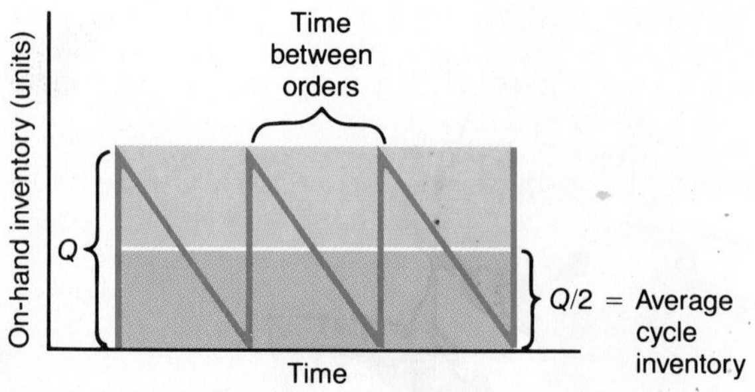

Figure 12.2

Cycle-Inventory Levels.

Box 12.2

EVALUATING AN ORDER POLICY

One of the top-selling items in the container group at the museum's gift shop is a birdfeeder. It is especially designed to prevent even the most clever squirrel from stealing any of the bird feed. Lois Henry estimates that weekly sales are 18 feeders, which translates into 936 per year [or (18 feeders/wk)(52 wk/yr)]. The purchase cost is $60 per unit, and Lois estimates that it costs 25 percent of an item's value to hold one unit in inventory for a year or, in this case, that it costs $15 [or $60(0.25)]. The supplier gives no quantity discounts. The cost of placing an order is estimated to be $45.

The current policy is to place an order every five months, which translates into an average Q of 390 units [or 936(5/12)]. The total annual cost of this policy is

$$C = \frac{Q}{2}(H) + \frac{D}{Q}(S)$$

$$= \frac{390}{2}(\$15) + \frac{936}{390}(\$45)$$

$$= \$3033.$$

Box 12.2 contains data on the cost of birdfeeders carried by the gift shop at the Columbus Museum of Natural History. Figure 12.3 shows the effects of changing the lot size on total cost for the birdfeeder item.* It is obvious that reducing the current lot size policy ($Q = 390$) can result in significant savings.

Calculating the Economic Order Quantity

The economic order quantity minimizes total holding and ordering or setup costs. One way to find the EOQ is to try a range of values for Q, plot the costs as shown in Fig. 12.3, and select the one that minimizes total cost.

A more efficient way is to recognize that the EOQ is the order quantity that results in equal annual holding costs and ordering or setup costs. Note that the total cost is lowest when these two costs are equal (Fig. 12.3). Solving for the best Q, subsequently termed EOQ, is straightforward:

$$\text{Annual holding costs} = \text{Annual ordering or setup costs,}$$

* It usually is convenient to express the total cost on an annual basis, although this is not necessary. Any time horizon can be selected, so long as D and H are defined the same way. If the total cost is computed on a monthly basis, D must be monthly demand and H must be the cost to hold a unit for a month rather than a year.

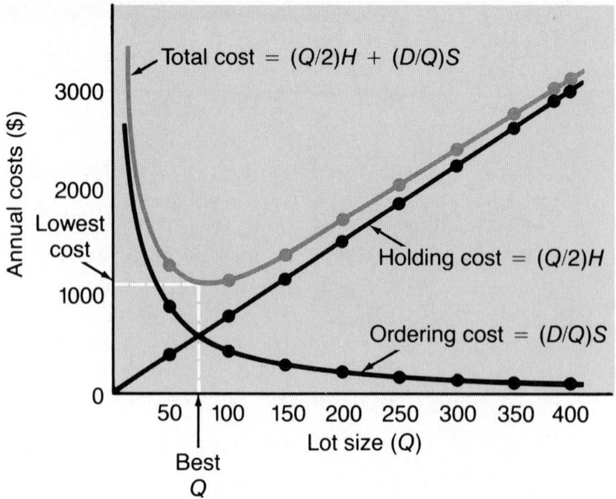

Figure 12.3

Total Inventory Cost Function for Birdfeeder.

or

$$\frac{QH}{2} = \frac{DS}{Q}$$

$$Q^2H = 2DS$$

$$Q^2 = \frac{2DS}{H}$$

$$Q = \sqrt{\frac{2DS}{H}} = \text{EOQ}.$$

This formula was developed by F. W. Harris more than 70 years ago.* For the birdfeeder example in Box 12.2,

$$\text{EOQ} = \sqrt{\frac{2DS}{H}} = \sqrt{\frac{2(936)(45)}{15}}$$

$$= 74.94 \quad \text{or} \quad 75.$$

Lois should order 75 feeders at a time, which translates into placing an order almost once every month, or

* The EOQ formula can also be derived by taking the first derivative of the total cost function with respect to Q and setting it equal to zero.

$$\text{Time between orders} = \frac{\text{Number of months per year}}{\text{Number of orders per year}}$$
$$= \frac{12 \text{ mo/yr}}{(936 \text{ feeders/yr})/(75 \text{ feeders/order})}$$
$$= 0.96 \quad \text{or} \quad 1 \text{ mo.}$$

The cost of using this policy would be \$1124 [or (75/2)(\$15) + (936/75)(\$45)]. This cost is much less than the \$3033 cost of her current policy of placing an order every 5 months.

Sensitivity Analysis

Subjecting the EOQ formula to sensitivity analysis can give us valuable insights into the management of inventories. We systematically substitute different values into the numerator or denominator of the formula and note the results. Sensitivity analysis can be used to help answer questions such as:

1. *What should happen to cycle inventory if the demand rate increases?* Since D is in the numerator, the EOQ (and therefore the best cycle inventory level) increases in proportion to the square root of the annual demand. We therefore should increase lot sizes when demand rises, but at a slower rate than actual demand. For example, if demand goes up by 25 percent, the new demand equals $1.25D$. The new lot size, however, should be only 1.118 (the square root of 1.25) times as large as the old lot size. Consequently, cycle inventory increases only 11.8 percent. This is one reason why higher repeatability, such as that gained from more part commonality or less product flexibility, helps reduce costs.
2. *What happens to lot sizes if setup costs decrease?* Reducing S reduces the EOQ and, consequently, reduces the average cycle inventory. Smaller lot sizes are now economic to produce, which is why manufacturers are so concerned about cutting setup time and costs. When setups become trivial, a major impediment to small-lot production is removed.
3. *What happens if interest rates drop?* Interest, or the cost of capital, is one component of the holding cost. (See Chapter 10.) Since H is in the denominator, the EOQ increases when H decreases. Larger lot sizes are justified by lower holding costs. The cycle inventory varies inversely with the square root of H.
4. *How critical are errors in estimating D, H, and S?* Since the EOQ is a function of the square root of these variables, it is rather insensitive to errors in estimating. Suppose that we incorrectly estimate the holding costs to be double their true value. That is, we calculate EOQ using $2H$, instead of H. This 100 percent error deflates the EOQ by a factor of 0.707, the square root of $\frac{1}{2}$. This is a 29.3 percent decrease in the lot size, from 75 to 53 units.

Total costs, however, increase only about 6 percent from \$1124 to about \$1192. This is a relatively small penalty for a 100 percent error in estimating holding costs.

Limitations

The economic order quantity is optimal only when the five assumptions presented earlier are satisfied. This constraint would seem to invalidate use of the EOQ, since very few situations are so simple and well-behaved. In fact, different lot-sizing approaches *are* needed to reflect quantity discounts, uneven demand rates, or interactions between items, some of which we introduce briefly later in this chapter. In the meantime, it is reassuring to know that the EOQ is often a reasonable first approximation of average lot sizes, even when several of the assumptions do not quite apply.

CONTINUOUS REVIEW SYSTEM

With these guidelines on the average size of new orders, we can now consider some of the inventory control systems commonly used. One of the best known systems is the **continuous review system,** in which an item's inventory status is supposedly reviewed each time a withdrawal is made from inventory. In practice, however, these reviews may only be done frequently, rather than continuously, such as on a daily basis rather than upon each withdrawal. At each review, a decision is made about an item's **inventory position** (IP), which, if judged to be unsatisfactory, triggers a new order. The inventory position is defined as

$$IP = n_{\mathrm{OH}} + n_{\mathrm{SR}} - n_{\mathrm{BO}}$$

where

IP = Inventory position of the item (in units);

n_{OH} = Number of units in on-hand inventory;

n_{SR} = Scheduled receipts (open orders); and

n_{BO} = Number of units either back ordered or allocated.

Recall that a back order is an unfilled customer order or commitment. It is an immediate (or past due) demand for an item that is out of stock. Shortages are filled later rather than being lost sales. *Allocated inventory* is on-hand inventory set aside or earmarked to meet past demands. For example, some of a component's on-hand inventory may be allocated for a parent's

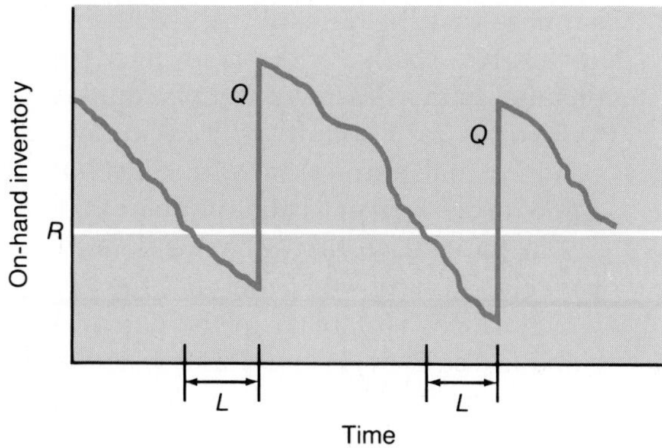

Figure 12.4

Illustration of a *Q* System.

order even though inventory has yet to be physically removed from the storeroom.

The inventory position therefore measures the ability to satisfy *future* demand, relying only on scheduled receipts and on-hand inventory. A mistake made frequently is to ignore scheduled receipts and back orders, which causes erratic inventory behavior.

The continuous review system, sometimes called a **reorder point system**, fixed order quantity system, or Q system, can be described as follows:

> Whenever a withdrawal brings the inventory position down to the reorder point R, place an order for Q units.

The Q system has just two parameters: Q and R. Each new order is of the same size, Q units, and Q can be based on the EOQ, a price-break quantity, a container size, or some other value selected by management. Figure 12.4 shows how the system operates. On-hand inventory (n_{OH}), rather than the inventory position (IP), is shown on the y-axis; n_{OH} and IP are identical except during the lead time (L), when there is a scheduled receipt. During the lead time, IP exceeds n_{OH} by the amount ordered (Q).* We now consider how to select the reorder point (R).

Selecting the Reorder Point

Recall the assumption made in calculating the EOQ: there is no uncertainty in demand, lead time, or supply. For the example at the Museum gift shop,

* This condition is true if the lead time is less than the elapsed time between orders. Otherwise, more than one scheduled receipt could be due.

suppose that the demand for feeders is always 18 per week, the lead time is always two weeks, and the supplier always ships the exact amount ordered on time. In this ideal world, Lois could wait until the inventory position drops to 36 units [or (18 units/wk)(2 wk)] to place a new order. Thus the reorder point R equals the *demand during lead time*, with no allowance for safety stock; a new order arrives at the moment that inventory drops to zero.

In the real world, behavior is not so predictable. Demand is a random variable. At best, we know that the *average* demand is 18 feeders per week, which causes variability in the demand during lead time. Suppose Lois decides to set R at 46 units and places orders in advance of when they are typically needed. This approach creates a safety stock of 10 units (or 46 − 36) to buffer against uncertain demand.*

More formally, the reorder point is

$$R = \overline{D}_L + B,$$

where

R = Reorder point;

$\overline{D}_L$ = Average demand during lead time L; and

B = Safety stock or buffer.

Since $\overline{D}_L$ is externally determined, the real decision to be made when selecting R concerns the safety stock level B. Deciding on a small or large B is a trade-off between customer service and inventory holding costs. Cost minimization models can be used to find the best B, but they require an estimate of stockout or back-order costs. This task is difficult and is not usually done. The usual approach is for management to judgmentally set a reasonable service level policy and then determine the safety stock level that satisfies this policy. Managers express service levels in a variety of ways, such as:

1. The desired probability of not running out of stock in any one inventory cycle, often called the **cycle-service level.**
2. The preferred proportion of annual demand (in units, customer orders, or dollars) instantaneously filled from stock, commonly called the **fill rate.**
3. The number of stockouts tolerated per year.
4. The preferred proportion of days in the year when an item is not out of stock.

* In this discussion we assume that demand is the only source of uncertainty. If lead time were also a random variable, the variability in demand during lead time would be even higher. If there were supply uncertainty, *IP* would also become a random variable, since the number of units actually received from scheduled receipts would be uncertain. These additional uncertainties would mandate higher safety stock.

For simplicity we will consider only the first two of these measures, beginning with cycle-service level.

Choosing an Appropriate Service Level Policy

Cycle-Service Level. Establishing a policy based on the cycle-service level is natural, since a stockout can occur only at the end of an inventory cycle (during the lead time). Even if a large withdrawal suddenly depletes inventory, causing a stockout or back order, it happens at the beginning of the lead time; a replenishment order would be placed immediately.

To understand how a cycle-service level is translated into *R*, consider the data in Box 12.3. For that probability distribution for demand during lead time and a 90 percent cycle-service level (9 out of 10 cycles), Lois concludes that *R* should be 50 units. With this choice, she will face a stockout only when the

Box 12.3

TRANSLATING CYCLE-SERVICE LEVEL INTO THE REORDER POINT

Lois Henry is considering using a *Q* system to control the inventory of birdfeeders. She has already settled on a *Q* of 75 feeders but now must decide on the reorder point *R*.

Based on the past records and her judgment, she believes that the following probability distribution accurately represents the demand during lead time (DDLT). She assumes a two-week lead time and an average demand of 18 feeders per week. She added the last column to compute the average demand during lead time $\bar{D}_L$.

DDLT (units)	Probability	DDLT × Probability
10	0.10	1.0
20	0.15	3.0
30	0.20	6.0
40	0.25	10.0
50	0.20	10.0
60	0.10	6.0
	1.00	$\bar{D}_L$ = 36.00

Based on this distribution and her judgment of the importance of a stockout versus the cost of holding inventory, she wants to avoid stockouts in 9 out of 10 cycles. What *R* should she select and how much safety stock will have to be carried?

demand during lead time (DDLT) is 60 units, or 10 percent of the time. Thus R will be greater than or equal to DDLT for 90 percent of the cycles, which conforms to Lois's cycle-service level policy. We calculate the safety stock B as follows:

$$R = \overline{D}_L + B$$
$$50 = 36 + B$$
$$B = 14 \text{ units.}$$

We can use this same general approach with other types of DDLT probability distributions. Instead of approximating DDLT with a specific probability distribution, as in Box 12.3, we can use the normal distribution, which is shown in Fig. 12.5. The first step is to obtain estimates of $\overline{D}_L$ and the standard deviation σ_L, either from past history or based on judgment. The next step is to compute the safety stock:

$$B = z\sigma_L,$$

where

z = Number of standard deviations above the mean needed to implement the cycle-service level; and

σ_L = Standard deviation of DDLT probability distribution.*

The higher the value of z, the higher will be B and the cycle-service level. If z is 0, there is no safety stock and stockouts will occur during 50 percent of the cycles. Note also the implications for forecasting. (See Chapter 3.) The better the job of forecasting demand and lead times, the smaller will be the values of σ_L and B. Lower safety stocks are one reward for improved forecasting techniques.

Returning to the birdfeeder example, suppose that Lois estimates $\overline{D}_L$ at 36 and σ_L as 15; she also believes that DDLT is normally distributed. Consulting the normal distribution table in Appendix D.3, we find that approximately 1.28 standard deviations to the right of the mean places 90 percent of the area under the curve to the left of that point. The 90 percent probability matches Lois's cycle-service level policy. We then calculate B and R:

$$B = z\sigma_L = 1.28(15) = 19.2 \quad \text{or} \quad 19;$$
$$R = \overline{D}_L + B = 36 + 19 = 55.$$

Fill Rate. Instead of setting a policy based on the cycle-service level, management may set a policy based on the fill rate of the inventory. The fill rate is

* Some inventory planners prefer to work with the mean absolute deviation (MAD), rather than the standard deviation because it is easier to calculate. To convert MAD to the standard deviation, simply multiply the MAD value by 1.25 and proceed as usual to calculate B.

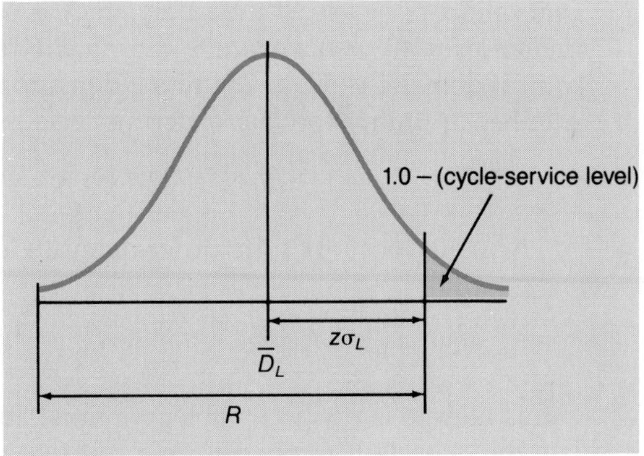

Figure 12.5

DDLT Probability Distribution.

the percentage of the *total* time (not just the cycle time) that inventory satisfies demand. For a given safety stock level, the fill rate is

Number of units short per year = (Expected number of units short per cycle)(Number of cycles per year),

or

$$(1 - F)D = n_S \left(\frac{D}{Q}\right)$$

$$1 - F = \frac{n_S}{Q}$$

$$F = 1 - \frac{n_S}{Q},$$

where

F = Fill rate, expressed as a proportion;

D = Annual demand;

n_S = Expected number of units short per cycle for a certain safety stock level; and

Q = Order quantity.

To illustrate the process for finding the fill rate, we return to the example in Box 12.3. Suppose that we want to find the fill rate for a safety stock of 4 units (that is, $R = 40$ units). We begin by calculating the expected number of units short per cycle. If the safety stock is 4 units, we will be able to satisfy a demand for 40 or fewer units during the reorder cycle. We will be short 10 units if demand is 50, or 20 units if demand is 60. Consequently, the expected number of units short per ordering cycle is

$$n_S = 10(0.20) + 20(0.10) = 4 \text{ units.}$$

Now suppose that the order quantity is 36 units. The fill rate is

$$F = 1 - \frac{4}{36} = 0.89 \quad \text{or} \quad 89\%.$$

If this fill rate is not acceptable, we must adjust the safety stock and recalculate the expected number of units short.

Comparing the Cycle-Service Level to Fill Rate. Choosing a service level involves a trade-off between improving customer service by reducing stockouts and decreasing inventory holding costs with smaller safety stocks. Often this trade-off is made with only some implicit notion of the costs involved. It is very important to be aware of the definition of service level that is being used, as demonstrated in Table 12.1. It shows what happens when Lois increases the reorder point for birdfeeders from 40 to 50 and 60 units. For each R we can calculate the safety stock, cycle-service level, and expected number of units short per cycle (n_S). Finally, we can find the fill rate (F) for different levels of Q. For example, when $R = 50$ and $Q = 78$ we get

$$F = 1 - \frac{1}{78} = 0.99 \quad \text{or} \quad 99\%.$$

The table shows clearly that the fill rate depends on the number of orders placed per year. The lower the number of orders per year, the higher the fill

Table 12.1

Comparing a Cycle-Service Policy to a Fill-Rate Policy for Birdfeeder Inventory

Reorder Point (R)	Safety Stock ($B = R - 36$)	Cycle-Service Level	Expected Number of Units Short per Cycle (n_S)	$Q = 36$ Annual Orders (D/Q)	$Q = 36$ Fill Rate (F)	$Q = 78$ Annual Orders (D/Q)	$Q = 78$ Fill Rate (F)	$Q = 234$ Annual Orders (D/Q)	$Q = 234$ Fill Rate (F)
40	4	70%	4.0	26	89%	12	95%	4	98%
50	14	90	1.0	26	97	12	99	4	99
60	24	100	0.0	26	100	12	100	4	100

rate for a specific level of safety stock. For example, if the order quantity were 234 units, we would have a fill rate of 98 percent, with only 4 units of safety stock. This is surprisingly high, considering that the cycle-service level is only 70 percent!

We need to make two points here. First, a low cycle-service level does not mean that the fill rate will be low. In fact, depending on the number of orders per year, it may be economical to have a low cycle-service level. Second, adjusting the cycle-service level has an increasing impact on fill rates as the number of orders per year increases. Note in Table 12.1 that for only 4 orders per year, the effect of increasing the safety stock is slight; for 26 annual orders, the impact is much greater. Consequently, in addition to considering inventory holding costs and stockout costs, choosing the appropriate safety stock level involves an understanding of (1) the relationship between service level measures such as cycle-service level and the fill rate; and (2) the impact of the annual number of orders on the effectiveness of safety stocks.

Calculating the Standard Deviation in Demand During Lead Time

Sometimes, the standard deviation in demand is estimated over a time interval different from the lead time. For example, records may report only daily demand. The standard deviation of daily demand can be readily calculated, but the lead time may be *several* days. Fortunately, the following conversion is possible:

$$\sigma_L = \sigma_t \sqrt{\frac{L}{t}},$$

where

σ_t = Known standard deviation of demand over some time interval t; and

σ_L = Standard deviation of demand during lead time (which must be calculated in order to find the safety stock).

When using this formula, make sure that both L and t are expressed in the same time measure. If t is in weeks, so must be L. Suppose that the standard deviation in demand per week ($t = 1$) is estimated from past records to be 50 units. If the lead time is four weeks ($L = 4$), then

$$\sigma_L = 50 \sqrt{\frac{4}{1}} = 50(2)$$

$$= 100.$$

After applying this conversion formula, you use the resulting σ_L as before to find the safety stock B.*

Putting It All Together

Let's consider a new example to bring together all the concepts of a Q system. A regional warehouse purchases hand tools from various suppliers and then distributes them on demand to retailers in the region. The warehouse operates 5 days per week and 52 weeks per year. Only when it is open can demand be experienced or orders received. The following data are estimated for $\frac{3}{8}''$ hand drills with double insulation and variable speeds.

Average daily demand = 100 drills.

Standard deviation of daily demand (σ_t) = 30 drills.

Lead time (L) = 3 days.

Holding cost (H) = \$9.30 per unit per year.

Ordering cost (S) = \$35 per order.

Cycle-service level = 92%.

Let's assume that Q will be set equal to the EOQ.† The only information that we still need for the EOQ formula is the annual demand. Since the daily demand is 100 units and there are 260 work days per year [or (52 wk)(5 work days/wk)], the annual demand D is 26,000 units [or (100 units/day)(260 days/yr)]. We can now calculate the EOQ:

$$\text{EOQ} = \sqrt{\frac{2DS}{H}} = \sqrt{\frac{2(26{,}000)(35)}{9.30}}$$
$$= 442.39 \quad \text{or} \quad 442 \text{ drills.}$$

The next step is to calculate B and R. Appendix D.3 shows that a 92 percent cycle-service level corresponds to a z of approximately 1.40. Multiply-

* This formula comes from basic statistics. The standard deviation of the sum of two or more identically distributed independent random variables is the square root of the sum of their variances. Here, the demand for each week in the lead time is an independent random variable. Therefore

$$\sigma_L = \sqrt{50^2 + 50^2 + 50^2 + 50^2},$$

which simplifies to $50\sqrt{4} = 100$.

† Theoretically, Q and R should be determined simultaneously. Recall our discussion of service levels and the effect of the number of orders per year on these variables. We chose to simplify the discussion by calculating Q and R sequentially, an approach often used in practice.

ing this by σ_L gives us B. Simultaneously calculating σ_L from the standard deviation of daily demand, we get

$$B = z\sigma_L = z\sigma_t\sqrt{\frac{L}{t}} = 1.40(30)\sqrt{\frac{3}{1}}$$
$$= 72.75 \quad \text{or} \quad 73 \text{ drills.}$$

We add this value of B to the average demand during lead time to obtain

$$R = \overline{D}_L + B = 100(3) + 73$$
$$= 373 \text{ drills.}$$

We have now specified the Q system for the hand drill. A new order is triggered whenever the inventory position IP drops to 373 drills. Each new order Q is for 442 drills. We simulated this system in Table 12.2 for a 21-day period. In this simulation:

Table 12.2

Simulation of *Q* System for Hand Drills (*Q* = 442 drills and *R* = 373 drills)

Work Day	Beginning Inventory	Orders Received	Daily Demand	Ending Inventory	Inventory Position	Amount Ordered
1	113	442	143	412	412	—
2	412	—	82	330	330	442
3	330	—	103	227	669	—
4	227	—	127	100	542	—
5	100	—	85	15	457	—
6	15	442	60	397	397	—
7	397	—	94	303	303	442
8	303	—	87	216	658	—
9	216	—	102	114	556	—
10	114	—	42	72	514	—
11	72	442	123	391	391	—
12	391	—	148	243	243	442
13	243	—	85	158	600	—
14	158	—	67	91	533	—
15	91	—	83	8	450	—
16	8	442	123	327	327	442
17	327	—	108	219	661	—
18	219	—	88	131	573	—
19	131	—	120	11	453	—
20	11	442	138	315	315	442
21	315	—	74	241	683	—

1. The beginning inventory is the ending inventory from the prior day. For day 1, it is 113 units.
2. The orders that are received at the beginning of the day can be used to satisfy demand during that day. They arrive three *full* days after ordered. For example, the order placed at the *end* of day 2 is received at the *end* of day 5. This order arrives too late to satisfy demand in day 5, so it is not available until day 6. At the beginning of the simulation, there is only one scheduled receipt. It is for 442 units and due the first day.
3. Demand is normally distributed, with a mean of 100 drills per day and a standard deviation of 30.
4. Ending inventory equals the sum of the beginning inventory and orders received minus the day's demand. Back orders are not allowed, so the inventory position is the ending inventory plus any scheduled receipts due on a subsequent day.

Using the beginning inventory on day 1, the scheduled receipts for the next four weeks (only one, due on day 1), and the daily demand shown for all 21 days, you should be able to reproduce the rest of the data in Table 12.2. Note that five new orders are placed during the 21-day period. This frequency is as expected because the lot size corresponds to about a four-day supply [or 442 units/(100 units/day)]. Also understandable is the fact that there are no stockouts; the *Q* system was designed to have insufficient stock in only 8 percent of the order cycles.

PERIODIC REVIEW SYSTEM

Another popular inventory control system is the **periodic review system,** in which an item's inventory position is reviewed periodically rather than continuously. A new order is placed at the end of each review, and the number of periods (*P*) between orders is fixed. Demand is a random variable, so the total demand between reviews varies, and the lot size *Q* changes from one order to the next. Note the differences between this system and the *Q* system, in which *Q* is fixed and the time between orders varies. The periodic review system is similar to that used by Lois Henry in the gift shop example. Another example is a soft-drink supplier who makes weekly rounds of grocery stores. Each week, store inventory positions are reviewed and restocked, supposedly with enough items to meet demand until the next week.

In this section, we carry forward unchanged the first four assumptions for deriving the EOQ, but relax the fifth one to allow for demand uncertainty. The periodic review system, also called the *P* system, periodic order system, fixed interval reorder system, or periodic reorder system, works as follows:

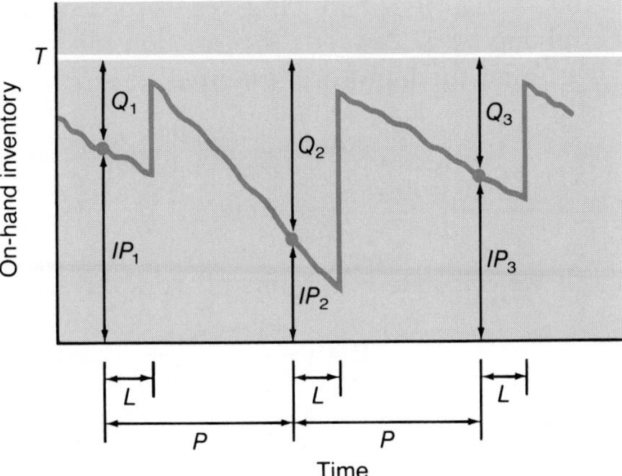

Figure 12.6

Illustration of the *P* System.

> Review the item's inventory position *IP* every *P* time periods. Place an order equal to $(T - IP)$ where *T* is the target inventory, that is, the desired inventory position just after a new order has been placed.

A *P* system is illustrated in Fig. 12.6.* The lot size for the first order (Q_1) is smaller than the one for the second order (Q_2). Why? Because the inventory position (IP_1) at the first review is greater than it is at the second review (IP_2), meaning that less must be ordered to bring the inventory position up to *T*.

Selecting the Reorder Interval

The *P* system also has just two parameters: *P* and *T*. Let's first consider *P*. It can be a convenient interval, such as each Friday or every other Friday. Another option is to base *P* on the cost trade-offs of the EOQ. For example, if *P* is expressed in weeks and there are 52 work weeks in a year, we get

$$P = \frac{\text{EOQ}}{D}(52).$$

* For ease of illustration, the situation in Fig. 12.6 does not have any scheduled receipts or back orders at the time of the two reviews. This makes the inventory position equal to on-hand inventory at those times.

Dividing the EOQ by D gives us the fraction of a year between orders. Multiplying by 52 converts this fraction into weeks.

For the hand drill example,

$$P = \left(\frac{442 \text{ units}}{26{,}000 \text{ units/yr}}\right)(52 \text{ wk/yr})$$
$$= 0.88 \text{ wk}.$$

If we calculate P in terms of work days, we get

$$P = \left(\frac{442 \text{ units}}{26{,}000 \text{ units/yr}}\right)(260 \text{ work days/yr})$$
$$= 4.4 \quad \text{or} \quad 4 \text{ days}.$$

Selecting the Target Inventory Level

Now let's consider how to calculate the target inventory T. If you look closely at Fig. 12.6, you will discover that an order must be large enough to make the inventory position IP last beyond the next review, or P periods away. Scheduled receipts do not arrive from the *next* order until $P + L$ time periods have elapsed. Therefore T must be at least equal to the expected demand during $P + L$. This level does not allow for safety stock protection. When B is added, it should be enough to protect against the uncertainty of demand during the review interval P and one lead time L. Since a Q system requires safety stock to cover uncertainty in demand during just the lead time, you should conclude that the safety stock must be higher for P systems. Thus

$$T = \overline{D}_{P+L} + B = \overline{D}_{P+L} + z\sigma_{P+L},$$

where

$\overline{D}_{P+L}$ = Average demand until the next review in P periods plus the average demand during one lead time of L periods;

σ_{P+L} = Standard deviation of demand during $P + L$ time periods; and

z = Number of desired standard deviations to implement the cycle-service level (same as for a Q system).

Let's now return to the hand-drill example and design a P system instead of a Q system. Suppose that P is set at 4 days to maintain comparability with the Q system. The safety stock is

$$B = z\sigma_{P+L} = 1.40(30)\sqrt{\frac{(4+3)}{1}}$$
$$= 111.12 \quad \text{or} \quad 111 \text{ drills}.$$

For a P system, B must be increased to 111 drills from the 73 drills needed for a Q system. Demand uncertainty must be absorbed for $P + L$ time periods, rather than just for L. Knowing B, we now calculate

$$T = \overline{D}_{P+L} + B = 100(4 + 3) + 111$$
$$= 811 \text{ drills.}$$

Table 12.3 shows a simulation of this P system based on the starting conditions and daily demand shown in Table 12.2 for the Q system. Assume that the next review will take place at the end of day 2. The simulation results are similar to those for the Q system in that five orders are placed and no stockouts occur. While this need not be the case, it is not unexpected. Recall that we set P to achieve the same average time between orders and selected B to implement the same cycle-service level. There are also some differences between the two systems. The time between orders is now constant in the P

Table 12.3

Simulation of *P* System for Hand Drills (*P* = 4 days and *T* = 811 drills)

Work Day	Beginning Inventory	Orders Received	Daily Demand	Ending Inventory	Inventory Position	Amount Ordered
1	113	442	143	412		—
2	412	—	82	330	330	481
3	330	—	103	227		—
4	227	—	127	100		—
5	100	—	85	15		—
6	15	481	60	436	436	375
7	436	—	94	342		—
8	342	—	87	255		—
9	255	—	102	153		—
10	153	375	42	486	486	325
11	486	—	123	363		—
12	363	—	148	215		—
13	215	—	85	130		—
14	130	325	67	388	388	423
15	388	—	83	305		—
16	305	—	123	182		—
17	182	—	108	74		—
18	74	423	88	409	409	402
19	409	—	120	289		—
20	289	—	138	151		—
21	151	—	74	77		—

Table 12.4

Comparison of *Q* and *P* Systems

Advantages of *P* System	Advantages of *Q* System
Fixed replenishment intervals	Can individualize the replenishment intervals
Can combine orders to same supplier	More suited for quantity discounts or capacity limitations
Perpetual inventory system not mandatory	Less safety stock

system but varied from 4 days to 5 days in the *Q* system. The lot size *Q* now varies, whereas it was constant at 442 units in the *Q* system.

Comparative Advantages of the *Q* and *P* Systems

Knowing the basics of both the *Q* and *P* systems, we can now identify the relative merits of each one. Neither is best in all situations, as shown in Table 12.4. It lists three *P*-system advantages, which must be traded off against three *Q*-system advantages. The advantages for one system are implicitly disadvantages for the other one.

***P*-System Advantages.** The first advantage of *P* systems is that replenishments can be made at fixed time intervals. This procedure can be administratively convenient, particularly if inventory control is but one of several duties of an employee. Some employees prefer to set aside a day or part of a day on a regular basis to concentrate on this particular task. Fixed replenishment intervals are also better for certain transportation systems, where the time of pickups (or deliveries) is fixed on a daily, weekly, or even monthly basis. For example, bread deliveries to a particular grocery store are usually made on a fixed schedule, which allows the route between stores to be standardized.

The second advantage shown for *P* systems is that orders for multiple items can be combined.* Suppose that similar items are being ordered at the same time from the same supplier. They can be combined into just one purchase order, resulting in a "family contract" that can lead to a pricing advantage. Even without a price break, combining orders can save the buyer some paperwork and reduce ordering cost. This procedure makes follow-up of open orders easier. When buyers call their suppliers to check on the status of one item, they can also ask about the others listed on the family contracts. Suppliers may also prefer combined orders. For example, all items in the

* Combining orders is also possible with a modified *Q* system. Each item is assigned a reorder point *R* as well as a higher *can-order* point. Whenever the first item in the group reaches *R*, it is ordered along with all other items that have reached their can-order points.

order might be shipped out at the same time, reducing transportation costs and increasing truck utilization.

A third advantage of *P* systems is that the inventory position *IP* needs to be known only when a review is made. This differs from a *Q* system, where inventory records must be updated continuously. When inventory records are always up-to-date, the system is called a **perpetual inventory system**.

Since the next replenishment decision can be required at any time in a *Q* system, management cannot afford the luxury of infrequently updated records. Not needing a perpetual inventory system can be an advantage for small, manual applications. When a decision is made to computerize record keeping, with a transaction report for each receipt or withdrawal, this last advantage of *P* systems disappears.

Q-System Advantages. The first advantage shown in Table 12.4 for *Q* systems can be a disadvantage of *P* systems. In a typical *P* system, the periods between orders are the same for a large number (if not all) items. Although this procedure may be administratively convenient and allow orders to be combined, there is less flexibility to tailor the review frequency to each item. A compromise *P* must be selected, even though the trade-off between holding and ordering costs can be quite different from one item to the next. The net result of forcing many items to have the same *P* can be an increase in total costs.

A second advantage of *Q* systems is that fixed lot sizes are sometimes desirable or even mandatory, as in the case of quantity discounts for purchases exceeding a certain size. Physical limitations may also require a fixed lot size. Truckload capacities, materials handling methods, and furnace capacities are three examples.

The final advantage of *Q* systems, lower safety stocks, was addressed earlier. They must guard against demand uncertainty for just the lead time *L*. For a *P* system, demand uncertainty must be covered for a $P + L$ elapsed time. This extended coverage forces safety stock to be increased.

Summary. In summary, the choice between *Q* and *P* systems is not clear-cut. Which one is best depends on the relative importance of its advantages (Table 12.4) in various situations. Management must carefully weigh each alternative in selecting the best system.

HYBRID SYSTEMS

A variety of hybrid systems are also used in practice. They include some but not all the features of the *P* or *Q* systems. We briefly examine three such hybrid systems: optional replenishment, base stock, and visual.

The **optional replenishment system,** sometimes called the optional review, min-max, or s,S system, is much like the P system. Inventory positions are reviewed periodically. When a new order is placed, it is large enough to bring the inventory position up to a target inventory, similar to T for the P system. However, orders are not placed after a review unless the inventory position has dropped to a minimum level. The minimum level acts as the reorder point R in a Q system. Its effect is to ensure that a reasonable order quantity is placed. If the target is 100 and the minimum level is 60, the minimum order size is 40 (or 100 − 60). Since the optional review system also avoids continuous reviews, it seems particularly attractive when the costs of review and ordering are both significant.

In a **base stock system** (in its simplest form) a replenishment order is issued each time there is a withdrawal. The order quantity Q is equal to the amount of the withdrawal. If 10 units are removed from inventory to satisfy a customer order, a 10-unit replenishment order is placed. This one-for-one replacement policy maintains the inventory position at a base-stock level equal to the expected demand during the lead time plus safety stock. The base-stock level therefore is equivalent to the reorder point in a Q system. However, order quantities now vary to keep the inventory position equal to R at all times. Since this is the lowest IP possible to maintain a specified service level, the base stock system can be seen as a way to minimize cycle inventory. Many small orders are placed, which is appropriate for very expensive items. An example is replacement engines for jet airplanes, which are held at bases where the planes are being used. No more inventory is held than the maximum demand expected until a replacement order can be received.

In actual practice, the base stock system is often modified in one of two ways. First, replenishment orders may be accumulated, so that orders can be made at fixed time intervals, as with the P system. For example, a DC may receive shipments on a weekly basis from the central plant. The quantity shipped equals the total withdrawals at the DC since the prior week's shipment. Second, replenishment orders may be accumulated to achieve a fixed order quantity, as with a Q system. This second modification to the base stock system has come about recently with the introduction of the Kanban system by Toyota in Japan (Chapter 15). Small-lot production in standard lot sizes is achieved, leading to minimal inventory levels.

Visual systems are a third hybrid. They are easy to administer since records on the current inventory position are not kept. The historical usage rate can simply be reconstructed from past purchase orders. Visual systems are intended for use with low-valued items that have a steady demand, such as nuts and bolts. Overstocking is common, but the extra inventory holding cost is nominal because the items have such little value. The two basic approaches used are the single-bin system and the two-bin system.

With the **single-bin system,** a maximum level is established and visually marked at the storage location (a shelf or bin). The inventory level is then brought up to the mark periodically, say, once a week. Examples include storage tanks at a gas station and storage bins for small parts at a manufacturing plant. This method is essentially a P system, with the target inventory T and current IP established visually.

With the **two-bin system,** an item's inventory is stored at two different locations. The first bin is the first place to go to withdraw inventory. If it is empty, the second bin provides backup to cover demand until a replenishment order arrives. When the inventory in the first bin is exhausted, this is a signal to place a new order. Premade order forms may be placed nearby, so that one can be sent to purchasing or even directly to the supplier. When the new order arrives, the second bin is restored to its normal level and the rest is put in the first bin. The two-bin system is really a Q system, with the normal level in the second bin being the reorder point R. It can even be implemented with just one bin by putting a mark at the reorder point level. Sometimes the reorder point is even built into the product by the supplier. A desk calendar is a good example, with a notice inserted toward the end to remind us to reorder for the new year.

ONE-TIME DECISIONS

One of the decisions facing Lois Henry at the Columbus Museum of Natural History (Box 12.1) is how to handle the seasonal goods group. These items are in demand during only one season of the year. To make matters worse, some of these items are stylish or high-fashion goods and probably cannot be sold at full markup next year. Furthermore, the lead time can be longer than the selling season; there is no second chance to rush through another order to cover unexpectedly high demand. This type of situation is often called the "newsboy problem." If the newspaper seller does not buy enough papers to resell on the street corner, sales opportunities are lost. If the seller buys too many, the overage cannot be sold because nobody wants yesterday's newspaper. This dilemma is faced by many retailers.

It also can arise in manufacturing plants when (1) customized items (sometimes called *specials*) are made (or purchased) to order; *and* (2) there also are scrap problems. A special item is never intentionally held in stock; the demand for it is too unpredictable, and, in fact, it may never be needed again. This means that a manufacturer would like to make just the amount requested by the customer—no more and no less. The manufacturer also would like to satisfy an order in just one run to avoid an extra setup and to prevent a delay in delivering goods ordered. These two goals can conflict. Suppose that a customer places an order for 20 units. If we order 20 units from the shop (supplier if it is a purchased item), one or two of them may have to be scrapped. This shortage forces us to place a second (or even third) order to replace the defective units. Replacement can be costly if setup time is high and can also cause a late shipment to the customer. To avoid such problems, we could order more than 20 units the first time. If some units are left over, the customer may be willing to buy the extras, or we may find an internal use for them. For example, some manufacturing companies set up a special account for obsolete materials. These materials can be "bought" by departments within the company at less than their normal cost, as an incentive for using them.

The most straightforward way to analyze such problems and decide on the best order quantity is with a payoff matrix. In Box 12.4, we apply this approach to the museum problem. We need three types of information:

1. The profit per unit sold during the season.
2. The loss per unit disposed of after the season is over.
3. The probability distribution of demand.*

The payoff for any pairing of Q and D is equal to \$10 multiplied by the number of units sold during the season minus \$5 multiplied by the number of units disposed of after the season is over.†

Using the **payoff matrix** in Box 12.4, we can obtain the best order quantity Q. A reasonable approach is to pick the Q with the highest expected payoff. If Lois were to use this strategy for all items in the seasonal goods group over many selling seasons, she would maximize profits. The expected value is simply an arithmetic mean. We calculate it for a specific Q by (1) multiplying each payoff in the row by the demand probability associated with the payoff; and (2) adding these products. For example, the expected payoff if we select a Q of 30 is

$$0.2(0) + 0.3(\$150) + 0.3(\$300) + 0.1(\$300) + 0.1(\$300) = \$195.$$

Making these calculations for each row in the payoff matrix, we get

Order Quantity (Q)	Expected Payoff
10	\$100
20	170
30	195
40	175
50	140

* In Box 12.4 the probability estimates relate to a demand range, which is a common practice. The probability that the demand will be between 5 and 15 units is 0.2, with 10 selected as the midpoint of the range. Similarly, 20 is selected as representative of demand between 15 and 25.

† If you are well-grounded in economic principles, you may feel that the payoff matrix should be expressed in terms of opportunity costs, which recognizes lost sales opportunities. Fortunately, the approach we use here always leads to the same conclusion with respect to the best Q.

Box 12.4

A PAYOFF MATRIX FOR ONE-TIME DECISIONS

One group of items sold at the Columbus Museum of Natural History is Christmas ornaments hand carved from wood. Lois buys them for $10 each and plans to sell them for $20.50 each. Variable cost, such as for wrapping, is $0.50 per unit sold. Any merchandise left over at the end of the season will be sold at $5.50 each. Thus items are sold at a $10 profit per unit (or $20.50 − $10.50) during the season and at a $5 loss (or $5.50 − $10.50) after the season is over.

Lois has identified five demand levels as possible outcomes for the coming season. The levels, along with her probability estimates, are

Demand (D)	Demand Probability
10	0.2
20	0.3
30	0.3
40	0.1
50	0.1

Reasoning that each demand level is a candidate for best order quantity (Q), she decided to calculate the profits for each combination of Q and D. Her results are shown in the following payoff matrix.

Q \ D	10	20	30	40	50
10	$100	$100	$100	$100	$100
20	50	200	200	200	200
30	0	150	300	300	300
40	− 50	100	250	400	400
50	− 100	50	200	350	500

For all cases where the demand (D) was at least as large as the order quantity (Q), she multiplied Q by $10 to get the payoff. For example, if Q is 30 and actual demand D turns out to be 50, she will sell all 30 units at a total profit of $300 [or 30($10)]. The calculation is somewhat more complicated if Q exceeds D. Suppose that Q is 50 and D turns out to be only 20. The total profit would be $200 [or 20($10)] for the 20 units sold during the season minus $150 [or 30($5)] for the loss sustained in disposing of the 30 extra units after the season is over. This results in a net profit of only $50 (or $200 − $150).

The payoff matrix gives Lois considerable information to help her make a decision. If she orders just 10 units, she is assured of a $100 profit, regardless of actual demand. On the other hand, she could earn $500 if she orders 50 units and demand turns out to be this high. What should be her order quantity Q?

The expected payoffs show that the best choice is to order 30 ornaments for the season, since its expected payoff at $195 is higher than that for any other choice.

PRACTICAL ISSUES

Operating an inventory system in practice involves additional issues, such as (1) which items deserve management's tightest control; (2) how to handle price breaks; (3) how to maintain accurate records; and (4) what types of computer support might be advisable. Let's consider each of these issues, beginning with control.

ABC Analysis

Thousands of items are held in inventory by a typical organization, but only a small percentage of them deserve management's closest attention and tightest control. The management-by-exception principle, when applied to inventory, is called ABC analysis, in which items are divided into three classes according to their *dollar usage*. Class A items represent only about 20 percent of the items but account for 80 percent of the dollar usage. Class B accounts for another 30 percent of the items, which represent only 15 percent of the dollar usage. Finally, 50 percent of the items fall in Class C and represent a mere 5 percent of the dollar usage.

The ABC analysis involves a two-step process. The first step is to assign each item to a class. You begin by calculating the dollar usage for each item. An item's dollar usage is simply its annual demand rate multiplied by the dollar value (cost) of one unit. After ranking the items on the basis of dollar usage, you assign approximately the top 20 percent of the items to class A, the next 30 percent to class B, and the bottom 50 percent to class C. These dividing lines between classes are inexact, but you should not be surprised if class A items account for the bulk of the dollar usage.

The second step is for management to tightly control the inventory levels of class A items. Recall the levers for reducing inventory discussed in Chapter 10. Thus if a P system is being used, a manager should give close attention to forecasts of D_{P+L} when setting T for class A items; better forecasts reduce the amount of safety stock required. A manager can direct that class A items be reviewed more frequently, which reduces the average lot size. A manager can also demand more accurate inventory records. If the records show an on-hand balance of 100 units, while the actual balance is 200 units, costly inventory is being carried needlessly. If a class A item is bought outside the firm, purchasing may be able to reduce its cost through centralized buying, switching vendors, or more effective contract negotiation.

For class C items, on the other hand, much looser control is appropriate. A stockout of a class C item can be as critical as for a class A item, but the inventory holding cost of class C items tends to be low. This feature suggests that higher inventory levels should be tolerated and that more safety stock, larger lot sizes, and perhaps even a visual system may suffice for class C items.

Quantity Discounts

In the derivation of the EOQ, we assumed that the price (or value) of the item was fixed. In many situations, however, the price of the item may be a function of the purchase quantity and the supplier's price schedule. In such a situation, the decision about how much to order goes beyond the basics of the EOQ formula.

To illustrate the considerations involved in making quantity discount decisions, we return to the birdfeeder decision faced by Lois Henry, the museum's gift-shop manager, and the data in Box 12.2. However, suppose that the supplier has offered a price of $58.80 per unit (2 percent discount) for all units if 300 or more are purchased or a price of $57.00 per unit (5 percent discount) for all units if 500 or more are purchased each time. Should Lois revise her new ordering policy of 75 units (the EOQ) to take advantage of these discounts?

To answer this question, we must first recognize that the relevant costs are annual holding, ordering, *and* materials costs. Before, we assumed that the price or value of the item was independent of the order quantity. Every order quantity that we evaluated resulted in the same materials cost for the year, that is, Dp, where p is the price of the item. Since this cost was a constant, it was not included in the total cost function. Now, p varies as the order quantity changes, and we need a new approach.

We begin by calculating the EOQ for each price of interest on the schedule. If the EOQ is large enough to qualify for a discount, we may as well use it. Recall from Box 12.2 that the holding cost per unit is the price of the unit multiplied by the holding cost, expressed as a proportion of average inventory value (0.25 for our problem). For a price of $60 we have already calculated the EOQ (75 units). Unfortunately, for the other two prices, the EOQs are close to 75 units as well. This means that when we calculate annual costs, we will use the EOQ of 75 units at $60, 300 units at $58.80, and 500 units at $57.00. The EOQs for the latter two prices were too small to actually qualify for the discount price.

Next, we calculate the total costs, including annual materials costs. Table 12.5 shows the results of these calculations. It appears that the best order

Table 12.5

Quantity Discount Calculations for Birdfeeder Purchases

Price per Unit (p)	Order Quantity	Annual Holding Costs	Annual Ordering Costs	Annual Materials Costs	Total Costs*
$60.00	75	$ 562.50	$561.60	$56,160.00	$57,284.10
$58.80	300	$2,205.00	$140.40	$55,036.80	$57,382.20
$57.00	500	$3,562.50	$ 84.24	$53,352.00	$56,998.74

* The EOQ is used to calculate the costs if it is at least as large as the minimum order quantity for a given price per unit.

quantity is 500 units. The increases in annual holding costs are offset by the savings in annual materials costs. These savings would be even greater if we had considered safety stock because less would be needed with the larger order quantities. However, quantity discounts are not always best. The 2 percent discount ($58.80 per unit) actually increases total costs relative to the standard price per unit. The order quantity decision in light of price discounts must be based on careful consideration of the *overall* effect on total cost.

Inventory Records

Information on the amount of on-hand inventory and scheduled receipts is needed for both inventory management and accounting purposes. Sometimes, only periodic checks are made, as when a facility is shut down once a year for several days to count all inventory. At the other extreme are perpetual inventory records, in which a transaction report is made for each withdrawal and receipt. In manual systems, this information is posted to some type of written record.* In computerized systems, this information is maintained on disk or tape. In either case, on-hand and scheduled receipts balances are updated the same way. Suppose that a scheduled receipt of 300 units is received, but the supplier actually shipped only 295 units, owing to scrap losses. The buyer decides to accept the order as is, rather than requesting a second shipment of 5 units. The buyer will simply release the next order a few days earlier than usual. For this transaction, the correct adjustments would be (1) increase on-hand inventory by 295 units; and (2) delete the 300-unit scheduled receipts from the record.

* Forms of manual record keeping include Kardex, visirecord, rotary wheel files, books, and logs.

Considerable attention must be paid to maintaining accurate inventory records. One method of keeping track of inventory is to *assign responsibility* to specific employees for issuing and receiving materials and faithfully reporting each transaction. Inventory accuracy is their responsibility and they are held accountable for it. A second method is to have *closed stores*, whereby the inventory is actually secured behind locked doors or gates to prevent unauthorized or unreported withdrawals. This method also guards against storing new receipts in the wrong locations, where they can be lost for months. **Cycle counting** is a third method, whereby storeroom personnel physically count a small percentage of the total number of items each day, correcting errors when found. Class A items are counted the most frequently. A final method, for computer systems, is to make *logic error checks* on each transaction reported and fully investigate discrepancies. Examples of discrepancies are (1) receipts when there is no record of scheduled receipts; (2) disbursements that exceed the current on-hand balance; and (3) receipts with a nonexistent part number.

These four methods can hold inventory record inaccuracy within acceptable bounds. Accuracy pays off mainly through better customer service, although some inventory reductions can be achieved by improving accuracy. A side benefit is that auditors may not require end-of-the-year counts if records prove to be sufficiently accurate.

Computer Support

As you have discovered by now, managing inventories requires many calculations. Since massive data manipulation is where computers excel, it is not surprising that many companies are computerizing at least parts of their inventory systems. Several software packages are generally available, in addition to the in-house systems developed by individual companies. Five of the most common uses of such packages are for updating records, providing management reports, automatic reordering, generating exception reports, and recomputing decision parameters.

Updating Records. Calculations are made at the time of each transaction to update on-hand inventory and scheduled receipts balances. Other information also may be updated and displayed on request, such as recent demand rates, yield losses, price changes, lead times, and vendor performance.

Providing Management Reports. Top management can get reports on inventory investment, using such measures as dollar value of inventory, weeks of supply, and turns. These data are often compared to measures from prior periods and can be broken into separate categories. For example, individual departments in a department store usually act as autonomous profit centers, and periodic inventory reports for each one help top management assess performance. Other information important to management includes customer service measures (such as the number of stockouts) and the costs of operating the inventory system itself.

Automatic Reordering. The decision rules already described for the Q and P systems can be easily programmed to generate purchase or shop orders automatically. In some cases, as with class A items, it may be mandatory to have an inventory analyst review computer-generated notices before taking action. A computer can be programmed to generate action notices whenever a new order should be placed or when a scheduled receipt appears to be late. An inventory analyst reviews the situation before authorizing a new order or following up on an order. The computer still saves considerable time, since only certain types of items and actions are brought to the analyst's attention. After a decision is made, the computer can also be programmed to generate the paperwork for the purchase order or shop order.

Generating Exception Reports. The computer can generate an **exception report** for any unusual situation. For example, actual lead times or demand rates may be deviating considerably from those forecast. Perhaps a transaction report shows an impossibly large withdrawal, based on the current on-hand record. Such exceptions to normal conditions can be displayed on a computer screen or printed out as hard copy for the analyst to assess.

Recomputing Decision Parameters. A computer can be programmed to recompute periodically parameters such as Q and R for a Q system or P and T for a P system. Costs, lead times, or demands may have changed. Demand forecasts can be revised to recognize new trends. Lead times can be updated, based on recent experience. Current and proposed parameters (such as Q and R) can be simulated, much as done for Tables 12.2 and 12.3. Summary statistics on inventory and customer service levels projected by the simulation can be displayed or printed out.

CHAPTER HIGHLIGHTS

The inventory management approach used depends on the nature of demand. The two broad categories of demand are: independent and dependent. This chapter focused on the management of independent-demand inventory systems. Some of the highlights of the chapter are:

- Independent demand is generated directly by the customer. Total demand for independent-demand items is often more uniform than for dependent-demand items, necessitating different inventory control systems. All types of organizations maintain independent-demand inventories. In the service sector, wholesale and retail merchandise alone accounts for 40 percent of the inventory in the U.S. economy.

- A basic question in inventory management is whether to order infrequently in large quantities or frequently in small quantities. Calculation of the EOQ helps with this choice by providing the lot size Q that minimizes the sum of holding and ordering (including setup) costs. EOQ assumptions include: constant demand, receipts in full lots, only two relevant costs, single-item decisions, and no uncertainty.
- In the continuous review system (or Q system), the buyer places orders of a fixed lot size Q whenever the inventory position IP drops to the reorder point R. The reorder point answers the second basic question in inventory management: when to place the next order. The reorder point is equal to the expected average demand during the lead time $\overline{D}_L$ and safety stock B to handle demand uncertainties. The size of the safety stock depends on the desired service level. The inventory position IP is equal to on-hand inventory plus scheduled receipts minus any back ordered or allocated demand.
- The cycle-service level and the fill rate are two measures of the service level of inventories. Choosing the proper safety stock level involves an understanding of the relationship between these service level measures and the impact of the number of annual orders.
- In the periodic review system (or P system), the buyer places orders every P fixed time interval. The order quantity is the difference between the target inventory T and the current inventory position and can vary from order to order. T is established to cover expected demand and safety stock B over $P + L$ time periods.
- The choice between P and Q systems is not clear cut. Fixed replenishment intervals, combined orders, type of record keeping, individual replenishment intervals, quantity discounts, and safety stocks all have to be considered.
- Various hybrid inventory systems are used in practice, including optional replenishment, base stock, and visual systems. The base stock system is used to minimize cycle inventory by maintaining the inventory position at the base-stock level. Visual systems, such as single-bin and two-bin systems, are adaptations of the P and Q systems that eliminate the need for records.
- Retailers, as well as manufacturers of specials, often face one-time inventory decisions. Demand uncertainty can lead to ordering too much or too little, which can result in cost or customer-service penalties. The most straightforward approach to one-time inventory decisions is to calculate the expected payoff over a range of reasonable alternatives and choose the one with the best expected payoff.
- ABC analysis helps managers to focus on the significant few items that account for the bulk of inventory dollar usage. Class A items deserve the most attention, with less attention justified for class B and class C items.
- When quantity discounts are available, the total relevant costs include annual holding, ordering, and materials cost. Purchasing larger quantities to achieve price discounts is not always the best strategy.
- At a minimum, inventory levels must be measured annually. Records are likely to be maintained for on-hand inventory and the scheduled receipts balances. Clearly assigned responsibility, closed stores, cycle counting, and logic error checks are

methods used to maintain accurate records.

- Computer packages are available to assist in updating records, providing management reports, expediting automatic reordering, generating exception reports, and recomputing decision parameters.

KEY TERMS

base stock system
continuous review system
cycle counting
cycle-service level
economic order quantity (EOQ)
exception report
fill rate
inventory position (IP)
optional replenishment system
payoff matrix
periodic review system
perpetual inventory system
reorder point system
single-bin system
two-bin system
visual systems

STUDY QUESTIONS

1. What recommendations would you make to Lois Henry for managing inventory better at the Columbus Museum of Natural History? (See Box 12.1.)
2. When can the cost of materials paid to the supplier no longer be ignored in finding a reasonable lot size?
3. What is the relationship between an item's lot size and the frequency of placing orders for it?
4. How are the best lot size Q and reorder point R affected by
   (a) increases in demand?
   (b) decreases in setup costs?
   (c) increases in interest rates?
   (d) forecast errors in D, H, or S?
5. "Its assumptions are so unrealistic that the EOQ provides little guidance in managing inventories." Comment.
6. What should be considered in setting a service level policy?
7. Blood is collected for medical purposes at various sites (such as at mobile units), tested, separated into components, and shipped to a hospital blood bank. Each bank holds the components in inventory and issues them as needed to satisfy transfusion requests. There are eight major types of blood and each type has many components (such as red cells, white cells, and plasma). Each component has a different medical purpose and a different lifetime. For example, the lifetime for white cells is only 6 hours, but the lifetime for red cells is now 35 days. What type of management issues are involved in this particular type of inventory control? Does perishability require different records than for other situations? How?

8. When the service level policy is expressed in terms of the fill rate, why does the needed safety stock B depend on the lot size Q?
9. What two basic questions are answered by Q and R of the Q system? P and T of the P system?
10. Under what conditions would you prefer to use a Q system? P system? Base stock system? Visual system?
11. When do one-time inventory decisions arise? What information should be gathered in making a final choice?
12. What is the meaning and purpose of ABC analysis?
13. Suppose that you are a buyer of an important raw material. Rumor has it that a sizable price increase will take place in the near future. How might you decide whether to hedge against the price increase by buying more than usual with the next order?
14. What are the rewards and costs of having accurate inventory records? How can accuracy be increased?

PROBLEMS

1. A discount appliance store sells combination radio and tape cassette players for only $80 per unit. These hand-held units have exceptional sound quality and are in great demand. For these units:
   - Demand (D) = 60 units/wk.
   - Order cost (S) = $30/order.
   - Annual holding cost (H) = 25% of selling price.

   The store operates 52 weeks per year and orders in lot sizes of 360 units (that is, Q = 360). Based on this lot-size policy, determine
   (a) the average time in weeks between orders;
   (b) the annual holding cost; and
   (c) the annual ordering cost.
   (d) Based on your answers to parts (b) and (c), is the current lot size too small or too large? Explain.

2. For the item in Problem 1,
   (a) what is the EOQ?
   (b) how much are total costs reduced by switching from Q = 360 to the EOQ?

3. Consider once again the data in Problem 1.
   (a) Suppose that the weekly demand forecast of 60 units is incorrect, and that it will actually be only 30 units per week. How much higher will be total costs because of this forecast error?
   (b) Suppose that actual demand of 60 units is correct but that ordering costs are cut to only $5 under a blanket order arrangement. (See Chapter 10.) However, the buyer does not tell anyone, and the EOQ is not adjusted to reflect this reduction in S. How much higher will total costs be, compared to what they could be if the EOQ were adjusted?

4. Your firm uses a continuous review system (Q system), where the inventory position of each item is updated after every transaction. The firm operates 52 weeks per year. One of the items has the following characteristics.
   - Demand (D) = 19,500 units/yr.
   - Ordering cost (S) = $25/order.
   - Holding cost (H) = $4/unit/yr.

- Lead time (L) = 2 wk.
- Standard deviation in *weekly* demand = 120 units.
- Cycle-service level = 95%.

(a) Calculate the EOQ for this item.
(b) Find the safety stock B and reorder point R that provides a 95 percent cycle-service level.
(c) For these policies, what are the annual costs of
  (i) holding the cycle inventory?
  (ii) placing the orders?

5. Suppose instead that your firm uses a periodic review system (P system), but otherwise the data are the same as in Problem 4.
   (a) Calculate the P that gives approximately the same number of orders per year as the EOQ. Round your answer to the nearest week.
   (b) Find the safety stock B and the target inventory T that provide a 95 percent cycle-service level.
   (c) How much larger is the safety stock than with a Q system?

6. Suppose that you are a recent graduate who majored in operations management. Your boss has just asked you to review the company's current inventory policies for its continuous review system (Q system). You begin by checking out the current policies for a sample of items. The characteristics of one item are
   - Demand (D) = 10 units/wk. (Assume 52 weeks per year.)
   - Ordering and setup cost (S) = \$45/order.
   - Holding cost (H) = \$12/unit/year.
   - Lead time (L) = 3 wk.
   - Standard deviation in *weekly* demand = 8 units.
   - Cycle-service level = 70%.

   (a) What is the EOQ for this item?
   (b) What is the desired safety stock B?
   (c) What is the desired reorder point R?
   (d) Suppose that the current policy is Q = 80 and R = 150. If this item were typical, what would you recommend to your boss?

7. Using the same information as in Problem 6, develop the best policies for a periodic review system (P system).
   (a) What value of P gives the same approximate number of orders per year as the EOQ? Round to the nearest week.
   (b) What safety stock B and target inventory T provide a 70 percent cycle-service level?

8. Management has decided to maintain a safety stock of 20 units for a certain item having a one-week lead time from the vendor. The company operates 50 weeks per year, uses a Q system with $R = \overline{D}_L + B$, and has the following weekly demand distribution.

Demand	Probability
50	0.06
100	0.12
150	0.20
200	0.40
250	0.22
	1.00

   What is the fill rate if
   (a) the lot size is 300 units?
   (b) the lot size is 75 units?

9. Suppose that the demand during lead time (DDLT) distribution for a product is estimated to be

DDLT (units)	Probability
0	0.30
50	0.20
100	0.20
150	0.15
200	0.10
250	0.05
	1.00

(a) What reorder point R would result in an 85 percent cycle-service level?
(b) How much safety stock B is provided with this policy?
(c) Suppose that the order quantity is 400 units. What is the fill rate?

10. The Georgia Lighting Center stocks more than 3000 lighting fixtures, including chandeliers, swags, wall lamps, and track lights. The store sells at retail, operates six days per week, and advertises itself as the "brightest spot in town." One expensive fixture is selling at an average rate of 5 units per day. The reorder policy is $Q = 40$ and $R = 15$. The lead time is two full days, and new orders are placed at the end of the day. Thus a new order is available for use at the beginning of the third day after an order is placed.

    Simulate the performance of this Q system for the next three weeks (18 work days). Any stockouts result in lost sales (rather than back orders). The beginning inventory is 19 units, and there are no scheduled receipts. Demand is random and is shown for each of the next 18 days in Table 12.6. Fill in the rest of the table.
    (a) What is the average ending inventory over the 18 days?
    (b) How many stockouts occurred?

11. Simulate Problem 10 again, but this time use a P system with $P = 8$ and $T = 55$. Let the next review period be day 1. As before, the beginning inventory is 19 units and there are no scheduled receipts.
    (a) What is the average ending inventory over the 18 days?
    (b) How many stockouts occurred?

Table 12.6

Work Day	Beginning Inventory	Orders Received	Daily Demand	Ending Inventory	Inventory Position	Amount Ordered
1	19	—	5			
2		—	3			
3		—	4			
4			1			
5			10			
6			9			
7			7			
8			4			
9			2			
10			7			
11			3			
12			6			
13			10			
14			0			
15			5			
16			10			
17			4			
18			7			

12. Reggie Staggs is the chief buyer at Investment Clothiers, a retail store known for excellence in apparel. It is time to order merchandise for the Christmas season. During a recent trip to Hong Kong, Reggie spotted a particular men's shirt that should sell quite well. Based on past experience, Reggie expects the demand for such a shirt to range from 50 to 200. He estimates the probability distribution as

Season's Demand	Probability
50	0.20
100	0.30
150	0.30
200	0.20
	1.00

The total cost to Investment Clothiers would be $25 per shirt and the retail price set at $50. Any shirts left over after Christmas would be sold at $20 each. How many shirts should Reggie buy if he wants to maximize expected profits?

13. McKenzie Industries is considering using ABC analysis to focus attention on its most critical inventory items. A random sample of 20 items has been taken and the dollar usages have already been calculated as shown in Table 12.7. Rank the items and assign them to an A, B, or C class. On the basis of this sample, does it appear that ABC analysis will help management identify the significant few items?

Table 12.7

Item	Dollar Usage	Item	Dollar Usage
1	$ 9,200	11	$ 300
2	400	12	10,400
3	33,400	13	70,800
4	8,100	14	6,800
5	1,100	15	57,900
6	600	16	3,900
7	44,000	17	700
8	900	18	4,800
9	100	19	19,000
10	700	20	15,500

14. As inventory manager you must decide on the order quantity for an item that has an annual demand of 2000 units. It costs you $20 each time you place an order and your holding cost, expressed as a percentage of average inventory value, is 40 percent. Your supplier has provided the following price schedule.

Price per Unit	Minimum Order Quantity
$5.00	1
$4.90	400
$4.75	600
$4.50	2000

How much + when

What is your recommended ordering policy? You can assume that no safety stock is needed.

SELECTED REFERENCES

Bragg, Daniel Jay, "The Impact of Inventory Record Inaccuracy on Material Requirements Planning Systems." Unpublished dissertation, Ohio State University, 1984.

Buffa, Elwood S., and Jeffrey G. Miller, *Production-Inventory Systems: Planning and Control*, 3rd ed. Homewood, Ill.: Richard D. Irwin, 1979.

Fogerty, Donald W., and Thomas R. Hoffman, *Production and Inventory Management*. Cincinnati: South-Western, 1983.

Greene, James H., *Production and Inventory Control Handbook.* New York: McGraw-Hill, 1970.

International Business Machines Corporation, *Basic Principles of Wholesale IMPACT,* Publication E20-8105-1.

Johnson, Lynwood A., and Douglas C. Montgomery, *Operations Research in Production Planning, Scheduling and Inventory Control,* New York: John Wiley & Sons, 1979.

Love, Stephen F., *Inventory Control.* New York: McGraw-Hill, 1979.

Silver, Edward A. "Operations Research in Inventory Management: A Review and Critique," *Operations Research,* vol. 9, no. 4 (July–August 1981).

Silver, Edward A., and Rein Peterson, *Decision Systems for Inventory Management and Production Planning.* New York: John Wiley & Sons, 1984.

Starr, Martin K., and David W. Miller, *Inventory Control: Theory and Practice.* Englewood Cliffs, N.J.: Prentice-Hall, 1962.

Tersine, Richard J., *Principles of Inventory and Materials Management,* 2nd ed. New York: North Holland, 1982.

CHAPTER 13

MASTER PRODUCTION SCHEDULING

Some Managerial Issues

- How do our competitive priorities affect our approach to master production scheduling?
- How can we provide accurate shipping dates to our customers?
- Should we position inventory toward end items, purchased items, or somewhere in between?
- How can we get better estimates of cash flows and capacity requirements?

Chapter Outline

In Chapter 11, we discussed production planning, a process that defines generally the commitment of organizational resources needed to meet various production requirements over an extended period of time. Products, work forces, and time periods are aggregated to simplify the planning process. In this sense, the production plan is not operational because it only deals in aggregates. Ultimately, *specific* products must be produced to satisfy *specific* customer demand. A more detailed plan, which disaggregates the production plan into specific product schedules, is required. The master production schedule is such a plan.

WHAT IS A MASTER PRODUCTION SCHEDULE?

A **master production schedule (MPS)** expresses the operational plan of production by period for some planning horizon. The MPS is stated in terms of end items, that is, either finished, shippable products or the highest level assemblies from which these products are eventually built. You will see later in this chapter that there are a number of variations of master production schedules.

In order to gain a basic idea of their role in the planning process, let's consider master production scheduling for a bicycle manufacturer. The company does not accept orders for specially designed bicycles and therefore produces all its products to stock. For production planning purposes the entire line of products was grouped into several families, based on wheel diameter. One in particular, the 20-inch family, includes three different styles. *Alpha* is designed for those customers just learning to ride a bicycle and comes with training wheels. *Dirty Dan* is a dirt bike with racing decals and rugged tires. *Roadster* has hand-caliper brakes, polished aluminum fenders, and a rearview mirror. All three styles are basically the same bicycle with minor variations in accessories and color.

The production plan for the 20-inch family calls for 1000 units in January, 1500 units in February, and 2000 units in March. One possible master production schedule for this family is shown in Table 13.1.

Bill of Materials

Bicycles, like other products, are assembled from components. For a bicycle, the components are frames, wheels, handlebars, and many others. The relationship between the frames and the wheels, handlebars and other components is very precise because of the manner in which a bicycle is produced. That is, steel tubing must be purchased, cut to various lengths, and welded to make the frame. Then the frame and other manufactured components such as wheels, brakes, handlebars, pedals, and a seat must be assembled to make the bicycle.

Table 13.1

Weekly Master Production Schedule

	January				February				March			
	Week				Week				Week			
Product	1	2	3	4	5	6	7	8	9	10	11	12
Alpha	—	160	—	160	—	240	—	240	—	320	—	320
Dirty Dan	150	150	150	150	225	225	225	225	300	300	300	300
Roadster	40	—	40	—	60	—	60	—	80	—	80	—
Monthly Total	1000				1500				2000			

A **bill of materials (BOM)** is based on the notion of *parents* and *components*. (See Chapter 10.) The BOM in Fig. 13.1 shows that item A is made from items B and C. Item B, in turn, is made from D and E, and E is made from F. Items A, B, and E are parents, since they are made from other items by passing them through one or more operations. All items except A are also components, since they are needed to make a parent. The BOM also provides a second type of information: *usage quantities*, which are shown in parentheses in Fig. 13.1. Note that one unit of A is made from two units of B and one unit of C. All other usage quantities are one unit, except for the three units of F to make one unit of E.

A BOM introduces another useful set of terms: end, intermediate, and purchased items. Item A in Fig. 13.1 qualifies as an **end item** because it is a parent but not a component. For master production scheduling purposes, end items are often the final products sold to customers. However, major assemblies or components are considered end items in plants that are part of a vertically integrated company; these items are shipped to an assembly plant for final assembly. Inventory for end items is classified in financial statements

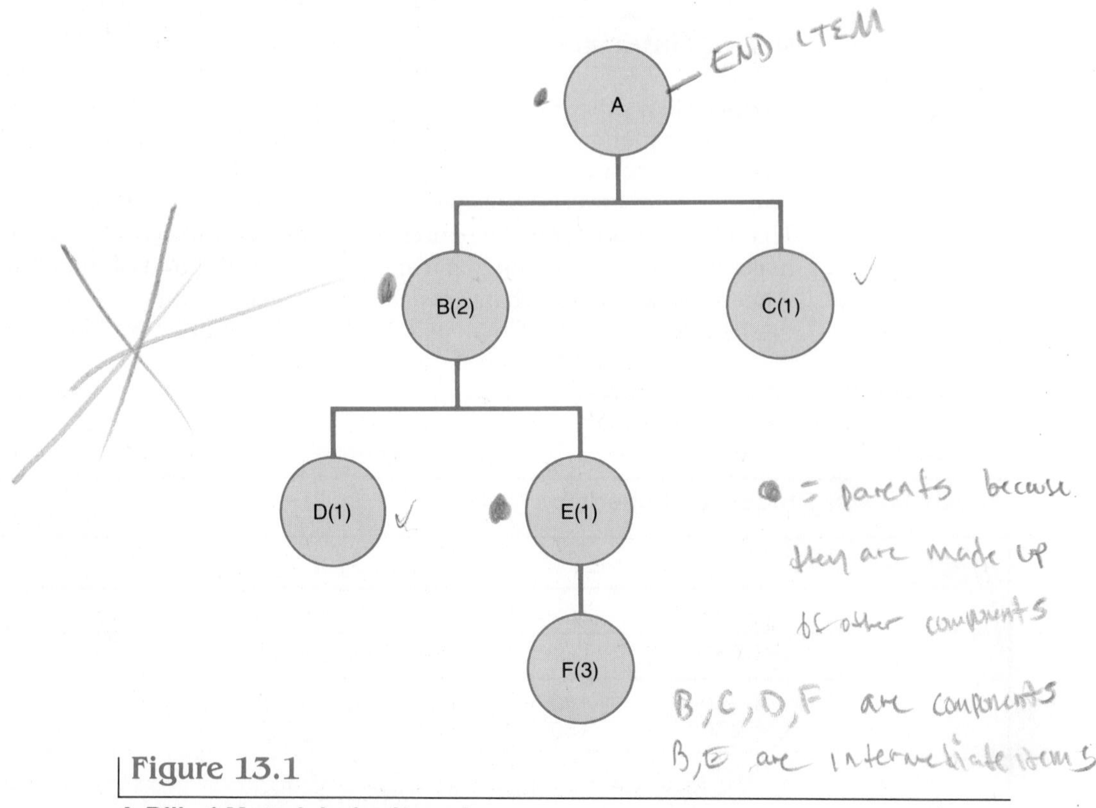

Figure 13.1

A Bill of Materials for Item A.

as either work-in-process (WIP) or finished goods. A lot still being produced for an end item and not yet through the final operation is WIP. The lot's status changes to finished goods inventory as soon as all operations on it are completed. An **intermediate item** is one that has at least one parent and at least one component. Both items B and E in Fig. 13.1 qualify as intermediate items. Manufacturing processes often have several levels of intermediate items, where the parent of one intermediate item is also an intermediate item. Inventory for intermediate items is either in its completed state or still on the shop floor as an open order. In either case, it is always classified as WIP. Examples of a **purchased item** are items C, D, and F in Fig. 13.1. Their distinguishing feature is that they have no components, yet have one or more parents. Inventory of purchased items is always treated as raw materials in financial statements.

Purposes of the Master Production Schedule

The master production schedule serves several purposes. First, by specifying the production lot sizes for end items for each period of the planning horizon, the MPS determines the requirements for all intermediate and purchased items. Here is where the bills of materials are important. For example, the schedule in Table 13.1 shows that 160 units of Alpha bicycles are scheduled for completion in week 2. This means that 160 Alpha main frames, 320 20-inch wheels, 160 training wheel sets, and specific quantities of many other parts must be produced in time to allow completion of 160 Alphas by then. We have more to say about the interface between the master production schedule and the function of inventory management in a dependent-demand environment in Chapter 14.

The second purpose of the MPS is to set due dates for the completion of production orders. In Table 13.1, the completion date for specific quantities of each product is shown in the schedule. For example, 40 units of Roadster are due in week 3. The setting of due dates is also important for products made to customer order. The master schedule identifies the date the product must be completed for shipment to the customer under a negotiated contract.

Finally, the MPS provides the basis for determining the resources required to support the production plan. Although the production plan provides for resources such as labor and subcontracting, they are stated in aggregate terms. The master production schedule is much more detailed and provides a more accurate picture of specific resource needs.

Typical Constraints

A master production schedule must satisfy several constraints. We discuss constraints further when we describe the master scheduling process later in this chapter. However, a brief discussion of them here will help you to understand what a master production schedule is. First, the sum of the master production schedule quantities must equal those of the production plan. The production quantities in Table 13.1 demonstrate two aspects of this constraint. Note that the total of the quantities for Alpha, Dirty Dan, and Roadster each month equals the production plan quantity for each month. In our example, we specified production plan quantities in units of the 20-inch family. If we had specified quantities in dollars or labor hours, we would have used a suitable conversion factor to convert MPS quantities to the same unit of measurement. However, master production schedules should be specified in units of *product* in order to be useful for inventory control purposes.

The second aspect of this constraint is that the total requirements for a product, as determined in the production plan, must be allocated over time in an efficient manner. For example, in Table 13.1 we plan to produce 320 units of Alpha, 600 units of Dirty Dan, and 80 units of Roadster, or a total of 1000 units for the family, in January. The specific product mix is selected on the basis of historical demand and marketing campaign and promotional considerations. After the mix has been determined, specific production quantities must be stated. In our example, the MPS is presented in weekly time periods, although in practice it could be in days or months, depending on the nature of the business or production process. The problem facing the scheduler for the 20-inch bicycle family is to select the production lot sizes for each specific product for each week in the master production schedule. This is done with consideration for the economics of the manufacturing process for the products, including the cost of production setups and inventory carrying costs.

The production lot size and timing decision is also subject to a second type of constraint: capacity limitations. Typically, several resources are crucial to the volume of production that can be achieved. These resources could be certain work stations that are typically short on capacity; storage space for components, assemblies, and finished products; or even working capital funds. The scheduler must acknowledge these limitations, recognizing that certain products require more of certain critical resources than others.

In general, these are the ways in which the master production schedule provides a link between the production plan and the scheduling and control of the myriad components a company manufactures. We now turn to a discussion of the process for developing acceptable master production schedules.

THE MASTER PRODUCTION SCHEDULING PROCESS

The master production scheduling process is shown in Fig. 13.2. This process begins where we left off in Chapter 11, with the authorized production plan. Using it as a basis, we develop a *prospective* master production schedule. You

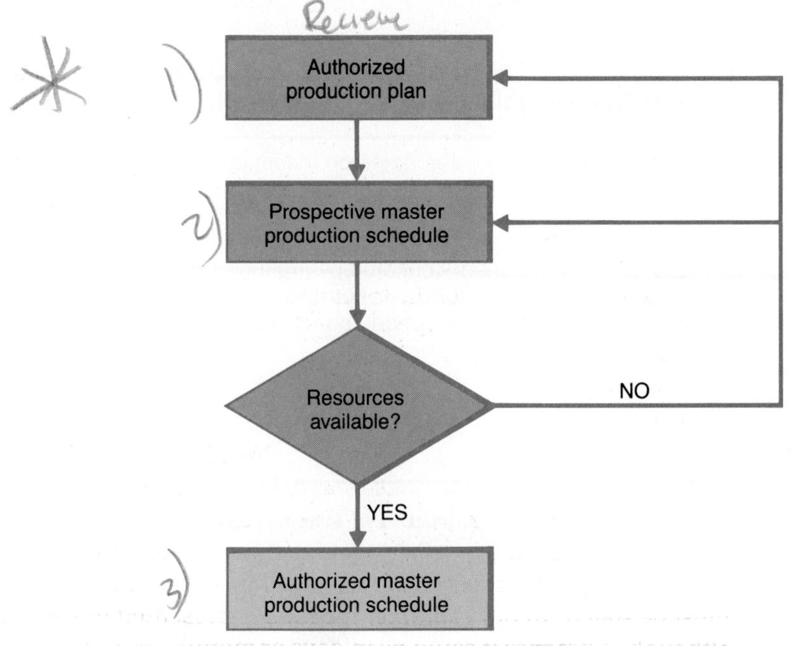

Figure 13.2

Master Production Scheduling Process.

can think of the prospective MPS as a trial balloon to see whether it can be accomplished within the machine capacities and the labor, overtime, subcontracting, or any other resource capacities provided by the production plan. If it cannot, we revise the MPS. We would continue to make revisions until either a schedule satisfying all resource limitations is found or we determine that a feasible schedule cannot be found. In that event, the production plan must be revised to either adjust production requirements or increase authorized resources. Ultimately, an acceptable prospective master production schedule emerges and is presented to management for authorization. The specific procedure for authorization differs from company to company.

In many manufacturing firms, a *master production scheduler* is responsible for developing a master production schedule that satisfies the intent of the production plan. Other responsibilities typically include those in Table 13.2. The master production scheduler makes minor changes to the authorized schedule or the product mix in some companies. Major changes affecting customer delivery dates or significant adjustments in delivery schedules or acquisition of materials may have to be authorized by the manager responsible for performance in those areas.

In summary, Fig. 13.2 shows that the master production scheduling process is iterative and requires feedback from the same functional areas that are

Table 13.2

Typical Responsibilities of a Master Production Scheduler

- Specify delivery promise dates on incoming orders and match actual requirements with the master production schedule.
- Evaluate the impact of "top-down" inputs, such as the introduction of new products in less than the normal lead time.
- Evaluate the impact of "bottom-up" inputs, such as anticipated shortage reports from manufacturing or purchasing indicating certain components will not be available as scheduled, or that planned production rates are not being attained.
- Revise the master production schedule when necessary for lack of material or capacity.
- Bring basic conflicts to the attention of the affected members of management for resolution.

Source: Oliver Wight, *Production and Inventory Management in the Computer Age.* Boston: Cahners Books, 1974, p. 69.

involved in the production planning process. In this way the master production schedule sets in motion the operations that will achieve the objectives of the production plan.

The process of developing prospective master production schedules and the format of MPS records may differ, depending on the firm and whether it has a product or a process focus. Thus the specific procedures and record formats that we present in the next two sections are *illustrative* of the types of procedures used in practice and may not apply to any specific firm. For those interested, details of specific master production scheduling processes used by eight firms are presented in the work by Berry, Vollmann, and Whybark (1979).

DEVELOPING A PROSPECTIVE MASTER PRODUCTION SCHEDULE

In this section we discuss the process of developing prospective master production schedules for a firm producing to stock. Later in this chapter we discuss considerations for other types of firms. First, we present the basic terminology of master production scheduling and some simple concepts for developing an MPS. Then, we show how to link the production plan and the MPS. Throughout, we emphasize the trial-and-error aspect of master production scheduling often found in practice.

Basic Concepts in Master Production Scheduling

Let's consider a valve manufacturer that produces a limited range of types and sizes of valves, all of which are made to stock. Management needs to develop a master production schedule for one of its products, the 3-inch gate valve. The marketing department has provided a demand forecast of 100 units for April and 160 units for May. These quantities can be considered **gross requirements** for the 3-inch gate valve because they do not take into account the amount of on-hand inventory. Management wants the master production schedule to be expressed in weekly time periods to enable closer control of component production. Figure 13.3 shows an allocation of the gross requirements equally over the weeks in each month. Other allocations are

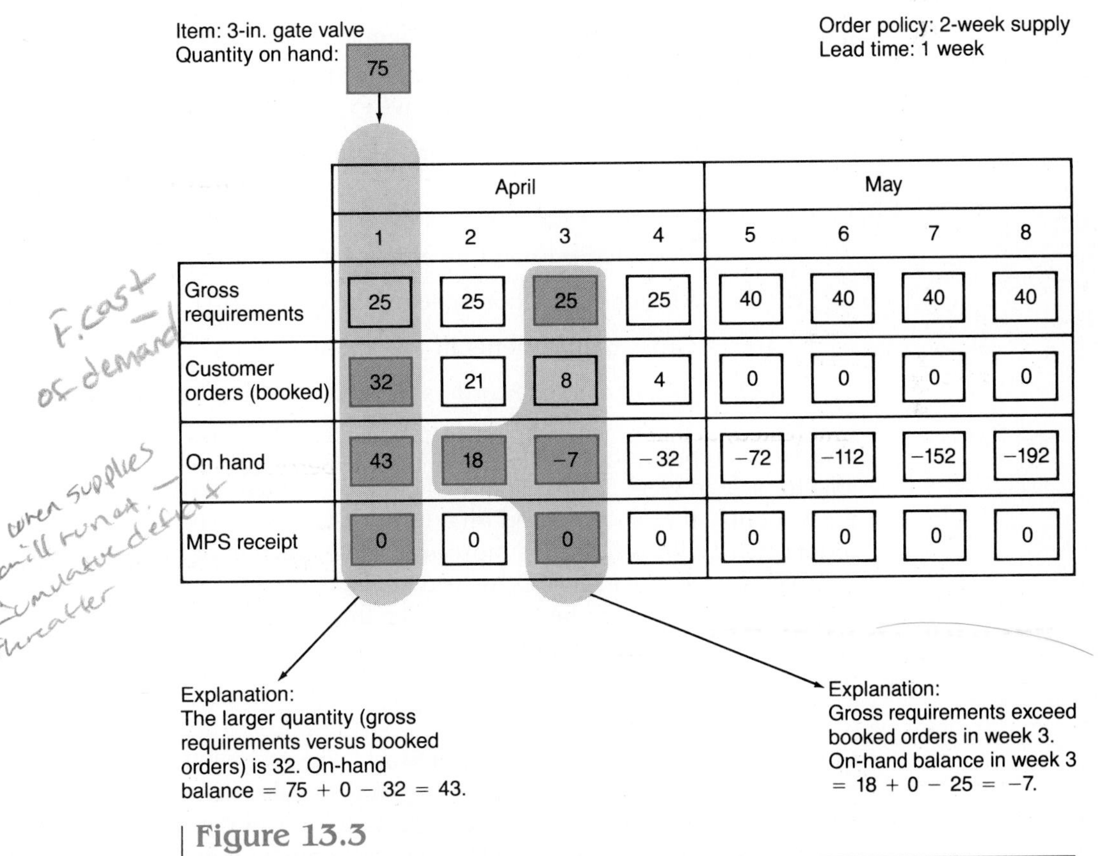

	April				May			
	1	2	3	4	5	6	7	8
Gross requirements	25	25	25	25	40	40	40	40
Customer orders (booked)	32	21	8	4	0	0	0	0
On hand	43	18	−7	−32	−72	−112	−152	−192
MPS receipt	0	0	0	0	0	0	0	0

Figure 13.3

Projected On-Hand Inventory Row for 3-inch Gate Valve.

also possible. For example, reliable *weekly* forecasts could be used directly for the gross requirements, which would then vary. Alternatively, the monthly forecasts could be allocated to each week based on the historical proportion of monthly demand experienced in each week of a given month, which would also vary.

Actual customer demand is shown in the week when the orders are promised for shipment. These entries represent actual orders received for the 3-inch gate valve. Keep in mind that the weekly *forecasts* of customer demand may be wrong. Figure 13.3 shows that actual customer orders for 32 valves exceeded the projected requirements of 25 valves for week 1, although total booked orders for the valve for the *month* are still within the forecasted gross requirements (65 versus 100).

Calculating On-Hand Balances. The projected **on-hand inventory row** of valves shows when the supply of valves will run out and the cumulative deficit for each week thereafter. It equals the on-hand balance last week (even if it is negative) plus MPS receipt during the current week minus the expected gross requirements *or* actual customer orders booked during the week, whichever is greater. Mathematically, we express this relationship as follows:

$$I_t = I_{t-1} + MPSR_t - \text{Greater of } [GR_t \text{ or } CO_t],$$

where

I_t = Projected on-hand inventory balance at the end of week t;

$MPSR_t$ = Master production schedule receipt during week t;

GR_t = Gross requirements in week t; and

CO_t = Actual customer orders booked for shipment in week t.

The $MPSR_t$ represents a quantity that is expected to be completed and available for sale in week t. We choose GR_t or CO_t, whichever is greater, because we recognize that GR_t is based on a forecast and is subject to error. If actual orders *exceed* GR_t, we obtain a more accurate projection of the on-hand inventory balance when we use CO_t instead of GR_t. Conversely, when GR_t exceeds CO_t, GR_t provides our best estimate of the requirements for week t. The calculation of I_t in Fig. 13.3 shows an expected shortage of seven valves in week 3. There are no MPS receipts, so the beginning on-hand inventory of 75 valves will only last for two weeks and part of a third.

Calculating MPS Receipts and MPS Start. Figure 13.4 shows a prospective master production schedule for the 3-inch gate valve. The timing and size of production quantities for the next eight weeks are shown in the MPS-receipt and MPS-start rows. The MPS also gives marketing an idea of the number of units that can still be promised to customers in the available-to-promise row. We discuss that calculation later in this section.

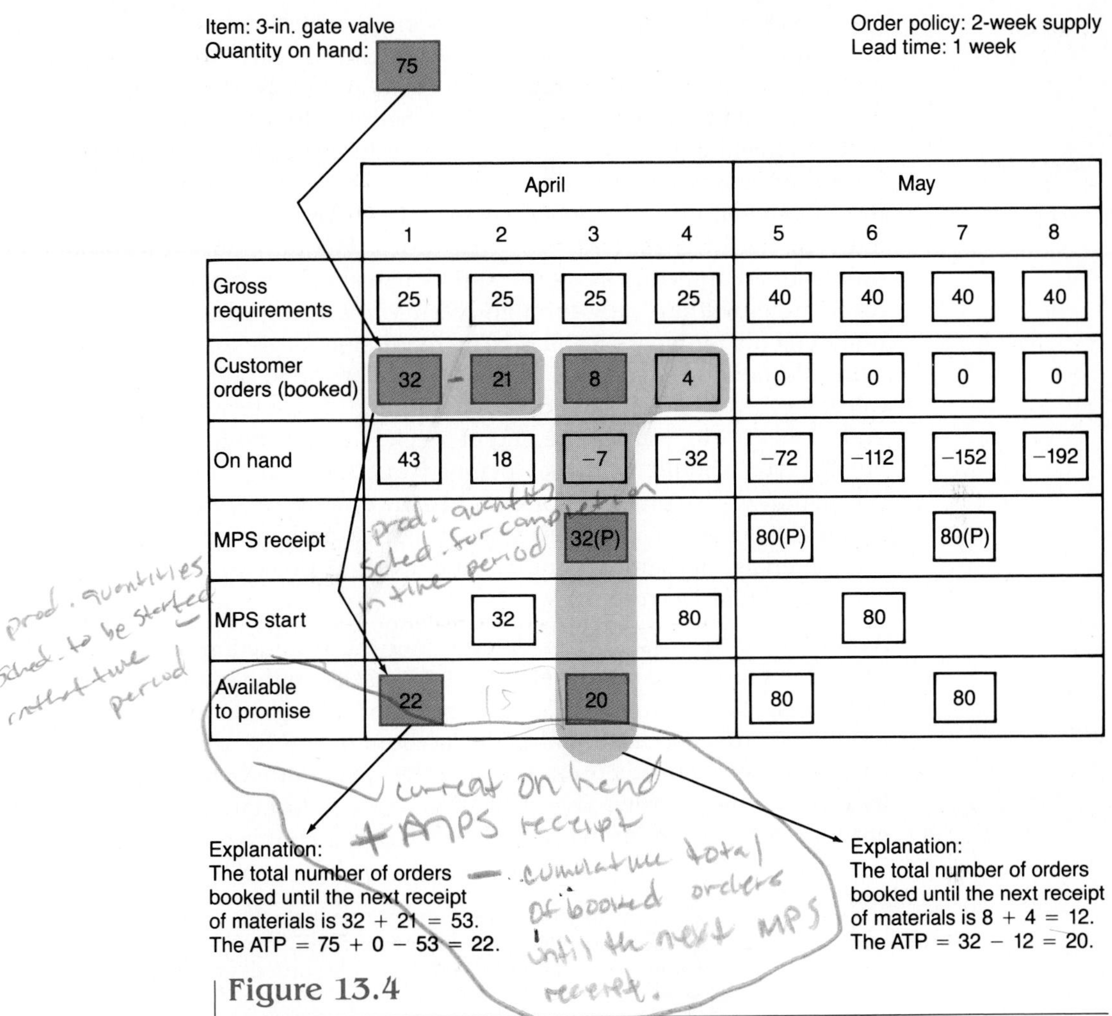

	April				May			
	1	2	3	4	5	6	7	8
Gross requirements	25	25	25	25	40	40	40	40
Customer orders (booked)	32	21	8	4	0	0	0	0
On hand	43	18	−7	−32	−72	−112	−152	−192
MPS receipt			32(P)		80(P)		80(P)	
MPS start		32		80		80		
Available to promise	22		20		80		80	

Figure 13.4

A Prospective Master Production Schedule.

The **MPS-receipt row** shows the production quantities scheduled for *completion* in the weeks indicated: 32 units in week 3 and 80 units each in weeks 5 and 7. The **MPS-start row** shows the production quantities of the valve scheduled to be *started* in the week indicated. Since the valve requires only one week to assemble, the start date for the 32 units is week 2 and for the 2 lots of 80 units, weeks 4 and 6. The entries in the MPS-start row are only planned because the production orders for those quantities have not yet been issued.

The ordering policy for the valve is to order a two-week supply.* We first

* Numerous lot-sizing techniques could be used. We present some of them in Chapter 14.

detect a need for replenishment in week 3, where the projected on-hand balance is −7 units. If we order a two-week supply each time, we must issue an order for 32 (or 7 + 25) units to prevent any stockouts during those two weeks. In addition, the order must be scheduled for completion in week 3 in order to avoid a stockout then. The (*P*) indicates that this is only a *planned* receipt of 32 units. If it were already in process, an (*R*) would indicate that the production order had been *released;* there would *not* be a corresponding entry in the MPS-start row for that order. We developed the production orders for 80 units due in weeks 5 and 7 in a similar manner. Since the order for 32 units will last only through week 4, the next order must cover gross requirements for weeks 5 and 6.* The requirements are for 40 units per week over that period, requiring a production order for 80 units. Another way to calculate the order size is to note the on-hand deficit grows from −32 at the end of week 4 to −112 at the end of week 6: this is a difference of 80 units. Finally, you should note that planned quantities are not included in the calculation of the projected on-hand balance; only released quantities enter into that calculation. In this way the projected on-hand balance reflects only the materials, on-hand inventory, and work in process, to which we have actually committed resources.

Available to Promise. After determining the production quantities in the MPS-receipt row, we can develop the information in the **available-to-promise (ATP) row.** This information is very useful for setting valid shipping dates for new valve orders because it takes into account the on-hand quantity of valves, customer orders already promised, and the master production schedule given by the MPS-receipt row. The calculation of this information is slightly different for the first (current) week of the schedule than it is for the other weeks.

> *First (Current) Week Calculation of ATP:*
>
> The available-to-promise quantity equals the current on-hand quantity *plus* the MPS receipt for the first week *minus* the cumulative total of booked customer orders until the next MPS receipt.

In Fig. 13.4, the ATP is 22 [or 75 + 0 − (32 + 21)] units, since there is no MPS receipt in week 1. The on-hand balance of 75 units can satisfy all booked orders until the next scheduled receipt of valves and still leave 22 units available for new orders.

We also calculate the ATP for other weeks having an MPS receipt. Here the ATP quantity equals the MPS receipt minus the cumulative total of booked customer orders until the next MPS receipt. We do not use the projected on-hand balance in this calculation because we already used the on-hand balance for the ATP quantity in the first week. In Fig. 13.4, the ATP

* In general, the next order would have to cover the greater quantity of either gross requirements or customer orders.

quantity in week 3 is 20 [or 32 − (8 + 4)] units. Since there are no more booked orders, the ATP quantities for weeks 5 and 7 equal the respective MPS-receipt quantities.

The information given by the available-to-promise quantities can be used to provide customer shipping dates for new orders. Figure 13.4 shows that marketing can promise new orders totaling 22 units for shipment in weeks 1 and 2. The next 20 units can be promised for delivery in weeks 3 and 4, the next 80 units in weeks 5 and 6, and so on. Thus, if *new* orders totaling 30 units arrive today, the first 22 units could be shipped this week and the remaining 8 units shipped in week 3.

Updating the Schedule. Suppose that the prospective MPS in Fig. 13.4 was approved and two weeks have passed, so that now we are at the beginning of week 3. Let's also assume that no new customer orders were booked and no other modifications to the schedule were made in the interim. The updated MPS, then, for the rest of April and May is shown in Fig. 13.5. The on-hand quantity at the beginning of week 3 is 22 units, since we shipped 53 (or 32 + 21) units in weeks 1 and 2 from the available inventory of 75 units in week 1. The ATP quantity in the current week (now week 3) is 42 [or 22 + 32 − (8 + 4)] units.

The planned production quantity for week 5 in the MPS-receipt row is now 76 units. Note that this quantity is 4 units less than the planned quantity in Fig. 13.4. There are two reasons for this result. First, we based the production quantity in Fig. 13.4 on the projected on-hand balance. At the end of week 2, we projected an on-hand balance of 18 units, but it actually turned out to be 22 units because 4 units of demand never materialized. Consequently, we can reduce the production quantity in week 5 by 4 units, since we have more inventory on hand than expected. The second reason for the change in quantity is the nature of the ordering policy we used. The policy of ordering a two-week supply allows changes to be made in production quantities each time new data are available. This type of policy can cause problems in scheduling components if there is too much instability in the size and timing of end-item production quantities. If we had the policy "order 80 units each time," we might achieve more stability in the MPS from week to week. However, we would have to carefully monitor actual customer orders to avoid building large amounts of inventory or creating large amounts of back orders.

Linking the Production Plan to the Master Production Schedule

The valve production example illustrates the development of a master production schedule directly from the forecast for the end item. We gave no consideration to the trade-offs associated with leveling production rates or the

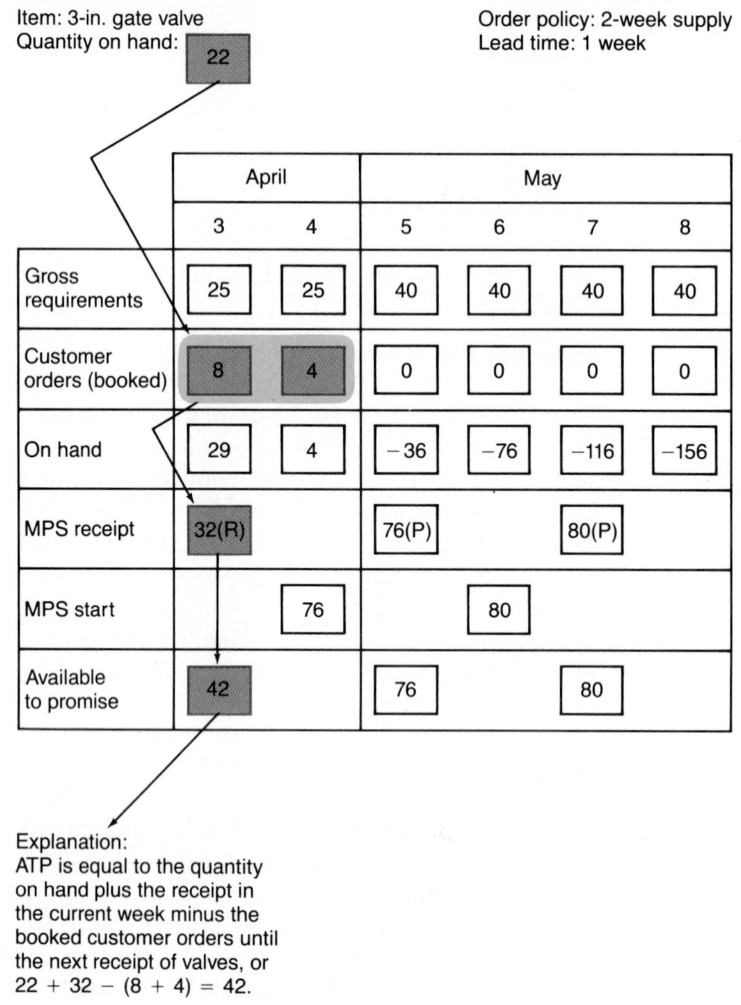

Figure 13.5

Updated Master Production Schedule.

work force, nor did we attempt to build any anticipation inventories. Whenever we ran out of inventory or released production quantities, the MPS simply became an accumulation of forecasts. However, as you saw in Chapter 11, the production plan *does* consider these trade-offs. The key to developing an acceptable MPS therefore is to link the production plan to it.

One way to incorporate a production plan into the master production scheduling process is to use **production requirements,** as opposed to gross requirements or forecasts, to determine production quantities. Let's consider two cases here: (1) a production plan specified in units of specific end items; and (2) a production plan specified in terms of product families. The former represents situations in which there are few end items, whereas the latter represents situations in which there are many end items.

Few End Items. The production plan gives us the desired production quantities, perhaps in monthly time periods, *net* of on-hand inventory. We can consider these monthly production quantities to be production requirements for specific products, since the firm only produces a small number of products; these quantities should be produced by the MPS. The production requirements can call for inventory buildups. For example, we plan to produce more now than we need to satisfy customer demand, so that we can build anticipation inventory for future high-demand periods.

Let's return to our 3-inch gate valve example, but this time let's suppose that the *production plan* specifies production quantities of 100 units for April and 160 units for May. The 75 units of on-hand inventory are already accounted for in the production plan. Consequently, our MPS receipt quantities should correspond as closely as possible to production plan quantities.

Table 13.3 shows one of many possible prospective master production schedules for the 3-inch gate valve. In the top row we replaced gross requirements with production requirements, the total of which equals the production plan quantity each month. We decided to divide the total monthly production requirements into two equal quantities and allocate them to weeks 2 and 4 and weeks 6 and 8, although we could have selected any of a large number of other allocations.*

The major difference between Table 13.3 and Fig. 13.4 is the manner in which the projected on-hand balance is calculated. The current on-hand quantity of 75 units is not included here because it has already been considered in determining production requirements. Booked customer orders are also ignored, so that the on-hand row becomes a projection of cumulative production requirements. Week 2 has a projected deficit of 50 units, which is why a planned order for 50 units is scheduled for completion in week 2. Note that the total quantity in the MPS-receipt row corresponds to the production plan quantity in each month because of our two-week ordering policy. MPS-start quantities would not change unless the production plan were revised. In this way inventories can be increased beyond immediate customer requirements and depleted later on, in accordance with management's overall operations plan. We calculate the quantities in the available-to-promise row in the same manner as before.

Many Products. As we discussed in Chapter 11, a company that produces a large number, perhaps thousands, of finished products aggregates these

* The timing and size of these production requirements could change when capacity limitations are considered.

Table 13.3

A Prospective Master Production Schedule Linked to a Production Plan

Quantity on hand: 75	April				May			
	Week				Week			
	1	2	3	4	5	6	7	8
Production requirements	—	50	—	50	—	80	—	80
Customer orders (booked)	32	21	8	4	0	0	0	0
On hand	—	−50	−50	−100	−100	−180	−180	−260
MPS receipt	—	50(*P*)	—	50(*P*)	—	80(*P*)	—	80(*P*)
MPS start	50	—	50	—	80	—	80	—
Available to promise	43	21	—	46	—	80	—	80

products into product families for purposes of the production plan. The master production scheduler now must **disaggregate** these product families—recognizing the desired product mix within each family—to arrive at production requirements for each specific end product.

As one approach to developing a prospective MPS for this type of situation, let's consider again the example of the bicycle manufacturer. The production plan in Table 13.1 calls for 1000 units of the 20-inch family in January. Using simple averages or a time series forecasting method, we could analyze the historical demand patterns for the three bicycle models and arrive at an average percentage of total demand for each model. This approach is called *planning* bill of materials.* Suppose that we found that Alpha historically represents 32 percent of total demand, Dirty Dan 60 percent, and Roadster only 8 percent. The estimated production requirements for Alpha would be 320 [or 0.32(1000)]. Similarly, they would be 600 [or 0.60(1000)] for Dirty Dan and 80 [or 0.08(1000)] for Roadster. We can now develop the MPS using the same approach we used in Table 13.3.

The percentages are really forecasts of product mix for the family, and you should take care to detect shifts in that mix; you can use tracking signals such as those discussed in Chapter 3. The production plan and/or the MPS may have to be updated. For example, let's say that each month (in the production planning process) management compares the actual inventory of

* The approach gets its name from the notion that the product family is the parent and the individual products within the family are components. The percentages of total demand for each product are similar to the usage quantities in a normal bill of materials.

the 20-inch family to the projected level and considers modifications to the plan. If one of the products is selling better than expected but total family sales are about as expected, adjusting the percentages to reflect the change in mix may be all that is necessary. However, if total sales have also increased, the percentages *and* the production plan for the family may have to be adjusted. In this way the planning process can help to reduce the effects of forecast uncertainties.

ROUGH-CUT CAPACITY PLANNING

After a prospective master production schedule has been developed, it must be checked for feasibility relative to the available resources of the firm, as shown in Fig. 13.2. Feasibility checks of the MPS in practice are done with rough-cut approaches. They are called rough-cut because they are intended to give only a rough approximation of actual resource requirements generated during the manufacture of products. In this section we describe only one of several approaches to **rough-cut capacity planning** called the method of overall factors. We chose it because it is simple and it demonstrates the *concept* of rough-cut capacity planning. (See Berry, Schmitt, and Vollmann, 1982, for other, more sophisticated, approaches.)

Developing Load Profiles

We can illustrate the method of overall factors using a company that produces three products, A, B, and C, to stock. The prospective master production schedule shown in Table 13.4 for the three items corresponds to the MPS-receipt row in each item's MPS record. To develop the load profile for this prospective schedule we need to (1) identify the critical work stations; (2) develop the direct labor factors for each item; and (3) develop the load factors for each critical work station.

Table 13.4

Prospective Master Production Schedule

	Week								
Item	1	2	3	4	5	6	7	8	Total Units
A	25	25	25	25	35	35	35	35	240
B	—	50	—	50	—	50	—	50	200
C	72	—	75	—	56	—	68	—	271

Critical Work Stations. Critical work stations are those that limit output because the need to use them frequently exceeds their capacity. Management tries to schedule time at these work stations as efficiently as possible in order to maximize their output. For example, if a critical work station has 200 hours of capacity per week and, for some reason, only 150 hours are used this week, the 50 hours of usage are lost; they cannot be used next week if 250 hours of usage are needed.

We can usually identify the critical work stations fairly easily by observation or from performance records. For our example, suppose that we have identified two critical work stations, which we call 0810A and 0820B for reference purposes. The hours that we schedule work for these stations are called *critical hours* because the acceptability of a prospective MPS will depend on the hours required at these work stations.

Direct Labor Factors. In the method of overall factors, we use time standards, or gross estimates if standards are not available, for the number of direct labor hours required at each work station to produce one unit of each item. We then aggregate the hours for the critical work stations to obtain one factor and the hours for the noncritical work stations to obtain a second factor. Table 13.5 shows these factors for our example.

Load Factors. In order to determine the number of hours required of each critical work station for a prospective MPS, we have to look at past records. Table 13.6 shows the number of direct labor hours worked at each critical work station last year and the percentage of the total number of critical hours this represents. For example, the hours reported for work station 0820B represent 66 percent of the total direct labor hours reported for all critical work stations. Thus in using the method of overall factors, we assume that work station 0820B will continue to get 66 percent of the load on the critical work stations.

Compiling a Load Profile. Let's now develop the load profile for the prospective MPS in Table 13.4. In the first week, 25 units of A and 72 units of C are scheduled. Using the factors shown in Table 13.5, we obtain a total plant

Table 13.5

Direct Labor Hours per Unit

Item	Critical Work Stations	Noncritical Work Stations	Total
A	1.60	0.00	1.60
B	6.07	8.00	14.07
C	5.04	4.00	9.04

Table 13.6

Direct Labor Hours Worked Last Year

Work Station	Quarter 1	2	3	4	Total	Percent
0810A	1,140	1,285	1,175	1,300	4,900	34
0820B	2,430	2,540	2,100	2,380	9,450	66
Total critical hours	3,570	3,825	3,275	3,680	14,350	100
Total noncritical hours	5,200	5,150	5,000	5,300	20,650	

direct labor requirement of 690.88 [or 25(1.60) + 72(9.04)] hours. Similarly, the total critical direct labor requirement is 402.88 [or 25(1.60) + 72(5.04)] hours. We can calculate the labor requirements for other weeks in a similar manner. The results (rounded to the nearest whole number) are shown in Table 13.7.

We allocate the total labor hours for the critical work stations to each critical station using the percentages in Table 13.6. For example, in the first week, the projected load for work station 0810A is 137.02 [or 0.34(403)] hours. We calculate the other projections similarly. The results are shown in Table 13.7.

The Role of Load Profiles in the Authorization Decision

Should the prospective master production schedule in Table 13.4 be authorized? The answer lies in a comparison of the projected load profile with the labor capacities approved in the production plan. Suppose that the production plan specified 780 total plant labor hours on regular time, including 370

Table 13.7

Load Profile Using Method of Overall Factors

Work station	Week 1	2	3	4	5	6	7	8	Total
0810A (34%)	137	117	142	117	115	122	136	122	1008
0820B (66%)	266	227	276	227	223	238	263	238	1958
Total critical hours	403	344	418	344	338	360	399	360	2966
Total noncritical hours	288	400	300	400	224	400	272	400	2684
Total labor hours	691	744	718	744	562	760	671	760	5650

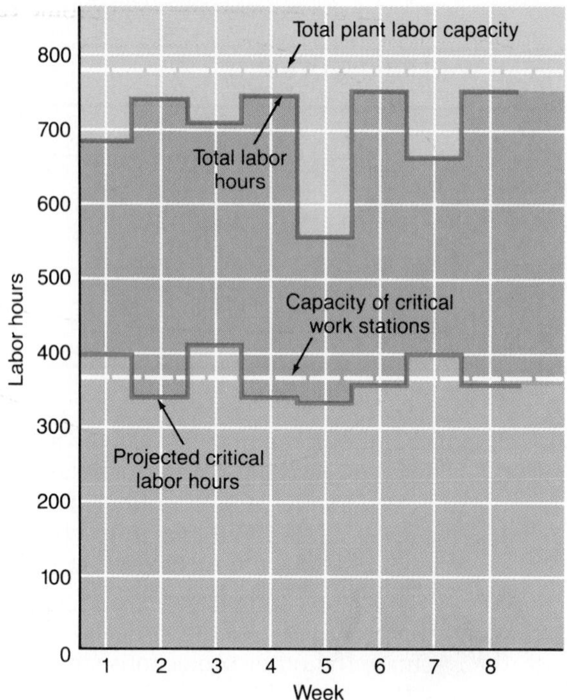

Figure 13.6

Graphic Display of Load Profile from Table 13.7.

labor hours in the critical work stations, for each week covered by the MPS. Figure 13.6 displays graphically the load profile in Table 13.7. From Fig.13.6 it is obvious that the schedule does not exceed the total plant labor capacity, since the peak load is 760 hours in weeks 6 and 8. Even so, it appears that the company will need to use overtime at the critical work stations; overtime will be needed in weeks 1, 3, and 7. Whether station 0810A, 0820B, or both need to work overtime depends on the specific amounts of capacity allocated to each from the 370 available hours. The projection of total overtime requirements is compared to the level authorized in the production plan for the period covered by the MPS. If the total overtime requirements fall within the authorized level, and the schedule is feasible in all other respects, the prospective MPS would be authorized. If not, the master production scheduler would have to come up with a better schedule.

Evaluation of the Method of Overall Factors

The method of overall factors is one of the simplest methods available for rough-cut capacity planning. The direct labor hours per unit of each end product used to calculate the load profile can be a gross estimate, based on accounting system data, or a more precise estimate, based on detailed files of time standards and item routings. In practice, gross estimates rather than precise estimates are used most often. Further, labor requirements are not specified by specific critical work station. They are proportioned to each work station on the basis of historical labor requirements. The assumption that historical requirements represent future requirements implies that the product mix does not change; otherwise, the requirements at a specific work station may change as a percentage of the total. Also, the method of overall factors will not reflect large swings in capacity requirements on a week-to-week basis for a specific work station because its assigned hours represent a fixed percentage of the total critical hours for a week. Nonetheless, the method can work reasonably well in situations where the MPS is fairly stable with respect to product mix on a week-to-week basis or the MPS is specified in monthly time periods and only a rough estimate of monthly labor requirements is needed.

MANAGERIAL ISSUES IN MASTER PRODUCTION SCHEDULING

The master production schedule is an important document since it provides a link between the top-level, strategic considerations incorporated in the production plan and the tactical plans needed to achieve the strategic objectives. So far we have focused on approaches to developing an MPS, including the use of rough-cut load profiles. However, the positioning of inventory in the factory, functional area interfaces, and the need for computers—and their effects on master production scheduling—are other important managerial issues.

Positioning Inventory

The issue of **positioning inventory** involves determining whether to concentrate inventory at the raw-materials, work-in-process, or finished-product level. Positioning of inventory has a bearing on the MPS approach used. Positioning of inventory also reflects the competitive priorities of the firm. Figure 13.7 shows inventories placed forward and backward.

Forward Positioning. Forward positioning holds most inventory toward the finished-product level. The main advantage of this approach is that customer response times are minimized. When a customer order is received, it can be responded to immediately. This is the approach used by product-focused firms because they typically use a **make-to-stock strategy.** Their product structure has the shape of a pyramid (without the peak) because there are relatively fewer finished products than intermediate and purchased items. Master production scheduling is done for the end-item level because demand

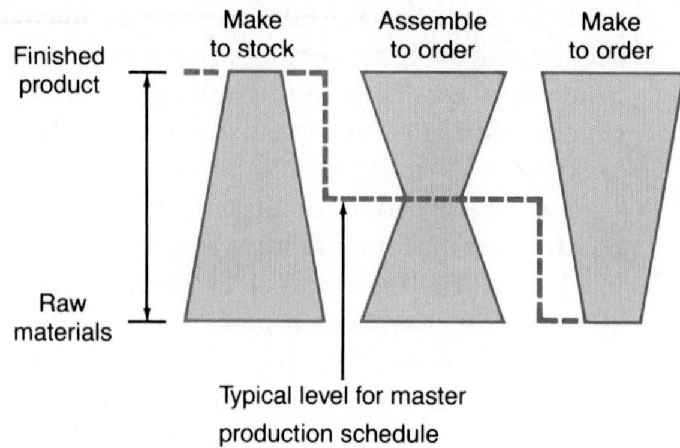

Figure 13.7

Relationship of Product Structure, Master Production Schedule Level, and Competitive Priorities.

forecasts are likely to be reasonably accurate, and the products are standardized.

Backward Positioning. At the other end of the spectrum, if the operations priority calls for high product flexibility, inventory should be positioned toward the purchased item level, as process-focused firms do. They use a **make-to-order strategy,** which produces many items from relatively few purchased items. Many of the intermediate items are also produced and assembled to customer specification, with minimal stocking of intermediate items. Backward positioning minimizes inventory and maximizes product flexibility. Master production scheduling in this case is typically done for the purchased-item level in the product structure because few of the manufactured components are standard. However, customer orders with sufficiently long delivery time promises for designing, purchasing, and manufacturing could be scheduled at the end-item level.

Intermediate Positioning. A compromise between forward and backward positioning, which is to create intermediate items, may be attractive. Intermediate positioning can often cut customer response times without risking slow-moving or obsolete inventory. This approach is taken by firms using an **assemble-to-order strategy,** whereby many end items are produced from relatively few intermediate items. For example, a customer purchasing an automobile has hundreds of options and accessories to choose from. An automobile manufacturer can literally produce millions of cars, no two alike, depending on the mix of options and accessories customers order. As Fig. 13.7 shows, the product structure in this environment looks more like an hour glass. Since there are far too many end items to forecast accurately, firms using the assemble-to-order strategy master schedule the major assemblies and components. Forecasting demand for these items is relatively easy because they are common to all the products produced. Then, when a customer order is received, the product is assembled with all the accessories specified by the customer.

To better understand the concept of intermediate positioning, consider the **operations process chart** in Fig. 13.8. It shows how product A is made from three raw materials, while passing through ten operations. For example,

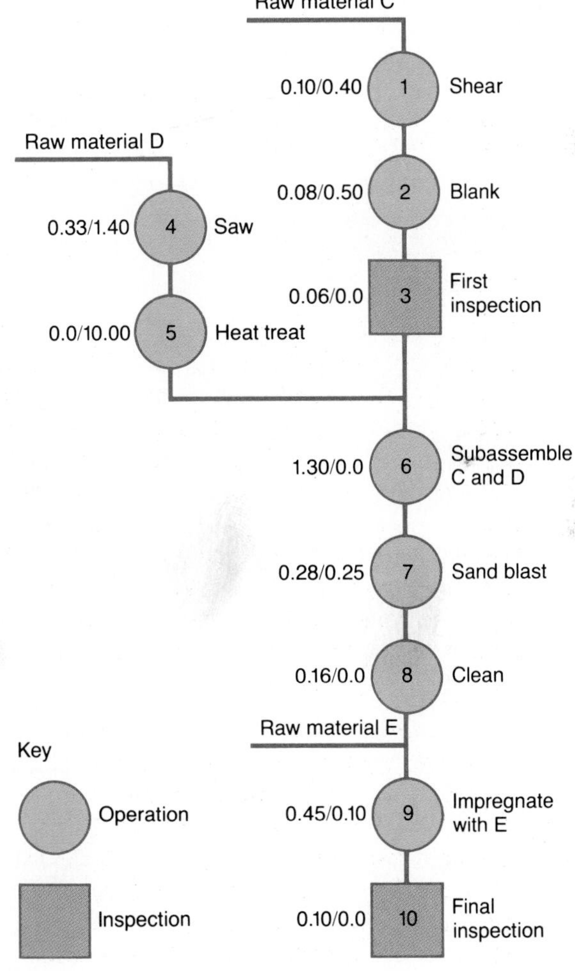

Figure 13.8

Operations Process Chart for Item A.

the first operation is shearing, using item C as raw material. The 0.10/0.40 notation means that it takes 0.10 hours to process each unit, while the setup time is 0.40 hours per lot; these are time standards. Note that the second raw material, item D, is not needed until the beginning of fourth operation.

Showing all this information on one chart can be tedious. It is usually replaced in practice by two documents: a routing and a bill of materials, which are shown in Fig. 13.9. The **routing** lists the sequence of operations to be performed, standard times, and required materials. It often shows other information such as tool requirements, crew sizes, or alternate sequences.

One of several options for creating intermediate items is shown in Fig. 13.10: Intermediate item B is created as a stocking point. When comparing Figs. 13.9 and 13.10, you can see that the manufacturing process is identical. All ten operations still must be done and all three raw materials are needed. However, creating item B changes both the routings and bills of materials.

Operation		Standard times (hours)		
Sequence no.	Description	Processing	Setup	Component
1	Shear	0.10	0.40	Raw material C
2	Blank	0.08	0.50	
3	First inspection	0.06	—	
4	Saw	0.33	1.40	Raw material D
5	Heat treat	—	10.00	
6	Subassemble C and D	1.30	—	
7	Sand blast	0.28	0.25	
8	Clean	0.16	—	
9	Impregnate with E	0.45	0.10	Raw material E
10	Final inspection	0.10	—	

(a)

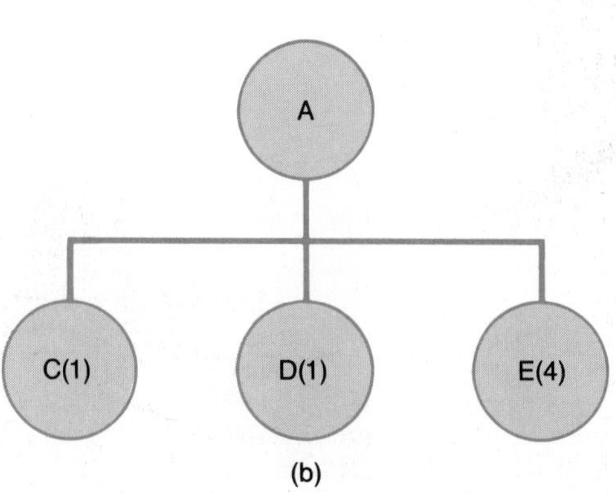

(b)

Figure 13.9

Item A: (a) Routing; (b) Bill of Materials.

Item A

Operation		Standard time (hours)		
Sequence no.	Description	Processing	Setup	Component
1	Impregnate with E	0.45 hr	0.10 hr	Items B and E
2	Final inspection	0.10	—	

Item B

Operation		Standard time (hours)		
Sequence no.	Description	Processing	Setup	Component
1	Shear	0.10	0.40	Raw material C
2	Blank	0.08	0.50	
3	First inspection	0.06	—	
4	Saw	0.33	1.40	Raw material D
5	Heat treat	—	10.00	
6	Subassemble C and D	1.30	—	
7	Sand blast	0.28	0.25	
8	Clean	0.16	—	

(a)

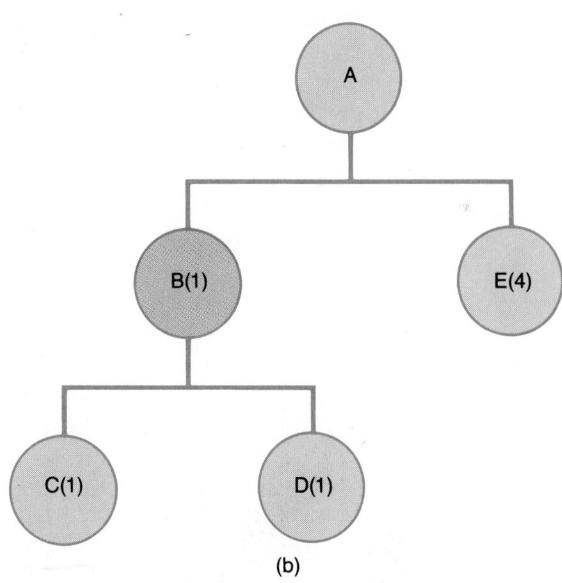

(b)

Figure 13.10

Intermediate Stocking Point with (a) New Routings; (b) Bill of Materials.

Item B needs a routing, and item A now has a shortened routing. Item A's bill of materials is also different now, since it has only two immediate components (B and E). Assuming that item B is stocked to be available when needed, we can now make item A in just two operations (rather than ten) and from only two components (rather than three).

Creating intermediate items as stocking points is more of an art than a science, but there are some guidelines:

1. Create an intermediate stocking point as close to the final operation as possible, making sure that the resulting intermediate item has sufficiently high demand. For example, suppose that many customized products may be made essentially the same way as item A in Fig. 13.8, except for the specific component added at the ninth operation. Varying this component creates a wide variety of products. It is better to add a stocking point *before* rather than after this operation, as done with item B in Fig. 13.10. Item B will have high part commonality and many parents. Having an intermediate item be a common component for many parents minimizes the risk of slow-moving or obsolete inventory. It also increases repeatability in the shop, which can enhance productivity. Perhaps even a group technology cell would become feasible. This approach is the rationale behind the assemble-to-order strategy.
2. Create a stocking point *after* an operation that is particularly time consuming, particularly if little value is added to the product by the operation and demand remains high. This minimizes customer response times without greatly increasing the inventory investment.
3. Create a stocking point *between* two operations, if the best lot size is small for one operation and large for the other. The best sizes can vary from one operation to the next, which provides motivation to decouple the operations, so that different lot sizes can be selected for each operation.
4. Create stocking points *before* bottleneck operations, so that their schedules are not disrupted because of unavailable components. This allows the bottleneck operation to be more closely scheduled, often using larger lot sizes to minimize the time lost to changeover from one job to the next.

Standards versus Specials. Managers make another choice that affects the positioning of inventory. Each item is treated either as a special or standard. A **special item** is made to order. If it is a purchased item, it is bought to order. Its lot size is just large enough to cover the latest customer order received. Cycle inventory is never created on purpose for it, which makes sense when inventory costs outweigh the benefits of larger lot sizes. For example, demand for an item may be so low and unpredictable that the risk of obsolescence is excessive if the item is stocked. Specials can be at any BOM level, but usually are concentrated at the top. A **standard item,** on the other hand, is made to stock. It has a sufficiently high demand that inventory can be built with little fear of obsolescence.

A particularly strong incentive for making an item a standard is to reduce customer delivery time, as illustrated in Fig. 13.11. The lead time required for each item is overlaid on the BOM for item A in Fig. 13.11(a). The customer response times for six stocking strategies are shown in Fig. 13.11(b). Strategy I treats all items as specials, which minimizes inventory holding cost but maximizes customer response time. A customer must wait 17 weeks after placing an order before it is shipped. This customer response time is found by adding the lead times along the longest path down to a standard item or the bottom of the BOM, whichever comes first. For strategy I, A–B–D is the longest path. It takes 5 weeks to buy D, another 11 weeks to make item B, and still another

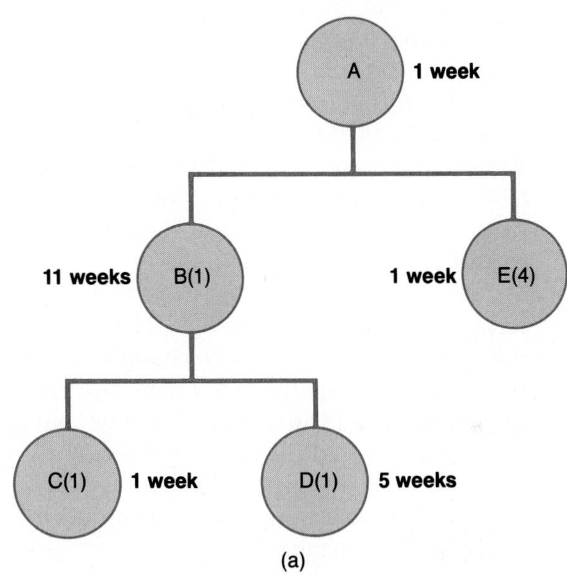

(a)

Strategy	Standard items	Longest path	Customer response time (weeks)
I	None	D – B – A	17 (5 + 11 + 1)
II	D	C – B – A	13 (1 + 11 + 1)
III	C and D	B – A	12 (11 + 1)
IV	B	E – A	2 (1 + 1)
V	B and E	A	1
VI	A	—	0

(b)

Figure 13.11

Reducing Customer Response Times: (a) BOM and Lead Times; (b) Strategies and Response Times.

week to assemble B and E to make A. Item E is not on the longest path; it can be bought in just one week, whereas it will be 16 weeks before B is ready.

Strategy II cuts the customer response time to 13 weeks by making item D a standard. Since item D now has inventory, which normally is available without any further delay, the longest path changes to A–B–C. The ultimate in minimizing customer response time is strategy VI. When item A is treated as a standard, customer response time normally is immediate.

Safety Stock Positioning. As you learned in Chapters 10 and 12, the need for safety stock arises from demand uncertainty. Positioning safety stock relative to the level in the BOM or product structure is related to the decision about the positioning of stocking points. Whether inventory is held at the end-item level, the purchased-item level, or somewhere in between, the decision to have a safety stock as a part of that inventory depends on costs, the amount of uncertainty about requirements, and on the policy for customer service. From a master production scheduling perspective, however, two considerations are worth emphasizing. The first is cost. Safety stock held at the end-item level is the most costly. However, if the market will bear waiting a little longer for the product when demand exceeds the forecast, safety stock held one or two levels lower in the BOM can reduce inventory holding costs considerably.

The second consideration is that allowing for safety stock in the MPS tends to stabilize the schedule. That is, when demand exceeds expectations, the MPS may not have to be changed so often if safety stocks were built into the schedule initially. Every time the MPS is changed, schedules for purchased items and intermediate items may have to be changed. These revisions can cause additional expediting and overtime costs or missing production due dates. Management must weigh the trade-offs involved in planning for safety stocks in the MPS (which may be very costly) and the costs associated with an unstable MPS.

Functional Interfaces

The master production scheduling process involves all the functional areas of a firm. As in the development of a production plan, inputs from various functional areas are needed to develop an MPS that achieves the objectives of the production plan and the goals of the organization. However, interaction with these various functional areas does not end with the inputs they provide. Finance can use the MPS to estimate budgets or cash flows by projecting pro-forma profit-and-loss statements. Marketing can use it to project the impact of product mix changes on the capability of the firm to satisfy customer demand and to better manage customer delivery schedules with the available-to-promise technique. Using rough-cut capacity planning, manufacturing can estimate the effects of MPS changes on loads at critical work stations. In general, the MPS is needed by all functional areas of the firm.

Computer-Assisted Master Production Scheduling

Applications of the techniques for master production scheduling and rough-cut capacity planning discussed in this chapter require the use of computers. When there are thousands of items, as is sometimes the case, developing the MPS manually is an enormous, if not impossible, task. Most major computer vendors and many more companies specializing in manufacturing systems software have developed software packages that perform the types of calculations that we have presented. These programs also provide managers with detailed reports that are useful for analyzing the MPS. With the surge in the use of personal computers that have excellent graphic capabilities, many MPS-related reports, such as the load profile in Fig. 13.6, can be made accessible to managers in readable and useful formats. Interfacing a personal computer with a mainframe computer allows managers to ask "what-if" questions about master production schedules and estimate MPS effects from the reports and graphics provided.

The techniques that we have presented in this chapter, and those offered by most of the commercial software packages, are *descriptive* in the sense that modifications to the schedule are left to the discretion of the master production scheduler. The techniques only project what may happen *if* the prospective MPS is implemented. They do not prescribe what *should* be done. In the supplement to Chapter 14 we discuss briefly one commercial software package that seeks to find the best master production schedule. It is called Optimized Production Technology (OPT),* and it addresses more than just the MPS. Other prescriptive approaches have been proposed, and, if you are interested, you can pursue some representative studies in the works of Hax and Meal (1975), Newson (1975), and others referred to at the end of this chapter.

* OPT is a registered trademark of Creative Output, Incorporated.

CHAPTER HIGHLIGHTS

In this chapter we addressed the concept of master production scheduling. We limited our discussion to techniques that, by and large, are descriptive rather than prescriptive. Some of the highlights of the chapter are:

- A master production schedule (MPS) expresses the operational plan of production for a specific period of time. It is stated in terms of end items, which may be either shippable products or the highest level assemblies used to build these products eventually.
- The master production scheduling process is iterative. A prospective MPS is developed within the overall guidelines of the production plan. If resources are available, the prospective schedule is authorized for implementation. If not, the prospective

MPS or the production plan has to be changed.

- The primary duty of the master production scheduler is to prepare the master production schedule. Other duties include specifying promise dates for incoming customer orders, evaluating the impact of changes in the MPS, revising the schedule as necessary, and communicating with managers when conflicts arise.
- The techniques used for master production scheduling depend on the competitive priorities of the firm. A master production schedule record for an item typically contains information on ordering policy and manufacturing lead time, as well as gross (or production) requirements, booked customer orders, on-hand inventory balances, available-to-promise quantities, and MPS-receipt and MPS-start quantities for a number of periods in the future. The MPS-receipt information is usually considered to be the master production schedule. The available-to-promise information helps to provide valid promise dates for new customer orders.
- In the rough-cut capacity planning method of overall factors, all direct labor hours for an item are accumulated. This figure multiplied by the master production schedule quantity for the item yields an estimate of overall plant load. The overall load is subdivided into critical and noncritical work station loads. Individual station loads are estimated using historically based percentages.
- Inventory can be positioned forward, backward, or in between, depending on the competitive priorities of the firm. Firms using a make-to-stock strategy typically position inventories at the end-item level, whereas firms using a make-to-order strategy position inventories at the purchased-item level. Firms using an assemble-to-order strategy position inventories at the level of major components or assemblies, to capitalize on commonality of parts for various end-item parents.
- The master production schedule is a useful input to the plans developed by finance and marketing, as well as manufacturing.
- Most major computer vendors and many software companies have developed software packages for the MPS techniques discussed in this chapter.

KEY TERMS

assemble-to-order strategy
available-to-promise (ATP) row
bill of materials (BOM)
disaggregate
end item
gross requirements
intermediate item
make-to-order strategy
make-to-stock strategy
master production schedule (MPS)
MPS-receipt row
MPS-start row
on-hand inventory row
operations process chart
positioning inventory
production requirements
purchased item
rough-cut capacity planning
routing
special item
standard item

STUDY QUESTIONS

1. How does a master production schedule (MPS) differ from a production plan?
2. What is a bill of materials? How is it relevant to master production scheduling?
3. What is the purpose of the MPS?
4. Briefly explain the master production scheduling process to your boss, who has not heard of it before. Why are the alternative schedules called prospective?
5. How can the available-to-promise information in an MPS record be used?
6. Why is the on-hand balance different from the available-to-promise quantity in any given period of time?
7. What are the advantages of linking the MPS to the production plan?
8. If you were a master production scheduler in a company using an assemble-to-order strategy, would you prepare a schedule for end items or some group of intermediate level items? Explain.
9. What are the underlying assumptions of the method of overall factors?
10. Why are inventory positioning and competitive priorities important considerations for master production scheduling?
11. With the help of Fig. 13.11 you found that making the end item a standard item provides the best customer response time. What are the cost implications of such a move?
12. What are the trade-offs in holding safety stock of end items in an MPS?

PROBLEMS

1. Complete the master production schedule record in Table 13.8 for a single item. The gross requirements are actually forecasts. At present there are 20 units in inventory. The production lead time is one week, and each order is for 40 units. No MPS receipts have been released to the shop.
2. The following data apply to an end item.
   - The gross requirements (forecasts) for the next 10 weeks are
     20, 10, 40, 10, 0, 0, 40, 20, 30, 10.
   - The current on-hand quantity is 55 units.
   - The booked customer orders, starting

Table 13.8

Quantity on hand: 20	Week							
	1	2	3	4	5	6	7	8
Gross requirements	10	10	15	15	25	25	30	30
Customer orders (booked)	5	12	4	3	6	0	0	0
On hand								
MPS receipt								
MPS start								
Available to promise								

with week 1, are

30, 20, 5, 8, 0, 0, 0, 0, 0, 0.

- The lead time for this item is 2 weeks.
- No orders for the item have been released.
- The order policy is "order a 2-week supply."

(a) Develop a prospective MPS and calculate the available-to-promise quantities.

(b) A customer needs 35 units of this item. What is the earliest shipping date you could give the customer?

3. The marketing department of NEVED Homehelp Products has forecasted the following demand for the company's two products.

	Jan	Feb	Mar
Home Energy Controller (HEC)	1000	1200	1400
Home Personal Robot (HPR)	120	200	160

The company has 280 units of HEC and 35 units of HPR on hand. Sixty units of HPR are scheduled to be received in the first week of January. The company orders a two-week supply and has a lead time of one week for each product. The company has received the following orders.

	Jan				Feb			
	1	2	3	4	1	2	3	4
HEC	—	260	100	—	400	—	400	370
HPR	45	25	—	—	10	60	—	—

Management likes to have the MPS expressed in weekly time periods and typically allocates monthly forecasts evenly over the weeks in the month. Assume that each month has four weeks.

(a) Develop a prospective MPS for each product.

(b) A potential customer is interested in buying 1000 units of HEC and 100 units of HPR. What is the earliest realistic date that marketing can promise delivery of the HEC units? The HPR units?

(c) The customer has decided to take delivery of the two products at the same time. What is the earliest date that marketing should promise to deliver 1000 units of HEC and 100 units of HPR to the customer?

4. The *production* requirements for a half-horsepower motor for the next 6 weeks are 0, 100, 0, 100, 75, and 75. Marketing has booked orders totaling 40 units in the first (current) week and 30 units in the third week. Currently, there are 50 units of the motor on hand. The ordering policy is to order exactly the quantity to meet production requirements each week. The lead time to assemble this motor from its major components is one week.

(a) Develop the MPS record for the half-horsepower motor.

(b) Suppose that a distributor of the motor places an order for 15 units. What is the appropriate shipping date for the entire order?

5. Complete the MPS record in Table 13.9. There are currently 5 units on hand and the order policy is to produce in lots of 60. The lead time is 2 weeks.

6. The following production plan has been approved for the seismic-sensory product family manufactured at the Hilliard facility of Sloan Automated, Inc.

	Oct	Nov	Dec
Production Plan	120	140	140

There are four products in this product family. The product mix ratio for products A, B, C, and D for the past two years has

Table 13.9

	Week							
Quantity on hand: 5	1	2	3	4	5	6	7	8
Production requirements	60	60	60	60	30	30	30	30
Customer orders (booked)	65	45	30	20	5	5	0	0
On hand								
MPS receipt	60(*R*)	60(*R*)						
MPS start								
Available to promise								

been 24 percent, 20 percent, 36 percent, and 20 percent, respectively. There are 20 units of product B on hand. The company orders a two-week supply and has a one-week lead time for product B. Assume that each month has 4 weeks, prepare a prospective MPS for product B, and calculate the available-to-promise information. The company has already accepted orders of 18, 8, 3, 6, 1, and 2 units of product B in weeks 1–6, respectively.

7. Item A has 6 components: B, C, D, E, F, and G. You have the following information about them.
   - Items D and E are purchased items. They both have a single parent: item B.
   - Items F and G are also purchased items. They both have a single parent: item C.
   - Items B and C are intermediate items. They both have a single parent: item A.

   (a) Draw the bill of materials for item A. Assume that all usage quantities are one-for-one.

   (b) Specify the customer response time in each of the situations (i)–(iii) for the following lead times.

   A: 1 week
   B: 2 weeks
   C: 3 weeks
   D: 3 weeks
   E: 6 weeks
   F: 4 weeks
   G: 3 weeks

   (i) All items are specials.
   (ii) Only item E is a standard.
   (iii) Only items E and F are standard.

8. Consider the bill-of-materials diagram in Fig. 13.12.

   (a) How many parents does item I have? How many parents does item E have?

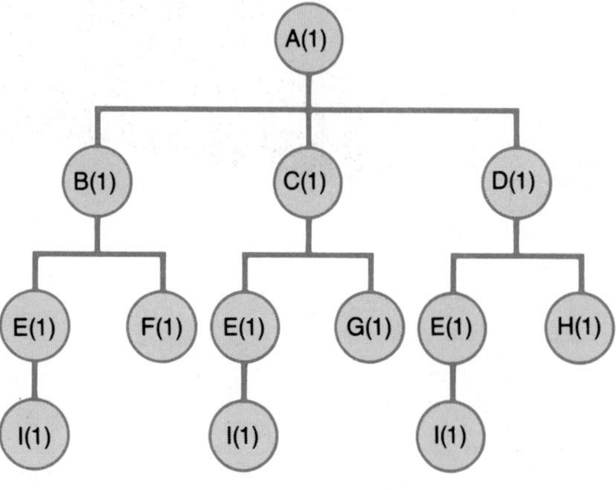

Figure 13.12

(b) How many unique components does item A have?
(c) How many purchased items does item A have?
(d) How many intermediate items does item A have?
(e) The items have the following lead times.

A: 2 weeks
B: 1 week
C: 3 weeks
D: 2 weeks
E: 4 weeks
F: 3 weeks
G: 5 weeks
H: 3 weeks
I: 2 weeks

What is the customer response time if
(i) all items are specials?
(ii) only items E and I are standard?
(iii) only items E, F, G, H, and I are standard?

9. The Acme Rocket Company produces two products. The harness rocket (HR) is designed for quick acceleration and low-level flying in the pursuit of winged delicacies. The shoe rocket (SR) is useful for high-speed chases over long, straight Arizona roads. The following prospective MPS has been proposed.

	Week					
Item	1	2	3	4	5	Total
HR	20	20	20	40	40	140
SR	30	—	30	—	30	90

The direct labor hours per unit are

Item	Critical Work Stations	Noncritical Work Stations	Total
HR	10.0	6.0	16.0
SR	7.2	3.5	10.7

The Acme Rocket Company has two critical work stations: Powder Packing (PP) and Wick Setting (WS). Historically, PP has had 70 percent and WS 30 percent of the critical work station hours.

(a) Create a load profile for weeks 1–5 based on the prospective MPS, using the method of overall factors.
(b) Do you see any potential problems with the prospective schedule? Suppose that the production plan specified a total of 680 labor hours per week, including 420 hours at the critical work stations. Propose a better schedule if you believe that there are problems with the proposed schedule.

Table 13.10

Master Production Schedule

	Month						
Item	Jan	Feb	Mar	Apr	May	Jun	Total
A	50	50	40	40	60	60	300
B	25	—	25	—	25	—	75
C	—	100	—	70	—	120	290

10. The master production scheduler at your company has developed a prospective MPS for the three products your company produces (Table 13.10). There are two critical work stations in the shop: WSA has recorded 40 percent of the hours at the critical work stations, while WSB has recorded the rest. The production plan that you devised has a constant work-force size that yields 820 hours per month, of which 240 hours total are at the critical work stations. Work station WSA has been allocated 96 hours per month, while WSB has been allocated 144 hours. Direct

labor hours per unit are shown in Table 13.11.

(a) Prepare a load profile for the prospective MPS using the method of overall factors. Comment on the feasibility of this schedule.

(b) Prepare an alternative MPS to the one proposed by the master production scheduler that satisfies the labor budget specified in the production plan. Assume that the master production scheduler was operating under the following guidelines.

Month	Cumulative Production Required by End of Month		
	A	B	C
Jan	0	25	0
Feb	100	25	100
Mar	100	50	100
Apr	180	50	170
May	180	75	170
Jun	300	75	290

For example, you need no As in January, but you need 100 by the end of February. Also, no As are needed in March, but by the end of April the cumulative production of A must be 180 because there is a need for 80 units in April. Note that the MPS proposed by the master production scheduler adheres to these guidelines.

Table 13.11

Direct Labor Hours per Unit

Item	Critical Work Stations	Noncritical Work Stations	Total
A	1.0	5.0	6.0
B	2.0	8.0	10.0
C	3.0	2.0	5.0

SELECTED REFERENCES

Bahl, H. C., and L. P. Ritzman, "An Empirical Investigation of Different Strategies for Material Requirements Planning," *Journal of Operations Management*, vol. 3, no. 2 (1983), pp. 67–77.

Berry, W. L., T. G. Schmitt, and T. E. Vollmann, "Capacity Planning Techniques for Manufacturing Control Systems: Information Requirements and Operational Features," *Journal of Operations Management*, vol. 3, no. 1 (November 1982), pp. 13–25.

Berry, W. L., T. E. Vollmann, and D. C. Whybark, *Master Production Scheduling: Principles and Practices*. Falls Church, Va.: American Production and Inventory Control Society, Inc., 1979.

Bitran, G. R., and A. C. Hax, "On the Design of Hierarchical Production Planning Systems," *Decision Sciences*, vol. 8, no. 1 (January 1977), pp. 28–25.

Chung, C. H., and L. Krajewski, "Planning Horizons for Master Production Scheduling," *Journal of Operations Management*, vol. 4, no. 4 (August 1984).

Everdell, R., and W. Chamberlain, "Master Scheduling in a Multi-Plant Environment," *Proceedings of the 23rd Annual American Production and Inventory Control Society Conference*. Los Angeles (October 14–17, 1980), pp. 421–429.

Hax, A. C., and H. C. Meal, "Hierarchical Integration of Production Planning and Scheduling." In M. A. Geisler (Ed.), *Studies in Management Sciences*, vol. 1, *Logistics*. New York: North Holland-American Elsevier, 1975, pp. 53–69.

Lasdon, L. S., and R. C. Terjung, "An Efficient Algorithm for Multi-Item Scheduling," *Operations Research,* vol. 19, no. 4 (July–August 1971) pp. 946–969.

Ling, R., "Master Scheduling in a Make-to-Order Environment," *Inventories and Production,* vol. 1, no. 3 (July–August 1981), pp. 17–21.

Mangiameli, P., and L. Krajewski, "The Effects of Workforce Strategies on Manufacturing Operations," *Journal of Operations Management,* vol. 3, no. 4 (August 1983), pp. 183–196.

Newson, E. P., "Multi-Item Lot Size Scheduling by Heuristic, Part I: With Fixed Resources; Part II: With Variable Resources," *Management Science,* vol. 21, no. 10 (June 1975), pp. 1186–1203.

Orlicky, J., *Material Requirements Planning.* New York: McGraw-Hill, 1975.

Proud, J. F., "Controlling the Master Schedule," *Production and Inventory Management,* vol. 22, no. 2 (Second Quarter 1981), pp. 78–90.

Wight, O., *Production and Inventory Management in the Computer Age.* Boston: Cahners Books, 1974.

Zoller, K., "Optimal Disaggregation of Aggregate Plans," *Management Science,* vol. 17, no. 8 (April 1971), pp. B533–B547.

CHAPTER 14

MATERIALS REQUIREMENTS PLANNING

Some Managerial Issues

- What information is available from MRP systems that will help us to manage materials better?
- Is MRP appropriate for our firm? Who benefits the most from MRP systems?
- What prerequisites do we have to meet to successfully implement MRP?
- Can we use MRP for nonmanufacturing inventories?
- How can we couple MRP with other decision areas?
- How important is our choice of lot sizing strategy?

Chapter Outline

Development and authorization of a master production schedule supposedly means that all needed materials and other resources can be made available at the right time to produce finished products on schedule. This is easier said than done because manufacturers may have to keep track of thousands of components, assemblies, and raw materials. These inventory items experience *dependent* demand because their demand is dependent on the production plans for their parent items. An order for a parent cannot be completed if even one of its components is missing. These parent–component relationships, which are expressed in bills of materials (see Chapter 13), introduce complexity into inventory management.

Your first thought might be that we could use the reorder point system to manage dependent-demand inventory. Recall, however, that in Chapter 12 we stated that the reorder point system (also called the continuous review or *Q* system) should be used only for *independent*-demand items. Many companies unadvisedly continue to use this system to manage dependent-demand items, and the outcomes are seldom happy, as the example in Box 14.1 shows.

SHORTCOMINGS OF REORDER POINT SYSTEMS

Reorder point systems have several shortcomings when applied to dependent-demand inventory. Let's begin with Fig. 14.1, which helps to explain the reorder point system shortcomings for King Manufacturing. Production orders to replenish the inventories of both items A and B are released whenever inventory levels reach the reorder points.* Note that the inventory level depletes at a uniform, predictable rate for these two items. However, the demand pattern for item C is much different. Demand appears in chunks of 120, 150, or 270 units at a time. The *average* is still 50 units per week, but in many weeks there is no demand. Consequently, item C inventory does not approach the reorder point slowly—it plunges right past the reorder point. In week 7, the quantity of item C falls precipitously from an inventory balance of 240 units to a stockout of 30 units. An order for item C is issued immediately, but it takes two weeks to complete. Item A is the parent item shortchanged in this instance. Production of A is delayed until week 9, when the components are finally available. It takes another week to produce the 150 units of A. Consequently, item A suffers a stockout as well.

What went wrong? First, the assumption of a uniform, continuous demand rate is unrealistic, as it is in most dependent-demand situations. Typically, component demand is lumpy because of production lot-size decisions made for parent items. Forecasting lumpy demand using statistical methods results in large forecast errors. Compensating for this lack of predictability by increasing safety stock is costly, and even then there is no guarantee that stockouts will be avoided.

Second, the assumption of independence among the inventory items is incorrect. Dependent-demand items are linked through bills of materials. Reorder point systems fail to recognize that the production schedules of parent items become the requirements schedules for the components, assemblies, and raw materials needed to make the parent items. Item C demand is based on the production schedules of its parents, A and B. Since the production schedules are set by management, why not use the information in them to manage the inventories of components or subassemblies such as item C? Reorder point systems do not use this information.

Finally the reorder point system provides no forward visibility for planning purposes. Recall that reorder points and safety stocks are derived by looking to the past and assuming that it is a good predictor of future requirements. Under this premise, no information beyond the present (such as an MPS) is available for planning purposes. Actually, if the demand for item C were uniform and predictable, there would be no need to look beyond the

* Since the lead time for stock replenishment is so short, on-hand inventory equals the inventory position (except during the lead time) in this example. No scheduled receipts are outstanding when an order is placed.

Box 14.1

A TRADITIONAL INVENTORY MANAGEMENT SYSTEM IN TROUBLE

King Manufacturing is privately owned and makes office furniture. Although a few products are made to customer order, virtually all the 5000 inventoried items at King are made to stock. During the last five years, King Manufacturing has added many new products, making inventory management more complex. Fred Neff, the new vice-president of operations, has become increasingly concerned about bloated inventories, long manufacturing lead times, an excessive number of past-due customer orders, and the amount of overtime being worked. To get at the core of the problem, Fred called a meeting with the production and inventory control (P&IC) manager and shop superintendent.

The Formal System

Fred's first question was, "How are production and purchase orders being placed?" Barbara Jones, the P&IC manager, explained the system, using some examples.

"We make many products, but let's take two desk chairs as examples. For simplicity, let's call them items A and B. The average demand for item A is 30 chairs per week. It takes one week to assemble all the components into the final product. Based on the demand-during-lead-time distribution, we have determined that a safety stock of 30 units will give us a fill rate of 95 percent. (See Chapter 12.) The economic order quantity for this product is 150 units. The reorder point is 60 or [30(1) + 30] units. Whenever inventory gets down to 60 units, we order 150 units.

"The logic for controlling item B is similar. Its average weekly demand is 20 units, the lead time to produce a batch of item B is also one week, and a safety stock of 20 units should give us a fill rate of 95 percent. The order quantity is 120 units. Whenever inventory gets down to 40 units, we order 120 units.

"Both items A and B require a pedestal assembly, called item C. Each unit of A or B requires one unit of C. Since the demand for A and B totals 50

present. Unfortunately, dependent-demand situations rarely allow this luxury. If Barbara had known the schedules for A and B, she could have predicted in week 1 that there would be trouble in week 7. Since the lead time for C is only two weeks, there would have been sufficient time to produce enough C to avoid the stockout.

Table 14.1 shows how Barbara could have calculated the on-hand inventory for item C had she made use of the production schedules of items A and B. What is needed is a better way to integrate the information already available, so that better estimates of future requirements for dependent-demand items can be made. Materials requirements planning is one such approach.

units per week and is fairly uniform, we have set up a reorder point for item C so that whenever the inventory gets down to 150 units, we order 230 units. The order quantity is based on the EOQ. The lead time to produce a batch of item C is two weeks. We figure that our system will give us a 95 percent fill rate for this item too.

"The system works in the following way. Whenever the reorder point for A is reached, we issue a requisition order for C in the amount of 150 units. We cannot start production of A until components for all 150 units are available. When C (and the other components of A) are available, we take one week to make the batch of item A. The process is similar for item B."

The Informal System

Fred Neff turned to the shop superintendent, Bill Hardy, asking whether he saw any problems with this approach. Bill launched into a heated explanation of how they *really* got production out.

"When the production orders for A and B are received, along with the routings and bills of materials (see Chapter 13), the components and raw materials are withdrawn from the stockroom. Almost invariably, several components are missing. A high priority is placed on getting these components into stock. Normally, these components have already been ordered and now it is a matter of expediting them. If the jobs are in the shop, a red tag is attached to the job order to indicate high priority. Unfortunately, most jobs on the shop floor have red tags. If the material is purchased, a call is made to the purchasing manager who in turn contacts the supplier. It seems like we are always expediting some order."

At the end of the meeting, Fred could not identify the real problem. Why didn't the reorder point system work? It seemed logical enough, but there apparently were many more stockouts than the 95 percent fill rates would imply. What could be wrong?

BASICS OF MATERIALS REQUIREMENTS PLANNING

During the past decade many manufacturing firms have switched from traditional reorder point systems to MRP systems. Impetus for change came from the American Production and Inventory Control Society, led by such pioneers as Joseph Orlicky (1975), George Plossl (1973), and Oliver Wight (1979). **Materials requirements planning** (MRP) is a computerized information system for managing dependent-demand inventory and scheduling stock replenishment

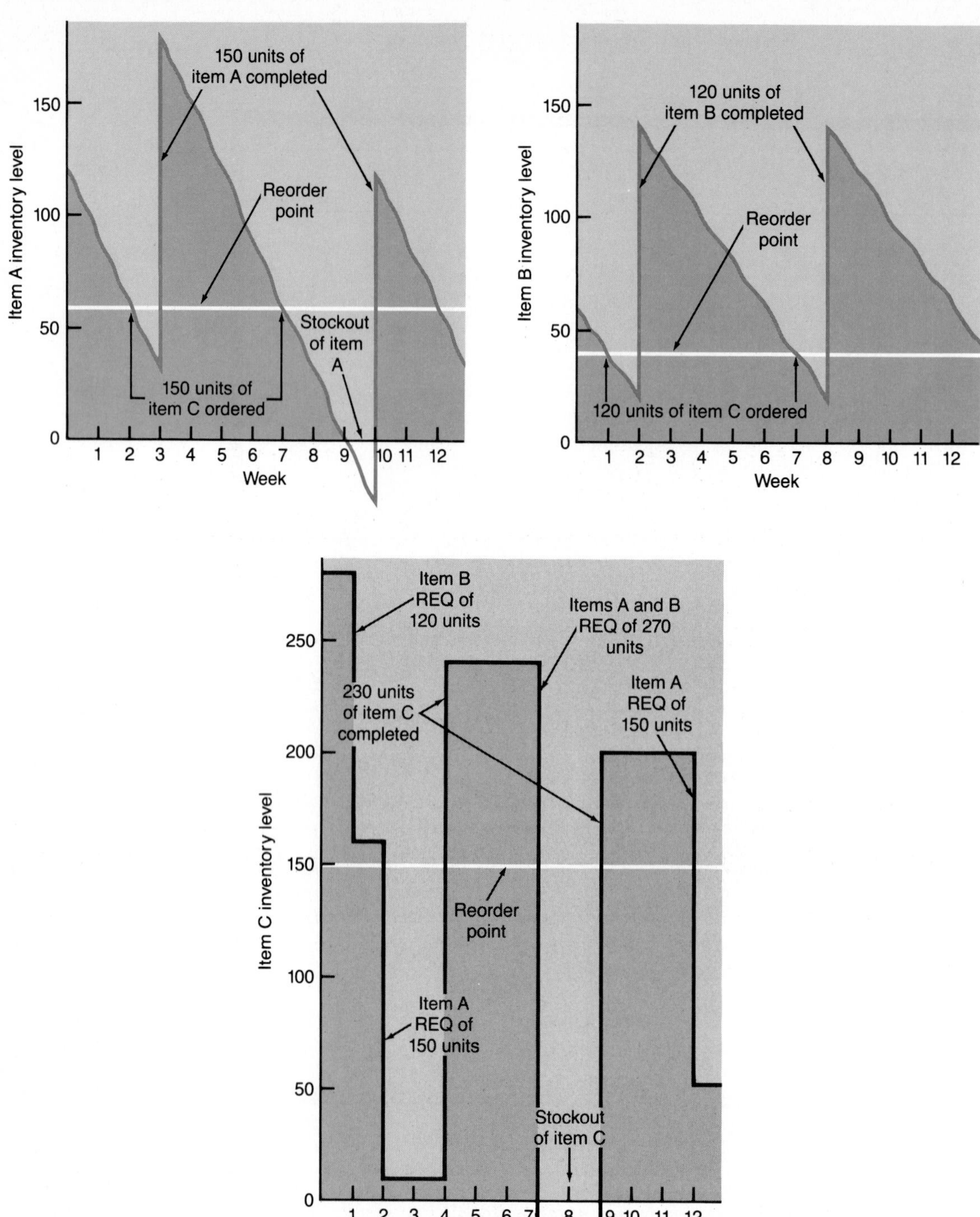

Figure 14.1

Application of the Reorder Point System to Dependent-Demand Inventory.

Table 14.1

Projecting the On-Hand Inventory for Item C

Week (t)	On-Hand Inventory in Week $t - 1$	+ Scheduled Receipts	− Scheduled Production of A and B in Week t	= On-Hand Inventory in Week t	Comments
1	50	230	120	160	Item B withdraws 120 units of C.
2	160	0	150	10	Item A withdraws 150 units of C. Order placed for 230 units of C.
3	10	0	0	10	No demand for C.
4	10	230	0	240	Order for C arrives.
5	240	0	0	240	No demand for C.
6	240	0	0	240	No demand for C.
7	240	0	−270	−30	Item B withdraws 120 units. Item A demands 150 units, but there is insufficient inventory.

orders. It is based on two principles that set it apart from reorder point systems:

1. Dependent demand for components, subassemblies, and raw materials is *calculated* from the production schedules of their parents, in contrast to the statistical forecasting methods used in reorder point systems.
2. Replenishment orders (production schedules, purchase orders) are *time phased* relative to the date they are needed. That is, if we need to replenish the stock of an item in week 5 to avoid a stockout and the lead time is 3 weeks, we would plan to issue the order in week 2. This is analogous to the determination of the MPS-start date in the master production schedule record. (See Chapter 13.) In reorder point systems, however, we wait until a reorder point is reached and then issue an order, oblivious to specific needs in the future.

We can best describe these two principles by examining the ways in which the inventory status of an item is recorded, a replenishment order is determined, and the item demand is computed.

Inventory Status Record

There is no standard format for an **inventory status record,** but the top of the record typically identifies the part number and describes the item. Two planning factors, the preassigned lead time and lot-sizing rule, are shown in the upper right corner. The main body of the record divides the future into several time periods, called *time buckets,* which normally represent weeks but could be expressed in days or months. The body of the record contains information about gross requirements, scheduled receipts, on-hand balances, net requirements, and planned order releases.

Gross Requirements. Figure 14.2 shows a partial inventory status record for a desk chair seat produced by King Manufacturing. The item has only two parent items, MZ104 and MY114, which are different styles of chairs. The master production schedule calls for production to start on 100 units of MZ104 and 50 units of MY114 in week 1. Since only one seat is required per chair, the gross requirements for the seat in week 1 is 150 units. Note that the gross

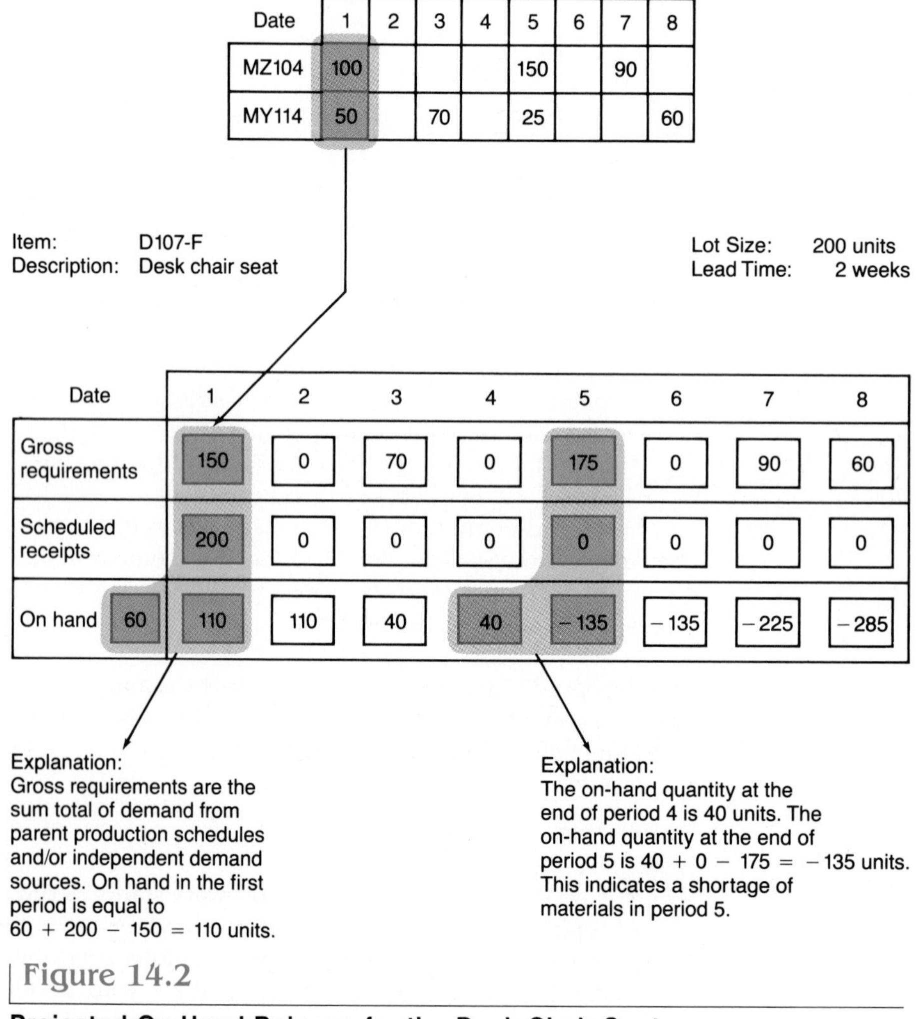

Figure 14.2

Projected On-Hand Balance for the Desk Chair Seat.

requirements for chair seats exhibit lumpy demand; inventory withdrawals are to be made in only five of the eight weeks.

Scheduled Receipts. If the item is purchased, the open order could be in one of several stages, such as being ordered by a buyer, being processed by the vendor, being in transit, or being inspected by the receiving department. If the item is made in-house, the open order would be on the shop floor being processed, waiting for components, waiting in queue, or waiting to be moved to its next operation. Figure 14.2 shows that there is one scheduled receipt for seats due in week 1. Since its lead time is two weeks, and it is due in the current week, the order probably was released two weeks ago by an inventory planner.

On Hand. The first entry of 60 units shows the beginning on-hand inventory.* This entry must be carefully updated with each new withdrawal and receipt, so as to avoid inaccurate records. The other entries reflect expected inventory levels in future weeks, if no additional orders are placed. The inventory in week t equals the beginning inventory (inventory balance in week $t - 1$) plus the quantity to be received (scheduled receipt in week t) minus the quantity to be withdrawn (gross requirement in week t). For example, the on-hand inventory in week 3 is 40 (or $110 + 0 - 70$) units. One unusual feature of the on-hand row is that it can contain negative quantities in later weeks. You should interpret these numbers as the cumulative deficit in inventory that will occur if we rely only on the current on-hand inventory and future scheduled receipts. For example, the deficit grows from −135 units in week 6 to −285 units in week 8 owing to the gross requirements in weeks 7 and 8. The projected cumulative deficit provides the inventory planner with an estimate of the total number of units that still must be produced or purchased, as the case may be.

Net Requirements. Figure 14.3 contains the complete inventory status record for the desk chair seat. The net requirements reflect distribution of the cumulative deficit to specific time periods. Computation of net requirements is based on two simple rules: (1) to find the first net requirement, scan the on-hand row to find the first deficit, eliminate the negative sign, and make this quantity the first net requirement; and (2) to find the net requirements in subsequent periods, merely equate them to the gross requirements in the same period.

Planned Order Releases. All the computations so far lead to the planned order releases row in the inventory status record. **Planned order releases** (PORs) indicate how we will cover projected net requirements. The POR row is important because (1) it indicates whether an order release is necessary

* In this example we assume that there is no safety stock. We discuss the procedure for incorporating safety stock in the inventory status record later in this chapter.

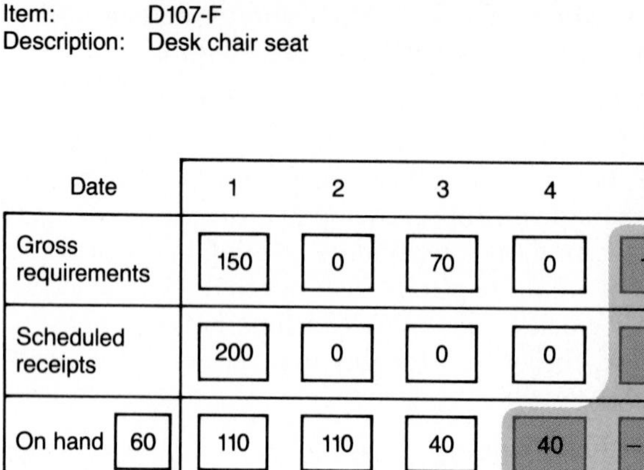

Item: D107-F
Description: Desk chair seat

Lot Size: 200 units
Lead Time: 2 weeks

Date		1	2	3	4	5	6	7	8
Gross requirements		150	0	70	0	175	0	90	60
Scheduled receipts		200	0	0	0	0	0	0	0
On hand	60	110	110	40	40	−135	−135	−225	−285
Net requirements						135		90	60
Planned order releases				200		200			

Explanation:
The first net requirement is in period 5. With a 2-week lead time, we will release the order in period 3. This order will cover the net requirements in periods 5, 6, and part of period 7.

Explanation:
Since there are 40 units of inventory but no scheduled receipts, net requirements are 175 − 40 = 135.

Explanation:
There is no inventory or scheduled receipts coming into period 7. Net requirements are equal to gross requirements.

Figure 14.3

MRP Inventory Record for the Desk Chair Seat.

before the next regular inventory review; and (2) it specifies the timing of gross requirements for any components in the same way the schedules for MZ104 and MY114 determined the gross requirements for D107-F in Fig. 14.2. This latter use of PORs is essential in identifying the requirements for dependent-demand items and lies at the heart of the first principle of MRP.

Two decisions are involved: the timing and the size of each new release. With respect to the timing decision, the first net requirement occurs in week 5, when a new POR must be *completed*. Since the lead time for seats is 2 weeks, the POR must be released in week 3. This approach is the *time phasing* referred to in the second principle of MRP. In this example we used the *midpoint convention* when doing our time phasing; that is, we assume that withdrawals and receipts occur at the middle of the week. If receipts tend to occur at the end of the week and withdrawals at the beginning, and this difference is not reflected in the lead-time estimate, we should move the timing of orders back one more week. For uniformity, we continue to use the midpoint convention for the remainder of this chapter.

Now that we have determined the timing of the first POR, the second decision concerns its size. The lot-sizing rule in Fig. 14.3 calls for each POR to be 200 units. This is one of several possible rules. Management feels that a lot size of 200 units is reasonable, for one of any number of reasons. We discuss other lot-sizing rules later in this chapter.

The final step is to plan for any additional PORs that might be needed. The first order of 200 units covers the cumulative deficit through week 6 (see the on-hand row) but falls 25 units short in week 7. A second order should be received in this week. Offsetting by the two-week lead time produces a second POR for week 5.

This completes the processing logic needed for the computer for a given inventory record. Each row is computed sequentially, but there is a temptation to recompute the scheduled receipts and on-hand rows after the PORs are planned. For example, we could show a scheduled receipt of 200 in week 5 and then revise the on-hand inventory balance in the same week to 65. This not only creates extra work but is misleading. The scheduled receipt in week 1 has actually been released. The POR planned for receipt in week 5 has not been released. It should not appear as a scheduled receipt until acted on by an inventory planner. Otherwise, there would be two apparently scheduled receipts and no need to release a new order in week 3.

Safety Stock

In our previous examples, we avoided the use of safety stock, but it can be easily incorporated into the inventory status record. Figure 14.4 illustrates how safety stock is handled by MRP logic. In this example a safety stock of 20 units is to be maintained. Net requirements and PORs are now computed to prevent the projected on-hand inventory from dropping below 20 units (rather than zero). The on-hand balance drops below 20 units in week 27, generating a net requirement of 15 units. This condition leads to a POR in week 24. Without a safety stock requirement, there would be no net requirement in week 27 or POR in week 24. Note also that the second POR must be released in week 28. Without its receipt in week 31, the inventory would drop to only 15 units (the 25-unit deficit shown in the on-hand row, plus the 40-unit POR planned for release in week 24).

Although the mechanics are available for including safety stock in the computations, the managerial issue is how much safety stock to build. The answer is not as clear as that for independent-demand items. (See Chapter 12.) Excessive safety stock for dependent-demand items, particularly for

Item: B149 Description: Table legs										Lot Size: 40 units Lead Time: 3 weeks Safety Stock: 20 units		
Date		21	22	23	24	25	26	27	28	29	30	31	32
Gross requirements		20		37				20				30	30
Scheduled receipts				40									
On hand	42	22	22	25	25	25	25	5	5	5	5	−25	−55
Net requirements								15				30	30
POR					40				40				

Figure 14.4

MRP Record with Safety Stock.

those with lumpy demand (gross requirements), is of little value. It is probably better to use safety stock only when there is considerable uncertainty about future gross requirements or the timing or size of scheduled receipts. The usual consequence of this policy is that safety stock would be provided for items mainly at the master production scheduling and purchasing levels. This approach protects against customer order uncertainties at the top of the product structure (the end item level) and unreliable vendors at the bottom (the purchased item level). For the remainder of this chapter we assume that no safety stock is required.

Lot-Sizing Strategies

The computer logic for MRP requires that a lot-sizing rule be preassigned to each item; only then can the POR row be computed. Many types of rules are possible, but we will examine only three basic ones: **fixed order quantity** (FOQ), **lot for lot** (L4L), and **periodic order quantity** (POQ). All such rules can be categorized as either *static* or *dynamic*.

Static Lot Sizing. The **static lot-sizing rules** are exemplified by the FOQ rule: Each new order is for the same number of units. The lot size could be predetermined by the economic order quantity (EOQ) formula. (See Chapter 12.) Alternatively, the lot size could be the container size dictated by materials handling constraints or by upper limits on equipment capacity, such as when a full lot must be loaded into a furnace at one time. For purchased items, the FOQ could be set at the quantity discount level, or it could be equal to a carload or truckload capacity.

Figure 14.5(a) shows the use of the FOQ logic for another item (a table top) produced by King Manufacturing. The FOQ is the economic order quantity for this item. The first net requirement occurs in week 3. Since the lead time is two weeks, the order for 70 units should be released in week 1. The supply from this order will satisfy net requirements through week 7, but will be 45 units short in week 8. That is why the second POR is scheduled for Week 6.

In some cases, the FOQ may not be sufficient to cover the net requirement in a week of heavy demand. The POR must be increased beyond the FOQ either to the net requirement level or possibly to an integer multiple of the FOQ.

Dynamic Lot Sizing. The **dynamic lot-sizing rules** make the order quantity equal to net requirements for a specified number of weeks. The rules are dynamic because the lot size can vary each time an order is placed. One such rule is the POQ rule. This rule makes the POR equal to P weeks of net requirements. One way to select a P value is to divide a desirable average lot size (such as the EOQ) by the average weekly demand.* In Fig. 14.5(b), gross requirements average 17.5 units per week. Dividing this volume into the EOQ of 70 units gives a P value of 4 weeks. Thus each POR has a lot size equal to the sum of the net requirements for 4 weeks, beginning with the week in which the POR must be received.† The first net requirement is for 5 units in week 3. The net requirements for weeks 3, 4, 5, and 6 sum to 45 units. The first order is scheduled for release in week 1 to reflect the two-week lead time. The next order covers weeks 7, 8, 9, and 10 and must be for 80 units. Note that the order quantities change from order to order.

A special case of the POQ rule is the L4L rule. Here, $P = 1$, which makes the POR the same as the net requirement of the single week it covers. In Fig. 14.5(c), the L4L rule results in six orders, one for each net requirement.

Comparison of Lot-Sizing Rules. Choosing a lot-sizing strategy can have important implications for inventory management. In Fig. 14.5, a new row, *net inventory available,* was added for comparative purposes. This row shows what the inventory balance should be if the order quantities are released and received as expected. Three conclusions can be drawn from this example:

1. The FOQ rule generates a higher level of average inventory because it creates inventory *remnants*. A remnant is inventory carried into a week but is of insufficient quantity to cover the week's net requirement. Remnants occur because the FOQ does not exactly match the net requirements.

---

* The reasons and methods for selecting P in this context are similar to some of those discussed in Chapter 12 regarding periodic review systems.

† A slightly different version of the POQ rule is to place an order every four weeks (even if the order comes in before it is needed). This approach equalizes the time between orders, but can result in somewhat higher inventory.

Item: C128-Z
Description: Table Top

Lot Size: 70 units
Lead Time: 2 weeks
Safety Stock: 0 units

Date	1	2	3	4	5	6	7	8	9	10	11	12	Total	Results
Gross req.	30		10		40		20	50		10		50	210	1. Three orders will be placed. 2. Average inventory of 26 units (310/12).
Sched. rec.													0	
On hand 35	5	5	−5	−5	−45	−45	−65	−115	−115	−125	−125	−175	−175	
Net req.			5		40		20	50		10		50	175	
POR	70					70				70			210	
Net inventory available	5	5	65	65	25	25	5	25	25	15	15	35	310	

(a)

Date	1	2	3	4	5	6	7	8	9	10	11	12	Total	Results
Gross req.	30		10		40		20	50		10		50	210	1. Three orders will be placed. 2. Average inventory of 14 units (170/12).
Sched. rec.													0	
On hand 35	5	5	−5	−5	−45	−45	−65	−115	−115	−125	−125	−175	−175	
Net req.			5		40		20	50		10		50	175	
POR	45				80					50			175	
Net inventory available	5	5	40	40	0	0	60	10	10	0	0	0	170	

(b)

Date	1	2	3	4	5	6	7	8	9	10	11	12	Total	Results
Gross req.	30		10		40		20	50		10		50	210	1. Six orders will be placed. 2. Less than 1 unit of average inventory. (10/12).
Sched. rec.													0	
On hand 35	5	5	−5	−5	−45	−45	−65	−115	−115	−125	−125	−175	−175	
Net req.			5		40		20	50		10		50	175	
POR	5		40		20	50		10		50			175	
Net inventory available	5	5	0	0	0	0	0	0	0	0	0	0	10	

(c)

Figure 14.5

Comparison of FOQ, POQ, and L4L Rules: (a) Using FOQ Rule for 70 Units; (b) Using POQ Rule for 4-Week Supply; (c) Using L4L Rule for 1-Week Supply.

2. The POQ reduces the amount of inventory on hand because it does a better job of matching the order quantity to net requirements. It increases lot sizes as requirements increase, or vice versa.
3. The L4L rule minimizes inventory investment but maximizes the number of orders placed. This rule is useful for expensive items or items having small ordering or setup costs.

In general, static lot-sizing rules create inventory remnants but introduce some stability into the production process. Inventory remnants can act as a buffer against unexpected scrap losses, capacity bottlenecks, inaccurate inventory records, or unstable gross requirements. Dynamic rules, in contrast, reduce inventory levels by avoiding remnants but can introduce instability by tying the lot-size decision closely to net requirements. If any net requirement changes, so must the lot size. This can cause trouble when you are trying to plan the gross requirements of a component.

Level-by-Level Processing

We can now be more specific about obtaining gross requirements. We can derive an item's gross requirements from three sources: the MPS-start row for parents in the MPS, the POR row for parents below the MPS level, and any other requirements not originating in the MPS. In order to accumulate the gross requirements for a particular component we must start at the master production schedule and work downward through the bills of materials, calculating the PORs of all items as we go, until all the PORs of the component's parents have been determined. This procedure is called **level-by-level processing.**

To effectively accomplish this procedure on a computer, we assign a number called a *level code* to each item. For example, all MPS items are assigned to level 0. Those components having an MPS item as an immediate parent are assigned to level 1. Their components are assigned to level 2, and so on. Sometimes, an item is found at different levels in a number of bills of materials. In that case the item is assigned to the *lowest level* (highest code number) found in any bill of materials. Each item has only one level code. The computer then proceeds level-by-level, each time checking to be sure that all items with lower code numbers (at higher levels) have been processed before accumulating the gross requirements for an item.

Figure 14.6 shows an example of level-by-level processing. Item A4, which is a shelf used in two wall units produced by King Manufacturing, exists at two levels: (1) as a component of G2, an MPS item; and (2) as a component of R1, which is itself a component. Consequently, we assign A4 a level code of 2. Thus we have to wait until the PORs of all level 1 items are processed before we can process A4. After we have accomplished this step

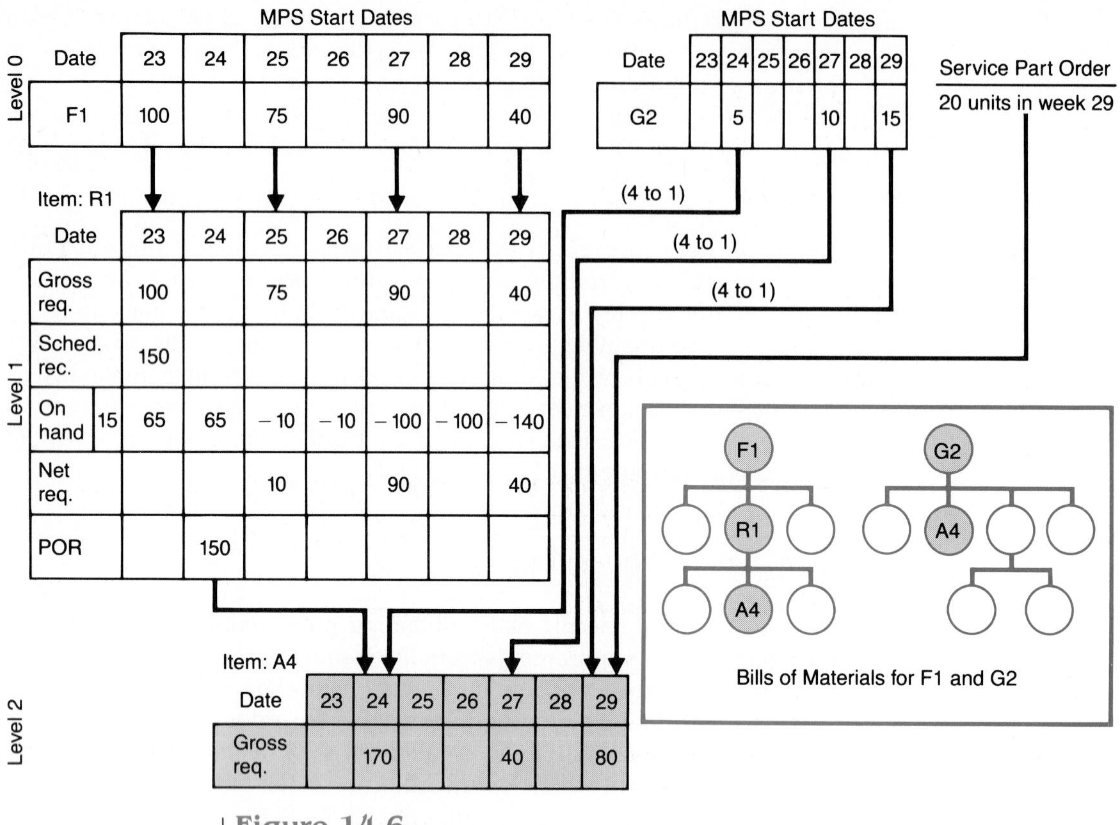

Figure 14.6

Deriving Gross Requirements for A4.

and have determined the POR of 150 in week 24 for R1, we can begin to compute the gross requirements for A4. Note that we need 4 units of A4 for each unit of G2. There is also a service-part order for A4 of 20 units in week 29. Combined, they result in the gross requirements shown for A4.

MATERIALS REQUIREMENTS PLANNING AS AN INFORMATION SYSTEM

Knowing the basic concepts of MRP, we can now turn to its larger context: MRP is a computerized information system. Figure 14.7 shows that MRP translates four basic inputs into several outputs that aid decision making in a variety of materials management areas.

Inputs

The first input is the *authorized master production schedule,* which is the driving force of MRP. Materials requirements planning provides information needed for releasing new orders, adjusting priorities, and revising capacities to implement the master production schedule. The master production schedule, in turn, is linked to higher level plans for marketing and production strategies.

Inventory records are the second input. The basic building blocks for maintaining up-to-date records are inventory transactions. Planners make transactions when they release new orders or adjust due dates for scheduled receipts. Other transactions include reporting the completion of scheduled receipts, withdrawing inventory, canceling orders, correcting inventory inac-

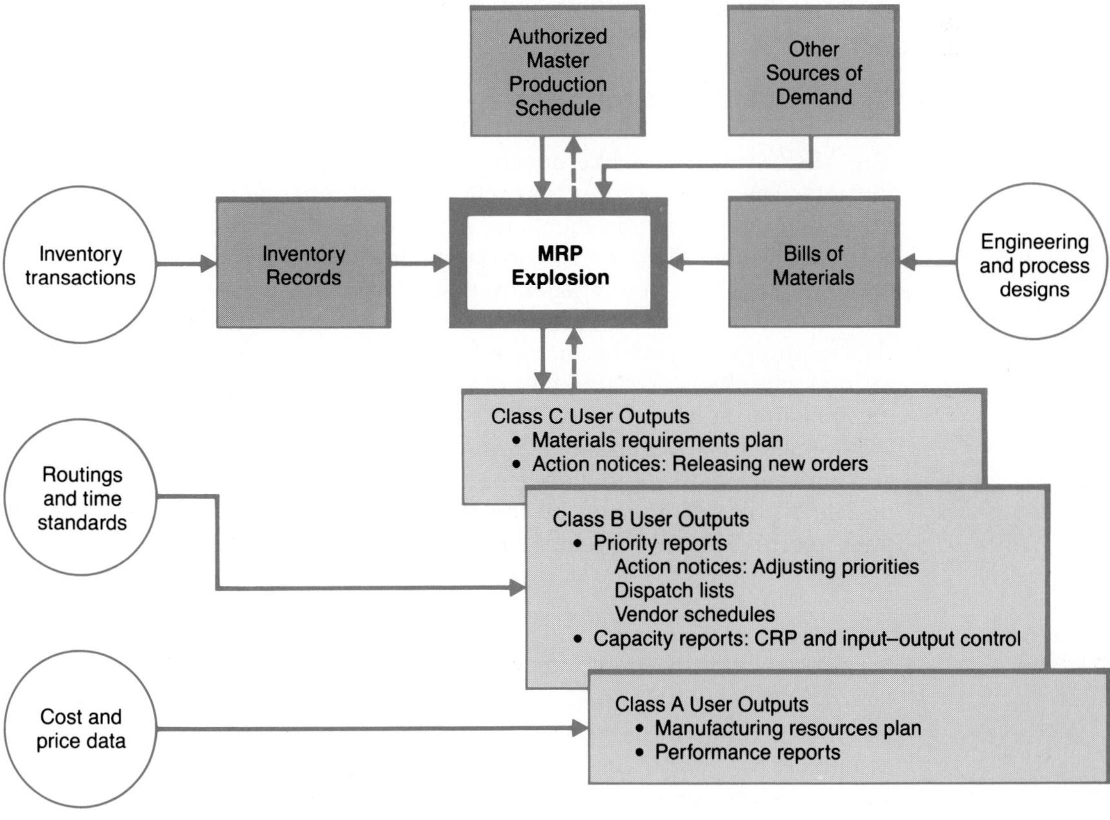

Figure 14.7

Overview of MRP Systems.

curacies, rejecting shipments, and verifying scrap losses and stock returns. The recording of such transactions is essential for keeping accurate records, particularly of on-hand inventory balances and the status of scheduled receipts. Without accurate records, an MRP system cannot be as effective.

Bills of materials, the third input, are derived from engineering and process designs. Materials requirements planning derives an item's gross requirements from the PORs of its parents, so BOM information about the item's parents and their usage quantities must be known.

Other sources of demand not reflected in the master production schedule are the final input. For example, items lower in the bills of materials are sometimes needed as service parts to replace worn-out parts in the field. This source of demand, in addition to the MPS, must be satisfied by the materials requirements plan. External orders from other plants or warehouses, or units needed for quality control purposes (such as destructive testing), may not be reflected in the master production schedule.

Types of MRP Systems

The MRP system acts like an engine to transform the inputs into usable outputs. The master production schedule and other sources of demand are translated into the requirements for all the components, assemblies, and raw materials needed to produce the required products. This process is sometimes called an *explosion.* In a **regenerative MRP system,** all inventory records are recomputed periodically, typically on a weekly basis. After a week, the materials requirements plan becomes outdated. A new explosion therefore is performed with the latest MPS, bills of materials, and information on scheduled receipts and on-hand balances. In a **net change MRP system,** the materials requirements plan is updated continuously. With each change in the MPS and with each new transaction, a partial explosion is executed immediately to update all records affected by the change. Net change systems tend to be preferred in the more dynamic manufacturing environments.

Outputs

Figure 14.7 shows that there can be several levels of outputs, depending on whether a company is a class C, class B, or class A user. Class C users essentially use MRP to determine when to release orders and for nothing else. They make no attempt to require the system to detect problems such as materials shortages caused by late receipt of vendor shipments.

Class B users strive to detect problems in the materials and capacity plans with *closed-loop control.* The dotted lines in Fig. 14.7 are feedback loops, representing planning activities that adjust the materials plan and, if necessary, the

MPS, to cope with difficulties not anticipated in the MRP logic. Closed-loop control is made possible by the *additional* outputs shown for class B users: priority reports and capacity reports.

Class A users are the most sophisticated users of MRP. In addition to priority reports and capacity reports, class A users require management reports that project the dollar value of shipments, product costs, overhead allocations, inventories, backlogs, and profits. Time-phased information from the MPS, scheduled receipts, and PORs can be converted into cash flow projections, broken down by product families. For example, MRP inventory records allow us to project the number of units to be held in inventory during future periods. We can then convert these projections into inventory dollars simply by knowing the per-unit cost of each item. We can then sum these amounts for all items belonging to the same product family. Similar computations are possible for other performance measures of interest to management.

Sometimes referred to as *MRP II* or *manufacturing resource planning* (see Wight, 1979), these additional outputs help tie the MRP system to the company's financial system. They give focus to meetings involving key managers of the firm representing manufacturing, purchasing, marketing, finance, or engineering. The reports help these managers to develop and monitor the overall business plan and recognize sales objectives, manufacturing capabilities, and cash flow constraints.

Since almost every MRP user makes use of some type of action notice and class A and B users make use of capacity reports, we will consider each of these outputs in more detail.

Action Notices. Inventory records (see Fig. 14.3) must be computed for each item appearing in the bills of materials. These records together represent the current *materials requirements plan.* Updating it is a massive data processing job, which is done by computer and typically takes 4–8 hours over each weekend. Thus the materials requirements plan is available at the beginning of the week to assist inventory planners make decisions during that week. A list of **action notices** can be generated for the items assigned to each planner, allowing the planner to focus on urgent problems and to manage by exception. One type of action notice is a basic feature of most MRP systems. It calls attention to those items for which a new order release is needed during the current period. A second type of action notice calls attention to those items for which scheduled receipts are arriving at the wrong time (too early or too late). Such action notices on misaligned due dates are a basic building block for priority planning, which is limited to class A and class B users.

With regard to the first type of action notices, the computer detects that it is time to release a new order simply by examining the first week's entry in the POR row. If there is a nonzero quantity in this time bucket, an action notice is printed out. An action notice would not be generated for the item in Fig. 14.3, but one would be issued for each case in Fig. 14.5.

Although the computer generates such action notices, the final *decision* rests with the inventory planner. The planner would first review the item's complete inventory record, along with those of its components. If component inventory is available to support the order, the planner would usually decide to release the order as planned. The planner would input an *inventory transaction* to change the computer record file by adding a new scheduled receipt with its quantity and due date. The next time the materials requirements plan is generated, this new order would show up in the scheduled receipts row. The planner also performs other activities when releasing a new order, such as preparing documentation for tool requisitions, routings, or parts lists. For purchased items, a requisition is sent to the appropriate buyer, who in turn places the order with a vendor. These purchasing activities also are often computer assisted.

At times the planner might deviate from the lot size or timing specified in this week's POR. For example, an action notice might be issued for the situation where the number of weeks to the first net requirement is less than the planned lead time for an item. In effect, an order should have been placed last week or even earlier. This undesirable condition should happen less frequently with MRP than with the system used at King Manufacturing. It can occur occasionally owing to unexpected scrap losses in open orders, last-minute changes in the MPS, or inaccurate inventory records. Figure 14.8 shows such a situation. The planner must determine whether the new order can be completed in less than the normal lead time. If so, the order would be released with a due date less than the normal lead-time offset; if not, the production schedules of its parents might have to be rearranged. Another

Item: A4 **Description:** Shelf

Lot Size: 200 units **Lead Time:** 2 weeks **Safety Stock:** 0 units

Date		23	24	25	26	27	28	29	30	31	32	33	34
Gross req.			170			40		80			120	60	
Sched. rec.			140										
On hand	20	20	−10	−10	−10	−50	−50	−130	−130	−130	−250	−310	−310
Net req.			10			40		80			120	60	
POR		200							200				

Comment: 60 units of the original scheduled receipt have been scrapped, so only 140 units now will be received. This creates a POR in week 23 with less than the normal lead time.

Figure 14.8

Action Notice for a Planned Release with Less Than the Normal Lead Time.

case requiring the planner to exercise judgment would be if capacity, tooling, or inventory of a component were insufficient to support the new order. The planner might release an order for a reduced quantity or even delay the order's release. Otherwise, component inventories would be tied up in an order that will be delayed anyway.

The second type of action notices is issued to expedite or delay a scheduled receipt. The computer detects this condition whenever the current due date assigned to a scheduled receipt no longer corresponds to when it is needed. Figure 14.9 shows how these adjustments are made. In case I (Fig. 14.9a) the computer would generate an action notice to expedite the scheduled receipt currently due in week 24. Its scheduled late arrival is detected from the on-hand balance in the *prior* week. If it is too low (negative or below the desired safety stock), the order should be rescheduled for earlier arrival. Releasing a new order to cover the deficit is unnecessary, since the scheduled receipt is sufficient if it is received earlier. The action notice would suggest changing the due date from week 24 to week 23.*

Case II (Fig. 14.9b) illustrates the condition when a scheduled receipt should be delayed. Completing it by week 24 builds up inventory with no apparent payoff in customer service; the scheduled receipt can be delayed until week 27. The need to delay the scheduled receipt is detected by comparing the size of the scheduled receipt with the on-hand balance in the *same* period. If the on-hand quantity exceeds it by an amount equal to the desired safety stock, the scheduled receipt can be delayed. Even without its receipt, inventory is sufficient. We defer a more detailed discussion of priority planning with MRP to Chapter 16.

Capacity Requirements Planning (CRP). We use **capacity requirements planning (CRP)** to project time-phased labor requirements for critical work stations. The capacity requirements report in Fig. 14.10 shows that these labor requirements come from two sources: (1) the *actual* column reflects the labor requirements for all scheduled receipts that still must be processed at the drying kilns station; (2) the *planned* column reflects the labor requirements for PORs, that is, orders projected for release by MRP logic at some future time. Note that the proportion of total capacity comes increasingly from PORs, as we project further into the future. Such forward visibility is a unique capability of MRP and was not possible with King Manufacturing's system. Computing these capacity reports requires more than a list of scheduled receipts and PORs. Routings and time standards are needed to identify which orders are

* There is no net requirement in week 23, even though the first negative on-hand balance occurs then. The reason is that the balance is not negative in the following week (week 24), which can happen only when a scheduled receipt is coming in too late. No net requirement is shown because the size of the order already released is sufficient; the only adjustment required is in the timing of the receipt. Late scheduled receipts are an exception to the two simple rules for computing net requirements.

Item:	**A4**									**Lot Size:**	**200 units**	
Description:	**Shelf**									**Lead Time:**	**2 weeks**	
										Safety Stock:	**0 units**	
Date		23	24	25	26	27	28	29	30	31	32	33	34
Gross req.		30	170			40		80			120	60	
Sched. rec.		←	200										
On hand	20	−10	20	20	20	−20	−20	−100	−100	−100	−220	−280	−280
Net req.						20		80			120	60	
POR				200					200				

Comment: A service part order for 30 units has just been received for week 23, creating a negative on-hand balance. There is no net requirement in week 23 because the deficit can be covered by the scheduled receipt if expedited.

(a)

Item:	**A4**									**Lot Size:**	**200 units**	
Description:	**Shelf**									**Lead Time:**	**2 weeks**	
										Safety Stock:	**0 units**	
Date		23	24	25	26	27	28	29	30	31	32	33	34
Gross req.			20			190		80			120	60	
Sched. rec.			200 →	→	→	→							
On hand	20	20	200	200	200	10	10	−70	−70	−70	−190	−250	−250
Net req.								70			120	60	
POR						200				200			

Comment: The POR for R1 has been delayed to week 27 (see Fig. 14.6). The scheduled receipt of A4 now is not needed until week 27, assuming no need for safety stock.

(b)

Figure 14.9

Action Notices for Adjusting Priorities: (a) Case I—Expedite Notice; (b) Case II—Delay Notice.

to be processed at the drying kilns and how long setup and processing will take for each order. Information on lead times and the current status of scheduled receipts help us to estimate the time periods when each order will be processed at this work station.

The capacity report for the drying kiln may cause us some concern. The current capacity of 320 hours per month will be exceeded in weeks 40–43 and weeks 48–51 unless something is done. At the same time, requirements for all other time periods are well below the capacity limit. Perhaps the best choice is

Date: 07/30/84 Plant 01 Dept. 03: Drying Kilns Station Capacity: 320 hours per month				Week 32
From Week	To Week	Planned Hours	Actual Hours	Total Hours
32	35	90	210	300
36	39	156	104	260
40	43	349	41	390
44	47	210	0	210
48	51	360	0	360
52	55	280	0	280

Figure 14.10

Capacity Requirements Report.

to release some orders earlier than called for by the materials requirements plan or MPS in weeks 36–39 and 44–47. This adjustment will help smooth capacity and alleviate the projected bottlenecks. Other options might be to change the lot sizes of some items, use overtime, subcontract, off-load to another work station, or even let the bottlenecks occur. The numbers in the *total* column of the capacity report give advance warning about potential problems only when they are compared to actual capacity constraints. The planner must make these comparisons and close the loop by resolving the capacity problems found.

Input–Output Control. An **input–output control report** is shown in Fig. 14.11 for the rough mill station. The information in this report helps us to check on whether a work station is performing as expected. The planned

Work station: Rough Mill Tolerance: ±25					Week 32
Week Ending	28	29	30	31	32
Inputs					
Planned	160	155	170	160	165
Actual	145	160	168	177	
Cumulative deviation	−15	−10	−12	+5	
Outputs					
Planned	170	170	160	160	160
Actual	165	165	150	148	
Cumulative deviation	−5	−10	−20	−32	

Figure 14.11

Input–Output Control Report.

input comes from previous CRP reports and shows that 155–170 hours per week of use were expected during weeks 28–31. The actual hours of use are also shown, so we can monitor deviations from the plan. The planned output shows 170 hours per week of use for weeks 28 and 29, followed by a cutback to 160 hours of use for the last three weeks. The reason for the higher level of planned use in weeks 28 and 29 could have been to reduce an excessive backlog that had developed.

Is there a capacity problem at the rough mill station? To help answer this question, let's assume that management has established a tolerance of ±25 hours. So long as the cumulative deviations do not exceed this threshold, there is no cause for concern. In our case, actual outputs fell behind planned outputs by a total of 32 hours in week 31. There are two possible reasons for the shortfall. The first is that inputs may have been insufficient to support the planned output rates. However, Fig. 14.11 shows that this is not the case because actual inputs are now running somewhat ahead of planned inputs. The second reason may be that absenteeism, equipment failures, insufficient staffing levels, or lower productivity rates caused output levels to slip below expectation. The specific cause should be identified and corrective action taken. It may also be necessary to use overtime to temporarily increase the planned output rate.

Summary. Figure 14.7 indicates that outputs such as those we have discussed require considerable data input. They can be important sources of information for the crucial short-term decisions that materials managers must continually make. Nonetheless, MRP itself does not recognize capacity limitations when the PORs are computed; *managers* must monitor the capacity with CRP and input–output reports. The materials requirements plan must be corrected by trial and error. Optimized Production Technology (OPT),* another production planning system, does recognize capacity when developing the material plan. It is described in the supplement to this chapter.

IMPACT OF MATERIALS REQUIREMENTS PLANNING

Although it has been beneficial to some firms, MRP is not the best system for all firms. In this section we consider its benefits, implementation issues, and situations in which MRP seems to be best suited, as well as the use of MRP concepts for distribution inventory.

Benefits

Box 14.2 contains reports of experiences of five companies that have successfully adopted an MRP system. At its best, MRP appears to be near miracu-

* OPT is a registered trademark of Creative Output, Incorporated.

Box 14.2

SOME SUCCESSFUL MRP USERS

American Sterilizer Company

The company's Hospital Products and Systems Group, since introducing MRP, has increased on-time customer deliveries from 70 percent to 95 percent, cut overtime by at least 50 percent, reduced component shortages by over 80 percent, lowered indirect labor by 24 percent, and reduced direct labor by 7 percent.

Carlyle Compressor Company

A division of Carrier Corporation, the company makes hermetic reciprocating compressors at a rate of more than 2500 per day on three major production lines. Since changing over to MRP late in 1977, inventory turns improved by 15 percent, and materials shortages dropped by 50 percent. There has been no improvement in customer service, but the plant now schedules much closer to maximum capacity, thereby improving labor and equipment utilization.

Bentley-Nevada

The company manufactures instruments that measure vibration in machinery and implemented MRP in less than 18 months. Past-due shipments are less than 3 percent of prior levels, and inventory turns have improved by 20 percent. While total shipments increased by 13 percent, labor requirements dropped by 21 percent.

Hill Rom Company

A maker of hospital beds, the company has found MRP's biggest payoff to be better on-time deliveries. Whereas the company was late on every third customer order, the manufacturing vice-president now is dissatisfied if one out of ten orders is late.

Hewlett-Packard

The Colorado Springs Division of H-P makes a variety of complex electronic instruments. It modified its MRP system to provide financial reports in step with operational plans. Predictions are quite good, with production costs (at standard) coming within 1 percent of projections for this MRP II system.

lous, helping to improve customer service, reduce inventory, lower overtime costs, and improve productivity. A comprehensive survey of industrial firms suggests that such benefits are not isolated examples (see Schroeder et al., 1981). Of the 679 firms responding, almost two-thirds were MRP users. Over 80 percent of these users had converted to MRP since 1971, indicating that it is a fairly recent development. The average user manages almost 13,000 items, some six levels in the bill of materials, and more than 450 employees.

Table 14.2 shows the average performance of these MRP users, both in terms of implementation costs and benefits. Implementation costs are one-time expenditures for buying or developing the computer software, preparing

Table 14.2

MRP Implementation Costs and Benefits

Annual Sales	Implementation Costs	
	Current cost ($000)	Eventual cost ($000)
Under $10 million	93	194
$11–25 million	210	385
$26–50 million	298	560
$51–100 million	511	912
$101–500 million	565	1800
Over $500 million	1633	2237

Performance Measure	Benefits		
	Pre–MRP estimate	Current estimate	Future estimate
Inventory turns	3.2	4.3	5.3
Delivery lead time (days)	71	59	44
Percent on-time deliveries	61%	76%	88%
Percent of "split" orders	32%	19%	9%
Number of expediters	10	6	5

Source: Roger G. Schroeder et al., "A Study of MRP Benefits and Costs," 1981 *Journal of Operations Management*, Journal of the American Production and Inventory Control Society, Inc. Reprinted with permission.

data files (particularly bills of materials and inventory files), and educating those in the company who need to know about the system. The average firm responding to the survey had already spent $375,000 to implement MRP, and expected the total to eventually reach $618,000. The reason for the eventual higher cost is that most users begin with class C outputs (Fig. 14.7), but intend to expand the system to include class B and class A outputs at a later date. Indeed, only 9 percent of the MRP users claim to be class A users, with 64 percent being at best class C users. Implementation costs are highly correlated with company size. Firms with larger annual sales spend considerably more to implement MRP because they must develop larger databases and train more employees; larger companies also tend to implement more sophisticated MRP systems, more likely being class A or class B users.

Although implementation costs were substantial, most users reported even larger benefits. The average company improved inventory turns from 3.2 to 4.3, and expected an eventual increase to 5.3. The average plant surveyed held about $6 million in inventory. An improvement of from 3.2 to 5.3 turns implies an annual savings of approximately $1 million per firm, assuming that holding costs are 30 percent of inventory investment. This savings alone produces a quick payback of implementation costs. Table 14.2 also shows significant improvement in customer service, as measured by on-time delivery, which enhances market penetration. The last two benefits, the number of split orders and number of expediters, also are revealing. When a production and inventory system is behaving poorly, component delays are more numerous. One symptom of component delays is the number of production orders that must be split (creating extra setups) because of insufficient component inventory. Another symptom is the need for a large number of expediters to rush late orders through the system. Both symptoms of poor performance diminished after firms installed MRP.

Implementation Issues

Although several thousand firms have tried MRP, not all have succeeded. A company can easily invest $500,000 in an MRP system, only to find that it is still plagued by high inventory and late customer deliveries. What has gone wrong? One possible explanation is that the MRP system was poorly implemented. Success is not automatic but must be achieved by the efforts of all concerned. A second possible explanation, which we cover in the next section, is that the company's manufacturing environment does not give MRP a distinct advantage over other systems.

There are four main prerequisites to successful implementation of an MRP system:

1. Computer support.
2. Accurate and realistic input data.
3. Management support.
4. User knowledge and acceptance.

Each week the average firm computes the time-phased records for 13,000 items, with each record having more than 38 time periods in its horizon (see Schroeder et al., 1981). This is a massive amount of data manipulation, requiring both a computer and an accompanying software package for almost all MRP applications. For most companies, having access to a computer no longer presents an obstacle. Furthermore, more than 40 commercial software packages are available, and, in addition, many companies have developed computer programs for their own use.

Any decision support system such as MRP rests on valid input data. You saw in Fig. 14.7 that MRP relies on many data inputs. The three principal ones are the master production schedule, bills of materials, and inventory records. The inventory record, in turn, requires the current on-hand inventory balance, lead-time estimates, and lot-sizing rules. Class B or class A outputs also rely on routing, time standard, and cost data. When MRP fails to live up to expectations, look first at these inputs. Are they accurate and realistic? If not, little progress can be made. Data accuracy makes a major difference in whether MRP implementation is successful or unsuccessful (see White et al., 1982).

The third element to successful implementation is management support. Converting to a new system challenges long-established habits and prerogatives of the people involved, whether they are managers, planners, buyers, marketing specialists, or shop supervisors. Resistance to change is normal and predictable. Overcoming this resistance begins with top management, who should convey to others the importance of success. Being actively involved in implementing and operating MRP, top management can motivate others.

The last prerequisite is to have knowledgeable users at all levels of the company. They must understand how they will be affected and what is required of them to make the system work. Such understanding helps to replace resistance with enthusiasm. Training programs often involve employees throughout the organization. The Tennant Company, an $80 million producer of industrial maintenance equipment, gave 525 of its 575 employees at least some MRP training. Usually, a people problem, such as lack of training, inadequate management support, or gaining acceptance for the change, is the single most important impediment to MRP success (see White et al., 1982).

Favorable Environments for MRP

Some companies do not adopt an MRP system, or are disappointed with its results when they do, because their manufacturing environment does not give MRP a distinct advantage over other systems. Four characteristics of the environment are particularly important:

1. Number of BOM levels.
2. Magnitude of lot sizes.
3. Volatility.
4. Manufacturing's positioning strategy.

You have seen that one of MRP's unique advantages is the way in which it handles lumpy demand for dependent-demand items. Dependent-demand items are most numerous when there are many levels in the bills of materials. The greatest number of MRP users are in the fabricated metals, machinery, and electric/electronic industries, which tend to have many BOM levels. It is no coincidence that the average user has more than six BOM levels (see Schroeder et al., 1981). Even with many levels, dependent-demand patterns need not be lumpy. The other variable is the magnitude of lot sizes. Our own simulation studies bear out these conclusions: The relative superiority of MRP increases with more levels and larger lot sizes. When lot sizes are extremely small, as achieved by some Japanese manufacturers, changing over to MRP is less attractive.

A highly volatile manufacturing environment, which management cannot stabilize, is also less of a candidate for large MRP savings. A basic MRP assumption is that projections of gross requirements, scheduled receipts, and PORs are realistic. This assumption is not valid when there are high scrap rates, capacity bottlenecks, last-minute rush jobs, and unreliable vendors.

Finally, MRP seems to be most attractive for firms that have positioned themselves with an intermediate strategy. (See Fig. 2.7 in Chapter 2.) They produce in batches, experience low to medium demand volumes, tend to offer a number of options with their products, and make products that have relatively short life cycles. These characteristics are not necessary for successful MRP, but they give us an idea of the sort of environment in which the capabilities of MRP can be best utilized. Firms with a process focus or product focus find that MRP is less valuable. In process-focused firms, the annual demand for items is small, and the number of customized products is large. Products are often expensive and require advance engineering, which make lead times long and uncertain. Maintaining files on bills of materials is complex; lot sizes are small. In product-focused firms (such as a paper mill) there tend to be few BOM levels, high capital intensity, and tight constraints on equipment capacity. Here the focus of managerial concern is with the master production schedule. This is an *input* to MRP, rather than an output. Only 12 percent of MRP users operated continuous processes, which are indicative of a product focus (see Schroeder et al., 1981).

Distribution Inventories

The principles of MRP can also be applied to distribution inventories. Consider the distribution system in Fig. 14.12. The top echelon represents retail stores at various locations throughout the country. At the middle level, we see regional distribution centers (DCs) that replenish retail store inventories on request. The bottom level consists of one or more plants that supply the DCs. In the past, plants tended to schedule production to meet the forecasted demand patterns of the DCs. These forecasts were likely to be derived from past usage, as is done for independent-demand items. DCs, in turn, replenished their inventories based on past demand patterns of the retail stores. In short, reorder-point logic was used at all three levels.

To illustrate the deficiency of this approach, let's suppose that customer demand for a product suddenly increases by 10 percent. What will happen? Since the retailers carry some inventory (for safety stock and to minimize the number of orders they have to place), there will be some delay before the full 10 percent increase is felt by the DCs. Then, more time passes before the full increase is reflected as higher demand from the DCs to the plants. In other

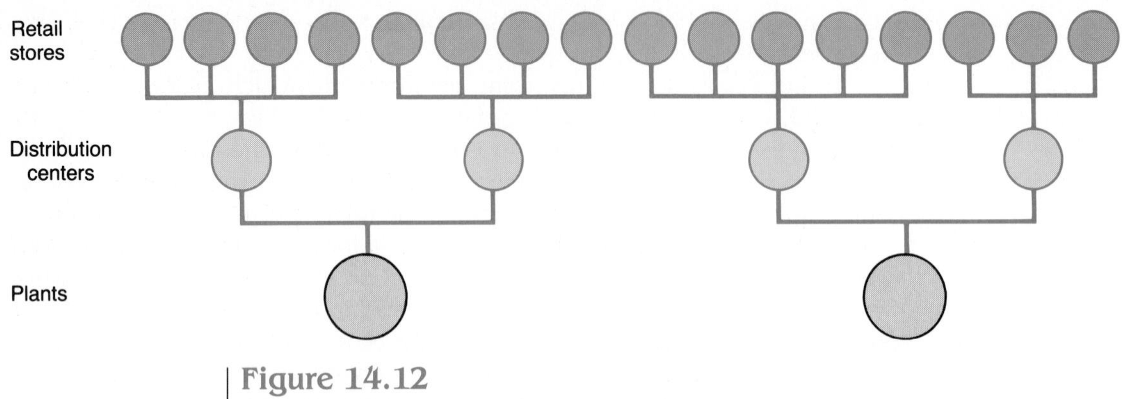

Figure 14.12

A Multi-Echelon Distribution System.

words, months can pass with plants underproducing at a 10 percent rate. When this deficiency finally becomes apparent, the plants must increase output by much more than 10 percent to replenish inventory levels.

Distribution requirements planning (DRP) helps to avoid such self-induced swings in demand. An inventory record is maintained for each item at each location. The PORs projected at the retail level are used to derive the gross requirements for each item at the DC level, using standard MRP logic and bills of materials. After next computing PORs at the DC level, the gross requirements for the plant level can be derived. This information provides the basis for updating the master production schedule at the plant.

Use of DRP requires an integrated information system. If the manufacturer operates its own DCs and retail stores (forward integration), this poses no particular problem. If operations in each echelon are owned by different firms, all need to agree to convey PORs from those at one level to those at the next. Open communication between firms need not stop at the plant level. More and more manufacturers are conveying POR data to their suppliers, giving them a better idea of future demand. Reducing demand uncertainty pays off either in lower inventories or better service.

CHAPTER HIGHLIGHTS

In this chapter, we focused on materials requirements planning (MRP), a computerized information system useful for managing dependent-demand inventories. Some of the highlights of the chapter are:

- The shortcomings of using reorder point systems in a dependent-demand environment are that (1) the assumption of a uniform, continuous demand rate is unrealistic; (2) items are assumed to be independent of each other when in reality they are not; and (3) they provide no forward visibility for planning purposes.

- The basic principles of MRP are that (1) dependent demands should be calculated, not forecasted; and (2) replenishment orders should be time phased.
- The materials requirements plan is prepared from the most recent inventory records of all items. The basic elements in each record are the gross requirements, scheduled receipts, on-hand inventory, net requirements, and PORs.
- Several parameters must be preassigned to each inventory record, including the lot-sizing rule, planned lead time, and desired safety stock. A variety of static and dynamic lot-sizing rules are available.
- The planned order releases of a parent, modified by usage quantities, become the gross requirements of its components. This procedure involves level-by-level processing, starting at the MPS level.
- MRP is a computerized information system having three basic inputs: the master production schedule, inventory records, and bills of materials. A fourth input, demand from sources other than the MPS, is also possible.
- Action notices allow management by exception, bringing to a planner's attention only those items for which new orders need to be released or that have open orders with misaligned due dates. Decisions based on the notices are normally made by the planner.
- There are three classes of MRP users. Class C users rely on the system only to release new orders. Class B users require additional outputs to help achieve closed-loop control. These outputs deal with priority and capacity questions. Class A users also require management reports, which help them integrate and monitor production, marketing, and financial plans.
- MRP implementation is widespread but relatively new. Significant inventory, customer service, and productivity benefits have been reported by many firms. Prerequisites to successful implementation are computer support, accurate databases, management support, and user knowledge and acceptance.
- The relative benefits of MRP depend on the number of BOM levels, the magnitude of lot sizes, environmental volatility, and positioning strategy.
- The principles of MRP can be used to manage distribution inventory with a system called distribution requirements planning (DRP).

KEY TERMS

action notices
capacity requirements planning (CRP)
distribution requirements planning (DRP)
dynamic lot-sizing rules
fixed order quantity (FOQ)
input–output control report
inventory status record
level-by-level processing
lot for lot (L4L)
materials requirements planning (MRP)
net change MRP system
periodic order quantity (POQ)
planned order releases (PORs)
regenerative MRP system
static lot-sizing rules

STUDY QUESTIONS

1. How does independent demand differ from dependent demand?
2. How does reorder point logic account for lead times and demand forecasts? How does MRP logic account for them?
3. Define *gross requirements, scheduled receipts, net requirements,* and *planned order releases.*
4. Would you agree with the P&IC manager at King Manufacturing, if she stated that its formal system for releasing orders is adequate? Why or why not?
5. With MRP logic, a component's gross requirements are derived from the PORs of all its parents. Why does this necessitate a top-down processing of records?
6. How is safety stock handled by MRP? How much should be carried? At what levels?
7. Why do priority and capacity reports of class B users help to close the loop? Why isn't it always wise to implement the materials requirements plan without change?
8. What potential problem do you detect from the data in the input–output control report in Fig. 14.13? What is the source of the problem and what can be done to resolve it?
9. Comment on the statement: "It is impossible to put together realistic marketing and financial plans without being able to set and achieve production plans."
10. How can MRP users report *simultaneous* improvements in inventory, customer service, and productivity? Isn't there a fundamental trade-off, where improvements in one come at the expense of another? Explain.
11. Why do some companies fail to achieve any measurable improvements after adopting MRP?
12. Suppose that a manufacturer decides to share POR information with its suppliers. What benefits can accrue to both parties? Can there be disadvantages?
13. Why can the reliability of time-phased gross requirements be decreased by the following shocks: last-minute changes in the master production schedule, unex-

Work Station: Chair Assembly **Tolerance: ±50**					**Week 49**
Week Ending	**45**	**46**	**47**	**48**	**49**
Inputs					
Planned	300	300	300	300	310
Actual	305	275	280	260	
Cumulative Deviation	+5	−20	−40	−80	
Outputs					
Planned	300	300	300	300	320
Actual	310	290	270	260	
Cumulative Deviation	+10	0	−30	−70	

Figure 14.13

pected scrap losses, late vendor shipments, unexpected capacity bottlenecks, or inaccurate inventory records.

14. The relative advantage of MRP over the current system at King Manufacturing does not hold for small lot sizes and lead times. Do you agree? Disagree? Why?

PROBLEMS

1. The dependent demand for a standard item at King Manufacturing has averaged 10 units per week during the last year. Suppose that the actual dependent demand for the next five weeks is that shown in Table 14.3.
   (a) Complete Table 14.3. Begin by making three sets of forecasts for weeks 2–5. The first forecasting technique uses the past average of 10 units for all future weeks. The last two update the forecast weekly with simple exponential smoothing, using smoothing parameter α (see Chapter 3) of either 0.10 or 0.20. Finally, calculate the mean absolute deviation (MAD) for each forecasting technique.
   (b) Judging from the MAD values obtained:
      (i) Does the adaptiveness of exponential smoothing help with forecasting dependent demand?
      (ii) Would you say that the MAD value is small or large, relative to a weekly demand of 10 units?
      (iii) How can such forecasting errors be eliminated?
   (c) Suppose that 35 units of this item are on hand, desired safety stock is 10 units, lead time is 2 weeks, and there are no scheduled receipts or back orders.
      (i) If demand is forecast at 10 units per week, would a new order be

Table 14.3

Week	Actual Dependent Demand	Three Forecasts			Forecast Errors		
		Simple average	Exponential smoothing		Simple average	Exponential smoothing	
			$\alpha = 0.10$	$\alpha = 0.20$		$\alpha = 0.10$	$\alpha = 0.20$
1	0	10	10	10	10	10	10
2	40						
3	0						
4	0						
5	20						
				MAD =			

Item:	H10-A	Lot Size:	80 units
Description:	Chair seat assembly	Lead Time:	4 weeks
		Safety Stock:	0 units

Date		31	32	33	34	35	36	37	38	39	40
Gross requirements				75		40			25		60
Scheduled receipts		80									
On hand	20	100	100	25	25	-15	-15	-15	-40	-40	-100
Net requirements						15			25		60
Planned order releases		80					80				

Figure 14.14

released this week using reorder point logic?

(ii) For the same demand forecast, would a new order be released using MRP logic?

2. The inventory record in Fig. 14.14 has been partially completed, showing gross requirements, scheduled receipts, and on-hand inventory balance. Parameters for lead time and safety stock are also given. Item H10-A is produced in the plant (not purchased).
   (a) What is the source of the information already shown for gross requirements and scheduled receipts?
   (b) Fill in the last three rows of the record, using an FOQ of 80 units.
      (i) Will there be any action notices?
      (ii) If there are action notices, what would you consider in reacting to them?
   (c) Revise the POR row using the L4L rule.
   (d) Revise the POR row again, this time using the POQ rule and a value of P that will give an average lot size of 80 units. Assume that the *average* weekly demand will be 20 units for the foreseeable future when computing P.
3. Repeat Problem 2, except that the scheduled receipt of 80 units is due in week 33; safety stock is set at 10 units; and the nonzero gross requirements change to 60 units in week 32, 35 units in week 36, 45 units in week 38, and 60 units in week 40.
4. In the master production schedule for product A, the MPS-start row calls for 200 units in week 6. Develop the materials requirements plan for the next six weeks for items B, C, and D. The BOM is shown in Fig. 14.15, and data from the inventory records are shown in Table 14.4. The numbers in parentheses in the BOM are usage quantities. For example, two units of C are needed for each unit of parent B. In deriving C's gross requirements, double the PORs from B. Assume that next week is week 1. After completing the plan, identify any action notices that would be brought to a planner's attention. *Hint:* The record for item D must be completed first, followed by B and then C. An

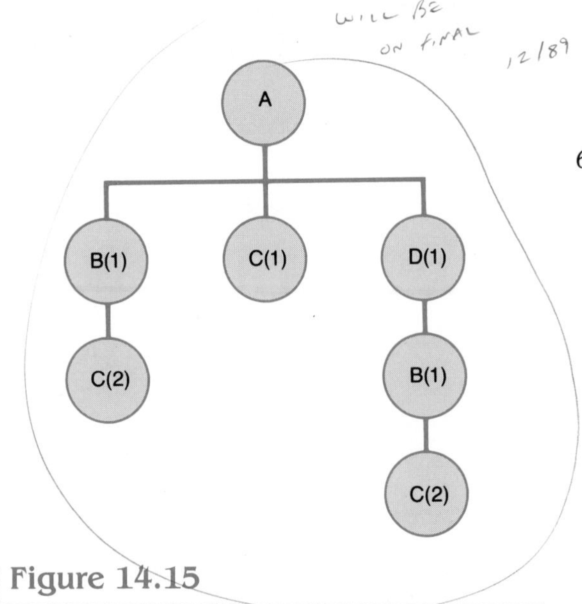

Figure 14.15

BOM for Product A.

item's gross requirements cannot be derived without knowing the PORs of all its parents.

5. The MPS for product A calls for 50 units in week 2 and 60 units in week 6; the MPS for product B calls for 200 units in week 4. Develop the materials requirements plan for the next six weeks for items C, D, E, and F, identifying any action notices that would be provided. The BOMs are shown in Fig. 14.16, and data from the inventory records are shown in Table 14.5.

6. Product A is made from two units of B and one unit of C. Item B is assembled from one unit of D and two units of E. Item C is fabricated from two units of D. All lead times are one week except for E, which requires two weeks. In order to minimize inventory, items B, C, and D have L4L lot-sizing rules. Purchased item E must be ordered in lots of 300 because of transportation costs. Only item B has a scheduled receipt, which is for 40 units due in this week. On-hand inventory for B and C is 0; for D, 40 units; and for E, 60 units. No item has a safety stock requirement.
   (a) Draw a product tree (as in Problems 4 and 5) to represent the BOM.
   (b) The MPS calls for orders of 20 units of A to be released in weeks 2, 4, and 6. Develop a materials requirements plan for the next six weeks for items B, C, D, and E.
   (c) Would any action notices be generated? If so, what are they?

7. Repeat Problem 6 but with the following changes.
   - The master production schedule calls

Table 14.4

Selected Data from Inventory Records

Data Category	Item B	Item C	Item D
Lot-size rule	L4L	FOQ = 600	L4L
Lead time	1	3	2
Safety stock	0	0	0
Scheduled receipts	None	600 (week 1)	None
Beginning inventory (on hand)	0	200	40

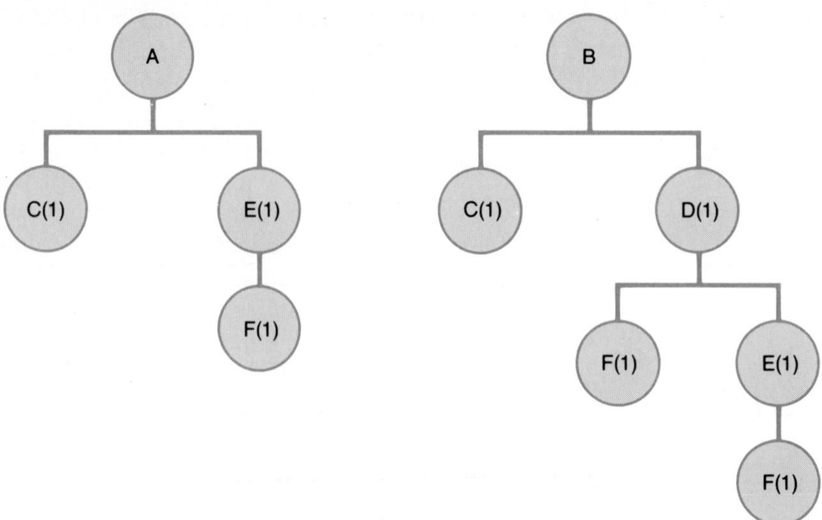

Figure 14.16

BOMs for Products A and B.

for 20 units of A to be released in week 1 and 40 units in week 6.

- Item C is not just produced to make A. It is also produced to meet the forecasted demand for service parts. Past usage for service parts has been 5 units per week. *Hint:* Add 5 units per week to C's gross requirements, in addition to those coming from A.
- There are 31 units of C on hand, and the safety stock requirement is 10.
- Use the POQ lot-sizing rule for C, with $P = 3$.
- Only one unit of D is needed to make C.

8. Items A and B are dependent-demand items. Item B's only parent is A. Four units of B are needed to make one unit of

Table 14.5

Selected Data from Inventory Records

Data Category	Item C	Item D	Item E	Item F
Lot-size rule	FOQ = 250	FOQ = 400	L4L	POQ (P = 2)
Lead time	3	2	3	2
Safety stock	50	0	0	0
Scheduled receipts	250 (week 2)	None	50 (week 3)	None
Beginning inventory (on hand)	60	300	0	0

Item: A Description: Leg assembly							Lot Size: 80 units Lead Time: 1 week Safety Stock: 0 units
Date	**1**	**2**	**3**	**4**	**5**	**6**	**7**
Gross requirements	70		60			85	50
Scheduled receipts	80						
On hand 15	25	25	−35	−35	−35	−120	−170
Net requirements			35			85	50
Planned order releases		80			80	80	

Figure 14.17

A. The current materials requirements plan for A is shown in Fig. 14.17, and that for B is shown in Fig. 14.18.

(a) Today the planner responsible for items A and B learned some good news and some bad news. Although the scheduled receipt of 80 units of A has been finished (the good news), only 50 units were put in the storeroom; the other 30 were scrapped (the bad news). Recalculate the two inventory records, reflecting this event. *Hint:* A scheduled receipt should no longer be shown for A, but its on-hand balance now is 65.

(b) Are there any action notices relative to the new materials requirements plan? If so, what are they?

Item: B Description: Leg							Lot Size: L4L Lead Time: 3 weeks Safety Stock: 0 units
Date	**1**	**2**	**3**	**4**	**5**	**6**	**7**
Gross requirements		320			320	320	
Scheduled receipts		320					
On hand 0	0	0	0	0	−320	−640	−640
Net requirements					320	320	
Planned order releases		320	320				

Figure 14.18

Date: 1/31/84 Plant 01 Dept. 05: Inspection Capacity: 160 Hours Per Month				Week 1
Week From	Week To	Planned Hours	Actual Hours	Total Hours
1	4			

Figure 14.19

9. Repeat Problem 8, except that the only news is that A's on-hand balance is incorrect. There are actually 55 units of A, rather than 15, in the storeroom. Recalculate the materials requirements plan and identify any new action notices.
10. Fill in the rest of the row in the CRP report (Fig. 14.19) for the inspection station, using the PORs and scheduled receipts in the inventory records in Problem 8. Assume that only the inspection operation remains to be done for A's scheduled receipt and that all of its PORs will be completed in the week of their release. As for B, assume that its scheduled receipt will be inspected in week 2 and all planned orders will remain one week at each operation. For example, the POR to be released in week 2 will not reach its third operation until week 4. Routings and time standards for A and B are shown in Table 14.6.

Table 14.6

Item	Operation	Work Station	Setup Time per Batch (hr)	Processing Time per Unit (hr)
A	10	Assembly	0.4	2.5
	20	Inspection	0.2	0.5
B	10	Rough mill	0.1	0.3
	20	Finishing	2.1	0.8
	30	Inspection	0.0	0.1

SELECTED REFERENCES

Aquilano, Nicholas J., and Dwight E. Smith, "A Formal Set of Algorithms for Project Scheduling with Critical Path Scheduling/Material Requirements Planning," *Journal of Operations Management*, vol. 1, no. 2 (November 1980), pp. 57–67.

Benton, W. C., and D. Clay Whybark, "Material Requirements Planning (MRP) and Purchase Discounts," *Journal of Operations Management,* vol. 2, no. 2 (February 1982), pp. 137–143.

Biggs, Joseph R., Chan K. Hahn, and Peter A. Pinto, "Performance of Lot-Sizing Rules in an MRP System with Different Operating Conditions," *Academy of Management Review,* vol. 5, no. 1 (1980), pp. 89–96.

Blackburn, J., and R. Millen, "Improved Heuristics for Multi-Stage Requirements Planning Systems," *Management Science,* vol. 28, no. 1 (January 1982).

Carlson, J. M., "The Control of Change in a Net Change MRP Environment." *Proceedings of the 23rd Annual Conference,* American Production & Inventory Control Society, Falls Church, Va, October 1980, pp. 177–181.

Graves, S. C. "Multi-Stage Lot Sizing: An Iterative Procedure." In L. Schwarz (Ed.), *Multi-level Production/Inventory Systems: Theory and Practice.* New York: North-Holland, 1981.

Harl, Johannes E., and Larry P. Ritzman, "A Heuristic Algorithm for Capacity Sensitive Lot Sizing," *Journal of Operations Management,* vol. 5, no. 3 (May 1985), pp. 309–326.

Honeywell, Inc., *Manufacturing IMS/66 (Extended) Systems Handbook,* DE80, rev. 1, June 1977.

International Business Machines Corporation, *Communications Oriented Production Information and Control Systems.* Publications G320-1974–G320-1981.

Miller, Jeffrey, G., and Linda G. Sprague, "Behind the Growth in Material Requirements Planning," *Harvard Business Review* (September–October 1975), pp. 83–91.

Orlicky, Joseph, *Material Requirements Planning.* New York: McGraw-Hill, 1975.

Plossl, George W., *Manufacturing Controls—The Last Frontier for Profits.* Reston, Va.: Reston Publishing Company, 1973.

Ritzman, Larry P., Barry E. King, and Lee J. Krajewski, "Manufacturing Performance—Pulling the Right Levers," *Harvard Business Review* (March–April 1984), pp. 143–152.

Ritzman, Larry P., and Lee J. Krajewski, "Comparison of Material Requirements Planning and Reorder Point System." In Haluk Bekiroglu (Ed.), *Simulation for Production and Inventory Control.* La Jolla, Ca.: Society for Computer Simulation, 1983.

Schroeder, Roger G., John C. Anderson, Sharon E. Tupy, and Edna M. White, "A Study of MRP Benefits and Costs," *Journal of Operations Management,* vol. 2, no. 1 (October 1981), pp. 1–9.

Steinberg, Earle E., Basheer Khumawala, and Richard Scamell, "Requirements Planning Systems in the Health Care Environment," *Journal of Operations Management,* vol. 2, no. 4 (August 1982), pp. 251–259.

Steinberg, Earle E., William B. Lee, and Basheer M. Khumawala, "A Requirements Planning System for the Space Shuttle Operation Schedule," *Journal of Operations Management,* vol. 1, no. 2 (November 1980), pp. 69–76.

"The Trick of Material Requirements Planning," *Business Week,* June 4, 1979.

White, Edna M., John C. Anderson, Roger G. Schroeder, and Sharon E. Tupy, "A Study of the MRP Implementation Process," *Journal of Operations Management,* vol. 2, no. 3 (May 1982), pp. 145–153.

Whybark, D. Clay, "MRP: A Profitable Concept for Distribution," *Research Issues in Logistics,* 1975, pp. 82–93.

Wight, Oliver W., "MRP II: Manufacturing Resource Planning," *Modern Materials Handling* (September 1979).

SUPPLEMENT

OPTIMIZED PRODUCTION TECHNOLOGY

The need for **optimized production technology** (OPT)* was based on the premise that businesses have spent literally billions of dollars on production and inventory control systems but have fallen short of achieving even modest goals for these systems. Many reasons for the general lack of success have been suggested: poor data accuracy, lack of management support, inadequate education, and others; however the developers of OPT claim that the main reason is the faulty assumptions used in these systems to arrive at production schedules. Recall that MRP, for example, does not recognize capacity constraints when generating planned order releases. Planners must intervene manually, using additional methods such as capacity requirements planning and input–output control to manage the schedule. Even so, the scheduling problem is very complex because, typically, at any one time there are many shop orders in progress that require the same critical work stations. Arriving at valid schedules that remain valid for more than a short time is difficult, if not impossible, to do manually.

The general idea behind OPT is to look at the production and inventory control problem from a systems viewpoint. Order release and production schedules take into consideration the capacity bottlenecks in the system. The goal of OPT is to find schedules that *simultaneously* increase throughput and decrease inventory and operating expenses. This approach differs from those of the users of MRP and reorder point systems, who develop their schedules *sequentially,* first identifying the timing and size of order releases and then making adjustments to account for capacity constraints.

* OPT is a registered trademark of Creative Output, Incorporated.

CONCEPTS

The basic concepts of the OPT approach fall into two major categories: capacity and inventory. Capacity considerations are pivotal to OPT, so we begin with them.

Capacity

Optimized production technology recognizes two types of resources in a manner similar to the method used in capacity requirements planning (CRP) with MRP systems. A **critical resource** is one for which the requirements are equal to or exceed its capacity over a specified period of time. A **noncritical resource** is one for which the requirements are less than its capacity. A resource is any element, such as people, machines, or space, needed to produce a product. Optimized production technology distinguishes between these two types of resources because the critical resources determine the amount of output from the manufacturing system.

Scheduling Noncritical Resources. Suppose that we had a very simple two-machine manufacturing system. Machine X has average requirements of 96 hours per month and machine Y has average requirements of 160 hours per month. Both machines have 160 hours of potential capacity per month. Consequently, machine Y is the critical resource.

We need to consider two scenarios. If we activate machine X to 100 percent of its capacity and it feeds machine Y, the only result will be a buildup of inventory at machine Y because the output of machine Y cannot be increased. Alternatively, if machine Y feeds machine X, machine Y again dictates the output of the system because machine X will be starved for material. In either situation, machine Y, the critical work station, dictates the output of the system. Thus OPT recognizes that resources such as machine X should not be activated at a level greater than that needed to accommodate the throughput capabilities of the critical resources or the level of market demand.

Slack at Critical Resources. The resource capacities in a plant should not be so closely balanced that there is no slack in the system. The rationale behind this concept is that often there are dominant flows of materials in a plant, and the output from one station becomes the input to another. The processing times at each station are rarely constant. Therefore allocating resources and scheduling each work station to its limit using average processing times is doomed to failure. Any delay caused by materials problems, machine downtime, behavioral factors, and the like at one work station will be transmitted to the work station it feeds. If a station falls behind, it is very difficult, if not impossible, to get the station back on schedule without using additional resources. Thus OPT looks at the entire manufacturing system and carefully schedules the critical resources at a level slightly less than actual capacity and judiciously assigns buffer stock to minimize the effects of processing time variations.

Lead-Time Effects. When MRP determines the lead time for an item, it simply computes the longest time path through the bill of materials. It cannot recognize that two or more of the components may need the same production process. In this case, the planned lead time is a function of the *sequencing* of components on the critical resources. This condition is called process dependency. It is not too difficult to understand that when there is process dependency, fixed lead times (as in MRP) can cause poor schedule performance (if they are too short) or excessive work-in-process inventories (if they are too long). Thus OPT attempts to simultaneously determine the release dates for orders and the sequencing of their components, recognizing the capacity constraints of the resources. In this respect, OPT tries to incorporate the sequential planning process of MRP users into a simultaneous process of lead-time planning, sequencing, and capacity planning.

Inventory

Whereas MRP formally recognizes only one lot size for an item, OPT recognizes two basic types of lot sizes. A **transfer batch** is the quantity of an item that moves from station to station. A station will not begin to process an item until there are sufficient parts to process a transfer batch. Also, parts will be released from the station for further processing only in transfer batch quantities. The size of the transfer batch is determined by a managerial parameter that specifies the *processing time* to be spent on transfer batches at each station. For a given time, the *quantity* of parts in a transfer batch at one station may be different from the quantity of parts in the transfer batch at another station because the processing times per unit are different.

The other type of lot sizes recognized by OPT is the **process batch,** which is the total number of units of an item processed at one time at a particular station. The process batch consists of an integral number of transfer batches, and its size depends on setup time and capacity constraints.

There are several advantages in using the concept of process batches and transfer batches. First, as soon as a transfer batch is completed, it can be taken to its next station before the rest of the process batch is completed. This improves materials flow by reducing the lumpiness of requirements and increasing the uniformity of flow. Second, transfer batches at one station need not be the same as those at any other station. They can be designed to best match capacity and demand requirements. Finally, the process batches at the *critical* work stations can be chosen to minimize setup time. This increases the throughput of materials through the bottleneck areas. Saving an hour of setup time at a critical work station gains an hour of processing capacity for the system; saving an hour of setup time at a noncritical work station accomplishes nothing.

THE SYSTEM

The basic concepts regarding capacity and inventory have been incorporated into a complex software package for production and inventory control. Figure S14.1 shows the major elements.

The *data inputs* for OPT are similar to those for MRP. Bills of materials, item routings, inventory status, and demand requirements are all used by the system. These files must be continually updated to reflect engineering changes, schedule performance, forecast changes, and the like.

The *Buildnet* module converts input data into a product–process network. The network is a mathematical model of the manufacturing system, which describes how a product is made, the competition for resources, and the interrelationships between parts going into an assembled product.

After the network model of the manufacturing facility has been constructed, *Serve* computes the average utilization of each resource, using the demand requirements for each product. It then sorts them by rank order from the most heavily loaded to the lightest. The bottleneck resources are those for which utilization is at least 100 percent. *Serve* is essentially a modified MRP system.

The *Split* module divides the network into two parts: (1) those resources that are affected by the output of the bottleneck operations; and (2) those that are unaffected. The splitting of resources is important because it reduces the effort needed to arrive at schedules. Recall that only the critical resources determine the throughput of the manufacturing system.

The *Brain* module is the heart of the OPT system. Although the term *optimized* is used in the system's name, the schedules for the critical resources generated by this module are not truly optimal. In a practical sense that would not be possible because of the enormity of the problem. However, *Brain* is a noninteractive algorithm that solves the scheduling problem within some defined range short of the optimum. It determines process batch sizes, production sequences, and buffer stocks for the critical resources, based on their capacity limitations, to maximize throughput.

The output from *Brain* is used by *Serve* to develop schedules for noncritical resources. Driven by the schedules for the critical resources, *Serve* tends to schedule production at noncritical resources in smaller quantities. This requires more setups but provides a better mix of parts to downstream stations. Also, it schedules noncritical resources with *safety capacity*, or planned idle

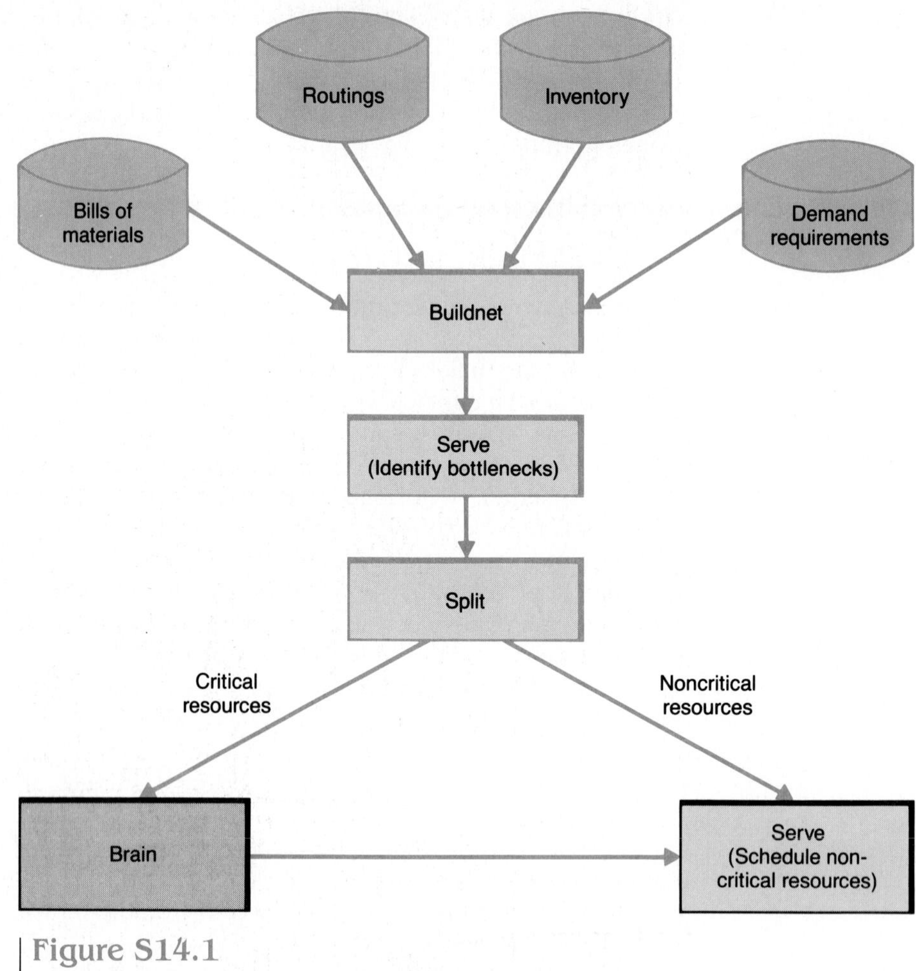

Figure S14.1

The Optimized Production Technology (OPT) System.

time, so that the effects of uncertainty in process times or requirements can be minimized.

The end results of the OPT process are a complete set of materials requirements for the planning time horizon and a detailed production schedule for each work station.

MANAGERIAL CONSIDERATIONS

Every system such as OPT has certain advantages and disadvantages. Table S14.1 shows the advantages of OPT, and Table S14.2 shows the disadvantages. We have already addressed all but the last two advantages. OPT enables management to fine-tune schedules by using a number of managerial input parameters designed to control the sizes of transfer batches and buffer stock. In addition, the system can be used to analyze "what-if" questions associated with issues such as changing the factory load, changing the processing sequences or amount of resources, and modifying management policies on delivery performance.

Several disadvantages should also be mentioned. Perhaps the greatest potential disadvantage is that the mechanics of the system—the generation of schedules and materials requirements—are proprietary and essentially unknown to the user. In particular, the heart of OPT, the *Brain,* is like a "black box," which takes certain inputs and provides certain outputs. The user cannot alter any of the logic in the system. This prohibition means that the user must rely heavily on the developers of OPT when problems arise. This situation is in stark contrast to systems such as MRP, which is the subject of many books and articles. A company can develop its own MRP software package if it wants to. Not so with OPT. Also, a basic assumption of OPT is that a network model can be developed to truly represent the conditions and interactions that are crucial to the scheduling of manufacturing operations. Conceivably, some manufacturing environments cannot be adequately modeled with this approach.

The use of OPT may require some changes in typical managerial philoso-

Table S14.1

Advantages of OPT

- Differentiates and identifies critical and noncritical resources.
- Specifies a schedule for each resource.
- Simultaneously determines order releases and planned lead times.
- Allows for transfer batches that are not equal to process batches.
- Allows for varying process batches.
- Enables management to fine-tune schedules.
- Can be used to analyze "what-if" questions.

Table S14.2

Disadvantages of OPT

- The "black-box" syndrome.
- Assumes that the manufacturing process can be accurately modeled.
- Requires changes in typical manufacturing philosophy.
- Potential for system nervousness.
- Does not specifically address costs.

phies. The changes could be warranted, but might cause considerable internal strife. For example, OPT forces a total systems viewpoint, which means that it may be best to leave some resources with slack capacity. Traditional cost accounting practices, however, may view the underutilized resources as a liability, and the foremen in charge of these resources may be pressured to increase their use. This could undermine the performance of the OPT system.

There is also a potential for system nervousness with OPT. This term means that plans are unstable and in a constant state of flux. In effect, OPT develops dynamic lot sizes and production sequences that are based on demand requirements and capacity constraints. In an uncertain environment, the process batches and sequences could change each time a new schedule is developed, presumably weekly. The OPT system tries to circumvent these problems by using buffer stock and safety capacity at selected operations; however, this approach can be costly if not properly controlled. The OPT system also relies on the values of the managerial parameters for this control, not some overall cost function. In fact, costs are not specifically addressed in *any* of the OPT modules. The system attempts to maximize the throughput of materials, which typically results in fewer setups and longer production runs at the critical work stations. The only way that inventory investment and operating costs can be controlled is by the trial-and-error manipulation of the managerial parameters.

It is probably safe to say that OPT represents the first of many proprietary scheduling systems that will be developed by software vendors in the future.

KEY TERMS

critical resource
noncritical resource
optimized production technology (OPT)
process batch
transfer batch

SELECTED REFERENCES

Fox, R. E., "MRP, Kanban or OPT—What's Best?" *Inventories and Production,* vol. 2, no. 4 (July–August 1982).

———, "OPT, An Answer for America: Part II," *Inventories and Production,* vol. 2, no. 6 (November–December 1982).

———, "OPT, An Answer for America: Part III," *Inventories and Production,* vol. 3, no. 1 (January–February 1983).

———, "OPT, An Answer for America: Part IV, Leapfrogging the Japanese," *Inventories and Production,* vol. 3, no. 2 (March–April 1983).

———, "OPT vs. MRP: Thoughtware vs. Software," *Inventories and Production,* vol. 3, no. 6 (November–December 1983).

Jacobs, F. R., "The OPT Scheduling System: A Review of a New Production Scheduling System," *Production and Inventory Management,* vol. 24, no. 3 (1983).

CHAPTER 15

HIGH-VOLUME PRODUCTION SYSTEMS

Some Managerial Issues

- Under what circumstances could we use a just-in-time system effectively?
- Should we consider the limitations of process capacity on our manufacturing system?
- Which factors should we consider in choosing an appropriate manufacturing system for a process-industry firm?
- Can we make all types of manufacturing systems work equally well in a given environment?
- What environmental factors affect the performance of our manufacturing system?

Chapter Outline

Firms engaged in high-volume or continuous production cannot always take advantage of materials requirements planning systems. They are most useful in situations involving intermediate volume batch production. In these situations, the requirements are lumpy, and the lead times for component production or purchased items are long. In MRP, we time phase requirements, so that inventory can be replenished on a timely basis. However, many firms in the United States use **repetitive manufacturing** or **continuous flow manufacturing** systems. Both types of manufacturing involve high volumes; however, repetitive manufacturing produces standard, discrete products in relatively small lot sizes, whereas in the process industries continuous flow manufacturing produces long runs of products in a linear flow to effectively utilize the large capital investment required. In either of these cases, MRP is not the only planning and scheduling alternative available, and, under certain conditions, other systems could work as well or better. In this chapter we will address systems suitable for high-volume production.

JUST-IN-TIME SYSTEMS

Not so long ago, many U.S. industries enjoyed a competitive edge in technology and inexpensive resources and the prospects of a bright future in expanding markets. More recently, a significant number of companies in the chemical, steel, electronics, and automotive industries have lost that competitive advantage. One of the most notable competitive challenges came from the Japanese in the automotive industry. Japanese cars were made better and priced lower in many cases than comparably sized and equipped American cars. This prompted U.S. managers to study Japanese methods of repetitive manufacturing management and control.

What they learned, in retrospect, is not all that surprising, although it is most revealing. The Japanese used no single, magic formula to achieve their success. Their geographic and cultural environment, managerial practices, support of the work force, and automation all played a role.

The core of Japanese productivity improvement in repetitive manufacturing is the **just-in-time (JIT) system.** The purpose of JIT is simple: produce (or deliver) the right items in the quantities needed by subsequent production processes (or customers) at the time needed. The intent is to eliminate the buildup of work-in-process inventory by coordinating the flow of materials between production processes. The JIT system also strives to coordinate the final assembly rate with the customer demand rate to eliminate the need for finished goods inventory. The system can have substantial economic payoffs, as shown in Box 15.1.

Figure 15.1 illustrates the JIT concept, showing a schematic flow of materials in repetitive manufacturing. The process consists of two standard machine groups, three group technology cells, and a final assembly line. The schedule for the assembly line is coordinated with the market demand rate. Suppose that the assembly line works on lot sizes equivalent to 25 percent of the daily demand requirements. Consequently, every two hours the assembly line gets materials from cells 4 and 5 for the next two hours of assembly. This action prompts cell 5 to get materials from machine group 1 and cell 3, so that it can manufacture the items needed next on the assembly line. Similarly, cell

Box 15.1

GENERAL MOTORS USES JUST-IN-TIME SYSTEM

The Buick assembly plant in Flint, Michigan, is getting a second lease on life. On the brink of being permanently closed because of outdated production technology and troubled labor relations, a new concept was developed in which the workers would do their own inspections and just-in-time delivery would be used. The plant operates with minimal in-plant inventories, and some suppliers have located nearby to provide deliveries on frequent schedules. The $300 million renovation and the move to just-in-time deliveries will save an estimated 35 percent in assembly costs.

Source: "The Empire Strikes Back" by Thomas M. Rohan, *Industry Week* (April 15, 1985), pp. 40–48.

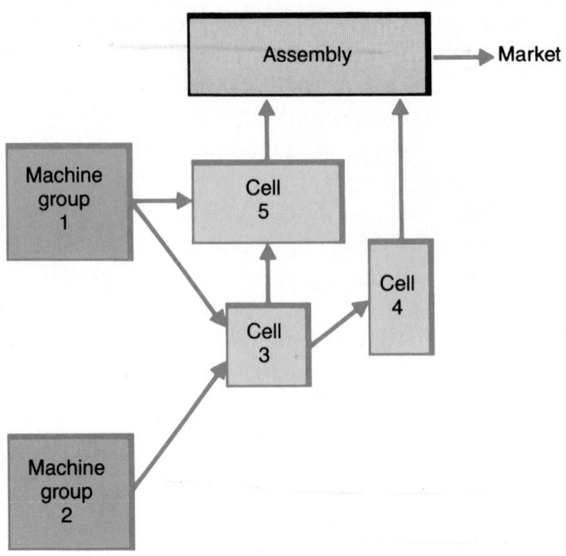

Figure 15.1

Flow of Materials in Repetitive Manufacturing.

4 gets more materials from cell 3. Finally, cell 3 must get materials from machine groups 1 and 2 to support the next request from cells 4 and 5. Machine groups 1 and 2 must get more raw materials. Even though this is an oversimplified example of JIT in practice, it demonstrates the degree of coordination in production that has contributed to significant reductions in inventory levels and increases in productivity for its users. In general, JIT is a *pull system,* in which a production process pulls material from a prior process in support of the final assembly schedule.

The JIT concept will not work without the proper environment. Most of the firms that have successfully implemented JIT have the following characteristics in common.

1. *Uniform assembly schedules.* The use of JIT in repetitive manufacturing requires a stable assembly schedule. A uniform, continuous need for parts and components is essential.
2. *Group technology.* Utilizing group technology cells takes advantage of high-volume production, even when the specific demand for parts produced at the cells is low per unit of time.
3. *Flexible work force.* The ability to utilize workers at a variety of operations helps to alleviate bottleneck operations and maintain a uniform flow of products.
4. *Short setup times.* Short setup times permit small-lot production, which is essential for low inventory investment.

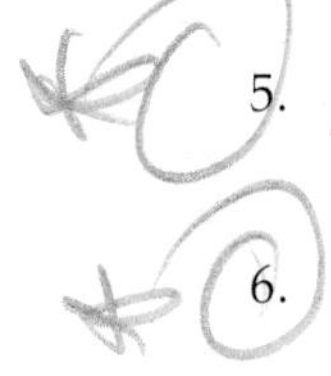

5. *Low rates of machine failure.* Machine failure disrupts the production process in a JIT system because of the low levels of inventory used to decouple the operations.
6. *Low rates of yield loss or rework.* Both yield losses and rework disrupt the uniform flow of materials through the manufacturing process.

The total JIT system environment, as practiced by the Japanese, entails more than these six characteristics. We emphasize them here because they are relevant to this chapter. Other characteristics involve organizational and behavioral norms, managerial practices, and automation. We discuss these characteristics, along with the six already mentioned, more fully in Chapter 20 when we present the JIT system as an example of using manufacturing strategy as a competitive weapon.

Toyota's Kanban System

Perhaps the most publicized just-in-time system is Toyota's kanban system. The word ***kanban*** means card or visible record in Japanese. As the system's name suggests, Toyota uses cards to control the flow of production through the factory. Although there are many different types of cards, the two main types used by Toyota are the *withdrawal* kanban and the *production-ordering* kanban. The withdrawal kanban specifies the item and the quantity the subsequent process should withdraw from the preceding process and the stocking locations for each process. The production-ordering kanban specifies the item and production quantity the preceding process must produce, the materials required and where to find them, and where to store the finished item. The cards are attached to containers representing approximately 10 percent of the daily requirements for the item. This implies that production lot sizes as small as one-tenth the average daily requirements appear to be economical.

Figure 15.2 shows how the two cards are used to control production flow. The two processes shown are similar to cell 4 and the assembly line in Fig. 15.1. In all, eight steps are required:

Step 1. Accumulated withdrawal kanban and the empty containers are taken to storage location A.

Step 2. The empty containers are exchanged for full containers. The production-order kanban on each full container is detached and placed on the kanban receiving post.

Step 3. The contents of the full containers are checked against the specifications on the withdrawal kanban, and, if satisfactory, a withdrawal kanban is attached to each full container. The containers are moved to the inbound stocking location of the subsequent process.

Step 4. When work begins on a container at the subsequent process, the withdrawal kanban is detached and placed on the post.

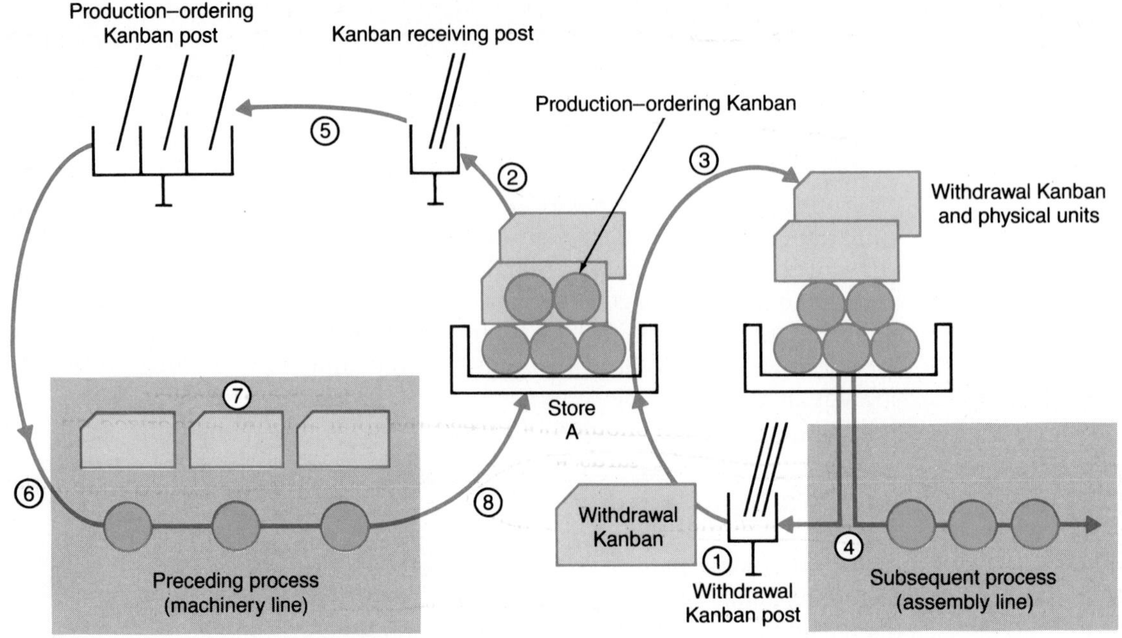

Figure 15.2

The Flow of Kanban System Cards.

Source: Y. Monden, "Adaptable Kanban System Helps Toyota Maintain Just-in-Time Production," Reprinted from *Industrial Engineering,* May 1981, p. 33. Copyright © Institute of Industrial Engineers, 25 Technology Park/Atlanta, Norcross, Georgia 30092.

Step 5. The production sequence at the preceding process begins with the removal of the production-order cards from the kanban receiving post. They are reviewed and sorted before placing them on the production-ordering kanban post.

Step 6. The parts are produced in the sequence of the production-order kanban on the post.

Step 7. The production-order kanban and the container move as a pair during processing.

Step 8. In the last step the finished units are transported to storage location A to support the production requirements of the subsequent process.

All work stations and suppliers are coordinated in a similar way to provide just-in-time quantities of materials.

General Operating Rules. The operating rules for the kanban system are simple and are designed to facilitate the flow of materials, while maintaining control of inventory levels:

1. Each container must have a kanban.
2. The *subsequent* process must always go to the preceding process to get the materials it needs. The preceding process must never move the parts to the subsequent process because, sooner or later, it will be supplying parts that are not yet needed for production.
3. Containers of parts must never be removed from a storage area without an authorizing kanban.
4. The containers should always contain the same number of good parts. The use of nonstandard containers or irregularly filled containers disrupts the production flow of the subsequent process.
5. Defective parts should never be passed along to the subsequent process. Not only is material wasted, but the time of workers at the downstream work stations who process the defective parts is also wasted.
6. Total production should not exceed the total amount authorized on the production-order cards in the system. Similarly, the quantity of parts withdrawn by the subsequent process should not exceed the total amount authorized on the withdrawal cards in the system.

Determining the Inventory Level. The amount of inventory (on-hand plus scheduled receipts) of each part is equal to the authorized number of parts in each container multiplied by the number of cards for that part. The number of production-order cards is given by the following equation.

$$k = \frac{\text{Average demand during lead time plus safety stock}}{\text{Size of a container}}$$

$$= \frac{d(\bar{w} + \bar{p})(1 + \alpha)}{c};$$

where

k = Number of production-order cards for a given part;

d = Expected daily demand for the part, in units;

$\bar{w}$ = Average waiting time during the production process for the part plus materials handling time per container in decimal fractions of a day;

$\bar{p}$ = Average processing time per container in decimal fractions of a day;

c = Quantity in a standard container of the part (not more than 10 percent of the daily demand); and

α = Policy variable of not more than 10 percent, which reflects the efficiency of the work stations producing and using the part.

The container quantity c and the efficiency factor alpha are variables that management can use to control inventory. Adjusting c changes the lot sizes, and adjusting alpha changes the amount of safety stock. The kanban system is actually a special form of the base stock system that we described in Chapter 12. In this case, the stocking level is $d(\bar{w} + \bar{p})(1 + \alpha)$ and the order quantity is fixed at c units. Each time a container of parts is removed from the base stock, authorization is given to replace it.

Table 15.1 shows two sample calculations. The average lead time per container is given by $(\bar{w} + \bar{p})$. With a lead time of 0.10 days, we need 10 cards. However, if improvements in the facility layout reduce the materials handling time and waiting time $(\bar{w})$ to 0.06 days, we would need only 8 cards. The maximum authorized inventory of a part is kc units. In the first example, the maximum authorized inventory is 220 units; in the second, it is only 176 units. Reducing $\bar{w}$ by 25 percent has reduced the inventory of the part by 20 percent.

It took Toyota ten years to perfect its system. Over the years the company worked at reducing inventory levels on a trial-and-error basis. Figure 15.3 characterizes the philosophy behind the kanban system. The water level represents the inventory level, including buffer and work-in-process inventories. When the water level is high enough, the ship passes over the rocks, symbolizing good customer service. To the Japanese manager, clear sailing implies too much inventory and waste, and the order is given to reduce the number of authorized cards. Lowering the water level ultimately means that the ship will hit a rock, which represents one of the many problems encountered in manufacturing. This step is intentional because the problem becomes obvious, and the workers, supervisors, engineers, and analysts make every effort to demolish the exposed rock. For example, the Kawasaki plant in Nebraska periodically cuts buffers to almost zero. Problems are exposed, recorded, and later assigned as improvement projects. After the tops of the rocks are shaved off, inventory buffers are permanently cut. This is the trial-and-error process that the Japanese have used to shape their manufacturing environment to provide more efficient manufacturing operations.

Table 15.1

Calculations of the Number of Kanban System Cards

- *Example 1:* Lead time equals 0.10 days.

$$d = 2000 \text{ units/day} \quad \bar{p} = 0.02 \text{ days} \quad \alpha = 0.10 \quad \bar{w} = 0.08 \text{ days} \quad c = 22 \text{ units.}$$

$$k = \frac{2000(0.08 + 0.02)(1.10)}{22} = \frac{220}{22} = 10 \text{ cards.}$$

- *Example 2:* Lead time equals 0.08 days.

$$d = 2000 \text{ units/day} \quad \bar{p} = 0.02 \text{ days} \quad \alpha = 0.10 \quad \bar{w} = 0.06 \text{ days} \quad c = 22 \text{ units.}$$

$$k = \frac{2000(0.06 + 0.02)(1.10)}{22} = \frac{176}{22} = 8 \text{ cards.}$$

Figure 15.3

Philosophy Behind the Kanban System.

Final Assembly Schedule

It is obvious from our discussion of the Toyota system that the **final assembly schedule** drives the entire system. Such a system does not work well if the workload of individual work centers fluctuates on a day-to-day basis. The Japanese achieve a uniform flow at the work centers by assembling the same type and number of units each day. This creates a uniform daily demand at all feeder work stations. Techniques of capacity planning, which recognize capacity constraints at critical work stations, and line balancing are used to develop the monthly assembly schedule. For example, at Toyota there may be a need to produce 4500 Corollas per week for the next month, working two full shifts, five days a week. This means that 900 Corollas, or 450 per shift, must be produced per day. Three models of Corollas are produced: 4-door sedans (S), 2-door coupes (C), and wagons (W). Suppose Toyota needs 200 4-door sedans, 150 2-door coupes, and 100 wagons per shift to satisfy market demand. To produce 450 units in one shift of 480 minutes, the company must produce a Corolla every 480/450 = 1.067 min.

Note that the production requirements are in the ratio of 4 S's to 3 C's to 2 W's, found by dividing model production requirements by the greatest common divisor, 50. If the Toyota planner develops a production cycle consisting of 9 units, of which 4 are 4-door sedans, 3 are 2-door coupes, and 2 are wagons, the cycle would have to be completed in 9(1.067) = 9.60 min. Consequently, given the requirements per shift for each model and adequate capacity, Toyota's planner can balance the mixed-model assembly line for the month's production schedule. Table 15.2 shows the data for this problem and a possible production cycle for the models. Note that the production is not batched by grouping all models of one type. Instead (in this example) the cycle would be repeated 50 times per shift [or 50(9.60 min.) = 480 min.]. This

Table 15.2

A Production Cycle for Corolla Models

Model	Production Requirements per Shift	Number Required in One Cycle
4-door sedan (S)	200	4
2-door coupe (C)	150	3
Wagon (W)	100	2
Total	450	9

Cycle

S–W–S–C–S–C–S–W–C

Table 15.3

Advantages of Just-in-Time Systems

- Reduce space requirements.
- Reduce inventory investment in purchased parts, raw materials, work-in-process, and finished goods.
- Reduce manufacturing lead times.
- Increase the productivity of direct labor employees, indirect support employees, and clerical staff.
- Increase equipment utilization.
- Reduce paperwork and require only simple planning systems.
- Set valid priorities for production scheduling.
- Encourage the participation of the work force.
- Increase product quality.

repetition generates a steady rate of component requirements for the various models and allows the use of small lot sizes. Consequently, the capacity requirements of feeder work stations are greatly smoothed. These requirements can be compared to actual capacities during the planning phase, and modifications to the cycle, production requirements, or capacities can be made as necessary.

Managerial Considerations

Although JIT systems have worked well in some large companies, they cannot treat all manufacturing ills. Let's examine some of the managerial considerations regarding JIT systems.

Advantages of JIT Systems. Table 15.3 contains a list of some of the advantages of JIT systems. One of the goals of these systems is to drive setup times down so low that production of one unit or a part becomes economical. Although this goal is rarely achieved, the focus is still on small-lot production. In addition, constant attention is given to cutting safety stock and WIP inventory between manufacturing processes. The result is to reduce the amounts of storage space and inventory investment. Smaller lot sizes and smoothed flows of materials help to reduce manufacturing lead times and increase work-force productivity and equipment utilization. The kanban system is simplicity itself. Product mix or volume can be changed by adjusting the number of cards in the system. The priority of each production order is obvious, since the only time a production-order card can be posted is when a container of a part is withdrawn. The sequence of production-order cards on the post reflects the priority of the jobs associated with those cards.

Just-in-time systems also involve a considerable amount of work-force participation in decision making on the shop floor. Small-group interaction sessions held by workers encourage participation and have resulted in improvements in many aspects of manufacturing, not the least of which is product quality. Overall, the advantages of JIT systems experienced by the companies using them have caused many managers to reevaluate their own systems and consider adapting their plant operations to the JIT philosophy.

Disadvantages of JIT Systems. Table 15.4 contains a list of some of the disadvantages of JIT systems. Most of them relate to system requirements that may pose problems for many firms in the United States.

From a behavioral perspective, the workers and first-line supervisors must now take on responsibilities formerly assigned to middle managers and support staff. Activities such as scheduling, expediting, and productivity improvements become part of the duties of personnel much lower in the organizational structure than before. Consequently, a reorientation of the organization is needed, requiring close cooperation and mutual trust between the work force and management. Such cooperation and trust may be difficult to achieve, particularly with the typical adversarial positions taken by labor and management in the past.

Certain other aspects of JIT systems may preclude their use generally. The firm must have a product focus and daily production schedules must be stable for extended periods. At Toyota, the master production schedule is stated in daily time periods for three months and revised only once a month. The first month of the schedule is frozen in order to avoid disruptive changes in the daily production schedule for each work station; the work stations execute the same work schedule each day of the month. At the beginning of each month

Table 15.4

Disadvantages of Just-in-Time Systems

- Require workers and first-line supervisors to take responsibility for shop-floor production control and productivity improvements.
- Require an atmosphere of close cooperation and mutual trust between the work force and management.
- Require daily production schedules that are virtually identical for extended periods.
- Require actual daily production to closely approximate the daily schedule.
- Cannot respond rapidly to changes in product design, product mix, or large demand volumes.
- Require a large number of production setups and frequent shipments of purchased items from suppliers.
- Require parts to be produced and moved in the smallest containers possible.
- Not well-suited for irregularly used parts or specially ordered products.

cards are reissued for the new daily production rate. Stable schedules are needed, so that production lines can be balanced and new assignments found for employees who would otherwise be underutilized. The JIT system cannot respond quickly to changes in the schedules because there is little slack inventory or capacity to absorb these changes.

If the inventory advantages of JIT systems are to be realized, the firm must perform a large number of setups, so that container sizes can be kept as small as possible. This objective requires efforts to reduce setup times significantly. In some cases, small setup times will not be possible, and large-lot production will still have to be used. Also, if frequently scheduled, small shipments of purchased items cannot be arranged with suppliers, large inventory savings for these items cannot be realized. Such arrangements may be difficult in many cases in the United States because of the geographical dispersion of suppliers. Finally, even though cards can be assigned to irregularly used parts, the policy variable α must be larger to provide more safety stock. This precaution is necessary because JIT systems do not provide forward visibility of requirements as does, for example, MRP. Tomorrow's requirements are assumed to be the same as today's. Also, if the firm produces any items specifically to customer order, JIT systems can only be used for those parts or raw materials that have reasonably stable requirements. In most cases these items would be low in the product structure and most of the advantages of JIT production would be lost in relation to other considerations.

Use of Just-in-Time Systems in the United States

The use of just-in-time production concepts is becoming more common in the United States. However, initial attempts faced a number of obstacles. At General Motors, for example, a plan to reduce stock at one plant ran into trouble because the production superintendent refused to cut back production of unneeded parts; his salary was based on the amount of production at his plant.

The realignment of reward systems was not the only initial hurdle. Labor contracts have consistently reduced management's flexibility in reassigning workers as the need arises. At Toyota, management deals with only one company union, and there are only eight different labor classifications in a typical plant. A comparable automobile plant in the United States has dozens of labor classifications. In order to gain more flexibility, management in some cases has negotiated union concessions, and in other cases it has relocated the production facility to take advantage of nonunion labor.

Even the layout of many plants had to be changed. For example, many plants receive raw materials and purchased parts by rail. To get smaller, more frequent shipments, truck deliveries are preferable. Loading docks had to be reconstructed or expanded and certain operations relocated to accommodate the changes in transportation mode and quantities of the arriving materials. Finally, the ability to manage purchased item inventory is related to the number of suppliers with which the company must deal. At one time, General Motors had more than 3500 suppliers just for its assembly operations. In contrast, Toyota has only 250. General Motors has significantly reduced its number of suppliers. This change placed more reliance on fewer suppliers, which had its own risks, but contracts were worked out to ensure dependable delivery of high-quality materials.

Obstacles such as these were overcome by many firms. The automobile industry offers some good examples. Chrysler uses a JIT system and found that by changing to reusable containers for moving parts it could save $9 million in cardboard packaging. Ford and GM also use JIT systems. In particular, GM designed its new Saturn complex in Tennessee to incorporate on-site component production and assembly operations. Many other suppliers are planning to locate nearby. Parts suppliers will be linked directly to the plant's central computer, enabling them to monitor production schedules and better time their shipments. Of course, Japanese firms locating in the United States use JIT concepts, including Nissan in Smyrna, Tennessee, Honda in Marysville, Ohio, Toyota in Fremont, California, and Mazda in Flat Rock, Michigan.

Just-in-time concepts are also being used in other repetitive manufacturing industries. The name used at IBM is "continuous flow manufacturing" and at Hewlett-Packard, "stockless production." Motorola, Honeywell, Westinghouse, Black and Decker, Briggs and Stratton, John Deere, Bendix, Rockwell, and Tennant all use JIT concepts at some of their operations. The particular form used by companies in the United States may not be a mirror image of the JIT systems used in Japan; however, these companies have utilized key elements of the JIT system to their advantage.

MANUFACTURING IN THE PROCESS INDUSTRIES

Firms in the process industries have a different environment than firms in the repetitive manufacturing or fabrication and assembly industries, where MRP or JIT systems are applicable. Process industry firms can be characterized as having high-volume production and a product focus, such as those found in industries making major chemicals, paper, beer, oil, steel, and forest products. They often have a flow-shop orientation, utilizing product layouts with high capital intensity. However, some process industry firms have hybrid flow shop-job shop orientations because their products are highly differentiated. These industries include drugs and specialized chemicals.

The process industries are more capital intensive than the fabrication and assembly industries. Taylor et al., (1981) found that the process industries have a ratio of $1.8 of sales to $1 of gross plant investment, compared to a ratio of 3:1 for the fabrication and assembly industries. Process industry

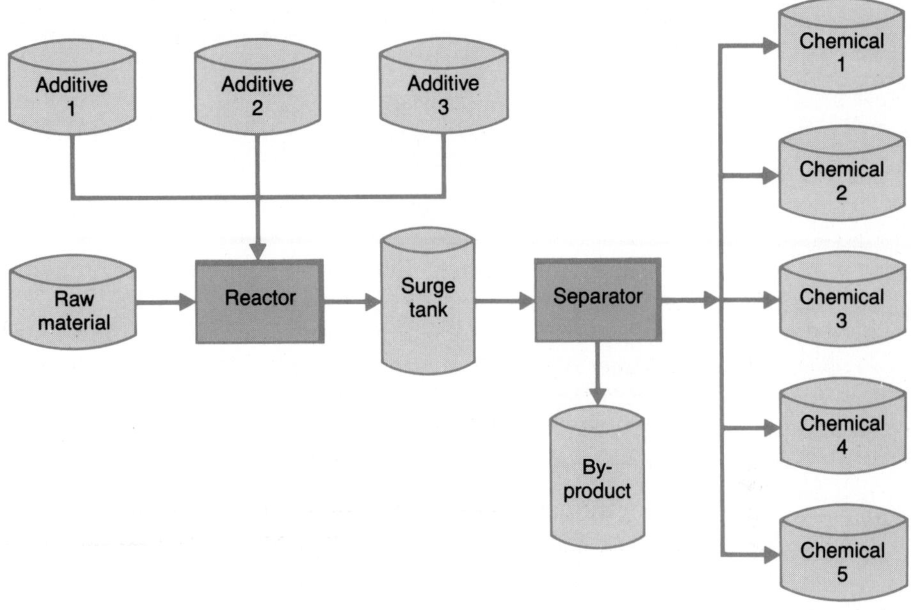

Figure 15.4

Chemical Process Example.

plants are designed for a specific throughput, and the equipment typically operates seven days a week, three shifts per day. Thus production and inventory management systems must be capacity-oriented because the capacity cushion is very small and it is impossible to significantly increase capacity with extra overtime or shifts.

Lot-Size Considerations

Consider Fig. 15.4, which depicts two chemical manufacturing processes: reaction and separation. A surge tank separates the two processes and can absorb minor variations in process flow, although its capacity is insufficient to decouple the reactor schedule from that of the separator. Consequently, we will treat the system as a single process, which uses one raw material and three additives to produce five chemicals and one by-product.

Plant Load. Suppose that the plant produces the five chemicals in a predetermined cycle. That is, the chemicals are produced 1–2–3–4–5 in each cycle, and the cycles are repeated enough times to satisfy annual demand for the chemicals. For chemical i, the total number of days of production per year T_i is

$$T_i = N_i t_{si} + D_i t_{pi},$$

where

N_i = Number of cycles per year for chemical i;

t_{si} = Setup time in days for chemical i;

D_i = Annual demand for chemical i; and

t_{pi} = Process time in days per unit of chemical i.

The factor T_i is actually a measure of *load*. The only unknown variable in the relationship for T_i is N_i. By changing N_i, the time required for setups changes, while the total time required to produce the annual demand remains the same. Also, by changing N_i, the lot size for chemical i changes because the lot size is equal to D_i divided by N_i. Small values of N_i create large lots, and large values create small lots. Consequently, some value of N_i minimizes annual setup and inventory holding costs.

Total Annual Costs. If we assume that the demand for each chemical is constant and uniform throughout the year, we can use a modified version of the total cost equation for the economic order quantity discussed in Chapter 12, or

$$C_i = \text{Annual setup costs} + \text{Annual holding costs},$$

or

$$C_i = \frac{D_i s_i}{Q_i} + \left(\frac{Q_i}{2}\right)\left(1 - \frac{r_i}{p_i}\right)H_i,$$

where

C_i = Total cost per year for chemical i;

D_i = Annual demand for chemical i;

s_i = Cost to set up the process for one lot (batch) of chemical i;

Q_i = Lot size in units (barrels);

r_i = Constant daily demand for chemical i;

p_i = Daily production rate of chemical i for the common processes; and

H_i = Cost to hold one unit (barrel) in inventory for one year.

Also, $Q_i = D_i/N_i$, where N_i is the number of cycles per year for chemical i. The factor that modifies the annual holding costs, $1 - r_i/p_i$, comes from the assumption that demand for the chemical occurs continuously throughout the year, but that production is no longer instantaneous as assumed in calculating the EOQ. Consequently, inventory is being consumed even as it is produced.

Constraints. Two constraints must be satisfied in order to have a feasible schedule. Recall that we said that the choice of N_i affects the total setup time and the load on the production process. Consequently, the values of N_i, or the lot sizes Q_i, generated from a production and inventory control system should satisfy the following constraint.

Total load on the facility in days of production and setup	$\leq$	Total number of production days available for the year,

or

$$\sum_{i=1}^{m} T_i \leq T_A,$$

where

T_i = Total setup plus processing days needed for chemical i;

T_A = Total number of production days for the year; and

m = Total number of chemicals (products).

The other constraint is called the **schedule interference constraint.** If the total time required to produce one cycle exceeds the stock depletion time for any one of the chemicals, that chemical will suffer a stockout. Therefore

Total time to produce one cycle in days	$\leq$	Minimum number of days to deplete the stock of any chemical,

or

$$\sum_{j=1}^{m} (t_{sj} + Q_j t_{pj}) \leq \min_i \left[\frac{Q_i}{r_i}\right] \quad \text{for} \quad i = 1, 2, \ldots, m.$$

The risk of violating this constraint is greatest when the "best" lot size is determined for each product independently of its effect on the others and all the products must be processed on the same equipment.

Developing a Feasible Schedule

One way to overcome the problem of schedule interference is to find a common number of cycles N per year to produce each chemical; that is, to make all $N_i = N$. We could do this by trial and error for various values of N, making sure each time that capacity is not exceeded. We would then choose the value of N that minimizes the total cost, summed over all chemicals.

Consider Table 15.5, which contains data for our chemical plant problem. Using these data, we generated Table 15.6, which contains the total load and

Table 15.5

Data for the Chemical Plant Scheduling Problem

	Demand		Production Data			Costs	
Chemical (i)	Annual (barrels) (D_i)	Daily (barrels) (r_i)	Daily (barrels) (p_i)	Process time per barrel (days) (t_{pi})	Setup time (days) (t_{si})	Holding (H_i)	Setup (S_i)
1	10,500	30	190	0.005	1.00	$0.21	$200
2	2,100	6	25	0.040	0.50	0.52	150
3	5,950	17	71	0.014	2.00	0.40	300
4	17,850	51	245	0.004	0.33	0.15	100
5	3,150	9	100	0.010	1.50	0.32	250

total cost for various choices of N. Suppose that the total number of production days available is 350. Thus we can satisfy the total capacity constraint if the value of N does not exceed 5 (for $N = 5$, the total load on the plant is 349.35 days). The value of N that minimizes total cost is 2 cycles per year.

The solution $N = 2$ also satisfies the schedule interference constraint, which we verify in the following manner. Since all $N_i = N$, each chemical has the same stock depletion time of $\frac{1}{2}$ year, or 175 days. We multiply the lot size for each chemical by its process time per barrel, sum them, and add the total setup time to get the total cycle time, t_c, in days. For $N = 2$,

$$\begin{aligned} t_c &= 5250(0.005) + 1050(0.040) + 2975(0.014) + 8925(0.004) \\ &\quad + 1575(0.010) + 5.33 \\ &= 166.68 \text{ days.} \end{aligned}$$

Consequently, since the total cycle time for the production of the chemicals is less than the depletion time of the chemicals, we should not experience any stockouts.

Process Industry Production and Inventory Control Systems

We have generated what might be called a master production schedule for the chemical plant. Using a bill of materials for each chemical, we can determine the need for raw materials and additives. However, we must keep in mind the yield loss in the form of a by-product (see Fig. 15.4). The requirements for the raw materials and additives must be adjusted for this loss in output. Bolander and Taylor (1983) suggest a scheduling technique for solving such problems

Table 15.6

Effects of Lot Size on Load and Total Cost for the Chemical Plant Scheduling Problem

Chemical (i)	Cycles Per Year														
	$N = 1$			$N = 2$			$N = 3$			$N = 5$			$N = 10$		
	$Q_i = \frac{D_i}{N}$	Load (T_i)	Total cost (C_i)	$Q_i = \frac{D_i}{N}$	Load (T_i)	Total cost (C_i)	$Q_i = \frac{D_i}{N}$	Load (T_i)	Total cost (C_i)	$Q_i = \frac{D_i}{N}$	Load (T_i)	Total cost (C_i)	$Q_i = \frac{D_i}{N}$	Load (T_i)	Total cost (C_i)
1	10,500	53.50	$1,128.42	5,250	54.50	$ 864.21	3,500	55.50	$ 909.47	2,100	57.50	$1,185.68	1,050	62.50	$ 2,092.84
2	2,100	84.50	564.96	1,050	85.00	507.48	700	85.50	588.32	420	86.50	832.99	210	89.00	1,541.50
3	5,950	85.30	1,205.07	2,975	87.30	1,052.53	1,983	89.30	1,201.64	1,190	93.30	1,681.01	595	103.30	3,090.51
4	17,850	71.73	1,160.07	8,925	72.06	730.03	5,950	72.39	653.36	3,570	73.05	712.01	1,785	74.70	1,106.01
5	3,150	33.00	708.64	1,575	34.50	729.32	1,050	36.00	902.88	630	39.00	1,341.73	315	46.50	2,545.86
Total		328.03	$4,767.16		333.36	$3,883.57		338.69	$4,255.67		349.35	$5,753.42		376.00	$10,376.72

called *time phased forward scheduling* (TPFS). This system schedules capacity forward through each operation from the first bottleneck operation. Completion of the final production process determines the completion date of the product. After the capacity has been scheduled, materials requirements are checked to ensure that there are enough to support the schedule. Bills of materials and time-phased inventory records are used to keep track of materials.

Another technique often used for production planning in the process industries is linear programming. Problems such as product mix and plant loading can be analyzed with the help of linear programming. Appendix C addresses linear programming and its applications.

CHOOSING A PRODUCTION/INVENTORY MANAGEMENT SYSTEM

We conclude this chapter with a brief comparison of the various production/inventory management systems for discrete item production systems. In Chapter 12, we presented the reorder point system (ROP) and in Chapter 14, the material requirements planning system (MRP). In the supplement to Chapter 14 we discussed optimized production technology (OPT)* and in this chapter, the just-in-time (JIT) system. Obviously, there are several systems to choose from, and many more will become available in the future. Do all these systems work equally well in a given environment? To this question we respond: absolutely not. In our research of these systems (see references at the end of this chapter) we found that MRP outperforms ROP as the number of levels in bills of materials increase. Also, the larger the lot sizes, the greater is the advantage of MRP over ROP, which does not recognize product structure. The kanban system works well in high-volume, repetitive manufacturing environments with small lot sizes and short setup times. But if you take the kanban system out of that environment, it will perform poorly. For example, MRP or a hybrid of MRP with kanban, might work better when the company produces items to customer order, as well as to stock. However, OPT may outperform MRP because capacity considerations are directly incorporated in requirements planning, although more experience with this system is needed before we will know whether it is really better than MRP. In general, although there are many environments in which several systems could work well, there are also some environments where the systems would not work well. The choice of a system can have an effect on inventory levels and customer service. High inventory levels put a strain on financial resources and may limit the capability of the company to invest in needed capital improvements. Poor customer service affects market share and the

* OPT is a registered trademark of Creative Output, Incorporated.

ability of the company to compete in the marketplace. An inappropriate choice of system could be an expensive mistake.

Which specific aspects of manufacturing affect system performance? We have identified a number of factors that affect inventory investment, productivity, and customer service, but, by and large, the production/inventory management system does not have an overriding impact on any of these criteria. From our studies we concluded that reducing lot sizes and setup times have the greatest impact, followed by reducing yield losses and increasing worker flexibility. Other aspects of manufacturing, such as capacity slack or safety stock, product structure, facility design, and supplier performance, had less impact on performance. Nonetheless, our philosophy is that firms should "get their house in order" by working to improve these environmental factors for whatever production/inventory system is in use. For example, reducing lot sizes and setup times will improve inventory investment and customer service, regardless of the system being used. The point is that any production/inventory system used will not by itself set things right, but significant improvements in performance *can* be achieved by shaping the manufacturing environment properly.

CHAPTER HIGHLIGHTS

In this chapter, we discussed production systems for high-volume situations: repetitive manufacturing and continuous flow manufacturing. Some of the highlights of the chapter are:

- The purpose of JIT systems is to produce or deliver the right items in the quantities needed by subsequent production processes or customers at the time needed. The intent is to coordinate production flows to reduce the need for inventories.
- Toyota's kanban system uses withdrawal cards and production-ordering cards to control production flow. The withdrawal card specifies the item and quantity the subsequent process should withdraw from the preceding process and where to find the item. The production-ordering card specifies the item and quantity that the preceding process must produce each time, where to store the finished item and input materials, and where to find them.
- Material cannot be withdrawn without a withdrawal card. Production cannot begin without a production-ordering card. The produced items are placed in containers, which should always have the same standard number of parts in them. The authorized inventory of a part is a function of the number of authorized cards for that item. The number of cards depends on average demand during manufacturing lead time, the container size, and a policy variable to adjust for unexpected occurrences.
- JIT systems have many advantages, including reductions in inventory, space requirements, and paperwork, and increases in productivity, worker participation, machine utilization, and quality. JIT systems also have disadvantages, such as requiring stable schedules for extended periods of

time and not being well-suited for irregularly used parts or specially ordered products.

- Process industries can be characterized as having a flow-shop orientation, high-volume demand, and high capital intensity. Lot size determination must be capacity sensitive. When a number of products must be processed in a common facility, the lot size must be chosen to avoid stockouts during the production cycle. The total load on the facility must also be checked to ensure schedule feasibility.
- TPFS is a forward scheduling system that recognizes capacity when determining the schedule of a process-oriented plant. It maintains feasibility with respect to capacity and uses principles similar to MRP, except that it has the capacity of phasing requirements forward for selected items.
- For a given manufacturing environment, the choice of a production/inventory system can make a difference. Also, certain environmental factors, if improved, can result in significant improvements in inventory investment, customer service, and productivity, regardless of the system in use.

KEY TERMS

continuous flow manufacturing
final assembly schedule
just-in-time (JIT) system
kanban
repetitive manufacturing
schedule interference constraint

STUDY QUESTIONS

1. Explain the purpose of just-in-time systems. Why is JIT considered a *pull system*?
2. Toyota's kanban system utilizes two main types of cards that authorize certain actions. Explain the purposes of these cards and describe how they are used.
3. Consider the formula for the number of kanban system cards for an item. If the process for that item is *inefficient*, which parameters in the equation might be larger than desirable? Why? Suppose that a supervisor wanted to increase the safety stock. Which parameter would be adjusted?
4. It took Toyota ten years to perfect its kanban system. Why? How can the system be used to identify areas for improvement?
5. Why is the final assembly schedule critical to the Toyota kanban system? What characteristics must the schedule have?
6. Consider the following statement: "The just-in-time system is a total managerial concept, whereas the kanban system and systems like it are merely information systems designed to provide the basis for the timing and sizing decisions of production quantities." Do you agree or disagree? Why?
7. What factors should management consider when deciding whether to use a JIT system in a given manufacturing environment?
8. Which aspects of JIT systems have been troublesome for U.S. manufacturers to date? Why?
9. Which factors make process industries

different from fabrication and assembly industries? Why is their consideration important in choosing a production/inventory system?

10. What constraints should be considered when determining lot sizes in the process industry?

11. Why does the choice of a production/inventory system have implications for the firm as a whole?

12. What is meant by "shaping the environment"?

PROBLEMS

1. A certain Japanese automobile manufacturer operates an assembly plant in the United States. The plant uses a kanban system to control production and inventory. You have been put in charge of a certain machine group that manufactures a tie-rod assembly. The daily demand rate for tie-rods is 1000 units. The average waiting time for containers of parts in your machine group is 0.5 days, and the average processing time per container of tie-rods is 0.1 days. Each container holds 100 tie-rods. You have decided that you should allow 10 percent of the average waiting time and processing time per container for unexpected contingencies. How many cards would you suggest for controlling production of the tie-rods?

2. A company using a kanban system has a machine group that is not very efficient. For example, the daily demand for part L105A is 3000 units. The average waiting time for a container of parts is 0.8 days. The processing time for a container of L105A is 0.2 days, and a container holds 270 units. There are presently 20 kanban production cards for this item.
   (a) What is the implicit value of the policy variable α?
   (b) What is the total planned inventory (work in process and finished products) for item L105A?
   (c) Suppose that the policy variable α was set equal to zero. How many cards would be needed now? What is the effect of the policy variable in this example?

3. A manufacturer of plastic pipe recently purchased a used extruding machine. The company plans to produce two products on the machine. Product 1 is a one-inch diameter pipe and product 2 is a two-inch diameter pipe. The current capacity of the extruder is 250 feet of pipe per day, regardless of the diameter. The company plans to use the extruder 350 days per year. Specific production data are

Data Category	Product 1	Product 2
Demand (ft/yr)	35,000	70,000
Setup time (days)	3	4
Current lot size	18,708	30,550

   (a) Will the company violate the schedule interference constraint with the current lot sizes? Explain.
   (b) Will the annual machine time capacity be exceeded? Explain.

4. Again consider the extruding machine situation in Problem 3. Suppose that the engineers have been able to increase the maximum output capability of the extruder to 350 feet of pipe per day. In addition, you now have the following data.

Product	Setup Cost	Holding Cost (per ft per yr)
1	$300	$0.10
2	200	0.15

Find the common number of cycles for the products that minimizes cost and does not violate capacity and schedule interference constraints.

5. A candy manufacturer produces three varieties of chocolate. The processing system can be thought of as a single machine that must be cleaned and inspected between each batch of chocolate. The company produces the products in the sequence 1–2–3 and operates 250 days per year.

Product	Annual Demand (lb)	Setup Time (days)	Process Time (days/lb)
1	50,000	2	0.001
2	20,000	2	0.003
3	10,000	3	0.010

(a) The company is interested in keeping inventories low. Find the largest number of cycles per year, N, such that the total number of production days per year is not exceeded.

(b) What are the batch sizes for each product?

(c) Based on your recommendation in part (a), what are the effective daily production rates for each product? Do they depend on the number of cycles per year?

6. A chemical plant produces four chemical solvents used in the manufacture of wall coverings. The plant operates 250 days per year. The plant scheduler has suggested lot sizes for the items, which all must be produced in common facilities. Production data are shown in Table 15.7.

(a) Will the application of the suggested lot sizes cause any product stockouts if the production sequence is 1–2–3–4? Which ones? Explain.

(b) Determine the least-cost lot sizes such that each item is set up the same number of times per year and show that you have a feasible schedule.

7. A company processes five products on the same equipment. The data for these items is given in Table 15.8. Assume 250 working days per year.

(a) The master scheduler for this company has developed the scheduled lot sizes and plans to sequence the products 1–2–3–4–5. Which products will suffer stockouts if this approach is used?

Table 15.7

Product	Annual Demand (gal)	Daily Production Rate (gal)	Setup Time (days)	Setup Cost	Holding Cost (per gal per yr)	Suggested Lot Size (gal)
1	10,000	320	1	$40	$1.00	956
2	15,000	240	2	80	0.25	3578
3	60,000	720	2	30	0.50	3286
4	5,000	100	1	100	0.30	2041

Table 15.8

Product	Annual Demand (gal)	Daily Production Rate (gal)	Setup Time (days)	Annual Holding Cost	Setup Cost (per run)	Scheduled Lot Size (gal)
1	5,000	100	2	1.60	$40	559
2	10,000	400	1	1.40	25	630
3	7,000	350	3	0.60	30	872
4	15,000	200	1	1.15	27	1,003
5	4,000	100	1	1.65	80	679

(b) Calculate the minimum-cost lot sizes for each item for a common-cycle approach. Will this schedule be feasible? Why?

8. Two managers of a chemical processing plant are having a disagreement over the scheduling of three products that must be processed on a certain bottling machine. Simon Kingly claims that his schedule, which makes use of a lot-size formula for each product separately, will minimize setup and carrying costs for the products. Ignatius Withet, however, claims that Kingly's schedule will not work because it will result in stockouts. Production data are shown in Table 15.9. The bottling machine operates 4000 hours per year.

(a) Analyze Kingly's claim and determine whether there will be a stockout problem if the products are bottled in 1–2–3 order in each cycle.

(b) If there is a stockout problem, develop a plan that will work, based on the sequence 1–2–3 for each cycle. Specify the production quantities that you would recommend and show that your proposal will work.

(c) Compare your plan to Kingly's plan.

9. A mustard manufacturer makes five varieties of mustard on the same machines. Management believes that each variety should be produced in sequence in each cycle. It takes one-half day to set up for a change from one variety to the next. Production data are

Table 15.9

Product	Demand (gal/yr)	Hourly Production Rate (gal)	Annual Holding Cost (per gal)	Changeover Cost	Changeover Time (hr)	Kingly's Lot Size (gal)
1	200,000	125	1/6 dollar	$400	4	40,000
2	100,000	100	2/3 dollar	250	3	10,000
3	600,000	500	1/7 dollar	300	5	60,000

Variety	Daily Demand (cases)	Daily Prod. Rate (cases)	Annual Carry Cost $/case	Setup Cost
1	10	50	$5.00	$100
2	5	25	6.00	75
3	15	100	7.00	50
4	20	100	5.00	125
5	50	250	6.67	150

The company works 200 days per year. Prepare a master production schedule for the facility for the next 50 days that is feasible from a capacity standpoint and will not incur stockouts. You may assume that on-hand inventory will cover requirements until you begin processing each item for the first time. Your goal should be to find a schedule that is as cost effective as possible.

SELECTED REFERENCES

Bolander, S. F., and S. C. Taylor, "Time-Phased Forward Scheduling: A Capacity Dominated Scheduling Technique," *Production and Inventory Management* (First Quarter 1983), pp. 83–96.

Haglund, E. A., "Primary Metals—We're Different," *Production and Inventory Management* (Third Quarter 1981), pp. 21–26.

Hahn, Chan K., Peter Pinto, and Daniel Bragg, "Just-in-Time Production and Purchasing," *Journal of Purchasing and Materials Management* (Fall 1983), pp. 2–10.

Hall, R. W., *Driving the Productivity Machine.* Falls Church, Va.: The American Production and Inventory Control Society, 1981.

Krajewski, L. J., B. King, L. P. Ritzman, and D. S. Wong, "Kanban, MRP and Shaping the Manufacturing Environment." To appear in *Management Science.*

Melynk, S., and P. Carter, "Viewing Kanban as an (s,Q) System: Developing New Insights into a Japanese Method of Production and Inventory Control." In Sang M. Lee and Gary Schwendimen (eds.), *Management by Japanese Systems.* New York: Praeger, 1982.

Monden, Y., "Adaptable Kanban System Helps Toyota Maintain Just-in-Time Production," *Journal of Industrial Engineering* (May 1981), pp. 29–46.

Monden, Y., "What Makes the Toyota Production System Really Tick?" *Journal of Industrial Engineering* (January 1981), pp. 36–46.

Nelleman, D. O., and L. Smith, "Just-in-Time vs. Just-in-Case Production/Inventory Systems Concepts Borrowed Back from Japan," *Production and Inventory Management* (Second Quarter 1982), pp. 12–20.

Rice, J. W., and T. Yoshikawa, "A Comparison of Kanban and MRP Concepts for the Control of Repetitive Manufacturing Systems," *Production and Inventory Management* (First Quarter 1982), pp. 1–13.

Ritzman, Larry P., Barry E. King, and Lee J. Krajewski, "Manufacturing Performance—Pulling the Right Levers," *Harvard Business Review* (March–April 1984), pp. 143–152.

Ritzman, L. P., and L. J. Krajewski, "Performance Comparisons Between MRP and Reorder Point Systems." In H. Bekrioglu (ed.), *Simulation and Inventory Control.* La Jolla, Ca.: Society for Computer Simulation, 1983.

Schonberger, R. J., *Japanese Manufacturing Techniques.* New York: The Free Press, 1982.

Smith-Daniels, Vicki, "The Lot Sizing and Sequencing Problem in Process Industries." Unpublished Ph.D. dissertation, Ohio State University, 1983.

Taylor, S. C., "Production and Inventory Management in the Process Industries: A State of the Art Survey," *Production and Inventory Management* (First Quarter 1979), pp. 1–16.

Taylor, S. C., S. M. Seward, S. F. Bolander, and R. C. Heard, "Process Industry Production and Inventory Framework: A Summary," *Production and Inventory Management* (First Quarter 1981), pp. 15–32.

Taylor, S. C., S. M. Seward, and S. F. Bolander, "Why the Process Industries are Different," *Production and Inventory Management* (Fourth Quarter 1981), pp. 9–24.

CHAPTER 16

WORK-FORCE AND OPERATIONS SCHEDULING

Some Managerial Issues

- Which of our customers or jobs should have top priority?
- What information do we need for effective operations and work-force scheduling?
- If we have a staff plan, how can we develop an effective work-force schedule?
- How important is our choice of priority dispatching rules to the effectiveness of the operating system?

Chapter Outline

Scheduling is the allocation of resources over time to accomplish a set of specific tasks. Poor scheduling decisions can damage an organization, but, in the overall scheme of things, it is of secondary importance to a number of other managerial decisions. For example, the management of a manufacturing company must make decisions about the products it will produce, competitive priorities, and strategy focus; choose an appropriate process design and layout; and commit the level of capital and labor required for the level of production desired—all before it makes sense to schedule the various tasks to be performed. Similarly, the planning of emergency services such as fire protection first requires an analysis of the best location for fire stations, decisions about the type and quantity of fire-fighting equipment at each location, and a staffing plan for each station. Only then can decisions such as specific work schedules for each employee be determined. Consequently, the process of scheduling becomes important *after* the nature of the tasks to be performed and the available resources have been determined.

WORK-FORCE SCHEDULING

Work-force scheduling involves the specification of on-duty and off-duty time periods for each employee over a certain time horizon. For example, work-force scheduling is concerned with assigning employees such as postal clerks, nurses, or machinists to specific day and shift work periods. In this sense we address the planning aspect of work-force scheduling. Another aspect of scheduling is assigning workers to specific tasks during their on-duty time periods. We address that issue when we discuss operations scheduling.

Purpose of the Work-Force Schedule

Consider the situation explained in Box 16.1. The schedule posted by the manager is shown in Table 16.1. Work-force schedules such as this one translate the staffing plan (see Chapter 11) into operational schedules of work for each member of the work force. The staffing plan for APS calls for ten employees in the time period covered. The work-force schedule for these employees must specify the days of the week that each employee will be on duty. This would not be a problem if the company worked only one eight-hour shift, five days a week, but that is not the case here. In Table 16.1, the X's denote the days the employees are on duty. For example, Jones is off duty on Tuesday and Saturday each week.

Box 16.1

AMALGAMATED PARCEL SERVICE

The Amalgamated Parcel Service (APS) is a family-owned company that delivers packages by truck to most cities and towns in the state of Ohio. There are two main parcel processing centers—one located in Columbus and the other in Mansfield.

The centers are open seven days a week and can be operated with a minimum number of employees. Any of the employees can perform the typical tasks such as loading and unloading trucks and sorting the packages by destination. The centers are not unionized, and management is very interested in good employee relations. The Columbus center, however, recently had some grievances filed regarding work schedules. A new work schedule had been posted, and five employees immediately complained.

John Tower, Columbus center manager, explained the scheduling procedure. "We went into our records and estimated the number of employees we need each day of the week. These estimates turned out to be quite stable from week to week. We have ten employees, each of them working a five-day week. We just went down the list of employees, assigning them to work days until all the daily requirements were covered. When we got to the bottom of the list there were still some employees who did not have five work days assigned. We kept two constraints in mind when assigning these excess days of work. We tried to spread the excess capacity evenly throughout the week, and we made sure that there were no excess workers on Sunday. Excess employees can be put to work on maintenance activities."

Table 16.1

Posted APS Work-Force Schedule

Employee	Monday	Tuesday	Wednesday	Thursday	Friday	Saturday	Sunday	
Jones	X	Off	X	X	X	Off	X	
Smith	X	Off	X	X	X	Off	X	
Carter	X	X	X	X	X	Off	Off	
Johnson	X	X	X	X	X	Off	Off	
Kramer	X	X	X	X	X	Off	Off	
Farley	Off	X	X	X	X	X	Off	
Whitcomb	Off	X	X	X	X	X	Off	
Anderson	X	Off	X	X	X	X	Off	
Booth	X	X	Off	X	X	X	Off	
Bell	X	Off	X	X	X	X	Off	
								Total
Capacity (C)	8	6	9	10	10	5	2	50
Requirements (R)	6	4	8	9	10	3	2	42
Slack ($C - R$)	2	2	1	1	0	2	0	8

Determining the periods of duty for each employee in itself does not make the staffing plan operational. The daily work-force requirements must be satisfied. These requirements were stated in the aggregate in the staffing plan. Thus for an APS staffing plan specifying an expected overall requirement of 168 employee-days per month, or 42 employee-days per week, Table 16.1 shows the daily expected requirements. The work-force schedule must determine the periods of duty for each employee, so that daily requirements are met or no more than the amount of backlogged demand specified in the staffing plan is allowed. The work-force capacity available each day must meet or exceed daily requirements. If it does not, the schedule must be changed by rearranging the off-duty periods of the work force until these requirements are met. If such a schedule cannot be found, the staffing plan may have to be changed to provide for more employees, overtime hours, or authorization for larger backlogs.

Finally, work-force schedules provide the basis for day-to-day reallocation of the employees as requirements change. Suppose that the manager at the APS center in Columbus finds out that some special shipments will arrive on Sunday, requiring two more employees than usual. In the schedule in Table 16.1, you can see that there are three days having a slack capacity of two employees. To resolve his problem, the manager could ask Carter and Johnson, for example, to work Sunday in exchange for a day off on Monday.

Constraints

From the technical standpoint, the constraints imposed on the work-force schedule amount to living within the resources provided by the staffing plan and meeting the requirements placed on the operating system. However, there may be numerous other constraints, involving legal and behavioral considerations. For example, a hospital may be required to have at least a minimum number of registered nurses on duty on each floor at all times. Similarly, a minimum number of fire and safety personnel must be on duty at a fire station at all times. These constraints limit management's flexibility in developing work-force schedules, but the constraints imposed by the psychological needs of the work force can be even more complex. Some of these constraints are written into labor agreements. For example, an employer may agree to give employees a certain number of consecutive days off per week or limit employees' consecutive work days to a certain maximum. Other provisions might govern the allocation of vacations, days off for holidays, or rotating shift assignments. In addition, the preferences of the employees themselves need to be considered. All of these considerations complicate work-force scheduling tremendously.

One way to deal with certain undesirable aspects of scheduling is to use a **rotating schedule**. In such a schedule, employees rotate through a series of workdays and/or hours, so that each person has the same opportunity to have weekends or holidays off and to work days, as well as evenings and nights. For example, the schedules in Table 16.1 could be rotated by giving each employee the next employee's schedule the following week. For example, Jones takes Smith's schedule, Smith takes Carter's, and so forth. After 10 weeks, Jones would have the first schedule again. In contrast, a **fixed schedule** calls for each employee to work the same days and hours each week. A fixed schedule at APS would require some employees to always have split days off.

Developing a Work-Force Schedule

Let's take a closer look at the APS scheduling problem described in Box 16.1. Five employees objected to the posted schedule because they did not get two consecutive days off. Obviously the manager did not consider this constraint in his approach. In this section we will demonstrate the technique developed by Browne (1979, 1980) that recognizes this constraint.

The object of the method is to identify the two consecutive days off for each employee that will minimize the amount of total slack capacity. The work schedule for each employee is simply the five days that remain after the two days off have been determined. After an employee has been scheduled, the requirements satisfied by the employee are netted from the total requirements, and the process is repeated for the next employee.

In order to identify days off for a specific employee, we begin by observing the schedule of net requirements for the week. We find the highest requirement, the next highest, and so on, until we can identify a unique pair of days off that includes the minimum level requirements and has the lowest total requirements for the two days. We assign this pair of days as days off for the employee. This method reduces the amount of slack capacity assigned to days having low requirements and forces us to schedule first the days having high requirements. If a tie occurs, we arbitrarily choose one of the pairs. For example, we could give preference to Saturday–Sunday combinations.

Now let's apply this method to the APS problem. The schedule of requirements is

M	T	W	Th	F	S	Su	Employee
6	4	8	9	10	3	2	Jones

The unique pair of minimum requirements is S–Su. Therefore Jones is scheduled to work Monday–Friday.

We must now reduce the requirements for the period M–F to recognize that Jones will be on duty. Note that the requirements for S–Su are carried forward because these were employee days off in the last step. This results in the following net requirements.

M	T	W	Th	F	S	Su	Employee
5	3	7	8	9	3	2	Smith

The unique minimum again is on S–Su, so we assign Smith to a Monday–Friday schedule. After recognizing the net requirements, the minimum requirement is now on T and Su; however, the consecutive-day pair with the lowest total requirements is S–Su. Thus Carter gets the same work schedule as Jones and Smith.

M	T	W	Th	F	S	Su	Employee
4	2	6	7	8	3	2	Carter

The net requirements now indicate that the unique minimum pair is M–T, so Johnson's work week begins on Wednesday and ends on Sunday.

M	T	W	Th	F	S	Su	Employee
3	1	5	6	7	3	2	Johnson

Table 16.2 shows the results for the rest of the APS work force. We invoked the tie-breaking rule three times, giving preference to weekends off whenever possible.

The schedule for all the APS employees is shown in Table 16.3. Since there is a considerable amount of slack capacity, the schedule is not unique. Booth, for example, could have Su–M, M–T, or T–W off without causing a shortage of capacity. Indeed, it seems as though we could get by with one less

Table 16.2

Day Off Assignments for the Remainder of the APS Employees

Net Requirements								
M	T	W	Th	F	S	Su	**Employee**	**Comments**
3	1	4	5	6	[2]	[1]	Kramer	S–Su has the lowest total net requirements.
[2]	[0]	3	4	5	2	1	Farley	M–T is the unique minimum.
2	0	2	3	4	[1]	[0]	Whitcomb	S–Su has the lowest net requirements.
1	0	1	2	3	[1]	[0]	Anderson	S–Su is arbitrarily chosen.
[0]	[0]	0	1	2	1	0	Booth	M–T is arbitrarily chosen.
0	0	0	0	1	[0]	[0]	Bell	S–Su is arbitrarily chosen.

employee because of the total of 8 slack days of capacity. However, we need all 10 employees on Fridays. If we were willing to get by with only 9 employees on Fridays, we would not need Bell. You can see this condition in Table 16.2; the net requirements left for Bell to satisfy amount to only one day, Friday.

Table 16.3

APS Work-Force Schedule, Imposing the Two Consecutive Days Off Constraint

Employee	Monday	Tuesday	Wednesday	Thursday	Friday	Saturday	Sunday	
Jones	X	X	X	X	X	Off	Off	
Smith	X	X	X	X	X	Off	Off	
Carter	X	X	X	X	X	Off	Off	
Johnson	Off	Off	X	X	X	X	X	
Kramer	X	X	X	X	X	Off	Off	
Farley	Off	Off	X	X	X	X	X	
Whitcomb	X	X	X	X	X	Off	Off	
Anderson	X	X	X	X	X	Off	Off	
Booth	Off	Off	X	X	X	X	X	
Bell	X	X	X	X	X	Off	Off	
								Total
Capacity (C)	7	7	10	10	10	3	3	50
Requirements (R)	6	4	8	9	10	3	2	42
Slack ($C - R$)	1	3	2	1	0	0	1	8

Examples of Work-Force Scheduling for Services

In this section we discuss several work-force scheduling problems to demonstrate the variety of situations in which these problems arise, particularly as they relate to providing services. Methods of scheduling service providers can be very sophisticated and depend on the specific nature of each service.

Telephone Operators. Buffa, Cosgrove and Luce (1976) developed a scheduling system for telephone operators that has been implemented in several hundred General Telephone and Electronics (GTE) operator offices. These offices operate 24 hours a day, 7 days a week, and demand for services measured by the volume of calls throughout the day is highly variable. The company has stringent standards for service, which require that calls must be answered within 10 seconds 90 percent of the time.

Scheduling of the operators is done weekly. The first step is to forecast the requirements for service. The total daily call volume for a day of the week is forecasted with a time series model. Next, the total operator-hours required for the day are estimated from average call duration and operator efficiency records. This total is then distributed by half-hour time increments throughout the day by using exponentially weighted percentages of the total represented by each half-hour increment. This process is then repeated for each day of the week, which yields the requirements profile.

The next step is to schedule the shifts. Shifts were established to provide flexibility yet conform to state and federal laws and union agreements. Shift lengths vary, as do start times, length of lunch times, and number of nonwork hours imbedded in the middle of the shift. A heuristic algorithm is used to assign shifts to each day, so that the absolute difference between the requirements profile and the scheduled operators is minimized. The result is a schedule of shifts that must be staffed for each day.

Finally, individual operators must be assigned to shifts. This is a two-step process. First, the days-off assignments are made for each operator. A number of constraints are recognized: (1) all shifts must be worked; (2) each operator gets at least one day off per week; (3) each operator works at least 5 consecutive work days; (4) consecutive days off are maximized; and (5) weekend days off are rotated. A computer algorithm was designed for this purpose. Second, based on seniority, the operators select the shifts they will work each day. Each operator makes a list of shifts in order of preference. A computer program then makes the assignments. After using the system for one year, GTE realized a net annual savings of $170,000 in clerical and supervisory costs and a 6 percent increase in productivity.

Police Deployment. Many police departments in the United States schedule their manpower evenly over 24 hours. Although this policy simplifies the scheduling problem, it ignores the fact that requirements for police services vary considerably throughout the day. Needs can be as much as 8 times greater in the 10–11 P.M. time period than they are in the 5–6 A.M. time period. A patrol car allocation model (PCAM) has been designed to allocate a given number of cars to shifts, where a shift is defined as a specific tour (normally 8 hours) on a particular day for a specific precinct (see Chaiken and Dormont, 1978). The model can also handle overlay tours, which begin during one normal tour and end during the following tour.

This model has proven to be quite versatile. It can be used during budget preparation to determine the total number of patrol officers a department needs to meet stated performance standards. It can also be used to allocate officers to precincts and tours of duty. It can even be used to study the effects of changes in performance standards or priorities for calls for service. Various police departments have used PCAM, including those in Los Angeles, San Diego, Virginia Beach, Seattle, Atlanta, Toledo, Minneapolis, Wilmington, and New Brunswick, N.J.

Airline Crew Scheduling. The scheduling of crews in the airline industry is a complicated problem. The process used by Flying Tiger Airlines has been described by Marsten, Muller, and Killion (1979). The process begins with the flight schedule, which lists all the *basic legs* that must be flown. A basic leg is one takeoff and landing and has an associated frequency of service. The basic legs are linked to form *resolved legs,* or a sequence of basic legs during which the crew has no opportunity to change planes. The resolved legs are then linked to form *trips,* or a sequence of resolved legs that can be flown in one duty period. A number of factors must be considered at this step, including (1) admissible starting and ending cities for trips; (2) minimum and maximum number of flying hours in a duty period; (3) number of plane changes allowed; (4) minimum time required for a plane change; (5) maximum waiting time between flights; and (6) cost limits for layovers and deadhead flights (crew riding as passengers) to reposition the crew.

The next step is to link trips to form *pairings,* which are sequences of trips forming a round trip, beginning and ending at a crew base. Flying Tiger has three crew bases: Los Angeles, San Francisco, and Seattle. In order to determine the pairings, a number of conditions must be specified, including (1) admissible crew bases; (2) admissible layover cities; (3) minimum and maximum time allowed for a duty break; (4) maximum number of trips in a single pairing; and (5) cost limits for layovers and deadhead flights for a single pairing.

The final step is to group pairings into *bid lines,* which constitute a complete set of flying assignments for a month. Certain constraints must be acknowledged in the generation of bid lines. For example, the pilots' contract specifies a certain number of days off, and at least some minimum number of those days must be a block of three consecutive days off. Other factors that must be recognized are (1) the minimum time between pairings; (2) the maximum number of pairings in a single bid line; and (3) the minimum and maximum number of flying hours in a single bid line. Several mathematical computer program models were developed to solve this problem. Using this process to schedule crews for just their 747 aircraft results in about $300,000 in savings per year for Flying Tiger.

OPERATIONS SCHEDULING

Operations scheduling differs from work-force scheduling in several important ways. First, work-force scheduling addresses the problem of assigning people to on-duty and off-duty periods of time, whereas **operations scheduling** assigns people to jobs or assigns jobs to machines during some time period. Operations scheduling determines what workers should do while on duty. Second, work-force scheduling actually determines the amount of labor capacity that is available each time period, whereas operations scheduling begins with a known capacity and focuses on how to best use that capacity. Finally, work-force scheduling must often deal with myriad legal, behavioral, and psychological considerations and constraints, whereas operations scheduling typically deals with technical constraints that are directly related to the production of the product or service.

Our treatment of operations scheduling focuses on situations in which a number of jobs, such as production orders, bundles of checks, or people, must be processed at (or served by) one or more facilities, such as lathes, check encoding machines, or physicians. Typically, each facility can perform a variety of tasks, depending on the job requirements, and there is the potential for queues to develop. In the remainder of this chapter we discuss several approaches to the problem of operations scheduling and their managerial implications.

Gantt Charts

Consider Box 16.2. John Thompson's problem is a typical operations scheduling problem. The current situation is shown in Fig. 16.1, in which the scheduled start date of each order is shown and the progress of each order is compared to its scheduled delivery date. The current date is April 21, designated by the ∨ in the chart. It is clear that the Ford order is behind schedule, while the Plymouth order is on schedule and the Pontiac order is slightly ahead of schedule. This type of chart, called a **Gantt chart,** was first devised by Henry L. Gantt in 1917 and is useful in monitoring the progress of jobs.

To help resolve his problem, John could use another form of the Gantt chart. All three jobs are ready for processing on the Watterson grinder and then must be processed on the polisher. Figure 16.2 shows one of several

Box 16.2
THE POLAND AUTO PARTS COMPANY

The Poland Auto Parts Company, located in Poland, Ohio, manufactures automobile parts to customer specifications. The customers of Poland include the big-three automobile manufacturers, as well as many smaller companies that specialize in performance accessories for standard cars. The products manufactured by Poland range from rack-and-pinion steering assemblies to specially designed engine blocks. John Thompson, owner and general manager, has just received a call from the procurement manager of the Ford Motor plant at Dearborn. In no uncertain way, she reminded John that the order for cam shafts was due before the end of the day tomorrow, Friday, April 22, and if Ford did not receive the shipment by Tuesday, April 26, a portion of its operations would have to shut down. John had received similar calls from other automobile manufacturers recently. The company had always strived to give good customer service, and special care had been taken to assure adequate capacity over the long term.

John decided to check the status of the Ford order. He found that it is at the Watterson grinder, waiting be processed along with two other jobs. All three jobs must be processed on the polisher next. Which job should be scheduled next? The Ford job will take three days on the grinder and then a day on the polisher before it will be ready for shipping. If the Ford job is done next, the other jobs will fall behind. In addition, the longer these other jobs wait, the larger will be the investment in work-in-process inventory. Alternatively, if another job is processed first, is there enough time to get the Ford job completed before the Ford plant must shut down? John pondered his problem awhile. He knew that he would have to authorize overtime for the weekend. He realized that the problem involved more than just keeping the Watterson grinder busy. The real issue was making sure that the right order was being processed at the right time.

possible schedules for the two machines that John decided to use. This form of the Gantt chart depicts the sequence of work for each machine and can also be used to monitor progress. The chart notation shown in Fig. 16.1 is also used here. On April 23, the chart shows that the Ford job is on schedule (with respect to the new schedule) and that the polisher has already finished a job for Dodge. However, comparing actual progress to the originally scheduled completion dates in Fig. 16.1 shows that all three jobs will be past due but that the Ford plant will not have to shut down. If John had chosen to process the orders in the sequence Plymouth–Pontiac–Ford, the Plymouth and Pontiac orders would have been completed on time. However, the Ford plant would have suffered a shutdown. These consequences can be seen by working with the Gantt chart, juggling the schedules by trial and error until a satisfactory one is found.

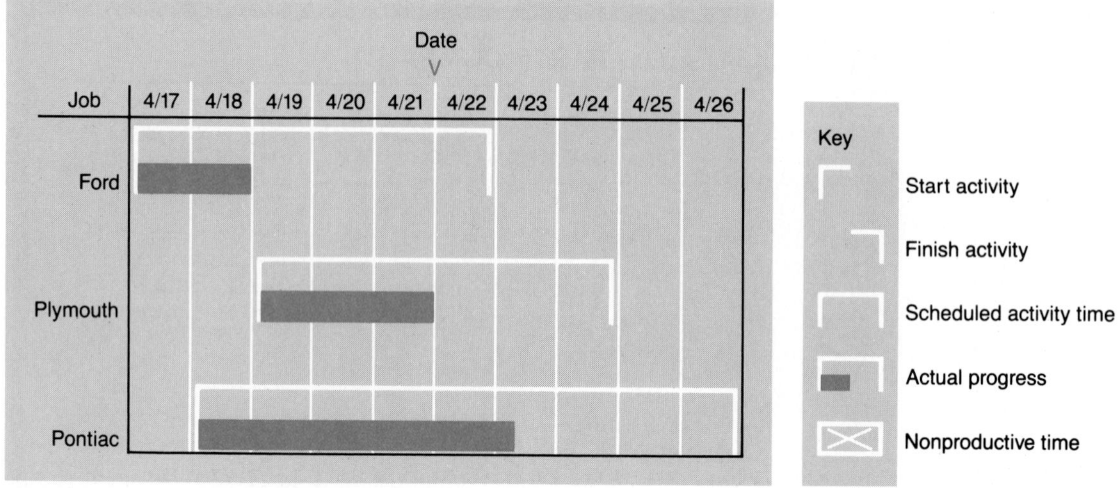

Figure 16.1

Gantt Chart of Job Progress for the Poland Auto Parts Company.

Performance Measures

Technically speaking, there were 36 schedules to consider for the two machines at Poland Auto Parts. For each of the 3! (that is, $3 \times 2 \times 1$) ways to sequence the Watterson grinder, there were 3! ways to sequence the polisher. In general, for n jobs, each requiring m machines, there are $(n!)^m$ possible

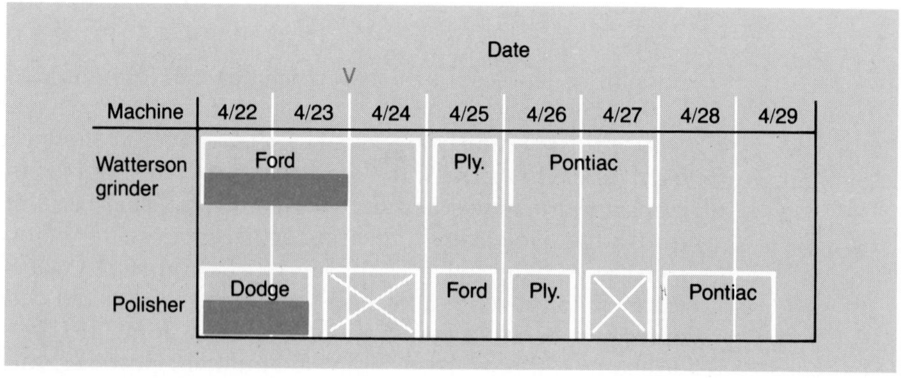

Figure 16.2

Gantt Chart for Machines at the Poland Auto Parts Company.

schedules. Some may not be feasible because of individual job routings or because some jobs may depend on the completion of others before they themselves can be scheduled. Even so, there are typically thousands of ways to schedule a number of jobs on a given set of machines. From a managerial perspective, it is important to identify the performance measures to be used in selecting a schedule. In a job shop, for example, hundreds of scheduling decisions are made every day. If the overall goals of the organization are to be achieved, the schedules should reflect managerially acceptable performance measures.

Many different performance measures could be used in operations scheduling. The following identifies and describes the more commonly used measures, some of which will be familiar to you already. Many others are derivatives, or variants, of these measures.

- *Job flow time:* Sometimes called *cycle* time, **job flow time** is the amount of time the job spends in the shop and is the sum of the moving time between operations, waiting time for machines or work orders, process time (including setups), and delays resulting from machine breakdowns, component unavailability, and the like. It is the difference between the time of completion and the time the job is available for its first processing operation.
- *Makespan:* The total amount of time required to complete a given *group* of jobs is called **makespan**. It is the difference between the start of the first job and completion of the last job.
- *Past due:* The **past due** measure can be expressed as the amount of *time* a job missed its due date, or the *percentage* of the total jobs processed over some period of time that missed their due dates.
- *Work-in-process inventory:* Any job in a queue, moving from one operation to the next, being delayed for some reason, being processed, or residing in component or sub-assembly inventories is considered to be **work-in-process (WIP) inventory.** It is a special case of *transit* inventory, in which the item is produced rather than purchased. This measure can be expressed in individual item units, number of jobs, dollar value for the entire system, or weeks of supply.
- *Total inventory:* The sum of scheduled receipts and on-hand inventories is the **total inventory**. This measure could be expressed in weeks of supply, dollars, or units (individual items only).
- *Utilization:* The percentage of productive time spent by a machine or worker is called **utilization**. It can be aggregated for more than one machine or worker. If there are fewer workers than machines, utilization can be calculated separately for each resource.

Each of these measures can be expressed as a statistical distribution having a mean and a variance, but the performance measures are not entirely independent of each other. For example, minimizing the mean job flow time tends to reduce work-in-process inventory and increase utilization. In a flow-shop setting, minimizing the makespan for a set of jobs also tends to increase the utilization of the facilities required by those jobs. We present examples of these interactions later in this chapter. We mention them here to point out that sometimes, when scheduling individual jobs or groups of jobs, it is easier to work with criteria such as job flow time, makespan, and past due—provided that their relationships to inventory and utilization are understood.

Dispatching

Just as there are many feasible schedules for a specific group of jobs on a particular set of work stations, there are also many ways to generate schedules. They range from straightforward manual methods, such as manipulating Gantt charts, to sophisticated computer methods for developing optimal schedules. We will concentrate on one class of schedule generating procedures called **dispatching procedures.** Simply stated, these procedures allow the schedule for a given work station to evolve over a period of time because the decision about which job to process next, or to let the station remain idle, is made at the time the work station becomes available for further processing. One advantage of this approach over others is that last-minute information on operating conditions can be incorporated into the schedule as it evolves.

Typically, these decisions are made with the help of **priority sequencing rules.** When a number of jobs are waiting in line at a work station, priority rules specify the job processing sequence. These rules can be used manually by a worker to select the next job, or they can be incorporated into a computerized scheduling system that generates a dispatch list of jobs and priorities that the supervisor can use to assign jobs to work stations. We will discuss and later demonstrate with examples the following priority sequencing rules, which are those commonly used in practice.

- *Critical ratio* (*CR*): Job priorities are calculated by dividing the time remaining to a job's due date by the total shop time remaining, including the operation being scheduled. A ratio of less than 1.0 implies that the job is behind schedule, and a ratio of greater than 1.0 implies that the job is ahead of schedule. The job with the *lowest* CR is scheduled next.
- *Slack per remaining operation* (*S/RO*): Slack is the difference between the time remaining to the job's due date and the total shop time remaining, including the operation being scheduled. A job's priority is determined by dividing the slack by the number of operations remaining, including the one being scheduled. The job with the *lowest* S/RO is scheduled next.
- *Earliest due date* (*EDD*): The job with the earliest due date is scheduled next.
- *First-come, first-served* (*FCFS*): The job that arrived at the machine first has the highest priority.

- *Shortest processing time (SPT)*: The job requiring the shortest processing time at the work station to be scheduled is processed next.

Priority rules can be classified as local or global. **Local priority rules** base a job's priority assignment only on information represented by the jobs in the individual work station queue. For example, EDD, FCFS, and SPT are local rules. By contrast, **global priority rules** base a job's priority assignment on information from other work stations, in addition to the one being scheduled. Examples of global rules are CR and S/RO. It may seem that global rules would always be the best. However, they may not provide enough benefit in a given situation to outweigh the added cost of the increased information requirements. Let's look at how the local and global rules can be used.

Local Priority Rules

Local priority rules can be used to schedule any number of work stations. For the purpose of introducing the concepts of dispatching, we will focus on the scheduling of a single operation. Consider a situation in which five vehicles are waiting to have engine work done at the service department of a new-car dealership. The company has only one engine expert who can do this type of work on duty at any time. The engine problems of each vehicle have been diagnosed, and standard times for each job have been estimated. The customers also have said when they expect the work to be completed. Table 16.4 shows the situation as of Monday morning.

Suppose that the service manager decides to use SPT to schedule the engine expert. Table 16.5 shows the resulting schedule. The flow time for each job equals the waiting time plus the processing time. For example, the Ranger had to wait 9 hours before the engine expert started to work on it. Since the standard time for the job is 8 hours, its flow time is 17 hours.

We calculate the average work-in-process inventory by dividing the sum

Table 16.4

Scheduling Data for Engine Repair Jobs

Vehicle	Standard Time, Including Setup (hr)	Scheduled Customer Pickup Time
Ranger	8	10
LTD Wagon	6	12
Bronco	15	20
Econoline 150	3	18
Thunderbird	12	22

Table 16.5

Shortest Processing-Time Schedule for Engine Repair Jobs

Vehicle Sequence	Begin Work	Process Time (hr)	End Work	Flow Time (hr)	Scheduled Customer Pickup Time	Actual Customer Pickup Time*	Hours Early	Hours Past Due
Econoline 150	0	3	3	3	18	18	15	
LTD wagon	3	6	9	9	12	12	3	
Ranger	9	8	17	17	10	17		7
Thunderbird	17	12	29	29	22	29		7
Bronco	29	15	44	44	20	44		24
Total				102		120	18	38
Average				20.4			3.6	7.6

Average work-in-process $= \frac{102}{44} = 2.32$ vehicles. Average total inventory $= \frac{120}{44} = 2.73$ vehicles.

* We have assumed that customers will never pick up their vehicles before the scheduled pickup time and, if there is a delay, they pick up their vehicles immediately when they are finished.

of the individual job flow times by the makespan. You might think of the sum as the total *vehicle-hours* that have been spent by the vehicles waiting for the engine expert and being processed.* Dividing this sum by the total elapsed time required to complete work on all the vehicles provides the average work-in-process inventory.

We calculate the average total inventory similarly. Total inventory is the sum of the work-in-process inventory and the completed jobs waiting to be picked up by customers. The average total inventory is equal to the sum of the *actual* pickup times divided by the makespan. The sum is the total vehicle-hours spent waiting for the engine expert, being processed, and waiting for pickup. For example, the first vehicle to be picked up is the LTD wagon, which spent 12 hours in the system. Then the Ranger is picked up at time 17 and consequently has spent 17 vehicle-hours in the system. The time spent by any vehicle in the system is merely its actual customer pickup time because all were available for processing at time zero. When we divide this sum by the total elapsed time, we get the average total inventory. In our example, the averages were 2.32 vehicles in work-in-process and 2.73 vehicles in total inventory. This implies an average of 0.41 (or 2.73 − 2.32) vehicles in finished inventory, waiting for customer pickup.

Suppose that the service manager instead had used the EDD priority rule. Table 16.6 shows the resulting schedule. Comparing these results to those in

* In this example there are no component or sub-assembly inventories, so WIP consists only of those vehicles waiting in queue or being processed.

Table 16.5, you can see that the SPT schedule provided a lower average flow time and lower work-in-process inventory. The EDD schedule gave better customer service, as measured by the average hours past due, and a lower *maximum* hours past due (22 versus 24). It also provided a lower total inventory because fewer vehicle-hours were spent waiting for customers to pick up their cars after they had been completed. The SPT priority rule will push jobs through the system and get them to the completed state more quickly than the other rules. Speed can be an advantage *if* jobs can be delivered sooner than promised and revenue collected earlier. If they cannot, as we assumed in our example, the completed job must stay in the finished inventory, canceling the advantage of minimizing the average work-in-process inventory. Consequently, the manner in which work is scheduled affects criteria that may be of concern to management. In our example, SPT and EDD provided schedules that resulted in different values for the criteria. Interestingly, both schedules have the same makespan of 44 hours. This result will always occur in single-operation scheduling for a *fixed* number of jobs available for processing, regardless of the priority rule used.

We can also use local priority rules to schedule more than one operation. We treat each operation independently of the others. When the work station becomes idle, we apply the priority rule to the jobs waiting for that operation and select the one with the highest priority. When the job is finished it is moved to the next operation in its routing, where it waits until it has the highest priority in that waiting line. At any work station, the jobs in the waiting line change over a period of time. The choice of a priority rule can make quite a difference in this case, too. Using simulation models of job-shop

Table 16.6

Earliest Due Date Schedule for Engine Repair Jobs

Vehicle Sequence	Begin Work	Process Time (hr)	End Work	Flow Time (hr)	Scheduled Customer Pickup Time	Actual Customer Pickup Time*	Hours Early	Hours Past Due
Ranger	0	8	8	8	10	10	2	
LTD wagon	8	6	14	14	12	14		2
Econoline 150	14	3	17	17	18	18	1	
Bronco	17	15	32	32	20	32		12
Thunderbird	32	12	44	44	22	44		22
Total				115		118	3	36
Average				23.0			0.6	7.2

Average work-in-process $= \frac{115}{44} = 2.61$ vehicles. Average total inventory $= \frac{118}{44} = 2.68$ vehicles.

* We have assumed that customers will never pick up their vehicles before the scheduled pickup time and, if there is a delay, they pick up their vehicles immediately when they are finished.

Table 16.7

Generalizations about the Performance of Selected Local Rules

Rule	Comments
Earliest due date (EDD)	Performs well with respect to the percentages of jobs past due and the variance of hours past due. For a given set of jobs to be processed on a single machine, it minimizes the maximum of the past due hours of any job in the set. It is popular with firms that are sensitive to due date changes, although it does not perform very well with respect to flow time, work-in-process inventory, or utilization.
First come, first served (FCFS)	Even though this rule is considered fair to the jobs (or customers), it performs poorly with respect to all performance measures. It is actually a random rule with respect to operating performance measures.
Shortest processing time (SPT)	Often referred to as the "world champion," it tends to minimize mean flow time, work-in-process inventory, and percentage of jobs past due and to maximize shop utilization. However, it could increase total inventory value because it tends to push all work to the finished state. In addition, it tends to produce a large variance in past due hours because the larger jobs might have to wait a long time for processing. Also, it provides no opportunity to adjust schedules when due dates change. The advantage of this rule over others diminishes as the load on the shop increases.

systems, researchers have studied the implications of various priority sequencing rules on various performance measures. In most of these studies, all jobs were considered independent, and the assumption was made that capacity was generally available. Some generalizations about the performance of the local priority rules that we have used as examples are stated in Table 16.7. Later in this chapter we discuss priority planning and the role that rules such as these play in managing schedules of *interdependent* jobs.

Global Priority Rules

Global rules take into account information about succeeding operations before setting the priority of a job in a particular waiting line. Therefore these rules apply to the scheduling of two or more facilities. Before discussing the more general case, we will first look at a special case.

Two-Facility Flow Shop. Suppose that we have a situation in which a number of jobs are ready for processing on two facilities and that the routings of all jobs are identical. In situations like this, the makespan criterion becomes important. Recall that the makespan for a group of jobs in a single-facility scheduling problem is the same, regardless of the sequence chosen. That is no longer true for scheduling two or more facilities. Minimizing the makespan for a group of jobs to be processed on two facilities in a flow shop has the advantage of minimizing the idle time of the *second* facility because the first facility will be utilized continuously until it processes the last job.

Johnson (1954) developed a procedure to minimize makespan in scheduling a group of jobs on two facilities. He showed that the sequence of jobs at the two facilities should be identical. Therefore the priority assigned to a job should be the same at both facilities. His procedure assumes there is a known set of jobs, all of which are available to begin processing on the first facility. In this sense it is not a dispatching procedure, but the procedure does assign priorities to jobs based on their operation times at both facilities.

We can illustrate Johnson's procedure with a problem faced by the plant manager of the Morris Machine Company. A recent fire in one of its shops damaged five machines. The machines will be recovered in the following manner.

Operation 1: Unbolt the machine from the floor, move it to the repair shop, and dismantle it.

Operation 2: Clean or replace parts, test the machine, make adjustments, and reinstall it in the shop.

The estimated time for each machine is shown in Table 16.8. Each operation will be performed by a separate crew of maintenance and engineering personnel. Since the shop is inoperable until all the machines are back in place, the plant manager is interested in minimizing the makespan and has authorized round-the-clock operations until the machines have been repaired.

The procedure is shown in Table 16.9, along with the solution for the Morris Machine Company problem. Machine 2 is the first to be processed by

Table 16.8

Estimated Times for the Morris Machine Company Repairs

	Time (Hours)	
Machine	Operation 1	Operation 2
1	12	22
2	4	5
3	5	3
4	15	16
5	10	8

Table 16.9

Application of Johnson's Procedure to Morris Machine Company Repairs

Procedure	Result
1. Scan the process times in the two columns. Find the shortest process time of those jobs not yet scheduled. If there is a tie, choose one arbitrarily.	The shortest process time is 3 hours for machine 3 on the second operation.
2. If the shortest process time appears in the operation 1 column, schedule the corresponding job as early as possible. If the shortest process time appears in the operation 2 column, schedule the corresponding job as late as possible.	Since the shortest process time is in the operation 2 column, machine 3 is scheduled last. [| | | | 3]
3. Eliminate the last job scheduled from further consideration. Repeat 1 and 2 until all jobs are scheduled.	Eliminate machine 3's times from Table 16.8. The next shortest process time is 4 hours for machine 2 on operation 1. Therefore, we schedule it first. [2 | | | | 3] The remaining steps are: [2 | | | 5 | 3] [2 | 1 | | 5 | 3] [2 | 1 | 4 | 5 | 3]

the crew assigned to operation 1. Machine 1 is next, followed by machines 4, 5, and 3. Even though the choice of the next machine to schedule was unique for each step in our example, ties can be broken arbitrarily. No other sequence of machines will produce a lower makespan. In order to determine the makespan, we have to draw a Gantt chart like that in Fig. 16.3. In this case, it will take 65 hours to refurbish and reinstall all five machines.

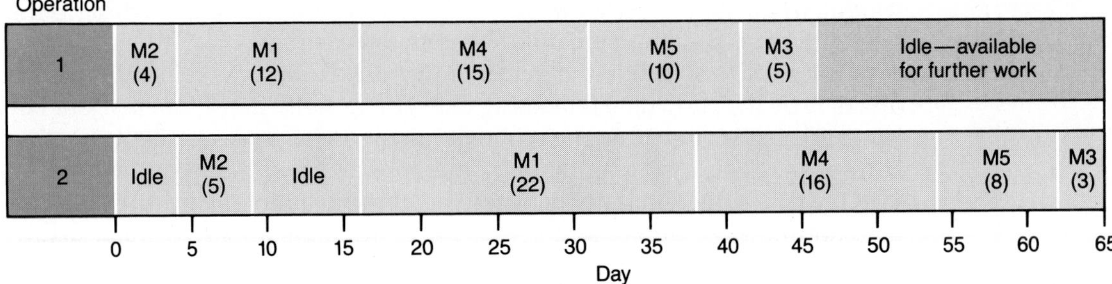

Figure 16.3

Gantt Chart of the Morris Machine Company Repair Schedule.

Multiple-Facility Scheduling. We can also use global rules to schedule many facilities using the dispatching procedure. Although many global rules have been devised, we will use the critical ratio (CR) and slack per remaining operation (S/RO) as examples of this type of priority rule. Consider Table 16.10, which contains the information available for a set of four jobs presently

Table 16.10

Operating Data for Four Jobs and the Resulting Schedules Based on CR and S/RO

Job	Operation Time at Engine Lathe (hr)	Time Remaining to Due Date (days)	Number of Operations Remaining, Including Engine Lathe	Shop Time Remaining, Including Engine Lathe (days)
1	2.3	15	10	6.1
2	10.5	10	2	7.8
3	6.2	20	12	14.5
4	15.6	8	5	10.2

Critical Ratio			Slack/Remaining Operation		
Job	Priority Index	Sequence on Engine Lathe	Job	Priority Index	Sequence on Engine Lathe
1	2.46	Fourth	1	0.89	Third
2	1.28	Second	2	1.10	Fourth
3	1.38	Third	3	0.46	Second
4	0.78	First	4	−0.44	First

waiting in queue at an engine lathe. A number of operations, including the one at the engine lathe, remain to be done on each job.

Using CR to schedule the machine, we divide the time remaining to the due date by the shop time remaining to get the priority index for each job. For job 1, this is 15/6.1 = 2.46. The sequence of jobs to be processed by the engine lathe is 4–2–3–1, assuming that no other jobs arrive in the meantime. Using S/RO, we take the difference between the time remaining to the due date and the shop time remaining and divide it by the number of remaining operations. For job 1, this is (15 − 6.1)/10 = 0.89. The sequence of jobs is 4–3–1–2. Note that the two priority rules yield two different schedules. By way of comparison, the SPT schedule, using the operation times at the engine lathe only, is 1–3–2–4. No preference is given to job 4 in the SPT schedule, even though it may not be finished by its due date.

Labor-Limited Environments

Two basic types of environments affect the complexity of operations scheduling. In **machine-limited environments** the limiting capacity is the number of machines or facilities available. The assumption is that a job never has to wait for lack of a worker, which we made in our discussion of local and global priority rules. Perhaps more typical, however, is the situation in which the number of workers is less than the number of machines or facilities. Workers are trained to work on a variety of machines or tasks, increasing the flexibility of the operating system to produce a wide variety of products or services. Thus in the **labor-limited environment,** the capacity constraint is the amount of labor available, not the machines or facilities.

Labor-limited environments add another dimension to operations scheduling. Not only must we decide which job to process next at a particular work station, but we must also decide at which work station a worker should work next. We can use a dispatching procedure to make these decisions as the situation arises, similar to the way we scheduled the machines in the preced-

Table 16.11

Examples of Labor Assignment Rules

- Assign personnel to the work station having the job in queue that has been in the system the longest time.
- Assign personnel to the work station having the most jobs in queue.
- Assign personnel to the work station having the largest standard work content in its queue.
- Assign personnel to the work station having the job in queue that has the earliest due date.

ing examples. In labor-limited environments, the labor-assignment policies, as well as the dispatching priority rules, have an impact on performance. Table 16.11 lists some examples of labor-assignment rules. Rules such as these are useful after work-force schedules have already been developed.

A SYSTEMS APPROACH TO OPERATIONS SCHEDULING

The dispatching procedure for generating operations schedules works well if the job priorities reflect management's objectives. What happens when the priority system breaks down? The problems at Maket Manufacturing Company described in Box 16.3 show what happens when the formal priority system fails.

Priority Planning

Although the priority system at Maket Manufacturing Company seems odd, it essentially mirrors common practice at many companies and serves to highlight the importance of priority planning. Judging from the large number of red tags, capacity seems to be the problem; however, in this case the problem lies with the priority system itself. Scheduling the wrong jobs on bottleneck machines can create apparent capacity problems. Valuable machine time is used for the wrong jobs, and schedule performance relative to job due dates suffers. Such was the case when Casey Randall processed an order for pinions, when the gear for the order was going to be late anyway. Priorities were not updated to reflect the current status of parent item or component orders.

Valid Priorities. The key to effective priority planning is to strive to maintain valid priorities. An order has a **valid priority** if its due date matches its *need date*. The due date could be a delivery date promised to a customer or a shop due date that identifies the scheduled start time of a parent item for an order. At the time an order is issued, the due date and the need date are the same. However, as time passes, either the due date or the need date may change for a variety of reasons. For example, customers cancel orders, new customer orders are put into the schedule, machines fail and cause component delays, vendor shipments arrive late, and changes are made to the bill of materials for a product. The Maket Manufacturing Company tried to cope with disturbances such as these by using expediters and red tags. However, not all schedule changes were communicated in time, which left many of the scheduling decisions to the machine operators, who had to work with limited, often faulty information.

Priority Dependency. In order to maintain valid priorities, we must recognize the **priority dependency** of jobs in a manufacturing system where there

Box 16.3

MAKET MANUFACTURING COMPANY

The Maket Manufacturing Company produces matched gear and pinion sets for truck axles. Each gear must be processed on ten machines and each pinion on seven machines. Then gears must be matched to the pinions in the final two operations. The company uses a reorder point system to issue replenishment orders to the shop for gears and pinions. Each time an order is released a due date is given to the order, which reflects the average manufacturing lead time for the item. The due date and other processing information are put on a green tag and attached to the container of materials assembled for the order. The shop processes the orders using the earliest due date (EDD) rule.

Yancey Knott, production and inventory manager, was proud of the system because the lead times and reorder points were scientifically determined with the help of a local consultant. He could not understand why the priority system, suggested by Cindy Johnson, production supervisor, was necessary. Under Cindy's system, a job that is on schedule has a green tag. One that is behind schedule has a red tag. If it is "urgent" the red tag has two black stars on it, and if it is "critical" the tag has three black stars on it. Finally, if it is an "emergency," it has "Mr. Maket really needs this" in big black letters on the red tag. The backbone of the system was the cadre of expediters, whose job was to make sure that the right materials got to the right place at the right time. They were the ones who put red tags on the orders. Casual observation of the shop floor revealed a sea of red tags with expediters scurrying about carrying more red tags.

Cindy pointed out that the system was far from perfect but that something had to be done because of numerous schedule changes. Her system sometimes broke down because of the intensity of the problem. For example, the assembly schedule for gear and pinion set GP502 was canceled because the customer canceled the order. Casey Randall had worked two days overtime to process the pinions for that order only to have them put into stock for a future order. In another case, Randall processed pinions for a certain order only to find out that the gears for that order would be three weeks late because of materials shortages. He could have processed another order that could have met its schedule. Now both orders were late. Cindy explained that the due dates on the green tags could not be used because a few days after they are issued they are obsolete. "We would be working to a schedule we know is wrong. At least we are trying to do what management wants with this system."

are several levels in the bills of materials. In *vertical priority dependency,* the priority of a component order depends on the priority of the parent order, as when the order for item GP502 was canceled. The due date for the pinions that Casey Randall processed should have been revised to reflect the new need date for those pinions. In *horizontal priority dependency,* the priority of a component order is dependent on the priority of another component order.

For example, Randall processed the order for pinions when the gears for the same order were going to be delayed three weeks. If the due date for the pinions had been revised to reflect the new date, Randall could have processed other orders that could have met their due dates. A formal system for priority planning should recognize these dependencies, so that the priorities make sense to the people who must process the orders. Otherwise, an informal system like the one at Maket Manufacturing Company will flourish.

A Formal System

Figure 16.4 shows how a materials requirements planning system can be used to plan priorities. Based on an authorized master production schedule,

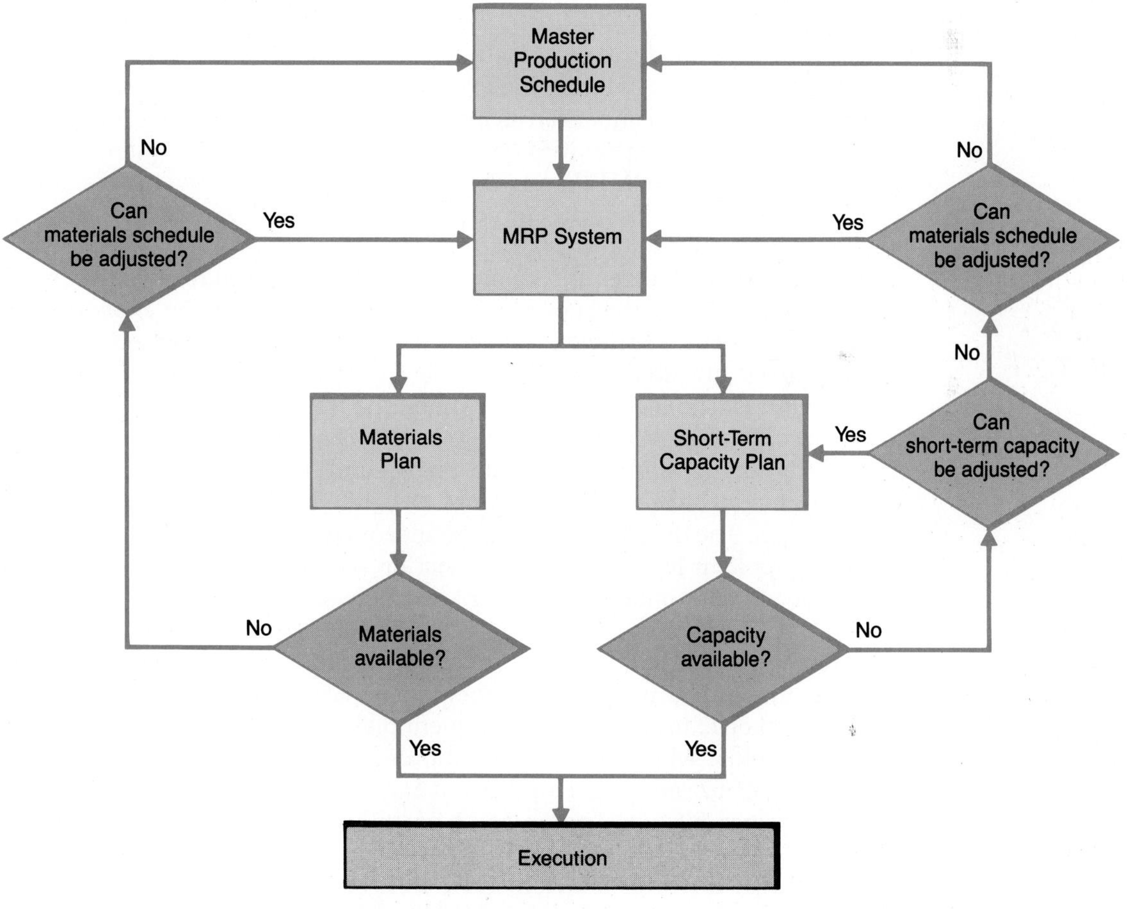

Figure 16.4

A Formal Scheduling System.

the MRP system generates a detailed materials requirements plan, complete with planned order releases for all purchased materials, components, and assemblies. If an unanticipated disturbance will lead to a materials shortage, the MRP system issues action notices indicating the problems that need to be resolved. Management can then determine the extent to which the original due dates for the affected open orders have diverged from their need dates. If there is sufficient capacity, adjustments can be made accordingly.

In Fig. 16.5, we illustrate the process of adjusting the materials schedule for item GP502, the gear and pinion set produced at the Maket Manufacturing Company, and its two components. Below each component inventory status record is a **peg record,** which indicates for each week the quantity needed for each parent item. Note that the gear has several parents and that the gross requirements of 22 units in week 8 are split between two different parent items. The peg record gives us the *upward visibility* we need to adjust schedules, if necessary.

Another useful device is called a **firm planned order.** This technique enables the planner to override the fixed parameters of the MRP system on an exception basis. The planner can change lead times and/or lot sizes and adjust schedules to make the priorities on the shop floor valid. Subsequent replanning sessions with the MRP system will not change the timing or size of the firm planned orders. Examples of priority planning with an MRP system are shown in Table 16.12.

The schedule changes shown are not the only ways to resolve the problems caused by the disturbances. Whenever orders have to be expedited or planned lead times shortened, capacity feasibility must be checked. Each of the examples in Table 16.12 should be considered independently of the others, with Fig. 16.5 as the base situation. The results in Table 16.12 become apparent only after recomputing the records. The first two disturbances are caused by changes in parent-item plans, and the component schedule changes amount to realigning the due dates and need dates of certain scheduled receipts. The third disturbance, an unavoidable delay in G500, originates at the component level and has an effect on parent-item plans. We use the peg record to determine which parent item(s) will be affected, which in this case is GP502 only. The inventory record for GP502 indicates that its gross requirements could still be met if the planned order release in week 2 were reduced to 42. The inventory of component G500 is sufficient to cover a requirement of 42 in week 2. A subsequent planned order of 52 can be scheduled for week 3, when the component order is to be available. This lot-size change for GP502 can be accomplished using the firm planned order method. Note that since P002 has no on-hand inventory, the due date for its open order in week 2 has not diverged from its need date.

The last disturbance shown in Table 16.12 also requires the use of the peg record and the firm planned order. In this case, the lead time for the planned order of GP502 in week 4 is shortened to three weeks. A subsequent replan-

Item:	**GP502**						**Lot Size:**	**POQ—2 weeks**		
Description:	**Gear and pinion set**						**Lead Time:**	**4 weeks**		
Week		1	2	3	4	5	6	7	8	9	10
Gross req.		20	45	13	31	10	48	52	37	18	63
Sched. rec.		60		57							
On hand	8	48	3	47	16	6	−42	−94	−131	−149	−212
POR			94		55		63				

Item:	**G500**						**Lot Size:**	**100**		
Description:	**Gear**						**Lead Time:**	**7 weeks**		
Week		1	2	3	4	5	6	7	8	9	10
Gross req.			94		55		63		22	30	
Sched. rec.			100				100				
On hand	50	50	56	56	1	1	38	38	16	−14	−14
POR			100								

Peg Record G500

Week	Quantity	Parent
2	94	GP502
4	55	GP502
6	63	GP502
8	12	GP507
8	10	GP509
9	30	GP504

Item:	**P002**						**Lot Size:**	**100**		
Description:	**Pinion**						**Lead Time:**	**3 weeks**		
Week		1	2	3	4	5	6	7	8	9	10
Gross req.			94		55		63				
Sched. rec.			100		100						
On hand	0	0	6	6	51	51	−12	−12	−12	−12	−12
POR				100							

Peg Record P002

Week	Quantity	Parent
2	94	GP502
4	55	GP502
6	63	GP502

Figure 16.5

An Example of Priority Planning.

Table 16.12

Examples of Priority Planning with an MRP System

Source of Disturbance	Resulting Schedule Changes	
1. Customer cancelation of gross requirement of 52 units of GP502 in week 7. (This change reduces the planned order release in week 2 to only 42 units.)	G500: Delay the open order in week 2 until week 4. Remove the planned order release in week 2.	P002: Delay the open order in week 4 until week 6. Remove the planned order release in week 3.
2. Increase in customer order for GP502 in week 9 by 15 units. (The planned order release in week 4 now becomes 70 units.)	G500: Expedite open order in week 6 to week 4.	P002: No change.
3. Machine failures delay the open order for G500 in week 2. (It is now expected to be completed in week 3.)	GP502: Change the planned order release in week 2 to 42 units. Create a new planned order release for 52 units in week 3.	P002: No change.
4. Temporary labor shortages delay the open order for P002 in week 4. (It is now expected to be completed in week 5.)	G500: No change.	GP502: Compress the lead time of the planned order release in week 4 to three weeks. This moves the planned order release to week 5.

ning session with MRP will move the gross requirements of 55 units to week 5 for both components, thus avoiding any unplanned materials shortages.

Shop-Floor Control Systems

The priority planning that we did with the help of the MRP system is of no use unless we transmit the changes in the scheduled-receipt due dates to the shop floor. We can do so with a **shop-floor control system.** The diagram in Fig. 16.6 shows the typical inputs and functions of such a system. The input files used here are similar to those used in materials requirements planning and capacity requirements planning systems. The order file contains the details of all planned order releases and scheduled receipts. The scheduled-receipts data enable the user to track the progress of any open order and are updated by the shop-floor control system as changes to their status are recorded.

We can perform four major functions with shop-floor control systems. We use the *order release* function to adjust the release date of planned orders to correspond to the capacity constraints revealed by capacity requirements planning and to check for component availability. Orders are released only if components are available, unless the check is overridden. As part of this function, we also initiate all the paperwork that authorizes the start of the

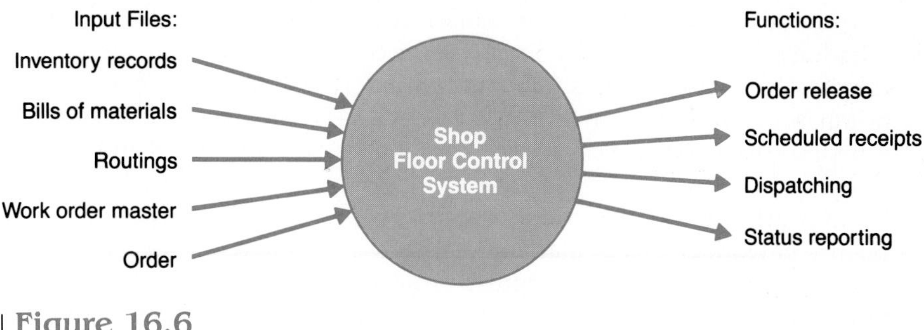

Figure 16.6

Typical Shop-Floor Control System.

order, requisitions materials, and specifies moves between operations and routings.

We use the *scheduled-receipt maintenance* function to provide an accurate database for each order. Our major source of information is the report of daily shop-floor transactions that gives us the status of the scheduled receipts. This function also covers order splitting and adding more operations to a routing because of rework.

In performing the *dispatching* function, we generate a work center list that specifies the status of jobs in each work center and ranks them in order of priority. We use dispatching rules that make use of due dates, such as critical ratio, slack per remaining operation, or earliest due date, to transmit priorities to the shop floor. We can revise the work list daily to reflect the latest changes in priorities of scheduled receipts.

In performing the *status reporting* function, we generate a variety of reports from the database needed in the shop-floor control system. For example, we can generate reports detailing the status of scheduled receipts for a specific customer order or the status of any work center showing the orders currently being processed there and the load expressed in standard hours.

Thus the realignment of due dates and need dates in a formal scheduling system can be translated into action by the shop-floor control system. These methods are useful for converting the various plans and schedules of operations management into the production of goods in order to achieve the overall goals of the organization.

CHAPTER HIGHLIGHTS

Scheduling is the allocation of resources over a period of time to accomplish a specific set of tasks. In this chapter, we addressed the topics of work-force and operations scheduling. Some of the highlights of the chapter are:

- A work-force schedule translates a staffing plan into an operational schedule of work for each member of the work force. Typical considerations encountered in work-force scheduling include capacity limits, service targets, consecutive days off, maximum number of workdays in a row, type of schedule (fixed or rotating), and vacation time.

- Gantt charts are useful for depicting the sequence of work at a particular work station, as well as monitoring the progress of jobs in the system.
- There are many ways to schedule multiple jobs on a set of facilities. Performance measures that can be used to develop an acceptable schedule include average job flow time, makespan, percentage of jobs past due, average amount of time past due per job, average work-in-process inventory, average investment in total inventory, and utilization of equipment and workers.
- Dispatching procedures for schedule generation allow a schedule to evolve because the decision about which job to process next at a work station, or for it to remain idle, is made when the work station becomes available for further processing. Priority rules are used to make these decisions. *Local priority rules* assign priorities on the basis of information concerning only the jobs in the individual work station queue. Examples of these rules are EDD, FCFS, and SPT. *Global priority rules* assign priorities on the basis of information from other machines or facilities, in addition to the one being scheduled. Examples of these rules are CR and S/RO. The choice of priority rule can affect the schedule performance measures that are of concern to management.
- Labor-limited systems add another dimension to the operations scheduling problem. Not only must a decision be made about which job to process next at a work station, but also about which work station an operator should work at next.
- The key to effective priority planning in manufacturing is to maintain valid priorities by striving to maintain order due dates that correspond to the order need dates. Horizontal and vertical priority dependencies need to be recognized. Priority planning with an MRP system can be aided by the use of peg records and firm planned orders.
- Shop-floor control systems transmit the changes in open-order due dates to the shop floor and make use of priority rules to control the scheduling process. They also involve the functions of order release, scheduled-receipt maintenance, and status reporting.

KEY TERMS

dispatching procedures
firm planned order
fixed schedule
Gantt chart
global priority rules
job flow time
labor-limited environment
local priority rules
machine-limited environment
makespan
operations scheduling
past due
peg record
priority dependency

priority sequencing rules
rotating schedule
shop-floor control system
total inventory
utilization
valid priority
work-in-process (WIP) inventory
work-force scheduling

STUDY QUESTIONS

1. Work-force schedules have a number of uses. Discuss these uses within the context of a service operation familiar to you.
2. In the Amalgamated Parcel Service example, we assumed we had 10 employees to schedule. Can Browne's method be used to find the minimum number of employees needed to cover all requirements, subject to the constraint that each employee gets two consecutive days off per week? Explain.
3. Compare and contrast work-force scheduling with operations scheduling. Are they related in any way? If so, how are they related?
4. How does scheduling in general fit into overall operations management?
5. In the Poland Auto Parts example, John Thompson sequenced the jobs on the Watterson grinder in the order Ford–Plymouth–Pontiac. He used trial and error with Gantt charts. Specify a simple priority rule that would have yielded the same schedule in this case. You will want to use the information in Fig. 16.1.
6. What is the difference between the job flow time measure and the makespan measure? When does makespan become relevant?
7. Suppose that you have two alternative approaches for determining machine schedules. One is an optimizing approach that can be run once a week on the computer. The other is a dispatching approach that utilizes priority rules to determine the schedule as it evolves. Discuss the advantages and disadvantages of each approach and the conditions under which each approach is likely to be better.
8. On what basis would you make a choice between local priority rules and global priority rules?
9. The shortest processing time (SPT) rule has been criticized because it tends to produce schedules having a large variance in past due hours. That is, some jobs get through the production system quickly, whereas others (the ones that have long processing times) must spend considerable time in queue. Suggest a modification to the SPT rule to overcome this criticism.
10. It has been pointed out that there is a problem with S/RO when more than one job in queue has negative slack. For example, if job 1 has a slack of -1 with 1 operation remaining and job 2 has a slack of -2 with 10 operations remaining, S/RO would choose job 1 first because it has the smallest (most negative) ratio. Yet job 2 seems to be the one that should be processed next. Suggest a simple modification to the S/RO to overcome this difficulty.
11. Explain why management should be concerned about priority systems in manufacturing and service organizations.
12. Consider the Maket Manufacturing Company example. Explain why the reorder

point system does not provide the information necessary to maintain valid priorities.

13. Your company is considering the use of its MRP system for priority planning. Briefly explain the advantages and uses of peg records and firm planned orders to your boss.

PROBLEMS

1. Consider a machine shop that operates 24 hours per day and makes heavy use of a certain engine lathe. The load on the engine lathe is monitored, and no more than 24 hours of work is released to the lathe in any day. The data for a typical set of jobs is shown in Table 16.13. Management has been investigating scheduling procedures that would focus on customer service and inventory criteria. A current policy states that if a single job is in queue ready for processing and the machine is idle, the job should be processed on the machine regardless of the characteristics of that job. At 8:00 A.M. on Monday the engine lathe was idle.
   (a) Develop a schedule using each of the following priority rules and draw a Gantt machine chart for each schedule.
      (i) FCFS.
      (ii) SPT.
      (iii) EDD.
   (b) For each schedule in part (a), calculate the average past due hours per job and the average flow time per job. Keep in mind that the jobs are available for processing at different times.
   (c) Comment on the performance of the three rules regarding customer service and inventory criteria. What trade-offs should management consider in selecting among the rules for scheduling the engine lathe in the future?

2. The Neptune's Den Marina is located at Aldrich Lake in Northern Wisconsin. In addition to the myriad services the marina provides to avid fishermen, Rusty Botim, the owner and proprietor, services outboard motors. The typical motor brought in for service at this time of the year has been stored in a garage in Milwaukee for the winter and requires maintenance repair of the ignition system. Some motors

Table 16.13

Job	Release Time	Lot Size	Process Time (hr/unit)	Setup Time (hr)	Due Time
1	8:00 A.M. Monday	100	0.020	3	5:00 P.M. Monday
2	8:30 A.M. Monday	50	0.060	1	6:00 A.M. Tuesday
3	8:40 A.M. Monday	200	0.010	5	6:00 P.M. Monday
4	9:10 A.M. Monday	500	0.008	2	11:00 P.M. Monday

require the replacement of broken parts, while others need a complete overhaul. Presently there are five motors with varying problems waiting to be serviced. Rusty's best estimate for the labor time involved and the number of days from today the customer is expecting to pick up the motor are shown in the following table. Customers usually do not pick up their motors early.

Motor	Estimated Labor Time (days)	Promise Date (days from now)
50 hp Evinrude	5	8
7 hp Chrysler	4	15
100 hp Mercury	10	12
4 hp Sportsman	1	20
75 hp Nautique	3	10

(a) Develop two schedules using the SPT and EDD rules.
  (i) What is the average flow time for each schedule?
  (ii) What is the percentage of past due jobs for each schedule?
  (iii) Which schedule minimizes the maximum past due days for any motor?
(b) For each schedule in part (a), calculate the
  (i) average work-in-process inventory (in motors);
  (ii) average total inventory (in motors).
(c) Comment on the performance of the two rules relative to these performance measures.

3. Consider the Gantt machine chart in Fig. 16.7.
  (a) Suppose that a routing requirement is that each job must be processed on machine A first. Can the makespan be improved? If so, draw a Gantt chart with the improved schedule. If not, state your reason.
  (b) Suppose that there is no routing restriction on machine sequence. Jobs can be processed in any sequence on the machines. Can the makespan in the chart be improved in this case? If so, draw a Gantt chart with your schedule. If not, state your reasons.

4. Boynton Smith, operations manager at the Westerville Tool and Die Company, called Ignatius Katt and Primus Dogg to his office. Katt is the supervisor of department 4 and Dogg is the supervisor of department 8. Katt and Dogg were arguing over the scheduling of a group of jobs for

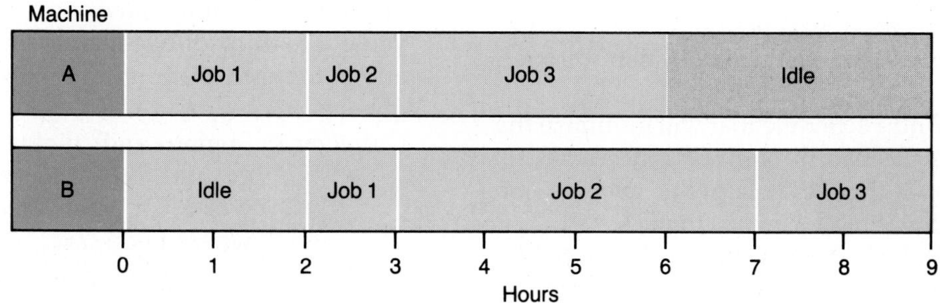

Figure 16.7

the Kramer Company. All six jobs were now in Katt's department waiting for processing. They had to be routed to Dogg's department next. Katt was adamant about processing the jobs according to the shortest processing times for the operation in his department. "I want to minimize my work-in-process inventory these days, given the high cost to carry inventory," he hissed. Dogg barked, "You should be less selfish. If we worked together, we could get those six jobs to Kramer earlier. We should think of the customer in all of this." Jack Kramer had recently called Boynton Smith and told him that the order represented by the six jobs was critical. He also reminded Boynton that the Kramer Company was a big customer.

	Process Times (days)	
Job	Department 4	Department 8
1	5	7
2	6	2
3	2	1
4	4	10
5	10	6
6	3	4

(a) Use Katt's plan to determine a schedule for the operation in each department. That is, use SPT for department 4, and use the same sequence for department 8.
   (i) What is the average job flow time for department 4?
   (ii) What is the makespan through both departments?

(b) Find a schedule that will minimize the makespan through both departments and then calculate the average job flow time for department 4.

(c) Discuss the trade-offs represented by these two schedules. What implications do they have for centralized scheduling?

5. The data in the following table were reported by the shop-floor control system at your company for order processing at the edge grinder. The current date is week 150. The number of remaining operations and the total work remaining includes the operation at the edge grinder. All orders are available for processing and none has been started yet.

Current Order	Process Time (hr)	Due Date (wk)	Remaining Operations	Total Work Remaining (wk)
A101	10	162	10	9
B272	7	156	4	6
C105	15	152	1	1
D707	4	170	8	18
E555	8	154	5	8

(a) Specify the priorities for each job, if the shop-floor control system uses:
   (i) SPT.
   (ii) EDD.
   (iii) S/RO.
   (iv) CR.

(b) For each priority rule, calculate the average flow time per job at the edge grinder.

(c) Which of these priority rules would work best for priority planning with an MRP system? Why?

6. Treetop Airlines needs to schedule 10 aircraft of various designs for maintenance. From a scheduling standpoint, it is convenient to think of two maintenance operations for each plane in the following sequence.

   Operation 1: Engine and flight systems ground checks, replacing worn or damaged parts where necessary.

   Operation 2: Flight tests and final safety checks.

   Based on flight records and the specific

Table 16.14

Aircraft	Operation 1	Operation 2
1	3	1
2	4	4
3	3	2
4	6	1
5	1	2
6	3	6
7	2	4
8	4	8
9	8	2
10	1	1

design of each aircraft, management has estimated that each operation will require the amount of time (in days) shown in Table 16.14.

(a) Suppose that one of management's objectives is to minimize the total length of time all 10 aircraft are without maintenance. This objective can be translated as minimizing the makespan of the 10-aircraft fleet. First, find a schedule that minimizes the makespan. (There are multiple optimal solutions to this problem, so just choose one.) Then, calculate the average job flow time on an aircraft through the two operations, assuming that all 10 are available for maintenance now. What is the total elapsed time to maintain all 10 aircraft?

(b) Now suppose that one of management's objectives is to maximize the number of aircraft in service that have received maintenance. This can be translated as minimizing the average job flow time of the 10 aircraft through the two operations, assuming that once the plane has completed the second operation it immediately returns to service. First, devise a schedule using SPT. This can be accomplished by adding the operation times for each aircraft and scheduling the aircraft as if there were only one operation. The resulting sequence is used for both operations. Then, calculate the average flow time per aircraft. What is the total elapsed time to maintain all 10 aircraft with your schedule?

(c) Discuss the solutions to parts (a) and (b), including the trade-offs that must be made between the schedules and other factors that you would consider in scheduling the aircraft for maintenance.

7. Your company uses an MRP system to do priority planning. Consider the information presented in Fig. 16.8 concerning three of the items the company manufactures. Item X1 has two components, Y1 and Y2; both Y1 and Y2 have more than one parent. Your job is to have materials in the right place at the right time. You are interested in maintaining valid priorities and satisfying customer demand, as evidenced by the gross requirements for item X1.

State why situations (a) and (b), taken independently of each other, would (or would not) cause a problem in priority validity for the components and how you would resolve the problem, assuming sufficient capacity.

(a) A customer cancellation of an order for X1 causes its gross requirement in week 6 to become 28 units instead of 82 units.

(b) A good customer asks you to ship an unplanned order of 100 units of X1 in week 5. This increases the gross re-

Item: X1 Description: Rotor housing									Lot Size: 100 Lead Time: 2 weeks	
Week		1	2	3	4	5	6	7	8	9	10
Gross req.		50		33			82	70	40		52
Sched. rec.		100									
On hand	22	72	72	39	39	39	−43	−113	−153	−153	−205
POR					100	100			100		

Item: Y1 Description: Armature									Lot Size: 150 Lead Time: 3 weeks	
Week		1	2	3	4	5	6	7	8	9	10
Gross req.		25		18	133	110		40	100		20
Sched. rec.		150			150						
On hand	10	135	135	117	134	24	24	−16	−116	−116	−136
POR					150						

Item: Y2 Description: Rotor housing									Lot Size: 120 Lead Time: 6 weeks	
Week		1	2	3	4	5	6	7	8	9	10
Gross req.			30		133	110			100		20
Sched. rec.			120			120					
On hand	50	50	140	140	7	17	17	17	−83	−83	−103
POR			120								

Peg Record Y1

Week	Quantity	Parent
1	25	Z3
3	18	Z3
4	33	Z8
4	100	X1
5	10	Z8
5	100	X1
7	40	Z3
8	100	X1
10	20	Z8

Peg Record Y2

Week	Quantity	Parent
2	30	Z4
4	33	Z8
4	100	X1
5	10	Z8
5	100	X1
8	100	X1
10	20	Z8

Figure 16.8

quirement of X1 in week 5 to 100 units. Top management agrees to make the shipment but does not compensate for it by adjusting the gross requirements of X1 in other weeks.

8. Consider the MRP information in Problem 7. State why situations (a)–(d), taken independently, would (or would not) cause a problem in priority validity or materials coverage for X1, Y1, or Y2 and how you would resolve the problem, assuming sufficient capacity. If more than one approach seems reasonable to you, discuss each one in terms of its relative advantages and disadvantages.
   (a) Suppose that Y1 is a purchased item and the supplier tells you that the scheduled receipt you expected in week 4 will now arrive in week 5. There is no way to expedite the scheduled receipt to have it arrive as previously planned. There are no other suppliers who can get Y1 to you by week 4. You must now accept the fact that the order will arrive in week 5.
   (b) Suppose instead that Y1 is a manufactured part. The gross requirement of 25 units in week 1 have been canceled.
   (c) The requirement for item Z8 has increased in week 4 from 33 to 43.
   (d) A new machinist working on the order for Y2 scheduled for week 5 irrevocably damaged 50 percent of the lot. The quantity now expected in week 5 is 60 units.

9. Tom Rash is a young entrepreneur in Steubenville, Ohio, who saw the need for a private refuse collection service. Apartment complexes and businesses would be the primary customers. The unique aspect of this service would be collections each day of the week, including Sundays. In addition, each customer would have specially designed refuse bins to allow the use of only one person per truck. Customers could also schedule special pickups for unexpectedly heavy refuse accumulations. The trucks would be pleasantly decorated with a base color of gray and "The T. Rash Company" proudly displayed in brilliant scarlet letters.

   Tom surveyed a number of prospective customers and arrived at the following estimate of the number of refuse collectors he would need for each day of the week.

Day	M	T	W	Th	F	S	Su
Requirements	12	10	7	8	6	4	3

   Collection requirements would be higher on Mondays and Tuesdays to accommodate businesses that do much of their business on weekends. The owners prefer not to have refuse collection on weekends because of the increased traffic and shortage of parking space around their establishments.
   (a) Find the minimum number of refuse collectors required, if each employee works five days a week and has two consecutive days off.
   (b) Specify the work schedule for each employee. How much slack does your schedule generate for each day?
   (c) Suppose that Tom Rash can smooth the requirements by offering special rates for pickups Wednesday–Sunday. The requirements would be 8 on Monday and 7 on the other days of the week.
      (i) How many employees would be needed now?

(ii) Does this analysis have implications for capital investment in this business? If so, what are they?

10. The Food Bin grocery store operates 24 hours per day, 7 days per week. Fred Bulgebottom, the store manager, has been analyzing store operations recently, particularly with respect to efficiency and productivity. For example, at present there are 10 checkout clerks on the first shift from 8:00 A.M. to 5:00 P.M. However, Fred has noticed a considerable amount of slack capacity on certain days of the week. Granted, these clerks could be used to bag groceries, but their wages are higher than those of the bagging clerks who should be doing that chore. Consequently, Fred decided to observe the need for checkout clerks on the first shift for a period of one month. Each time the queue in front of a cash register exceeded three customers, he recorded the need for another register to open. At the end of the month, he calculated the average number of checkout registers that should be open during the first shift each day. His results showed that his peak needs are on Saturdays and Sundays.

Day	M	T	W	Th	F	S	Su
Requirements:	3	4	4	3	4	7	8

Fred now had to come up with a work-force schedule that guaranteed each checkout clerk two consecutive days off but still covered all requirements.

(a) Develop a work-force schedule that covers all requirements while giving two consecutive days off to each clerk. How many clerks do you need?

(b) Specify the work schedule for each checkout clerk.

SELECTED REFERENCES

Baker, K. R., *Introduction to Sequencing and Scheduling*. New York: John Wiley & Sons, 1984.

Berry, W. L., and V. Rao, "Critical Ratio Scheduling: An Experimental Analysis," *Management Science*, vol. 22, no. 1 (October 1975), pp. 192–201.

Browne, J. J., "Simplified Scheduling of Routine Work Hours and Days Off," *Industrial Engineering* (December 1979), pp. 27–29.

Browne, J. J., and J. Prop, "Supplement to Scheduling Routine Work Hours," *Industrial Engineering* (July 1980), p. 12.

Buffa, E. S., M. J. Cosgrove, and B. J. Luce, "An Integrated Work Shift Scheduling System," *Decision Sciences*, vol. 7, no. 4 (October 1976), pp. 620–630.

Chaiken, J. M., and P. Dormont, "A Patrol Car Allocation Model: Capabilities and Algorithms," *Management Science*, vol. 24, no. 12 (August 1978), pp. 1291–1300.

Conway, R. W., "Priority Dispatching and Job Lateness in a Job Shop," *Journal of Industrial Engineering*, vol. 16, no. 4 (July 1965).

Day, James E., and Michael P. Hottenstein, "Review of Sequencing Research," *Naval Research Logistics Quarterly*, vol. 27, no. 1 (March 1970), pp. 11–39.

Fryer, J. S., "Operating Policies in Multiechelon Dual-Constraint Job Shops," *Management Science*, vol. 19, no. 9 (May 1963), pp. 1001–1012.

Hill, A. D., J. D. Naumann, and N. L. Chervany, "SCAT and SPAT: Large-Scale Computer-Based Optimization Systems for the Personnel Assignment Problem," *Decision Sciences*, vol. 14, no. 2 (April 1983), pp. 207–220.

Johnson, S. M., "Optimal Two Stage and Three Stage Production Schedules with Setup Times Included," *Naval Logistics Quarterly*, vol. 1, no. 1 (March 1954), pp. 61–68.

Kanet, J. K., and J. C. Hayya, "Priority Dispatching with Operation Due Dates in a Job Shop," *Journal of Operations Management*, vol. 2, no. 3 (May 1982), pp. 167–175.

Krajewski, L. J., and L. P. Ritzman, "Shift Scheduling in Banking Operations: A Case Application," *Interfaces*, vol. 10, no. 2 (April 1980), pp. 1–8.

LeGrande, E., "The Development of a Factory Simulation System Using Actual Operating Data," *Management Technology*, vol. 3, no. 1 (May 1963).

Mabert, V. A., "Static vs. Dynamic Priority Rules for Check Processing in Multiple Dispatch-Multiple Branch Banking," *Journal of Operations Management*, vol. 2, no. 1 (May 1982), pp. 187–196.

Marsten, R. E., M. R. Muller, and C. L. Killion, "Crew Planning at Flying Tiger: A Successful Application of Integer Programming," *Management Science*, vol. 25, no. 12 (December 1979), pp. 1175–1196.

Nelson, R. T., "Labor and Machine Limited Production Systems," *Management Science*, vol. 13, no. 9 (May 1967), pp. 648–671.

Saladin, Brooke A., "A Methodology for the Allocation of Police Patrol Vehicles." Unpublished dissertation, The Ohio State University, 1980.

CHAPTER 17

PROJECT SCHEDULING AND CONTROL

Some Managerial Issues

- How can we avoid costly project delays?
- Which activities in our large project determine the duration of the entire project?
- Do network planning methods increase our potential to control costs and provide better customer service?
- How can we determine the effect of limited resources on the duration of the project?
- How can we incorporate uncertainty in the time estimates for various activities into project planning?

Chapter Outline

You probably saw some or all of the pageantry and excitement of the 1984 Olympic Games. Have you ever wondered what goes on behind the scenes to produce such an event? Try to imagine the myriad interrelated activities that must be completed before, during, and after the games. For example, the Olympic Planning Committee for the 1988 Olympic Winter Games in Alberta, Canada must plan for events in 55 major sports (some of which will be held simultaneously in different locations), each one consisting of several tasks that must be carried out in a logical sequence. Housing and logistics for the teams must be arranged, as well as security for the athletes while they are in Alberta. Transportation and accommodations for approximately 1.5 million spectators must be planned. Arrangements for press and TV coverage are also part of the Olympic Committee's duties, as are contingency plans for bad weather. Delays caused by poor management are intolerable, not only to the athletes but also to the millions of people who follow the games on TV or in the press. Even cleaning up after the games must be scheduled. In this chapter we consider methods for managing projects that involve a large number of interrelated tasks.

MANAGING PROJECTS

The planning problem faced by the Olympic Committee involves the scheduling and control of a large project. A **project** is a set of activities, with a definite starting and ending point, that results in a unique product or service. Some activities must be completed before others can start, and some activities can be performed simultaneously with other activities, so long as resources permit. Usually the activities to be performed—and there can be thousands of them—are unique to the product or service. The degree of difficulty in scheduling projects is a function of the number of activities, their sequence, and their timing. Table 17.1 shows some examples of large projects.

The Steps in Project Management

Managing a project, whether it is a large one like the Olympic Games or a smaller in-house one such as moving a department of 10 people to a different location, involves the following steps.

Table 17.1

Examples of Large Projects

- Oil pipeline construction.
- Organization of a trade exposition.
- Renovation of a blighted urban area.
- Relayout of a plant or office.
- Design and production of prototypes for aircraft, ships, locomotives, or missiles.
- Organization of a state fair.
- Construction of buildings, roads, and dams.
- Large computer system installation.
- New-product introduction.
- Advertising campaign design.
- Maintenance schedules.
- Space shuttle launch.
- Crane installation.

1. Describe the project.
2. Develop a network model.
3. Incorporate time estimates.
4. Analyze the model.
5. Develop the project plan.
6. Periodically assess the progress of the project and repeat steps 2–6 as needed.

Describe the Project. The first step is to describe the project in a way that all involved can understand. Included in this description should be a clear statement of the endpoint of the project (for example, a cleaned Olympic City, with all temporary facilities removed). In addition, the following elements must be carefully defined.

- *Activities:* An **activity** is recognizable work effort in a project and consumes time and resources.
- *Precedence Relationships:* The **precedence relationships** between activities indicate sequencing constraints; that is, an activity cannot start until a certain preceding activity has been completed.*

For example, consider the project described in Box 17.1, which we use as an example throughout this chapter. The activities and the precedence relationships have been defined. What constitutes an activity for inclusion in the project description can become an issue. An activity should be defined as the smallest unit of work effort to be scheduled and controlled by the project manager. Judy Kramer, as project manager in this example, is not concerned primarily with the myriad details of constructing the hospital (activity H). But she is concerned about the completion of that activity as a whole, so that the total project—making the hospital operational—can be completed on time. However, when she assigns responsibility to someone for the hospital construction activity, that person will want to specify all the details of constructing the hospital. In general, the activities in the project description should represent the level of detail most useful for scheduling and resource allocation decisions.

Develop a Network Model. A network planning model depicts a project graphically showing all its activities and their relationships to each other. The model is represented by a **network diagram,** which consists of nodes and arcs. The interpretation of nodes and arcs differs, depending on the specific modeling technique used. One approach is the so-called **activity-on-arc** (AOA) **network.** For this approach, we must define another project element.

* Precedence relationships are important also in the entirely different context of assembly line balancing, as discussed in Chapter 9.

Box 17.1

A HOSPITAL ON THE MOVE

Judy Kramer, executive director for the board of St. Adolf's Hospital, must prepare for a hearing of the Central Ohio Hospital Board (COHB) next week. In the interest of better serving the public in Benjamin County, St. Aldolf's has decided to relocate from Christofer to Northville, a large suburb of Christofer, which at present has no major medical facility. The COHB oversees the deployment of medical facilities in Central Ohio to guard against excessive duplication of costly services, unwarranted increases in the number of hospital beds, and inequitable distributions of standard hospital services. St. Adolf's must justify its move to the COHB and any interested citizens who may show up at one of the open-door sessions of the proceedings.

The move to Northville would mean construction of a new hospital and the accomplishment of a number of other interrelated activities needed to make the new hospital operational. One part of the hearings will involve the specifics of the total project, including time estimates for the completion of the project and the cost. With the help of her staff, Judy identified 11 major activities in the project. She also specified the immediate predecessors (those activities that must be done just before the given activity can begin) for each activity. The results are as follows:

Activity	Description	Immediate Predecessor(s)
A	Select administrative and medical staff.	None
B	Select site and do site survey.	None
C	Select equipment.	A
D	Prepare final construction plans and layout.	B
E	Bring utilities to the site.	B
F	Interview applicants and fill positions in nursing, support staff, maintenance, and security.	A
G	Purchase and take delivery of the equipment.	C
H	Construct the hospital.	D
I	Develop an information system.	A
J	Install the equipment.	E, G, H
K	Train nurses and staff.	F, I, J

Judy realized that each activity could be broken down into more detailed work elements but that this level of detail would not be necessary for the hearings. She also knew that she would have to supply time and cost estimates for the activities. Then, she would have to use this information to answer questions such as

- Can the project be completed in 72 weeks?
- Which activities are crucial to completing the project on schedule?
- Considering total project costs, what is the minimum-cost schedule?

Judy had heard that other hospitals used network planning techniques to help plan and schedule major projects such as this one. She decided to use these techniques for this project.

- *Event:* An **event** is a specific, definable accomplishment in a project, recognizable at a particular point in time, that does not consume time or resources.

The network is constructed with arcs representing activities and nodes representing events. The precedence relationships, depicted by arcs going into and out of event nodes, require that an activity cannot start until the preceding event has occurred and that an event cannot occur until all activities preceding it have been completed.

Another approach is the **activity-on-node** (AON) **network.** Here, activities are the nodes of the network and arcs represent precedence relationships. Consequently, AOA networks are *event-oriented* and AON networks are *activity-oriented.* Top management is typically more interested in the achievement of events or milestones (major events), whereas operating-level managers are more interested in activities. We provide an example of each type of network in this chapter to demonstrate the difference between the two approaches.

Incorporate Time Estimates. Regardless of the method chosen for modeling the network, project managers must decide whether to use probabilistic (uncertain) or deterministic (certain) time estimates for activities. This decision leads to the choice of one of two different network planning methods. If there is uncertainty in the time estimates for activities, the project management system to use is the **program evaluation and review technique** (PERT). This system was developed in the late 1950s for the Polaris missile project. The project involved 3000 separate contractors and many activities that had never been performed before. Since there was considerable uncertainty in the time estimates, PERT was developed to cope with the uncertainty, and the system is generally credited with reducing the completion time of the project by at least 18 months.

If the times for project activities can be estimated accurately, the system to use is the **critical path method** (CPM). This system was developed by J. E. Kelly of Remington-Rand and M. R. Walker of DuPont at about the same time (in 1958) that PERT was developed. In its original application, CPM was used to schedule maintenance shutdowns at chemical processing plants. The maintenance projects were routine, and reasonably accurate time estimates for activities were available.

Before PERT and CPM, project managers used Gantt charts to schedule and control projects. We introduced Gantt charts in Chapter 16 (see Figs. 16.1 and 16.2) and showed how they can be used to schedule jobs (or activities). However, for large projects, Gantt charts become difficult to work with because they do not directly recognize precedence relationships between activities. In addition, Gantt charts do not indicate those activities that are crucial to the completion of the project on time. Both PERT and CPM were developed to overcome these difficulties and to provide managers with more relevant information about their projects.

Analyze the Model. Project network models can be used to identify the activities that are crucial to the completion of the project and to estimate the probability of completing the project on time. In addition, they can be used to find those activities that, if expedited, could reduce the time to complete the entire project and reduce total costs. Later in this chapter, we demonstrate how PERT and CPM can be used to analyze the hospital project described in Box 17.1.

Develop the Project Plan. When the network has been modeled, a schedule can be developed for each activity in the project. Activities that have been found to be crucial to the completion of the project on time will be given preference in light of resource constraints. After the start of the project, re-

Box 17.2

PROJECT DELAYS CAN CAUSE MANAGERIAL HEADACHES

The late introduction of new products is costly to manufacturing firms in the personal computer market:

- Gavilan Computer Corporation promised delivery of a new portable computer in April 1983 but did not ship until June 1984. The company entered Chapter 11 bankruptcy proceedings in October 1984 after selling only 3000 units.
- Osborne Computer Corporation also filed for Chapter 11 protection in 1983 after a premature announcement and delay of its second-generation computer dried up the sales of its first product.
- VisiCorp, a software company, announced the introduction of a new software series in November 1982 but did not ship until early 1984. Because of the financial losses, VisiCorp agreed to merge with a smaller company in October 1984.

In August 1983 the Florida Power and Light Company accomplished a rare feat—it finished building a nuclear power plant in just over six years, only four months beyond the schedule set in 1977. On the average it takes 10–12 years to build such a complex project. Special teams were set up to handle specific problems, and managers made sure that vendors upheld their contractual commitments. A computer kept track of the progress on each of the 20,000 tasks needed to finish the plant. For each *month* such a plant is finished beyond schedule, it is estimated that (1) 770,000 barrels of oil would be used at a cost of \$23 million to rate payers; and (2) the capital cost of the plant would increase by \$13 million, which would cost the rate payers an annual increase of \$2.5 million dollars over the life of the plant.

Sources: "In Personal Computers, Delays in Production Take an Industry Toll," by Dennis Kneale, *Wall Street Journal*, January 8, 1985; "Utility Cuts Red Tape, Builds Nuclear Plant Almost on Schedule," by Ron Winslow, *Wall Street Journal*, February 22, 1984.

ports are generated to show the current status of all activities relative to their planned completion dates.

Update the Project Plan. Periodically, there will be a need to add more information to the planning process. Perhaps an activity took longer than expected, more activities have been identified, or the precedence relationships between several activities have changed. This information requires changes in the network or the time estimates and, ultimately, the project plan itself.

The Importance of Effective Project Management

Project managers must be on top of the project at all times, if schedules are to be met and costs are to remain within the budget. However, Murphy's law—"If something can go wrong, it will."—applies to projects better than to anything else. Unexpected problems can cause delays in project schedules, necessitating replanning of schedules and reallocation of resources, and often resulting in severe financial repercussions. The examples in Box 17.2 demonstrate the penalties associated with project delays. Frequently, decisions must be made quickly and on the basis of only partial information. In order to stay in control, project managers need techniques that provide the capability to replan schedules, answer "what-if" questions regarding the timing of project activities, and evaluate the time and cost implications of resource trade-offs. Network planning models are very useful for these purposes.

NETWORK MODELING WITH THE PROGRAM EVALUATION AND REVIEW TECHNIQUE

Let's return to the St. Aldolf's Hospital project, for which Judy Kramer has already identified the activities and their precedence relationships. In this section, we focus on those activities and use the following PERT procedures to analyze them.

1. Diagraming the AOA network.
2. Estimating activity times.
3. Calculating time statistics.
4. Determining the critical path.
5. Analyzing probabilities.

Diagraming the Activity-on-Arc Network

In order to diagram a project as a network, we first need to identify the precedence relationships between activities. We do so by going through the list of activities and identifying those activities that must immediately precede each activity listed. In a complex project, this task can be tedious, but it is important because incorrect or omitted precedence relationships will result in project delays.

Now, let's develop an AOA network for the hospital project, based on the activities and precedence relationships shown in Box 17.1. Recall that in AOA networks nodes (circles) are events and directed arcs (arrows) are activities. Figure 17.1 shows some of the activities and events for the St. Adolf's Hospital project. Event 1 is the start of the project, and activities A and B emanate from event 1 because they have no immediate predecessors. Event 2 signals the completion of activity A. Since activities C, F, and I all require the completion of activity A, the arrows representing these activities leave the node representing event 2. Similarly, the arrows for activities D and E leave the

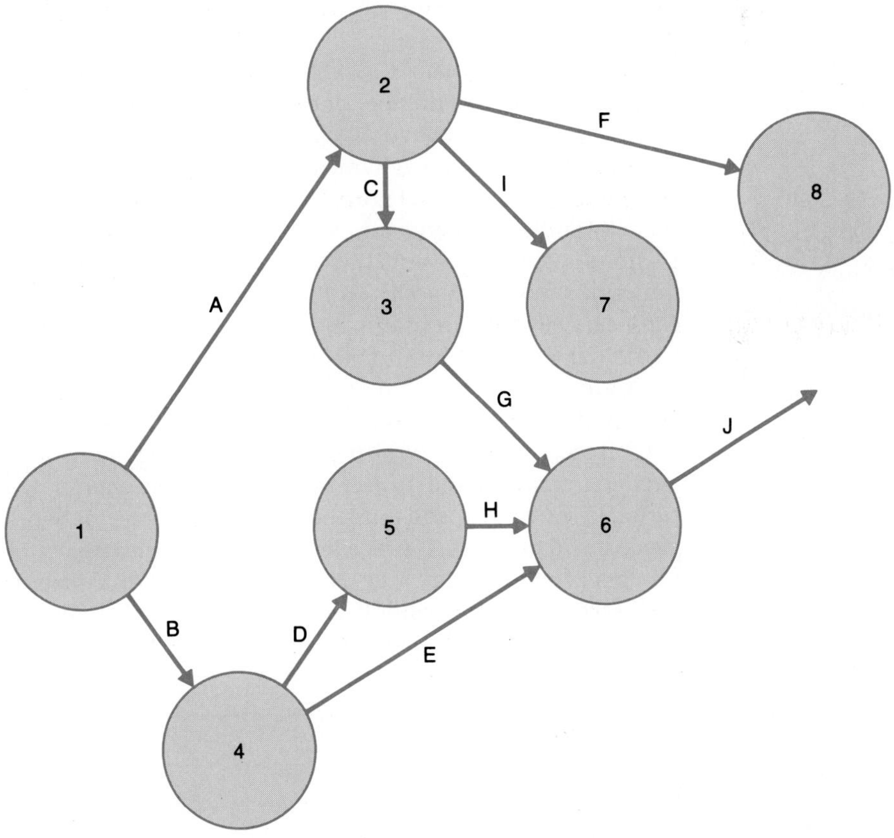

Figure 17.1

Partial PERT Network for the St. Adolf's Hospital Project.

node for event 4, which signals completion of activity B. The arrow for activity G leaves event 3, signaling completion of activity C. Event 6 ties activities G, H, and E together for activity J.

Until now, the diagraming of the hospital project network has been straightforward. We drew the diagram in such a way that each activity is represented by a unique ordered pair of events (i, j), where i is the beginning event and j is the ending event. For example, we can represent activity E by the ordered pair of events (4, 6). This is important because computer algorithms can distinguish between different activities only on the basis of their beginning and ending event numbers. Two activities with the same ordered pair of events would be considered the same activity. In Fig. 17.1, we have avoided this problem so far; however, activity K poses a dilemma. It requires the completion of activities F, I, and J. If we eliminate event 7 and connect activities F, I, and J to event 8, we would have an event node from which to start activity K. However, activities F and I would have the same beginning and ending event nodes and would no longer be distinguishable from each other.

We can overcome this difficulty by introducing a *dummy activity*. A dummy activity has no time or resource requirements and is used to maintain the uniqueness of activity definitions, to represent the proper precedence relationships between activities, and to recognize the existence of competing resource requirements. Figure 17.2 shows the use of a dummy activity for the hospital project. It connects event 7 (completion of activity I) to event 8 (completion of activities F and J). Now all activities are uniquely defined and the network shows that activities F, I, and J must be completed before activity K can begin. Event 9 indicates the completion of the project. Figure 17.3 shows two other uses for dummy activities.

Care must be taken to ensure the network diagram accurately represents all activities and precedence relationships. The network diagram is the basis for project analysis, which provides management with the information needed to manage the project to successful completion. For example, it would certainly not make sense to have a loop in the network, where activity S precedes activity T, T precedes U, and U precedes S. At a minimum, the process of modeling a large project as a network is useful in itself because it forces management to identify all the necessary activities and to recognize the precedence relationships between them.

Estimating Activity Times

The PERT system was originally designed for situations in which there was little direct experience with many of the activities and thus little basis for time estimates. To overcome this difficulty, the people responsible for each activity are asked to provide three time estimates for the activities under their control.

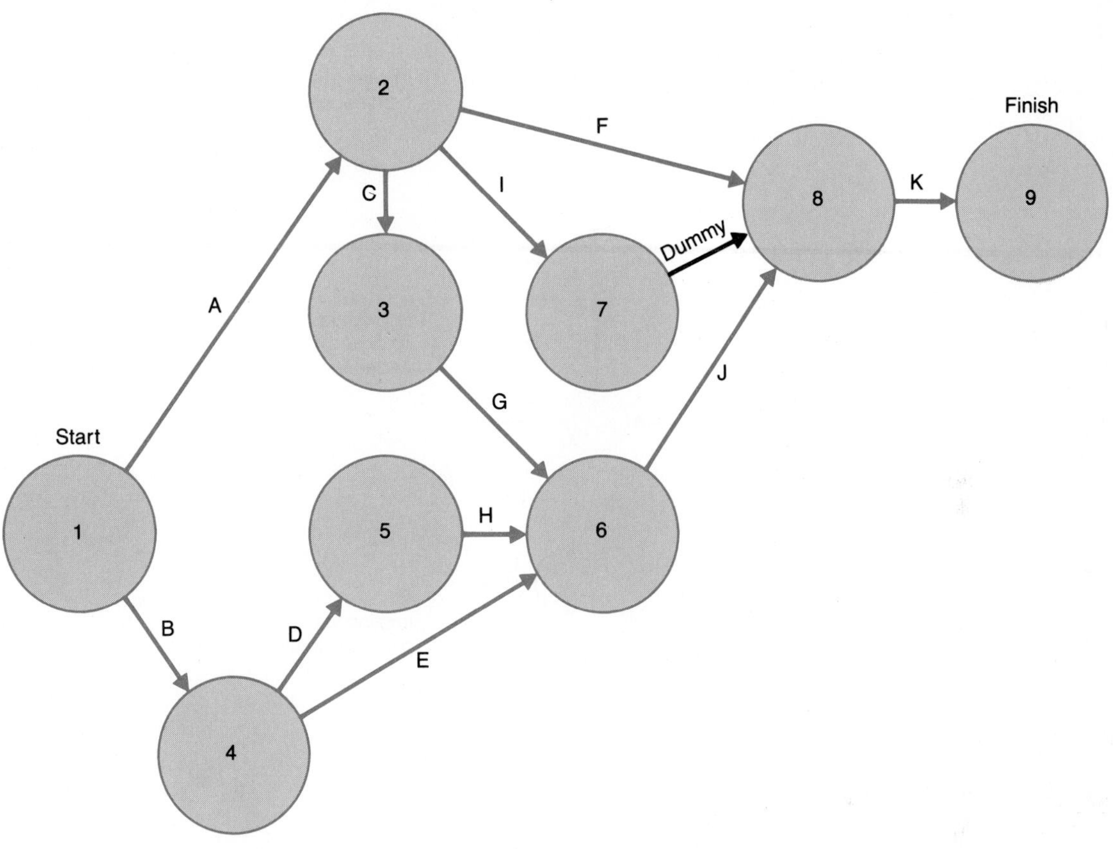

Figure 17.2

PERT Network for the St. Adolf's Hospital Project Showing the Use of a Dummy Activity.

- *Most optimistic time, a:* The shortest time in which the activity can be completed, if everything goes exceptionally well. The probability that the activity can be completed in a *shorter* period of time is estimated to be no more than one chance in a hundred.
- *Most likely time, m:* The mode of the distribution of the time required to perform an activity. This time would be expected to occur most often, if the activity could be repeated many times under similar circumstances.
- *Most pessimistic time, b:* An estimate of the longest time required to perform an activity, assuming that everything that could go wrong actually does go wrong. The probability that the activity would require *more* time than this projection is estimated to be no more than one chance in a hundred.

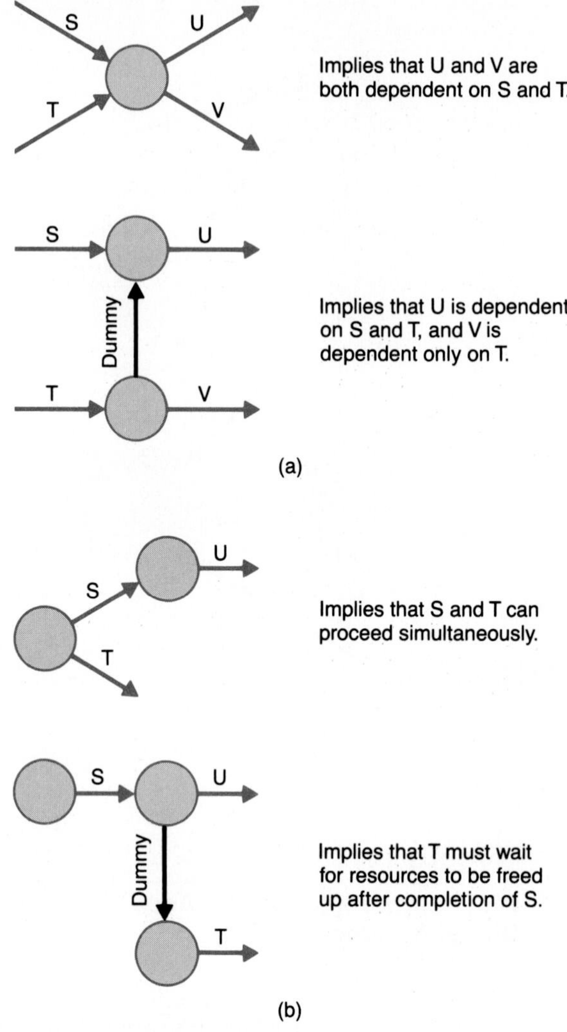

Figure 17.3

Additional Uses for Dummy Activities.

These time estimates should be based on the assumption that all resources necessary to accomplish the activity in its most likely time are available during a normal work period. With the exception of dummy activities that recognize competing resources, the use of PERT does not directly consider resource limitations.

Calculating Time Statistics

The three time estimates for each activity provide enough information to estimate the mean and variance of a probability distribution for each activity. The probability distribution chosen by the developers of PERT is the beta distribution. The primary reason for choosing this distribution is that it can take on a variety of shapes, allowing the mode (most likely time estimate) to fall anywhere between the end points (most pessimistic and most optimistic time estimates). This condition is not possible with just any distribution. For example, the normal distribution is symmetrical, requiring the mode always to be equidistant from the end points. This condition would be unduly restrictive.

The estimate for the mean of the beta distribution is given by the following weighted average of the three time estimates.

$$t_e = \frac{a + 4m + b}{6}$$

Note that the most likely time is weighted four times greater than the most pessimistic or most optimistic time estimate.

Table 17.2 shows the expected times for each activity in the hospital project. For example, the expected time for activity B is

$$t_e = \frac{7 + 4(8) + 15}{6} = \frac{54}{6}$$

$$= 9 \text{ wk.}$$

The expected time does not have to equal the most likely time for an activity. They will be equal only when the most likely time is equidistant from the most optimistic and most pessimistic times.

The variance of the beta distribution for each activity is given by the following formula.

$$\sigma^2 = \left(\frac{b - a}{6}\right)^2$$

The variance increases as the difference between the most pessimistic and most optimistic time estimates increases. This implies that the less certain a person is in estimating the actual time for an activity, the greater will be the variance.

Table 17.2 also contains the estimates of the variances for each activity. For activity B, the variance is

$$\sigma^2 = \left(\frac{15 - 7}{6}\right)^2 = \left(\frac{8}{6}\right)^2 = 1.78.$$

Table 17.2

Time Estimates and Activity Statistics for the St. Adolf's Hospital Project

	Time Estimates (weeks)			Activity Statistics	
Activity	Most optimistic (a)	Most likely (m)	Most pessimistic (b)	Expected time (t_e)	Variance (σ^2)
A	11	12	13	12	0.11
B	7	8	15	9	1.78
C	5	10	15	10	2.78
D	8	9	16	10	1.78
E	14	25	30	24	7.11
F	6	9	18	10	4.00
G	25	36	41	35	7.11
H	35	40	45	40	2.78
I	10	13	28	15	9.00
Dummy	0	0	0	0	0.00
J	1	2	15	4	5.44
K	5	6	7	6	0.11

In the hospital project, the greatest uncertainty lies with the time estimate for activity I, followed by activities E and G. Both the expected times and the variances for each activity will be useful in performing the analysis in the next two steps.

Determining the Critical Path

One of the crucial aspects of project management is time of completion. If we add the expected times for each activity in Table 17.2, we get 175 weeks for the hospital project. This amount of time is based on the assumption that we could work on only one activity at a time. However, in PERT or CPM we assume that we have the resources to work on various activities simultaneously and that we need to consider only the precedence relationships and the expected times in scheduling activities. Indeed, Fig. 17.2 recognizes these assumptions, and it is apparent that we can finish the project in much less time than 175 weeks.

In order to determine the earliest completion time of a project, we must find the critical path. The **critical path** is the sequence of activities, from the start to the finish of a project, having the greatest cumulative elapsed time. The critical path also has the minimum slack time at each event along the path. The slack for event i is defined as the difference between the latest allowable achievement date TL_i and the earliest expected achievement date TE_i for the event. We will develop these concepts further with the help of Fig. 17.4.

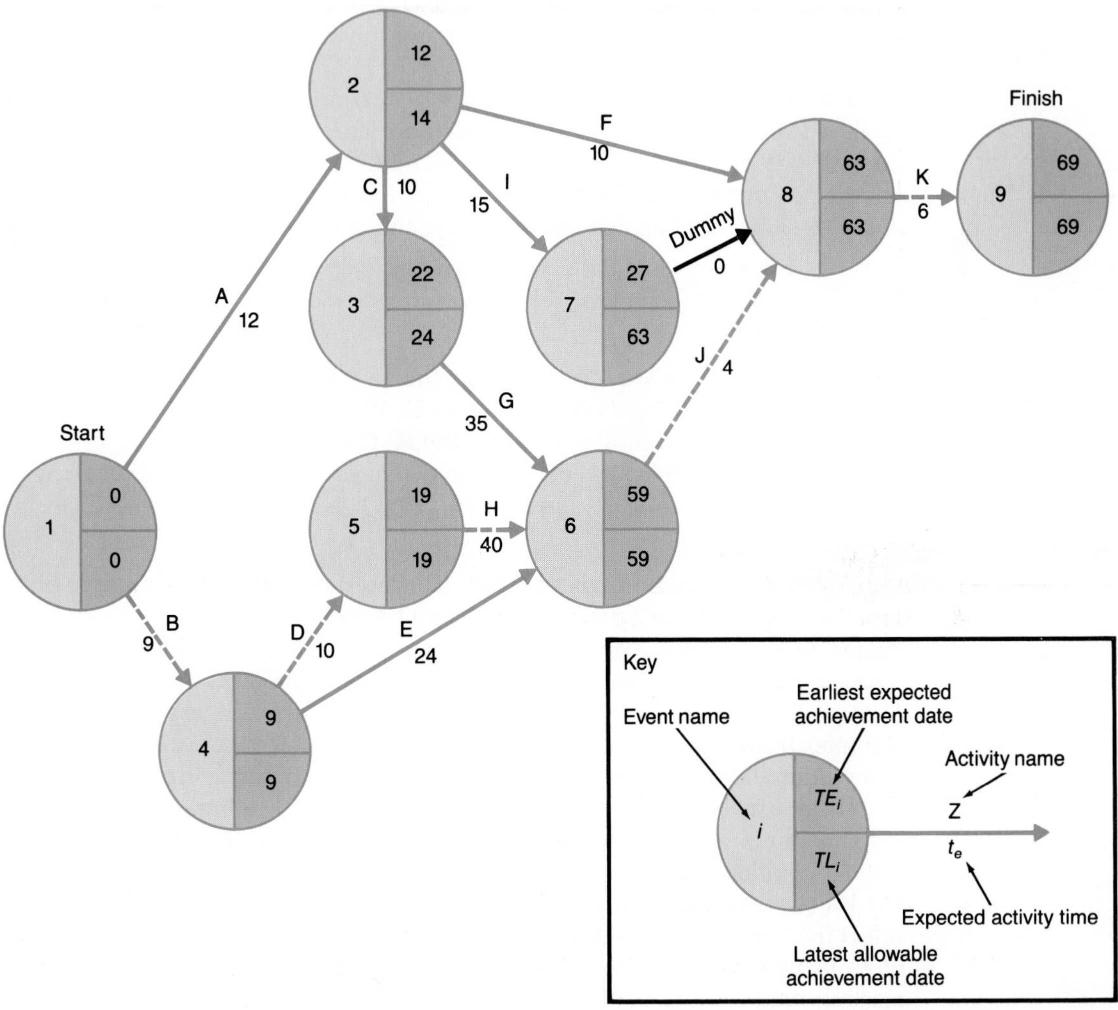

Figure 17.4

Network for the St. Adolf's Hospital Project Showing Earliest Expected Achievement Dates, Latest Allowable Achievement Dates, and the Critical Path.

Earliest Expected Achievement Date. We begin the calculation of the earliest expected achievement date for each event at the start node and proceed to the finish node, recognizing the precedence relationships. For convenience, we arbitrarily begin with $TE_1 = 0$ for the start node, although we could have used the actual start date of the project. Thereafter, to get the earliest expected achievement date for any node with only one entering activity arrow, we simply add the earliest expected achievement date for the preceding event to the expected activity time. For example, $TE_2 = 0 + 12 = 12$. Similarly, $TE_3 = 12 + 10 = 22$. These calculations are straightforward because each node has only one entering activity.

When more than one activity enters an event node the calculation for the earliest expected achievement date is more complicated. In this case, the earliest that an event can be achieved is the date when *all* entering activities have been completed. Mathematically, it is the *maximum* of the expected completion dates of all activities entering the event node. For example,

$$TE_6 = \max[9 + 24, 19 + 40, 22 + 35]$$
$$= 59.$$

Thus the earliest that we can expect to achieve event 6 is week 59 because the earliest that we can begin activity H is week 19, and it takes 40 weeks. Activities E and G can be completed earlier, but all three must be completed before we can say that event 6 has been achieved. The earliest expected achievement dates for all the events are shown in Fig. 17.4. Note that the project can be completed in 69 weeks.

Latest Allowable Achievement Date. The latest allowable achievement date for an event is the latest date that the event can be achieved and still allow the project to be completed on time. To calculate the latest allowable achievement date for an event, we begin at the finish node and proceed backward to the start node. The TL_i for any event i is dictated by the longest time path of activities from that event to the finish event node. Since the earliest expected completion date of the hospital project is week 69, we start with $TL_9 = 69$.* To get TL_i for any event i having only one activity arrow leaving it and terminating at event j, we subtract the activity time from TL_j. For example, $TL_8 = 69 - 6 = 63$. Similarly, $TL_6 = 63 - 4 = 59$, and $TL_3 = 59 - 35 = 24$.

When more than one activity leaves an event node we must take care to select the longest time path from the event to the finish event as the basis for our calculations. Since the achievement date of an event node signals the starting date for any activity leaving it, we must find the minimum of the expected starting dates of all activities leaving the event node. For example,

* In general, if the project has a specific due date, it could be used for determining TL for the finish event node.

$$TL_2 = \min[63 - 10,\ 63 - 15,\ 24 - 10]$$
$$= 14.$$

The latest that we could achieve event 2, start activity C, and still complete the project in week 69 is week 14. Activities F and I could start much later; however, before *any* of the activities can be started we must first achieve event 2. Activity C is on the longest path of activities from event 2 to the finish event. The remaining *TL*s are shown in Fig. 17.4.

Event Slack. The slack for any event is merely the difference between *TL* and *TE* for the event. For example, the slack for event 3 is 2 (or 24 − 22) weeks. This means that the achievement of event 3 could be delayed no more than 2 weeks without jeopardizing completion of the project in week 69. Slack information is useful to project managers because it helps them make decisions regarding reallocation of resources. Some resources could be taken from activity C and given to activity D if it is behind schedule, so long as the time required to do activity C is not extended by more than two weeks. It is important to note, however, that the slack at an event depends on the performance of activities leading to it. If the time for activity A turned out to be 14 weeks instead of 12 weeks, the slack for events 2 *and* 3 would be zero. We discuss slack further when we present the critical path method. The slack for each event in the hospital project is shown in Table 17.3.

Critical Path. We can now identify the critical path. All events on the critical path have minimum slack. The event string 1–4–5–6–8–9 constitutes the critical path for the hospital project. Since each activity has unique starting and ending nodes, the event string indicates that activities B–D–H–J–K are on the critical path. The critical path is important because it defines the com-

Table 17.3

Event Slack for the St. Adolf's Hospital Project

Event	*TL* (weeks)	*TE* (weeks)	Slack (weeks)	Critical Path
1	0	0	0	Yes
2	14	12	2	No
3	24	22	2	No
4	9	9	0	Yes
5	19	19	0	Yes
6	59	59	0	Yes
7	63	27	36	No
8	63	63	0	Yes
9	69	69	0	Yes

Table 17.4

Network Paths for the St. Adolf's Hospital Project

Path	Expected Time (weeks)
A–F–K	28
A–I–Dummy–K	33
A–C–G–J–K	67
B–D–H–J–K	69 (Critical)
B–E–J–K	43

pletion time of the project, and any delays in the activities along the critical path cause a delay in project completion. Adding the expected times for each activity along the critical path, we determine that the expected time to complete the hospital project is 69 weeks. Management should focus more attention on these activities in managing the project, although if activity A or C were to fall behind by two weeks they and activity G would be on the critical path as well. Using up slack could result in more than one critical path in a project.

Rather than calculating event slack first, we could have found the critical path by enumerating all the activity paths in the network and identifying the one having the longest cumulative time. Table 17.4 shows this solution, mainly to demonstrate that the path having the minimum slack is also the *longest* time path in the network. Although finding the critical path in this way is easy for small projects, the usual approach used by computer routines is to calculate event slack because the slack information is desired by project managers anyway, and identification of the critical path is a by-product of that information.

Analyzing Probabilities

Since the time estimates for activities in a PERT network involve some uncertainty, it is useful to provide a measure of the probability of achieving any event in a specific amount of time. In order to do this, we must define the probability distribution of achievement dates for an event. Managers focus most often on the completion date of the entire project, so we will use the *finish* event as an example.

In order to specify the probability distribution of achievement dates for the finish event, we must determine a mean and a variance. It seems reasonable to use the sum of the expected activity times on the critical path as the mean of the distribution. For the hospital project, the earliest expected achievement date for the finish event TE_9 is 69 weeks.

Similarly, we use the sum of the variances of the activities on the critical path as the variance of the project time distribution. From Table 17.2, the variance would be $1.78 + 1.78 + 2.78 + 5.44 + 0.11 = 11.89$.

If we assume that the probability distributions for each activity on the critical path are independent, we can use the normal probability distribution to find the probability of achieving a given due date for the project. We can use the z-transformation formula as follows:

$$z = \frac{T' - TE}{\sqrt{\Sigma\sigma^2_{CP}}},$$

where

T' = Due date for the project;

TE = Earliest expected completion date for the project; and

$\Sigma\sigma^2_{CP}$ = Sum of the variances on the critical path.

The procedure for assessing the probability of achieving any event in a project by a given date T' is similar to that which we just discussed. However, instead of the critical path, we would use the longest time path of activities from the start node to the event in question.

Let's now return to the hospital project. Recall that one of the questions raised was whether the hospital could become operational in 72 weeks. With a length of the critical path of 69 weeks and a variance along the critical path of 11.89, we can calculate the z-value as follows:

$$z = \frac{72 - 69}{\sqrt{11.89}} = \frac{3}{3.45}$$
$$= 0.87.$$

Using the normal distribution table in Appendix D.3 we find that the probability of completing the project in 72 weeks or less is 0.8078. Alternatively, there is about a 20 percent chance that the project will exceed 72 weeks. This probability is shown graphically in Fig. 17.5.

Thus we can use the uncertainty in activity time estimates to make statements about the chances of completing a project on schedule. The analysis hinges on the identification of the critical path. We calculated the critical path

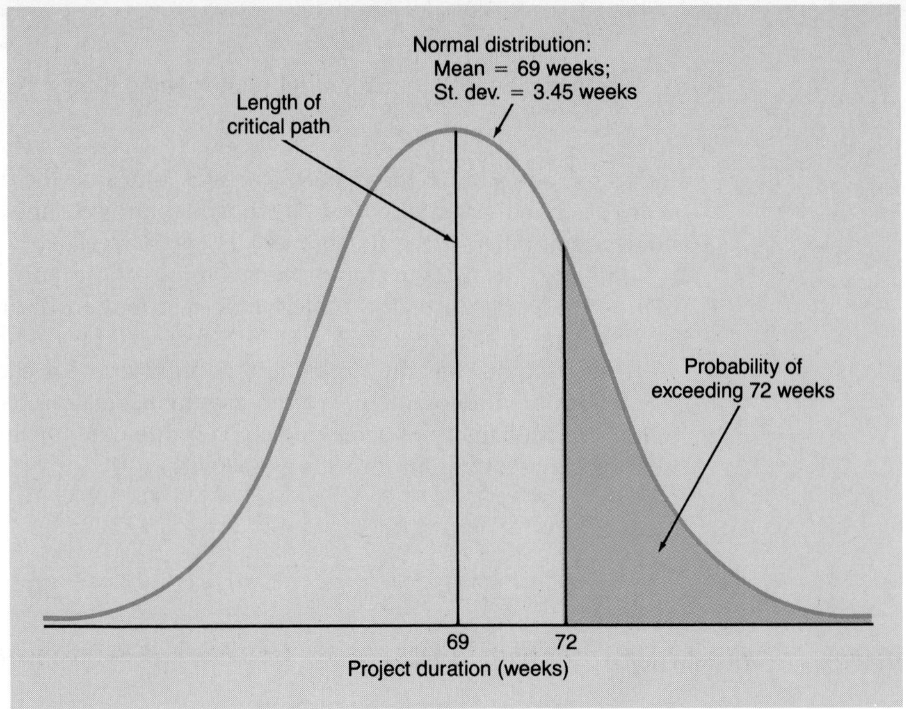

Figure 17.5

Probability of Exceeding 72 Weeks for the St. Adolf's Hospital Project.

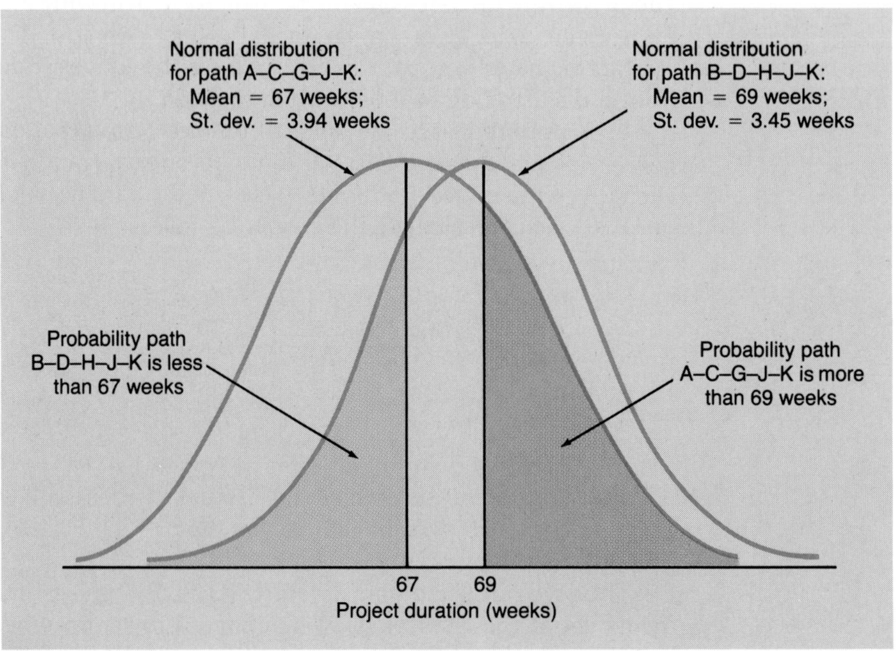

Figure 17.6

Probability Distributions for the Critical Path and Next Longest Path for the St. Adolf's Hospital Project.

on the basis of the expected times for each activity and disregarded the variances. Conceivably, one or more network paths for a project may be shorter in length than the critical path but have enough variance in activity time estimates to actually become the critical path sometime during the project. Such is the case in the hospital project. In Table 17.4 you can see the path A–C–G–J–K is 67 weeks long, or only two weeks shorter than the critical path. The sum of the variances along that path is 15.55.

This situation is shown in Fig. 17.6. Path A–C–G–J–K will be the critical path if its length equals or exceeds 69 weeks *or* if the length of path B–D–H–J–K equals 67 weeks, or less. Fig. 17.6 shows that there is a considerable overlap between the probability distributions for these two paths.* Close attention to activities A, C, and G, in addition to activities B, D, H, J, and K seems warranted.

THE CRITICAL PATH METHOD AND MINIMUM-COST SCHEDULES

The critical path method was designed for projects in which activity times are known with certainty, or at least they can be safely assumed to be certain. In this section, we discuss the concepts of AON network modeling but focus on the use of CPM to find minimum-cost project schedules.

Diagraming the Activity-on-Node Network

The process for developing an AON network diagram is similar to that for an AOA network diagram. The precedence relationships between project activities must be identified and then incorporated in a network. The advantage of AON networks is that dummy activities are not needed, simplifying network construction.

Figure 17.7 shows the AON network diagram for the hospital project. The arrows in the diagram represent only the precedence relationships between activities. In the AOA diagram, the arrows represented both activities and precedence relationships. The activities in the AON network are on the nodes, along with activity times. The start and finish nodes have been added to tie the entire network together.

We used the t_e values from our PERT analysis for the activity times in Fig. 17.7. In practice, CPM is typically used for projects that are repetitive, and,

* Computing the probability that path A–C–G–J–K will be critical requires the estimation of the joint probability that path A–C–G–J–K $\geq$ 69 weeks *and* path B–D–H–J–K $\leq$ 67 weeks in addition to the shaded areas in Fig. 17.6. Since the two paths are dependent on each other (share common activities), the calculation of the joint probability requires computer simulation.

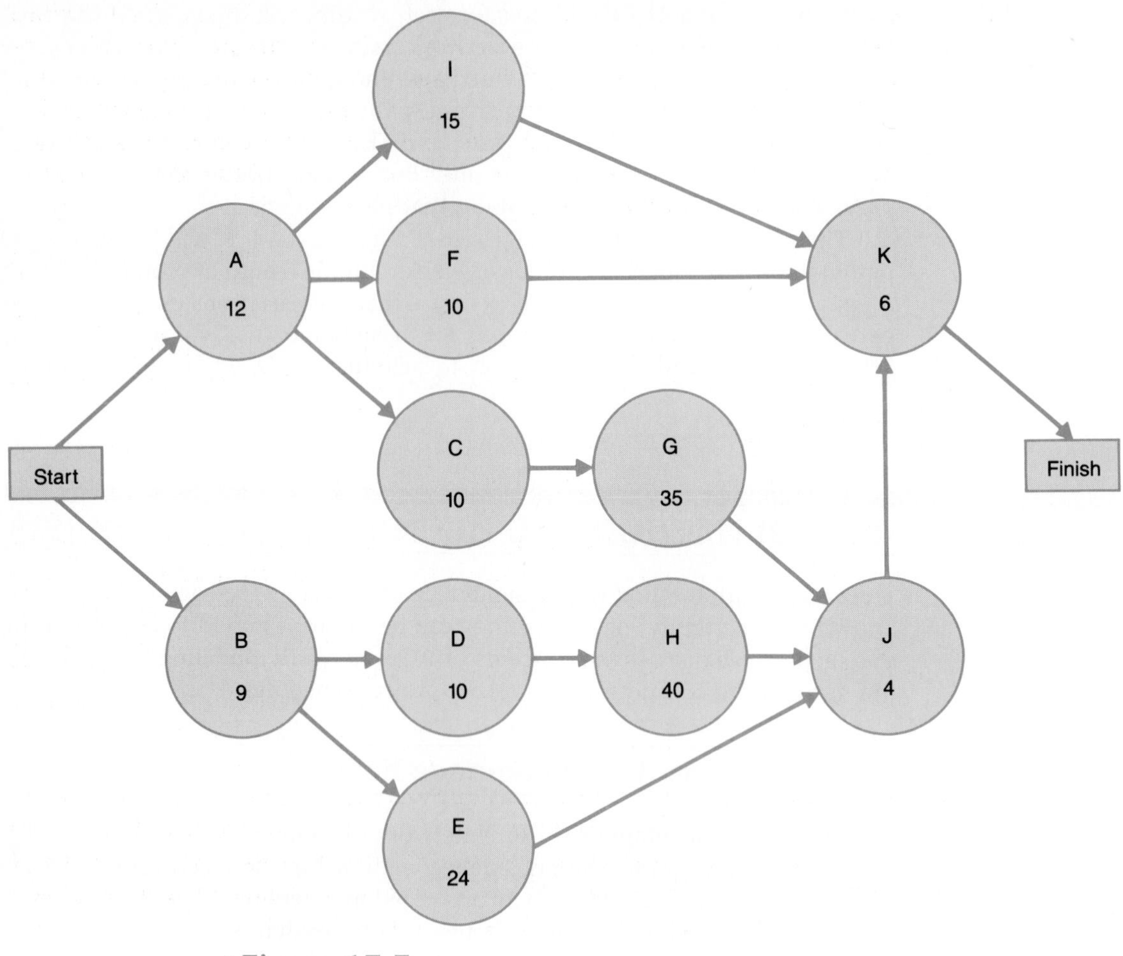

Figure 17.7

CPM Network Diagram for the St. Adolf's Hospital Project.

consequently, the activity times can be estimated from prior experience. Any reasonable method for estimating activity times can be used, including the method we used for PERT. A basic CPM assumption, however, is that the estimates have no statistical variance.

Calculating Slack and the Critical Path

We can find the critical path by enumerating all paths from the start node to the finish node and identifying the path having the longest cumulative elapsed time. In Fig. 17.7, the critical path is Start–B–D–H–J–K–Finish with a total length of 69 weeks, as we found in our PERT analysis. In practice, the critical path is found by computing the slack for each activity and finding the path of activities that have minimum slack. In PERT, we identified the critical path by calculating the slack for each event because we used an AOA network. In order to calculate activity slack for an AON network, we need to calculate four time values for each activity:

1. *Earliest start time* (*ES*), which is the earliest possible beginning time for an activity.
2. *Latest start time* (*LS*), which is the latest possible beginning time for an activity that will allow the project to be completed on schedule.
3. *Earliest finish time* (*EF*), which is the earliest start time plus the time needed for the activity.
4. *Latest finish time* (*LF*), which is the latest possible completion time for an activity that will not delay the entire project.

Earliest Start and Earliest Finish Times. Figure 17.8 shows these time values for the hospital project. To calculate the earliest start and earliest finish times, we begin at the start node and assume that the project can be started at time zero. Since activities A and B have no predecessors, the earliest start times for these activities are also zero. We find the earliest finish times for each activity by adding the activity time to the earliest start time. The only thing that we have to watch out for is when more than one arrow enters an activity node. The earliest start time for that activity is the *latest* of the *earliest finish* times of the activities that must immediately precede it. Consider activity J in Fig. 17.8. The earliest finish times are week 57 for activity G, week 59 for activity H, and week 33 for activity E. The earliest start time for activity J must be week 59 because all three activities must be completed before activity J can be started. A similar situation exists for activity K.

Latest Start and Latest Finish Times. To calculate the latest start and latest finish times, we start at the finish node and assume that the project is to be completed at the earliest finish time of the last activity. Alternatively, we could choose the contract due date. For the hospital project, we set the latest finish time of activity K at week 69. We calculate the latest start time for an activity by subtracting the time needed for the activity from its latest finish time. We have to be careful at an activity node having more than one arrow leaving it. The latest finish time for that activity is the *earliest* of the *latest start* times of those activities immediately following it. For example, the activities immediately following activity A are C, F, and I. The earliest of the latest start times for these activities is week 14 for activity C. Consequently, the latest finish time for activity A is week 14 because activity C cannot begin until activity A is completed, and we have already determined that the latest start time for activity C is week 14, if the project is to be completed by week 69.

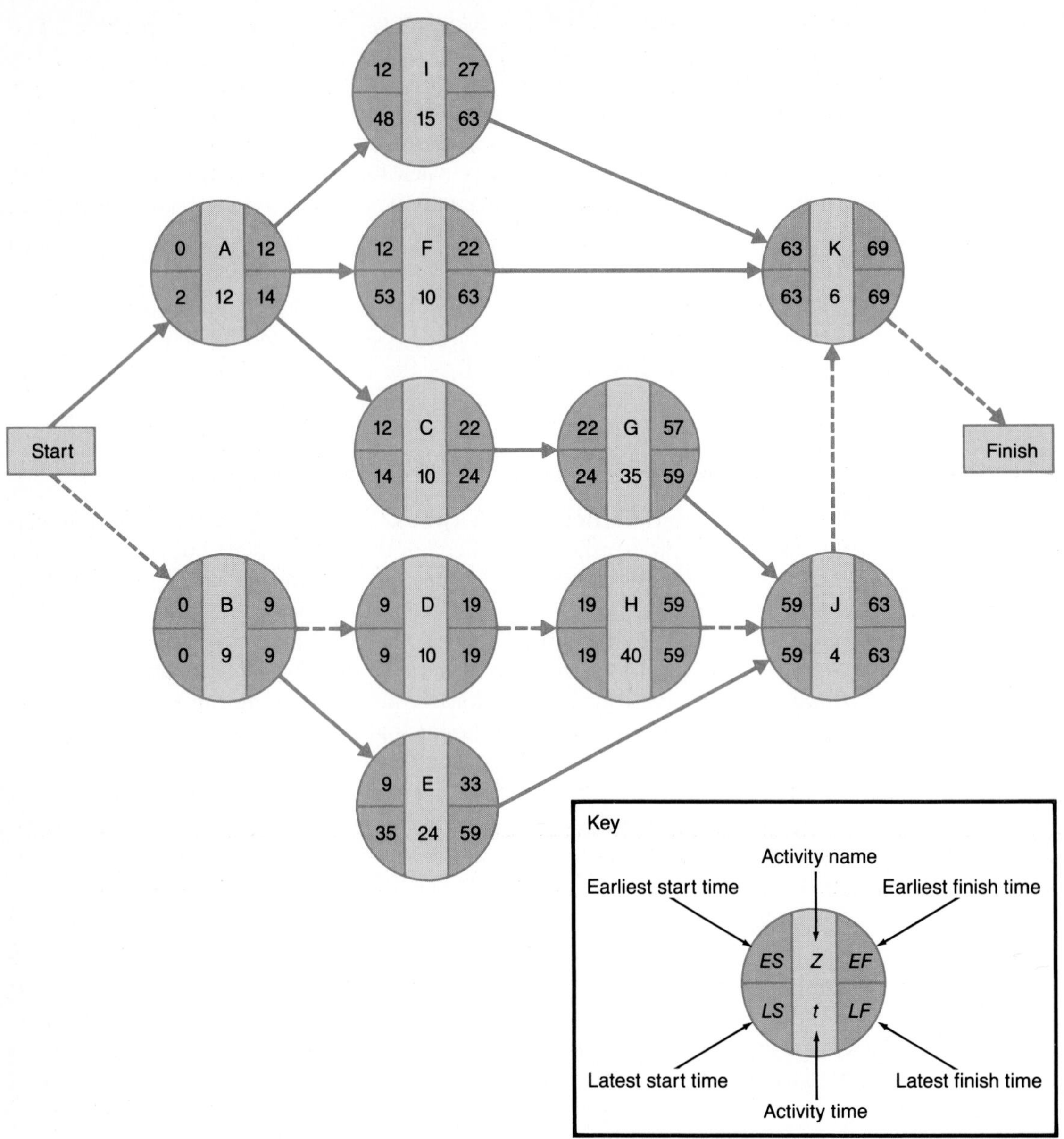

Figure 17.8

CPM Diagram Showing All Time Values Needed to Calculate Activity Slack for the St. Adolf's Hospital Project.

Slack. Table 17.5 shows the activity slacks for the hospital project. **Total slack** for an activity is simply the difference between its latest and earliest start times ($LS - ES$) or the difference between its latest and earliest finish times ($LF - EF$). It specifies the maximum time that an activity can be delayed without delaying the entire project. The distinguishing feature of total slack is that it is shared with other activities. For example, in Table 17.5, activity G has a total slack of 2 weeks. Note that activities A and C also have total slacks of 2 weeks. In Fig. 17.8, activities A, C, and G are linked by precedence constraints. Thus if activity A is delayed and uses the two weeks of slack, C and G no longer have slack available. This relationship reflects the nature of the *event slacks* we calculated for PERT.

Free slack is also shown in Table 17.5 and indicates the time that an activity can be delayed without delaying the *ES* of any other activity. Free slack is the difference between the *EF* for an activity and the earliest of the *ES* times of all the activities that immediately follow it. Activity G has a free slack of 2 weeks. Its earliest finish time is week 57 whereas its only successor, activity J, has an earliest start time of week 59. Activity G could be delayed 2 weeks without affecting the earliest start time of any other activity. The same cannot be said for activity A because each of its successors has an earliest start time of 12 weeks, the same as the *EF* for activity A. Any slippage in the schedule for A will affect the slack of any of its successors.

Critical Path. The critical path is identified by those activities with minimum *total* slack. This principle is the same as that for AOA diagrams. In Table 17.5, the critical path is Start–B–D–H–J–K–Finish, and its length is 69 weeks.

Table 17.5

Activity Slacks for the St. Adolf's Hospital Project

		Start		Finish				
Node	**Duration**	Earliest	Latest	Earliest	Latest	**Total Slack**	**Free Slack**	**Critical Path**
Start	0	0	0	0	0	0	0	Yes
A	12	0	2	12	14	2	0	No
B	9	0	0	9	9	0	0	Yes
C	10	12	14	22	24	2	0	No
D	10	9	9	19	19	0	0	Yes
E	24	9	35	33	59	26	26	No
F	10	12	53	22	63	41	41	No
G	35	22	24	57	59	2	2	No
H	40	19	19	59	59	0	0	Yes
I	15	12	48	27	63	36	36	No
J	4	59	59	63	63	0	0	Yes
K	6	63	63	69	69	0	0	Yes
Finish	0	69	69	69	69	0	0	Yes

Monitoring Project Progress

Even the best laid plans can go awry, and so it is with PERT or CPM. Progress of a project must be monitored, so that schedule delays can be readily identified. A *slack-sorted report* on a weekly basis (or some other suitable schedule) is helpful in this regard. Suppose that in the hospital project 16 weeks have passed and that activity A has just been completed. Consequently, activity A was completed 4 weeks late (see Fig. 17.8). Also suppose that activity B took 10 weeks instead of the expected 9 weeks. Table 17.6 shows a slack-sorted report as of the sixteenth week of the project. Activities A and B are not shown because they have already been completed.

Note that activities C, G, J, and K now have negative slack and replace activities D and H on the critical path. The activities at the top of the report are more critical than those at the bottom. If the original completion target of week 69 is still valid, management would try to make up two weeks of time somewhere along path C–G–J–K. However, to make the deadline, they will also have to make up one week along path D–H. If they are successful, there will be two critical paths: C–G–J–K and D–H–J–K. Slack-sorted reports such as this one can be used more conveniently than a network diagram by managers. Most managers work with this type of computer report and never see a network diagram.

Analyzing Costs with the Critical Path Method

Our previous discussion focused on the management of project time. The implicit assumption was that if the project was kept on schedule, total project costs would be acceptable. The reality of project management, however, is that there are always trade-offs between time and cost. Total project costs are the sum of *direct costs, indirect costs,* and *penalty costs.* Direct costs include labor, materials, and any other costs directly related to the activities of the project. Indirect costs include administration and other variable overhead costs that can be avoided by reducing the total time of the project. Penalty costs may be incurred if the project extends beyond some specific date. In some cases a bonus may be provided for early completion. Consequently, when a project manager considers total project costs, or total profits, the best schedule may include some expedited activities to reduce the overall project completion time.

Direct Costs and Times. Direct costs can be subdivided into *normal costs* and *crash costs* for each activity. Associated with these costs are a *normal time* and a *crash time.*

1. *Normal Time, NT:* The time to complete the activity under normal conditions.

Table 17.6

Slack-Sorted Computer Report for the St. Adolf's Hospital Project after 16 Weeks

Activity	Duration	Earliest Start	Latest Start	Total Slack	Free Slack*	Critical Path
C	10	16	14	−2	0	Yes
G	35	26	24	−2	0	Yes
J	4	61	59	−2	0	Yes
K	6	65	63	−2	0	Yes
D	10	10	9	−1	0	No
H	40	20	19	−1	1	No
E	24	10	35	25	27	No
I	15	16	48	32	34	No
F	10	16	53	37	39	No

* The free-slack calculation is based on the revised earliest start times of the activities immediately following the given activity.

2. *Normal Cost, NC:* The expected activity cost associated with the normal time.
3. *Crash Time, CT:* The shortest possible time to complete the activity.
4. *Crash Cost, CC:* The cost to achieve the minimum activity time.

Cost Assumptions. In our CPM cost analysis, we assume that there is a *linear* increase in costs as the activity time is reduced from its normal time. For example, suppose that the normal time for activity C is 10 weeks at a direct cost of $4000. If the crash time is 5 weeks at a crash cost of $7000, the net time reduction is 5 weeks at a net cost increase of $3000. We assume that it costs $600 (or $3000/5) per week to crash activity C. This assumption of linear marginal costs is shown in Fig. 17.9. Also shown is a hypothetical actual-cost curve. Thus if activity C were expedited by 2 weeks, the estimated direct costs would be $5200 even though actual costs would be much less in this example.* Table 17.7 contains direct cost and time data for the hospital project. The amounts in the last column were calculated as follows:

$$\text{Cost to crash per week} = \frac{CC - NC}{NT - CT}.$$

Indirect and Penalty Costs. Suppose that there are project indirect costs of $8000 per week. In addition, suppose that after week 65 St. Adolf's incurs a

* PERT and CPM do not require the assumption of linear cost increases. Nonlinear relationships can be used, but the linear assumption is usually adequate.

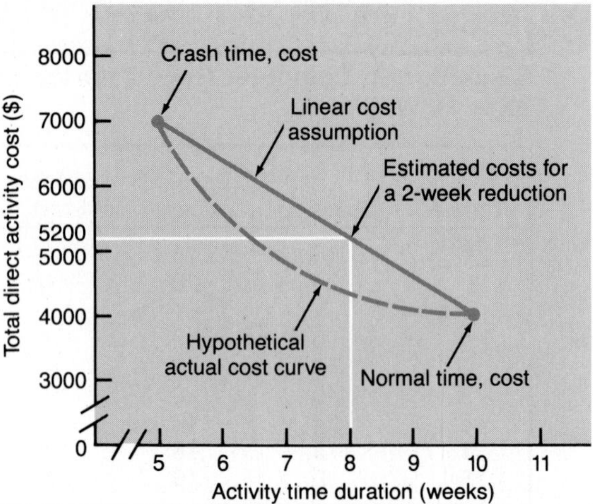

Figure 17.9

Cost–Time Relationships in a CPM Cost Analysis.

penalty cost of $20,000 per week if the hospital is not fully operational. With a critical path completion time of 69 weeks, it appears that St. Adolf's faces some major expenses. As the figures in Table 17.7 indicate, any activity in the project could be expedited for a certain increase in direct costs. For every week that the project duration is shortened, to week 65, St. Adolf's saves one

Table 17.7

Direct Cost and Time Data for the St. Adolf's Hospital Project

Activity	Normal Time (*NT*)	Normal Cost (*NC*)	Crash Time (*CT*)	Crash Cost (*CC*)	Maximum Time Reduction (weeks)	Cost to Crash Per Week
A	12	$ 12,000	11	$ 13,000	1	$ 1,000
B	9	50,000	7	64,000	2	7,000
C	10	4,000	5	7,000	5	600
D	10	16,000	8	20,000	2	2,000
E	24	120,000	14	200,000	10	8,000
F	10	10,000	6	16,000	4	1,500
G	35	500,000	25	530,000	10	3,000
H	40	1,200,000	35	1,260,000	5	12,000
I	15	40,000	10	52,500	5	2,500
J	4	10,000	1	13,000	3	1,000
K	6	30,000	5	34,000	1	4,000
Total		$1,992,000		$2,209,500		

week of penalty *and* indirect costs, or $28,000. For decreases beyond week 65, the savings are only the weekly indirect costs of $8000. Our objective is to determine the target project completion time that minimizes total project costs.

Normal and Rational Crash Schedules. From the perspective of project completion time, the normal time schedule and the minimum-time schedule provide the limits for our search for the minimum-cost schedule. Finding the cost for the normal time schedule is straightforward. Table 17.7 shows that the total direct cost is $1,992,000. The indirect costs would be $8000 per week, or $552,000. There would also be four weeks of penalty costs, or $80,000. Thus the total cost for a 69-week project is $2,624,000.

The first step in finding the cost of the minimum-time schedule is to find the minimum project duration by crashing all the activities in the project and finding the length of the critical path. Figure 17.10 shows the CPM network with the crash times for each activity. The critical path is B–D–H–J–K, with a total completion time of 56 weeks. The total direct cost for this schedule, as shown in Table 17.7, is $2,209,500. The indirect costs would be $448,000 [or 56($8000)]. Since there are no penalty costs, the total project cost would be $2,657,500.

The minimum-time schedule that we just evaluated crashed all activities to their limits. However, the minimum time of 56 weeks can be achieved *without* crashing all the activities. Table 17.8 shows how to derive the *rational crash schedule* for the hospital project. We begin by finding the activity not on the critical path that is the most expensive to crash. We then relax it as much as possible, without exceeding its normal time or increasing the length of the total project. This activity is E. We can return it to its normal time and save $80,000 relative to the total crash schedule. The next most expensive noncritical activity is G. Its normal time is 35 weeks; however, we can relax it only 9 weeks because, at an adjusted time of 34 weeks, path A–C–G–J–K is also 56 weeks long. Activities I and F can both be returned to their normal times, but all other activities remain at their crash times. The total savings relative to the total crash schedule is $125,000. Consequently, the total project cost for the rational crash schedule is $2,532,500 (or $2,657,500 − $125,000).

Finding the Minimum-Cost Schedule. So far we have established an upper limit for total project costs of $2,532,500 for the rational crash schedule. Thus we would not accept an intermediate schedule between 56 and 69 weeks that costs more than $2,532,500. In evaluating intermediate schedules, we will use a heuristic procedure that starts with the normal time schedule and crashes activities along the critical path in such a way that the added crash costs are less than the savings in indirect and penalty costs.* The procedure involves the following steps.

* This same procedure could be used for AOA networks.

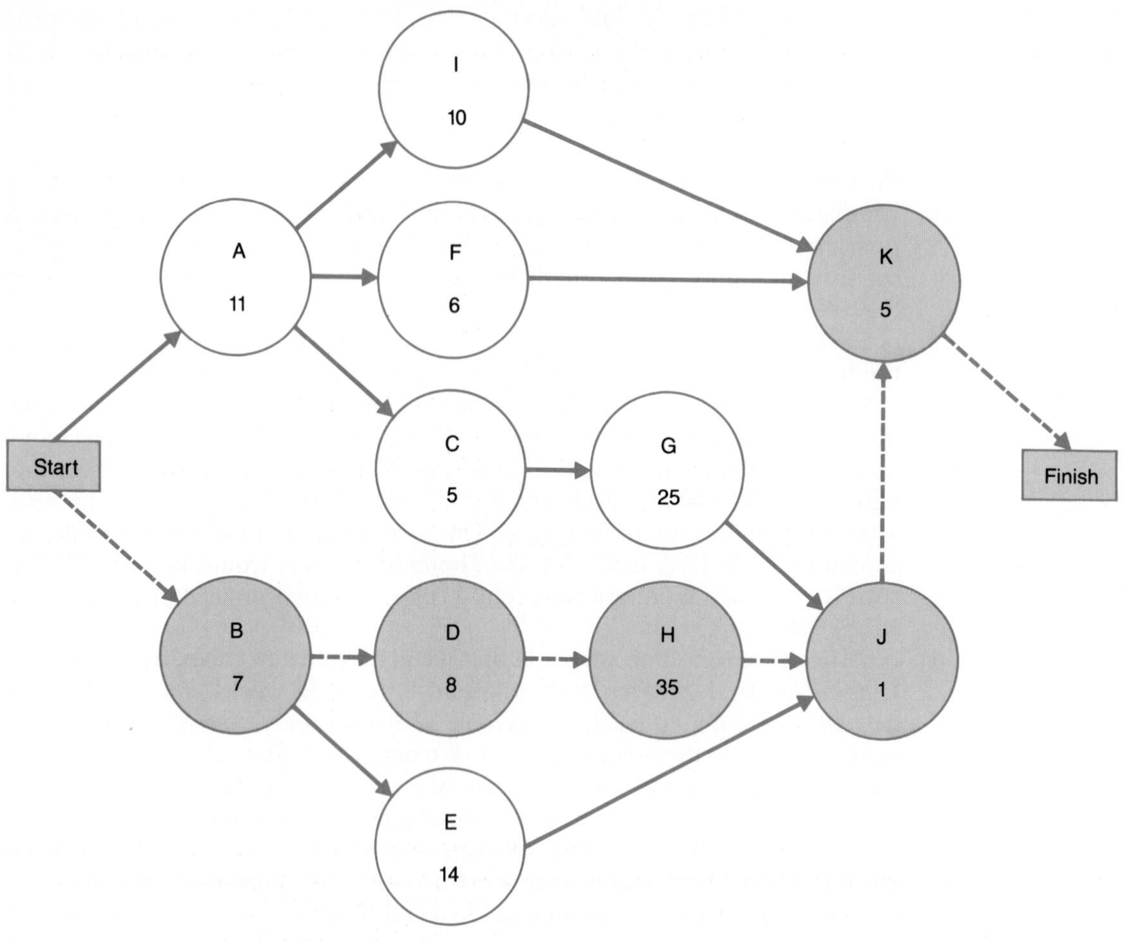

Figure 17.10

Network Showing Crash Times and the Critical Path for the St. Adolf's Hospital Project.

1. Determine the critical path(s) in the project.
2. Find the activity (activities) on the critical path(s) that is (are) cheapest to crash per week.
3. Reduce the time for this activity until (a) it cannot be further reduced; (b) another path becomes critical; or (c) the increase in direct costs exceeds the savings that result from shortening the duration of the project. If more than one path is critical, it may be necessary to reduce the time for an activity on each path simultaneously.
4. Go back to step 1 and repeat the procedure, so long as the increase in

Table 17.8

Deriving the Rational Crash Schedule for the St. Adolf's Hospital Project

Noncritical Activity	Cost to Crash per Week	Crash Time (weeks)	Maximum Relax Time (weeks)	Adjusted Time (weeks)	Savings Relative to Total Crash Schedule
E	$8000	14	10	24	$ 80,000
G	3000	25	9	34	27,000
I	2500	10	5	15	12,500
F	1500	6	4	10	6,000
Total					$125,500

direct costs is less than the savings generated by shortening the duration of the project.

Table 17.9 summarizes the application of the procedure for the hospital project. You will find it helpful to refer to Fig. 17.8 and Table 17.7 as we proceed. Activity J was chosen for trial 1 because it is the activity on the critical path B–D–H–J–K (see Table 17.7) that is the cheapest per week to crash. The crash cost of $1000 per week is much less than the potential savings in indirect and penalty costs of $28,000 per week. Activity J is crashed to its limit because the critical path remains unchanged. The box around activity J in Table 17.9 indicates that we have crashed it to its limit and cannot reduce it further.

In trial 2, activity D is the next least expensive of the activities on the critical path to crash after trial 1. We crash it to its limit of two weeks because first-week savings are $28,000, while second-week savings are $8000. After week 65, there are no more penalty costs. Note that after crashing D, we now have two critical paths.

In trial 3 and beyond, two critical paths must be considered. *Both* paths must be shortened to realize any savings in indirect project costs. If one is shortened and the other is not, the length of the project remains unchanged. Our alternatives are to crash one of the following combinations of activities, (A, B), (A, H), (C, B), (C, H), (G, B), (G, H), or to crash activity K, which is on both critical paths. The cheapest of these alternatives is activity K, so we choose it for trial 3.

The next least expensive alternative is to simultaneously crash activities B and C, at a cost of $7600 per week. This amount is still less than the savings of $8000 per week in indirect costs. In trial 4, we can reduce the time of these activities by only two weeks because that is the limit for activity B. (See Table 17.7.) Any other combination of activities will result in a net increase in total project costs because the crash costs exceed the weekly indirect costs. Thus

Table 17.9

Cost Analysis for the St. Adolf's Hospital Project

Trial	Crash Activity	Resulting Critical Path*	Time Reduction (weeks)	Project Duration (weeks)	Total Project Direct Costs at Last Trial	Crash Costs Added This Trial	Total Indirect Costs	Total Penalty Costs	Total Project Costs
0	—	B–D–H–J–K	—	69	$1,992,000	$ —	$552,000	$80,000	$2,624,000
1	J	B–D–H–[J]–K	3	66	1,992,000	3,000	528,000	20,000	2,543,000
2	D	A–C–G–[J]–K B–[D]–H–[J]–K	2	64	1,995,000	4,000	512,000	0	2,511,000
3	K	A–C–G–[J]–[K] B–[D]–H–[J]–[K]	1	63	1,999,000	4,000	504,000	0	2,507,000
4	B, C	A–C–G–[J]–[K] [B]–[D]–H–[J]–[K]	2	61	2,003,000	15,200	488,000	0	2,506,200

* A [ ] indicates that the activity has been crashed to its limit.

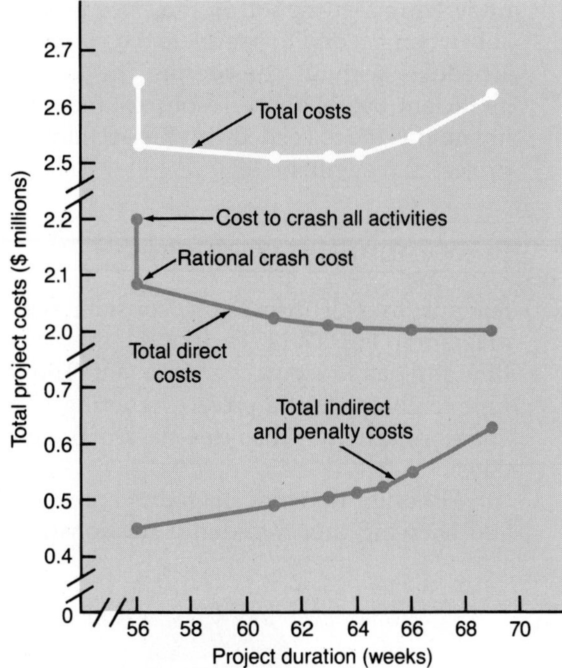

Figure 17.11

Cost Curves for the St. Adolf's Hospital Project.

the minimum-cost schedule is 61 weeks, with a total cost of $2,506,200. In this schedule, we crash activities B, D, J, and K to their limits and activity C to 8 weeks. The other activities remain at their normal times. This schedule costs about $26,300 less than the rational crash schedule.

Figure 17.11 shows the cost curves for the hospital project. The curves consist of a series of straight-line segments because of our assumption that marginal costs are linear. Our heuristic procedure stopped at 61 weeks; however, we could have continued crashing more activities (even though total costs would have increased) until week 56 and plotted the costs along the way to get a better approximation of the cost curves in that range. Of course, because the procedure is heuristic, we have no guarantee that the schedule developed is the optimal minimum-cost schedule.

RESOURCE CONSIDERATIONS IN PROJECT MANAGEMENT

The project management models that we have discussed so far consider only activity times in determining the overall project duration and critical path. An underlying assumption in their use is that sufficient resources will be available when needed to complete the various activities on schedule. Developing schedules without considering the load placed on resources can result in inefficient use of those resources and even cause project delays if capacity limitations are exceeded. In this section we explore resource implications for project management.

Smoothing the Workload

For purposes of discussion, consider the project represented by the AON diagram in Fig. 17.12. Each of the five activities involves a certain amount of time and has a resource requirement. The critical path is A–B–E, and the total time to complete the project, ignoring resource limitations, is nine days. In addition, activity C has free slack of 3 days and activity D has free slack of 2 days.

Although network diagrams are useful for displaying an entire project and showing the precedence relationships between activities, they are not

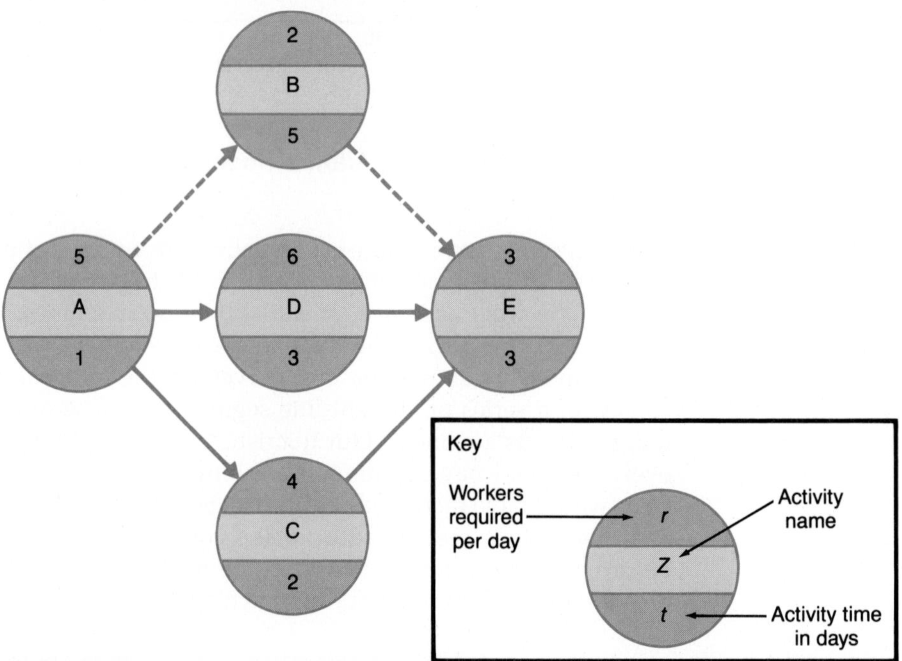

Figure 17.12

AON Diagram Showing Resource Requirements and Critical Path.

very useful for showing the implications of resource requirements for a schedule of activities. Gantt charts (see Chapter 16) are more useful in this regard. Figure 17.13 shows two schedules and their resource implications for our example project. Both schedules recognize the precedence relationships shown in Fig. 17.12 and maintain the project completion date of day 9. The *left-justified schedule* shows all activities starting at their earliest start dates, and the *right-justified schedule* shows all activities starting at their latest start dates. These two schedules represent extremes in terms of the timing of resource requirements. Note that the peak of 12 workers per day comes in days 2 and 3 for the left-justified schedule and in days 5 and 6 for the right-justified schedule. In long projects where the time value of money is a concern, right-justified schedules may be desirable because the expenditures for the heavier use of resources can be put off until much later in the project.

Most often, however, project managers are interested in smoothing the work-force load with their schedules rather than creating peak work-force requirements. The benefits of this approach include reduced overtime expenditures and hiring and firing costs. Figure 17.14 shows two schedules that reduce the peak requirement from 12 workers to only 8 workers, without extending the completion date of the project. These schedules take advantage of the slack for activities C and D. In schedule 1, the start time for activity D is delayed until its latest starting date, consuming its slack and making it a critical activity. The reverse is true for schedule 2. By manipulating the slacks of various activities, project managers can generate alternative schedules and choose the one that is the most effective. In this trial-and-error approach, we assume that the project completion date, as determined by standard CPM or PERT methods, is not to be changed and that we have the resources (or the commitment to acquire them) to accomplish any schedule that results.

Handling Resource Limitations

With resource limitations, the concept of activity slack changes. We must now generate the schedule with these resource constraints, as well as the precedence relationships between activities, in mind. For demonstration purposes, suppose that we are limited to a maximum of six workers per day in our example problem. Although we could use an optimizing approach, such as linear programming (see Appendix C), to derive a schedule under these conditions, a more useful approach in practice is to use a heuristic procedure such as the one developed by Weist (1966):

1. Start on the first day of the project and schedule all activities possible, considering precedence relationships and resource limitations. Continue with the second day, and so on, until all activities are scheduled.
2. When several activities compete for the same resources, give preference

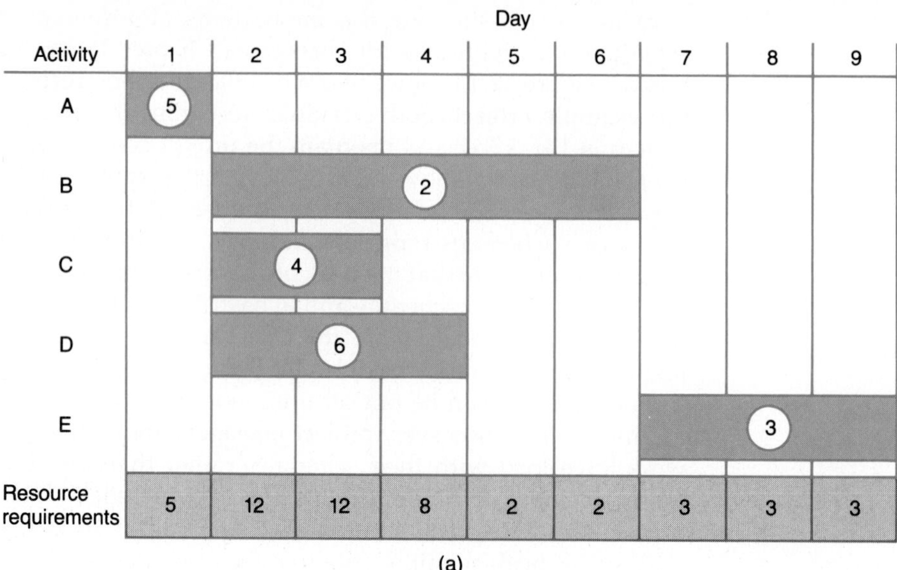

(a)

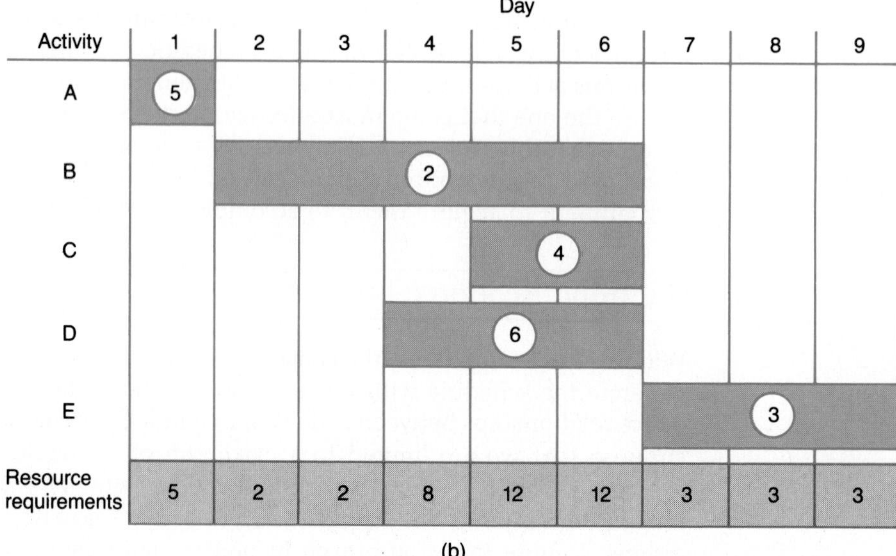

(b)

Figure 17.13

Two Schedules Showing the Extremes in the Timing of Resource Requirements: (a) Left-Justified Schedule; (b) Right-Justified Schedule.

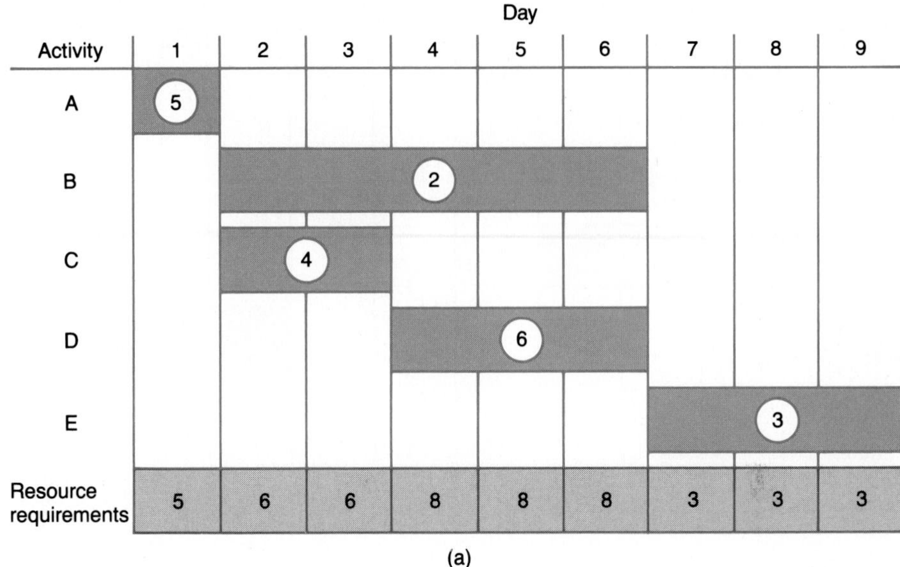

(a)

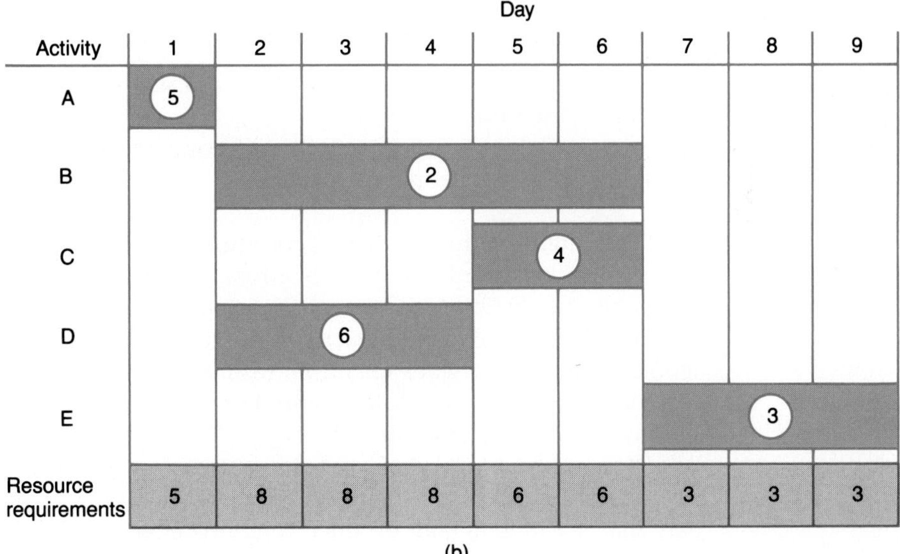

(b)

Figure 17.14

Two Schedules That Smooth the Workload: (a) Schedule 1; (b) Schedule 2.

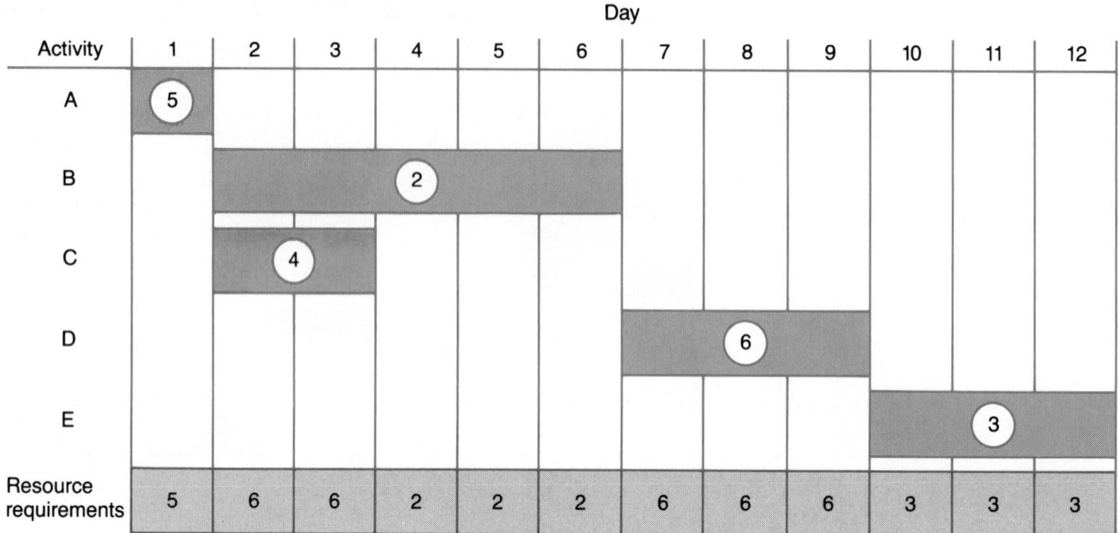

Figure 17.15

Resource-Constrained Schedule.

to the activities with the least slack, as calculated using standard CPM or PERT methods.

3. Reschedule noncritical activities, if possible, to free resources for scheduling critical or nonslack activities.

The intent of this heuristic procedure is to minimize total project time, subject to constraints on the resources. Figure 17.15 shows the results of using the heuristic procedure for the example problem. Activity A has to be scheduled first, followed by activity B, which has no slack. Next, we have a choice between activities C and D; resource limitations force us to schedule activity C first. We schedule activity D next because of precedence considerations. Finally, we can schedule activity E, and we now have a 12-day schedule. This schedule results in the shortest project time possible; however, the use of the heuristic procedure will not always be so successful. We can only say that it will generally produce solutions close to, but not necessarily, the optimum.

COMPUTERIZED PROJECT SCHEDULING AND CONTROL

The use of network planning models can simplify project management. These models supply the information necessary to plan and control projects having complex activity interdependence and resource requirements. However, the manual use of these models is limited to only the smallest of projects. Calculating slack times, updating networks, and calculating cost–time trade-offs, probability estimates, resource allocations, and other factors require the use of computers. Software packages equipped to provide spreadsheets, network diagrams, PERT-milestone charts, critical path activity reports, and Gantt charts are readily available (Davis, 1973). Software producers have begun to offer the same capabilities to users of microcomputers. Some of these packages can handle more than 60,000 activities per project and any number of resources per activity, limited only by disk capacity (Fawcette, 1984). They can also handle a number of different projects.

CRITIQUE OF PERT AND CPM SYSTEMS

In this chapter, we have demonstrated the benefits that PERT and CPM offer to project managers. We now address the criticisms of PERT and CPM because, if nothing else, they serve to emphasize the assumptions and limitations of these methods.

Network Diagrams

Both PERT and CPM are based on the assumption that project activities having clear beginning and ending points can be identified. In addition, it is assumed that activity sequence relationships can be identified at the start of the project and specified in a network diagram. However, there are situations in which these assumptions are too restrictive. For example, PERT and CPM network diagrams do not show that two activities, where one must precede the other, can be overlapped and worked on simultaneously. One activity must be shown to precede the other in the network diagram. Also, project content can change, and a network diagram developed at the start of a project may limit the project manager's flexibility to handle changing situations later in the project. In other situations, the actual precedence relationships cannot be specified beforehand. The sequencing of some activities is contingent on the result of certain other activities. In situations such as these, PERT or CPM may not be very useful.

Control

The major underlying assumption in PERT or CPM is that managerial attention should focus on the activities along the critical path. However, as we pointed out earlier in this chapter, attention also should be paid to *near-critical* paths. The reason is that these near-critical paths could easily become critical, if one or more of the activities along these paths slips relative to its schedule. Project managers who overlook this possibility often complain that using PERT or CPM did not help them complete their projects on time. This shortcoming is not that of either PERT or CPM itself, but rather is the result of an incomplete understanding of the concepts involved.

Time Estimates

In PERT, the assumption is that activity times follow the beta distribution, with the variance of the total project time equaling the sum of the variances along the critical path. This aspect of PERT has brought a variety of criticism. First, the formulas used to calculate the mean and variance of the beta distribution are only approximations and are subject to error. Errors on the order of 10 percent for the mean and 5 percent for the variance can be expected. Second, it is very difficult to arrive at a single time estimate, let alone three estimates, for an activity that has never been performed before. A single time estimate, the most likely time, is preferred by many project managers because they feel that the pessimistic time estimates often are inflated and vary to a greater extent from the most likely time estimate than do the optimistic time estimates. They argue that some managers use these pessimistic time estimates as an excuse for failure. Perhaps a more harmful by-product of inflated pessimistic time estimates is the inflation of *expected* activity times, which builds a cushion of slack into the schedule. Finally, the choice of the beta distribution was somewhat arbitrary, and the use of another distribution would result in different expected times and variances for each activity.

Summary. Although the application of PERT and CPM to project management has shortcomings, effective management includes knowing their limitations. These shortcomings have not precluded their widespread use in practice. The Department of Defense actually requires the use of PERT or CPM by major contractors. Other notable users include the Ford Motor Company for retooling assembly lines, the Chrysler Corporation for building a new assembly plant, and a large number of organizations representing a broad spectrum of applications, including Brigham and Women's Hospital in Boston, the San Francisco Opera Association, Walt Disney Corporation, and Procter & Gamble. While network planning models are not perfect, the skillful use of these models can be a significant aid to project managers.

CHAPTER HIGHLIGHTS

Most organizations, whether in manufacturing or service, must undertake large projects at one time or another. In this chapter, we presented some of the issues of project management and tools that can be used to manage large projects efficiently. Some of the highlights of the chapter are:

- PERT and CPM are similar network modeling systems that are useful in project management. The major difference between them is that PERT allows for uncertainty in activity time estimates.
- In AOA networks, arcs (arrows) represent both activities and precedence relationships, and nodes represent events. In AON networks, nodes represent activities, and arcs (arrows) represent precedence relationships only.
- Three time estimates are needed for each activity in PERT. Actual activity times are assumed to follow a beta distribution.
- PERT and CPM focus attention on the critical path, that is, the sequence of activities having the greatest cumulative amount of time. Any delays in these activities will delay the entire project.
- PERT can be used to assess the probability of finishing the project by a certain date.
- CPM can be used to find the minimum-cost schedule, with the assumption that marginal costs are linear.
- When resource capacity is considered, activity slack can be used to smooth the workload while holding to the scheduled project completion date. If there are specific resource constraints, heuristics can be used to schedule the project.
- A number of criticisms have been leveled at PERT and CPM. Although these methods have some shortcomings, PERT and CPM are widely used in practice.

KEY TERMS

activity
activity-on-arc (AOA) network
activity-on-node (AON) network
critical path
critical path method (CPM)
event
free slack
network diagram
precedence relationships
program evaluation and review technique (PERT)
project
total slack

STUDY QUESTIONS

1. Briefly describe the differences between PERT and CPM. When would each be the most appropriate tool to use in managing a project?
2. What information is needed to construct the network diagram for a project? Can any project be diagramed as a network?
3. A certain advertising agency is preparing a bid for a promotional campaign of a type never before attempted. The project consists of a large number of interrelated activities. Explain how you would arrive at a single time estimate for each activity, so that you can use a network planning model to assess the chances that the project can be completed when the sponsor wants it.
4. Why was the beta distribution chosen over the normal distribution for PERT analyses?

5. Why is the critical path of such importance in project management? Can it change during the course of the project? If so, why?
6. What is the major advantage of activity-on-node networks over activity-on-arc networks?
7. Explain the difference between total slack and free slack. Why is this distinction important to project managers?
8. Suppose that your company has accepted a project of a type it has completed many times before. Any activity can be expedited with an increase in costs. There are weekly indirect costs, and there is a weekly penalty if the project exceeds a certain date. Identify the data that you would need and explain the analytic process that you would use to determine a minimum-cost schedule. What assumptions would you make in doing such an analysis?
9. Suppose that you are trying to convince management that project planning techniques such as PERT or CPM would be useful to them. Some of the managers have voiced the following concerns.
   (a) There is a tendency for technicians to handle the operation of PERT or CPM; consequently, management will not use it very much.
   (b) It puts pressure on managers because everyone knows where the critical path is. Managers of activities along the critical path are in the spotlight, and if their activities are delayed, the cost of the delay is on their shoulders.
   (c) The introduction of network planning techniques may require new communication channels and systems procedures.

   Comment on each of these concerns.

PROBLEMS

1. Recently, you were assigned to manage a project for your company. Having heard of a technique called PERT, you identified the various activities and drew a network diagram of the project (Fig. 17.16). In addition, you asked various managers and subordinates to estimate the amount of time that they would expect each of the activities to take. Their responses are shown in Table 17.10.

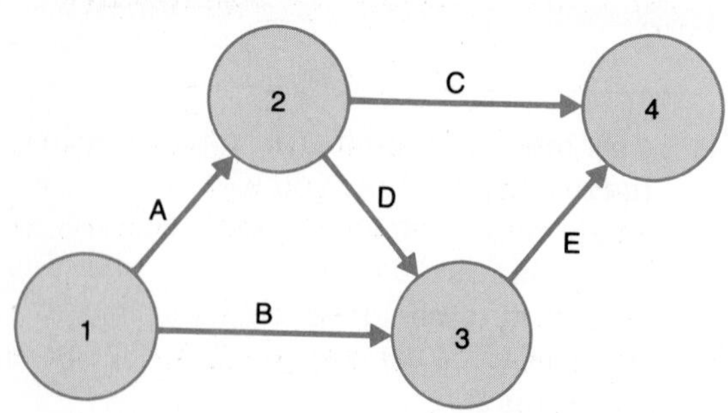

Figure 17.16

Table 17.10

Activity	Time Estimates (days) Optimistic	Most likely	Pessimistic
A	3	5	13
B	10	12	14
C	4	5	8
D	6	8	16
E	1	3	5

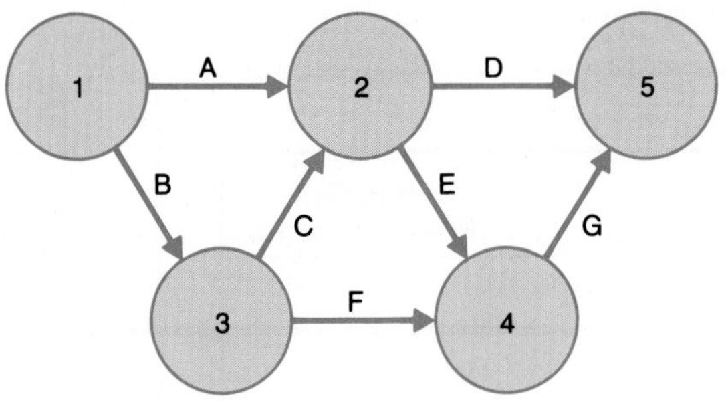

Figure 17.17

(a) What is the expected completion time of the project?
(b) Suppose that the optimistic times prevail during the project. What is the earliest the project could be completed?

2. An advertising project manager has developed the AOA diagram shown in Fig. 17.17 for a new advertising campaign. In addition, the manager gathered the time information for each activity shown in Table 17.11.
(a) Find the critical path for this project.
(b) What is the probability of completing the project within 18 weeks?

Table 17.11

	Time Estimates (weeks)		
Activity	Optimistic	Most likely	Pessimistic
A	1	2	3
B	4	6	8
C	3	3	3
D	2	8	10
E	3	6	9
F	1	8	15
G	4	5	6

3. The following information has been gathered for an AON network.

Activity	Time (weeks)	Immediate Predecessor(s)
A	4	—
B	8	A
C	2	A
D	6	A, C
E	9	B, C
F	5	E, D

(a) Draw the AON diagram.
(b) Calculate the total slack for each activity and determine the critical path. How long will the project take?
(c) Do any of the activities have *free* slack?

Table 17.12

Activity	**Time (weeks)**	**Immediate Predecessor(s)**
A	3	—
B	4	—
C	9	—
D	4	A, B
E	5	B
F	6	D, C
G	6	E, C
H	10	F, G

4. Consider the information about a project shown in Table 17.12.
(a) Draw the AON diagram for this project.
(b) Specify the critical path(s).
(c) Compute the total slack for activities A and D.
(d) What happens to the slack for D if A takes 5 days?

Table 17.13

Activity	Description	Immediate Predecessor(s)
A	Design brochure and course announcement.	—
B	Identify prospective teachers.	—
C	Prepare detailed outline of course.	—
D	Send brochure and student applications.	A
E	Send teacher applications.	B
F	Select teacher for course.	C, E
G	Accept students.	D
H	Select text for course.	F
I	Order and receive texts.	G, H
J	Prepare room for class.	G

5. Consider the following data for a project never before attempted by your company.

Activity	Expected Time, t_e (weeks)	Immediate Predecessor(s)
A	2	—
B	3	—
C	5	A
D	7	B
E	4	C, D
F	3	D

   (a) Draw the AOA diagram for this project.
   (b) Identify the critical path and estimate the duration of the project.
   (c) Calculate the slack for each event.

6. The director of continuing education at Bluebird University has just approved the planning for a sales-training seminar. Her administrative assistant has identified the various activities that must be done and their relationships to each other, as shown in Table 17.13. Since there is typically a considerable amount of uncertainty in planning a new course such as this, the assistant also supplied several time estimates for each activity, as shown in Table 17.14. The director wants to conduct the seminar 45 working days from now. What is the probability that this can be done?

Table 17.14

Activity	Time Estimates (working days) Optimistic	Most likely	Pessimistic
A	3	5	7
B	2	3	6
C	1	2	3
D	15	20	25
E	10	12	16
F	2	3	4
G	1	2	3
H	3	6	7
I	10	15	20
J	1	1	1

7. An AON diagram (Fig. 17.18) has been prepared for the production of a certain item specially ordered by a good customer. Nonetheless, starting on the thirteenth day from now, your firm will expe-

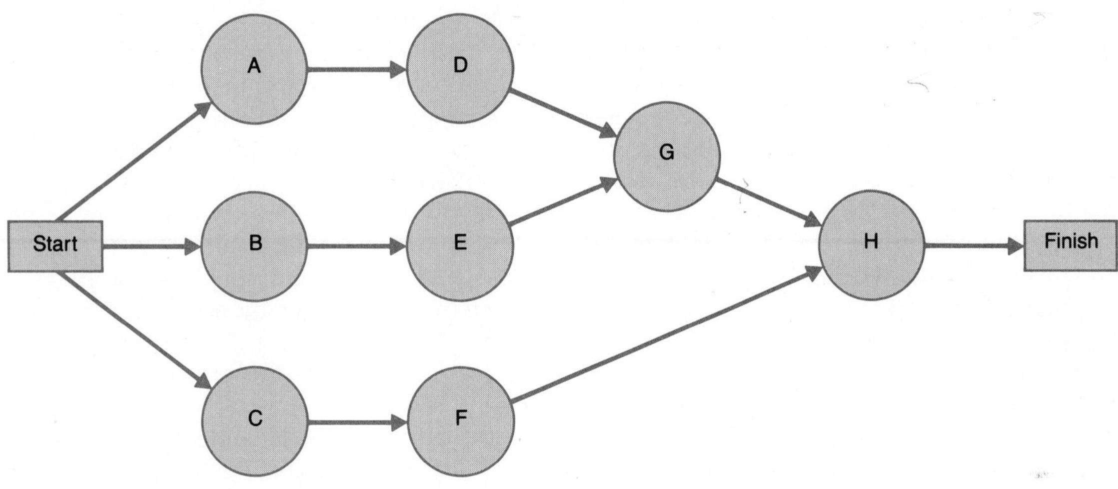

Figure 17.18

rience a penalty of $100 per day if the job is not completed. Indirect project costs amount to $200 per day. The direct cost and time data gathered by the project manager are shown in Table 17.15.

(a) What completion date would you recommend?

(b) What is the critical path?

Table 17.15

Activity	Normal Time (days)	Normal Cost	Crash Time (days)	Crash Cost
A	4	$1000	3	$1300
B	7	1400	4	2000
C	5	2000	4	2700
D	6	1200	5	1400
E	3	900	2	1100
F	11	2500	6	3750
G	4	800	3	1450
H	3	300	1	500

Table 17.16

Activity	Maximum Crash Time (days)	Cost to Crash (per day)
A	0	—
B	1	$150
C	1	100
D	2	200
E	2	100
F	2	200
G	2	400
H	2	400

8. You have been given the additional data shown in Table 17.16 for the project in Problem 4. Shorten the project by 2 days, using the heuristic procedure for finding a minimum-cost schedule. Assume that project indirect costs and penalty costs are negligible. Use the heuristic procedure to identify activities to crash, minimizing the additional crash costs.

9. Hamilton Berger, district manager for Gumfull Foods, Inc., is in charge of opening a new fast-food outlet in the college town of Senility. His major concern is the hiring of the manager of the outlet and a cadre of hamburger cooks, assemblers, and dispensers. He also has to coordinate the renovation of a building that previously was owned by a pet-supplies retailer. Realizing that he could manage this project using PERT, he gathered the data shown in Table 17.17.

   Top management has told Berger that the new outlet is to be opened as soon as possible. Every week that the project can be shortened will save the firm $1000 in lease costs. Hamilton thought about how to save time during the project and came up with two potential ways:

   - Employ Amazon, Inc., a local employment agency, to locate some good prospects for the manager's job. This approach would save 2 weeks in activity A and cost Gumfull Foods $1200.
   - By adding a few workers, he could shorten the time for activity B by 1 week, at an additional cost of $1700.

   Help Ham Berger by answering the following questions.

   (a) How long is the project expected to take?
   (b) Suppose that Hamilton has a personal goal of completing the project in 11 weeks. What is the probability of this happening?
   (c) What additional expenditures should be made to reduce the project dura-

Table 17.17

Activity	Description	Immediate Predecessor(s)	Time (weeks) *a*	*m*	*b*
A	Interview at college for new manager.	—	3	5	7
B	Renovate building.	—	4	6	20
C	Place ad for employees and interview applicants.	—	2	5	14
D	Visit by new-manager prospects.	A	1	2	3
E	Purchase equipment for new outlet and install.	B	2	4	6
F	Check references for employee applicants and make final selection.	C	1	1	1
G	Check references for new manager and make final selection.	D	1	1	1
H	Hold orientation meetings and do paperwork to get manager and employees on payroll.	E, F G	1	1	1

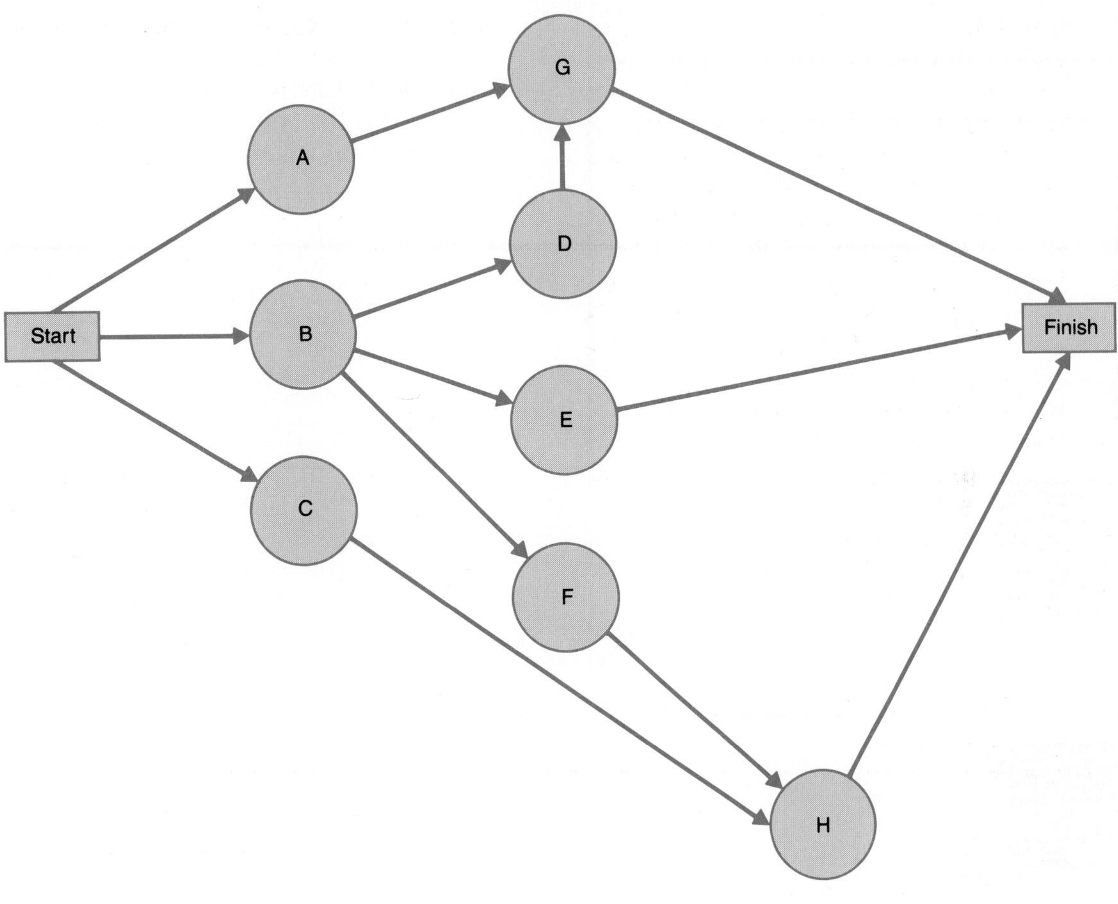

Figure 17.19

tion? Use the PERT expected times for each activity as if they were certain.

10. The CPM diagram in Fig. 17.19 was developed for a project that you are managing. Suppose that you are interested in finding ways to speed up the project at minimal additional cost. Determine the schedule that results in project completion in 26 days at minimum cost. There are no penalty costs or project overhead costs worth considering. Alternative time and cost data for each activity are shown in Table 17.18.

11. A maintenance crew at the Woody Manufacturing Company must do scheduled maintenance of machines in the fabricating department. A series of interrelated activities must be accomplished, requiring a different number of workers each day. The following information is available.

Table 17.18

Activity	Time (days)	Cost	Time (days)	Cost
A	18	$ 4,300	15	$ 5,200
B	9	3,000	7	4,400
C	12	3,100	9	4,900
D	11	2,400	9	3,600
E	20	3,200	14	5,600
F	6	4,000	3	5,200
G	12	4,300	10	5,700
H	10	1,200	6	3,200
Total		$25,500		$37,800

Activity	Immediate Predecessor(s)	Time (days)	Workers Required (per day)
A	—	3	4
B	A	2	3
C	A	4	6
D	C	2	4
E	B, C, D	2	5

(a) Draw the AON diagram for this project.
(b) Determine the critical path and duration of the project.
(c) Find a schedule that smooths the workload requirements, without delaying project completion. Draw a Gantt chart for your schedule.

12. Consider Problem 11 further. Suppose that the Woody Manufacturing Company can only devote a maximum of 6 maintenance workers per day to this project. Use Weist's heuristic procedure to find a new schedule and draw a Gantt chart for it.
    (a) What is the critical path?
    (b) How long will the project take?

13. A crew of linemen for the Alphabet Telephone Company must install some cable in a rural area. The following data are available for the project.

Activity	Immediate Predecessor(s)	Time (days)	Crew Members Required (per day)
A	—	2	10
B	A	2	3
C	A	3	4
D	A	5	7
E	D	2	8
F	B, C, E	1	9

(a) Disregarding capacity limitations, determine the critical path and calculate the total slack for each activity. How long will the project take?
(b) Specify a work schedule that smooths the workload of the crew, without delaying the project. Draw a Gantt chart for your schedule.
(c) Suppose that there are only 10 crew members. Use Weist's heuristic procedure to find a schedule that does not exceed 10 workers per day on the project.
    (i) What is the critical path now?
    (ii) What are the slacks for each activity?
    (iii) How long will the project take now?

SELECTED REFERENCES

Aquilano, N. J., and D. E. Smith, "A Formal Set of Algorithms for Project Scheduling with Critical Path Scheduling–Material Requirements Planning," *Journal of Operations Management*, vol. 1, no. 2 (November 1980), pp. 57–67.

Britney, R., "Bayesian Point Estimation and the PERT Scheduling of Stochastic Activities," *Management Sciences,* vol. 22, no. 9 (May 1976), pp. 938–948.

Davis, E. W., "Project Scheduling under Resource Constraints—Historical Review," *AIIE Transactions,* vol. 5, no. 4 (December 1973), pp. 297–311.

Fawcette, J. E., "Choosing Project Management Software," *Personal Computing,* vol. 8, no. 10 (October 1984), pp. 154–167.

Martin, C. C. *Project Management: How to Make It Work,* New York: AMACOM, a Division of American Management Associations, 1976.

Weist, J. D., "Heuristic Programs for Decision Making," *Harvard Business Review* (September–October 1966), pp. 129–143.

Weist, J. D., and F. K. Levy, *A Management Guide to PERT/CPM,* 2nd ed. Englewood Cliffs, N.J.: Prentice-Hall, 1977.

CHAPTER 18

QUALITY MANAGEMENT

Some Managerial Issues

- How can we best meet the quality levels dictated by our competitive strategies?
- What organizational design best achieves our quality goals?
- What can we do to reduce the high costs of poor quality?
- What do we consider to be acceptable scrap rates? Vendor quality levels?

Chapter Outline

Placing the topic *quality management* near the end of the text seems to imply that it is of marginal importance to operations managers. Nothing could be further from the truth. Recall in Chapter 2 (Fig. 2.4) that North American manufacturers put all four dimensions of quality at the top of their priority list for the future. This emphasis does not mean that important trade-offs between cost, quality, and flexibility should be ignored. It is obvious, however, that good quality has become a competitive weapon, and the challenge for top managers today is to produce products or services efficiently and of the quality demanded by consumers. Managerially, this requires decisions regarding the level and reliability (or consistency) of quality to provide. Viewed in this manner, quality management encompasses virtually every topic that we have discussed so far. It puts operations managers squarely in the middle of top-management policy and goal setting because it is the operations function in cooperation with the other functional areas in an organization, that must meet the challenge.

The issue of quality has not always been considered a top-management problem. Not too long ago quality was in the hands of first-line supervisors—and sometimes the workers—with no top-management support. Quality

Box 18.1

QUALITY IS MANAGEMENT'S RESPONSIBILITY

Folklore has it in America that quality and production are incompatible: that you cannot have both. It is either or. Insist on quality, and you will fall behind in production. Push production and you will find that your quality has suffered.

The fact is that quality is achieved by improvement of the process. Improvement of the process increases uniformity of output of product, reduces mistakes, and reduces waste of manpower, machine-time, and materials.

Reduction of waste transfers man-hours and machine-hours from the manufacture of defectives into the manufacture of additional good product. In effect, the capacity of a production line is increased. The benefits of better quality through improvement of the process are thus not just better quality, and the improvement in the long-range market-position that goes along with it, but greater productivity and much better profit as well. Improved morale of the work force is another gain: they now see that the management is making some effort themselves, and not blaming all faults on the production-workers.

Source: W. Edwards Deming, "Improvement of Quality and Productivity Through Action by Management," *National Productivity Review,* 1(1): 12–13, Winter 1981–82.

problems, when detected, were dealt with on a fire-fighting basis. Too often the focus was on the worker and not on the process itself. The extract from an article by W. Edwards Deming, a noted consultant in the area of quality management, in Box 18.1 provides some insights into the responsibilities of management. In this chapter, we emphasize the managerial issues associated with providing products and services of good quality.

WHAT IS QUALITY?

Defining *quality* is not a simple matter because the definition depends on the perspective from which quality is viewed. Basically, there are two perspectives: internal to the organization (producer) and external to the organization (consumer).

Internal Perspective

Internal to the organization, quality typically means *conformance to specifications.* In precision manufacturing, it would seem that every part produced would be identical, but such is not the case. For example, measurements will show that no two cylindrically shaped wrist pins, which tie the connecting rod to the piston of an automobile engine, are identical, even though both were made by the same operator on the same machine. One wrist pin may be slightly larger in diameter, or the two may differ in roundness. For this reason, tolerances are specified for critical dimensions, and the quality of a part is measured relative to its conformance to these specifications. Parts not meeting the specifications are either reworked or scrapped. The assumption is that, if all parts of a product conform to specifications, the entire product will be of good quality.

External Perspective

Viewing quality as merely conformance to specifications may be a useful guide for operations, but it is a very narrow view. It neglects the customer's perception of quality. Customers typically define quality as *value* or *fitness for use,* which involves expectations the customer has for the product. However, in assessing value or fitness for use, the customer may look at several different aspects of product quality, as shown in Table 18.1.

Hardware. In the provision of services, hardware quality relates to the interior and exterior aesthetics of the location where a service is provided and the

Table 18.1

Examples of Consumer Perceptions of Quality

Quality Aspect	Service	Manufacturing
Hardware	Style and appearance of tableware at a restaurant Age of equipment in a dentist's office	Visible appearance of the product Ease of installation and use of the product
Product or service support	Number of errors in bank statements Responsiveness to expressed or implied warrantees	Accuracy of billing procedures and ease of correcting errors Truthfulness in advertising
Promptness	Time spent in queue at a fast-food shop Response time for emergency services	Availability of product when demanded Length of lead time to the customer due date
Psychological impressions	Courtesy of the bellman at a hotel Sympathy of the clerk at the customer complaints desk of a retail store	Knowledge of the salesperson regarding product performance Reputation of the brand name

condition of the equipment that is used to provide the service. In manufacturing, hardware quality refers to product characteristics such as appearance, style, durability, reliability, craftsmanship, longevity, and maintainability. Thus both workmanship and product design are judged by the consumer.

Support. Often the product or service support provided by the company is just as important as the quality of the product or service itself. Customers can get very upset with a company if financial statements are incorrect, responses to warranty claims are delayed, or advertising is misleading. Often, good product support can partially offset deficiencies in hardware quality. For example, a customer who just had a brake job would be understandably upset if the brakes began squealing again only one week later. A reputable brake shop will give a warranty to redo the work at no additional charge. If it also has a policy of following up with a call to each customer to find out whether he or she is satisfied, the company makes very clear its intent to satisfy the customer.

Promptness. Another aspect of quality from the perspective of the customer is the promptness of response to a demand. The quality of police services is often measured in terms of response time to the scene of a crime or accident. A customer in a McDonald's restaurant may measure the quality of service by the length of time it takes to get to the front of the line. In manufacturing and distribution, the positioning of inventories and the size of safety stock affect the length of time required to satisfy customer demand for a product. The closer that inventories are positioned to the customer, the quicker will be the response time to the customer. Larger safety stock at the end-item level will provide better customer service.

Psychological Impressions. Not to be overlooked is the psychological aspect of quality. In the provision of services, where the customer is in close contact with the provider, the appearance and actions of the provider are very important. Nicely dressed, courteous, hospitable, and sympathetic employees can affect the customer's perception of the quality of the service. For example, rumpled, discourteous, or grumpy bellhops can undermine a hotel's best efforts to provide high-quality service; the guests who encounter them may form lasting impressions of the hotel from these encounters.

In manufacturing, product quality is often judged on the basis of contact with salespersons or advertisements. The knowledge and personality of salespersons, as well as the product image presented in advertisements, create an impression of product quality in customers.

From this discussion of the external perspective of quality, it should be apparent that defining quality is no easy task. To make things worse, consumers change their perceptions of quality. Taking automobiles as an example, consumer preferences shifted from styling in 1970 to fuel economy in 1975 to quality of design and performance in 1980. Changes in consumer lifestyles and values in response to the economic conditions during that time drastically changed the meaning of automobile quality. Today, a buyer is more inclined to invest in a long-lasting product, even if it means paying more for it at the outset. By not identifying these trends and responding to them quickly, companies lose opportunities to maintain or increase their market shares relative to foreign competition.

Summary

In this section we have discussed the definition of quality for manufacturing and service organizations. It should be apparent that the internal definition of quality—conformance to specifications—is inadequate. In order to improve the quality of products or services, managers must supplement the internal perspective with two additional considerations: (1) the accuracy of their perceptions of customer expectations; and (2) the degree to which the process and product or service designers have bridged the gap between consumer expectations and the operations system.

IMPORTANCE OF QUALITY MANAGEMENT

Quality is an issue that pervades an entire organization. Poor quality affects the performance of an organization and therefore should be of concern to management. It erodes the ability of the firm to compete in the marketplace and increases the costs of producing a product or service and warranty work later.

Market Implications

In the past, price was considered to be the key factor in gaining market share, but this is no longer true. Quality has also become a strategic weapon for gaining an increased market share. Consumers are much more quality-minded and in many cases would prefer to spend more for a product if it can provide longer service. A recent survey of 2000 business units conducted by the Strategic Planning Institute of Cambridge, Massachussetts, indicated that the degree of product quality affects a firm's chances of increasing its market share. If product quality is stable, a high-quality product has a much better chance of gaining a larger share of the market than does a low-quality product. If quality is perceived to be improving, the chances of increasing market share are better, regardless of the level of product quality.

Good quality can also pay off in a higher profit margin. High-quality products can be priced higher than comparable lower quality products and yield a greater return for the sales dollar. In addition, as you will see later in this chapter, good quality can reduce costs, which in turn increases the profit margin. Management then has more flexibility to compete on price as well as on quality.

Cost Implications

The costs of poor quality go beyond the obvious costs of scrap or rework. In Box 18.2, we show an example of the costs of poor quality in the credit-card

Box 18.2

COSTS OF POOR QUALITY IN A BANK

The following data describe the credit-card operation of a bank.

- 100,000 statements per month are prepared.
- Each inquiry costs the bank $5 to process.
- The average monthly profit per credit card is $10.
- There is a 10% error rate, of which

 5% are financial errors, causing the customers to inquire about their statement; and
 5% are nonfinancial errors, but only one-half of these customers will call to resolve the confusion.

Direct Costs
The error rate will cause 5000 customers to call because of financial errors and 2500 customers to call because of confusion. The monthly direct costs are

$$\text{Direct costs} = (5000 + 2500)(\$5) = \$37{,}500.$$

Indirect Costs
Of the 100,000 customers, 92,500 were completely satisfied and will continue to use the credit card. Of the 2500 who were confused by their statements, historical experience indicates that only 80 percent will continue to use the card. Of the 5000 customers who had financial errors in their statements, only one-half will use the card again. Since the monthly profit per card is $10, the monthly indirect costs are

$$\begin{aligned}\text{Indirect costs} &= [2500(0.20) + 5000(0.50)](\$10)\\ &= \$30{,}000.\end{aligned}$$

Loss of Future Customers
Consumer surveys have indicated that a satisfied customer will talk positively about the credit card service to four other people, whereas a dissatisfied customer will talk negatively about the service to ten other people. Since there are 7500 dissatisfied customers, the bank has lost the potential of 75,000 customers—each month.

operation of a bank. Not only are there the direct costs of responding to the telephone inquiries (rework costs), but there are also the costs of immediate and future lost profits. Ignoring the lost future profits for a moment, the bank earned only 100,000($10) − ($37,500 + $30,000) = $932,500, instead of the $1 million it could have earned with no defective statements. In the extreme case of zero defects, the bank's profits would increase by $67,500/$932,500 = 7.2 percent. The positive impact on future profits could be even greater, if negative publicity from dissatisfied customers were reduced or eliminated.

Historically, managers' perceptions of losses caused by poor quality were lower than actual losses, and they were content to accept a relatively large percentage of defectives. For many years, the work of consultants such as Joseph Juran and W. Edwards Deming has demonstrated the costs of poor quality to managers in Japan and the United States, but only recently have managers in the United States begun to take action. The examples in Box 18.3 are notable. The result is a conscious effort to reduce the level of defective products and services.

Four major categories of cost are associated with quality management and are defined in Table 18.2. **Prevention costs** increase as the level of quality (as measured by product or service design or average delivery time) or the reliability of quality (as measured by conformance to specifications or on-time

Box 18.3

REACTIONS TO POOR QUALITY

Borg-Warner

A quality program at the Automotive Components Group has initially focused on management, as opposed to blue-collar workers, because it is believed that quality improvement must begin at the top of the organization. The company has been spending 20 percent of sales to correct quality problems. Reducing that 20 percent represents an excellent opportunity to increase profitability.

Hewlett-Packard

At one division it has been estimated that a "zero-defects" program could result in a 33 percent reduction in workers, a 25 percent reduction in required floor space, and a 66 percent decrease in inventories.

Westinghouse

A quality center has been built for $7.5 million and staffed with 250 engineers and technicians. In addition, the push to reduce inventories will force vendors and divisions to improve quality. Defective levels as low as one defective part per 100 will no longer be acceptable.

Source: "Quality: The U.S. Drives to Catch Up," *Business Week*, November 1, 1982, pp. 66–67.

Table 18.2

Costs Associated with Quality Management

- Prevention costs are the costs associated with preventing defects before they happen. Included in this category are the costs of process design, product design, employee training, and vendor programs.
- Appraisal costs are the costs incurred in assessing the level of quality attained by the operating system. The costs of quality audits and statistical quality control programs are included in this category.
- Internal failure costs result from yield losses and the need to rework products or services because of defects incurred during production.
- External failure costs include costs of warranty repairs, loss of market share, and lawsuits arising from injury or property damage from use of the product or services.

delivery performance) increases. That is, quality improvement requires the allocation of resources and effort.

Appraisal costs decrease as quality level or quality reliability increases. Quality appraisal helps management to determine where quality problems exist. As quality is improved through preventive measures, fewer resources are needed for quality inspections and the subsequent search for the causes of problems when they are detected. The Japanese have the philosophy that no worker should pass a defective unit downstream to the next work station. This is known as *quality at the source* and is a good way to reduce the appraisal costs of quality management.

Internal failure costs decrease as the level or reliability of quality increases. Various preventive measures can be used to reduce the number of rejects and thereby reduce scrap, rework, and a number of other costs, including overtime, machine failure, and inventory costs. We cover this issue in more detail later in this chapter.

Finally, **external failure costs** also decrease as the level or reliability of quality increases. Not only do warranty repair costs and losses in market share decrease, but also legal liability for injury or damage resulting from the use of the product or service will decrease.

The implication seems to be that improving quality by increasing expenditures for preventive measures is a good investment for any organization. However, it depends on whether we are talking about quality level or quality reliability. If we are trying to increase the quality *level* by better product and process design, for example, we are actually addressing business objectives and trade-offs among the *competitive priorities* of price (cost), quality, and flexibility in the hope of doing better in the marketplace. In this situation, we cannot completely offset the increased prevention costs by reductions in the other quality costs. As a result, we may have to raise the price of the product or service, moving closer to a competitive priority of quality rather than price. That is why a Mercedes Benz costs more than a Ford, and a night at a Hilton Hotel costs more than a night at a Howard Johnson's motel.

Alternatively, if we are trying to increase quality *reliability* by better conformance to specifications, the added prevention costs may be more than offset by the reduced appraisal, internal failure, and external failure costs. For the same set of product or service specifications, less waste is created, and savings can be enormous. That is why the firms described in Box 18.3 are spending large sums of money to improve quality. The overwhelming evidence is that improving quality reliability makes the trade-off between prevention costs and other quality costs worthwhile.

In the remainder of this chapter, we discuss prevention, internal failure costs, and external failure costs in more detail. We then discuss quality appraisal in Chapter 19.

PREVENTING QUALITY PROBLEMS

Any effort to improve quality requires the support of top management. The reason is that improving quality raises issues for the entire organization, involves employee considerations, has product and process design implications, and affects purchasing considerations.

Organizational Issues

One of the ways to improve quality is to demolish the organizational barriers between departmental empires and force managers in different functional areas to work together to design and produce more reliable products or services. This is easier said than done; however, several alternatives intended to move organizations in this direction are being tried.

Quality Assurance Groups. Sometimes, organizational barriers between departments encourage the development and testing of products or services in a vacuum without interaction with other departments. This may lead to premature introduction of products or services into the market. One way to increase the likelihood of a rational approach to the design and testing of new products is to have a quality assurance group.

Quality *assurance* is broader than quality *control.* **Quality assurance** is concerned with the prevention of quality problems, as well as the detection of the problems themselves. A quality assurance group confirms through rigorous testing that necessary corrective actions have been taken. In this way, management can be assured that problems have been corrected prior to marketing the product or service. The group should be staffed by people who have the respect of the various departmental managers. In a manufacturing company, the group determines the cause of actual problems with the product encountered by the consumer, identifies potential problems, and initiates corrective actions. To help the group discover design or workmanship problems, it may even be given a budget allotment to buy back products that have been in service a long time or products that have prematurely failed. In service organizations as well as manufacturing companies, the quality assurance group assists management in establishing or updating quality standards, developing information feedback systems, developing quality cost data, and performing quality improvement studies.

Setting Goals for Quality Performance. Successfully improving quality and reducing quality problems in the future require an appropriate set of goals. Typically, goals become more specific at lower levels in the organization; what starts out as a general statement by top management about the need for quality improvement may end up as a specific, quantifiable goal at the lowest level in the organization. Fig. 18.1 shows such a set of goals for an electric-hoist manufacturer.

The quality characteristics desired by the customer must be stated clearly so that the respective goals for various segments of the production system can be specified. For example, if customers are looking for an electric hoist that has high reliability, a high-priced model with low maintenance costs will

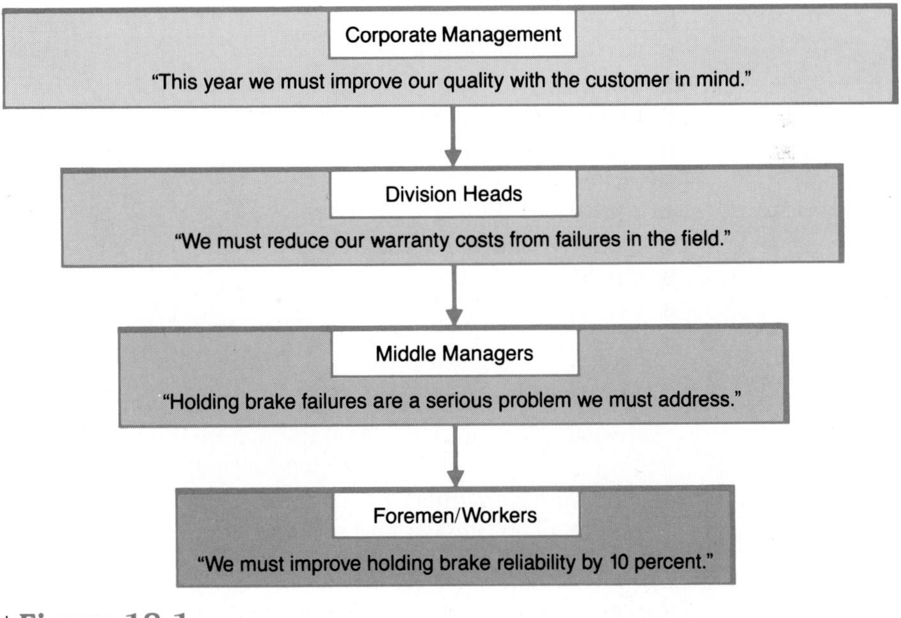

Figure 18.1

A Hierarchy of Goals for a Manufacturer of Electric Hoists.

probably compete favorably against another firm's product that is priced lower but requires a high level of maintenance. Incorrectly specifying quality goals can result in lost market opportunities.

Marketing Interface. The situation of the electric-hoist manufacturer has implications for marketing. Marketing managers must contribute information about customers' perceptions of quality, if reasonable quality goals are to be developed. In addition to providing this type of information, marketing can help improve the quality of new products by not pressuring for premature release of the product. Suppose, for example, that a new model of the electric hoist is being tested before release. The testing is still in progress, so potential design and quality problems still exist. However, the published date of availability for the product is rapidly approaching, and there is not enough time to thoroughly test the new product. Pressure from marketing to release the product on time could result in marketing a product that will experience a high rate of failure in actual use.

Employee Considerations

The field of quality management draws on a wide variety of skills. The following are examples of job titles used by various manufacturing and service organizations.

- Quality Engineer
- Reliability Engineer
- Technician
- Inspector
- Product Specialist
- Tester
- Auditor
- Quality Assurance Manager
- Quality Control Manager
- Lab Technician
- Chemist

However, employees such as these are not the only ones who must be concerned about quality. Quality must be the concern of all employees, from the top manager to the hourly worker on the assembly line. The challenge of quality management is to instill an awareness of the importance of good quality in all employees and provide an environment in which employees are motivated to improve product quality.

Career Progression. A well-designed career progression program can help instill a high degree of company loyalty and pride in employees, which often translates into improved quality. These programs prepare employees for promotion to higher paying jobs by providing courses to improve employee communication and technical skills and to inform the employee about broader company policies and procedures. Such a program has been developed for the employees of Marriott Corporation. Initially designed for underprivileged minority-group employees, the program is now open to any employee who has a positive attitude and the aptitude. In addition to courses in hotel operations, the participants take courses designed to improve their basic reading, writing, and mathematical skills. The program has enabled many employees to earn promotions not otherwise achievable. Even if an employee has no desire to enroll, the knowledge that the program exists strengthens positive attitudes toward the company. In the hotel industry, where there is a high degree of direct contact with the customer, a positive attitude can greatly improve the quality of the service.

Individual Development. On-the-job training programs related directly to specific jobs can also help to improve quality. Programs aimed at new work methods for experienced workers or short courses for new employees in current practices can help to improve productivity and reduce the number of product defects. Some companies also train workers on related jobs, so that they can better understand the work of other employees, recognize the problems caused for others if their own work contains defects, and propose remedial action when defects occur. Top management can also benefit from training programs. Texas Instruments initiated a quality improvement program in which 300 top executives attended an outside training program on quality management and 20,000 other employees later attended a 16-hour, in-house course.

Monetary Incentives. Some of the incentive for improving quality can come from merit pay and bonuses. Some companies tie monetary incentives directly to quality improvement, while others do not. The Marriott Corporation, for example, has a profit-sharing plan whereby employees can elect to contribute at least 5 percent of their earnings, and the company makes a contribution from profits; in the past, company contributions have more than equaled the amount of employee contributions. Presumably, as the quality of service increases, profits increase and employees are rewarded. Texas Instruments take a more direct approach. Top managers are ranked by the quality of the products they produce. Pay increases and bonuses are based on this ranking.

Quality Circles. Another way to promote employee participation and improve quality is to develop quality circles. A **quality circle** is a small group composed of supervisors and employees who meet to identify, analyze, and solve production and quality problems. The philosophy behind quality circles is that most employees will take more pride and interest in their work if they are allowed to make meaningful contributions to it. Typically, participation in a quality circle is voluntary, and sometimes the group meets after normal working hours. The groups are kept small, perhaps 6–10 employees, to afford the greatest amount of interaction between members. Consequently, a company may have a large number of quality circles. For example, one IBM facility has 800 quality circles.

One quality circle can generate hundreds of ideas for improvement in a year. Many may be minor, and some may prove to be infeasible. However, management must commit itself to giving serious attention to these ideas, if the concept of quality circles is to work. Benefits in the form of improved quality, productivity, and cost savings can be substantial.

Product and Process Design Implications

Preventing quality problems involves more than solving people problems. Proper design of the product and the process is also very important.

Product Design. In order to reduce quality problems product designs should be stable. Typically, the more design changes there are, the greater the defect rates are. If design changes result from customer considerations, there is no easy answer to this problem. If the company tries to minimize the number of changes, it may lose competitiveness in the marketplace. If the changes are in response to the introduction of new products, an approach often used by Japanese manufacturers is to emphasize reliability engineering and careful shakedowns of new designs. Often, a product design is changed to better conform to process capability. The trade-off here is better quality and competitiveness for the added time and cost required to check the product thoroughly before it is introduced.

Process Design. Prevention of quality problems can also lead to the purchase of new machinery. Suppose that the design specification for the distance between two holes in a metal plate is 3.000 inches ± 0.0004. Thus the standard is 3 inches, but there also is an acceptable range, or tolerance, of deviation from the standard. The present machinery is capable of producing the metal plate with holes 3.000 inches ± 0.0005 apart, resulting in some defective parts that fall outside the design specification. Now suppose that we want to reduce the percentage of defective parts produced by the process. One way to accomplish this objective would be to purchase new machinery that has the capability to produce metal plates with holes 3.000 inches ± 0.0003 apart. The percentage of defective parts would be reduced and hence the degree of conformance to the design specifications increased. However, process costs would be greater. Box 18.4 shows an application of automation to improve conformance to specifications at International Harvester.

The design of the production process also has quality management implications. In Chapter 2, we described a continuum of positioning strategies, ranging from a process focus to a product focus. Firms with a process focus are more likely to compete on the basis of high-performance design quality

Box 18.4

THE USE OF ROBOTS TO ENSURE QUALITY

A production cell at International Harvester's Farmall Division uses a robot to improve the consistency in producing castings. The robot takes rough castings and produces finished, inspected parts. After the rough casting has been processed on a turning center, the robot takes it to an automatic gauging station. If the part is within tolerance the robot moves it to the second turning center. The finished casting is then removed and the process repeats itself.

Source: "Inspection: A New Role for Robots," *Quality Progress,* vol. 15, no. 8 (August 1982), pp. 50–53.

and rely largely on employee involvement in ensuring quality. At the other extreme, firms with a product focus are more likely to compete on the basis of consistent quality, utilize quality specialists, and have more formal controls. Automated inspection becomes more likely. In some cases, such as with breweries, much of the quality is designed into the process itself, and periodic sampling is used to check quality levels. Consequently, the approach taken to quality management depends on the organization's positioning strategy.

Linking Product Design to Process Design. Over and above the need to ensure conformance to product design specifications, management should be concerned with linking each aspect of quality prized by the customer to the raw materials, parts, assemblies, and process steps that collectively contribute to building a particular attribute into the product. Blueprints show parts and assemblies and how they are to be put together. However, they do not help to pinpoint a problem in product design that needs to be corrected in order to satisfy a customer's particular quality concern. One way to accomplish this is to develop a **fishbone diagram,** which relates a product defect to the potential contributing factors, so that customer complaints can be readily traced to the operations involved. If a certain production operation cannot contribute to a particular defect, the operation is not shown on the fishbone diagram for that defect.

For example, consider Fig. 18.2, which shows a fishbone diagram for one quality problem related to the manufacture of castings: fractured surface of the cast metal (identified as the main arrow of the diagram). In this example, four factors are considered critical: casting temperature, mold coating, composition of molten metal, and mold temperature. These factors are identified as the main connecting arrows of the fishbone. Subfactors are identified as the secondary arrows. The subfactors should be checked if a critical factor is

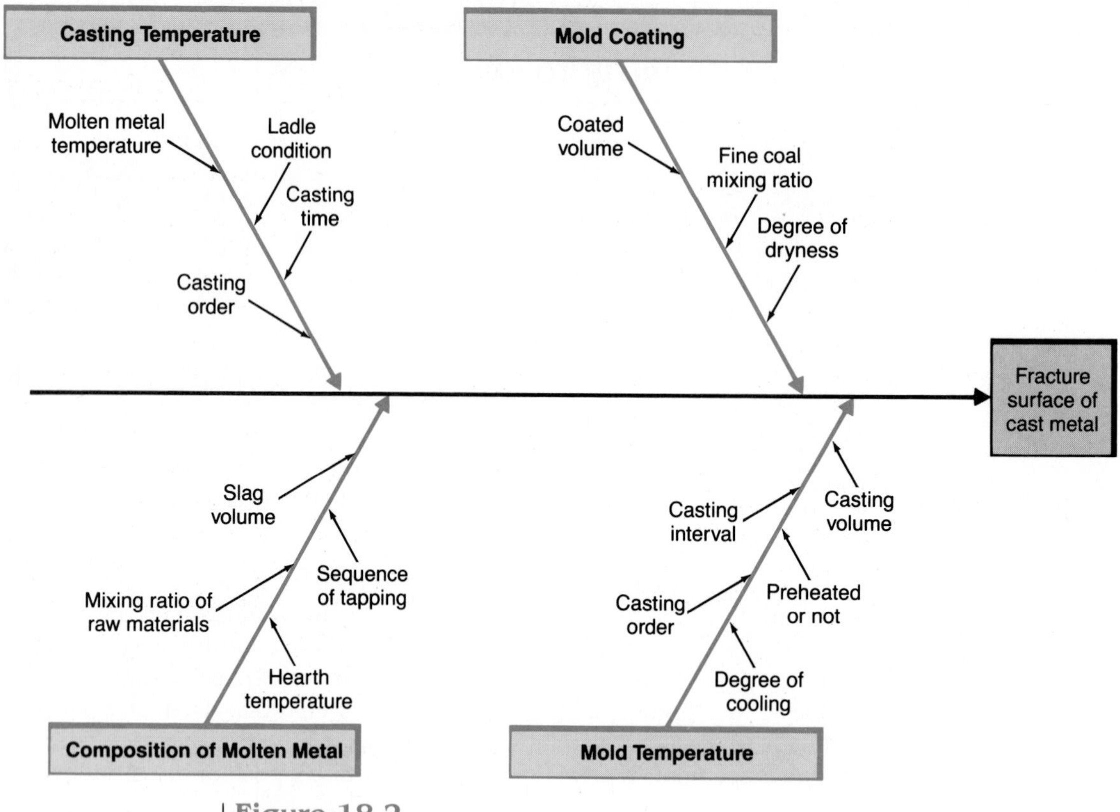

Figure 18.2

A Fishbone Diagram.

Source: Reprinted with permission of The Free Press, a division of Macmillan, Inc., from *Japanese Manufacturing Techniques: Nine Hidden Lessons in Simplicity* by Richard J. Schonberger, p. 72. Copyright © 1982 by Richard J. Schonberger.

suspected of causing the quality problem. For example, if mold coating is suspected, we would check the subfactors of coated volume, fine-coal mixing ratio, and degree of dryness to see whether any of these operations is causing the problem. The benefits of fishbone diagrams go beyond the identification of potential causes of a problem. The process of constructing a fishbone diagram itself calls to managerial and worker attention the critical factors affecting product quality.

Purchasing Considerations

Since the production of most goods and services requires the input of some raw materials or purchased items, we should not overlook the quality of these inputs. Large companies have hundreds and even thousands of suppliers, some of which supply the same parts, and quality assurance for the items they supply is an enormous task. The example in Box 18.5 demonstrates the cost of poor supplier quality.

Regardless of the number of suppliers involved, the buyer's approach and style and specification management are two key methods for controlling supplier quality. From the standpoint of the buyer for a company, positive reports of money saved, orders placed, and on-time delivery performance of suppliers will override negative reports on quality performance unless top management places a high priority on quality. In a survey of the air-conditioning industry, companies with the highest quality reported that they placed quality above price when evaluating supplier contracts (see Garvin, 1983). Operating under such a priority, a good buyer will identify supplier capabilities and concentrate on those suppliers and products that offer an opportunity for quality improvement at a reasonable cost. From a technical standpoint, this is no easy task; however, after these suppliers have been identified, the buyer's approach and style become important parts of quality improvement. The buyer should work with the supplier to obtain essentially defect-free parts by examining and evaluating trade-offs, handling problems of off-specification materials firmly but diplomatically, and participating in corrective-action efforts. Patience, understanding, and trust are qualities needed in a buyer.

Specification management is also important. The specifications for purchased parts and materials must be clear and *realistic*. Sometimes, specifications are set arbitrarily to a tight limit to protect the designer in case something goes wrong. In other cases, the specifications make the product uneconomical to produce or service later. Specifications have implications for the buyer, who is trying to identify quality standards for suppliers and keep

Box 18.5

THE IMPORTANCE OF GOOD VENDOR QUALITY

Poor quality of purchased parts can have a devastating effect on a company with a product focus. On September 17, 1984 the Ford Motor Company halted production at its Kansas City, Missouri, and Oakville, Ontario, plants because of a faulty part purchased from an outside supplier. Upon testing, some gears lost a few teeth, apparently caused by the defective part. Approximately 5500 hourly workers were temporarily laid off. In addition, Ford loses about 10,000 cars for each week that production is stopped.

Source: "Ford Halts Production of 2 Compact Models, Cites an Engine Part," *Wall Street Journal*, September 25, 1984.

Box 18.6

EXAMPLES OF PROGRAMS TO IMPROVE THE QUALITY OF PURCHASED ITEMS

Whirlpool Corporation
The top priority of a newly initiated total quality assurance organization is to help suppliers deliver better parts. Nearly 40 percent of all failures can be traced to purchased parts.

Xerox Corporation
Suppliers are getting involved in the design phase of new products. In addition, suppliers are awarded contracts for the lifetime of the product, if they can prove they can deliver defect-free parts. In the process, the number of suppliers has dwindled from 3000 to 500.

General Motors Corporation
The 3500 suppliers that deliver parts and components to GM assembly plants have been told that eventually they will have to demonstrate their ability to control quality statistically. This is expected to reduce the number of suppliers.

Source: "Quality: The U.S. Drives to Catch Up," *Business Week,* November 1, 1982, pp. 66–80.

costs down. As a check on specifications, buyers in some companies initiate a *process capability study* for key products. This study amounts to a trial run of a small product sample to ensure that all components, including the raw materials and purchased parts, work together to form a product having the desired quality level. Analysis of study results may lead to the identification of unrealistic specifications and, consequently, to some changes in them.

Top management also has some responsibilities regarding supplier quality. If it wants the purchasing department to identify several low-cost, qualified suppliers, top management must allow purchasing enough time to obtain and analyze the information. An unrealistic deadline can cause mistakes in selecting suppliers because of incomplete information about supplier qualifications. In addition, top management can help tear down organizational barriers that hamper communication between purchasing and other departments, such as engineering and quality control. Some of the information needed to assess a supplier's qualifications requires sampling of products and detailed analysis of the supplier's manufacturing process, a task usually performed by quality control personnel and engineers in cooperation with the supplier's technical staff. This effort requires cooperation between purchasing and the other departments. The examples in Box 18.6 describe what three companies are doing to improve the quality of supplier inputs.

INTERNAL FAILURE COSTS

Internal failure costs result from defects generated during the production of a good or service and fall into two major cost categories. *Yield losses* are incurred if a defective item has to be scrapped. Sometimes, the material can be reused, but the item must be completely remanufactured. The other cost category is *rework costs.* In manufacturing, the item is rerouted to some previous operation(s) for correction of the defect. In the case of a service, the customer calls or returns in person to have the defect corrected.

Yield Losses

Your first thought when someone mentions yield losses may be about the cost of the materials lost. While this is an important part of yield losses, you should also learn to recognize a number of hidden costs. For example, consider the simple four-operation process depicted in Fig. 18.3. Each operation generates a certain percentage of defects, as shown in Table 18.3. The operating requirement is to produce 100 defect-free units per day. Consider two possible ways to detect and correct defective units: (1) let the inspector find the defects at the end of the production line; or (2) do not pass a defective unit to the next operation.

Let Inspectors Find the Defects. Too many companies feel that inspectors should earn their pay by catching all the defects generated by the process. Let's look at the costs involved in this approach. Table 18.3 shows us that we need 114 units at the start of the line to get 100 defect-free units at the end. Consequently, there are 14 units of scrap, which amount to a 14 percent increase in raw-material cost to cover the yield losses. In addition, work-in-process costs are increased because more material must flow between the operations, and, at each operation, value is added to the semifinished product regardless of whether it will be scrapped later.

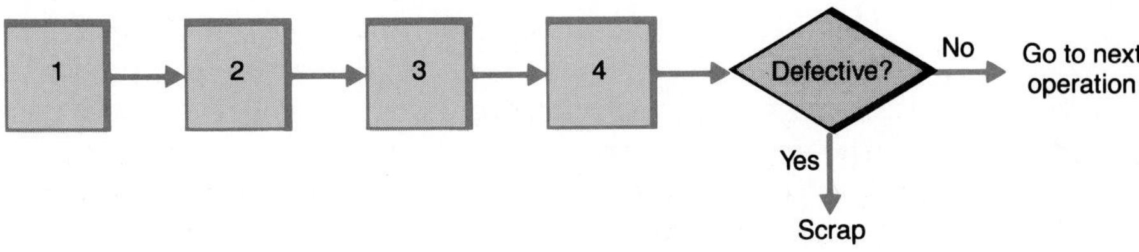

Figure 18.3

A Four-Operation Flow Shop.

Table 18.3

The Effects of Yield Loss on a Four-Machine Flow Shop

Operation	Percentage of Units Defective	Units Processed	Number of Defective Units Added by Operation*	Number of Good Units Passed to Next Operation
1	1	114	1	113
2	4	114	5	108
3	2	114	2	106
4	6	114	6	100
Total number of defective units produced			14	

* Rounded to the nearest number of whole units. The number of defective units is equal to the number of good units passed to the operation by the previous operation multiplied by the percentage of defectives generated at the operation. For operation 2, for example, 113(0.04) = 5 defective units.

Poor yields also result in other costs. More labor and machine hours are required to produce the same quantity of product as a defect-free process. For example, each operation must process 114 units each day. If no defectives were generated, each operation would only have to process 100 units per day. Thus we must spend 14 percent more for labor and machine costs because of the yield losses. The increase in machine-hours could also cause failures and increase machine downtime. In addition, since we need to process more material to get the required daily quantities of the product, the product cycle time will increase. The implications for customer service are an increase in the percentage of orders past due and, ultimately, lost future sales. Finally, this approach is based on the assumption that inspectors will catch all the defects generated by the process. If not, downstream operations incur additional costs such as those already discussed. Letting inspectors find all the defects can be very costly.

Quality at the Source. Rather than trying to "inspect quality into the product," as in the previous example, the Japanese approach is to ensure "quality at the source." In other words, an employee does not pass defective units to the next operation.

To demonstrate some of the advantages of this approach, let's return to Table 18.3. Suppose that each operator passed only good units to the next operation. For example, operation 1 passes only 113 units to operation 2, 108 units to operation 3, and so on. The graph in Fig. 18.4 shows a comparison of the labor and machine hours required for the same amount of defect-free output using the two approaches to quality assurance. We still need capacity for 114 units per day at operation 1, but now we only need capacity for 113 units at operation 2, 108 at operation 3, and 106 at operation 4. Consequently, we do not need as many machine and labor hours (regular and overtime) to produce the 100 units needed. Also, assuming no delays for machine or worker availability, the cycle time is significantly reduced because the process times per batch at operations 2, 3, and 4 are less. Further, there is less wear and tear on the equipment, which reduces maintenance and downtime costs. Even though the costs of the scrapped materials are the same, there is a savings in the work-in-process inventory investment; no value is added to materials made defective at an early operation only to be scrapped at the end of the production line. In total, the savings can be significant.

Summary. Obviously, the ideal solution is to produce no defective units because this quality level can significantly reduce operating costs. Recognizing that this condition may not be practical or economical, we contend that ensuring quality at the source can result in significant savings, regardless of

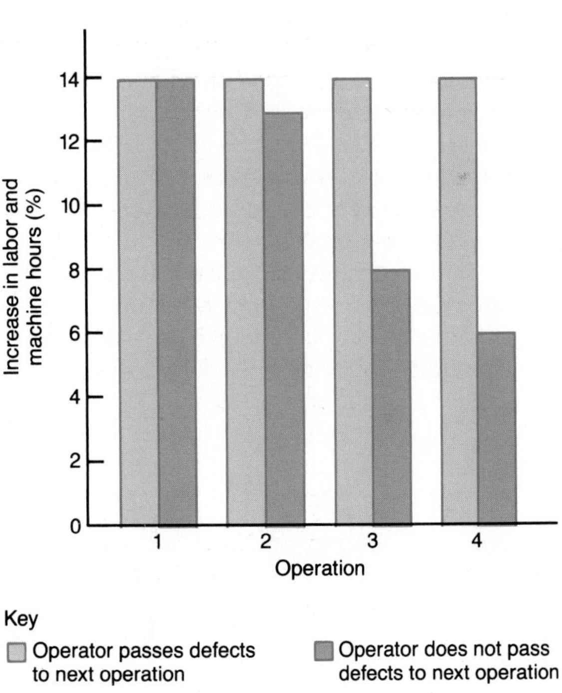

Figure 18.4

Implications of Yield Losses in a Four-Machine Flow Shop.

the percentage of defective units generated at each operation. This approach can also reduce the need for inspectors and thereby reduce appraisal costs. Inspecting quality into the product is an expensive proposition and should not be considered.

Rework Costs

Sometimes, when a defective part or production lot is discovered, it can be sent back to a previous work center to be corrected. Let's consider our simple four-operation example again, except that this time there is no scrap. Instead, let's suppose that the product is produced in lots of 10 and that an entire lot can be defective. We still require 100 defect-free units at the end of the day. Units are inspected after operation 3, and there is a 10 percent chance that operation 3 will produce a defective lot; if it does, the lot must be sent back for rework. This situation is shown in Fig. 18.5.

Table 18.4 shows how this situation affects the operation of the system. Since we have to process 10 lots in a day, we would expect to encounter one lot that needs rework. This means that operation 3, and inspection would be expected to process at least 110 units per day. However, the lot that has to be processed again has a 10 percent chance of being defective again. If the chances of rework are independent of whether the lot has already been reworked, there is a 1 percent chance [or $0.10(0.10) = 0.01$] that the lot will have to be reworked twice. Consequently, the average number of units processed per lot is $10[1.0 + 0.1 + (0.1)^2 + (0.1)^3 + \cdots]$, or approximately 11.1 units, including the first time every lot must be processed. Thus the expected number of units per day worked by operation 3 and inspection is 111 units over an extended period of time.

Let's consider the costs associated with rework. Obviously, we would need more labor- and machine-hours at operation 3 and inspection, or, in this example, an 11 percent increase over the case of no rework. In addition, most situations involving rework involve an increase in the number of setups, even if only a portion of a lot must be reworked. Furthermore, work-in-process

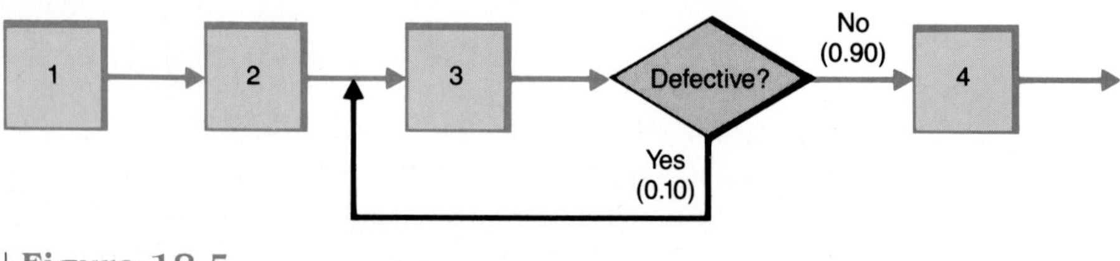

Figure 18.5

An Example of Inspection and Rework in a Four-Operation Flow Shop.

Table 18.4

The Effects of Rework on a Four-Operation Flow Shop

Operation	Probability of Rework per Lot	Operation to Route to	Average Number of Units Processed per Lot*	Average Number of Units Processed per Day†
1	0	—	10	100
2	0	—	10	100
3	0	—	11.1	111
Inspection	0.10	3	11.1	111
4	0	—	10	100

* The average number of units processed per lot equals $10[1.0 + 0.1 + (0.1)^2 + (0.1)^3 + \cdots]$, or approximately 11.1.

† Since 10 lots per day are required, the average number of units processed per day equals 10 times the average number of units processed per lot.

inventory levels increase because the material that must be reworked stays in a semifinished state longer. The value of that inventory also increases because of the added labor and machine costs needed to produce it correctly. Finally, the manufacturing cycle time for the average production lot increases because of the possibility that it may have to be rerouted to a previous work center for rework. Consequently, promised due dates may not be met, or the lead time for customer delivery may have to be increased to such an extent that the company can no longer compete in the marketplace.

Rework problems are not restricted to manufacturing processes. For example, the service department of an automobile dealer performs many maintenance and repair services for car owners. The customers bring their coughing, choking, wheezing, rattling, smoking, or abnormally smelling cars to the service department for repair. If the mechanic does not correct the problem, or creates a new one, the customer must bring the car back to get the job done right. The costs of shoddy service include the additional labor and diagnostic-machine time and the ill will of the car owner. Sometimes, the service system comes to the customer and rework costs involve the added labor and travel time. Such is the case of the TV repairman who must return to a customer's home to correct a problem that should have been corrected on the first trip.

The cost implications of using a quality-at-the-source approach as opposed to an inspect-quality-into-the-product approach are the same in the case of rework as they are in the case of yield losses. If operator 3 processes units correctly the first time in our example, operating costs for the whole system can be significantly reduced.

EXTERNAL FAILURE COSTS

External failure costs arise from product or service failures at the customer level. We differentiate them from internal failure costs because these costs are incurred to correct defective products or services that somehow escaped internal checks and controls. When a *customer,* as opposed to a firm's worker or quality inspector, finds a defect, this situation has a number of implications for the company that produced the defective product or service. The most obvious implication is the loss of market share or future profits because bad news travels fast. Dissatisfied customers tell their friends, who in turn tell others, and so on. The potential impact on future profits is difficult to assess, but, obviously, poor quality erodes market share and profits. The loss of market share or future profits is not the only external failure cost. There are also costs of warranty service and litigation.

Warranty Costs

A warranty is a written guarantee of the integrity of a product or service and of the producer's responsibility to replace or repair defective parts or to reperform the service to the customer's satisfaction. Usually, a warranty is given for some specified time period. For example, television repairs are usually guaranteed for 90 days and new automobiles for one year or 12,000 miles, whichever comes first.

Encountering defects and correcting them after the product is in the customer's hands is costly. The example in Box 18.7 vividly demonstrates this point. As Fig. 18.6 shows, the place to catch the defect is where it occurs: in

Box 18.7

WARRANTY COSTS IN THE AIRCRAFT INDUSTRY

The Navy temporarily stopped buying F-18 jet fighters from McDonnell-Douglass Corporation because of tail defects. Flight restrictions were issued for the plane because mountings for the plane's two vertical tails were cracking under extreme stress. In no uncertain terms the Navy told McDonnell that it expected the company to pay for all the repairs. The Navy and the Marine Corps have 156 F-18's and the Canadian government has 38. The cost to repair the defective tail mountings could be as much as $25 million.

Source: "McDonnell to Fix F-18 Flaws at Cost Up to $25 Million," *Wall Street Journal,* August 3, 1984.

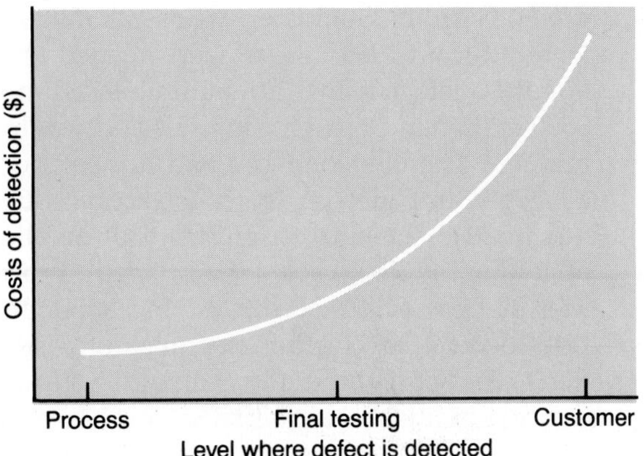

Figure 18.6

The Costs of Detection as a Function of the Level at Which a Defect Is Detected.

the production process. The closer a product is to its finished state, the costlier it is to find defects and correct them. When the product has finally been shipped to the customer, the cost to fix a defective part skyrockets. It is very expensive to send a customer engineer from IBM to a remote computer installation to find out what is wrong and fix it. Similarly, the cost of sending a team of electrical engineers to India to diagnose and repair a problem with a switch gear in an electric power station is prohibitive. In Box 18.2, we showed clearly the nature of costs incurred by a bank as a result of sending defective credit-card statements to customers.

Litigation Costs

Unfortunately, defective products can cause injury and even death to the consumers who purchase them. In this regard, a defect could mean poor product design and/or nonconformance to specifications. An increasing number of states are adopting *strict liability laws* that force companies to pay damages—often in large amounts—to injured plaintiffs, even when they have not proved that the manufacturer was negligent in designing the product. All that needs to be shown is that a product was defective and that it caused injury. At present there is no nationwide, uniform code on product liability. Each state can have its own set of rules, which creates a chaotic situation for companies that sell their products in more than one state.

Chaotic as the situation may be, its one common element is the high cost of litigation in the courts. More and more frequently, lawsuits brought on behalf of injured plaintiffs are spotlighted in the news media. For example, the Ford Motor Company, whose 23 million automatic transmissions manufactured from 1968 to 1980 were alleged to slip from park into reverse if the engine is left running, at one time faced more than 1000 lawsuits exceeding $500 million in claims for injuries and death supposedly caused by the transmission. The Firestone Tire and Rubber Company, whose Firestone 500 tire allegedly had defects in construction causing premature wear, resolved nearly 8000 lawsuits arising from these allegations and spent $180 million, including recalls, to solve the problem. Procter & Gamble's Rely tampon and Merrell-Dow Pharmaceuticals, Inc.'s Bendectin, the latter alleged to cause birth defects, are further examples of costly litigation and media notoriety. Regardless of whether the company is judged to be at fault in a court of law, the cost of litigation in terms of legal fees and bad publicity is enormous.

TOTAL QUALITY CONTROL

Our discussion of quality management would not be complete without presenting the concept of **total quality control (TQC).** The Japanese have successfully implemented TQC to improve quality reliability, and top management in Western companies would do well to take note. Total quality control was first introduced by A. V. Feigenbaum in 1961, but it was the Japanese who made it work at the level of the individual worker. Under TQC, quality is a responsibility that must be shared by all the people in an organization, especially the workers who actually make a product. In Japan, the foreman and the workers, not a quality control department, have primary responsibility for quality reliability. Everyone else is expected to contribute to the overall improvement of quality—from the secretary who avoids typing errors to the salesperson who properly presents the product to the customer, to the engineers who build automatic error-checking devices, to managers who approve funding for quality improvement projects. In other words, TQC involves all the functions that relate to a product or service.

In TQC, all personnel share the view that quality control is an end in itself. Errors or defects should be caught and corrected (if possible) at the source. The cost advantages of quality at the source were apparent in our discussion of internal failure costs. In TQC, quality at the source becomes a way of life, and workers even have the authority to stop a production line if they see quality problems. At Kawasaki's U.S. plant, lights of different colors strung along the assembly lines indicate the severity of the quality problem detected. Workers activate a yellow light to indicate that a problem has been detected and a red light when the problem is serious enough to stop the production line. If the line is stopped, the problem must be resolved quickly because each lost minute results in less output. In TQC, quality reliability or consistency has a higher priority than the level of output.

Total quality control starts with top management. In 1981, W. Edwards

Deming, who is considered to be the father of quality control in Japan, suggested the TQC activities for top management shown in Table 18.5. Deming urges a company to have a definite strategic plan of where it is going and how it will get there. Management should embrace the philosophy that mistakes, defects, and unsuitable materials are no longer acceptable and should be eliminated. The quality of supervision should be improved by allowing more time for supervisors to work with employees and providing them with the tools they need to do the job. Management should also create an environment in which employees will not fear reporting problems or recommending improvements. Such fear usually results from the perceived effects of such communication on a worker's own job or the jobs of fellow workers. This behavior can also apply to quality inspectors who incorrectly report the result of an inspection for fear of exceeding the quota of allowable defectives for the work force.

Deming also is against the use of slogans, such as *Quality Is Everyone's Job*, or *Let's Have Zero Defects Today*. Slogans typically only create frustration because the support of management in terms of equipment and training is usually lacking. Furthermore, work standards (see Chapter 6) should not be defined only as numbers or quotas but should include some notion of quality to promote the production of *good* output. Management also has the responsibility to train (or retrain) employees in new skills to keep pace with changes in the workplace.

Table 18.5

TQC Suggestions for Top Management

- Create a strategic plan for the company.
- Embrace the philosophy that defects are no longer acceptable.
- Require statistical evidence of process control along with that for incoming critical parts.
- Use statistical methods to find the sources of trouble.
- Use statistical techniques to determine whether further job training is needed.
- Improve supervision.
- Create an environment in which people are not afraid to report problems.
- Encourage open communication among departments.
- Do not rely solely on slogans to improve productivity and quality.
- Create work standards that take quality into account.
- Institute training programs in simple but powerful statistical methods.
- Train employees in new skills to keep up with changes in model style, materials, and machinery.

Source: W. Edwards Deming, "Improvement of Quality and Productivity Through Action by Management," *National Productivity Review*, vol. 1, no. 1 (Winter 1981–1982), pp. 12–22.

Management must develop the proper tools to manage quality. Such tools are not only the machines or hand tools that help to gauge the quality of a produced item, but also statistical methods to control processes or incoming materials and to help identify the sources of quality problems. Statistical methods can even be used to determine whether more worker training is needed. Deming believes that statistical methods are the backbone of management's arsenal of tools for managing quality. We explore some of these methods in Chapter 19.

CHAPTER HIGHLIGHTS

Good quality is a competitive weapon, and the challenge for operations managers is how to produce products or services efficiently and with the aspects of quality demanded by customers. In this chapter, we focus on the management of quality. Some of the highlights of the chapter are:

- Quality can be defined from an internal perspective as conformance to specifications and from an external perspective as value or fitness for use. Value, or fitness for use, may be judged on the basis of hardware quality, product or service support, promptness, or psychological impressions.
- Quality management is important because of the impact on market share, price and profits, and the costs of poor quality. The four major cost categories associated with quality management are prevention, appraisal, internal failure, and external failure costs.
- Prevention costs increase as the level or reliability of quality increases. Appraisal, internal failure, and external failure costs all decrease as quality is improved through preventive measures.
- Increasing prevention expenditures to increase the quality *level* through better product and process design may involve tradeoffs among the competitive priorities of price (cost), quality, and flexibility. Increasing prevention expenditures to obtain better conformance to specifications may be offset by savings in appraisal, internal failure, and external failure costs. Better quality reliability *and* a reduction in total costs may be possible.
- The prevention of quality problems can be addressed organizationally by using quality assurance groups, setting consistent quality goals, and fostering close cooperation between the operations and marketing functions.
- Fmployee-related strategies for preventing quality problems include designing well-defined career progressions, instituting employee training, providing adequate monetary incentives, and initiating quality circles. Quality problems can also be prevented by having product and process designs that are stable and that foster quality reliability. Linking product design to process design can increase quality reliability. One useful technique is the fishbone diagram, which relates a particular quality problem to its possible causes.
- With regard to purchasing practices, the role of the buyer in identifying supplier capabilities and working with suppliers to achieve higher levels of quality is as important as managing the specifications for purchased parts and materials.

- The costs of internal failure arise from yield losses and rework. In addition to the cost of scrapped material, yield losses and rework increase the costs of labor- and machine-hours, machine failure, and work-in-process inventory. Cycle times also increase, which has an impact on future sales.
- The quality-at-the-source approach dramatically reduces yield loss and rework costs when compared to the inspect-quality-into-the-product approach.
- External failure costs consist of warranty and litigation costs. These costs can be extremely large but can be significantly reduced with effective quality management.
- Total quality control (TQC) has been successfully implemented in Japan. Its basic tenet is that producing a quality product is a responsibility that must be shared by all the people in an organization, especially the workers who actually make the product. TQC begins with top management.

KEY TERMS

appraisal costs
external failure costs
fishbone diagram
internal failure costs
prevention costs
quality assurance
quality circle
total quality control (TQC)

STUDY QUESTIONS

1. Your company manufactures Christmas-tree lights. Define *quality* from both an internal and external perspective by giving examples of conformance to specifications and factors that influence the consumer's perceptions of product quality.
2. You own a small company that provides an income-tax preparation service. Define *quality* from both an internal and external perspective by giving examples of conformance to specifications and factors that influence the consumer's perceptions of service quality.
3. Suppose that you are the proprietor of an independently owned motel located at the intersection of two interstate highways. Give an example of each of the four aspects of quality (Table 18.1) for your motel service.
4. What are the implications of quality management for the marketing function of an organization?
5. Explain why poor quality can be expensive for companies manufacturing a product or producing a service.
6. What role does a quality assurance group play in the prevention of quality problems?
7. As a manager, what can you do for your employees to improve the quality of output?
8. What are the implications of *product* design for quality management? Of *process* design?
9. Suppose that you are the purchasing manager of a company that buys raw materials from hundreds of suppliers, some of which supply the same raw materials.

You are convinced that the quality of these materials, as measured by conformance to specifications, can be improved. Disregarding sampling plans, what can you do as a purchasing manager to improve the quality of the raw materials your company needs? Do the engineering group and top management also have some responsibilities? Explain.

10. Why are internal failure costs so expensive?
11. Explain why the costs of detecting quality problems increase proportionally with the distance from the source of the problem.
12. What is the essence of the total quality control concept? Do you think that it can be easily applied in the United States?

PROBLEMS

1. The Crampton Electric Company manufactures semiconductors for the electronics industry. Although the company produces a wide variety of semiconductors, one of its products requires only four operations. The raw material is a silicone bar, 3 inches in diameter. The bar is sliced on the first operation, and the slices are processed on three more machines to complete the product. However, each of the four machines generates a certain percentage of defective units:

Operation	Machine	Percent Defectives
1	Saw	2
2	Scrubber	1
3	Edge grinder	5
4	KOH	3

   (a) The demand rate for the product is 1000 slices per day. How many slices must the saw cut in order to ensure 1000 units of acceptable output come from KOH?
   (b) Assume that all defects are discovered after each operation. What is the implication for the quantity of silicone bar needed?
   (c) What is the percentage of extra capacity required at each machine owing to the defect rates of the machines?
   (d) Why is the percentage of extra capacity required more than the defect percentage at the saw, scrubber, and edge grinder machines?
   (e) Besides extra capacity costs, what other costs increase because of poor quality in this case?

2. Consider a three-operation flow shop. After the last operation, an inspector determines whether an entire lot must be reworked. Historically, 20 percent of the lots have to be reworked. If rework is required, the entire lot is moved back to operation 2, and the lot must also go through operation 3 again. The size of each production lot is 50 units, and the daily requirement is 200 units. Estimate the average extra capacity per day required at operations 2, 3, and inspection.

SELECTED REFERENCES

Aubrey, C. A., and L. A. Eldridge, "Banking on High Quality," *Quality Progress*, vol. 14, no. 12 (December 1981), pp. 14–19.

Deming, W. Edwards, "Improvement of Quality and Productivity Through Action by Management," *National Productivity Review,* vol. 1, no. 1 (Winter 1981–1982), pp. 12–22.

Feigenbaum, A. V., *Total Quality Control: Engineering and Management.* New York: McGraw-Hill, 1961.

Garvin, David A., "Quality on the Line," *Harvard Business Review* (September–October 1983), pp. 65–75.

Hostage, G. M., "Quality Control in a Service Business," *Harvard Business Review* (July–August 1975), pp. 89–106.

Ishikawa, Kaoru, *Guide to Quality Control.* Tokyo: Asian Productivity Organization, 1972.

Juran, J. M., "Japanese and Western Quality: A Contrast in Methods and Results," *Management Review* (November 1978), pp. 26–45.

Reddy, Jack, and Abe Berger, "Three Essentials of Product Quality," *Harvard Business Review* (July–August 1983), pp. 153–159.

Schonberger, Richard J., *Japanese Manufacturing Techniques.* New York: The Free Press, 1982.

Takeuchi, Hirotaka, and John A. Quelch, "Quality Is More than Making a Good Product," *Harvard Business Review* (November–December 1981), pp. 14–19.

CHAPTER

19

QUALITY CONTROL

Some Managerial Issues

- How can we devise a system to monitor quality reliability and help us to identify the sources of problems?
- Of the various acceptance sampling methods available, which one can we best use in a given situation?
- What trade-offs are involved if we use attribute measurements instead of variable measurements of quality?
- What are the implications of our narrowing the control limits in a process control chart?
- Where should we put our inspection stations?

Chapter Outline

In this chapter we discuss several methods for appraising the quality offered to a firm by its suppliers or generated by its own operations system. Because of our discussion of quality management in Chapter 18, you may be wondering why we need to devote a chapter to quality control techniques. Effective quality management requires that suppliers show evidence that they can meet specified quality standards for the items they supply. Therefore why should a firm be concerned with quality control techniques that help a buyer decide whether to accept or reject a shipment from a supplier? Also, the concept of quality at the source, which requires that no employee pass a defective product to the next process or the customer, greatly reduces the amount of defective products or services generated by the operations system. Why does a company need statistical process control systems to monitor quality reliability or conformance to specifications?

There are two parts to the answer to these questions. First, the business world in general has not yet awakened to the advantages of quality reliability. Even if they have, some companies simply are not in a position to require evidence that their suppliers have quality under control. To be sure, large companies such as GM, IBM, or Westinghouse can demand such compliance and can rely on the quality of their vendors. Many other companies do not have the economic clout and, consequently, must monitor the quality of incoming materials. Someday, perhaps in the near future, every company will be able to boast that they have quality under control. Until then, the use of quality control methods is necessary.

The second part of the answer to the questions relates to process control. Statistical process control methods are used to identify problems in quality reliability and help to prescribe a remedy. These methods provide the *evidence* needed to ensure customers quality is under control. Statistical process control methods can be used not only to appraise the degree of quality reliability but also to prevent quality problems by early detection of process irregularities.

ACCEPTANCE SAMPLING

Acceptance sampling is a statistical procedure used to determine whether a quantity of goods conforms to specifications or should be rejected. The goods may have been produced either by a supplier or internally. The issues raised in the situation described in Box 19.1 are typical of those encountered in acceptance sampling.

We can assess the quality of goods in one of two ways. We can take a random *sample* from a quantity of goods and make a decision based on the sample results. In that case, we assume that a random sample of adequate size is representative of the quality of all the items. Sampling is appropriate when the cost of inspection is a major concern, which is the case in many industrial settings. This may be the case when special knowledge and skills are required to perform the tests or the testing requires high-cost equipment. Moreover, sampling is necessary *regardless of the cost* of inspection when the tests are destructive. For example, tests of tensile strength or product life require that the product be destroyed to judge its quality.

Our other alternative is complete inspection, which requires that each unit be inspected for quality. This approach is used when the cost of passing a defective item is high relative to the cost of inspection. For example, suppliers of components for the moon exploration project checked each component many times before shipping them to a contractor. The cost of a failure in such a situation greatly exceeded the cost of the inspection because it involved human life. Nonetheless, complete inspection will not always uncover all defects. Inspector fatigue or the monotony of the tests may allow some defects to pass unnoticed. In many situations, the cost of defects is not as high as for the moon exploration, and a well-conceived sampling plan can achieve the same degree of protection against defects that complete inspection can.

Quality Measurement

We can measure conformance to specifications in two ways. One way is to use **attribute measures**. We use them when we can easily recognize that one

Box 19.1

TYPICAL ISSUES TO RESOLVE IN ACCEPTANCE SAMPLING

The Mini-Kar Company manufactures replicas of Formula 1 race cars for use at miniature grand-prix tracks in amusement parks. John Birns, quality assurance manager, just received word that a shipment of 3000 wheel rims arrived at the receiving department yesterday. In the past, quality problems with the rims have caused delays on the assembly line and Sam Conners, the purchasing manager, has had to return portions of shipments to the supplier and get replacements on an expedited basis. Not only did this cause downtime along the assembly line and extra purchasing costs, it also caused late shipments to customers. Since the present shipment will not be needed for awhile, John feels that now is the time to set up a procedure for deciding about the acceptability of the rims before they go to the assembly line.

John set up a meeting with Sally Johnson, the manufacturing manager, and Jim Saunders, director of engineering. Sally said that the biggest problem with the wheel rims is the spacing of the lug holes. If a wheel rim is defective, it is usually because it cannot be mounted on the axle. Jim said that this attribute can be easily tested by placing the rim on a facsimile of the axle mounting and checking the alignment of the holes. If a rim does not fit properly, it would be considered defective.

John said, "It looks like we have a way to test for the aspect of quality we are most concerned with, but we must have some idea of what we consider good quality. We cannot expect to always get defect-free rims. If we accept only defect-free shipments, we may end up sending a lot of shipments back to the supplier, which will increase our lead time for manufacturing cars. On the other hand, how many defects per shipment are we willing to accept? We must be fair to the supplier, but we must also watch out for ourselves."

Sally brought up some other issues. "John, are you considering taking a sample of the shipment or inspecting each rim? Keep in mind that there are certain risks with sampling. There is a chance we will reject a shipment of rims with our definition of acceptable quality just because the sample we picked was not typical of the entire shipment. There is also a chance that we will accept a shipment of poor quality. How much risk are we willing to accept? It seems to me that there is a trade-off between the cost of inspecting each rim and the potential cost that can arise from sampling."

or more characteristics of the product or service are either acceptable or unacceptable, and a simple yes or no decision can be made for each item in the sample. For example, the wheel rims for Mini-Kar production (Box 19.1) could be quickly checked for lug hole spacing by using the facsimile of the axle mounting. The concern was not over the degree of deviation from the specification, but only whether the specification was met. Testing radios by turning them on as a final check also results in a simple yes or no decision regarding quality. Other examples of attributes are color (paint on a refrigerator), taste (wine), or smell (food at a restaurant). We often use attributes when the quality specifications are complex and all that we need to know is whether the *unit as a whole* is defective. This is the case with the radio: If it does not play when turned on, it is sent to the repair department to find out what specifically is wrong with it.

The other way to measure conformance to specifications is to use **variable measures**. This approach is useful when we want to measure the deviation from specifications on a continuous scale so that corrective action can be taken. The spacing between the lug holes on the rims at Mini-Kar could be measured and plotted to determine whether it adheres to the specification (within tolerances), or whether there are identifiable trends in the spacing from sample to sample. Sampling plans based on variable measures can be useful in assessing problems with the process used to produce the item.

Managerial Parameters

The procurement of materials involves two parties: the producer (or supplier) and the consumer (or buyer). Acceptance sampling plans are intended to provide the consumer decision guidelines that limit the risk of rejecting materials with good quality or accepting materials with bad quality. Consequently, it is the consumer, sometimes in conjunction with the producer, who specifies the parameters of the plan.*

Two levels of quality should be specified in the design of an acceptance sampling plan. The first, is the **acceptable quality level (AQL),** or the quality level acceptable to the consumer. It is the quality level that the producer of the item is aiming for. The probability of rejecting a lot with AQL or better quality is called the **producer's risk (α),** or the risk that the sampling plan will fail to verify the acceptable quality of a lot. The consumer is interested in designing a plan that minimizes the producer's risk because sending material back to the supplier (1) is disruptive of the production process and increases the likelihood of materials shortages; (2) unnecessarily adds to the lead time for finished products; and (3) causes poor relations with the supplier when the materials actually are of acceptable quality.

The second level of quality that must be specified is the **lot tolerance proportion defective (LTPD),** which identifies the worst level of quality that the consumer will accept. Recognition of the high cost of defects when identified at the consumer level has caused management to be more cautious about

* Any company can be both a producer and a consumer. It can be a producer of products purchased by another company and it can be a consumer of raw materials supplied by another company.

Table 19.1

Decisions in Acceptance Sampling

Decision	Comments
Sampling versus complete inspection	The trade-off of inspection cost versus the potential cost of passing a defective item is important. Destructive testing requires a sampling plan. Fatigue and the monotony of the testing procedure should be considered.
Attribute versus variable measures	Attribute measures involve a simple yes–no decision about a quality characteristic. Variable measures involve measurement of quality characteristics of an item on a continuous scale to quantify the amount of deviation from specifications.
If sampling is chosen:	
Acceptable quality level (AQL); risk of rejecting lot of AQL or better quality (α) Lot tolerance proportion defective (LTPD); risk of accepting LTPD quality or worse (β)	These parameters quantify risks to the producer and the consumer. They provide the basis for determining the specifics of a sampling plan.
Design of the sampling plan	The design is derived from the specification of AQL, α, LTPD, and β.

accepting materials of poor quality from suppliers. Thus sampling plans now tend to have lower LTPD values than in the past. The probability of accepting a lot with LTPD quality or worse is called the **consumer's risk (β).**

Table 19.1 summarizes the decisions that must be made with regard to acceptance sampling.

The Single-Sample Plan

Let's now turn to a simple attribute plan: the **single-sample plan.*** As its name implies, this method involves a decision to accept or reject a lot based on the results of one random sample from the lot. To begin, we let

n = Sample size, randomly selected from the lot to be judged;

* Single-sample plans can also be devised for variable measurements.

c = Acceptable number of defective items in the sample; and

d = Actual number of defective items found in the sample.

Then, we select values for n and c.

Procedure. The procedure is to take a random sample of size n from the lot and inspect each item. If $d \leq c$, we accept the lot; if $d > c$, we reject the lot.

For example, suppose that we have a lot of 5000 items and decide to sample 200 of them (or $n = 200$). When we inspect the 200 items, we find 4 that are defective (or $d = 4$). If the acceptance number for this plan is 5 defective items (or $c = 5$), we would decide to accept the lot of 5000 because the actual number of defective items is less than the acceptance number for the plan (or $d < c$).

Derivation of a Single-Sample Plan. We can illustrate the derivation of a single-sample plan using the acceptance decision at Mini-Kar. Three thousand wheel rims are on the receiving dock. Suppose that John Birns, the quality assurance manager, has decided to use an acceptance sampling plan for attribute measures with the following specifications.

Acceptable quality level (AQL)	= 0.01.
Producer's risk (α)	= 0.05.
Lot tolerance proportion defective (LTPD)	= 0.06.
Consumer's risk (β)	= 0.10.

We must now determine the appropriate values for the sample size n and the acceptance number c. If the shipment of rims has AQL or better quality, we want to find values for n and c such that the probability of acceptance of the lot is $1.0 - \alpha = 0.95$. If the shipment has LTPD quality or worse, we want the plan to yield a probability of acceptance of $\beta = 0.10$. In order to find the values of n and c that satisfy these two conditions we can use Table 19.2. We can best explain the contents of the table by referring to a specific row. Let's take an acceptance number of $c = 1$. Now suppose that the lot of wheel rims actually has AQL quality, that is, the proportion p of defectives is only 1 percent. For $c = 1$ and AQL quality, we find the appropriate sample size by dividing the value in column 1 by AQL. In our example, $n = 0.36/0.01 = 36$, as shown in column 2. This means that if

$$c = 1, \quad p = 0.01, \quad \text{and} \quad n = 36,$$

the probability of accepting the lot is 95 percent. Since the value in column 1 is the expected number of defectives in the sample, the expected number of defectives per sample would be 0.36, if we were to repeatedly take random samples of size 36.

Table 19.2

Single-Sample Planning Table for $\alpha = 0.05$ and $\beta = 0.10$*

	When the Lot Proportion Defective, *p*, Equals AQL		When the Lot Proportion Defective, *p*, Equals LTPD	
	(1)	(2)	(3)	(4)
Acceptance Number (c)	Expected number of defectives in sample (*np*)	Implied sample size† [col. (1)/AQL]	Expected number of defectives in sample (*np*)	Implied sample size‡ [col. (3)/LTPD]
0	0.05	5	2.30	38
1	0.36	36	3.89	65
2	0.82	82	5.32	89
3	1.37	137	6.68	111
4	1.97	197	7.99	133
5	2.61	261	9.28	155
6	3.29	329	10.53	176
7	3.98	398	11.77	196
8	4.70	470	13.00	217
9	5.43	543	14.21	237
10	6.17	617	15.41	257

* Table values in columns 1 and 3 are based on the Poisson approximation to the binomial distribution.
† AQL = 0.01 for this example. In general, use the AQL appropriate for the problem.
‡ LTPD = 0.06 for this example. In general, use the LTPD appropriate for the problem.

Unfortunately, $c = 1$ and $n = 36$ do not satisfy the second condition that the probability of accepting a lot of LTPD quality or worse is only 0.10. You can see that the condition has not been met by referring to columns 3 and 4 of Table 19.2. Suppose that the lot of wheel rims actually has LTPD quality: that is, the proportion p of defectives is 6 percent. For $c = 1$ and LTPD quality, we find the required sample size by dividing column 3 by LTPD, or $n = 3.89/0.06 = 65$, which is shown in column 4. This means that if

$$c = 1 \quad \text{and} \quad p = 0.06,$$

we need a sample size of 65 to be sure that we will find enough defectives to reject the lot. A sample size of 65 provides an acceptance probability of 10 percent for lots that have such poor quality.

Thus we are left in a quandary about which sample size to use. Our first impulse might be to look for the acceptance number that results in the smallest difference between the implied sample sizes. The smallest difference between columns 2 and 4 in Table 19.2 occurs for $c = 2$. However, $c = 2$ would be the wrong choice. Note that the values in column 2 start out smaller than those in column 4, but end up much larger. At $c = 2$, the sample size in column 2 is less than that in column 4, but at $c = 3$ the reverse is true. (See the highlighted rows in Table 19.2.) Since we must choose one value for c and one value for n, let's examine the implications of these choices.

Four alternative plans are shown in Table 19.3. We used the cumulative Poisson exponential probability curves in Appendix D.4 to estimate α and β for each plan. Estimating β amounts to finding the probability of acceptance (P_a) for p = LTPD while estimating α amounts to finding $(1.0 - P_a)$ for p = AQL. To find the value of P_a, we

1. select a value for p;
2. multiply p by the sample size n;
3. find the value of np along the horizontal axis of the chart;
4. move up the chart to the curve for the appropriate value of c; and
5. move horizontally to the left-hand side of the chart and read the value for P_a from the vertical axis.

For example, let's estimate β for Plan 1 with $c = 2$ and $n = 82$. If $p = 0.06$, we multiply by n and get $82(0.06) = 4.92$. Moving up to the curve for $c = 2$ and over to the vertical axis, we read $P_a = 0.12$.

You can see in Table 19.3 that if we choose $c = 2$, the risk will be *greater* than desired for either α or β, and if we choose $c = 3$ the risk will be *less* than desired for either α or β. This leads us to the following guideline for the design of a single-sample plan for attributes measures.

> Assuming that the specifications for α and β must be met, choose the lowest acceptance number c for which the implied sample size for LTPD quality is less than the implied sample size for AQL quality. This ensures the smallest sample size that meets the requirements.

In our example, we would choose $c = 3$ and some sample size between 111 and 137, depending on the trade-offs we would be willing to make between inspection cost and the potential cost of passing defective items. Of

Table 19.3

Alternative Single-Sample Plans for Mini-Kar

Plan	Acceptance Number (c)	Sample Size (n)	Producer's Risk (α)	Consumer's Risk (β)
1	2	82	0.05	0.12
2	2	89	0.07	0.10
3	3	137	0.05	0.03
4	3	111	0.03	0.10

Table 19.4

Values for the Operating Characteristic Curve with n = 111 and c = 3

(1) Proportion Defective (p)	(2) Value of np*	(3) Probability of c or Less Defects (P_a)†	Comments
0.01 (AQL)	1.11	0.970	Implies $\alpha = 0.03$
0.02	2.22	0.820	
0.03	3.33	0.560	
0.04	4.44	0.350	
0.05	5.55	0.200	
0.06 (LTPD)	6.66	0.100	$\beta = 0.10$
0.07	7.77	0.050	
0.08	8.88	0.020	
0.09	9.99	0.010	
0.10	11.10	0.004	

* Column (1) times 111.
† Column (3) is estimated from the chart in Appendix D.4, with $c = 3$. First, locate the Column 2 value on the horizontal axis. Then, move up the chart to the curve for $c = 3$. Finally, move horizontally to the vertical axis and read the value for P_a.

course, if we were willing to relax our specifications for α and β, we could save some on inspection costs by choosing $c = 2$.

Operating Characteristic Curves. Changing n or c in a single-sample plan affects the probability of lot acceptance for a specific p. A graphic display of the performance of a sampling plan, as expressed by the probability of acceptance for a range of lot proportion defectives, is called an **operating characteristic (OC) curve**. OC curves can be used to depict the implications of changes in the sample size or acceptance number on the probability of acceptance.

To demonstrate the construction of an OC curve, we can use plan 4, which specified $n = 111$ and $c = 3$. We need to determine the probability of acceptance (P_a) for each of a series of values of the proportion of lot defective p over some reasonable range. We can use the same procedure we used for Table 19.3.

Table 19.4 shows the value of P_a for a range of P values. Note that in this plan the value of the producer's risk is only 0.03, while the consumer's risk is 0.10.* This supports our earlier discussion of Table 19.3. Figure 19.1 shows the shape of the resulting OC curve.

* Appendix D.4 can also be used to find n. Start with P_a on the vertical axis of Appendix D.4. Move horizontally to the curve for the appropriate value of c. Then find the value of np along the horizontal axis and divide it by p.

Now, let's consider the effect of changing the sample size while holding $c = 3$. Figure 19.2 shows that increasing the sample size improves the consumer's risk (β becomes smaller), but the producer's risk increases because it is easier to reject a lot of good quality. Increasing n gives us more chance to find c defective items. The ultimate is complete inspection in which case the acceptance number of 3 no longer applies. We would reject the lot if more than 1 percent of the wheel rims in the shipment are defective.

You can also see the effects of changing the acceptance number by examining a series of curves. Figure 19.3 shows what happens as c is changed from 1 to 4, holding $n = 111$. As c increases, the producer's risk *decreases,* while the consumer's risk *increases.* Increasing c while n is fixed requires that more defective items be found before the lot can be rejected. Operating characteristic curves such as those in Fig. 19.2 and 19.3 enable management to choose a plan that fits the situation best.

Other Attribute-Sampling Plans

The single-sampling plan is the simplest of acceptance sampling plans. Other plans that may be appropriate under certain conditions include the double-sample plan and the sequential-sample plan. In a **double-sample plan,** we

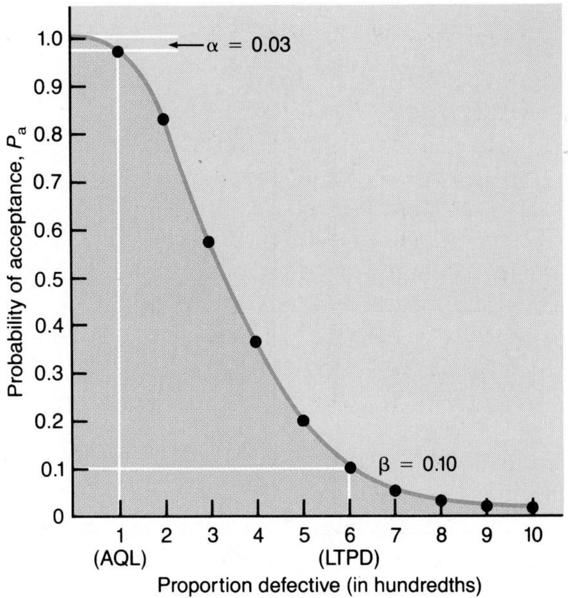

Figure 19.1

Operating Characteristic Curve for $n = 111$ and $c = 3$.

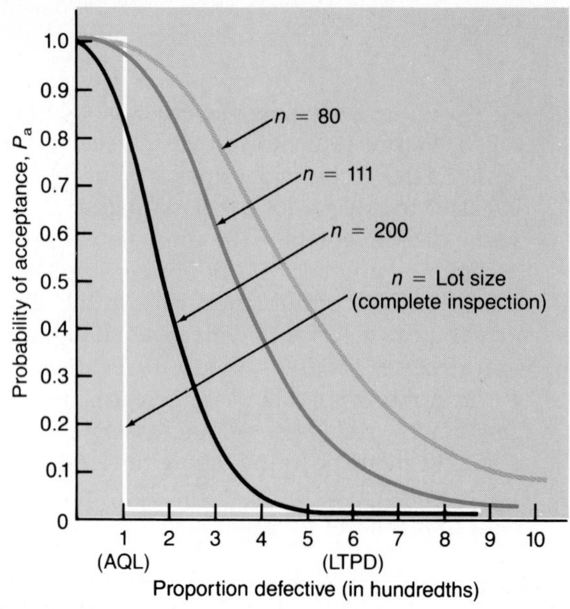

Figure 19.2

Effects of Changing the Sample Size (Holding c = 3 Constant).

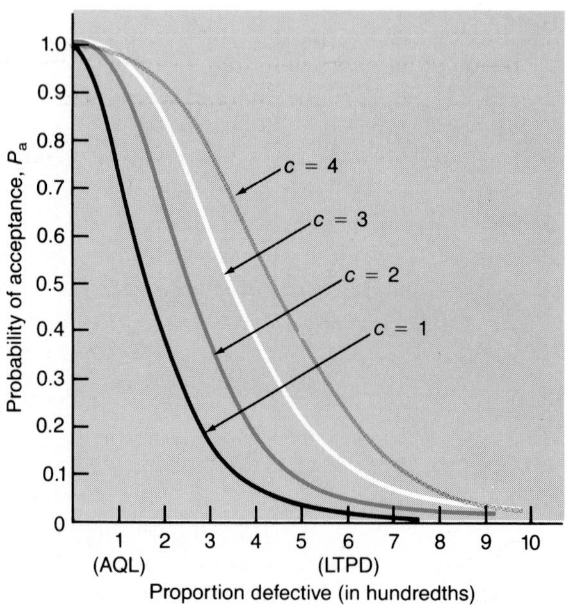

Figure 19.3

Effects of Changing the Acceptance Number (Holding *n* = 111 Constant).

specify two sample sizes (n_1 and n_2) and two acceptance numbers (c_1 and c_2). The procedure is as follows:

1. Take a random sample of size n_1 and determine d_1, the number of defectives in the sample.
2. If $d_1 \leq c_1$ accept the lot; if $d_1 > c_2$ reject the lot.
3. If $c_1 < d_1 \leq c_2$, take another random sample of size n_2 and determine d_2, the number of defectives in the second sample.
4. If $(d_1 + d_2) \leq c_2$, accept the lot; otherwise, reject the lot.

For example, suppose that there is a shipment of 10,000 items on the receiving dock. Suppose also that $n_1 = 200$, $c_1 = 4$, $n_2 = 250$, and $c_2 = 9$. When we examine the first sample of 200, we find 6 defective items ($c_1 < d_1 \leq c_2$). Therefore we must take a second sample of 250 items. In the second sample we find 4 more defective items. On the basis of our double sample plan, we must reject the shipment because the combined total number of defective units ($d_1 + d_2 = 10$) exceeds the second acceptance number ($c_2 = 9$). If, in our first sample we had found only 4 defectives, we would have accepted the lot without taking the second sample. Alternatively, if we had found 10 defectives in our first sample, we would have rejected the lot outright.

One of the major advantages of the double-sample plan is that the average number of items inspected (ANI) can be less than that of a single-sample plan with a comparable OC curve. The advantage depends on whether complete inspection is performed. With *complete inspection,* after a sample has been taken, every item in the sample is inspected even if enough defects have been found to warrant rejection. With *curtailed inspection,* however, the inspection process is stopped when a decision can be made. Figure 19.4 shows that, even with complete inspection, the double-sample plan results in inspecting fewer items when the lot proportion defective is either very small or very large. The reason is that n_1 is smaller than the single-sample size, and under these extreme conditions a decision can usually be made on the basis of the first sample. For intermediate proportion defective values both samples are usually needed, and the combined samples ($n_1 + n_2$) are typically larger than the comparable single-sample plan. Curtailed inspection, however, generally results in inspecting fewer items, regardless of the proportion defective.

The Sequential-Sample Plan. If we extend the concept of the double-sample plan to its limit, we obtain the item-by-item **sequential-sample plan**. Each time an item is inspected a decision is made to (1) reject the lot; (2) accept the lot; or (3) continue sampling, based on the cumulative results so far. We can plot the total number of defectives against the cumulative sample size, and, if the number of defectives is greater than a certain acceptance number (c_u), we reject the lot. If the number is less than another acceptance number (c_L), we accept the lot. If the number is somewhere between the two, we inspect another item.

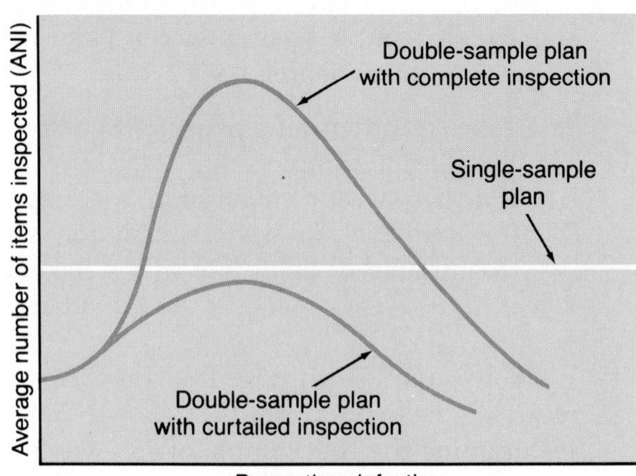

Figure 19.4

The Effects of the Choice of Sampling Plan on the Average Number of Items Inspected.

The two acceptance numbers c_u and c_L are functions of the cumulative sample size, AQL, α, LTPD, and β, and can be plotted as two parallel lines on a chart. We can use tables that are generally available and easily calculate the lines.* Figure 19.5 is an example of a sequential-sample chart and shows that we would have to sample at least 26 items before we *accept* the lot, but we could *reject* the lot much sooner. Whenever the cumulative number of defectives enters the region above the line for c_u, we can reject the lot. If we enter the region below the line for c_L, we can accept the lot but not until the twenty-sixth item in this case. All we need to do is plot the cumulative number of defectives as we discover them and continue sampling until we make a decision. In our example, we decide to reject the lot after sampling 41 items at random.

The average number of items inspected (ANI) in the sequential plan is generally lower than that for any other form of acceptance sampling. At extreme values of the proportion defective, no other plan with a comparable OC curve will have a lower ANI. It is possible, although not likely, that a sequential plan will have a larger ANI than a comparable single- or double-sample plan for intermediate values of the proportion defective. In general, the sequential-sample plan may reduce ANI to approximately 50 percent of that required by a comparable single-sample plan. Consequently, substantial inspection costs can be saved by using a sequential-sample plan.

* Such tables can be found in a publication of the Statistical Research Group, Columbia University, *Sequential Analysis of Statistical Data: Applications.* New York: Columbia University Press, 1945.

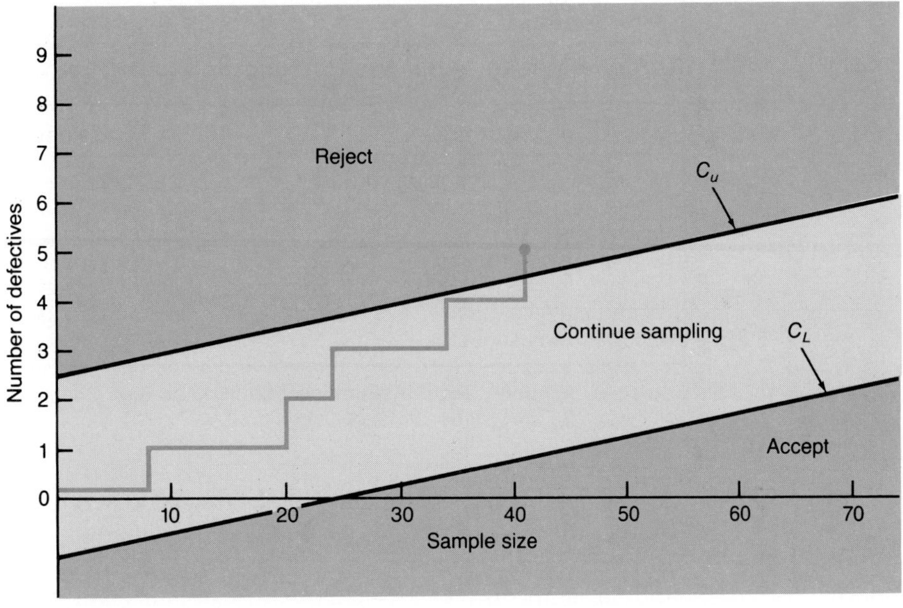

Figure 19.5

Sequential Sample Chart.

Although we have concentrated on acceptance sampling using attribute measures, plans based on variable measures can also be designed. The procedures for designing these plans parallel those already discussed. For example, a single-sample plan could be based on the average weight of the items in a lot. A random sample of size n is collected and the average weight per item ($\overline{w}$) is computed. If $\overline{w} \leq w_a$, the acceptance weight for this item, we accept the lot. Otherwise, we reject it. The main advantage of plans based on variable measures is that the required sample size is usually less than that for an attribute plan having a comparable OC curve. However, it may take more time to measure the variables. In addition, if an item has more than one quality characteristic, it may be necessary to have more than one variable inspection plan for the item. Conversely, it may be possible to accept or reject the item on the basis of a single attribute measure. Management should carefully consider the trade-offs between attribute and variable plans.

PROCESS CONTROL METHODS

Process control methods are used to monitor quality characteristics during the manufacturing or service production process. These methods are useful in (1)

Table 19.5

Attribute Measures for the Booking Services Department of a Bank

Attribute	Population
Wrong account number recorded	Total number of deposits
Nonendorsed deposits	Total number of deposits
Missing items	Total number of statements
Stop-payment transaction incorrect	Total stop-payment transactions
Misfiled items	Total checks and debits
Wrong statement sent	Total number of statements
Incorrect adjustments	Total number of statements

Source: C. A. Aubrey and L. A. Eldridge, "Banking on High Quality," *Quality Progress*, vol. 14, no. 12 (December 1981), pp. 14–19.

measuring the current quality of products or services; and (2) detecting whether the *process* itself has changed in a way that will affect quality. Regardless of the specific method used, the basic procedure is generally the same. A random sample is taken from a quantity of items, and the quality characteristic is measured. If the sample measurement is found to be outside an *upper control limit* (*UCL*) or a *lower control limit* (*LCL*), the process is checked for the cause (such as a faulty machine setting, an inexperienced operator, or poor raw materials).*

The reason for upper and lower control limits is that no two products or services can be produced *exactly* alike. For example, consider a manufacturing process for producing bearings. Although the average diameter of the bearing is 1.00 inch, we cannot expect that every bearing will have exactly a 1.00-inch diameter. Variation in a process is to be expected, and the issue to be addressed by process control is whether the observed variation is abnormal or normal. Abnormal variation can be caused by machine, operator, or materials factors. The UCL and LCL are chosen so that abnormal variation can be detected.

Control Charts for Attribute Measures

A commonly used control chart for measuring attributes is the ***p*-chart** for the population proportion defective. To illustrate the development of a *p*-chart, we can use the booking services department of a bank. Table 19.5 shows some of the attribute measures that are of concern to the department's manager. We could construct a *p*-chart for each attribute, but will use only the attribute *wrong account number recorded* for our example.

* Process industries such as paper, chemical, and oil use process control equipment that continuously monitors the production process. We only focus on sampling methods in this chapter.

Suppose that historically the proportion of wrong account numbers recorded (total number of wrong account numbers recorded divided by the total number of deposits) is 0.005, and management believes that this represents good performance. We will call this value $\bar{p}$. Now suppose that each week we take a random sample of 2500 deposits and record the number of times the account number was incorrectly recorded. The results for the past 12 weeks are shown in Table 19.6. Is the process out of control?

We cannot answer that question until we determine the nature of the normal variation that we would expect in such a process. Since sampling with attribute measures involves a yes–no decision, the underlying statistical distribution is the binomial distribution. However, the distribution of *estimates* of the population proportion defective calculated from each sample (number of defectives divided by the sample size) will tend to be normal, with a standard deviation of

$$s_p = \sqrt{\frac{\bar{p}(1 - \bar{p})}{n}},$$

where n is the sample size and $\bar{p}$ is the historical average population proportion defective. We can use this measure of the variation to arrive at the following upper and lower control limits for a p-chart.

$$UCL = \bar{p} + k\sqrt{\frac{\bar{p}(1 - \bar{p})}{n}} \quad \text{and} \quad LCL = \bar{p} - k\sqrt{\frac{\bar{p}(1 - \bar{p})}{n}},$$

Table 19.6

Observed Number of Wrong Account Numbers Recorded in 12 Samples of 2500 Each

Sample Number	Wrong Account Numbers	Proportion of Sample
1	15	0.0060
2	12	0.0048
3	19	0.0076
4	2	0.0008
5	19	0.0076
6	4	0.0016
7	24	0.0096
8	7	0.0028
9	10	0.0040
10	17	0.0068
11	15	0.0060
12	3	0.0012

where $\bar{p}$ is the process average, or central line of the chart, and k is the number of standard deviations from the process average. Typically, the upper and lower control limits are set at ± 3 standard deviations ($k = 3$), allowing 99.74 percent of the variation to fall within the control limits. (See the normal probability table in Appendix D.3.) Thus the probability is very small that a sample proportion defective that falls outside these limits will have come from a population with a mean proportion defective equal to $\bar{p}$.

In our example, $\bar{p} = 0.005$, so

$$UCL = 0.005 + 3\sqrt{\frac{0.005(0.995)}{2500}} = 0.00923,$$

and

$$LCL = 0.005 - 3\sqrt{\frac{0.005(0.995)}{2500}} = 0.00077.$$

The control chart and the results obtained for the 12 samples are shown in Fig. 19.6. You can see that sample 7 exceeded the upper control limit. Thus we can say that the process is out of control and that we should determine the reasons for the poor performance that week. We might find that the account

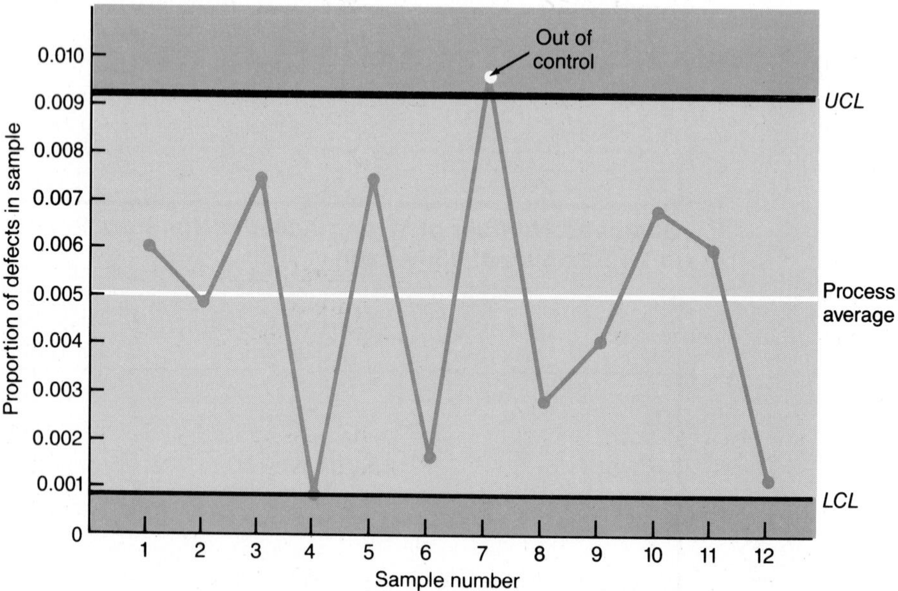

Figure 19.6

Control Chart for Wrong Account Numbers.

numbers were incorrectly entered into the computer by a trainee or an encoding machine was defective. We would then correct the problem, returning the process to statistical control. Of course, there is a slight chance that we might not find any assignable causes for the problem. The value of p in sample 7 could have been due to chance causes alone. Nonetheless, the p-chart provides us with a tool to not only measure the quality of the product or service, but also to indicate when the process needs adjustment.

Control Charts for Variable Measures

Two control charts for variable measures frequently used in tandem are the *range chart*, or **R-chart**, and the *average chart*, or **$\bar{x}$-chart.** Recall that the term *variable measures* means that the quality characteristic to be controlled (such as distance, weight, or response time) is measured on a continuous scale. A sample is taken and two values are calculated: the sample mean of the quality characteristic and the range. The range is calculated by subtracting the smallest from the largest measurement in each sample. These values are used to develop an R-chart for the process variability and an $\bar{x}$-chart for the process average. Both the process variability and the process average must be in control before we can say that the process is in control.

Range Chart. The process variability must be in control before we can construct a valid chart for the process average. The reason is that a measure of process variability is required to determine the control limits for the $\bar{x}$-chart. If the process variability is out of control, the control limits for the $\bar{x}$-chart will be incorrect.

The control limits for the R-chart are

$$UCL_R = D_4\bar{R} \quad \text{and} \quad LCL_R = D_3\bar{R}$$

where $\bar{R}$ is the average of several past R values (and the central line of the control chart), and D_3 and D_4 are constants that provide three standard deviation (3σ) limits for the range for a given sample size. Values for D_3 and D_4 are contained in Table 19.7.

Average Chart. When the process variability is in control, we can construct an $\bar{x}$-chart to control the process average. The control limits for the $\bar{x}$-chart are

$$UCL_{\bar{x}} = \bar{\bar{x}} + A_2\bar{R} \quad \text{and} \quad LCL_{\bar{x}} = \bar{\bar{x}} - A_2\bar{R}$$

where $\bar{\bar{x}}$ is the average of several past $\bar{x}$ values (and the central line of the control chart), or a target value that management has set for the process. The values for the constant A_2 provide three standard deviation (3σ) limits for the process average and are contained in Table 19.7. Note that the control limits

Table 19.7

Factors for Calculating 3σ Limits for $\bar{x}$-Chart and *R*-Chart

Size of Sample (n)	Factor for *UCL* and *LCL* for $\bar{x}$-Charts (A_2)	Factor for *LCL* for *R*-Charts (D_3)	Factor for *UCL* for *R*-Charts (D_4)
2	1.880	0	3.267
3	1.023	0	2.575
4	0.729	0	2.282
5	0.577	0	2.115
6	0.483	0	2.004
7	0.419	0.076	1.924
8	0.373	0.136	1.864
9	0.337	0.184	1.816
10	0.308	0.223	1.777

Source: 1950 *ASTM Manual on Quality Control of Materials*, copyright © ASTM. Reprinted with permission.

use the value of $\overline{R}$, which, again, is the reason for constructing the $\bar{x}$-chart *after* the process variability is in control.

Using the *R*-Chart and $\bar{x}$-Chart. We can demonstrate the use of the *R*-chart and the $\bar{x}$-chart by considering the manufacture of a certain type of metal screw. A quality characteristic of concern to management is the diameter of

Table 19.8

Data for the *R*-Chart and $\bar{x}$-Chart

Sample Number	Observations of Screw Diameter in Sample (Inches)				Sample Average $\bar{x}$*	Sample Range *R*†
	1	2	3	4		
1	0.51	0.63	0.39	0.35	0.47	0.28
2	0.50	0.56	0.42	0.64	0.53	0.22
3	0.68	0.49	0.53	0.62	0.58	0.19
4	0.45	0.33	0.47	0.55	0.45	0.22
5	0.70	0.58	0.64	0.68	0.65	0.12

* The value of $\bar{x}$ is the sum of the observations in each sample divided by 4.
† The value of R is the difference between the largest and smallest observation in a sample. In sample 1, for example, $R = 0.63 - 0.35 = 0.28$.

the screw. Historically, the process average $\bar{x}$ has been 0.500 inches and the average range $\bar{R}$ has been 0.18 inches. We first construct the R-chart. Suppose that our sample size is 4. Using Table 19.7, we find that the control limits for the R-chart are

$$UCL_R = 2.282(0.18) = 0.411 \text{ in.},$$

and

$$LCL_R = 0(0.18) = 0 \text{ in.},$$

where $D_3 = 0$, and $D_4 = 2.282$ for $n = 4$.

Table 19.8 shows the data for the last five samples of the metal screw. The value of the range for each sample is then plotted on the R-chart, as shown in Fig. 19.7. None of the sample ranges fall outside the control limits. Consequently, we can say that the process variability is in control. If any of the sample ranges had fallen outside the limits (the range can never be negative, of course), we would have had to search for the cause of the excessive variability.

We can now proceed to construct the $\bar{x}$-chart for the process average. Using $\bar{x} = 0.500$ and Table 19.7, we find that the control limits for the $\bar{x}$ chart are

$$UCL_{\bar{x}} = 0.500 + 0.729(0.18) = 0.631 \text{ in.},$$

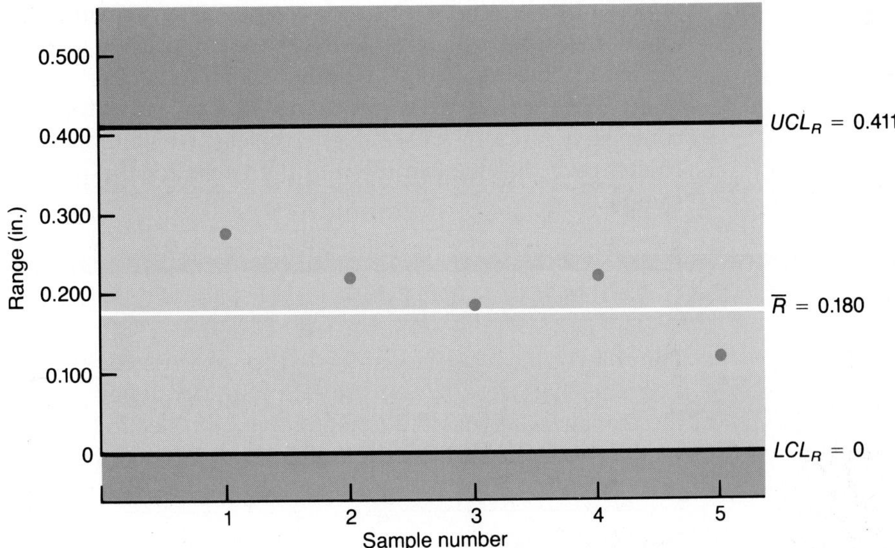

Figure 19.7

Range Chart for the Metal Screw.

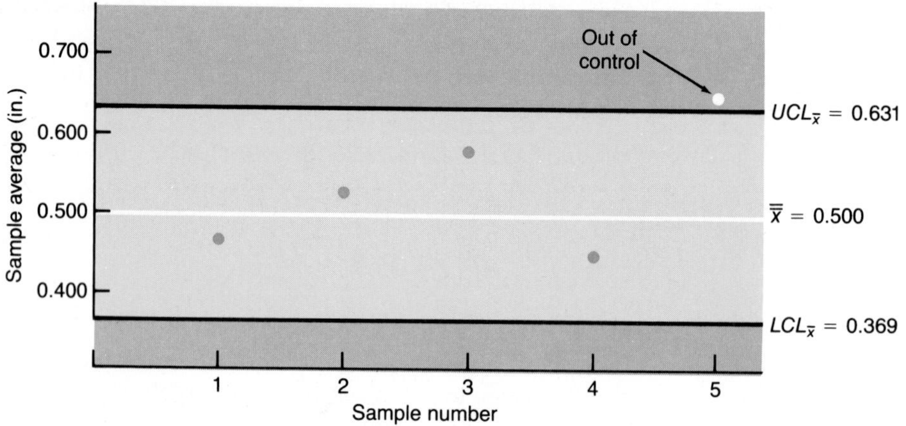

Figure 19.8

Average Chart for the Metal Screw.

and

$$LCL_{\bar{x}} = 0.500 - 0.729(0.18) = 0.369 \text{ in.},$$

where $A_2 = 0.729$ for $n = 4$.

We plotted the values for $\bar{x}$ for the last five samples (Table 19.8) on the $\bar{x}$-chart in Fig. 19.8. The value for sample 5 falls above the upper control limit, which indicates that the process average is out of control and that we should look for assignable causes. Perhaps we could use a fishbone chart (see Chapter 18) to help determine whether machines, operators, or materials are at fault. There is always a slight chance that the value for $\bar{x}$ for sample 5 is due to completely random causes. Nevertheless, we would make the search because chances are that we can identify the cause for the poor performance in that sample.

MANAGERIAL CONSIDERATIONS FOR PROCESS CONTROL

The three critical decisions needed for process control charts are the sample size, the chart design, and the sampling frequency. We now turn to some of the managerial considerations involved in selecting these parameters. In this section, we also address the issue of inspection station locations.

Sample Size

The ultimate in process control is to test each item to make sure that it satisfies design specifications. Often, this is not possible, particularly when the test involves the destruction of the item or the test is very technical and time-consuming. Consequently, the choice of sample size has economic as well as control implications.

p-Charts Versus $\bar{x}$-Charts. Earlier we said that p-charts are based on attribute measures and are useful in situations where quality can be easily checked and the acceptance decision is a simple yes or no. The ease of measuring quality characteristics (compared to variable measures) is accompanied by the requirement for larger sample sizes. The magnitude of the difference varies, but an attribute control chart may require as much as 4–100 times the sample size of that required for a variables control chart. Typical $\bar{x}$-charts use sample sizes of 4 or 5, whereas the sample size for a p-chart must be large enough to detect at least one defective item on the average. For example, the population proportion defective in our banking services example was 0.005, requiring a bare minimum sample size of 200. The reason that we can use smaller sample sizes for $\bar{x}$-charts is that we can derive much more information from the variable measures. Consequently, unless variable measures take far more effort than attribute measures, variable control charts are usually less expensive to operate.

Degree of Control. Another consideration is the effect of sample size on degree of control. Recall that the standard deviation for the p-chart has n in the denominator. Also note that in Table 19.7 the value of A_2 decreases as the sample size increases. This relationship implies that, as the sample size increases, the control *limits* on the control charts move closer to the central line, or target process average. Thus we are more likely to detect a shift in the process average. For example, when we use an $\bar{x}$-chart, sample sizes of 4 or 5 are usually sufficient to detect a relatively large shift in the process average (say, 2 standard deviations). However, we would need a sample size of 3–5 times larger to detect shifts of only 1 standard deviation. Here again, management must balance the cost of inspection against the cost of not detecting a shift in the process average.

Homogeneity. We should choose a sample size that represents subgroups of output that are as homogeneous as possible. When significant deviations occur and we can identify assignable causes, we want the causes to show up as differences between subgroups and not as differences between members of a subgroup. For example, suppose that we have a two-shift operation, with each shift capable of producing 500 units. If we choose a sample size of 2000, we could be masking one of the assignable causes of quality problems: differences in output quality by shift. It might be better in this case to take samples that are homogeneous by shift, so that we can determine whether the problems occur during one particular shift.

Japanese $n = 2$ Philosophy. Some Japanese companies reduce the sample size to only two units, regardless of the quality characteristic to be measured. For each lot produced, only the first unit and the last unit are inspected. The assumption is that, if production of the first and last units is under control, the intervening production is also under control. Even though the samples are not random, the method works well in repetitive manufacturing situations with small-lot production. Definite starting and ending points (discrete lot production) are needed, along with a process that, if it goes out of control during the production of the lot, will stay out of control until the end of the lot. Small-lot production is needed because, otherwise, a large amount of defective items can be produced before the problem is detected.

Chart Design

Two decisions that affect degree of control are the choices of the center line for the chart and the spread in the control limits.

Selecting the Central Line. We have two possible choices for the central line of a control chart. One is to use the average of past averages ($\bar{\bar{x}}$) of the quality characteristic. This approach would be useful if we consider past performance to be under control and want to continue to monitor quality from that benchmark.

The other possibility is to use a value specified by management to achieve certain goals. In other words, the central line could be related to a desired machine or process setting but with some design specifications in mind. For example, Fig. 19.9 shows the relationship of the central line to the design specifications for the weight of a box of cereal. Since the net weight printed on the product's box is 18 ounces, the lower tolerance level is 18 ounces. To avoid too much waste, the upper tolerance level is set at 18.0500 ounces. The machine that fills the boxes has some natural variability. Note that the range of natural process variability is within the design tolerance range in this example. If this were not the case, the product designers would have designed a product that the production process would not be able to produce consistently. The machine is set to fill boxes with 18.0250 ounces of cereal. Consequently, the central line of the $\bar{x}$-chart corresponds to the machine setting. The control limits are closer to the central line than are the limits of the process variability because the control limits are for *averages* of a sample of boxes, whereas process variability relates to individual boxes.

Control Limit Spread. In our examples of control charts we used control limits that were three standard deviations from the central line. We could have chosen other control limits. Figure 19.10 shows the effects of changing k in a p-chart. You can see that as we change from $k = 3$ to $k = 2$, we increase the probability of detecting a shift in the process average, but we also increase the probability of looking for an assignable cause when the process average has not shifted. Our choice of k would depend on the cost of looking for assignable causes when none exist versus the cost of not detecting a shift. In general, charts with $k = 1.5$ or $k = 2$ are more economical than those with $k = 3$, if

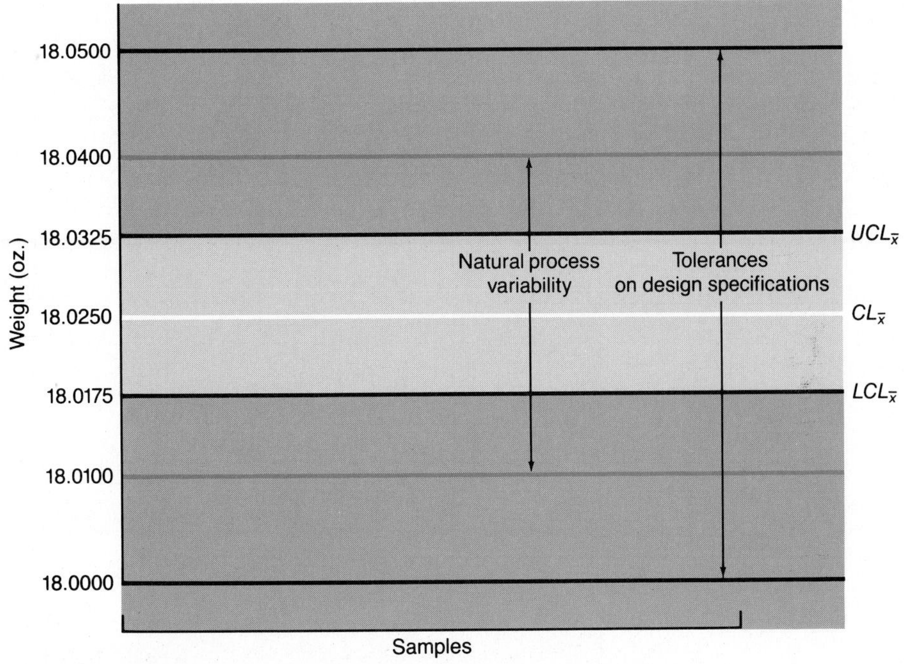

Figure 19.9

Setting the Central Line Relative to Design Specifications.

we can determine inexpensively and quickly whether something is wrong. If the cost of looking for the cause of a problem is high, charts with $k = 3$ or $k = 4$ might be more useful and economical.

Frequency of Inspection

Another managerial consideration is the frequency of inspection. Generally speaking, large samples taken frequently afford the best protection against shifts in the process average, but such plans are costly. The practical trade-off is typically between large samples taken less frequently and small samples taken more frequently. If a shift causes a high loss rate, it is usually best to take small samples on a frequent basis, so that the larger samples do not mask the change that is occurring in the process shift.

Interrelationships

It is obvious from our discussion that sample sizes, control limits, and the frequency of inspection are not independent decisions. Sample sizes affect the control limits and, for a given sample size, our choice of control limit

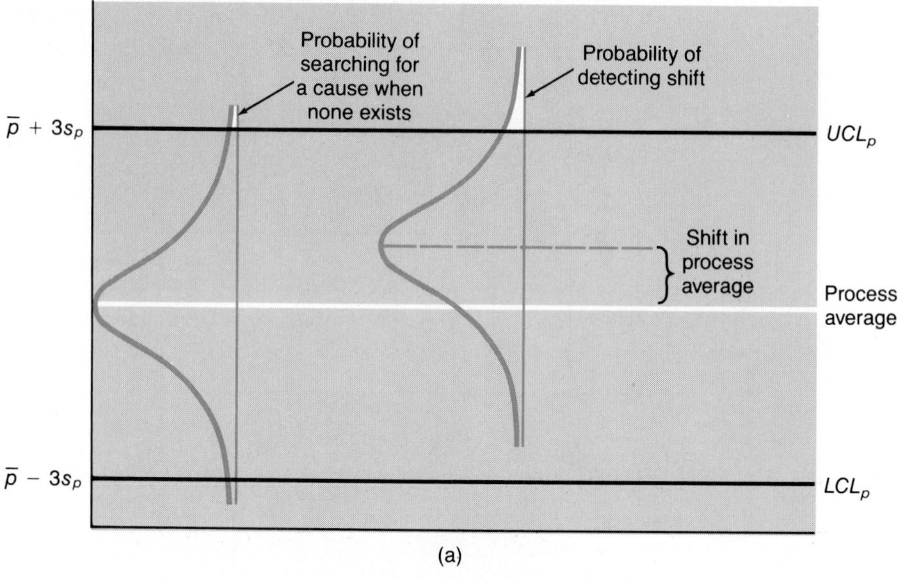

(a)

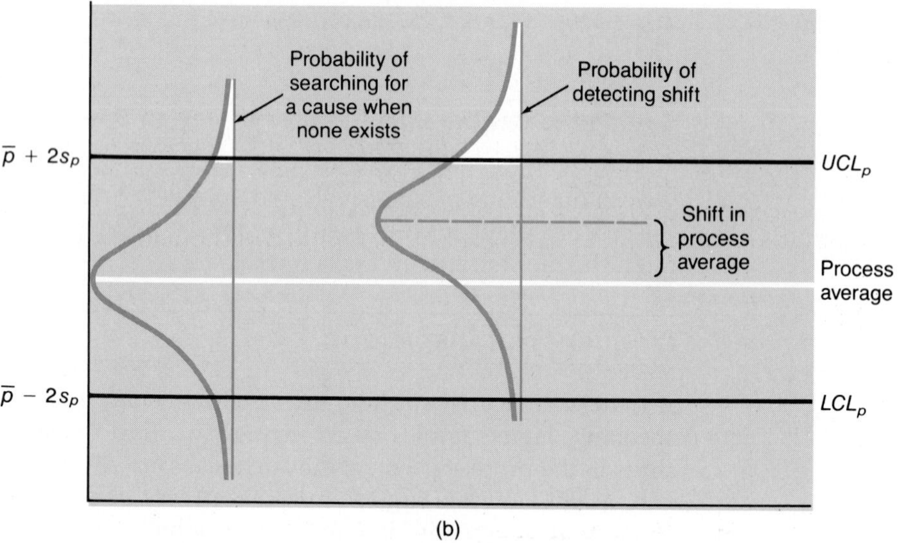

(b)

Figure 19.10

Effects of Changing *k* in a *p*-Chart: (a) *k* = 3; (b) *k* = 2.

spread affects the probability of detecting shifts or searching for causes when none exist. The frequency of inspection depends on the sample size and the control limits. An effective process control system requires the careful consideration of these three interdependent control chart parameters.

Location of Inspection Stations

Before any decisions regarding the location of inspection stations can be made, the aspects of quality important to the consumer and the steps in the production process that affect those characteristics must be identified. A fishbone chart (see Chapter 18) is a good way to identify the critical steps in the process that relate to the important quality characteristics. These critical steps occur in three different stages of the total process: raw-material inputs, work-in-process, and finished products or services.

The inspection of purchased materials is important to ensure the proper quality of the inputs to the production process. At this early stage of the process, various acceptance-sampling plans could be used (such as the ones we discussed earlier in this chapter).

The location of inspection stations is usually more involved at the work-in-process stage. Conceivably, we could put an inspection station after each step in the process, but this would be very costly. Testing can require highly skilled inspectors or expensive technology. A *zero-defects* program, which has the goal of not passing defective materials from one step in the process to the next, requires discipline in the work force but greatly reduces the need for inspection stations. In deciding on the number and location of inspection stations, we have to remember that we cannot inspect quality into the product; we can only detect that the process is not operating according to our specifications and then take corrective action. Thus, even with a zero-defects program, we would need to have some inspection stations. Using a fishbone chart or a process flow chart, we can identify the steps in the process where we should check important quality characteristics. We should also check quality just prior to the steps that involve costly operations. The cost of inspecting materials at any location should be balanced against the cost of passing defective materials to the next step.

Final inspections are made after the product or service has been finished. In the case of manufacturing systems, the inspections are made just prior to stocking the finished product or shipping it to the customer. Product failures discovered at this point result in (1) scrapping the defective items or batch; (2) routing the defective items or batch to a previous step in the process for rework; or (3) routing the defective items or batch to a special area for diagnosis and correction of the defects. Final inspections in service systems involve similar considerations; however, in many cases, the customer plays a major role in the inspection process. Table 19.9 contains some examples of final inspection procedures used in manufacturing and service processes.

Table 19.9

Examples of Final Inspection Procedures

• Semiconductor manufacturing	Semiconductors are tested for their conformance to specifications. Those that do not meet the specifications but are above some minimal performance level can be sold as a different, lower grade product. Those that fall below the minimal performance level are scrapped.
• Plastic bottle manufacturing	Plastic bottles that do not conform to specifications on wall thickness or neck diameter are shredded and reused as raw material in the production of new bottles.
• Glue manufacturing	Batches of glue are pumped from the reactor to holding vessels where they are checked for viscosity, percentage solids, ph level, and amount of grit. A chemist checks the batch and may order adding water, removing water, or filtering the batch in the holding vessel.
• Automotive repair	The mechanic test-drives the car before returning it to the customer. If problems remain, previous repair procedures may have to be repeated. The customer may also request some rework.
• TV repair	The TV repairperson tests the TV before returning it to the customer. Premature failure of replaced components results in the customer returning the set for more repair.
• Hair styling	The hairstylist works with the customer until the customer is satisfied.
• Hotels	Most hotels have customer-survey cards in each room, which allow the customer to grade the quality of service provided by the hotel.

CHAPTER HIGHLIGHTS

Acceptance-sampling plans and statistical process control methods are useful for appraising the degree of quality performance and identifying where problems exist in quality reliability. Some of the highlights of the chapter are:

- Acceptance sampling is concerned with the decision to accept or reject a certain quantity of goods. The design of the acceptance-sampling process includes decisions about sampling versus complete inspection, attribute versus variable measures, AQL, α,

LTPD, β, the sample size, and the acceptable number of defective items in the sample.

- Sampling using attribute measures can be done with single-sample, double-sample, or sequential-sample plans. Double-sample and sequential-sample plans have an advantage over single-sample plans because the average sample size needed to make a decision is less when the lot proportion defective is either very low or very high. Management can select the best plan (choice of sample size n and acceptance number c) by using an operating characteristic curve.
- Process control charts are useful for measuring the current quality generated by the process and for detecting whether the process has changed to the detriment of quality. The use of p-charts and $\bar{x}$-charts can help to identify abnormal variations in the process average. If abnormal variation is present, a search for assignable causes is initiated. The use of R-charts can help to define abnormal variations in the process variability.
- The process variability should be in control before process average control charts are constructed. The reason is that the average range is used in the calculation of control limits for process average control charts. Crucial decisions in the design of control charts are the sample size, the central line of the control chart and control limits, and the frequency of sampling. All three decisions are interrelated.
- The use of p-charts requires a larger sample size than do $\bar{x}$-charts, but the measurement of attributes may be easier than the measurement of variables. Larger samples provide greater protection in detecting a shift in the process average than do smaller samples. Also, the sample should be homogeneous with respect to potential causes of quality problems.
- The central line of a control chart can be the average of past averages of the quality measurement or a management target related to the design specifications of a product. The spread in control limits affects the chances of detecting a shift in the process average or range, as well as the chances of looking for assignable causes when none exist.
- In practice, a decision must be made between small samples taken frequently versus large samples taken less frequently.
- Inspection stations should be located at the point where incoming materials are received, at selected points in the process, and at the end of the process. The cost of inspection should be weighed against the cost of passing defective items downstream in the process and defective products to the customer.

KEY TERMS

acceptable quality level (AQL)
acceptance sampling
attribute measures
consumer's risk (β)
double-sample plan
lot tolerance proportion defective (LTPD)
operating characteristic (OC) curve
p-chart
producer's risk (α)
R-chart
sequential-sample plan
single-sample plan
variable measures
$\bar{x}$-chart

STUDY QUESTIONS

1. Using sampling to determine conformance to quality specifications involves certain risks. What are they?
2. Explain the trade-offs that are made in choosing the sample size n and the acceptance number c in a single-sample plan for attributes.
3. What are the considerations involved in choosing between sampling and complete inspection? Between variable and attribute measures?
4. How can an operating characteristic curve help management settle on the design parameters for a single-sample plan?
5. For a given AQL and LTPD, what is the effect on α and β in a single-sample plan of increasing the acceptance number c while holding the sample size n constant? Explain.
6. For a given AQL and LTPD, what is the effect on α and β in a single-sample plan of increasing the sample size n while holding the acceptance number c constant? Explain.
7. Compare and contrast single-sample plans, double-sample plans, and sequential-sample plans. What are the implications for inspection costs?
8. What is the rationale for having upper and lower control limits in process control charts?
9. What are the critical design parameters that must be specified for control charts? Are they interrelated? Explain.
10. What factors should be considered regarding the location of inspection stations?

PROBLEMS

1. An inspection station has been installed between two production processes. The feeder process, when operating correctly, has an acceptable quality level of 0.03. The consuming process, which is expensive, has a specified lot tolerance proportion defective of 0.08. The feeding process produces in batch sizes and, if a batch is rejected by the inspector, the entire batch must be checked and the defective items reworked. Consequently, management wants no more than a 5 percent producer's risk and, because of the expensive process that follows, no more than a 10 percent chance of accepting a lot with 8 percent defectives or worse.
   (a) Specify a single-sample plan for this inspection station.
   (b) Explain how the inspector should use your plan.

2. The Lustre-Potion Shampoo Company purchases the label that is pasted on each bottle of shampoo it sells. The label contains the company logo, name of the product, a decorative design, and directions for the use of the product. Sometimes the printing on the label is blurred or the colors are not right. The company would like to design an acceptance sampling plan for the purchased item. The acceptable quality level is 0.03, while the lot tolerance proportion defective is 0.10. Management would like to find a plan where the producer's risk is 0.05 or less and the consumer's risk is 0.10 or less.

Specify a plan that satisfies these directives.

3. Consider a certain raw material for which a single-sample plan using attribute measures is needed. The AQL is 0.014 and the LTPD is 0.050. Two plans have been proposed:

Plan 1	Plan 2
$n = 100$ $c = 3$	$n = 200$ $c = 6$

Are the two plans equivalent? Substantiate your response by determining the producer's and consumer's risks for each plan. Use the chart in Appendix D.4.

4. The Webster Chemical Company produces mastics and caulking for the construction industry. The product is blended in large mixers and then pumped into tubes and capped. The company is concerned about the possibility of underfilling the tubes, thereby short-changing the customer. Twenty samples of 200 tubes each had the record of underfilled tubes shown in Table 19.10.

(a) Construct a p-chart for this situation. You may use $k = 3$ and the historical average proportion defective in Table 19.10 as the central line of the chart.

(b) Comment on the process average proportion defective, given the samples in Table 19.10.

5. The data processing department of the Westerville Bank has 5 keypunch operators. Each day a random sample of 250 cards is verified for accuracy. A card containing one or more errors is considered defective and must be redone. The results of the last 25 samples are shown in Table 19.11.

(a) Based on this historical data, set up a p-chart using $k = 3$.

(b) Samples for the next four days were as follows:

Sample	Number of Defective Cards
26	17
27	15
28	22
29	21

Table 19.10

Sample Number	Number of Underfilled Tubes	Sample Number	Number of Underfilled Tubes
1	12	12	20
2	16	13	4
3	8	14	8
4	24	15	16
5	20	16	8
6	4	17	24
7	16	18	8
8	12	19	16
9	28	20	12
10	8	Total	284
11	20		

Table 19.11

Sample	Number of Defective Cards	Sample	Number of Defective Cards
1	7	14	4
2	5	15	11
3	19	16	8
4	10	17	12
5	11	18	4
6	8	19	6
7	12	20	11
8	9	21	17
9	6	22	12
10	13	23	6
11	18	24	7
12	5	25	13
13	16	Total	250

What is your assessment of the keypunch process? Explain.

6. The Emerald Dormer is a luxury hotel in Key West, Florida. The manager of the hotel was interested in the overall quality of service the hotel was providing to its customers. A unique customer survey system was developed to collect data and help the manager to make a judgment. Each customer was given a survey card and a blank envelope. The survey card contained a number of specific questions about various services and asked the customer to score the overall service on a scale from 0 to 100, with 100 considered excellent. The customer could fill out the card anonymously and put it in the envelope. If it was given to the desk clerk at checkout, the customer received a 5 percent discount on the bill. The program was very successful, and only a negligible number of customers ever turned in blank cards.

   The manager of the hotel considered a score of 75 on the overall evaluation the breakpoint between acceptable and unacceptable service. Each week, 100 envelopes were picked at random, opened, and examined. If the overall score on a card was less than 75, the card was considered "defective." The manager felt that an average proportion defective of 0.20 meant that service was in control (that is, 80 percent of the customers thought service was good or better).

   (a) Specify the control limits of a *p*-chart for the manager of the hotel. Since service is considered so important, $k = 2$ is desired. The cost of searching for service quality problems is far outweighed by the cost of a shift in overall customer satisfaction with the service received.

(b) The following are the results of the past 5 weeks of sampling.

Sample	Score of <75
March 1	17
March 8	10
March 15	18
March 22	30
March 29	25

Suppose that you are in charge of recording the results of the samples. What would you tell the manager about the overall service quality of the hotel? Would you make any recommendations?

7. The Stosh Motor Company purchases engine bolts for its model X-350 high performance racing engine. If defective, the bolts typically have damaged threads or improper diameters. A defect can be easily discovered by threading the bolt into a block of steel having a hole of correct threading and diameter. Although the test is simple, thousands of bolts have to be checked each time a shipment arrives. If a defective bolt is passed to the assembly line there is a chance that the threads in the engine block hole will be damaged or that the bolt may work itself loose during operation of the engine.

Stosh management has specified in the purchase agreement with the bolt supplier that good quality is considered to be 2 percent or less defectives. Stosh management decided that shipments with 7 percent or more defectives should not be accepted because of the costs involved. The producer's risk should be 0.05, and the consumer's risk should be 0.10. Find the single-sample plan having the smallest sample size that meets or exceeds these specifications.

8. The Mega-Byte Academy is an exclusive school for teaching the fine art of computer programming. Only those students who have impeccable scholastic records and a high aptitude for programming are admitted. In an attempt to judge and monitor the quality of instruction, the administration devised an examination to test students on the basic concepts that all should have learned. The test is not a final examination for graduation; the results are used for tracking the output of this educational facility.

Each year, a random sample of 10 graduating students is selected for the test. The average score is used to track the quality of the educational process. Prior experience with this exam indicates that the average range of student scores is 20. Test results for the past 10 years are

Year	Sample $\bar{x}$	Year	Sample $\bar{x}$
1975	80.31	1980	80.62
1976	74.37	1981	75.00
1977	78.12	1982	81.87
1978	80.00	1983	74.06
1979	81.25	1984	77.50

(a) Set up an $\bar{x}$-chart using this historical information.

(b) This year the exam was given again. Scores for individual students were

59 60 90 85 72

63 71 57 68 74

What comments would you make to the administration of Mega-Byte Academy?

9. Consider a production line that produces a part every minute. The critical quality characteristic is the diameter of the part, measured in thousandths of an inch. Management would like to detect any shift in the process average diameter from 0.0025 in. Management considers the variance of the process to be in control. His-

torically, the average range has been 0.004 in., regardless of the process average. You have been asked to design an $\bar{x}$-chart to control this process. The center line of the chart should be 0.0025 in. and the control limits should be 3 σ from the central line. The sample size and the frequency of sampling was left to you to analyze.

In order to test your design, management has provided the results of 80 minutes of output from the production line (Table 19.12). During this 80 minutes the process average changed once. All measurements are in thousandths of an inch.

(a) Set up an $\bar{x}$-chart with $n = 4$. The frequency should be sample 4, then skip 4. Thus your first sample would be for minutes 1–4, the second would be for minutes 9–12, and so on. When would you stop the process to check for a change in the process average?

(b) Set up an $\bar{x}$-chart with $n = 8$. The frequency should be sample 8, then skip 4.
   (i) When would you stop the process now?
   (ii) What can you say about the desirability of large samples on a frequent sampling interval?

10. Using the data from Problem 9, continue your analysis of sample size and frequency by trying the following plans.
   (a) Using the $\bar{x}$-chart for $n = 4$, try the frequency sample 4, then skip 8. When would you stop the process in this case?

Table 19.12

Minute	Diameter	Minute	Diameter	Minute	Diameter	Minute	Diameter
1	22	21	28	41	27	61	26
2	27	22	26	42	26	62	29
3	29	23	27	43	25	63	25
4	25	24	24	44	32	64	33
5	23	25	21	45	30	65	26
6	28	26	30	46	25	66	28
7	26	27	23	47	23	67	32
8	30	28	22	48	29	68	30
9	26	29	21	49	31	69	26
10	26	30	28	50	24	70	29
11	21	31	27	51	29	71	33
12	24	32	31	52	27	72	24
13	25	33	23	53	32	73	25
14	28	34	27	54	28	74	27
15	23	35	29	55	25	75	32
16	24	36	30	56	29	76	28
17	25	37	28	57	32	77	29
18	26	38	27	58	27	78	30
19	25	39	25	59	30	79	31
20	20	40	29	60	24	80	26

(b) Using the $\bar{x}$-chart for $n = 8$, try the frequency sample 8, then skip 8. When would you consider the process out of control?

(c) Using your results from parts (a) and (b), what trade-offs would you consider in choosing between them?

11. The Watson Electric Company produces a certain brand of incandescent light bulb. The following data on the number of lumens for each light bulb were collected when the process was in control.

	Observation			
Sample	1	2	3	4
1	604	612	588	600
2	597	601	607	603
3	581	570	585	592
4	620	605	595	588
5	590	614	608	604

Since the time that those data were collected, some new employees were added to the work force. A new sample was taken and had the following readings: 570, 603, 623, and 583. Is the process still in control?

SELECTED REFERENCES

Charbonneau, Harvey C., and Gordon L. Webster, *Industrial Quality Control.* Englewood Cliffs, N.J.: Prentice-Hall, 1978.

Crosby, Philip B., *Quality is Free: The Art of Making Quality Certain.* New York: McGraw-Hill, 1979.

Dodge, Harold F., and Harry G. Romig, *Sampling Inspection Tables—Single and Double Sampling,* 2d ed. New York: John Wiley & Sons, 1959.

Duncan, Acheson, J., *Quality Control and Industrial Statistics,* 4th ed. Homewood, Ill.: Richard D. Irwin, 1974.

Feigenbaum, A. V., *Total Quality Control: Engineering Management.* New York: McGraw-Hill, 1961.

Fetter, Robert B., *The Quality Control System.* Homewood, Ill.: Richard D. Irwin, 1967.

Ishikawa, Kaoru, *Guide to Quality Control.* Tokyo: Asian Productivity Organization, 1972.

Juran, J. M., and F. M. Gryna, *Quality Planning and Analysis.* New York: McGraw-Hill, 1970.

Saniga, Erwin M., and Larry E. Shirland, "Quality Control in Practice—A Survey," *Quality Progress,* May 1977, pp. 30–33.

Wald, A., *Sequential Analysis.* New York: John Wiley & Sons, 1947.

CHAPTER 20

OPERATIONS AS A COMPETITIVE WEAPON

Some Managerial Issues

- How can we make operations an effective competitive weapon?
- What are other companies doing to meet the competitive challenge?
- How should we link our positioning strategy with the other decision areas in operations?
- How much of the *Japanese approach* makes sense for our industry?
- How can we diagnose problems in operations and monitor its vital signs?
- What are our high-leverage opportunities for improvement?

Chapter Outline

We now come full circle, pulling together the various topics covered into a unified view of operations management. It is also time to return to the troubling productivity trends presented in Chapter 1: U.S. manufacturers have not been doing well in terms of productivity, and the record for the service industry is as bad or worse. Our concern in operations management is to improve productivity in both segments of the economy. It seems obvious to us that the decision to improve productivity is mandatory, not optional.

British, Japanese, and U.S. executives agree on one point: Among all the functions in business, operations management is the most important source of productivity improvements (McInnes, 1984). A strategic approach to operations, backed by careful analysis, is fundamental to such improvements. Three points on operations strategy, first stated in Chapter 1, need repeating here:

1. Operations can be either a competitive weapon or a millstone.
2. Fundamental (and strategic) choices must be addressed first, but success also depends on tactical choices.
3. Decisions in operations should be linked.

In this chapter, we address each of these points. We begin by presenting examples of what various companies are doing to make operations a competitive weapon. These examples show that many things, ranging from fundamental choices such as competitive priorities to tactical choices such as scheduling, must be done well. This information underscores the first two points. We address the third point, linking decisions in a consistent way, in two ways by: (1) describing how decisions in operations relate to positioning strategy; and (2) examining the linkage of elements in the *Japanese approach*. We conclude with discussion of a diagnostic approach for gaining a competitive advantage.

WHAT INDUSTRY IS DOING

What is the best avenue for making operations a competitive weapon? The examples in Box 20.1 give us considerable insight into how firms contend with the competitive challenge. The relevant decision areas of operations management are identified in parentheses in each example. Productivity is essentially the ratio of the value of outputs to the value of inputs. The steps taken by the J. C. Penney Company remind us that productivity improvement is not limited to cost reduction (the ratio's denominator). Productivity can improve even when the value of inputs rises, so long as the value of outputs rises even faster. The steps taken by GM and by Black and Decker cover practically every decision area in operations management: competitive priorities, quality management, product design, process design, work-force management, location, inventory, and scheduling. The same story emerges from approaches taken by hospitals, Pan Am, United Airlines, and Marriott. Some types of productivity improvement are particularly fashionable these days. They include computerized information systems, new technological options (such as message exchange systems, robots, and FMS), and programs enhancing the firm's human resources (such as quality circles and supervisory training). However, many companies are achieving excellence by doing many little things well, not looking for a single cure or magic formula. Low productivity can be only partially blamed on government regulation (such as EPA), a strong dollar, or an intractable union. The ultimate responsibility lies with management and the work force.

DECISION LINKAGES

Making operations management a competitive weapon means that decisions about designing and operating the production system should be consistent and linked. If the decisions are inconsistent and independent, they can act at cross-purposes and hurt overall productivity. Results of surveys suggest that the lack of consistent, linked decisions is a key factor in lagging productivity (Judson, 1982). Most productivity improvement efforts are disjointed reactions to the latest symptoms of productivity problems. Only one-third of the firms surveyed link their efforts to improve productivity with their competitive priorities and positioning strategy. Achieving more agreement between corporate strategy and operations can result in higher profits (Richardson et al., 1985).

The process of linking decisions is depicted in Fig. 20.1. The cube repre-

Box 20.1

PRODUCTIVITY IMPROVEMENT AT SELECTED FIRMS

J. C. Penney plans to modernize 550 of its largest stores. The $1 billion price tag aims at renovating existing stores, rather than opening new ones (*capacity* and *location*). There will be a more stylish look, ranging from potted plants to striking graphics (*layout*). Some lines are dropped and others expanded (*product plans*), with an increased emphasis on quality (*competitive priority*). The sales at one of the first renovated stores rose almost 40 percent.

General Motors' "Project Saturn" was named after the U.S. effort to overcome Russia's early lead in space for a moon landing. It also is a come-from-behind effort, this time to eliminate the $2000-a-car cost differential now enjoyed by Japanese manufacturers. The new GM subsidiary aims at becoming one of the world's lowest-cost producers of small cars (*competitive priority*). Its $5 billion facility (*capacity*) located in Tennessee will have almost all major parts built in the immediate vicinity (*location*). A process called "simultaneous engineering" allows for better integration between product design engineers, manufacturing engineers, and marketers as the product is designed (*product design*) and the manufacturing process selected (*process design*). The new, highly integrated production process will be modernized in various ways, including intelligent robots and an innovative casting process (*technological choices*). The goal is to pare down from 175 labor-hours per car to only 30. Parts are to be assembled into larger modules (*positioning inventory*), and workers will perform a wider variety of tasks (*job design*). Purchases will be concentrated in fewer suppliers (*materials management*), with an expectation that they also will modernize, improve quality, and assume the burden of carrying inventory. The labor contract is innovative (*work-force management*), with increased union influence on operations in exchange for flexibility in seeking ways to improve productivity. Blue-collar workers will be paid salaries instead of hourly wages, and 20 percent of regular pay is tied to meeting productivity goals. A "consensus decision-making" structure has been added to the traditional grievance system. The union views the new president of the Saturn subsidiary as a people-oriented manager who makes workers feel important. Finally, GM is looking carefully at its joint venture with Toyota for new ways to reduce inventory (*inventory systems*) and improve quality (*quality management*).

The American Hospital Association reports that outpatient surgery rose 77 percent in 5 years, while inpatient operations dropped 7 percent.

sents the firm, which consists of various functional areas. Each function is represented by a vertical slice of the cube, and each involves a different set of decisions. The operations function is shown in front, so that you can see the specific decision areas assigned to it (listed on the nearest face of the cube). These decision areas were first introduced in Chapter 1 (Table 1.3). We then

This trend reflects a push to cut health-care costs, the growth of so called "free-standing surgery centers," (*product plans*) and advances in medical technology (*process design*).

Black and Decker is struggling to meet Japanese competition head-on. It spent $256 million to modernize plants, with strong interest in robots and flexible machining (*process design*). It dropped the chain-saw business while adding new products such as the hand-held vacuum sweeper (*product plans*). Some plants have been closed (*capacity*), while others have been carefully rearranged to minimize the distance traveled by components through the plant (*layout*). Workers are divided into teams at its Hampstead facility (*work-force management*), hoping to inspire pride and greater quality-consciousness (*quality management*). One of the pioneers in introducing materials requirements planning in the 1970s (*inventory systems*), the firm is truly international, with operations in 55 different countries (*location*).

Airline companies have made several changes to improve operations. Pan Am took steps to relieve the bottleneck at Kennedy airport, which handled 43 percent of its capacity (*capacity* and *location*). Its schedule of connecting flights (*scheduling*), baggage transfer system (*process design* and *layout*), and flying on time (*competitive priority*) were concerns. United Airlines has moved from long-haul flights with big jets to traffic hubs and shorter spoke routes with midsized jets (*scheduling* and *capacity*). It cut its work force by 20 percent and seeks wage concessions from unions (*work-force management*).

J. Willard Marriott, Jr., chief executive officer of the Marriott Corporation, logged 200,000 miles to visit in one year more than 100 of the chain's hotels and resorts. He believes that productivity improvement comes from direct contact with customers and employees (*work-force management*). He even makes spot-checks at all hours (*quality management*) of conditions ranging from dishes to laundry facilities to lobby appearance. This attention to detail communicates the importance of each person's role in the organization.

Sources: "Gearing Down," *Wall Street Journal*, May 14, 1984; "Black and Decker Meets Japan's Push Head-On in Power-Tool Market," *Wall Street Journal*, February 18, 1983; "Pan Am Conducts Major Shake-Up to Improve Its Weak Performance," *Wall Street Journal*, April 26, 1984.

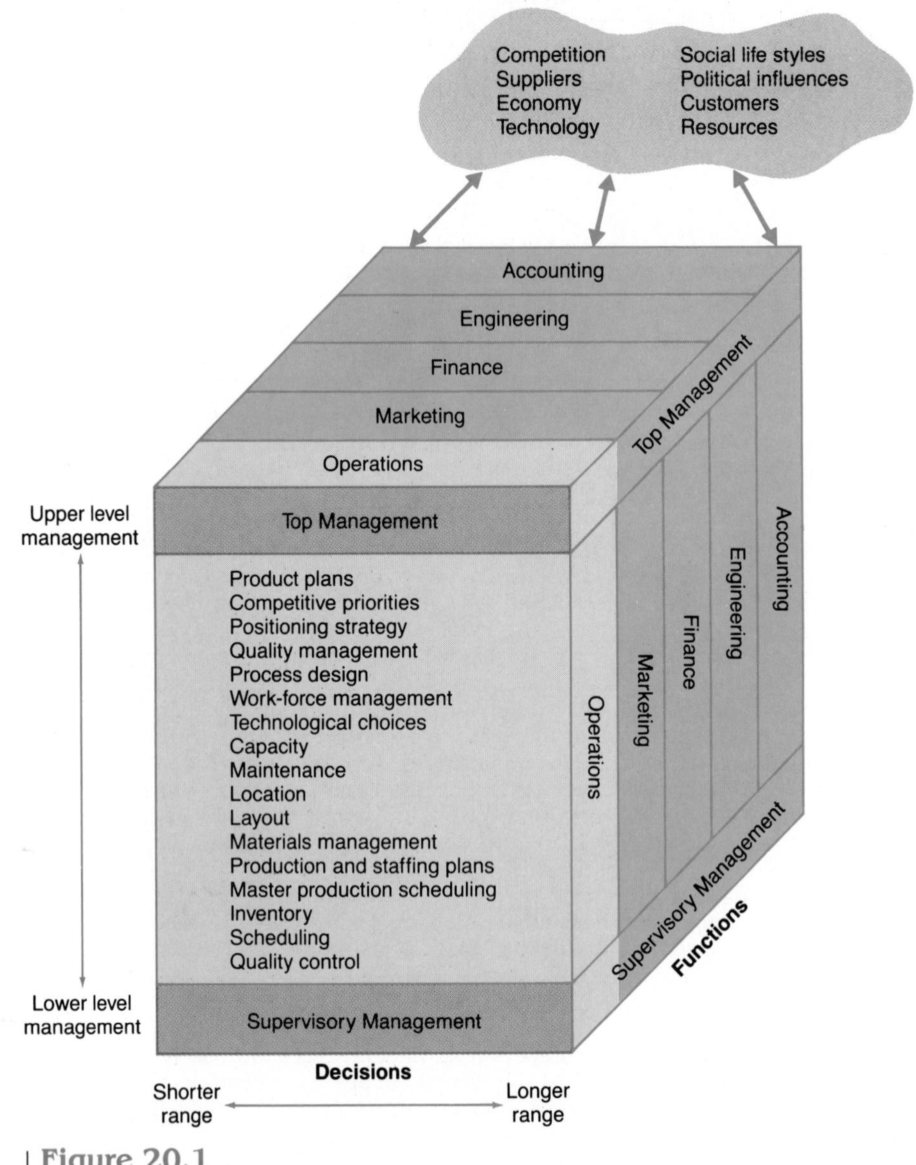

Figure 20.1

Linking Decisions to Corporate Strategy.

Source: We are indebted to Aleda V. Roth for much of this representation.

covered each one in subsequent chapters.* Collectively, they are the essence of operations management. The more strategic long-range decision areas extend downward from the top, while the more tactical short-range decisions extend upward from the bottom. The sequence of chapters was based on this hierarchy.†

Figure 20.1 shows top management at the top of the cube, with supervisory-level management at the bottom. Top management monitors the external environment (the cloud at the top), such as for changes in competition, suppliers, customers, and technology. Changes in the environment eventually lead to changes in corporate strategy. Top management ultimately is responsible for making sure that decisions at the functional-area level are linked to and support the revised corporate strategy.

Linking decisions within the operations function was emphasized in many of the preceding chapters. The next several sections summarize the linking process, as represented in Fig. 20.2, at four decision levels.

- Level 1: Positioning decisions.
- Level 2: Design decisions.
- Level 3: Capacity and location decisions.
- Level 4: Operating decisions.

Figure 20.2 shows that positioning decisions serve as the basis for decisions at the other levels. If positioning decisions are properly linked to other decisions, operations becomes a competitive weapon. For example, a high-volume commodities manufacturer is unlikely to compete successfully on cost, if it has a process focus and general-purpose equipment; the flexibility is not needed and efficiency is lessened. The patterns described in the following sections are *tendencies* rather than unbreakable rules, and many exceptions can be found. For example, some assembly lines have a product focus but are labor intensive. In other cases, facilities offer customized products, but they all follow the same production-line flow, as in some plants that make adhesives and glues (where only the formula changes from one customized order to the next). Specific relationships are complex, but our only purpose is to present general patterns.

Level 1: Positioning Decisions

Corporate strategy connects with operations through positioning decisions. A *process focus* strategy means jumbled flows of products (or customers) through

---

* Forecasting (Chapter 3) and work measurement (Chapter 6) are not shown. They are best viewed as part of the management information system, which, along with important information from accounting, support decisions made by operations managers.

† The only exception is quality management, which was discussed later to lead into the chapter on quality control.

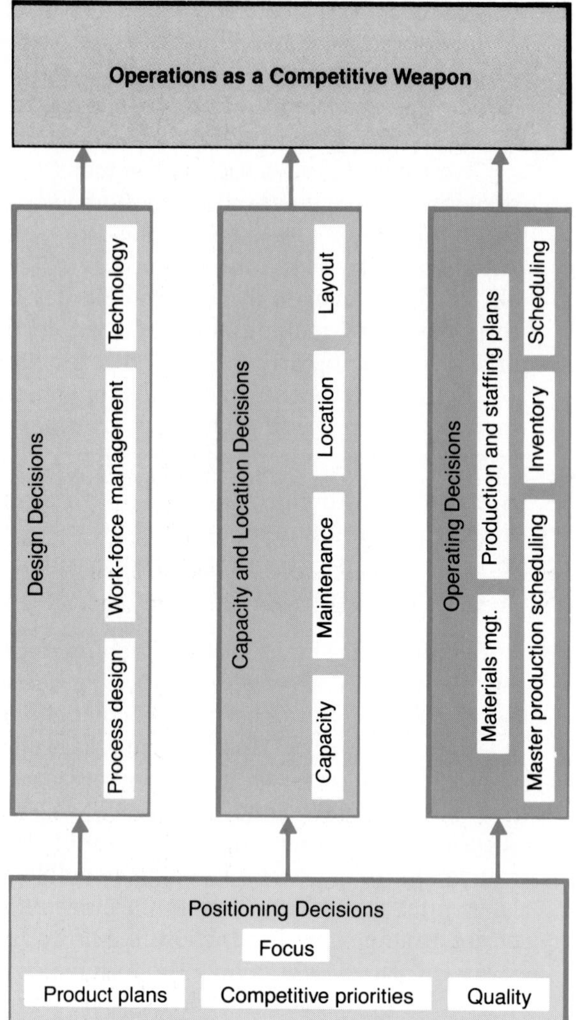

Figure 20.2

Linking Decisions within Operations Management.

the system. Flexibility is maximized by organizing resources around the process (or function performed). A *product focus* strategy is just the opposite, trading off flexibility to achieve standard routings, line flows, and resources organized by product. The best focus for a specific company depends on its product plans, competitive priorities, and quality choices, as shown in Table 20.1.

Product Plans and Competitive Priorities. Table 20.1 shows the linkage of positioning strategy with product plans and competitive priorities. When *product plans* call for more customized products, prices will be high and volumes low. Life cycles are shorter, and products tend to be in the earlier stages of their cycles. With such flux in product plans, it is unwise to dedicate resources to specific products. A process focus is best. Its flexibility handles the changing product mix, but at higher unit costs. This means that the *competitive priority* must not be cost. Product flexibility, superior quality, and volume flexibility are the other choices. They differentiate the product from others, preventing head-on cost competition. Fast delivery times are unlikely with a process focus. Customized products must be made from scratch, rather than held on the shelf awaiting demand that may never come. The emphasis is on meeting due date promises, rather than giving quick deliveries.

Quality Management. Table 20.1 also shows the linkage of positioning strategy to quality management. Reliable quality, which means consistently meeting product specifications, is important to all firms because scrap and rework are costly. The most important link with positioning strategy lies with the product specifications themselves. A firm choosing top-of-the-line quality as its competitive priority is likely to have a process focus. Prices must be higher,

Table 20.1

Linking Focus with Product Plans, Competitive Priorities, and Quality Management

Decision Area	Positioning Strategy: Process focus	Positioning Strategy: Product focus
Product planning	More customized products, with low volumes Shorter life cycles Products in earlier stages of life cycle An entrance–exit strategy favoring early exit	More standardized products, with high volumes Longer life cycles Products in later stages of life cycle An entrance–exit strategy favoring late exit
Competitive priorities	More emphasis on product and volume flexibility Long delivery times	More emphasis on low price Short delivery times
Quality management	High-performance design quality More work-force involvement Informal procedures	Consistent quality More automated inspection Formal procedures

resulting in lower product volumes. This approach rules out a product focus because resource utilization would be too low. There is another link: Firms choosing product or volume flexibility as a competitive priority are likely to be small and have a process focus. Their quality control procedures are less formal, and they depend largely on the work force to achieve reliable quality. Such was the case with Longhorn Products. (See Chapter 2.) High-volume firms with a product focus tend to have more staff specialists and inspectors, and the inspection operation might even be automated. They have formal procedures for monitoring incoming materials, process yields, and outgoing products. Scrap and rework are particularly disruptive to the line flows in a product-focused plant.

Level 2: Design Decisions

Designing the production system, both in terms of processes and the work force, should fit the positioning strategy. Table 20.2 shows these linkages.

Table 20.2

Linking Focus with Process Design Decisions and Work-Force Management

Decision Area	Positioning Strategy: Process focus	Positioning Strategy: Product focus
Process design	General purpose, flexible equipment	Specialized equipment dedicated to a few products
	Labor intensive, with less automation	Capital intensive, with more automation
	Attention on labor costs	Attention on facility utilization and overhead costs
	Less vertically integrated	More vertically integrated
Work-force management	Flexible work force	Specialized work force
	Enlarged jobs	Specialized jobs
	Informal promotion channels	Formal promotion channels
	Frequent two-way communication with supervisors	Less frequent two-way communication with supervisors
	Fewer staff specialists	More staff specialists

Process Design and Technology. A process focus means more general-purpose (and less efficient) equipment. Operations are more labor intensive, gaining flexibility but giving up rock-bottom costs. We discussed these differences in Chapter 2, using the process-focused Longhorn Products and the product-focused Suds Brewery as examples. Longhorn had an investment of about $10,000 per employee in equipment, but the Suds investment was almost $0.5 million per employee. A survey of 150 firms showed that the average capital investment for those having more of a process focus was only $17,000 per employee (Taylor, 1980). Those firms having more of a product focus had an average investment almost four times as large. Capital intensity and automation require high production volumes for effective equipment utilization. Typically, in the automotive industry, a new automated line was introduced with each model change. The cost was more than $20 million, which was quite a disincentive for frequent product changes. Only recently has the relationship between product volumes and capital intensity been broken in certain situations. Group technology, reprogrammable robots, and flexible machining can mean higher capital intensity, even with low product volumes and short life cycles.

Since a process-focused production system is more labor intensive, managers are particularly concerned about labor costs. Continuing attention is given to efficiency losses caused by setups, materials handling, and component delays. With a product focus, attention shifts to obtaining effective facility utilization because of the high capital intensity. Controlling the various overhead costs gains more and more management attention.

A final link is with vertical integration. With a process focus, where volumes are low and unit costs are high, a firm tends to rely more on outside suppliers to manufacture parts and assemblies for its products. Suppliers can achieve economies of scale by pooling the requirements of several process-focused firms. On the other hand, firms with a product focus have the option of doing more work in-house by integrating backward (make rather than buy) and forward (toward the customer).

Work-force Management. A process focus also favors a more flexible work force. Workers have more cross-training, in order to help out with the capacity imbalances and frequent shocks at a process-focused facility. This creates enlarged, broader jobs, which often serve to motivate workers. Small, process-focused firms have less formalized promotion channels and are less likely to be unionized. Until recent innovative contracts such as that at GM's Saturn facility, unions have favored narrow job boundaries and more formal promotion channels. Filling one opening sets off a chain reaction of bumping under the provisions of most labor contracts.

The unpredictability of day-to-day production requirements of a process focus places great importance on two-way communication between workers and supervisors to identify which work to do next and how it should be done.

Fewer supervisory tasks are diverted to task specialists. For example, forward scheduling of equipment is less critical (owing to lower capital intensity) and even less possible (owing to unpredictability). When equipment investment reaches $1 million per worker, as is true with some product-focused processes, more staff specialists can be justified for production planning and work design.

Level 3: Capacity and Location Decisions

Table 20.3 shows how positioning strategy fits with capacity, maintenance, location, and layout decisions.

Capacity. The most obvious link is the capacity cushion. (See Chapter 7.) It must be larger with a process focus because of low capital intensity (which reduces the cushion's cost), shifting product mixes (creating capacity imbalances), increased demand and supply uncertainties, greater scheduling complexity, and more uneven demands (peaks and valleys). Since capacity often comes in chunks, expanding by even the minimum increment can cre-

Table 20.3

Linking Focus with Capacity, Maintenance, Location, and Layout

	Positioning Strategy	
Decision Area	Process focus	Product focus
Capacity	Large capacity cushion	Small capacity cushion
	Large capacity imbalances	Small capacity imbalances
	Difficult to measure	Easy to measure
	Less of a management preoccupation	More of a management preoccupation
	Small economies of scale	Large economies of scale
Maintenance	Less maintenance intensity	More maintenance intensity
Location	Single facility	Multiple facilities
	Expand on site or relocate nearby	Expand by adding new facilities, possibly overseas
	More local or regional markets	More national or international markets
	Transportation costs not a primary location factor	Transportation costs sometimes a primary location factor
Layout	Process layouts	Product layouts
	Flexible	Inflexible
	Variable-path materials handling	Fixed-path, automated materials handling

ate a large cushion with the small volumes of a process focus. One study in particular confirms the link between positioning strategy and the capacity cushion (Taylor, 1980). Firms with more of a process focus averaged 10 shifts per week, whereas those with a product focus averaged 17. The maximum number of shifts possible is 21 per week [or 3 shifts/day (7 days/wk)].

Table 20.3 shows three other links to capacity. First, capacity is particularly difficult to measure with a process focus, since multiple products share the same equipment. Changing product mixes create imbalances and floating bottlenecks. Second, managers at facilities with a process focus are less preoccupied with capacity decisions. Equipment costs are low, and lead times to buy new, general-purpose equipment are shorter. Management does not need to plan so far ahead for capacity changes, and unit costs depend less on high utilization. Finally, economies of scale are less dramatic. With the facility's smaller size, it benefits less from spreading fixed costs (which are lower anyway) and from avoiding setups by dedicating resources to products.

Maintenance. Managers are less concerned about equipment failures when there is a process focus. There is less automation, and the cost of breakdown maintenance is not so high. Work stations tend to be decoupled from each other because of larger capacity cushions and substantial work-in-process inventories. Since equipment is more general purpose, jobs often can be rerouted to another piece of equipment. Disabling one work station does not shut down others, at least in the short run. Conversely, with line processes, failure at one operation can quickly shut down the entire line. This situation not only idles the work force, but it could also cause lost business opportunities. At some facilities with a product focus, this loss is as much as $300,000 per day.

Location. The most striking link is simply the number of facilities. Low-volume producers choose a process focus out of necessity. Since they are small, they usually have just one facility. They expand either on-site or by relocating nearby. They appeal to a local or regional market, which makes transportation costs less of a primary location factor. Even for distant customers, the product is not standardized enough to avoid costly direct shipments. High-volume producers, on the other hand, create multiple facilities, including a system of warehouses. Each facility can focus on product, market area, or process.

Layout. The layout translates positioning strategy into concrete form with either a *process layout* for a process focus or a *product layout* for a product focus. With a process layout, employees and equipment are grouped by function or process. All grinding is done by the grinding department, all bill processing by the accounts payable section, and all budget apparel displayed in the department store's basement. This approach makes supervision easier, helps foster worker flexibility, and improves responses to changing product mixes.

The jumbled routings, however, result in less efficient materials handling methods. Variable-path devices, such as carts, forklift tractors, and overhead cranes, must be used. Only with the line flows of a product focus can efficient fixed-path devices (such as conveyors) be utilized.

Level 4: Operating Decisions

Positioning strategy must also link with tactical decisions about operating (rather than designing) the facility. These linkages are shown in Table 20.4.

Materials Management. With a process focus, low repeatability and jumbled routings cause complexity. Last-minute changes by customers and vendors, imprecise time standards, and difficulties in predicting capacities create uncertainty. Because of the complexity and uncertainty, plans cannot be made far in advance. Planning is done more at a local, decentralized level to adapt to the latest conditions. Greater work-force and inventory cushions are tolerated because of the dynamic environment. A process focus also involves less formal relationships with suppliers. No long-term contracts are negotiated with key vendors. Raw-material volumes are low, so the firm has less control over suppliers, who naturally cater to larger customers. On the outbound side, distribution channels are less formal. Markets are likely to be local or regional, and an elaborate network of distribution centers is not needed. Products are more likely to be specials, which rules out positioning finished goods inventory at warehouses close to the customer. Direct shipments from the plant to the customer are the norm.

A final link with materials management deals with information requirements. With a process focus, information tends to be oriented to the bidding process and specific customer orders. Output plans are communicated by releasing jobs with detailed routing information. With a product focus, information is oriented more to demand forecasts and current inventory positions, rather than individual customer orders.

Production and Staffing Plans. A process focus allows more volume flexibility and changes in the output rate to meet seasonal or cyclical demand. One study showed that changing the output rate by using overtime, subcontracting, and extra shifts is about twice as common with a process focus (Taylor, 1980). A product focus is accompanied by a *level strategy,* letting anticipation inventory build during the slack season. A firm may even have enough clout to require customers take early delivery of the inventory. It is also better positioned for aggressive alternatives. The last resort for a product-focused firm is to shut down one of its plants entirely. There are five reasons for these links to a product focus:

Table 20.4

Linking Focus with Operating Decisions

Decision Area	Positioning Strategy: Process focus	Positioning Strategy: Product focus
Materials management	More complexity and uncertainty	Less complexity and uncertainty
	Shorter-range plans	Longer-range plans
	Higher tolerance for cushion of extra workers and inventory	Lower tolerance for cushion of extra workers and inventory
	Informal vendor and customer relationships	Formal vendor and customer relationships
	Information oriented to orders	Information oriented to forecasts
Production and staffing plans	More volume flexibility	Less volume flexibility
	Relies on overtime, subcontracting or extra shifts	Relies on anticipation inventory and aggressive alternatives
Master production scheduling	Inventory positioned lower in BOM	Inventory positioned higher in BOM
	Less stable MPS	More stable MPS
Inventory	Short runs	Long runs
	Longer cycle times and more WIP	Shorter cycle times and less WIP
	Component shortages	Capacity shortages
	Lot sizing and sequencing loosely coupled	Lot sizing and sequencing tightly coupled
	MRP system	JIT system
Scheduling	Fluid and changing	Stable
	Planned just a few days ahead	Planned many days ahead
	Decentralized decisions	Centralized decisions
	Labor-limited environment	Machine-limited environment

1. Overtime and extra shifts tend to be infeasible options, since the plant is more likely to be operating with three shifts already in order to maximize facility utilization.
2. A product focus implies low variable costs, making the extra cost of subcontracting prohibitive. Too much is lost by going outside to have the work done. It is also unlikely that a subcontractor can be found to supply the necessary volumes when business is booming.
3. Products are more standardized, making it possible to build anticipation inventory without fear of obsolescence.
4. Line processes are more rigid and tend to be set at specific output rates. Rebalancing a line means changing the jobs of many individuals. It is simpler to temporarily shut down a whole line when demand falls.
5. A high-volume producer is more likely to be able to influence the market or add new products as aggressive alternatives to level out the uneven demand pattern.

Master Production Schedule. The product flexibility of a process focus means that inventory must be created lower in the bills of materials. Inventory is not created by plan at higher levels because of low turnover and the fear of obsolescence. More intermediate items are likely to be produced to help increase part commonality, keep customer delivery times at acceptable levels, cut losses owing to setups, and buffer against bottlenecks. Another link is that the master production schedule is less stable with a process focus. There is a greater willingness to change the MPS to satisfy last-minute requests. Products are more likely to be custom-engineered, which raises the possibility of delays before the job is released to production because engineering changes are more frequent. Another cause of unstable schedules is that a small, process-focused firm such as Longhorn Products has much less clout with customers than the product-focused Suds Brewery. (See Chapter 2.)

Inventory. The positioning strategy also links with inventory decisions. Low volumes mean short runs, and at the extreme, special customer orders are matched with shop orders on a one-for-one basis. The shorter runs do not necessarily mean lower turnover, since demand is also lower. A 100-unit batch may represent a six-month supply in a job shop, but just a one-day supply with the high volumes of a product focus.

Items at a process-focused facility are routed through many work stations. Each station is a potential bottleneck and has a long waiting line. Lead times (or cycle times) are long and variable, which requires more work-in-process (WIP) inventory and more safety stock. For example, firms with a process focus reported that 36 percent of their inventory is WIP (Taylor, 1980). This level drops to only 18 percent with a product focus.

Table 20.4 shows three other links with inventory. Product flexibility and low-volume production make component availability the key concern of inventory planners at a process-focused facility. With the capital intensity of a product focus, the concern shifts to capacity shortages. Achieving plans that provide for adequate capacity forces inventory and sequencing decisions to be more highly integrated. Finally, product diversity lends itself to an order-based system such as MRP. Its logic is particularly appropriate for ensuring component availability. The repetitiveness of high-volume production indicates the need for a system such as JIT.

Scheduling. Process-focused facilities have fluid and changing schedules because both demand and supply are less certain. Reactive, crisis-oriented scheduling is not as apparent with a product focus. Instead, scheduling and monitoring of day-to-day performance is more elaborate. Because of the high cost of idle resources, schedules are developed further into the future, often on a more centralized basis. When inventory decoupling operations are stripped away, more attention must be given to scheduling in order to maximize facility utilization and customer service. In some cases, lead times to customers might even have to be extended to get better utilization. At medical facilities, for example, attempts are made to achieve better utilization by an appointment system. Patients are scheduled well in advance of when the service is to be provided, except for emergency cases.

Finally, Table 20.4 shows that a process focus normally means a labor-limited scheduling environment with a more flexible work force. Both labor assignment policies and dispatching priority rules are needed. The machine-limited environment of a product focus is simpler in this respect. However, it is not without its challenges. Capacity constraints must be recognized and schedules developed to maximize facility utilization.

DECISION LINKAGES IN JAPANESE MANUFACTURING

Linking operations management decisions to the positioning strategy is one way to understand how to make consistent decisions. Another way is to review the decisions made by Japanese automobile manufacturers. Japan has almost no natural resources or domestic energy supply, which was accentuated by the oil crisis in 1973. Most raw materials must be imported. The country is also quite densely settled. Space is at a premium, with an acre of land costing as much as $1.5 million. Transportation lead times to foreign markets rule out quick response times for automobiles customized to individual preferences.

Corporate Strategy

Top management recognized the country's environmental obstacles and sought better ways to compete. A corporate strategy to achieve the lowest delivered cost position, anchored by high volumes, consistent quality, and a fuel-efficient car, emerged. Distinctive competencies for Japanese manufacturers are work-force characteristics and vendor proximity. The work force comes from a closely knit culture that encourages group consciousness, and suppliers locate near assembly plants because of the country's size and geography.

Operations Strategy

The operations strategy to achieve that corporate mission centers on dramatic improvements in (1) inventory turnover; and (2) labor productivity. The strategy might best be characterized as making the manufacturing environment so tranquil that only minimal inventory is justified. The way in which decisions are linked to low inventory and high productivity is shown in Table 20.5. Since inventory policies are the key, let's begin there.

Inventory. Inventory is viewed as the root of all evil, which wastes assets and masks solvable problems. In Chapter 15, we showed that the kanban

Table 20.5

How Japanese Automobile Manufacturers Link Operations Decisions

Decision Area	Choice
Inventory	Minimize the lot sizes and safety stock.
Competitive priorities	Emphasize low cost and consistent quality.
Positioning strategy	Have a product focus.
Process design	Minimize setup times. Reduce the frequency of setups through product layouts, group technology, and one-worker–multiple-machines. Automate as much as possible. Have a flexible work force.
Work-force management	Seek a flexible, cooperative work force through job enlargement, consensus management, and training.
Capacity	Minimize capacity cushions.
Maintenance	Minimize the frequency and duration of breakdowns.
Materials management	Have a cooperative orientation with vendors.
Master production scheduling	Maintain the same daily output rate for a whole month.
Quality	Put quality control at the source.

system is a simple inventory system for small-lot production. Its real value is that of a catalyst, exposing problems standing in the way of further inventory reduction. Inventory reduction results from smaller lot sizes and smaller safety stocks. The Japanese aim for lot sizes considerably less than a one-day supply. Small lot sizes reduce cycle inventory. Less inventory helps cut lead times, which in turn cuts pipeline (WIP) inventory. Safety stock is reduced by having fewer cards for each item. Such reductions are made at a risk, since inventory protects against unexpected demand for components and capacity. Inventory is a buffer, absorbing shocks from the environment. The rest of the choices in operations, in effect, aim at eliminating those shocks.

Competitive Priorities. Low cost and consistent quality are the two priorities given top emphasis. Superior features (Rolls-Royce quality), volume flexibility, and quick delivery time get less emphasis. As for product flexibility, the Japanese offer a variety of cars through choice of color and options. However, production for overseas markets is not customized to individual customer orders. End items are standards rather than specials, preproduced to inventory and pushed forward into distribution channels. The erratic demand and last-minute rush jobs of customized products do not link well with low inventory buffers.

Positioning Strategy. A product focus is chosen to achieve high-volume, low-cost production. Workers and machines are organized around product flows, which are arranged to conform to the necessary sequence of work operations. With line flows, a unit finished at one station goes almost immediately to the next one, which reduces inventory. Process repetition makes opportunities for methods improvement more visible.

Process Design. Small lot sizes can severely hurt productivity because setups are more frequent; large amounts of human and capital resources can be lost. This situation is particularly true in fabrication operations, where components are made for the final assembly line. One solution to this problem is to design the process to minimize setup times. It can take three to four hours to change dies on the large presses that form automobile hoods and fenders. The Japanese responded simply by cutting die-change time to less than 10 minutes. They call this *single-digit setup* and use a variety of techniques, including conveyors for die storage, simpler dies, machine controls, microcomputers to automatically feed and position work, and preparing for changeover while the current job is being processed.

The other solution is to reduce setup frequency. A product focus helps here, particularly if volumes are high enough to dedicate a group of machines and workers to one product or a mix of similar products. A product layout can eliminate setups entirely. If volume is insufficient to keep a line busy with similar products, a second tactic is to use group technology. Components with common attributes and enough collective volume are manufactured on what is essentially a small production line. Changeovers from one component in the family to the next are minimal. A final tactic for eliminating setups is to use the one-worker–multiple-machines approach, which essentially is a one-person line. A single worker operates several machines, with each machine advancing the item one more step in the process. This is common in feeder operations, where a worker runs as many as five machines simultaneously. The same product is made over and over, so setups are eliminated. This approach avoids half-automation, where a worker just monitors a machine's performance.

Another link with process design is automation. Sakichi Toyoda, the founder of Toyota, says, "Whenever there is money, invest it in machinery." Automation is a key to low-cost production. For example, Japan is a world leader in using robots, which have the lowest wage rate of all. The relentless reduction of inventory frees money for automation. In contrast, in the U.S. economy, more than two times as much money is held in inventory as is invested each year in plant modernization and capacity expansion. The final link is a flexible work force, which helps to absorb shocks without inventory buffers. Workers are able and willing to respond to capacity bottlenecks. Job boundaries are broader and workers multiskilled. They can help co-workers and often even change to a different job to alleviate bottlenecks. A considerable investment in education and training is required, but it builds quick response to problems and job variety into the system.

Work-Force Management. Several aspects of the Japanese operations strategy require a flexible and cooperative work force. How can this be achieved, when the high-volume production of a product focus creates the potential of repetitive, monotonous work? They have three answers: job enlargement, consensus management, and training.

Workers participate in some decisions reserved in many U.S. companies for middle management. Quality circles provide one kind of job enlargement. Small, voluntary groups meet periodically to find ways to improve operations in their work areas. They are team-oriented and generate many ideas for productivity improvement. Job enlargement also involves rotating employees among jobs, having them help co-workers with temporary capacity bottlenecks, and doing their own inspection and maintenance.

Two distinctive features of Japanese culture are a strong group orientation and a desire for harmony (called *wa*). Consistent with these features, while making jobs more satisfying, is *consensus management*. Managers seek consensus before making changes, fostering a sense of equality. Managers also often go onto the plant floor to help solve problems. There are fewer visible status differences. The new Honda plant in Ohio has an *open office* layout. No partitions, doors, or status symbols separate top management from other employees.

Workers are carefully selected, training begins immediately, and training continues as part of the job until the employee retires. This approach creates and maintains a knowledgeable work force. Considerable attention is given to job security, which helps to retain the educational investment in human resources. It also reduces the fear of methods improvements and technological change, which are keys to productivity improvements.

Capacity. Having extra labor and equipment capacity helps handle unexpected bottlenecks. The Japanese view these cushions as waste, which must be eliminated to increase productivity. The lack of cushions links well with a low-cost position, so long as the shocks they guard against are minimized.

Maintenance. One type of shock is equipment failure. A disruption at one station quickly affects many other work stations when inventory is not available to decouple them. The Japanese response is to find ways to reduce the frequency and duration of breakdowns. One tactic is to allow three hours between shifts for periodic preventive maintenance. Another is to make the workers responsible for routine maintenance of their equipment. Employees pride themselves in keeping their machines in top condition.

Materials Management. One aspect of purchasing is vendor relations. Here Japan has another distinctive competency. Domestic suppliers are located in close proximity to plants. Frequent, small shipments are possible, without paying excessive penalties in transportation costs. Considerable attention is given to achieving a close, harmonious relationship with vendors. Purchases are concentrated in a smaller number of suppliers than is done in the United States. This makes a plant more vulnerable to supply disruptions, but increases the incentive for suppliers to avoid them. One expectation is just-in-time deliveries, which links to the goal of minimal inventory.

Master Production Scheduling. Two steps are taken to minimize disruptions that would impede inventory reduction. First, components are standardized as much as possible. For example, even though a Japanese elevator manufacturer customizes its final products, many of the parts going into the final product have been standardized. Such part commonality increases volumes, which tends to reduce inventory and increase productivity. Second, the master production schedule is stable, and lot sizes for end items are very small. The daily output rate for each end item stays the same for an entire month. After a month, it is adjusted for forecast errors and inventory imbalances among models. Lot sizes are small, with output rotating frequently from one model to the next, which eliminates lumpy demand for components and reduces capacity bottlenecks. Both results help to reduce inventory and increase productivity.

Quality. Scrap and rework are inconsistent with an operations strategy aimed at low inventory, high productivity, and consistent quality. The Japanese make quality everyone's concern. Quality is controlled at the source, with workers acting as their own inspectors. Defective units are immediately returned to the worker responsible for them. Workers are encouraged to stop the entire assembly line if a quality problem arises. This is a costly action but brings the problem to everyone's attention, rather than masking it. Quality circles also help here, in addition to being part of a program for job enlargement.

A DIAGNOSTIC APPROACH

A strategic approach to operations management answers two fundamental questions:

1. What should we be doing?
2. How are we doing?

The first question has a *planning orientation*, which has been our main perspective. We started with corporate strategy and positioning decisions and then linked them to planning in the various functional areas of operations management. The second question has a *control orientation* (see Ruefli and Sarrazin, 1981). The purpose of control is to monitor performance, identify problems, and diagnose causes of problems. Managers can then make corrections and steer operations in the desired direction. Since both orientations help to make operations a competitive weapon, we conclude with a brief description of two control methods: audits and ongoing reports.

Operations Audit

One important diagnostic tool is an **operations audit,** or special study of operations. Checklists for service systems (Chase and Aquilano, 1985) and manufacturers (Skinner, 1978) are available. They contain a variety of dimensions on which to evaluate operations. Two scores are assigned to each dimension, one for current performance and one for the goal. Large negative differences represent planning and/or production problems. An audit begins with competitive priorities and works down through each decision area shown in Figure 20.1. Starting from the top ties the audit to strategic planning and evaluation of decision consistency. Dimensions for evaluating process design include

- degree of capital intensity;
- extent of equipment specialization;
- degree of worker flexibility;
- degree of vertical integration;
- degree of customer involvement in the process;
- frequency of process innovations; and
- work-force involvement in process design.

A similar list can be developed for the other decision areas in operations, tailoring the choices to the needs of the individual firm.

Ongoing Reports

Another diagnostic tool is ongoing reports on multiple measures. Some measures are traditional accounting data on costs (broken into various categories), profits, and return on investment. Over the years, manufacturing management has been evaluated primarily on the basis of direct labor (actual versus time standard) costs. There is growing recognition that such measures are insufficient and can actually restrain production systems. An excessive financial orientation makes efficiency or short-term profits the overriding priority. New technologies or improvements in the quality of work life are ignored, since many of their benefits are long-term and difficult to quantify. While extremely useful, short-term financial measures must be kept in perspective.

Recognizing that no single measure of productivity is adequate, the logical approach is to use multiple tracking devices. The examples listed in Table 20.6 help managers to monitor the *vital signs* of the production system. Such

Table 20.6

Some Vital Signs for Operations Management

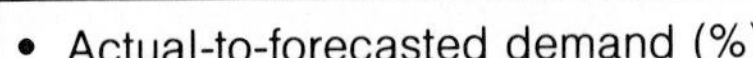

- Actual-to-forecasted demand (%)
- Returned merchandise ($)
- Scrap rate (%)
- Nursing hours to patient hours (%)
- Ratio of sales $ to payroll $ (%)
- Number of grievances
- Voluntary quits
- Overhead ($)
- Facility utilization (%)
- Preventive maintenance ($)
- Leased truck utilization (%)
- Open orders ($)
- Purchase prices (% of prior prices)
- Seasonal inventory ($)
- New orders booked ($)
- Stockouts
- Total inventory (weeks of supply)
- WIP inventory (% of total)
- Transaction volume (number)
- Capital intensity ($ per worker)
- Training (hr/wk)
- Number of products produced per machine
- Change in sales and profit margins over last year (life cycle position)
- Rework labor (% of direct labor)
- Materials costs (% of total)
- Direct labor (actual versus standard)
- Absenteeism
- Tooling cost ($)
- Number of quality circle projects
- Equipment breakdowns (hr lost)
- Ratio of maintenance hours to direct labor hours (%)
- Purchase orders (% placed in 3 days)
- Late deliveries from suppliers (% of orders)
- Overtime ($)
- On-time delivery (% orders)
- Order backlog ($)
- Inventory ($)
- Book-to-cycle count accuracy (%)
- Cycle time (days)
- Transaction costs ($)
- Customer return rate (%)
- Variation in monthly production rate
- Number of production orders per month

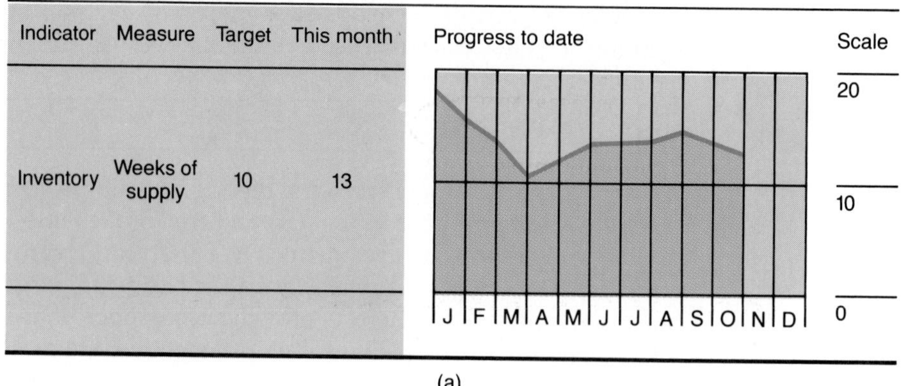

(a)

Indicator	Measure	Target	This month	Year to date	Past year	Range: Past 12 months	
						High	Low
Inventory	Weeks of supply	10	13	14	17	18	11

(b)

Figure 20.3

Two Display Formats: (a) Format with Graph; (b) Format with Trend Measurements.

Source: The concepts displayed here are discussed in more detail in Robert L. Janson, "Graphical Indicators of Operations," *Harvard Business Review* (November–December 1980), pp. 164–170.

measures are tailored to specific operations and change from time to time. A pyramid approach is used, in which department managers pick five or ten measures that best fit their operations. Each manager passes a few to his or her supervisor, and so on. Thus a vice-president of operations might end up with 20 or 30 indicators. Figure 20.3 suggests two possible formats for displaying each measure. The report should show a target, the latest performance, and some index of the year-to-date performance.

ABC analysis is particularly valuable here to focus management's attention on the relatively few areas that are the key problems. The management-by-exception concept applies equally well to inventory (by type or department), equipment failures (by machine or department), customer goods returned (by product line or department), scrap or rework (by work station), or employee absenteeism (by department).

Finally, we have to remember that this monitoring is but a means to an end. The end is improving performance and linking operations with corporate strategy. Managers must draw on a knowledge of operations and an awareness of their environment in seeking remedies. If inventory is too high, for example, the cause can rest with any number of factors. Large lot sizes, high forecast errors, long lead times, uneven or seasonal demand, unstable master production schedules, or inaccurate records are all possible causes. Managers must dig deep for remedies for the symptomatic problems uncovered by ongoing reports.

CONCLUSION

Throughout this book we have stressed that the operations function, whether in manufacturing or services, can and must be managed better. Operations can become a competitive weapon, rather than being a millstone, as proved by Japanese manufacturers. We also emphasized that each decision area in operations can make a difference in efforts to improve productivity. Operations management must be approached strategically, but with careful attention to tactical decisions and analytic methods. As current or future managers, the response to the competitive challenge lies in your hands.

CHAPTER HIGHLIGHTS

- Making operations management a competitive weapon depends on doing many things well, rather than seeking a magic solution.
- A strategic approach is needed to productivity improvement, so that decisions are linked and consistent. Management's positioning strategy is the starting point for making consistent operations decisions. The choice of process focus or product focus must be linked with the other decision areas in operations.
- At the highest decision levels, a process focus links with customized products, low volumes, short life cycles, and an entrance–exit strategy favoring early exit.
- For design decisions, a process focus links with flexible resources, labor intensity, less vertical integration, enlarged jobs, informal promotion channels, frequent two-way communication, and fewer staff specialists.
- For capacity and location decisions, a process focus links with large capacity cushions, smaller economies of scale, less maintenance intensity, single-site locations, local or regional markets, process layouts, and variable-path materials handling.
- For operating decisions, a process focus means more complexity and uncertainty, shorter-range plans, higher tolerance for inventory cushions, informal vendor and customer relationships, more volume flexibility, positioning inventory lower in the BOM, short runs, long cycle times, more WIP, potential component shortages, and decentralized scheduling.
- The Japanese approach to manufacturing aims at low cost and consistent quality.

Much of their operations strategy aims at achieving extremely low inventory, which is viewed as the root of all evil. Small lot sizes, a product focus, single-digit setups, infrequent changeovers, automation, worker flexibility, job enlargement, consensus management, preventive maintenance, good vendor relationships, stable master production schedules, and quality at the source all link to small inventory buffers.

- An operations audit helps to diagnose problems in operations by systematically evaluating a variety of dimensions. It starts with competitive priorities and works down through the various decision areas.
- Ongoing reports are another diagnostic tool for managers. Since there is no single measure of productivity, multiple measures are needed. When problems are identified, managers must draw on their knowledge of operations and awareness of the environment in order to solve the problems.
- Operations management needs a strategic orientation, but with full attention to analysis and tactical decisions.

KEY TERM

operations audit

STUDY QUESTIONS

1. "The only real answer to the productivity challenge is relocating facilities to where labor rates are cheap." Do you agree or disagree with this statement? Why?
2. What product plans and competitive priorities link well with a process focus? Why?
3. Why is a product-focused facility more likely to be capital intensive? Place more emphasis on equipment utilization? Have a larger staff?
4. Why does the choice of materials handling equipment depend on positioning strategy?
5. Why are inventories stocked at more forward positions with a product focus?
6. "The Japanese have successfully challenged all the traditional thinking and beliefs of U.S. operations managers. We can expect widespread adoption of their approaches in the next decade." Do you agree or disagree with this statement? Why?
7. "The Japanese approach cuts down on wasteful cushions by minimizing the shocks to the production system." Do you agree or disagree? Why?
8. How do Japanese approaches to workforce management fit other decisions and their environment?
9. Comment on the statement: "Annual profits and efficiency are the only true measures of a production system."
10. What dimensions for an operations audit would you suggest for layout? Inventory?

SELECTED REFERENCES

Buffa, Elwood S., *Meeting the Competitive Challenge,* Homewood, Ill.: Dow Jones-Irwin, 1984.

Burnham, John M., "Improving Manufacturing Performance—Management's Vital Challenge," *Production and Inventory Management,* vol. 25, no. 2 (Second Quarter 1984), pp. 1–20.

Chase, Richard B., and Nicholas J. Aquilano, *Production and Operations Management,* Homewood, Ill.: Richard D. Irwin, 1985.

Hayes, Robert H., and Kim B. Clark, "Explaining Observed Productivity Differentials Between Plants: Implications for Operations Research," *Interfaces,* vol. 15, no. 6 (November–December 1985), pp. 3–14.

Janson, Robert L., "Graphic Indicators of Operations," *Harvard Business Review* (November–December 1980), pp. 164–170.

Judson, Arnold S., "The Awkward Truth about Productivity," *Harvard Business Review* (September–October 1982), pp. 93–97.

Kendrick, John W., *Improving Company Productivity,* Baltimore: The Johns Hopkins University Press, 1984.

McInnes, J. Morris, "Corporate Management of Productivity—An Empirical Study," *Strategic Management Journal,* vol. 5 (1984), pp. 351–365.

Miller, Jeffrey G., and Thomas E. Vollmann, "The Hidden Factory," *Harvard Business Review* (September–October 1985), pp. 142–150.

Richardson, P. R., A. J. Taylor, and J. R. M. Gordon, "A Strategic Approach to Evaluating Manufacturing Performance," *Interfaces,* vol. 15, no. 6 (November–December 1985), pp. 15–27.

Ritzman, Larry P., Barry E. King, and Lee J. Krajewski, "Manufacturing Performance—Pulling the Right Levers," *Harvard Business Review* (March–April 1984), pp. 143–152.

Ruefli, Timothy, and Jacques Sarrazin, "Strategic Control of Corporate Development under Ambiguous Circumstances," *Management Science,* vol. 27, no. 10 (October 1981), pp. 1158–1170.

Schonberger, Richard L., *Japanese Manufacturing Techniques: Nine Hidden Lessons in Simplicity.* New York: The Free Press, 1982.

Skinner, Wickham, *Manufacturing in the Corporate Strategy,* New York: John Wiley & Sons, 1978.

Taylor, Sam G., "Are Process Industries Different?" *23rd Annual Conference Proceedings.* American Production and Inventory Control Society, Los Angeles, October, 1980, pp. 94–96.

Wheelwright, Steven C., "Japan—Where Operations Really Are Strategic," *Harvard Business Review* (July–August 1981), pp. 67–74.

Wheelwright, Steven C., and Robert H. Hayes, "Competing through Manufacturing," *Harvard Business Review* (January–February, 1985), pp. 99–109.

APPENDIX

FINANCIAL ANALYSIS

Some Managerial Issues

- What types of tools can we use to evaluate investments?
- Are we overlooking some investments of great strategic importance because their returns seem to be lower than the hurdle rate?
- How can we avoid *managing by the numbers?*

Appendix Outline

Many decisions in operations management involve large capital investments. Automation, vertical integration, capacity expansion, layout revisions, and installing a new MRP system are but some examples. Most of a firm's assets are tied up in the operations function. Therefore the operations manager should seek high-yield capital projects and then assess their costs, benefits, and risks. Such projects typically are subjected to one or more types of financial analysis. In this appendix, we present a brief overview of basic financial analyses.

TIME VALUE OF MONEY

An important concept underlying many financial analysis techniques is that a dollar in hand today is worth more than a dollar to be received in the future. A dollar available today can be invested to earn a return, so that more than one dollar will be available in the future. This concept is known as the **time value of money.**

Future Value of an Investment

If \$5000 is invested at 10 percent interest for one year, at the end of the year the \$5000 will have earned \$500 in interest, and the total amount available will be \$5500. If the interest earned is allowed to accumulate, it also earns interest, and the original investment will grow to \$12,970 in 10 years. The process by which interest on an investment accumulates and then earns interest itself for the remainder of the investment period, is known as **compounding interest.** The value of an investment at the end of the period over which interest is compounded is called the **future value of an investment.**

In order to calculate the future value of an investment, we first express the interest rate and the time period in the same units of time as the interval at which compounding occurs. Let's assume that interest is compounded annually, so we express all time periods in years and use annual interest rates. To find the value of an investment one year in the future, we multiply the amount invested by the sum of one plus the interest rate (expressed as a decimal). The value of a \$5000 investment at 12 percent per year one year from now is

$$\$5000(1.12) = \$5600.$$

If the entire amount remains invested, at the end of two years we have

$$\$5600(1.12) = \$5000(1.12)^2 = \$6272.$$

In general,

$$F = P(1 + r)^n,$$

where

F = The future value of the investment at the end of n periods;

P = The amount invested at the beginning, called the principal;

r = The periodic interest rate; and

n = The number of time periods for which the interest compounds.

Present Value of a Future Amount

Let's look at the opposite problem. Suppose that we want to make an investment now that will be worth \$10,000 in one year. If the interest rate is 12 percent, and P represents the amount invested now, this problem can be expressed as

$$F = \$10,000 = P(1 + 0.12).$$

Solving for P gives us:

$$P = \frac{F}{(1 + r)} = \frac{10,000}{(1 + 0.12)}$$
$$= \$8,929.$$

The amount to be invested now is called the **present value of an investment.** The process of finding the present value of an investment, when the future value and the interest rate are known, is called **discounting** the future value to its present value. If the number of time periods n for which discounting is desired is greater than one, the present value is determined by dividing the future value by the nth power of the sum of one plus the interest rate. The general formula for determining the present value is

$$P = \frac{F}{(1 + r)^n}.$$

The interest rate is also called the **discount rate.**

Present Value Factors

Although we can calculate P from its formula in a few steps with most pocket calculators, we can use a table instead. Note that we can write the present value formula another way:

$$P = \frac{F}{(1 + r)^n} = F\left[\frac{1}{(1 + r)^n}\right]$$

Let $[1/(1 + r)^n]$ be the *present value factor*, which we call pf and can be found in Appendix D.1. This table gives you the present value of a future amount of \$1 for various time periods and interest rates. To use the table, locate the column for the appropriate interest rate and the row for the appropriate period. The number in the body of the table where this row and column intersect is the pf value. Multiply it by F to get P. For example, suppose that an investment will generate \$15,000 in 10 years. If the interest rate is 12 percent, we find in Appendix D.1 that $pf = 0.3220$. Multiplying it by \$15,000 gives us the present value, or

$$\begin{aligned} P &= Fpf = \$15{,}000(0.3220) \\ &= \$4830. \end{aligned}$$

Annuities

An **annuity** is a series of payments of a fixed amount for a specified number of years. We treat all payments as happening at the end of a year. Suppose that we want to invest an amount at an interest rate of 10 percent, so that we may draw out \$5000 per year for each of the next four years. We could determine the present value of this \$5000 four-year annuity by treating the four payments as single future payments. The present value of an investment needed now, in order to receive these payments for the next four years, is the sum of the present values of each of the four payments. That is,

$$P = \frac{\$5000}{1 + 0.10} + \frac{\$5000}{(1 + 0.10)^2} + \frac{\$5000}{(1 + 0.10)^3} + \frac{\$5000}{(1 + 0.10)^4}$$
$$= \$4545 + \$4132 + \$3757 + \$3415$$
$$= \$15{,}849.$$

A much easier way to calculate this amount is to use Appendix D.2. Look for the factor in the table at the intersection of the 10% column, and the fourth period row and find 3.1699. For annuities, we call this present value factor *af*, to distinguish it from the present value factor for a single payment. We determine the present value of an annuity by multiplying its amount by *af*. For our example, we get

$$P = Aaf = \$5000(3.1699)$$
$$= \$15{,}849$$

where

P = The present value of an investment;

A = The amount of the annuity received each year; and

af = The present value factor for an annuity.

TECHNIQUES OF ANALYSIS

We can now apply these concepts to the financial analysis of proposed investments. Two basic financial analysis techniques are

1. net present value method; and
2. payback method.

Both methods are based on cash flows. Our first step, then, is to calculate the cash flows resulting from the investment (project).

Determining Cash Flows

We have to estimate as accurately as possible the cash that will flow into and out of the organization because of the project. **Cash flow** includes revenues, costs, and changes in assets and liabilities. We illustrate this process with the salad bar project in Box A.1. It is important to remember two points when determining cash flows for any project:

1. Consider only the amounts of cash flows that will change if the project is undertaken. These amounts are called incremental cash flows and are the difference in the cash flows with the project and without it.

Box A.1

A SALAD BAR: TO FUND OR NOT TO FUND

A local restaurant is considering adding a salad bar. The investment required to remodel the dining area and add the salad bar will be $16,000. Other information about the project is as follows:

1. The price and variable cost per salad are $3.50 and $2.00, respectively.
2. Annual demand should be about 11,000 salads.
3. Fixed costs, other than depreciation, will be $8000, which covers the energy to operate the refrigerated unit and another part-time employee to stock the salad bar during peak business hours.
4. The project is expected to last four years and have no salvage value at the end of that time. The straight-line depreciation method is used.
5. The tax rate is 50 percent.
6. Management wants to earn a return of at least 14 percent on the project.

Should the salad bar project be funded?

2. Cash flows should be converted to *after-tax* amounts before applying the net present value or payback method to them. This step introduces taxes and depreciation into the calculations.

Depreciation. In this type of analysis, **depreciation** is relevant for only one reason: It acts as a tax shield.* Taxes must be paid on before-tax cash inflows *minus* the depreciation associated with the proposed investment. We will use the *straight-line method* of calculating annual depreciation, since it is simplest.† First, subtract the estimated salvage value from the amount of investment required at the beginning of the project, then divide by the number of years of life. If the item can be sold for cash at the end of its life, it has a salvage value greater than zero. For the salad bar, the annual depreciation is

$$D = \frac{(I - S)}{n} = \frac{\$16{,}000 - \$0}{4}$$

$$= \$4000,$$

where

* Depreciation is not a legitimate cash flow because it is not cash that is actually paid out each year. On the other hand, depreciation does affect how an accountant calculates net income, against which the income-tax rate is applied. Therefore, depreciation enters into the calculation, as a tax shield, only when we have to figure our tax liability.

† For a discussion of other depreciation methods, see Kieso and Weygandt (1983).

D = Annual depreciation;

I = The amount of the investment;

S = The salvage value; and

n = The number of years of project life.

Tax Considerations. The income-tax rate varies from one state or country to another. We will use an income-tax rate of 50 percent, assuming that all relevant federal, state, and local income taxes are included in this rate. When you are doing a financial analysis you may want to use an average income-tax rate based on the firm's historical tax rate over the past several years, or you may want to base the tax rate on the highest tax bracket that applies to the taxpaying unit. The one thing you must never do is ignore taxes in your analysis.

After-Tax Cash Inflows. We are now ready to determine the after-tax cash flows for each year of the project's life. We calculate the amount of taxes in four steps:

1. Contribution margin = Revenue − Variable cost.
2. Before-tax cash inflow = Contribution margin − Fixed costs.
3. Taxable cash inflow = Before-tax cash inflow − Depreciation.
4. Additional taxes = Taxable cash inflow × Tax rate.

In some investment projects, revenues are unaffected. The before-tax cash inflow is really a cost savings, such as might come from an automation project. They are the equivalent of the before-tax cash inflow of step 2. In such cases we would begin with step 3.

Now, we simply subtract the additional taxes (step 4) from the before-tax cash inflow (step 2), or

$$\text{After-tax cash inflow} = \text{Before-tax cash inflow} - \text{Additional taxes.}$$

Salvage Values. If the project has a **salvage value** in the last year of its life, this amount is a cash inflow in the final year. Adding it to the after-tax cash flow, you arrive at the total cash flow for the year. If an item has a negative salvage value, which can happen if you must pay to dispose of something, you subtract this amount from the after-tax cash flow to obtain the net cash flow for the year. Gains or losses on disposition of property must be carefully evaluated for tax effects in order to determine the cash flow actually resulting from them. Only the after-tax values are relevant to cash-flow determination.*

* Disposal of property often results in an accounting gain or loss that can increase or decrease income tax and affect cash flows. These tax effects should be considered in determining the actual cash inflow or outflow from disposal of property.

We will assume that all salvage values are net of their tax effects for this example.

Net Present Value Method

The **net present value** (NPV) **method** simply takes the time value of money into account when we total after-tax cash flows. Table A.1 shows the calculations for the salad bar project, with after-tax cash inflows of $6250 per year. Figure A.1 shows these cash inflows graphically, along with the initial investment (cash outflow) of $16,000. While the $16,000 is already a present value, the four $6250 inflows are not. They are equivalent to a four-year annuity. Since management wants to earn a return of at least 14 percent on its invest-

Table A.1

Cash Flows and NPV for the Salad Bar Project

	Year				
Item	1987	1988	1989	1990	1991
Initial information					
Annual demand (salads)		11,000	11,000	11,000	11,000
Investment	$16,000				
Interest (discount) rate	0.14				
Cash flows					
Revenue		$38,500	$38,500	$38,500	$38,500
Minus variable cost		−22,000	−22,000	−22,000	−22,000
Contribution margin		16,500	16,500	16,500	16,500
Minus fixed cost		− 8,000	− 8,000	− 8,000	− 8,000
Before-tax cash inflow		8,500	8,500	8,500	8,500
Minus depreciation		− 4,000	− 4,000	− 4,000	− 4,000
Taxable cash inflow		4,500	4,500	4,500	4,500
Taxes @ 50%		2,250	2,250	2,250	2,250
Before-tax cash inflow		8,500	8,500	8,500	8,500
Minus taxes		− 2,250	− 2,250	− 2,250	− 2,250
After-tax cash inflow		$ 6,250	$ 6,250	$ 6,250	$ 6,250

Present value of cash flows

1988: $6250(0.8772) = $5482

1989: $6250(0.7695) = $4809

1990: $6250(0.6750) = $4219

1991: $6250(0.5921) = $3701

NPV of project = ($5482 + $4809 + $4219 + $3701) − $16,000
= $2211

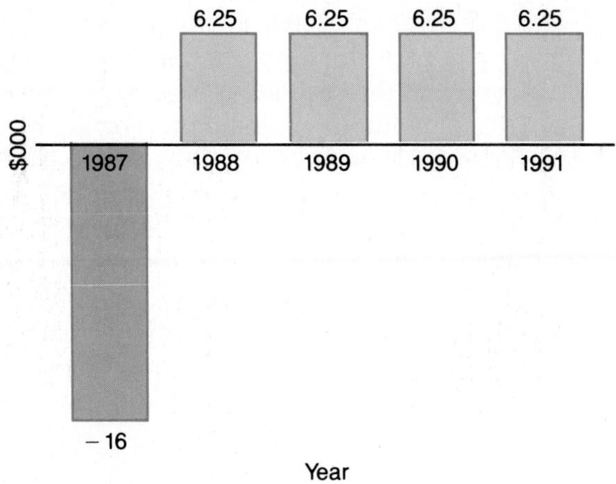

Figure A.1

After-Tax Cash Flows for the Salad Bar Project.

ment, we use that rate to find the *af* value in Appendix D.2 to be 2.9137. The net present value of the inflows minus outflows is

$$\begin{aligned} \text{NPV} &= \$6250(2.9137) - \$16{,}000 \\ &= \$2211. \end{aligned}$$

We can obtain the same result by discounting each year's after-tax cash flow to its present value and adding all the present values. This method is shown at the bottom of Table A.1.

If the net present value is positive for the discount rate used, the investment earns a rate of return higher than the discount rate. If the net present value is negative, the investment earns a rate of return lower than the discount rate. Most firms set the discount rate equal to the lowest desired return on investment. If a negative net present value results, the project is not approved. The discount rate is thought of as a hurdle over which the investment must pass, and is often referred to as the **hurdle rate.** Since the NPV in Table A.1 is positive, the return on the salad bar exceeds the hurdle rate.*

Payback Method

The other commonly used method of evaluating projects is the **payback method.** Once again we use *after-tax* cash flows. The difference is that this

* A related technique is called the *internal rate of return* (IROR). Using trial and error, we find the discount rate that makes the present value of the after-tax inflows equal to the outflows. The IROR makes the NPV of a project equal to zero. Multiple projects can be ranked from best to worst using IROR.

method determines the amount of time that will elapse before these cash flows pay back the initial investment. Using after-tax cash flows from Table A.1, you add the cash flows for each year until you get to as close as possible to $16,000, without exceeding it. For the years 1988 and 1989, cash flows are $6500 + $6500 = $13,000. The payback method assumes that cash flows in evenly throughout the year, so that in 1990 only $3000 must flow in before the payback point is reached. Since $3000/$6500 is 0.46, the payback period is 2.46 years.

The payback method continues to be widely used, particularly at lower management levels, even though it is scorned by many academics. Its advantages are that it is quick and easy to apply. It also gives decisionmakers some idea of how long it will be until investment funds are recovered. Uncertainty surrounds every investment project. The costs and revenues on which analyses are based are really best estimates, not actual values. If an investment project has a quick payback, it is not considered as risky as when the payback is longer. The payback method also has drawbacks. A major criticism is that it encourages managers to focus on the short run. A project that takes a long time to develop, but generates excellent cash flows later in its life, is usually rejected by the payback method. The payback method has also been criticized for its failure to consider the time value of money. For these reasons, we recommend that payback analysis be combined with a more sophisticated method such as NPV in analyzing the financial implications of a project.

Managing by the Numbers

The precision and analytical detachment that come from using the NPV or payback method can be deceiving. American business has been accused of *managing by the numbers,* with a preference for short-term results from low-risk projects (see Hayes and Abernathy, 1980, and Skinner, 1984). Part of the problem lies with managers who are on the fast track to the top of their organizations. They occupy a rung on the ladder for a short time and then move up. They perceive it to be in their career interests to favor investments that give quick results. They establish short paybacks and high hurdle rates. They ignore or forego long-term benefits from technological advances, innovative product plans, and strategic capacity additions. Over the long haul, this narrow vision jeopardizes the firm's competitive advantage—and even survival.

Managing by the numbers has a second cause. Projects with the greatest strategic impact are also likely to be riskier and have more qualitative benefits, which cannot be easily quantified. Consider an investment in some of the newer types of flexible automation. (See Chapter 5.) Benefits can include better quality, quicker delivery times, higher sales, and lower inventory. The equipment might be reprogrammed to handle new products not yet conceived of by the firm. Enough might be learned with the new technology that subsequent investments will pay off at an even higher rate of return. The mistake is to ignore these benefits simply because they cannot be easily quantified. It is far better to bring in the risks and qualitative factors as part of the analysis, rather than to ignore them. The proliferation of microcomputers and the corresponding use of computer spreadsheets to perform financial analyses have made possible the rapid evaluation of many different alternatives relating to a project. These are referred to as "what if" analyses and allow an analyst to look at what would happen to cash flows if certain events, or combinations of events, were to occur. Using a preference matrix may also help to give more explicit recognition to qualitative factors.

The message is clear. The techniques of financial analysis are a valuable tool for evaluating investment projects. However, they never replace the insight that comes from "hands-on" experience. Managers must use their judgment, taking into account not only NPV or payback data, but also how the project fits operations and corporate strategy.

APPENDIX HIGHLIGHTS

- Many financial techniques, such as the net present value (NPV) method, take into account the time value of money. The present value of a future amount, or annuity of several amounts, can be found by using formulas or by using values from tables.
- Only cash flows that change if the project is undertaken need to be considered. They should be converted to *after-tax* amounts before a financial technique is applied to them. Depreciation is relevant to the analysis because it is a tax shield.
- The NPV method converts after-tax cash flows to their present value equivalent, using a hurdle rate established by management as the discount rate.
- The payback method determines the amount of time that will elapse before the after-tax cash flows pay back the initial investment. While a popular technique, it encourages a short-run focus and does not consider the time value of money.
- American business has been accused of managing by the numbers and favoring low-risk projects that promise good short-term results. Over the long term, this approach can jeopardize a firm's competitive position and even its chances for survival.

KEY TERMS

annuity
cash flow
compounding interest
depreciation
discount rate
discounting
future value of an investment
hurdle rate
net present value (NPV) method
payback method
present value of an investment
salvage value
time value of money

STUDY QUESTIONS

1. Give one example in each decision area of operations management that could require a capital investment.
2. Why does the payback method encourage projects with short-run results? Why might it be the method of choice for managers who are averse to risk?
3. How can we take advantage of financial techniques without falling into the trap of managing by the numbers?

PROBLEMS

1. Another option instead of the salad bar (Box A.1) is to assemble, store and sell preassembled salads. In order to do so, an investment outlay of $6000 to remodel the kitchen would be required. The price and variable cost of each salad would drop to $2.25 and $1.50, respectively. Fixed cost (excluding depreciation) would be $900, since there is no longer a need to hire someone to keep the salad bar stocked. The other assumptions about total demand, project life, tax rate, hurdle rate, salvage value, and depreciation method remain unchanged.
   (a) Based on the NPV method, is the salad bar or preassembled salad option best?
   (b) What is the payback period for each option?
   (c) What other factors might influence your decision?

2. Suppose that the demand estimate for salads in Problem 1 is revised upward to 36,000 salads per year.
   (a) Evaluate both options using the NPV method.
   (b) Evaluate both options using the payback method.
   (c) Does the higher demand estimate change any of your conclusions?

3. Valley Memorial Hospital is considering two different computerized information systems to improve nurse productivity. The first alternative is a portable computer system. It will require a one-time investment in computer hardware, computer software, and employee training of $150,000. After-tax cash flows attributable to this investment are expected to be $30,000 per year for the next 10 years. These estimated savings would accrue from increased employee productivity and the value of having timely and accurate information. The second alternative is to install a mainframe computer linked to bedside terminals. This system will require an investment of $350,000 but is expected to generate after-tax cash flows of $45,000 per year for 10 years. The hospital must earn 12 percent on its investments. Assume that both systems will have no salvage value at the end of 10 years.
   (a) Calculate the net present value and payback periods for each alternative.
   (b) Based on your financial analysis, what do you recommend?
   (c) Are there any valid considerations other than financial?

4. Dr. Wilson, an orthodontist, is considering the expansion of his office from four to

six chairs. Each chair requires an investment of $200,000. He will have to hire one new technician at $18,000 per year. Other additional costs are expected to be negligible. The two new chairs will allow him to expand his practice by 200 more patients. Each new patient is expected to bring in $1,500 per year in before-tax revenue. Dr. Wilson will depreciate the chairs over a 5-year period, and at the end of that time the chairs are expected to have no value. Assume that Dr. Wilson is in the 50 percent tax bracket and requires a return of 20 percent on an investment. Calculate the following:

(a) The incremental after-tax cash flows attributable to the two new chairs.
(b) The net present value of the investment.
(c) The payback period.
(d) The number of new patients Dr. Wilson will have to add in order to break even (before taxes) on an annual basis.

5. Joan Ruiz designs and makes custom jewelry, which she sells at craft shows on weekends. If Joan purchases a new kiln, she can add ceramic earrings and necklaces to her product line. Based on previous experience, she would only produce this line of jewelry for about four years before she or her customers tire of it. The kiln she wants costs $2400, but Joan estimates that it would be worth $800 in salvage value at the end of four years. If she buys the kiln, she will also have to invest $600 in additional inventory, for a total investment of $3000. At the end of four years, she would liquidate the inventory and get the $600 back. Joan thinks she can sell pairs of earrings or necklaces for $6.00 apiece. She estimates her variable costs at $4.50 per item (a pair of earrings count as one item). The cost to run the kiln, $300 per year, is her only incremental fixed cost, except for depreciation. Joan believes that she can sell 50 of these items at every craft show. She goes to 20 craft shows every year. Joan wants this investment to earn at least 16 percent. Assume that her tax rate is 50 percent. Calculate the following and make a recommendation concerning her potential investment.
   (a) Annual after-tax income.
   (b) After-tax cash flows for four years.
   (c) Net present value of this investment.
   (d) Payback period.

6. Suppose that Joan's jewelry (Problem 5) becomes extremely popular, and she is able to sell 100 items at every craft show for $8.00 apiece. Recalculate your answers in Problem 5. Do these new figures change your recommendation? Explain.
7. Suppose Joan (Problem 5) can lease a kiln for $800 per year. Assume that her additional fixed costs are $400 a year. Use the variable costs and sales price from Problem 5 and calculate Joan's break-even point in number of units sold. Which option, leasing or buying the kiln, gives Joan more flexibility?
8. A grocer is thinking of adding an in-store bakery, which would require an investment of $35,000. The grocer expects the bakery to generate incremental after-tax cash flows of $12,000 for each of the next 6 years. What is the present value of the stream of expected cash flows? (Use 18 percent for the interest rate.)
   (a) What is the net present value?
   (b) What is the payback period?
   (c) What advice would you give the grocer about this investment project?
   (d) What other issues should the grocer consider?

SELECTED REFERENCES

Hayes, Robert H., and William J. Abernathy, "Managing Our Way to Economic Decline," *Harvard Business Review* (July–August 1980), pp. 67–77.

Hodder, James E., and Henry E. Riggs, "Pitfalls in Evaluating Risky Projects," *Harvard Business Review* (January–February 1985), pp. 128–135.

Kieso, Donald E., and Jerry J. Weygandt, *Intermediate Accounting,* 4th ed. New York: John Wiley & Sons, 1983.

Skinner, Wickham, "Operations Technology: Blind Spot in Strategic Management," *Interfaces,* vol. 14, no. 1 (January–February 1984), pp. 116–125.

Weston, J. Fred, and Thomas E. Copeland, *Managerial Finance,* 8th ed. Chicago: Dryden, 1986.

Woodward, Herbert N., "Management Strategies for Small Companies," *Harvard Business Review* (January–February 1976), pp. 113–121.

APPENDIX B

QUEUING AND SIMULATION ANALYSIS

Some Managerial Issues

- How should we arrange the service facilities in a queuing situation to gain the most efficiency in operation?
- What is the best priority system for us to use in a given situation?
- What is the impact on operating characteristics if we increase the productivity of the servers in a queuing situation?
- What role must we as managers play in a simulation analysis?
- What should we know about the limitations of a queuing or simulation analysis?

Appendix Outline

- Structure of Queuing Problems
  Input source ▪ Queues ▪ Priority discipline ▪ Service facilities ▪ Decision variables ▪ Operating characteristics
- Application of Queuing Models to Operations Management
  Analyzing different service rates ▪ Increasing capacity by adding facilities ▪ Analyzing different work methods
- Simulation
  What is simulation? ▪ Reasons for using simulation ▪ A simulation example ▪ Computers and simulation
- Appendix Highlights
- Key Terms
- Study Questions
- Problems
- Selected References

Anyone who has had to wait in line for service has experienced the dynamics of queues, or waiting lines.* We find queues everywhere in our daily lives. We wait at stoplights, stand in line at McDonald's, and bear the agony of waiting to pay registration fees at the registrar's office on the last day before late-payment penalties are assessed. With all these frustrations, you might wonder whether anyone is managing these queues. Actually, queuing analysis is closely associated with operations design, capacity planning, spatial planning, inventory management, and scheduling—many of the topics covered in this text. Perhaps one of the best examples of effectively managing queuing problems is that at Walt Disney World. During slack periods, an average of 15,000 customers per day visit the park, while on busy days the average is 65,000. This requires careful analysis of process flows, technology for people-mover (materials handling) equipment, capacity, and layout to keep the waiting lines to acceptable levels.

Queuing situations are not associated only with service operations. Those in a queue can be inanimate objects such as machines, production orders, or inventory items. Thus queuing situations are prevalent in operations management, both in manufacturing and service settings.

---

* The word *queue* is a British term for *waiting line.* We will use the two terms interchangeably in this appendix.

Recognizing that a situation can be formulated as a queuing problem is one thing, but solving it to achieve the desired performance characteristics of the system is quite another. In this appendix, we discuss some simple models that have been derived from queuing theory. While these are useful models, they are based on stringent assumptions about the operating environment. More complex queuing problems, as well as many nonqueuing problems, can be analyzed by the use of *simulation*. In this appendix, we will also demonstrate the usefulness of simulation for analyzing operations problems.

STRUCTURE OF QUEUING PROBLEMS

Analysis of queuing problems begins with a description of the basic elements of the queuing phenomenon as they relate to the specific situation to be analyzed. Figure B.1 shows these basic elements, which are common to all queuing problems. An **input source** generates potential customers for the **service system,** which consists of one or more queues, a priority discipline, and some service facilities. Some customers may decide not to enter the system (*balking* customers). Other customers enter a queue or waiting line. Some of these customers may elect to leave the system (*reneging* customers). A **priority discipline** selects the next customer to be served by the **service facilities**. The system can include one or more facilities, each consisting of a person (or crew), a machine (or group of machines), or both. After the service has been performed, the served customers leave the system. The situations in Table B.1

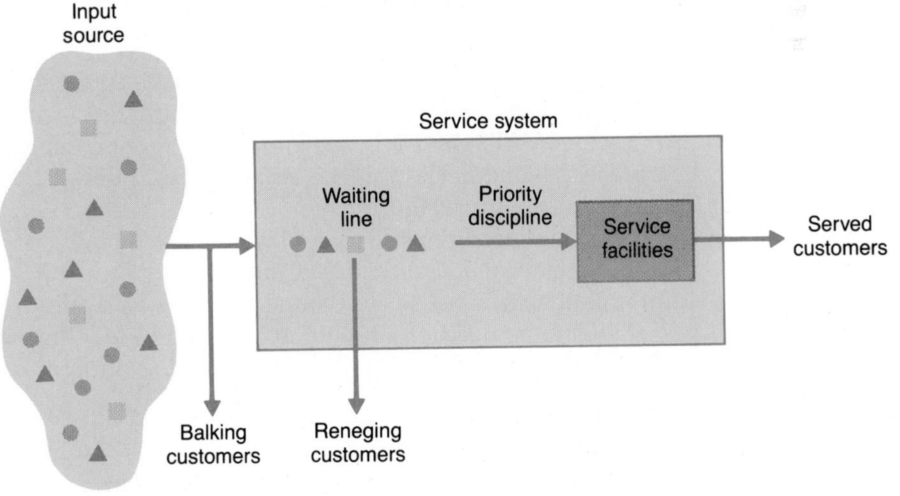

Figure B.1

Basic Elements of Queuing Problems.

Table B.1

Examples of Queuing Problems

Situation	Customers	Priority Discipline*	Server
Loading/unloading dock	Trucks and vans	Varied	Conveyor and/or dock employees
Warehouse inventory	Orders for product	Varied	Stockpicking system and/or warehouse employees
Theater ticket sales	Theatergoers	FCFS	Ticket seller
Toll highway	Cars and trucks	FCFS	Toll booth attendant
Grocery store	Shoppers	FCFS	Checkout clerks
Banking	Bank patrons	FCFS	Bank tellers
Machine maintenance	Machines needing repair or maintenance	Varied	Maintenance crew
Job shop	Job order	Varied	Work station
Typing pool	Reports	Varied	Secretaries and word processors
Medical clinic	Patients	Varied	Physicians and nurses
Airport	Airplanes	Varied	Air traffic controller
Telephone exchange	Telephone calls	FCFS	Switchboard operator and/or electronic switching apparatus
Judicial system	Court cases	Varied	Judges
Check processing	Checking account transactions	Varied	Bank clerks and/or computers

* FCFS means first come, first served.

suggest the wide range of queuing problems found in operations management. In many such situations, the traditional priority discipline *first come, first served* (FCFS) is used, while in others more complex priority disciplines are used. Nonetheless, all the situations in Table B.1 have the same basic elements shown in Figure B.1.

Besides describing the basic elements of a queuing problem, we must also identify relevant *decision variables* and the *operating characteristics*. We need this information in order to determine whether an appropriate queuing theory model is to be used or whether a simulation model must be developed. We discuss the basic elements, decision variables, and performance measures in this section.

Input Source

An input source is the population of potential customers for the service system. It can be described by its size, the distribution of customer arrivals, and the disposition of the customers.

Size. The input source can be either a *finite* or *infinite* population of potential customers. This distinction is based on the relative proportion of the input source that can be in the service system at any one time. If the rate (customers per unit of time) at which the input source generates new customers for the service system is appreciably affected by the number of customers already in the system, the input source is said to be finite. For example, suppose that a company has ten machines that periodically need to be repaired by a maintenance crew. If three machines have failed and are currently in the maintenance service system being repaired or waiting to be repaired, there are only seven machines left that could fail and enter the service system. That is a 30 percent reduction in the size of the input source, and it could have an appreciable effect on the rate at which the input source will generate more customers for the maintenance crew.

Alternatively, an infinite input source is one in which the number of customers in the system does not affect the rate at which the input source generates new customers. Bank patrons transacting business with a bank teller is a case in point. The rate at which the input source generates more patrons needing the services of the bank teller is not appreciably affected by the number of customers already in the system. Banks may have thousands of customers, but only a small percentage of them are in the bank lobby at any one time.

Arrival Distribution. The distribution of customer arrivals is a probability distribution that describes either the number of arrivals per unit of time or the time between successive arrivals, called the **interarrival time**. A *Poisson distribution* is often used to describe customer arrivals per unit of time. Let A_T be the number of customers arriving during an interval of time 0, T. If λ is the mean number of customer arrivals per unit of time, the probability that there will be exactly n arrivals during the time interval 0, T is

$$P(A_T = n) = \frac{(\lambda T)^n}{n!} e^{-\lambda T} \qquad \text{for } n = 0, 1, 2, \ldots$$

The mean of the Poisson distribution is λT, and the variance also equals λT.

The Poisson distribution is a discrete distribution; that is, the probabilities are for a specific number of arrivals per unit of time. For example, suppose that customers arrive at a complaint desk in a large department store at the rate of two customers per hour ($\lambda = 2$). The probability that four customers will arrive in the next hour ($n = 4$, $T = 1$) is

$$P(A_1 = 4) = \frac{[2(1)]^4}{4!} e^{-2(1)} = \frac{16}{24} e^{-2}$$
$$= 0.090.$$

The entire distribution for $\lambda T = 2$ is shown in Fig. B.2. If we want to determine the distribution of arrivals for an 8-hour work day, T would equal 8, and the parameter for the Poisson distribution would be $\lambda T = 16$.

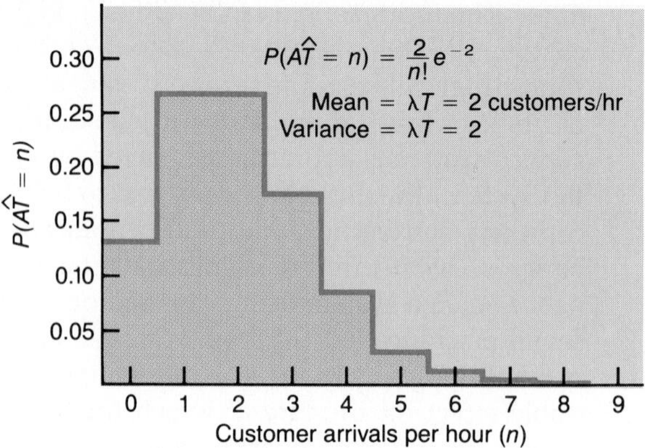

Figure B.2

Distribution of Customer Arrivals.

It may be more convenient to specify the arrival distribution in terms of customer interarrival times. If the input source generates customers according to a Poisson distribution, we can use the *exponential distribution* to describe the probability that the next customer will arrive in the time interval $(0, T)$. The mean of the distribution is $1/\lambda$ and the variance is $(1/\lambda)^2$. We will defer further discussion of the exponential distribution until we address the service time distribution.

Customer Disposition. Customers in queuing situations can be either *patient* or *impatient*. In this regard, patience has nothing to do with the colorful language a customer may use while waiting in line for a long time on a hot day. A patient customer is one who enters the system and remains there until being served. For example, drivers of cars arriving at a highway toll booth must wait until they are served by the toll booth attendant. There is no other place for them to go. Similarly, machines needing repair in a production system will wait patiently in queue to be served by the maintenance crew.

An impatient customer is one who either estimates the waiting time and decides not to enter the system (balking) or enters the queue but leaves the system before being served (reneging). For example, a customer driving past the lobby of a bank may balk at entering the system after noting that the waiting line in front of the automatic teller machine (ATM) has 15 customers in it. Another customer, standing in line for the ATM service for 20 minutes, may decide to leave the queue and return at some later time. For the models in this chapter, we make the simplifying assumption that all customers are patient.

Queues

Queues may be described by their size limitations and the number of lines.

Size Limitations. The queue size can be *limited* or *unlimited.* A limited queue is constrained to be no larger than some finite number of customers. For example, the line of theatergoers waiting to see a Broadway play that has been "sold out" is limited to the seating capacity of the theater. Only those who have tickets will wait for the doors to open. Those without tickets have to leave and return for another performance.

Unlimited queues are found in those situations where space or other resource limitations do not impose a limitation on queue length. A catalog sales department, for all practical purposes, could entertain unlimited queue sizes because the customers (orders to be processed) take up little space, and the queue can be very large relative to the capacity of the order-processing system at any time.

Number of Lines. Queues can be designed to be *single line* or *multiple lines.* Figure B.3 shows an example of each arrangement. When multiple servers are available and each one can handle general transactions, the single-line arrangement has the advantage of maintaining the utilization of servers at a high level and giving the customer a sense of fairness. Customers have the feeling that they are being served on the basis of when they arrived, not on how well they guessed their waiting time when selecting a particular line, as in the multiple-line arrangement. Banks often use the single-line arrangement for these reasons.

The multiple-line design is best when some of the servers provide a limited set of services. Grocery stores or discount department stores set up checkout counters with restrictions such as "cash only" or "10 items or less" to provide faster service to those with lower expected transaction times.

Sometimes, queues are not organized neatly into "lines." Machines that need repair on the production floor of a factory remain right where they are when they fail and wait for the maintenance crew to come to them. Nonetheless, we can think of the machines forming a single line or multiple lines, depending on the number of repair crews and their specialties.

Priority Discipline

When a waiting line forms, the question then becomes one of which customer to serve next. Most service systems that the average person encounters in daily life use the first-come, first-served (FCFS) rule. The customer at the head of the waiting line has the highest priority, and so on, to the customer who last arrived. However, this rule is only one of many priority disciplines used in queuing systems. Accident victims are served in an emergency ward at a

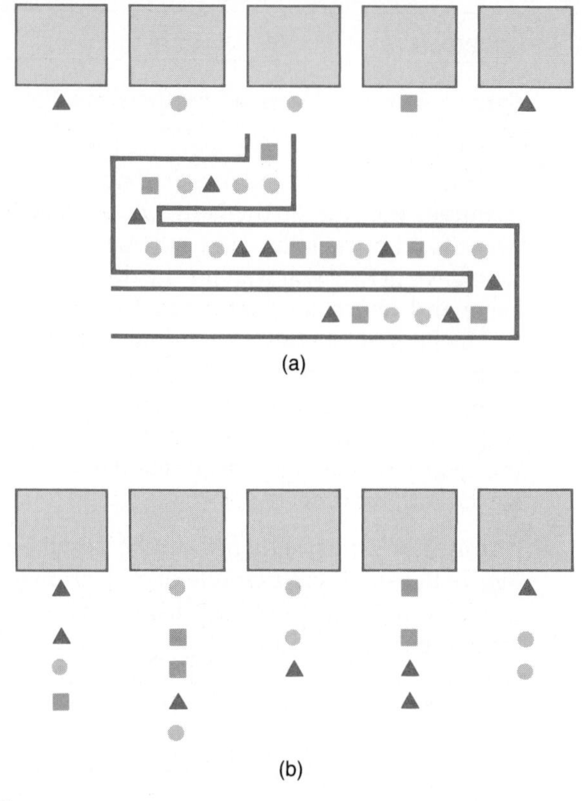

Figure B.3

Waiting-Line Arrangements: (a) Single Line; (b) Multiple Lines.

hospital on the basis of the severity of their injuries. The check-processing department in a bank may choose to process the checks of highest denomination first. In production systems, the jobs to be processed next on a particular machine may be chosen on the basis of their due dates or their expected processing times. Air traffic controllers give planes low on fuel priority over others waiting for permission to land.

The service system may even invoke a **preemptive discipline.** Preemption takes place when a customer of higher priority interrupts the service of another customer. For example, a production order that is far behind schedule may be allowed to interrupt the processing of another order on a particular machine in the interest of completing the late order as soon as possible. Modeling queuing systems having complex priority disciplines is difficult, and, most often in practice, these situations are analyzed with simulation.

Service Facilities

Service facilities consist of the personnel and/or equipment necessary to perform the service for the customer. They can be characterized by their arrangement and service time distribution.

Arrangement. Figure B.4 shows examples of the five basic types of service facility arrangements. The choice of arrangement is a function of customer volume and the nature of the services that are to be performed. Some services require a sequence of steps, while others require only a single step.

The *single-channel, single-phase* system is the simplest of all queuing problems. It is based on the assumption that all services demanded by a customer can be performed by a single-service facility. An example of this arrangement is an automatic teller machine at a bank.

The *single-channel, multiple-phase* arrangement is used when the services are best performed in sequential order by more than one facility, yet customer volume or other constraints limit the design to one channel. This arrangement is used for many production assembly lines. Primary concerns include allocating the total work to be performed to the various facilities and deciding whether queues will be allowed between facilities. A semiautomatic car wash system is an example where, typically, no intermediate queues are allowed when the vacuuming–washing–window cleaning–final inspection process is started.

Window tellers serving bank customers or work crews unloading semitrailer rigs at a receiving dock in a factory are examples of a *multiple-channel, single-phase* arrangement. Figure B.4 shows a single-line queue for the multiple-channel arrangements. The multiple-channel, single-phase arrangement is used when the demand volume is large enough to warrant providing the same service at more than one facility or when the services offered by the facilities are different.

The *multiple-channel, multiple-phase* arrangement is just an extension of the preceding arrangement. In some cases, customers cannot switch channels after service has begun, while in others they can. For example, if the facilities in each phase perform the same services, customers completing one phase can choose whichever facility is free for the next phase. Such is the case in a laundromat, where customers first use a washing machine and then a dryer.

The most general (and complex) facility arrangement is the *mixed* arrangement. In this situation, each customer has a specific routing between service facilities and, consequently, service cannot be neatly described in phases. Queues can develop in front of each facility. The arrival times at each facility are a complex function of variations in processing times and move times between facilities, as well as the priority disciplines and capacities of the other facilities. A production job shop using a process layout is an example of this arrangement.

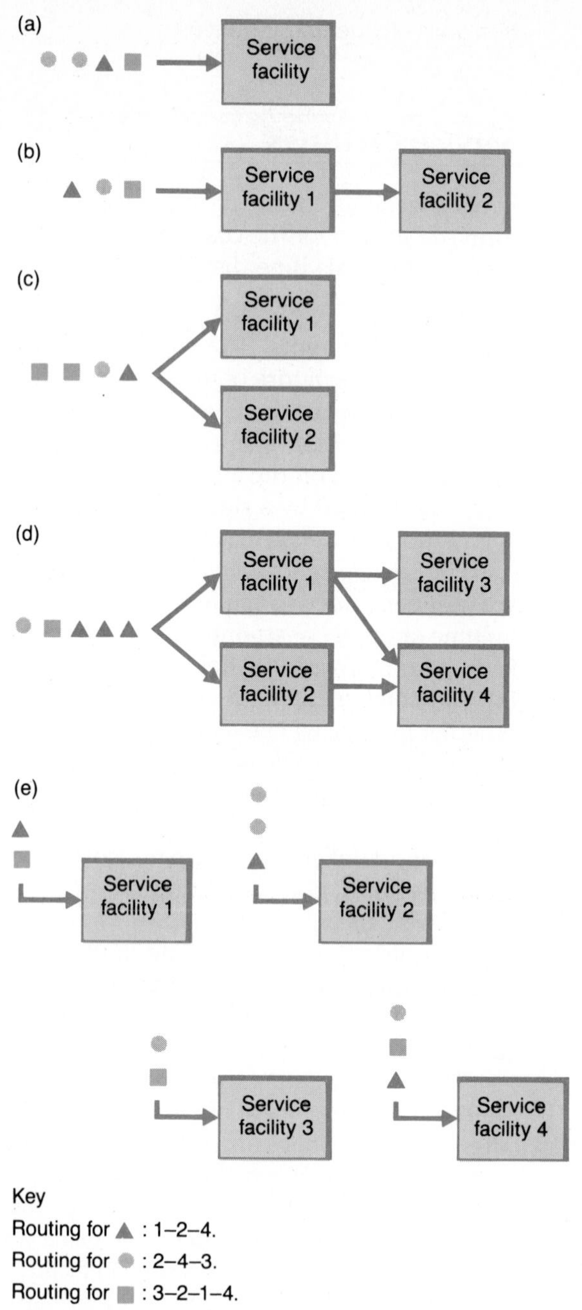

Figure B.4

Examples of Service Facility Arrangements: (a) Single Channel, Single Phase; (b) Single Channel, Multiple Phase; (c) Multiple Channel, Single Phase; (d) Multiple Channel, Multiple Phase; (e) Mixed.

Service-Time Distribution. The service-time distribution describes the probability that the service time of the customer at a particular facility will be no more than T time periods. A distribution that has been found to be useful in practice is the *exponential distribution*:

$$P(t \leq T) = 1 - e^{-\mu T},$$

where μ is the mean number of customers completing service per unit of time t. The mean of the service-time distribution is $1/\mu$ and the variance is $(1/\mu)^2$. For example, suppose that the clerk at a customer complaint desk can serve an average of three customers per hour. Thus the mean of the service distribution is 1/3 hr (or 20 min). Figure B.5 shows the exponential distribution for this example: As T increases, the probability that the customer will receive complete service approaches 1.0. Specific values can be read from the graph.

Some characteristics of the exponential distribution do not always conform to an actual situation. An underlying assumption is that each service time is independent of those that preceded it. Consequently, it does not allow for any learning about the work performed and resulting productivity improvements. Another underlying assumption is that very small, as well as very large, service times are possible. This assumption does not hold in situations for which there is a fixed start-up time or some cutoff on total service time. For example, an automatic teller machine has a fixed start-up time of almost fifteen seconds to get the user code number and the type of transaction desired. Service times less than fifteen seconds are not possible. Also, there are situations where the service time is constant, or nearly so, as, for example,

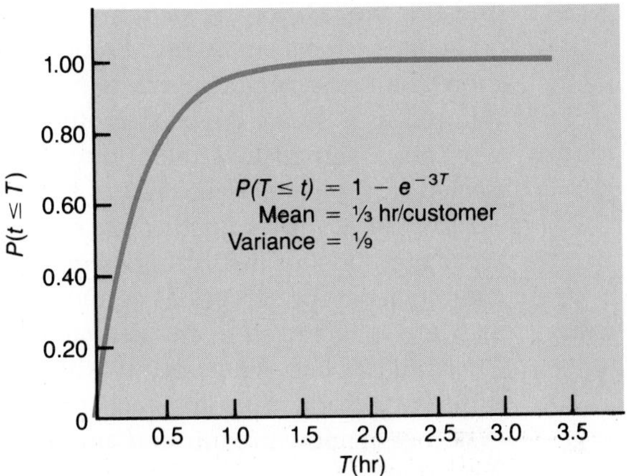

Figure B.5

Service-Time Distribution.

with automatic car washes, certain video games, and subway trains. Nonetheless, there are many practical settings where the exponential distribution is a good approximation of actual service times.

Decision Variables

The analysis of queuing problems involves making decisions in one or more of the following areas.

1. *Arrival rates.* Often, the rate of customer arrivals (λ) can be affected by management. Advertising or differential pricing such as that used by a telephone company for long-distance calls after 5:00 P.M. can affect the rate of demand for services.
2. *Number of service facilities.* The number of tool cribs, toll booths, or bank tellers has to be determined. Whether some facilities in a phase should perform a unique set of services has to be decided. These decisions relate to the number of facilities in a particular phase of the service system and, consequently, to the capacity of the system.
3. *Number of phases.* This decision involves the allocation of service tasks to sequential phases of the facility arrangement. At some point, also, two sequential service facilities may be more efficient than one. In the assembly-line problem discussed in Chapter 9, the decision concerned the number of phases needed along the assembly line. Determining the number of workers needed on the line also involves assigning a certain set of work elements to each one. In addition to affecting the facility arrangement, this decision also affects the service rate (μ) of each facility and the capacity of the system.
4. *Number of servers per facility.* Sometimes, a service facility is operated by more than one person. Such would be the case when a single facility is defined as a work crew or group of workers (such as the number of workers assigned to a telephone line repair crew). This decision is reflected in the service rate (μ) of the service facility.
5. *Server efficiency.* By adjusting the capital-to-labor ratio, devising improved work methods, or instituting incentive programs, management can affect the efficiency of servers assigned to a service facility. Decisions in this area are reflected in μ, the service rate of the service facility.
6. *Priority discipline.* The priority rule to be used and whether to have a different priority rule for each service facility are important decisions. Whether to allow preemption and, if so, under what conditions is equally important.
7. *Queue arrangement.* Whether to have a single-line queue or a line for each facility in a given phase of service has to be decided.

Although we presented these decision areas as though they are independent of each other, they are obviously interrelated. Adjusting the customer arrival rate λ might have to be accompanied by an increase in the service rate μ in some way. Decisions about the number of facilities, the number of phases, and queue arrangement are also related.

Operating Characteristics

Queuing models enable the analyst to study the effects of manipulating decision variables on the operating characteristics of a service system. Some of the more common operating characteristics considered are:

1. *Queue length.* The number of customers in the waiting line reflects one of two conditions. Short queues could mean either good customer service or too much capacity. Similarly, long queues could indicate either low server efficiency or the need to increase capacity.
2. *Number of customers in system.* The number of customers in queue and being served also relates to service efficiency and capacity. Large values imply congestion, potential customer dissatisfaction, and a need for more capacity.
3. *Waiting time in queue.* Long lines do not reflect long waiting times, if the service rate is fast. However, when waiting time seems long to customers, they perceive that the quality of service is poor. Long waiting times may indicate a need to adjust the service rate of the system or change the arrival rate of customers.
4. *Total time in system.* The total elapsed time from entry into the system until exit from the system may indicate problems with customers, server efficiency, or capacity. If some customers are spending too much time in the service system there may be a need to change the priority discipline, increase productivity, or adjust capacity in some way.
5. *Service facility utilization.* The collective utilization of the service facilities reflects the percentage of time the facilities are busy. Management is interested in maintaining high utilization, but this objective may have an adverse impact on the other operating characteristics.

The effect of various alternatives to be analyzed for a queuing problem can be expressed in terms of the operating characteristics. If operating characteristics and alternatives can be related to dollars, the effects of an alternative can be expressed in dollars. However, it is difficult to place a dollar figure on certain characteristics (such as the waiting time of a shopper in a grocery store). In such cases, an analyst must weigh the cost of implementing the alternative under consideration against a subjective effect on operating characteristics.

APPLICATION OF QUEUING MODELS TO OPERATIONS MANAGEMENT

We now turn to some examples of the application of queuing theory models to operations management. To simplify the presentation, we will use the notation contained in Table B.2. In this section, we analyze problems requiring the single-server, multiple-server, and finite input-source models, all of which are single phase. More advanced models can be found in the references at the end of this appendix.

Analyzing Different Service Rates

The manager of a grocery store in Sunnyville is interested in providing good service to the senior citizens who shop in his store. Presently, the store has a separate checkout counter for senior citizens. The senior citizens arrive at the counter at an average of 30 per hour, according to a Poisson distribution, and

Table B.2

Notation for Queuing Models

λ = Mean arrival rate (customers per unit of time).

μ = Mean service rate per server (customers per unit of time).

$\frac{1}{\lambda}$ = Mean time between arrivals.

$\frac{1}{\lambda_0}$ = Mean time between arrivals for a finite input source.

$\frac{1}{\mu}$ = Mean time per customer served.

ρ = Average utilization of the service facility. Sometimes called the traffic density. (Defined as λ/μ or $\lambda/s\mu$.)

$\bar{L}$ = Average number of customers in the service system.

$\bar{L_q}$ = Average number of customers in the waiting line.

$\bar{W}$ = Average time spent in the system (including service).

$\bar{W_q}$ = Average waiting time in line.

n = Number of customers in the service system.

P_n = Probability that there are n customers in the system.

N = Number of customers in the input source (for the finite input-source case).

s = Number of servers.

Table B.3

Single-Server Model

Assumptions	Operating Characteristics
Input source: infinite; no balking or reneging. Arrival distribution: Poisson; mean arrival rate = λ. Service distribution: exponential; mean service time = $1/\mu$. Queue: unlimited length; single line. Priority discipline: FCFS. Number of servers: 1. Number of phases: 1.	$\rho = \frac{\lambda}{\mu}$ $P_n = (1 - \rho)\rho^n$ $\overline{L} = \frac{\lambda}{\mu - \lambda}$ $\overline{L_q} = \rho\overline{L}$ $\overline{W} = \frac{1}{\mu - \lambda}$ $\overline{W_q} = \rho\overline{W}$

are serviced at an average rate of 35 customers per hour, with exponential service times. The *single-server model* in Table B.3 is appropriate. Find the average

1. utilization of the checkout clerk;
2. number of customers in the system;
3. number of customers in line;
4. time spent in the system; and
5. waiting time in line.

Using the equations for the operating characteristics of a single-channel, single-phase system in Table B.3, we can calculate the average characteristics as follows:

1. The average utilization of the checkout clerk is

$$\rho = \frac{\lambda}{\mu} = \frac{30}{35} = 0.857 \quad \text{or} \quad 85.7\%.$$

2. The average number of customers in the system is

$$\overline{L} = \frac{\lambda}{\mu - \lambda} = \frac{30}{35 - 30} = 6 \text{ customers.}$$

3. The average number of customers in line is

$$\overline{L_q} = \rho\overline{L} = 0.857(6) = 5.14 \text{ customers.}$$

4. The average time spent in the system is

$$\overline{W} = \frac{1}{\mu - \lambda} = \frac{1}{35 - 30} = 0.20 \text{ hr} \quad \text{or} \quad 12 \text{ min.}$$

5. The average time spent waiting in line is

$$\overline{W_q} = \rho\overline{W} = 0.857(0.20) = 0.17 \text{ hr} \quad \text{or} \quad 10.28 \text{ min.}$$

The manager would like to address the following questions: (1) What service rate would be required to have customers average only 8 minutes in the system? (2) For that service rate, what is the probability of having more than 4 customers in the system? and (3) What service rate would be required to have only a 10 percent chance of exceeding 4 customers in the system?

Question 1. We need to use the equation for the average time in the system and solve for μ.

$$\overline{W} = \frac{1}{\mu - \lambda}$$

$$8 \text{ min} = 0.133 \text{ hr} = \frac{1}{\mu - 30}$$

$$0.133\mu - 0.133(30) = 1$$

$$\mu = 37.52 \text{ customers/hr.}$$

Question 2. The probability that there will be more than 4 customers in the system is equal to 1 minus the probability that there are 4 or less customers in the system.

$$P = 1 - \sum_{n=0}^{4} P_n$$

$$= 1 - \sum_{n=0}^{4} (1 - \rho)\rho^n \qquad \text{where } \rho = \frac{30}{37.52} = 0.80$$

$$= 1 - 0.2(1 + 0.8 + 0.8^2 + 0.8^3 + 0.8^4)$$

$$= 1 - 0.672$$

$$= 0.328.$$

Therefore there is a nearly 33 percent chance that more than 4 customers will be in the system.

Question 3. We use the same logic as in Question 2, except that μ is now a decision variable. It is easier to first find the correct average utilization by trial and error and then solve for the service rate.

$$P = 1 - (1 - \rho)(1 + \rho + \rho^2 + \rho^3 + \rho^4).$$

Try $\rho = 0.7$:

$$0.10 \overset{?}{=} 1 - (0.3)(1 + 0.7 + 0.49 + 0.343 + 0.240)$$
$$0.10 \neq 0.168.$$

Try $\rho = 0.6$:

$$0.10 \overset{?}{=} 1 - (0.4)(1 + 0.6 + 0.36 + 0.216 + 0.1296)$$
$$0.10 \neq 0.078.$$

Try $\rho = 0.63$:

$$0.10 \overset{?}{=} 1 - (0.37)(1 + 0.63 + 0.3969 + 0.2500 + 0.1575)$$
$$0.10 \approx 0.099.$$

Therefore, for a utilization rate of 63 percent, the probability of more than 4 customers in the system is 10 percent. For $\lambda = 30$, the service rate must be

$$\frac{30}{\mu} = 0.63$$
$$\mu = 47.62 \text{ customers/hr.}$$

The manager must now find a way to increase the service rate from 35 per hour to approximately 48 per hour. He can increase the service rate in a number of different ways, ranging from employing a high school student to help bag the groceries to incorporating electronic point-of-sale equipment that reads the prices from barcoded information on each item.

Increasing Capacity by Adding Facilities

The management of the American Parcel Service terminal in Poland, Ohio, is concerned about the amount of time the company's trucks are idle, waiting to be unloaded. Presently the terminal operates with 4 unloading bays, although the terminal actually has 5 bays. The fifth bay was never used because management thought that the cost of adding the two employees required to operate the bay would exceed the benefits in reduced idle truck time. Adding a crew of two employees would cost \$30 per hour, while the estimated cost of an idle truck is \$50 per hour. Trucks arrive at an average rate of 3 trucks per hour, according to a Poisson distribution. A crew of two employees can unload a semitrailer rig in an average of one hour, with exponential service times. The *multiple-server model* in Table B.4 is appropriate.

Four-Bay Design. In order to find the total cost of labor and idle trucks, we must calculate the average waiting time in the system and the average num-

Table B.4

Multiple-Server Model

Assumptions	Operating Characteristics
Input source: infinite; no balking or reneging. Arrival distribution: Poisson; mean arrival time = λ. Service distribution: exponential; mean service time = $1/\mu$. Queue: unlimited length; single line. Priority discipline: FCFS. Number of servers: s. Number of phases: 1.	$\rho = \frac{\lambda}{s\mu}$ $P_0 = \left[\sum_{n=0}^{s-1} \frac{(\lambda/\mu)^n}{n!} + \frac{(\lambda/\mu)^s}{s!}\left(\frac{1}{1-\rho}\right)\right]^{-1}$ $P_n = \begin{cases} \frac{(\lambda/\mu)^n}{n!} P_0 & 0 < n < s \\ \frac{(\lambda/\mu)^n}{s!s^{n-s}} P_0 & n \geq s \end{cases}$ $\overline{L_q} = \frac{P_0 (\lambda/\mu)^s \rho}{s!(1-\rho)^2}$ $\overline{W_q} = \frac{\overline{L_q}}{\lambda}$ $\overline{W} = \overline{W_q} + \frac{1}{\mu}$ $\overline{L} = \lambda \overline{W}$

ber of trucks in the system. However, we first need to calculate the average number of trucks in queue and the average waiting time in queue.

The average utilization of the four bays is

$$\rho = \frac{\lambda}{\mu s} = \frac{3}{1(4)} = 0.75 \quad \text{or} \quad 75\%.$$

For this level of utilization, we can now compute the probability of no trucks in the system.

$$P_0 = \left[\sum_{n=0}^{s-1} \frac{(\lambda/\mu)^n}{n!} + \frac{(\lambda/\mu)^s}{s!}\left(\frac{1}{1-\rho}\right)\right]^{-1}$$

$$= \frac{1}{\left[1 + 3 + \frac{9}{2} + \frac{27}{6} + \frac{81}{24}\left(\frac{1}{1-0.75}\right)\right]}$$

$$= 0.0377.$$

The average number of trucks in queue is

$$\overline{L_q} = \frac{P_0(\lambda/\mu)^s\rho}{s!(1-\rho)^2}$$

$$= \frac{0.0377(3/1)^4(0.75)}{4!(1-0.75)^2}$$

$$= 1.53 \text{ trucks.}$$

The average waiting time in queue is

$$\overline{W_q} = \frac{\overline{L_q}}{\lambda} = \frac{1.53}{3}$$

$$= 0.51 \text{ hr.}$$

The average time spent in the system is

$$\overline{W} = \overline{W_q} + \frac{1}{\mu} = 0.51 + \frac{1}{1}$$

$$= 1.51 \text{ hr.}$$

Finally, the average number of trucks in the system is

$$\overline{L} = \lambda\overline{W} = 3(1.51)$$

$$= 4.53 \text{ trucks.}$$

Consequently, the number of trucks in the system averages 4.53 at all times. We can now calculate the hourly costs of labor and idle trucks as follows:

$$\begin{aligned} \text{Labor cost} &= \$30(s) = \$30(4) &&= \$120.00 \\ \text{Idle truck cost} &= \$50(\overline{L}) = \$50(4.53) &&= \underline{\$226.50} \\ && \text{Total hourly cost} &= \underline{\underline{\$346.50}} \end{aligned}$$

Five-Bay Design. The logic for the five-bay design is the same as that for the four-bay design.

$$\rho = \frac{3}{1(5)} = 0.60 \quad \text{or} \quad 60\%.$$

$$P_0 = \frac{1}{\left[1 + 3 + \frac{9}{2} + \frac{27}{6} + \frac{81}{24} + \frac{243}{120}\left(\frac{1}{1-0.60}\right)\right]} = 0.0466$$

$$\overline{L_q} = \frac{0.0466(3/1)^5(0.60)}{5!(1-0.60)^2} = 0.354 \text{ trucks}$$

$$\overline{W}_q = \frac{0.354}{3} = 0.12 \text{ hr}$$

$$\overline{W} = 0.12 + \frac{1}{1} = 1.12 \text{ hr}$$

$$\overline{L} = 3(1.12) = 3.36 \text{ trucks.}$$

The hourly costs for the five-day bay design are

$$\begin{aligned} \text{Labor cost} &= \$30(5) &&= \$150.00 \\ \text{Idle truck cost} &= \$50(3.36) &&= \underline{\$168.00} \\ \text{Total hourly cost} &= &&\underline{\underline{\$318.00}} \end{aligned}$$

Based on this analysis the company would save \$28.50/hr by adding the fifth bay.

Analyzing Different Work Methods

The Worthington Gear Company had installed a bank of ten robots about three years ago. The robots have greatly increased the labor productivity of the firm. However, recent attention has been directed to the maintenance function. The firm does no preventive maintenance on the robots because of the high variability in the breakdown distribution. Each machine has an exponential breakdown (or interarrival) distribution with the average time between failures equal to 200 hours ($\lambda_0 = 0.005$ breakdowns per hour). Each machine-hour lost to downtime costs \$30, which means that the firm has to react quickly to machine failure. The firm currently employs one maintenance person, who takes an average of 10 hours to fix a robot ($\mu = 0.10$). Actual maintenance times have been observed to be exponentially distributed. The wage rate for the maintenance person is \$10 per hour and he can be productively put to work elsewhere when not fixing robots.

The industrial engineering department has developed a proposal to increase the productivity of the robot maintenance person. It would entail purchasing new diagnostic equipment at a cost of \$6000. In addition, a skilled robot mechanic would be hired for \$15 per hour. With these new resources, the procedure for repairing robots would be improved by 20 percent to an average of 8 hours per robot ($\hat{\mu} = 0.125$). Repair times would still follow an exponential distribution.

The *finite-source model* in Table B.5 is appropriate for analyzing the proposal for improving work methods because there are only ten machines in the input source and the other assumptions are satisfied.

Current Method. In order to calculate the cost of the current method to compare with the proposal, we need only to estimate $\overline{L}$, the average number

Table B.5

Finite Source Model

Assumptions	Operating Characteristics
Input source: finite; equals N customers.	$P_0 = \left[\sum_{n=0}^{N} \frac{N!}{(N-n)!}\left(\frac{\lambda_0}{\mu}\right)^n\right]^{-1}$
Arrival distribution: exponential interarrival times; mean = $1/\lambda_0$.	$\rho = 1 - P_0$
Service distribution: exponential; mean service time = $1/\mu$.	$\overline{L_q} = N - \frac{\lambda_0 + \mu}{\lambda_0}(1 - P_0)$
Queue: no more than $N - 1$; single line.	$\overline{L} = N - \frac{\mu}{\lambda_0}(1 - P_0)$
Priority discipline: FCFS.	$\overline{W_q} = \overline{L_q}[(N - \overline{L})\lambda_0]^{-1}$
Number of servers: 1.	$\overline{W} = \overline{L}[(N - \overline{L})\lambda_0]^{-1}$
Number of phases: 1.	

of machines in the maintenance system. However, to demonstrate the use of the finite-source model, we will compute all the operating statistics.

The probability that the maintenance system is empty is

$$P_0 = \left[\sum_{n=0}^{N} \frac{N!}{(N-n)!}\left(\frac{\lambda_0}{\mu}\right)^n\right]^{-1} = \frac{1}{\sum_{n=0}^{10} \frac{10!}{(10-n)!}\left(\frac{0.005}{0.10}\right)^n}$$

$$= 0.538.$$

The average utilization of the maintenance person is

$$\rho = 1 - P_0$$
$$= 1 - 0.538 = 0.462 \quad \text{or} \quad 46\%.$$

The average number of robots waiting to be repaired is

$$\overline{L_q} = N - \frac{\lambda_0 + \mu}{\lambda_0}(1 - P_0) = 10 - \frac{0.005 + 0.10}{0.005}(1 - 0.538)$$
$$= 0.30 \text{ robots.}$$

The average number of robots in queue and being repaired is

$$\overline{L} = N - \frac{\mu}{\lambda_0}(1 - P_0) = 10 - \frac{0.10}{0.005}(1 - 0.538)$$
$$= 0.76 \text{ robot.}$$

The average waiting time of robots for the maintenance person is

$$\overline{W}_q = \overline{L}_q[(N - \overline{L})\lambda_0]^{-1} = \frac{0.30}{(10 - 0.76)(0.005)}$$
$$= 6.49 \text{ hr.}$$

Finally, the average time that a failed robot spends waiting for service and being repaired is

$$\overline{W} = \overline{L}[(N - \overline{L})\lambda_0]^{-1} = \frac{0.76}{(10 - 0.76)(0.005)}$$
$$= 16.45 \text{ hr.}$$

The daily cost of labor and robot downtime is

Labor cost = ($10/hr)(8 hr/day) = $ 80.00
Idle robot cost = (0.76 robot)($30/robot-hr)(8 hr/day) = $182.40
Total daily cost = $262.40

Proposed Method. The operating characteristics with $\hat{\mu} = 0.125$ robot per hour are compared to those of the present method in Table B.6. Note that a 20 percent increase in the service rate results in disproportionate changes in the operating characteristics. The new methods would reduce the utilization of the maintenance person by 17.4 percent. However, the number of robots in the maintenance system will be reduced by more than 27 percent and the total downtime of a robot will be reduced by 20 percent. The daily cost of labor and robot downtime for the proposal is

Labor cost = ($15/hr)(8 hr/day) = $120.00
Idle robot cost = (0.55 robot)($30/robot-hr)(8 hr/day) = 132.00
Total daily cost = $252.00

The net savings of the proposal over the current method is $262.40 − $252.00 = $10.40/day. If the company operates 250 days a year, the annual

Table B.6

Comparison of Operating Characteristics with Current and Proposed Methods

Condition	ρ	$\overline{L}_q$	$\overline{L}$	$\overline{W}_q$	$\overline{W}$
Current method ($\mu = 0.10$)	0.46	0.30	0.76	6.49	16.45
Proposed method ($\hat{\mu} = 0.125$)	0.38	0.17	0.55	3.60	11.64
Percentage change	−17.4%	−43.3%	−27.6%	−44.5%	−29.2%

savings is 250($10.40) = $2600. Suppose that the tax rate is 50 percent, the estimated life of the equipment is 10 years, and the straight-line depreciation method is used. Since the investment in equipment for the new repair method is $6000, the depreciation is $600 per year and the after-tax cash flow would be $1600 (see Appendix A). The payback period is

$$P = \frac{\text{Investment}}{\text{Annual savings after tax}} = \frac{6000}{1600} = 3.75 \text{ yr.}$$

The management of the Worthington Gear Company can now judge whether a payback of 3.75 years warrants an outlay of $6000 for the new equipment.

SIMULATION

For the problems just analyzed with the use of queuing theory models, we were fortunate that the arrivals had a Poisson distribution (or exponential interarrival times) and that the service times had an exponential distribution. The service facilities had a simple arrangement and the priority discipline was first come, first served. Many more models have been developed with queuing theory (see, for example, Cooper, 1972; And Saaty, 1961). However, they get very complex as we deviate from our earlier simplifying assumptions. Many times, the nature of the input source, the constraints on the queue, the priority discipline, the service time distribution, and the arrangement of the facilities are such that queuing theory is no longer useful. In these cases, simulation is often used.

What is Simulation?

Simulation is the act of reproducing the behavior of a system. A **descriptive model** of the system is developed, and certain variables are manipulated to measure their effects on the operating characteristics of interest. A descriptive model, unlike a linear programming model, for example (see Appendix C), merely describes the system and cannot prescribe what should be done about the problem. It can be used to estimate the operating characteristics of the system under study for alternative solutions to the problem. The alternatives are systematically used in the model and the relevant operating characteristics are recorded. After trying all the alternatives, we choose the best one based on the simulation.

The queuing theory models we presented earlier are actually descriptive models because they describe the operating characteristics of the queuing situation. The difference with simulation, however, is that we do not know the equations for the operating characteristics. We must actually generate customer arrivals, put customers in queues, select the next customer to be served using some priority discipline, serve that customer, and so on. We actually keep track of the number in queue, waiting time, and the like during the simulation and calculate the averages and variances at the end.

Simulation can also be used in analyzing nonqueuing problems. Consider a flight simulator for a major airline company. Pilots are tested on the flight simulator periodically. The cockpit of the simulator is identical to that of a real airplane. Through the use of computer graphics and other visual and mechanical effects, the pilot feels as though he or she is actually flying the airplane. However, the entire process takes place inside a large laboratory. Table B.7 shows some other examples of the use of simulation in queuing and nonqueuing situations.

Table B.7

Examples of the Use of Simulation in Operations Management

- **Process design and choice of technology**
  Airport design
  Clerical system design
  Library operations design
- **Capacity and location**
  Airline maintenance
  Ambulance location
  Court system resource allocation
  Harbor design
  Steel furnace maintenance
  Warehouse and plant location
- **Layout**
  Assembly-line design
  Manufacturing process layouts
  Parking facility design
  Pharmaceutical center layout
- **Inventory management**
  Aerospace inventory systems
  Aircraft maintenance inventories
  Hospital inventories
  Mail system distribution networks
  Manufacturing inventories
  Military logistics
- **Production and staff planning**
  Insurance staffing
  Mail system staffing
  Police patrol staffing
  Production output planning
- **Operations scheduling and control**
  Air traffic control
  Aircraft maintenance
  Aircraft parts manufacturing
  Aircraft schedules and routes
  Ambulance and other emergency vehicle dispatching
  Bank courier routing
  Bank teller scheduling
  Bus scheduling
  Iron-ore mine scheduling
  Job-shop scheduling
  Metals forming
  Multishift worker scheduling
  Nurse scheduling
  Personnel scheduling for spacecraft trips
  Rail freight-car dispatching
  Shipyard scheduling
  Taxi dispatching
  Work-in-process control
- **Quality management**
  Location of inspection staff
  Semiconductor yield loss

Reasons for Using Simulation

We have already said that we would use simulation in queuing situations for which queuing theory models become too complex or are not available. There are also other reasons for using simulation for analyzing operations management problems. First, many practical problems cannot be solved with optimizing methods. The relationship between the variables may be nonlinear and very complex. In addition, there may be too many variables and/or constraints to handle with current optimizing approaches. A simulation model may be the only way to estimate the operating characteristics or objective function values and analyze the problem.

Second, simulation models can be used to conduct experiments without disrupting real systems. Experimenting with a real system can be very costly. It would be unreasonable to go through the expense of purchasing and installing a new flexible manufacturing system without first estimating its benefits in detail from an operating perspective. A simulation model can be used to conduct experiments for a fraction of the cost of installing such a system. Also, the model could be used to evaluate different configurations or processing decision rules. To try any of these methods while attempting to maintain a production schedule would be virtually impossible.

Third, simulation models can be used to obtain operating characteristic estimates in much less time than required to gather the same operating data from a real system. This feature of simulation is called *time compression*. For example, a simulation model of airport operations can generate statistics for a year on airplane arrivals, landing delays, and terminal delays in a matter of minutes on a computer. Alternative airport designs can be analyzed and decisions made quickly.

Finally, simulation is useful in sharpening managerial decision-making skills through gaming. A descriptive model that relates managerial decisions to important operating characteristics (such as profits, market share, and so on) can be developed. For a set of starting conditions, the managers make periodic decisions with the intention of improving one or more operating characteristics. In such an exercise, a few hours "play" can simulate a year's time. Management games also enable managers to experiment with new ideas without disrupting normal operations.

Despite these reasons for using simulation, many practitioners still think of simulation as the method of last resort. Mathematical analysis is still preferred by management scientists because it provides the "best" solution for the problem, whereas simulation requires the analyst to try various alternatives. If the "best" alternative is not on the list of alternatives, only a suboptimal solution will be obtained. In addition, simulation modeling is usually very expensive because of the detail required in the computer model. It is not uncommon for thousands of hours to be spent on programming and debugging complex models. Optimizing approaches, if they apply, are usually less expensive. Nonetheless, simulation is used extensively in practice. Christy and Watson (1983) surveyed nonacademic members of the Institute of Management Sciences and the Operations Research Society of America and found that 89 percent of the firms responding used simulation. Of those using simulation, the largest category of use was in production (59 percent), followed by corporate planning (53 percent) and engineering (46 percent). It would seem that the so-called last resort is an option often used in practice.

A Simulation Example

To demonstrate the concept of simulation we will analyze a capacity planning problem at the Specialty Steel Products Company. The company produces items such as machine tools, gears, automobile parts, and other specialty items in small quantities to customer order. Since the products represent such a wide variety, demand is measured in machine-hours. Whenever an order for a certain quantity of product comes in, it is translated into required machine-hours using time standards for each operation.

Data Collection. Historical records indicate that the demand for the lathe department varies from week to week in the following way:

Weekly Production Requirements (hr)	Relative Frequency
200	0.05
250	0.06
300	0.17
350	0.05
400	0.30
450	0.15
500	0.06
550	0.14
600	0.02
	1.00

To gather this data, all weeks with requirements of 175.00–224.99 hours were grouped in the 200-hour category; all weeks with 225.00–274.99 hours, in the 250-hour category; and so on. The average weekly production requirements for the lathe department are

$$200(0.05) + 250(0.06) + 300(0.17) + \cdots + 600(0.02) = 400 \text{ hr.}$$

Presently, employees in the lathe department work 40 hours per week on 10 machines. However, the number of machines actually available during any week may be less than 10. Machines may need repair or a worker may not show up for work. Historical records indicate that actual machine-hours were distributed as follows:

Regular Capacity (hr)	Relative Frequency
320 (8 machines)	0.30
360 (9 machines)	0.40
400 (10 machines)	0.30

The average number of machine-hours available in a week is 320(0.30) + 360(0.40) + 400(0.30) = 360 hours.

The Specialty Steel Products company has a policy of completing each week's workload on schedule, using overtime and subcontracting if necessary. The maximum amount of overtime authorized in any week is 100 hours, and any excess requirements over 100 hours are subcontracted to a small machine shop in town. Lathe operators receive $10 per hour for regular time. However, management estimates that it costs $25 per hour per employee for overtime work, which includes premium-wage, variable overhead, and supervision costs. Subcontracting costs $35 per hour, exclusive of materials costs.

Management is considering adding another machine and a worker to the lathe department. In order to justify the new machine, management estimates that weekly savings should be at least $650. These savings would cover the cost of the additional worker and provide for a reasonable return on machine investment. Prior experience with the uncertainty in available capacity each week is reflected in the estimated distribution of weekly capacity hours with 11 machines:

Regular Capacity (hr)	Relative Frequency
360 (9 machines)	0.30
400 (10 machines)	0.40
440 (11 machines)	0.30

Should management authorize the purchase of the new lathe?

Random-Number Assignment. Before we can begin to analyze this problem with simulation, we must specify a way to generate demand and capacity each week. Suppose that we want to simulate 100 weeks of lathe operations with 10 machines. We would expect that 5 percent of the time (or five weeks of the hundred) we would have a demand for 200 hours. Similarly, we would expect that 30 percent of the time (or 30 weeks of the hundred) we would have 320 hours of capacity. What about starting our simulation with a demand of 200 hours for the first five weeks, 250 hours for the next six weeks, and so on? Or, using a capacity of 320 hours for the first 30 weeks? The reason for not doing our simulation in this manner is that the real system does not operate that way. Demand may be 200 hours one week but 550 hours the next. However, we certainly want our simulation to generate a demand of 200 hours for 5 percent of the time, as stated in the demand distribution. Simi-

Table B.8

Table of Random Numbers

71509	68310	48213	99928	64650	13229	36921	58732	13459	93487
21949	30920	23287	89514	58502	46185	00368	82613	02668	37444
50639	54968	11409	36148	82090	87298	41396	71111	00076	60029
47837	76716	09653	54466	87987	82362	17933	52793	17641	19502
31735	36901	92295	19293	57582	86043	69502	12601	00535	82697
04174	32342	66532	07875	54445	08795	63563	42295	74646	73120
96980	68728	21154	56181	71843	66134	52396	89723	96435	17871
21823	04027	76402	04655	87276	32593	17097	06913	05136	05115
25922	07122	31485	52166	07645	85122	20945	06369	70254	22806
32530	98882	19105	01769	20276	59401	60426	03316	41438	22012
00159	08461	51810	14650	45119	97920	08063	70819	01832	53295
66574	21384	75357	55888	83429	96916	73977	87883	13249	28870
00995	28829	15048	49573	65277	61493	44031	88719	73057	66010
55114	79226	27929	23392	06432	50200	39054	15528	53483	33972
10614	25190	52647	62580	51183	31338	60008	66595	64357	14985
31359	77469	58126	59192	23371	25190	37841	44386	92420	42965
09736	51873	94595	61367	82091	63835	86858	10677	58209	59820
24709	23224	45788	21426	63353	29874	51058	29958	61220	61199
79957	67598	74102	49824	39305	15069	56327	26905	34453	53964
66616	22137	72805	64420	58711	68435	60301	28620	91919	96080
01413	27281	19397	36231	05010	42003	99865	20924	76151	54089
88238	80731	20777	45725	41480	48277	45704	96457	13918	52375
57457	87883	64273	26236	61095	01309	48632	00431	63730	18917
21614	06412	71007	20255	39890	75336	89451	88091	61011	38072
26466	03735	39891	26361	86816	48193	33492	70484	77322	01016

larly, we want to generate a capacity of 320 hours for 30 percent of the time, but not sequentially.

We can obtain the effect we want by using a random-number table to determine the amount of demand and capacity each week. A random number is a number that has the same probability of being selected as any other number. Table B.8 contains 5-digit random numbers for our use.

The events in the simulation can be generated in an unbiased way if random numbers are assigned to the events in the same proportion as their probability of occurrence. We expect a demand of 200 hours for 5 percent of the time. If we have 100 random numbers (00–99), we can assign 5 numbers (or 5 percent of them) to the event "200 hours demanded." Thus we can assign the numbers 00–04 to that event. If we randomly choose numbers in the range 00–99 enough times, we would expect that 5 percent of the time they would fall in the range 00–04. Similarly, we can assign the numbers 05–10 to the event "250 hours demanded." In Table B.9, we show the allocation

97314	03944	04509	46143	88908	55261	73433	62538	63187	57352
91207	33555	75942	41668	64650	38741	86189	38197	99112	59694
46791	78974	01999	78891	16177	95746	78076	75001	51309	18791
34161	32258	05345	79267	75607	29916	37005	09213	10991	50451
02376	40372	45077	73705	56076	01853	83512	81567	55951	27156
33994	56809	58377	45976	01581	78389	18268	90057	93382	28494
92588	92024	15048	87841	38008	80689	73098	39201	10907	88092
73767	61534	66197	47147	22994	38197	60844	86962	27595	49907
51517	39870	94094	77092	94595	37904	27553	02229	44993	10468
33910	05156	60844	89012	21154	68937	96477	05867	95809	72827
09444	93069	61764	99301	55826	78849	26131	28201	91417	98172
96896	43760	72890	78682	78243	24061	55449	53587	77574	51580
97523	54633	99656	08503	52563	12099	52479	74374	79581	57143
42568	30794	32613	21802	73809	60237	70087	36650	54487	43718
45453	33136	90246	61953	17724	42421	87611	95369	42108	95369
52814	26445	73516	24897	90622	35018	70087	60112	09025	05324
87318	33345	14546	15445	81588	75461	12246	47858	08983	18205
08063	83575	25294	93027	09988	04487	88364	31087	22200	91019
53400	62078	52103	25650	75315	18916	06809	88217	12245	33053
90789	60614	20862	34475	11744	24437	55198	55219	74730	59820
73684	25859	86858	48946	30941	79017	53776	72534	83638	44680
82007	12183	89326	53713	77782	50368	01748	39033	47042	65758
80208	30920	97774	41417	79038	60531	32990	57770	53441	58732
62434	96122	63019	58439	89702	38657	60049	88761	22785	66093
04718	83199	65863	58857	49886	70275	27511	99426	53985	84077

Table B.9

Random-Number Assignments to Simulation Events

Event: Weekly Demand (hr)	Probability	Random Numbers	Event: Existing Weekly Capacity (hr)	Probability	Random Numbers
200	0.05	00–04	320	0.30	00–29
250	0.06	05–10	360	0.40	30–69
300	0.17	11–27	400	0.30	70–99
350	0.05	28–32			
400	0.30	33–62			
450	0.15	63–77			
500	0.06	78–83			
550	0.14	84–97			
600	0.02	98–99			

of the 100 random numbers to the demand events in the same proportion as the probability of their occurrence. We assigned random numbers to the *capacity* events for 10 machines in a similar fashion. The capacity events for the 11-machine simulation would have the same random number assignments, except that the events would be 360, 400, and 440, hours respectively.

The Simulation Process. In our example, we will simulate 20 weeks of lathe department operations. We will use the first two rows of random numbers in Table B.8 for the demand events and the third and fourth rows for the capacity events. Since these are five-digit numbers, we will use only the first two digits of each number for our random numbers. The choice of the rows in the random number table was arbitrary. The important point is that we must be consistent in drawing random numbers, and we should not repeat the use of numbers in any one simulation.

To simulate a particular capacity level, proceed as follows:

1. Draw a random number from Table B.8 from the first two rows. Start with the first number in the first row, then go to the second number in the first row, and so on.
2. Find the random-number interval for production requirements associated with the random number.
3. Record the production-hours (PROD) required for the current week.
4. Draw another random number from Table B.8 from row 3 or row 4. Start with the first number in row 3, then go to the second number in row 3, and so on.
5. Find the random-number interval for capacity (CAP) associated with the random number.
6. Record the capacity-hours available for the current week.
7. If CAP $\geq$ PROD, then IDLE HR = CAP − PROD.
8. If CAP $<$ PROD, then SHORT = PROD − CAP. If SHORT $\leq$ 100, then OVERTIME HR = SHORT and SUBCONTRACT HR = 0. If SHORT $>$ 100, then OVERTIME HR = 100 and SUBCONTRACT HR = SHORT − 100.
9. Repeat steps 1–8 until you have simulated 20 weeks.

This process is known as *Monte Carlo simulation* because of the random numbers used to generate the simulation events.

Simulation Analysis. Table B.10 contains the simulations for the two capacity alternatives. We used a unique random-number sequence for weekly production requirements for each capacity alternative and another one for the existing weekly capacity in order to make a direct comparison between the capacity alternatives.

Table B.10

20-Week Simulations of Alternatives for Specialty Steel Products Company

				10 Machines				11 Machines			
Week	Demand RN	Weekly Prod (hr)	Capacity RN	Existing weekly capacity (hr)	Idle hours	Overtime hours	Sub-contract hours	Existing weekly capacity (hr)	Idle hours	Overtime hours	Sub-contract hours
1	71	450	50	360		90		400		50	
2	68	450	54	360		90		400		50	
3	48	400	11	320		80		360		40	
4	99	600	36	360		100	140	400		100	100
5	64	450	82	400		50		440		10	
6	13	300	87	400	100			440	140		
7	36	400	41	360		40		400			
8	58	400	71	400				440	40		
9	13	300	00	320	20			360	60		
10	93	550	60	360		100	90	400		100	50
11	21	300	47	360	60			400	100		
12	30	350	76	400	50			440	90		
13	23	300	09	320	20			360	60		
14	89	550	54	360		100	90	400		100	50
15	58	400	87	400				440	40		
16	46	400	82	400				440	40		
17	00	200	17	320	120			360	160		
18	82	500	52	360		100	40	400		100	
19	02	200	17	320	120			360	160		
20	37	400	19	320		80		360		40	
Total					490	830	360		890	590	200
Weekly average					24.5	41.5	18.0		44.5	29.5	10.0

Based on the 20-week simulations, we would expect average weekly overtime hours to be reduced by 12 hours (or 41.5 − 29.5) and subcontracting hours to be reduced by 8 hours (or 18 − 10) per week. The average weekly savings would be

$$\begin{aligned} \text{Overtime} &= (12\text{ hr})(\$25/\text{hr}) = \$300 \\ \text{Subcontracting} &= (8\text{ hr})(\$35/\text{hr}) = \underline{280} \\ \text{Total savings per week} &= \underline{\underline{\$580}} \end{aligned}$$

This amount falls short of the minimum required savings of $650 per week. Does this mean that we should not add the machine and worker? Before we answer that question, let's look at Table B.11 which shows the results of a *1000-week* simulation for each alternative. These results are quite different from those of the 20-week simulations. Now the savings are estimated to be $692 (or $1851.50 − $1159.50) and exceed the minimum required savings for the additional investment. This result emphasizes the importance of selecting the proper run length for a simulation analysis. We must run the simulation long enough to achieve stable results before we begin calculating operating characteristics. Typically, operating characteristics fluctuate widely for short run lengths and stabilize for longer run lengths. We can use statistical tests to check for stability.

Simulation analysis can be viewed as a form of hypothesis testing, whereby the results of a simulation run provide sample data that can be analyzed statistically. When the simulation has achieved stability, data can be recorded and compared with the results from other simulation runs. Statistical tests can also be made to determine whether differences in the alternative operating characteristics are statistically significant. Commonly used statistical methods include *analysis of variance, t-tests,* and *regression analysis.* These techniques require replication of each simulation experiment. For example, if we wanted to test the null hypothesis that the difference between the total weekly costs is zero, we would have to run the simulation model several times for each capacity alternative. Each time, a different set of random num-

Table B.11

Comparison of 1000-Week Simulations for Specialty Steel Products Company

	10 machines	11 machines
Idle hours	26.0	42.2
Overtime hours	48.3	34.2
Subcontract hours	18.4	8.7
Cost	$1851.50	$1159.50

bers would be used to generate weekly production requirements and weekly existing capacity. The number of replications is analogous to the sample size in statistical terminology. If we can show that the weekly cost for 11 machines is significantly different (in a statistical sense) from the weekly cost for 10 machines, we can be more confident in the estimate of the difference between the two.

Even though a difference between simulation experiments may be statistically significant, it may not be *managerially* significant. For example, suppose that we developed a simulation model of a car-wash operation. We may find, by changing the speed of the car wash from 3 minutes per car to 2.75 minutes per car, that we can reduce the average waiting time per customer by 0.20 minutes. Even though this may be a statistically significant difference in the average waiting time, the difference is so small that it may not even be noticeable by the customers. What is managerially significant is often a judgment decision.

Computers and Simulation

It does not take much imagination to recognize that analyzing simulation models requires a computer for virtually all real problems. Simulation programming can be done in a variety of computer languages. General-purpose programming languages such as BASIC, FORTRAN, or PASCAL can be used. The advantage of general-purpose programming languages is that they are available on most computer systems. A number of special simulation languages, such as GPSS, SIMSCRIPT, GASP, and GERT, are also available. These languages have the advantage of simplifying programming because they have macro instructions for the commonly used elements of simulation models. These macro statements automatically generate a series of computer instructions needed to accomplish certain tasks. For example, generating arrivals, keeping track of queues, and calculating the statistics on the operating characteristics of a queuing problem is relatively simple with these special languages.

APPENDIX HIGHLIGHTS

In this appendix, we addressed queuing and simulation as methods for analyzing operations management problems. Some of the highlights of the appendix are:

- Queuing problems consist of an input source that generates customers, a queue (or waiting line), a priority discipline for choosing the next customer to be served, and the service facilities. Examples of queuing problems in operations management are numerous. Customers can be human, or they can be inanimate objects, such as machines or production orders.

- Two distributions found useful in practice for defining customer arrivals and the time required for serving a customer are the Poisson and the exponential distributions, respectively. However, many queuing situations do not satisfy the assumptions of these distributions.
- Decision variables in a queuing analysis include arrival rates, number of service facilities (channels), number of phases, number of servers per facility, server efficiency, priority discipline, and queue arrangement. Operating characteristics include queue length, number of customers in the system, waiting time in queue, total time in the system, and service facility utilization.
- Under simplifying assumptions, queuing equations can be formulated to provide the mean values for operating characteristics. These equations become more complex as the complexity of the service system increases, or customer arrivals or service times diverge from the Poisson or exponential distributions. Many real queuing situations defy derivation of queuing equations mathematically.
- Simulation is the act of reproducing the behavior of a system, using a descriptive model. Simulation is used (1) when optimizing methods cannot be used; (2) to evaluate alternatives without disrupting the real system; (3) to take advantage of time compression in gathering and analyzing data; and (4) to sharpen managerial decision-making skills through gaming.
- Monte Carlo simulation involves data collection, generating random numbers, assignment of random numbers to simulated events, collecting statistics on operating characteristics, and analyzing the results.
- Computers are essential for practical simulation analysis.

KEY TERMS

descriptive model
input source
interarrival time
preemptive discipline
priority discipline
service facilities
service system

STUDY QUESTIONS

1. Describe the input source, waiting line, priority discipline, and service facilities for each of the following:
   (a) Drive-in window at a fast-food restaurant.
   (b) Gas station.
   (c) Pediatrics clinic with three doctors.
2. Why is it useful to identify and characterize the basic elements of a particular queuing problem?
3. Suppose that you had a queuing situation in which the arrival distribution of customers per hour is

$$P(A_1 = n) = \frac{(4)^n}{n!} e^{-4},$$

and the service time distribution is

$$P(t \leq T) = 1 - e^{-3T}.$$

What do you suppose will happen to the queue length in this situation? Why?

4. Explain how each of the queuing decision variables (a)–(d), taken independently, could be expected to affect *queue length, waiting time in queue*, and *service facility utilization*.
   (a) Mean arrival rate.
   (b) Number of phases.
   (c) Number of channels.
   (d) Queue arrangement.
5. Suppose that someone said to you, "Queuing theory is too esoteric for practical use. The assumptions that must be made are too limiting to result in anything useful." Discuss this statement in light of the material in this appendix and your understanding of the complexity of queuing problems.
6. Priority systems involve priority rules. Discuss some of the priority rules that a hospital emergency ward might use to process patients. What trade-offs must be considered by hospital management?
7. It is often said that simulation is the "technique of last resort." Explain.
8. Suppose that you want to simulate the operation of loading semitrailer trucks at a distribution warehouse. The trucks arrive empty and are loaded manually with products ordered by retail outlets. Specify the data you would need to do the simulation study. How would you get the data?
9. You are a consultant working on a simulation study of a manufacturing operation. The manager of the operation is not familiar with simulation techniques. Part of your study involves making a change in the manufacturing process in the model and estimating the resulting benefits. Explain how you would convince the manager to accept your model's benefit estimates if the change was implemented.
10. What is a random number? Why are random numbers useful in simulation studies?

PROBLEMS

1. The Kramer Company employs a large number of salespersons. Although many of them are on the road at any one time, they generate an average of 1.5 sales documents per hour. These documents have to be typed and Kramer employs one typist for this sales force who can type and proof them at an average rate of 2 per hour.
   (a) What is the average utilization of the typist?
   (b) What is the probability that more than three documents are waiting or being typed?
   (c) What is the average number of documents waiting to be typed?
   (d) What is the average waiting time for documents in queue?
2. The son of a local hamburger magnate is preparing to open a new fast-food restaurant called Hasty Burgers. He is presently designing the drive-in window operation. Based on arrival rates at his father's outlets, customers are expected to arrive according to a Poisson distribution with a mean of 25 customers per hour. The service rate is flexible, since the work methods are yet to be designed; however, the service times are expected to follow an exponential distribution. The drive-in window is a single-server operation.
   (a) What service rate is needed to keep the average number of customers in the service system (line plus being served) to 5?
   (b) For the service rate from part (a),

what is the probability that more than 5 customers are in line and being served?

(c) For the service rate from part (a), what is the average waiting time in queue for each customer? Does this seem satisfactory for a fast-food business?

3. The Lone Star Company has a stockroom that utilizes an automatic stock picker. Workers arrive at the stockroom with production orders requiring various purchased parts and raw materials. The clerk feeds the information into a computer and the order is picked by a mechanical device and returned to the clerk. Workers arrive at the stockroom at the rate of 20 per hour. The automatic stock picker can be adjusted for speed, although actual service times for a given order depend on the nature of the materials in the order. Setting the machine too fast causes more failures, whereas setting it too slow causes delays on the shop floor. Answer the following questions, assuming that the single-server queuing model is appropriate.
   (a) If the time required for the clerk to enter the order is negligible, what average service rate should the stock picker be set at to ensure only a 30 percent chance that 3 or more workers are in queue or being served?
   (b) What is the average time a worker spends in the system?
   (c) What is the average number of workers waiting to be served?

4. The manager of the Lucky Lode Casino is concerned about the number of slot machines that are down for repair. Three employees in the maintenance department are responsible for repairing slot machines. A maintenance worker can fix one slot machine per hour on the average, with an exponential distribution. A recent study revealed that an average of 2.7 machines failed per hour according to a Poisson distribution. Each machine that is down costs the casino $60 per hour in lost profits. A new maintenance worker would cost $40 per hour, including wage, fringe benefits, and tools. The manager is not sure whether any new personnel should be added. If some should be added, the manager must also determine how many. Up to this point you have enjoyed being a blackjack dealer. Since you had written on your resume that you are familiar with the multiple-server model, the manager has asked you to help with the analysis. What would you recommend to the manager, based on your analysis?

5. The Hairy Knoll is a discount barbershop where the students from the Kingston Barber School serve their apprenticeship. There are only three barber chairs, each manned by an eager student. An instructor oversees the operation and gives guidance as needed. Patrons are served on a first-come, first-served basis and arrive at the rate of 10 customers per hour according to a Poisson distribution. The time required for a haircut averages 15 minutes according to an exponential distribution.
   (a) What is the probability that there will be no customers in the shop?
   (b) What is the probability that there will be five or more customers in the shop?
   (c) What is the average number of customers waiting in queue?
   (d) What is the average waiting time in queue?

6. Consider further the Hairy Knoll barber shop described in Problem 5. Suppose that it is desirable to have idle time for the

students so that they can sweep the floor and be given additional instruction in cutting hair. The dean of the Kingston Barber School believes that the added expense of remodeling the Hairy Knoll to have four barber chairs could be offset by slightly increased prices, if the average waiting time in queue per customer is less than five minutes. Assuming that the price change will not affect the rate of customer arrivals, should the Hairy Knoll be remodeled?

7. The College of Business and Public Administration at Acorn University has a copy machine on each floor for use by the department faculties. Heavy use of the five copy machines causes them to fail frequently. Maintenance records show that a machine fails every 2.5 days (or $\lambda_o = 0.40$ failures/day). The college has a maintenance contract with the authorized dealer of the copy machines. Since the copy machines fail so frequently, the dealer has assigned one person to the college to repair the machines. This person can repair an average of 2.5 machines per day. Answer the following questions using the finite-source model.
   (a) What is the average utilization of the maintenance person?
   (b) On the average, how many copy machines are being repaired and waiting to be repaired?
   (c) What is the average time spent by a copy machine in the repair system (queue plus repair)?

8. The cities of Abalone and Bennington are connected by a series of large lakes. Ships and barges going from the steel mill in Abalone to the manufacturing plants in Bennington must pass through the Bear Canyon locks and canal, which connect two of the larger lakes. A maximum of two ships or barges per day can traverse the locks and canal. However, vessels arrive at the canal according to the following probability distribution.

Vessels Arriving per Day		
Number	Probability	RN
1	0.33	00–32
2	0.34	33–66
3	0.33	67–99

If a vessel arrives at the canal but cannot pass through the system the same day, it must wait overnight in the holding area for passage the next day. Use the following random numbers.

47, 76, 09, 54, 87, 82, 17, 52, 17, 19

   (a) Simulate the arrival and passage of 10 vessels.
   (b) Determine the maximum number of vessels held overnight in any one day.

9. The Yellowstone Ferry takes cars from Creepy Hollow to Boynton Corners on the other side of Phantom Lake. The ferry has a capacity of five cars and takes exactly one hour to make the round trip from Creepy Hollow to Boynton Corners and back. If more than five cars arrive during the hour, the excess must wait until the next trip. In such an event, the price of the ticket is discounted 20 percent. The arrival distribution at Creepy Hollow is

Number of Cars per Hour	Probability
3	0.20
4	0.35
5	0.20
6	0.15
7	0.10

   (a) Suppose that the owner of the ferry charges \$5 per car. Disregarding any revenues that might be generated on the trip back from Boynton Corners to Creepy Hollow, estimate the average hourly revenue for the trip from Creepy Hollow to Boynton Corners. Base your estimate on a simulation of 10 hours using the following random numbers.

26, 03, 39, 26, 86, 48, 33, 70, 77, 01

(b) What is the average utilization of the ferry from Creepy Hollow to Boynton Corners?

10. The Canyon Del Oro Service Station performs maintenance and minor repairs to automobiles. Customers arrive early in the morning and leave their cars for the day, expecting to pick them up after work. There is a risk, however, that the work needed on a given car cannot be completed that day. It depends on the nature of the work to be performed on the other cars brought in the same day, as well as the specific work required for a particular car. Historically, an average of 2.5 cars had to be held over to the next day. The manager of the station is contemplating adding another mechanic to reduce that backlog. A simulation model was developed with the following distribution for customer arrivals per day.

Number	Probability	RN
8	0.10	00–09
9	0.25	10–34
10	0.30	35–64
11	0.25	65–89
12	0.10	90–99

With the addition of the extra mechanic, the maximum number of cars that could be serviced per day is

Number	Probability	RN
9	0.30	00–29
10	0.40	30–69
11	0.30	70–99

The number of cars that can be repaired varies from day to day because of the nature of the work to be done on the cars. In the simulation for a specific day, the number of cars needing service (NCNS) is determined first. Next, the maximum number of cars repaired (MNCR) is determined. If MNCR $\geq$ NCNS, all cars are repaired for that day. If MNCR $<$ NCNS, then MNCR $-$ NCNS cars must be held over until the next day. These cars must be added to the number of cars arriving the next day to obtain the NCNS for the next day. The simulation continues in this manner until a specific number of days has been simulated.

Assuming that the service station is empty at the start, simulate 15 days of operations using the following random numbers.

(73, 80), (25, 30), (86, 97), (48, 41), (30, 79), (79, 60), (53, 32), (72, 57), (83, 53), (44, 58), (82, 04), (12, 83), (08, 65), (53, 27), (77, 49).

For each pair of random numbers, the first determines the number of arrivals and the second the capacity. What is the average daily number of cars held overnight, based on your simulation?

SELECTED REFERENCES

Christy, David P., and Hugh J. Watson, "The Application of Simulation: A Survey of Industry Practice," *Interfaces*, vol. 13, no. 5 (October 1983), pp. 47–52.

Cooper, Robert B., *Introduction to Queuing Theory,* 2nd ed. New York: Elsevier-North Holland, 1980.

Ernshoff, J. R., and R. L. Serson, *Design and Use of Computer Simulation Models.* New York: Macmillan, 1970.

Hillier, F. S., and G. S. Lieberman, *Introduction to Operations Research,* 2nd ed. San Francisco: Holden-Day, 1975.

Meier, R. C., W. T. Newell, and H. L. Pazer, *Simulation in Business and Economics.* Englewood Cliffs, N.J.: Prentice-Hall, 1969.

Morse, P. M., *Queues, Inventories and Maintenance.* New York: John Wiley & Sons, 1958.

Naylor, T. H., et al., *Computer Simulation Techniques.* New York: John Wiley & Sons, 1966.

Saaty, T. L., *Elements of Queuing Theory with Applications.* New York: McGraw-Hill, 1961.

Solomon, Susan L., *Simulation of Waiting Lines.* Englewood Cliffs, N.J.: Prentice-Hall, 1983.

Watson, Hugh J., *Computer Simulation in Business.* New York: John Wiley & Sons, 1981.

APPENDIX

LINEAR PROGRAMMING

Some Managerial Issues

- What is the best product mix for our limited resources?
- What are our most valuable resources in generating profits or reducing costs?
- Which resources should we increase and by how much?
- What is the effect of adding a new plant on our total logistics system?

Appendix Outline

A recurring problem in operations management is that of allocating scarce resources to competing demands. We have defined capacity as the maximum output rate of an organization over some period of time. (See Chapter 7.) This definition implies that there are some critical resources that limit our ability to produce more output. In addition, the amounts of critical resources needed for various products or services produced by an organization differ. Thus the particular mix of products or services produced over a specific period of time can affect the output rate of the organization. Decisions regarding product mix are made to optimize specific organizational objectives, and these objectives can change because of market or economic conditions. Consequently, decisions on capacity expansion should take into consideration the optimal allocation of resources for the probable mix of products or services to be produced in the future.

In this appendix, we address two techniques that are useful for allocating scarce resources to competing demands. These techniques fall under the general heading of *mathematical optimization techniques.* The most general method we discuss is linear programming (LP), which seeks to optimize a linear objective function subject to a set of linear constraints. The product-mix problem, along with a number of others, can be analyzed with this method. We also discuss a variant of LP, the transportation method. The transportation method is useful in allocating plant shipments to distribution centers or warehouses and for selecting facility locations based on transportation costs.

BASIC CONCEPTS IN LINEAR PROGRAMMING

Consider the situation explained in Box C.1. Since the operations are focused in the Stratton Company and product lines do not share critical resources, the

Box C.1

THE STRATTON COMPANY

The Stratton Company produces plastic pipe, couplings, and fittings for the construction industry. To increase the efficiency of its operations, the company has focused its resources by major product lines. The couplings and fittings require specialized equipment and are often produced to satisfy specific needs of the customer. The plastic pipe, however, is more standard, and general-purpose equipment can be used. Two basic types of plastic pipe are produced and differ with respect to diameter, wall thickness, and strength.

John Fisher, the plant manager, recently received an updated demand forecast for the two types of pipe. Based on an examination of the resources needed to manufacture the two pipe products, it was obvious that the plant could not satisfy the demand. Three resources are critical to the output of pipe: extrusion hours, packaging hours, and a special additive to the plastic raw material to control strength and flexibility. John gathered the following data, which represent the situation for next week. All data are expressed in units of 100 feet of pipe.

	Product		
Resource Type	Type 1	Type 2	Resource Availability
Extrusion	4 hr	6 hr	48 hr
Packaging	2 hr	2 hr	18 hr
Additive Mix	2 lb	1 lb	16 lb

The contribution to profit and overhead per 100 feet of pipe is $34 for type 1 and $40 for type 2.

John was uncertain about how much of each type of pipe to produce in order to maximize contribution to profits and overhead. Also, if more funds were made available to expand capacity in the extrusion or packaging areas, would it pay to increase capacities there if it costs $8 per hour to increase extrusion capacity and $6 per hour to increase packaging capacity? Finally, would it pay to buy more additive mix?

product-mix decision regarding the two types of pipe can be made independently of decisions about the other product lines. Even though there are other operations in the manufacturing of plastic pipe, this company only has three resources that are considered critical to the output of the pipe. The product-mix decision should be made in light of these limitations.

Let's begin construction of the mathematical model by letting

x_1 = The amount of type 1 pipe to be produced, measured in 100-foot increments. For example, $x_1 = 2$ means 200 feet of type 1 pipe; and

x_2 = The amount of type 2 pipe to be produced, measured in 100-foot increments.

These are the decision variables to be determined by solution of the model. The values of these variables determine the product mix that the Stratton Company should implement. However, each unit of x_1 and x_2 produced consumes some of the critical resources. In the extrusion department, a unit of x_1 requires 4 hours, and a unit of x_2 requires 6 hours. For specific values of x_1 and x_2, we find the total amount of extrusion resources consumed by multiplying the number of units of each product produced by the resources consumed per unit and adding them. The total must not exceed the 48 hours of resources available. Thus we have the first constraint for our model:

$$4x_1 + 6x_2 \le 48 \qquad \text{(extrusion)}.$$

Similarly, we can formulate the constraints imposed by the packaging resource and the supply of additive mix, or

$$2x_1 + 2x_2 \le 18 \qquad \text{(packaging);}$$

$$2x_1 + 1x_2 \le 16 \qquad \text{(additive mix).}$$

These three constraints impose restrictions on our choice of values for the decision variables. The values we choose for x_1 and x_2 must satisfy all the constraints, but an infinite number of values for x_1 and x_2 will satisfy these constraints. For example, $x_1 = 1$, $x_2 = 1$; $x_1 = 2.01$, $x_2 = 4.03$; and $x_1 = -4$, $x_2 = -10$ all satisfy the constraints in our problem. The negative values for x_1 and x_2 do not make sense, so we add so-called nonnegativity restrictions to the model as follows:

$$x_1 \ge 0 \quad \text{and} \quad x_2 \ge 0 \qquad \text{(nonnegativity restrictions).}$$

However, we are still left with an infinite number of possible solutions. In order to select the best values for x_1 and x_2, we need an objective function. The Stratton Company wants to maximize the contribution to profits and overhead. Since each unit of x_1 yields \$34 and each unit of x_2 yields \$40, we want to maximize $\$34x_1 + \$40x_2$, subject to the various constraints.

We can now state the entire model for the product-mix problem at the Stratton Company.

$$\begin{aligned} \text{Objective:} \quad & \text{Maximize } \$34x_1 + \$40x_2. \\ \text{Subject to:} \quad & 4x_1 + 6x_2 \leq 48; \\ & 2x_1 + 2x_2 \leq 18; \\ & 2x_1 + 1x_2 \leq 16; \\ & x_1 \geq 0 \quad \text{and} \quad x_2 \geq 0. \end{aligned}$$

The methods we will discuss can be used to solve this model for those values of x_1 and x_2 that maximize the contribution to profits and overhead.

The General Linear Programming Method

We can solve the model we developed for the Stratton Company by an optimizing process known as linear programming, which seeks values for the decision variables that satisfy the linear constraints (including nonnegativity) of the problem and optimize a linear objective function. The general linear programming method is

$$\begin{aligned} \text{Maximize:} \quad & c_1x_1 + c_2x_2 + \cdots + c_nx_2. \\ \text{Subject to:} \quad & a_{11}x_1 + a_{12}x_2 + \cdots + a_{1n}x_n \leq b_1; \\ & a_{21}x_1 + a_{22}x_2 + \cdots + a_{2n}x_n \leq b_2; \\ & \quad \vdots \\ & a_{m1}x_1 + a_{m2}x_2 + \cdots + a_{mn}x_n \leq b_m; \\ & x_1, x_2, \cdots, x_n \geq 0. \end{aligned}$$

In this problem there are n decision variables and m constraints (exclusive of the nonnegativity restrictions) where some of the constraints could be written as *greater than or equal to* ($\geq$) or *equals* ($=$), depending on the problem statement. The c_j, a_{ij}, and b_i values are given constants. Linear programming can also be used to *minimize* the value of the objective function.

Some important assumptions implicit in the formulation of linear programming problems are:

1. The objective function and constraint equations must be linear. Thus we can have no cross-products of decision variables, powers of x_j, or other types of nonlinear terms in the problem formulation. For the Stratton Company, this implies that one unit of x_1 contributes \$34 to profit and overhead, and two units contribute \$68, regardless of how much x_2 is

produced. Similarly, one unit of x_2 consumes 6 hours of extrusion time, and two units consume 12 hours. Production of x_1 does not affect the per-unit consumption of x_2 of any of the resources.

2. The decision variables can have fractional values. For example, $x_1 = 3.2$ in the Stratton Company example poses no problem, since it means 320 feet of pipe. However, in other problems the decision variables may be expressed in units such as workers, tables, or trucks that are not divisible. We can use a more advanced technique, called *integer programming*, in these situations if simply rounding off the linear programming solution, subject to satisfying the constraints, is unacceptable.
3. The constants are known with certainty. For example, each unit of x_1 requires 2 pounds of additive—no more, no less. The values of the constants cannot be statistical averages. They must be deterministic values that will not change when the solution to the problem is implemented.

Although these assumptions are quite restrictive, linear programming can provide a means to analyze complex resource allocation problems and several other benefits that are worth considering. First, the process of building the model forces managers to identify the important decision variables and constraints which can be useful in its own right. Identifying the nature and scope of the problem represents a big step toward solving it. Second, even though we assume that we know all the constants with certainty, we can use our best guess about their proper values and perform a *sensitivity analysis* of the constants that we suspect of violating our assumptions. Sensitivity analysis is a method whereby we systematically modify the value of critical constants in order to determine how the optimal solution is affected. For example, suppose that John Fisher at the Stratton Company was not sure about the number of packaging hours available next week; it could vary from 16 to 20 hours. John could use the linear programming model and first try 16 hours, then 20 hours.* If there is no significant difference in the resulting product mixes, the value for available resources in the packaging department is not critical in the range of 16 to 20 hours. A reasonable value, such as 18 hours, would do for planning purposes. However, if the product mix is sensitive to the amount of packaging resources in this range, John should try to estimate the amount of resources he will have next week. If the best he can do is specify a range of possible values, he may have to use a more sophisticated technique, such as *chance-constrained programming* or *stochastic programming* (see Wagner, 1975).

Finally, the solution to a linear programming problem is not necessarily the solution that management will actually use. Often, various nonquantita-

* Certain information about the range of values for c_j and b_i for which the optimal solution will not change can be derived by analyzing the algebraic information associated with the optimal solution itself without recalculating the entire solution each time. However, this analysis holds only for changes in the constants taken one at a time and not in combination with others.

tive factors must be considered. Nonetheless, the linear programming solution can be a good starting point for the final decision.

Graphic Analysis

Solutions to practical linear programming problems involve algebraic methods. However, considerable insight into linear programming concepts can be provided through the analysis of a simple two-variable problem using the **graphical method of linear programming.** We will use the Stratton Company product-mix problem as our example.

We begin by plotting the constraint equations, disregarding the inequality portion of the constraints ($<$) and assuming that each constraint is an equality ($=$). We let one variable equal zero and plot the axis intercept of the other variable. For the extrusion department, we have $4x_1 + 6x_2 = 48$. If $x_1 = 0$, then $x_2 = 8$. Similarly, if $x_2 = 0$, then $x_1 = 12$. We can connect the points (0, 8) and (12, 0) with a straight line, as shown in Fig. C.1. All points on the line *and* to the left of the line will satisfy the extrusion constraint because the original constraint was an inequality. We can plot the two other constraints in a similar manner.

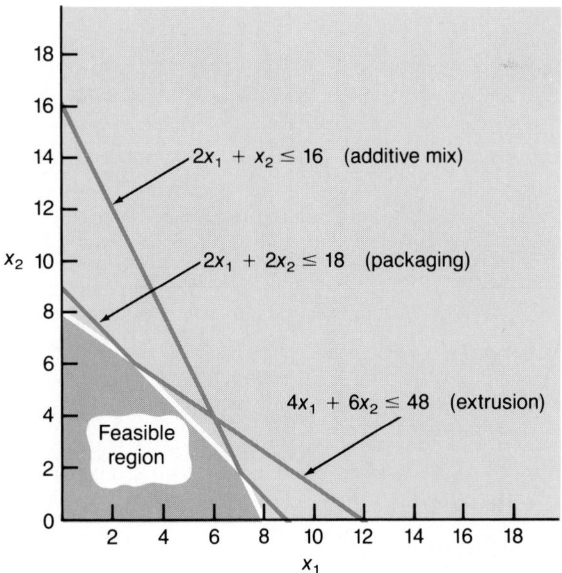

Figure C.1

Feasible Region for the Stratton Company Product-Mix Problem.

Each constraint helps to define the region of feasible solutions to the problem. The **feasible region,** shown as the shaded portion of Fig. C.1, contains the solutions that satisfy all the constraints simultaneously, including the nonnegativity restrictions. In our product-mix example, all the constraints were of the *less-than-or-equal-to* variety. Consequently, only the values of x_1 and x_2 in the lower left portion of the graph are feasible. In general, this condition is not always the case. For example, suppose that a linear programming model had the following constraints.

$$2x_1 + x_2 \geq 10;$$
$$2x_1 + 3x_2 \geq 18;$$
$$x_1 \leq 7;$$
$$x_2 \leq 5;$$
$$x_1, x_2 \geq 0.$$

Figure C.2 shows the feasible region in this case. The two *greater-than-or-equal-to* constraints provide lower limits that must be met or exceeded. Only the points on the line and to the right are feasible for these constraints.

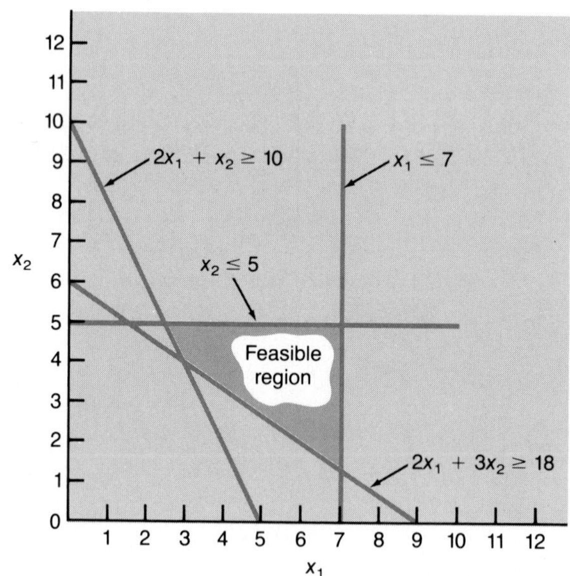

Figure C.2

Feasible Region with Lower Limits for the Stratton Company Product-Mix Problem.

After we have defined the feasible region for the Stratton Company, the problem becomes one of finding the solution that maximizes the contribution to profits and overhead. The optimal solution to a linear programming problem will be an extreme point (corner point) of the feasible region. In Fig. C.1, there are four corner points, excluding the origin, which would obviously be a poor solution. We could try each of these corner points in the objective function and select the one that maximizes its value. We may not be able to read these points from the graph accurately enough in some cases, and algebraically solving for all the corner points is inefficient when we have to calculate a large number of points.

The best approach is to plot the objective function on the graph of the feasible region for some arbitrary value of total contribution to profits and overhead. The line is called an *iso-profit* line because every point on that line will yield the same contribution. We can then draw a series of other iso-profit lines parallel to that line until we find the one farthest from the origin but still touching the feasible region. This point identifies the optimal solution to the problem.

We can use a similar procedure when we want to minimize the objective function. In this case we would draw an *iso-cost* line for an arbitrary value on the graph of the feasible region. We would then draw parallel iso-cost lines until we found the one which is *closest* to the origin but still touching the feasible region.

Suppose that we plot the objective function of our product-mix problem for an arbitrary value of $170 in the same manner as the constraint equations. This line is shown in Fig. C.3, along with two other iso-profit lines. It is obvious that the optimal solution to the problem occurs at the corner point represented by the intersection of the extrusion and packaging constraints. Simultaneously solving the two equations representing these constraints yields $x_1 = 3$ and $x_2 = 6$. This is the optimal product mix, which can be verified by looking at the graph. The Stratton Company should produce 300 feet of type 1 pipe and 600 feet of type 2 pipe next week.

There can be more than one optimal solution to a linear programming problem. This situation occurs when the objective function is parallel to one of the faces of the feasible region and would be the case if our objective function were $\$38x_1 + \$38x_2$. Both $x_1 = 3$, $x_2 = 6$ and $x_1 = 7$, $x_2 = 2$, as well as any other point on the line connecting these two corner points, would be optimal. When this situation occurs, management would probably base a final decision on nonquantifiable factors. The important point here, however, is that we only need to consider the corner points of the feasible region when optimizing an objective function. Even when there are multiple optimal solutions, there will always be a corner point that is the optimum. This feature enables us to use a technique capable of solving complex linear programming problems efficiently.

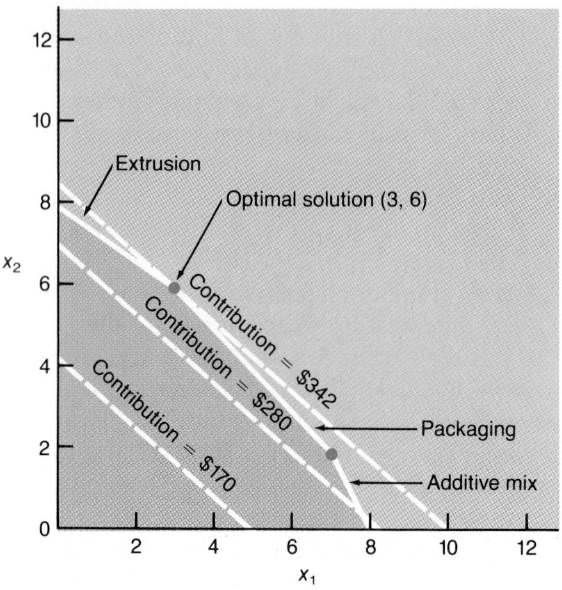

Figure C.3

Iso-Profit Lines and Solution to the Stratton Company Product-Mix Problem.

THE SIMPLEX METHOD

The **simplex method** is an iterative algebraic procedure for solving linear programming problems. Starting with an initial solution, the procedure systematically evaluates corner points of the feasible region in such a way that the objective function improves (or at worst stays the same) at each iteration. In practice, these problems are solved on computers, but we will solve manually the Stratton Company product-mix problem to demonstrate the logic of the approach.

Problem Formulation and Initial Tableau

Recall the model we developed for the Stratton Company product-mix problem.

$$\text{Maximize: } \$34x_1 + \$40x_2.$$

$$\text{Subject to: } 4x_1 + 6x_2 \leq 48;$$

$$2x_1 + 2x_2 \leq 18;$$

$$2x_1 + 1x_2 \leq 16;$$

$$x_1, x_2 \geq 0.$$

The simplex method involves the solution of linear equations, but the constraints in our model are expressed as inequalities. In order to use the simplex method, we have to transform the original model and express all constraints as equalities. We can do this by augmenting the model with *slack variables*, that is,

$$\begin{aligned} \text{Maximize:}\quad & \$34x_1 + \$40x_2 + \$0s_1 + \$0s_2 + \$0s_3. \\ \text{Subject to:}\quad & 4x_1 + 6x_2 + 1s_1 + 0s_2 + 0s_3 = 48; \\ & 2x_1 + 2x_2 + 0s_1 + 1s_2 + 0s_3 = 18; \\ & 2x_1 + 1x_2 + 0s_1 + 0s_2 + 1s_3 = 16; \\ & x_1, x_2, s_1, s_2, s_3 \geq 0. \end{aligned}$$

A slack variable for a given constraint takes up the difference between the total resource consumption implied by specific values of x_1 and x_2 and the total amount of the resource available. For example, consider the extrusion constraint for which s_1 is the slack variable and actually represents the amount of idle time in the extrusion department. If $x_1 = 2$ and $x_2 = 5$, s_1 would be 10 hours (or 48 − 38). Alternatively, if $x_1 = 3$ and $x_2 = 6$, s_1 would be zero. Slack variables must be nonnegative to ensure that they accurately measure the slack resources for a particular constraint. Also, since slack resources do not generate contributions to profit and overhead, they have coefficients of zero in the objective function. Insofar as the decision variables x_1 and x_2 are concerned, an optimal solution to the augmented model will also be an optimal solution to the original model.

The most convenient way to summarize the information needed to solve a linear programming problem using the simplex method is to use a tableau. Table C.1 shows the initial tableau for our product-mix problem. Most of it

Table C.1

Initial Tableau for the Stratton Company Product-Mix Problem

c_j		\$34	\$40	\$0	\$0	\$0	
	Solution Variables	x_1	x_2	s_1	s_2	s_3	Quantity
\$0	s_1	4	(6)	1	0	0	48 ←
\$0	s_2	2	2	0	1	0	18
\$0	s_3	2	1	0	0	1	16
	z_j	\$0	\$0	\$0	\$0	\$0	\$0
	$c_j - z_j$	\$34	\$40 ↑	\$0	\$0	\$0	

merely duplicates the c_j, a_{ij}, and b_i constants row-by-row from our augmented model. The first row of the tableau contains the objective function coefficients for each variable, including slack variables. This is the only row that does not change in subsequent tableaus. The first column shows the objective function coefficients for the variables in the current solution to the problem.

The variables (one for each constraint) chosen for the current solution are listed under *solution variables.* In the initial tableau the slack variables are chosen for the initial solution to the problem. In our example, we have three constraints; consequently, we list s_1, s_2 and s_3. The column labeled *quantity* shows the current value of the solution variables. In the initial tableau these values are merely the quantities on the right-hand side of the constraint equations. The initial tableau for our product-mix problem indicates that $s_1 = 48$, $s_2 = 18$, and $s_3 = 16$. By convention, the variables that are not in the current solution have values of zero. Thus $x_1 = 0$ and $x_2 = 0$. This solution corresponds to the origin (0, 0) in the graph of the feasible region shown in Fig. C.3.

All the variables in the problem are listed to the right of the solution-variables column. In the initial tableau, the coefficients of a particular variable in each constraint of the augmented model are listed under the variable name. These coefficients in the initial and subsequent tableaus have a special meaning. They indicate the *substitution rates* for a particular variable not in the solution, relative to those variables in the solution. For example, the 6, 2, and 1 in the x_2 column mean that for each unit of x_2 introduced into the solution, s_1 will be reduced by 6 units, s_2 will be reduced by 2 units, and s_3 will be reduced by 1 unit. In subsequent tableaus, these substitution rates will change. This information will be useful in determining how to improve the current solution at any iteration.

The final two rows of the tableau provide summary information about the trade-offs in introducing a variable into the solution. The z_j row shows the *profit foregone* by introducing 1 unit of variable j into the solution. To calculate the value of z_j, we need the substitution rates for variable j (in the column for variable j) and the profit contributions of the variables in the solution (the coefficients in the column labeled c_j on the far left side). Consider variable x_1. If we introduce 1 unit of variable x_1 into the solution, we must give up 4 units of s_1, 2 units of s_2, and 2 units of s_3. However, since slack variables provide no contribution to profits, the total profit foregone by the introduction of 1 unit of x_1 is $z_1 = \$0(4) + \$0(2) + \$0(2) = \$0$. All we are doing is giving up slack resources at this stage of the solution process. Similarly, $z_2 = \$0(6) + \$0(2) + \$0(1) = \$0$. The value for z_j in the *quantity* column shows the current value of the objective function. Since $s_1 = 48$, $s_2 = 18$, and $s_3 = 16$, we have $\$0(48) + \$0(18) + \$0(16) = \$0$.

The $c_j - z_j$ row shows the *net contribution* effect of introducing 1 unit of variable j into the solution. It is the difference between the profit contribution of variable j and the profit foregone by the introduction of 1 unit of variable j.

For x_1 we have $c_1 - z_1 = \$34$ (or $\$34 - \$0$), and for x_2 we have $c_2 - z_2 = \$40$ (or $\$40 - \$0$). The net contribution for any variable already in the solution will always be \$0 because the introduction of one more unit into the solution must be accompanied by the removal of 1 unit of the same variable to avoid violating one of the constraints.

It is apparent from the initial tableau that no resources are being used in production because only slack variables are in the solution. In addition, it also shows that the current solution can be improved. This is evident in the $c_j - z_j$ row where the net contributions by x_1 and x_2 are greater than zero.

Selecting the Entering Variable

In linear programming, we select one variable to enter the solution and one variable to leave the solution at each iteration until we find the optimal solution. The $c_j - z_j$ row tells us whether an improved solution is possible. In our problem, there is a positive net contribution of \$34 per unit of x_1 and \$40 per unit of x_2. Since we are interested in maximizing the contribution to profits and overhead, it would make sense to choose the variable that has the largest net contribution as the new variable to enter into the solution. This variable is x_2 in our product-mix problem. The column associated with the entering variable is designated with a vertical arrow in Table C.1.

Determining the Exiting Variable

Now that we have decided to introduce x_2 into the solution, we must determine the variable it is to replace. Consider Fig. C.1 again and the current solution, which is at the origin. To introduce x_2 into the solution, we proceed vertically along the x_2-axis. Since we want to have as much x_2 in the solution as possible without violating any constraints, our choices are 8, 9, and 16, as denoted by the intercepts of the equations for the constraints. It is obvious that if we want to satisfy *all* the constraints by our choice of x_2, we must be limited to the *smallest* increase, or $x_2 = 8$.

We can come to the same conclusion without the graph by using the substitution rates for the entering variable and the values in the quantity column of the tableau. We can find the value that the entering variable will have in the next solution and the variable in the current solution that will be replaced. For example,

$$s_1 \text{ row (extrusion):} \quad \frac{48}{6} = 8;$$

$$s_2 \text{ row (packaging)):} \quad \frac{18}{2} = 9;$$

$$s_3 \text{ row (additive mix):} \quad \frac{16}{1} = 16.$$

As we increase x_1 from zero, the first limitation that we encounter is the extrusion capacity, when $x_2 = 8$. If we go beyond that value we will violate the constraint. Also, since s_1 is associated with the first row, it will be at zero when $x_2 = 8$. This result makes intuitive sense because s_1 is the amount of idle resources in the extrusion department. When $x_2 = 8$, we are using all the extrusion capacity for the production of type 2 pipe because each unit of that product consumes 6 hours of extrusion time. Consequently, s_1 is the variable that exits the solution, and the row associated with s_1 is designated by a horizontal arrow, as shown in Table C.1.

To summarize the simplex method to this point, we have used two rules.

Entering rule: Select the variable with the largest value of $c_j - z_j$ to introduce into the solution in a maximization problem. In a *minimization* problem, select the variable with the largest *negative* value of $c_j - z_j$ because the objective function is to be as small as possible.

Exiting rule: Divide the substitution rates for the entering variable into the corresponding values in the quantity column. Consider only *positive* values for the substitution rates and select the row variable with the lowest ratio to be removed from the solution. This procedure is the same regardless of whether the objective function is to be minimized or maximized.

Transforming the Tableau

As we mentioned earlier, we use the simplex method to systematically evaluate corner points of a feasible region. Since the corner points are formed by the intersection of lines representing linear equations, we need to solve a system of linear equations. We will use a procedure called *Gaussian elimination* to transform the tableau to reflect a new solution to our problem. In the tableau, the coefficients in the column of a variable currently in the solution consist of a 1 in the row associated with that variable and zeroes in all the other rows. For s_1, our exiting variable, we have 1, 0, 0. The values in the column for x_2, our entering variable, are 6, 2, 1. The Gaussian elimination procedure will transform the column for x_2 into 1, 0, 0, thereby entering x_2 into the solution and replacing s_1. We make this transformation by performing various mathematical operations on the rows of the tableau. In a system of linear equations, we can multiply an entire equation by a constant and not change the nature of the relationship. We can also add two equations to form a third equation to replace one of them and not change the solution to the original set of equations. We now apply Gaussian elimination to transform our initial tableau.

Calculate the New Row for the Entering Variable. At the intersection of the entering-variable column and the exiting-variable row is a value called the *pivot element*. (See the circled value in Table C.1.) We replace the old s_1 row with a new row having a value of 1 for the pivot element. That is, we divide the values in the old s_1 row by the pivot element of 6 to create a new row for our next tableau:

	x_1	x_2	s_1	s_2	s_3	Quantity
Old s_1 row	4	6	1	0	0	48
New x_2 row	2/3	1	1/6	0	0	8

The new x_2 row replaces the first row in our tableau. Note that the new value for x_2 (in the quantity column) will be 8 in our next solution.

Transforming the Other Rows. We transform each of the other rows by selecting an appropriate constant, multiplying each element of the new x_2 row by this constant, and adding the result, element by element, to the row to be changed in such a way that we have a zero in the x_2 column. The appropriate constant in each case is the element in the x_2 column for the row to be transformed, multiplied by -1. For the s_2 row, the constant is -2, and for the s_3 row it is -1. Table C.2 shows the calculations for the transformed s_2 and s_3 rows.

The new tableau is shown in Table C.3. We calculated values for the z_j and $c_j - z_j$ rows as before, except that now some of the z_j values are greater than zero. At the end of this first iteration it is obvious that we can make further improvements in the solution, since $c_1 - z_1 = \$22/3$.

Table C.2

Transforming the s_2 and s_3 Rows in the Stratton Company Product-Mix Problem

	s_2 Row								s_3 Row							
Column	Old s_2 row	+	(Constant for s_2	×	New x_2 row)	=	New s_2 row	Old s_3 row	+	(Constant for s_3	×	New x_2 row)	=	New s_3 row
x_1	2	+	(−2	×	2/3)	=	2/3	2	+	(−1	×	2/3)	=	4/3
x_2	2	+	(−2	×	1)	=	0	1	+	(−1	×	1)	=	0
s_1	0	+	(−2	×	1/6)	=	−1/3	0	+	(−1	×	1/6)	=	−1/6
s_2	1	+	(−2	×	0)	=	1	0	+	(−1	×	0)	=	0
s_3	0	+	(−2	×	0)	=	0	1	+	(−1	×	0)	=	1
Quantity	18	+	(−2	×	8)	=	2	16	+	(−1	×	8)	=	8

Table C.3

Second Tableau for the Stratton Company Product-Mix Problem

c_j		$34	$40	$0	$0	$0	
	Solution Variables	x_1	x_2	s_1	s_2	s_3	Quantity
$40	x_2	2/3	1	1/6	0	0	8
$0	s_2	(2/3)	0	−1/3	1	0	2 ←
$0	s_3	4/3	0	−1/6	0	1	8
	z_j	$80/3*	$40	$20/3†	$0	$0	$320
	$c_j - z_j$	$22/3 ↑	$0	−$20/3	$0	$0	

* z_1 = $40(2/3) + $0(2/3) + $0(4/3) = $80/3.
† z_3 = $40(1/6) − $0(1/3) − $0(1/6) = $40/6 = $20/3.

Criterion of Optimality and the Solution to the Product-Mix Problem

The criterion for optimality in a linear programming problem can be stated as follows for

Maximization problems: If every entry in the $c_j - z_j$ row is zero or negative, the current solution is optimal.

Minimization problems: If every entry in the $c_j - z_j$ is zero or positive, the current solution is optimal.

Since our product-mix problem is a maximization problem, we have not met the criterion of optimality. Consequently, we must perform another iteration of the tableau. The entering variable is x_1, since it has the largest positive $c_j - z_j$ value. The exiting variable is s_2 because it had the lowest value when we divide the substitution rates in the x_1 column into the values in the quantity column. Thus

$$x_2 \text{ row: } 8/(2/3) = 12;$$
$$s_2 \text{ row: } 2/(2/3) = 3;$$
$$s_3 \text{ row: } 8/(4/3) = 6.$$

Consequently, x_1 will enter the solution and replace s_2. The pivot element for this iteration is 2/3. Dividing the values in the old s_2 row in Table C.3 by 2/3

Table C.4

Transforming the x_2 and s_3 Rows in the Stratton Company Product-Mix Problem

	x_2 Row								s_3 Row							
Column	Old x_2 row	+	(Constant for x_2	×	New x_1 row)	=	New x_2 row		Old s_3 row	+	(Constant for s_3	×	New x_1 row)	=	New s_3 row
x_1	2/3	+	(−2/3	×	1)	=	0		4/3	+	(−4/3	×	1)	=	0
x_2	1	+	(−2/3	×	0)	=	1		0	+	(−4/3	×	0)	=	0
s_1	1/6	+	(−2/3	×	−1/2)	=	1/2		−1/6	+	(−4/3	×	−1/2)	=	1/2
s_2	0	+	(−2/3	×	3/2)	=	−1		0	+	(−4/3	×	3/2)	=	−2
s_3	0	+	(−2/3	×	0)	=	0		1	+	(−4/3	×	0)	=	1
Quantity	8	+	(−2/3	×	3)	=	6		8	+	(−4/3	×	3)	=	4

yields the new x_1 row:

	x_1	x_2	s_1	s_2	s_3	Quantity
New x_1 row	1	0	−1/2	3/2	0	3

The calculations for transforming the x_2 and s_3 rows are shown in Table C.4, and the new tableau is shown in Table C.5. We have now satisfied the criterion for optimality. The Stratton Company should produce 300 feet of type 1 pipe and 600 feet of type 2 pipe. In so doing, the company will use all the available time for the extrusion and packaging ($s_1 = s_2 = 0$) and will have an extra 4 pounds of additive mix ($s_3 = 4$). You can verify the latter result by substituting $x_1 = 3$ and $x_2 = 6$ into the constraint for the additive mix.

The simplex process started at the origin and moved to the corner point $x_1 = 0$, $x_2 = 8$ because x_2 contributed the most to profits and overhead. It then moved to the intersection of the extrusion and packaging constraints (Fig.

Table C.5

Optimal Tableau for the Stratton Company Product-Mix Problem

c_j		$34	$40	$0	$0	$0	
	Solution Variables	**x_1**	**x_2**	**s_1**	**s_2**	**s_3**	**Quantity**
$40	x_2	0	1	1/2	−1	0	6
$34	x_1	1	0	−1/2	3/2	0	3
$0	s_3	0	0	1/2	−2	1	4
	z_j	$34	$40	$3	$11	$0	$342
	$c_j - z_j$	$0	$0	−$3	−$11	$0	

C.1) where the optimal solution was found. Note that the value of x_2 was reduced from 8 to 6 in the final iteration. By introducing 3 units of x_1, we were able to better utilize the available resources and generate more contribution to profits and overhead, even though we gave up 2 units of x_2.

Sensitivity Analysis

The simplex method provides more useful information than just the optimal solution to a linear programming problem. From the optimal tableau we can determine the value of each resource in terms of its contribution to profits and overhead. We can also determine the net benefit (or cost) of adjusting the amount of resources we have (the b_i quantities on the right-hand sides of the constraint equations). This information can be useful in making policy decisions about resource acquisition. Alternatively, if the b_i quantities must be forecasts, the information can be useful in determining the consequences of inaccurate forecasting. In this section we will discuss the sensitivity analysis concepts of shadow prices and right-hand-side ranging.

Shadow Prices. The relative value of a resource with respect to the objective function in a linear programming problem is called its **shadow price.** It is the amount of change in the objective function per unit change in its right-hand-side value. Since the slack variables measure the amount of idle resources, the shadow prices for the resources are found in the $c_j - z_j$ row for the slack variables (disregarding the negative signs). Thus, in Table C.5, the shadow price for extrusion capacity is \$3 per hour and is found in the s_1 column. Similarly, the shadow prices for packaging and the additive mix are \$11 per hour and \$0 per pound, respectively.

We can use the shadow prices for our product-mix problem in the following way. If we had an additional hour of packaging capacity next week, we could generate \$11 more in contribution to profits and overhead. If the added hour would cost less than \$11 to obtain, it would pay for us to add an hour to the packaging capacity. For example, if the additional hour cost \$7, the contribution to profits and overhead would increase by \$4. Similarly, if we had one *less* hour of packaging capacity next week, it would cost \$11 in lost contribution to profits and overhead. The trade-offs for extrusion capacity are similar, but the impact on profits and overhead per hour of capacity is much less. The shadow price of zero for the additive mix makes sense because we already have an extra 4 pounds that we cannot use. Adjusting the availability of that resource by a pound would have no effect on the value of the objective function.

We can now answer the questions posed by John Fisher in Box C.1. Since it costs \$8 per hour to expand extrusion capacity, he should not do it because the shadow price for that capacity is only \$3 per hour. However, it only costs \$6 per hour to expand packaging hours, and the shadow price is \$11 per hour. Therefore he should increase packaging capacity. Finally, it would not pay to buy more additive mix because there is already a surplus of 4 pounds; the shadow price is zero for that resource.

Right-Hand-Side Ranging. Knowing that the shadow price is greater than the cost of acquiring a given resource or less than the price we could obtain from selling it has only limited usefulness. We need to know *how much* resource we can buy or sell and retain an advantage. Put another way, we need the range of right-hand-side quantities (b_i's) over which the shadow price is valid for a given resource. This procedure is called **right-hand-side ranging,** and we start with the information in the optimal tableau.

For illustrative purposes consider packaging capacity, for which s_2 is the slack variable. The optimal tableau in Table C.5 shows that if we add one hour of s_2 into the solution, we will increase the production of x_2 by 1 unit (because the substitution rate is -1), decrease the production of x_1 by 3/2 units, and increase the slack amount of additive mix by 2 pounds (the substitution rate is -2). The profits and overhead contribution foregone would be \$11. However, *adding* one hour of s_2 is analogous to reducing the number of packaging hours (b_2) by one hour because it restricts the amount of resources available for x_1 and x_2. We can determine how many hours of packaging capacity we would be willing to sell (that is, how much s_2 we can introduce into the solution), provided that the price exceeds \$11, in the same way that we determined the exiting variable in the simplex procedure.

x_2 row: $6/(-1) = -6$ (negative, disregard);*

x_1 row: $3/(3/2) = 2$;

s_3 row: $4/(-2) = -2$ (negative, disregard).

Consequently, we can introduce two hours of s_2 (or equivalently, reduce packaging hours by 2, to 16 hours) before we will replace x_1 in the solution. The solution would then be $x_1 = 0$ and $x_2 = 8$, as shown in Fig. C.4. Every hour that we reduce capacity over this range will cost us \$11 in contribution to profits and overhead.

Now, we need to determine how much we can expand packaging capacity and still obtain a benefit of \$11 per hour. Again, we work with slack variable s_2 in the optimal tableau, but this time we reverse the signs of the

* A negative substitution rate means that the row variable actually increases as the entering variable increases. Therefore the exiting variable cannot be one that has a negative substitution rate with the entering variable.

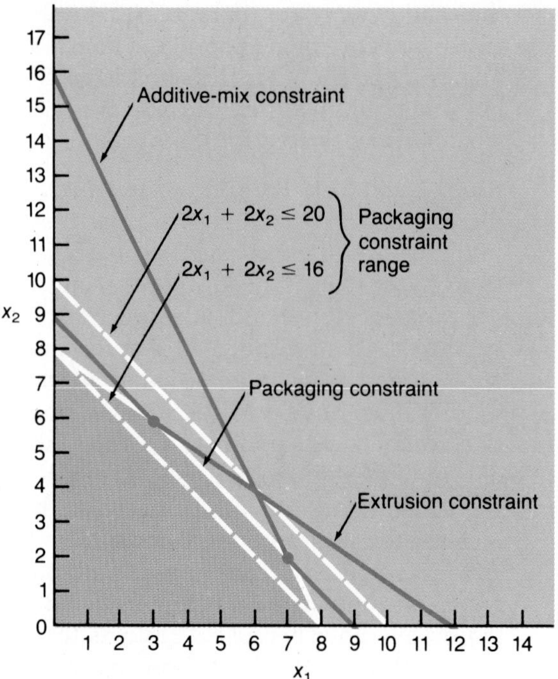

Figure C.4

Right-Hand-Side Ranging for the Stratton Company Packaging Constraint.

substitution rates. Intuitively, adding negative s_2 to the solution is analogous to adding packaging capacity. Proceeding as we did before, we have

$$
\begin{aligned}
x_2 \text{ row: } & 6/(1) = 6; \\
x_1 \text{ row: } & 3/(-3/2) = -2 \quad \text{(negative, disregard);} \\
s_3 \text{ row: } & 4/(2) = 2.
\end{aligned}
$$

As we increase packaging capacity we will ultimately run out of additive mix because s_3 will become the exiting variable. We can add only 2 hours before this will happen, making total packaging capacity 20 hours. The new solution would be $x_1 = 6$ and $x_2 = 4$ in Fig. C.4. The new value of the objective function would be \$364, or \$22 more than in our current solution, as we would expect. Consequently, the range in packaging hours over which the shadow price of \$11 would be valid is $16 \leq b_2 \leq 20$.

In a similar manner, we can find the range for extrusion capacity: $40 \leq$

$b_1 \leq 54$. With respect to the additive mix, the shadow price of \$0 will hold for any increase in supply. It will also hold for any reductions of up to 4 pounds because that is the amount of slack resource we have. Therefore the range for the additive mix is $12 \leq b_3 \leq \infty$.

Problem Formulation with Equality or Greater-Than-or-Equal-to Constraints

Suppose that our product mix problem had the requirement that all the additive mix be used in the production of x_1 and x_2. The constraint would now be

$$2x_1 + 1x_2 = 16.$$

Before, when the constraint was $2x_1 + 1x_2 \leq 16$, we added a slack variable to make the constraint an equality and to provide us with an initial solution to the problem. Now, the constraint does not allow slack, and we have no convenient initial solution. To overcome this difficulty we can add an *artificial variable* to the constraint equation, as follows:

$$2x_1 + 1x_2 + 1a_1 = 16.$$

Insofar as it gives us an initial solution, an artificial variable acts like a slack variable. However, unlike a slack variable, an artificial variable should not appear in the final solution to the problem. If a_1 has a positive value in the end, it would mean that $2x_1 + 1x_2 < 16$, which violates the constraint. To safeguard against this result, we insert a very large negative coefficient in the objective function for a_1. The objective function for our problem would then be

$$\text{Maximize:} \quad \$34x_1 + \$40x_2 + \$0s_1 + \$0s_2 - \$ma_1,$$

where m is a number such as \$1 million.* Since it has a negative sign, the simplex method will remove it from the solution before we find the optimal solution.

We also need to modify each greater-than-or-equal-to constraint. Suppose that we must use *at least* 16 pounds of additive mix. The constraint would become $2x_1 + 1x_2 \geq 16$. Adding a slack variable to make the constraint an equality will not work here. We have to subtract something from the left-hand

* In a minimization problem, an artificial variable has a large *positive* coefficient, m, in the objective function to ensure that it will not appear in the final solution.

side of the constraint to make it an equality, as follows:

$$2x_1 + 1x_2 - 1s_3 = 16.$$

The variable s_3, which must be nonnegative, is called a *surplus variable* and measures the amount by which the left-hand side exceeds the right-hand side of the constraint. Unfortunately, even though we now have an equality, we do not have an initial solution. We would have $s_3 = -16$, which violates the nonnegativity restrictions.

We can use an artificial variable to provide an initial solution here, as we did for the previous constraint equation. We write the constraint as follows:

$$2x_1 + 1x_2 - 1s_3 + 1a_1 = 16.$$

The objective function would now be

$$\text{Maximize:} \quad \$34x_1 + \$40x_2 + \$0s_1 + \$0s_2 + \$0s_3 - \$ma_1$$

Note that the surplus variable has a coefficient of zero in the objective function, just like a slack variable. Procedurally, the simplex method treats slack, surplus, and artificial variables identically; however, artificial variables have no economic meaning and must have a value of zero in the final solution.

Summary of the Simplex Method

Using the simplex method involves the following steps:

1. Formulate the problem in terms of a linear objective function and a set of linear constraints. Augment the formulation with slack, surplus, or artificial variables, as needed.
2. Set up the initial tableau with slack or artificial variables as the solution variables and calculate the z_j and $c_j - z_j$ quantities.
3. Determine the entering variable with the largest $c_j - z_j$ value in maximization problems or the smallest $c_j - z_j$ value for minimization problems.
4. Determine the exiting variable by finding the ratio of the value in the quantity column to the corresponding substitution rate in the entering-variable column for each row and selecting the smallest positive ratio.
5. Create a new tableau. Calculate the new row for the entering variable by dividing the old row for the exiting variable by the pivot element and placing it in the new tableau. Use Gaussian elimination to transform the values in the remaining rows and place them in the new array. Calculate the new z_j and $c_j - z_j$ values for the new tableau.
6. In maximization problems, if all $c_j - z_j$ values are zero or negative, the optimal solution has been found. In minimization problems, stop when all $c_j - z_j$ values are zero or positive. If these conditions do not hold, repeat steps 3–6.

THE TRANSPORTATION METHOD

You have seen that the simplex method is an efficient procedure for solving linear programming problems. Efficiency, however, is relative and is directly related to the computational effort required to solve the problem. In this

Box C.2

A FOOD PROCESSING COMPANY PLANT LOCATION PROBLEM

The Giant Farmer Company processes and cans vegetables and fruits for sale in discount food stores. Presently the company has two plants: one in Chicago and one in Houston. The company also owns and operates four warehouses, located in Miami, Denver, Lincoln, and Jackson. A recent forecast of demand at the warehouses indicated that it will exceed supply in the near future. In particular, a new plant with a capacity of 8000 cases per week is needed. The decision has been made to build a new plant, but the location still has to be selected.

An important factor in the location decision will be the cost of transportation from the plants to the warehouses. Two potential sites for the new plant have been identified: Buffalo and Atlanta. The following data on capacities, forecasted demand, and shipping costs have been gathered.

Plant	Capacity in Cases per Week (00)	Warehouse	Demand in Cases per Week (00)
Chicago	100	Miami	70
Houston	75	Denver	90
New Plant	80	Lincoln	45
Total	255	Jackson	50
		Total	255

Plant	Shipping Cost to Warehouse (per case)			
	Miami	Denver	Lincoln	Jackson
Chicago	$7	$2	$4	$5
Houston	3	1	5	2
Buffalo (alternative 1)	6	9	7	4
Atlanta (alternative 2)	2	10	8	3

The shipping cost data reflects the best arrangements that can be made from each plant to each warehouse, considering both the cost and the quality of service provided by the shipper. Management would like to determine the location for the new plant that minimizes the costs of shipping.

section we discuss a class of linear programming problems for which the solution method is more efficient than the simplex method. The transportation method is an iterative procedure for solving problems when we want to minimize the cost of shipping products from m plants or sources of supply to n destinations.* We can also use this method to analyze alternative plant or warehouse locations. (See Chapter 8.) A typical problem is presented in Box C.2.

The Initial Tableau

The initial tableau for the Giant Farmer Company problem is shown in Fig. C.5, for the Buffalo option, which we elected to evaluate first. Each cell in the tableau represents a decision variable in the problem. The cost to ship one unit from a plant to a warehouse is shown in the upper right-hand corner of the corresponding cell. In the transportation method, the sum of the allocations to a row must equal the capacity of that row; similarly, the sum of the allocations to a column must equal the requirements for that column. These two sets of constraints are called **rim conditions.** Note that the sum of the capacities equals the sum of the requirements in Fig. C.5, which must always be the case when we use the transportation method. However, in many real problems, capacity may exceed requirements or vice versa. If so, we can easily adjust the model to satisfy the conditions for the transportation method. If capacity exceeds requirements by r units, we create an additional *column* in the tableau representing a dummy warehouse with a demand for r units and make the shipping costs in the newly created cells $0. This approach is analogous to adding slack variables in a linear programming problem. Similarly, if requirements exceed capacity by r units, we create a new *row* representing a dummy plant with a capacity of r units. We assign shipping costs of $0 per unit in the new cells to reflect the addition of slack variables to the problem. After making these adjustments, we can use the transportation method to solve the problem.

Generating an Initial Solution

Like the simplex method, the transportation method requires an initial solution to get started. This step amounts to allocating quantities to cells so that we meet the rim conditions. We will present two procedures for specifying an initial solution: the northwest-corner approach and Vogel's approximation method (VAM).

* The same approach can be used for a profit maximization problem.

Plant	Warehouse				Capacity
	Miami	Denver	Lincoln	Jackson	
Chicago	7	2	4	5	100
Houston	3	1	5	2	75
Buffalo	6	9	7	4	80
Requirements	70	90	45	50	255 / 255

Figure C.5

Initial Tableau for the Giant Farmer Company Problem.

The Northwest-Corner Approach. The quickest way to arrive at an initial solution to a transportation problem is to use the *northwest-corner approach.* As you may surmise from the name, the procedure starts in the northwest corner of the tableau and allocates as many units as possible to that cell without exceeding the row capacity or the column requirement. This allocation will completely satisfy either the row or the column constraint. In our example, we can allocate 70 units to the Chicago–Miami route, which eliminates Miami from further allocations, as shown in Fig. C.6.

We continue to make allocations to satisfy each row or column quantity but do not exceed any of the rim conditions. Thus the sequence of our allocations would be to Chicago–Denver (eliminating the first row), Houston–Denver (eliminating the second column) Houston–Lincoln (eliminating the second row), and so on.

The total cost for this initial solution is $1095, as calculated at the bottom of Fig. C.6. In general, the northwest-corner approach does not yield low-cost initial solutions. This result is to be expected, since costs were not considered in the allocation process. Consequently, we usually must trade off quickness in arriving at an initial solution with added work later in finding the optimal solution.

Vogel's Approximation Method (VAM). Although **Vogel's approximation method (VAM)** requires more work than the northwest-corner approach, it normally provides an initial solution that, if not optimal, is close to optimal.

Plant	Warehouse				Capacity
	Miami	Denver	Lincoln	Jackson	
Chicago	70 (7)	30 (2)	(4)	(5)	100
Houston	(3)	60 (1)	15 (5)	(2)	75
Buffalo	(6)	(9)	30 (7)	50 (4)	80
Requirements	70	90	45	50	255 / 255

Total cost = 70($7) + 30($2) + 60($1) + 15($5) + 30($7) + 50($4) = $1095

Figure C.6

Initial Solution for the Giant Farmer Company Using the Northwest-Corner Approach.

The more useful initial solution results from inclusion of the objective function in making the allocations. Application of VAM to our problem is shown in Fig. C.7.

We begin by calculating a penalty cost for each row and column. The penalty cost for each row is the difference between the lowest cost element in a row and the *next largest* cost element in that row. We obtain the penalty cost for each column in the same manner. For example, in our problem the penalty cost for the first row is $4 − $2 = $2, and the penalty cost for the first column is $6 − $3 = $3.

In making our first allocation, we choose the row or column having the largest penalty cost because it is like an opportunity cost. That is, if we do not allocate as many units as possible now to the cell with lowest cost in that row or column, we may have to allocate units later to the cell with the next largest cost in that row or column. The largest cost penalty is $3, for column 1, so we allocate as many units as we can to the lowest cost cell in the first column. This is the Houston–Miami route, the allocation is for 70 units, and this allocation satisfies the Miami requirements. If we have a tie in penalty costs, we can arbitrarily choose from the tied rows or columns.

In the second iteration (and thereafter), we have to recalculate the penalty costs to determine whether any have changed because of the last allocation. In this case, only the third-row penalty cost changed because we have eliminated column 1. The $3 penalty cost for the third row is now the largest, so we allocate 50 units to the lowest cost cell. Even though 80 units of capacity are available in row 3 (Buffalo), the requirement in column 4 (Jackson) is only 50 units.

The rest of the iterations are straightforward. In iteration 3, row 2 has the highest penalty cost. However, we can only allocate 5 units to the lowest cost cell because we had previously allocated 70 units to that row and the capacity is 75 units. We can eliminate column 2 in the fourth iteration by allocating 85 units to the Chicago–Denver route. The final allocation is obvious at this point. Two cells need allocations, and their values are prescribed by the rim conditions. The total cost of this initial solution is \$855, which is \$240 less than the cost generated by the northwest-corner approach.*

Selecting the Entering Route

At each iteration, we select a nonallocated cell (or route) to introduce into the solution, an allocated cell (or route) to be removed from the solution, and transform the tableau to reflect the impact of this change on the allocations to all the cells. In so doing, we have to make sure that the value of the objective function is improved or at least stays the same. We will discuss the process of selecting the entering route first.

Although there are other approaches to selecting the entering route in a transportation problem, we will discuss the so-called *stepping-stone method* because it is the most intuitive of those available.† The method is named for the procedure utilized. In general terms, we begin by selecting a nonallocated cell to be evaluated. We hypothetically allocate 1 unit to the cell, then adjust the currently allocated cells to balance the affected row capacities and column requirements alternately, without violating the rim conditions. In this respect, the tableau is like a shallow pond of water, with the allocated cells as stepping stones. Starting with the nonallocated cell, we move from allocated cell to allocated cell, each time moving at a right angle to the last move, alternately subtracting 1 unit from and adding 1 unit to the allocated cells, until we end up at the nonallocated cell again. In so doing, we create a *loop* and satisfy all rim conditions. Fortunately, there is only one loop for each nonallocated cell. We can calculate the net cost advantage from this loop.

---

* Regardless of the method used for determining an initial solution, it is important that the number of allocated cells equals $m + n - 1$, where m = number of rows and n = number of columns. If we have more than that number it means that we did not allocate as much as we could to each cell at each step. If we have less than that number, we have a case called *degeneracy,* which we discuss later.

† Another approach, called the *modified-distribution* (MODI) *method,* actually requires less work but is based on concepts beyond the scope of this appendix. This approach is discussed in Krajewski and Thompson (1981).

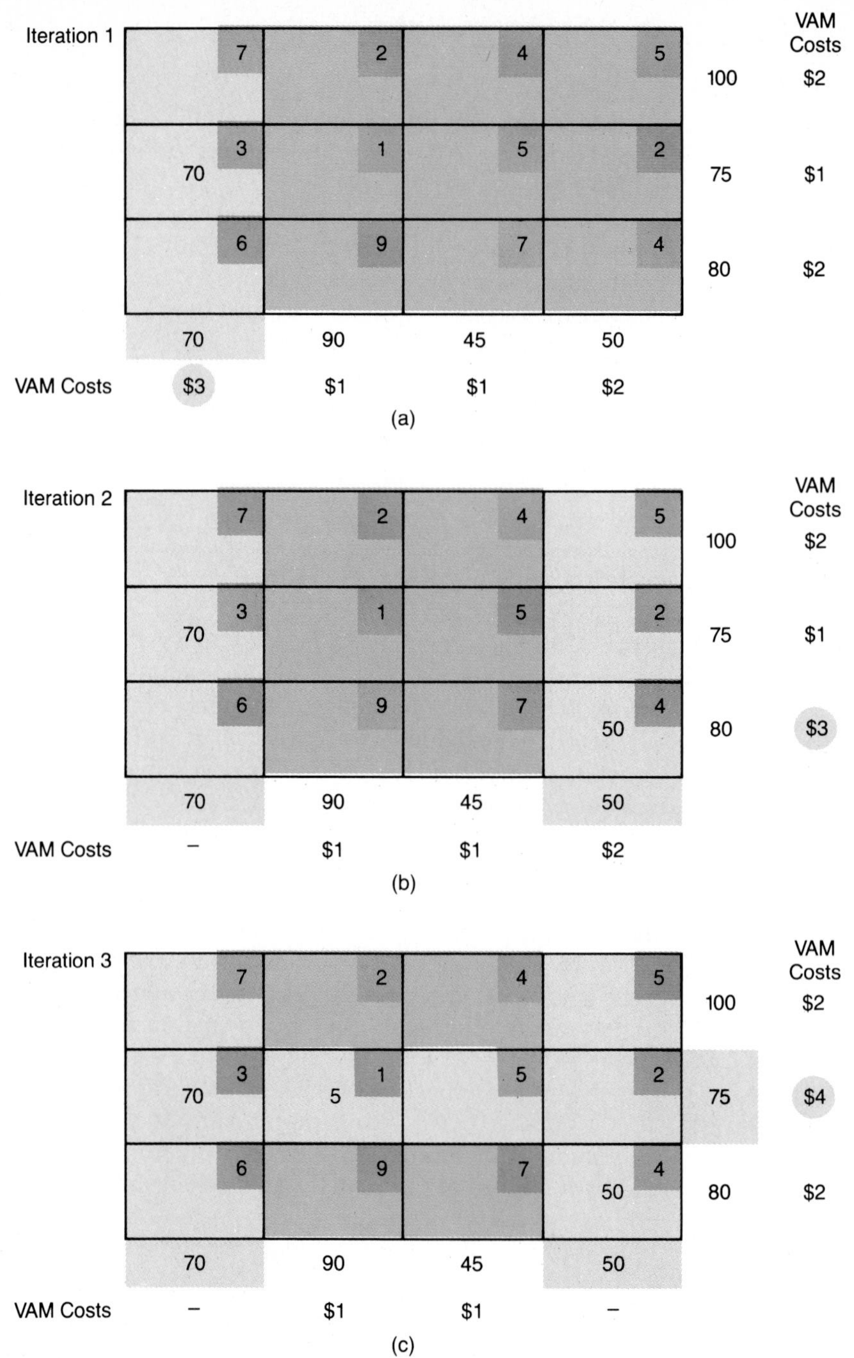

Figure C.7

Initial Solution for the Giant Farmer Company Problem Using VAM: (a) Iteration 1; (b) Iteration 2; (c) Iteration 3; (d) Iteration 4; (e) Final Allocation.

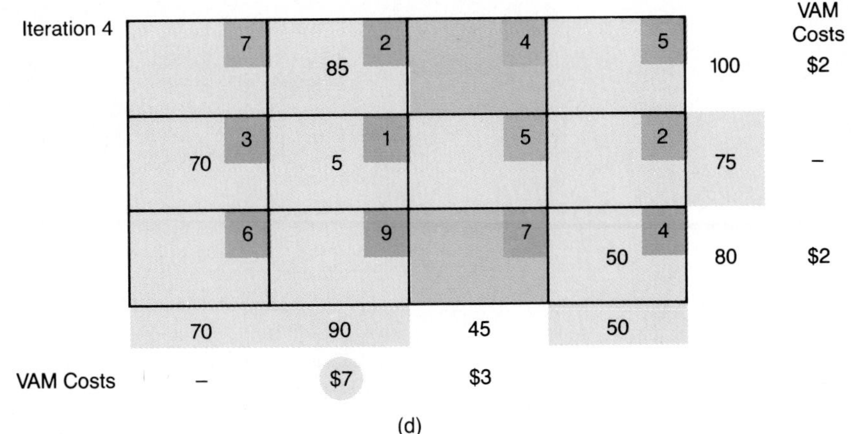

(d)

Final Allocation

Plant	Miami	Denver	Lincoln	Jackson	Capacity
	Warehouse				
Chicago	(7)	(2) 85	(4) 15	(5)	100
Houston	(3) 70	(1) 5	(5)	(2)	75
Buffalo	(6)	(9)	(7) 30	(4) 50	80
Requirements	70	90	45	50	255 / 255

Total cost = 70(\$3) + 85(\$2) + 5(\$1) + 15(\$4) + 30(\$7) + 50(\$4) = \$855

(e)

Consider Fig. C.8, which contains the initial solution derived from VAM in Fig. C.7. An ∗ indicates an allocated cell, and the □ indicates the nonallocated cell that we will evaluate first. The dashed line shows the loop for this cell. The cost of shipping 1 unit from Chicago to Jackson is \$5, but, since Jackson requires only 50 units, we must decrease the shipment from Buffalo to Jackson by 1 unit at a *savings* of \$4. This leaves Buffalo 1 unit short of its capacity of 80 units, but we know that all of its capacity will be needed because the total requirements from all warehouses equals the total plant capacity. Consequently, we add 1 unit to the Buffalo–Lincoln route, *increasing* costs by \$7. In so doing, we have allocated to Lincoln one more unit than it requires, so we

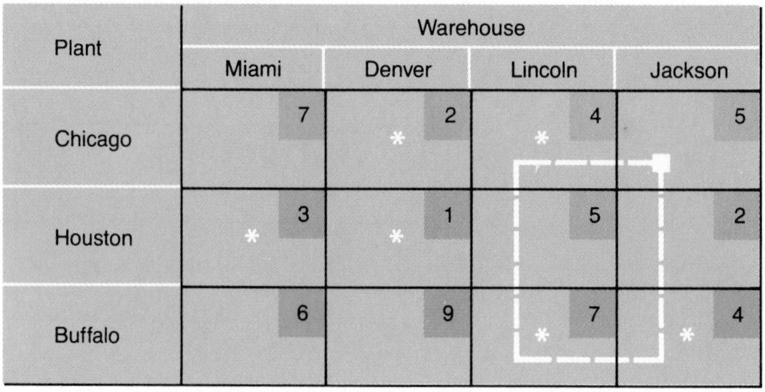

Plant	Warehouse			
	Miami	Denver	Lincoln	Jackson
Chicago	7	2 *	4 *	5
Houston	3 *	1 *	5	2
Buffalo	6	9	7 *	4 *

Net contribution to total costs per unit = \$5 − \$4 + \$7 − \$4 = \$4

Figure C.8

Loop for the Chicago–Jackson Route.

reduce the shipment from Chicago to Lincoln by 1 unit at a *savings* of \$4. This completes the loop and the net contribution to total costs is \$5 − \$4 + \$7 − \$4 = \$4. Since the net contribution is positive, opening a route from Chicago to Jackson is not profitable at this time. It would add \$4 to the total cost for each unit shipped.

Figure C.9 shows the loops for the remaining nonallocated cells, and Table C.6 shows the calculation of the net contributions for each one. Note that some loops are more complicated than others. The Houston–Jackson loop crosses itself, which is permissable so long as the intersection is at a right angle. The Buffalo–Denver loop passes over the Houston–Denver cell because, if we had stopped there, the only right-angle move would have been Houston–Miami. From that position, there is no right-angle move to an allocated cell. Finally, we should mention that loops can be traversed in two directions.

We can now identify the entering route for our problem. From Table C.6, it is obvious that the only route that would reduce costs is Buffalo–Miami. In general, we would pick the route with the largest negative net contribution.

Determining the Exiting Route and Transforming the Tableau

After we have determined the entering route, we allocate as many units to that route as possible. In order to maintain the same number of shipments (allocated cells) as before, this implies that one of the current shipments must

Table C.6

Net Contributions for the Remaining Nonallocated Cells in the Giant Farmer Company Problem

Shipment Change		Cost Change
Chicago–Miami		
Add 1 unit	Chicago–Miami	+$7
Subtract 1 unit	Houston–Miami	−$3
Add 1 unit	Houston–Denver	+$1
Subtract 1 unit	Chicago–Denver	−$2
Net contribution		+$3
Buffalo–Miami		
Add 1 unit	Buffalo–Miami	+$6
Subtract 1 unit	Houston–Miami	−$3
Add 1 unit	Houston–Denver	+$1
Subtract 1 unit	Chicago–Denver	−$2
Add 1 unit	Chicago–Lincoln	+$4
Subtract 1 unit	Buffalo–Lincoln	−$7
Net contribution		−$1
Buffalo–Denver		
Add 1 unit	Buffalo–Denver	+$9
Subtract 1 unit	Chicago–Denver	−$2
Add 1 unit	Chicago–Lincoln	+$4
Subtract 1 unit	Buffalo–Lincoln	−$7
Net contribution		+$4
Houston–Lincoln		
Add 1 unit	Houston–Lincoln	+$5
Subtract 1 unit	Chicago–Lincoln	−$4
Add 1 unit	Chicago–Denver	+$2
Subtract 1 unit	Houston–Denver	−$1
Net contribution		+$2
Houston–Jackson		
Add 1 unit	Houston–Jackson	+$2
Subtract 1 unit	Buffalo–Jackson	−$4
Add 1 unit	Buffalo–Lincoln	+$7
Subtract 1 unit	Chicago–Lincoln	−$4
Add 1 unit	Chicago–Denver	+$2
Subtract 1 unit	Houston–Denver	−$1
Net contribution		+$2

Chicago-Miami

	Miami	Denver	Lincoln	Jackson
Chicago		*	*	
Houston	*	*		
Buffalo			*	*

(a)

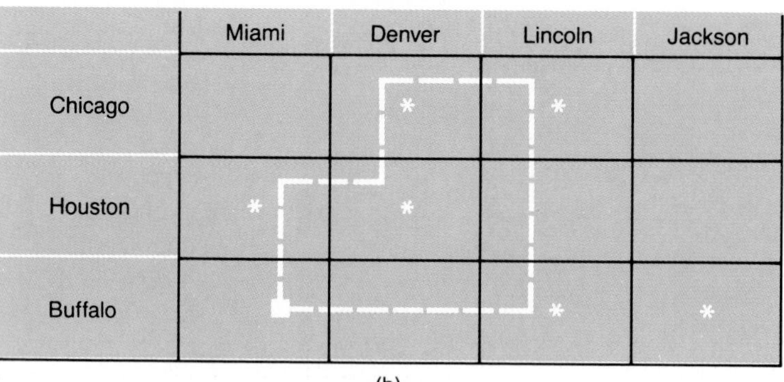

(b)

Buffalo-Denver

	Miami	Denver	Lincoln	Jackson
Chicago		*	*	
Houston	*	*		
Buffalo			*	*

(c)

Figure C.9

Loops for the Remaining Nonallocated Cells: (a) Chicago–Miami; (b) Buffalo–Miami; (c) Buffalo–Denver; (d) Houston–Lincoln; (e) Houston–Jackson.

Houston-Lincoln

	Miami	Denver	Lincoln	Jackson
Chicago		*	*	
Houston	*	*		
Buffalo			*	*

(d)

Houston-Jackson

	Miami	Denver	Lincoln	Jackson
Chicago		*	*	
Houston	*	*		
Buffalo			*	*

(e)

be reduced to zero.* We determine the maximum shipping quantity for the entering route and the route that will be removed from the solution by analyzing the loop for the entering route.

Figure C.10 shows the tableau for the initial solution that we developed using VAM and the loop for the Buffalo–Miami route. The (+) or (−) in the circle of each cell in the loop indicates that we must add a unit to or subtract a unit from that cell in order to satisfy the rim conditions. Note that each row and column affected has one positive cell and one negative cell. To determine the maximum quantity that can be shipped from Buffalo to Miami, we examine the negative cells because these are the cells for which shipping quantities will be reduced. In this example, they are Houston–Miami (70 units), Chicago–Denver (85 units), and Buffalo–Lincoln (30 units). Consequently, the maximum quantity that we can ship along the Buffalo–Miami route is the

* When more than one shipment is reduced to zero, a case of degeneracy results.

Plant	Warehouse				Capacity
	Miami	Denver	Lincoln	Jackson	
Chicago	7	2 / 85 (−)	4 / 15 (+)	5	100
Houston	3 / 70 (−)	1 / 5 (+)	5	2	75
Buffalo	6 / (+)	9	7 / 30 (−)	4 / 50	80
Requirements	70	90	45	50	255 / 255

Figure C.10

Loop for the Buffalo–Miami Route.

minimum of (70, 85, 30), or 30 units. To ship any more than 30 units would result in a negative quantity in the Buffalo–Lincoln cell and would violate the nonnegativity restrictions. Since Buffalo–Lincoln has the minimum allocation of the negative cells in the loop, we remove it from the solution. Figure C.11 shows the new solution to the problem after 30 units have been added to each positive cell and subtracted from each negative cell. The values in the circles are the net contributions for each nonallocated cell of Fig. C.11 and are calculated in the same manner as those in Table C.6.

The criterion for optimality in transportation problems can be stated in the following manner.

Minimization problems: If the net contributions of all nonallocated cells are zero or *positive,* the current solution is optimal.

Maximization problems: If the net contributions of all nonallocated cells are zero or *negative,* the current solution is optimal.

Consequently, the solution in Fig. C.11 is the optimal solution to the problem if we locate the new plant in Buffalo. The total transportation cost is $82,500. If one or more of the net contributions were still negative, we would have to do another iteration of the tableau.

Turning to alternative 2, locating the new plant in Atlanta, the solution to the transportation problem results in a total transportation cost of $57,500. We leave the solution of this problem to you, as Problem 8 at the end of this appendix. If transportation cost is the overriding consideration, the new plant should be located in Atlanta. However, management usually considers many other factors before making a final plant location decision. (See Chapter 8.)

Degeneracy

Whenever we have fewer than $m + n - 1$ allocated cells in a transportation problem we have **degeneracy.** It can occur in the derivation of an initial solution when we satisfy a row constraint and a column constraint simultaneously with one allocation, or when we introduce a new route into the solution and more than one negative cell in the loop has the same minimum allocation. We need to have $m + n - 1$ allocated cells so that we can create loops for each nonallocated cell.

The procedure for dealing with degeneracy involves the allocation of an infinitesimal quantity, ε, to as many nonallocated cells as necessary to bring the total number of allocated cells to $m + n - 1$. It is important that we choose only those nonallocated cells having loops that cannot be formed without the ε allocation. Since the value of ε is so small, it does not enter into the total cost of the solution or the shipping quantity for a given route; its only use is in calculating the loops for nonallocated cells. We treat the cell with ε as a typical allocated cell in our calculations, and we continue with the stepping-stone method until we reach the condition of optimality.

Plant	Warehouse				Capacity
	Miami	Denver	Lincoln	Jackson	
Chicago	7 / + $3	2 / 55	4 / 45	5 / + $3	100
Houston	3 / 40	1 / 35	5 / + $2	2 / + $1	75
Buffalo	6 / 30	9 / + $5	7 / + $1	4 / 50	80
Requirements	70	90	45	50	255 / 255

Total cost = 40($3) + 30($6) + 55($2) + 35($1) + 45($4) + 50($4) = $825

Figure C.11

Transformed Array Showing Optimal Solution to Giant Farmer Company Problem.

Table C.7

Typical Applications of Linear Programming Methods to Resource Allocation Problems in Operations Management

Problem Type	Description	Method*
Production planning	*Production:* Find the minimum-cost production schedule for a given work-force plan, taking into account inventory carrying, overtime, and subcontracting costs.	Transportation
	Production and work force: Find the minimum-cost production schedule, taking into account hiring and layoff costs as well as inventory carrying, overtime, and subcontracting costs, subject to various capacity and policy constraints.	Simplex
	Staffing: Find the optimal staffing plan for various categories of workers, subject to various demand and policy constraints.	Simplex
Distribution	*Shipping plans:* Find the optimal shipping assignments from factories to distribution centers or from warehouses to retailers.	Transportation
Inventory planning	*Stock control:* Determine the optimal mix of products to hold in inventory in a warehouse.	Simplex
	Supplier selection: Find the optimal combination of suppliers to minimize the amount of unwanted inventory.	Simplex
Location planning	*Plants or warehouses:* Determine the optimal location of a plant or warehouse with respect to total transportation costs between various alternative locations and existing supply and demand sources.	Transportation
Process control	*Stock cutting:* Given the dimensions of a roll or sheet of raw material, find the cutting pattern that minimizes the amount of scrap material.	Simplex
Product planning	*Mixes:* Find the optimal production quantities of a group of products, subject to resource capacity and market demand constraints.	Simplex
	Blends: Find the optimal proportions of various ingredients of products such as gasoline, paints, and foods, subject to certain minimal requirements.	Simplex
Scheduling	*Shifts:* Determine the minimum-cost assignment of workers to shifts, subject to varying demand.	Simplex
	Vehicles: Assign *m* vehicles to *n* products or jobs and determine the number of trips to make, subject to vehicle size, vehicle availability, and demand constraints.	Simplex
	Routing: Find the optimal routing of a product through a number of sequential processes, each with their own capacities and characteristics.	Simplex

* The simplex method could be used for any of the applications described in this table. The transportation method is more efficient in those cases for which it is listed under *method.*

APPLICATION OF LINEAR PROGRAMMING TO OPERATIONS MANAGEMENT

Linear programming has been applied to a wide variety of operations management problems, some of which are shown in Table C.7. Although linear programming is a powerful tool for solving complex resource allocation problems and can provide much information about the implicit values of various resources, we must emphasize that it is *only a tool* for decisionmakers. Linear programming does not make decisions—decisionmakers do. Linear programming is a method for solving a linear model that is a specification of the objectives and constraints of a particular problem. The assumption of linearity in all relationships in the model must be made. At best, in most applications this assumption yields only a good approximation of the real relationships. Consequently, the solution of the model can be regarded only as a good starting point for the overall solution of the problem. In this regard, the supplementary information generated, such as shadow prices of critical resources or right-hand-side ranges, could be more important than the solution itself.

Practical applications of linear programming are carried out with the help of a computer. Most major computer vendors have general-purpose software programs that solve very complex linear programming problems. Although the concepts we have presented in this appendix could be used for large-scale applications, the advanced procedures of computer programs and the computational speed of the computer dramatically reduce the amount of time required to solve problems. In addition, a complete sensitivity analysis of objective function coefficients and right-hand-side values is provided along with the solution. If a particular application, such as product mix or blending, must be repeated frequently, special-purpose programs can be developed. They have input generator routines that simplify the input of data and generate the objective function and constraints for the problem. These special-purpose programs also have output routines that prepare specially designed managerial reports.

APPENDIX HIGHLIGHTS

Linear programming is a powerful tool that can be used to help solve resource allocation problems. In this appendix, we presented the simplex method and the transportation method and showed how they can be used to analyze operations management problems. Some of the highlights of this appendix are:

- Linear programming is a method that can be used to optimize a linear objective function, subject to a set of linear constraints. It has been applied to a wide variety of resource allocation problems in practice.

- The simplex method is an iterative algebraic procedure for solving linear programming problems. It systematically evaluates corner points of the feasible region in such a way that the objective function improves (or at worst stays the same) at each iteration. The optimal simplex tableau can be used to do sensitivity analysis. The shadow prices of the resources are provided in that tableau. Also, right-hand-side ranging can be done to determine the sensitivity of the solution to changes in the amount of resources.
- The transportation method is useful for solving problems when the objective is to minimize the cost of shipping products from a group of sources to another group of destinations. The only constraints are stated in the form of rim conditions. It is an iterative method that avoids some of the computational difficulties of the simplex method for problems of this type.
- Linear programming methods such as the ones discussed in this chapter should be considered only as tools in the analysis of operations management problems. The final decision might differ from the solutions generated by these techniques after various nonquantitative factors are considered.

KEY TERMS

degeneracy

feasible region

graphical method of linear programming

right-hand-side ranging

rim conditions

shadow price

simplex method

Vogel's approximation method (VAM)

STUDY QUESTIONS

1. In solving resource allocation problems with the help of linear programming, what assumptions are you making about the relationships of variables and constants in the problems?
2. Explain the method of linear programming, as to your boss, in an intuitively appealing way.
3. In the simplex method, the exiting variable in any iteration is determined by calculating the ratios of the values in the quantity column to the corresponding substitution rates in the entering-variable column and selecting the row having the lowest positive ratio. Explain why you must choose the *minimum* ratio.
4. How can linear programming be used to study managerial policies regarding a particular operations management problem? What information can a linear programming analysis supply that is useful in assessing the impact of changing policies associated with the availability of resources?

5. What is a *slack* variable? What usefulness does it have in linear programming analysis?
6. What modifications to the simplex method are required for minimization problems? What role do *surplus* and *artificial* variables play? Might these variables be needed in a maximization problem?
7. Why is the transportation method more efficient than the simplex method for problems having the structural requirements of a transportation problem?
8. What are the trade-offs in choosing between the northwest-corner method and Vogel's approximation method for obtaining an initial solution in a transportation problem?
9. Explain the stepping-stone method in simple terms. Explain why total requirements must equal total supply to make it work. What modifications must you make if total requirements do not equal total supply?
10. What is *degeneracy* in a transportation problem? How can it be handled with the transportation method?

PROBLEMS

1. The plant manager of a plastic pipe manufacturer has the opportunity to use two different routings for a particular type of plastic pipe. Routing 1 uses extruder A and routing 2 uses extruder B. Both routings require the same melting process. The following table shows the time requirements and capacities of these processes.

	Hours per 100 Feet		
Process	Routing 1	Routing 2	Capacity (hours)
Melting	1	1	45
Extruder A	3	0	90
Extruder B	0	4	160

In addition, each 100 feet of pipe processed on routing 1 uses 5 pounds of raw material, whereas each 100 feet of pipe processed on routing 2 uses only 4 pounds. This difference results from differing scrap rates of the extruding machines. Consequently, the profit per 100 feet of pipe processed on routing 1 is \$60 and on routing 2 is \$80. A total of 200 pounds of raw material is available.

(a) Write the constraints and objective function for this problem.
(b) Use the graphic method to find the optimal solution.

2. Use the simplex method to solve Problem 1.
3. The Trim-Look Company makes skirts, dresses, and sport coats in a variety of lines for women. Recently it was suggested that the company reevaluate its South Islander line and allocate its resources to those products that would maximize contribution to profits and overhead. Each product must pass through the cutting and sewing departments. In addition, each product in the South Islander line requires the same polyester fabric. The following data were collected for the study.

	Process Time (hours)		
Product	Cutting	Sewing	Material (yards)
Skirt	1	1	1
Dress	3	4	1
Sport Coat	4	6	4

The cutting department has 100 hours of capacity, sewing has 180 hours, and there is 60 yards of material. Each skirt contributes \$5 to profits and overhead; each dress and sport coat contributes \$17 and \$30, respectively.

(a) Specify the objective function and constraints for this problem.

(b) Solve the problem using the simplex method.

4. Consider Problem 3 further.

(a) How much would you be willing to pay for

(i) an extra hour of cutting time?

(ii) an extra hour of sewing time?

(iii) an extra yard of material?

Explain your responses to each question.

(b) Determine the range of right-hand-side values over which the shadow price would be valid for each of the following constraints.

(i) Cutting.

(ii) Material.

5. The following is a linear programming model for analyzing the product mix of a company that produces three products.

Max. z:

$\$0.5x_1 + \$6x_2 + \$5x_3$ (Contribution to profits).

Subject to:

$4x_1 + 6x_2 + 3x_3 \leq 24$ (machine A time);

$1x_1 + \frac{3}{2}x_2 + 3x_3 \leq 12$ (machine B time);

$3x_1 + 1x_2 \leq 12$ (machine C time);

$x_1, x_2, x_3 \geq 0.$

Let s_1, s_2 and s_3 be the slack variables for the machine A, machine B, and machine C constraints respectively. The following is a partially completed optimal tableau for the problem.

Consider each of the following statements independently, state whether it is true or false, and explain each answer.

(a) If an added hour of capacity for machine A costs \$0.50, we could *add* 20 hours of machine A capacity at an expected increase in contribution to profits and overhead of \$5.56.

(b) We could *reduce* machine B capacity by 9 hours and reduce the contribution to profits and overhead by \$8, ex-

c_j		\$0.5	\$6	\$5	0	0	0	
	Solution Variables	x_1	x_2	x_3	s_1	s_2	s_3	Quantity
		2/3	1	0	2/9	−2/9	0	8/3
		0	0	1	−1/9	4/9	0	8/3
		7/3	0	0	−2/9	2/9	1	28/3
	z_j							
	$c_j - z_j$							

clusive of layoff and other incidental costs.

(c) We could *reduce* machine C capacity by 5 hours without any effect on the contribution to profits and overhead, exclusive of layoff and other incidental costs.

6. The Acme Company has four factories that ship products to five warehouses. The shipping costs, requirements, and capacities are shown in the following tables. Use the transportation method to find the shipping schedule that minimizes shipping costs.

	Shipping Costs ($/case) to				
From	W1	W2	W3	W4	W5
F1	1	3	4	5	6
F2	2	2	1	4	5
F3	1	5	1	3	1
F4	5	2	4	5	4

Requirements (000)	Capacities (000)
W1: 60	F1: 80
W2: 70	F2: 60
W3: 50	F3: 60
W4: 30	F4: 50
W5: 40	

7. Consider further the Acme Company situation described in Problem 6. Suppose that the company is contemplating the closing of F4 because of high operating costs. If this were done, 50,000 units of capacity would be added to F3. The logistics manager is worried about the effect of this move on transportation costs. Presently, F4 is shipping 50,000 cases to W2 at a cost of $2 per case. Since the shipping cost is $5 per case from F3 to W2, the manager estimated that closing F4 would increase transportation costs by $150,000.

(a) What is the potential flaw in the logistics manager's thinking?

(b) Determine a better estimate of the expected change in the transportation costs. Assume that current distribution costs total $410,000.

8. Consider the facility location problem at the Giant Farmer Company described in Box C.2. Find the minimum-cost shipping plan if the new plant were located in Atlanta.

9. The Pelican Company has four distribution centers (A, B, C, and D) that require 50,000, 40,000, 60,000, and 40,000 gallons of diesel fuel, respectively, per month for their long-haul trucks. Three fuel wholesalers (1, 2, and 3) have indicated their willingness to supply up to 80,000, 100,000, and 50,000 gallons of fuel, respectively. The total cost (shipping plus price) of delivering 1000 gallons of fuel from each wholesaler to each distribution center is shown in the following table.

	Distribution Center			
Wholesaler	A	B	C	D
1	1.70	1.60	1.60	1.60
2	1.50	1.80	1.60	1.70
3	1.80	1.50	1.80	1.60

Currently, wholesaler 1 is supplying 40,000 gallons to distribution center B and 10,000 gallons to C. Wholesaler 2 is shipping 50,000 gallons to A and 50,000 gallons to C. Wholesaler 3 is shipping 40,000 gallons to D. Does the present delivery arrangement minimize the cost to the Pelican Company? If not, find a plan that minimizes total costs.

10. The Kramer Corporation produces and markets a certain product, which it stocks in various warehouses throughout the country. Recently, its market research group compiled a forecast indicating that a significant increase in demand will occur in the near future, after which demand will level off for the foreseeable future.

The company has decided to satisfy this demand by constructing new plant capacity. The company already has plants in Boston and Chicago and has no desire to relocate those facilities. Each plant is capable of producing 800,000 units per year.

After a thorough search, the company has developed two alternative sites and three capacity alternatives. Alternative 1 is to build an 800,000-unit plant in Denver. Alternative 2 is to build an 800,000-unit plant in Houston. Alternative 3 is to build a 400,000-unit plant in Denver and a 400,000-unit plant in Houston.

The company has four warehouses that distribute the product to retailers. The market research study provided the following data:

Warehouse	Expected Future Annual Demand (units)
Cleveland (CL)	400,000
Los Angeles (LA)	900,000
San Francisco (SF)	500,000
St. Louis (St. L)	600,000

The logistics department compiled the following cost table that specified the cost per unit to ship the product from each plant to each warehouse in the most economical manner, subject to the reliability of the various carriers involved.

	Warehouse			
Plant	CL	LA	SF	St. L
Boston	$0.12	$0.52	$0.58	$0.20
Chicago	0.08	0.48	0.50	0.07
Denver	0.25	0.33	0.40	0.20
Houston	0.30	0.39	0.42	0.18

As one part of the location/capacity decision, management would like to estimate the total distribution cost for each alternative. Use the transportation method to calculate these estimates.

SELECTED REFERENCES

Asim, R., E. De Falomir, and L. Lasdon, "An Optimization-Based Decision Support System for a Product-Mix Problem," *Interfaces*, vol. 12, no. 2 (April 1982), pp. 26–33.

Hadley, G., *Linear Programming*. Reading, Mass.: Addison-Wesley, 1962.

Hillier, F. S., and G. J. Lieberman, *Introduction to Operations Research*, 2nd ed. San Francisco: Holden-Day, 1974.

Krajewski, L. J., and H. E. Thompson, *Management Science: Quantitative Methods in Context*. New York: John Wiley & Sons, 1981.

Markland, R. E., *Topics in Management Science*. New York: John Wiley & Sons, 1979.

Perry, C., and K. C. Crellin, "The Precise Management Meaning of a Shadow Price," *Interfaces*, vol. 12, no. 2 (April 1982), pp. 61–63.

Wagner, H. M., *Principles of Operations Research*, 2nd ed. Englewood Cliffs, N.J.: Prentice-Hall, 1975.

Zeleny, M., "On the Squandering of Resources and Profits via Linear Programming," *Interfaces*, vol. 11, no. 5 (October 1981), pp. 101–107.

APPENDIX D

FINANCIAL AND STATISTICAL AIDS

Appendix Outline

Appendix D.1

Present Value Factors for a Single Payment of $1, n Periods from Now

Number of Periods (*n*)	Interest Rate (*r*)																	
	0.01	0.02	0.03	0.04	0.05	0.06	0.08	0.10	0.12	0.14	0.16	0.18	0.20	0.22	0.24	0.26	0.28	0.30
1	.9901	.9804	.9709	.9615	.9524	.9434	.9259	.9091	.8929	.8772	.8621	.8475	.8333	.8197	.8065	.7937	.7812	.7692
2	.9803	.9612	.9426	.9246	.9070	.8900	.8573	.8264	.7972	.7695	.7432	.7182	.6944	.6719	.6504	.6299	.6104	.5917
3	.9706	.9423	.9151	.8890	.8638	.8396	.7938	.7513	.7118	.6750	.6407	.6086	.5787	.5507	.5245	.4999	.4768	.4552
4	.9610	.9238	.8885	.8548	.8227	.7921	.7350	.6830	.6355	.5921	.5523	.5158	.4823	.4514	.4230	.3968	.3725	.3501
5	.9515	.9057	.8626	.8219	.7835	.7473	.6806	.6209	.5674	.5194	.4761	.4371	.4019	.3700	.3411	.3149	.2910	.2693
6	.9420	.8880	.8375	.7903	.7462	.7050	.6302	.5645	.5066	.4556	.4104	.3704	.3349	.3033	.2751	.2499	.2274	.2072
7	.9327	.8706	.8131	.7599	.7107	.6651	.5835	.5132	.4523	.3996	.3538	.3139	.2791	.2486	.2218	.1983	.1776	.1594
8	.9235	.8535	.7894	.7307	.6768	.6274	.5403	.4665	.4039	.3506	.3050	.2660	.2326	.2038	.1789	.1574	.1388	.1226
9	.9143	.8368	.7664	.7026	.6446	.5919	.5002	.4241	.3606	.3075	.2630	.2255	.1938	.1670	.1443	.1249	.1084	.0943
10	.9053	.8203	.7441	.6756	.6139	.5584	.4632	.3855	.3220	.2697	.2267	.1911	.1615	.1369	.1164	.0922	.0847	.0725
11	.8963	.8043	.7224	.6496	.5847	.5268	.4289	.3505	.2875	.2366	.1954	.1619	.1346	.1122	.0938	.0787	.0662	.0558
12	.8874	.7885	.7014	.6246	.5568	.4970	.3971	.3186	.2567	.2076	.1685	.1372	.1122	.0920	.0757	.0625	.0517	.0429
13	.8787	.7730	.6810	.6006	.5303	.4688	.3677	.2897	.2292	.1821	.1452	.1163	.0935	.0754	.0610	.0496	.0404	.0330
14	.8700	.7579	.6611	.5775	.5051	.4423	.3405	.2633	.2046	.1597	.1252	.0985	.0779	.0618	.0492	.0393	.0316	.0254
15	.8613	.7430	.6419	.5553	.4810	.4173	.3152	.2394	.1827	.1401	.1079	.0835	.0649	.0507	.0397	.0312	.0247	.0195
16	.8528	.7284	.6232	.5339	.4581	.3936	.2919	.2176	.1631	.1229	.0930	.0708	.0541	.0415	.0320	.0248	.0193	.0150
17	.8444	.7142	.6050	.5134	.4363	.3714	.2703	.1978	.1456	.1078	.0802	.0600	.0451	.0340	.0258	.0197	.0150	.0116
18	.8360	.7002	.5874	.4936	.4155	.3503	.2502	.1799	.1300	.0946	.0691	.0508	.0376	.0279	.0208	.0156	.0118	.0089
19	.8277	.6864	.5703	.4746	.3957	.3305	.2317	.1635	.1161	.0829	.0596	.0431	.0313	.0229	.0168	.0124	.0092	.0068
20	.8195	.6730	.5537	.4564	.3769	.3118	.2145	.1486	.1037	.0728	.0514	.0365	.0261	.0187	.0135	.0098	.0072	.0053
21	.8114	.6598	.5375	.4388	.3589	.2942	.1987	.1351	.0926	.0638	.0443	.0309	.0217	.0154	.0109	.0078	.0056	.0040
22	.8034	.6468	.5219	.4220	.3418	.2775	.1839	.1228	.0826	.0560	.0382	.0262	.0181	.0126	.0088	.0062	.0044	.0031
23	.7954	.6342	.5067	.4057	.3256	.2618	.1703	.1117	.0738	.0491	.0329	.0222	.0151	.0103	.0071	.0049	.0034	.0024
24	.7876	.6217	.4919	.3901	.3101	.2470	.1577	.1015	.0659	.0431	.0284	.0188	.0126	.0085	.0057	.0039	.0027	.0018
25	.7798	.6095	.4776	.3751	.2953	.2330	.1460	.0923	.0588	.0378	.0245	.0160	.0105	.0069	.0046	.0031	.0021	.0014
26	.7720	.5976	.4637	.3607	.2812	.2198	.1352	.0839	.0525	.0331	.0211	.0135	.0087	.0057	.0037	.0025	.0016	.0011
27	.7644	.5859	.4502	.3468	.2678	.2074	.1252	.0763	.0469	.0291	.0182	.0115	.0073	.0047	.0030	.0019	.0013	.0008
28	.7568	.5744	.4371	.3335	.2551	.1956	.1159	.0693	.0419	.0255	.0157	.0097	.0061	.0038	.0024	.0015	.0010	.0006
29	.7493	.5631	.4243	.3207	.2429	.1846	.1073	.0630	.0374	.0224	.0135	.0082	.0051	.0031	.0020	.0012	.0008	.0005
30	.7419	.5521	.4120	.3083	.2314	.1741	.0994	.0573	.0334	.0196	.0116	.0070	.0042	.0026	.0016	.0010	.0006	.0004
35	.7059	.5000	.3554	.2534	.1813	.1301	.0676	.0356	.0189	.0102	.0055	.0030	.0017	.0009	.0005	.0003	.0002	.0001
40	.6717	.4529	.3066	.2083	.1420	.0972	.0460	.0221	.0107	.0053	.0026	.0013	.0007	.0004	.0002	.0001	.0001	.0000

$$P = \frac{F}{(1 + r)^n} = Fpf,$$

where

P = Present value of a single investment;

F = Future value of a single payment;

n = Number of periods for which P is to be invested;

r = The periodic interest rate; and

pf = The present value factor for \$1 = $1/(1 + r)^n$.

Appendix D.2

Present Value Factors of an Annuity of $1 for n Periods

Number of Periods (n)	Interest Rate (r)																	
	0.01	0.02	0.03	0.04	0.05	0.06	0.08	0.10	0.12	0.14	0.16	0.18	0.20	0.22	0.24	0.26	0.28	0.30
1	0.9901	0.9804	0.9709	0.9615	0.9524	0.9434	0.9259	0.9091	0.8929	0.8772	0.8621	0.8475	0.8333	0.8197	0.8065	0.7937	0.7812	0.7692
2	1.9704	1.9416	1.9135	1.8861	1.8594	1.8334	1.7833	1.7355	1.6901	1.6467	1.6052	1.5656	1.5278	1.4915	1.4568	1.4235	1.3916	1.3609
3	2.9410	2.8839	2.8286	2.7751	2.7232	2.6730	2.5771	2.4869	2.4018	2.3216	2.2459	2.1743	2.1065	2.0422	1.9813	1.9234	1.8684	1.8161
4	3.9020	3.8077	3.7171	3.6299	3.5460	3.4651	3.3121	3.1699	3.0373	2.9137	2.7982	2.6901	2.5887	2.4936	2.4043	2.3202	2.2410	2.1662
5	4.8534	4.7135	4.5797	4.4518	4.3295	4.2124	3.9927	3.7908	3.6048	3.4331	3.2743	3.1272	2.9906	2.8636	2.7454	2.6351	2.5320	2.4356
6	5.7955	5.6014	5.4172	5.2421	5.0757	4.9173	4.6229	4.3553	4.1114	3.8887	3.6847	3.4976	3.3255	3.1669	3.0205	2.8850	2.7594	2.6427
7	6.7282	6.4720	6.2303	6.0021	5.7864	5.5824	5.2064	4.8684	4.5638	4.2883	4.0386	3.8115	3.6046	3.4155	3.2423	3.0833	2.9370	2.8021
8	7.6517	7.3255	7.0197	6.7327	6.4632	6.2098	5.7466	5.3349	4.9676	4.6389	4.3436	4.0776	3.8372	3.6193	3.4212	3.2407	3.0758	2.9247
9	8.5660	8.1622	7.7861	7.4353	7.1078	6.8017	6.2469	5.7590	5.3282	4.9464	4.6065	4.3030	4.0310	3.7863	3.5655	3.3657	3.1842	3.0190
10	9.4713	8.9826	8.5302	8.1109	7.7217	7.3601	6.7101	6.1446	5.6502	5.2161	4.8332	4.4941	4.1925	3.9232	3.6819	3.4648	3.2689	3.0915
11	10.3676	9.7868	9.2526	8.7605	8.3064	7.8869	7.1390	6.4951	5.9377	5.4527	5.0286	4.6560	4.3271	4.0354	3.7757	3.5435	3.3351	3.1473
12	11.2551	10.5753	9.9540	9.3851	8.8633	8.3838	7.5361	6.8137	6.1944	5.6603	5.1971	4.7932	4.4392	4.1274	3.8514	3.6059	3.3868	3.1903
13	12.1337	11.3484	10.6350	9.9856	9.3936	8.8527	7.9038	7.1034	6.4235	5.8424	5.3423	4.9095	4.5327	4.2028	3.9124	3.6555	3.4272	3.2233
14	13.0037	12.1062	11.2961	10.5631	9.8986	9.2950	8.2442	7.3667	6.6282	6.0021	5.4675	5.0081	4.6106	4.2646	3.9616	3.6949	3.4587	3.2487
15	13.8651	12.8493	11.9379	11.1184	10.3797	9.7122	8.5595	7.6061	6.8109	6.1422	5.5755	5.0916	4.6755	4.3152	4.0013	3.7261	3.4834	3.2682
16	14.7179	13.5777	12.5611	11.6523	10.8378	10.1059	8.8514	7.8237	6.9740	6.2651	5.6685	5.1624	4.7296	4.3567	4.0333	3.7509	3.5026	3.2832
17	15.5623	14.2919	13.1661	12.1657	11.2741	10.4773	9.1216	8.0216	7.1196	6.3729	5.7487	5.2223	4.7746	4.3908	4.0591	3.7705	3.5177	3.2948
18	16.3983	14.9920	13.7535	12.6593	11.6896	10.8276	9.3719	8.2014	7.2497	6.4674	5.8178	5.2732	4.8122	4.4187	4.0799	3.7861	3.5294	3.3037
19	17.2260	15.6785	14.3238	13.1339	12.0853	11.1581	9.6036	8.3649	7.3658	6.5504	5.8775	5.3162	4.8435	4.4415	4.0967	3.7985	3.5386	3.3105
20	18.0456	16.3514	14.8775	13.5903	12.4622	11.4699	9.8181	8.5136	7.4694	6.6231	5.9288	5.3527	4.8696	4.4603	4.1103	3.8083	3.5458	3.3158
21	18.8570	17.0112	15.4150	14.0292	12.8212	11.7641	10.0168	8.6487	7.5620	6.6870	5.9731	5.3837	4.8913	4.4756	4.1212	3.8161	3.5514	3.3198
22	19.6604	17.6580	15.9369	14.4511	13.1630	12.0416	10.2007	8.7715	7.6446	6.7429	6.0113	5.4099	4.9094	4.4882	4.1300	3.8223	3.5558	3.3230
23	20.4558	18.2922	16.4436	14.8568	13.4886	12.3034	10.3711	8.8832	7.7184	6.7921	6.0442	5.4321	4.9245	4.4985	4.1371	3.8273	3.5592	3.3254
24	21.2434	18.9139	16.9355	15.2470	13.7986	12.5504	10.5288	8.9847	7.7843	6.8351	6.0726	5.4509	4.9371	4.5070	4.1428	3.8312	3.5619	3.3272
25	22.0232	19.5235	17.4131	15.6221	14.0939	12.7834	10.6748	9.0770	7.8431	6.8729	6.0971	5.4669	4.9476	4.5139	4.1474	3.8342	3.5640	3.3286
26	22.7952	20.1210	17.8768	15.9828	14.3752	13.0032	10.8100	9.1609	7.8957	6.9061	6.1182	5.4804	4.9563	4.5196	4.1511	3.8367	3.5656	3.3297
27	23.5596	20.7069	18.3270	16.3296	14.6430	13.2105	10.9352	9.2372	7.9426	6.9352	6.1364	5.4919	4.9636	4.5243	4.1542	3.8387	3.5669	3.3305
28	24.3164	21.2813	18.7641	16.6631	14.8981	13.4062	11.0511	9.3066	7.9844	6.9607	6.1520	5.5016	4.9697	4.5281	4.1566	3.8402	3.5679	3.3312
29	25.0658	21.8444	19.1885	16.9837	15.1411	13.5907	11.1584	9.3696	8.0218	6.9830	6.1656	5.5098	4.9747	4.5312	4.1585	3.8414	3.5687	3.3317
30	25.8077	22.3965	19.6004	17.2920	15.3725	13.7648	11.2578	9.4269	8.0552	7.0027	6.1772	5.5168	4.9789	4.5338	4.1601	3.8424	3.5693	3.3321
35	29.4086	24.9986	21.4872	18.6646	16.3742	14.4982	11.6546	9.6442	8.1755	7.0700	6.2153	5.5386	4.9915	4.5411	4.1644	3.8450	3.5708	3.3330
40	32.8347	27.3555	23.1148	19.7928	17.1591	15.0463	11.9246	9.7791	8.2438	7.1050	6.2335	5.5482	4.9966	4.5439	4.1659	3.8458	3.5712	3.3332

$$P = \frac{A}{(1 + r)} + \frac{A}{(1 + r)^2} + \cdots + \frac{A}{(1 + r)^n} = A \sum_{j=1}^{n} 1/(1 + r)^j = Aaf,$$

where

P = Present value of a single investment;

A = Amount of annuity to be received at the end of each period;

n = Number of periods for which the annuity is received.

r = The periodic interest rate; and

af = The annuity factor for an annuity of $1 = $\sum_{j=1}^{n} 1/(1 + r)^j$.

Appendix D.3

Cumulative Probabilities of the Normal Distribution (Areas under the Standardized Normal Curve from $-\infty$ to z)

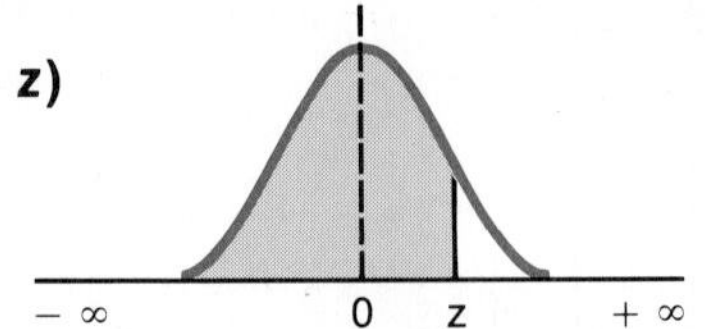

z	.00	.01	.02	.03	.04	.05	.06	.07	.08	.09
.0	.5000	.5040	.5080	.5120	.5160	.5199	.5239	.5279	.5319	.5359
.1	.5398	.5438	.5478	.5517	.5557	.5596	.5636	.5675	.5714	.5753
.2	.5793	.5832	.5871	.5910	.5948	.5987	.6026	.6064	.6103	.6141
.3	.6179	.6217	.6255	.6293	.6331	.6368	.6406	.6443	.6480	.6517
.4	.6554	.6591	.6628	.6664	.6700	.6736	.6772	.6808	.6844	.6879
.5	.6915	.6950	.6985	.7019	.7054	.7088	.7123	.7157	.7190	.7224
.6	.7257	.7291	.7324	.7357	.7389	.7422	.7454	.7486	.7517	.7549
.7	.7580	.7611	.7642	.7673	.7704	.7734	.7764	.7794	.7823	.7852
.8	.7881	.7910	.7939	.7967	.7995	.8023	.8051	.8078	.8106	.8133
.9	.8159	.8186	.8212	.8238	.8264	.8289	.8315	.8340	.8365	.8389
1.0	.8413	.8438	.8461	.8485	.8508	.8531	.8554	.8577	.8599	.8621
1.1	.8643	.8665	.8686	.8708	.8729	.8749	.8770	.8790	.8810	.8830
1.2	.8849	.8869	.8888	.8907	.8925	.8944	.8962	.8980	.8997	.9015
1.3	.9032	.9049	.9066	.9082	.9099	.9115	.9131	.9147	.9162	.9177
1.4	.9192	.9207	.9222	.9236	.9251	.9265	.9279	.9292	.9306	.9319
1.5	.9332	.9345	.9357	.9370	.9382	.9394	.9406	.9418	.9429	.9441
1.6	.9452	.9463	.9474	.9484	.9495	.9505	.9515	.9525	.9535	.9545
1.7	.9554	.9564	.9573	.9582	.9591	.9599	.9608	.9616	.9625	.9633
1.8	.9641	.9649	.9656	.9664	.9671	.9678	.9686	.9693	.9699	.9706
1.9	.9713	.9719	.9726	.9732	.9738	.9744	.9750	.9756	.9761	.9767
2.0	.9772	.9778	.9783	.9788	.9793	.9798	.9803	.9808	.9812	.9817
2.1	.9821	.9826	.9830	.9834	.9838	.9842	.9846	.9850	.9854	.9857
2.2	.9861	.9864	.9868	.9871	.9875	.9878	.9881	.9884	.9887	.9890
2.3	.9893	.9896	.9898	.9901	.9904	.9906	.9909	.9911	.9913	.9916
2.4	.9918	.9920	.9922	.9925	.9927	.9929	.9931	.9932	.9934	.9936
2.5	.9938	.9940	.9941	.9943	.9945	.9946	.9948	.9949	.9951	.9952
2.6	.9953	.9955	.9956	.9957	.9959	.9960	.9961	.9962	.9963	.9964
2.7	.9965	.9966	.9967	.9968	.9969	.9970	.9971	.9972	.9973	.9974
2.8	.9974	.9975	.9976	.9977	.9977	.9978	.9979	.9979	.9980	.9981
2.9	.9981	.9982	.9982	.9983	.9984	.9984	.9985	.9985	.9986	.9986
3.0	.9987	.9987	.9987	.9988	.9988	.9989	.9989	.9989	.9990	.9990
3.1	.9990	.9991	.9991	.9991	.9992	.9992	.9992	.9992	.9993	.9993
3.2	.9993	.9993	.9994	.9994	.9994	.9994	.9994	.9995	.9995	.9995
3.3	.9995	.9995	.9995	.9996	.9996	.9996	.9996	.9996	.9996	.9997
3.4	.9997	.9997	.9997	.9997	.9997	.9997	.9997	.9997	.9997	.9998

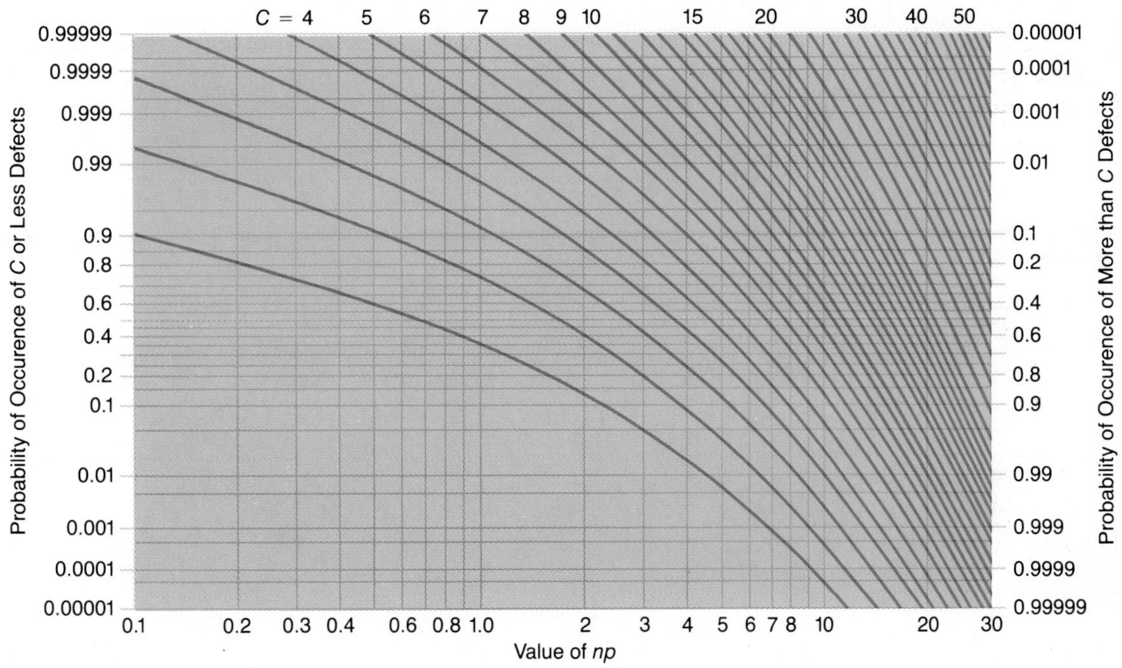

Appendix D.4

Poisson Chart

Source: Harold F. Dodge and Harry G. Romig, *Sampling Inspection Tables,* 2d ed., copyright © 1959, New York: John Wiley & Sons and copyright © 1959, Bell Telephone Laboratories, Inc. Reprinted with permission.

GLOSSARY

ABC analysis The process of dividing inventory items into three classes on the basis of dollar usage.

Acceptable quality level (AQL) The quality level acceptable to the consumer and the quality level the producer aims for.

Acceptance sampling A statistical procedure, based on one or more samples, used to determine whether a quantity of goods conforms to specifications and should be accepted or rejected.

Action notices Computer-generated memos indicating to inventory planners the need to release an order or adjust the priority of a scheduled receipt.

Activity A recognizable segment of work in a project that consumes time and resources.

Activity-on-arc (AOA) network A network in which the arcs represent activities and depict precedence relationships, and the nodes represent events.

Activity-on-node (AON) network A network in which the nodes represent activities and the arcs represent precedence relationships.

Aggregate inventory value The total value of all units held in inventory for a group of items, calculated by multiplying the number of units of each item on hand by its per-unit value and adding the amounts for all items.

Aggressive alternatives Actions in a production planning or staffing problem that seek to change customer demand and consequently resource requirements to achieve efficient operations.

Annual plan The equivalent of a business plan for service organizations.

Annuity A series of payments of a fixed amount for a specified number of years.

Anticipation inventory Inventory used to help absorb uneven rates of supply or demand.

Appraisal costs Costs associated with assessing the level of quality attained by an operating system and determining where quality problems exist.

Assemble-to-order strategy A strategy of assembling end items having many options from a relatively few major assemblies and components after the customer order is received.

Assembly line A labor-intensive production system arranged serially so that assembly work progresses from one work station to the next in line.

Assembly-line balancing The process of determining the number of work stations and the work assignments for those stations that minimize total idleness along the assembly line.

Attribute measures Characteristics of a product or service that can be checked quickly and a simple yes or no decision can be made about acceptable quality.

Automated layout design program (ALDEP) A computerized heuristic method that makes use of a REL chart to find a good layout for a facility.

Automation A system, process, or piece of equipment that is self-acting or self-regulating, substituting mechanical or electronic devices for human observation, effort, and decision making.

Available-to-promise (ATP) row The row in a master production schedule that shows the quantities of end items that can be promised for delivery on the dates indicated.

Backlog An accumulation of customer orders that have been promised for delivery on specific future dates.

Back order A customer order that is not ready when promised or demanded.

Bar coding The process of putting information on products as thin black bars and spaces that can be quickly read by an optical scanner.

Base stock system An inventory system in which a replenishment order is issued in the amount of the withdrawal each time a withdrawal is made.

Bill of materials (BOM) A diagram, or record, that shows all the components for an item, their parent–component relationships, and their usage quantities.

Bottleneck operation An operation that limits output; also referred to as a *critical resource.*

Break-even analysis The process of determining the product volume needed to make revenues equal to total costs, or the total costs equal for two alternatives, in a decision problem.

Business plan A projected statement of income, costs and profits, bringing together the plans and expectations of operations, finance, and marketing managers.

Capacity The maximum rate of output for a facility; also measured as the maximum input rate or number of input units.

Capacity cushion The amount by which the average utilization rate falls below 100 percent.

Capacity requirements planning (CRP) A technique for projecting resource requirements for critical work stations, generated from scheduled receipts and planned order releases.

Capital budgeting The process of allocating scarce funds among competing investment alternatives.

Capital intensity The mix of equipment and human skills in a production process.

Cash flow The flow of funds into and out of an organization, including revenues, costs, and changes in assets and liabilities.

Causal method A mathematical method that expresses the relationships between dependent variables and independent variables.

Chase strategy A planning strategy that adjusts production rates or staff levels to closely match demand requirements over the planning horizon.

Coincident indicators Time series having turning points that generally match those of the general business cycle.

Compensation The pay and employee benefits provided by an organization.

Competitive priorities The emphasis placed on low price, high-performance design, fast delivery time, consistent quality, on-time delivery, product flexibility, and volume flexibility.

Complementary products Products having similar resource requirements but different demand cycles.

Component An item that must be assembled with others to make another item or an item that must be transformed by the manufacturing process into another item.

Compounding interest The process by which interest on an investment accumulates and each period's interest earned is calculated on the principal plus accumulated interest to that time.

Computer numerical control (CNC) machines Numerical control machines that are controlled by a computer.

Computer-aided design (CAD) A computerized process useful in designing and testing new parts or products or in making changes to existing ones.

Computer-aided manufacturing (CAM) A computerized method aimed at integrating the manufacturing of parts through computer-controlled automatic processes.

Computer-integrated manufacturing (CIM) The total integration of product design, engineering, process planning, and manufacturing through complex computer systems.

Computerized relative allocation of facilities technique (CRAFT) A heuristic method that uses a From–To matrix and seeks a good layout by a series of paired exchanges of departments.

Consumer's risk (β) The probability of accepting a lot with LTPD or worse quality.

Continuous flow manufacturing The high-volume production of products in long runs in a linear flow to effectively utilize a large capital investment in plant and equipment.

Continuous review system An inventory control system in which an item's inventory status is checked each time a withdrawal is made from inventory, and an order for a predetermined quantity is placed if the inventory position has reached a certain minimum level; also referred to as *reorder point system.*

Corporate strategy A specification of an organization's central purpose, how to acquire and allocate resources to carry out the mission, and the objectives against which actual performance can be measured.

Critical path The sequence of activities from the start of a project to its completion having the greatest cumulative elapsed time, thereby determining the time duration of the entire project.

Critical path method (CPM) A project planning method that is based on the assumption that all activity times are known with certainty.

Critical resource A resource for which the requirements equal or exceed its capacity over a specified period of time.

Customer involvement How much and in what ways the customer becomes part of the production process.

Cycle counting Verifying the accuracy of inventory status records by physically counting a small percentage of the total number of inventory items each day.

Cycle inventory Inventory of an item held during the time interval between orders, exclusive of safety stock, averaging approximately one-half the order quantity.

Cycle time In assembly-line balancing, the maximum amount of time allowed for work on a unit at each work station; in scheduling, the time that elapses between job start and completion (also referred to as *flow time* or even *lead time*).

Cycle-service level The desired probability of not running out of stock during the time between inventory replenishments.

Degeneracy A situation in which fewer than $m + n - 1$ cells in a transportation problem are allocated non-zero values or a solution variable in a linear programming problem has a zero value.

Delphi method A qualitative approach to forecasting whereby a group of experts participates in an iterative process of making projections and getting feedback from other group members and ultimately arrives at a consensus.

Demand management The process of influencing the timing and volume of demand or adapting to the undesirable effects of unchangeable demand patterns.

Dependent demand Demand for an item that results from the production decisions for its parent items.

Dependent variable A variable that is to be estimated or forecasted, having a value that is determined by that of one or more other variables.

Depreciation An allowance recognizing the consumption of capital used to offset income when calculating taxes.

Descriptive model A set of relationships between dependent and independent variables designed to describe the operations of a productive system.

Disaggregate The process of determining the production quantities or staffing levels of individual items or workers by breaking down an aggregated total.

Discount rate The interest rate used in a present value analysis.

Discounting The process of finding the present value of an investment when the future value and interest rate are known.

Dispatching procedures Procedures used to construct a schedule for a work station by assigning priorities to the jobs in queue and deciding which job to process next when the work station becomes available for further processing.

Distinctive competencies The unique resources and strengths which should guide the formulation of corporate and operations strategies.

Distribution Management of the outbound flow of materials from manufacturing to customers, involving the storage and transportation of products.

Distribution requirements planning (DRP) An inventory control and scheduling technique that applies the principles of MRP to distribution inventories.

Double exponential smoothing A forecasting method whereby the estimate for the average of a series and the estimate for a trend are smoothed.

Double-sample plan An acceptance sampling plan in which a decision to accept or reject a lot can be made on the first sample but, if it is not, a second sample is taken and a decision is made on the basis of the combined samples.

Dynamic lot-sizing rules Procedures for determining order quantity that allow a change in size each time an order is issued, with the quantity equal to net requirements for a specified number of weeks.

Economic order quantity (EOQ) The order quantity that minimizes total annual inventory holding costs plus ordering (or setup) costs, given certain assumptions.

Economies of scale The concept that increasing a facility's size will reduce the average unit cost of production.

Electronic data interchange (EDI) systems Integrated systems in which computers in one organization exchange information directly with computers in another organization.

Electronic mail system A system allowing users to exchange messages through computers, with others who have access to the same computer network.

Electronic spreadsheets A popular analytical tool with microcomputers whereby many rows and columns of data are entered and manipulated mathematically.

End item The item scheduled in a master production schedule that typically is the final product sold to a customer but could be a major assembly in companies using a final assembly schedule.

Entrance–exit strategy A product planning strategy for determining when to enter a market and when to exit it.

Euclidean distance measure The straight-line distance between two points, used in location or layout analyses.

Event A specific, definable project accomplishment, recognizable at a particular point in time, that does not consume time or resources.

Exception report A computer-generated report indicating the need for some type of action regarding inventory items.

External failure costs Costs of warranty repairs, loss of market share, and lawsuits resulting from defective products or services.

Facility location The geographic site at which a productive facility is situated.

Feasible region The set of solutions to a linear programming model that satisfy all its constraints simultaneously.

Fill rate The proportion of annual demand instantaneously filled from stock.

Final assembly schedule A schedule that determines the due dates for major assemblies and components so that the final product can be assembled when promised.

Firm planned order A technique that enables a planner to override an MRP system and change the timing and/or size of any planned order.

Fishbone diagram A diagram that relates a product defect to the potential contributing factors so that customer complaints can be readily traced to the operations involved.

Fixed automation Automation arranged in flow lines designed to produce one type of part or product.

Fixed order quantity (FOQ) A lot-sizing rule under which the lot size is a predetermined, fixed quantity.

Fixed schedule The assignment of an employee to the same days and hours of work each week.

Fixed-position layout A layout where the product remains fixed in place and workers, along with their tools and equipment, come to the product to work on it.

Flexible manufacturing system (FMS) A manufacturing system with several CNC machines, a computer-controlled transport system, and loading and unloading stations.

Flexible work force A group of workers, each of whom is capable of working at a variety of operations.

Flow diagram A diagram of the flows of people, equipment, or materials through a process.

Flow shop See *Product-focused strategy.*

Focus forecasting A forecasting method whereby several time-series forecasting models generate forecasts for each period and the model that generated the best prediction for the last period is used to make the forecast for the current period.

Focused facilities The concept that narrowing the range of demands on a facility will lead to better performance.

Forecasts Predictions about future events based on historical data.

Free slack The time by which an activity can be delayed without delaying the earliest start time of any other activity.

From–To matrix A table showing the number of trips (or some other measure of materials movement) between each pair of departments in a layout analysis.

Future value of an investment The value of an investment at the end of the period over which interest is compounded.

Gantt chart A chart that shows the scheduled start date and the progress of each job compared to its scheduled delivery date.

General-purpose plant A plant that maximizes product and resource flexibility.

Global priority rules Sequencing rules that base the priority assignment on information about other work stations (job routings, queue sizes, and the like), in addition to the one being scheduled.

Goal programming models Models that incorporate conflicting objectives and are solved using a procedure based on ordinary linear programming.

Graphical method of linear programming The process of solving small linear programming problems by plotting the constraints and objective function on a graph.

Gross requirements Demand requirements before netting out on-hand inventory and scheduled receipts.

Group technology (GT) A manufacturing technique by which products or parts with similar characteristics are grouped into families and machines are grouped into cells in such a way that high levels of repeatability are achieved.

Heuristics Solution guidelines, or rules of thumb, which find good solutions to problems, but not necessarily the best.

Hurdle rate The discount rate in a net present value analysis that represents the lowest desired return on investment.

Hybrid layout An arrangement of a facility with some portions designed as a product layout and other portions designed as a process layout.

Independent demand Demand for an item that is influenced by market conditions and not related to the production decisions for any other item held in stock.

Independent variable A variable that determines the values of one or more dependent variables.

Industrial robots A type of programmable automation involving machines that have an arm, hand, and sometimes fingers and a sensing device similar in function to an eye.

Input source The population of potential customers for the service system in a queuing problem.

Input–output control report A report that compares planned input with actual input and planned output with actual output, so that management can determine whether a capacity problem exists at a work station.

Interarrival time The time between successive customer (job) arrivals.

Intermediate item An item that has at least one parent and one component.

Internal failure costs Costs resulting from yield losses and rework of defective parts or services.

Inventory A stock of materials created to satisfy some eventual demand.

Inventory holding cost The cost of interest, storage and handling, taxes, insurance premiums, and shrinkage.

Inventory position (IP) The inventory on hand plus scheduled receipts minus back orders.

Inventory status record MRP record that shows an item's gross requirements, scheduled receipts, on-hand balance, net requirements, and planned order releases.

Inventory turnover The number of business weeks in a year divided by the weeks of supply.

Job design Specification of the content of a job and determination of the skills and training an employee will need in order to perform the job.

Job enlargement The process of assigning a greater variety of tasks to workers, including allowing workers more involvement in self-supervision.

Job flow time The elapsed time between the release of a job or production order to the shop and completion of the job or order; also referred to as *cycle time.*

Job shop See *Process-focused strategy.*

Just-in-time (JIT) systems Production and inventory control systems designed to produce small lots and to produce the right items in the quantities needed by subsequent production processes at the right time.

Kanban A Japanese word for *card,* which is often used to describe Toyota's just-in-time system.

Knowledge workers Employees who generate and disseminate information, including many nonclerical white-collar workers, nonmanagerial professionals, and managers.

Labor standard The time required for a trained worker to perform a given task using a prescribed work method with normal effort and skill.

Labor-limited environment A situation in which the limiting capacity is the number of workers.

Lagging indicators Time series having turning points that generally follow behind those of the general business cycle.

Layout planning Determining the physical arrangement of centers of economic activity within a facility.

Leading indicators Time series having turning points that precede those of the general business cycle.

Learning curve A curve displaying the relationship between the total direct labor per unit and the cumulative quantity of a product produced.

Level strategy A planning strategy that

maintains a level production rate or staff level over the planning horizon.

Level-by-level processing A procedure used in MRP to determine the gross requirements for each dependent-demand item.

Life-cycle audit An evaluation, based on changes in sales and profits, of whether a product is in the introductory, growth, maturity or decline stage.

Linear programming A mathematical technique that is used to optimize a linear objective function, subject to a set of linear constraints.

Load–distance method Using a mathematical model for finding the location of a single facility when the objective is to minimize the total load to each destination multiplied by the distance traveled.

Local priority rules Sequencing rules that base a job's priority assignment only on information represented by the jobs in queue at the work station.

Lot for lot (L4L) A lot-sizing rule under which the order quantity equals the net requirements of a single period.

Lot tolerance proportion defective (LTPD) The worst level of quality that the consumer will accept.

Machine-limited environment A situation in which the limiting capacity is the number of machines or facilities available.

Make-to-order strategy A strategy of making end items to individual customer specifications.

Make-to-stock strategy A strategy of holding end items in stock for immediate availability.

Makespan The total amount of time required to complete a particular group of jobs.

Market research A systematic approach used to create and test hypotheses about the marketplace, usually involving surveys.

Market-area plant A plant that produces all or most of the products for its assigned market area.

Master production schedule (MPS) An expression of the operational plan of production by period, indicating the timing and size of end-item quantities.

MPS-receipt row The row in a master production schedule that shows the quantities of an end item scheduled for completion by specific dates.

MPS-start row The row in a master production schedule that shows the dates production is to begin for the quantities of end items specified.

Materials handling processes The moving, packaging, and storing of materials or products.

Materials management The managing of supplies, production levels, staffing patterns, inventories, schedules, and distribution.

Materials requirements planning (MRP) A computerized information system for managing dependent-demand inventory and scheduling stock replenishment orders.

Mean absolute deviation (MAD) A measure of forecast error whereby the absolute value of the forecast errors are averaged.

Methods time measurement (MTM) A predetermined data approach for setting time standards whereby the normal times for micromotions are stored in a database so that the normal time for a task can be developed by reference to the data.

Mixed-model assembly line An assembly line capable of producing a number of different items belonging to the same product family.

Moving average method A forecasting method whereby the forecast for each period is made by taking the simple average of a fixed number of the most recent past demand levels.

Multiple activity chart A chart similar to a process chart, which shows the activities performed by or on several subjects over some time period.

Multiplicative seasonal method A forecasting method whereby the estimated average demand for a period is multiplied by a seasonal factor for that period.

Net change MRP system An MRP system in which changes to the master production schedule and the item inventories initiate updates of the affected inventory records only.

Net present value (NPV) method A method of determining the desirability of an investment that compares the present value of the after-tax cash flows with the original investment amount.

Network diagram A diagram consisting of arcs and nodes that depicts the relationships between activities or tasks in a project or job.

Noncritical resource A resource for which the requirements are less than its capacity over a specified period of time.

Numerical control (NC) machines Large machine tools that can be reconfigured to produce a wide variety of parts by changing the instructions stored on a punched card or tape.

On-hand inventory row The inventory balance at the end of the preceding period plus scheduled receipts minus total expected requirements.

On-the-job training The process by which employees learn jobs by actually performing them.

One-worker–multiple-machine (OWMM) concept An arrangement whereby one worker operates several different machines at a time to achieve a line flow.

Open orders See *Scheduled receipts.*

Operating characteristic (OC) curve A curve depicting the probability of acceptance of a lot for a range of lot proportion defectives for specific parameters of an acceptance sampling plan.

Operations audit The process of assessing the need for change in an operating system by comparing current performance to goals on a variety of dimensions.

Operations management The systematic direction and control of the processes that transform inputs into finished goods or services.

Operations process chart A diagram showing the materials and sequence of operations needed to manufacture a product.

Operations scheduling The assignment of people to jobs or jobs to machines, for specific labor and/or machine capacities.

Operations strategy A specification of how to achieve organizational goals and carry out the corporate strategy within the operations function.

Optimized Production Technology (OPT) A technique for production scheduling and inventory control that recognizes capacity constraints.

Optional replenishment system An inventory control system in which the inventory status is checked at fixed intervals of time and, if the inventory position has dropped to a predetermined level, an order of variable size is issued to cover expected needs.

Order entry sequence The steps taken to confirm a customer's order, typically including (1) receipt of information about desired quantity and delivery date; (2) check of customer credit and preparation of documentation; (3) check on availability of capacity and materials; and (4) notification to the customer of the quantity and scheduled shipping date.

Ordering cost The cost incurred in preparing an order to a supplier or the shop, regardless of the size of the order.

***p*-chart** A process control method for attribute measurements whereby the sample proportion defective is plotted on a chart to determine whether the process is in control.

Parent An item that has one or more components.

Part commonality The degree to which components have more than one parent.

Past due The amount of time by which a job missed its due date or the percentage of all jobs processed over some period of time that missed their due dates.

Payback method A method of determining the desirability of an investment that determines how much time will elapse before the total of after-tax cash flows will equal the initial investment.

Payoff matrix A table showing the profits or benefits for each alternative for different levels of demand.

Peg record An MRP record that indicates for each week the component quantity needed by each parent item.

Periodic order quantity (POQ) A lot-sizing rule under which the order quantity equals the total net requirements for a specified number of periods.

Periodic review system An inventory control system in which the inventory status of an item is checked at predetermined intervals and an order of variable size is placed on the basis of expected needs.

Perpetual inventory system A continuous review system in which the inventory records are always up-to-date.

Piece rate A pay plan in which compensation is based on the number of units processed during a day or week.

Pipeline inventory Inventory in transit, moving from point to point in the materials flow system.

Planned order releases (PORs) The dates on which orders for specified quantities of an item are planned for issue to the shop or a supplier.

Planning horizon The length of time for which plans or schedules are made.

Plant charter A statement of the responsibilities of a particular plant, relative to others in a multiplant system.

Positioning inventory The act of determining whether to concentrate inventory at the raw-material level, work-in-process level, or finished goods level.

Positioning strategy The decision about how to organize a production system, ranging from a process focus to a product focus, recognizing product or service volume and the flow pattern of the products or services.

Precedence relationships Sequencing constraints on the activities in a project.

Preemptive discipline A priority rule that allows a customer or job with higher priority to displace another one presently being served.

Preference matrix A table in which alternative ideas are judged against a series of criteria, with each one weighted according to its importance, and a total score for each alternative is obtained.

Present value of an investment The amount of money that must be invested now to accumulate to a certain amount in the future at a specific rate of interest.

Prevention costs Costs associated with preventing quality defects before they happen.

Preventive maintenance (PM) Activities directed at preventing machine breakdowns and poor performance.

Priority dependency A situation in which a job's priority is dependent on the progress or priority of another job in the shop.

Priority discipline A rule that selects the next customer to be served by the service facilities.

Priority sequencing rules Rules that specify the job to be processed next from a queue of jobs at a work station.

Process batch The total number of units of an item processed at one time at a particular work station.

Process chart An organized way of recording all the activities performed by a person or machine, at a work station, or on materials.

Process design The selection of inputs, operations, work flows, and methods used to produce goods and services.

Process layout The arrangement of a facility where the work stations or departments are grouped according to the functions they perform.

Process plant A plant that is assigned responsibility for only a certain segment of the total production process.

Process-focused strategy Equipment and work force are organized around a production process; often called a *job shop.*

Producer's risk (α) The probability of rejecting a lot with AQL or better quality.

Product family A group of products or services that have similar demand requirements and common processing, labor, and materials requirements.

Product flexibility The ability of an organization to accommodate changing product designs or highly customized products.

Product layout The arrangement of a facility where the work stations or departments are arranged in a line devoted to producing individual products.

Product life cycle The stages of product life, including product planning, introduction, growth, maturity, and decline.

Product planning The process of generating new ideas for goods and services and introducing them into the market, revising existing products, and dropping old products.

Product plant A plant that specializes in a certain product line or family.

Product-focused strategy Equipment and work force are organized around the product; often called a *flow shop.*

Production line A capital-intensive production system utilizing specialized equipment arranged serially.

Production plan A managerial statement of time-phased production rates, workforce levels, and inventory investment, which takes customer requirements, and capacity limitations into consideration.

Production requirements Desired production quantities, net of on-hand inventory in the master production schedule.

Productivity Total output per hour worked or the value of outputs divided by the value of inputs.

Program evaluation and review technique (PERT) A project planning method in which uncertainties in the time estimates for activities are explicitly recognized.

Programmable automation Automatic processes that can be programmed to handle a variety of product configurations.

Project A set of activities, having a definite starting and ending point, that results in a unique product or service.

Purchased item An item that has no components but has one or more parents.

Purchasing The process of acquiring inputs, including decisions about which vendors to use, contract negotiation, and decisions about whether to buy locally or centrally.

Qualitative techniques Techniques that use managerial judgment, expert opinions, and/or survey methods to convert qualitative information into quantitative estimates.

Quality assurance The process of preventing, detecting, and correcting quality problems.

Quality circle A small group composed of supervisors and employees who meet to identify, analyze, and solve production and quality problems.

Quantity discounts An incentive to order larger quantities for which the price per unit drops if the order is sufficiently large.

Queue A line of people or inanimate objects waiting for service.

***R*-chart** A process control method for variable measures whereby the sample range is plotted on a chart to determine whether the process variability is in control.

Reactive alternatives Actions in a production planning or staffing problem that take demand requirements as a given quantity.

Rectilinear distance measure A measure of the distance between two points where it is assumed that the trip is made with a series of 90° turns, as along city blocks.

Redundancy Backup equipment used to reduce the effects of machine breakdowns, or equipment designed with extra components in parallel.

Regenerative MRP system An MRP system in which all records are periodically recomputed by completely exploding the master production schedule, and other sources of demand, taking into account changes to the status of the item inventories.

REL chart A chart used for layout planning that reflects the qualitative judgments of managers regarding the importance of proximity in locating each possible pair of departments.

Reliability The probability that a component or system will be working at any time.

Reorder point system See *Continuous review system.*

Repeatability The degree to which a task repeats itself, such as through job specialization or standardized products and parts.

Repetitive manufacturing The high-volume production of standard, discrete products in relatively small lot sizes.

Resource flexibility The ease with which equipment and employees can handle a wide variety of products, output levels, duties, and functions.

Right-hand-side ranging The process of determining the range of values that a right-hand-side quantity in a linear program can have while the shadow price is still valid.

Rim conditions In a transportation model, the sum of the allocations to a row must equal the capacity of that row; and the sum of the allocations to a column must equal the requirements for that column.

Rolling planning horizon A procedure whereby the plan for the entire planning horizon is updated and extended at the beginning of each period but only that portion of the plan covering the first period is implemented.

Rotating schedule The process of rotating employees through a series of weekdays and/or hours so that each person has the same opportunity to have weekends or holidays off and to work days, as well as evenings and nights.

Rough-cut capacity planning An approach intended to give only a rough approximation of actual resource requirements generated by a master production schedule.

Routing A list showing the sequence of operations through which an item must pass, the standard times, and required materials.

Safety stock inventory Inventory used to protect against uncertainties in supply, lead time, and demand.

Salvage value The amount received from the disposal of used plant and equipment.

Schedule interference constraint A stipulation that the total time required to produce a group of items cannot exceed the time to deplete the stock for any one item.

Scheduled receipts Orders that have been issued to the shop or supplier but not yet received; also referred to as *open orders.*

Scientific management A philosophy based on the assumption that any operation can be improved by breaking it into components, measuring the work content of the components, and seeking ways to improve work methods.

Search decision rule A heuristic method using a computer search method that finds values of the production rate and workforce level that minimize costs.

Sensitivity analysis A method whereby critical parameters in a model are systematically modified to determine the effects on the solution.

Sequential-sample plan An acceptance sampling plan in which each time an item is inspected a decision is made to accept the lot, reject the lot, or continue sampling.

Service facilities The personnel and/or equipment to perform a service.

Service system One or more queues, a priority discipline, and service facilities.

Setup cost Cost incurred in changing over a machine to produce a different item, regardless of the lot size.

Shadow price The relative value of a resource with respect to the objective function in a linear programming problem.

Shop-floor control system An information system used to track scheduled receipts, generate dispatch priority lists, and monitor the status of work stations.

Simplex method An iterative algebraic procedure used to solve linear programming problems.

Simulation The act of reproducing the behavior of a system.

Single exponential smoothing A forecasting method whereby the forecast is made on the basis of only three pieces of data: the calculated average demand for the preceding period, the estimated demand for the current period, and a smoothing parameter alpha.

Single-bin system A simple inventory control system in which a desired maximum inventory level is marked on a bin and the bin is periodically filled to that mark.

Single-sample plan An acceptance sampling plan in which the decision to accept or reject a lot is made on the basis of a single sample.

Special item An item made to order.

Staffing plan A managerial statement of time-phased staff sizes and labor-related capacities that takes customer requirements and machine-limited capacities into consideration.

Standard item An item made to stock.

Static lot-sizing rules Lot-sizing rules with

which the order quantity remains the same each time an order is issued.

Stockout Not satisfying the demand for a stock item when it occurs.

Subassembly An item made up of one or more components and, in turn, used as a component in a finished product.

Technological forecasting The process of predicting the direction and scope of certain technological advances.

Technology The automatic, manual, and mental processes, work methods, and raw materials that are used by an organization to convert input resources into goods or services.

Time series analysis A statistical approach that relies heavily on repeated observations, arranged in the order in which they actually occurred, to forecast future demand, recognizing both the historical trend and seasonality patterns.

Time study A method of setting time standards in which a stopwatch is used to time a trained worker while he or she performs a series of work elements for a number of work cycles.

Time value of money The concept that a dollar in hand today is worth more than a dollar to be received in the future.

Total inventory The sum of scheduled receipts and on-hand inventory quantities.

Total quality control (TQC) An approach involving the concept that producing a quality product is a responsibility to be shared by everyone in the organization, especially those making the product or service.

Total slack The maximum time by which an activity in a project can be delayed without delaying the entire project.

Tracking signal A measurement that indicates whether a forecast has any built-in biases over a period of time.

Transfer batch The quantity of an item that moves between work stations.

Transportation method An iterative technique, based on linear programming, for solving shipping problems from m sources of supply to n destinations.

Two-bin system A simple inventory control system in which the inventory is held in two bins, one of them containing the reorder point quantity and the other, when empty, signaling the need to place a replenishment order.

Utilization The percentage of total work hours spent productively by a machine or worker.

Valid priority A priority where the due date and the need date for an order match.

Variable measures Characteristics of a product or service that can be measured on a continuous scale.

Vertical integration The degree to which a firm's own production system handles the supply chain from raw material to final customer.

Visual systems Inventory control systems for which the inventory status is checked visually rather than with inventory records.

Vogel's approximation method (VAM) A technique for finding the initial solution to a transportation model which considers the objective function in making the allocations.

Volume flexibility The ability to quickly accelerate or decelerate the rate of production to meet large fluctuations in demand.

Weeks of supply An inventory measure obtained by dividing aggregate inventory value by sales per week at cost.

Weighted moving average method A forecasting method whereby each demand in the average can have its own weight, provided that the sum of the weights equals 1.

Word processing system A system allowing documents to be created, filed, retrieved, altered, and stored electronically.

Work sampling A method of work measurement for estimating the proportions of time spent (by people and machines) on various activities.

Work-in-process (WIP) inventory Materials in queue, moving from one operation to another, being delayed or processed, or residing in component or subassembly inventories.

Work-force scheduling Specifying the on-duty and off-duty time periods for each employee over a certain period of time.

$\bar{x}$-chart A process control method for variable measures whereby the sample mean is plotted on a chart to determine whether the process average is in control.

INDEX

B

C

M

N

O

Q

T